GATEWAYS TO ART

Debra J. DeWitte | Ralph M. Larmann | M. Kathryn Shields

University of Texas
at Arlington, TX

University of Evansville, IN

Guilford College, NC

GATEWAYS TO ART

UNDERSTANDING THE VISUAL ARTS

FOURTH EDITION

with 1896 illustrations

Gateways to Art © 2012, 2015, 2018, and 2023
Thames & Hudson Ltd, London

Text © 2012, 2015, 2018, and 2023 Debra J. DeWitte, Ralph M. Larmann, and M. Kathryn Shields

Designed by Christopher Perkins and Rowena Alsey

First published in 2012 in paperback in the United States of America by Thames & Hudson Inc., 500 Fifth Avenue, New York, New York 10110

Fourth edition 2023

Library of Congress Control Number 2011922637

Paperback: ISBN 978-0-500-84506-6
Instructor's copy, Not for Sale: ISBN 978-0-500-84486-1
Looseleaf/3-Hole-Punch: ISBN 978-0-500-84507-3

Printed and bound in Canada by Transcontinental Printing

Be the first to know about our new releases, exclusive content and author events by visiting
thamesandhudson.com
thamesandhudsonusa.com
thamesandhudson.com.au

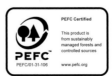

Contents

*See overleaf for a more
detailed list of the contents
of each chapter*

Part 1 Fundamentals

Part 2 Media and Processes

Part 3 History and Context

Part 4 Themes

Preface

Organization and How to Use this Book

Gateways to Art is an introduction to the visual arts, divided into four parts: Part 1, Fundamentals, the essential elements and principles of art that constitute the visual language of artworks; Part 2, Media and Processes, the many materials and processes that artists use to make art; Part 3, History and Context, the forces and influences that have shaped art throughout human history; and Part 4, Themes, the major cultural and historical themes that have motivated artists to create. Each of these parts is color-coded to help you move easily from one section to the next.

Gateways to Art gives you complete flexibility in finding your own pathway to understanding and appreciating art. Once you have read the Introduction, which outlines the core knowledge and skills you will need to analyze and understand art, you can read the chapters of our book in any order. Each chapter is entirely modular, giving you just the information you need when you need it. Concepts are clearly explained and definitions of terminology in the margins ensure that you are never at a loss to understand a term; and Portal features use thumbnail images to make direct links to related artworks throughout the book (see p. 15 for how to use Portals and glossary definitions in the margins).

This means that you can learn about art in the order that works best for you. You can, of course, read the chapters in the order that they appear in the book. This will tell you all you need to know to appreciate art. But you can also choose your own path. For example, the Introduction discusses how we define art and what it contributes to our lives. Next you might read Chapter 2.6, The Tradition of Craft, which deals with media that artists have used for centuries to create artworks, but which some cultures today consider less important than fine art, such as painting and sculpture. Then the discussion of Japanese art in Chapter 3.3, Art of India, China, Japan, Korea, and Southeast Asia, reveals how the traditional tea ceremony or a carefully raked Zen garden are appreciated just as much as a painting.

In *Gateways to Art* you will discover the pleasure of looking at great artworks many times and always finding something new because there are many ways of seeing and analyzing art. That is why our book takes its title from its unique feature, the Gateways to Art (introduced on p. 15). Through eight iconic works of world art, we invite you to continually return to these Gateways to discover something different: about the design characteristics of the work; the materials used to make it; how history and culture influenced its creation; or how the work expressed something personal. Sometimes we compare the Gateway image with another artwork, or consider what it tells us about the great mysteries of our existence, such as spirituality or life and death. We hope to encourage you to revisit not only our Gateways, but also see that other works can be viewed through multiple lenses.

Our Gateways to Art are just one of numerous features we provide to help you in your studies. In many chapters you will find Perspectives on Art features, in which artists, art historians, critics, and others involved in the world of art explain how diverse people engaged in art think and work. Other features will, for example, help you to focus in depth on a single artwork, or to compare and contrast artworks that deal with a similar subject or theme. Explore Further pages at the end of every chapter perform a similar function to the Portals in the margins: they group together relevant artworks from throughout the book according to the themes or topics discussed in the chapter, and allow you to make interesting connections across time periods, themes, and media.

New in this Edition

- More than 150 artworks have been added to this edition, including works by Abdoulaye Konaté, Abie Loy Kemarre, Amrita Sher-Gil, Cai Guo-Qiang, Elizabeth Catlett, Harriet Powers, Tom Lea, William Eggleston, and many others.
- Increased coverage of race and the history of enslavement, including works by Deana Lawson, Sondra Perry, Kerry James Marshall, Mark Bradford, and Dustin Klein.

- Contemporary issues of climate change, social justice and migration, and state violence and censorship are addressed in works by Elizabeth Demaray, Ronald Rael and Virginia San Fratello, Félix González-Torres, Ai Weiwei, Doris Salcedo, Eduardo Kobra, Mona Hatoum, Anila Quayyum Agha, and Xena Goldman, Cadex Herrera, and Greta McLain.
- The eight Gateway to Art features have been refreshed with three works: April Greiman's *Does It Make Sense?*; Kara Walker's *Insurrection! (Our Tools Were Rudimentary, Yet We Pressed On)*; and a *nkisi nkondi* figure—a late nineteenth-century Yombe sculpture. Five Gateways have been retained from the previous edition: Frida Kahlo's *The Two Fridas*; Raphael's *The School of Athens*; Ai Weiwei's *Dropping a Han Dynasty Urn*; Hokusai's "The Great Wave off Shore at Kanagawa"; and the Taj Mahal.
- Our e-media package has been expanded with new features and improvements for both instructors and students: see the following sections for more information.

Resources for Instructors and Students

We have developed a range of digital resources to support teaching and learning, and have enhanced and added new resources for this fourth edition in response to user feedback. Resources can be found at https://digital. wwnorton.com/gateways4. For assistance, contact your W. W. Norton representative.

- The authors have revised the Instructor's Manual to include updated chapter outlines, active learning exercises, suggested readings, lecture ideas, and discussion questions. Transition guides facilitate the updating of syllabi.

- The authors have also updated the Test Bank of more than 1,600 questions, now available in TestMaker.
- The Lecture PowerPoints are fully customizable, featuring images and bullet points of key topics from each section for in-class presentation.
- The interactive e-book includes dozens of embedded videos, animations, and panoramas, as well as the audio glossary. The e-book also includes new concept-check questions to assess students' understanding of key themes in each section as they read.
- InQuizitive, the easy-to-use adaptive learning tool that helps students to master key concepts, has been thoroughly revised and updated for this edition. Featuring visual prompts with images from the text, InQuizitive questions are linked directly to the relevant e-book page to support students' reading and comprehension.
- Other student resources have been revised and updated: terminology and image flashcards; chapter outlines; a full glossary and an audio glossary to aid pronunciation of non-English terms and artists' names; and interactive exercises demonstrating key concepts.
- The *Gateways to Art Journal for Museum and Gallery Projects* is now available as an e-book, and has been updated to address current issues that museums face, such as online community outreach, diversity and inclusion, and colonialism and decolonization, with a new exercise on provenance and repatriation.

Videos, Animations, and Images

The following interactive elements in the e-book are also available separately for classroom use:
- Videos exclusive to Thames & Hudson, including in-the-studio videos that demonstrate how art is made; videos that introduce and analyze key works of world art; and

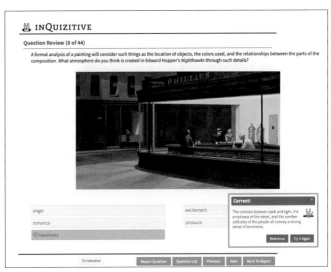

A sample search result in the Gateways Global Gallery shows how you can create your own image collections to download and use in your teaching.

A sample InQuizitive question shows answer feedback for the student.

- the Looking More Closely series, which examines details in larger works, such as Bosch's *Garden of Earthly Delights*.
- Videos by author Ralph Larmann, with discussions of elements and principles such as line, rhythm, and form, as well as in-depth analysis of key artists and artworks.
- Licenses with major museums offer an expanded range of videos.
- A variety of interactive animated exercises to demonstrate the elements and principles of art. Thames & Hudson's own animations include the Making It Real series, which explains processes such as metal casting, engraving, and marquetry, and line art animations that explore site and floor plans in a dynamic way to help students visualize ancient architecture.
- For instructors, image files of all the available artworks for use in lectures are available as high-quality jpg files, and in PowerPoint slides with captions, organized by chapter.
- More than 6,500 additional image files are also available in the Gateways Global Gallery, which is searchable as well as indexed to the chapters of the fourth edition.

The Authors

Debra J. DeWitte has a PhD in aesthetics from the University of Texas at Dallas. She now teaches at the University of Texas at Arlington, where she has devised an award-winning online art appreciation course.

Ralph M. Larmann has a BFA from the University of Cincinnati and an MFA from James Madison University. He currently teaches at the University of Evansville and is a past President of Foundations in Art: Theory and Education.

M. Kathryn Shields has a PhD in art history from Virginia Commonwealth University. She is Professor of Art History at Guilford College, where she also serves as Co-Chair of the Art Department and Associate Academic Dean.

Acknowledgments

The publisher would like to thank the following for their generous advice and feedback during the preparation of this new edition:

Naomi Slipp, Auburn University; Cynthia Mills, Auburn University at Montgomery; Ronnie Wrest, Bakersfield College; Jennifer Rush, Central New Mexico Community College; Carolyn Jacobs and Mary Kilburn, Central Piedmont Community College; Laura Stewart, Daytona State College; Brenda Hanegan, Delgado Community College; Barbara Armstrong, El Centro College; Susan Dodge, Frostburg State University; David Cook, Georgia Gwinnett College; Megan Levacy, Georgia Perimeter College; Marion de Koning and Malia Molina, Grossmont College; Melanie Atkinson, Hinds Community College; Jenny Ramirez, James Madison University; Anita Rogers and Eric Sims, Lone Star College System; Buffy Walters, Marion Military Institute; Terrell Taylor, Meridian Community College; Errol Alger, Midlands Technical College; David Hamlow, Minnesota State University–Mankato; Mano Sotelo, Hirotsune Tashima, and Michael Nolan, Pima Community College; Karene Barrow, Pitt Community College; Debra Schafter, San Antonio College; Patricia Ballinger, South Texas College; Christian deLeon, Kristina Elizondo, and Sharon Covington, Tarrant County College; Alice Ottewill Jackson, University of Alabama at Birmingham; Patti Shanks, University of Missouri; Kurt Rahmlow, University of North Texas; Marta Slaughter, University of South Florida; Perry Kirk, University of West Georgia.

The publisher would like to thank the following contributors to the student and instructor resources: Jill Foltz, Dallas College, El Centro Campus; Lucy Holland, Grossmont College; Malia Molina, Grossmont College; Carissa Nicholson, University of Florida; and Aaron Smith, Palo Alto College.

The publisher also gratefully acknowledges the following contributors: Wafaa Bilal, Mel Chin, Gabriel Dawe, Molly Gochman, April Greiman, Zahi Hawass, Hyo-In Kim, Darian Leader, the late Loongkoonan, Howard Risatti, Richard Serra, Cindy Sherman, Spencer Tunick, and Bill Viola.

Debra J. DeWitte would like to thank the following for their scholarly assistance: Richard Brettell, University of Texas at Dallas; Annemarie Carr, Southern Methodist University; Jenny Ramirez, James Madison University; Beth Wright, University of Texas at Arlington (Museum Guide); and for their patience and support she would like to thank her family: Bill Gibney, Jaclyn Jean Gibney, and Connie DeWitte.

Ralph M. Larmann would like to thank the following for their scholarly assistance and support: Ella Combs-Larmann, independent scholar and artist; Dr. Heidi Strobel, University of Evansville; University of Evansville, Office of Academic Affairs, Office of Alumni Relations, University Library, Department of Art; and for their patience and understanding: Ella, Allison, and Tip.

M. Kathryn Shields would like to thank the following people for specific insights and general support: Laura M. Amrhein, University of North Carolina School of the Arts; Damon Akins, Guilford College; Scott Betz, Winston-Salem State University; Maria Bobroff, Boston University; Frank Boyd, Higher Education Data Sharing Consortium; Maia Dery and our Riding the Waves/Waves to Wisdom friends; Jenny Ramirez, James Madison University and Mary Baldwin University; Eric Steginsky, independent artist; Antoine Williams, Guilford College. She extends love and gratitude to Barry Bell, Gillian Denise Shields Bell, Alden Emmerich Shields Bell and honors the memory of Nancy Shields and Denise Wolf.

How to Use the Gateways to Art and Other Features

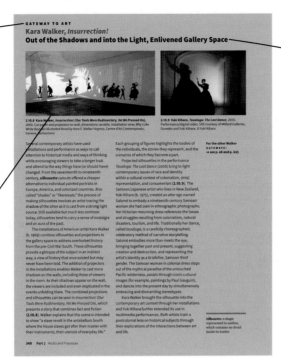

GATEWAY TO ART
Kara Walker, *Insurrection!*
Out of the Shadows and into the Light, Enlivened Gallery Space

The Gateway Artworks

To help you develop the important skills of looking at, analyzing, and interpreting works of art, we have selected eight iconic works—the Gateways to Art—that you will encounter several times as you read this book.

A Different View

Every time you look at a great work of art, it will have something new to say to you—and this is explored through the eight Gateway artworks, which each recur three times throughout the book.

If you consider in Part 1 the way an artist designed the work, you may notice something about the use of color or contrast that had not struck you before. In Part 2, you will learn more about the materials and processes involved in creating the artwork, and how the artist used these to communicate visual ideas. In Part 3 we take a historical point of view: how does this work reflect the circumstances and the society in which it was created? Does it express the values of those who held political and economic power, or could it tell us something about the status of women at the time? In Part 4, we will ask whether the work touches on very big questions, such as the nature of the universe, or life and death. Or how it engages with such concerns as gender, sexuality, race, and our own identities.

Compare and Contrast

You can learn more about one work by studying another and comparing the two. For example, Kara Walker and Yuki Kihara's artworks both transform the gallery space, but in different ways: Walker uses installation, while Kihara's piece exists as a multimedia performance. Both artists employed the nostalgic media of silhouettes and shadows to encourage viewers to take a longer look, and to evaluate historical subjects such as race, identity, and oppression through a postcolonial lens.

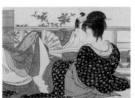

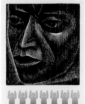

Portals

Portals help you make direct connections and encounter new works. The authors have selected Portals that create interesting comparisons or contrasts: each one shows a thumbnail image of a related artwork, along with a short explanation of its relevance to the current chapter. Each Portal artwork's page and figure number indicate its main position in the book, so you can turn to that chapter to see the work in full and find out more.

Glossary Terms in Margins

Terminology is defined in the margin of the spread on which the term first appears (which is also bold in the text), so you can build your artistic vocabulary as you read—without having to navigate to the complete glossary at the back of the book.

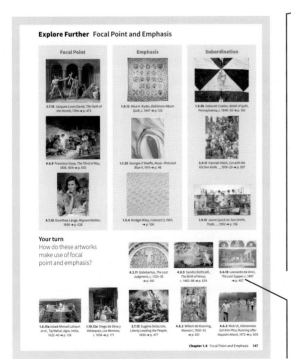

Explore Further

Explore Further pages conclude each chapter with a gallery of related images that make connections across chapters and themes.

Introduction

The Visual World

When we look at an artwork, we often assume that it was created entirely from the artist's own ideas and inspirations. But art is part of a wider **context** of things we experience, including the visual culture in which we live, which includes all of the images that we encounter in our lives. Think about how many images you saw on your way to class today. They may have included traffic signs, roadside billboards, and the logos of businesses. On campus, you may have seen posters informing you of an upcoming event, the logo of the coffee shop, informational signs about college policies, or maps directing you to where your class takes place. Online you are inundated with emojis, selfies, and ads for the latest games. Public art and street art provide even more examples of the fact that artworks can be found wherever we go, such as *Etnias*

(**0.0.1**), the largest public **mural** in the world at 30,000 sq. ft. It was created by the Brazilian mural artist Eduardo Kobra (b. 1975) for the 2016 Summer Olympics in Rio de Janeiro. The mural features colorful portraits of Indigenous people from five different continents, emphasizing the connection between humans around the world.

What Is Art?

The Japanese artist Katsushika Hokusai (1760–1849) is said to have created a painting titled *Maple Leaves on a River* by dipping the feet of a chicken in red paint and letting the bird run freely on a sheet of paper he had just covered in blue paint. Although we know that Hokusai was an unconventional character, this painting has not yet been found today, and we cannot be certain that the story is true. If we think about this curious anecdote for a while,

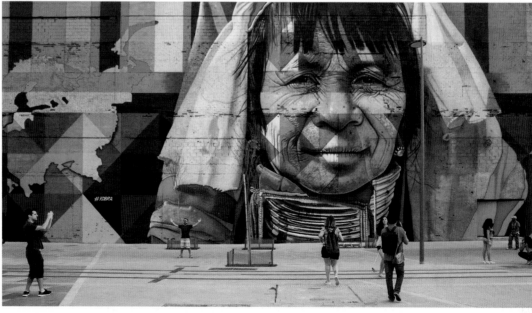

0.0.1 Eduardo Kobra, *Etnias*, 2016, Rio de Janeiro, Brazil

however, we can begin to understand the most basic question addressed in this book: What is art? This is not an easy question to answer, because people define art in many ways. In Hokusai's case, *Maple Leaves on a River* would have captured the peaceful sensations of a fall day by a river, without showing what an actual river and real leaves look like. In this instance, art primarily communicates a sensation.

Marcia Smilack's (b. 1949) striking image of water (**0.0.2**) is similar to Hokusai's lost painting in that it captures the essence of the movement of water. But Smilack used more than her sense of sight to create this work. She experiences life through **synesthesia**, the physical process whereby stimulation of one sense causes experiences in a different sense—such as visualizing color when hearing music. Smilack describes her experience:

> The way I taught myself photography is to shoot when I hear a chord of color...I hear with my eyes and see with my ears.

Of the photograph *Cello Music*, Smilack says:

> I walked by the water and heard cello...I couldn't resist the sound so I gave in and aimed my camera at what had elicited it. As soon as I let go of my thoughts, the texture of the water washed over me in synch with

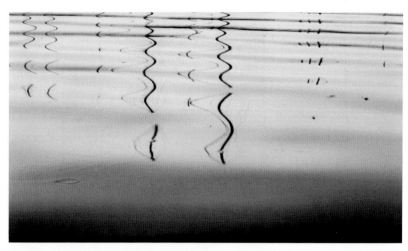

0.0.2 Marcia Smilack, *Cello Music*, 1992. Photograph, 12¾ × 24″. Collection of the artist

the sound and turned to satin on my skin. When I felt myself climb into the shadows between the folds, I snapped the shutter. I hear cello every time I look at it today, though I discovered that if I turn it upside down, it becomes violin.

Thomas Cole's (1801–1848) *View from Mount Holyoke, Massachusetts, after a Thunderstorm—The Oxbow* views the twisting Connecticut River from afar as it carves through the landscape (**0.0.3**). Cole was the founder of the Hudson River School, a group of **Romantic** American painters who painted landscapes to represent pride in the expansion of the developing

Synesthesia: when one of the five senses perceives something that was stimulated by a trigger from one of the other senses

Romantic, Romanticism: a movement in nineteenth-century European culture, concerned with the power of the imagination and greatly valuing intense feeling

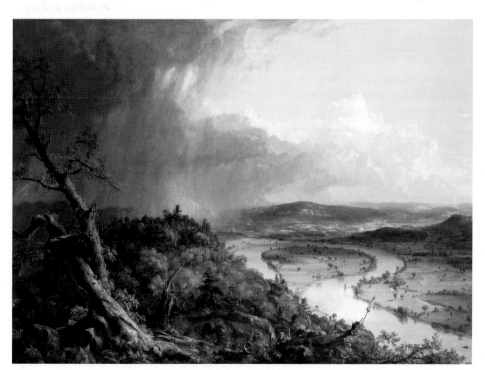

0.0.3 Thomas Cole, *View from Mount Holyoke, Massachusetts, after a Thunderstorm—The Oxbow*, 1836. Oil on canvas, 4′3½″ × 6′4″. Metropolitan Museum of Art, New York

Sublime: a feeling of awe or terror, provoked by the experience of limitless nature and the awareness of the smallness of an individual

Subject, subject matter: the person, object, or space depicted in a work of art

Style: a characteristic way in which an artist or group of artists uses visual language to give a work an identifiable form of visual expression

Conceptual art: a work in which the ideas are most important to the work

Ceramic: fire-hardened clay, often painted, and normally sealed with a shiny protective coating

Renaissance: a period of cultural and artistic change in Europe from the fourteenth to the seventeenth century

Calligraphy: the art of emotive or carefully descriptive hand lettering or handwriting

Middle Ages: the time period roughly between the fall of the Roman empire and the start of the Renaissance

Oil paint(ing): paint made of pigment suspended in oi

Classical: Greek art of the period *c.* 480–323 BCE

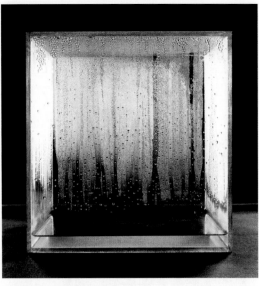

0.0.4 Hans Haacke, *Condensation Cube*, 1963–65. Clear acrylic, distilled water, and climate in area of display, 12 × 12 × 12″

American nation. These landscapes embody the idea of the **Sublime**, where the awe-inspiring power of nature overwhelms the smallness of humans. In this painting a tree in the foreground has been battered by weather, while the river is far below in the valley. Above are fierce thunderclouds, but in the distance we can see the sky after the storm has passed. The only trace of people in this scene is the artist, wearing a hat. We can just glimpse him, engulfed by the grandeur of the landscape, in the lower center of the canvas.

Rather than depicting a perception of water, like Smilack and Hokusai, or showing the dominance of water in the landscape, like Cole, Hans Haacke (b. 1936) analyzed the physical properties of water in his *Condensation Cube* (**0.0.4**). Both a work of art and a scientific experiment, Haacke's cube is a sealed plexiglass box filled with one centimeter of water. The way the artwork looks is dependent upon its surroundings, such as the temperature and moisture levels of the room. As these environmental aspects change, so does the degree of condensation on the cube. The box is a metaphor for the building in which it resides and the water within the box represents the art housed in the museum. In this sense, the artist is acknowledging the delicate engineering needed for museums to protect works of art from damp or from drying out.

If we go back to our original question, what is art?, can our consideration of these four very different works help us to find a quick and simple definition that will tell us whether we are looking at something called art? Although they have the same **subject matter**—water—these four works certainly do not have much in common in terms of their appearance, **style**, or even their materials. (The definition of art needs to include a range of materials: in fact, art can be made from almost anything.) Nor do these works share a common purpose. Cole's painting portrays a dramatic landscape but also carries a powerful message of nationalism. Smilack's work is a photograph that captures her sensations of water, whereas Hokusai captured more universal sensations of a riverside scene. In Haacke's sculpture, water becomes one of the materials used to make the work; his work is **conceptual** in nature.

What these works do have in common is the fact that they all communicate an idea by visual means that can help us see the world in new and exciting ways and strengthen our understanding. In other words, art is a form of language.

Fine Art, Craft, and the Commercial Arts

There is no simple definition that allows us to tell who is an artist and who is not. If we take a global view, we certainly cannot define artists by what they made. The terms we choose to label things, such as fine or high art, often tell us more about our own attitudes and stereotypes than about the object under consideration. But while such labels can be misused, they can nonetheless reflect cultural judgments and sometimes lead to ways of identifying, categorizing, and understanding art.

The term craft typically includes furniture, textile-making, **ceramics**, and other objects that require great manual skill to make. Fine art usually refers to a work of art (traditionally a painting, drawing, carved sculpture, and sometimes a print) that is pleasing or beautiful to look at and was believed, incorrectly, to be made through more intellectual effort than the manual labor of craftspeople. Therefore, those things became status symbols of the rich and powerful. The value placed on art objects has also shifted over time, and differs around the world. In Europe during certain eras of history, particularly the **Renaissance**, painting and sculpture were considered to be the most important categories of art (high art), while others, such as ceramics and furniture, were once considered less important. This distinction arose partly because artworks were often valued based on the cost of the materials used (such as precious stones or metals), and according to the amount of skilled labor needed to make them. In other cultures, the relative importance of various forms of art was quite different. The people of ancient Peru, for example, placed special value on wool, and the artists who made fine woolen textiles were likely considered as skillful as a painter would have been in the Renaissance. In China the art of **calligraphy** (elegantly painted lettering, and painting with ink using similar brushstrokes) was considered one of the highest forms of art. Some famous calligraphy painters found in this book include Ma Yuan and Wang Meng.

The art of quilting, going back to at least the **Middle Ages**, has been practiced throughout Europe, Asia, and the Americas. While quilts were treasured for their complexity and the skill used to make them, traditionally quiltmaking has been considered a craft because of the textiles used, the fact that they are made by hand, and the fact that quilts were most often made by women—an example of how, in the past, women were offered limited opportunities to make a living through their artistic talents. By mid-nineteenth-century America, most quilts were made in a block style. The *Bible Quilt* (**0.0.5**) was made by Harriet Powers (1837–1910), an enslaved person born in Georgia. She lived to see the abolition of enslavement in the US in 1865, and sold her quilts to help support her nine (or more) children. The eleven panels of the quilt illustrate biblical stories and figures such as Adam and Eve with the serpent (upper left), Satan and seven stars (upper right), and the crucifixion (lower left).

A typical example of the nineteenth-century European category of fine art is *Flaming June* (**0.0.6**) by Sir Frederic Lord Leighton (1830–1896). Leighton studied and traveled throughout Europe and became a member of the Royal Art Academy in London. The luscious beauty of the painting highlights his skill with **oil paint** and the woman's pose alludes to Greek **Classical** sculpture and the work of the Renaissance master Michelangelo, both of whom were greatly admired by those who were wealthy enough to purchase fine art, and who mistakenly believed that only the wealthy were capable of appreciating it. While today the painting is one of the most famous pieces

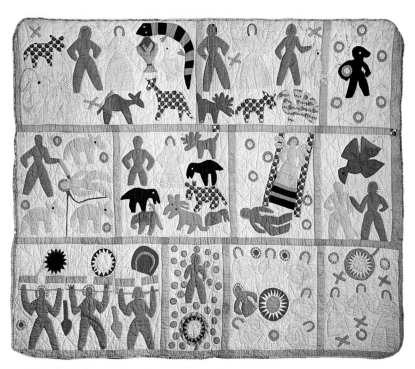

0.0.5 Harriet Powers, *Bible Quilt*, 1885–86. Cotton, 75 × 89".
National Museum of American History, Smithsonian Institution, Washington, D.C.

of Victorian art in the world, when it was first rediscovered in a shop in the 1960s, it was not initially regarded as valuable until it was acquired by a museum in Puerto Rico.

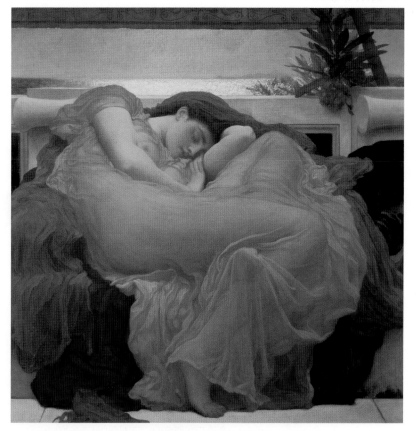

0.0.6 Frederic Lord Leighton, *Flaming June*, 1895. Oil on canvas, 47½ × 47½".
Museo de Arte de Ponce, Ponce, Puerto Rico

Historically, the graphic arts (those made by a method that enables reproduction of many copies of the same image) were also considered less important, and perhaps less accomplished, than the fine arts. While Leighton's painting is unique, made with an exclusive group of powerful, upper-class viewers in mind, works of graphic art are made to be available to many people and are in that sense potentially much more democratic, which is considered an advantage by many artists and viewers. Graphic art includes a wide range of **media**: books, magazines, posters, advertising, signage, television, computer screens, and social media.

Graphic design is a commercial art, the essence of which is communication. For example, consider the apparent simplicity of a **logo** created in 1994 to identify the global brand of the logistics company FedEx (**0.0.7**). The designer of the logo, Lindon Leader, discovered that the company's name at the time, Federal Express, gave customers the impression that it operated only in the United States, rather than internationally. In addition, everybody simply called the company FedEx. Leader's task was to design a logo that could be used on package labels, advertisements, trucks, and planes to identify FedEx as a dynamic, global organization. The solution was a design that retained the colors (slightly modified) of the existing logo, but shortened the company name to FedEx. The type was arranged so that the white space between the E and x formed a white arrow that suggested speed and precision.

The design seems very simple, but we should be careful not to assume that it required less skill and effort than a painting. Leader and his colleagues held focus groups to research the public's impressions of the company and developed about 200 concepts before they settled on their chosen design. Then they made protoypes of planes, vans, and trucks to test it. Leader's logo has won more than forty design awards.

Where Is Art?

You almost certainly have some art in your home: perhaps a painting in the living room, a poster in your bedroom, or a beautifully made flower vase; and there are sculptures and memorials in parks or other public spaces in most cities. You have probably also figured out that art can be found in many places: in the form of a **tapestry**, as a corporate logo, in a book, and, of course, in an art museum.

Our word "museum" comes from the ancient Greek *mouseion*, meaning a temple dedicated to the arts and sciences. The mouseion of Alexandria in Egypt, founded about 2,400 years ago, collected and preserved important objects—still a key function of museums today. Many great art museums

FedEx ® Express

0.0.7 Federal Express logo

Medium (plural **media**): the material on or from which an artist chooses to make a work of art

Graphic design: the use of images, typography, and technology to communicate ideas for a client or to a particular audience

Logo: a unique graphic image used to identify an idea or entity

Tapestry: hand-woven fabric—usually silk or wool—with a non-repeating, usually figurative, design woven into it

0.0.8 Louvre Museum, Paris, France. Glass pyramid designed by Ieoh Ming Pei, 1998

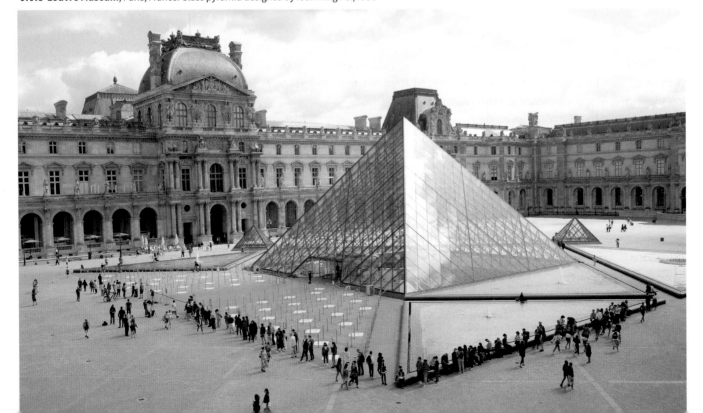

began as private collections. For example, the famous Louvre Museum in Paris, France, was originally a fortress and then a royal palace where the king kept his personal art collection. After the French Revolution (1789–99), the king's collection was opened to the public in the Louvre (see **0.0.8**).

Some of the collections in museums were purchased or looted during times of war. For example, some works in the Louvre were acquired during the Napoleonic Wars of the early nineteenth century. Today, museums are frequently asked to repatriate—or return—works of art that were taken during times of societal upheaval or war. The Greeks have asked for the marble sculptures that were once atop the Parthenon to be returned. These marbles are in museums around the world, but the majority are in the British Museum and the Louvre. The Benin bronzes (a collection of more than 1,000 plaques and sculptures that once adorned the palace of the Kingdom of Benin) are gradually being returned by museums in Germany, France, and England, and a new museum is being built in Benin City, Nigeria to house the sculptures (see p. 609). Museums are also being held responsible for artworks taken from Jews during the Second World War, even if the museum was not aware of that history when it originally acquired the work (see **0.0.14**).

Since the twentieth century, the architecture of museums continues to be as much a reason to visit as the collections held within. In Paris, a 71-foot-tall glass-and-metal pyramid (designed by the Chinese-American architect Ieoh Ming Pei), was constructed in 1988 in the main courtyard of the Louvre Palace, and now serves as the museum's main entrance (**0.0.8**). The pyramid and its underground lobby were designed to handle the increasing number of museum visitors. However, its modern architecture attracted some criticism in France, due to its sharp contrast with the Louvre Palace's French Renaissance style. In China, the Ordos Museum, designed by Ma Yansong, is made in the shape of **abstract**, **organic forms** inspired by the sand dunes of the Gobi desert.

Most art museums hold permanent collections of artworks that are regularly displayed, although some can show only a portion of the works in their large collections. Museums also organize **exhibitions** of works on loan from other institutions. They often have **conservation** departments to care for

and restore the artworks. In recent years, and propelled even more by the global COVID-19 pandemic, museums have found ways to reach the public through websites, online tours and activities, and socially interactive projects. Although nothing can replace seeing a work of art in person, museums understand that one of their primary responsibilities is to teach the public about art, even if in some circumstances that can occur only remotely.

Many artworks were made to be used, rather than displayed where they cannot be touched. For example, quilts (such as Harriet Powers's, **0.0.5**) have often been used as a cover for a bed, and in **Medieval** Europe, tapestries were hung on walls to keep a room warmer. Beautifully and thoughtfully crafted tea bowls were to be used as part of a Japanese tea ceremony, involving other fine objects, good conversation, and, of course, excellent tea. The tea bowl was valued because it formed part of a ritual that had social and spiritual significance, and was designed to be appreciated slowly as the user sipped tea. This bowl, made during the Edo period by Hon'ami Koetsu (**0.0.9**), would have been prized for its subtle variations of color, the pleasant tactile sensations of its slightly irregular surface, and its shape. Japanese artists followed with supreme skill the established methods of working and making.

Similarly, African artists made masks that originally formed part of costumes that were used in a ceremonial performance involving other costumed figures, music, and dancing. In other words, masks often had spiritual significance for their creators and performers, but they would have regarded them as holding this value only when used as intended, not when displayed in isolation in a museum.

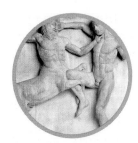

About one-third of the Parthenon's marble sculptures were taken by Lord Elgin between 1801 and 1805 and are now in the British Museum, London:
→ see **3.1.25**, p. 364

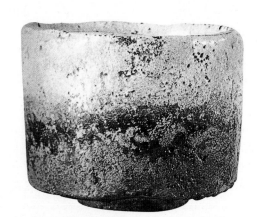

0.0.9 Hon'ami Koetsu, Tea bowl (called Mount Fuji), Edo period, early 17th century. Raku ware, height 3⅜". Sakai Collection, Tokyo, Japan

Abstract: an artwork the form of which is simplified, distorted, or exaggerated in appearance.

Organic: having irregular forms and shapes, as though derived from living organisms

Form: an object that can be defined in three dimensions (height, width, and depth)

Exhibition: the display of art objects, often only for a limited time

Conservation: scientific efforts to preserve artworks

Medieval: relating to the Middle Ages; in Europe, roughly, between the fall of the Roman empire and the start of the Renaissance

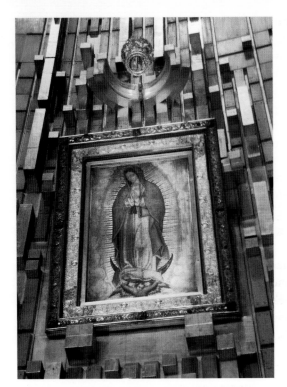

0.0.10 *The Virgin of Guadalupe*, 1531. Tempera on linen. Basilica of St. Mary of Guadalupe, Mexico City, Mexico

If we consider only works that are displayed in museums and galleries, we ignore many works that are placed in communal or religious spaces. Street art, such as Kobra's *Etnias* (**0.0.1**), is an example of communal art that is in a public space where people can interact with it on a daily basis. One of the most enduring examples of a religious work is the painting of the Virgin of Guadalupe (**0.0.10**). According to Catholic tradition, in December 1531 the Virgin Mary appeared several times to a local Indigenous man, Juan Diego, with the first appearance occurring on Tepeyac Hill (in present-day Mexico City). The Virgin was believed miraculously to have imprinted her own image on his cloak made of cactus fiber. (Historical evidence, however, suggests that the Virgin was painted in **tempera** on linen.) The Virgin became the symbol of the Mexican nation, not just for Mexicans of Indigenous descent but also for all citizens of the country— and not only for devout Catholics. Today, the original painting of the Virgin is housed in the National Basilica of St. Mary of Guadalupe at the base of Tepeyac Hill, which receives hundreds of thousands of pilgrims annually.

Art and Creativity

Consider the role of creativity in our own lives: making images is an ever-present activity in our world. We make our own photos and videos, and share them through social-networking services or using our cell phones. These activities, so common now, show how people naturally respond to images and seek to express themselves visually. In other words, most of us instinctively relate to human creativity. An essential reason we value art is because it has the power to tell us something important about ourselves. Art is an effective means of self-expression because it enables us to give physical shape or form to thoughts and sensations and to see them for what they are.

The seventeenth-century Dutch painter Judith Leyster (1609–1660) expressed her creativity through the way she presented herself as an artist. In her self-**portrait** (**0.0.11**) Leyster revels in what she does, thoroughly enjoying the act of painting and raising her tool (the paintbrush) as if to echo the joy of the violin player on the canvas beside her. Leyster painted this self-portrait while applying to become a master at the Saint Luke's Guild of Haarlem, which was rare for a woman at the time. She portrays herself in a lace-trimmed collar and dress that seem designed to impress, despite the fact that they would have been impractical

Tempera: a fast-drying painting medium made from pigment mixed with water-soluble binder, such as egg yolk

Portrait: image of a person or animal, usually focusing on the face

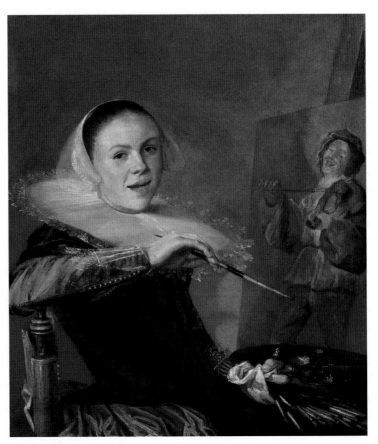

0.0.11 Judith Leyster, *Self-Portrait*, *c.* 1630. National Gallery of Art, Washington, D.C.

clothing for a painter's studio. Her expression and pose are confident and relaxed, perhaps conveying a sense of pride in her identity and success as a female painter. Until the twentieth century, male painters far outnumbered their female counterparts. In addition, historians frequently attributed to men works that were in fact made by women. Leyster's paintings were often thought to have been made by either her husband or Frans Hals, until 1893, when the Louvre Museum found Leyster's monogram signature hidden underneath a false Hals signature. Since then, several more paintings have been reattributed as works by Leyster.

Who Makes Art?

Who decides what an artwork looks like? The simple answer might seem to be the artist who makes it. But in many cases, works were not created by just one person. We know that art has been made for thousands of years: at least since humans first painted images on the walls of caves, and probably long before then. Ancient artworks were often communal efforts in which spirituality and notions of the cycle of life were common themes. As time progressed, artists have addressed social issues (war and social conscience) and created more individual expressions of their identity (gender and race).

The great temples in Egypt, Mexico, and Southeast Asia were certainly not made single-handedly, and in some cases, we cannot tell if their overall design was the idea of a lone individual. **Archaeologists** have discovered near the Valley of the Kings in Egypt an entire village, Deir el-Medina, which was occupied by artisans who made the tombs that we admire today. The temples Angkor Wat and Templo Mayor, or the cathedrals of medieval Europe, were the result of the skills of many different artists and artisans: stone carvers, the makers of **stained-glass** windows, and carpenters who made the furniture. These skilled workers remain mostly anonymous, except for a very few whose names have been found in **manuscripts** or carved on works of art. But though we may never identify these early artists, it is clear that humans have always wanted to create art. This urge is part of our nature, just like our need to eat and sleep.

The idea, popular in much of today's society, of individuals creating their own art to express something very personal, was first explored during the Renaissance due to artists' efforts to elevate their profession as a liberal art.

For example, the Italian Renaissance artist Leonardo da Vinci (1452–1519) became famous in an era that not only prized tradition, but also highlighted individual achievement and ingenuity. He was a supremely talented artist whose visionary interests and inventions extended far beyond the visual arts, to engineering and science. Between 1503 and 1506 he created a portrait that is now probably the most famous painting in the world, although in his own time the work was virtually unknown because it was not commissioned by an important **patron**. Leonardo was not content simply to create a likeness of the subject (Lisa Gherardini, wife of a silk merchant in Florence). The *Mona Lisa* smiles and looks out at the viewer, inviting us to seek in her face, her pose, and the surrounding landscape a meditation on the human soul (**0.0.12**).

In the nineteenth and twentieth centuries it became more common for artists to determine individually the appearance and **content** of their own work, and, in their search for new forms of self-expression, to make art that was often very controversial. This remains true today. But for many centuries before this, very few artists worked alone. Even Renaissance

Stained glass: colored glass used for windows or decorative applications

Manuscripts: handwritten texts

Patron: an organization or individual who sponsors the creation of works of art

Content: the meaning, message, or feeling expressed in a work of art

Archaeology: the study of human history and prehistory by excavating sites of habitation to analyze artifacts and other cultural remains

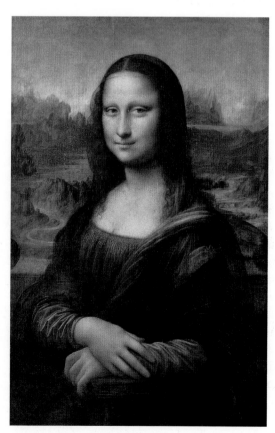

0.0.12 Leonardo da Vinci, *Mona Lisa, c.* 1503–6. Oil on wood, 30⅜ × 20⅞". Musée du Louvre, Paris, France

artists who promoted the idea of creative genius operated workshops staffed by artist assistants who carried out most of the effort involved in turning their master's design into a work of art. In nineteenth-century Japan, the eccentric Katsushika Hokusai was famous around the world for his prints, but he could not have made them alone. A wood carver cut Hokusai's designs into blocks from which a printer manufactured copies. Today, many artists employ a workshop of assistants to help them.

As early as the tenth century in Africa, Asia, and Europe, art objects were frequently made by monks, nuns, or other religious figures. Such objects were believed to be spiritual in nature, and so it makes sense that those people who were believed to have a closer connection to their culture's god would be the makers of these works. Training was passed down from a skilled expert to their students. Later, the rise of the merchant class led to the development of workshops—called **guilds** in Europe—for specializing in art-making skills, such as guilds of painters, glassmakers, and goldsmiths. The system in Europe changed in the sixteenth century. Schools called **academies** were organized (first in Italy) to train artists in a very strict curriculum devised by specialized teachers. In modern Europe and North America, most practicing artists are trained in art schools, often part of a university or college that teaches many subjects. The training of artists also helps to determine who makes art and what is shown in galleries and museums. It would be a mistake, however, to assume that artists must be formally trained: non-professional, self-taught artists (sometimes referred to as "naïve" or "outsider" artists) produce art that is just as admired. Indeed, the Dutch painter Vincent van Gogh (1853–1890) was principally self-taught and received little **formal** art training. In his ten years as an active artist, Van Gogh produced about 1,000 drawings, sketches, and watercolors, as well as around 1,250 other paintings. Very few people saw his work in his lifetime, however; he received only one favorable notice in a newspaper; his work was shown in only one exhibition; and he sold only one painting. Yet today his work is extraordinarily famous, it sells for millions of dollars, and in his native Netherlands an entire museum is devoted to his work.

We must also consider that artworks are not only the result of the work of those who made them, but are also often influenced by the input of others: patrons who employ an artist to make an artwork; a company that commissions a work of graphic design; the collectors who buy an artwork and the dealers and gallery owners who sell it; or the needs of customers who buy crafted pieces to be used in the home. In contemporary times, both the publicist who presents artworks and the critic who reviews them help to make an artist's work well known and desirable. All of these people, not just the artist, help to determine what art we see, and to some extent they can influence what we consider to be art. By controlling access to those who buy art, the places where art is displayed, what artistic content is selected to be shown, and the media that inform the public about art and artists, they also often influence what kind of art an artist actually produces.

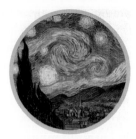

Although he is one of the best-known artists today, Vincent van Gogh was not famous during his lifetime: → see **3.8.19**, p. 495

The Value of Art

In our contemporary society, art is often valued by its sale price, but there are many

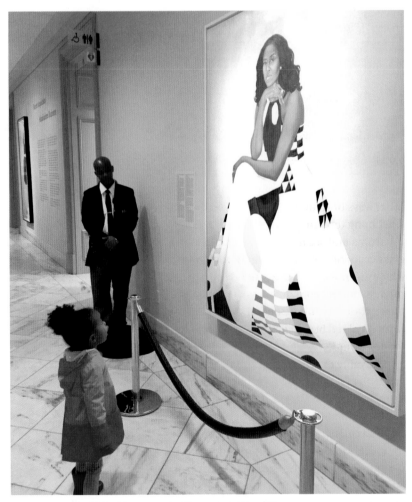

0.0.13 **Photograph of Parker Curry looking at Amy Sherald's** *Portrait of Michelle Obama*, 2018.

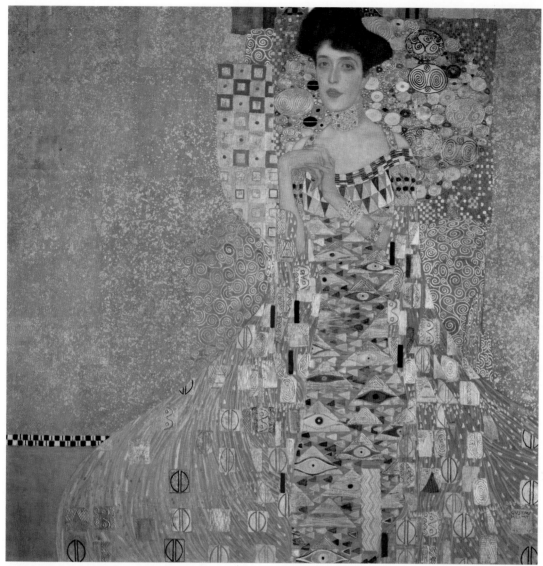

0.0.14 Gustav Klimt, *Portrait of Adele Bloch-Bauer I*, 1907. Oil and gold leaf on canvas, 54⅜ × 54⅜". Neue Galerie, New York

other ways of valuing it (see Perspectives on Art: Loongkoonan, p. 26). When we visit art museums and see artworks displayed inside glass cases or at a distance from the viewer, who must not touch, the care taken to preserve them in perfect condition is an indication that these works are highly valued. Sometimes a work is valued because it is very old or rare, or indeed unique.

The value of art can be found in the personal way it can move people. Two-year-old Parker Curry was photographed by a stranger as she admired Amy Sherald's (b. 1973) *Portrait of Michelle Obama* (**0.0.13**), staring at the painting for much longer than one might expect from someone so young. The image spread quickly online as it demonstrated the importance of having the first African American presidential family in the White House. This young girl had

not seen many images of people who looked like her as she wandered through the museum. The photograph became its own work of art, as people watching the girl enthralled by the painted portrait imagined her mind opening up to the possibilities of what she herself could become.

The value of Gustav Klimt's (1862–1918) *Portrait of Adele Bloch-Bauer I* (**0.0.14**) derives not only from the beauty of the work, but also from its legacy of ownership. The dramatic portrait portrays a wealthy Jewish patron of the arts in Vienna, Austria. Bloch-Bauer (1881–1926) stated in her will that she would like the paintings by Klimt that she and her husband owned to go to the Galerie Belvedere for the people of Vienna to enjoy. Her husband Ferdinand (1864–1946), however, willed his entire estate to his family members. Ferdinand

Guilds: medieval European associations of artists, craftspeople, or tradespeople

Academies: institutions training artists in both the theory of art and practical techniques

Formal: in art, refers to the visual elements and principles in a work

Perspectives on Art: Loongkoonan
The Value of Art to Keep Alive Knowledge and Culture

Loongkoonan (c. 1910–2018) was a Nyikina elder and artist from Western Australia who started painting in her nineties, depicting with complexity and beauty the land she lives in. Her paintings *won several prestigious awards in Australia, and exhibitions of her work were shown as far away as the United States. The nonagenarian (90–99-year-old) wrote these words explaining her art.*

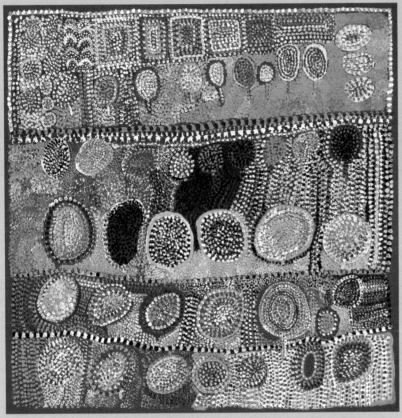

0.0.15 Loongkoonan, *Bush Tucker Nyikina Country*, 2006. Acrylic on canvas, 35⅛ × 35⅛". Collection of Diane and Dan Mossenson, Perth, Western Australia

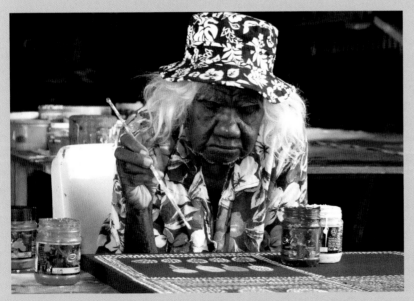

0.0.16 Loongkoonan at work in her studio in Derby, Western Australia, 2007

I am Loongkoonan and I am an elder of the Nyikina people. I am a proper Nyikina, one of the Yimadoowarra or riverside people. I am only Nyikina, not mixed up with anything else. My grandfather was proper Nyikina too. He died at Udialla. I was born at Mount Anderson Station near the Fitzroy River. When I was born, no one worried much about recording the births and deaths of Indigenous people, or teaching us to read or write. Research by my niece Margaret suggests that I am aged in my late nineties, but I am still very lively.

My parents worked on stations, and I was a good-sized girl when I started work mustering *kookanja* [sheep] and cooking in stock camps. Later on, I rode horses and mustered cattle too. Wet season was our holiday time for footwalking Nyikina Country with my grandparents….I have been a busy person all my life, no drinking, no smoking, just bush medicine….I had a good life on the stations, and three husbands.

Footwalking is the only proper way to learn about the Country, and remember it. That is how I got to know all of the bush tucker [wild food] and medicine. Nowadays I show young people how to live off the Country, and how to gather spinifex wax, which is our traditional glue for fixing stone points to spear shafts, patching *coolamons* [shallow vessels with curved sides], and making all kinds of things. Nyikina spinifex wax is really strong. It was so well known in the olden days that it was traded all over the Kimberley and desert….I still enjoy footwalking my country, showing the young people how to chase *barni* [goannas] and how to catch fish.

I was always used to working hard, and the chance came up for me to start painting with my friends, so I thought that I would give it a try….In my paintings I show all types of bush tucker—good tucker that we lived off in the bush….I paint Nyikina Country the same way eagles see Country when they are high up in the sky. I paint the bush foods and fruits and rivers of Nyikina Country.

I am happy that people like my paintings and that they get to understand more about Nyinkina Country and my life. I am happy to be an example for my community and people.

outlived Adele but had to flee the city, leaving his art collection behind, when Vienna was annexed by the Nazis. After the war, many paintings looted from Vienna by the Nazis were returned to the Galerie Belvedere, including this portrait of Adele.

It was not until later in the twentieth century that museums in Europe and America began to research whether works in their own collections had originally been stolen by Nazis from Jewish families. Because many works of art in museums are purchased through dealers or donated, their history of ownership, or **provenance**, is not always recorded or easily found. In 1998, The Austrian government stated in the Art Restitution Act that all museums must return any works confiscated from Jews during World War II to their descendants. Maria Altmann (1916–2011), niece of Adele and Ferdinand, contacted the Galerie Belvedere, but the institution argued that Adele Bloch-Bauer had originally wanted the paintings to go to the museum. Altmann sued the Austrian government and, in 2006, was awarded this and four other Klimt paintings that had been owned by her family. The painting has since become a symbol of pride for the people of Vienna, and many Viennese hoped Altmann would still allow the painting to remain in the city, but Adele's niece instead sold the work for $135 million. Today it is owned by the Neue Galerie in New York, available for the public to see.

The monetary value given to a work of art fluctuates and can depend on current trends, name recognition of the artist, and whether any intriguing context can be associated with the work, as was the case with the *Portrait of Adele Bloch-Bauer I*. The commercialism of the **art market**, where only the wealthy have access to art, has been criticized by the anonymous artist known as Banksy, who paints stencils in public places. When a printed stencil of one of his best-known subjects—a young girl holding a red balloon—was sold for $1.4 million at an **auction** at Sotheby's in October of 2018, the artwork began to self-destruct (**0.0.17**). Banksy had hidden a shredder in the frame and when the hammer went down to finalize the sale of his work, the artwork fell through the shredder. While the audience was at first shocked, the event became an acknowledged work of performance art and the buyer kept the shredded artwork, the value of which has doubled. Today, artists are able to assert more

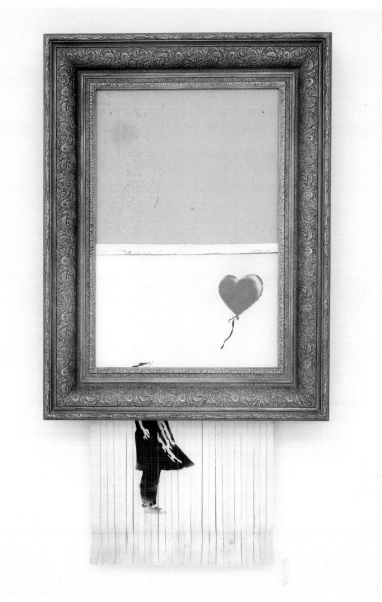

0.0.17 Banksy, *Love Is in the Bin*, 2018. Aerosol paint, acrylic paint, canvas, board, 40 × 31 × 7″. Originally titled *Girl with Balloon*, 2006, shredded October 5, 2018 at a live Sotheby's auction in London, England

financial control over their digital artworks through certification: buyers purchase a cryptographic token, called the non-fungible token (NFT), of a digital work of art. Owning an NFT is proof that you have purchased an original, non-reproducible image. NFTs therefore function in a similar way to a limited **edition** of prints, by artificially limiting the number of copies of an artwork that exist.

Power and the Social Role of Art

Art has the power to reflect societal issues and can, as in the case of the mural of George Floyd (**0.0.18**, p. 28), become a touchpoint for protest and mourning. The mural was painted by a group of artists, Xena Goldman, Cadex Herrera,

Provenance: The history of ownership of a work

Art market: the economic space in which artworks are bought and sold

Auction: an event in which artworks are sold to the highest bidder

Edition: all the copies of a print made from a single printing

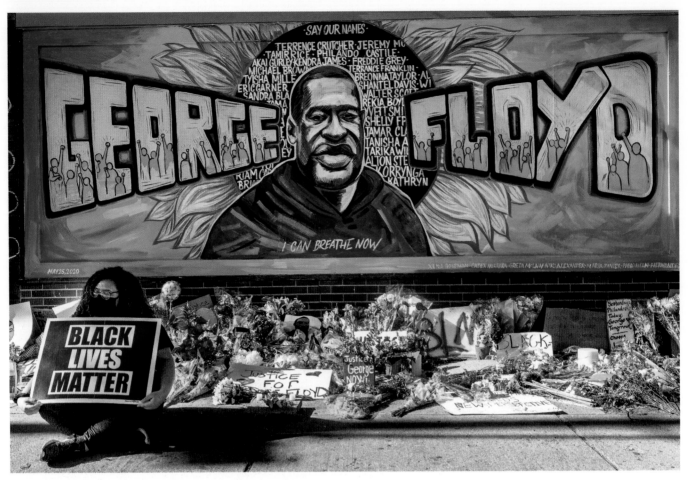

0.0.18 Xena Goldman, Cadex Herrera, and Greta McLain, with Niko Alexander and Pablo Hernandez, *George Floyd*, 2020. Mural, 20 × 6.5 ft. Minneapolis, Minnesota

and Greta McLain, at the site of the murder of George Floyd, who in 2020 suffocated when a Minneapolis police officer deliberately kneeled on his neck for over nine minutes. George Floyd is depicted in the center with the words, "I can breathe now," written on his chest, recalling the words he spoke as he was dying, "I can't breathe!" Surrounding him, written in white on a black backdrop, are the names of other African American victims of police violence, inscribed under the words, "Say our names." In the letters of Floyd's name are figures pumping their fists into the air, signifying the Black Lives Matter movement (founded in 2013).

The site has functioned as a memorial, as a backdrop for news stories about Floyd's murder, and as a hub for protests. The mural is recognizable worldwide and has taken on the power of being a rallying cry to fight racial injustice. Along with the video showing Floyd's suffocation, the mural has urged society never to forget what happened. In June 2021, former police officer Derek Chauvin was convicted for Floyd's murder and sentenced to twenty-two-and-a-half years in prison, and other officers are expected to go on trial in 2022.

As we see from this mural, art can be a powerful form of expression that inspires discussion and even instigates social change. Artists frequently make statements through their art, highlighting issues in society or making calls for activism. Keith Haring (1958–

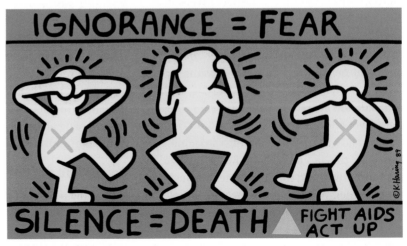

0.0.19 Keith Haring, *Ignorance = Fear*, 1989. Poster, 24 × 43 ¼". Keith Haring Foundation

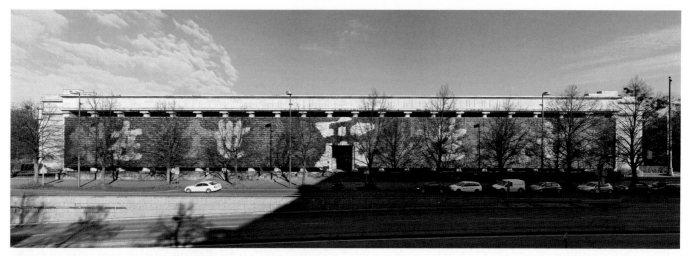

0.0.20a **Ai Weiwei**, *Remembering*, 2009. Backpacks and metal armature, 30'4" × 347'11" × 4". Haus der Kunst, Munich, Germany

1990), whose fame arose from drawings he made in and around New York City subways, protested many social injustices. Haring defended the rights of LGBTQ+ people and in *Ignorance = Fear* (**0.0.19**) was fighting for government and community support to fight HIV, the virus that can lead to AIDS. By the end of 1990, the United States had over 100,000 AIDS cases, but many saw the disease as a form of divine punishment that targeted only homosexuals or drug addicts. Haring's poster highlights how the public need to educate themselves on how the disease spreads and speak out against homophobia. Haring died one year later of AIDS-related complications. The Keith Haring Foundation continues his work to prevent the spread of HIV/AIDS, fight stigma toward LGBTQ+ people, and enrich the lives of underprivileged children through art.

Probably the most famous contemporary living artist who has suffered for his work and his opinions is the Chinese artist Ai Weiwei (b. 1957). Ai's father was a revered poet and a member of the ruling Communist Party, and Ai was involved in the design of the stadium for the Beijing Olympics in 2008. He was therefore in some ways an establishment figure in China. But 2008 was also the year of a devastating earthquake in southwestern China, which killed at least 69,000 people and left 4.8 million homeless. Several schools collapsed due to poor construction, which the government tried to hide. Ai visited the sites, met with the parents, wrote a blog criticizing the government, and posted the names of the 5,385 children who died. In 2009, Ai made a memorial out of 9,000 brightly-colored backpacks, exhibited

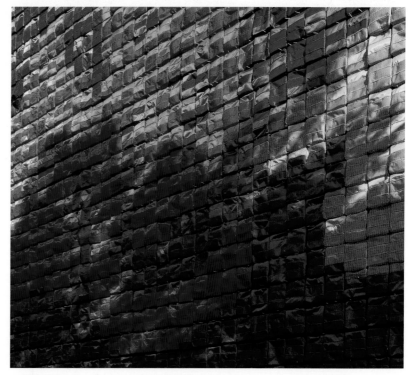

0.0.20b **Ai Weiwei**, *Remembering* **(detail),** 2009. Backpacks and metal armature, 30'4" × 347'11" × 4". Haus der Kunst, Munich, Germany

in Münich, Germany (**0.0.20a** and **0.0.20b**). The packs are arranged to spell out, "She lived happily for seven years in this world"—a quote from a letter from a mourning mother. Later in 2009, Ai was beaten severely by the police, receiving injuries that required emergency brain surgery. In January 2011 Chinese government officials ordered the demolition of his studio and in April he was arrested for "economic crimes." After serving 81 days in prison, he was not allowed to leave the country until 2015. He currently resides in England; his work is banned from being shown in China.

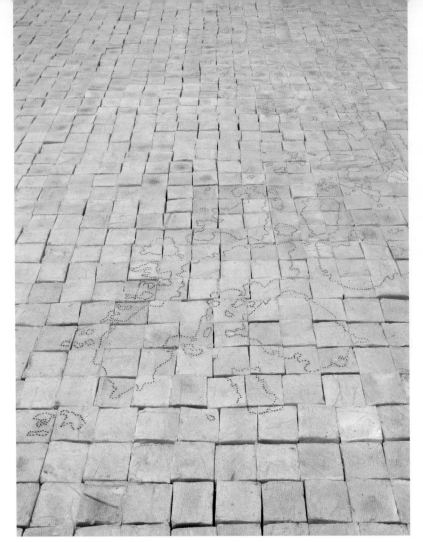

0.0.21 Mona Hatoum, *Present Tense*, 1996 (detail). Installation photo, Mona Hatoum exhibition, Room 5, Tate Modern, London, UK, 4 May–21 August, 2016

Grid: a network of horizontal lines; in an artwork's composition, the lines are implied

Interpretation: explaining the meaning of an artwork

Formal analysis: a visual study that includes careful description of the artwork and its use of elements and principles

Representational: art that depicts figures and objects so that we recognize what is represented

Non-objective: art that does not depict a recognizable subject

Abstraction: the degree to which an image is altered from an easily recognizable subject

The British-Palestinian artist Mona Hatoum (b. 1952) addresses current social issues in many of her works. In *Present Tense* (1996, **0.0.21**), she has used 2,200 blocks of pure olive-oil soap to create a large **grid**, on the surface of which she has pressed red glass beads to re-create the lines of the territories meant to be given to the Palestinians under the Oslo Accords of 1993. The territories are disjointed, with many not connected to the whole, which highlights the way Palestinians have often felt as if they were separated from one another. This soap has been made in the city of Nablus since the tenth century and is integral to Palestinian economic and social culture. The use of this material shows the strength of the Palestinian people. The fact that soap dissolves easily in water was meant to give a temporary status to the borders shown. The title of the work references its complexity and creativity: "Present" can refer to both the stating of information and to the current moment in time. "Tense" can also refer

to time (such as past or future tense) as well as the degree of anxiety in a situation.

Studying Art

Why take a course that teaches you how to look at art? Surely we all see the same thing when we look at a work of art, so we can decide what we like or dislike about it? In fact, it is not quite that simple. Our **interpretations** of works of art may differ from other people's, according to our perceptions, beliefs, and ideas. Art is also a form of language, one that can communicate with us even more powerfully than written language. Art communicates so directly with our senses (of sight, touch, even smell and sound) that it helps us to understand our own experiences. By learning to look more closely, we experience new sensations and ideas that expand our horizons beyond our daily lives.

Art, as we have already seen, is a form of communication using visual language. All communication has a purpose, a message—in other words, content. In art, content is rarely just about subject matter, but instead also concerns underlying meanings expressed in the way the subject is shown. To understand the content of a work of art, one must first identify its subject, consider the context in which the artwork was made, and then perform a **formal analysis** (study the work's arrangement of the visual elements and principles.)

Subject Matter

The subject matter of a work offers preliminary information about its content. As we have seen, although the four works of art at the beginning of this chapter all had water as their subject, the content and purpose of each work was different. Of course, there are many artworks in which the subject matter itself is not clear, and many have no title (indeed, there are artworks that the artist specifically designates as "Untitled")—but such artworks still possess content. This point will be clearer if we understand the concepts of **representation**, **non-objectivity**, and **abstraction**. Works of art may be representational (depicting objects or people so that we can recognize them), or non-objective (depicting subject matter that is unrecognizable). Most, however, lie somewhere in between, depending on their degree of abstraction. These concepts help us to analyze what the artist had in mind or wished to communicate to us when creating the work.

For example, Michelangelo's sculpture (**0.0.22**) is representational because everyone looking at it would agree that it shows a heavily draped woman holding a man in her lap. Even if one does not recognize that these are Christian figures and that the woman is shown in the form of a *pietà* (the moment when the Virgin Mary is mourning the death of her son Jesus), we can all agree that we recognize the human forms. Representational artworks are also called objective, meaning that everyone agrees on the subject matter.

Non-objective works of art are deliberately not recognizable as something we might be able to identify in the world around us. Eva Hesse's (1936–1970) *Untitled (Rope Piece)* (**0.0.23**) is an example of non-objective art. The materials used to make the artwork, especially the rope, may be identifiable, but the subject matter is not. Non-objective art is, by definition, subjective: without contextual information about the artist's intentions or experiences, we each determine our own interpretations of what the artwork means or communicates—or whether it means anything at all.

The concepts of representational and non-objective may be thought of as two

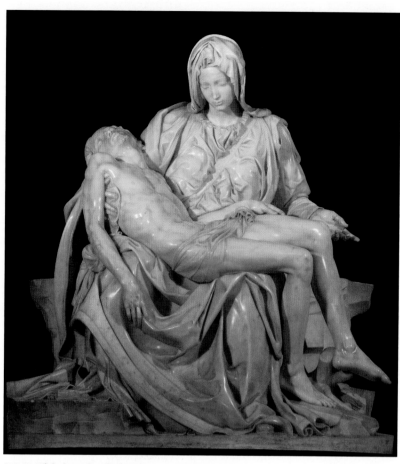

0.0.22 **Michelangelo**, *Pietà*, 1498–99. Carrara marble, 68½ × 76¾". St. Peter's Basilica, Vatican City, Rome, Italy

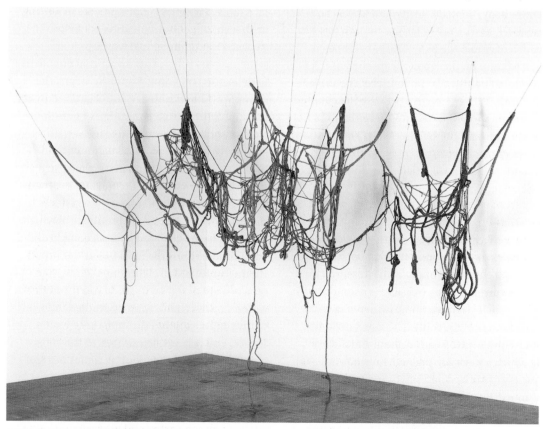

0.0.23 **Eva Hesse**, *Untitled (Rope Piece)*, 1969–70. Latex, rope, string, and wire, dimensions variable. Whitney Museum of American Art, New York

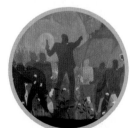

Aaron Douglas's painting *Aspects of Negro Life...* is representational, but also involves a considerable degree of abstraction:
→ see **3.9.24**, p. 514

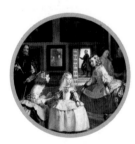

endpoints in a continuum of abstraction. "To abstract" means to extract something or to emphasize it. Abstraction in art refers to the ways artists can emphasize, distort, simplify, or arrange the formal (visual) elements of an artwork. A representational work, such as *Reverie* (**0.0.24**) by the Chiricahua Apache artist Allan Capron Houser (or Haozous), contains some degree of abstraction, while Eva Hesse's work is highly abstract.

In Houser's sculptures, we can recognize two faces, one larger and one smaller. We also interpret the swoop of the form downward from the larger face to be a back, and that the smaller face probably represents a baby being held in its mother's arms. The mother's entire body (her back, arms, and knees) is, however, abstracted to be one smooth form in which to cradle the baby. The baby's body is just a bump on the lap of the mother, as if it is swaddled tightly. We can interpret the subject and form of the sculpture because the detailed representation of the figures' faces enables us to see a mother holding her baby. The implied connection between mother and child is strong in both Houser's and Michelangelo's work, but Michelangelo's is less abstracted.

0.0.24 Allan Houser, *Reverie*, 1981. Bronze, 25 × 23 × 13", edition of 10. Allan Houser Archives

For a complete formal analysis of *Las Meninas* by Diego Velazquez:
→ see **1.10.12a**, p. 171

→ see **1.10.12a**, p. 171

Elements of art: the basic vocabulary of art—line, shape, form, volume, mass, texture, value (lightness/darkness), space, color, and motion and time

Principles of art: the principles, or grammar of art – contrast, unity, variety, balance, scale, proportion, focal point, emphasis, pattern, and rhythm—describe the ways the elements of art are arranged in an artwork

Context

How can we interpret a work that is several centuries old and comes from a completely different culture than our own? Research into the culture and the artist's circumstances will help us to learn more about an artwork by understanding its context. Context includes, for example, information about the society in which a work was created: how was the society organized and ruled, and who ruled it? Context also includes information about the economics and religion of the people who made the work, such as whether they had freedom of expression; specific details about the person who ordered it made; and the status of the artist who created it.

If we know more about the context in which a work of art was made, we can learn more about it than we probably expected at first glance. Context often helps to enrich even more our understanding of non-objective works, which may not be easy to decipher otherwise. For example, when Hesse was creating *Untitled (Rope Piece)*, she had recently been diagnosed with a brain tumor, from which she died later that year. Elements of her works were often seen as relating to parts of the human body, and *Untitled (Rope Piece)* does look like the intestines, veins, or other inner elements. As in this piece, she frequently used latex, which feels like human skin. Latex deteriorates, just as the human body does. Hesse described this work as representing the chaos of life and death. As you can see, even if you are not able to identify the subject matter in a work of art, studying the context in which it was made can still help you understand its meaning.

Formal (Visual) Analysis

Art communicates with the viewer through vision. The arrangement of the visual **elements** and **principles** of an artwork helps us to analyze its content. When we communicate in writing or speech, our communication consists of a vocabulary of individual words that are structured by rules of grammar that enable us to determine meaning. Similarly, in art, the elements (like vocabulary) are organized by the principles (the visual equivalent of grammar). In Part 1 of this book we will teach you, through in-depth examination of the elements and principles of art, the language artists use. Part 2 describes the materials (media) and processes used to make works of art. Part 3 considers the historical and geographical contexts in which artworks have been made. Part 4 compares art from different places and times under broad themes universal to all humans. These four sections are designed to guide you through the different ways that art can be studied. All works of art can be explored through these various lenses, and you are encouraged to travel back and forth through the book as topics intrigue you, while considering multiple ways to examine and experience each work of art. At the end of each chapter, a page of related images will inspire you to explore more artworks that relate to what you just read. Enjoy the journey!

Part 1 Fundamentals

Art is a form of visual language, and much as we use vocabulary and grammar to communicate verbally, artists use a visual vocabulary (the elements of art) and rules similar to grammar (the principles of art). When we study an artwork, we can use the same elements and principles to analyze the work: a process called visual analysis. In this part you will learn about the elements and principles, and will be shown how to apply them in a visual analysis. You will also learn how to use two other concepts when you analyze a work of art: style and content.

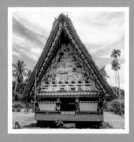

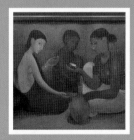

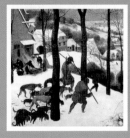

1.1
Line, Shape, and the Principle of Contrast

Elements of art: the basic vocabulary of art—line, shape, form, volume, mass, texture, value (lightness/darkness), space, color, and motion and time

Principles: the principles, or grammar of art—contrast, unity, variety, balance, scale, proportion, focal point, emphasis, pattern, and rhythm—describe the ways the elements of art are arranged in an artwork

Line: a mark, or implied mark, between two endpoints

Shape: a two-dimensional area, the boundaries of which are defined by lines or suggested by changes in color or value

Two-dimensional: having height and width

Three-dimensional: having height, width, and depth

Contrast: a drastic difference between such elements as color or value (lightness/darkness) when they are presented together

Engraving: a printmaking technique where the artist gouges or scratches the image into the surface of the printing plate

Just as we use the principles of grammar to turn vocabulary into sentences, so the language of art consists of **elements** (the basic vocabulary of art) and **principles** (the grammar that artists apply to turn the elements into art). The principles of design are a set of rules that explain how the elements of a work of art are organized.

In this chapter we will look at **line** and **shape**, which are basic elements of any kind of artwork, and we will principally consider how they function in examples of **two-dimensional** art. (In Chapter 1.2, we will focus more on **three-dimensional** art.) We will then see how to apply them to the understanding of works of art by using the principle of **contrast**.

Two-dimensional art is a remarkably elegant way to express ideas and share our mental pictures of the world. Two-dimensional art is made on a flat surface, and can be measured only by height and width—for example, a drawing of a triangle. It can be made very simply, with a pencil on paper. The first plans for the grandest of designs can be drawn up on a napkin with a few squiggles of a pen. As well as drawing and painting, two-dimensional arts include the graphic arts: printmaking, graphic design, and photography. In contrast to two-dimensional art, three-dimensional art can be measured by height, width, and *depth*, and it exists in real space. Because two-dimensional art has only height and width, any depth that we see when we look at a flat artwork—for example, a drawing of a pyramid—is an illusion: it exists solely in our imagination.

Line

Lines are the most fundamental element that artists use. They exist in almost every work of

art or design. Lines organize the visible world. Without line, an artist hardly knows where to begin.

The ancient designs known as the Nazca Lines on the high desert plains of Peru include some of the most unusual drawings in the world. They show us much about line and shape. In the monkey "drawing," lines define the shape onto the landscape at such an enormous scale that it can be seen in full only from the sky (**1.1.1**). (In fact, the Nazca Lines were first discovered in modern times by overflying commercial aircraft.)

Unlike most drawings, the Nazca Lines cannot be rolled up in a tube or carried off in a portfolio. First of all, they are too huge: the monkey shown here is 330 ft. across, or about the length of a football field. Second, they are hardly drawings at all. Instead, they were made by scraping off the layer of dark gravel that covers the flat Nazca plain to expose the white gypsum that lies just beneath the surface. In this sense, they are a sort of incision or **engraving**.

The lines are mysterious. Why would such enormous designs, so huge they can hardly be understood at ground level, be made? What was their purpose? The designs resemble symbolic decorations found on local pottery made at least 1,300 years ago. We do not know what they were used for, but their size suggests they played an important part in the lives of the people who made them. How were they made? There are postholes found at intervals along their edges—perhaps strings from post to post formed guidelines for the scraping of the pathway. Notably, the Nazca Lines do not cross over themselves. The lines define the **outline** of the shape.

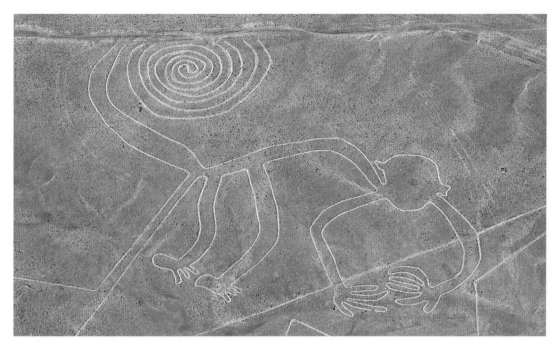

1.1.1 **Monkey**, *c.* 500 BCE–500 CE. Approximately 190 × 330′. Nazca, Peru

Definition of Line

The variety of different types of line is virtually infinite. A line can be a mark that connects two points, like the strings that must have run from post to post at Nazca. Artists can use lines to define the boundaries between **planes** in a two-dimensional work of art: notice how the lines at Nazca divide one area of the gravel surface of the land from another. In two-dimensional art, line can also define shapes (in this case, the shape of a giant monkey). A line may direct our eyes to look at something the artist particularly wants us to notice. Finally, line can convey a sense of movement and energy, even the movement of a giant monkey.

In figure **1.1.2a** we see drawings, or **blueprints**, for a geodesic **dome**, and in **1.1.2b** a photograph of the finished geodesic dome house in Carbondale, Illinois. The dome was designed by the architect and visionary R. Buckminster Fuller (1895–1983) as his personal home. Architect Thad Heckman made the technical drawings in 2011 when the dome was undergoing restoration. The drawings use line to visualize the finished architectural form.

Although line is two-dimensional, by using it, the artchitect points out where one plane meets another, and implies three dimensions. Line is thus a tool for describing, in a simple way and in two dimensions, the boundaries and edges of three-dimensional surfaces.

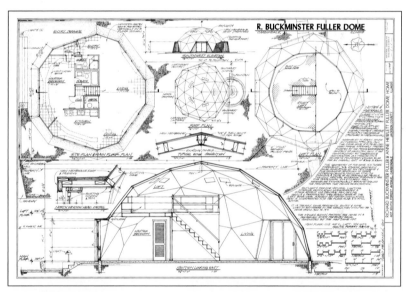

1.1.2a **Thad Heckman**, Pen and ink rendering of R. Buckminster Fuller & A. Hewlett Fuller Dome Home, Carbondale, Jackson County, Illinois, 2011

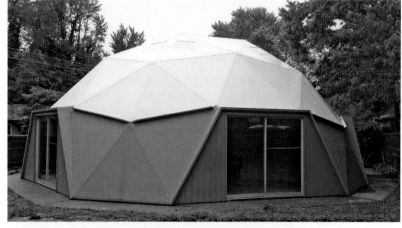

1.1.2b **Buckminster Fuller**, *R. Buckminster Fuller and Anne Hewlett Dome Home*, Carbondale, Jackson County, Illinois, built 1960; photo post-restoration (phase 1)

For example, Heckman's drawings use line (rather than lightness, darkness, or **texture**) to define where the **tetrahedrons** come together to form the dome. He was thus creating a visual record so that others could see, in detail, how the dome was designed.

In the photo of the *R. Buckminster Fuller and Anne Hewlett Dome Home*, we see the dividing lines between the tetrahedrons because of the changes in line, lightness, darkness, and texture. The lines in the blueprints therefore represent the places where, in the real building, the different planes meet. In architecture, blueprint drawings are used to visualize future buildings, and are then passed on to builders so that they can become a reality.

The following sections of this chapter will show us some of the different types, functions, and expressions of line:

Types of line:
- contour line
- implied line

Functions of line:
- directing the viewer's gaze
- communicating an idea

Different feelings or ideas that can be expressed by line:
- lines can regulate and control
- lines can express freedom and passion
- lines can be regular or irregular

Types and Functions of Line

Contour Line A contour is an edge or **profile** of an object, but is not necessarily the complete outline of a shape. Contour lines can suggest a **volume** in **space** by giving us clues about the changing character of a surface.

Woman Seated in an Armchair, by the French artist Henri Matisse (1869–1954), is drawn almost entirely using contour lines (**1.1.3**). The confident line that sets the boundary between the figure and the **background** represents one kind of contour line, marking the edge of the figure's overall shape. Although contour drawing is a methodical and measured process, here Matisse creates an impression of spontaneity that gives the work a fresh, relaxed feeling. He has paid close attention to the lines that define the woman's face. Contour lines are also used to describe the surface of her dress as it falls across her figure. Matisse, a master of artistic simplicity and directness, uses solid continuous lines to reveal complex three-dimensional shapes and surfaces. He used bold, simple lines and shapes deliberately to put viewers at ease, as if they, too, were sitting in a comfortable armchair.

Contour drawing is a process that requires an artist's focused attention on a surface edge. Imagine focusing your stare on a single point, perhaps on the top of a forehead in profile, then moving your eye painstakingly slowly around the tip of the nose and on along the roundness of the lips and around the chin until it meets the neckline. If you carefully follow that edge and move your pencil along a sheet of paper, recording your progress across the page in a long continuous line, then you are engaging in contour drawing. This type of drawing helps to develop eye–hand coordination and reveal subtle changes in a subject.

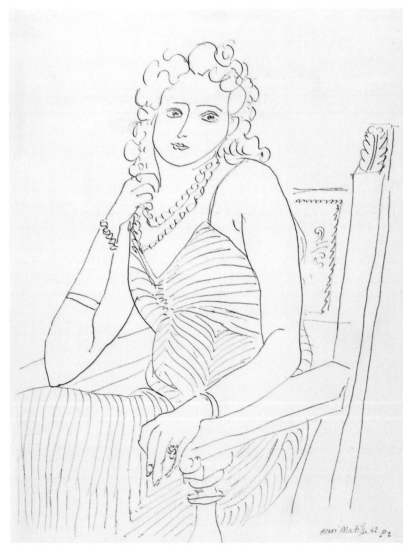

1.1.3 Henri Matisse, *Themes and Variations*, series P, *Woman Seated in an Armchair*, pl. 2, 1942. Pen and ink, 19¾ × 15¾". Musée des Beaux-Arts, Lyons, France

The Spanish artist Pablo Picasso (1881–1973) was famous for his ability to describe the shapes and planes that make up an object. In his line drawing *Blonde Woman in Profile*, the artist uses a continuous line that follows the contours of the profile (**1.1.4**). The pencil line wraps around the outer edge of the subject, a woman's head, describing the undulating texture of the hair. By giving the viewer clues resembling the kind of curves found in real life, these contour lines communicate shape and indicate some depth using directional changes only. Picasso is often associated with the **Cubist style**, a way of representing, simultaneously, all aspects of a three-dimensional object on a flat, two-dimensional surface.

Implied Line The lines we have discussed so far can be clearly seen as continuous marks. We can call these lines **actual lines**. But line can also be implied by a series of marks. An **implied line** is an illusion: it gives us the impression we are seeing a line where there is no continuous mark (**1.1.5**).

Implied line is important in the creation of a **calligram**: a design created using carefully arranged writing. At first glance, the drawing of a person wearing a hat in **1.1.6** (see p. 38) appears to have been created using an irregular scribbled line. In fact, the line is a series of words that Guillaume Apollinaire (1880–1918) has used to describe his lover. If we look at the text more carefully, it becomes obvious there is no actual line at all; rather, it is an implied line created by the skillful arrangement of the letters. The scribbled text becomes a way for Apollinaire to depict his lover using image and word at the same time.

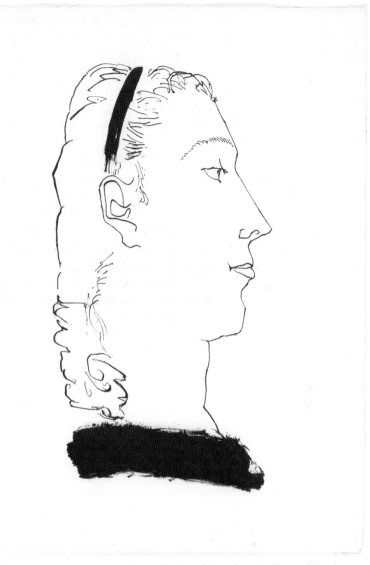

1.1.4 Pablo Picasso, *Blonde Woman in Profile*, plate, folio 16 from the illustrated book *Vingt poëmes*, 1947. Lift ground aquatint, 11⅞ × 6½". MoMA, New York

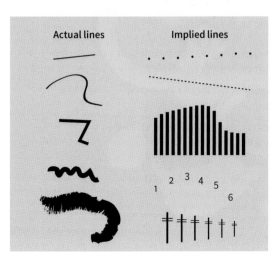

1.1.5 Actual and implied lines

Texture: the surface quality of a work, for example fine/coarse, detailed/lacking in detail

Tetrahedron: a pyramid shape in which all four faces are equally sized triangles

Profile: the outline of an object, especially a face or head, represented from the side

Volume: the space filled or enclosed by a three-dimensional figure or object

Space: the distance between identifiable points or planes

Background: the part of a work depicted furthest from the viewer's space, often behind the main subject matter

Cubism, Cubist: twentieth-century movement and style in art, especially painting, in which perspective with a single viewpoint was abandoned and use was made of simple geometric shapes, interlocking planes, and, later, collage; the Cubists were artists who formed part of the movement. "Cubist" is also used to describe their style of painting

Style: a characteristic way in which an artist or group of artists uses visual language to give a work an identifiable form of visual expression

Actual line: a continuous, uninterrupted line

Implied line: a line not actually drawn but suggested by the positions of elements in the work, for example, an aligned series of dots

Calligram: a word or piece of text that is laid out so that it creates a visual image related to the meaning of the word or piece of text

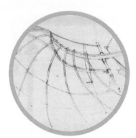

Leonardo da Vinci's *Drawing for a wing of a flying machine* is an example of lines that organize and illustrate an idea:
→ see **2.1.1**, p. 178

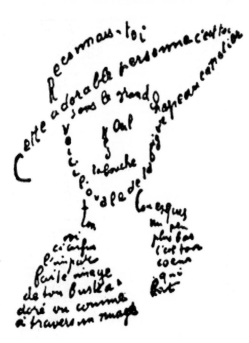

1.1.6 Guillaume Apollinaire, Calligram of lover from *Calligrammes: Poems of Peace and War 1913–1916*, published 1918

Implied line is used in a more varied way in the work by Sauerkids, the Dutch graphic designers Mark Moget (b. 1970) and Taco Sipma (b. 1966). *The Devil Made Me Do It* uses implied line to influence visual **rhythms** that add to

the excitement of the design (**1.1.7**). The many dashes and the **grid** of dots at the bottom of the work imply vertical and horizontal lines. Even the title of the work is spelled out using implied line.

Directional Line As well as demarcating boundaries, indicating depth, and noting surface changes, line can also communicate direction and movement. Artists can use line to direct our attention to something they want us to notice. An example of directional line occurs in the American artist James Allen's (1894–1964) **etching** of Depression-era construction workers. They are depicted working in New York City on the Empire State Building, which was to become the tallest building in the world at the time.

In *The Connectors*, the steel girders appear to be slightly closer together at the bottom of the picture than at the top. As a result, the girders direct the viewer's eye downward in order to accentuate their great height (**1.1.8**). The narrowing lines showing the buildings in the background of the print help reinforce the same effect.

When an artist uses line to direct the viewer's eye to more than one area in a composition, a sense of movement is

Rhythm: the regular or ordered repetition of elements in the work

Grid: a network of horizontal and vertical lines; in an artwork's composition, the lines are implied

Etching: an intaglio printmaking process that uses acid to bite (or etch) the engraved design into the printing surface

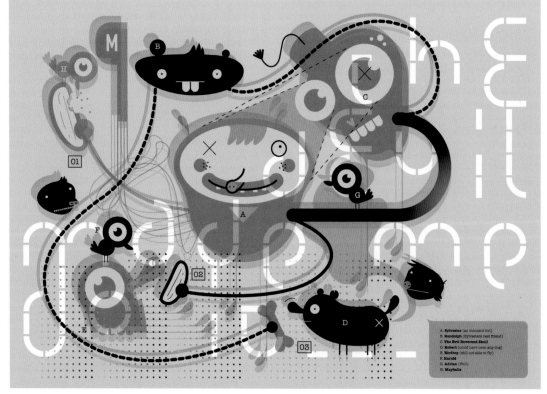

1.1.7 Sauerkids, *The Devil Made Me Do It*, 2006. Digital image, 16½ × 8¼"

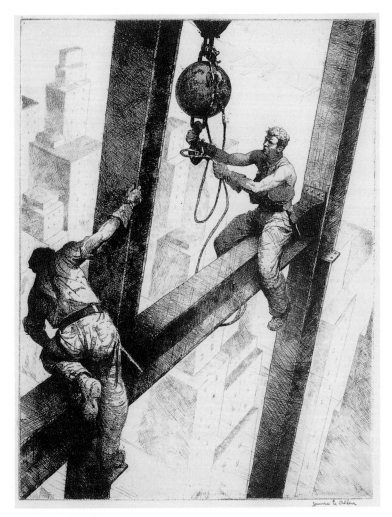

1.1.8 James Allen, ***The Connectors***, 1934. Etching, 12⅞ × 9⅞".
British Museum, London, England

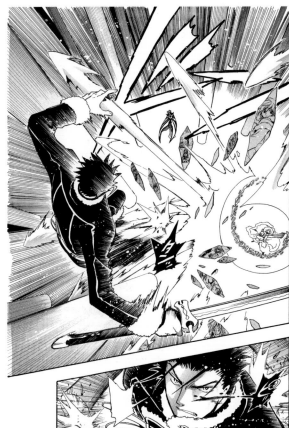

1.1.9 CLAMP, page from the *Tsubasa RESERVoir CHRoNiCLE*, volume 21, page 47, 2007

communicated as the eye darts from place to place. The page from the manga (Japanese comic/cartoon book) *Tsubasa RESERVoir CHRoNiCLE* (**1.1.9**) is divided into two major sections. A close-up view of a character is compressed into the bottom, and a larger action scene occupies the upper two-thirds of the page. In this section, directional lines converge on a light area in the upper right of the page, then our attention is redirected to the left, where a figure is being blasted away by an explosion. The mangaka (group of manga artists) CLAMP has cleverly used the strong diagonals to add an intense feeling of movement to the page.

Communicative Line The directions of lines (whether they go up, across, or diagonally) both guide our attention and suggest particular feelings. Vertical lines tend to communicate strength and energy; horizontal lines can suggest calmness and passivity; diagonal lines are associated with action, motion, and change (**1.1.10**).

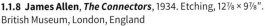

Vertical lines communicate strength, stability, and authority

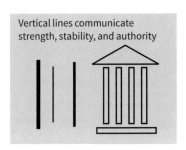

Horizontal lines communicate calm, peace, and passiveness

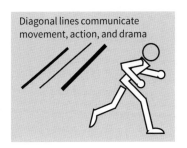

Diagonal lines communicate movement, action, and drama

1.1.10 Communicative qualities of line

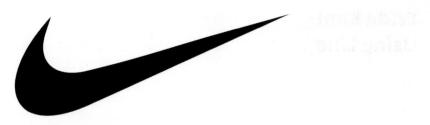

Logo: a unique graphic image used to identify an idea or entity

Color: the optical effect caused when reflected white light of the spectrum is divided into separate wavelengths

Value: the lightness or darkness of a plane or area

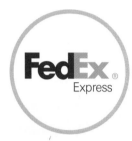

The FedEx logo suggests speed and precision:
→ see **0.0.7**, p. 20

1.1.11 Carolyn Davidson, Nike Company logo, 1971

Graphic designers use the communicative qualities of directional line when creating **logos**. To convey the strength of government or the stability of a financial institution, they may choose verticals. Logos for vacation resorts often feature horizontal lines to communicate peaceful repose. Diagonals can express the excitement and energy of athletic activity. For example, Carolyn Davidson's (b. *c.* 1943) distinctive Nike "swoosh" conveys action with a stylized, diagonal line (**1.1.11**).

Line gives an unsettling energy to a painting of the bedroom (**1.1.12**) of the Dutch artist Vincent van Gogh (1853–1890). Most of the lines that make up the room are strong verticals. This suggests that Van Gogh's bedroom was not a calm place of rest, as horizontal lines might imply. The floor also nervously changes **color** and **value**. The varying width of the vertical lines communicates the anxiety Van Gogh may have felt in the months leading up to his suicide in 1890.

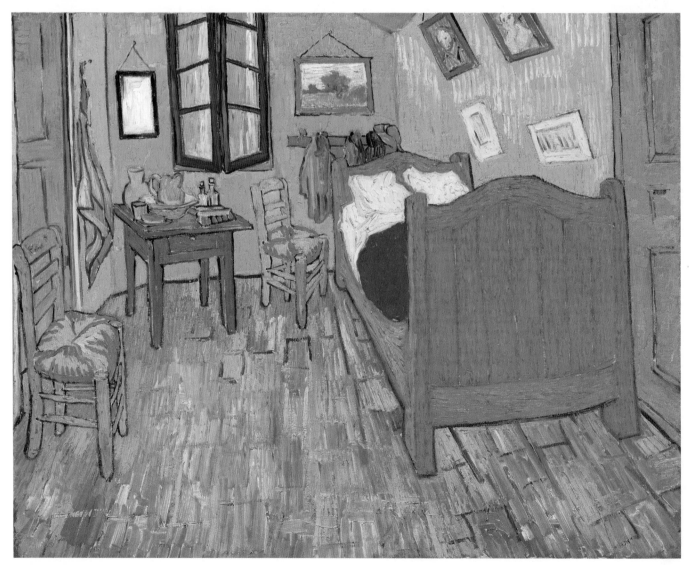

1.1.12 Vincent van Gogh, *The Bedroom*, 1889. Oil on canvas, 28¾ × 36¼". Art Institute of Chicago, Illinois

Frida Kahlo, *The Two Fridas*
Using Line to Connect and Direct a Viewer's Attention

For the other Kahlo
GATEWAYS:
→ see p. 190 and p. 643

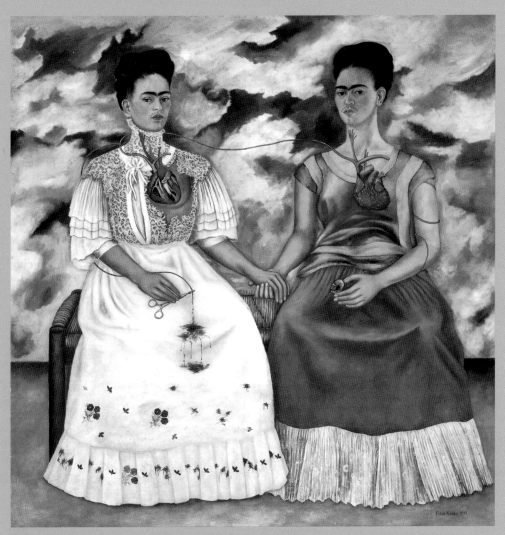

1.1.13 Frida Kahlo, *The Two Fridas*, 1939. Oil on canvas, 5'8" × 5'8". Museo de Arte Moderno, Mexico City, Mexico

In *The Two Fridas*, line plays an important role in connecting areas of the painting and directing the viewer's attention. Connections were important in the life of the Mexican artist Frida Kahlo (1907–1954). The artist's connections to her family lineage, to her husband, and to her history of physical suffering are all encapsulated in this work.

The line created by the vein that connects the two images of Frida (**1.1.13**) makes reference to her lineage (or bloodline) as it winds from the Frida on the right, in traditional Tehuana (from Tehuantapec, Mexico) clothing, to the Frida on the left, in white European dress. It refers to her Spanish-Native Mexican and European parents and links the two. The vein sometimes disappears behind or inside the clothing, implying a continuous but hidden line. On the European figure, the vein alludes to Frida's recent divorce

from her husband, fellow Mexican artist Diego Rivera (1886–1957), because it directs us to her broken heart. The Mexican Frida holds in her hand a small picture of Rivera.

The vein continues to wrap around and meander throughout the figures. It also tells us about the lifelong pain that Frida endured after being badly injured in a traffic accident when she was eighteen years old. She had many surgeries, as symbolized here by the scissor-like surgical clamp on the left, which almost stops the blood flow—though drips of her life essence still stain the white dress. This red line becomes the main element in expressing the story of Frida's life. Other lines that contribute to the overall composition are the strong crisp outlines of the figures and the soft irregular lines of the clouds. Each gives character to this story of strength in the face of hardship.

Chapter 1.1 Line, Shape, and the Principle of Contrast   **41**

Conceptual art: a work in which the communication of an idea or group of ideas is most important to the artwork

The strength of the verticals combined with the agitation of the emphatic diagonals makes for a powerful sense of unease. Yet Van Gogh may also have been trying to ground himself in the here and now by painting the simple room in which he slept.

Lines to Regulate and Control Whether straight or curved, a line can be regular and carefully measured. Regular lines express control and planning, and impart a sense of cool-headed deliberation and accuracy. Such lines are effective for communicating ideas that must be shared objectively by groups of people, such as the plans an architect provides to guide builders.

The American **conceptual artist** Mel Bochner (b. 1940) uses ruled line in his work *Vertigo* (**1.1.14**). By using a regular line drawn with the aid of a straightedge, Bochner speaks in the language of mechanical planning. He seems to contradict the use of regular line to convey a sense of control, however. The repetitious diagonal movement and hectic crossing and overlapping of his lines impart a sense of motion in disarray, as if his machine has somehow gone out of whack.

The British sculptor Barbara Hepworth (1903–1975) used regulated line in the preliminary drawings she made for her sculptures. The lines are crisp and clear, and they combine to represent feelings or sensations that Hepworth wants to make visible in her sculpture. Hepworth said, "I rarely draw what I see. I draw what I feel in my body."

In **1.1.15**, the artist has projected four views of a future sculpture. As she rotates this imaginary work in her mind's eye, the precision of her line helps her comprehend the complexity of her sensations. Like a dancer who responds to the rhythm of music, Hepworth has revealed the kind of lines that she feels, rather than sees, and has translated them into a visual "dance." Like an architect preparing the blueprints of a real building, Hepworth uses regulated line to translate her feelings into drawing and then, finally, into a real sculpture.

Lines to Express Freedom and Passion Lines can also be irregular, reflecting the wildness of nature, chaos, and accident. Such lines—free and unrestrained—seem passionate and full of feelings otherwise hard to express. Some artists decide to use irregular lines to reflect

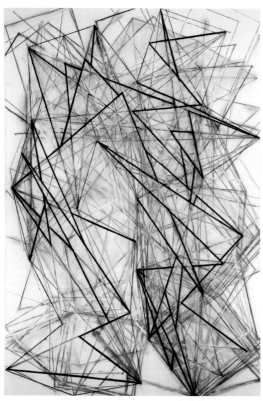

1.1.14 Mel Bochner, *Vertigo*, 1982. Charcoal, Conté crayon, and pastel on canvas, 9′ × 6′2″. Albright-Knox Art Gallery, Buffalo, New York

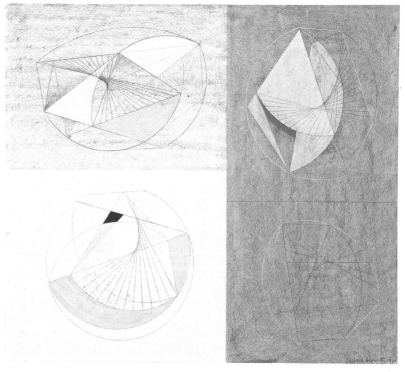

1.1.15 Barbara Hepworth, *Drawing for Sculpture (with color)*, 1941. Pencil and gouache on paper mounted on board, 14 × 16″. Private collection

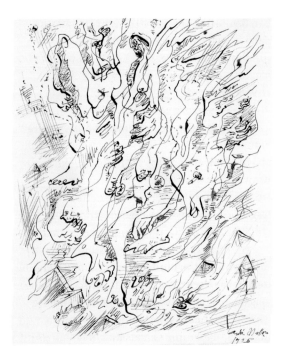

1.1.16 André Masson, *Automatic Drawing*, 1925–26. Ink on paper, 12 × 9½". Musée National d'Art Moderne, Centre Georges Pompidou, Paris, France

their drawing and thinking process. French artist André Masson (1899–1987) wanted to create images that expressed the depths of his subconscious. Sometimes he would go for days without food or sleep in an attempt to force himself to explore deeper-rooted sources of creativity and truth. His **automatic** drawings look spontaneous and free, and also perhaps unstructured and rambling (**1.1.16**).

The drawings of British nineteenth-century artist and spiritualist Georgiana Houghton (1814–1884) share André Masson's uninhibited style. The lines appear irregular and loose, yet repetitious. At first sight, *Glory Be to God* may seem chaotic and unpredictable, but, according to the artist, the overall composition is systematically organized by spiritual forces (**1.1.17**). Houghton was one of the first artists to derive her ideas and images from non-visual sources and depict them in a non-representational way. She chose to interpret her spiritual experiences and create visual representations of them, introducing viewers to a unique world that they would never otherwise have been able to encounter.

Regular and Irregular Lines Although line can be either regular or irregular, most art exhibits a combination of both. The American artist George Bellows (1882–1925) uses both varieties of line in his work *Woodstock Road, Woodstock,*

Automatic: suppressing conscious control to access subconscious sources of creativity and truth

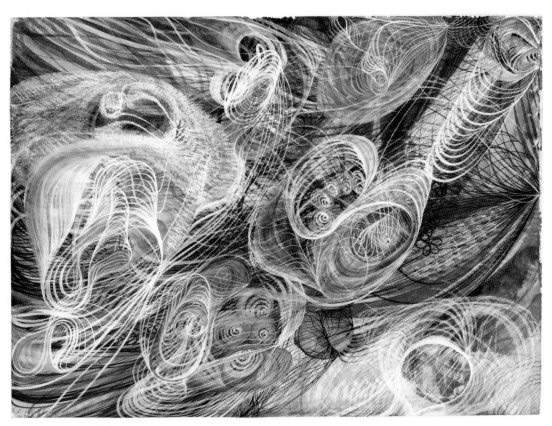

1.1.17 Georgiana Houghton, *Glory Be to God*, 1864. Pencil, watercolor, and ink on paper, 9⅜ × 12⅞". Victorian Spiritualists Union, Melbourne

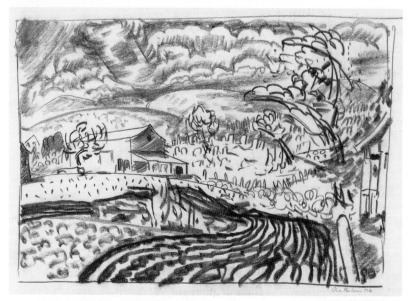

1.1.18 **George Bellows**, *Woodstock Road, Woodstock, New York, 1924*, 1924. Black crayon on wove paper, image 6⅛ × 8⅞"; sheet 9¼ × 12⅜". National Gallery of Art, Washington, D.C.

can be used to suggest depth. In art, shape is a basic, two-dimensional element that can be used to define space.

Geometric and Organic Shapes

Shapes can be classified into two types: geometric and organic. Geometric shapes are composed of regular lines and curves. Organic shapes, however, as the examples on the right of **1.1.20** show, are made up of unpredictable, irregular lines that suggest the natural world. Organic shapes may seem unrestrained and sometimes chaotic, reflecting the constant change characteristic of living things.

Geometry is a branch of mathematics dating back more than 2,000 years. It is concerned with space, area, and size. Traditionally defined, a geometric shape is mathematically regular and precise. The simple shapes we know—circle, square, triangle—are all examples of geometric shapes. These can be created by plotting a series of points and connecting them with lines, or simply enclosing a space using regulated and controlled line. Although artists can draw by hand something similar to a geometric shape, they often use tools to control and regulate the precision of the line. For example, an artist may use a ruler to create perfectly straight lines, or alternatively, a computer graphics application can be used to generate a clean, sharp edge. In both cases the artist adds a layer of control that gives the shape greater predictability.

While line may be the most fundamental element of art, often shape is the element we see most clearly. The **collage** by Canadian-born feminist artist Miriam Schapiro (1923–2015) illustrates differences between geometric and organic shapes (**1.1.21**). In *Baby Blocks*—also the name of a traditional quilting **pattern**—images of flowers and children's clothes overlap a tiling of orange, blue, and black diamond shapes that create an illusion of cubes. The organic shapes of the flowers are clearly distinct from the hard geometric shapes of the blocks and the red frame; they overflow the boundaries of both. The stylized floral designs, derived from old-

New York, 1924 (**1.1.18**). He contrasts the natural and organic lines of landscape and sky with the restrained and regular line of the human-made and architectural features. It seems that Bellows made this drawing as a preliminary sketch for another work. In the center at the bottom is the inscription, "all lights as high as possible/get color out of shadows." He wrote this to remind himself later of ideas he had while sketching the scene.

Shape

A shape is a two-dimensional area, the boundaries of which are defined by lines or suggested by changes in color or value. In **1.1.19** we can see the central circular shape because its edges are defined by the sudden transition from white to medium gray. Two-dimensional figures can be defined only by their height and width: they have no depth. As a result, they can function as a simple concept (for example, circles, squares, triangles) used to organize what we see. So a three-dimensional object, such as a sphere, can be drawn using a circle shape; then an artistic device, such as shading,

Another example of geometric shape can be found in Gerrit Rietveld's Schröder House, which is made up of rectangles:
→ see **3.9.34**, p. 520

Collage: a work of art assembled by gluing materials, often paper, onto a surface. From the French *coller*, to glue

Pattern: an arrangement of predictably repeated elements

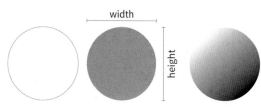

1.1.19 Two-dimensional circular shapes

1.1.20 Geometric and organic shapes

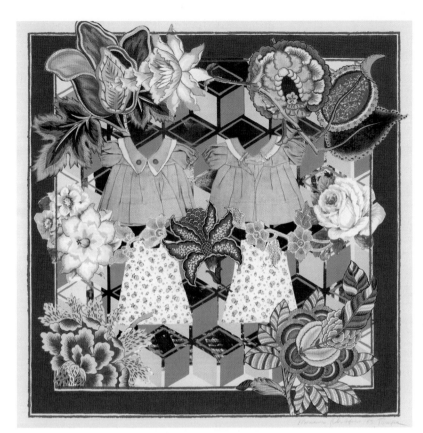

1.1.21 **Miriam Schapiro**, *Baby Blocks*, 1983. Collage on paper, 29⅞ × 30″.
University of South Florida Collection, Tampa

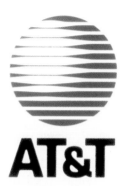

1.1.23 **Saul Bass**, **Bass & Yager**, **AT&T logo**, 1984

boundary exists. Just as line can be implied, so can shape (**1.1.22**). The AT&T logo, created in the 1980s by American graphic designer Saul Bass (1920–1996), uses horizontal lines to imply a sphere or globe (**1.1.23**). Twelve horizontal lines are trimmed to form a circle. By constricting the width of nine of these lines, a **highlight** appears on the circular shape, implying the swell of a globe. This logo communicates the idea of an expansive telecommunication network operating all over the world. The image is simple, creating a meaningful and readily recognizable symbol for a global company.

Contrast

When artists use two noticeably different states of an element, they are applying the principle of contrast. For example, lines can be both regular and irregular, or shapes can be both geometric and organic. Strong differences in the state of an element can be a very useful effect for an artist; it is especially effective to use opposites.

Positive Shape and Negative Space

In everyday life, positive and negative are opposites: one needs the other for contrast and comparison. Without positives, negatives would not exist, and vice versa. When we speak of positive and negative in visual form, they are most often represented by black and white. The words on this page, for example, are **positive shapes** in black that we can see on the **negative space** of the white background. The space, which is the ground area where such shapes are present, supports the solidity of the placement of the words or shapes. Although black and white are common examples of positive and negative, any color combination can work the same way. Sometimes, the lighter color becomes the positive shape.

We can see the interlocking of positive shape and negative space in the work of Russian

fashioned wallpaper and upholstery patterns, are simplified representations of real flowers. Even so, the shapes have an irregularity that reflects the kind of shapes we find in living things. By contrast, the interlocked blue and yellow blocks are so predictable and regular that we can envision the pattern even where it disappears behind the flowers. This geometric regularity acts as a foil to the organic shapes casually arranged on it. By incorporating doll clothes, home decorations, and sewing materials into her "femmages" (homages to the work of women), Schapiro opens our eyes both to the remarkable artistry of much traditional so-called women's work, and to the cultural forces that undervalue it.

Implied Shape

Most shapes are defined by a visible boundary, but we can also see a shape where no continuous

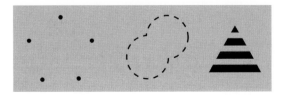

1.1.22 Implied shapes

Highlight: an area of lightest value in a work

Positive shape: a shape defined by its surrounding empty space

Negative space: an unoccupied or empty space that is created after positive shapes are positioned in a work of art

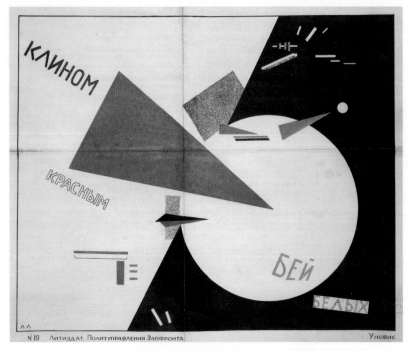

1.1.24 El Lissitzky, *Beat the Whites with the Red Wedge (The Red Wedge Poster)*, 1919. Lithograph, 18⅛ × 22 in. Private collection.

designer and architect El Lissitzky (1890–1941). In *Beat the Whites with the Red Wedge* (**1.1.24**), the red and black features and the blank white space both contrast with and complement each other, intensifying the **abstract** design. As a poster artist, Lissitzky needed a strong impact, to catch his audience's attention quickly as they passed by. In this case, the image is an abstract design that symbolizes the victory of the Bolshevik Red Army, a revolutionary political party which later became the Communist Party, over the anti-Communist White Russians in such a direct way that the message is immediately recognizable. The diagonally oriented, sharp red wedge pierces the white circle as if it were a strategic movement drawn on a military map. Lissitzky's graphic style was derived from other early Russian painters and designers who sought simple and direct ways to communicate an idea to a viewer.

The works of the American artist Georgia O'Keeffe (1887–1986) often play upon the

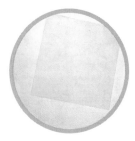

El Lissitzky was a Russian Suprematist artist. Another example of this style is Kazimir Malevich's *Suprematist Composition: White on White*:

→ see **3.9.19**, p. 512

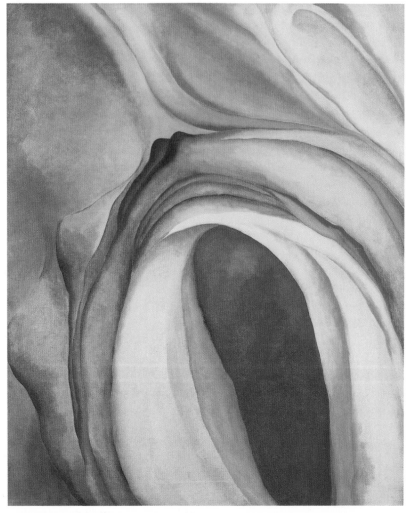

1.1.25 Georgia O'Keeffe, *Music—Pink and Blue II*, 1919. Oil on canvas, 35 × 29⅛". Whitney Museum of American Art, New York

relationship between positive and negative shape. Her abstract shapes derive from a close observation of organic objects. In the painting *Music—Pink and Blue II*, O'Keeffe puts emphasis on the negative blue shape in the bottom right of the picture (**1.1.25**). That negative shape initially draws our attention into a deep interior, so that the positive shape of the pink arc above it carries us back to the surface through a maze of tender folds. O'Keeffe's paintings are inspired by landscape and flower shapes to make associations with objects that live and grow. The interplay of positive and negative space becomes symbolic of the natural ebb and flow of life.

Sometimes illustrators use negative shape to convey information in a more integrated way. For example, the Israel-born illustrator and designer Noma Bar (b. 1973) cleverly combined complementary symbols to superimpose two connected ideas. In his illustration *Gun Crime* (**1.1.26**), Bar uses a silhouette of a handgun to create the positive, or black, shape on the lighter tan background. But in the area where the trigger has been drawn, we see a small crescent shape and a vertical swatch of red. When we consider the image by looking at the negative tan space in this area, we see a simple image of a head with blood running from its mouth. The alternation of positive and negative shape communicates the act of gun crime and its terrible result in a single image.

In the **woodcut** *Sky and Water I* (**1.1.27**), the Dutch artist M. C. Escher (1898–1972) applies many of the concepts we have been exploring in this chapter. The negative shape changes from white in the upper part of the picture to black in the lower. The most refined version of each animal occurs at the top and bottom extremes of the image. As we follow each transition upward or downward, each animal becomes

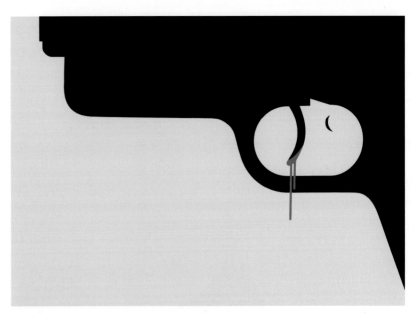

1.1.26 Noma Bar, ***Gun Crime***, 2009. Digital, dimensions variable

more simplified until it forms part of the background negative shape. Strong geometric patterns change into the organic shapes of animals. The woodcut method, where removed material prints as white and preserved material prints as black, is conducive to exploring **figure–ground reversal**, which is the very essence of Escher's technique here.

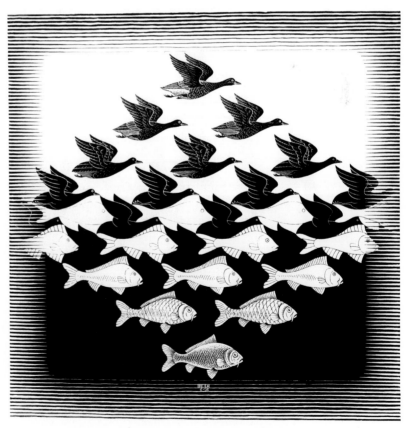

1.1.27 M. C. Escher, ***Sky and Water I***, 1938. Woodcut, 17⅛ × 17⅜". The M. C. Escher Company, The Netherlands

Abstract: art imagery that departs from recognizable images of the natural world

Woodcut: a relief print made from a design cut into a block of wood

Figure–ground reversal: the reversal of the relationship between one shape (the figure) and its background (the ground), so that the figure becomes background and the ground becomes the figure

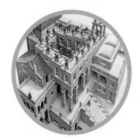

Another example by M. C. Escher can be found in his work *Ascending and Descending*:
→ see **1.3.23**, p. 82

Kara Walker, *Insurrection! (Our Tools Were Rudimentary, Yet We Pressed On)*
The Projected Shape of Things

For the other Walker
GATEWAYS:
→ see p. 340 and p. 625

The African American artist Kara Walker (b. 1969) projects the shape of racial stereotypes in her work *Insurrection! (Our Tools Were Rudimentary, Yet We Pressed On* (**1.1.28**). These organic and representational shapes serve as a kind of storybook of fictional characters that might exist in the mind of viewer. Walker's exaggerated **caricatures** of the antebellum South come alive in the form of a twisted dark cartoon comedy about forced human enslavement.

As she focuses on these subjects, Walker uses organic shape as an important device in her projection to describe the distorted frailties of humanity. Walker exploits the irregularities and unexpected nature of biological **silhouettes** by pushing the extremities further than they would be seen in nature. She arranges the various black figures to contrast against the lighter background of trees draped with Spanish Moss and thick foliage, like that found in a swamp. These contrasts support Walker's intent to create a cast of unworldly characters that reflect an awful reality. The artist's use of exaggerated organic shape reveals uncomfortable truths through a fictional realm.

Caricature: a picture of a person in which certain striking characteristics are exaggerated in order to create a comic or grotesque effect

Silhouette: a solidly colored-in shape represented in outline, which contains no detail inside its border

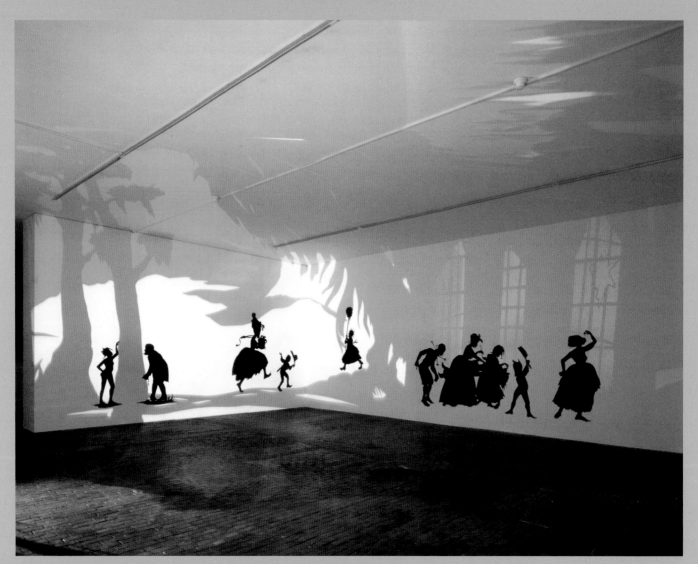

1.1.28 Kara Walker, *Insurrection! (Our Tools Were Rudimentary, Yet We Pressed On)*, 2000. Cut paper and projection on wall, dimensions variable. Installation view, *Why I Like White Boys, an Illustrated Novel by Kara E. Walker Negress*, Centre d'Art Contemporain, Geneva, Switzerland

Explore Further   Line, Shape, and the Principle of Contrast

Line

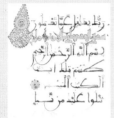

3.2.10 Page from the Koran, probably late 13th century → p. 379

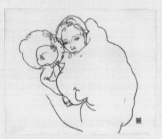

2.1.26 Egon Schiele, *Mother and Child*, 1918 → p. 192

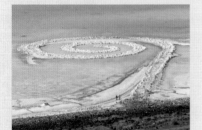

2.4.15 Robert Smithson, *Spiral Jetty*, 1969–70 → p. 238

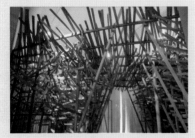

1.2.12 Carol Mickett and Robert Stackhouse, *In the Blue (Crest)*, 2008 → p. 57

Shape

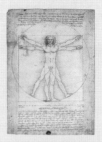

4.4.1 Leonardo da Vinci, *Vitruvian Man*, c. 1490 → p. 580

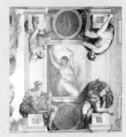

2.4.8 Michelangelo, *Separation of Light and Darkness*, 1508–10 → p. 232

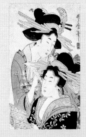

3.8.10 Kitagawa Utamaro, *Two Courtesans*, second half of 18th century → p. 488

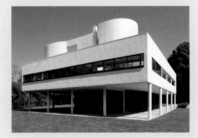

2.5.31 Le Corbusier, Villa Savoye, 1928–31 → p. 262

Contrast

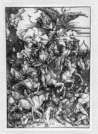

2.3.2 Albrecht Dürer, "The Four Horsemen," 1498 → p. 213

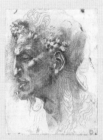

3.3.20 Yin and yang symbol → p. 404

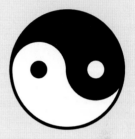

1.3.8 Michelangelo, *Head of a Satyr*, c. 1520–30, → p. 70

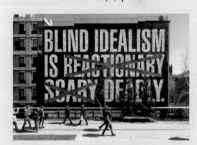

2.10.2 Barbara Kruger, *Untitled (Blind Idealism is …)*, New York, 2016–17 → p. 336

Your turn
How do these works relate to line, shape, and contrast?

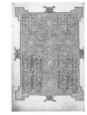

3.2.11a Cross-and-carpet page, Lindisfarne Gospels, 1508–10 → p. 380

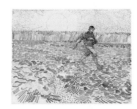

2.1.23 Vincent van Gogh, *Sower with Setting Sun*, 1888 → p. 191

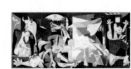

4.6.10 Pablo Picasso, *Guernica*, 1937 → p. 611

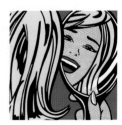

3.9.31 Roy Lichtenstein, *Girl in Mirror*, 1964 → p. 518

1.2
Form, Volume, Mass, and Texture

Three-dimensional: having height, width, and depth

Elements of art: the basic vocabulary of art—line, shape, form, volume, mass, texture, value (lightness/darkness), space, color, and motion and time

Form: an object that can be defined in three dimensions (height, width, and depth)

Volume: the space filled or enclosed by a three-dimensional figure or object

Mass: a volume that has, or gives the illusion of having, weight, density, and bulk

Texture: the surface quality of a work, for example fine/coarse, detailed/lacking in detail

Two-dimensional: having height and width

Shape: a two-dimensional area, the boundaries of which are defined by lines or suggested by changes in color or value

3-D modeling: a computer-generated illusion that emulates an object in three dimensions; it can be modified to show visual movement

Space: the distance between identifiable points or planes

Scale: the size of an object or artwork relative to another object or artwork, or to a system of measurement

In 1802 a French artist and archaeologist described his impression of the great pyramids of Egypt:

> On approaching these colossal monuments, their angular and inclined form diminishes the appearance of their height and deceives the eye...but as soon as I begin to measure...these gigantic productions of art, they recover all their immensity...
>
> (Vivant Denon, *Travels in Upper and Lower Egypt*)

The massive structures that so impressed Denon have, like every object in our world, three dimensions, which can be expressed as their height, width, and depth (**1.2.1**). Because the pyramids can be measured in these three dimensions they are classified as **three-dimensional** works of art, and like all the art discussed in this chapter they possess four of the visual **elements**: **form**, **volume**, **mass**, and **texture**. We need to understand these terms in sequence so that we can analyze and understand three-dimensional art.

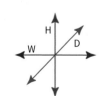

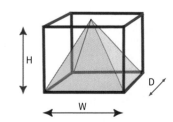

1.2.1 Three dimensions: height, width, and depth

Form

A **two-dimensional** object, such as a drawing of a triangle, is called a **shape**. Shapes are flat and do not have depth, mass, or volume, although they can be made to give an illusion of actual depth.

Shapes that have the illusion of three dimensions are an integral part of **3-D modeling** and animation: a computer-generated image is made using mathematical calculations that enable it to emulate the appearance of an object in real **space**. The digital environment makes it easier to visualize what something might look like in real life (modeling), and users are even able to give their creations the illusion of movement (animation).

An actual three-dimensional object, such as a pyramid, is called a form. A form occupies three-dimensional space and exists in a real and solid way. Some forms are so tiny they cannot be seen with the naked eye, while others are as large as a galaxy. When artists and designers create forms, they consider how we will experience them in three dimensions. Architects usually make buildings that accord with our physical size, in proportions that are convenient and easy to live in, but sometimes they might build to a larger **scale** in order to leave us in awe. A jeweler makes objects at a small scale that few people can experience at once: we are drawn closer to examine the work more intimately.

Forms have two fundamental attributes: volume and mass. Volume is the amount of actual space a form occupies. Mass describes the concept that volume is solid and occupies space, whether it is enormous, such as a pyramid, or relatively small, such as a piece of jewelry.

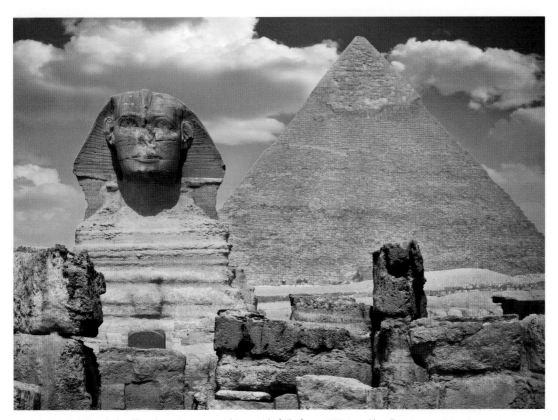

1.2.2 Great Sphinx of Giza (front), *c.* 2500 BCE, and Pyramid of Khafre, *c.* 2570 BCE, Giza, Egypt

The surface of a form can be cool and slick, rough and jagged, soft and warm. Such sensations arise from the texture of the form. Texture can be experienced directly, but we can also imagine how the surface of a form may feel simply by looking at it. Some hand-made objects, such as ceramics or basketry, attract our touch naturally. They were touched by the hands that formed them, and they fit in our hands just as they used to fit in the hands of the artist. Some machine-made forms reflect the crisp precision of mechanical perfection; their smooth, shiny forms seduce our senses. Artists and designers create forms with the full knowledge that they can evoke our memories of other three-dimensional objects in the world and allow us to experience our own world in a richer way.

The forms created by artists in the ancient world reflected the everyday experiences of people of that time. For example, stone was a common material in ancient Egypt, easily accessible and so durable that artists must have thought it would last for a very long time—a correct assumption, as we can still see.

The Great Sphinx guards the tombs of the Egyptian kings at Giza, near Cairo (**1.2.2**). It is the largest carving in the world made from a single stone. The sculpture stands as a symbol of the power to change our surroundings. The Egyptians who created this work changed the very earth by sculpting the living rock. We do not know what the Egyptians called this half-man, half-lion, but we now call it a sphinx after the creature from Greek mythology with the body of a lion, the wings of an eagle, and the head of a human. The Great Sphinx's face is believed to be a likeness of the Egyptian king Khafre.

There are two types of form: **geometric** and **organic**.

Geometric Form

Geometric forms are regular and are readily expressible in words or mathematics: cubes, spheres, cylinders, cones, and pyramids are simple examples. The Pyramid of Khafre, which is guarded by the Great Sphinx of Giza in **1.2.2**, is a stunning example of geometric form in architectural design because of the straight, controlled **planes** that articulate the four sides. The crisp regularity of the pyramids derives from attention to detail. For example, the base of another of the pyramids, Khufu's, is level to within less than an inch, and the greatest difference in the length of its sides is 1¾ in. The emphasis on precise mathematical proportion reflects an ordered culture in

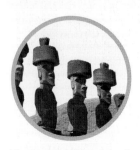

The Rapa Nui (Easter Island) *moai* ancestor figures are examples of artistically accentuated organic forms: → see **3.5.19**, p. 439

which artists were governed by a canon, or set of rules, that imposed strict controls on how artists worked and the images that they created.

The American sculptor David Smith (1906–1965) also relied on geometric forms to create his compositions. In *Cubi XIX*, made of stainless steel, Smith uses cubes, cuboids, and a thick disk (**1.2.3**). Smith learned welding in an automobile factory and became expert while fabricating tanks of thick armor plate during World War II. The late works of his *Cubi* series combine geometric forms in angular relationships. The diagonal angles imply

movement, giving these basic geometric forms a visual energy. Smith burnished their surfaces to create a counterpoint between industrial and natural form.

Organic Form

The form of most things in the natural world is organic: it is irregular and unpredictable. Living things, such as plants and animals, change constantly, and their forms change too. Artists accentuate the irregular character of organic form for expressive effect.

The human figure gives an artist a subject that can communicate the rich experience of humanity and organic form in a way we can all understand. The human body, like other organic forms, constantly changes in concert with its surroundings. Forms representing the human figure can provide the artist with a subject conveying **symmetry** and balance. But by visually contradicting such order, an artist can make a work seem uneasy or uncomfortable to look at. The unknown artist who carved the Christian *Pieta Roettgen* in the fourteenth century expresses the agony of death and grief by making the bodies of Jesus and the Virgin Mary irregular, awkward, and distorted (**1.2.4**). The suffering of torture is made shocking by the disjointedness of the lifeless

1.2.3 David Smith, *Cubi XIX*, 1964. Stainless steel, 113¼ × 21⅝ × 20⅝". Tate Gallery, London, England

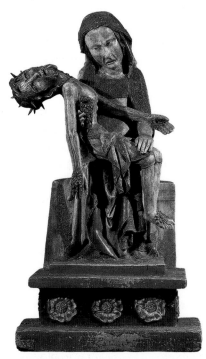

1.2.4 *Roettgen Pietà* (*Vesperbild*), Middle Rhine region, *c.* 1330. Wood, height 34½". Rheinisches Landesmuseum, Bonn, Germany

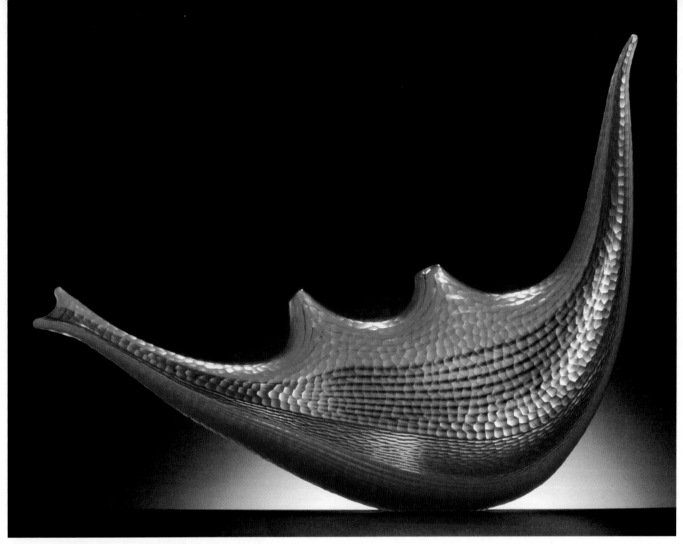

1.2.5 Lino Tagliapietra, *Batman*, 1998. Glass, 11½ × 15½ × 3½"

Jesus. Stiffly angular, he is stretched across the lap of his mother Mary. Prickly thorns, gushing wounds, and crumpled drapery give texture to pain and anguish. The disproportionate size of Mary's twisted face makes her unbearable sorrow all the more inescapable.

The expression of vigor and uplift in Italian glass artist Lino Tagliapietra's *Batman* (**1.2.5**) **contrasts** with the expression of death and despair in the *Pieta Roettgen.* Tagliapietra (b. 1934) wanted to convey the idea of "a creature who emerges from his dark cave to share goodness and light." He has enhanced the positive emotion of this **abstract** image by using bright **color** and stretching the extreme edges upward as if this were a growing, living object. Rather than producing hard, angular distortions, the artist uses a form that is lively and organic. The natural energy of light is captured in the glowing transparency of the glass. Tagliapietra, a master of glassblowing technique, wants the form to allude, without making a literal reference, to the idea behind

the character Batman. Thus we are free to revel in the life, energy, and power of the superhero through an expressive form, rather than a carefully depicted, lifelike representation. Tagliapietra says of the work, "I imaged pieces that allow the viewer to see both the reality and fantasy of Batman's world."

Form in Relief and In-the-Round
An artist who works with three-dimensional form can choose to create a work in **relief** or **in-the-round**. A relief is a work in which forms project from a flat surface. It is designed to be viewed from one side only. A form in-the-round can be seen from all sides.

Forms in relief combine aspects of two-dimensional and three-dimensional works of art. Like a two-dimensional work, a relief can be mounted on a wall or other surface. Although relief may appear to limit the work's potential visual impact, the sculptor can create the illusion of a three-dimensional space with dramatic results.

Symmetry: the correspondence in size, form, and arrangement of items on opposite sides of a plane, line, or point that creates direct visual balance

Contrast: a drastic difference between such elements as color or value (lightness/darkness) when they are presented together

Abstract: art imagery that departs from recognizable images of the natural world

Color: the optical effect caused when reflected white light of the spectrum is divided into separate wavelengths

Relief: a sculpture that projects from a flat surface

In-the-round: a freestanding sculpted work that can be viewed from all sides

Facade: any side of a building, usually the front or entrance

Composition: the overall design or organization of a work

Foreground: the part of a work depicted as nearest to the viewer

High relief: a carved panel where the figures project with a great deal of depth from the background

Bas-relief (low relief): a sculpture carved with very little depth: the carved subjects rise only slightly above the surface of the work

Stela (plural stelae): an upright stone slab decorated with inscriptions or pictorial relief carvings

Pictographic: conveys meaning through resemblance to physical shape

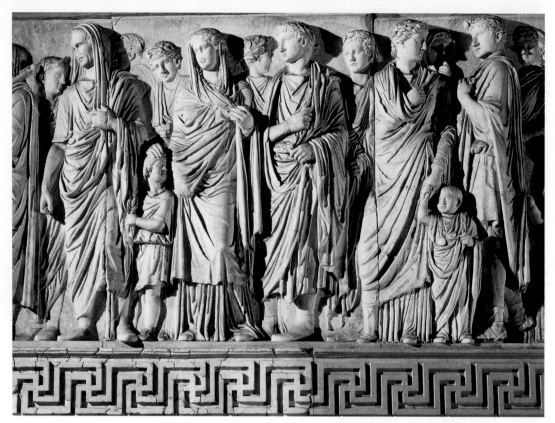

1.2.6 Imperial Procession from the *Ara Pacis Augustae*, 13 BCE. Marble altar, Museo dell'Ara Pacis, Rome, Italy

In the relief sculptures on the south **facade** of the Ara Pacis Augustae (Latin for Altar of Peace of Augustus) in Rome, Italy, a sculptor chose to fit many figures into a limited space (**1.2.6**). The unknown artist uses the depth of the carvings to suggest that some areas of the **composition** are further away from us than others. The figures in the **foreground** are deeply carved (in **high relief**) so that the folds in their togas are strongly delineated by shadows. But the artist wanted to imply a large crowd rather than just a line of people. The figures behind those in the foreground are also carved in relief, but not quite so deeply. They appear to be further away because there is less shadow defining their shape. The artist suggests greater depth by using a third group of figures who are carved in shallow relief, so that there is no shadow at all to make them stand out. This effect is clear in the upper left-hand corner, where the carving overlaps and diminishes in height.

The Maya artist who carved **1.2.7** in **bas-relief** worked in a tradition quite different from that of the Roman sculptor of the Ara Pacis, with its deeply incised figures. On the Maya **stela** all of the carving is carefully arranged on the same plane. The sculptor has created a series of glyphs, or **pictographic** symbol, describing the

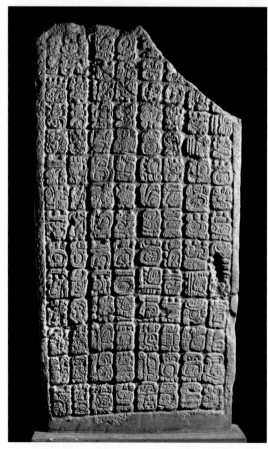

1.2.7 Limestone stela with Mayan glyphs, Pusilhà, Belize, c. 600–800 CE. Limestone, 86¼ × 45⅔ × 7″. British Museum, London, England

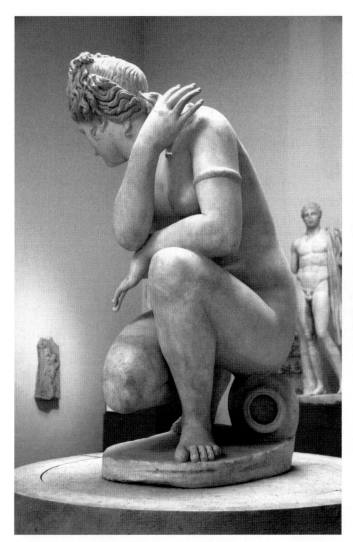
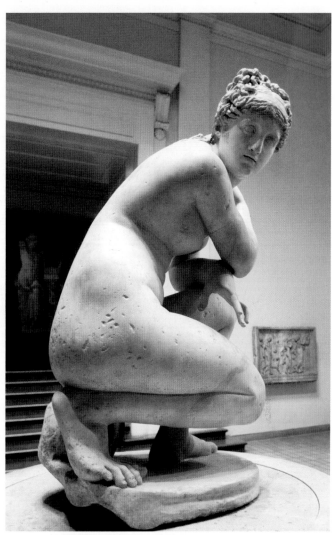

1.2.8a and **1.2.8b** *Naked Aphrodite Crouching at Her Bath* (*Lely's Venus*). Marble, Roman, 2nd century CE; copy of lost Greek original of the late 3rd/2nd century BCE, height 44⅛". British Museum, London, England (on loan from Her Majesty the Queen)

reign of the ruler K'ak' U' Ti' Chan. The figures of Mayan writing are organized with equal visual weight; the sculptor intended the viewer to read every element of the composition.

A sculpture is no longer a relief when the work can be viewed from all sides: this kind of form is known as in-the-round. Such **freestanding** works of art occupy space in the same way that other real-life objects do. When artists compose works that are designed in-the-round, they consider how viewers will interact with the works. In the ancient Roman statue *Naked Aphrodite Crouching at Her Bath*, also known as *Lely's Venus*, the artist rewards the viewer who walks around the work by constantly changing the elements of the design (**1.2.8a** and **1.2.8b**). You can see that the figure's face is turned away from a forward-looking position, and the body is slightly twisted. So, if a viewer moves from one side to another, there will be new surface changes and interesting

angles from which to look, enlivening the experience and holding the viewer's attention. Each time the viewer moves, the design of the work reveals a different aspect, and their perception of it changes. From the view in **1.2.8a**, you are encouraged to move to the opposite side to view Aphrodite's face (**1.2.8b**). The artist has effectively designed the work so that you feel compelled to look further and experience it more fully, while the sculpture's form remains satisfying from every viewpoint. This is one important attribute of good three-dimensional design.

Volume

Three-dimensional objects necessarily have volume. Volume is the amount of space occupied by an object. Solid objects have volume; so do objects that enclose an empty space. Mass, by contrast, suggests that something is solid and occupies space (**1.2.9,** see p. 56). Architectural

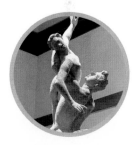

Giambologna's freestanding *Rape of a Sabine* has been sculpted for the viewer to experience in-the-round:
→ see **2.4.2**, p. 229

Freestanding: any sculpture that stands separate from walls or other surfaces so that it can be viewed from a 360-degree range

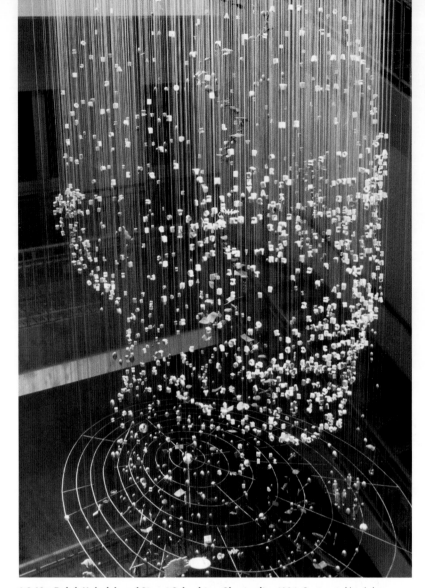

1.2.10a Ralph Helmick and Stuart Schechter, *Ghostwriter*, 1994. Cast metal/stainless cable, 36 × 8 × 10′. Evanston Public Library, Illinois

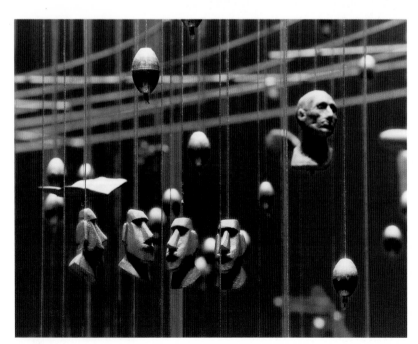

1.2.10b Detail of *Ghostwriter*

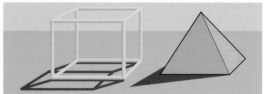

1.2.9 Volume (left) and mass (right)

forms usually enclose a volume of interior space to be used for living or working. For example, some hotel interiors feature a large, open atrium that becomes the **focal point** of the lobby. Some sculptures accentuate weight and solidity rather than openness. Such works have very few open spaces that we can see. The presence of mass suggests weight, gravity, and a connection to the Earth. The absence of mass suggests lightness, airiness, flight. Asymmetrical masses—or masses that cannot be equally divided on a central **axis**—can suggest dynamism, movement, change.

Open Volume

An open volume can occur when artists imply a form by using separate pieces, organized so that they create a recognizable structure. In *Ghostwriter*, Ralph Helmick (b. 1952) and Stuart Schechter (b. 1958) use carefully suspended pieces of metal to make an open volume that, when looked at as a whole, creates the image of a large human head (**1.2.10a** and **1.2.10b**). The small metal pieces, which represent letters of the alphabet, little heads, and other objects, are organized so that they delineate the shape of the head but do not enclose the space. In the stairwell where the piece hangs, the empty space and the head are not distinct or separate, but the shape is nonetheless implied.

The Russian artist Vladimir Tatlin's (1885–1953) *Monument to the Third International* was intended to be a huge tower housing the offices and chamber of delegates of the Communist International. It was going to commemorate the triumph of Russia's Bolshevik Revolution. Although never built, it would have been much higher than the Eiffel Tower in Paris, France. In its planned form, the spiraling open volume of the interior, and its proposed novel use of such materials as steel and glass, symbolize the modernism and dynamism of Communism (**1.2.11**). Tatlin believed that art should support and reflect the new social and political order.

Open volume can make a work feel light. *In the Blue (Crest)*, a collaborative work by

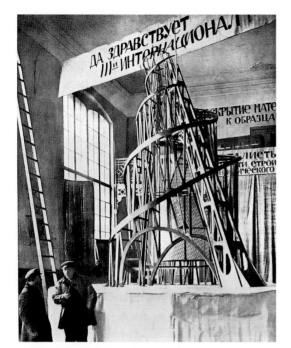

1.2.11 Vladimir Tatlin, Model for *Monument to the Third International*, 1919

American sculptors Carol Mickett (b. 1952) and Robert Stackhouse (b. 1942), was created to imply the presence of water (**1.2.12**). By creating **negative space** (the openings between the wooden slats) with crowds of horizontal struts, the artists made the work seem to float. Mickett and Stackhouse also curved the pieces and placed them at irregular intervals to create many subtle changes in direction. This arrangement gives a feeling of motion, like the gentle ripples of flowing water. The artists hope that viewers experience a sensation of being surrounded by water as they walk through the passage.

Negative space, like that used in *In the Blue (Crest)*, illustrates the importance of leaving areas of a work visually empty. These openings allow light to become a more active part of the work by adding light and dark contrasts. Negative space is also common in two-dimensional work, in which emptiness contrasts with the positive shapes and lines.

Mass

Mass suggests that a volume is solid and occupies space. Every substance has mass. Our perception of mass influences how we react to and what we feel about that substance. We can feel the weight of a pebble in the palm of our hand, or the heaviness of a chair as we pull it away from a table. Our perception of mass in large objects is derived from our imagination,

Focal point: the center of interest or activity in a work of art, often drawing the viewer's attention to the most important element

Axis: an imaginary line showing the center of a shape, volume, or composition

Negative space: an unoccupied or empty space that is created after positive shapes are positioned in a work of art

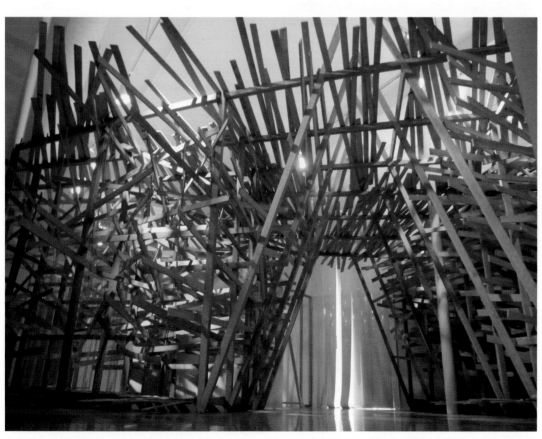

1.2.12 Carol Mickett and Robert Stackhouse, *In the Blue (Crest)*, 2008. Painted cypress, 24 × 108 × 11'. Installation at St. Petersburg Art Center, Florida

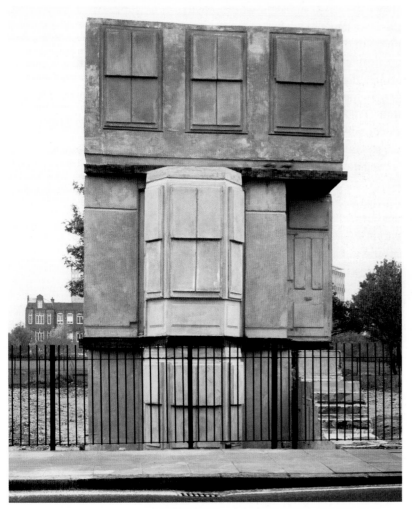

1.2.13 Rachel Whiteread, *House*, 1993. Concrete. Bow, London, England (demolished 1994)

of its former self. Whiteread took the volume of this building's interior and transformed it into a memorial of the lives of the people who used to live in it, and in other houses just like it. We comprehend not only the weight of the concrete, but also the related associations of life and death, memory and change.

The sculpture of Father Damien by the Venezuelan-born American artist Marisol (b. Maria Sol Escobar, 1930) stands as an immovable object against an irresistible force (**1.2.14**). It depicts the courage of a humanitarian hero. Father Damien was a Catholic missionary who supervised a leper colony on the Hawaiian island of Molokai during the nineteenth century. His steadfast compassion is suggested by the four-square mass of Marisol's work, while his unwavering determination is reflected in its vertical lines—in the cane, in the cape, and in the straight row of buttons. The stout form communicates stability and determination. Father Damien, who himself died of leprosy while serving its victims, exemplified such heroism that the Hawaiian legislature voted to place this memorial to him in front of the State Capitol Building in Honolulu.

our previous experience with smaller objects, and our understanding of the forces of nature. Artists tap into these various intuitions when they create a work of art.

Mass can suggest weight in a three-dimensional object. Some artists imply mass (without it necessarily being there) to give us the impression that the object we are looking at is very heavy. In movies, special-effect artists use illusion to create the impression of great weight; for instance, boulders that look crushingly heavy (and real) but that are actually made of foam. Mass does not necessarily imply heaviness—only that a volume is solid and occupies space.

The mass of British sculptor Rachel Whiteread's *House* suggests great weight and solidity (**1.2.13**). To create this work, Whiteread (b. 1963) filled the interior space of a house with tons of concrete before demolishing the exterior. The empty volume that was once filled with the happy and sad moments of domestic life was thus turned into a commemoration

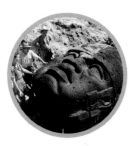

Another example of mass can be found in the colossal Olmec head from Veracruz, Mexico: → see **3.4.9**, p. 416

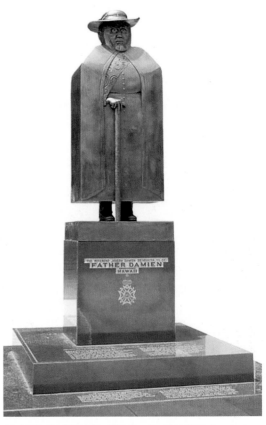

1.2.14 Marisol (Escobar), *Father Damien*, 1969. Bronze, height 7'. State Capitol Building, Honolulu, Hawaii

Brancusi and Rodin
Using Mass to Describe Love

Mass is an element of art that deals with solidity in three-dimensional objects. We can see how two artists working in the same medium—carved stone—can manipulate its mass to create two very different interpretations of romantic love.

The Romanian-born French sculptor Constantin Brancusi (1876–1957) used the element of mass to support his idea about the nature of love and its permanence. In his work *The Kiss* (**1.2.15**) Brancusi carves directly into a block of limestone to express the idea of two lovers unified in their relationship with each other. Stone is a material that implies a heavy mass, and it is associated with some of the oldest human-made monuments in human history. By fusing the separate figures into one solid stone mass, Brancusi communicates a transcendent and timeless love that is not bound by the human body and its limited time on Earth, but becomes symbolic of something ancient and lasting.

In comparison to Brancusi's *The Kiss* is a work of the same name by the French sculptor Auguste Rodin (1840–1917). Considered a true example of a modern sculptor, Rodin dismissed Classical sculpture and traditional poses. Instead, he used live models and depicted energetic and passionate figures. Rodin's *The Kiss* (**1.2.16**) also depicts two lovers, but in a more literal and realistic way than that of Brancusi's work. The

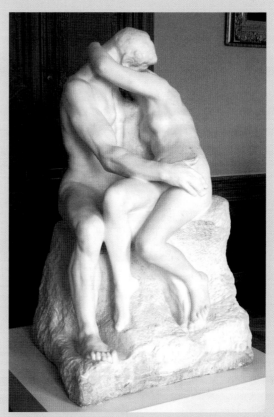

1.2.16 Auguste Rodin, *The Kiss*, c. 1882. Marble, 71½ × 44⅜ × 46". Musée Rodin, Paris, France

figures closely resemble real human bodies, and the artist portrays the inner feelings of the couple by emphasizing their muscles and anatomy. The couple was originally conceived to be part of Rodin's *Gates of Hell*, two large bronze doors depicting scenes from a masterpiece of medieval Italian literature, Dante's *Divine Comedy*. *The Kiss* is based upon the story of Paolo and Francesca (wife of Paolo's brother). Rodin did not include the figures in the final composition of the Gates, and instead made several copies of *The Kiss*, one of which was a marble commissioned by the French government.

Although both artists chose to work in the same medium, Rodin decided to carve a naturalistic image of two figures embracing, with much less remaining of the original block of stone than in Brancusi's work. Rodin downplayed the role of the material, instead creating a lighter expression of mass and revealing the form and texture of the human body to communicate the power of real, physical love. Brancusi symbolized the strength, permanence, and depth of love by associating the image with the timelessness of the original stone.

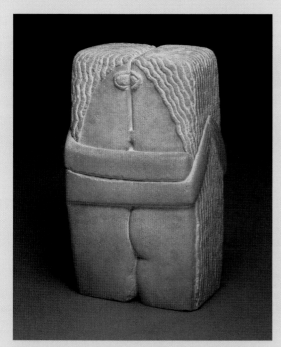

1.2.15 Constantin Brancusi, *The Kiss*, 1916. Limestone, 23 × 13¼ × 10". Philadelphia Museum of Art, Pennsylvania

The Guggenheim Museum, Bilbao

The American architect Frank Gehry (b. 1929) designed the Guggenheim Museum, located between a river and a motorway, in Bilbao, Spain; it was completed in 1997 (**1.2.17**). Bilbao was once a center for shipbuilding, and the powerful curves of Gehry's creation suggest ships and ship construction. Gehry's design uses contrasts in geometric and organic form. Historically, architectural design has relied on geometric form. Organic forms, by comparison, are more difficult to visualize and plan in advance; curved and irregular structures are difficult to survey, measure, plumb, and level. But Gehry used computer programs originally invented for aerospace design to plan buildings that contradict our preconceived ideas about architecture as geometric form. Most of the walls of the Guggenheim Museum consist of irregular, curving, organic forms that rise and fall unpredictably. The undulating surfaces give a sense of movement and life to the structure. This could make some visitors feel disoriented,

but Gehry counters this at critical junctures by using strongly geometric form. At the entrance, for instance, the reassurance of geometric form encourages even the most apprehensive visitor to enter the building.

Gehry employs both sculptural relief and in-the-round forms. The surfaces of the organic portion of the building are covered with titanium tiles. The subtle changes to the surfaces of this material resemble an abstract bas-relief. But the entire building is also like a sculpture in-the-round that the viewer can stroll around to appreciate its unexpected juts and curves.

Gehry's museum has reshaped its location. The interior space, designed to meet the changing needs of art and artists in the future, can also be extended or reduced, creating interesting exhibition opportunities. The complex shapes of the building extend into space like a huge boat, emphasizing its relationship to the nearby River Nervión. When it was first constructed, the building

1.2.17 Frank Gehry, **Guggenheim Museum**, 1997, Bilbao, Spain

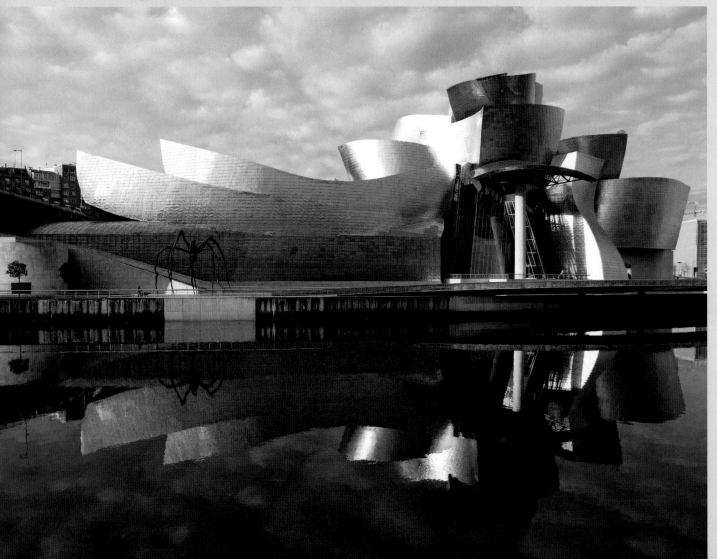

stood in stark contrast to the surrounding urban landscape. It was designed to offer an optimistic vision in what was at that time a deteriorating industrial district, and has done so in the most extraordinary way: inspired by Gehry's creation, this part of the city has been transformed into the vibrant cultural and commercial area it is today.

The shimmering titanium tiles of Gehry's building are complemented by a sculpture that stands beside the museum, *Maman* (**1.2.18**; meaning "Momma" in French), by French artist Louise Bourgeois (1911–2010). The Guggenheim's apparently solid mass is contrasted with the spindly form and open volume of *Maman*. The negative space surrounding the spider's legs and body imparts lightness. The subtle variations of angle in the legs imply movement. The wobbly vulnerability of the spider contrasts with the massive solidity of the building. Even though this spider is made of bronze, the effect is one of lightness. By suspending below the central body a container of marble spheres, like an egg sac, Bourgeois suggests both the tenderness and fierce protectiveness of motherhood.

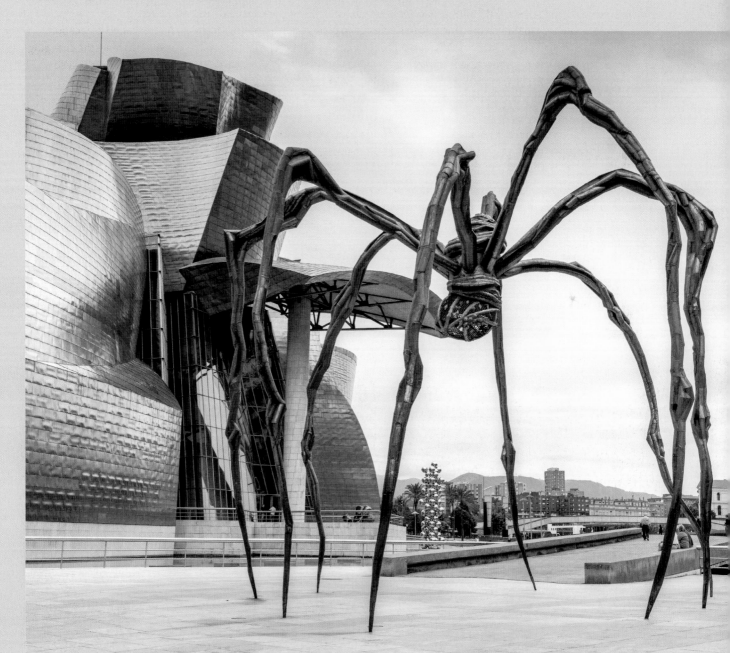

1.2.18 Louise Bourgeois, *Maman*, 1999 (cast 2001). Bronze, stainless steel, and marble, 29' 4⅜" × 32' 9⅛" × 38' 1". Guggenheim Museum, Bilbao, Spain

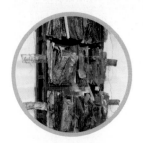

Anselm Kiefer's *Breaking of the Vessels* is an example of an extremely rough texture:
→ see **4.6.11**, p. 611

Texture

Any three-dimensional object that can be touched and felt has actual texture—the tactile sensation we experience when we physically encounter a three-dimensional form. (Two-dimensional images have *implied* texture, which means the artist creates an effect that reminds us of our tactile memory of an actual texture.) Textures vary, from the slick, cold surface of a finely finished metal object, to the rough-hewn splintery character of a broken branch, to the pebbly surface of a rocky beach.

We mostly rely on the impressions we receive from our hands when we think of texture, and these tactile experiences influence the way we look at art. Viewers of Indian-born British artist Anish Kapoor's (b. 1954) sculpture *Cloud Gate* experience actual texture when they see and touch the work (**1.2.19**). We understand the tactile sensation of touching a smooth, stainless-steel surface. Kapoor presents us with a highly polished, organic (bean-like) form that literally reflects the city of Chicago and the surrounding activity as it takes place. By providing such an invitingly slick surface, he wants the viewer to interact with the sculpture in visual and tactile ways. A viewer feels welcome to touch the work, knowing that it will feel cool and slippery: the invitation would not be as clear, or as appealing, if a rougher surface had been presented. The sleek actual texture of this work influences the actions of those viewers who encounter it.

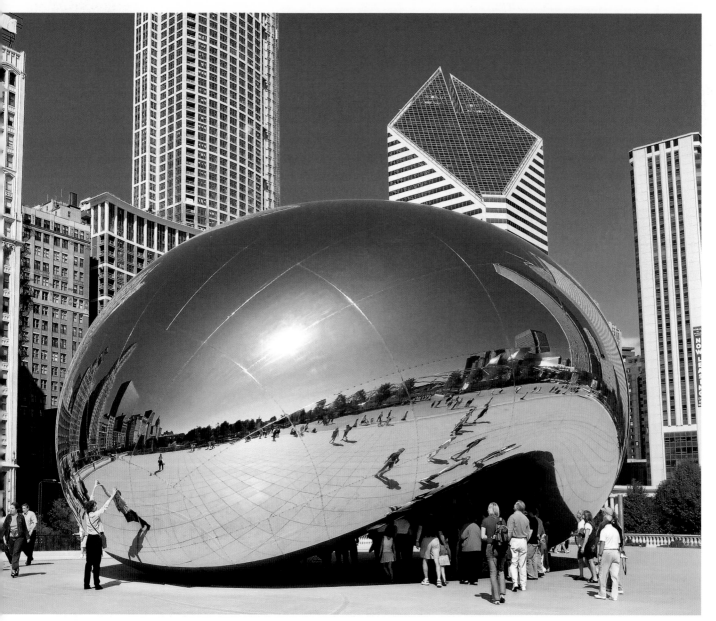

1.2.19 Anish Kapoor, *Cloud Gate*, 2004. Stainless steel, 32' 9" × 65' 7" × 41' 12". Millennium Park, Chicago, Illinois

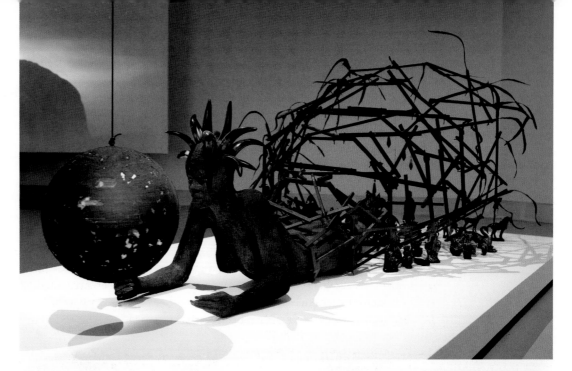

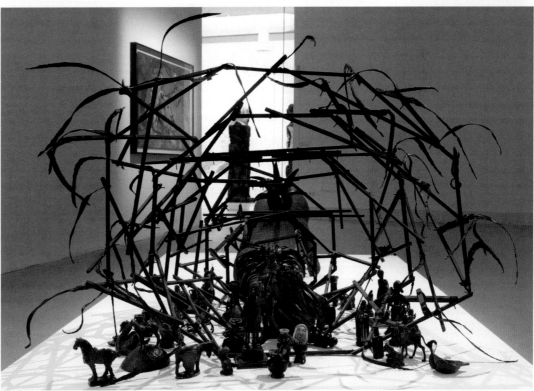

1.2.20a (top) and 1.2.20b (above) Wangechi Mutu, *She's Got the Whole World in Her*, 2015. Mannequin, paper, wax, and lights, 9′ × 5′ × 3′5″

Even if we do not touch three-dimensional works of art, we can still think of them as having actual texture. This is an association we can make based on our previous experience of touching objects that have similar surfaces. We know what polished stone feels like (cool and smooth), so when we look at a highly polished marble sculpture, we can imagine how its texture feels. Although viewers are not encouraged to handle the works of

contemporary African-born artist Wangechi Mutu (b. 1972), texture is still an effective element. In the sculpture *She's Got the Whole World in Her* (**1.2.20a** and **1.2.20b**), Mutu employs a wide variety of organic textures derived from such transient materials as paper and wax to symbolize issues of gender, colonialism, and other concerns unique to people in Africa or of African descent. Textured objects are used to express the changing role

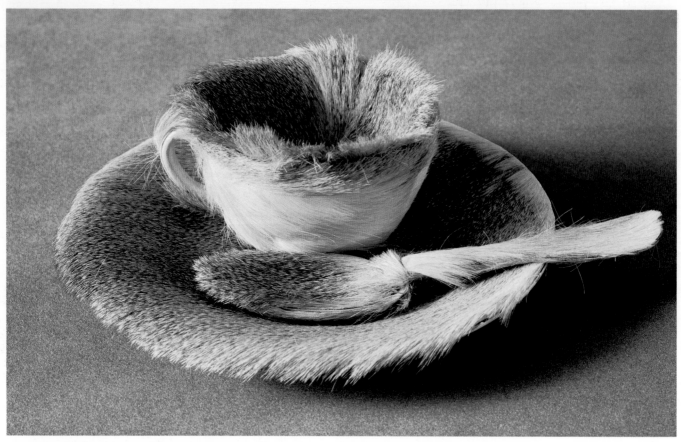

1.2.21 Méret Oppenheim, *Object*, 1936. Fur-covered cup, saucer, and spoon, height 2⅞". MoMA, New York

Surrealism, Surrealist: an artistic movement in the 1920s and later; its works were inspired by dreams and the subconscious

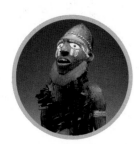

Traditional African art often uses texture to enhance the richness of viewer experience, as in the *nkisi nkondi* figure:
→ see **2.4.11**, p. 235

of African women, from traditional agrarian responsibilities to careers in business and government, as well as modern society in general. This work features a female figure surrounded by natural textures—wood, animal horns, and rough papier mâché—gazing at a lighted globe. Feathers protrude from the rear of the body, which is encased in a basket-like space where small models of animals and figures are placed. The light of the globe and the soft texture of the feathers allude to the elegant and dignified feminine figure, in contrast to the hardness of the horns and the rough construction of the basket-like skirt that imprisons the body.

Subversive Texture

A subversive texture contradicts our previous tactile experience. For example, some types of cactus appear to have a soft, furry covering, but touching them will be painful. Artists

and designers use the contradictions and contrasts of subversive texture to invite viewers to reconsider their preconceptions about the world around them.

In the early twentieth century, artists calling themselves **Surrealists** created work that drew on ideas and images from dreams and the unconscious mind. The Swiss Surrealist Méret Oppenheim (1913–1985) used texture to contradict the conscious logical experiences of viewers. In her sculpture *Object*, Oppenheim takes a cup, saucer, and spoon, normally hard and cool to the touch, and instead makes them soft and furry (**1.2.21**). The idea of sipping tea from this object conjures the unexpected sensation of fur tickling our lips. The artist is counting on our tactile memory to conflict with the actual experience of sipping tea from a shiny teacup. In this case, the form is recognizable, but not the associated experience.

Explore Further Form, Volume, Mass, and Texture

Form

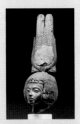

4.5.7 Queen Tiye of Egypt portrait, *c.* 1355 BCE → p. 598

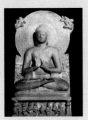

3.3.5 Seated Buddha from the Gupta period, (5th century CE), India → p. 393

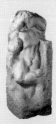

2.4.7 Michelangelo, *Awakening Slave*, 1519–20 → p. 232

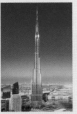

2.5.29 Adrian Smith and Bill Baker, Burj Khalifa, Dubai, 2010 → p. 260

Volume

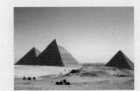

3.3.8 Ritual vessel (*guang*), late Shang Dynasty, *c.* 1700–*c.* 1050 BCE → p. 396

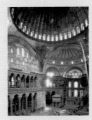

2.5.17 Hagia Sophia, Istanbul, Turkey, 532–35 → p. 253

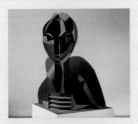

2.4.16 Naum Gabo, *Constructed Head No. 2*, 1916 → p. 239

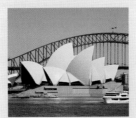

2.5.30 Jørn Utzon, Sydney Opera House, Australia, 1973 → p. 261

Mass

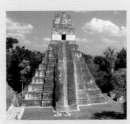

3.1.13 Pyramids at Giza, Egypt, *c.* 2500 BCE → p. 355

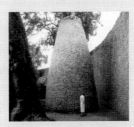

2.5.3 Maya Temple, Tikal, Guatemala, *c.* 300–900 → p. 246

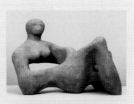

3.5.11 Conical Tower, Great Zimbabwe *c.* 1350–1450 → p. 434

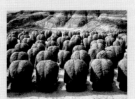

4.8.17 Henry Moore, *Recumbent Figure*, 1938 → p. 642

Texture

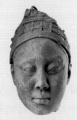

4.8.6 Head, possibly an Ife king from West Africa, 12th–14th century → p. 634

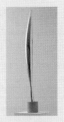

3.9.20 Constantin Brancusi, *Bird in Space*, *c.* 1928 → p. 512

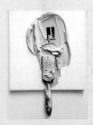

1.10.7 Magdalena Abakanowicz, *80 Backs*, 1976–80 → p. 166

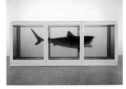

1.7.2 Golsa Golchini, *the lazy pink*, 2020 → p. 131

Your turn

How do these works relate to form, volume, mass, and texture?

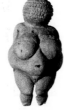

4.8.1 Woman from Willendorf, *c.* 24,000–22,000 BCE → p. 630

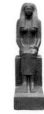

2.4.1 Sculpture of the Lady Sennuwy, 1971–1926 BCE → p. 229

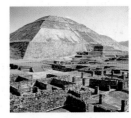

3.4.11 Pyramid of the Sun, Teotihuacan, *c.* 225 → p. 417

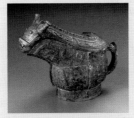

2.4.17 Damien Hirst, *The Physical Impossibility of Death...*, 1991 → p. 239

1.3
Implied Depth: Value and Space

Three-dimensional: having height, width, and depth

Two-dimensional: having height and width

Value: the lightness or darkness of a plane or area

Space: the distance between identifiable points or planes

Perspective: the creation of the illusion of depth in a two-dimensional image by using predictable principles

Isometric perspective: a system using diagonal parallel lines to communicate depth

Reality is merely an illusion, albeit a very persistent one.

(Albert Einstein, physicist and Nobel Prize winner)

When Albert Einstein (1879–1955) suggested that not everything we see is real, he probably did not have art in mind. But artists readily understand his remark, because when they create a picture of real space on a flat surface, they know they are creating an illusion. When we watch a magician perform a trick, we instinctively wonder how the magic was achieved. In this chapter we will reveal some of the secrets that artists rely upon to create the appearance of **three-dimensional** depth in a **two-dimensional** work of art.

The techniques artists use to imply depth—**value**, **space**, and **perspective**—evoke our past visual experiences and the way we see. Value, the lightness or darkness of a surface, emulates the effects of light and shadow, and can be used to suggest solidity. Artists use a variety of techniques based on the optics of vision to create the illusion of pictorial space. One of these is called atmospheric perspective, a method that mimics our visual perceptions of color, clarity, and form at a distance (see p. 73). **Isometric** and **linear perspective** (also explained on pp. 74–78) are drawing methods that can express the idea of three-dimensional space on a two-dimensional surface. In this chapter we will introduce these methods of creating the illusion of space and discuss why some artists choose to use them.

In *The Treachery of Images*, Belgian **Surrealist** artist René Magritte (1898–1967) uses value and perspective to imply depth (**1.3.1**). The pipe is painted in varying values (light and dark tones), which create the appearance of shadows that suggest depth. The top of the pipe bowl is composed of two concentric ellipses, which is how circles appear in perspective. We know what a real pipe looks like in real space, and Magritte understands our habits of visual perception. He paints a picture of a pipe that feels solid, but then playfully invites us to re-examine our habits of mind.

In this painting, Magritte tells us that painting is a visual trick. By writing *"Ceci n'est pas une pipe"* ("This is not a pipe"), Magritte wants us to recognize that what appears to be a pipe is not really a pipe: it is an illusion, nothing more than paint on a flat surface. Magritte confirmed this when someone asked him about the painting once. He replied that it obviously

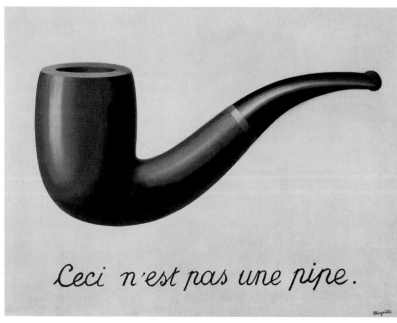

1.3.1 René Magritte, *The Treachery of Images ("This Is not a Pipe")*, 1929. Oil on canvas, 23¾ × 32". Los Angeles County Museum of Art (LACMA), California

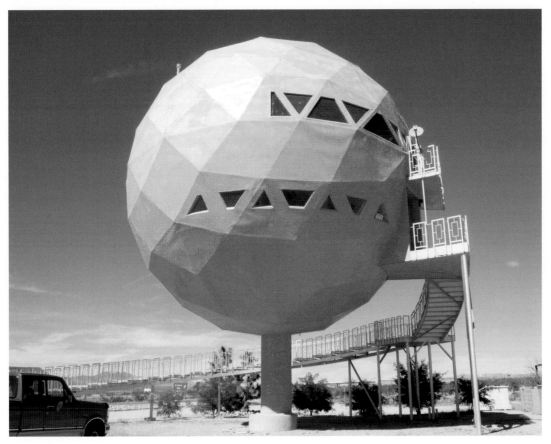

1.3.2 Dinesphere, Yucca, Arizona

Linear perspective: a system using converging imaginary sight lines to create the illusion of depth

Surrealism, Surrealist: an artistic movement in the 1920s and later; its works were inspired by dreams and the subconscious

Style: a characteristic way in which an artist or group of artists uses visual language to give a work an identifiable form of visual expression

Plane: a flat, two-dimensional surface on which an artist can create a drawing or painting. Planes can also be implied in a composition by areas that face toward, parallel to, or away from a light source

was not a real pipe, as anyone who tried to fill it with tobacco would discover.

Value

Value refers to lightness and darkness. An artist's use of value can produce a sense of solidity and can influence our mood. For example, detective movies of the 1940s were filmed in such dark tones that they had their own **style** called *film noir*, French for "black film." The serious mood of these mysteries was enhanced by the filmmaker's choice of dark values. Artists use dark and light values as tools for creating depth.

Artists learn to mimic the appearance of things by observing the effects of light as it illuminates a surface. The Dinesphere—a geodesic structure erected in Yucca, Arizona—demonstrates the effect of light on **planes** in varying locations (**1.3.2**). Many triangular planes make up the sphere's surface. Each plane has a different value, the relative degree of lightness or darkness of the plane depending upon the amount of light shining on it. The light source (high and to the left of the sphere here) hits some of the triangular planes of the Dinesphere more directly than others. The planes that have a lighter value are facing the light source; the darker ones are facing away.

Value changes often occur gradually. If you look at the Dinesphere, you will notice that the relative dark values increase as the planes get further away and face away from the light (**1.3.3**). These changes occur on any

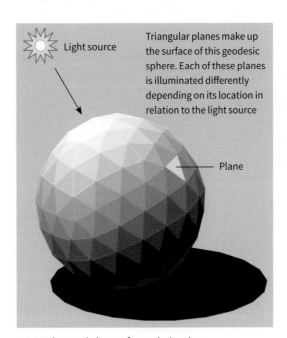

Light source

Triangular planes make up the surface of this geodesic sphere. Each of these planes is illuminated differently depending on its location in relation to the light source

Plane

1.3.3 Values and planes of a geodesic sphere

Chiaroscuro: the use of light and dark in a painting to create the impression of volume

Renaissance: a period of cultural and artistic change in Europe from the fourteenth to the seventeenth century

Highlight: an area of lightest value in a work

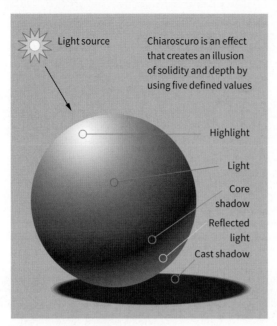

Light source

Chiaroscuro is an effect that creates an illusion of solidity and depth by using five defined values

Highlight

Light

Core shadow

Reflected light

Cast shadow

1.3.4 Diagram of chiaroscuro

object. There are subtle value changes even in a white object.

A value range refers to a series of different values. In the image of the geodesic sphere there is a value range of black, white, and eight values of gray. Black and white are the values at the extreme ends of this range.

Chiaroscuro

Chiaroscuro (Italian for "light-dark") is a method of applying value to a two-dimensional piece of artwork to create the illusion of a three-dimensional solid form (**1.3.4**). The illusion of solidity and depth in two dimensions can be achieved by using an approach devised by artists of the Italian **Renaissance**. Using a sphere as their model, Renaissance artists identified five distinct areas of light and shadow. A **highlight** marks the point where the object is most directly lit. This is most often depicted as bright white. From the highlight, moving toward the shadow, progressively less light is cast on the object until the point is reached where the surface faces away from the light. At this point there is a more sudden transition to darker values, or core shadow. At the bottom of the sphere a lighter value is produced by shadow mixed with light reflected from the surrounding environment. This lighter value defines the bottom edge of the sphere. In contrast, the sphere casts a shadow away from the direction of the light source. Near the edge of the cast shadow, as light from the surrounding environment increases, the shadow becomes lighter.

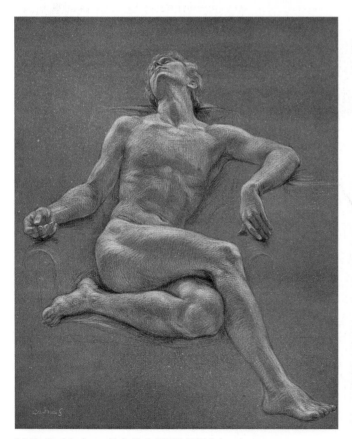

1.3.5a Paul Cadmus, *Male Nude NM32*, 1967. Colored crayons on hand-toned paper, 19½ × 16⅛″

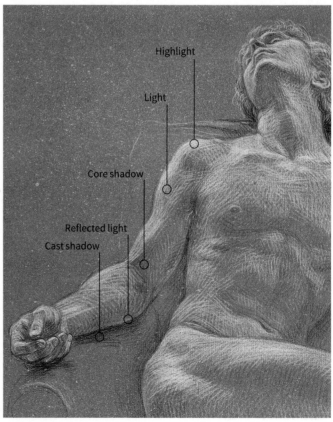

Highlight

Light

Core shadow

Reflected light

Cast shadow

1.3.5b Chiaroscuro annotations on Paul Cadmus, *Male Nude NM32*, (detail)

In *Male Nude NM32*, the American artist Paul Cadmus (1904–1999) uses chiaroscuro to draw a male figure (**1.3.5a**). If you look carefully at the figure's arm (**1.3.5b**), you can see that the chiaroscuro is used just as it is in **1.3.4**. There is an area of highlight on the shoulder transitioning to the lighted left side of the arm. Under the bicep there is a strong core shadow: reflected light can be seen on the right side of the arm. This light is accentuated by the dark cast shadow under the forearm. Cadmus's use of brown, red, and white chalk on tan-toned paper allows him to accentuate the lightest and darkest areas, the chiaroscuro.

Dramatic and beautiful effects can be achieved through the use of chiaroscuro, especially if it is exaggerated. *The Calling of St. Matthew* by the Italian artist Caravaggio (1571–1610) uses strongly contrasting values to convert a quiet gathering into a pivotal and powerful event (**1.3.6**). This extreme type of chiaroscuro, often referred to as **tenebrism**, relies on a single light source and broad areas of darkness or shadow. The intense difference between lights and darks places extra **emphasis** on Christ's hand as he singles out Matthew, who points to himself in response. The light also frames Matthew and highlights the

Tenebrism: dramatic use of intense darkness and light to heighten the impact of a painting

Emphasis: the principle of drawing attention to particular content in a work

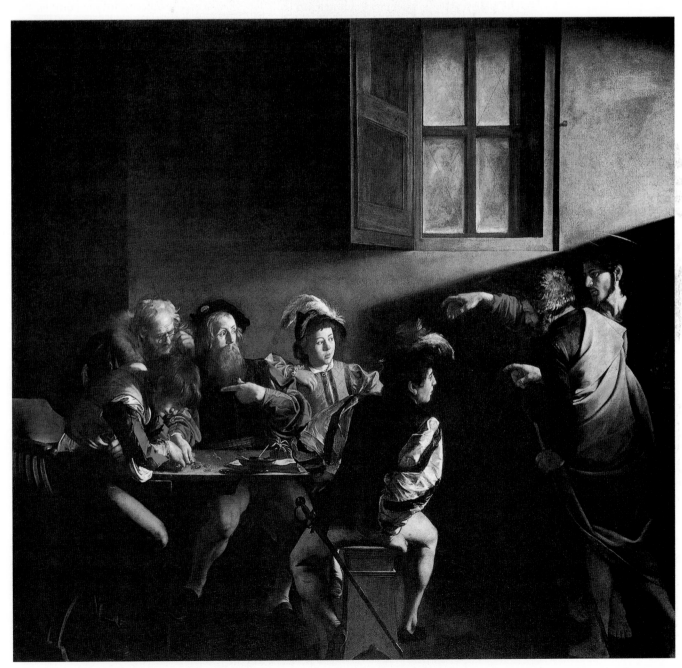

1.3.6 Caravaggio, *The Calling of St. Matthew*, *c.* 1599–1600. Oil on canvas, 11'1" × 11'5". Contarelli Chapel, San Luigi dei Francesi, Rome, Italy

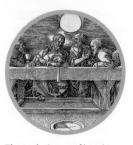

The techniques of hatching and cross-hatching can be found in Albrecht Dürer's version of the *Last Supper*:
→ see **3.6.19**, p. 458

surprised looks of the others in the room as he is called to become one of Christ's disciples.

Hatching and Cross-Hatching

Artists also use a method called **hatching** to express value (**1.3.7**). Hatching consists of a series of lines, close to and parallel to each other. **Media** that demand a thin line, for example **engraving** or pen-and-ink drawing, do not allow much variation in the width of the line. Here an artist may choose hatching or **cross-hatching** (a variant of hatching in which the lines overlap) to suggest values that create a greater sense of form and depth.

The Italian artist Michelangelo Buonarroti (1475–1564) uses cross-hatching in his pen and ink drawing *Head of a Satyr* (**1.3.8**). Cross-hatching gives the face of the satyr solidity and depth. By building up layers of brown ink, Michelangelo overcomes the restrictions of the

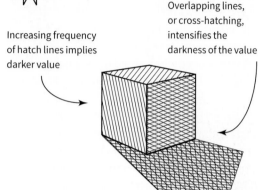

Increasing frequency of hatch lines implies darker value

Overlapping lines, or cross-hatching, intensifies the darkness of the value

1.3.7 Creating value using hatching and cross-hatching

pen's thin line. For example, if we look carefully at the cheekbone of the satyr it appears to be jutting out toward us. This effect is created by hatching and cross-hatching. The bright white highlight uses no lines; the surrounding hatch lines define the transition from bright light to a darker value.

As we move our gaze downward and to the right of the highlight, we notice that a second layer of overlapping hatching lines intersects the diagonals bordering the highlight. Then, as we continue to scan downward and to the right, we see more layers of hatching lines crossing over the previous ones. As the hatching lines cross over and over, the value appears to get darker. Michelangelo communicates three-dimensional depth using narrow and two-dimensional lines.

Space

Value is just one of a variety of techniques artists use to create a sense of depth and the illusion of space in a work of art. We will now explain some other methods.

Size, Overlapping, and Position

In a work of art, the size of one **shape** compared to another often suggests that the larger object is closer to us. Another way to create the illusion of depth is to overlap shapes. If one shape appears to overlap another, the shape in front seems closer than the shape that is partially covered. Position in the **picture plane** is also an effective device for implying depth. A shape lower in the picture plane appears to be closer.

The Finnish artist Beda Stjernschantz (1865–1910) uses all of these devices—relative

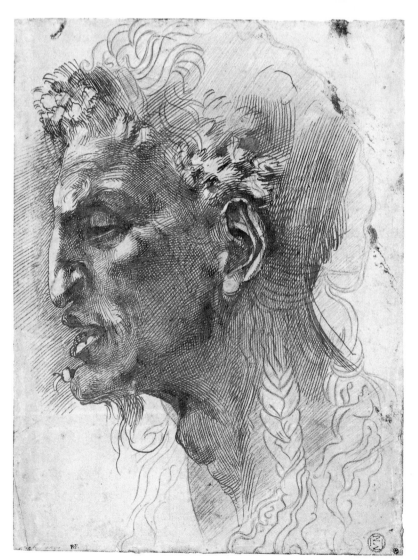

1.3.8 Michelangelo, *Head of a Satyr*, c. 1520–30. Pen and ink on paper, 10⅝ × 7⅞". Musée du Louvre, Paris, France

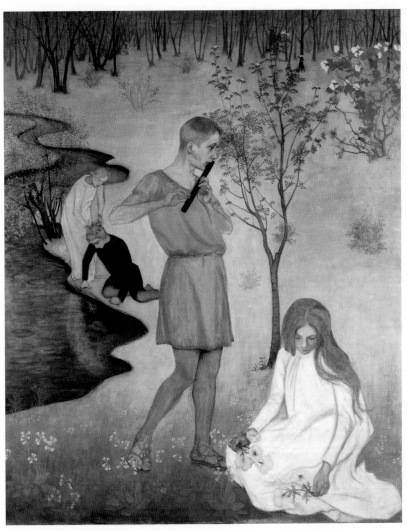

1.3.9 **Beda Stjernschantz,** *Pastoral (Primavera)*, 1897. Oil on canvas, 49⅝ × 41¾".
K. H. Renlund Museum, Kokkola, Finland.

Hatching: the use of non-overlapping parallel lines to convey darkness or lightness

Medium (plural **media**): the material on or from which an artist chooses to make a work of art, for example canvas and oil paint, marble, engraving, video, or architecture

Engraving: a printmaking technique where the artist gouges or scratches the image into the surface of the printing plate

Cross-hatching: the use of overlapping parallel lines to convey darkness or lightness

Shape: a two-dimensional area, the boundaries of which are defined by lines or suggested by changes in color or value

Picture plane: the surface of a painting or drawing

Relative placement: the arrangement of shapes or lines to form a visual relationship to one another in a design

Foreground: the part of a work depicted as nearest to the viewer

Middle ground: the part of a work between the foreground and the background

Background: the part of a work depicted furthest from the viewer's space, often behind the main subject matter

size, overlapping, and strategic positioning of shapes in the picture plane—to create an illusion of depth in her work *Pastoral (Primavera)* (**1.3.9**). The passive, idyllic scene draws us into a landscape that does not exist, but we feel a sense of depth because the artist makes it possible for us to be imaginatively transported there. In the painting there are two pairs of figures; one is larger than the other, which informs the viewer's understanding of space. The two figures in the center left of the image, who are positioned near a river, are notably smaller than those that dominate the lower right corner of the work. We see the larger figures as closer because of this difference in size.

Stjernschantz also implies depth by positioning the larger figure with the flute in a way that conceals the foot of one of the smaller figures. Similarly, we interpret the woman in the white dress as being closest to us because she partly obscures the left foot of the flute player. The artist further enhances the illusion of depth by placing the figure in white against the bottom of the work and setting the smaller pair of figures higher in the composition.

In using such **relative placement**, the artist invites us to saunter visually from the **foreground** (where the two largest figures are placed) to the **middle ground** (where the smaller group of figures is set), and continue on our visual journey along the softly curving river and into the beckoning woods in the **background** (the uppermost area of the work). Even though there are no noticeable value differences between the groups, Stjernschantz uses enough placement strategy and size change to imply depth to a viewer.

Alternating Value and Texture

The illusion of depth in two dimensions is often influenced by the arrangement of value

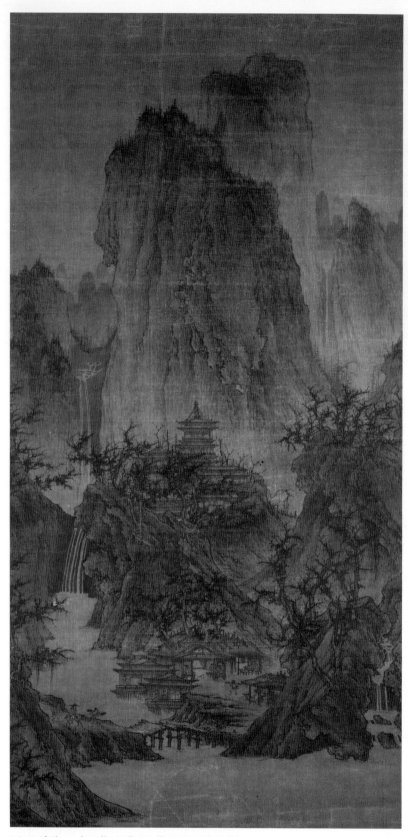

1.3.10 Li Cheng (attributed), *A Solitary Temple Amid Clearing Peaks*, Northern Song Dynasty, *c.* 960–1127. Hanging scroll, ink, and slight color on silk, 44 × 22". Nelson–Atkins Museum, Kansas City, Missouri

and **texture**. Artists intersperse value and visual texture to create a sense of **rhythm**. Look at *A Solitary Temple Amid Clearing Peaks* (**1.3.10**), attributed to Chinese painter Li Cheng (*c.* 919–967). From the bottom up, we first confront a section of water, perhaps the shoreline of a lake, followed by a small bridge and then some architectural structures set amongst a rocky, tree-filled landscape. Moving upward we see a light area—immediately behind and above the solitary temple that gives this work its name—after which the values gradually darken as our view climbs the face of the mountain. Finally, as we reach above the peaks, the sky is again lighter, completing the alternating rhythm from bottom to top. Each area of light and dark occupies different amounts of space, making the design more interesting. We can also note the change in visual texture from bottom to top. The texture appears to be extremely rough and detailed near the bottom, with craggy rocks and gnarled trees dominating the foreground. From this point it progressively becomes less precise: as Li's landscape rises, it also appears to recede behind the soft mist, then reappear with great vertical strength. The trees at the top of the scroll have lost the gnarled texture and now look soft and fuzzy as they crown the mountain crest. These visual layers create a sense of depth as they accentuate differences in both value and texture.

Brightness and Color

Brightness and color can both be used to suggest depth in a work of art. Lighter areas seem to be closer as dark areas appear to recede. This is especially true of color. For example, we are more likely to think that a green that is very pure and intense is closer to us than a darker green. The American painter Thomas Hart Benton (1889–1975) used brightness and color to create and manipulate our sense of distance in his painting *The Wreck of the Ole '97* (**1.3.11**). Benton wanted the viewer to be a witness to one of the most notorious train disasters in American history, in which several people died. In the green areas we see the bright, pure greens come forward as the darker, less intense greens fall away. The greens in the lower central portion of the work are more intense than the greens on the far left. Because we perceive color that is more intense as being closer, this difference in color **intensity** helps us to feel that we are *just* at enough

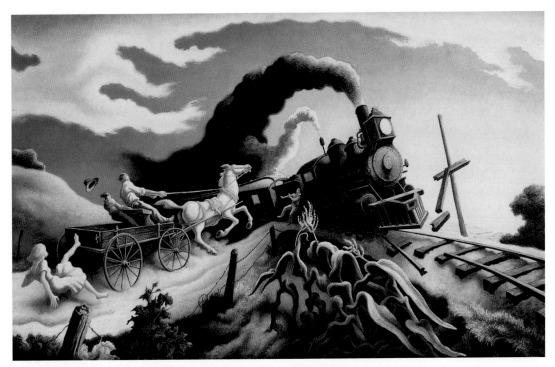

1.3.11 **Thomas Hart Benton**, *The Wreck of the Ole '97*, 1943. Egg tempera on gessoed masonite, 28½ × 44½". Hunter Museum of Art, Chattanooga, Tennessee

distance to witness the terrible train wreck without becoming another of its casualties. Yet by painting the engine steaming ahead, at an angle that suggests it is about to hit the broken rail in the foreground and head straight out of the picture, hurtling inevitably toward us, Benton simultaneously manages to convey a fearful sense of danger.

Perspective

Artists, architects, and designers who wish to suggest the illusion of depth on a two-dimensional surface use perspective. They have the choice of several ways to do this, of which three are the most common. Atmospheric perspective modifies value, color, and texture to create the sense that some parts of an image are situated further away than others. Isometric perspective uses diagonal parallels to communicate depth, while linear perspective relies on a system where lines appear to converge at points in space. All these forms of perspective tap into some of the ways we see the world and think about space.

Atmospheric Perspective Some artists use **atmospheric perspective** to create the illusion of depth. Distant objects lack **contrast**, detail, and sharpness of focus, because the air that surrounds us is not completely transparent. The effect makes objects with strong color take

on a blue-gray middle value as they get further away: the atmosphere progressively veils a scene as the distance increases. Contemporary filmmakers use this atmospheric effect to give the illusion of great depth, just as traditional artists have always done.

In **1.3.12** the Greek temple to the left appears to be closer to the viewer than the other temples because its colors are brighter and its shape is more sharply defined. The smallest temple

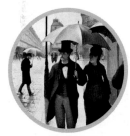

Caillebotte's *Paris Street, Rainy Day* is an example of atmospheric perspective:
→ see **3.8.14**, p. 491

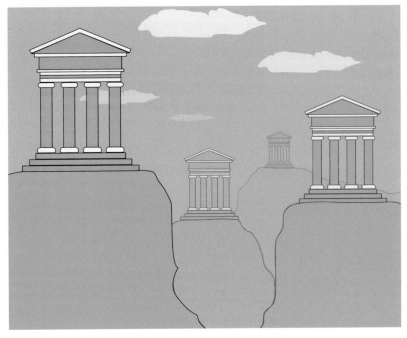

1.3.12 The effects of atmospheric perspective

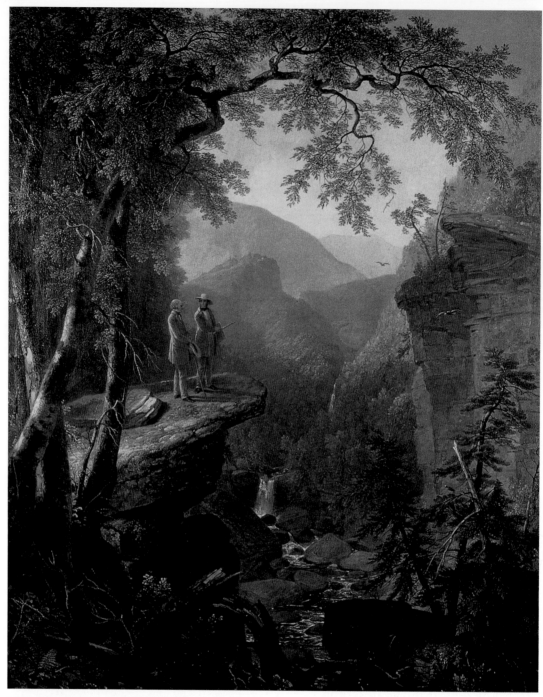

1.3.13 Asher Brown Durand, *Kindred Spirits*, 1849. Oil on canvas, 44 × 36″.
Crystal Bridges Museum of American Art, Bentonville, Arkansas

lacks detail and is tinged blue-gray, making it seem the furthest away. The American Asher Brown Durand (1796–1886) used comparable effects in his painting *Kindred Spirits* (**1.3.13**). The trees in the foreground are detailed and bright green, but as the trees recede into the landscape behind the two figures, they become a lighter gray and increasingly out of focus. Lines and shapes also become less distinct as the illusion of distance increases. By using atmospheric perspective, Durand conveys an impression of the vastness of the American landscape.

Isometric Perspective Isometric perspective arranges parallel lines diagonally in a work to give a sense of depth. The word isometric derives from the Greek meaning "equal measure." The system has been used by artists in China for more than a thousand years. It was particularly suitable for painting on scrolls, which can be examined only in sections.

Since Chinese landscape painters were not generally interested in portraying space from a single viewpoint—they preferred to convey multiple viewpoints simultaneously—isometric perspective was their chosen technique to convey the illusion of space in the structural lines of architecture and other rectilinear objects. A section from the painting *The Qianlong Emperor's Southern Inspection Tour, Scroll Six: Entering Suzhou and the Grand Canal* by Xu Yang shows this system in action (**1.3.14**). The parallel diagonal lines that define the small L-shaped building in the lower right of the work suggest a three-dimensional object (**1.3.15**). Xu Yang, a Chinese artist working in the 1770s, uses this method to give the architecture along the Grand Canal the illusion of depth. This method of implying depth is not **realistic** according to the Western tradition, but the artist makes use of other spatial devices to help us understand how the space is structured. For example, the diminishing size of the trees as they recede into the distance reinforces the sense of depth.

Realism: an artistic style that aims to represent appearances as accurately as possible

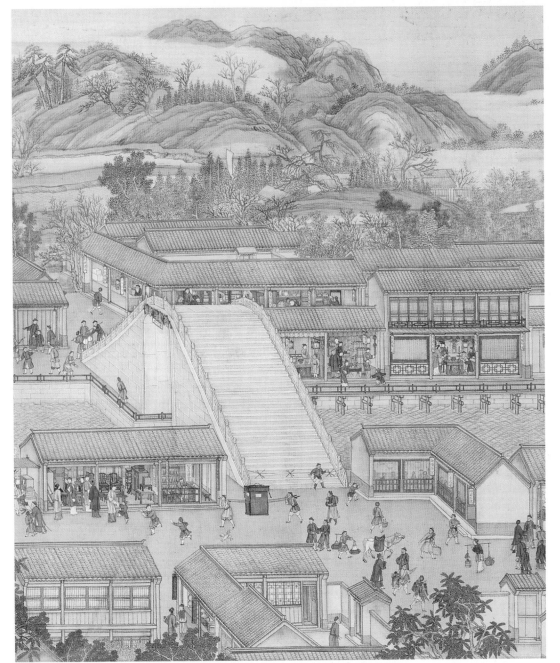

1.3.14 Xu Yang, *The Qianlong Emperor's Southern Inspection Tour, Scroll Six: Entering Suzhou and the Grand Canal*, Qing Dynasty, 1770 (detail). Hand scroll, ink and color on silk, 2'3⅛" × 65'4½". Metropolitan Museum of Art, New York

Lines are drawn parallel and diagonal to create depth in isometric perspective

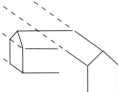

1.3.15 Graphic detailing isometric perspective in scroll image

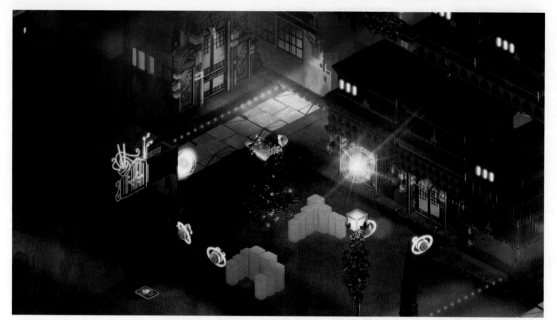

1.3.16 Supergiant Games, screenshot from *Transistor*, 2014. Art Director, Jen Zee

Isometric perspective is now common in contemporary computer graphics as well. The computer and video console game *Transistor* (**1.3.16**) is designed to express depth using a perspective method similar to the one Xu Yang used in 1770. The designers have created the architecture of the game with parallel diagonal lines so that the playing area consists of small rectangular graphic images that are known as tiles. The tiles allow uniform objects to remain the same size, yet as the objects are moved around the game environment, they still imply depth. The game designers' choice of isometric perspective allows players to move from level to level and space to space without distortion because the individual tiles remain the same size.

Linear Perspective Linear perspective is a mathematical system that uses lines to create the illusion of depth in a two-dimensional artwork. (The lines can be **actual lines**, for example of buildings, or **implied lines** of figures or shapes.) The linear perspective systems used by artists are based on observation of space in the world we see around us. For example, the two sides of a straight railway line or road appear to converge as they recede into the distance, even though in reality they are parallel. This system, created through the use of line, emulates the observed effect of diminishing size that naturally occurs where distant identical objects appear smaller than those nearby.

Like many ideas in human history, linear perspective was developed with knowledge acquired over centuries. Mozi, a Chinese philosopher working in the fifth century BCE; Alhazen, an Arab mathematician from around the year 1000; and Leon Battista Alberti (1404–1472), an Italian Renaissance architect: each contributed ideas that helped artists to understand light and its properties more fully. Knowledge of light's properties led other Renaissance artists to use a projection device called a camera obscura (Latin for "dark room") to explore the possibilities of naturalistic illusion and the re-creation of reality. The device consisted of a small dark box, which would conduct sunlight through a little pinhole and allow a real, full-color, upside-down image of the objects outside the device to be projected with light onto a surface. The artist could then draw the projected image, or trace it directly onto paper or canvas. Images created using this device revealed recurring ways in which lines could be arranged, and this influenced the artist and architect Filippo Brunelleschi (1377–1446) to create a practical way of expressing the theories of depth using linear perspective.

Because Brunelleschi, as an architect, was interested in the realistic representation of buildings, he began to work with ideas about perspective and the idea that light enters the eye. He combined this with use of the camera obscura to prove that reality could be re-created in art using a system of lines. It had been demonstrated that an image projected onto a

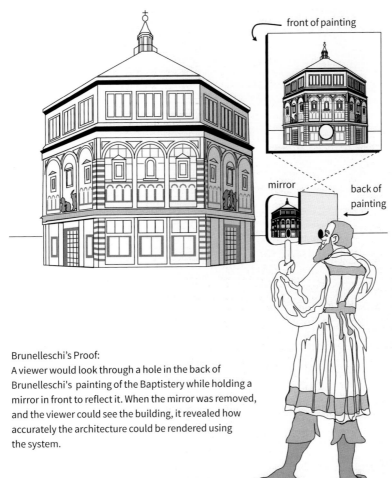

front of painting

mirror | back of painting

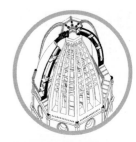

Brunelleschi's main vocations were sculpture and architecture. See a diagram of his design for the dome of Florence Cathedral:
→ see **3.6.5**, p. 445

Brunelleschi's Proof:
A viewer would look through a hole in the back of Brunelleschi's painting of the Baptistery while holding a mirror in front to reflect it. When the mirror was removed, and the viewer could see the building, it revealed how accurately the architecture could be rendered using the system.

1.3.17a Brunelleschi's proof of the accuracy of linear perspective

surface in a camera obscura could be traced to produce a convincing illusion of depth, but this did not explain exactly how the illusion of depth was created. Brunelleschi took this discovery one step further by formulating rules of linear perspective to allow an artist to depict realistically something observed without the aid of a camera obscura. To prove his point, Brunelleschi painted an image of the Florence Baptistery (**1.3.17b**), applying his set of rules, on a polished piece of silver. He then drilled a small hole in the silver plate so that a viewer could look through the back of it and, holding a mirror up in front of it, could see the painted image of the Baptistery reflected in the mirror (**1.3.17a**). The viewer could then compare the degree of realism of the painting with the real Baptistery itself by removing the mirror to confirm that Brunelleschi's rules worked. Although many artists had effectively approximated linear perspective, Brunelleschi was the first to define it formally as a practical system.

Brunelleschi's discovery became, for hundreds of years, a standard systematic process for creating an impression of realistic

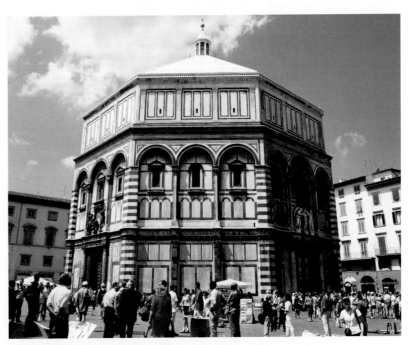

1.3.17b The Baptistery, Florence, Italy

depth. The British artist Edith Hayllar (1860–1948) exhibited many works at the Royal Academy (a rare honor for a woman artist at the time) between 1882 and 1897. The enhanced

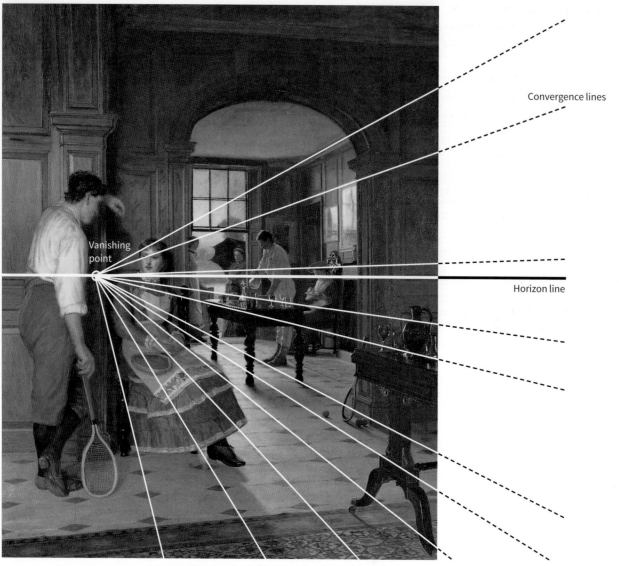

Convergence lines

Vanishing point

Horizon line

1.3.18 The effect of convergences: **Edith Hayllar**, *A Summer Shower*, 1883. Oil on panel, 21 × 17⅜".
Private collection

photograph of her painting *A Summer Shower* shows the basis for linear perspective (**1.3.18**). The converging lines represent planes that are parallel to each other in reality. Notice how, if we were to draw lines from the right side of the image and continue them until they intersect, these parallel lines would appear to converge on one single point, on the horizon line, in front of the male tennis player on the left of the painting. This is the **vanishing point**. These converging parallel lines are also known as **orthogonals**; the artist uses them here to create a composition that reflects the orderly life of upper-middle-class Victorian England.

There are a number of variations of linear perspective—**one-point**, two-point, and multiple-point—depending on the effect the artist wants to achieve. These formal approaches to conveying a sense of depth are important tools, so we will now look at each one in some detail to see how they function and the different kinds of effects they produce.

One-Point Perspective Brunelleschi created his painting of the Florence Baptistery using one-point perspective, but the one-point perspective system has some limitations. Although the system makes it possible to represent real space, certain rules have to be followed. Since one-point perspective relies on a single vanishing point, the scene must be directly in front of the artist and receding. The effect is something like standing on an empty highway facing an underpass (**1.3.19**). The sides of the road and the inside of the underpass appear to follow converging paths to a single point on the horizon. But if you redirect your gaze to the right or left of the underpass, the edges of the roadway and underpass are out of direct sight and it is not as easy to see the recession of space.

One of the first artists to use one-point perspective was the Italian painter Masaccio (1401–1428). In his **fresco** of the Christian Holy Trinity, Masaccio places the horizon line, an imaginary line that mimics the horizon, at the viewer's eye level (note the figure) and centers the vanishing point in the middle of that line (**1.3.20**). The horizon line represents our eye level and is the basis for the setting-out of a perspective drawing. The orthogonals create an illusion that the background is an architectural

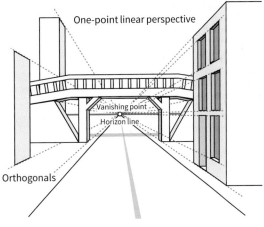

1.3.19 Applying one-point perspective technique

Vanishing point(s): the point or points in a work of art at which imaginary sight lines appear to converge, suggesting depth

Orthogonals: in perspective systems, imaginary sight lines extending from forms to the vanishing point

One-point perspective: a perspective system with a single vanishing point on the horizon

Fresco: a technique where the artist paints onto freshly applied plaster. From the Italian *fresco*, "fresh"

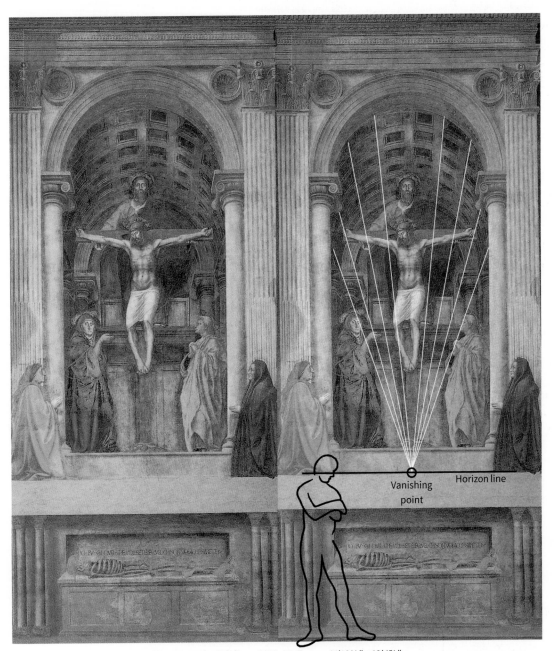

1.3.20 Use of one-point perspective: **Masaccio**, *Trinity*, *c.* 1425–26. Fresco, 21'10½" × 10'4⅞". Santa Maria Novella, Florence, Italy

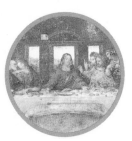

Another famous example of one-point linear perspective is Leonardo da Vinci's *The Last Supper*: → see **3.6.18**, p. 457

Raphael, *The School of Athens*
The Illusion of Depth

For the other Raphael
GATEWAYS:
→ see p. 180 and p. 448

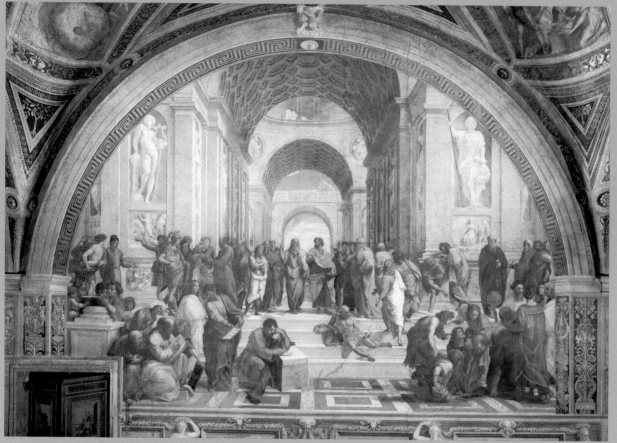

1.3.21a Raphael, *The School of Athens*, 1510–11. Fresco, 16'8" × 25'. Stanza della Segnatura, Vatican City, Italy

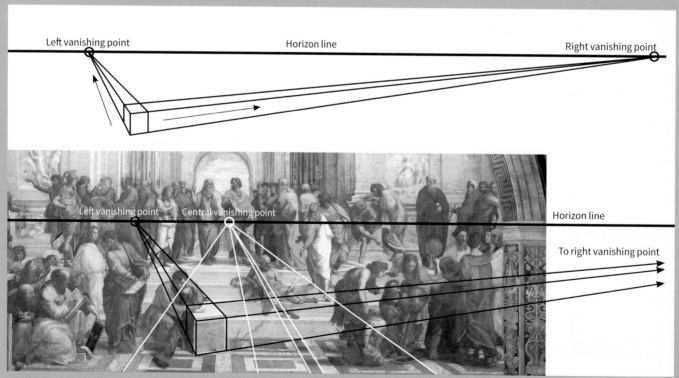

1.3.21b Applying two-point perspective: **Raphael, *The School of Athens* (detail)**

The Italian artist Raphael (1483–1520) painted *The School of Athens* on one of the walls of the library of Pope Julius II in the Vatican, in Rome, to create the illusion of an architectural space that was separate from the actual room. This wall was designed as part of a larger program including three other paintings, an intricately tiled floor, and a painted ceiling, all choreographed thematically as a backdrop for Pope Julius II's library. The Pope's hundreds of books were laid on shelves built directly under the paintings on each of the four walls (these shelves have since been removed).

The School of Athens highlights the development of learning in the ancient world, focusing on the great philosophers Plato and Aristotle, who are the central figures in the painting.

In *The School of Athens* Raphael combines one-point perspective and two-point perspective in a single composition (**1.3.21a** and **1.3.21b**). The figure in the foreground is leaning against an object set at an angle that is not perpendicular and parallel to the rest of the architectural setting. Consequently, it cannot depend on the central vanishing point that has been determined following the rules of one-point perspective, or it will be distorted. Raphael deals with this situation by introducing two additional vanishing points. Notice that both of these fall on the horizon line, following the established rules of perspective (vanishing points must fall on the horizon line). One vanishing point is positioned to the left of the central vanishing point that anchors the architecture, and the right vanishing point is outside of the picture. The block in the center is the only object in the composition that uses these two vanishing points, because the viewer is not perpendicular or parallel to it. Since it is turned at an angle, Raphael had to integrate another level of perspective into the work. All of the objects and architectural spaces depicted in this painting rely on one of these two perspective points.

setting. The end result is an effective illusion of depth on a two-dimensional surface that must have amazed visitors at the church of Santa Maria Novella in Florence, Italy. Masaccio's work was innovative for its time and influenced other significant artists of the Renaissance, including Michelangelo.

Two-Point Perspective The one-point perspective system worked for Masaccio because his composition relied on the viewer standing directly in front of the vanishing point. But if the vanishing point is not directly (or near directly) in front of a viewer, or if the objects in the work are not all parallel, one-point perspective does not create a believable illusion of depth. The Italian artist Raphael (1483–1520) dealt with this problem in his famous painting *The School of Athens* (**1.3.21a** and **1.3.21b**).

Multiple-Point Perspective As artists discovered the many possibilities of linear perspective for creating illusions of space, they began to expand on the idea of multiple-point perspective systems. Any object that exists in our cone of vision—the area we can see without moving our head or eyes—can usually be depicted using vanishing points on the horizon line (**1.3.22**). But if we are looking at an object from a position other than ground level, then we will need points *away* from the horizon line and other variations on perspective.

Objects and spaces that have right angles make it easy to work out where vanishing points should be: we can use one-point perspective. Unfortunately, many objects are made up of multiple angles that need even more vanishing points. As more of these are incorporated into a design, the artist can more readily reflect the complexities of the real world.

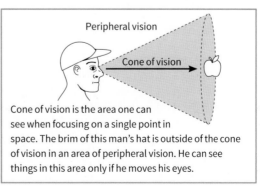

Peripheral vision

Cone of vision

Cone of vision is the area one can see when focusing on a single point in space. The brim of this man's hat is outside of the cone of vision in an area of peripheral vision. He can see things in this area only if he moves his eyes.

1.3.22 Cone of vision

The most common multiple-point perspective system is **three-point perspective**: here a vanishing point is placed above or below the horizon line to accommodate a high or low angle of observation. Whether this third vanishing point is above or below the horizon depends on whether the viewer has a worm's-eye (looking up) or bird's-eye (looking down) view. The Dutch graphic artist M. C. Escher (1898–1972) uses a third vanishing point in *Ascending and Descending*; we can see three distinct vanishing points (**1.3.23**). Two of the vanishing points are placed on the horizon line, but one is well below it. This gives us a bird's-eye view of the structure that allows us to see its sides while looking down on it as if from above.

Foreshortening

Foreshortening results when the rules of perspective are applied to represent unusual points of view. An illustration of Superman for DC Comics illustrates foreshortening (**1.3.24**). The figure of Superman is oriented so that his fist is in the extreme foreground, with the rest of his body receding into space. The artist makes the fist on the right side larger than Superman's head, exaggerating the depth. The entire figure is vertically shortened, compared to a frontal standing position, because of the oblique angle from which we are viewing the character. Like the linear perspective in the city below, foreshortening has the effect of grabbing our interest. It looks as if Superman is blasting toward us through the air over downtown Metropolis, on his way to save the day.

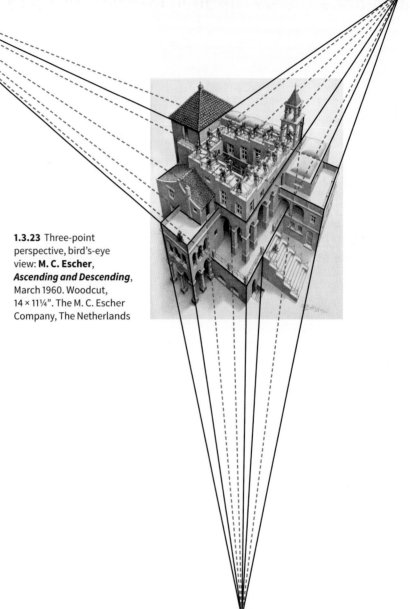

1.3.23 Three-point perspective, bird's-eye view: **M. C. Escher**, ***Ascending and Descending***, March 1960. Woodcut, 14 × 11¼". The M. C. Escher Company, The Netherlands

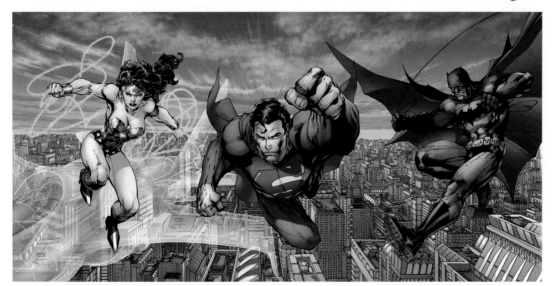

1.3.24 Wonder Woman, Superman, and Batman, pages from *Trinity: Volume 1*, ™ and © DC Comics

Three-point perspective: a perspective system with two vanishing points on the horizon and one not on the horizon

Foreshortening: a perspective technique that depicts a form—often distorting or reducing it—at an angle that is not parallel to the picture plane, in order to convey the illusion of depth

Explore Further   Implied Depth: Value and Space

Value

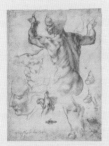

2.1.15 Michelangelo, *Studies for the Libyan Sibyl*, 1510–11 ➔ p. 186

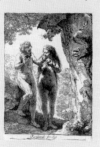

2.3.10 Rembrandt van Rijn, *Adam and Eve*, 1638 ➔ p. 218

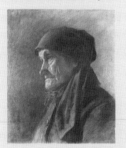

2.1.13 Léon Augustin Lhermitte, *An Elderly Peasant Woman*, c. 1878 ➔ p. 185

Space

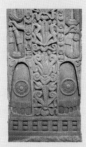

3.3.3 Detail of North Gate, Great Stupa, Sanchi, India, 1st century BCE ➔ p. 392

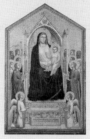

3.2.27 Giotto, *Virgin and Child Enthroned*, c. 1310 ➔ p. 388

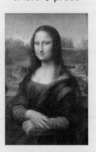

0.0.12 Leonardo da Vinci, *Mona Lisa*, 1503–6 ➔ p. 23

Perspective

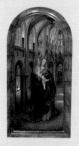

1.7.5 Jan van Eyck, *Madonna in a Church*, 1437–38 ➔ p. 133

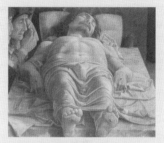

4.3.12 Andrea Mantegna, *Dead Christ*, c. 1480 ➔ p. 576

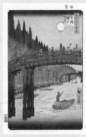

1.8.11 Ando Hiroshige, "Riverside Bamboo Market, Kyo-bashi," 1857 ➔ p. 146

Your turn

How do these works relate to value, space, and perspective?

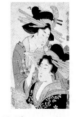

1.10.12a Diego de Silva y Velázquez, *Las Meninas*, c. 1656 ➔ p. 171

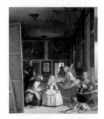

3.8.10 Kitagawa Utamaro, *Two Courtesans*, second half of 18th century ➔ p. 488

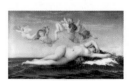

3.8.1 Alexandre Cabanel, *Birth of Venus*, 1863 ➔ p. 481

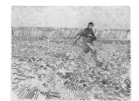

2.1.23 Vincent van Gogh, *Sower with Setting Sun*, 1888 ➔ p. 191

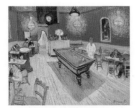

1.4.28 Vincent van Gogh, *The Night Café*, 1888 ➔ p. 99

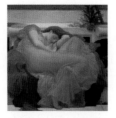

0.0.6 Frederic Leighton, *Flaming June*, 1895 ➔ p. 19

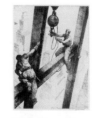

1.1.8 James Allen, *The Connectors*, 1934, ➔ p. 39

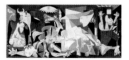

4.6.10 Pablo Picasso, *Guernica*, 1937 ➔ p. 611

1.4
Color

The first colors that made a strong impression on me were bright, juicy green, white, carmine red, black and yellow ochre. These memories go back to the third year of my life. I saw these colors on various objects which are no longer as clear in my mind as the colors themselves.

(Vasily Kandinsky, Russian painter)

Color is the most vivid element of art and design. By its very essence, color attracts our attention and excites our emotion. Just as personality and mood vary from one person to the next, our perceptions of color are personal and subjective. Few other phenomena touch our innermost feelings as deeply and directly. Due to its complex nature, it is useful to approach the subject by focusing first on the science of color and second on its psychological effects. It is important to note the difference between these two aspects: color as a scientific phenomenon, and the idea of color.

Color and Light

Scientists understand a great deal about how we perceive color, although, because it is a complicated element, there are dimensions of color that are not yet fully explained. But the science of color is the best place to begin to understand the role of color in art.

Science tells us that we cannot perceive color without light. Light consists of energy that travels in waves, much as water forms waves. The distance between the peak of each wave of this energy is its **wavelength**. If white or normal daylight passes through a **prism** we see that it is composed of constituent colors of light, which have different wavelengths (**1.4.1**). Therefore, the colors of light make up the **spectrum** of potential visible colors. But if we need light in order to perceive color, and daylight is white, how is it that we can see individual colors (blue, red, and so on) when we look at particular objects? Our perception of the color of objects is the result of the interaction between light and something in the surface of an object that we call **pigment**. Light is necessary to activate the color of an object, but light alone does not determine the color that we perceive. This depends on light and pigment.

Color and Pigment

We see a blue sweater as blue only when light strikes it. If light consists of all the colors of the spectrum, not just blue, how is it that we perceive only the blue portion of the spectrum when we look at the sweater? This occurs because the colors we see in objects are those portions of the light spectrum that a surface fails to absorb, and instead reflects. So, if the

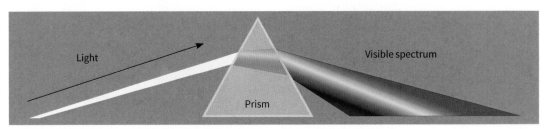

1.4.1 White light can be separated into the visible spectrum using a prism

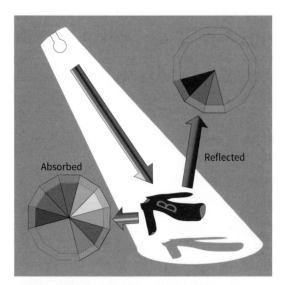

1.4.2 White light reaches a blue object and blue light is reflected

Additive and Subtractive Color

Although light and pigment are both essential for the perception of color, when colors of light are mixed, the result is not the same as when colors of pigment are mixed. This is because pigment is a solid material and light is made from transient waves of energy. When white light strikes a particular pigment, a color is reflected back to the eye. Spectral light is created when naturally occurring white light is divided; for example, by a prism. Like white light, spectral light can be perceived only when it strikes a surface. Imagine that we take two flashlights with different colored lenses. If we shine the two colored beams of light onto the same spot on a white surface, the resulting color appears brighter than the original two. Because combining the two colors *increases* the brightness of the color, this mixture is termed **additive** (and adding more and more colors will eventually lead to white light).

The brilliant illuminated color of a video display is a seductive **medium** for computer artists (see **1.4.3**). The digital artist Charles Csuri (b. 1922) has been creating imagery on computers since 1963. A pioneer in the merging of art with scientific innovations in computer technology, Csuri has explored and helped develop the digital realm as a viable art medium. In *Wondrous Spring* (**1.4.3**), only

surface of the sweater contains blue pigment, when white light reaches that surface, all the other colors in the spectrum are absorbed by the pigment, and only the blue is reflected back. Physiologists explain that our visual perception of reflected colors begins when the reflected color excites the nerve cells that line the back of our eyes. These nerve signals are processed and interpreted as color in the brain. Thus, when we see someone wearing a blue sweater, the blue we see is the portion of the spectrum that is reflected back to our eyes; the rest of the light is absorbed by the sweater (**1.4.2**).

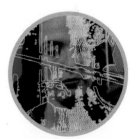

An example of computer-generated art is that of Nam June Paik and John J. Godfrey's *Global Groove*:
→ see **2.9.19**, p. 331

Additive color: the colors produced from light

Medium (plural **media**): the material on or from which an artist chooses to make a work of art, for example canvas and oil paint, marble, engraving, video, or architecture

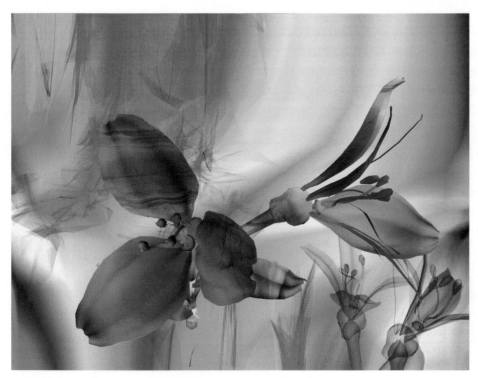

1.4.3 Charles Csuri, *Wondrous Spring*, 1992. Computer image, 4′ × 5′5″

red, green, and blue phosphors, or tiny light emitters in the monitor, are used to create a dazzling illuminated array of colors reminiscent of a modern-day stained-glass window. The entire spectrum of color that makes the work so lustrous was made visible by numerous additive combinations of red, green, and blue light. The computer creates an almost infinite range of color by systematically turning off and on the phosphors to create the various additive color mixtures present in the work.

Although our perception of the colors of pigment depends on the reflection of the colors of light to our eyes, when we mix pigments together, they do not behave in the same way as when we mix colors of light. Since paint is made of pigment mixed with a **binder**, if two different-colored paints, containing different-colored pigments, are mixed, the result is not brighter but tends to be duller. This is called **subtractive color** because in such a pigment mixture, more of the spectrum is absorbed (or subtracted) from the light that hits the pigmented surface.

Color Wheels

As we have seen, different results occur when artists mix colors of light (for example, in televisions and computer monitors, or beams of different-colored light from flashlights) and when artists mix colors of pigment (such as paint). Artists are faced with many ways of mixing color to achieve different effects. In addition, our eyes can perceive a total of 360 colors. These two factors, taken together, mean that predicting and managing the effectsof color mixing is often an important aspect of an artist's work—and it is at this stage that a tool called a color wheel can be of assistance.

A color wheel displays important information about **hue** relationships. Hue is a way we identify a color group, such as reds, rather than a specific color, for example blood red. A color wheel acts as a kind of color map that allows us to assess the attributes of hues as they relate to each other. There are many color wheels that chart color combinations, but three basic wheels are most commonly used. The first two that we will study show the fundamental hues of pigment-based color, that is, the color that we associate with colored objects. These two wheels are maps or models of subtractive color combinations. The third

color wheel maps out the ways that colors of light combine with one another. There are different color wheels for the hues of light and the hues of pigment because the two types of hues react and are perceived independently of each other. As we have seen, when pigments are mixed, the result is referred to as subtractive color, as the blended hues tend to be less intense than in their original, unmixed state. When color in spectral light is blended, the resulting hues tend to be lighter, and this is referred to as additive color. We will start by discussing color wheels used to manage the mixing of hues of pigment as they occur in white light.

Since the eighteenth century, scientists and color theorists have produced color wheels that artists have used (and continue to use today) to manage the mixing of paint and any other pigment-based medium. The hues of this color wheel are the building blocks of most color combinations (**1.4.4**). "Artist's colors" are the traditional **primary colors**—red, yellow, blue. They are called primary because they cannot be created by mixing any other two colors. The **secondary colors** can be produced by mixing two primary colors. They are the hues orange (that can be created by blending red and yellow), green (a blend of yellow and blue), and violet (a blend of red and blue). In this color wheel, the secondary colors are located between the primary ones because they naturally fall between them in the visible spectrum. The remaining hues in the wheel are called **tertiary colors** and can be created by blending a primary and a secondary color: for

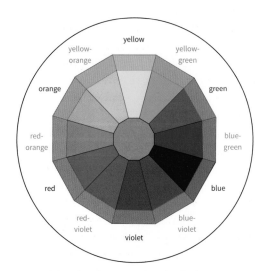

1.4.4 Traditional twelve-step color wheel using "artist's colors"

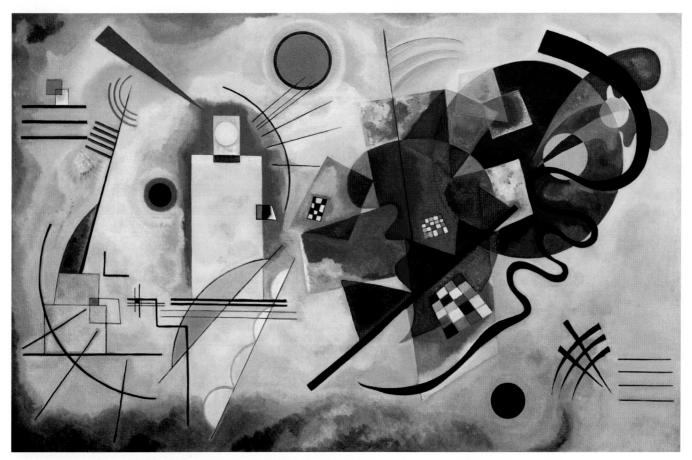

1.4.5 Vasily Kandinsky, *Yellow-Red-Blue*, 1925. Oil on canvas, 50⅜ × 79¼".
Musée National d'Art Moderne, Centre Georges Pompidou, Paris, France

example, red-violet is (as its name suggests) a blend of red and violet.

One work that uses the traditional combination of primary red, yellow, and blue is a painting by the Russian artist Vasily Kandinsky (1866–1944) (**1.4.5**). Appropriately titled *Yellow-Red-Blue*, this work utilizes the basic colors of the traditional color wheel, along with black and white. Kandinsky advocated the use of these fundamental elements to simplify and celebrate art and design in their purest sense. Since no primary can be mixed from any other two colors in this wheel, the three he chose exemplified the purest and simplest color available.

If you look again at the color wheel in figure **1.4.4**, you will notice the gray in the center. In theory, a perfect subtractive mix of the primary colors of red, yellow, and blue should result in a perfect black, which absorbs all the colors of the spectrum. In practice, however, if an artist mixes the primaries as they are arranged on this color wheel, the result is not black but a brownish gray. These colors mix to a brownish gray because the traditional primary triad, red, yellow, and blue, are not true primaries, but

an approximation. This is not a problem for artists who are accustomed to working with this color wheel; their past experience with color and their knowledge of their own personal preferences enable them to create the colors they need. But for graphic designers working on materials that need to be printed using layers of transparent printing inks in a very exact way, it is necessary to be able to create more accurate color mixtures that conform to universal rules. Modern research has therefore provided a new set of primary colors that are better suited to producing specific blended colors when these are printed.

Although the colors red, yellow, and blue have traditionally been accepted as the basic hues of pigment, scientific discoveries in physics have provided a new set of primaries that can be combined into a subtractive mix that enables designers to produce a real (true) black for printing purposes. If we mix these primaries—cyan (a slightly greenish light blue), magenta (a pinkish light violet), and yellow—their color combination results in black (**1.4.6** and **1.4.7**, p. 88). The entire spectrum of white light is absorbed (subtracted) in the

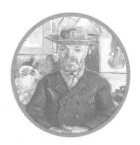

Commercial printers use cyan, magenta, and yellow, and mix colors by overlapping:
→ see **2.7.22**, p. 297

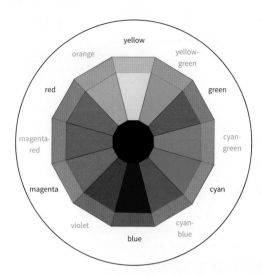

1.4.6 Cyan, magenta, yellow (CMY) pigment twelve-color wheel with black center

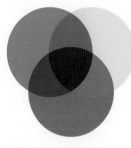

1.4.7 Subtractive color mixtures using CMY primaries. When the three colors are perfectly layered together, the result is black

combination of cyan, magenta, and yellow pigments, so not a single segment of the spectrum is reflected.

Like Kandinsky, the contemporary Argentine-born artist Analia Saban (b. 1980) also works with primary colors to distill art and design to their purest state. But in her work *Layer Painting (CMY): Flowers* (**1.4.8**), Saban wants to "debunk the mysteries of contemporary art." To do this she has adopted the scientifically proven primary combination of cyan, magenta, and yellow to paint a **still life** of flowers. In so doing, Saban challenges traditional beliefs about color. Red, considered a primary color since the eighteenth century, can now be mixed from the two colors magenta and yellow. Although Saban is questioning

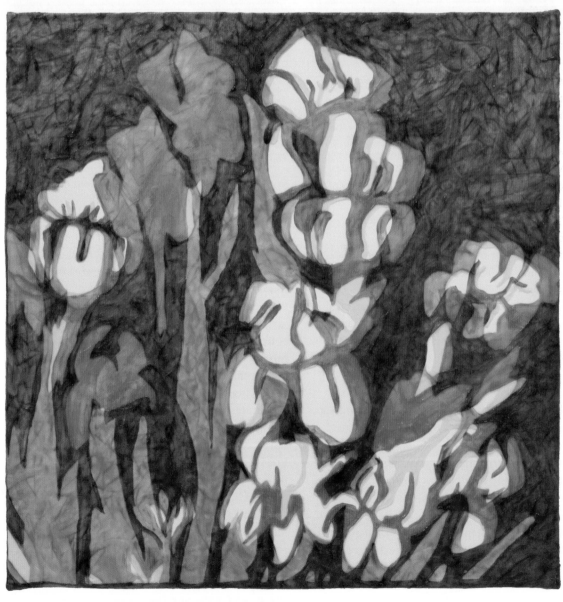

1.4.8 Analia Saban, *Layer Painting (CMY): Flowers*, 2008. Acrylic and screen printing ink on canvas, 36 × 36 × 1½". Thomas Solomon Gallery

ideas about color in painting, the CMY primaries are already the accepted colors used in most visual communication design and commercial printing (**1.4.7**).

These two subtractive color wheels are used to manage the mixing of pigments and to help artists predict the results (**1.4.6** and **1.4.7**). They are useful for painters who mix paints, graphic designers who design for the mixing of printing inks, and for anyone making color combinations of any pigment-based medium. But subtractive color wheels are not useful for artists who work with **spectral color**. For this, an additive color wheel is required.

Additive color is not generated from pigment, like the traditional or subtractive hue combinations, but from light. For example, an artist who creates an installation consisting of different spectral lights in a room painted white needs to understand how the colors of the different lights combine. Digital artists use the color combinations of red, green, and blue that make up the matrix for color in computer monitors (see, for example, Charles Csuri, *Wondrous Spring*, **1.4.3**, p. 85).

Although white light contains the entire spectrum, it is useful to divide light into individual colors so that we can manage combinations as simply as possible (**1.4.9**). The primary hues of light are red, green, and blue. When colors of light are mixed, we call the mixture additive color, because each time a color is added, the blended mix gets lighter, until eventually it results in white (**1.4.9**). The secondary colors of light are cyan, yellow, and magenta and are created by mixing two

primaries (**1.4.10**). As in the pigment color wheels, tertiary colors in light are derived from combinations of a primary and a secondary color.

Dynamics of Color
Color wheels place hues in a visual arrangement that can be a guide to the many attributes of color and how to use them. We will now consider two other important aspects of color that can be clearly understood by looking at color wheels.

Complementary Color Complementary colors can be found on opposite sides of a color wheel. For example, in the **CMY** subtractive color wheel (**1.4.6**), magenta is the complement of green. For an artist or designer, understanding the juxtaposition of these two colors on the color wheel can be very helpful.

When complementary colors are mixed, they produce gray (or black); they tend to dull one another. But when two complementary colors are painted side by side, these "opposite" colors create visual anomalies: they intensify one another. This happens because complementary colors have markedly different wavelengths, creating an illusion (in the photoreceptors of the eye) of vibrating movement where their edges meet (**1.4.11**). When the eye tries to compensate for the different wavelengths of two complementary colors, we tend to see each color more intensely than when we see them separately. So when red is present, greens tend to appear more vibrantly green.

American landscape painter Frederic Edwin Church (1826–1900) used complementary colors for dramatic effect. In *Twilight in the Wilderness* (**1.4.12**, p. 90), the intense red-orange clouds complement swathes of the blue-green evening sky, creating magnificence within a

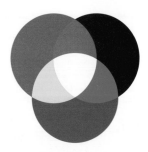

1.4.10 Additive color mixtures using red, green, and blue (RGB) primaries

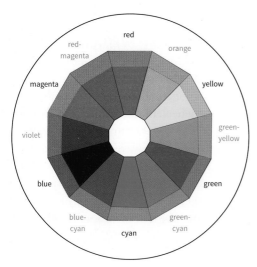

1.4.9 Red, green, blue (RGB) light twelve-color wheel with white center (primary mixture)

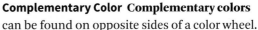
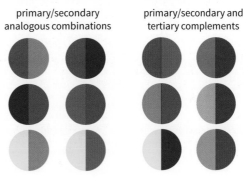

primary/secondary analogous combinations

primary/secondary and tertiary complements

1.4.11 Color combinations and color complements in pigment

CMY: the primary colors used in inkjet printing: cyan, magenta, and blue

Still life: a scene of inanimate objects, such as fruits, flowers, or dead animals

Spectral color: a color in the visible light spectrum

Complementary colors: colors opposite one another on the color wheel

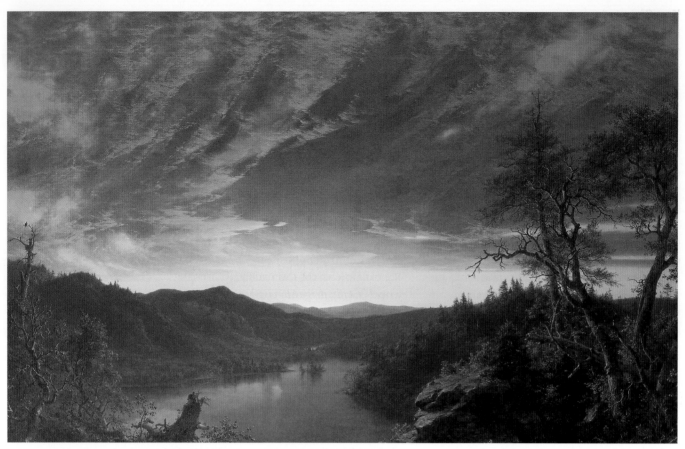

1.4.12 Frederic Edwin Church, *Twilight in the Wilderness*, 1860. Oil on canvas, 40 × 64".
Cleveland Museum of Art, Ohio

quiet landscape. The powerful color of the sky and its reflection in the water below reveal Church's awe and respect for the American landscape.

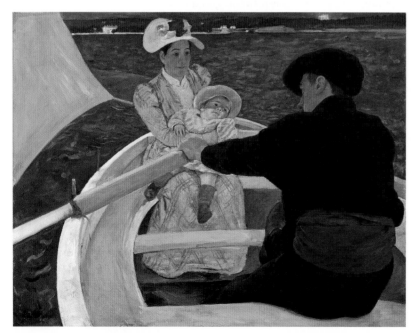

1.4.13 Mary Cassatt, *The Boating Party*, 1893–94. Oil on canvas, 35⅜ × 46⅛".
National Gallery of Art, Washington, D.C.

Analogous Color Analogous colors fall adjacent to each other on a color wheel and are similar in wavelength, so they do not create optical illusions or visual vibrations the way complementary colors do. Painters use analogous color to create color unity and harmonies that steer viewers toward a particular attitude or emotion. By keeping the color within a similar range, artists avoid jarring, contrasting combinations of colors and moods.

In *The Boating Party* by Mary Cassatt (1844–1926), her color palette creates a harmonious effect (**1.4.13**). This is the result of using analogous colors that are next to one another on the color wheel. In this painting, yellows, greens, and blues predominate. These colors have relatively similar wavelengths and do not intensify one another when placed in close proximity. Cassatt's color seems relaxed, reinforcing her theme. Cassatt was one of the few female members of the **Impressionists**, a group of artists who shared an interest in the effects of light and color on the natural world, which they depicted in their paintings of everyday life.

Key Characteristics of Color

Because of the wide range of attributes associated with color, artists and designers use specific terms to be more descriptive. We will now identify these terms as we examine the main properties of color.

Properties of Color

All colors have four basic properties: hue, **value**, **chroma**, and **tone**. By manipulating these four properties, artists and designers can achieve an endless range of visual effects.

Hue When many of us refer to "the color orange", we are really referring to the hue orange. Hues represent the individual color ranges of the spectrum, that is, red, yellow, blue, green, orange, and violet. Orange is therefore a hue that describes a broad color range, while cocoa-pod orange (**1.4.14**) refers to a specific single point in the spectrum of that overall hue family.

For the sake of reference, we associate a hue with an ideal version of a given color. For example, the hue orange is usually associated with a bright, warm, intense orange color of the kind we might see in sports jerseys and industrial surfaces, such as farm equipment. So, when we use the term "hue," we most often are making associations to a brilliant color, or at least one as strong as it can be.

Color is such an important aspect of a coffin created by the African sculptor Kane Kwei (1922–1992) that the work is sometimes nicknamed *Coffin Orange* (**1.4.14**). Kwei's coffin

is painted with a brilliant mid-hue orange color, that of a half-ripened cocoa pod. While ripening cocoa pods do generally turn some sort of orange hue, the specific color chosen by the artist for this coffin is intentionally bright and exaggerated.

In Ghana, Kwei's native country, funerals are celebratory, loud affairs where bright color adds to the festive mood. Ghanaians believe that having lots of happy people at a funeral gives solace to the family of the deceased, reminding them that they still have many friends. Kwei got started in his career when his dying uncle asked the artist to build him a boat-shaped coffin. It was such a hit in the community that others began to ask for coffins made in interesting shapes. *Coffin in the Shape of a Cocoa Pod* was commissioned by a cocoa farmer who wanted to tell everybody about his lifelong passion at his last party on Earth.

Value Each hue has a value, meaning its relative lightness or darkness compared to another hue. For example, a pure yellow has a light value, and a pure blue has a dark value. Similarly, different colors of the same hue vary in terms of their value: there are light reds and dark reds. **Tints** are colors that are lighter than their basic hue, implying that they have been mixed with white; **shades** are colors that are darker and imply that they have been mixed with black.

Figure **1.4.15** (p. 92) shows relative values of red, blue, and yellow. The purest values, compared with those visible in the spectrum, are indicated by a black square behind them.

Analogous colors: colors adjacent to each other on the color wheel

Impressionism, Impressionist: in the visual arts, a late nineteenth-century style conveying the fleeting impression of the effects of light; Impressionists were artists working in this style

Value: the lightness or darkness of a plane or area

Chroma (also known as saturation): the degree of purity of a color

Tone: a color that is weaker than its brightest, or most pure, state

Tint: a color lighter in value than its purest state

Shade: a color darker in value than its purest state

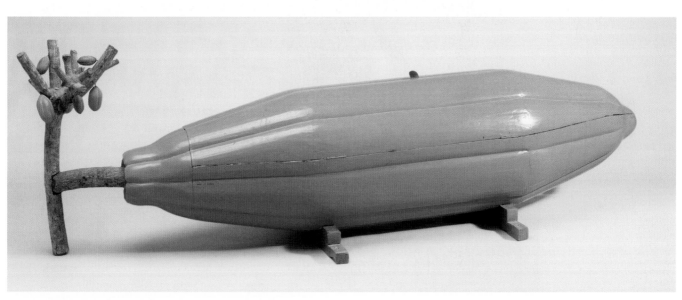

1.4.14 Kane Kwei, ***Coffin in the Shape of a Cocoa Pod (Coffin Orange)***, *c.* 1970. Polychrome wood, 2'10" × 8'6" × 2'5". Fine Arts Museums of San Francisco, California

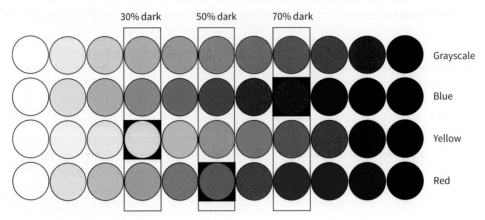

1.4.15 Color–value relationships

Figure **1.4.15** also shows the grayscale values; these are described as **neutral**, meaning there is an absence of color.

A work that uses only one hue is called **monochromatic**. An artist can give variety to such a work by using a range of values. Creating dramatic differences in the values of a color allows for ordered transitions from one value to another. Many of American Mark Tansey's (b. 1949) large paintings are monochromatic. In *Picasso and Braque*, Tansey depicts two figures, whom he calls "Orville and Wilbur," a reference to aviators the Wright Brothers

(**1.4.16**). He is also referring wryly to Pablo Picasso's (1881–1973) and Georges Braque's (1882–1963) habit of calling each other Orville and Wilbur during the pioneering days of **Cubism**. The two figures here have created a flying machine that resembles an early Cubist **collage**. The monochromatic **palette** is reminiscent of the black-and-white photos of the Wright Brothers' experiments with flight, and the blue tone refers to an early **style** of Picasso's known as his Blue Period.

Picasso's *Old Guitarist* (**1.4.17**) was painted during this period (1901–4); it was a time of

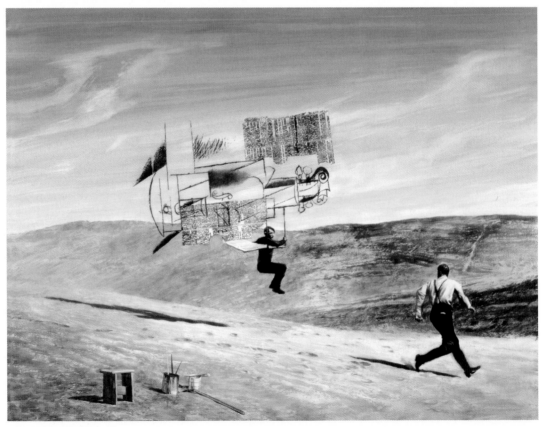

1.4.16 Mark Tansey, *Picasso and Braque*, 1992. Oil on canvas, 5'4" × 7'. LACMA, Los Angeles, California

poverty and personal depression after the suicide of a good friend. This artwork is characteristic of the color palette of blues, browns, and grays that Picasso was using during this time. Limiting himself to only a few colors, he relies heavily on value to suggest depth and the solidity of the guitar, figure, and its surroundings. The colors chosen by the artist create a sad and somber mood (see also p. 98 for more about the psychology of color) and the use of different values to create a realistically modeled figure increases the viewer's empathy for the hunched old man—we feel a part of his sorrowful song.

Chroma When we think of the color yellow, we often imagine something strong, bright, and intense. Many shades of yellow exist, but we tend to associate a color with its purest state, or its highest level of chroma. The color mustard yellow, which has a brownish tone, has a weaker chroma, because the intensity of the color is less than the purest hue. Chroma is sometimes described as **saturation**, chromaticness, or intensity, but these terms all generally refer to the strength of color.

Such works as *Vir Heroicus Sublimis* (Latin for "heroic sublime man") by the American painter Barnett Newman (1905–1970) rely, for their visual impact, on value and strong chroma (**1.4.18**). The differing colors of the vertical lines (which Newman calls "zips") break up a broad red **plane**. The white zip makes a gap, while

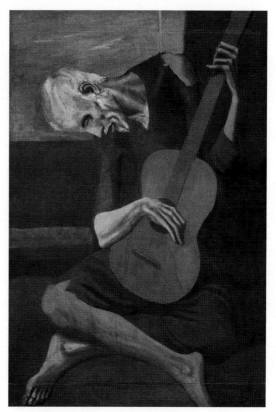

1.4.17 Pablo Picasso, *The Old Guitarist*, 1903–4. Oil on panel, 48⅞ × 32½", Art Institute of Chicago, Illinois

Saturation (also known as chroma): the degree of purity of a color

Plane: a flat, two-dimensional surface on which an artist can create a drawing or painting. Planes can also be implied in a composition by areas that face toward, parallel to, or away from a light source

the maroon zip melds into the red field. Subtle variations in the red hues create the sensation that parts of the work are separately lit.

Newman wants viewers to stand close to the canvas, engulfed by color, meeting the artwork as one might another person. The square area in the center of this painting suggests

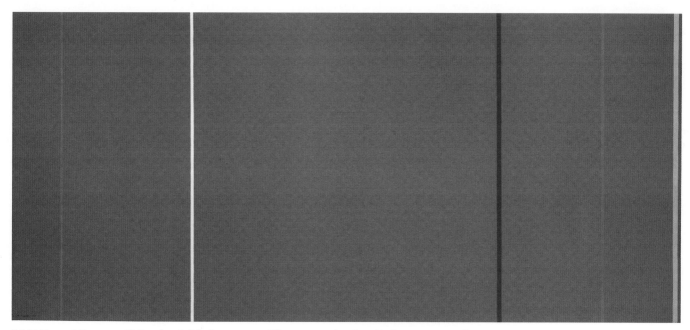

1.4.18 Barnett Newman, *Vir Heroicus Sublimis*, 1950, 1951. Oil on canvas, 7'11⅜" × 17'8¼". MoMA, New York

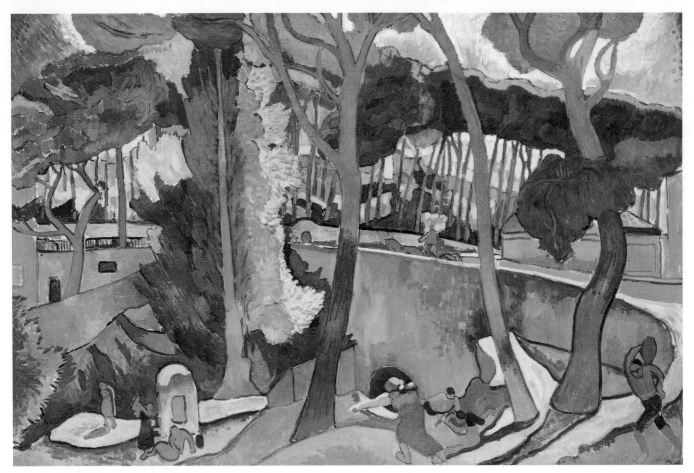

1.4.19 André Derain, *The Turning Road, L'Estaque*, 1906. Oil on canvas, 4′3″ × 6′4¾″. Museum of Fine Arts, Houston, Texas

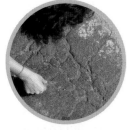

An example of high chroma used to accentuate an artwork is the *Red Sand Project*:

→ see **2.10.13**, p. 343

Newman's idealistic vision of the perfectibility of humankind.

The French painter André Derain (1880–1954) was a great advocate of strong chroma. In his work *The Turning Road, L'Estaque*, his use of vivid, bright color makes the entire scene glow with energy and vitality (**1.4.19**). Derain was a member of an artistic movement known as the **Fauves** (French for "wild beasts"). The Fauves delighted in using the new and brighter-colored pigments made available by advances in industrial manufacturing. They used colors in their purest and strongest states as an act of defiance against the Academy, a state-sponsored school of art that set rigid rules and standards for art and artists at the turn of the twentieth century. Although today it might seem as though the Fauves' subjects and colors are tame by comparison with those of contemporary artists, in their day they were perceived as revolutionary and fierce, challenging the Academy as well as Western artistic conventions generally and earning the artists their nickname. Derain's painting is energized by high chroma and color complements that intensify adjacent colors when seen close together.

Tone Chroma is a term that also describes the purity of a hue derived from the spectrum of pure white light. A green at its highest chroma is closest to its pure state in the spectrum of light (**1.4.20**), and when a color is in its strongest chromatic state, it has no tints or shades. Yet green, for example, can also be a very muted hue. The weaker chromatic states of any hue are known as tones. Tone is a property of any color that is not at its highest chroma within its value range. A hue that is almost gray is a tone because it has been dulled from its most intense chromatic state, even though it may be similar in *value* to the hue at its highest chroma. Therefore a muted tone, whatever its hue, is less intense as it gets further from the purity of its spectral origin. A pastel-green tone and a dark-green tone would each have a restricted value of green, but a grayed-green hue that is just as dark as the original green would also have a low chroma.

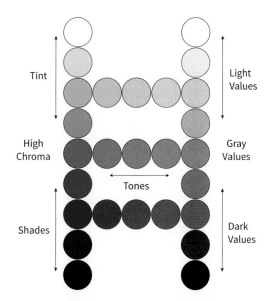

Tint

Light Values

High Chroma

Gray Values

Tones

Shades

Dark Values

1.4.20 Sampling of chroma, tone, shades, and tints in green hue

Many artists have used the tonal qualities of color and associated them with sound. In the painting *Ancient Sound* (**1.4.21**) by the Swiss artist Paul Klee (1879–1940), varying tones of green and orange are organized so that a viewer might make associations with sounds, for example seeing the yellows as similar to bright, high-pitched noises, and the darks as similar

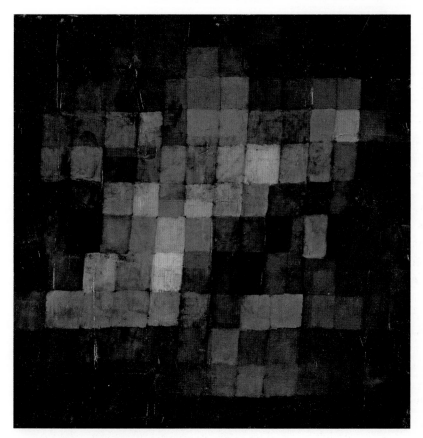

1.4.21 Paul Klee, *Ancient Sound*, 1925. Oil on cardboard, 15 × 15″. Kunstmuseum Basel, Switzerland

to deep, low sounds. Klee, who excelled as both artist and accomplished violinist, organized a grid full of colors that varied from an extremely light tone of yellow-orange to greens and browns that nearly become black in value. The tones are carefully darkened and lightened to take full advantage of the adjacent colors to increase or decrease the **contrast**. Like the changing notes in a piece of music, the chroma of these colors rises and falls as if they are notes that have been unleashed through a voice or musical instrument.

The Sensation of Color

Our sensations of color are both evocative and physical. Some colors are associated with emotional states: if we say we are feeling "blue," we are describing a psychological state of mind. Blue is also associated with cold, and red with hot: an association that can be referred to as color **temperature**. Color temperature is relative to other surrounding colors, and its interpretation is highly subjective.

Color can also affect the way we see. Because of the difference in color wavelengths, our eyes cannot fully comprehend all the colors at the same time, so our brain translates (or distorts) the incoming information. This is the basis of an illusion known as optical color. Our interpretation of color can also be completely inaccurate because of the limitations of our optical senses.

Color Temperature

We associate color with temperature because of our previous experiences. We may have been burned by something red-hot, or chilled by cool blue water. Our perception of the temperature of a color can be altered if it is placed next to an analogous, or similar, color. For example, green, a color we might associate with coolness, can seem warm if we see it next to a cooler color, such as blue. A yellow-green would be warmer than a blue-green. Color temperature is relative to the other colors nearby. Artists use such associations to communicate physical and emotional states.

The colors chosen for the underglaze-painted lamp from the Islamic shrine the Dome of the Rock, in Jerusalem, are blue and green, on a white **ground** for contrast (**1.4.22**, p. 96). They reflect the kind of color influence valued in the meditative atmosphere of a holy place. The choice of colors is cool and peaceful. Many people associate green and blue with water, plant life, or a clear sky. Our life experiences with blue and green things can easily be associated with passive environments. The color green has positive associations in Islamic art and supports the peacefulness of prayer.

Optical Color

Sometimes our brains receive so much information that they simplify it. Optical colors are colors our minds create based on the information we can perceive. In **1.4.23**, the square on the left contains so many red and blue dots that our brain interprets them as a violet color. In the square on the right, red and yellow dots are interpreted as an orange tone.

The French painter Georges Seurat (1859–1891) used the optical qualities of color to create a new style of painting, called **pointillism** because it relied on small dots (or points) of

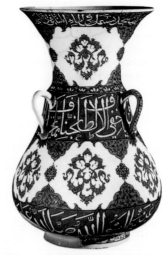

1.4.22 Mosque lamp from the Dome of the Rock in Jerusalem, 1549. Iznik pottery, height 15". British Museum, London, England

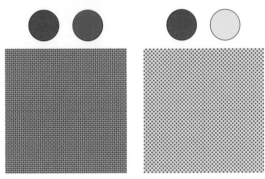

1.4.23 Two squares, one filled with red and blue dots and the other with red and yellow dots to create optical color mixing effect

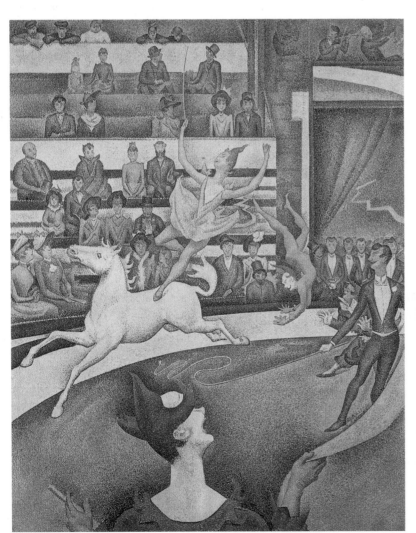

1.4.24a Georges Seurat, *The Circus*, 1890–91. Oil on canvas, 6'7⅞" × 4'11⅞". Musée d'Orsay, Paris, France

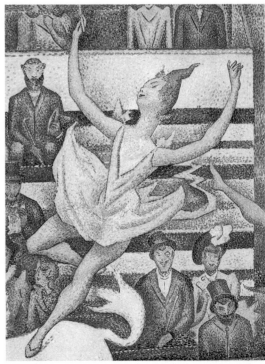

1.4.24b Detail of Georges Seurat, *The Circus*

color. In *The Circus*, Seurat paints a scene of lively entertainment, imbued with bright color and texture through the use of small dots (**1.4.24a** and **b**). Because these dots are so close together, the colors we see are different from the actual colors of the dots.

This optical mixing makes the colors more intense because they have retained their individual intensity, whereas if they were mixed on the palette they would appear more subdued. *The Circus*'s jewel-like diffusion of light and the illusion of vibrations between the colors make it visually exciting.

Color Theory and Deception

Researchers called color theorists experimented and observed the many attributes of perception and interaction. Two significant theorists were Johannes Itten (1888–1967) and Josef Albers (1888–1976). Itten was a painter, designer, and teacher who worked on finding ideal color combinations while at the Bauhaus, a school of art in twentieth-century Germany that focused on **Modernist** ideas. Some theorists found that we can be deceived by a color because of the influences of color adjacent to it. As we see from optical color mixtures that can imply colors that are not actually present, color can trick our perception. Itten's contemporary, Albers, described some color deceptions in his experiments. In **1.4.25a** and **1.4.25b**, Albers, a teacher of **color theory** and design at the Bauhaus, Black Mountain College, and Yale, has created an illustration of how one color can look like two. If you look at state A, the brown squares on either side of the horizontal center stripes look distinctly different, but when the

blue and yellow center stripes are removed in state B, we see that the different browns are actually exactly the same. Albers realized that color is relative to its surroundings and that by changing the adjacent colors, he could change how a color is perceived.

Interpreting Color Symbolism

Color can affect how we think and feel. Studies by Faber Birren (1900–1988), a color psychologist, indicate that when people are constantly exposed to red light they can often become loud and argumentative, and eat voraciously: it appears that red can influence aggression in our behavior.

Colors also have traditional **symbolic** values. As we have seen, green traditionally has positive associations for Muslims; Buddha wore yellow or gold; Jews and Christians associate the color blue with God (the Virgin Mary is most frequently depicted wearing blue in Christian art). Our cultural beliefs about color also affect the way we think and feel.

In China there are five particular colors that stand out in traditional history, derived from Wu Xing, the Theory of Five Elements or Five Virtues. Wu Xing was a philosophy that sought to explain how change affects the cosmos through five elements: water, metal, fire, earth, and wood. Black, white, red, yellow, and green-blue (sometimes called "qing") were established as the basic colors representing these five elements. Each color also stood as a symbol that had multiple associations (see **1.4.26**). For example, black represented water, the direction north, winter, and more. Hence, particular colors communicate particular ideas to others who share the same cultural understanding and history. For instance, black was chosen by the founder of the Qin empire as a color that represented the north, and all who lived during that period passed this cultural

Pointillism: a late nineteenth-century painting style using short strokes or points of differing colors that optically combine to form new perceived colors

Modernism, Modernist: a radically new twentieth-century art and architectural movement that embraced modern industrial materials and a machine aesthetic

Color theory: the understanding of how colors relate to one another, especially when mixed or placed together in close proximity

Symbolism: using images or symbols in an artwork to convey meaning; often obvious when the work was made but requiring research for modern viewers to understand

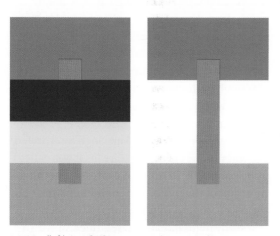

1.4.25a (left) **Josef Albers, *Two Colors Look Like One, State A**. From Interaction of Color*, Ch. IV, plate 1
1.4.25b (right) **Josef Albers, *Two Colors Look Like One, State B**. From Interaction of Color*, Ch. IV, plate 2

	Black	White	Red	Green-Blue	Yellow
Element	water	metal	fire	wood	earth
Direction	north	west	south	east	center
Emotion	winter	autumn	summer	spring	"fifth season" (late summer)
State	fear	sorrow	joy	anger	desire
Animal	tortoise	unicorn	phoenix	dragon	human

1.4.26 Chart of the colors, representative of the Five Virtues and other associated symbols

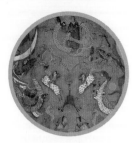

An example of the elemental colors of ancient China can be found in the painted banner from the tomb of Lady Dai:

→ see **3.3.9**, p. 396

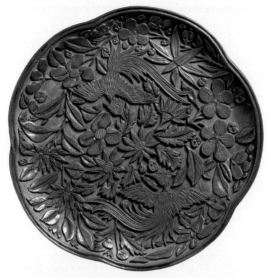

1.4.27 Tray in the form of a plum blossom with birds and flowers, China, Late Southern Song Dynasty, *c.* 1200–1279. Carved red lacquer on wood core, diameter 7⅜". LACMA, California

knowledge on to future generations. The color red represents fire and the direction south; it is also symbolic of warmth, good luck, and happiness. Because of this, red would never be worn to a funeral in China, but it is a popular color for brides because of its associations with joy and life-giving.

The color red is used for this lacquer tray from China dating to the Song Dynasty (**1.4.27**). Lacquer is made from tree sap, and it is a very laborious substance both to produce and to apply. Several colored pigments can be added to lacquer, but red and black are by far the most common. During the Song Dynasty (from 960 to 1279 CE) the ideas of Wu Xing were well established, and this tray features some of the traditional symbols associated with red. The two long-tailed birds could be phoenixes; they may also remind us of the Vermillion Bird, one of four symbols of the constellations in the night sky. The Vermillion Bird is linked with summer and the south, as is the color red.

The Psychology of Color

Although science explains how light can be separated or refracted so that we can experience it, and books and treatises can tell us of the symbolic color associations practiced in different cultures, color is also experienced in ways that are non-objective— that is, dependent on our individual character, background, and nature. Ancient Greek philosophers speculated that color might

be a state of mind and that the color we see is a unique experience for every person, because our interpretations of color are deeply associated with the psychological and social aspects of our lives.

Color affects us because it can alter the way we feel and react. In Western cultures, we associate love and danger with red, and sadness with blue. The potential impact of color on our sense of well-being is such that some ancient cultures, such as the Egyptians and Chinese, used colors for healing. The ancient Persian philosopher Avicenna (980–1037) created a chart that associated color with medical symptoms and their treatment. For example, it was believed that a bleeding open wound would be aggravated by the presence of red, but if the patient was exposed to blue (by simply looking at it), the effect would be beneficial.

Artists understand that color affects the way we think and react to the world. Some of these reactions are culturally biased: in the United States blue is paired with masculinity, but in China it is associated with the feminine. As we have seen, red (which we can easily associate with blood) can arouse feelings not only of anxiety, aggression, and anger, but also of passion, eroticism, and vitality. Green, a color we associate with growing plant life, encourages restfulness, but it also suggests decay and illness.

The Dutch painter Vincent van Gogh (1853–1890) was enormously affected by color, and studied its psychological effects. Van Gogh was plagued by periods of deep depression and was hospitalized on many occasions; through his treatment he learned a great deal about psychology. The colors in his painting *The Night Café* are not taken from life, but were carefully chosen to elicit emotional responses from viewers (**1.4.28**). In a letter to his brother Theo, Van Gogh writes about the work, "I have tried to express with red and green the terrible passions of human nature."

Like any skilled artist, Van Gogh interpreted the color of the Café de la Gare (as it was called) as he painted it, in order to express something more about the place. The color intensifies the psychological implications of the scene, in a seedy nightspot in Arles, France, as we wander visually into this menacing place as outsiders. By choosing fierce and oppressive red, a feverish yellow, and the rather bilious or

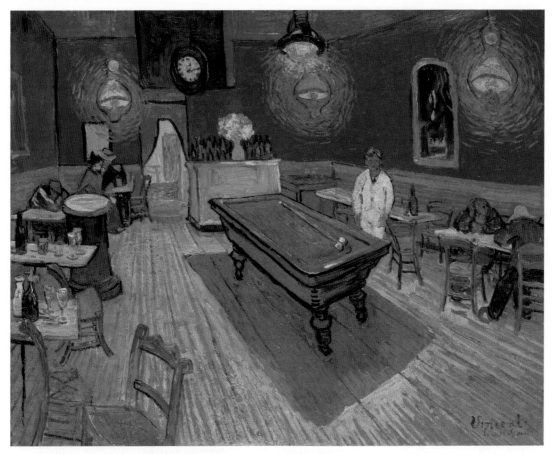

1.4.28 Vincent van Gogh, *The Night Café*, 1888. Oil on canvas, 28½ × 36¼".
Yale University Art Gallery, New Haven, Connecticut

sickly green, Van Gogh expresses his sense that this nightspot had a detrimental psychological influence on its patrons. The almost lurid hues convey a strong feeling of unease and sorrow, and the strange, lurching perspective in the room opens up irregular spaces that intensify the painting's lonely atmosphere.

The color green has different associations for the Puerto Rican artist Chemi Rosado-Seijo (b. 1973) and the people of Naranjito, Puerto Rico. The term "green" often refers to things that are environmentally friendly, and this is the idea reflected in Rosado-Seiji's *El Cerro* (**1.4.29**), which is a collaboration between the artist and the local community. An entire neighborhood began painting houses and other buildings in the El Cerro district of Naranjito in 2002. The residents decided to paint their homes different shades of green, showing respect for the surrounding mountainous environment. The work helped to unify the community and promote programs that support positive changes, such as the creation of a space that is both a museum and classroom, as well as the establishment of a community center.

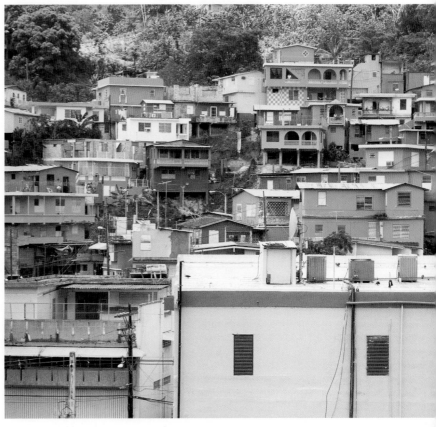

1.4.29 Chemi Rosado-Seijo, *El Cerro*, 2003 (started 2002).
Collaboration, Naranjito, Puerto Rico

Expressive Aspects of Color

Such artists as Van Gogh wanted viewers to "feel" artworks, rather than merely understand them. Color in particular can express a wide range of emotions—for example, the bright yellow of a happy-face symbol attracts our attention and lifts our spirits. Artists and designers can use color to engage the viewer, whether by using blue around the image of a political candidate to suggest traditional values, or green to imply environmental awareness.

Henri Matisse (1869–1954) was a French artist who was a great and influential practitioner of the expressive use of color. He and the artists of the Fauve movement focused especially on using color as intensely as they could to reveal the rich possibilities of painting. For example, in Matisse's *Open Window, Collioure* (**1.4.30**), the artist uses pairs of complementary colors to enhance the painting. In this scene we see such combinations as the orange and blue boats, through the window, and the red-pink wall on the right paired with the greenish-blue one on the left. Since complementary colors influence each other, the resulting experience is a brilliant expression of vibrant color.

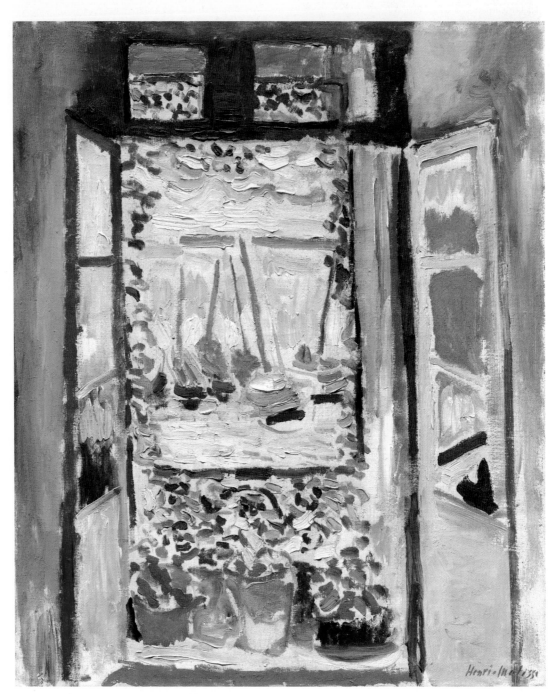

1.4.30 Henri Matisse, ***Open Window, Collioure***, 1905. Oil on canvas, 21¾" × 18⅛". National Gallery of Art, Washington, D.C.

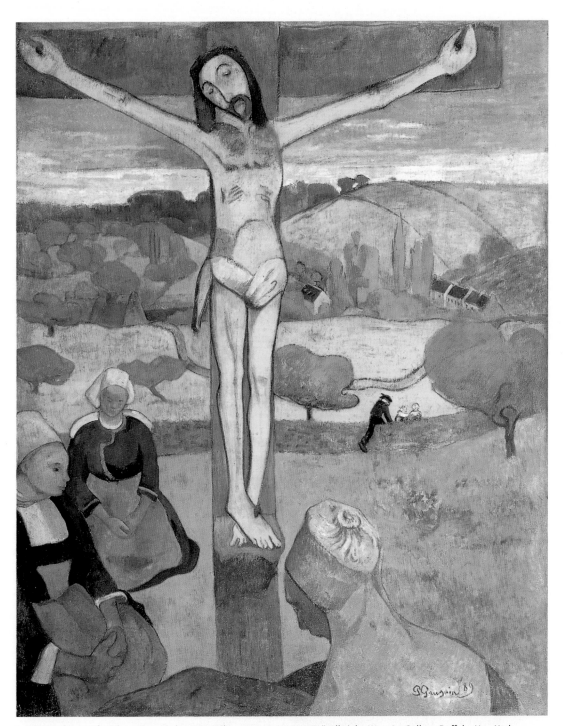

1.4.31 Paul Gauguin, *The Yellow Christ*, 1889. Oil on canvas, 36¼ × 27⅞". Albright-Knox Art Gallery, Buffalo, New York

The French painter Paul Gauguin (1848–1903) used yellow for its uplifting associations when he painted *The Yellow Christ* (**1.4.31**). Gauguin painted this scene—a deliberately populist portrayal of folk spirituality—while in Brittany, France. In it, three women in traditional Breton dress appear to attend the crucifixion of Jesus Christ. Although Gauguin is known to have been inspired by a woodcarving in a local chapel, his choice of color is primarily symbolic. Through color he connects the crucifixion to the seasons of Earth and the cycle of life. Yellows and browns correspond to the colors of the surrounding autumnal countryside, harvested fields, and turning leaves. Gauguin's color palette relates the background natural world to the body on the cross, so that our gaze too is drawn in and upward. By using bright color, Gauguin creates a simple and direct emotional connection with the viewer. While depicting death, Gauguin chose colors that nonetheless express the optimism of rebirth.

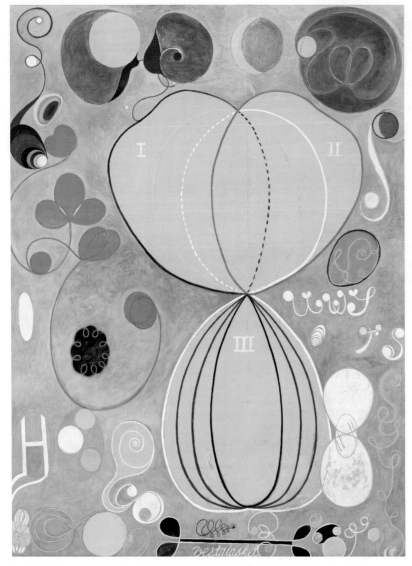

1.4.32 Hilma af Klint, *Group IV, No. 7, Adulthood*, 1907. Tempera on paper mounted on canvas, 10'4½" × 7'8½". Moderna Museet, Stockholm, Sweden

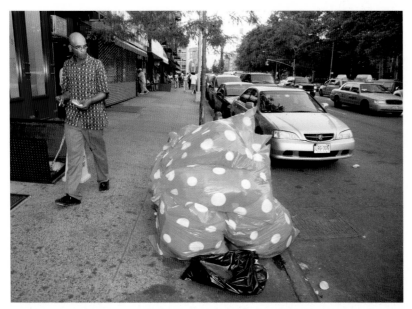

1.4.33 Adrian Kondratowicz, *TRASH maximalism NYC (Harlem)*, *TRASH project*, 2008–ongoing

While some expressions of color can be experienced in the same way by entire groups of people or societies, others are intensely personal, and can hold meanings that are known fully only to the individual concerned. Swedish artist Hilma af Klint (1862–1944) used color to create her own visual vocabulary. She was a prolific artist and created many hundreds of paintings inspired by her spiritual experiences.

According to Af Klint, the designs and colors in a number of her works were directed by a spirit guide whom she contacted during séances. Many of her works are painted in an **abstract** style: the **subject matter** is not immediately recognizable. The artist also felt that certain colors symbolized particular meanings; for example, yellow was "the splendid color of light, of the foundation of knowledge." The strong yellow in her work *Group IV, No. 7, Adulthood* (**1.4.32**) represents light and the knowledge that one achieves with adulthood. Af Klint may not have intended for viewers to understand completely her paintings and their symbolism—in fact, she requested that her spiritual works not be shown publicly until twenty years after her death.

Color has always been used expressively by artists and designers, sometimes to change the way that viewers feel about their surroundings. Take for example a project by the Polish-born New York artist Adrian Kondratowicz (b. 1984), where he asked his Harlem neighbors to look at trash a bit differently (**1.4.33**). Adrian, as he is known locally, distributed bright pink, rodent-repellent, biodegradable trash bags to his community. When these pink polka-dotted bags were used, they subverted the standard black and elicited a positive emotion from the community.

Abstract: art imagery that departs from recognizable images of the natural world

Subject matter, subject: the person, object, space, or topic depicted in a work of art

Explore Further Color

Sensation and Color

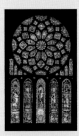

2.6.7 Rose window and lancets, Chartres Cathedral, France, 13th century → p. 273

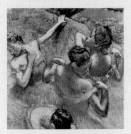

3.8.12 Edgar Degas, *Blue Dancers*, c. 1898 → p. 489

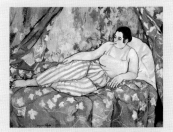

1.9.2 Suzanne Valadon, *The Blue Room*, 1923 → p. 149

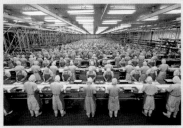

2.8.17 Edward Burtynsky, *Manufacturing #17…*, 2005 → p. 310

Psychology of Color

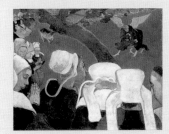

3.8.18 Paul Gauguin, *The Vision after the Sermon*, 1888 → p. 494

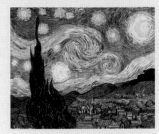

3.8.19 Vincent van Gogh, *Starry Night*, 1889 → p. 495

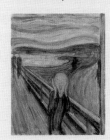

1.10.11 Edvard Munch, *The Scream*, 1893 → p. 170

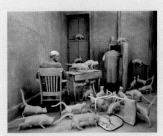

2.8.16 Sandy Skoglund, *Radioactive Cats*, 1980 → p. 309

Key Properties of Color

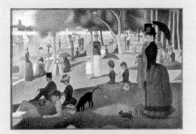

4.4.12 Georges Seurat, *Sunday on La Grande Jatte*, 1884–86 → p. 587

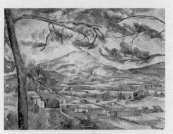

3.8.17 Paul Cézanne, *Mont Sainte-Victoire*, c. 1886–88 → p. 493

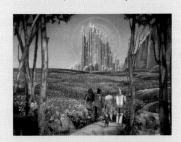

2.9.7 Victor Fleming, still from *The Wizard of Oz*, 1939 → p. 322

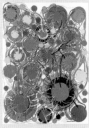

1.6.6 Atsuko Tanaka, *Work*, 1968 → p. 120

Your turn

How does color function in these artworks?

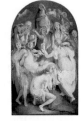

3.6.14 Jacopo da Pontormo, *Deposition*, 1525–28 → p. 454

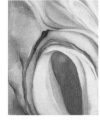

3.9.3 Henri Matisse, *Joy of Life*, 1905–6 → p. 502

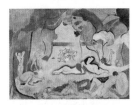

1.1.25 Georgia O'Keeffe, *Music—Pink and Blue II*, 1919 → p. 46

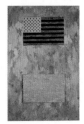

4.4.13 Jasper Johns, *Flags*, 1965 → p. 588

1.5
Motion and Time

Motion: the effect of changing placement in time

Medium (plural **media**): the material on or from which an artist chooses to make a work of art, for example canvas and oil paint, marble, engraving, video, or architecture

Futurism, Futurist: an artistic movement originating in Italy in 1909 that violently rejected traditional forms in favor of celebrating and incorporating into art the energy and dynamism of modern technology; Futurists were artists working in this style

Moving images are part of our daily experience of life in the twenty-first century. We see them on our TV and computer screens, on displays in stores, and on the street. In an age where we can see highly sophisticated and dynamic movies in 3-D, and we know that what we are seeing are brilliant illusions and special effects created through technological wizardry, it is difficult to imagine how astonished, even afraid, audiences were when they first watched footage of objects hurtling through space. But such reactions are understandable. If we could travel back in time little more than a century, our visual experience would be quite different: all art images were still.

Motion and time are closely linked elements of art. Most of the traditional art **media** are inherently motionless and timeless. Paintings, for example, are static, holding a moment so that it can be experienced through the ages. But artists who work in static media have found imaginative ways to indicate the passage of time and the appearance of motion. Film and video have overturned the conventions of traditional art, as new technology and media allow artists to capture motion and time.

Motion

> The aim of every artist is to arrest motion, which is life, by artificial means and hold it fixed so that a hundred years later, when a stranger looks at it, it moves again since it is life.
>
> (William Faulkner, American novelist)

Faulkner tells us that an artist can make even a still image move and come to life. Motion occurs when an object changes location or position. Because this process occurs as time

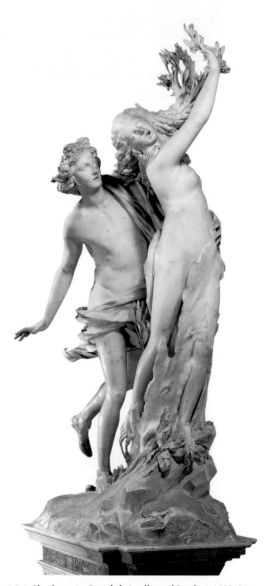

1.5.1 Gianlorenzo Bernini, *Apollo and Daphne*, 1622–24. Carrara marble, height 8′, Galleria Borghese, Rome, Italy

passes, motion is directly linked to time. To communicate motion without actually making anything move, artists can choose to imply time or alternatively, create the illusion of it.

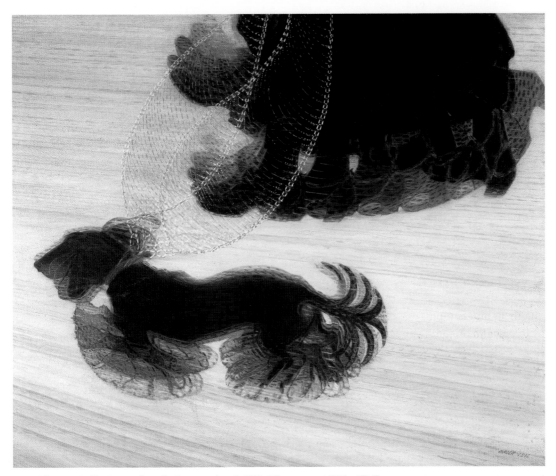

1.5.2 Giacomo Balla, *Dynamism of a Dog on a Leash*, 1912. Oil on canvas, 35⅜ × 43¼".
Albright-Knox Art Gallery, Buffalo, New York

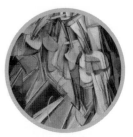

Another great example of implied motion is *Nude Descending a Staircase, No. 2* by Marcel Duchamp:
→ see **3.9.17**, p. 511

Implied Motion

When artists imply motion, they give us clues that a static work of art portrays a scene in which motion is occurring or has just occurred. In the case of implied motion, we do not actually see the motion happening, but visual clues tell us that it is a key aspect of the work.

The seventeenth-century Italian sculptor Gianlorenzo Bernini (1598–1680) emphasizes implied motion in many of his marble sculptures. *Apollo and Daphne* illustrates a story from ancient Greek mythology in which the sun god Apollo falls madly in love with the wood nymph Daphne (**1.5.1**). Terrified, she runs from him and begs her father, the river god Peneius, to save her. As Apollo reaches Daphne, Peneius transforms his daughter into a bay laurel tree. To convey the action, Bernini uses diagonal lines in the flowing drapery, limbs, and hair. Daphne's fingers sprout leaves as bark encases her legs. At the pivotal moment in the story, the scene is suddenly frozen in time. Since she could not be Apollo's wife, Daphne became his tree, and he made the laurel wreath his crown.

The Italian **Futurist** Giacomo Balla (1871–1958) uses a different method of implying motion in his painting *Dynamism of a Dog on a Leash* (**1.5.2**). Balla paints a series of repeating marks to give the impression that we are seeing motion as it happens, as if we are viewing several separate moments at once. He paints the dog's tail in eight or nine different positions to communicate movement. Its feet are merely indicated by a series of strokes that give a sense of very rapid motion. The leash, a white implied line created by the artist using small dotted brush strokes in close proximity, is also repeated in four different positions. The composition gives viewers a sense of ongoing forward motion even though the paint on the canvas is perfectly still.

The Illusion of Motion

In the works by Bernini and Balla, the artists *imply* motion: we do not actually see it occurring, but visual clues tell us that the works, although static, portray motion. Artists can also communicate the idea of motion by creating an

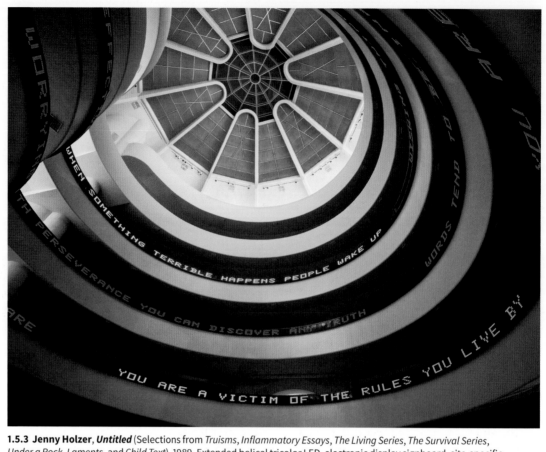

1.5.3 Jenny Holzer, *Untitled* (Selections from *Truisms*, *Inflammatory Essays*, *The Living Series*, *The Survival Series*, *Under a Rock*, *Laments*, and *Child Text*), 1989. Extended helical tricolor LED, electronic display signboard, site-specific dimensions. Solomon R. Guggenheim Museum, New York

1.5.4 Bridget Riley, *Cataract 3*, 1967. PVA on canvas, 7'3¾" × 7'3¾". British Council Collection, England

illusion of it. Artists create this illusion through visual tricks that deceive our eyes into believing there is motion as time passes, even though no actual motion occurs.

The American artist Jenny Holzer (b. 1950) uses the illusion of motion to enhance her text-based presentations. Her untitled 1989 **installation** in the Guggenheim Museum, New York, displays messages as text (**1.5.3**). Although the text does not actually move, it appears to spiral up the ramped circular atrium of the museum as the tiny LED lights are illuminated and then switched off in an automated sequence. This creates the impression that the text is moving as time elapses. The intermittent flashing of lights creates a scrolling series of letters and words, like the flashing lights of the casinos on the Las Vegas Strip. Holzer uses this illusion to invigorate her messages and critiques of society.

Another illusion of motion that deceives the eye forms the basis for **Op art** (short for Optical art). During the 1960s, Op art painters experimented with discordant **positive– negative** relationships. There is a noticeable sense of movement when we look at *Cataract 3*

(**1.5.4**), by the British artist Bridget Riley (b. 1931). If we focus on a single point in the center of the work, it appears there is an overall vibrating motion. This optical illusion grows out of the natural physiological movement of the human eye; we can see it because the artist uses sharp contrast and hard-edged graphics set close enough together that the eye cannot compensate for its own movement. Riley understands that the natural oscillation of the eye combined with the passage of time makes us feel a sense of motion.

Stroboscopic Motion

When we see two or more repeated images in quick succession, they tend visually to fuse together. The illusion of motion created is attributed to the theory of persistence of vision, which explains how visual sensations persist even after they are no longer in sight. For example, when a lightstick or sparkler is waved about, there is a visible trail of light that remains. Artists today still use this theory to make amazing impressions of motion.

The American sculptor Gregory Barsamian (b. 1953) creates spinning sculptures that are intended to be viewed in an environment with strobe (intermittently flashing) lighting. The resulting illusion of motion is achieved by the visual interruptions created by the flashing lights, which make a series of sculptural **forms** appear to move. Barsamian's work *Drum 52* (**1.5.5**) is a **kinetic**, or moving, sculpture and also an installation that depends on the surrounding lighting to complete the viewer's experience. When the work is spinning, the viewer sees an illusion that consists of green liquid spheres rising out of a vat until caught by a series of hands that turn upward and then disappear as the cycle starts again.

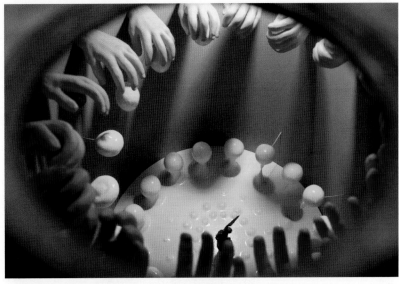

1.5.5 Gregory Barsamian, *Drum 52*, 2013. Kinetic sculpture/installation: steel, ureathane foam, sculpy, strobe light, motor. Artist's collection

If the viewer's vision was not interrupted by the pulsing effect of the strobe, the image would disappear into a blur of motion and the individual steps would be lost. Hence, persistence of vision is here aided by the flickering light.

Cartoon animation grew out of early stroboscopic experiments, and **stop-motion** animation follows the same principle. Wes Anderson's (b. 1969) *Isle of Dogs* is compiled from individual frames of hand-sculpted puppets and backgrounds (**1.5.6**). Anderson, like many other animators, begins the process by drawing a storyboard, or visual plan that anticipates the movement and interactions of the characters. The animator makes subtle changes to the sculpted puppets. Individual frames are captured in sequence on film, and are then played in rapid succession to create the idea of movement in the mind of the viewer. This succession of images is combined with

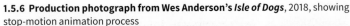

1.5.6 Production photograph from Wes Anderson's *Isle of Dogs*, 2018, showing stop-motion animation process

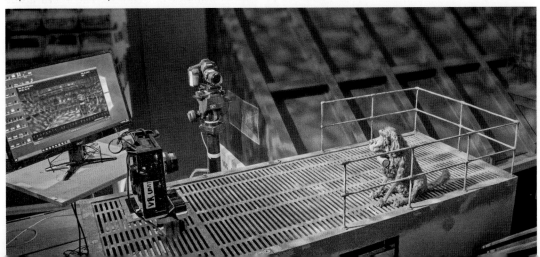

other scenes and eventually committed to film—or, more commonly, digital media—for distribution to movie theaters.

"Movie" is an abbreviation of "moving picture," and during the twentieth century movies became the dominant mode of artistic expression in motion. Film relies on individual frames played in quick succession. Similar advanced forms of stroboscopic motion have been developed to stream digital video on the Internet. Files with a series of multiple images (and sound files) are played in rapid succession on a computer, much like a film.

Such films as Tom Tykwer's (b. 1965) *Run Lola Run* (**1.5.7**) experiment with the notion of story and time. Set in 1990s Berlin, the story revolves around a young woman, Lola, who receives a panicked call from her boyfriend, Manni. If she does not get him 100,000 Deutschmarks (approximately $60,000) within twenty minutes, he will be forced to rob a grocery store in order to escape being killed by the mobster who is threatening him. Lola, desperate to save his life, does everything in her power to obtain the money, but only gets shot herself.

We discover, however, that the scope of the storyline extends beyond the everyday passage of time. Lola refuses to die, and so the story reboots and begins again, this time with a new set of circumstances, some of which Lola is now prepared for from the first version of events. In all, she does three runs: in each, the time allowed for the run is the same, but the action takes a different course.

The film's reinterpretation of time engages the viewer and helps to explore the characters in greater depth with each reset. The director thus uses stroboscopic motion as a tool to question the nature of time, and to demonstrate the impact that a few seconds' difference can make.

Motion graphics are designs, especially those including type, that are imbued with an illusion of motion. This type of visual communication, sometimes called **kinetic typography**, uses the attributes of time and

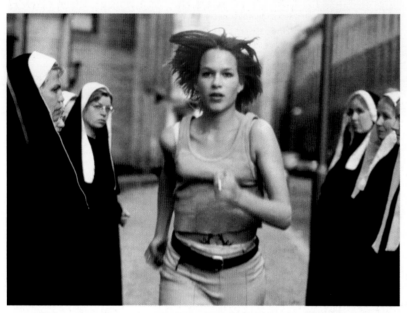

1.5.7 Still from *Run Lola Run*, 1998. Duration 81 minutes. Director Tom Tykwer, X-Filme Creative Pool/WDR/Arte

Kinetic typography: An animation design process that features moving text

Performance art: a work involving the human body, usually including the artist, in front of an audience

Space: the distance between identifiable points or planes

Mobile: suspended moving sculptures, usually impelled by natural air currents

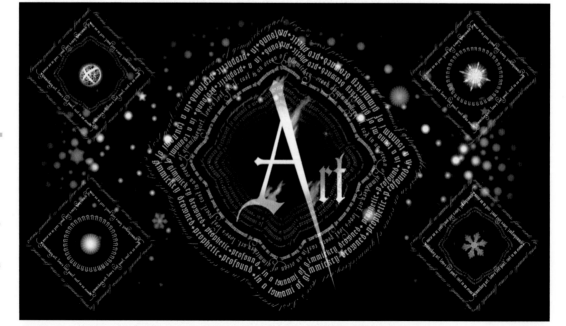

1.5.8 Oliver Harrison, still from *Apocalypse Rhyme*, 2012 (remastered 2014). Kinetic typography, 3 minutes

motion to support a message. In his work *Apocalypse Rhyme* (**1.5.8**), Oliver Harrison creates an expressive animation primarily by using type that has been formed into shapes and textures that support a poem about the inevitability of extensive change. Harrison uses the beauty of poetry fused with type design and rhythmic movement to intensify the impact of the text.

Actual Motion

We perceive actual motion when something really changes over time. We see it in **performance art** and in kinetic art, when objects physically move and change in real **space** and time. Performance art is theatrical; the artist's intention is to create not an art object, but an experience that can exist only in one place and time in history. Kinetic art plays out the passage of time through an art object, usually a sculpture, that moves.

Performance art emerged as a specific form of visual art during the twentieth century, when such artists as the German Oskar Schlemmer (1888–1943) began to expand the range of visual art by presenting works as live events. The Bauhaus, where Oskar Schlemmer worked as a teacher, challenged artists to experiment and invent new ways of integrating visual design into everyday life. His crowning achievement was the *Triadic Ballet* (**1.5.9**) which integrated costume, dance, and music into an improvised performance in which only three dancers appeared on stage at one time. The work had no plot, and unfolded as the dancers rhythmically explored the stage and their own cast shadows.

Performance artists need not focus on a social or political issue. For example, since 1984 the touring entertainment act Cirque du Soleil (French for "Circus of the Sun") has performed in ways that integrate music and acrobatics, enacted before a live audience (**1.5.10**). In order to keep the show continuous and seamless, transitions between different acts are choreographed into the show and set changes are done by the performers.

In performance art, the motion we see is made by a person, or people, whereas kinetic sculpture can appear to move of its own accord, unaided by human action. The earliest kinetic artwork is credited to French artist Marcel Duchamp (1887–1968), who mounted a bicycle wheel on a barstool so that the wheel could be spun. Later, the American sculptor Alexander

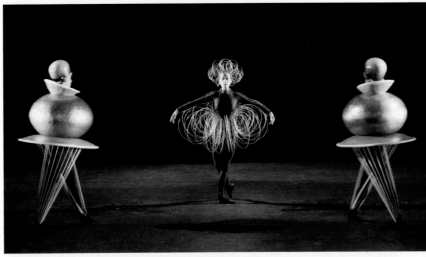

1.5.9 Oskar Schlemmer, *Triadic Ballet*, 1922. Reconstruction and choreography by Gerhard Bohner, 1977. New staging commissioned by the Akademie der Künste, Berlin and performed by the Bavarian Junior Ballet Munich, 4th June 2014, Reithalle, Munich, Germany

Calder (1898–1976) invented the **mobile**, taking the name from a suggestion by Duchamp. The mobile relies on air currents to power its movement, and Calder's kinetic sculptures were so finely balanced that even the smallest breeze would set them in motion. His final sculpture is the huge aluminum-and-steel mobile suspended in the National Gallery of Art in Washington, D.C. (**1.5.11**, p. 110). It resembles its predecessors in being made up

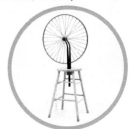

Marcel Duchamp was one of the first artists to create kinetic sculptures:
→ see **3.9.10**, p. 506

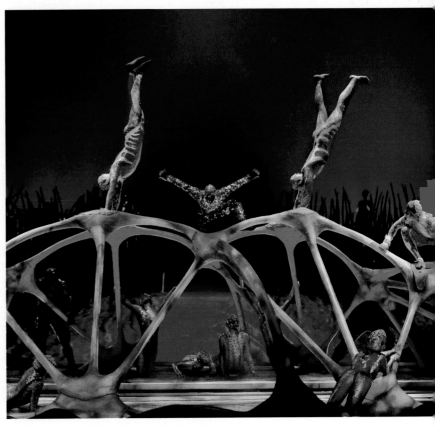

1.5.10 Cirque du Soleil performing *Totem* in Montreal, Quebec, July, 2010

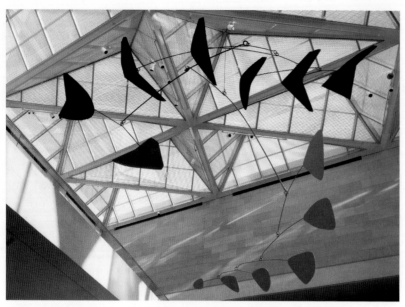

1.5.11 Alexander Calder, *Untitled*, 1976. Aluminum and steel, 29'10⅜" × 75'11¾". National Gallery of Art, Washington, D.C.

"Strandbeests," or beach animals (**1.5.12**). These sculptures, made primarily out of plastic pipe, are engineered so that they appear to walk as the wind catches their outstretched sails. Jansen incorporates bicycle pumps that compress air into plastic bottles using the wind power supplied by sails on the Strandbeests. The compressed air then pushes back, supplying a countermovement that allows the system to reset. The result gives the object the remarkable appearance of continuous movement that looks like an animal walking. Both Calder and Jansen use kinetic sculpture to enliven the environments in which these works are displayed. Calder's work energizes the Atrium of the National Gallery and Jansen's "beasts" are free to roam the beaches, when released.

Time

Since events necessarily take place over time, any artwork that deals with events must show how time goes by. Writers use chapters and other tools to give us a sense of how stories unfold. Artists also find ways to communicate the passage of time and to remind us of its influence on our lives. Motion can exist only because connected images, actions, and the ideas that they conjure in the mind of the viewer cannot be conceived of without time as a measure.

of counterbalanced organic shapes that move independently of one another. This is made possible by balancing the parts on points of equilibrium so that they can easily move. The result is a constantly changing visual form.

Sculptures by the Dutch artist Theodorus Gerardus Jozef "Theo" Jansen (b. 1948) have been carefully designed to appear to move by themselves, as if they were living beings. Jansen builds moving sculptures that he calls

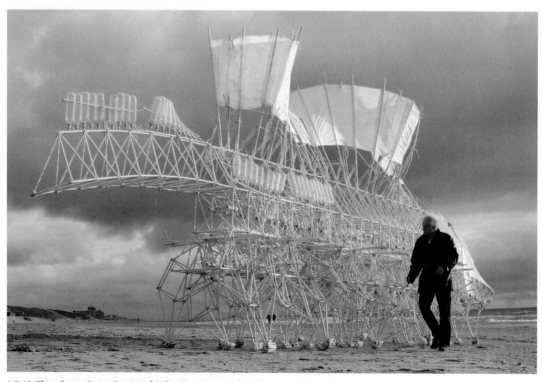

1.5.12 Theodorus Gerardus Jozef "Theo" Jansen, *Animaris Umeris (Strandbeest #48)*, 2009.
Recycled plastic bottles, plastic tubing, PVC pipe, wood, and fabric. Scheveningen Beach, The Netherlands

The Passage of Time

In **1.5.13**, *The Meeting of St. Anthony and St. Paul*, painters in the workshop of the fifteenth-century artist known as the Master of Osservanza solved the problem of how to tell a story in a single painting by merging a series of episodes into one picture. The Christian story begins in the upper left-hand corner, where St. Anthony sets out across the desert to seek the hermit St. Paul. In the upper right, St. Anthony encounters a mythical creature called a centaur—half-man, half-horse—which was associated with the Greek god of wine, Bacchus. This symbol of earthly temptation does not deter St. Anthony. He continues on his lone journey through thick forest until he finally meets and embraces St. Paul: their meeting is the culminating incident in the foreground. The entire painting signifies a pilgrimage on the long and winding road of time, rather than merely a single moment. This linear method is still used by artists, comic-book writers, and designers as a story-telling device and as a way of expressing the passing of time.

The American artist Nancy Holt (1938–2014) examines cycles of time in her works. Many of Holt's sculptures intertwine the passage of time with the motion of the sun. Her *Solar Rotary*, at the University of South Florida, Tampa, is designed to express meaning from shadows cast by the sun throughout the year (**1.5.14**). The work features an aluminum sculptural "shadow caster" perched on eight poles high above the center of a circular concrete plaza. The shadow caster—a ring with eight serpentine arms—is oriented so that shadows cast by its central ring encircle notable dates set into the surrounding concrete. The different angles of the sun at different times of the year make

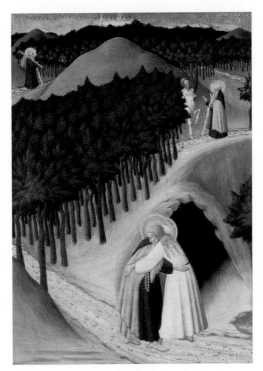

1.5.13 Workshop of the Master of Osservanza (Sano di Pietro?), *The Meeting of St. Anthony and St. Paul*, c. 1430–35. Tempera on panel, 18½ × 13¼". National Gallery of Art, Washington, D.C.

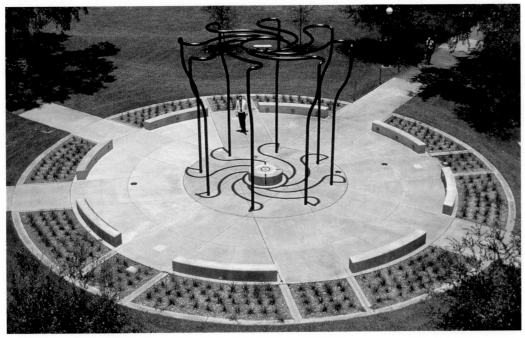

1.5.14 Nancy Holt, *Solar Rotary*, 1995. Aluminum, bronze, concrete, electric light, plants, approx. height 20', approx. diameter 24'. University of South Florida, Tampa

Ai Weiwei, *Dropping a Han Dynasty Urn*
Motion and Reproduction as a Metaphor for Time

For the other Ai Weiwei
GATEWAYS:
→ see p. 398 and p. 620

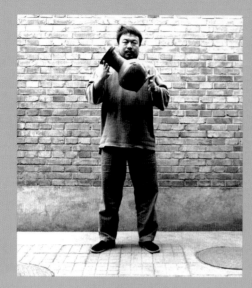

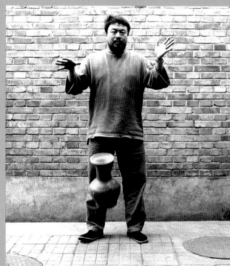

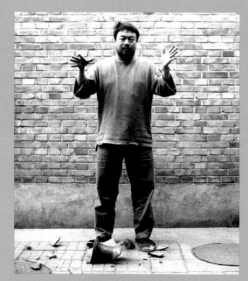

1.5.15 Ai Weiwei, *Dropping a Han Dynasty Urn*, 1995. Three black-and-white photographs, each 53½ × 42⅞"

The act of changing the understanding and perspective of an object, or reworking an established concept, disrupts its stability and makes it questionable.

—Ai Weiwei

In 1995 Chinese artist Ai Weiwei (b. 1957) created a time-based work that sparked great controversy: he was photographed dropping a 2,000-year-old Chinese urn (**1.5.15**). The act of destruction, and its photographic record, raised a furor not only because he had smashed an ancient artifact, but also for his seeming lack of concern. Yet, through the use of the elements of time and motion, the artist was actually acknowledging both the antiquity and importance of the object.

The three large-scale photographic panels are documentation of the passage of time as the artist committed the irreversible act of destruction. The first panel shows the artist holding the vase somewhat carelessly. The second shows the vase falling to the ground and the artist's hands boldly (or shamelessly) in the air. The third photo captures the vase smashing on the ground without any reaction on his part.

The images link the old and the new in Chinese art and culture. Chinese ceramics are symbols of centuries-long innovation and ingenuity. Ai himself emphasizes a Chinese look, with his traditional slippers and a beard that recalls the appearance of an ancient emperor. As an artist, he also symbolizes modern Chinese ingenuity with this action, which both challenges and draws attention to the prominence of Chinese tradition.

Important artifacts, such as the one that Ai is here seen, shockingly, smashing on the ground, and the ones he painted over, were—and still are—frequently damaged by government-run demolition and construction projects. Ai's seemingly emotionless expression, as he withdraws any responsibility for preserving this urn and lets it fall to the ground, references the Chinese government's similar lack of care and preservation of ancient objects. Through the elements of time and motion, *Dropping A Han Dynasty Urn* sparked a renewed interest in ancient objects that were being taken for granted by the Chinese government and society as a whole.

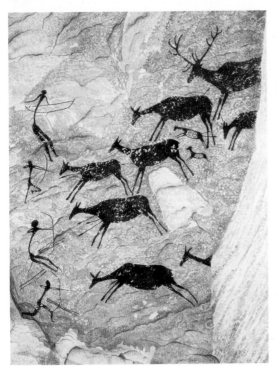

1.5.16 Hunting scene, painting from Cova dels Cavalls (Horses' Cave), Mesolithic period. Valltorta, Valencia, Spain

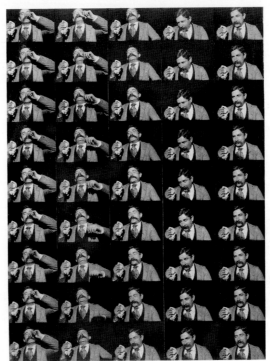

1.5.17 Thomas Edison and W. K. Dickson, *Fred Ott's Sneeze*, 1894. Still frames from kinetoscope film. Library of Congress, Washington, D.C.

shadows at different locations in the sculpture. For example, on March 27 a circle shadow surrounds a marker that records the day in 1513 when the Spanish explorer Juan Ponce de León first sighted Florida. In the center, a concrete circular bench, into which a meteorite has been set, is encircled by the shadow at noon on the summer solstice, the longest day of the year (in the northern hemisphere), when the sun reaches its northernmost point. The meteorite symbolizes the connection between our world and the larger universe.

Depicting time in art is not a concept that exists only in the modern world. The most ancient pieces of art that we know, cave paintings, show the passage of time. Cave paintings at Valltorta Gorge, Spain, show, variously, bow hunters as the bow is aimed; the arrows in flight; and arrows piercing deer (**1.5.16**).

The Attributes of Time

Time is the fourth measurable dimension of a work of art after width, height, and depth. Time-based arts, such as film, embody six basic attributes of time: duration, tempo, intensity, scope, setting, and chronology. All of these attributes exist in one of the first American movies, *Fred Ott's Sneeze*, made by Thomas Edison and W. K. Dickson in 1894 (**1.5.17**). Since

we measure time in seconds, minutes, hours, and days, the duration, or length, of this film is 5 seconds. Duration provides a standard measurement that can be shared by others to ensure uniformity in the editing process. The tempo, or speed, is 16 frames per second. Contemporary filmmakers set tempo at 24 frames per second (or faster) for a smoother effect. The intensity, or level of energy, is high because the activity is sudden and strong. Since a viewer has to perceive and then process the perception of movement, moments with less change in the image are regarded as having less intensity. This film has a limited scope, or range of action, because it is confined to a simple activity. If the film were presented from multiple viewing angles it would have a broader scope. The setting, or context, is Thomas Edison's studio. The chronology, or order of events, can be seen in the still frames as Fred Ott appears to be placing some snuff in his nose, recoiling, then jerking forward as he sneezes. Art that uses motion is sometimes called **temporal art** because it exists only within the passage of time.

Natural Processes and the Passage of Time

Some artistic media—such as aluminum or stone—will last for centuries, or even millennia, whereas others change states or

Temporal art: an artist's image or action that is transitory, existing in a passage of time

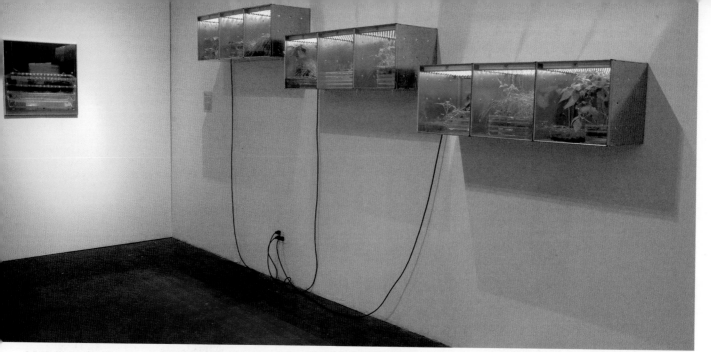

1.5.18 Suzanne Anker, *Astroculture (Shelf Life)*, 2009. Aluminum, plastic, red and blue LED lights, plants, water, soil, and no pesticides. Dimensions variable. Vegetable-producing plants grown from seed using LED lights. Installation view at Corpus Extremus (LIFE+), Exit Art, New York

begin to degrade almost immediately, for example artworks that are made from organic or biological materials. **Bioart** is art that reflects the passage of time through the natural processes of growth and decay that organic materials undergo. Thus, work by bioartists is always changing. In her work *Astroculture (Shelf Life)* (**1.5.18**), the American bioartist Suzanne Anker (b. 1946) experiments with how plants might react in such artificial conditions as those necessary to sustain life in outer space. In this case, the artist has used red and blue LED lights to provide the equivalent of the nourishing rays of sunlight, reducing the amount of light and energy required. Even though the leaves would appear green if under normal light, in this environment they appear to be a strong magenta color. The artificial conditions eliminate the need for insecticide and result in lower carbon emissions, and are therefore a practical option for artificial growing conditions in outer space. Anker's work blurs the lines between science and art, contributing to our understanding of the universe while delivering interesting and colorful visual forms.

Natural processes also dominate the work of American sculptor Ron Lambert (b. 1975), for whom the water cycle illustrates the passage of time. For *Sublimate (Cloud Cover)* he created a large transparent plastic environment in which water endlessly evaporates and condenses

(**1.5.19**). Lambert draws attention to our immediate environment as he shows how the rhythms of nature become a measure of natural time that we gauge by how long we have to wait for the next rain.

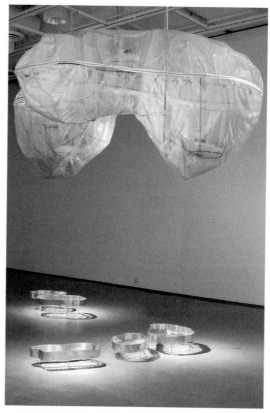

1.5.19 Ron Lambert, *Sublimate (Cloud Cover)*, 2004. Water, vinyl, humidifiers, steel, aluminum, and acrylic, dimensions variable

Bioart: art that is created with living, changing organisms

Explore Further Motion and Time

Actual Motion

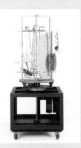

2.4.21 László Moholy-Nagy, *Light Prop for an Electric Stage*, 1929–30 ➔ p. 241

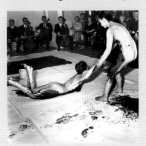

4.8.13a Yves Klein, *Anthropométries de l'époque bleue*, 1960 ➔ p. 638

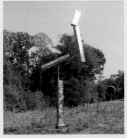

2.4.20 George Rickey, *Breaking Column*, 1986 (completed 2009) ➔ p. 241

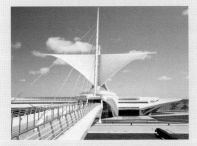

2.5.35 Santiago Calatrava, *Quadracci Pavilion*, Milwaukee Art Museum, 2001 ➔ p. 265

Implied Motion

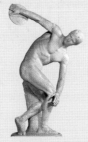

4.8.4 Myron, *Discus Thrower (Discobolos)*, c. 450 BCE ➔ p. 633

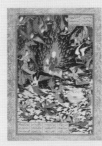

3.2.13 *The Ascent of the Prophet Muhammad*, from Nizami's *Khamsa*, 1539–43 ➔ p. 381

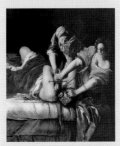

1.8.1 Artemisia Gentileschi, *Judith Decapitating Holofernes*, c. 1620 ➔ p. 140

1.1.11 Carolyn Davidson, Nike Company logo, 1971 ➔ p. 40

Stroboscopic Motion

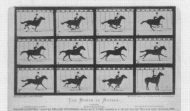

2.9.3 Eadweard Muybridge, *The Horse in Motion*, 1878 ➔ p. 320

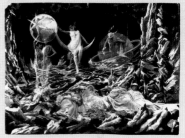

2.9.4 Georges Méliès, still from *A Trip to the Moon*, 1902 ➔ p. 320

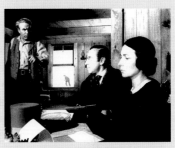

2.9.6 Orson Welles, still from *Citizen Kane*, 1941 ➔ p. 321

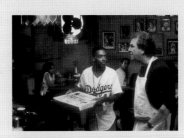

4.9.12 Spike Lee, still from *Do the Right Thing*, 1989 ➔ p. 656

Your turn

How do these works relate to motion and time?

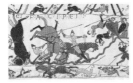

4.6.6 Detail of the Battle of Hastings, *Bayeux Tapestry*, c. 1066–82, ➔ p. 608

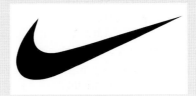

3.7.3 Jean-Honoré Fragonard, *The Swing*, 1766, ➔ p. 468

3.9.16 Umberto Boccioni, *Unique Forms of Continuity in Space*, 1913 ➔ p. 510

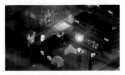

1.3.16 Supergiant Games, screenshot from *Transistor*, 2014, ➔ p. 76

1.6
Unity, Variety, and Balance

Unity: the appearance of oneness or harmony in a work of art: all of the elements appearing to be part of a cohesive whole

Variety: the diversity of different ideas, media, and elements in a work

Balance: a principle of art in which elements are used to create a symmetrical or asymmetrical sense of visual weight in an artwork

Principles of art: the principles, or grammar of art—contrast, unity, variety, balance, scale, proportion, focal point, emphasis, pattern, and rhythm—describe the ways the elements of art are arranged in an artwork

Elements of art: the basic vocabulary of art—line, shape, form, volume, mass, texture, value (lightness/darkness), space, color, and motion and time

Composition: the overall design or organization of a work

Medium (plural **media**): the material on or from which an artist chooses to make a work of art, for example canvas and oil paint, marble, engraving, video, or architecture

Grid: a network of horizontal and vertical lines; in an artwork's composition, the lines are implied

Gestalt: complete order and indivisible unity of all aspects of an artwork's design

Unity, **variety**, and **balance** are central **principles** that artists use to create visual impact. Unity—creating order or wholeness, the opposite of disorder—is central in the creation of a work of art or design. Unity refers to the imposition of order and harmony on a design. It is the sense of visual harmony that separates the work of art from the relative chaos of the surrounding world. Unity refers to the oneness or organization of similarities between **elements** that make up a work of art. Artists use the principle of unity to make choices that link visual elements to each other in a **composition**.

By comparison, variety is a kind of visual diversity that brings many different ideas, **media**, and elements together in one composition. It is expressed in contrast and difference, which create visual interest and excitement. Sometimes artists will use the discordance of variety to create uneasy relationships between visual elements. Sometimes, too, this lack of similarity between elements can actively create a sense of unity when an artist imposes on the work a **grid** or other visual structure.

Balance refers to the distribution of elements, whether unified or varied, within a work. The number and distribution of different elements influence the composition. Balance in visual art is much like the balance we experience in real life. If we carry a large heavy bucket in one hand, it pulls us to one side and we orient our body to offset its weight. In art, the visual elements in one half of a work are offset by the elements on the opposite side. By making sure that the elements are distributed in an organized way, artists create balance.

It is possible for an artist to depict an unbalanced design. Such a design is usually

created to carry a message or create an unsettled feeling in the viewer. To create an unbalanced composition the artist or designer will intentionally violate the guidelines for good design for a specified effect.

Unity

Unity provides an artwork with its cohesiveness and helps to communicate the visual idea it embodies. Artists face a communication challenge: to find a structure within the chaos of nature and to select and organize materials into a harmonious composition. An artist will identify specific elements in a scene and use them to create unity. Artists are concerned with three kinds of unity: compositional, conceptual, and **gestalt**.

Compositional Unity
An artist creates compositional unity by organizing all the visual aspects of a work. This kind of harmony is not easy to achieve. The three similar diagrams in **1.6.1** illustrate the idea of compositional unity. Although A is unified, it lacks the visual interest of B. While C is a unified work, its visual variety feels incoherent and chaotic. These diagrams show how too much similarity of shape, color, line, or any single element or principle of art can be

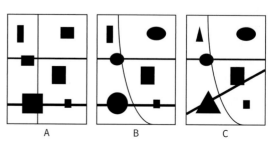

1.6.1 Three diagrams of compositional unity

Katsushika Hokusai, "The Great Wave off Shore at Kanagawa" A Masterpiece of Unity and Harmony

For the other Hokusai
GATEWAYS:
→ see p. 215 and p. 404

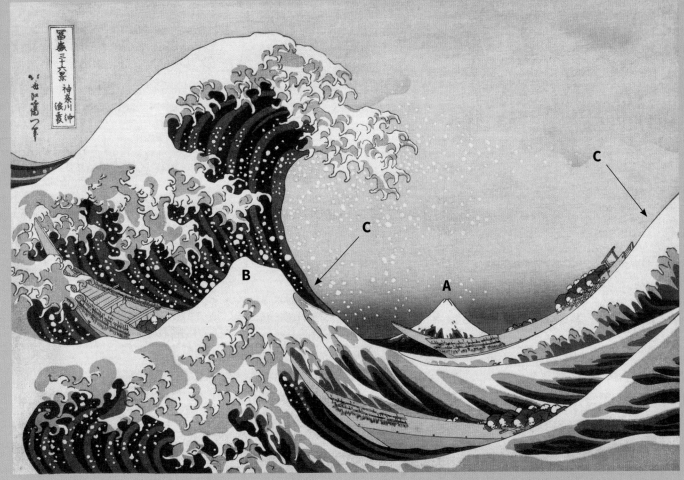

1.6.2 Katsushika Hokusai, "The Great Wave off Shore at Kanagawa," from *Thirty-Six Views of Mount Fuji*,
1826–33 (printed later). Print, color woodcut. Library of Congress, Washington, D.C.

In his print "The Great Wave off Shore at Kanagawa," Japanese artist Katsushika Hokusai (1760–1849) created a unified composition by organizing repetitions of shapes, colors, textures, and patterns to create a visual harmony, even though the scene is chaotic (**1.6.2**). These repetitions visually link different parts of the picture. Even Mount Fuji (A), in the middle of the bottom third of the work, almost blends into the ocean: because whitecaps on the waves (B) mimic the snow atop Mount Fuji, the mountain's presence is felt and reiterated throughout the composition. The shape and placement of the boats also create a pattern amongst the waves. Because the great wave on the left is not repeated, it has a singular strength that dominates the scene. Hokusai has also carefully selected the solids and voids in his composition to create opposing but balancing areas of interest. As the solid shape of the great wave curves around the deep trough below it (C), the two areas compete for attention, neither one possible without the other.

The words unity and harmony suggest peaceful, positive coexistence in a chaotic world. A skillful artist can depict unity and harmony even in a work portraying a scene that in reality would be chaotic and threatening. Here, Hokusai has organized a group of visual elements into a structure that makes sense because it has been simplified and ordered.

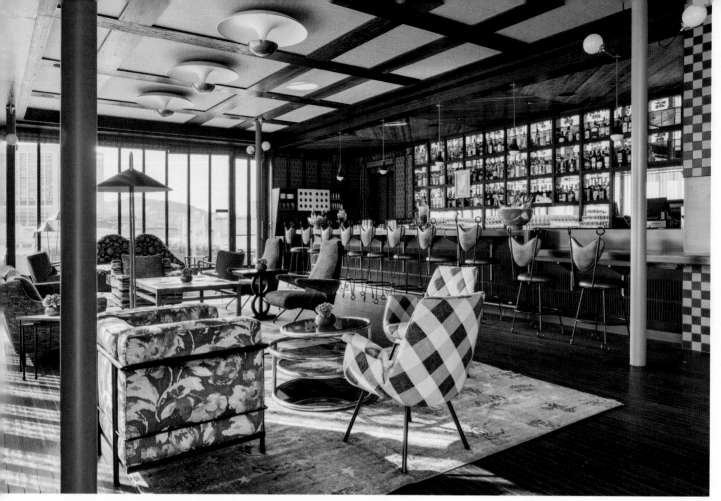

1.6.3a Charmaine's Bar at San Francisco Proper, California, with interiors by Kelly Wearstler. Opened September 2017

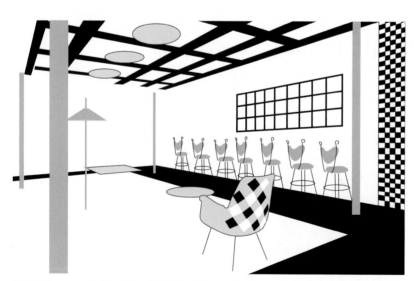

1.6.3b Linear evaluation of interior design elements in Charmaine's Bar design

monotonous and make us lose interest. Too much variety can lead to a lack of structure and the absence of a central idea. Experienced artists learn to restrict the range of elements: working within limitations can be liberating.

The interior of Charmaine's Bar at the San Francisco Proper hotel, designed by Kelly Wearstler (b. 1967) (**1.6.3a**), closely reflects the design in **1.6.3b**. The interior has a series of rectangular grids and orange highlights that complement each other. The grid and checker patterns repeat (black and white) on the walls, ceiling, and some furniture. Other oval and organic shapes are distributed throughout the scene, especially visible in the row of barstools. The composition appears harmonious without being boring.

In the work of Russian artist Marie Marevna (1892–1984), the unifying features are the angular lines and flat areas of color or pattern (**1.6.4**). Marevna was one of the first female members of the **Cubist** movement; here her Cubist **style** breaks apart a scene and re-creates it from a variety of different angles. In this image, she shows us the seltzer bottle from the side, while we look down at the tabletop from above. The entire work becomes unified, however, because the artist paints a variety of different viewing angles using flat areas of color and pattern throughout, rather than relying on a more realistic representation. Even though we view the **still life** from many different angles, the artist was able to unify the composition

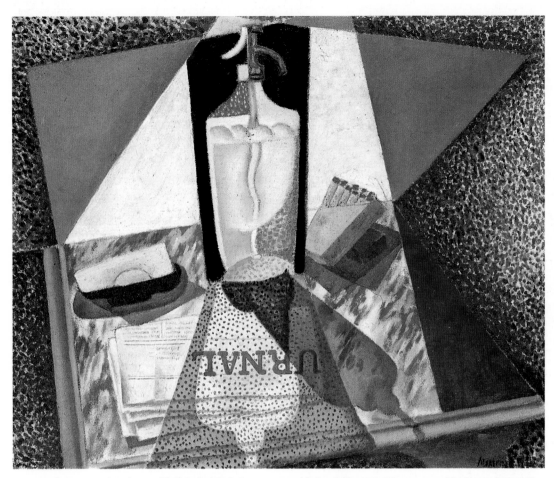

1.6.4 **Marie Marevna (Marie Vorobieff-Stebelska)**, *Nature morte à la bouteille*, 1917. Oil on canvas with plaster, 19¾ × 24″

by using similar elements. The texture of the paint, the hard diagonal angular lines, and the dominant gray-brown color all work together to counteract the potentially excessive variety that could have come from the many points of view presented.

As demonstrated opposite, artists add unity to a design by matching visual similarities, but connected ideas can help support that principle as well. The Gutai group was a collection of Japanese artists working in the 1950s and 1960s that experimented with different kinds of artistic expression. The term Gutai is formed of the words "gu," which translates as "tool," and "tai," meaning body—and this represents the physical methods of many of the group's artists, who used their own bodies in their works in ways that anticipated **performance art** of the 1960s and 1970s in the US and Europe. One of the notable members of the Gutai group was Atsuko Tanaka (1932–2005). Tanaka had traditional training as an artist, but she found new creative outlets when she joined the group in 1965. She is best remembered for *Electric Dress* (**1.6.5**), which she wore to exhibition

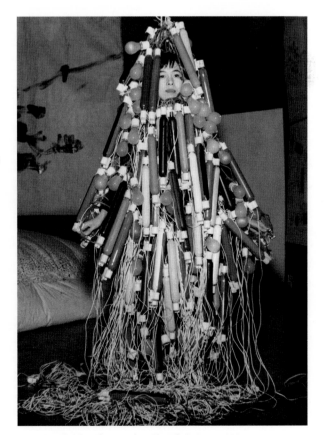

1.6.5 **Atsuko Tanaka wearing *Electric Dress***, *c.* 1956.

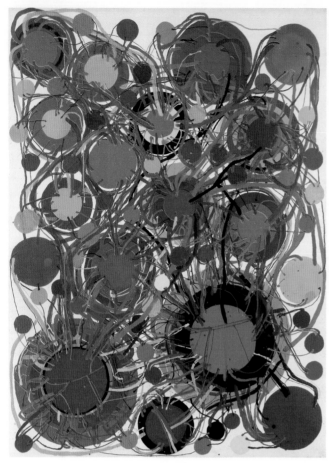

1.6.6 Atsuko Tanaka, *Work*, 1968. Synthetic polymer paint on canvas, 51½ × 38¼". Private collection

openings. She derived her idea from a neon pharmaceutical sign that would turn off and on sporadically. Tanaka's painting *Work* (**1.6.6**) reflects the sensibilities of *Electric Dress*. Both the dress and her painting are **abstract** works that together find unification in the repeated **motifs** of lines and circular shapes presented in a variety of bold colors. The circular shapes visually connect with the light bulbs of the dress, while the curved lines can be associated with the wires that provide electricity to this living sculpture.

Some artists create compositional unity while gathering together bits and pieces of visual information. The African American artist Romare Bearden (1911–1988) captures the unity of New York in the fragments that make up his **collage** *The Dove* (**1.6.7**). In this work we see snippets of faces and hands, city textures of brick walls and fire escapes, and other associated images assembled into a scene that, at first glance, seems frenetic and chaotic. We may feel this pace of life when we visit a big city, but if we look beyond our first impressions, we often notice the orderly grid of streets and the organization that underpin city life.

Bearden reflects this order in an underlying grid of verticals and horizontals in the street

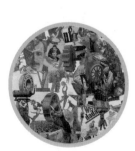

Another great example of compositional unity and collage is *Cut with the Kitchen Knife through the Last Weimar Beer-Belly Cultural Epoch of Germany*, by Hannah Höch:
→ see **3.9.11**, p. 507

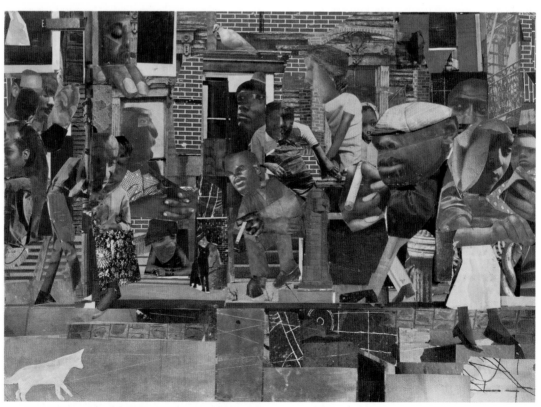

1.6.7 Romare Bearden, *The Dove*, 1964. Cut-and-pasted printed papers, gouache, pencil, and colored pencil on board, 13⅜ × 18¾". MoMA, New York

below, and in the vertical street posts and buildings in the upper section of the work.

The hectic composition is subtly coordinated by an implied triangular shape that runs from the cat in the lower left and the woman's feet in the lower right to the dove (hence the title) at the top center. These three points create a sense of depth while stabilizing the lively image of a bustling street scene.

Conceptual Unity

Conceptual unity refers to the cohesive expression of ideas within a work of art. Ideas can come to us in haphazard and unpredictable ways. Sometimes the expression of these ideas may not look organized, but an artist can still communicate them effectively by selecting images that conjure up a single notion. For example, an artist wishing to communicate the feeling of flight can use such symbols as feathers, kites, or balloons. Each of these has different visual attributes, but they all have an idea in common. That common idea is emphasized when they are placed together in the same work. The artist links images that, although different—perhaps even drastically different—in their appearance, have an idea, symbol, aspect, or association in common. Sometimes, on the other hand, an artist may deliberately break or contradict linkages between ideas in order to freshen up our tendency to find conventional—even boring—connections between them.

Artists bring their own intentions, experiences, and reactions to their work. These ideas—conscious and unconscious—can also contribute to the conceptual unity of a work and are understood through the artist's style, attitude, and intent. In addition, the conceptual links that artists make between symbols and ideas derive from the collective experiences of their culture: this too influences both the means that artists use to create unity and the viewer's interpretation of the work.

American **Surrealist** sculptor Joseph Cornell (1903–1972) created boxes that contain compositions of **found objects**. His works seem to suggest mysterious ideas and elusive feelings. The diverse shapes, colors, and other characteristics of everyday things come together to form distinctive images. Cornell's works are like a complex game with the viewer, a game that reveals and conceals—just as in a dream or **psychoanalysis**—the artist's personality. In

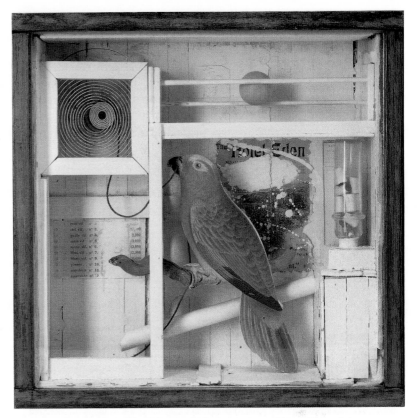

1.6.8 Joseph Cornell, *Untitled (The Hotel Eden)*, 1945. Assemblage with music box, 15⅛ × 15⅛ × 4¾". National Gallery of Canada, Ottawa

Untitled (The Hotel Eden), Cornell has collected objects from life and sealed them in a box (**1.6.8**). Although the interior of the box is a protected place, the bird is caged and unable to get out. A yellow ball sits trapped on two rails that limit its freedom of movement to roll back and forth. Neither the bird nor the ball is free. Placed together, all the different objects in the box make an idea greater than any one of them could create on its own. The artist has fused (and deliberately confused) his memories, dreams, and visualizations; the resulting artwork is a rich and complex visual expression of Cornell's personality and methods.

Gestalt Unity

Gestalt, a German word for form or shape, refers to something (here a work of art) in which the whole seems greater than the sum of its parts. The composition and ideas that make up a work of art—as well as our experience of it—combine to create a gestalt. We get a sense of gestalt when we comprehend how compositional unity and conceptual unity work together.

We can discover the many faces of gestalt by examining the ancient Hindu relief *Vishnu Dreaming the Universe* (**1.6.9**, p. 122). In this

Abstract: art imagery that departs from recognizable images of the natural world

Motif: a design or color repeated as a unit in a pattern

Collage: a work of art assembled by gluing materials, often paper, onto a surface. From the French *coller*, to glue

Surrealism, Surrealist: an artistic movement in the 1920s and later; its works were inspired by dreams and the subconscious

Found image or object: an image or object found by an artist and presented, with little or no alteration, as part of a work or as a finished work of art in itself

Psychoanalysis: a method of treating mental illness by making conscious the patient's subconscious fears or fantasies

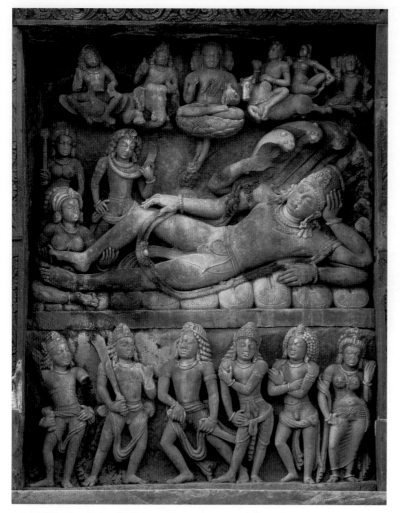

1.6.9 *Vishnu Dreaming the Universe*, c. 450–500 CE. Relief panel. Temple of Vishnu, Deogarh, Uttar Pradesh, India

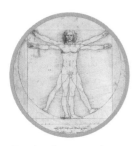

Gestalt unity connecting human proportions and architecture can be found in Leonardo's *Vitruvian Man: Study of the Human Body*:
→ see **4.4.1**, p. 580

Value: the lightness or darkness of a plane or area

Texture: the surface quality of a work, for example fine/ coarse, detailed/lacking in detail

stone carving, an abundance of human figures surrounds a much larger reclining figure; this is the god Vishnu dreaming. The repetition of the human shapes that attend Vishnu creates compositional unity: these similar shapes are linked visually.

According to some texts written in the ancient Indian language known as Sanskrit, the existence of the universe, and its creation, are directly dependent on the god Vishnu, who is sheltered by the great serpent Ananta and sleeps on the Cosmic Sea. Through his sleep, the universe is reborn over and over into eternity. Hindu pantheism (the unity of many gods as one) is elegantly illustrated in this work. Brahma is the upper figure seated on a lotus that sprouted from Vishnu's navel. Here he becomes the active agent of creation. The god Shiva, riding a bull (Nandi), is at Brahma's left. Lakshmi, Vishnu's wife, attends her sleeping husband. Their unity of male and female creates a partnership that results in the birth

of a new universe and many other universes into eternity. The dualities of male/female, life/death, good/evil are illustrated in the complex stories of the gods. Shiva, for example, is both creator and destroyer, destruction being necessary for creation—yet another unifying duality.

As is often the case, a religious idea provides profound conceptual unity. The image, the religious idea that the image illustrates, and the fervent belief of the artist who created the work interconnect through a symbolic representation in carved stone. As we come to appreciate how these aspects combine so completely in an artwork, we experience a sense of gestalt, an awakened understanding of the whole. This is a goal in any artwork.

Variety

If variety is the spice of life, it is also the spice of the visual world. In art, variety is a collection of ideas, elements, or materials that are fused together into one design. Inasmuch as unity is about repetition and similarity, variety is about uniqueness and diversity. Artists use a multiplicity of **values**, **textures**, colors, and so on to intensify the impact of a work. It is unusual to see a good composition that has just one type of value, shape, or color. Variety can invigorate a design. The example in **1.6.10** shows a composition of shapes set into a rectangle on a grid. Even though the grid structure is predictable, the variety of shapes and values counteracts the rigid structure. Many artists use this kind of variety to express an energy that would be lost if there were too much unity. Variety is the artist's way of giving a work of art a jolt.

The American Robert Rauschenberg (1925–2008) used variety to energize his artwork and challenge his viewers. In the work

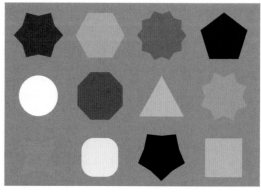

1.6.10 Variety of shapes and values set into a grid

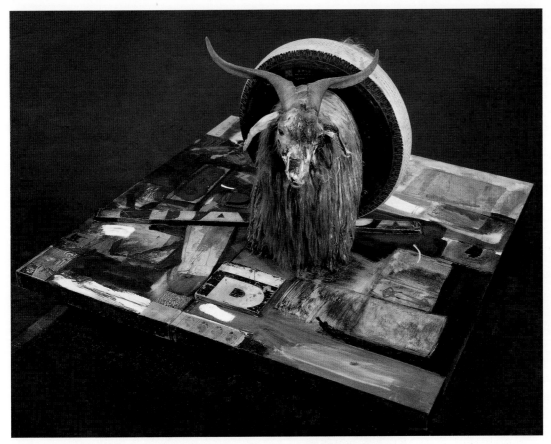

1.6.11 Robert Rauschenberg, *Monogram*, 1955–59. Mixed media with taxidermy goat, rubber tire, and tennis ball, 42 × 63¼ × 64½″. Moderna Museet, Stockholm, Sweden

Monogram, Rauschenberg has used all kinds of different things to form his composition (**1.6.11**). The work features a stuffed goat with a tire around its middle standing on a painting. By combining these objects, Rauschenberg creates an outlandish symbol of himself as a rebel and outcast. The goat, an ancient symbol of male lust and a Christian symbol of souls cast out from salvation, becomes the totem of Rauschenberg's own provocative behaviors and his violation of art-world conventions. The stuffed goat penetrates the tire and stands atop a symbol of the established art world (painting) while defecating a dirty tennis ball onto it (not visible in this image). For the first time in modern art, too, Rauschenberg breached the divide between painting and sculpture and took painting off the wall. By using a variety of non-traditional art materials and techniques, the work becomes a transgression against traditional art and morals.

Using Variety to Unify

Although it might seem contradictory, variety can be unifying. This can be seen in Baltimore album quilts (**1.6.12**) created by nineteenth

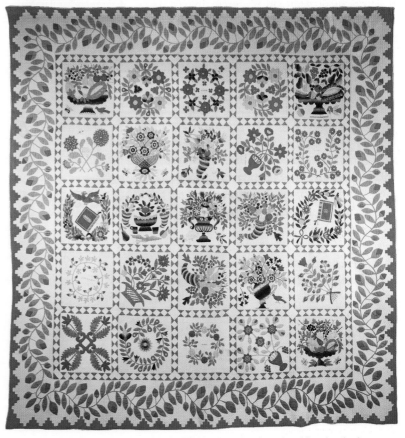

1.6.12 Alice A. Ryder, *Baltimore Album Quilt*, *c.* 1847. Pieced, appliquéd and quilted cotton with ink, 123⅝ × 123⅝″, American Museum and Gardens, Bath, England

century women. These carefully sewn quilts are named after the scrapbooks kept by Baltimore girls, although rather than being constructed from scraps of leftover material, as many quilts are, these fiber works were made from new pieces of fabric, a reflection of the wealth of this port city. Like a scrapbook, however, these quilts use a variety of images and fuse them together into a finished work. Because a strong structure is imposed on the many different shapes through the use of a grid, the work holds together as a unified whole. The quilted surface is an arrangement of shapes that, although they include a variety of different motifs and colors, form a unified composition that displays visual harmony.

Balance

Just as real objects have physical weight, parts of a work of art can have visual weight, or impact; these need to be balanced to achieve a sort of visual equilibrium. We can identify visual balance in a form or composition, just as we can with weighted objects, by noting differences between the two halves we are looking at. If the amount of visual weight does not have a reasonable counterweight on the opposite side, the work may appear to be unsuccessful or unfinished. If there are reasonable visual counterweights the work seems complete, and balance has been achieved. Even placing a visual weight in the center of a composition can impose a strong balance on a design.

Finding visual weight and counterweight is a challenge for the artist; balance in a work is not always easy to define. But there are some situations that often arise. For example, dark and light, although opposites, can act as counterbalances. Large shapes or forms can be countered by groups of smaller shapes or forms. For many artists this process is intuitive; they make decisions about the work based on what looks right, rather than on a rigid set of rules.

Symmetrical Balance

If a work can be cut in half and each side looks exactly (or nearly exactly) the same, then it is **symmetrically balanced**. Near-perfect symmetry exists in the human body. For example, each side of our face has half a nose, half a mouth, half a chin, and so on. The same is true for most animals and a number of

geometric shapes, such as circles and squares. Because it is a part of our physical body, symmetry can seem very natural and we can make natural connections to it.

Artists of ancient Ireland designed religious crosses that exhibit symmetry. Muiredach's High Cross (**1.6.13**) displays a bilateral balance

Symmetrical balance: an image or shape that looks exactly (or nearly exactly) the same on both sides when cut in half

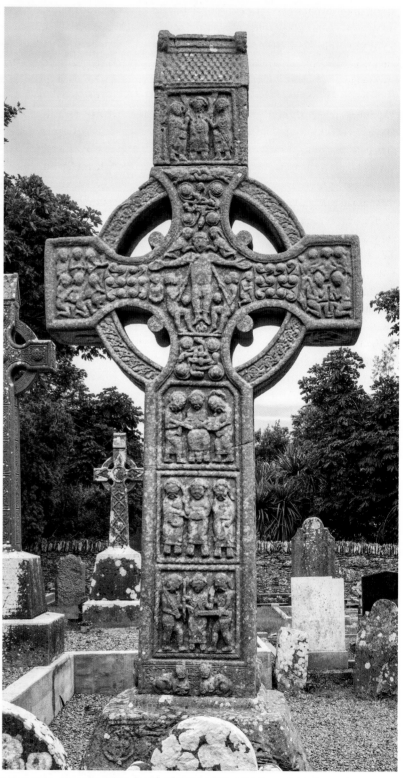

1.6.13 Unknown artist, Muiredach's High Cross (West face), *c.* 10th century. Sandstone, height 19′. Monasterboice, County Louth, Ireland.

because both sides of the object are nearly identical. This 19-ft-tall freestanding sculpture and memorial to an important person named Muiredach marks a burial location in Monasterboice, in County Louth, Ireland. The surfaces are covered with Christian symbols in the panels on each side. The west side (shown in **1.6.13**) features the crucifixion of Christ at the juncture of the vertical and horizontal parts with multitudes of people in the crossbar. Symmetry often appears in religious symbols because its predictable order suggests harmony and balance.

Asymmetrical Balance

On an old-fashioned scale, the kind with a long arm centered on top of a vertical support, a single heavy object on one side can be balanced by several lighter objects on the other side as long as the weight on both sides is the same. Similarly, when artists organize a composition they often use different visual weights on each side of the composition. This is asymmetrical balance, also called dynamic balance; it applies when the elements on the left and right sides are not the same, but the combination of elements counter one another.

Chinese artists have long used asymmetrical balance to reflect on life and the landscape. The twelfth/thirteenth-century academic painter Ma Yuan (1160–1225) expresses balanced asymmetry in his work *Walking on a Mountain Path in Spring* (**1.6.14**). In this painting, dark, light, and the placement of elements in the composition are not distributed evenly between the left and right sides. Ma Yuan is intentional in the way he positions shapes and figures on each side of the central **axis**. On the left are the large, dark shapes of trees, two figures, and distant mountains, which place a heavy visual weight on that side. On the right there are few shapes and a great deal of light, open space. Ma Yuan brilliantly counteracts the visual heaviness of the left side by placing the poetic inscription at the top right as a counterweight that leads the viewer's eye down to a small branch and some little rocks. For many Chinese artists, the use of brush and ink was a form of meditation, through simple, thoughtful actions, in search of higher knowledge. Yuan's asymmetrical design, with mostly empty space on the right, reminds the viewer of the expansive unknown that eludes discovery.

Radial Balance

Radial balance (or symmetry) is achieved when all elements in a work are equidistant from a central point and repeat in a symmetrical way from side to side and top to bottom. Radial

Axis: an imaginary line showing the center of a shape, volume, or composition

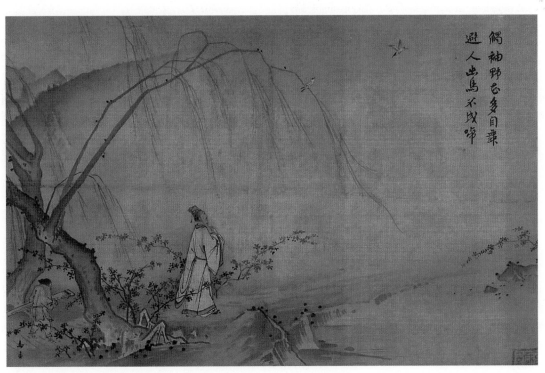

1.6.14 Ma Yuan, *Walking on a Mountain Path in Spring*, Song Dynasty (960–1279). Album leaf, ink and color on silk, 10¾ × 17". National Palace Museum, Taipei, Taiwan

The Taj Mahal
Love and Perfection

For the other Taj Mahal
GATEWAYS:
→ see p. 256 and p. 578

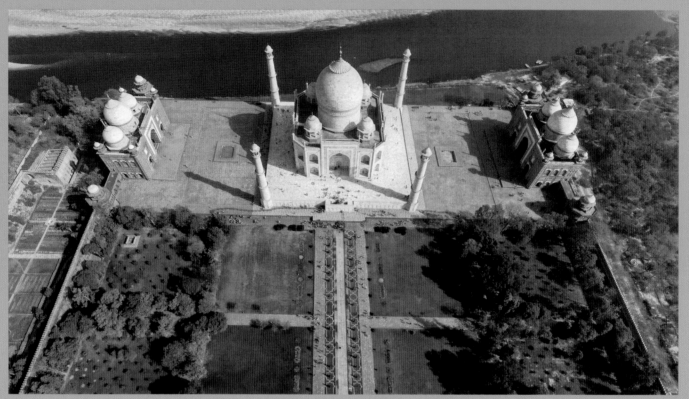

1.6.15a **The Taj Mahal, designed by Ustad Ahmad Lahauri, Abd al-Karim Ma'mur Khan, and Makramat Khan**; commissioned by Shah Jahan, 1632–43. Marble architecture. Agra, India

The building that we know as the Taj Mahal is an exemplary and enduring study in pure symmetry (**1.6.15a**). It was commissioned by the grieving Shah Jahan (1592–1666), the fifth Mughal Emperor of India, as a memorial to his third and beloved wife, Mumtaz Mahal (1593–1631). She and Shah Jahan were devoted to each other, and in recognition of their love and as an expression of his admiration for her, he sought after her death to create a building that would, through its visual perfection, honor her memory and stand as a testament to the transcendent power of timeless love.

In art, symmetrical balance is created when harmony unites all the elements, just as Shah Jahan and Mumtaz felt united in their relationship based on mutual love. A stable visual form is achieved when opposite sides of a design mirror each other exactly, creating this perfect balance. In most cases symmetry suggests pleasing tranquility, order, and numerical perfection to the viewer, so its use in the proportions and design of the Taj Mahal carries associations of beauty and stability.

The Taj Mahal uses both bilateral and radial symmetry in the design of the central tomb building (**1.6.15b**) and the surrounding complex in which it stands. The entire complex includes the central mausoleum and four **minarets**, a meeting house, a mosque, two pavilions, a gatehouse, two plaza areas, and a grand garden (**1.6.16a**), all of which can be bisected to reveal identical components on the opposite side. There are even some additional areas adjacent and across the Yamuna River that

Minaret: a tall slender tower, particularly on a mosque, from which the faithful are called to prayer

1.6.15b Plan of the tomb of Mumtaz Mahal

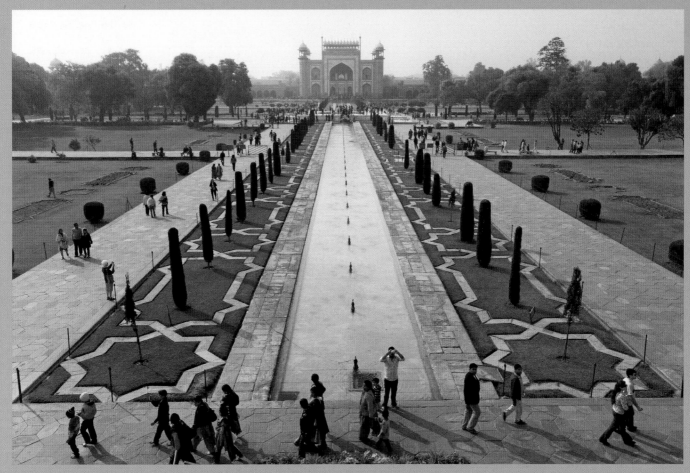

1.6.16a Mughal gardens and the South Gate of the Taj Mahal, Agra, India

also share the same characteristics. The entire plan, if bisected parallel to its longest axis, would find an exact replication in its opposite side. The carefully apportioned symmetrical balance in this plan expresses a sense of perfection.

Radial balance exists in both the main building and the adjacent *charbagh* (Mughal garden) (**1.6.16b**). Both are planned in such a way that each design element is repeated equidistant to a central point. So the symmetry exists along not only the bilateral axis, but also the principal intersecting axis. The multiple repetition of this balance in the design is a deliberate affirmation, in its sustained artistry, of the depth of Shah Jahan's love. Similarly, the complete design itself reflects his overarching commitment to perfection, shared by his architects Ustad Ahmad Lahauri, Abd al-Karim Ma'mur Khan, and Makramat Khan, as an expression, and indeed a proof, of the timelessness of true love.

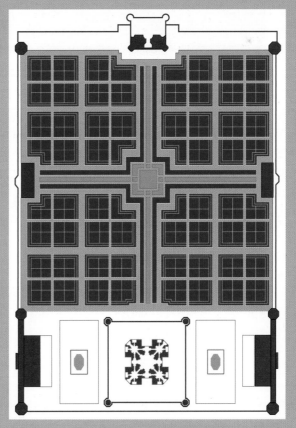

1.6.16b Plan of the charbagh (Mughal garden)

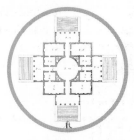

Another example of radial balance is the Villa Rotonda by Andrea Palladio:
→ see **3.6.17b**, p. 456

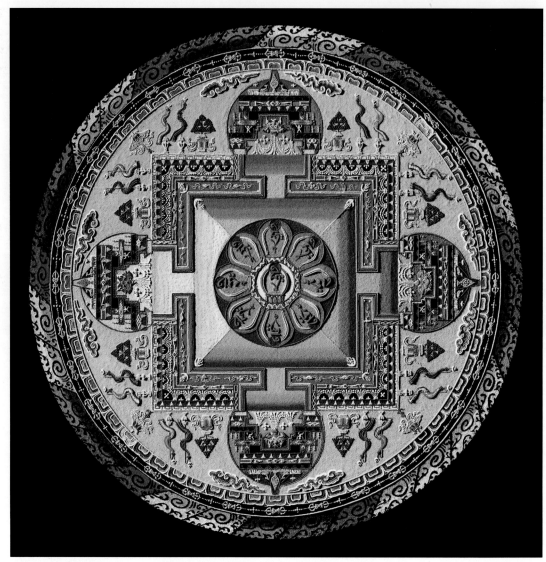

1.6.17 Amitayus Mandala created by the monks of Drepung Loseling Monastery, Tibet

Mandala: a sacred diagram of the universe, often involving a square and a circle

symmetry can imply circular and repeating elements. Although the term "radial" suggests a round shape, in fact any geometric shape can be used to create radial symmetry. Artists can employ this kind of balance when it is necessary to depict an element more than twice. It is sometimes used in religious symbols and architecture where repetition plays an important role in the design.

The Tibetan sand painting shown in **1.6.17** is a diagram of the universe (also known as a **mandala**) from a human perspective. The Tibetan Buddhist monks who created this work have placed a series of symbols equidistant from the center. In this mandala the colors vary but the shapes pointing in four different directions from the center are symmetrical. The square area in the center of the work symbolizes Amitayus, or the Buddha of long life, and surrounds a central lotus blossom. The creation of one of these sand paintings is an act of meditation that takes many days, after which the work is destroyed. The careful deconstruction of the work after it has been completed symbolizes the impermanence of the world.

Explore Further   Unity, Variety, and Balance

Unity

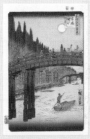

1.8.11 Ando Hiroshige, "Riverside Bamboo Market, Kyo-bashi," 1857 → p. 146

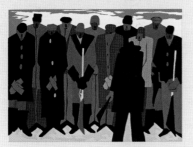

1.8.7 Jacob Lawrence, "John Brown Remained a Full Winter…," 1977 → p. 143

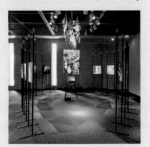

3.10.9 Jolene Rickard, *Corn Blue Room*, 1998 → p. 527

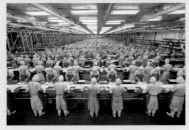

2.8.17 Edward Burtynsky, *Manufacturing #17…*, 2005 → p. 310

Variety

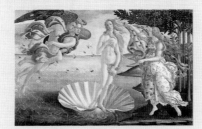

4.8.5 Sandro Botticelli, *The Birth of Venus*, c. 1482–86 → p. 634

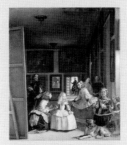

1.10.12a Diego de Silva y Velázquez *Las Meninas*, c. 1656 → p. 171

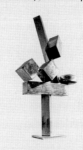

1.2.3 David Smith, *Cubi XIX*, 1964 → p. 52

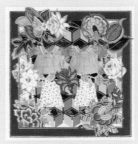

1.1.21 Miriam Schapiro, *Baby Blocks*, 1983 → p. 45

Balance

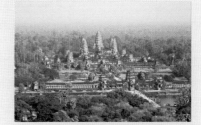

3.3.22 Angkor Wat, Siem Reap, Cambodia, 12th century → p. 406

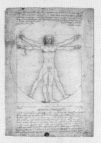

4.4.1 Leonardo da Vinci, *Vitruvian Man*, c. 1490 → p. 580

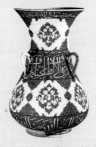

1.4.22 Mosque lamp from the Dome of the Rock, Jerusalem, 1549 → p. 96

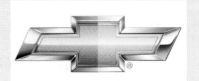

2.7.9 Chevrolet logo, first used in 1913, → p. 288

Your turn
How do these works relate to unity, variety, and balance?

2.4.1 Sculpture of the Lady Sennuwy, Egypt, 1971–1926 BCE → p. 229

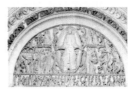

3.3.23 *Vishnu Churning the Ocean of Milk*, Angkor Wat → p. 407

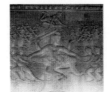

4.2.11 Gislebertus, *The Last Judgment*, c. 1120–35 → p. 561

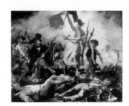

3.7.15 Eugène Delacroix, *Liberty Leading the People*, 1830 → p. 477

1.7
Scale and Proportion

Scale: the size of an object or artwork relative to another object or artwork, or to a system of measurement

Proportion: the relationship in size between a work's individual parts and the whole

Principles: the principles, or grammar of art—contrast, unity, variety, balance, scale, proportion, focal point, emphasis, pattern, and rhythm—describe the ways the elements of art are arranged in an artwork

Elements of art: the basic vocabulary of art—line, shape, form, volume, mass, texture, value (lightness/darkness), space, color, and motion and time

Monumental: having massive or impressive scale

Unity: the appearance of oneness or harmony in a work of art: all of the elements appearing to be part of a cohesive whole

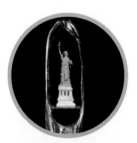

Scale is an important attribute in Willard Wigan's miniature *Statue of Liberty*:
→ see **4.4.9**, p. 585

The nineteenth-century French poet Charles Baudelaire wrote that "All that is beautiful and noble is the result of reason and calculation." Baudelaire was speaking of cosmetics and makeup, and not referring specifically to works of art, but his statement neatly summarizes the care with which artists determine **scale** and **proportion**. Artists use these key **principles** of design to control how they implement the basic **elements of art**, just as grammar controls how words work in a sentence.

We perceive scale in relation to our own size. Art objects created on a **monumental** scale appear larger than they would be in normal life. In a work created on a human scale, its size corresponds to the size of things as they actually exist. Work at this scale often surprises us. Small-scale objects appear smaller than our usual experience of them in the real world. Often, scale is used to indicate importance, yet this is not always the case: sometimes the smallest thing is the most significant.

Proportion is a core principle in the **unity** of any art object. Usually, an artist ensures that all the parts of an object are in proportion to one another. Alternatively, an artist can create a contradiction by portraying objects or figures out of proportion. For example, a cartoonist may portray a figure with disproportionately large nose or ears to exaggerate the distinctive, prominent facial features of a famous personality. Careful proportion is a sign of technical mastery; discordant proportions can express a wide range of meanings.

Scale

The scale of a work of art communicates ideas. A small work communicates something very different than a larger one does. Small-scale pieces force viewers to come in close to experience the artwork. A small-scale work implies intimacy, like whispering in someone's ear or admiring a ring on his or her finger. Large-scale works can be experienced by groups of viewers, and usually communicate big ideas directed at a large audience. Artists and designers make conscious choices about the scale of a work when they consider the message they want to convey.

Artists may also consider scale while they make more practical choices about a work. Considerations of cost, the time it will take to execute the piece, and the demands that a specific location may place on the work all come into play in decisions about scale.

Scale and Meaning

Usually, a monumental scale indicates heroism or other epic virtues. War monuments, for example, often feature figures much larger than lifesize in order to convey the bravery and heroism of the warriors. The Swedish-born artist Claes Oldenburg (b. 1929), however, uses monumental scale to poke fun while expressing admiration for the little things of everyday life.

Oldenburg believes that items from mass culture, no matter how insignificant they might seem, express a truth about modern life. So he restyles small, often overlooked objects on a monumental scale, giving clothespins and ice-cream cones a grandeur and significance they do not usually have. In the process, Oldenburg transforms the essence of these everyday things as he magnifies their sculptural form. Look at, for example, the enormous planting trowel, or *Plantoir*, in **1.7.1**,

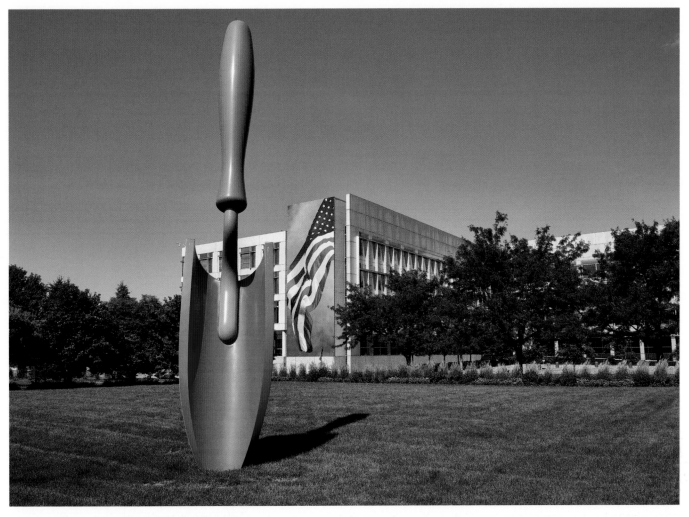

1.7.1 Claes Oldenburg and Coosje van Bruggen, *Plantoir*, 2001. Steel, aluminum, and fiber-reinforced plastic, height 23′. Collection Meredith Corporation, Des Moines, Iowa

a collaboration between Oldenburg and his wife, the Dutch-born sculptor Coosje van Bruggen (1942–2009).

The Iranian-born Italian painter Golsa Golchini (b. 1986) uses small scale to challenge our sense of scale. Golchini likes to create her figural paintings within **impasto** daubs of paint. In *the lazy pink* (**1.7.2**) the artist contrasts a highly detailed figure looking out of a window with a heavily painted canvas, leaving the artist's brush as a permanent appendage. The miniature scale of Golchini's work—only one person at a time can see it properly—forces us to come closer; looking at it becomes an intimate experience.

The scale of a work can add meaning in profound ways. In the French artist Jean-François Millet's (1814–1875) first major work, *The Gleaners* (**1.7.3**, p. 132), the artist uses scale to comment on the class system in nineteenth-century France. In the **foreground**, Millet shows three poor women who are pulling the

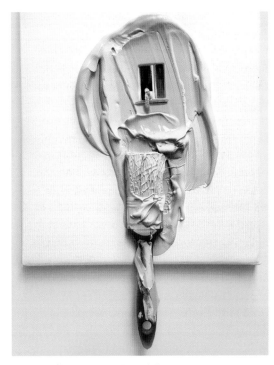

1.7.2 Golsa Golchini, *the lazy pink*, 2020. Mixed media and brush on canvas, 9¾× 13⅝″

Impasto: paint applied in thick layers

Foreground: the part of a work depicted as nearest to the viewer

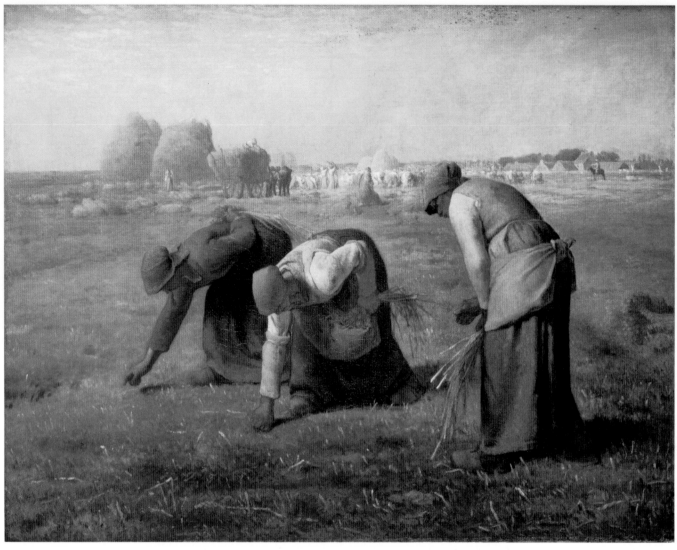

1.7.3 Jean-François Millet, *The Gleaners*, 1857. Oil on canvas, 2′9″ × 3′8″. Musée d'Orsay, Paris, France

last stubble from a recently harvested wheat field, while in the background members of the middle class harvest straw. In the upper right, a man on horseback—probably a representative of the wealthy landowner—supervises the activities in the field. In other artworks of the time, and in previous artistic periods, large-scale portraits were typically reserved for depicting religious subjects, royalty, and other figures of political or cultural importance. In this work, however, the artist chooses as his main focus three lower-class subjects. The suggestion that the poor, and their backbreaking labors, were worthy of pictorial honor ignited hostile responses from Millet's contemporaries. Simply by depicting these figures on a heroic scale, Millet adds a deeper meaning to the painting, commenting on the divides in the society in which he lives.

Relief: a sculpture that projects from a flat surface

Gothic: a Western European architectural style of the twelfth to sixteenth century, characterized by the use of pointed arches and ornate decoration

Surrealism, Surrealist: an artistic movement in the 1920s and later; its works were inspired by dreams and the subconscious

Hierarchical Scale

Artists can use size to indicate the relative importance of figures or objects in a composition: almost always, larger means more important, and smaller means less important. Hierarchical scale refers to the deliberate use of relative size in a work in order to communicate differences in importance. In **1.7.4** we can see the use of hierarchical scale in a **relief** sculpture from the ancient Maya. In this type of artwork, the king is depicted as the largest figure because he had the highest status in the social order. This is exemplified here, where the central figure represents the ruler Tajal Chan Ahk; he is visually more dominant than the others (sajal and aj-k'uhun nobles) and is depicted as a water lord in a cave.

The Flemish artist Jan van Eyck (c. 1395–1441) uses hierarchical scale to communicate spiritual importance. In his painting *Madonna*

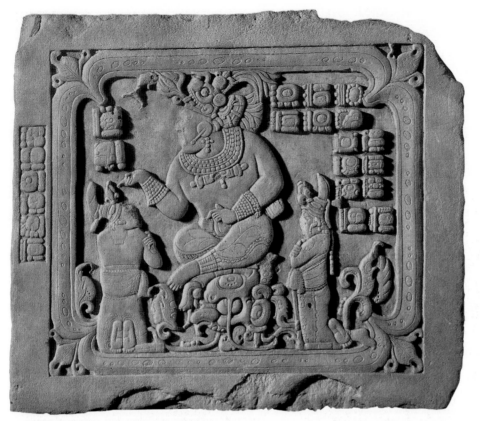

1.7.4 Panel 3 from the Maya city of Cancuén portraying the ruler Tajal Chan Ahk, *c.* 8th century. Cancuén, Guatemala. Limestone, 22⅝ × 26⅛ × 2½". Museo Nacional de Arqueología y Etnología, Guatemala City, Guatemala

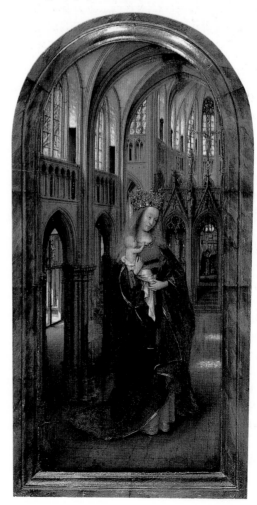

Hierarchical scale can also be seen in an Egyptian relief, the Palette of Narmer:
→ see **4.6.5b**, p. 607

in a Church, Van Eyck enlarges the scale so that the mother and child fill the enormous space of a **Gothic** church (**1.7.5**). In his effort to glorify the spiritual importance of Mary and the Christ child, Van Eyck also separates them from normal human existence. Their gigantic appearance, relative to the interior, makes these figures appear to be larger than normal human beings. Van Eyck has scaled them to symbolize their central importance in the Christian religion.

Distorted Scale

An artist may deliberately distort scale to create a supernatural effect. In the twentieth century, artists known as **Surrealists** created works that use dreamlike images to subvert our conscious experiences. The American Surrealist artist Dorothea Tanning (1910–2012), in *Eine Kleine Nachtmusik*, paints a sunflower at a scale that contradicts its surroundings (**1.7.6**, p. 134).

The flower seems huge in relation to the interior architecture and the two female figures standing on the left. By altering our ordinary experience of scale, Tanning invites us into a world unlike the one we know: a realm of childhood dreams and nightmares where

1.7.5 Jan van Eyck, *Madonna in a Church*, 1437–38. Oil on wood panel, 12⅝ × 5½". Gemäldegalerie, Staatliche Museen, Berlin, Germany

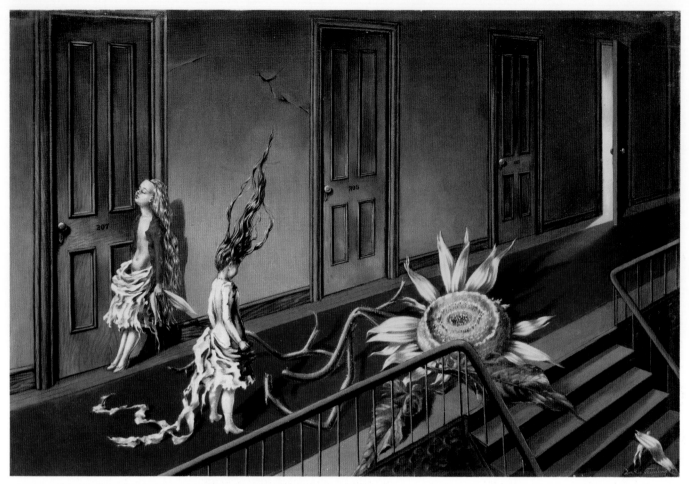

1.7.6 **Dorothea Tanning**, *Eine Kleine Nachtmusik*, 1943. Oil on canvas, 16⅛ × 24″. Tate, London, England

odd things happen, such as the strangely alive sunflower and the unexplained wind that lifts the hair of one figure. The title, *Eine Kleine Nachtmusik* ("A Little Night Music"), derives from a lighthearted piece of music by the eighteenth-century Austrian composer Wolfgang Amadeus Mozart, but ironically Tanning's scene exhibits a strange sense of dread.

Proportion

The relationships between the sizes of different parts of a work make up its proportions. By controlling these size relationships, an artist can enhance the expressive and descriptive characteristics of the work.

As size relationships change, so do proportions. For example, **1.7.7** (A) shows the profile of a Greek vase. If we change the width (B) or the height (C), the overall proportions are altered. Each of these vase profiles communicates a different feeling simply because the ratio of height to width is different. When the width is reduced, the vase seems elegant and light. Reducing the height produces

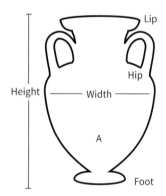

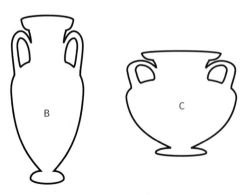

1.7.7 Examples of how proportion changes on vertical and horizontal axes

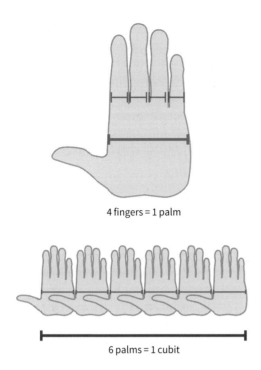

4 fingers = 1 palm

6 palms = 1 cubit

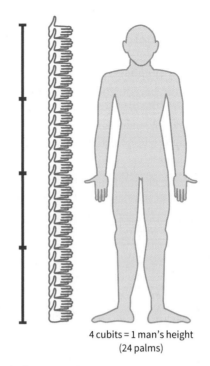

4 cubits = 1 man's height
(24 palms)

1.7.8 Ancient Egyptian system using the human hand as a standard unit of measurement

the opposite effect: the vase seems sturdier and weightier than the original profile (A).

For a two-dimensional work, the artist chooses an area, or **format**, on which to make a drawing, painting, print, or design. The format's dimensions—its height and width—dictate a great deal about what kind of image can be created. For example, a format that is only 2 in. tall and 10 in. across will require an image that is short and wide. Artists must plan ahead and choose the format that best fits their intended image.

Human Proportion

As we saw when discussing **1.7.7**, carefully chosen proportions can make an art object seem pleasing to the eye. As it happens, the parts of a vase are given names based on the human body: the lip, hip, and foot. Just as the body of a vase can have more compact or lengthy proportions, the same is true of the human body.

In ancient Egypt, the palm of the hand was a unit of measurement (**1.7.8**). Six palm widths equaled a unit of measurement called a cubit. The height of an average man was estimated at 4 cubits or 24 palms: the proportion of the man's palm to the height of his body was therefore 24:1.

The ancient Greeks were especially interested in proportion. Greek mathematicians investigated, in the visual arts and in other art forms, such as music, the mathematical basis of beauty and of ideal proportions. The Greek sculptor Polykleitos wrote a treatise describing how to create a statue of a human being with ideal or perfect proportions. In the first century BCE the Roman writer Vitruvius wrote his book *On Architecture*, in which he claimed to set out the rules that Greeks and Romans applied to the design of architecture.

The Greeks sought an ideal of beauty in the principle of proportion. Figures made during the **Classical** period of Greek sculpture share similar proportions. To the Greeks, these proportions embodied the perfection of the gods. In contrast, fifteenth-century African sculptors preferred to show status and individuality through their use of proportion. Pictured in **1.7.9** is a sculpture of the Oni of Ife in **cast** brass. The Oni, or Monarch, of the Ife Dynasty of the Yoruba people is shown standing in full regalia (ceremonial clothing and adornments). The Oni is the most powerful and important figure in this culture, yet his proportions here are neither realistic nor idealized. The head—about a quarter of the entire figure—is large; the Yoruba believe that the head is the seat of

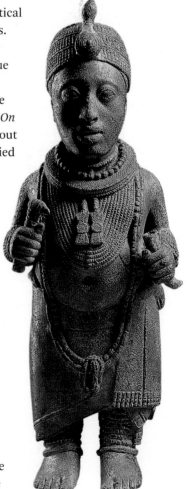

1.7.9 Nigerian Ife artist, *Figure of Oni*, early 14th–15th century. Brass with lead, height 18⅜″. National Museum, Ife, Nigeria

a divine power from whence a life source emanates to control personality and destiny. This figure, like Ife kings, represents a direct descendant of Oduduwa, the heroic leader whose children became the great leaders of the Yoruba. The facial features are idealized, suggesting that a personal heritage shapes one's destiny as a great leader. Many African sculptures exaggerate the head and face as a way to communicate status, destiny, and a connection to the spiritual. Both the Yoruba and the Greeks were concerned with creating a connection to the spiritual world, but African artists celebrated the importance of history (inheritance) and one's unique affiliation or office, while the Greeks sought an impersonal, ideal model.

Rule of Thirds

The English painter J. M. W. Turner's (1775–1851) sensitivity to proportion reflects his pursuit of perfection, an ideal of many traditional artists. Turner indicated the importance of his masterpiece by creating it on a significant scale: it measures 3 × 4 ft. (35.7 × 47.9 in.) (**1.7.10**). The scene depicts one of the last remaining ships from the naval Battle at Trafalgar, being towed to its final destination.

An analysis of the dimensions of *The Fighting Temeraire* provides some insight into how proportion plays a role in the creation of a design. Because this work measures exactly 3 × 4 ft., it can be visually subdivided, horizontally, into three 1⅓-ft. increments from left to right (1, 2, 3). When the work is

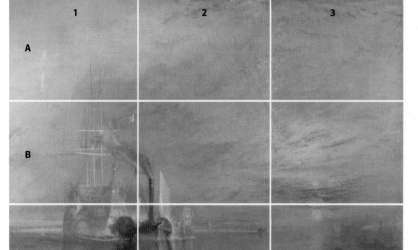

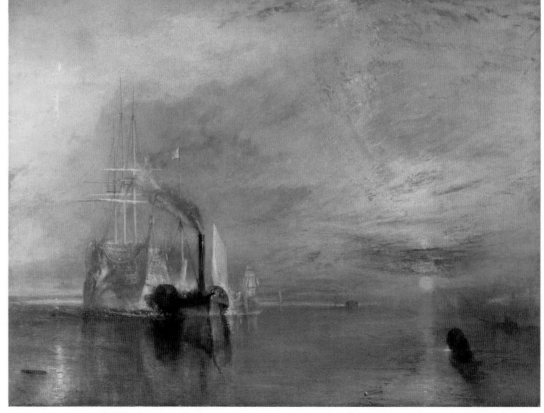

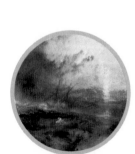

J. M. W. Turner's *Slave Ship* is another example of a work featuring a ship that uses the Rule of Thirds:
→ see **3.7.17**, p. 478

1.7.10 Joseph Mallord William Turner, *The Fighting Temeraire tugged to her last berth to be broken up, 1838*, 1839. Oil on canvas, 35¾ x 47⅞". National Gallery, London, England. Above: Overlaid diagram showing proportional structure

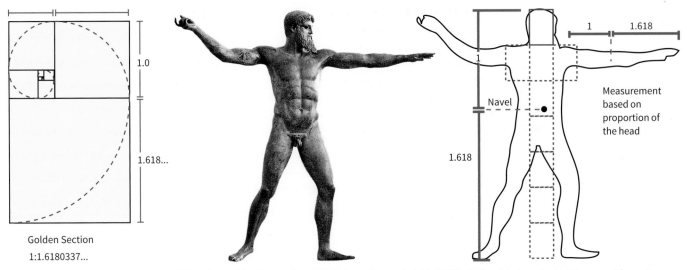

Golden Section
1:1.6180337...

Golden Section
1:1.6180337...

1.7.12a (above) ***Poseidon (or Zeus)***, *c.* 460–450 BCE. Bronze, height 6'10½". National Archaeological Museum, Athens, Greece
1.7.12b (above right) Diagram of proportional formulas used in the statue

1.7.11 Diagram of the Golden Section

subdivided in this way, we can perceive some recognizable divisions in the composition.

For example, the tall mast flying a white flag set at the point where the two ships overlap separates section 1 from 2, set one-third from the left edge. Another interesting correlation is made when we subdivide the work into thirds vertically (A, B, C). When we view the vertical divisions, it appears that the line of the horizon lies just beneath the separation between B and C, leaving emphasis on the evening sky.

These clear divisions seem intentional and suggest that Turner was working with a proportional system when he first designed *The Fighting Temeraire*. The format appears to reflect a system that some artists call the Rule of Thirds because it organizes the spatial area of a composition according to regular units of one- or two-thirds. The Rule of Thirds is used by artists, designers, photographers, and architects to provide pleasing proportional associations.

The Golden Section

The Greeks' interest in the use of mathematical formulas to determine perfect proportions has fascinated artists ever since. One of the best-known formulas is what has become known since the **Renaissance** as the **Golden Section** (**1.7.11**) (also referred to as the Golden Mean or Golden Ratio), a proportional ratio of

1:1.618, which occurs in many natural objects. It turns out that real human bodies do not have exactly these proportions, but when the ratio 1:1.618 is applied to making statues, it gives naturalistic results.

It is likely that Greek sculptors used much simpler methods than the Golden Section to calculate the proportions of their sculptures, but the resulting proportions are often very close to the Golden Section. The sculpture of Poseidon (some art historians say it is Zeus) is a famous example (**1.7.12a**). As a Greek god, he had to be portrayed with perfect proportions. The sculptor applied a conveniently simple ratio, using the head as a standard measurement. In **1.7.12a** and **1.7.12b** you can see that the body is three heads wide by seven heads high.

Proportional Ratios

Artists have learned other ways to apply proportional formulas to organize their compositions and ensure that their work is visually interesting. One such technique is known as Golden Rectangles, because it is based on a succession of rectangles, nesting inside each other, based on the 1:1.618 proportions of the Golden Section. The shorter side of the outer rectangle becomes the longer side of the smaller rectangle inside it, and so on. The result is an elegant spiral shape.

In 1858, the English photographer Henry Peach Robinson (1830–1901), one of the great innovators of the photographic arts, used this idea to compose a photograph titled

Renaissance: a period of cultural and artistic change in Europe from the fourteenth to the seventeenth century

Golden Section: a unique ratio of a line divided into two segments so that the sum of both segments (a + b) is to the longer segment (a) as the longer segment (a) is to the shorter segment (b). The result is 1:1.618

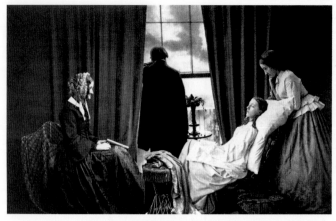

1.7.13a Henry Peach Robinson, *Fading Away*, 1858. Combination albumen print, 9½ × 15½". George Eastman House, Rochester, New York

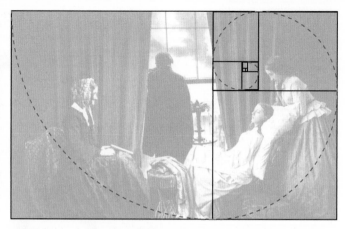

1.7.13b Proportional analysis of the photograph

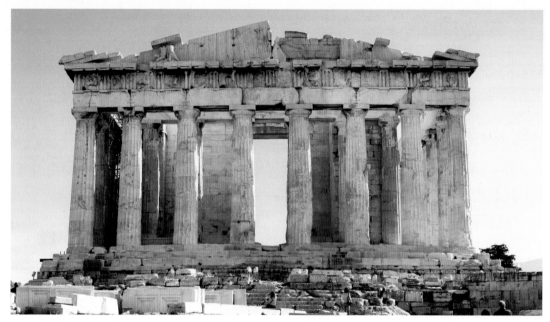

1.7.14a Iktinos and Kallikrates, **Parthenon**, 447–432 BCE, Athens, Greece

Fading Away (**1.7.13a** and **1.7.13b**). Robinson was well known for his work in fusing many different **negatives** to create a new image. This image shows his attention to the coordinated ratios in artistic composition. Notice how the right-hand drape divides the photograph into two Golden Rectangles and how the spiral draws our eye to the dying young woman.

The Greeks applied their proportional systems to architecture as well as to sculpture. By applying the idealized rules of proportion for the human body to the design of the Parthenon, a temple of the goddess Athena, the Greeks created a harmonious design. As it happens, the proportions correspond quite closely to the Golden Section (**1.7.14a**). The vertical and horizontal measurements work together to create proportional harmony (**1.7.14b**).

1.7.14b The use of the Golden Section in the design of the Parthenon

Negative: a reversed image, in which light areas are dark and dark areas are light (opposite of a positive)

Explore Further Scale and Proportion

Scale

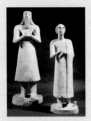

1.10.5 Votive Figures, Temple of Abu (Tell Asmar), Iraq, *c.* 2700 BCE → p. 163

1.3.10 Li Cheng (attrib.), *A Solitary Temple Amid Clearing Peaks*, *c.* 960–1127 → p. 72

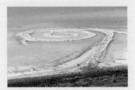

2.4.15 Robert Smithson, *Spiral Jetty*, 1969–70 → p. 238

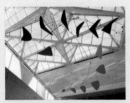

1.5.11 Alexander Calder, *Untitled*, 1976 → p. 110

Proportion

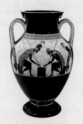

3.1.28 Exekias, amphora with Achilles and Ajax playing dice, *c.* 530 BCE → p. 366

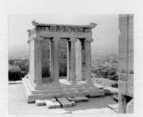

2.5.8 Kallikrates, Temple of Athena Nike, Athens, Greece, *c.* 421–415 BCE → p. 248

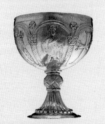

2.6.10 Chalice with Apostles venerating the cross, Syria, *c.* 600 → p. 275

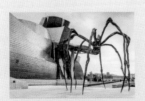

1.2.18 Louise Bourgeois, *Maman*, 1999 (cast 2001) → p. 61

Human Proportion

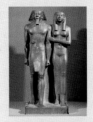

4.8.3b *Menkaure and His Wife, Queen Khamerernebty*, Egypt, *c.* 2520 BCE → p. 632

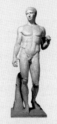

3.1.20 Polykleitos, *Doryphoros* (Roman version), 120–50 BCE → p. 361

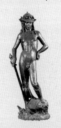

3.6.22 Donatello, *David*, *c.* 1430 → p. 460

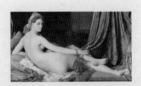

1.10.8 Jean-Auguste-Dominique Ingres, *Grande Odalisque*, 1814 → p. 167

Hierarchical Scale

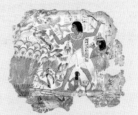

3.1.18 Fowling scene from tomb of Nebamun, Egypt, *c.* 1350 BCE, → p. 359

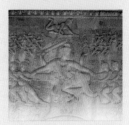

3.3.23 *Vishnu Churning the Ocean of Milk*, Angkor Wat → p. 407

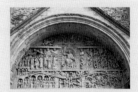

3.2.22 Tympanum of the west portal of Sainte-Foy, Conques, *c.* 1130–46 → p. 386

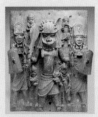

4.6.8 Benin plaque with warrior and attendants, 16th–17th century → p. 609

Your turn

How do these works relate to scale and proportion?

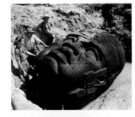

3.4.9 Colossal Olmec head, *c.* 800–400 BCE → p. 416

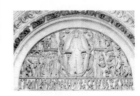

4.2.11 Gislebertus, *The Last Judgment*, *c.* 1120–35 → p. 561

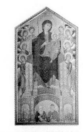

3.2.26 Cimabue, *Virgin and Child Enthroned*, *c.* 1280 → p. 388

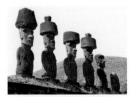

3.5.19 *Moai* ancestor figures, Rapa Nui, before 15th century → p. 439

1.8
Focal Point and Emphasis

When we emphasize something, we draw attention to it. This is a valuable part of communication that allows us to set some things apart. In art, **emphasis** is the **principle** by which an artist draws attention to particular content. An entire work, a broad area within a work of art, multiple areas, and even specific points can be emphasized. The term **focal point** can be used to describe a specific place of visual

emphasis in a work of art or design, which, similarly to emphasis, is a way of highlighting certain locations in a work.

An artist can emphasize focal points through the use of **line**, **implied line**, **value**, **color**—in fact, any of the **elements of art** can help to focus our interest on specific areas. In a way that is similar to the effect of the bull's-eye on a target, focal points concentrate our attention. Even though our field of vision is fairly wide, at any given moment we can focus our vision only on a small area. The physiology of vision underlies the principle of focal point.

The opposite of emphasis is **subordination**: subordination draws our attention away from certain areas of a work. Artists choose carefully—in both two- and three-dimensional works—which areas to emphasize or subordinate in order to heighten the impact of their artworks. Focal point and emphasis usually accentuate concepts, themes, or ideas the artist wants to express: they signal what the artwork is about.

Focal Point

In any **composition**, a focal point is the place in an area of emphasis to which the artist draws our eye. They can do so by using line, implied line, or **contrast**. These techniques focus our gaze on that point in the work. We can see an intensely dramatic use of focal point in Artemisia Gentileschi's (1593–*c.* 1656) ferocious painting, *Judith Decapitating Holofernes* (**1.8.1**). The painting depicts the story from the Old Testament of the Israelite heroine Judith killing the Assyrian general Holofernes, who had been sent by his king to punish the Israelites for not supporting his reign. Holofernes had conquered Judith's city and tried to seduce

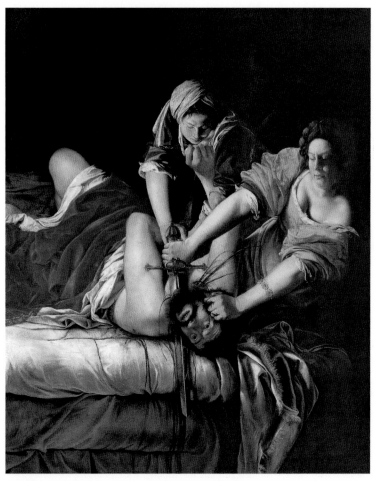

1.8.1 Artemisia Gentileschi, *Judith Decapitating Holofernes*, *c.* 1620. Oil on canvas, 6′6⅜″ × 5′3¾″. Uffizi Gallery, Florence, Italy

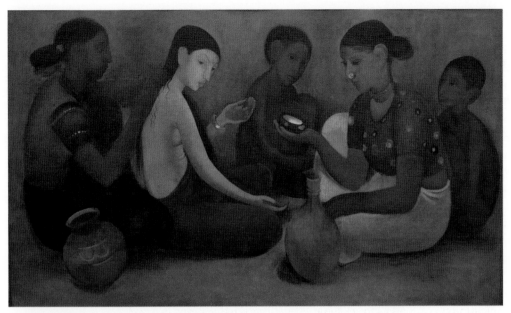

1.8.2 Amrita Sher-Gil, *Bride's Toilet*, 1937. Oil on canvas, 57½ × 35″. National Gallery of Modern Art, New Delhi, India

her; in consequence, she murdered him as he lay sleeping after becoming intoxicated at a banquet in his tent. Through Gentileschi's use of directional line and contrasting values, we are drawn irresistibly to the point where the climax of the story is unfolding. Bright light emphasizes Judith's arms and those of her maidservant (visually connected to the sword itself) as they stretch toward the dark values of their victim's head. The light values of the five bare arms create strong directional lines that lead to the focal point, where blood spurts from the violent attack on Holofernes' neck. This double emphasis (contrast of values and directional line) fixes our stare upon the fatal blow, even as it obscures it in darkness.

Portraiture often uses focal point to keep the attention of the viewer on a particular important person. The modern Indian artist Amrita Sher-Gil (1913–41) uses contrast to place the viewer's gaze on the principal figure in the painting *Bride's Toilet* (**1.8.2**). Sher-Gil, whose work reflected everyday life in early twentieth-century India, uses lighter values on the bride-to-be to draw attention to her. The bride's strangely melancholy expression and the somber mood of the scene are accentuated by the darkened area around the main figure.

Contemporary designers also rely on the power of focal point to bring home a message. The American graphic designer Milton Glaser (b. 1929) introduced a simple and powerful message when he used two hearts and a skull to represent the letter 'W' on this poster for the World Health Organization (**1.8.3**). Glaser was tasked with creating a poster for the WHO's Special Programme on AIDS in 1987 as part of a worldwide effort to prevent transmission. The bright blue skull against the red of the hearts results in a dramatic focal point, while highlighting the cultural unease surrounding the virus at the time. Glaser also designed New York State's official I ♥ NY logo: by replacing the word 'love' with a heart icon, he ushered in

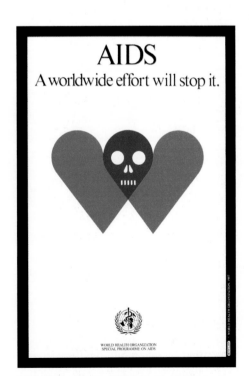

1.8.3 Milton Glaser, *AIDS: A Worldwide Effort Will Stop It,* 1987. Poster commissioned by the World Health Organization.

Emphasis: the principle of drawing attention to particular content in a work

Principles of art: the principles, or grammar of art—contrast, unity, variety, balance, scale, proportion, focal point, emphasis, pattern, and rhythm—describe the ways the elements of art are arranged in an artwork

Focal point: the center of interest or activity in a work of art, often drawing the viewer's attention to the most important element

Line: a mark, or implied mark, between two endpoints

Implied line: a line not actually drawn but suggested by the positions of elements in the work, for example, an aligned series of dots

Value: the lightness or darkness of a plane or area

Color: the optical effect caused when reflected white light of the spectrum is divided into separate wavelengths

Elements of art: the basic vocabulary of art—line, shape, form, volume, mass, texture, value (lightness/darkness), space, color, and motion and time

Subordination: the opposite of emphasis; it draws our attention away from particular areas of a work

Composition: the overall design or organization of a work

Contrast: a drastic difference between such elements as color or value (lightness/darkness) when they are presented together

a new wave of **pictographic** imagery that still exists in the form of emojis.

In his painting *The Fall of Icarus*, Marc Chagall (1887–1985) draws attention to, and illustrates, a critical moment from a haunting story from Greek mythology (**1.8.4**). Icarus and his father Daedalus had been imprisoned on the island of Crete by its ruler, Minos. In order to escape, Daedalus fashioned two sets of wings from feathers and wax. As father and son flew away from their prison, Icarus became overly exuberant. Although his father had warned him not to, Icarus, recklessly enjoying his new wings, flew too high and close to the sun. The wax in his wings melted, and he fell to his death in the sea below.

In Chagall's version, Icarus is the focal point, distinctly set apart from the light sky not only by his position at the top and center of the work, but also by the use of bold red, yellow, and blue **primary colors** to depict the flailing figure. Using the contrast between the brightly colored wings and the dull, pale-gray sky isolates and draws attention directly to the poor boy, whose futile fluttering is captured in Chagall's energetic brushstrokes. Even though there are many figures in this work, the main emphasis is clearly on the tumbling one in the sky. The Icarus story has proved a compelling one for artists and writers. Four centuries before Chagall created his painting, Pieter Bruegel the Elder (*c.* 1525/30–1569) took a very different approach to depicting Icarus's plunge into the sea (see p. 144).

Emphasis

Sometimes an artist is interested in emphasizing an entire work in its wholeness. When they want to do this, the artist will intentionally create a composition that does not have a dominant area of emphasis. For example, *Untitled (Ocean)* by Latvian-born American artist Vija Celmins (b. 1938) has an overall field of undulating value changes with no singular point to which the eye is drawn (**1.8.5**). Celmins's parents brought her to the United States when she was ten years old, eventually settling in Indianapolis, Indiana. In the work *Untitled (Ocean),* Celmins creates a photorealistic drawing of the ocean surface, calling attention to the vast and repetitive character of the sea. The resulting effect allows us to immerse ourselves in the work, as if it were a place for reflective meditation.

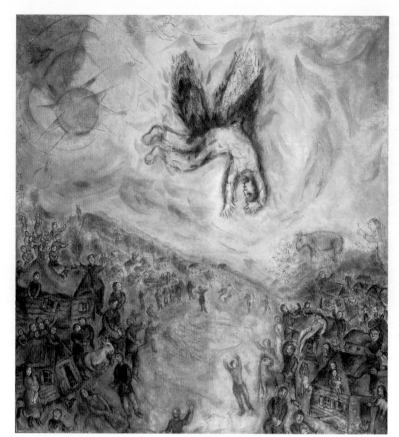

1.8.4 Marc Chagall, ***The Fall of Icarus***, 1975. Oil on canvas, 6'11⅞" × 6'6". Musée National d'Art Moderne, Centre Georges Pompidou, Paris, France

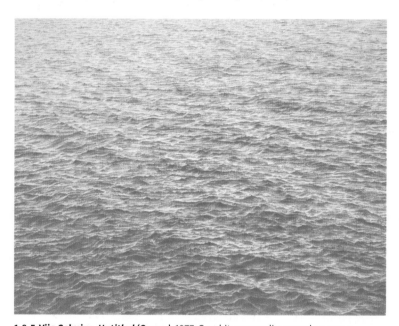

1.8.5 Vija Celmins, ***Untitled (Ocean)***, 1977. Graphite on acrylic ground on paper, 10 × 12⅞". San Francisco Museum of Modern Art, California

Emphasis can also be used to draw attention to a large portion of a work. Sometimes an artist wants the emphasis to encompass a significant area, but not quite the entire surface. The African American sculptor Martin Puryear (b. 1941) makes connections between a nineteenth-century trading company and

Pictographic: conveys meaning through resemblance to physical shape

Primary colors: three basic colors from which all others are derived

African masks in his work *C.F.A.O.* (**1.8.6**). The CFAO (Compagnie Française de L'Afrique Occidentale) was a company that connected Europe to ports in Sierra Leone in Africa, where Puryear also worked as a member of the Peace Corps. Using pine strips and a discarded wheelbarrow as a backdrop, Puryear directs our attention to the elongated white, blank, mask-like shape in the center. The wheelbarrow and the pine structure, with their rigid vertical and horizontal lines, emphasize the organic mask shape through contrast with its white color and smooth surface. Puryear created the mask to mimic the designs of the Fang tribe of Gabon, West Africa, and the piece is intended to recall French colonialism in the region by associating it with the CFAO. It invites viewers to lift the wheelbarrow and peer through the two eye-holes in the mask, encouraging them to see things from the point of view of, or assume the role of, the colonized instead of the colonist.

Emphasis can occur broadly over a large section when there are multiple elements within a work but where no one element dominates. For example, in a print from the series *The Life of John Brown* by the African American artist Jacob Lawrence (1917–2000), each of the twelve figures shown (one facing away from the viewer) attracts enough attention so that none stands out as most significant (**1.8.7**). The John Brown to whom Lawrence refers in the title is the Civil War-era abolitionist who believed that enslavement could be eradicated only through armed insurrection. Brown is not depicted in the image, but the solemn poses of the figures imply homage to this anti-enslavement militant who was hanged for leading a violent revolt against the US government at Harpers Ferry, West Virginia. In the print, Lawrence's visual balancing of the figures is complemented by his creation

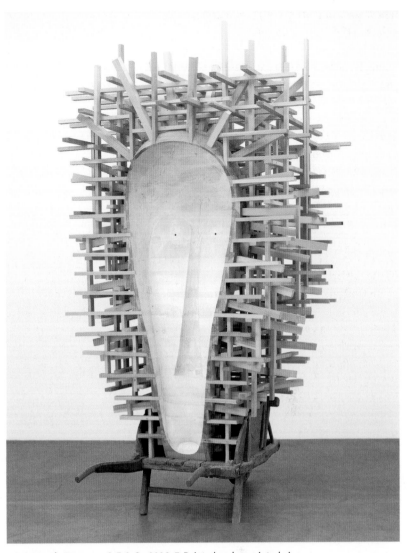

1.8.6 Martin Puryear, *C.F.A.O.*, 2006–7. Painted and unpainted pine and found wheelbarrow, 8'4¾" × 6'5½" × 5'1". MoMA, New York

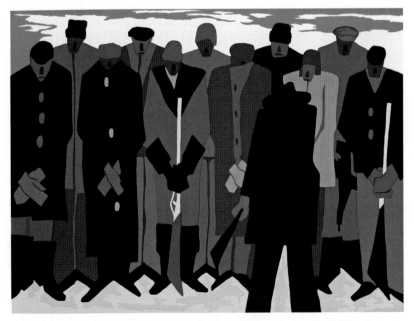

1.8.7 Jacob Lawrence, "**John Brown Remained a Full Winter in Canada, Drilling Negroes for His Coming Raid on Harpers Ferry (no. 17)**," from *The Life of John Brown* (22 prints), 1977. Gouache and tempera on paper, 20 × 14"

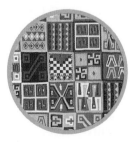

We can also see overall emphasis in the design of this Inca tunic:
→ see **3.4.6**, p. 414

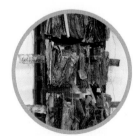

Another work that places emphasis on a large area of the work is Anselm Kiefer's *Breaking of the Vessels*:
→ see **4.6.11**, p. 611

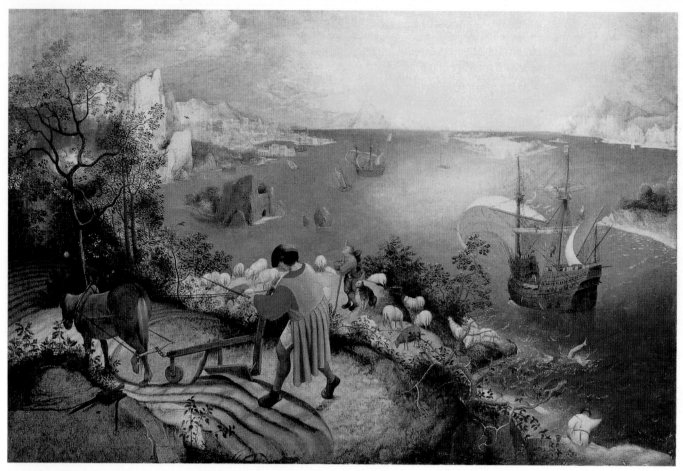

1.8.8 Pieter Bruegel the Elder, *Landscape with the Fall of Icarus*, *c.* 1555–58. Oil on canvas, mounted on wood, 29 × 44⅛". Musées Royaux des Beaux-Arts de Belgique, Brussels, Belgium

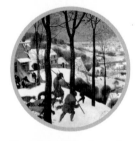

The painter Pieter Bruegel expertly used emphasis and focal point in his many paintings, like *Hunters in the Snow*: → see **1.9.7**, p. 152

of separate areas of emphasis. For example, the figure on the right in the yellow coat is immediately emphasized in contrast to the dark figure in the **foreground**, as is the white rifle held by the figure in brown on the left side of the work. These areas are also evenly balanced by size and contrasting values, unifying all of the parts into a larger whole with no strong single focal point. This methodical counter-balancing is critical to the composition because it implies equality amongst the men, thus subtly supporting the ideals for which John Brown fought and died.

Subordination

Subordination is a technique used to draw the viewer's attention away from a particular part of a composition. We are so attuned to looking for emphasized areas and focal points that artists can cleverly use this technique to redirect our attention from one area of an artwork to another. Subordination does not emphasize, but deliberately reduces the impact of certain details. In direct contrast to Marc Chagall, whose painting places the attention of

the viewer on Icarus as he fell to Earth (**1.8.4**, p. 142), in the work *Landscape with the Fall of Icarus,* Flemish artist Pieter Bruegel the Elder diverts our attention so that we scarcely notice Icarus plunging to his doom (**1.8.8**).

In Bruegel's version of this story, our attention is drawn first to the figure in the foreground, in his eye-catching scarlet shirt, plowing his field, unaware of the tragedy. As the painting's title suggests, several other areas of emphasis—the tree on the left, the sunset, the fanciful ships—also capture our interest. We hardly notice poor Icarus, whose legs are disappearing into the sea just in front of the large ship on the right, his feet barely distinguishable from the whitecaps and the tiny seabirds circling near the vessel. Because Bruegel has gone to such lengths to draw attention away from the plight of his subject, art historians think he is illustrating the Flemish proverb, "No plough stands still because a man dies." Or, as we might say, "Life goes on." Either way, it is a brilliant example of using emphasis and subordination to direct and control the way in which the viewer perceives the painting.

Foreground: the part of a work depicted as nearest to the viewer

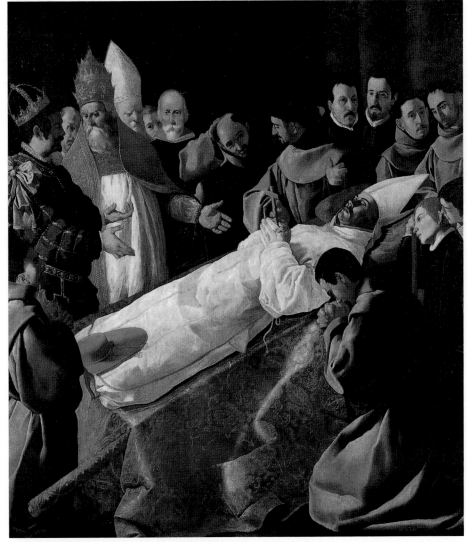

1.8.9 Francisco de Zurbarán, *The Funeral of St. Bonaventure*, 1629.
Oil on canvas, 8′2″ × 7′4″. Musée du Louvre, Paris, France

Focal Point and Emphasis in Action

Artists can use direction, dramatic contrasts, and placement relationships to organize the elements in a work and draw our attention to areas of emphasis and to focal points.

Contrast

Artists look to create effects of contrast by positioning elements next to one another that are very different, for example areas of different value, color, or size. Value is an effective and frequently used means of creating emphasis and focal point. It also has the advantage that it can be used in subtle ways. In *The Funeral of St. Bonaventure*, a painting by Spanish artist Francisco de Zurbarán (1598–1664), most of the lightest values are reserved for the clothing adorning the dead body of the thirteenth-century theologian St. Bonaventure (**1.8.9**). They create a central focal point that stands out in contrast to the surrounding dark values. We are drawn to the whiteness (symbolic of Bonaventure's chaste and spotless reputation) before we look at the surrounding characters. Enough light value is distributed to the other figures to allow our eyes to be drawn away from Bonaventure's body, making the composition more interesting.

Line

Line is an effective way to focus our attention in an artwork. In Mughal India (the period from 1526 until the mid-nineteenth century), a garden was considered a work of art, one that symbolized the promise of paradise. Zahir ud-Din Muhammad bin Omar Sheikh, nicknamed Babur, founded the Mughal empire in India when he conquered most of Central Asia and northern India. In **1.8.10** (p. 146), the gardener/artist Babur is pointing to a feature

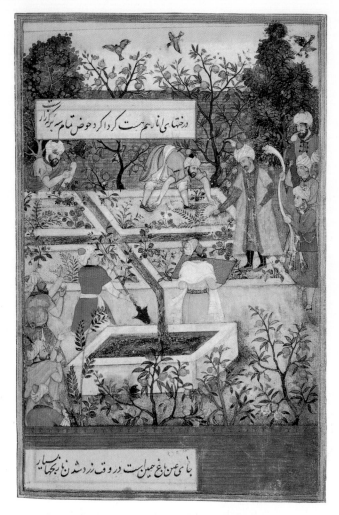

1.8.10 *The Emperor Babur Overseeing His Gardeners*, India, Mughal period, *c.* 1590. Tempera and gouache on paper, 8¾ × 5⅝″. Victoria and Albert Museum, London, England

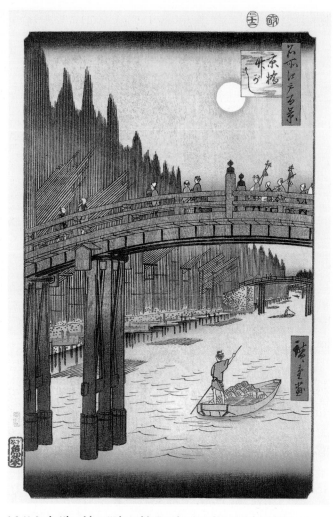

1.8.11 Ando Hiroshige, "Riverside Bamboo Market, Kyo-bashi," from *One Hundred Famous Views of Edo*, 1857. Woodblock print, 15 × 10⅜″. James A. Michener Collection, Honolulu Academy of Arts, Hawaii

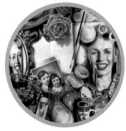

Audrey Flack use placement of elements to support multiple focal points:
→ see **4.3.9**, p. 573

Rhythm: the regular or ordered repetition of elements in the work

Outline: the outermost line or implied line of an object or figure, by which it is defined or bounded

Woodcut: a relief print made from a design cut into a block of wood

that channels water in four directions. The life-giving properties of water and the four cardinal directions were important symbols of life and eternity. Because the garden was based on the perfect geometry of a square, it could be expanded an infinite number of times without disturbing the original plantings. In this image of the garden, water is the focal point, both conceptually and visually.

We tend to notice diagonal lines because they appear to be more visually active than either horizontal or vertical lines. The strong diagonal of the channel draws our attention to the water as it runs toward us. The central cross-shaped confluence of the waters in the middle of the garden becomes the focal point of the composition.

Placement

The placement of elements within a composition controls **rhythm** and creates multiple focal points. In the print "Riverside Bamboo Market, Kyo-bashi," the Japanese artist Ando Hiroshige (1797–1858) has oriented three shapes, all visually independent of each other (**1.8.11**). The positions of the moon, the bridge, and the figure in a boat form three separate focal points. Each shape commands our attention and draws more of our focus to the right side of the work. Even though the bridge is the largest shape, the light value and hard geometry of the moon divert our gaze, and the moon becomes a secondary focal point. We look at the figure under the bridge because of its careful placement under the moon, and because it has a definite **outline** that contrasts strongly with the flat color of the water. The varying distances between the three focal points also create rhythm, which adds visual interest. Hiroshige, a master of **woodcut** printing, uses placement to emphasize specific points in the work and enliven the composition.

Explore Further Focal Point and Emphasis

Focal Point	Emphasis	Subordination

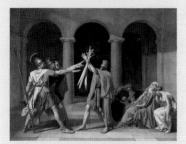

3.7.10 Jacques-Louis David, *The Oath of the Horatii*, 1784 → p. 473

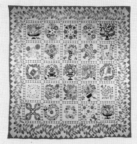

1.6.12 Alice A. Ryder, *Baltimore Album Quilt*, c. 1847 → p. 123

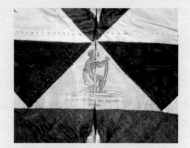

1.9.5b Deborah Coates, detail of quilt, Pennsylvania, c. 1840–50 → p. 150

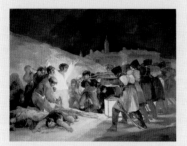

4.6.9 Francisco Goya, *The Third of May, 1808*, 1814 → p. 610

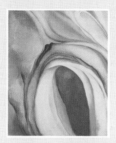

1.1.25 Georgia O'Keeffe, *Music–Pink and Blue II*, 1919 → p. 46

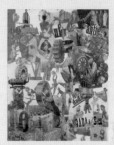

3.9.11 Hannah Höch, *Cut with the Kitchen Knife…*, 1919–20 → p. 507

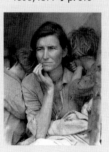

4.7.10 Dorothea Lange, *Migrant Mother*, 1936 → p. 626

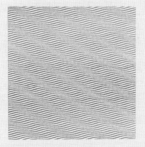

1.5.4 Bridget Riley, *Cataract 3*, 1967, → p. 106

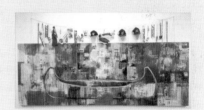

1.9.15 Jaune Quick-to-See Smith, *Trade…*, 1992 → p. 156

Your turn

How do these artworks make use of focal point and emphasis?

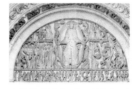

4.2.11 Gislebertus, *The Last Judgment*, c. 1120–35 → p. 561

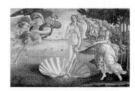

4.8.5 Sandro Botticelli, *The Birth of Venus*, c. 1482–86 → p. 634

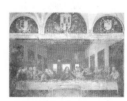

3.6.18 Leonardo da Vinci, *The Last Supper*, c. 1497 → p. 457

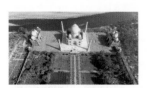

1.6.15a Ustad Ahmad Lahauri et al., Taj Mahal, Agra, India, 1632–43 → p. 126

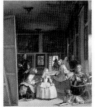

1.10.12a Diego de Silva y Velázquez, *Las Meninas*, c. 1656 → p. 171

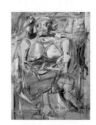

3.7.15 Eugène Delacroix, *Liberty Leading the People*, 1830 → p. 477

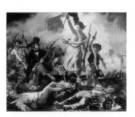

4.8.2 Willem de Kooning, *Woman I*, 1950–52 → p. 631

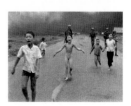

4.6.3 Nick Ut, *Vietnamese Girl Kim Phuc Running after Napalm Attack*, 1972 → p. 605

1.9
Pattern and Rhythm

Pattern: an arrangement of predictably repeated elements

Rhythm: the regular or ordered repetition of elements in the work

Space: the distance between identifiable points or planes

Elements of art: the basic vocabulary of art—line, shape, form, volume, mass, texture, value (lightness/darkness), space, color, and motion and time

Unity: the appearance of oneness or harmony in a work of art: all of the elements appearing to be part of a cohesive whole

Composition: the overall design or organization of a work

Variety: the diversity of different ideas, media, and elements in a work

Shape: a two-dimensional area, the boundaries of which are defined by lines or suggested by changes in color or value

Value: the lightness or darkness of a plane or area

Color: the optical effect caused when reflected white light of the spectrum is divided into separate wavelengths

Background: the part of a work depicted furthest from the viewer's space, often behind the main subject matter

Each day the sun rises and sets; we believe it will do so again tomorrow. **Patterns** and **rhythms** in nature help us make sense of the world. They express the order and predictability of our lives. Artists use pattern and rhythm to bring order to **space** and to create a dynamic experience of time.

When events recur, this creates a pattern. But other patterns are more regular, more predictable. In art, we can see patterns as the recurrence of an art **element**. In a work of art, the repetition of such patterns provides a sense of **unity**.

Rhythm arises through the repetition of pattern. It adds cohesiveness in artistic **composition** because it links elements together. Rhythm affects our vision as we study a work of art. The rhythm of a series of linked elements guides the movement of our eyes across and through a design. The artist can also use rhythm to add **variety**.

Pattern

The use of repetition in a work of art usually results in the creation of a pattern. These patterns are sometimes based on occurrences in nature, such as the regular repetition of fish scales, or the pattern created by the cracks that open as mud dries in the desert. Other patterns may be derived from the repeated **shapes** of mass-produced human-made objects, such as stacked tin cans or the warp and weft of woven cloth. Artists often create unity in works of art by repeatedly using a similar shape, **value**, or **color**, for example.

An artist can use repetition of a pattern to impose order on a work. But simple repetition can become more complex and make a work even more interesting when the pattern changes. Sometimes artists use alternating patterns to make a work more lively. The area covered by pattern is called the field; changes in the field can invigorate visual forms. The pattern in **1.9.1** shows a series of star shapes set on alternating black and white **backgrounds** on a rectangular field. The drastic difference in value combined with the active shape causes a visual vibration.

A variety of different colors and patterns enlivens work by the French painter Suzanne Valadon (1865–1938). In *The Blue Room*, she includes three **contrasting** patterns (**1.9.2**). In the blue bed covering (shown in the lower portion of the painting) Valadon has used an **organic** pattern of leaves and stems. The green-and-white striped pattern in the woman's pajama bottoms dominates, in direct contrast to the blue bed covering. Above the figure is a mottled pattern on the wall, which again contrasts with the other two. The differences between these patterns energize the work.

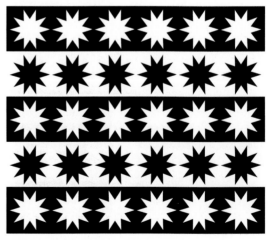

1.9.1 Vertical alternating pattern

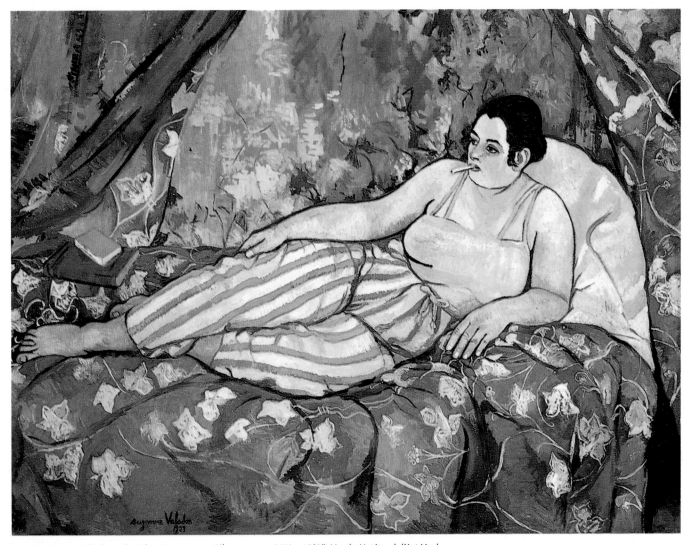

1.9.2 Suzanne Valadon, *The Blue Room*, 1923. Oil on canvas, 35½ × 45⅝". Musée National d'Art Moderne, Centre Georges Pompidou, Paris, France

Motif

A design repeated as a unit in a pattern is called a motif. Motifs can represent ideas, images, and themes that can be brought together through the use of pattern. An artist can create a strong unified design by repeating a motif.

A single motif can be interlaced with others to create complex designs. Many Islamic works use complex interlaced motifs, as this work created in seventeenth-century India demonstrates. The huqqa base (a huqqa is a water pipe used for smoking) in **1.9.3** may at first glance appear to use little repetition. Nevertheless, as we study the overall design we discover that elements, such as the flowers and leaves of the plants, recur at intervals.

Motif is a common occurrence in traditional quilting. By unifying a series of simple patterns into a repeatable motif, a quilter could connect a series of blocks into a cohesive design. One such traditional pattern, called "Birds in the

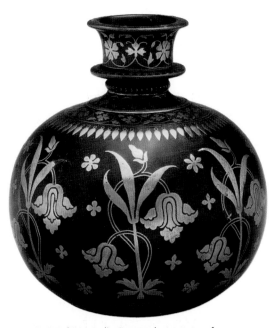

1.9.3 Huqqa base, India, Deccan, last quarter of 17th century. Bidri ware (zinc alloy inlaid with brass), 6⅞ × 6½". Metropolitan Museum of Art, New York

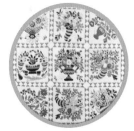

The artist has used pattern and motif to structure the floral forms in this nineteenth-century quilt from Baltimore:
→ see **1.6.12**, p. 123

Contrast: a drastic difference between such elements as color or value (lightness/darkness) when they are presented together

Organic: having irregular forms and shapes, as though derived from living organisms

Abstract: art imagery that departs from recognizable images of the natural world

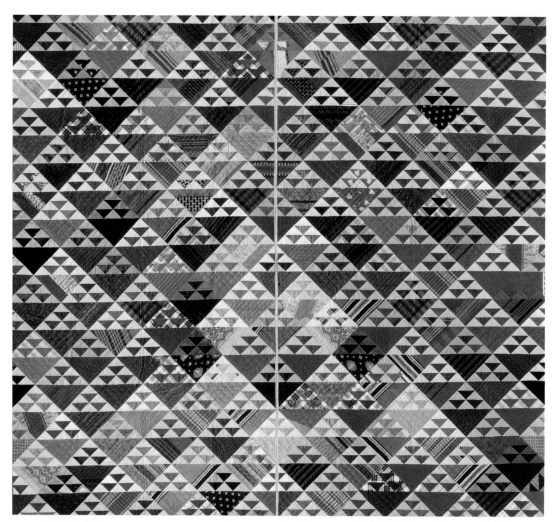

1.9.5a Deborah Coates, quilt, *c.* 1840–50. Pieced silk with stamp work, 96½ × 89″. Heritage Center Museum: Lancaster Quilt and Textile Museum, Lancaster, Pennsylvania

1.9.4 Diagram of block quilt pattern known as "Birds in the Air"

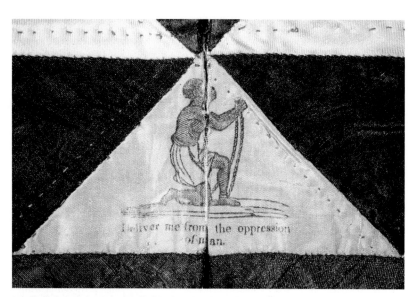

1.9.5b Deborah Coates, detail showing stamp work on quilt

Air" (**1.9.4**), was used as the integral component for a quilt design by the early American quilter Deborah Coates (1801–1888). Coates, the wife of the famed abolitionist (anti-enslavement campaigner) Linley Coates, created abolitionist quilts to raise awareness and funding to free enslaved people. Such quilts as **1.9.5a** were sold at popular quilting fairs in northern cities and were often inscribed with messages similar to the one in the detail, "Deliver me from the oppression of man," in **1.9.5b**. The choice of "Birds in the Air" was probably because the design, which implies the freedom of birds to fly away at will, was especially appropriate to the anti-enslavement cause.

The American artist Chuck Close (1940–2021) uses motif to unify his paintings. Repeated organic concentric rings, set into a diamond shape, are the basic building blocks for his large compositions. These motifs, which appear as **abstract** patterns when viewed closely, visually solidify into realistic portraits of the model. In his *Self-Portrait*, there is a distinct difference between a close-up view of the painting and the overall effect when we stand back from this enormous canvas (**1.9.6a**–**1.9.6c**). The motif

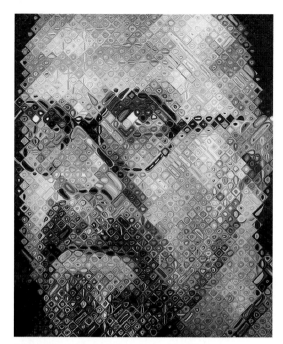

1.9.6a Chuck Close, *Self-Portrait*, 1997. Oil on canvas, 8'6" × 7'. MoMA, New York

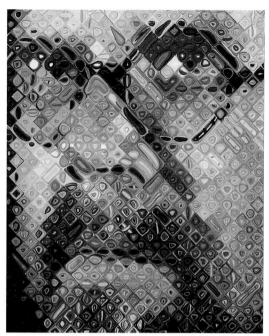

1.9.6b Chuck Close, *Self-Portrait*, detail

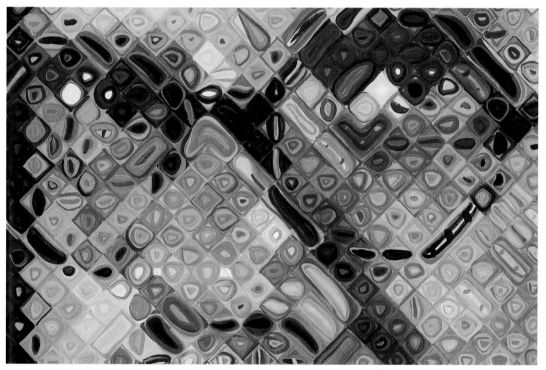

1.9.6c Chuck Close, *Self-Portrait*, detail

unifies the work and allows Close the freedom to control the color, **texture**, and value. In this case, the motif that Close uses is the result of a technical process. When applied to the larger image, however, it almost disappears because each unit that makes up the whole is so tiny in size. A grid that subdivides the entire image organizes the placement of each cell. In this way, Close uses an intricate system of patterns within patterns to achieve a dramatic effect.

Rhythm

Rhythm is something you either have or don't have, but when you have it, you have it all over.

(Elvis Presley)

Rock-and-roll icon Elvis Presley might as well have been speaking about visual art when he was talking about musical rhythm. Rhythm is something that visual art has "all over."

Texture: the surface quality of a work, for example fine/coarse, detailed/lacking in detail

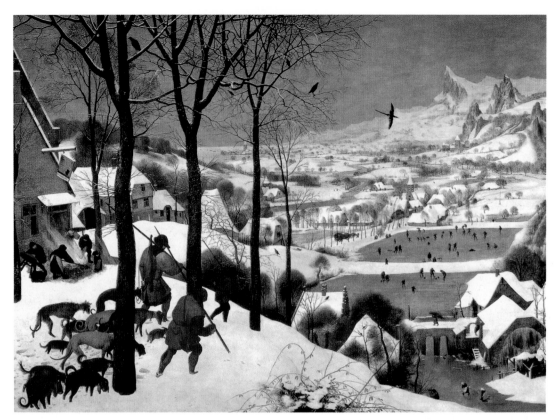

1.9.7 Pieter Bruegel the Elder, *Hunters in the Snow*, 1565. Oil on panel, 46 × 63¾".
Kunsthistorisches Museum, Vienna, Austria

Rhythm gives structure to the experience of looking, just as it guides our eyes from one point to another in a work of art. There is rhythm when there are at least two points of reference in an artwork. For example, the horizontal distance from one side of a canvas to the other is one rhythm, and the vertical distance from top to bottom is another. So, even the simplest works have an implicit rhythm. But most works of art involve shapes, colors, values, **lines**, and other elements too; the intervals between them provide points of reference for more complex rhythms.

In Flemish painter Pieter Bruegel's work, we see not only large rhythmic progressions that take our eye all around the canvas, but also refined micro-rhythms in the repetition of such details as the trees, houses, birds, and colors (**1.9.7**). Together, these repetitive elements create a variety of rhythms "all over."

In *Hunters in the Snow*, the party of hunters on the left side first draws our attention into the work. Their dark shapes contrast with the light value of the snow. The group is trudging over the crest of a hill that leads to the right; our attention follows them in the same direction, creating the first part of a rhythmic progression. Our gaze now traverses from the left **foreground** to the **middle ground** on the right, where figures appear to be skating on a large frozen pond. Thereafter, the color of the sky, which is reflected in the skaters' pond, draws our attention deeper into the space, to the horizon. We then look at the background of the work, where the recession of the ridgeline pulls the eye to the left and into the far distance. As a result of following this rhythmic progression, our eye has circled round and now returns to re-examine the original **focal point**. We then naturally inspect details, such as the group of figures at the far left making a fire outside a building. As our eye repeats this cycle, we also notice subsidiary rhythms, such as the receding line of trees. Bruegel masterfully orchestrates the winter activities of townspeople in sixteenth-century Flanders (a region now divided between Belgium, The Netherlands, and part of northern France) in a pulsating composition that is both powerful and subtle at the same time.

Rhythm is evident in the work of **installation** artists, who design areas for a set period and immerse their audience in the experience. The Pakistani-born artist Anila Quayyum Agha (b. 1965) creates three-dimensional objects with pattern, which are lit from inside and project rhythmic shadows on the walls of the surrounding gallery. In her work *This Is NOT a Refuge! 2* (**1.9.8**) the artist has used a geometric house-like structure and superimposed plant-like cutout patterns on each side. When lit from inside, in a darkened gallery, the work repeats the organic patterns so that it surrounds a viewer. Each face of the structure provides a pattern or motif that, when projected together, become rhythms. Each installation of this work is accompanied by an ambient soundscape that includes the voices of immigrants and refugees. The house-shaped lantern is an inviting image of shelter, but can never provide refuge as it is just a transient illusion. Her intent is to portray, in a compassionate way, a sense of the migrant experience that is both alienating and transient at the same time.

Simple Repetitive Rhythm

Artists create repetition by using the same shape, color, size, value, line, or texture over and over again. A repeating pulse of similar elements sets up a visual rhythm that a viewer can anticipate. Such regularity communicates reassurance (**1.9.9**), just as other types of rhythm may imply excitement or energy.

The design of buildings is often intended to reassure us about the stability and durability of the structure. Stability was so important to the ancient Romans that when the builders finally removed the temporary support structures for archways, the architects who had designed them were made to stand underneath. If the **arch** failed, the architect would be crushed. In common with Roman architects, we also want reassurance that our structures will endure. For this reason, architectural designs often incorporate simple repetition.

The main hall of the Great Mosque of Córdoba in Spain is full of seemingly endless rows of identical columns and arches made from alternating red and white **voussoirs** (stone wedges that make up the arch) (**1.9.10**). Each of these repeating elements—**columns**, arches, and voussoirs—creates its own simple rhythm. These repetitions also enhance the function of the space and become a part of the activity of worship, like prayer beads, reciting the Shahada (profession of faith), or the five-times-a-day call to prayer. Our trust in the permanence of architecture is combined with the timelessness of prayer in the repetitions of the Great Mosque of Córdoba.

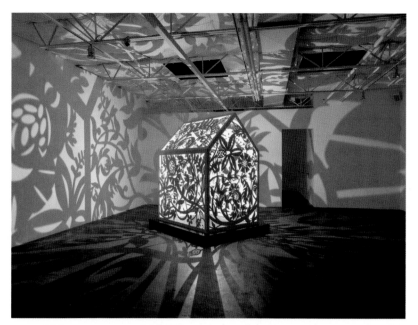

1.9.8 Anila Quayyum Agha, *This Is NOT a Refuge! 2*, 2019. Laser-cut, resin-coated aluminium, light bulb, 93 × 58 × 72″. Installation as part of solo show "Itinerant Shadows" at Talley Dunn Gallery, Dallas, Texas

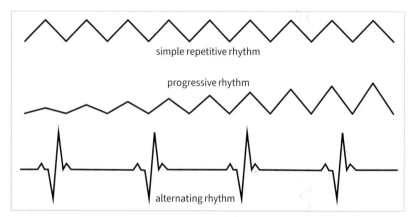

simple repetitive rhythm

progressive rhythm

alternating rhythm

1.9.9 Three types of rhythm

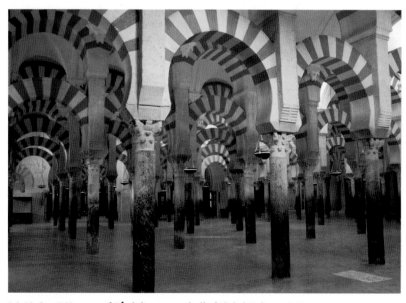

1.9.10 Great Mosque of Córdoba, prayer hall of Abd al-Rahman I, 784–86. Córdoba, Spain

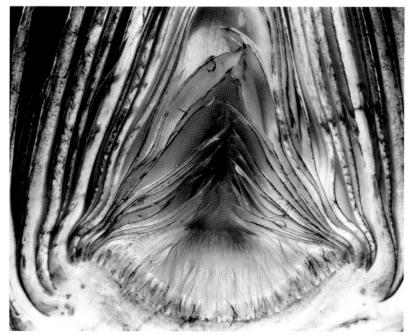

1.9.11 Edward Weston, *Artichoke Halved*, 1930. Silver gelatin print, 7⅜ × 9⅜″. Collection Center for Creative Photography, University of Arizona, Tucson

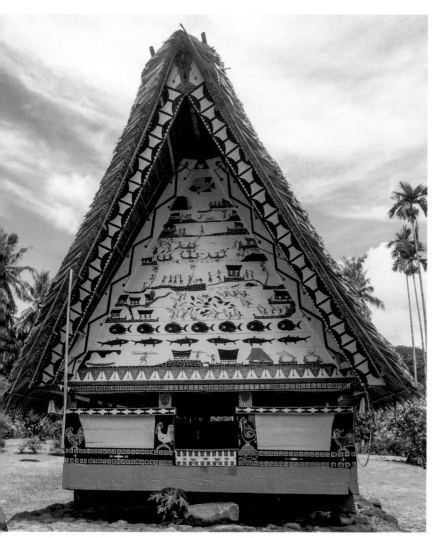

1.9.12 Bai-ra-Irrai, originally built *c.* 1700 and periodically restored, Airai village, Airai State, Republic of Palau

Progressive Rhythm

Repetition that regularly increases or decreases in frequency creates a progressive rhythm as the eye moves faster or slower across the surface of the work. In the photograph *Artichoke Halved*, by American Edward Weston (1886–1958), the outer layers (bracts) of the artichoke bud are closer together nearer the center (**1.9.11**). Then, as they form the triangular center of the bud, a second progressive rhythm begins and the small bracts below the triangle form a third rhythm. The highly focused close-up view and strong photographic contrasts of black and white accentuate the sense of speeding up.

Alternating Rhythm

Artists can intertwine multiple rhythms until they become quite complex. The addition and alternation of rhythms can add unpredictability and visual excitement. In Palau, an island group in the western Pacific, a traditional men's meeting house called the *bai* serves as a place for assembly and ritual (**1.9.12**). The imagery above the entry of this *bai* begins at the bottom, with the regular rhythms of horizontal lines of fish, but the images above become irregular as each higher row tells a new story. In each of the upper tiers, figures are interspersed with boats, buildings, and land masses to recall stories from the local tradition. The edges of the roof display a regular series of symbolic icons that, together with the building's horizontal beams, frame the composition and give the building's **facade** a dynamic feel.

Rhythmic Design Structure

The idea of rhythmic structure helps us understand how artists divide visual space into different sections to achieve different kinds of effects. In her 1849 painting *Plowing in the Nivernais: The Dressing of the Vines*, the French artist Rosa Bonheur (1822–1899) creates a horizontal structure that leads our eye in sequence from one group of shapes to the next (**1.9.13a** and **1.9.13b**). Bonheur expertly organizes the composition, emphasizing the cumulative effect of the rhythm of the groupings as they move from left to right. Because the composition is so horizontal, the design **emphasis** directs our gaze sideways using a linear direction and rhythm. By changing the width of the gaps between the animals, Bonheur suggests their irregular movement as they plod forward, drawing the

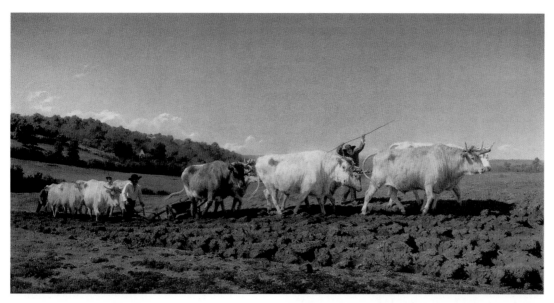

1.9.13a Rosa Bonheur, ***Plowing in the Nivernais: The Dressing of the Vines***, 1849. Oil on canvas, 4'4¾" × 8'6⅜". Musée d'Orsay, Paris, France

heavy plow. Each group also has a different relative size and occupies a different amount of space, creating a visual rhythm and energy that pulls our attention from left to right.

The careful composition and rhythmic structure in such paintings give an air of respectability and nobility to laborers of the field and the hard work they had to do. Bonheur may have been sympathetic toward those who worked outside of the stuffy social order of the time, since her gender may have been a disadvantage in a traditionally male profession. Yet her effort to bring respectability to such lives and labor did not seek to glamorize her subject: in this painting she insistently reminds us of the slow physical rhythms created by the sheer strength of these beasts and the irregularity of the plowmens' steps as all of them, men and cattle, work together to turn the weighty soil.

The Spanish painter Francisco Goya (1746–1828) uses differing visual rhythms to denote ideas of good and evil in the work *The Sleep of Reason Produces Monsters* (**1.9.14**) from the **series** "The Caprices" (*Los Caprichos*). Long considered one of the most significant Spanish painters, Goya established an expressive painting style and is well known for chronicling the harsh realities of the Napoleonic occupation of Spain. "The Caprices," however, is a strange, intriguing, and sometimes disturbing series of eighty **etchings** and **aquatints** depicting subjects as various as the clergy, witches, and prostitutes.

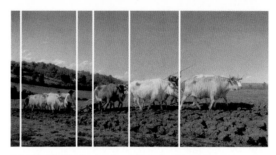

1.9.13b Rhythmic structural diagram of **1.9.13a**

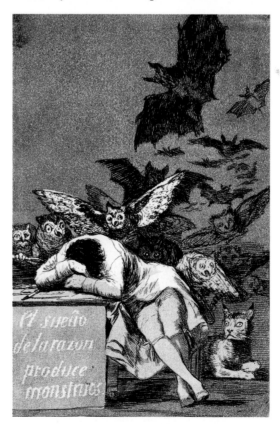

1.9.14 Francisco Goya, *The Sleep of Reason Produces Monsters:* **plate 43 from** "The Caprices" *(Los Caprichos)*, 1799. Etching, aquatint, drypoint, and burin, 8⅞ × 5⅞". Metropolitan Museum of Art, New York

Facade: any side of a building, usually the front or entrance

Emphasis: the principle of drawing attention to particular content in a work

Series: a group of related artworks that are created as a set

Etching: an intaglio printmaking process that uses acid to bite (or etch) the engraved design into the printmaking surface

Aquatint: an intaglio printmaking process that uses melted rosin or spray paint to create an acid-resistant ground

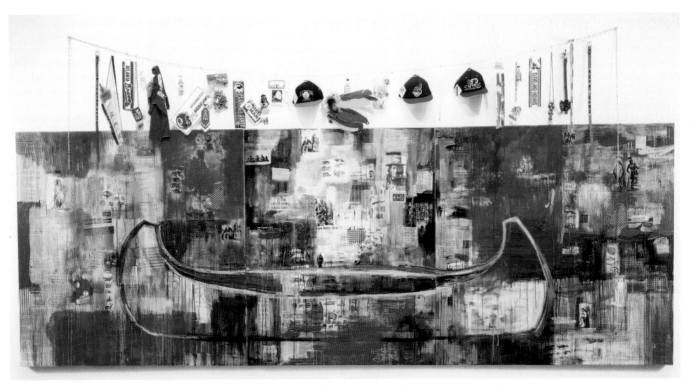

1.9.15 Jaune Quick-to-See Smith, *Trade (Gifts for Trading Land with White People)*, 1992. Oil paint and mixed media, collage, objects, canvas, 5' × 14'1⅝". Chrysler Museum of Art, Norfolk, Virginia

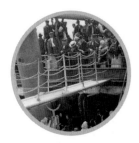

Another example of rhythmic structure can be seen in Alfred Stieglitz's photograph *The Steerage*:
→ see **2.8.25**, p. 314

Triptych: an artwork comprising three panels, normally joined together and sharing a common theme

Collage: a work of art assembled by gluing materials, often paper, onto a surface. From the French *coller*, to glue

The use of aquatint particularly heightens the contrast between dark and light, creating a shadowy, mysterious quality. The focus of the series is fantasy and invention, or the artist's imaginative powers. In **1.9.14** (see p. 155) particularly, he depicts the artist's dream (this is indicated in the inscription at lower left). But as the title suggests, the image is more than just a fantastical vision: it seems probable that the artist is expressing a belief that without rationality there is a danger that life would descend into chaos and irrational prejudices and superstition.

The two conflicting forces in the picture are skillfully contrasted: the box in the lower left corner stabilizes and anchors the image by means of the straight and regular lines of a square. The visual rhythm created through the vertical and horizontal lines is predictable and logical, symbolizing reason as a guarantee of safety and goodness. The monsters that dominate the upper portion of the image are more haphazard, active, and threatening in their placement within the work, rising as if to overwhelm the sleeper below.

The Native American artist Jaune Quick-to-See Smith (b. 1940) also used a rhythmic structure as she created the work *Trade (Gifts for Trading Land with White People)* (**1.9.15**). The work, created in 1992, was a reaction to the celebration of the five-hundredth anniversary of Columbus's landing in the Caribbean. Smith uses multiple rhythmic elements to communicate a reaction against the mistreatment of Native Americans that began with the arrival of Europeans. Two major components interact in this composition: a **triptych**, or three-panel artwork, in this case on canvas, and a hanging collection of objects. The three panels of the canvas are equal and create a simple repetitive rhythm that is unified by a nearly lifesize painted canoe. The surface of the painting is made up of **collaged** printed images of the many generalized ways in which Native people have been depicted. The hanging objects, a collection of stereotypical commercial images of Native Americans (mostly sports-team mascots), dangle above and in front of the canvas. The changing size and shape of the suspended objects establishes an alternating rhythm in real space. Additionally, the presence of real objects alongside the flat, collaged surface implies a connection between the past and present, and the notion that misconceptions from the past have led to distorted realities that persist today.

Explore Further Pattern and Rhythm

Pattern	Motif	Rhythm

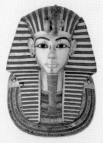

3.1.17 Funerary mask of Tutankhamun, Egypt, 1333–1323 BCE → p. 358

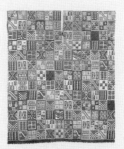

3.4.6 Inca tunic, Andes, *c.* 1500 → p. 414

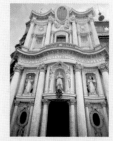

3.6.25a Francesco Borromini, San Carlo alle Quattro Fontane, Rome → p. 462

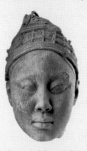

4.8.6 Head, possibly an Ife king, West Africa, 12th–14th century → p. 634

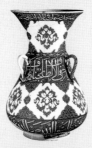

1.4.22 Mosque lamp from the Dome of the Rock, Jerusalem, 1549 → p. 96

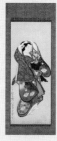

4.8.7 Kaigetsudō Dohan, *Beautiful Woman*, Edo Period, Japan, 18th century → p. 635

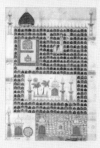

3.2.18 *View of the Sanctuary at Medina*, 17th or 18th century → p. 384

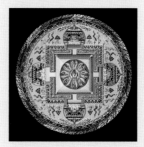

1.6.17 Amitayus Mandala, Drepung Loseling Monastery, Tibet → p. 128

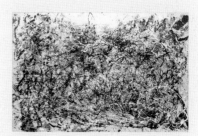

3.9.28 Jackson Pollock, *Number 1A*, 1948 → p. 516

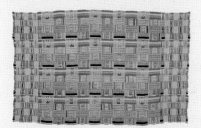

3.5.4 Asante textile wrapper (*kente*), Africa, 20th century → p. 430

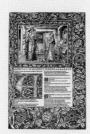

2.7.11 William Morris and Edward Burne-Jones, page from *Chaucer*, 1896 → p. 289

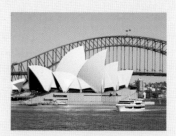

2.5.30 Jørn Utzon, Sydney Opera House, Australia, 1973 → p. 261

Your turn

How do pattern and rhythm function in these works?

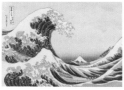

2.3.5 Katsushika Hokusai, "The Great Wave Off Shore at Kanagawa," 1826–33 → p. 215

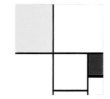

3.9.18 Piet Mondrian, *Composition with Yellow and Blue*, 1932 → p. 511

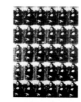

3.9.30 Andy Warhol, *Thirty Are Better than One*, 1963 → p. 517

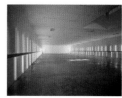

3.9.33 Dan Flavin, *Untitled* (installation), 1996 → p. 519

1.10
Engaging with Form and Content

Analysis: a detailed examination of the structure of an artwork

Critique: a detailed assessment or evaluation of an artwork

Content: the meaning, message, or feeling expressed in a work of art

Interpretation: explaining the meaning of an artwork

Primary sources: immediate or first-hand accounts of an artwork

Secondary sources: sources that are one step removed from primary references; give access to primary accounts

Elements of art: the basic vocabulary of art—line, shape, form, volume, mass, texture, value (lightness/darkness), space, color, and motion and time

Principles of art: the principles, or grammar of art—contrast, unity, variety, balance, scale, proportion, focal point, emphasis, pattern, and rhythm—describe the ways the elements of art are arranged in an artwork

Formal analysis: a visual study that includes careful description of the artwork and its use of elements and principles

Artworks communicate visual ideas, just as speaking and writing communicate verbal ideas. In order for viewers to engage with art more deeply than through personal response alone (like/dislike), we must interpret the visual language of the artist. We use a combination of various methods, such as description, **analysis**, and **critique**, to understand the appearance and meaning—or **content**—of a work. Careful looking and research contribute to effective analysis. We can also apply our own viewpoints, or critique. In this chapter we look at the interpretive methods that are most frequently used and are most effective (see: Types of Analysis and Critique, p. 164).

Analysis, Research, Critique, and Interpretation

Analysis involves careful consideration and discussion of specific aspects of an artwork. Some aspects of an artwork can be accessed by close observation, while others are best understood after some research. The strongest **interpretations** of an artwork combine the viewer's formal analysis, factual evidence from **primary** and **secondary sources**, and support from the work of specialists who know about the topics being covered.

In research, primary sources are connected most closely to the art and the artist, including the artwork itself; the artist's words (a statement or interviews); and accounts of direct contact with the artwork or artist (correspondence, exhibition reviews, etc.). Secondary sources are references that include indirect information about an artwork or data that was collected by someone else, such as reference books; scholarly articles or books; book reviews; and official artist or museum

websites. Internet research is a crucial way to access information about an artwork in order to analyze it, but the legitimacy of the source must be confirmed. In general, websites are unreliable if it is unclear who wrote the information or what contributors' qualifications are. Many of the great museums around the world have their own websites, however, which are excellent and trustworthy sources of fascinating information. These websites are generally considered secondary sources, but may include primary source information, too.

Interpretations of artworks may include analysis or critique (or both) based on various types of information, usually a balance of fact and opinion. Critiques of artworks often highlight the ideas, opinions, and experiences of the viewer. Art criticism, meaning a critical review or commentary, includes judgment, but it does not have to result in a negative opinion.

Formal Analysis

Artists have many tools at their disposal, which we call the **elements** and **principles** of art (discussed throughout Part I of this book). The elements include line, form, shape, volume, mass, color, texture, space, motion and time, and value. Artists use the principles, such as contrast, balance, unity, variety, rhythm, emphasis, pattern, scale, proportion, and focal point, to organize the elements. A work of art is therefore a product of the dynamic interrelationships between the various art elements and principles.

The process of analyzing the elements and principles used by the artist is called **formal analysis**. Making a formal analysis—a visual study—of a work of art involves careful

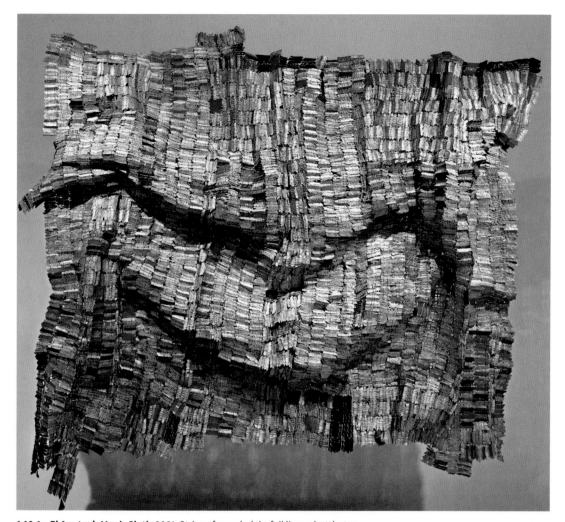

1.10.1a El Anatsui, *Man's Cloth*, 2001. Strips of recycled tin-foil liquor bottle-top wrappers stapled together with wire, 93 × 58 × 72″. British Museum, London, England

Kente cloth is also made using strips woven into patchwork patterns, but with silk fabric instead of aluminum:

→ see **3.5.4**, p. 430

observation. This practice not only helps us understand artworks but also helps us build skills that can be applied to other endeavors where description is important.

A formal analysis describes in specific detail how each element and principle is utilized within it. In this chapter we will focus on specific visual aspects of the chosen works in order to highlight the ways that elements and principles are used by the artists. We will look at the varying ways that artists convey underlying meaning, and the role of the viewer in interpreting the artworks. Toward the end of the chapter we will see examples of several, more complete formal analyses within a combined analysis (pp. 170–175).

In order to analyze a **three-dimensional** artwork fully, you need to see the piece from multiple views. Contemporary Ghanaian artist El Anatsui (b. 1944) makes large-scale **sculptures** that look very different far away than they do up close. From a distance, *Man's Cloth* (**1.10.1a**) looks like a multicolored sheet

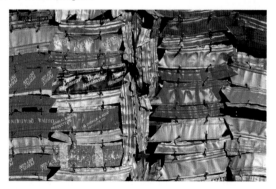

1.10.1b El Anatsui, *Man's Cloth* (detail)

of material, its texture crumpled in places and draped down a wall. The overall form is fully three-dimensional, but because it is displayed against the wall, we can see only one side. The outer edges of the sculpture create a roughly square shape with irregular, not straight or **symmetrical**, sides. The color of the piece is mixed, with small areas of silver, red, black, and gold throughout. Upon closer inspection (**1.10.1b**), we see that the sculpture was made

Three-dimensional: having height, width, and depth

Sculpture: a work of art created by carving, chiseling, casting, or modeling

Symmetry: the correspondence in size, form, and arrangement of items on opposite sides of a plane, line, or point that creates direct visual balance

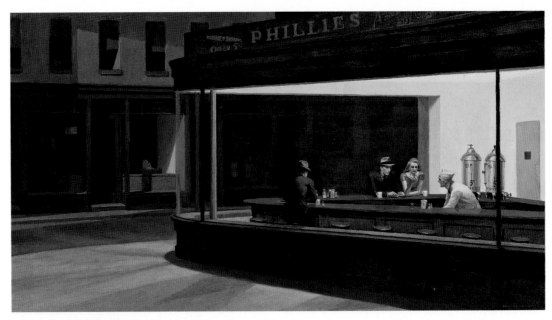

1.10.2 Edward Hopper, *Nighthawks*, 1942. Oil on canvas, 33⅛ × 60″.
Art Institute of Chicago, Illinois

Additive (sculpture): a sculpting process in which the artist builds a form by adding material

Assemblage: artwork made of three-dimensional materials, including found objects

***Kente* cloth:** African textile made of interwoven strips of silk and cotton fabric; native to the Asante and Akan groups of Ghana and traditionally worn by royalty and state officials

Composition: the overall design or organization of a work

Light: depicting a light source, applying contrasts of light and dark, or manipulating the emission of light in an artwork

Background: the part of a work depicted furthest from the viewer's space, often behind the main subject matter

Foreground: the part of a work depicted as nearest to the viewer

using an **additive** technique, by putting together smaller metal pieces. This process further contributes to the rough texture. *Man's Cloth* is in fact an **assemblage** of found liquor-bottle caps that have been cut, stretched flat, punctured, and sewn into rows with copper wire. The various colors correspond to the packaging, and some brand names are visible: Liquor Headmaster in black with gold letters and Quadrina in red with silver letters.

In our daily lives, we do not usually take note of visual details to this degree. When we do, they can lead us to ask questions about the reasons behind the formal choices and the meaning of the artwork. The technique that Anatsui uses recalls the traditional Ghanaian **kente cloth** made professionally by his father and brother (see Portal, p. 159). Anatsui chose bottle tops as his material because European traders bartered alcohol for African goods. Enslaved people were shipped from Ghana to the sugar plantations of the Caribbean; then in turn, rum was shipped from there back to Africa. El Anatsui's bottle tops thus remind us of the trade in enslaved people, as well as highlighting the scale of waste produced by modern consumerism.

When making a formal analysis of a two-dimensional work, such as a painting, useful aspects you can consider are the locations of objects, the colors used, and the relationships between the parts of the **composition**. The first thing we see when we look at *Nighthawks* (**1.10.2**), by the American artist Edward Hopper

(1882–1967), is a brightly lit diner on a dark, empty street. This contrast makes the room a particular area of emphasis in the picture. The **light** further draws our attention to the people inside, seated at a counter near a brilliant yellow wall. The brightness around them exposes them clearly to us, showing how isolated they are from one another, physically and psychologically. The stark contrasts in the colors of their clothing—the woman's red dress and hair, the black suits and hats of the two male customers, and the white uniform of the waiter—make the figures more distinct, both within the scene and from one another.

Some details that are not as obvious help contribute to the impact and underlying message of the painting. In this scene, we see a darkened building in the **background**, with large shop windows on the bottom floor and five tall windows on the red-brick upper story. Together, these areas form repeated dark gulfs that communicate a sense of hollowness and vacancy. We notice that even though the scene takes place in a city, the streets around are devoid of people and activity, creating a slightly eerie sense of stillness and quiet. In front of this building, the sidewalk in the left **foreground** wraps around the curved diner on the street corner, and the glass windows on the right side of the composition separate us from the group of people inside. The struts dividing the panes, and the solid walls above and below, create a strong framework through which we focus on the four figures.

Despite being gathered together, the figures are not smiling and have very little interaction with one another; these individuals appear to be alone in their own thoughts. One cannot tell whether the man and woman sitting together are a couple—they do not look at each other: he stares ahead, while her eyes are downcast. Their hands are close, but do not touch. These figures echo the two drink urns to the right: set very nearly together, but apart. The man and woman are further separated visually by the line of her right arm. The waiter is enclosed on his own within the triangular space of the bar, and the other customer sits with his back to us, surrounded by six empty barstools. Although the waiter is in an active pose, it appears that time has stopped. This stillness only further enhances the sense of quiet, as if these lives are frozen, sealed off in their separate loneliness. The artist remarked some time after finishing the work, "Unconsciously, probably, I was painting the loneliness of a large city," and if we look closely, within this careful use of formal devices we see that he intensifies the painting's effect through his choice of specific details.

Stylistic Analysis

We recognize **style** in our own lives: the way we dress and arrange our hair reflects our personal style. Artworks also have style, or specific characteristics that make them look the way they do. Style allows us to recognize that an artwork was made by a particular artist. A group of artists might share a style because they all used similar techniques, worked at the same time, or studied in the same place. The characteristics that contribute to style include the use of formal elements (line, shape, color, texture, and so on), the use of design principles (symmetry or asymmetry, for example), and the level of abstraction or representation used. Style can be related to the brushstrokes or marks an artist makes, the way light shines brightly on one part of the composition while the rest is in darkness, or the consistent use of a particular color in a certain way.

Style can be individual or shared by a group, school, time period, or movement. Analyzing style allows us to make connections between artworks. We can use style as a way to categorize them or to identify who made a work of art, where it came from, or when it was created.

Known for his unique style, Netherlandish artist Hieronymus Bosch (*c.* 1450–1516) is most famous for his painted **triptych** *The Garden of Earthly Delights* (**1.10.3**). Unlike many other artists working in Europe in the sixteenth century, Bosch was not interested in convincing **realism** or perfect proportion. His works are known for their fantastical quality: humans, fruits, and futuristic-looking objects (all in various distorted sizes) mingle in odd,

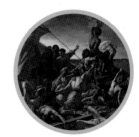

Raft of the Medusa is a work from the Romanticism movement; its style combines detailed realism with idealized form, emphasizing imagination and emotional content:
→ see **4.7.1**, p. 619

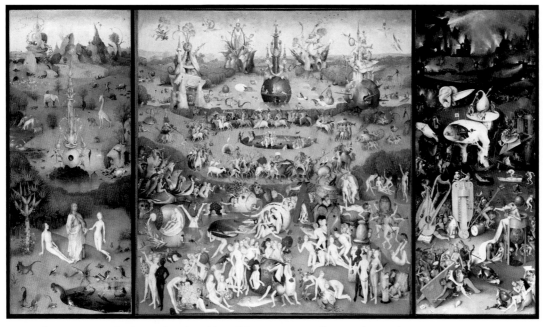

1.10.3 Hieronymus Bosch, ***The Garden of Earthly Delights***, 1500–1505. Oil on wooden panel, central panel 7'1⅝" × 6'4¾", wings 7'1⅝"× 38¼". Museo Nacional del Prado, Madrid, Spain

Style: a characteristic way in which an artist or group of artists uses visual language to give a work an identifiable form of visual expression

Triptych: an artwork comprising three panels, normally joined together and sharing a common theme

Realism: a nineteenth-century artistic style that aimed to depict nature and everyday subjects in an unidealized manner. Realism is also used to describe a historical movement from the same period, which tried to achieve social change and equality by highlighting, in art and literature, the predicament of the poor

erotic, and nonsensical ways. The specific meanings of the activities in Bosch's work are uncertain, but on the whole scholars agree that he is expressing a religious condemnation of immorality, particularly in regard to sexual behavior. In this sense his style has something in common with **medieval** biblical sermons and folkloric sources, which also suggested that sinful actions are reflected in distortions of human anatomy. As a Spanish monk, José de Sigüenza, wrote upon studying the work in 1605, "other artists depicted people as they appear outwardly, but only Bosch had the audacity to paint them as they are on the inside."

The left panel of *The Garden of Earthly Delights* shows God's presentation of Adam and Eve before the Fall; the center panel shows elongated nude figures inhabiting the false paradise of Earth, seduced by the ephemeral pleasures of frolicking and eroticism. The right panel shows the consequences of their behavior, with endless forms of tortured damnation for the sinners. Bosch's distinctive style may look quite modern in some ways, but he was an artist of the late medieval period.

1.10.4a Hans Holbein the Younger, *Jean de Dinteville and Georges de Selve ("The Ambassadors")*, 1533. Oil on oak, 6'9½" × 6'10⅓". National Gallery, London, England

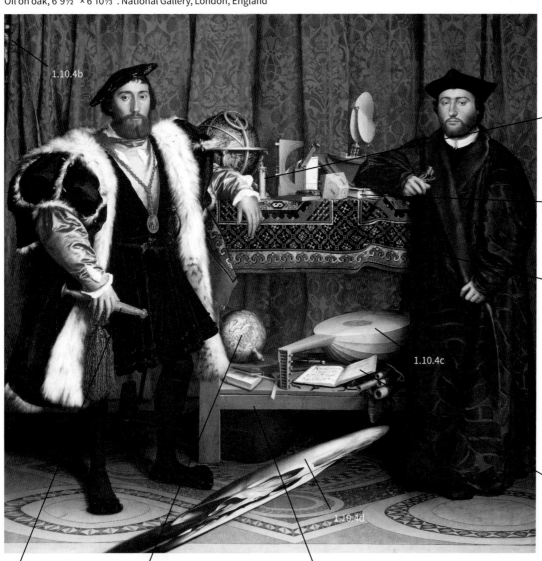

The cylindrical sundial gives the date (April 11, 1533) on which the painting was completed

The number 25, the age of de Selve, is inscribed along the outer edges of the pages of the book he is leaning on

The upper shelf, symbolically nearer to Heaven, features devices to understand the heavens and measure time, including a celestial globe, sundial, and compasses. These objects indicate how learned these men are and that they are well-traveled, as their occupation would demand

The hymn book, which is so exactly painted that it is possible to read the verses by Martin Luther, the German pioneer of Protestantism, inscribed on its pages, may be included to encourage the restoration of religious concord

The number 29, the age of Dinteville, is engraved on his dagger

The center of the globe on the lower shelf shows Rome, hub of the Catholic faith

The lower shelf, which is concerned with more earthly matters, includes—painted in meticulously precise detail—secular and religious objects including musical instruments, a hymn book, a mathematical book, and a terrestrial globe

Iconographic Analysis

When we identify and interpret the **symbolic** meanings of the objects and elements in artworks through research, we often find unexpected insights into their content. *The Ambassadors*, by German artist Hans Holbein the Younger (1497–1543), was painted while the artist was at the court of King Henry VIII of England and is extraordinarily rich in symbolic significance (**1.10.4**). We can begin by identifying the broader meanings of what the work includes. It shows Jean de Dinteville and the bishop Georges de Selve, French diplomats who served as ambassadors to England. In 1533, when the work was made, England was on the brink of breaking with the Catholic Church and becoming a Protestant country, and art historians who have been able to study the painting closely have revealed how its **iconography** reflects this religious

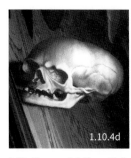

In the upper left corner, partially concealed by the green curtain, is a crucifix

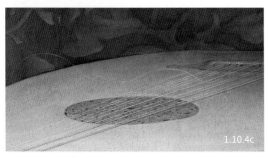

The lute has a broken string: this may be a reference to the religious discord that was occurring at the time—harmony (hence the musical instrument) was a key idea in the sixteenth century

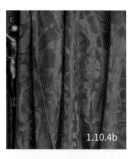

The large, distorted skull in the foreground, painted using **anamorphosis**, a type of optical illusion, signifies human mortality. This skull looks realistic only when the viewer stands in one specific spot, in front and to the right of the canvas

1.10.4b, c, and d Hans Holbein the Younger, *Jean de Dinteville and Georges de Selve ("The Ambassadors")*, 1533 (details)

predicament: the globe, hymn book, crucifix, and lute all carry specific religious meanings (**1.10.4a–1.10.4c**).

Most symbolic of all is the large, distorted skull in the foreground, which signifies human mortality, and the inclusion of which indicates that the painting as a whole is what is known as a **memento mori**—a symbolic reminder of the inevitability of death (**1.10.4d**). Despite the ambassadors' success, wealth, and youth, they are aware of the fleeting nature of life. The strange, haunting form of the skull, facing away from their worldly possessions and toward the half-hidden crucifix, affirms that the men believe their salvation, and eternal life, depend on God.

Contextual Analysis

The content, or meaning, of a work of art varies greatly between artworks. Both artists and viewers play roles in providing this meaning. An artwork may convey a particular message to those who view it in the context in which it was made, but the same artwork may convey a different meaning to someone living in another time and place. To understand the context of a work of art fully, you will usually have to undertake some research, in addition to looking very closely at the artwork itself. There are numerous types of contextual analysis that you can use to decipher the meaning of a work of art by gathering information (sometimes from multiple sources).

Analysis of Religious Context
The powerful feelings behind religious beliefs have often motivated the creation of art. Sumerian (4000–1000 BCE) rituals included bringing offerings for the gods to their temples. A dozen small praying figures were found under a Sumerian temple in modern-day Iraq; the two largest ones are shown here (**1.10.5**). Because the figures were found in a temple, we know they were created and used in a religious context. Their wide-eyed upward gaze and clasped hands, together with inscriptions on some of them, tell us that they are in eternal prayer. All the figures have similar conical forms, their

Medieval: the time period roughly between the fall of the Roman empire and the start of the Renaissance

Symbolism: using images or symbols in an artwork to convey meaning; often obvious when the work was made but requiring research for modern viewers to understand

Iconography: study of the symbolic meaning of an artwork or the general study of symbolism

Memento mori: Latin phrase that means "remember that you must die." In artworks, such symbols as skulls, flowers, and clocks are used to represent the transient nature of life on Earth

Anamorphosis: the distorted representation of an object so that it appears correctly proportioned only when viewed from one particular position

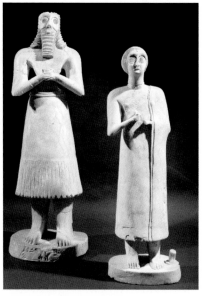

1.10.5 Votive Figures from the Temple of Abu, Eshnunna (Tell Asmar), *c.* 2700 BCE. Gypsum, male figure (left) height 28⅜", female figure (right) height 23¼". Iraq Museum, Baghdad, Iraq

Types of Analysis and Critique

There is no single right way to examine a work of art, and, as we shall see later on in this chapter, different methods can be combined to develop a more complete interpretation. Here is a summary of some important types of analysis.

Certain kinds of analysis (for example feminist, gender, or race studies) may be used when describing and explaining a set of ideas in the work of art itself, ideas related to beliefs held by the artist, or the context of the time period. Critique moves beyond the artist's biography, intentions, and the direct content to include contextual information (such as the historical treatment of women, considerations related to gender, or the way that race impacts a work of art) and highlights beliefs held by the person interpreting an artwork.

FORMAL ANALYSIS

Formal analysis involves looking closely and in detail at the work in order to consider how the formal elements and principles of art are used to create it and to convey meaning, and then carefully describing them.

STYLISTIC ANALYSIS

Style in art is the particular combination of characteristics that make a work (or works) of art distinctive. Stylistic analysis focuses on these characteristics in a way that clearly identifies how they typify the work of an individual, are shared by a group of artists to create a movement, or are concentrated in a particular place or time period.

ICONOGRAPHIC ANALYSIS

Iconography—"image writing" or "writing with images"—examines the visual images and symbols used in a work of art and leads to an interpretation of the work's meaning. Iconographic analysis identifies objects and figures in an artwork as signs or symbols that can reflect religious or historical contexts. The meaning of these symbols was often more directly understood at a particular time by a specific culture, but may now be less apparent to us.

CONTEXTUAL ANALYSIS

Contextual analysis looks at the making and viewing of the work in its context: it studies the atmosphere and ideas, often from a particular time or culture, which the artwork itself includes and reflects. Various aspects of context can be considered; for example, religious, historical, and biographical analysis are all types of contextual analysis.

Religious analysis considers the artwork in relation to the religious context in which it was made; this method often includes identification of narratives, key symbolism, and important figures.

Historical/social analysis considers historical events, either past or present, and the way they appear in an artwork.

Biographical analysis considers whether the artist's personal experiences and opinions may have affected the making or meaning of the artwork in some way.

FEMINIST ANALYSIS AND CRITIQUE

Inspired—as the name suggests—by feminism, feminist interpretations consider the role of women in an artwork as its subjects, creators, patrons, and viewers. A feminist approach can reflect the intentions of an artist, the perspective of a viewer, the interpretation of a critic, or a combination of two or three of these.

GENDER STUDIES ANALYSIS AND CRITIQUE

Gender studies analysis expands the considerations raised by feminist analysis to explore ways in which the work reflects experience based on a person's gender. This method of interpretation can also reflect the intentions of an artist, the perspective of a viewer, the interpretation of a critic, or all three.

ANALYSIS OF RACE IN SOCIETY AND CULTURE

This method of interpretation critically examines society and culture as it intersects with race, power, and institutional practices. It can also reflect the intentions of an artist, the perspective of a viewer, the interpretation of a critic, or all three.

PSYCHOLOGICAL ANALYSIS

This type of analysis investigates an artwork by considering the state of the artist's mind. Sometimes such interpretations make use of important psychological studies, such as those of Sigmund Freud or Carl Jung (1875–1961).

faces stoically forward with hands intertwining slightly above the waist. Yet each is unique: the size, hairstyle, and gender varies. While they are not precise portraits, each figure represents the person who brought it to the temple. The figures all hold a goblet for a votive—an offering made in accordance with a vow—to the gods, and would remain in the temple to offer continual prayer when the people represented by the statues could not be there.

Analysis of Historical Context

In the 1920s and 1930s, African American history, cultural traditions, and ways of life were widely explored in literature, music, and the visual arts. The **Harlem Renaissance**, an intellectual and creative revival centered on black identity to support political liberation and recognition for crucial cultural contributions, was promoted by such prominent individuals as Alain Locke (1886–1954, a philosopher and art patron) and W. E. B. DuBois (1868–1963, a scholar and activist). Harlem, New York, and other northern U.S. cities became important centers for African American cultural growth because many African Americans had moved there from the rural south to escape persecution.

Such artists as American Palmer Hayden (1890–1973; see **1.10.6**) wanted to celebrate

Harlem Renaissance: a movement in literature, music, and the visual arts from the end of WWI into the 1930s, celebrating black experience and culture

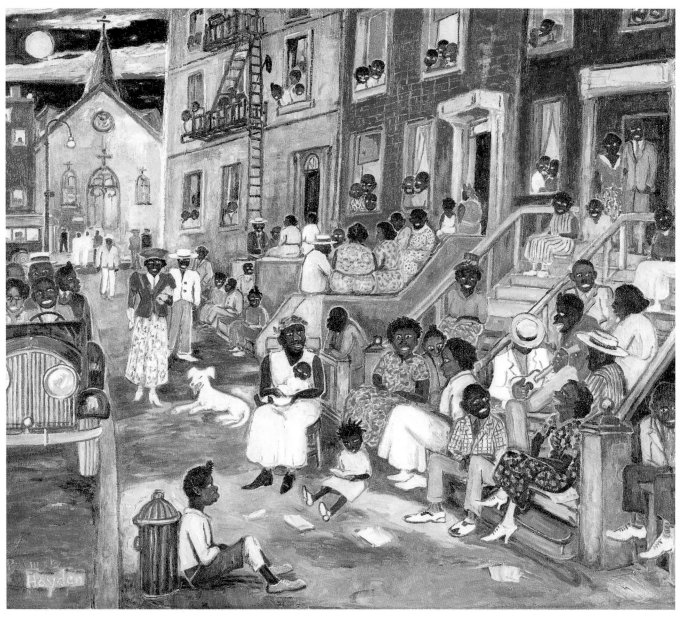

1.10.6 Palmer Hayden, *Midsummer Night in Harlem*, 1936. Oil on canvas, 25 × 30″.
Museum of African American Art, Los Angeles, California

their thriving communities. In *Midsummer Night in Harlem* (1936), he highlights the strong sense of community in his **subject matter** by showing people in the neighborhood gathering on stoops and sticking their heads out of apartment windows. Most people are shown as lively, with large smiles and bright eyes (**1.10.6**, p. 165). The prominent location of the church at the end of the street to our left, and the dresses and hats people are wearing, indicate that they have just returned from an evening at church. The artist makes this, one of many everyday-life scenes he painted, accessible by emphasizing realistic details of the gathering, such as the clothing, the car, the fire hydrant, and the fire escape. Hayden captures the time and place of this New York community by depicting joyful activity and the bonding of the people collectively under the full moon. At the same time, his use of flat, bright **hues** is a deliberate reference to the colors commonly found in traditional African art and also in the modern artworks that the artist had encountered during his training in Paris in the late 1920s.

Analysis of Biographical Context

Polish artist Magdalena Abakanowicz (1930–2017) based her artworks on her personal life experiences, Polish heritage, and imagery inspired by life in Poland during World War II. We can understand her work much better if we know about her life. When she was nine years old, at the beginning of World War II, her village was occupied by invading German troops. She witnessed at first hand the violent consequences of the occupation. At the end of the war, Poland spent the next forty-five years as a Soviet-Union-dominated Communist state. Abakanowicz chose to become a weaver, which meant she would not make realistic depictions of heroic workers even though that style of art was the one demanded by the ruling Soviet Union. Later she made **abstract** sculpture that explores issues of dignity, courage, and a will to survive under a totalitarian government. In *80 Backs* (**1.10.7**), the fragile, perishable fiber materials reflect her keen awareness of human vulnerability, to which she was often exposed during the war and its aftermath. She also used

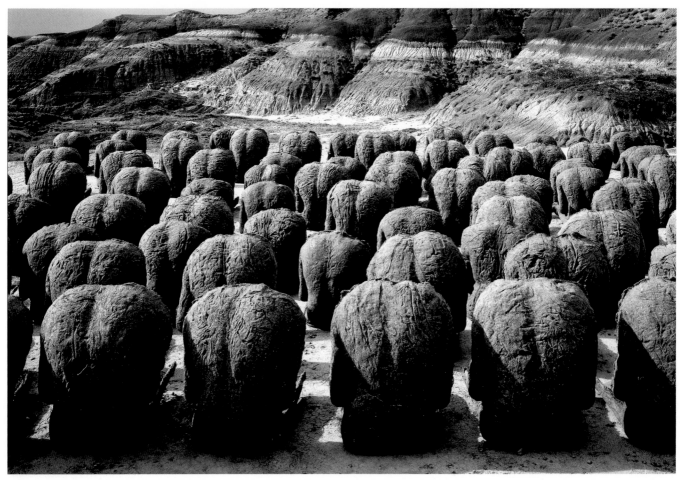

1.10.7 Magdalena Abakanowicz, *80 Backs*, 1976–80. Burlap and resin, height 24–27″; depth 19½–22″; width 21½–26″. Museum of Modern Art, Pusan, South Korea

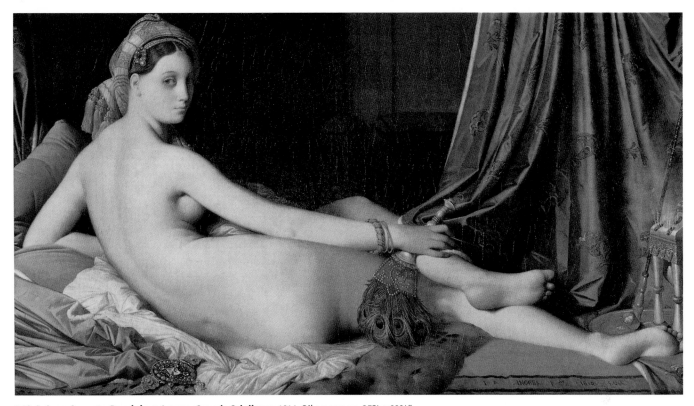

1.10.8 Jean-Auguste-Dominique Ingres, *Grande Odalisque*, 1814. Oil on canvas, 35⅞ × 63¾".
Musée du Louvre, Paris, France

this material because in the early years of her career she had no conventional materials from which to sculpt: burlap sacks were among the few things available to her. She had no studio in which to work at that time, and the soft, pliable materials could be easily folded and stored.

Abakanowicz has often created works involving multiple, repeated figures. This reflects her experience of the Communist regime's emphasis on the collective over the individual, and its attempts to control personal expression. In *80 Backs*, the burlap fabric is shaped into recognizable but abstracted human forms without heads or faces. A few years after making *80 Backs*, Abakanowicz said, "A human being turned into a crowd loses his human qualities. A crowd is only a thousand-times duplicated copy, a repetition, a multiplication. Amongst such a great number, one person is extremely close and at the same time terribly distant."

Analyzing Meaning

Feminist Analysis and Critique

Biographical analysis usually takes gender, race, and societal position into account. Feminist analysis is a subset of biographical analysis when it studies the life experience of women artists in relation to their work.

Feminist analysis has been expanded to include gender studies, and feminist critique additionally considers viewers' perspectives toward gender, the treatment of women as subjects, and the role of women at the time the artwork was made.

Grande Odalisque by the French artist Jean-Auguste-Dominique Ingres (1780–1867) was made in 1814 for a male French audience (**1.10.8**). Feminist analysis might compare this artwork to others made at the time and find that female nudes were often depicted as objects of desire and beauty. The woman is dressed as an odalisque (a woman in a harem), and so a feminist analysis might study the French view of women in Turkish society, who were considered fascinating for their perceived exotic sensuality. Feminist analysis could seek an explanation for the interest in harem women in art during this period, and might find that women in France were demanding equal rights, causing men to pine for docile females.

A feminist might also study this subject's demure gaze, whereby she accepts her status as an object of beauty. At the time the picture was painted, critics complained that the figure's body parts were disproportionate: her back was too long, and her hips too wide. A feminist analysis would point out that Ingres imposed

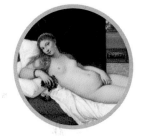

The tradition of reclining nudes began during the Renaissance and continued to influence later artists:
→ see **4.8.8**, p. 635

his male ideals onto the female body. He believed that the back was a very sensual part of a woman's body, and he claimed that he could not stop himself, when painting, from adding what appear to be extra vertebrae.

Feminist and Gender Studies Analysis/Critique

The American artist Robert Mapplethorpe (1946–1989) used his own life as inspiration for his photographs. The issue of gender affects his imagery because he chose subjects that were highly sexualized and often related to his own identity as a gay man. His photographs are carefully composed, elegantly lit, and technically perfect, making subjects that might previously have been seen as deviant appear normal, even beautiful. A national controversy was sparked by the exhibition of Mapplethorpe's work that traveled to several museums across the US shortly after the artist died of an AIDS-related illness in the late 1980s. Some museum officials and politicians considered the graphic sexual nature of some of Mapplethorpe's photographs to be problematic because the artist had been awarded a grant from public funds. Mapplethorpe, however,

did not see a significant difference between a flower, a Classical sculpture, or a nude male figure.

Mapplethorpe's subversion of binary gender distinctions can be seen in his 1980 *Self-Portrait (#385)* (**1.10.9**). The feminine appearance of the eyeshadow, blush and lipstick on his face contrasts with the masculine anatomy of his bare chest. Mapplethorpe's appearance raises many questions about the assumptions we make based on the way people look. It also reveals the degree to which gender is a construction and suggests that the conventional distinctions between the sexes are more fluid. Mapplethorpe photographed what he wanted to see, the things that he considered visually interesting but did not find elsewhere in the art world. Interpreting Mapplethorpe's photograph from the perspective of gender studies encourages us to take his intentions into account, and to think about how gender affects our experience.

Analysis of Race in Society and Culture

Art can also be interpreted through the lens of race, by examining society and culture as they reflect the ways in which the law and legal institutions reflect an inherently racist bias, as well as the ways race is a social construct that supports oppressive systems. Interpreting an artwork in this way takes into account the biography and life experience of the artist, the artist's intended meaning, and contextual cultural practices.

American artist Kerry James Marshall (b. 1955) grew up amidst the Civil Rights and Black Power movements, which he says helped instill a sense of social responsibility into his practice. His "unequivocally, emphatically black figures" have influenced a whole generation of younger artists and viewers. *Past Times* (**1.10.10**) builds on the Western European tradition of painting, while at the same time, it carries forward a view centered on African American experience through locations and scenarios that resonated for the artist as a Black American.

Marshall pursued painting as his **medium** because it was a dominant force in museums. His visual references range from Renaissance and Baroque banners to scenes of leisure characteristic of French Impressionism (see Portal, right). According to the artist, he used "**collage** as a logic" to bring various traditions

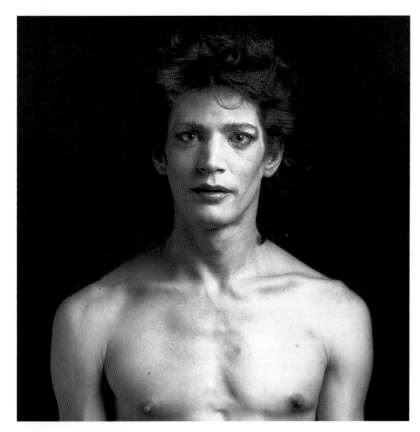

1.10.9 Robert Mapplethorpe, *Self-Portrait (#385)*, 1980. Gelatin silver print, 20 × 16″

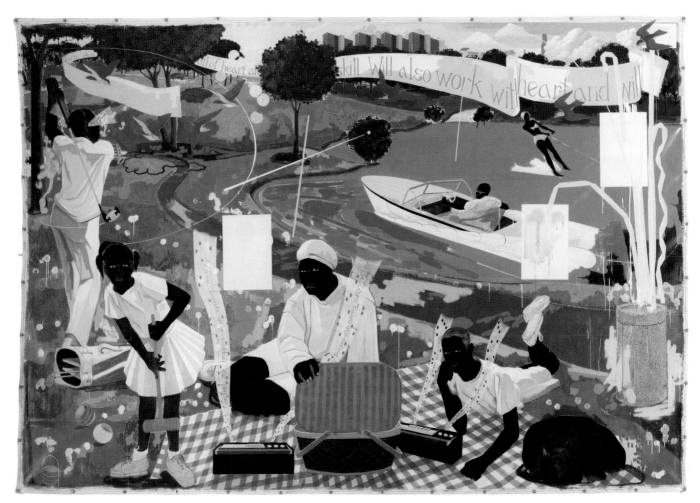

1.10.10 Kerry James Marshall, *Past Times*, 1997, acrylic and collage on canvas, 108¼ × 157". Private collection

together into a new expression. The paint splatters and unfinished areas of the painting allow us to see the artist's process while referencing both **Abstract Expressionist** brush strokes and graffiti.

At once special and mundane, this idyllic depiction begins to offset the omission of Black experience from the mainstream canon of art history. On a grassy hill overlooking a lake with a city skyline in the distance, we see three figures on a red-and-white checkered picnic cloth looking out towards us. The young girl to our left holds a croquet mallet while the older person seated in the center opens a picnic basket. A young boy to the right listens to music and, beside him, a dog curls up to rest. On the left-hand side, behind this group, a man swings a golf club and, in the lake off to the right, we see a man boating and a woman waterskiing. The color white is a unifying element in the composition: the figures' clothing, the banners, and the empty squares floating through the composition, as

if posters had been adhered to the painting's surface. Sound is evoked by the scrolls flowing from two boomboxes on the picnic cloth. The printed lyrics of songs by Black musicians, The Temptations' *Just My Imagination* and Snoop Dogg's *Gin and Juice*, hint at imagination, lived moments, and expectant futures that might be possible.

Psychological Analysis

Psychological analysis considers the artist's state of mind when creating an artwork. The Norwegian artist Edvard Munch (1863–1944) used the realm of his own mind as inspiration for *The Scream* (**1.10.11**, p. 170). As a child he endured the death of his mother and sister, and throughout his life he suffered from physical illness and depression. These tragic experiences and psychological disturbances motivated his work. Munch reported that he felt psychologically driven to make art. His painting *The Scream* presents a ghoul-like figure on a bridge, with a vibrant red sky in

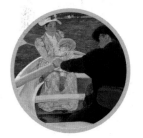

Marshall's painting references Impressionist scenes, such as Cassatt's *Boating Party*:
→ see **1.4.13**, p. 90

Collage: a work of art assembled by gluing flat materials, often paper, onto a surface. From the French *coller*, to glue

Abstract Expressionism: a mid-twentieth-century artistic style characterized by its capacity to convey intense emotions using non-representational images

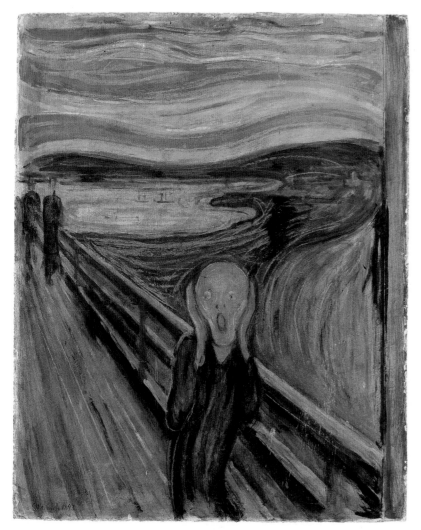

1.10.11 Edvard Munch, ***The Scream***, 1893. Casein and tempera on cardboard, 35⅛″ × 29⅛″. Munch Museum, Oslo, Norway

Expressionism, Expressionist: an artistic style at its height in 1920s Europe, devoted to representing subjective emotions and experiences instead of objective or external reality

Implied line: a line not actually drawn but suggested by the position of elements in the work, for example, an aligned series of dots

Vanishing point(s): the point or points in a work of art at which imaginary sight lines appear to converge, suggesting depth

Linear perspective: a system using converging imaginary sight lines to create the illusion of depth

the background. At first glance it appears to be a fictional scene. Entries in Munch's diary, however, indicate that the painting in fact represents his interpretation of an actual event. While walking on an overlook road with two friends (the figures looming in the distance), Munch saw the sky turn red and he froze with anxiety. Some scholars suggest that Munch witnessed an extraordinarily intense sunset caused by dust thrown into the atmosphere by a volcanic eruption that had occurred years before he made the painting. Others believe he experienced an attack of agoraphobia (fear of open spaces). Like many **Expressionist** artworks, this painting does not depict what Munch actually saw, but what he felt.

Combined Analysis in Historical and Contemporary Art

While it is rare to be able to use every method discussed in this chapter for every artwork,

we can often consider one work in many ways. Using these modes of analysis, we can arrive at a better and more rounded understanding both of famous pieces that have been studied by scholars for a long time and of more recent artworks that the artists themselves help us to understand through their statements and explanations.

Form and Content in Las Meninas

A *formal* analysis considers what the artist has communicated using a visual language. This kind of detailed description often enhances our awareness of the appearance of a work of art. *Las Meninas* (*The Maids of Honor*) by Diego de Silva y Velázquez (1599–1660) shows members of the court of the Spanish King Philip IV gathering in a room in the Alcázar Palace (**1.10.12a**). The painter depicts himself on the left, painting a large canvas. The Princess Margarita is posed in the center, with her ladies-in-waiting ("las meninas") surrounding her. Court workers, including dwarfs, are also present.

The **implied lines** suggested by the black frames on the right wall and the ceiling fixtures converge on the chest of the man standing in the doorway. This is the **vanishing point** required in **linear perspective** to create an illusion of **depth**, as if the viewer is looking into a real room. All the figures in the painting have a realistic sense of volume and are arranged to emphasize further the illusion of looking into a real space. Notice how they overlap one another, and that those toward the back of the room are smaller than those at the front. The painting is more than 10 ft. tall, which allows Velázquez to make the figures lifesize, further reinforcing the illusion of three-dimensional space. Finally, most of the colors in the painting are **neutral**. The **palette** of brown, gray, beige, and black creates the impression of a dark space, the depth of which is emphasized by the light coming in from a window on the right and the door at the back.

Velázquez highlights several areas he wants to emphasize. The young princess is in the central foreground (the part of the painting nearest to us), well lit, and shown attended by her maids. In the background, the mysterious male figure is emphasized because his black form contrasts with the light coming through the doorway. The painter himself stands proudly at his work. And we notice the mirror

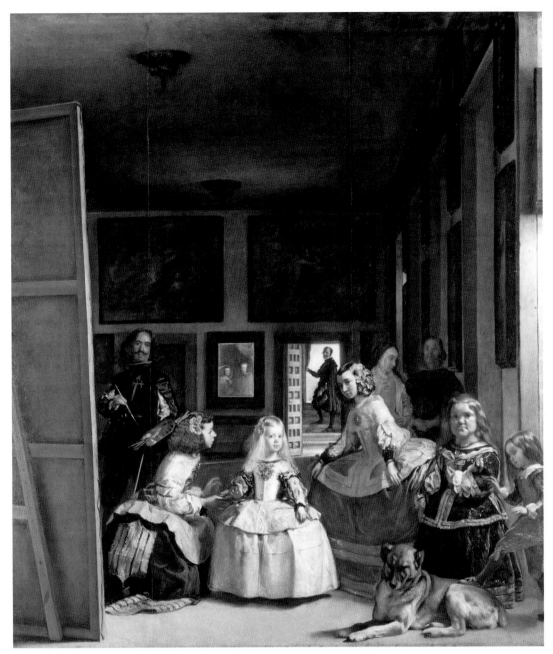

1.10.12a Diego de Silva y Velázquez, *Las Meninas, c.* 1656. Oil on canvas, 10'5¼" × 9'¾".
Museo Nacional del Prado, Madrid, Spain

on the back wall because of its blurry shiny surface: whom does it reflect? (**1.10.12b**, p. 172). Touches of red lead our eye around the painting to significant points of interest: from Margarita's flowers, to the cross on Velázquez's chest, to the red curtain in the mirror on the back wall.

The painting is balanced in various ways (**1.10.12c**, p. 172). All of the figures are placed in the lighter bottom half of the canvas, balanced by the sparseness of the wall and darker ceiling that take up the top half. While the figures at first appear to be arranged chaotically, they are actually placed in several stable pyramidal arrangements. One triangle highlights three of the composition's focal points: the mirror, Margarita, and the man in the doorway. The figures are of different heights and arranged so that our eye is led in a rhythmic line from Velázquez on the left through to the right of the painting: if you trace the heads of the figures in the foreground with your finger, you will sense the visual rhythm.

A *contextual* analysis gives us a better understanding of the content of the work of art by providing information about the time in which it was made. The young girl is the Spanish princess Margarita Habsburg; the

Depth: the degree of recession in perspective

Neutral: colors (such as blacks, whites, grays, and dull gray-browns) made by mixing complementary hues

Palette: the range of colors used by an artist

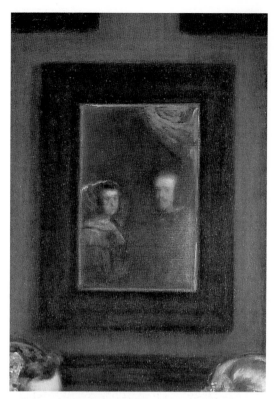

1.10.12b Detail of Diego de Silva y Velázquez, *Las Meninas*

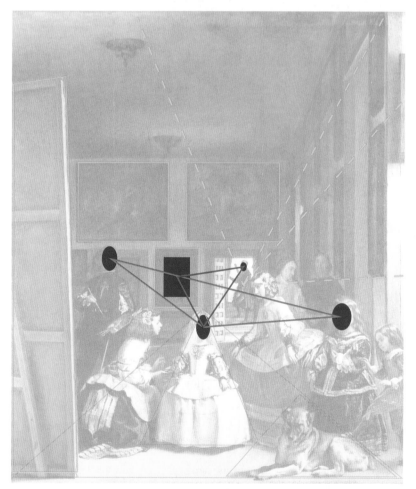

1.10.12c A formal analysis of Las Meninas reveals that the artist carefully organized the objects and people in his painting. Yellow lines show us the balance of shapes in the composition, and the two triangles connect various focal points (picked out in blue)

couple in the mirror are her parents, King Philip IV of Spain and Marianna of Austria. The mysterious man in the doorway is Nieto, the queen's chamberlain. Velázquez uses the mirror and this portrayal of an essential aide to the queen subtly to indicate the presence of the royal couple without violating etiquette, which did not permit showing the king and queen in a portrait with lesser court members.

A *biographical* analysis may explain why Velázquez placed himself in a painting that obliquely shows the presence of the king. One reason was that he was the king's favorite painter and assistant. It was extremely bold of him to paint himself into a scene with the royal family; by doing so, he wished to show his closeness with the king, and to raise his own status.

An *iconographic* analysis focusing only on the cross Velázquez wears, the cross of the Order of Santiago, tells us a lot about the symbol and about the times. Velázquez had a lifelong ambition to become a knight of the order, but the order challenged his membership for decades because he was not a noble, he had some Moorish (Muslim) ancestry, and he was considered a craftsman. The members saw painting as simply a manual craft rather than a liberal (or high-minded) art. In truth, Velázquez did not meet any of the criteria, but after hundreds of supportive interviews, and with the backing of both the king and the pope, the artist was finally knighted in 1659, three years after he painted *Las Meninas*. Historians have found evidence that the king ordered the cross to be painted on after Velázquez's death, to honor the artist for having achieved his lifelong goal.

What Is the Meaning of *Las Meninas*? After considering the various methods of analysis discussed above, scholars have arrived at a hypothesis as to what Velázquez wanted to say. They suggest that the artist was defending the nobility of painting itself. In order to be accepted as a knight, he needed to prove that his skill was not mere craft, but also an intellectual endeavor. Therefore Velázquez created a brilliant illusion of space through his mastery of atmosphere and perspective. Even more boldly, he included the king in a painting that also featured a self-portrait of the artist, demonstrating the king's clear support for the painter. Velázquez's painting is an intentional effort to raise the status of painters, and to raise his own status in Spanish society.

The Influence of *Las Meninas* Artists often study and copy the work of artists they admire, and may use such studies to create works in their own individual style. The Spanish painter Pablo Picasso (1881–1973) reimagined *Las Meninas* many times.

Pablo Picasso did not come to admire Velázquez until late in his own career, when he began to set his skills against the great artists of the past. At the age of seventy-six, Picasso locked himself in a room with a poster of *Las Meninas* and created forty-five paintings in response to Velázquez's masterpiece. In the first work in the **series**, Picasso alters the size of the canvas (**1.10.13**). While mimicking Velázquez, he uses the elements and principles differently. For example, although Picasso does not use linear perspective, he creates a sense of depth by making Nieto small in scale and placing his dark figure in the bright doorway. Velázquez now appears to be floating up to the ceiling, leaving his paintbrushes and palette below. Is Picasso removing the old master to make room for himself?

Other figures are mere suggestions of the forms they were in the original painting. Picasso has broken them down into abstract parts. Margarita is outlined with no sense of volume, and the heads of the figures on the right are just black lines on white circles. The play of light on the figures is similar to the original, but Picasso's approach is more abstract: on the right, he lines up a row of windows that shine a bright white on the figure there (which correlates to the male dwarf in the original). Margarita, highlighted in Velázquez's painting, is of a much lighter value

Series: a group of related artworks that are created as a set

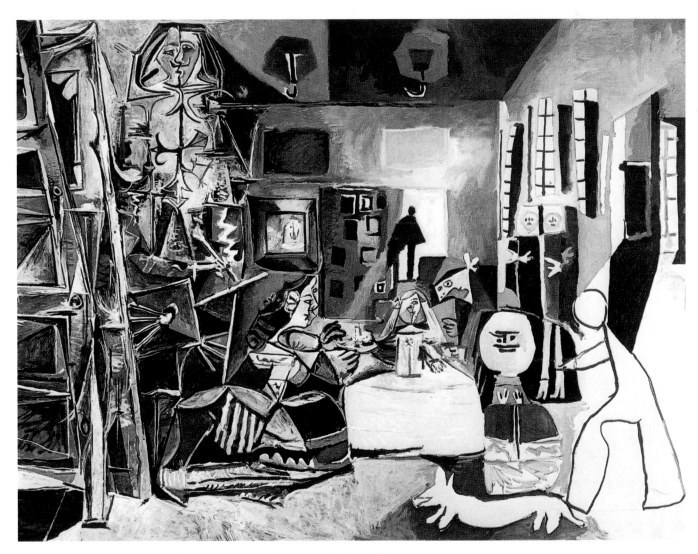

1.10.13 Pablo Picasso, ***Las Meninas***, first in a series, 1957. Oil on canvas, 6′4⅜″ × 8′6⅜″. Museo Picasso, Barcelona, Spain

than the other figures in Picasso's version, emphasizing that she is the most important person in the group. The majority of the rest of the series, in fact, are studies of Margarita specifically. This may relate to Picasso's own life. He first saw *Las Meninas* as a boy, just after his younger sister had died; she had been about the same age as Margarita here. Picasso has totally reinterpreted this artwork to make it his own; he has even replaced the large mastiff in Velázquez's painting with his own dog.

Form and Content in "Chaos Machine"

The drawing "Chaos Machine," *from The Chaos Series* by the Welsh contemporary artist Clive King (b. 1944), is much more abstract than the **representational** painting *Las Meninas*, but its imagery can similarly be accessed through description and analysis. After examining both artworks more fully, we come to a deeper understanding. With *Las Meninas* we initially see imagery we recognize as people in a room, but we do not actually know who those individuals are, the circumstances of their gathering, or the meaning of the symbolism until we have analyzed the imagery and conducted research. Similarly, the lines and shapes in "Chaos Machine" may at first seem meaningless to us and it may be hard to make sense of the drawings (**1.10.14**). As we learn more about the piece, though, this imagery

opens up to tell a story of the artist's memories from an intense childhood experience.

What do we see when we look at "Chaos Machine"? A formal analysis reveals three panels with a **monochromatic** palette. We will be looking at the triptych as a unified whole, but each part could also be considered a separate work on its own. Each section contains similar curving lines in varying densities: smaller and more ribbon-like on the left, larger and more scroll-like in the middle, and smallest and most confetti-like on the right. We also see a repeated ladder shape from varying distances: far away and more fully included on the left, closer and less complete in the middle, closest and most obscure on the right. The ladder functions as a kind of focal point in each panel, surrounded by curving lines filling the space around it. The composition of each panel uses **symmetrical balance**, with matching elements on the left and right sides.

King uses the medium of drawing, specifically pen and ink. The artist feels that drawing allows him to involve the viewer in an "equal physical and emotional engagement" through scale, depth, and intensity. Because each paper is 6 ft. 6 in. tall, somewhat larger than the artist, he works from inside the picture. As he is making the marks, they surround and overwhelm him, much as they do viewers when they look at the piece. The forms

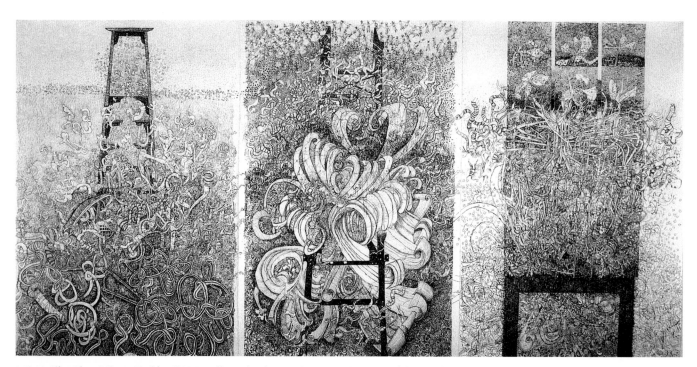

1.10.14 Clive King, "Chaos Machine," 2015–16 (from *The Chaos Series*, an ongoing series of drawings). Black ink on paper, three drawings, each 6'6" × 4'8"

build up over time and create dense areas at the bottom of the left panel, throughout the entire middle panel, and down the center of the right panel.

What Is the Meaning of "Chaos Machine"? A contextual analysis of "Chaos Machine" would include a historical event the artist experienced when he was twelve years old. King grew up near a Welsh coal-mining village called Aberfan (pronounced "ab-air-van"). As a byproduct of the mining, millions of tons of debris from the Merthyr Valley Colliery were deposited on the side of the ridge directly above Aberfan, called Mynydd Merthyr (pronounced "munnith murthur"). These deposits, called spoil heaps or tips, consisted of loose rock and earth. At Mynydd Merthyr the ridge was located over several underground springs. On October 21, 1966 the ground shifted and the tip collapsed, causing a landslide of waste coal and debris that destroyed everything in its wake. The Pantglas Junior School was located in the village below and 116 of its students and 5 teachers were tragically killed in the catastrophe. The timing was especially sad because minutes before the collapse, the students had not been in their classrooms and, had the landslide happened several hours later, they would have already left for the half-term holiday.

Very few people were recovered from the rubble right after the collapse. In total, 144 people died from impact and suffocation, including virtually all the village's children: an entire generation disappeared in the blink of an eye. Residents and school officials had raised complaints and concerns about the dangers associated with the tip for years. The National Coal Board, which operated the mine, was blamed for extreme negligence and paid compensation to families for loss, trauma, and destruction of property. Following the accident, new legislation from Parliament created safety regulations in consultation with mines and quarries.

A *biographical* analysis helps us understand that these drawings represent the artist's memories of the Aberfan disaster. For more than forty years he tried unsuccessfully to interpret his feelings of the experience through figurative approaches. Using a more abstract approach allowed the artist to suggest what he had seen rather than represent it literally. With "Chaos Machine" (and several later artworks), King felt that he had finally come up with a workable solution to express his experience appropriately.

In addition to autobiographical events, King's work explores the uneasy relationships between landscape and industry, and cultural erosion and evolution, by suggesting a chaotic sense of place. An *iconographic analysis* helps us understand the symbolism the artist created. The left panel shows the top of the winding tower, or headframe (the structure above an underground mine), with the debris from the tip rising from below like an explosion. In the center, we are engulfed by the momentum of the coal tip collapsing. On the right, we see wreckage inspired by the crunched-up mess, including windows and doorways, which the artist witnessed during secret visits to the inside of some of the houses and the school after the disaster.

By synthesizing the visual and contextual, biographical, and iconographic information we have gathered about "Chaos Machine," we can suggest an explanation of what King was trying to say. The symbolism in "Chaos Machine" combines the horrors of factual information and personal experience into a vision of a tragedy resulting from human error. After decades of attempting to do this subject justice through realism, the artist found that the ephemeral and suggestive nature of abstraction produced a more fitting expression of both the event and his experience. The simultaneous whimsy, visual intrigue, and violence of the **organic** shapes interweaving through the industrial frame of the mine equipment and exploding around the architecture, create a beautiful and powerful memorial to the victims and the historical moment when their lives were lost.

Organic: having irregular forms and shapes, as though derived from living organisms

Explore Further Engaging with Form and Content

Formal Analysis

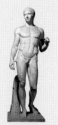

3.1.20 Polykleitos, *Doryphoros* (Roman version), *c.* 120–50 BCE → p. 361

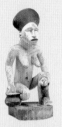

4.3.10 Kneeling female figure, Yombe, late 19th/early 20th century → p. 574

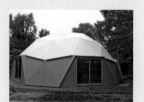

1.1.2b Buckminster Fuller and Anne Hewlett, *Dome Home*, Carbondale, Illinois, 1960 → p. 35

Iconographic Analysis

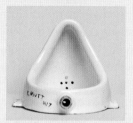

3.6.10a Jan van Eyck, *The Arnolfini Portrait*, 1434 → p. 450

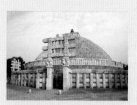

3.10.1 Marcel Duchamp, *Fountain*, 1917 (replica) → p. 523

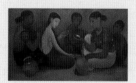

1.8.2 Amrita Sher-Gil, *Bride's Toilet*, 1937 → p. 141

Contextual Analysis

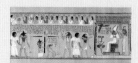

4.2.10 *Book of the Dead of Hunefer*, Egypt, *c.* 1275 BCE → p. 560

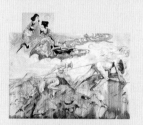

3.3.2 Great Stupa, 3rd century BCE (enlarged *c.* 150–50 BCE) Sanchi, India → p. 392

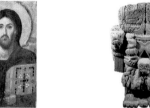

2.2.17 Hung Liu, *Interregnum*, 2002 → p. 204

Analyzing Meaning

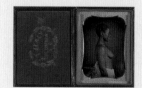

2.8.19 J. T. Zealy, *Delia, country born…*, 1850 → p. 311

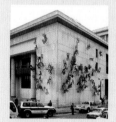

2.10.12 Félix Gonzàlez-Torres, *"Untitled" (Fortune Cookie Corner)*, 1990 → p. 342

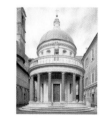

3.4.7 Doris Salcedo, *Noviembre 6 y 7*, 2002 → p. 415

Your turn:
What methods would you use to analyze/critique these artworks?

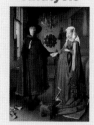

3.2.7 Christ icon, Egypt, 6th century → p. 377

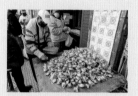

3.4.16 *The Mother Goddess, Coatlicue*, Aztec, *c.* 1487–1520 → p. 419

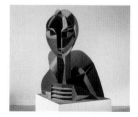

2.5.21 San Pietro in Montorio, Italy, *c.* 1502 → p. 255

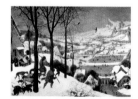

1.9.7 Pieter Bruegel, *Hunters in the Snow*, 1565 → p. 152

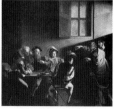

1.3.6 Caravaggio, *The Calling of St. Matthew*, *c.* 1599–1600 → p. 69

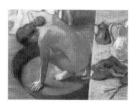

2.1.16 Edgar Degas, *The Tub*, 1886 → p. 187

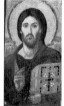

2.4.16 Naum Gabo, *Constructed Head No. 2*, 1916 → p. 239

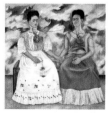

1.1.13 Frida Kahlo, *The Two Fridas*, 1939 → p. 41

Part 2 Media and Processes

Art is a form of visual communication: artists make art because they want to express something. Just as writers consider carefully the form that best expresses what they want to say (a long novel, a brief poem, a play or film script, for example), artists consider carefully the materials and processes available to communicate their visual ideas. In fact, art can be made from almost anything: one contemporary artist has used elephant dung in his paintings. There are certain media and processes that have been commonly used by artists, some of them for thousands of years, but others that have been developed more recently. In this part you will learn how most of the art that you will encounter has been made.

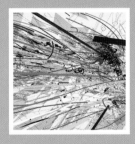

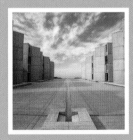

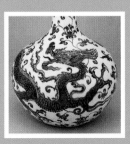

2.1
Drawing

Line: a mark, or implied mark, between two endpoints

Sketch: a rough preliminary version of a work or part of a work

Medium (plural **media**): the material on or from which an artist chooses to make a work of art, for example canvas and oil paint, marble, engraving, video, or architecture

He who pretends to be either painter or engraver without being a master of drawing is an imposter.

(William Blake, English artist and poet)

As William Blake suggests, drawing—defined as the depiction of shapes and forms on a surface, primarily by means of **lines**—is a fundamental artistic skill. Even before we learn to write, we learn to draw; we draw the shape of a cat before we can write the word. Drawing is spontaneous, a convenient way for us to "make our mark" on the world. Like the instinctive crayon marks children make as they explore and develop their fine motor skills, drawing provides a primal outlet for artistic energy and ideas.

Artists draw for many reasons: to define their ideas, to plan for larger projects, to resolve design issues in preparatory **sketches**, and to record their visual observations. Of course, drawings can also be finished works of art in their own right. Drawing is the basis of all visual communication. Most artists and designers continue to develop their drawing skills throughout their lives.

Functions of Drawing

Because drawing is a fundamental skill it is used, to some degree, in every artistic **medium**. Leonardo da Vinci (1452–1519) used drawing to examine the world. His sketchbooks are full of ideas and images, illustrating both his speculative thought and his careful

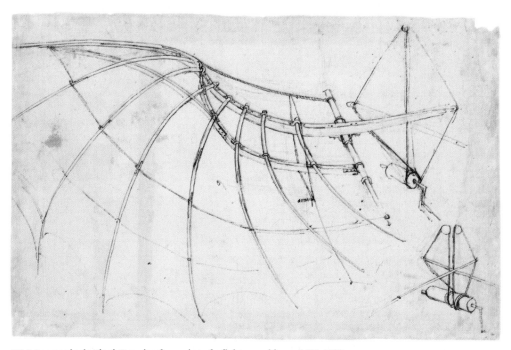

2.1.1 Leonardo da Vinci, *Drawing for a wing of a flying machine*, c. 1478–1480. From the *Codice Atlantico*, fol. 858r. Pen and ink. Biblioteca Ambrosiana, Milan, Italy

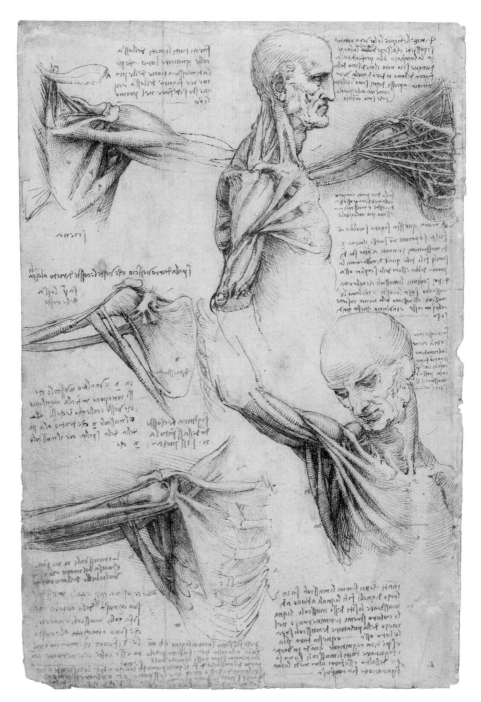

2.1.2 Leonardo da Vinci, *The muscles of the shoulder*, *c.* 1510. Pen and ink with wash over black chalk on paper, 11½ × 7⅞″. Royal Collection, London, England.

observations. Amongst his explorations, Leonardo dissected human bodies and then drew what he saw. He also studied the works of other artists, and observed the effects of light and shadow on a form. He investigated the mechanics of a bird's wing, and considered whether humans might also be able to fly if such mechanics were re-created on a human scale. His drawing of a flying machine illustrates a concept that had never been considered in this way before (**2.1.1**). Drawing enabled Leonardo to express his ideas beyond what could be said in words. Some of Leonardo's most revolutionary drawings depict the interior anatomy of the human body (**2.1.2**). These drawings are especially rare because the Catholic Church banned all acts that desecrated the body, including dissection. Leonardo may have been allowed to record his observations because he practiced his drawing methodically and with great care. Some speculate that the Church was interested in Leonardo's observations as possible evidence of how the human soul resides in the body.

Raphael, *The School of Athens*
Drawing in the Design Process

For the other Raphael
GATEWAYS:
→ see p. 80 and p. 448

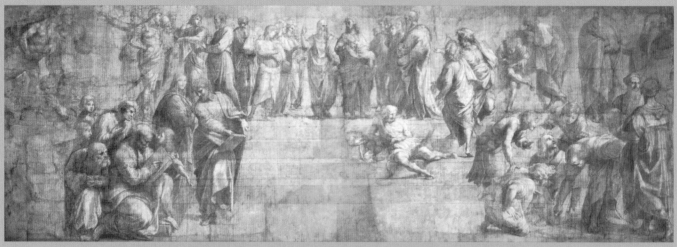

2.1.3a Raphael, Cartoon for *The School of Athens*, *c.* 1509. Charcoal and chalk, 9'4¼" × 26'4⅝".
Biblioteca Ambrosiana, Milan, Italy

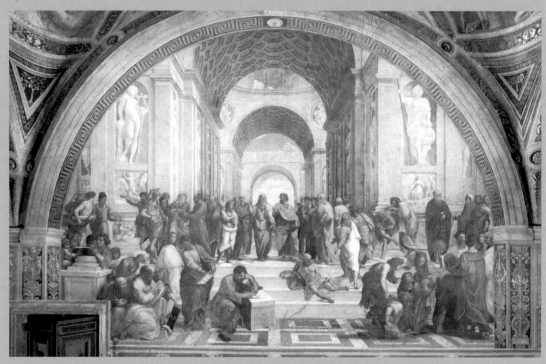

2.1.3b Raphael, *The School of Athens*, 1510–11. Fresco, 16'8" × 25'.
Stanza della Segnatura, Vatican City, Italy

When the Italian painter Raphael (1483–1520) prepared to paint *The School of Athens*, he drew the image in advance (**2.1.3a**), practicing before he tackled the larger work (**2.1.3b**). Raphael's preliminary drawings allowed him to refine his ideas and perfect the image at a smaller scale before investing in the more expensive painting materials he used for the final version.

The artist began the painting process by creating a large drawing of the work, almost the same size as the final painting, to use as the design for a mural. This design, called the **cartoon**, was perforated with small pinholes all along where the lines were drawn. It was then positioned on the wall where Raphael intended to paint the work, and powdered charcoal dust was forced through the small holes in the cartoon's surface, leaving behind an impression of the original drawing. These marks would aid Raphael in drawing the image onto the wall. He applied a thin layer of plaster, re-powdered the charcoal dust through the cartoon if necessary, and then began to paint *The School of Athens*.

Cartoon: a full-scale preparatory drawing for a painting or tapestry; from the Italian *cartone*, meaning "large sheet of paper"

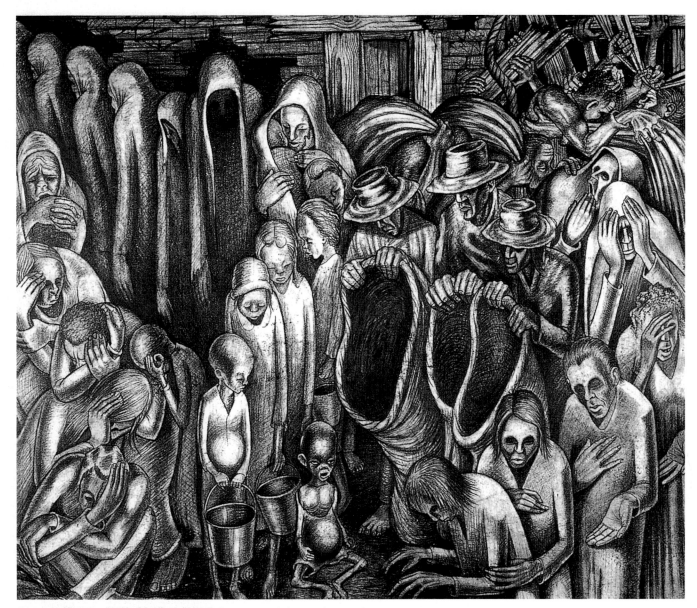

2.1.4 **John Biggers**, *Night of the Poor*, 1949. Preparatory study for mural, Pennsylvania State University

All artists draw for the same reasons as Leonardo: as an end in itself, to think, and to prepare and plan other works. Drawing played an essential role in Raphael's planning of his **fresco** *The School of Athens* (see Gateway: Raphael, **2.1.3a** and **2.1.3b**).

Like Raphael, contemporary artists still use drawing as a way to prepare for larger, more involved works. African American artist John Biggers (1924–2001) used pencil drawing in his preparation process, leading to large, permanent mural works. Such works as *Night of the Poor* (**2.1.4**) highlight how denial of education to the poor has a chilling effect on their future prospects. The finished painting was installed in Burrowes Hall, where Penn State's School of Education is housed. Even though it is a preparatory drawing, Biggers

approached it with the same energy and resolve that an artist might reserve for a grand painting, so the drawing stands as a great work in its own right.

Although most works that are generally considered drawings are done on paper, some notable exceptions exist. For example, watercolor is sometimes classified as a drawing, because it is executed on a heavy paper. **Pastel**, which is sometimes drawn on a rough panel, is occasionally referred to as painting. The surface on which a drawing is executed can affect how it is categorized.

The Materials of Drawing: Paper

Before the invention of paper, drawings were made on papyrus (a plant material), cloth, wood, and animal hide (parchment and

Fresco: a technique in which the artist paints onto freshly applied plaster. From the Italian *fresco*, "fresh"

Pastel: a powdered pigment mixed with gum and used in stick form for drawing

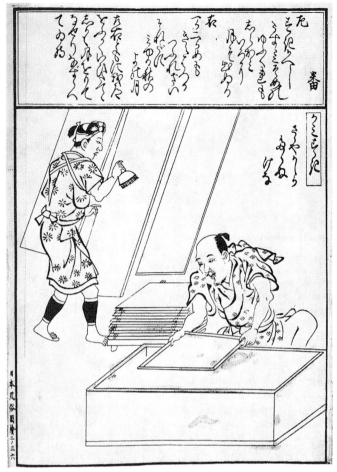

2.1.5 Hishikawa Moronobu, *Papermaking in Japan*, showing the vatman and the paper-drier, 1681. Woodblock print from the four-volume *Wakoku Shōshoku Edzukushi*, 1681

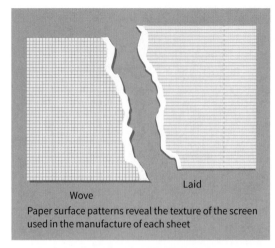

Wove

Laid

Paper surface patterns reveal the texture of the screen used in the manufacture of each sheet

2.1.6 Surface texture of wove and laid paper

Renaissance: a period of cultural and artistic change in Europe from the fourteenth to the seventeenth century

Ground: the surface or background onto which an artist paints or draws

Value: the lightness or darkness of a plane or area

Hatching: the use of non-overlapping parallel lines to convey darkness or lightness

Cross-hatching: the use of overlapping parallel lines to convey darkness or lightness

vellum). Paper was invented in China from around the end of the first century CE by a court official of the Han Dynasty, Cai Lun, who manufactured it from pounded or macerated plant fibers. The image in **2.1.5**, even though it was made more than 1,500 years later, shows how this was done. The fibers are suspended in water and then scooped up into a flat mold with a screen at the bottom, so that the water can escape. The fibers are now bonded enough to each other to keep their shape when they are taken out. The sheet is then pressed and dried.

Over the centuries, improvements were made to the construction of the mold to speed up the process of papermakers flipping out molded sheets of paper to reuse the mold. Hand-made papers are still manufactured this way in many countries, mostly from cotton fiber, although papers are also made of hemp, abaca (a leaf-based fiber derived from a banana-like plant), flax, and other plant fibers.

Papers are also classified by their surface texture and weight. Depending on the construction of the mold, the paper usually has a surface texture described as either wove or laid. The laid texture derives from a screen (bottom of the mold) composed of many parallel rods, like a bamboo mat, whereas the wove texture derives from the use of a grid-like mesh of metal wire or cloth (see **2.1.6**).

Paper in bulk is normally measured by the ream (a quantity of 500 sheets). The standard measurement for defining the character of paper is its weight per ream in the paper's basic sheet size. (For cotton rag paper, the sheet size is usually 17 × 22 in.) For example, if 500 sheets of 17 × 22-in. paper weigh 20 lbs., the paper is referred to as "20 lb." Heavier papers are stronger and usually better to work with, but cost more.

The Materials of Drawing: Dry Media

When creating a drawing, an artist must first choose whether to draw using dry media or wet media. Dry media offer the artist some unique and versatile properties.

Silverpoint

Almost every metal will leave a mark on a fibrous surface. Artists during the Italian **Renaissance** used lead, tin, copper, and silver to draw images. The most common of these drawing metals was silverpoint.

Silverpoint is a piece of silver wire set in some type of a holder, usually wood, to make the wire easier to grasp and control. The artist hones the end of the wire to a sharp point. Because of the hardness of the silver, artists can create finely detailed drawings. Historically, artists have drawn with silverpoint on wood primed with a thin coating of bone ash. This creates a white **ground** for the light **value** of the silver. Because silver tarnishes, the drawing becomes darker and the image more pronounced over time. Working on colored paper creates distinctive effects and was particularly popular in Renaissance Italy (*c*. 1400–1600).

In *Heads of the Virgin and Child*, a silverpoint drawing by Raphael, the artist uses **hatching** and **cross-hatching** to create a stronger dark value (**2.1.7**). Because silverpoint has such a light value and is usually drawn with very thin lines, much of the pale paper is exposed. By closely overlapping many parallel lines across each other, Raphael covers more of the paper, creating the illusion of a darker value. Many artists use this technique to darken values and create the effect of shading (**2.1.8**).

Pencil

Everyone knows what pencils are. We like them because we can erase and correct errors. This makes the pencil a valuable tool for artists as well. Most artists' pencils differ from those used for writing and are categorized by their relative hardness or softness.

A deposit of solid graphite—which looks and writes like lead, but without its weight—was discovered in the mid-1500s and gave rise to the manufacture of the basic pencil we know today.

Pencils have different degrees of hardness (**2.1.9**). The softer the pencil, the darker the mark, or grade, and the quicker the pencil loses its point. The B or black graphite pencils are softer and darker than the H series. Number 2 (HB to be precise) pencils are the writing tools used by nearly every American elementary-school student. The H or hard graphite pencils create a relatively light mark. This type of pencil is useful when an artist is doing layout work and does not want pencil lines to show in the final product. Artists carefully choose the grade of the pencil lead they use.

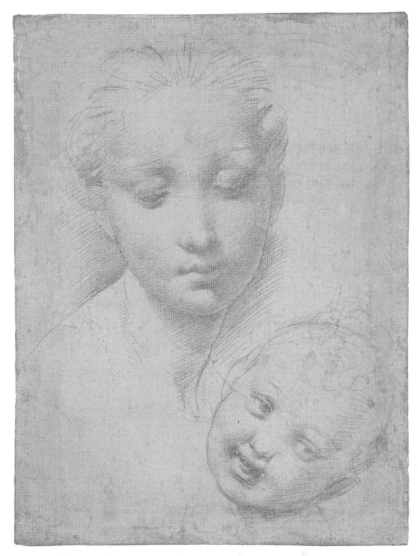

2.1.7 Raphael, ***Heads of the Virgin and Child***, *c*. 1509–11. Silverpoint on pink prepared paper, 5⅝ × 4⅜". British Museum, London, England

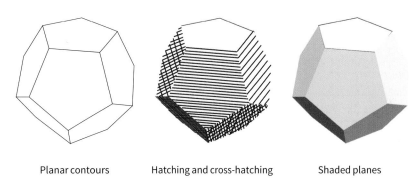

Planar contours　　　Hatching and cross-hatching　　　Shaded planes

2.1.8 How hatching and cross-hatching lines are used to create the effect of shading

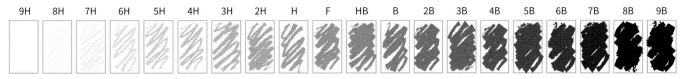

| 9H | 8H | 7H | 6H | 5H | 4H | 3H | 2H | H | F | HB | B | 2B | 3B | 4B | 5B | 6B | 7B | 8B | 9B |

2.1.9 Pencil hardness scale from 9H to 9B

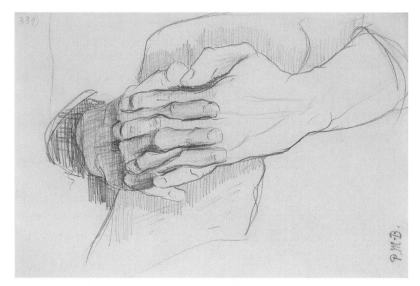

2.1.10 Paula Modersohn-Becker, *Gefaltete Hände* **(study),** 1897–98. Pencil, 10¼ × 15¼".

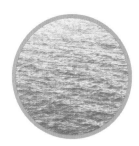

The possibilities of graphite drawing can be seen in Vija Celmins, *Untitled (Ocean),* 1977:

➔ see **1.8.5,** p. 142

The drawing of hands by the German artist Paula Modersohn-Becker (1876–1907) shows how an artist can vary the pressure of a pencil line to suggest **texture** and create **emphasis** in a drawing (**2.1.10**). Modersohn-Becker has used thick dark lines to imply darkness and thin light lines to suggest lightness. The dark value of the back of the hand on the left (from the viewer's vantage point), where the pencil has been pressed hard, concentrates our attention on that side of the image, while the different sets of straight overlapping light lines add depth. In further **contrast**, notice how differently the artist handles the graphite in the areas representing light compared with the shadowed areas. In this drawing, Modersohn-Becker sketches two intertwined hands with both delicacy and strength.

Color Pencil

Color pencil is manufactured much like the traditional graphite pencil, but the mixture that makes up the lead contains more wax and **pigment**. Color pencils are used just like graphite pencils, although their marks may be harder to erase or alter. The Mexican artist Martin Ramirez (1885–1963) exploits the richness of colored pencil when he creates a work. In *Untitled* (**2.1.11**) the artist pushes the waxy shaft of **color** into the fibers of the paper, along with some watercolor and crayon, to achieve a patterned scene of urban life.

Charcoal

Charcoal has long been an important material in the history of drawing: samples from cave

Texture: the surface quality of a work, for example fine/coarse, detailed/lacking in detail

Emphasis: the principle of drawing attention to particular content in a work

Contrast: a drastic difference between such elements as color or value (lightness/darkness) when they are presented together

Pigment: the colored material used in paints. Often made from finely ground minerals

Color: the optical effect caused when reflected white light of the spectrum is divided into separate wavelengths

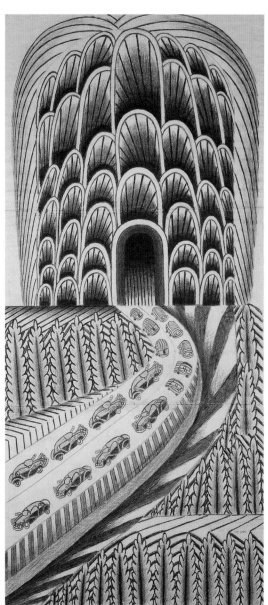

2.1.11 Martin Ramirez, *Untitled,* 1954. Graphite, colored pencil, watercolor, and crayon on paper, 52⅕ × 24". Solomon R. Guggenheim Museum, New York

drawings in France have been dated back to 30,000 BCE. Unlike pencils and silverpoint, charcoal smudges easily, creates lines that can be easily shaped and altered, usually has strong dark value, and is soft compared to metal-based drawing materials. Artists choose charcoal as a drawing material when they want to express strong dark tones, add interest to a surface, and make something look solid rather than linear.

Two types of charcoal are common. Vine charcoal is made from thin vine branches and is very soft and easily erased. Compressed charcoal, to which a binding agent, such as wax, is sometimes added, is much denser. To make charcoal, finger-length pieces of wood (often dried willow) are placed inside an airtight

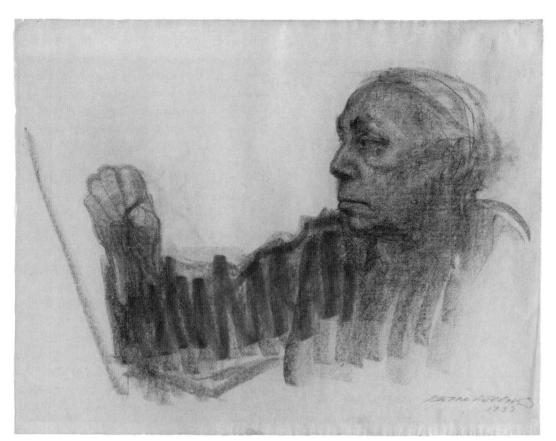

2.1.12 Käthe Kollwitz, *Self-Portrait, Drawing*, 1933. Charcoal on paper, 18¾ × 25".
National Gallery of Art, Washington, D.C.

Tooth: the textural quality of a paper surface, for holding drawing media in place

container (to prevent the loss of important binding chemicals) and heated in an oven until all the wood has been burned.

To draw with charcoal, an artist drags the stick across a fibrous surface, usually paper, leaving a soft-edged line. By using just the end, an artist can create thin strokes; by using the side, it is possible to cover a lot of surface quickly. The amount of pressure an artist exerts while drawing controls the lightness or darkness of the stroke. Sandpaper can be used to sharpen the stick for more detail. An artist can achieve a soft visual effect by rubbing the newly charcoaled drawing surface with a bare finger, some tissue paper, or a rolled-paper cone called a tortillon, made expressly for this purpose.

Charcoal is so soft that the texture of the paper's surface—even the drawing board's texture below the paper—profoundly affects the image. Charcoal works best on paper with a fairly rough texture (known as **tooth**), which catches the charcoal better in its fibers.

Charcoal portraits by the German artist Käthe Kollwitz (1867–1945) and the French artist Léon Augustin Lhermitte (1844–1925) show how artists work with the characteristics of the medium (**2.1.12** and **2.1.13**).

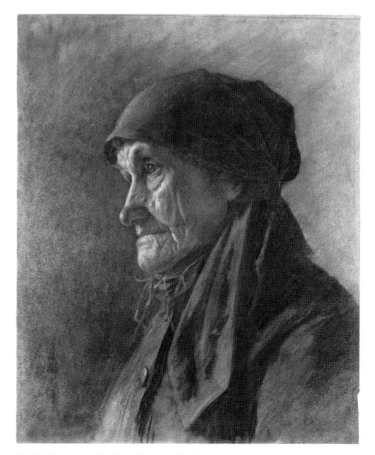

2.1.13 Léon Augustin Lhermitte, *An Elderly Peasant Woman*, c. 1878.
Charcoal on wove paper, 18¾ × 15⅝". National Gallery of Art, Washington, D.C.

In Kollwitz's self-portrait, we feel a sense of energy from the way she applies the charcoal. Although she renders her own face and hand realistically, in the space between we see the nervous energy connecting the eye to the hand. Kollwitz draws with a spontaneous burst of charcoal marks along the arm, in **expressive** contrast to the more considered areas of the head and hand.

In *An Elderly Peasant Woman*, Lhermitte works with the characteristics of charcoal to describe his **subject** carefully. Each line and blemish on this woman's face has been carefully rendered. The charcoal's dark value accentuates the contrast between the **highlights** in the face and the overall darkened tone of the work. It even carefully preserves the light reflected in her eye. Lhermitte has controlled charcoal's inherent smudginess to offer an intimate view of the effects of aging.

Although there is precise detail in both drawings, each artist allows the "personality" of the charcoal into the softened **background** through smudges and irregular soft marks.

The Chinese-born artist Zhang Chun Hong (b. 1971) has utilized both charcoal and graphite for dramatic effect in the work *Life Strands* (**2.1.14**). In this work, charcoal provides the deep, dark values that describe a long strand of braided hair. Because charcoal has a rich, dark softness, the tightly interlocked braid can cascade down the page into a scatter of gestural marks where the hair has been unleashed from its binding. The strand metaphorically represents the passage of time from the dark, full hair of childhood to the grayed and thinning hair of old age. In this drawing Zhang masterfully uses drawing on a long Chinese scroll to make parallels between life and art.

Chalk, Pastel, and Crayon

Sticks of chalk, pastel, and crayon are made by combining pigment and **binder**. Traditional binders include oil, wax, gum arabic, and glues. The type of binder gives each material a unique character. Chalks, pastels, and crayons can be prepared in any color. Chalk is powdered calcium carbonate mixed with a gum arabic (a type of tree sap) binder. Pastel is pigment combined with gum arabic, wax, or oil, while crayon is pigment combined with wax. Conté crayon, a variation invented by Nicolas-Jacques Conté (1755–1805), who was a French painter and army officer, is a heavily

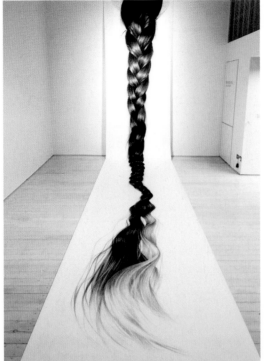

For the final result of Michelangelo's chalk study for *The Libyan Sibyl* in the Sistine Chapel:
→ see **2.2.6**, p. 197

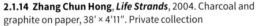

2.1.14 Zhang Chun Hong, *Life Strands*, 2004. Charcoal and graphite on paper, 38′ × 4′11″. Private collection

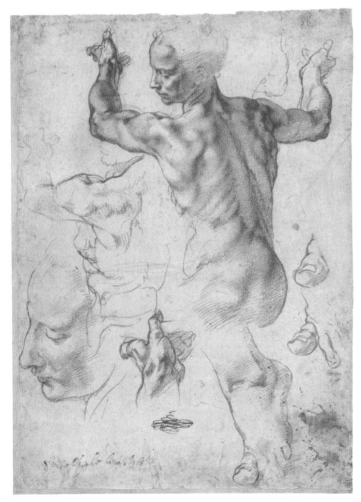

2.1.15 Michelangelo, *Studies for the Libyan Sibyl*, 1510–11. Red chalk, 11⅜ × 8⅜″. Metropolitan Museum of Art, New York

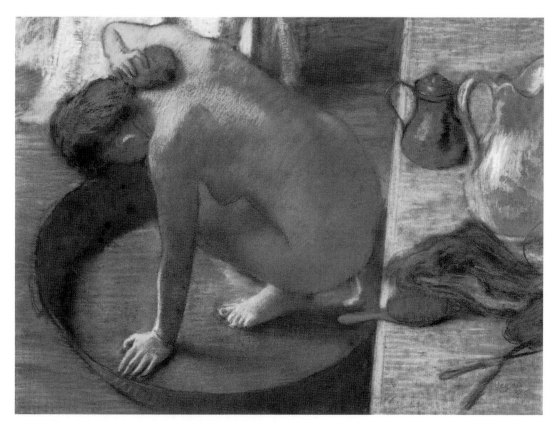

2.1.16 Edgar Degas, *The Tub*, 1886. Pastel, 23⅝ × 32⅝″. Musée d'Orsay, Paris, France

pigmented crayon sometimes manufactured with graphite.

For their preparatory sketches, artists of the Renaissance used colored chalks, in particular a red chalk known as sanguine. The Italian artist Michelangelo Buonarroti (1475–1564) used this red chalk for his *Studies for the Libyan Sibyl* (**2.1.15**), which he made in preparation for painting the Sistine Chapel ceiling in Rome. Michelangelo uses hatching and cross-hatching (**2.1.8**, p. 183) to build up the values and give the figure depth. The artist's study concentrates on the muscular definition of the back and on the face, shoulder, and hand, and gives repeated attention to the detail of the big toe. These details are essential to making this twisting pose convincing, and Michelangelo spent extra time refining them.

The French artist Edgar Degas (1834–1917) is noted for his pastel studies that stand as finished works of art. In *The Tub*, he lays down intermittent strokes of pastel in different colors (**2.1.16**). He takes advantage of the material's charcoal-like softness to blend the colors, thus giving them a rich complexity and creating a variety of contrasting textures. In pastel as in painting, Degas was a master of re-creating the effects of light and color seen in nature.

In the Conté crayon drawing *The Ploughing*, the French artist Georges Seurat (1859–1891) uses expressive marks to build up value and create depth (**2.1.17**). Seurat designates the **foreground** by using darker values; he allows the lightness of the paper to be more dominant

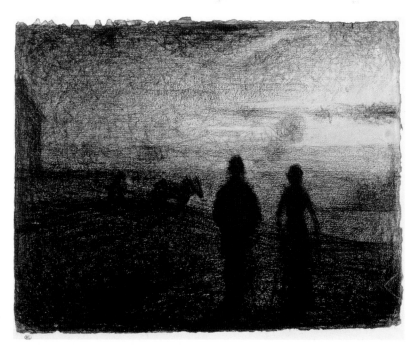

2.1.17 Georges Seurat, *The Ploughing*, 1882–83. Conté crayon, 9⅔ × 12½″. Musée D'Orsay, Paris, France

in areas he wants to recede into the distance. The shaded silhouetted figures in this work look as if they are the subjects of a dim nineteenth-century photograph. Seurat exploits the rich blackness available in dark Conté to add depth and dramatic contrast to his design.

Erasers and Fixatives

Erasers are not only used for correction but also to create light marks in areas already drawn. In this way the artist can embellish highlights by working from the dark to light.

Erasers can be used to create works of art by destroying the marks made by an artist. In 1953 the artist Robert Rauschenberg (1925–2008) created a new work of art by erasing a drawing by Willem de Kooning (**2.1.18**). Rauschenberg, a young, unknown artist at that time, approached the famous De Kooning (1904–1997) and asked if he could erase one of his drawings. De Kooning agreed, understanding what the younger artist had in mind. But, in order to make it more difficult, De Kooning gave Rauschenberg a drawing made with charcoal, oil paint, pencil, and crayon. It took Rauschenberg nearly a

month to erase it, but he did so, leaving a drawing on the back of the work intact. Some in the art world dubbed him "L'Enfant Terrible," which means a young person who behaves badly, but Rauschenberg's idea was to create a performed work of **Conceptual art** and display the result. Conceptual art, like Rauschenberg's modification of a De Kooning drawing, places emphasis on the idea, rather than the visual image. Since the drawing material in the work had been trapped in the fibers of the paper, minute parts of the image survived the erasure. This act created a new, collaborative work resulting from the original additive drawing by De Kooning and the subtractive method used by Rauschenberg.

A fixative is a type of coating that can be applied to a drawing to preserve its appearance by making the dry medium adhere to the surface of the paper. Once an artist has applied a dry medium and manipulated it by smudging, marking, or erasing, they can apply a fixative to set the image. Because artists usually need to make changes throughout the drawing process, most use a workable fixative that can be removed by erasing the surface of the coating. Most commercial fixatives used today are available in an aerosol can or spray bottle for easy and even application.

The Materials of Drawing: Wet Media

The wet media used in drawings are applied with brushes or pens. Wet media dry or harden as the liquid evaporates.

Ink

Ink is a favorite of artists because of its permanence, precision, and strong dark color. There are many types of ink, each with its own individual character.

Carbon ink, made by mixing soot with water and gum, has been in use in China and India since around 2500 BCE. This type of ink tended to discolor over time and could become smudged in moist or humid environments. A contemporary version of carbon ink, called India (or Indian) ink, is a favorite of comic-book artists.

Most European ink drawings from the Renaissance to the present day are made with iron gall ink. Gall ink is prized for its near-permanence and rich black color. It is manufactured from a mixture of tannin (from oak galls—parasitic growths on oak trees), iron

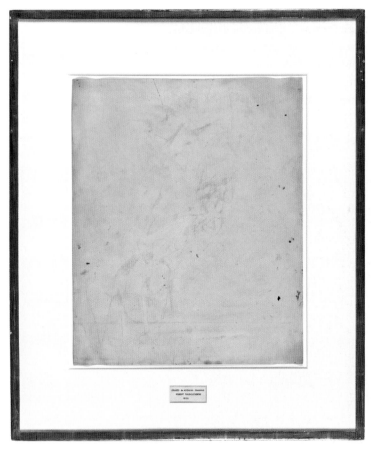

2.1.18 Robert Rauschenberg, *Erased de Kooning Drawing*, 1953. Traces of ink and crayon on paper, in gold-leaf frame, 25¼ × 21¾ × ½". San Francisco Museum of Modern Art, California

sulfate, gum arabic, and water. Gall ink is not entirely lightfast, however, and tends to lighten to brown after many years.

Other types of fluid media include bister, which is derived from wood soot and usually a yellow-brown color, and sepia, a brown medium that is derived from the secretions of cuttlefish.

Brush Drawing

Because ink is a liquid medium, it can also be applied with a brush. The ancient Chinese used brush and ink for both writing and drawing. Even today, children throughout East Asia who are learning to write must learn to control a brush effectively, in much the same way that students in Europe and the Americas learn to use pens and pencils.

East Asian artists use the same brush for writing and drawing. These brushes are made with a bamboo shaft and either ox, goat, horse, or wolf hair. Traditionally, Asian artists use a stick of solid ink that they hold upright and grind on a special ink stone with a small amount of water. As the ink reaches the desired consistency, it is pushed into a shallow reservoir at the rear of the stone. Artists wet the brush by dipping it into this reservoir, and then adjust the shape and charge of the brush by stroking it on the flat of the grinding stone. They can readily adjust the dilution of the ink with water to create an infinite range of grays. This is called a wash, and it allows the artist to control value and texture.

In **2.1.19** the fourteenth-century Chinese artist Wu Zhen (sometimes spelled Wu Chen) (1280–1354) uses brush, ink, and wash to create a masterpiece of simplicity. This finely planned design contains carefully controlled brushstrokes as well as loose, freer ink applications, thereby bringing together two opposing influences and reflecting the central principle of Daoism, a belief in the importance of balanced opposites. Because the artist uses only a few shapes, the arrangement of the bamboo leaves becomes like a series of letters in a word or sentence. Wu achieves the changing dark and light values by adding water to create a wash and lighten the ink. This work was intended as a model for Wu's son to follow as he learned the art of brushwork from his father.

In his **preparatory study** for a painting of the same name, *The Raising of Lazarus*, the Italian artist Guercino's (1591–1666) expressive brushstrokes give us a feeling of the power of the moment when, according to the Bible,

Preparatory study: a drawing or painting that was used to practice or to prepare for a larger artwork

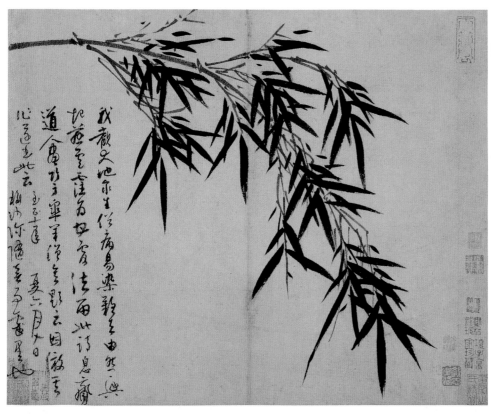

2.1.19 Wu Zhen, leaf from an album of bamboo drawings, 1350. Ink on paper, 16 × 21″.
National Palace Museum, Taipei, Taiwan

Frida Kahlo, *The Two Fridas*
Artist Sketchbooks

For the other Kahlo
GATEWAYS:
→ see p. 41 and p. 643

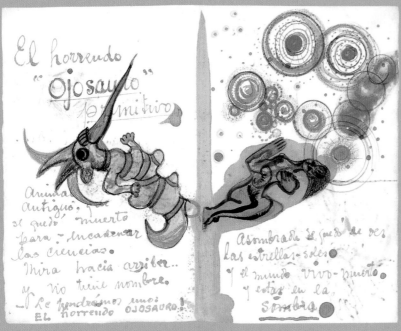

2.1.20 Frida Kahlo, pages from the artist's diary, c. 1944–54

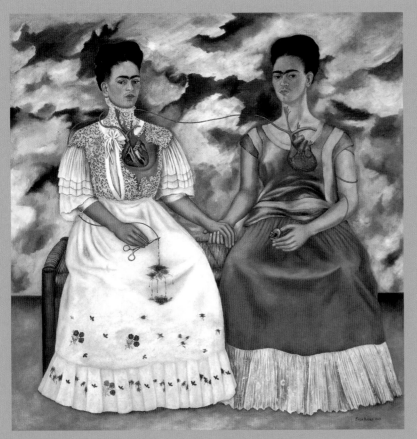

2.1.21 Frida Kahlo, *The Two Fridas*, 1939. Oil on canvas, 5'8" × 5'8". Museo de Arte Moderno, Mexico City, Mexico

While the Mexican painter Frida Kahlo (1907–1954) was suffering from the effects of childhood polio and a disabling back injury, she spent time reflecting on her life experiences in sketches she drew in a diary (**2.1.20**). Her diary was like many others in that she wrote about people she had met, relationship struggles, and expressed her opinions on a variety of issues. But Kahlo's diary was different because it was filled with richly colored drawings of the people she knew, influences in her life, and many self-portraits.

Like her double portrait *The Two Fridas* (**2.1.21**), Kahlo reveals her most intimate experiences through these sketches, which express the pain and happiness that permeated her life. These diary pages are titled "*El horrendo 'Ojosauro' primitivo*" (horrible, monstrous "Eyesaurus") and contain a sketch of an imagined Eyesaurus monster with a long, pointed snout. The sketched monster visually connects the two pages, much in the same way that the veins connect the two images of Frida. The horrible monster stands as a witness to, and a symbol of, the many painful operations and medical procedures that Frida endured during her forty-seven years of life. In *The Two Fridas*, Kahlo pushes the anatomy of the human heart to dominate the double portrait, accentuating the physiological dependence that her conflicting dual ethnic identity—European and Mexican—has had on her declining health. Like the Eyesaurus in her diary, the heart is an ominous reminder of the limitations of the flesh.

The Eyesaurus monster was created with watercolor, a favorite medium of Kahlo in her final decade of life. Because her health was failing, Kahlo's movement was limited, but she could still express her ideas through her diary. The sophisticated design of these pages reflects a mastery of watercolor sketches in combination with text and a vivid imagination that was both delightful and horrible.

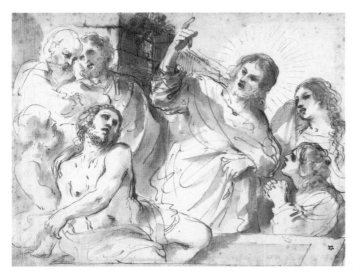

2.1.22 Guercino (Giovanni Francesco Barbieri), *The Raising of Lazarus*, 1619. Pen and brown ink, brush and brown wash, over traces of black chalk, 8 × 10⅔". Metropolitan Museum of Art, New York

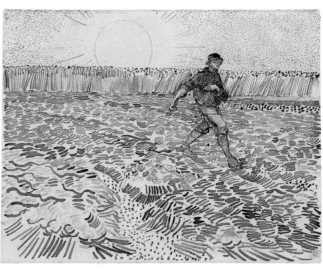

2.1.23 Vincent van Gogh, *Sower with Setting Sun*, 1888. Pen and brown ink, 9⅝ × 12⅝". Van Gogh Museum, Amsterdam, The Netherlands

Christ revives a dead man (**2.1.22**). The ink wash that Guercino uses creates a sense of depth by contrasting the dark values of the top middle with the glowing light surrounding the central figures.

Quill and Pen

Traditionally, a quill—the shaft of a bird's feather, or a similarly hollow reed—is carved to form a point, used to apply the ink. A slit, running parallel to the shaft, helps control its rate of flow. The modern version is a pen with a metal nib. The artist can control the flow of the ink by pressing harder or more softly. Apart from choosing different widths of nib, the artist can further increase or decrease the width of the drawn line by holding the pen at different angles. Often, pen-and-ink drawings employ hatching and cross-hatching to create variations in value (**2.1.8**, p. 183).

The Dutch artist Vincent van Gogh (1853–1890) uses a reed pen and brown ink for his *Sower with Setting Sun* (**2.1.23**). By changing the way he applies his pen strokes and by controlling their width, he creates an undulating, restless design. Van Gogh's emphatic direction of line expresses the characteristic energy of his work.

Life Drawing

Life drawing is the practice of drawing from a live model, as opposed to using photographs, plaster **casts**, or other existing artworks as source material. We associate this process with nude models, but life drawing can also involve animals, plants, and architecture. Life drawing is one of the core skills that art students learn. In addition to the extended study of live models, two types of introductory drawing methods are popular in the teaching of life drawing: gesture and **contour**.

Gesture Drawing

Gesture drawing aims to identify and react to the main visual and expressive characteristics of a form. Since artists often confront changing subjects and situations, capturing the energy and dynamics of the moment is the essential goal of gesture drawing.

The Swiss artist Alberto Giacometti (1901–1966) practiced gesture drawing in a way that exemplifies its function (**2.1.24**). Giacometti would capture a moment in time by focusing on the energy of the subject in front of him.

Cast: a sculpture or artwork made by pouring a liquid (for example molten metal or plaster) into a mold

Contour: an edge or outline that defines a form, but not necessarily the complete outline of a shape

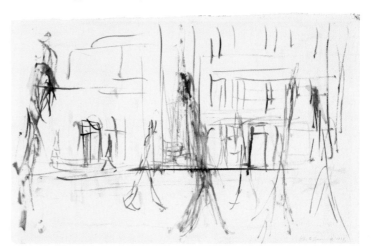

2.1.24 Alberto Giacometti, *The City Square*, 1949. Ink and colored ink on paper, 12⅜ × 20⅛". MoMA, New York

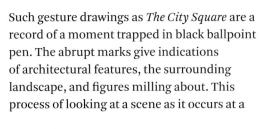

A vivid color ink drawing with gestural lines is Jiha Moon's *Mystery Myo—frustration is one of the great things in what you do*, 2010:
→ see **3.10.10**, p. 528

Such gesture drawings as *The City Square* are a record of a moment trapped in black ballpoint pen. The abrupt marks give indications of architectural features, the surrounding landscape, and figures milling about. This process of looking at a scene as it occurs at a precise moment challenges an artist to work holistically, capturing all related interacting parts of a scene. Giacometti would often execute these drawings in his sketchbook, or on scraps of paper that were to hand.

The energy of the human figure is evident in *Muscular Dynamism* (**2.1.25**), by the Italian artist Umberto Boccioni (1882–1916). In this gestural drawing, the movement of the body is implied by the undulating strokes of chalk and charcoal. The **rhythms** of the **composition** lead our eye through a series of changing curves and values that give us a sense of the figure's energy. Like Giacometti, Boccioni is primarily interested in capturing the essence of movement by reacting to the subject and employing gestural movement of the human hand.

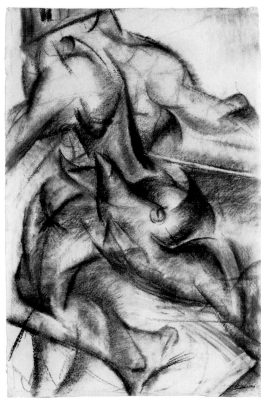

2.1.25 Umberto Boccioni, *Muscular Dynamism*, 1913. Pastel and charcoal on paper, 34 × 23¼". MoMA, New York

Contour Drawing

Contour drawing aims to register the essential qualities of three-dimensional form by rendering an edge, or contour, of an object. Artists use contour drawing to sharpen their hand–eye coordination and gain an intimate understanding of form, while increasing their sensitivity to essential detail. For example, contour drawing can help an artist copy the shape of a leaf as faithfully as possible by forcing them to focus on the subtleties of the object's shape. Because the artist concentrates their attention on a single point and incrementally progresses slowly along the visible edge, attributes of the subject may be slightly exaggerated, bringing attention to otherwise-overlooked visual cues. If the artist follows the edge with careful precision until it meets the starting point, they may create an **outline** of the object, rendering a complete shape. Contour drawing can also help an artist to identify the changing **planes** that make up the surface of a three-dimensional object.

A wonderful example of contour drawing is illustrated by **2.1.26**, *Mother and Child*, by the Austrian artist Egon Schiele (1890–1918). If you look carefully at the long line that describes the right side of the woman's back, you will see many subtle changes in line direction, indicating the stretching muscles that the mother is using as she embraces her child. The economy of this single line carries so much descriptive information that the artist brilliantly opts to allow it to support the entire right side of the composition.

2.1.26 Egon Schiele, *Mother and Child*, 1918. Black Conté crayon on paper, 11¾ × 14⅝"

Explore Further Drawing

Dry Media

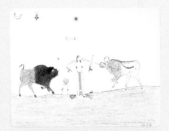

3.4.25 Wo-Haw, *Wo-Haw between Two Worlds*, c. 1875–77 → p. 424

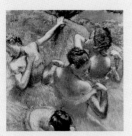

3.8.12 Edgar Degas, *Blue Dancers*, c. 1898, → p. 489

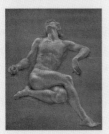

1.3.5a Paul Cadmus, *Male Nude NM32*, 1967 → p. 68

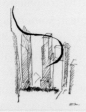

2.5.2 Fumihiko Maki, sketch of Four World Trade Center, 2006 → p. 245

Wet Media

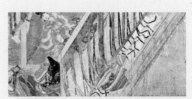

3.3.18 Scene from the *Tale of Genji*, first half of 12th century → p. 403

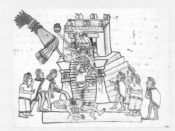

3.4.15 Aztec human sacrifice, from *Codex Magliabechiano*, 16th century → p. 419

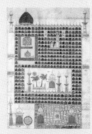

3.2.18 *View of the Sanctuary at Medina*, 17th or 18th century → p. 384

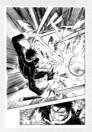

1.1.9 CLAMP, page from the *Tsubasa RESERVoir CHRoNiCLE*, 2007 → p. 39

Mixed Media

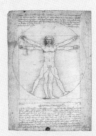

4.4.1 Leonardo da Vinci, *Vitruvian Man*, c. 1490 → p. 580

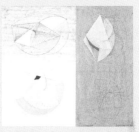

1.1.15 Barbara Hepworth, *Drawing for Sculpture*, 1941 → p. 42

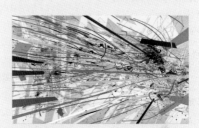

2.2.22 Julie Mehretu, *Excerpt (Suprematist Evasion)*, 2003 → p. 207

3.10.20b Mel Chin, *Operation Paydirt…* project, 2008 → p. 536

Your turn
How is drawing used in these works?

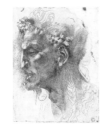

1.3.8 Michelangelo, *Head of a Satyr*, c. 1520–30 → p. 70

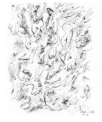

1.1.16 André Masson, *Automatic Drawing*, 1925–26 → p. 43

1.8.5 Vija Celmins, *Untitled (Ocean)*, 1977 → p. 142

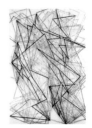

1.1.14 Mel Bochner, *Vertigo*, 1982 → p. 42

2.2
Painting

Medium (plural **media**): the material on or from which an artist chooses to make a work of art, for example canvas and oil paint, marble, engraving, video, or architecture

Color: the optical effect caused when reflected white light of the spectrum is divided into separate wavelengths

Scale: the size of an object or artwork relative to another object or artwork, or to a system of measurement

Pigment: the colored material used in paints. Often made from finely ground minerals

Binder: a substance that makes pigments adhere to a surface

Renaissance: a period of cultural and artistic change in Europe from the fourteenth to the seventeenth century

Lapis lazuli: a bright-blue semiprecious stone containing sodium aluminum silicate and sulphur

Polymer: a chemical compound commonly referred to as plastic

Oil paint: paint made of pigment suspended in oil

When most of us think of art, painting is the **medium** that most often comes to mind. Perhaps this is not surprising, since artists have painted surfaces of many kinds for tens of thousands of years. In prehistoric times, artists painted on the walls of caves. The temples of ancient Greece and Mexico were painted in bright **colors**, although what remains now is muted by comparison. About 500 years ago, artists began painting on linen cloth, a surface that was lighter and easier to handle. Modern muralists and graffiti artists also paint on walls. Of course, artists also paint on a much smaller and more intimate **scale**, on a stretched canvas or a sheet of paper. The artistic possibilities that paint offers are almost limitless, and the effects achieved are often amazing.

There are many kinds of paints, suitable for different purposes, but they all share the same components. Paint in its most basic form is composed of **pigment** suspended in a liquid **binder** that dries after it has been applied and holds pigment in place. Pigment gives paint its color. Traditionally, pigments have been extracted from minerals, soils, vegetable matter, and animal by-products. The color umber, for example, originated from the brown clay soil of Umbria in Italy. Ultramarine—from the Latin *ultramarinus*, beyond the sea—is the deep, luxurious blue favored for the sky color in some **Renaissance** painting; it was ground from **lapis lazuli**, a blue stone found in Afghanistan. In recent times, pigments have been manufactured by chemical processes. The bright cadmium reds and yellows, for instance, are by-products of zinc extraction.

Pigments by themselves do not stick to a surface. They need a liquid binder—a substance that allows the paint to be applied and then dries, leaving the pigment permanently attached. Just as there are many kinds of pigments, there are many binders: traditionally beeswax, egg yolk, vegetable oils and gums, and water; in modern times, art-supply manufacturers have developed such complex chemical substances as **polymers**. Painters also use solvents for different reasons, for example adding turpentine to **oil paint** to make it thinner.

Artists use many kinds of tools to help them paint. Brushes are the tools most commonly associated with painting. Traditionally made from animal hair, such as hog bristle or sable fur, it is now common to see brushes made of vinyl and polyester. Although historically brushes have been the most popular tools for paint, some artists have used compressed air to spray paint onto their chosen surface; others have spread it around with a palette knife as if they were buttering toast. Sometimes they have poured it from buckets, or have ridden across the canvas on a bicycle the wheels of which were covered in it; others have dipped their fingers, hands, or entire body in it so they can make their marks.

Paint is an attractive and versatile material with a long and fascinating history; artists have continually experimented with and developed it as a medium. In turn, such developments have reflected the changing pace and values in people's way of life. In the prehistoric era, with little scientific knowledge and no technology available to them, artists used saliva or animal fat to fix pigment made from colored mineral soil and ash from fires to mark and decorate their dwellings. As societies became more settled, domestic, and sophisticated, artists employed wax (**encaustic**) and egg (**tempera**) as binding agents for mineral pigments; eventually, artists who wanted their work to endure developed **fresco** techniques, using pigment with plaster to embed their paintings permanently in the walls of buildings. In East Asian countries, artists painted using the delicate medium of ink to express the complexities of human experience. In the fifteenth and sixteenth centuries, travel became more common and widespread due to, in part, the endeavors of the famous explorers of the era.

As travel became more accessible, European artists moved from painting principally on wood panels with tempera, to painting with oil on linen canvases, which could be transported much more easily and could support larger works. Oil was the dominant paint type used by artists until the quickening pace of the modern world and the industrialization of life encouraged artists to favor such quick-drying paint types as watercolor and **acrylic** (a modern, chemical invention), which proved both flexible in application and durable. This chapter will survey the most common forms of paint, and the many methods and tools used in creating paintings. It will also introduce some notable painters and paintings.

The First Paintings

Researchers have discovered that some images on a cave wall on the island of Sulawesi (**2.2.1**) Indonesia, were probably made of a pigment solution that was applied with a small tube. The application of this paint took place at least 45,500 years ago and the images are mostly of animals, although some human imagery is also present. The most detailed of these works, featuring hunters and some animals, may not have been painted by blowing an iron ore pigment solution. Because it is even more detailed than blown handprints that were found nearby, some researchers have even considered the possibility that a tool such as a brush may have been used, because there is such a high degree of detail. This

Encaustic: a painting medium that primarily uses wax, usually beeswax, as the binding agent

Tempera: a fast-drying painting medium made from pigment mixed with water-soluble binder, such as egg yolk

Fresco: a technique in which the artist paints onto freshly applied plaster. From the Italian *fresco*, "fresh"

Acrylic: a liquid polymer, or plastic, which is used as a binder for pigment in acrylic paint

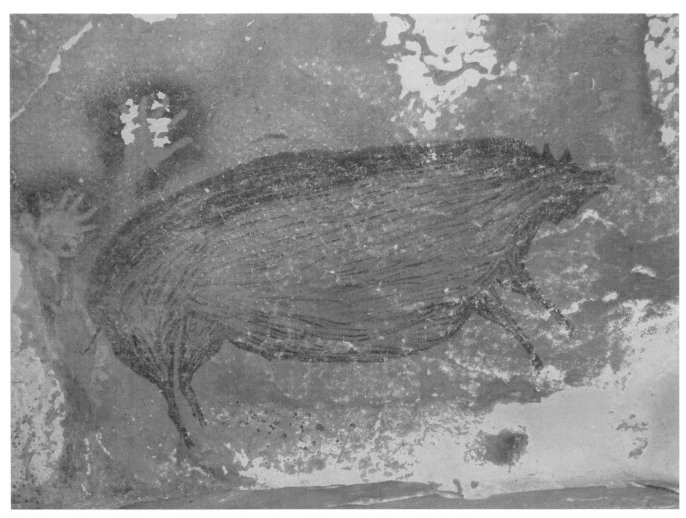

2.2.1 Cave paintings, *c.* 45,500 years ago. Red ocher pigment. Leang Tedongnge, South Sulawesi, Indonesia

representation of a warty pig appears to have been created from careful observation of a real animal because the artist depicts the texture of the hog's bristly body hair.

Encaustic

Another binding technique that was perfected many centuries ago is encaustic, a relatively semi-transparent paint medium that was used by the ancient Greeks and Romans. Encaustic continues to be chosen by some artists today because of the unique character of beeswax. To use encaustic, artists must mix pigments with hot wax and then apply the mixture quickly. They can use brushes (**2.2.2**), palette knives (**2.2.3**), or rags, or simply pour it. A stiff-backed **support**, such as a wooden panel or metal plate, is necessary because encaustic, when cool, is not very flexible and may crack. The Greeks and Romans typically painted encaustic on wood panel.

Ancient Roman painters showed great ability in controlling encaustic paint and produced beautiful results. The image of a boy in **2.2.4** was made by an anonymous artist during the second century CE in Roman Egypt. This type of portrait would have been used as a funerary adornment that was placed over the face of the mummified deceased or on the outside of the **sarcophagus**, above where the

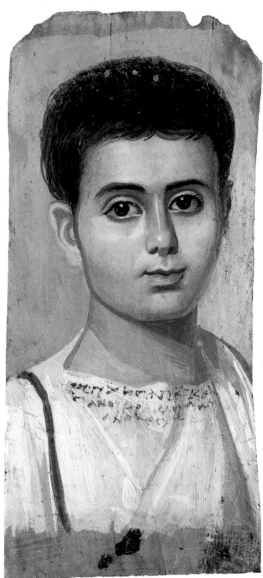

2.2.4 Portrait of a boy, *c.* 100–150 CE. Encaustic on wood, 15⅜ × 7½″. Metropolitan Museum of Art, New York

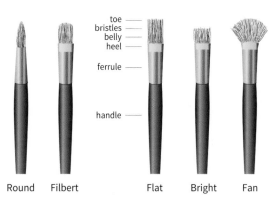

2.2.2 Commonly used brush types, and the parts of an artist's brush: **Round:** sketching and thinned paint application, can be rolled in hand for special effect; **Filbert:** applying color; short bristles for more control and softened edges; **Flat:** long, fluid strokes and sharp edges; **Bright:** controlled detailing and applying areas of color; **Fan:** blending slow-drying paint and softening edges

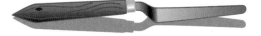

2.2.3 Palette knife, a tool that can be used by the painter for mixing and applying paint

head was positioned. The artist took great care to create a lifelike image and probably captured a fairly **naturalistic** likeness of the deceased boy. Encaustic portraits from this era are referred to as Fayum portraits, after the Fayum Oasis in Egypt where many of them were found.

The art of encaustic painting did not end in the ancient world, but has been adapted to contemporary trends in art. One such contemporary encaustic artist is the American Mary Black (b. 1948), who uses the medium exclusively. Black's experimental approach to encaustic painting can be seen in her use of the medium through a process of destruction, then creation, to build up layers of depth with the **translucent** wax and some added material. In her work *Natura 9* (**2.2.5**) the evidence of destruction then creation becomes a visible record of spontaneous reactions that the artist values in her work. The result is a visually rich surface of pocked and dripped paint with a strong physical presence.

Fresco

Fresco is a painting technique in which the artist paints onto freshly applied plaster. The earliest examples of the fresco method come from Crete in the Mediterranean (the palace at Knossos and other sites) and date to *c*. 1600–1500 BCE. Frescoes were also used later, to decorate the inside of Egyptian tombs. The technique was used extensively in the Roman world for the decoration of interiors, and its use was revived during the Italian Renaissance. The pigment is not mixed into a binder, as it is in other painting techniques. Instead, pigment mixed with water is applied to a lime-plaster surface. The plaster absorbs the color and the pigment binds to the lime as it sets. Once this chemical reaction is complete, the color is very durable, making fresco a very permanent painting medium.

There are two methods of fresco painting: *buon fresco* (Italian for "good fresco") and *fresco secco* ("dry fresco"). When artists work with buon fresco, they must prepare the wall surface by overlaying undercoats of rough plaster containing sand, gravel, cement, and lime. The artists add a further (but not final) layer of plaster and allow it to dry for several days; they then transfer onto it the design from a full-scale drawing (referred to as a **cartoon**) in preparation for the final painting. Next, they apply the last finishing layer of plaster, re-transferring onto it the required part of the cartoon. Onto this, they will paint pigment suspended in water. Because there are just a few hours before the lime plaster sets, only a portion of the wall is freshly plastered each day. If the artist makes a mistake, the plaster must be chiseled away and the procedure repeated. These technical challenges are offset by the brilliance of color for which fresco is renowned.

Many of the Renaissance fresco paintings were made to decorate the interiors of churches. The Italian artist Michelangelo Buonarroti (1475–1564) used the buon fresco method to decorate the ceiling of the Sistine Chapel in Rome (**2.2.6**). For this monumental undertaking, requiring four years to complete, Michelangelo needed to craft a strategic

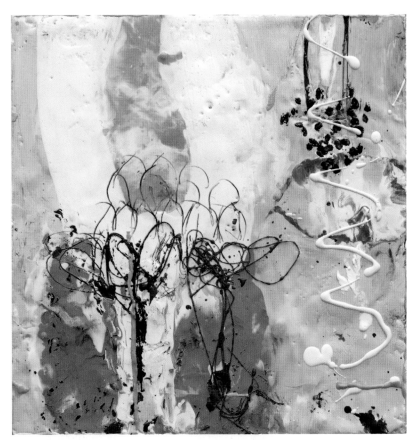

2.2.5 Mary Black, *Natura 9*, 2015. Encaustic, oil stick, graphite, ink, and Sheetrock tape on panel, 10 × 10″. Collection of the artist

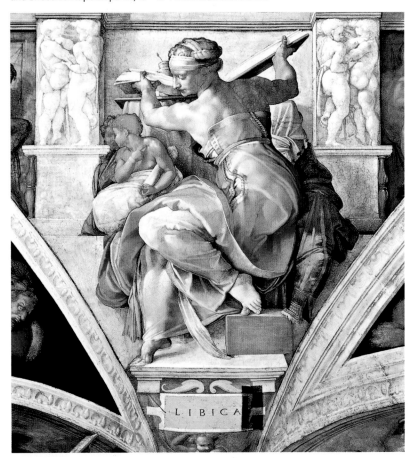

2.2.6 Michelangelo, *The Libyan Sibyl*, 1511–12. Fresco. Detail of the Sistine Chapel ceiling, Vatican City, Italy

Foreground: the part of a work depicted as nearest to the viewer

Value: the lightness or darkness of a plane or area

Trompe l'oeil: from the French meaning to "deceive the eye"; a visual illusion in art, in which a painted image appears as a three-dimensional object

Vaulted: covered with an arch-shaped ceiling or roof

Oculus: a round opening at the center of a dome

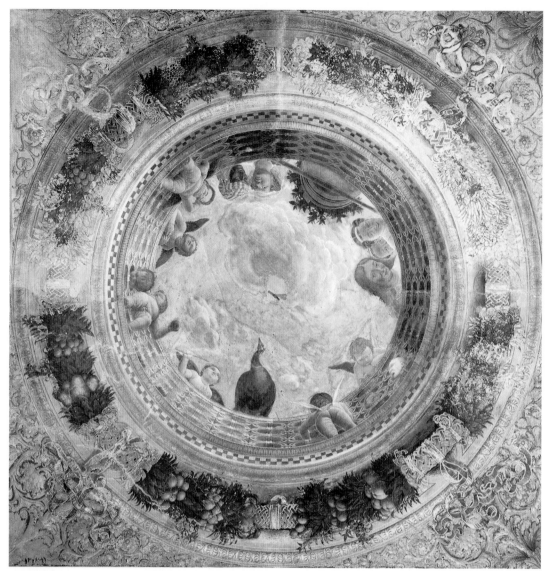

2.2.7 Andrea Mantegna, detail of central oculus, ceiling of the Camera degli Sposi.
Fresco, diameter 8′9″. Ducal Palace, Mantua, Italy

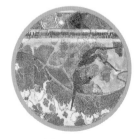

Some of the earliest examples of fresco are from the Minoan culture (in modern Crete):
→ see **3.1.7**, p. 351

approach in order to disguise the seams between separate days' work. For example, in one section, called *The Libyan Sibyl*, he plastered only the area where the leg in the **foreground** was to be painted (**2.2.6**, p. 197). This was probably a day's work, and the seam of the plaster could be camouflaged because the surrounding edges (the purple drapery in particular) change color and **value**.

Italian artist Andrea Mantegna (*c.* 1431–1506) also used the buon fresco method when he created **trompe l'oeil** paintings for an entire room of the palace of Ludovico Gonzaga, for the Duke of Mantua. The chamber, known as the Camera degli Sposi (Room of the Newlyweds), was used both to greet government officials and as a bedroom for the duke and his wife (**2.2.7**). In the **vaulted** ceiling, the artist painted the illusion of what seems to be an **oculus**

opening onto a blue sky, and surrounded it with figures looking down at the people below. Mantegna would have spent many hours on top of scaffolding to achieve the amazing detail in this work.

If an artist cannot finish painting a section within a day of plastering, or needs to retouch a damaged fresco, they employ the dry fresco method (fresco secco). To encourage absorbency, wet rags moisten the lime plaster that has already set, and the wall is then painted. The once-dry lime surface soaks up some of the pigment. Frescoes painted using the fresco secco method tend to be less durable than buon fresco, because the surface is less absorbent.

Although buon fresco is an ancient and temperamental art medium, many contemporary artists still choose to execute

Perspectives on Art: José Clemente Orozco
Fresco Painting Inspired by the Mexican Revolution

For more than thirty years Porfirio Díaz ruled Mexico as a dictator. This was a time of injustice and great divisions between the powerful rich and the poor masses. In 1911, the Mexican people rebelled and forced Díaz to resign. For ten years revolutionary groups led the fight for social justice, and from the 1920s to the mid-1930s, in an outpouring of national creativity, Mexican mural artists painted the walls of public buildings with works that expressed their aspirations for social justice and freedom, and revived the art of fresco painting. Subsequently, scholars termed this period the Mexican Mural Renaissance. One of the most famous mural painters of this time was José Clemente Orozco (1883–1949), who lost his left hand and had his sight and hearing damaged in an explosion during his childhood. Despite these disabilities, he went on to become a significant and radical artist who struggled for the rights of peasants and workers in revolutionary Mexico. His writings about art emphasize his interest in the medium of fresco painting and in its formal aspects: as he wrote, he saw art as visual poetry.

Fresco painting is free from the inconveniences of oils and varnishes, but the wall upon which the painting is done is subjected to many causes of destruction, such as the use of the wrong kind of building materials, poor planning, moisture from the ground or from the air, earthquakes, dive bombing, tanking or battleshipping, excess of magnesia in the lime or the marble dust, lack of care resulting in scratches or peeling off, et cetera. So, fresco must be done only on walls that are as free as possible from all these inconveniences.

There is no rule for painting al fresco. Every artist may do as he pleases provided he paints as thinly as possible and only while the plaster is wet, six to eight hours from the moment it is applied. No retouching of any kind afterwards. Every artist develops his own way of planning his conception and transferring it onto the wet plaster...Or the artist may improvise without any previous sketches.

A painting is a Poem and nothing else. A poem made of relationships between forms...

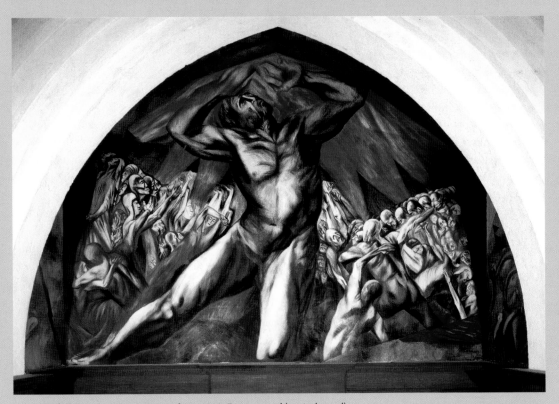

2.2.8 José Clemente Orozco, *Prometheus*, 1930. Fresco mural (central panel), approx. 20 × 28½′. Frary Hall, Pomona College, Claremont, California

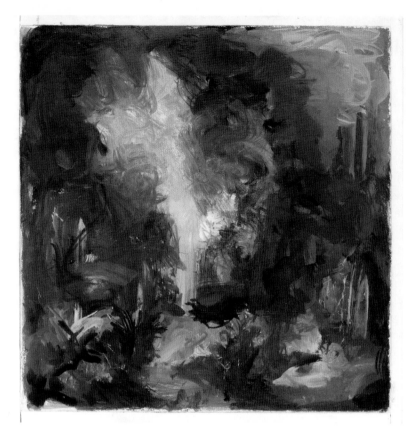

2.2.9 Walter O'Neill, *Untitled*, 2002. Fresco on wire mesh on wood, 24 × 24″. Courtesy Walter O'Neill

a brush and dries almost immediately. The earliest examples of egg tempera have been found in Egyptian tombs. From the fifth century onward, painters of Christian icons (**stylized** images of Jesus and saints) in what we know today as Greece and Turkey perfected the use of the medium and transmitted the technique to early Renaissance painters in Europe and West Asia.

As in many Italian paintings of the fourteenth century, the paint of the *Entry into Jerusalem*, from the back of the **altarpiece** called the *Maestà*, consists of pigment and egg yolk (**2.2.10**). For the *Maestà*, Duccio di Buoninsegna (*c.* 1255–1319) created a large, freestanding construction made up of many paintings that can be viewed from both front and back, with the latter comprising a series of images that depict important moments in the life of Christ, of which the *Entry into Jerusalem* is one. Although egg tempera can be challenging

their works using this process. The American artist Walter O'Neill (b. 1951) takes a more **painterly** and **abstract** approach to the buon fresco process in *Untitled* (**2.2.9**) by working in a loose **style** that suggests more traditional compositions. Since buon fresco demands that the paint be applied within hours of establishing the lime-plaster surface, the artist has taken advantage of this trait by using energetic gestural strokes that appear to have been executed quickly. O'Neill, a student of Renaissance fresco painting, captures the essence of ancient techniques and fuses them with the expressive character of modern and contemporary painting.

Tempera

If you have ever scrubbed dried egg off a plate while washing dishes, you know how surprisingly durable it can be. Painters who use egg tempera have different ideas about what parts of the egg work best for tempera painting, but many artists have favored the yolk. Despite its rich yellow color, egg yolk does not greatly affect the color of pigment; instead, it gives a transparent soft glow.

Tempera is best mixed fresh for each painting session. It is usually applied with

Painterly: a loosely executed style in which paint and brushstrokes are evident

Abstract: art imagery that departs from recognizable images of the natural world

Style: a characteristic way in which an artist or group of artists uses visual language to give a work an identifiable form of visual expression

Stylized: art that represents objects in an exaggerated way to emphasize certain aspects of the object

Altarpiece: an artwork that is placed behind an altar in a church

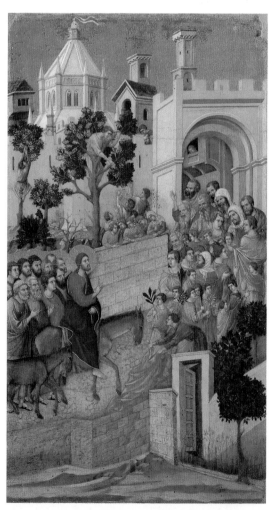

2.2.10 Duccio di Buoninsegna, *Entry into Jerusalem* (from the back of the *Maestà* altarpiece, Siena Cathedral), 1308–11. Tempera and gold leaf on wood, 3′4½″ × 1′9⅛″. Museo dell'Opera Metropolitana del Duomo, Siena, Italy

because it dries so quickly, Duccio's mastery of the medium, which demanded short, thin strokes, resulted in brilliant detail to enlighten a population of believers.

Islamic artists also enjoyed the sensitive detail that can be achieved with tempera, and some used tempera with gold leaf to create luxurious images for the ruling class. In *Two Lovers* by the Persian miniaturist Riza Abbasi (1565–1635), we see the rich gold-leaf finish combined with the high detail of tempera (**2.2.11**). Riza, who worked for Shah Abbas the Great, has used the transparency of the medium to make the plant life look delicate and wispy. The intertwined lovers stand out proudly from the softness of the plants in the **background**.

The appeal of tempera painting continues today. It has been used to create some of the most recognizable works in American art. Andrew Wyeth (1917–2009), loved by Americans for his sense of realism and high detail, chose tempera to create works that provide a glimpse into American life in the mid-twentieth century. The **subject** of *Christina's World* (**2.2.12**) is a neighbor of Wyeth's in Maine who had suffered from polio and could not walk. Wyeth has chosen to place her in a setting that expresses (in Wyeth's words) her "extraordinary conquest of life." The scene appears placid and bright,

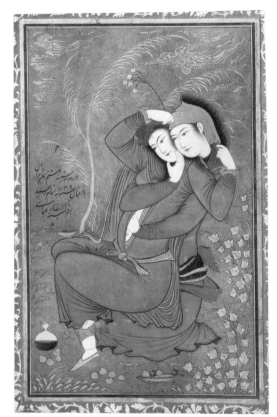

2.2.11 Riza Abbasi, **Two Lovers**, Safavid period, 1629–30. Tempera and gilt paint on paper, 7⅛ × 4¾". Metropolitan Museum of Art, New York

reflecting Wyeth's great admiration for her. The high degree of detail creates a sense of mystery that stimulates our imagination.

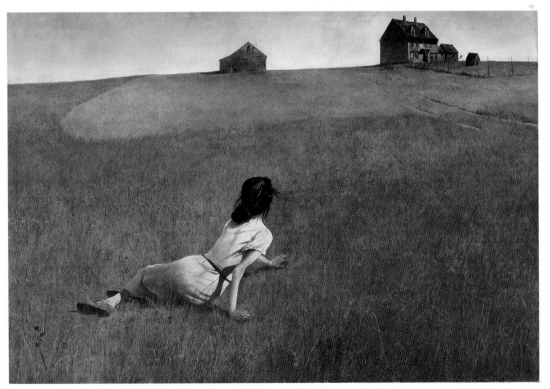

2.2.12 Andrew Wyeth, **Christina's World**, 1948. Tempera on gessoed panel, 32¼ × 47¾". MoMA, New York

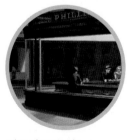

Edward Hopper's *Nighthawks* is a piece of realism that provides a snapshot of American life in the mid-twentieth century:
→ see **1.10.2**, p. 160

Background: the part of a work depicted as furthest from the viewer's space, often behind the main subject matter

Subject, subject matter: the person, object, or space depicted in a work of art

Oil

Painting with oil is a relatively recent invention compared to encaustic, tempera, and fresco. Artists used oil paint during the Middle Ages, but have done so regularly only since the fifteenth century, particularly in Flanders (modern-day Belgium, The Netherlands, and northern France). The oil used as a binder there was usually linseed oil, a by-product of the flax plant from which linen cloth is made. Giorgio Vasari, an Italian Renaissance writer and artist, credits the fifteenth-century Flemish painter Jan van Eyck (*c.* 1395–1441) with the invention of oil paint. In fact, Van Eyck did not invent it, but he is its most astonishing early practitioner. His virtuosity with the medium is apparent in his work known as *The Madonna of Chancellor Rolin* (**2.2.13**).

Because it is so flexible, oil paint readily adheres to a cloth support (usually canvas or linen), unlike encaustic, which is usually painted onto a stiff panel. Painters like oil paint because its transparency allows the use of thin layers of color called glazes. In the hands of such artists as Van Eyck, glazes attain a rich

luminosity, as though lit from within. This happens because many layers of transparent and semi-transparent color are applied, allowing light to pass through, then reflect light back, creating an impression that light is emanating from behind the glass-like paint. Because oil paint is slow drying, artists can blend it and make changes days after the initial coating has been applied, thereby achieving smooth effects and a high level of detail.

The use of transparent pigment in glaze painting also encouraged the use of **underpainting**. An underpainting is a preliminary layer of paint that is intended to support the final version of the work. It does this by setting up favorable conditions that allow the artist to achieve particular effects. For example, a **grisaille** (from the French term meaning to turn gray) is a black-and-white underpainting (similar to a black-and-white photograph in appearance) that establishes the light and dark values of the work. The French artist Jean-Auguste-Dominque Ingres (1780–1867) created a grisaille and did not add the finishing layers as an example for his students. The work, titled *Odalisque in Grisaille* (**2.2.14**) is made up entirely of gray values, then color was added in the next layer. A **verdaccio** (from the Italian word for green), or green underpainting, creates conditions that, for example, were well suited to realizing the light flesh tones often used in Renaissance portraiture. Although underpainting became more popular for use with oils, painters have used this technique with many other painting media. Grisaille can also be used as a technique to create a finished work of art rather than just for underpainting.

Oil painting gained another surge in popularity when the American artist John G. Rand (1801–1873) invented a new way of storing and transporting paint. In the late nineteenth century, the collapsible tube replaced the use of pig bladders as the favored container for oil paints. Whereas the pig bladder was sealed with string and the artist would poke a hole in it to access the paint, a collapsible tube could be reclosed using a screw-on cap, and was less likely to burst at inopportune moments. The French **Impressionist** movement, in particular, benefitted greatly from this advance, because it became much easier to transport a large variety of colors when painting outdoors.

Oil paint became a popular medium for **expressive** applications when used by artists

2.2.13 Jan van Eyck, *The Madonna of Chancellor Rolin*, 1430–34. Oil on wood, 26 × 24⅜". Musée du Louvre, Paris, France

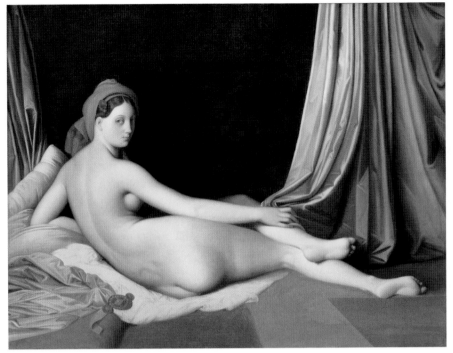

2.2.14 Jean-Auguste-Dominique Ingres, *Odalisque in Grisaille*, *c.* 1824–34.
Oil on canvas, 32¾ × 43″. Metropolitan Museum of Art, New York

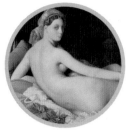

The finished version of Jean-Auguste-Dominique Ingres's *Grande Odalisque* uses grisaille to great effect:
→ see **1.10.8**, p. 167

who wanted to depict energetic scenes. One artist who exploited this energetic quality was Rosa Bonheur (1822–1899). Bonheur was the eldest child in a family of French artists. In her early life she was a disruptive student and was moved from one school to another until her father decided to educate her himself. She carried the same enthusiastic disdain for convention into her career as an artist. She

was best known in her time because she chose to wear pants and conduct her life as a man—although Bonheur said her dress was a matter of practicality because she was often working with animals, the main subject in most of her paintings. Her most famous work was *The Horse Fair* (**2.2.15**), an image derived from the horse market in Paris. All of her artworks address changing rhythms in order to communicate

Impressionism, Impressionist: in the visual arts, a late nineteenth-century painting style conveying the impression of the effects of light; Impressionists were painters working in this style

Expressive: capable of stirring the emotions of the viewer

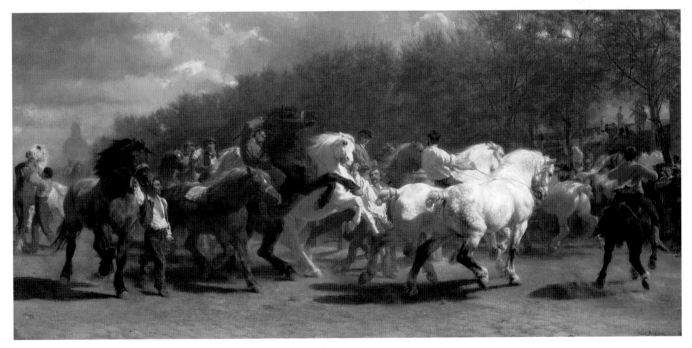

2.2.15 Rosa Bonheur, *The Horse Fair*, 1852–55. Oil on canvas, 8′ × 16′7½″.
Metropolitan Museum of Art, New York

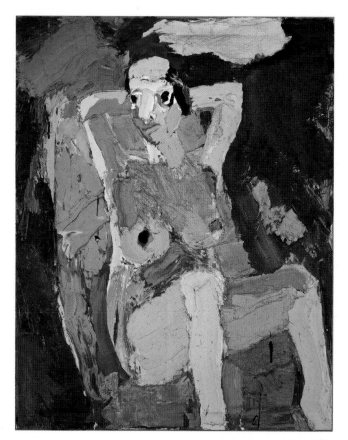

the animal biorhythms as they move in concert with their surroundings. The lively scene of horses rearing, trotting, and prancing is amplified by Bonheur's loose and vivacious oil brushwork.

Modern and contemporary artists have used oils to achieve quite different expressive effects. The San Francisco artist Joan Brown (1938–1990) used oil in an **impasto** (thickly painted) fashion (**2.2.16**). Because oil paint is normally thick enough to hold its shape when applied to a surface, the paint can pile up, giving Brown's work a **three-dimensional** presence.

The Chinese-born artist Hung Liu (b. 1948), who grew up in Communist China before immigrating to the United States, utilizes the different qualities of oil paint to achieve her own unique style. Hung's images express her Chinese roots. Her work *Interregnum* juxtaposes images and styles (**2.2.17**). The traditional Chinese style is used for the idyllic figures in the upper part of the work, in contrast with the back-breaking reality of life under Communist leader Mao Zedong in the lower part. Hung's work shows the discontinuity between reality and the ideal. It also reflects the meaning of the title: an interregnum is a period when normal government is suspended, especially between successive reigns or regimes.

2.2.16 Joan Brown, *Girl in Chair*, 1962. Oil on canvas, 5 × 4'. LACMA, California

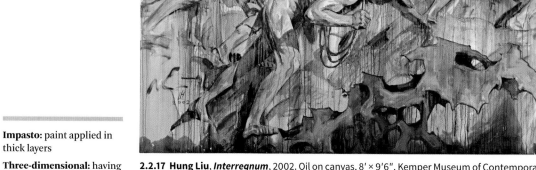

Impasto: paint applied in thick layers

Three-dimensional: having height, width, and depth

2.2.17 Hung Liu, *Interregnum*, 2002. Oil on canvas, 8' × 9'6". Kemper Museum of Contemporary Art, Kansas City, Missouri

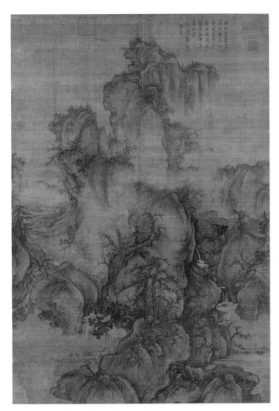

2.2.18 Guo Xi, *Early Spring*, 1072 (Northern Song Dynasty). Ink and color on silk, 62⅜ × 42½". National Palace Museum, Taipei, Taiwan

Ink Painting

Although artists often use ink with a pen on paper, they also use it for painting. Different surfaces require differences in ink. If you are drawing on a surface that is not fibrous enough, you need to modify the ink. Ink is commonly used on paper because the fibers hold the pigment, but a slicker surface needs an additional binder. Painting inks are slightly different from drawing inks because they have a binder, usually gum arabic, rather than simply being suspended in water.

Chinese **literati** painting grew out of the rich tradition of Chinese poetry. Any young aspiring government worker in ancient China was expected to be well-versed in the creation of poetry in a calligraphic style. The artistic influences of these two disciplines led artists to go beyond the decorative use of language into the visual form of ink painting. These paintings were initially images of people and animals, but by the time of the Song Dynasty (960–1279) an established academic painting style had evolved that was distinctively different than the calligraphic style that had been in use for hundreds of years. One of the great practitioners of academic landscape painting

was Guo Xi (1020–1090). Guo developed a process that he called "the angle of totality." This system enables artists to present a scene from many vantage points at the same time. The ink painting *Early Spring* (**2.2.18**) displays this kind of perspective, referred to as "floating perspective" because the viewer is not set in a fixed position, but can "move about" the scene to gain a stronger understanding of the landscape.

Watercolor and Gouache

Ink can be painted in much the same way as watercolor; artists sometimes incorporate it into their watercolor paintings to give extra richness and darker values. Watercolor and **gouache** suspend pigment in water with a sticky binder, usually gum arabic (honey is used for French watercolor), which helps the pigment adhere to the surface of the paper when dry. Watercolor is transparent, but an additive (often chalk) in gouache makes the paint **opaque**. Usually watercolor and gouache are painted on paper, because the fibers of the paper help to hold the suspended pigments in place. The portability of watercolor (all the artist needs is brushes, small tubes or cakes of paint, and paper) has made it vastly appealing, especially to artists who paint *en plein air*, or outdoors, using the landscape as subject matter. The American artist John Singer Sargent (1856–1925) sometimes worked en plein air, and such paintings as *Mountain Stream* (**2.2.19**) were executed outdoors, on location. As with other plein air artists, portraying

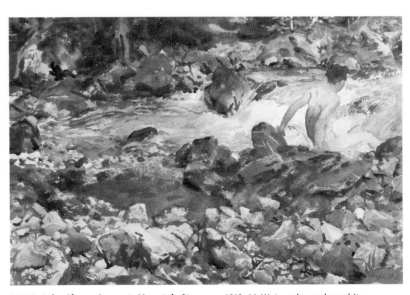

2.2.19 John Singer Sargent, *Mountain Stream*, *c.* 1912–14. Watercolor and graphite on off-white wove paper, 13¾ × 21". Metropolitan Museum of Art, New York

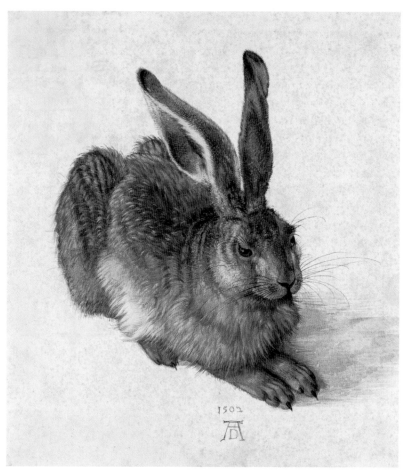

2.2.20 Albrecht Dürer, *A Young Hare*, 1502. Watercolor and gouache on paper, 9⅞ × 8⅞". Graphische Sammlung Albertina, Vienna, Austria

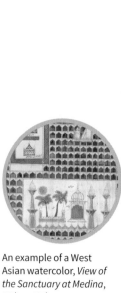

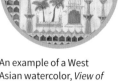

An example of a West Asian watercolor, *View of the Sanctuary at Medina*, 17th or 18th century:
→ see **3.2.18**, p. 384

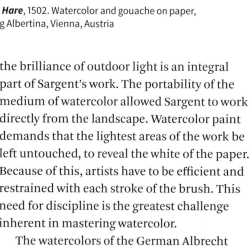

2.2.21 Sonia Delaunay, *Prose of the Trans-Siberian Railway and of Little Jehanne of France*, 1913. Watercolor and relief print on paper, support 77 × 14". Tate, London, England

the brilliance of outdoor light is an integral part of Sargent's work. The portability of the medium of watercolor allowed Sargent to work directly from the landscape. Watercolor paint demands that the lightest areas of the work be left untouched, to reveal the white of the paper. Because of this, artists have to be efficient and restrained with each stroke of the brush. This need for discipline is the greatest challenge inherent in mastering watercolor.

The watercolors of the German Albrecht Dürer (1471–1528) are noted for their masterful naturalism. Dürer's works, such as *A Young Hare*, reflect direct observation of a natural subject (**2.2.20**). But unlike plein air artists who focused on similar subject matter, Dürer opted to paint in his studio. Regardless of the location in which *A Young Hare* was created, the artist convincingly conveys a sense of the creature's soft, striped fur through a combination of watercolor with opaque white heightening.

The French artist Sonia Delaunay (1885–1979)—the first woman to have her work shown at the Louvre Museum in Paris, France, during her lifetime—mastered the art of watercolor. *Prose of the Trans-Siberian Railway and of Little Jehanne of France* (**2.2.21**), an **artist's book**, was part of a collaboration with the poet Blaise Cendrars (1887–1961). If all 150 copies of the first **edition** were placed end to end, it was intended that they would stretch the height of the Eiffel Tower. The book was also meant to be folded like a roadmap, and it recounts a trip from Russia to Paris. Delaunay's work is a "simultaneous book" in which her watercolor illustration on the left is set next to the Cendrars poem on the right. She used the bright colors that watercolor affords to create an illustration that progressively changes as the reader advances down the page.

Acrylic

Acrylic paints are composed of pigments suspended in an acrylic polymer resin. They dry quickly and can be cleaned up with relative ease. Latex house paint is made of acrylic polymer. These paints have been in use only since about 1950, but they have become popular with artists because of their versatility and practicality. Unlike oil paints, which dissolve only in turpentine or mineral spirits, acrylics can be cleaned up with water. When dry,

however, they have similar characteristics to those of oil paint, although they can also be used in ways that mimic the soft effects of watercolor. They also set easily on a variety of different artistic supports, from paper to canvas and wood.

Many professional artists, including the contemporary Ethiopian-born American artist Julie Mehretu (b. 1970), prefer acrylics as their primary painting medium. Mehretu uses them to better alternate between layers of the work, changing the traditional convention of drawing the design, then painting over. Mehretu will paint first, then add drawing, then return to painting again, a process that is best achieved in acrylic paint. This combination of layers was used to create the work *Excerpt (Suprematist Evasion)* (**2.2.22**). Because a shiny finish is easily achieved with acrylic, it is easier to draw on and integrates well with drawing media. Acrylic paint can also offer versatility to an artist because it is compatible with water-based media. This compatibility allows such artists as Mehretu to integrate other media they might need, for example ink or collage, for crisp sharp edges or quick-drying layers.

Artists will sometimes choose a painting medium that helps to support the idea being

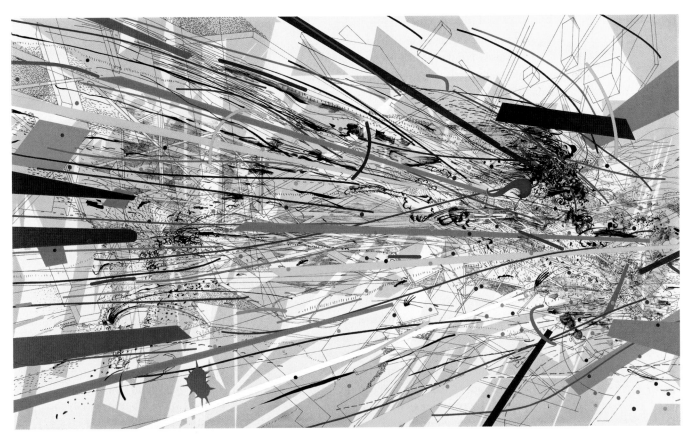

2.2.22 Julie Mehretu, *Excerpt (Suprematist Evasion)*, 2003. Ink and acrylic on canvas, 32 × 54"

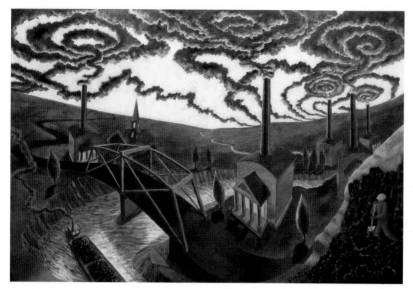

2.2.23 Ralph M. Larmann, *Coalopolis*, 2010. Acrylic on canvas, 40 × 60″. Collection Indiana State University, Terre Haute, Indiana

communicated in the work. Ralph M. Larmann (b. 1959) chose to use acrylic paint for his work, *Coalopolis* (**2.2.23**), because the **plastic** quality of the polymer reflects and is derived from contemporary manufacturing processes. In Larmann's industrial, menacing landscape, twisting clouds of coal soot rise in dark coils to fill the sky over a fictional town, emphasizing the uncomfortable relationship between economic progress and ecological damage. Even though this message of impending environmental disaster and the acrylic medium are contemporary, Larmann employs an old-fashioned glaze process that is similar to that of such early Dutch painters as Van Eyck, which in this case gives the image a strange glow or luminosity.

Mixed-Media Painting

The traditional boundaries between art media have been blurred as artists explore new ways to express themselves. **Mixed-media** and collage work have become popular ways of integrating imagery into a painted artwork. The best-known master of mixed-media painting was Robert Rauschenberg (1925–2008). Rauschenberg, an often controversial artist, approached art as if no boundaries existed between the different categories of media. He would often integrate painting, printmaking, drawing, and sculpture into the same work of art. He dubbed his early experiments into mixed media "combines," which are primarily a combination of painting and sculpture. In his iconic combine painting *Bed* (**2.2.24**),

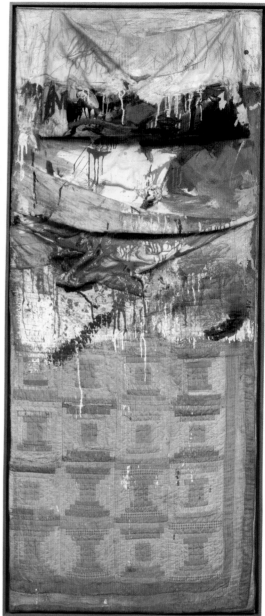

2.2.24 Robert Rauschenberg, *Bed*, 1955. Oil and pencil on pillow, quilt, and sheet on wood supports, 75¼ × 31½ × 8″. MoMA, New York

Rauschenberg uses sheets and other bedding material as his canvas, accentuating the physical nature of the cloth and pillows so that they stick out toward the viewer. The physicality of *Bed* is also emphasized in the manner in which the paint was applied by splattering it on the surface.

One of the first leading female practitioners of mixed-media painting was the American artist Jane Frank (1918–1986). In her work *Frazer's Hog Cay #18* (**2.2.25**) the artist incorporates oil paint and stones to create an association with a quiet Bahamian island. Even though Frank, who had studied under the abstract artist Hans Hofmann (1880–1966),

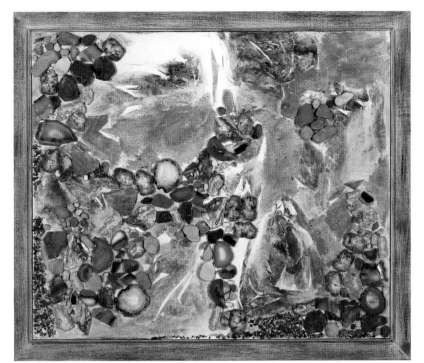

2.2.25 **Jane Frank**, *Frazer's Hog Cay #18*, 1968. Mixed media: oil paint and stones, 38 × 46″. Smithsonian American Art Museum, Washington, D.C.

Found image or object: an image or object found by an artist and presented, with little or no alteration, as part of a work or as a finished work of art in itself

Graffiti: markings that are scratched, scribbled, or sprayed on a wall without the consent of the owner

did not represent a recognizable landscape, she alludes to it through her use of **found objects**. The added natural sand and stones influence our senses so that we can more easily imagine the island where they may have been discovered.

Mural Art and Spray Paint

The Mexican Muralists, who espoused ideas about social justice and freedom in their works, believed that a painting should belong to all the people of a community, so they often worked outside, usually on a large scale so all could share (see Perspectives on Art: José Clemente Orozco, p. 199). This idea of collaborating on a painted work with an entire neighborhood has become an important tool for urban renewal and community. Judith Baca's (b. 1946) *Danza de la Tierra* (**2.2.26**), was painted in 2008 for an interior wall in the Dallas Latino Cultural Center. Baca created this work using influences from the surrounding community and local traditions. It is intended to offer the viewer a vibrant and energetic expression of Latino culture. Baca will often employ members of the local area to help create her wall paintings, encouraging strong community involvement.

Spray paint can be applied using a spray gun or spray can, a favorite of tag and **graffiti** artists. Graffiti artists prefer to use spray enamel, a commercially produced paint, packaged in an aerosol can and generally used for applying an even coating on a slick surface. A propellant forces the paint out in a fine mist when the user pushes down on the valve button. Graffiti artists often cut into the spray nozzle with a knife to

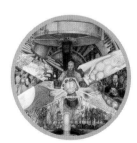

Diego Rivera, a Mexican muralist, was keenly aware of the important role art can play within local communities:
→ see **4.1.16**, p. 551

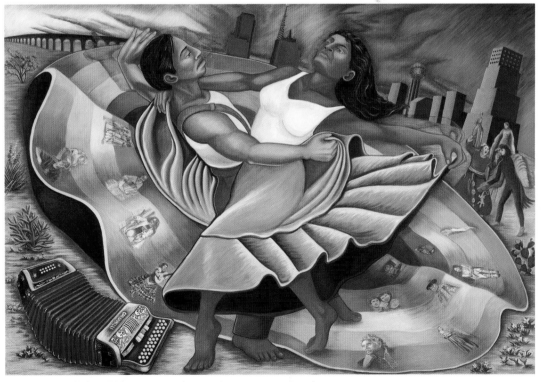

2.2.26 **Judith F. Baca**, *Danza de la Tierra*, 2008. Acrylic on canvas, 10 × 15′. Dallas Latino Cultural Center, Texas

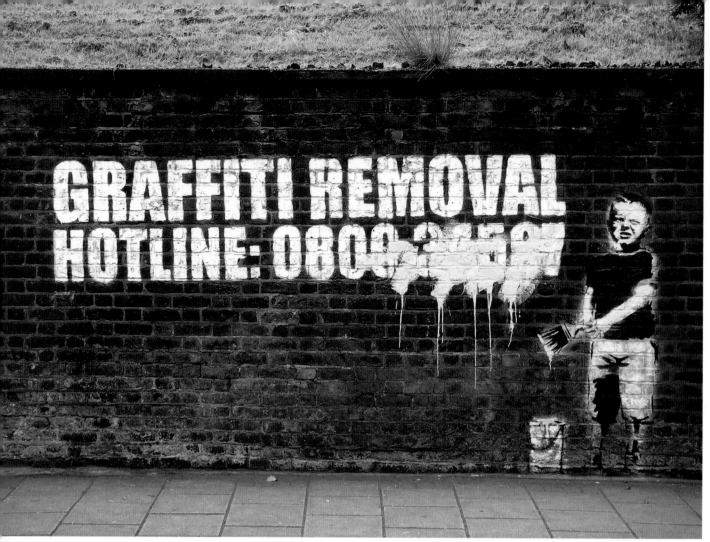

2.2.27 Banksy, *Graffiti Removal Hotline*, 2008. London, England

alter the spray stream, for example to spread a wider mist.

Practitioners of spray-painted graffiti art are considered vandals and criminals by local governments when they paint places without the permission of the property owners. Because of this, many keep their identity secret and sign their work with an alias, called a tag. Even so, many graffiti artists have become known and even celebrated.

The British graffiti artist known as Banksy (b. *c.* 1973) uses **stencils** as a quick way of transferring his designs to surfaces. (Speed of application is important to graffiti artists, who often risk being arrested for defacing private property.) In *Graffiti Removal Hotline*, Banksy, who carefully guards his identity and personal information, skewers and taunts the authorities who seek to curb his street art activities (**2.2.27**). Banksy's street art is full of such lampooning, and he often also points out the absurdity of modern life. In this work, the boy pictured on

the right has applied pink paint to "deface" a wall that carries a dull and rigid message. Banksy captures the irony of the moment by using pink, traditionally a passive color, as a tool of criminal vandalism.

As we have seen, the ancient artists who created the warty pig in a cave on Sulawesi (**2.2.1**, p. 195) did so by brushing and blowing a pigment solution through a small tube. Although today's spray paint comes in a can, the technique closely resembles that method, used 45,500 years ago. Because the spray spreads out in a fine mist, the ancient spray-paint artist, like today's spray painters, would **mask** out areas to create hard edges. Ancient artists may even have done this with the edge of their hand, covering the wall where they did not want the paint to fall. The contemporary street artist Banksy and the ancient people of Sulawesi may seem worlds apart, but they share a common technique, attesting to the timelessness of painting.

Stencil: a perforated template allowing ink or paint to pass through to print a design

Mask: in spray painting or silkscreen printing, a barrier the shape of which blocks the paint or ink from passing through

Explore Further Painting

Ancient Applications

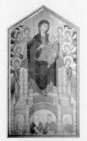

3.2.26 Cimabue, *Virgin and Child Enthroned*, c. 1280 → p. 388

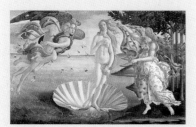

4.8.5 Sandro Botticelli, *The Birth of Venus*, c. 1482–86 → p. 634

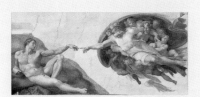

3.6.7b Michelangelo, detail of *Creation of Adam*, 1508–12 → p. 447

Traditional Applications

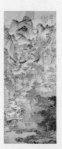

3.3.12 Wang Meng, *Ge Zhichuan Moving His Dwelling*, c. 1360 → p. 399

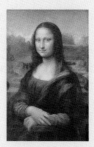

0.0.12 Leonardo da Vinci, *Mona Lisa*, c. 1503–6 → p. 23

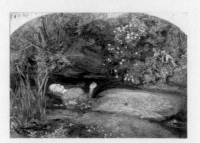

3.8.4 John Everett Millais, *Ophelia*, 1851–52 → p. 483

Contemporary Applications

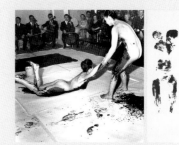

4.8.13a, **4.8.13b** Yves Klein, *Anthropométries de l'époque bleue*, 1960 → p. 638

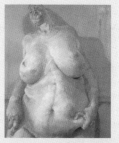

4.8.22 Jenny Saville, *Branded*, 1992 → p. 645

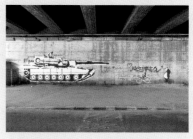

4.6.12 Ganzeer, *Tank vs. Bread-Biker*, 2011 → p. 612

Your turn
Which painting techniques are used in these works?

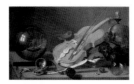

4.3.8 Pieter Claesz (attr.), *Vanitas (Still Life with Glass Globe)*, c. 1628 → p. 573

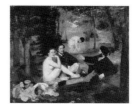

3.8.2 Édouard Manet, *Le Déjeuner sur l'Herbe*, 1863 → p. 481

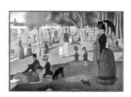

4.4.12 Georges Seurat, *Sunday on La Grande Jatte*, 1884–86 → p. 587

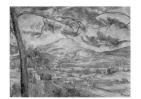

3.8.17 Paul Cézanne, *Mont Sainte-Victoire*, 1886–88 → p. 493

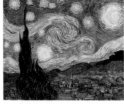

3.8.19 Vincent van Gogh, *Starry Night*, 1889 → p. 495

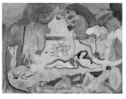

3.9.3 Henri Matisse, *Joy of Life*, 1905–6 → p. 502

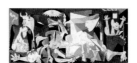

4.6.10 Pablo Picasso, *Guernica*, 1937 → p. 611

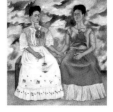

4.8.19 Frida Kahlo, *The Two Fridas*, 1939 → p. 643

2.3 Printmaking

Edition: all the copies of a print made from a single printing

Relief: a print process where the inked image is higher than the non-printing areas

Intaglio: any print process where the inked image is lower than the surface of the printing plate; from the Italian for "cut into"

Lithography, lithographic: a print process executed on a flat, unmarred surface, such as a stone, in which the image is created using oil-based ink with resistance to water

Serigraphy: printing that is achieved by creating a solid stencil in a porous screen and forcing ink through the screen onto the printing surface

Matrix: an origination point, such as a woodblock, from which a print is derived

Etching: an intaglio printmaking process that uses acid to bite (or etch) the engraved design into the printing surface

Woodblock: a relief print process where the image is carved into a block of wood

Woodcut: a relief print made from a design cut into a block of wood

Impression: an individual print, or pull, from a printing press

Incised: cut into a surface

Before the invention of printing, artists who wanted to have multiple copies of their work needed to copy it over by hand, one reproduction at a time. Printing with inks, first used in China to print patterns on fabrics in the third century CE, changed all that. Printing allowed the same designs to be more easily reproduced and distributed to many people. In the world of art, however, printmaking is much more than a way of copying an original. There are many different techniques, and each one gives a unique character to every work it creates. Artists may well choose a particular technique because they think it will suit the kind of effect they want to achieve.

Although artists may not always do the production work themselves, if they create the master image, supervise the process, and sign the artwork, it is considered an original print. This differs from a commercial reproduction of an artwork, where the artist may not be involved in the process. The production of two or more identical images, signed and numbered by the artist, is called an **edition**. When an artist produces only one print, it is called a monoprint. The method used to create a print may dictate the number of works that can be produced. There are four main printing processes: **relief**, **intaglio**, **lithography**, and **serigraphy**. Each process involves a different **matrix**, or the physical surface that holds the original image from which the print is derived—for example, the plate used in **etching**, or the **woodblock** used to make a **woodcut**.

In relief printmaking, the artist cuts or carves into a workable surface, such as wood or linoleum, to create the image. The printmaker rolls ink onto the raised surface that remains and presses a sheet of paper or

similar material onto the image to make what is known as an **impression**.

Intaglio printing requires the artist or printmaker to cut or scrape (in many different ways) into what is usually a metal plate. Ink is applied and then wiped off the surface, leaving ink in the lines or marks made by the artist. The pressure of the printing press transfers the image from the plate to the paper.

In the printing process known as lithography, the image is drawn with an oily crayon onto a special kind of limestone. The non-image area of the stone absorbs a little water, but enough so that when the printmaker applies oil-based ink to the whole stone, the ink remains only on the image area. In the printing press the image transfers to the paper.

Serigraphy, more commonly called silkscreen printing, physically blocks out non-image areas so that ink passes through the screen only where required.

As in any manufacturing process, traditional printmaking methods are being replaced by more efficient systems. Artists often rely on group workshops to reproduce images for commercial sale. The digital revolution has also introduced the means to create impressions in virtual environments that can be viewed electronically, printed two-dimensionally, or even three-dimensionally. Printmaking is experiencing a resurgence in the contemporary art world.

Context of Printmaking

Ancient Egyptian and Mesopotamian cultures reproduced images by rolling cylindrical **incised** stones across clay or pressing them into wax. These early relief impressions were used as a tamper-proof seal to show whether the contents of a sack had been opened. Elsewhere, in ancient China, craftspeople used wooden stamps to print patterned designs into textiles.

The earliest existing printed artworks on paper were created in China and date back to the eighth century CE (paper itself was invented in China in the second or first century BCE). By the ninth century, printed scrolls containing Buddhist *sutras* (scriptures or prayers) were being made across East Asia. Over the ensuing centuries, paper technology spread across the Islamic world as clever entrepreneurs created small prints that were sold as if they were handwritten charms. Woodblock printing and papermaking workshops became common throughout Europe by the beginning of the fifteenth century, and paper was no longer an expensive, exotic commodity.

While the woodblock print remained the primary vehicle for the development of the print in Asia (especially Japan), in Europe, a number of additional techniques developed over time.

Relief Printmaking

Relief prints are made by carving away a certain amount from a block of a suitably workable material, such as wood or linoleum, in order to create a raised image. The artist then applies ink to the raised surface and transfers the image to paper or similar material by applying pressure in a printing press (**2.3.1**). The areas of the block that remain print the image because the carved areas are recessed and are not inked. Traditionally, wood has been used for relief prints because it is readily available, familiar to work with, and holds up under the pressure exerted by the printing process; these prints are known as woodcuts. Today, for linocuts, printmakers use linoleum, an inexpensive material that cuts easily and can produce a clean, sharp image.

Series: a group of related artworks that are created as a set

Woodblock

The German artist Albrecht Dürer (1471–1528) combined images and the printed word (with text printed on the reverse) when he illustrated *The Apocalypse* with fifteen scenes from the final book of the Bible, the Book of Revelation. "The Four Horsemen" (**2.3.2**) is the most famous image in this **series** of illustrations and was made from a specially prepared woodblock. In this process, unlike cutting from a solid

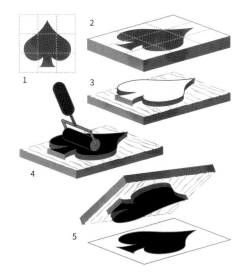

2.3.1 A brief overview of the relief printing process:
1. An image is designed and is prepared for transfer to the block surface.
2. The image is now transferred to the block.
3. The surface area that will not be printed is carved away.
4. The remaining protruding surface is carefully inked.
5. The raised inked area is transferred to the surface to be printed.

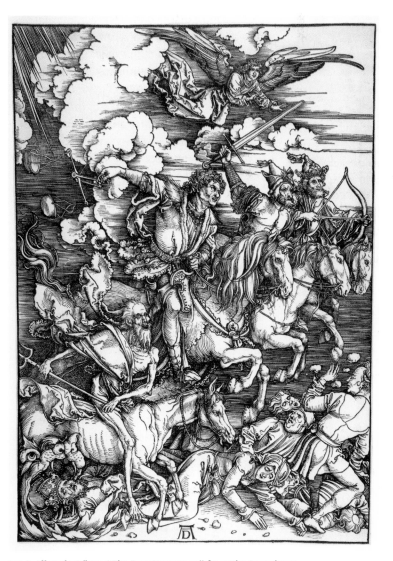

2.3.2 Albrecht Dürer, "The Four Horsemen" *from The Apocalypse*, 1498. Woodcut, 15¼ × 11″. Metropolitan Museum of Art, New York

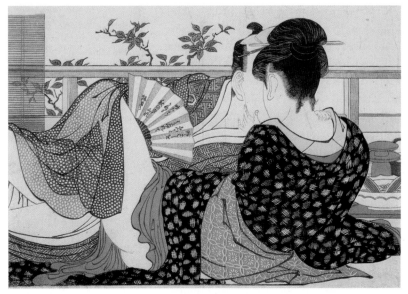

2.3.3 Kitagawa Utamaro, "Lovers in an Upstairs Room," from *Uta Makura (Poem of the Pillow)*, 1788. Color woodblock print, 10 × 14½". British Museum, London, England

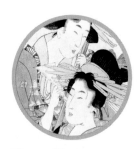

Kitagawa Utamaro woodcuts also influenced the work of Impressionists:
→ see **3.8.10**, p. 488

Color: the optical effect caused when reflected white light of the spectrum is divided into separate wavelengths

Ocher: a pigment found in nature containing hydrated iron oxide

Style: a characteristic way in which an artist or group of artists uses visual language to give a work an identifiable form of visual expression

Subject, subject matter: the person, object, or space depicted in a work of art

Composition: the overall design or organization of a work

block of wood, a print craftsman stacks and glues a series of thin, sliced layers of wood to create a more stable printing block (similar to plywood) that is less likely to splinter or crack. Dürer commissioned professional block cutters to perform the layering, and to cut the highly detailed lines of his original drawing into the block. This technique resulted in thin lines and detail that could withstand the compression of repeated printings. Because it required expert craftspeople, the labor was very expensive. But the series of works was so popular that it made Dürer wealthy. The Book of Revelation is a symbolic piece of writing that appears in the Christian Bible and prophesies the Apocalypse, or end of the world. The horsemen represent Death, Plague, War, and Famine.

Many great masters of woodblock printing were active in eighteenth- and nineteenth-century Japan. Kitagawa Utamaro's (1753–1806) print, entitled *Lovers in an Upstairs Room*, uses multiple **colors** and shows great graphic skill in controlling the crisp character of the print and the interplay of multiple blocks in different colors (**2.3.3**).

To create a color woodblock print, an artist must produce a separate relief block for every color. Utamaro uses at least three colors to create *Lovers in an Upstairs Room*: red ocher (a shade of red-brown), black, and green. In color woodblock printing, each block must be accurately carved and planned, because each individual color is printed in sequence on the same sheet of paper. Care must be taken to align each print color perfectly (this is called

registration); this is done by carving perfectly matching notches along two sides of each block to guide the placement of the paper. Utamaro is regarded as one of the greatest Japanese printmakers. He made images for the Japanese middle and upper classes, of figures, theaters, and brothels, in a **style** known as *ukiyo-e* printmaking. Ukiyo-e means "pictures of the floating world," a reference to a young urban cultural class who separated themselves from the agrarian life of traditional Japan by indulging in a fashionable and decadent lifestyle. The people of the "floating world" were the celebrities of their time.

In her woodcut *Man*, the American-Mexican artist Elizabeth Catlett (1915–2012) uses the natural character of the wood to suggest the hardships in the life of her **subject** (**2.3.4**). The crisp carving of the wooden block reveals the grain of the wood as it streaks the face of this indigenous Mexican man. The black and white portion of the print uses the hint of wood grain to reinforce the hardness of life that one might associate with working-class Mexicans. This print also demonstrates the use of linocut (linoleum) printmaking in the series of colorful figures printed at the bottom of the **composition**.

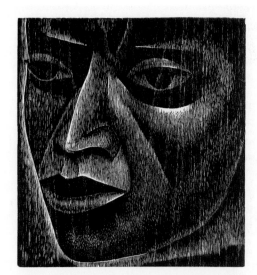

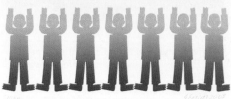

2.3.4 Elizabeth Catlett, *Man*, 2003. Woodcut, linocut in colors, 26 × 17¾"

Katsushika Hokusai, "The Great Wave Off Shore at Kanagawa" Using the Woodblock Printing Method

For the other Hokusai
GATEWAYS:
→ see p. 117 and p. 404

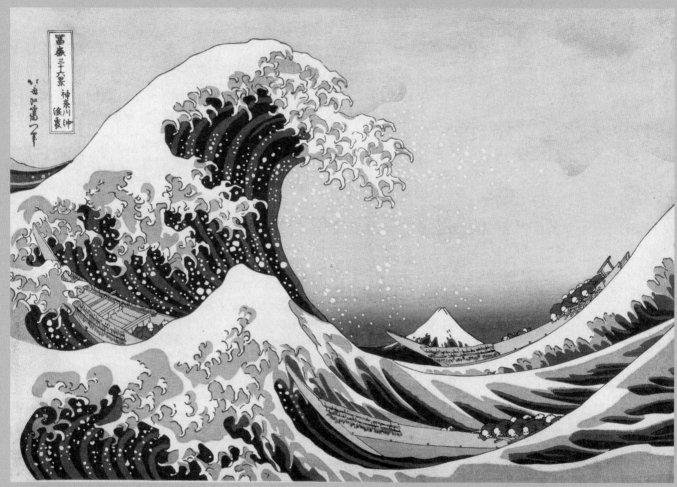

2.3.5 Katsushika Hokusai, "The Great Wave off Shore at Kanagawa," from *Thirty-Six Views of Mount Fuji*, 1826–33 (printed later). Print, color woodcut. Library of Congress, Washington, D.C.

Katsushika Hokusai's woodblock print "The Great Wave off Shore at Kanagawa" (**2.3.5**) uses multiple colors and shows great graphic skill. It is a fine example of the printmaker's art. Hokusai (1760–1849) was not solely responsible for the production of this print: he relied on skilled craftsmen. Hokusai made a drawing of his subject, which a print craftsperson then transferred face down onto a block of cherry wood. When the drawing was peeled away, the image remained, and the craftsperson then carved the image into the wood. To create a color woodblock print, a printer must produce a new relief block for each separate color. (Incidentally, "The Great Wave" was one of

ten prints in the series *Thirty-Six Views of Mount Fuji* to use a new blue color, imported from Europe, known as Prussian blue.) Nine blocks were used to print "The Great Wave." Each block had to be carefully carved, and the printmaker had to carry out the sequence of printing skillfully, because each new color was printed directly on top of the same sheet of paper. If all nine blocks were not printed in exactly the correct position, the print would be discarded because it would not match the others in the edition. The blocks of wood were used so many times that the carving eventually deteriorated. Although it is unknown how many prints were made, it is estimated there were more than 5,000.

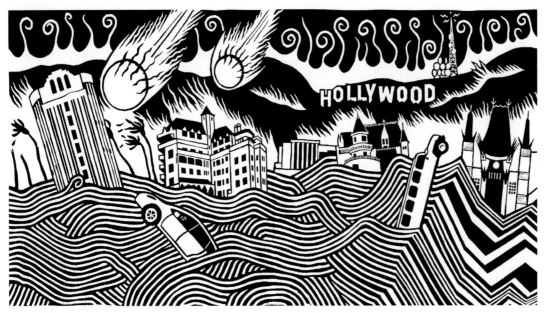

2.3.6 Stanley Donwood, "Hollywood Limousine," from the *Lost Angeles* series, 2012.
Black screenprint on a silver foil layer (based on an original linocut), 22 × 35¾"

Linocut

Linoleum ("lino") printmaking, similarly to the woodblock method, is done by carving into the surface of a material, then printing the raised surface left behind. The resulting prints are commonly known as linocuts. Because linoleum is softer than most woodblocks and does not show a wood grain, many contemporary printmakers prefer it for relief printing. One such artist is Stanley Donwood (real name: Dan Rickwood; b. 1968), who is best known for his creation of artwork for the rock band Radiohead. Donwood produced a series, or group of associated works, that depicts the last days of the city of Los Angeles, titled *Lost Angeles* (**2.3.6**). To create these works, he cut into sheets of linoleum to create the image, then printed the results on fine Japanese paper. The soft linoleum allowed Donwood to capture the myriad of fictional events in great detail, with the kind of clarity that a storybook illustration might have.

Intaglio Printmaking

Intaglio is derived from an Italian word that means "cut into" a surface. Usually the artist uses a sharp tool (a burin) to cut or gouge into a plate made of metal (or sometimes acetate or Plexiglas). Intaglio printing differs from relief printmaking because little of the base material is removed. The ink on the raised surface is also wiped away before printing, leaving ink in the scarred surface of the plate. The pressure of the printing press squeezes the plate against the

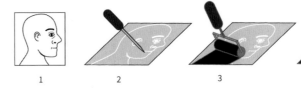

2.3.7 A brief overview of the engraving process (intaglio):
1. An image is designed for the plate.
2. Using a sharp tool, the artist incises the image into the plate.
3. The plate is inked.
4. The surface of the plate is wiped, removing all ink except in the grooves.
5. Paper is placed on the plate and it is pressed.
6. The paper lifts the ink out of the grooves and the ink is imprinted on the paper.
7. The final image is complete. (In most printmaking methods the final image is reversed from the plate or block.)

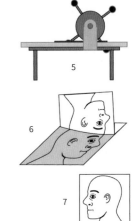

paper, transferring the ink. There are several variations of intaglio printing, all of which give the resulting artwork a different visual character (**2.3.7**).

Engraving

The intaglio **engraving** method is based on the careful scoring of a metal plate so that clean gouges are created in the surface. An engraving can achieve fine detail, making the resulting print more like the artist's original drawing.

Marcantonio Raimondi (1480–1534) chose to use engraving for his work, *Adam and Eve flanked by two trees, a town in the background* (**2.3.8**). This work, illustrating a story from

Engraving: a printmaking technique where the artist gouges or scratches the image into the surface of the printing plate

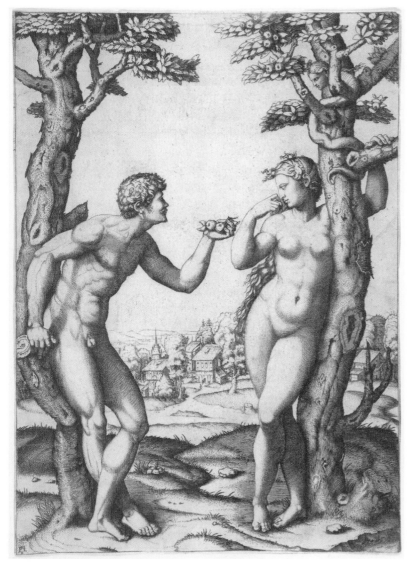

2.3.8 Marcantonio Raimondi, *Adam and Eve flanked by two trees, a town in the background*, 1512–14. Engraving on paper, 9½ × 7″. Metropolitan Museum of Art, New York

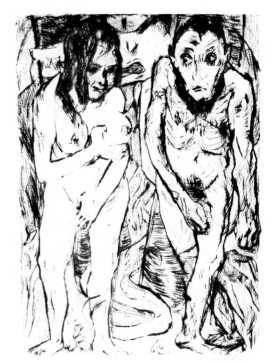

2.3.9 Max Beckmann, *Adam and Eve*, 1917, published 1918. Drypoint, 9⅜ × 7″. Private collection, New York

Drypoint: an intaglio printmaking process where the artist raises a burr when gouging the printing plate

Expressionism, Expressionist: an artistic style, at its height in 1920s Europe, devoted to representing subjective emotions and experiences instead of objective or external reality

Organic: having irregular forms and shapes, as though derived from living organisms

the Bible, was copied, with permission, from a painting by Raphael. Raphael supported Raimondi's copied engravings of his work by providing the preliminary drawings for his larger works. The two established a school of engraving that continued to make copies of his works, even after Raphael's death.

Drypoint

For his *Adam and Eve*, Max Beckmann (1884–1950) chose the **drypoint** intaglio method rather than engraving (**2.3.9**). In engraving, the burin is pushed across the surface, but in drypoint it is pulled, leaving a rough edge, or burr. When the plate is wiped the ink is caught under the burr. The result is a less precise line that has more irregularities. Artists can use this irregularity to add new dimensions to a work. For example, in Beckmann's *Adam*

and Eve the lines appear more irregular than those in Raimondi's version of the same subject. Beckmann, a German **Expressionist** artist, probably chose drypoint because its slightly uneven quality of line expresses unpredictability and an **organic** naturalness—two attributes that suit his choice of subject matter. In this image, Adam and Eve have eaten the apple from the Tree of the Knowledge of Good and Evil. We can tell this because they are beginning to express a sense of shame at being naked (in the Bible, they felt no shame before they had eaten from the tree, as nakedness was their natural state), covering their genitals with their hands. They know that they will be punished, and this uncertainty about their future, together with their growing worldliness, is captured in the rougher, less finished-looking lines created by using drypoint.

Etching

The Dutch artist Rembrandt Harmenszoon van Rijn (1606–1669) was a master of intaglio printmaking, especially etching. Etching is a process in which a metal plate is covered with an acid-resistant coating, into which the artist scratches the design. The plate is then immersed in a bath of acid. The acid "bites" into the metal where the covering has been removed, making grooves that hold the ink.

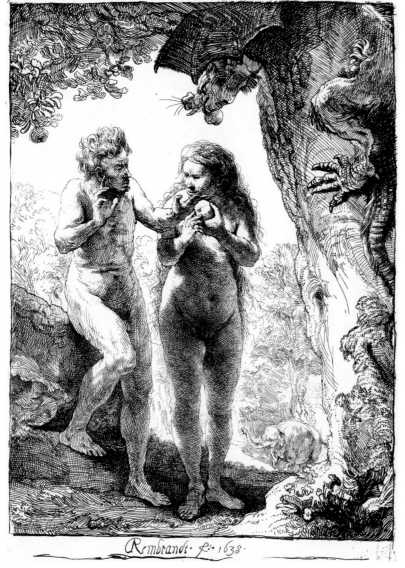

2.3.10 Rembrandt van Rijn, *Adam and Eve*, 1638. Etching, 9¾ × 7".
Rijksmuseum, Amsterdam, The Netherlands

the surface of the plate, creating a mottled, acid-resistant barrier into which the design is etched. Since the rosin leaves irregular areas of the plate exposed, a soft organic **texture** (similar to that created when one uses brush and ink) dominates the image. The artist can even use a brush to push around the dry rosin (before heating) to draw the original design, adding to the watery effect. Francisco Goya (1746–1828) utilizes the wash-like appearance of aquatint in his print *Giant* (**2.3.11**). Goya probably used a rosin box, a device that allows the artist to control the distribution and amount of powder that falls onto the plate, then he scraped away the heated rosin in the areas where he wanted the dark values of the final printed image to appear. The artist can progressively scrape more and more to get darker values. The **implied texture** of the aquatint print is soft and rich, giving a nuanced subtlety to the contours of the giant's body that communicate the sense of its being a fantastical, unreal creature.

Because each intaglio method leaves its own unique mark on the plate, many artists have opted to use more than one method when making a print. In his *Defense Worker*, the African American artist Dox Thrash (1893–1965) uses **mezzotint** over etched guidelines (**2.3.12**).

Unlike engraving and drypoint, the artist does not score a hard metal plate but makes small incisions, which allows for greater control in incorporating subtle changes of dark or light lines that affect **value**. In his etching *Adam and Eve*, Rembrandt brings out details by marring the plate surface more in the areas that will appear darker in the print (**2.3.10**).

Aquatint

Another process that requires the use of an acid bath to etch the surface of the plate is **aquatint** (from its Italian name *acqua tinta*, meaning "dyed water"). Despite the name, water does not play a role in aquatint printmaking. The image is created in a coating of powdered **rosin** (a tree sap), or spray paint, on the surface of the plate. When heated, the rosin melts onto

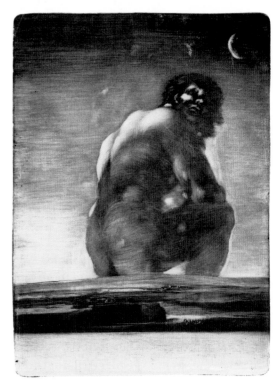

2.3.11 Francisco Goya, *Giant*, *c*. 1818. Burnished aquatint, first state, sheet size 11¼ × 8¼". Metropolitan Museum of Art, New York

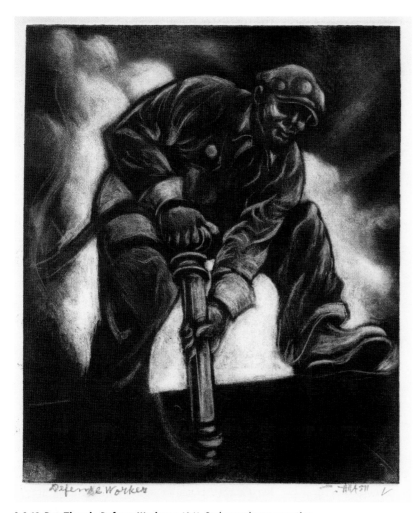

Value: the lightness or darkness of a plane or area

Aquatint: an intaglio printmaking process that uses melted rosin or spray paint to create an acid-resistant ground

Rosin: a dry powdered resin that melts when heated, used in the aquatint process

Texture: the surface quality of a work, for example fine/coarse, detailed/lacking in detail

Implied texture: a visual illusion expressing texture

Mezzotint: an intaglio printmaking process based on roughening the entire printing plate to accept ink; the artist smoothes non-image areas

Collagraphy, collagraphic, collagraph: a type of relief print that is created by building up or collaging material on or to a stiff surface, inking that surface, then printing

Collage: a work of art assembled by gluing materials, often paper, onto a surface. From the French *coller*, to glue

2.3.12 Dox Thrash, *Defense Worker*, *c*. 1941. Carborundum mezzotint over etched guidelines, 9¾ × 8″. Print and Picture Collection, Free Library of Philadelphia, Pennsylvania

Mezzotints often produce dark, rich values because the ink has many places to settle. To make a mezzotint, the entire surface is roughened with a heavy rocking tool, which is a metal object with a spiked, curved bottom. This can be rocked back and forth across the surface of the plate so that it is completely covered in burrs. The burrs are then smoothed in the areas where the printmaker wants the light tones. Ink is removed from the smoothed areas when the plate is wiped: the inked areas create dark tones, and the smoothed areas hold less ink, to create light tones. Thrash wanted to use this dark mood to reflect the drama and seriousness of the war effort at home. This work was sponsored by the Works Projects Administration, a government program originally created during the Great Depression to employ Americans at a time when jobs were hard to find. Artists, writers, musicians, and others contributed to American culture and infrastructure by applying their skills, first in support of rebuilding America and then, during World War II, in support of the war effort. Thrash, like other artists of the time, uses the dark values afforded by the medium to express the spirit and strength of the American worker.

Collagraphy

Relief and intaglio printmaking rely on a compromised surface—in a printmaking context, one that has been cut into in order to fashion an image. The ink is then applied to the surface and transferred to paper. But **collagraphic** prints are created by building up (rather than cutting into) a surface that can be inked for the purpose of transfer to paper. The artist glues materials to a rigid support, such as wood or heavy cardboard; this effectively **collages** the image to that surface. The image can then be printed by inking the materials with printing ink, and pressing paper onto them.

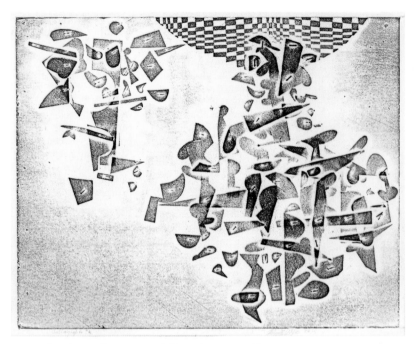

2.3.13 Glen Alps, *Roll-Up #2, 1956*. Collagraph, 26¼ × 32½"

The artist most closely associated with the development of the collagraph was Glen Alps (1914–1996), a longtime faculty member at the University of Washington in Seattle. Alps first used the term collagraph to describe the process. In his work *Roll-Up #2* (**2.3.13**), pieces of material are glued in a way that allows the printmaker more freedom because the surface can be easily manipulated. Although Alps did not invent the collagraphic technique, he was the first printmaker to succeed in mastering and promoting the process.

Lithography

Lithography (from the Greek for "stone writing") is traditionally done on stone. It is what is known as a **planographic** printmaking technique; that is, the print is made from an entirely flat surface, rather than one that is carved or otherwise modified. The German author Alois Senefelder (1771–1834), out of money and looking for a cheaper method to print his newest play, devised the lithographic printing process in 1796. The complex presses used nowadays by commercial printers for producing newspapers, magazines, and brochures (offset lithography) use thin sheets of zinc or aluminum instead of stone, but the basic principles are the same as Senefelder's original discovery.

Contemporary artists' lithographic prints are still made on the kind of stone used by Senefelder. Some artists like lithography because it allows them to draw a design in the same way they do a drawing. Successive stages in the process are illustrated in **2.3.14**. An artist first draws a design, using a grease pencil or other oil-based drawing material, directly onto a piece of specially selected, cleaned, and prepared limestone. Next, the artist applies a number of materials to the stone, including a gum arabic and nitric acid solution that makes the image more durable. Then they wipe the surface clean using kerosene. Even though the image appears to have been obliterated by the kerosene (this is a most unnerving moment for novice printmakers!), the stone is now ready to be printed. The surface is sponged with water, which is repelled by the greasy areas of the drawing, and rolled with oil-based ink. In the ungreased regions the water repels ink, leaving only the image covered with ink. At this point the artist carefully places paper over the stone and lightly presses down, usually by passing it through a printing press.

In 1834, the French artist Honoré Daumier (1808–1879) used his skills combined with the

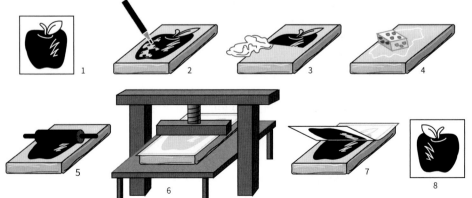

2.3.14 A brief overview of the lithography process:
1. The artist designs the image to be printed.
2. Using a grease pencil, the design is drawn onto the limestone, blocking the pores.
3. The stone is treated with acid and other chemicals that are brushed onto its surface. Then the surface is wiped clean with a solvent, such as kerosene.
4. The stone is sponged so that water can be absorbed into the pores of the stone.
5. Oil-based ink is repelled by the water and sits only on areas where the oil crayon image was drawn.
6. Paper is laid on the surface of the stone and it is drawn through a press.
7. The print is removed from the stone.
8. The completed image appears in reverse compared with the original design.

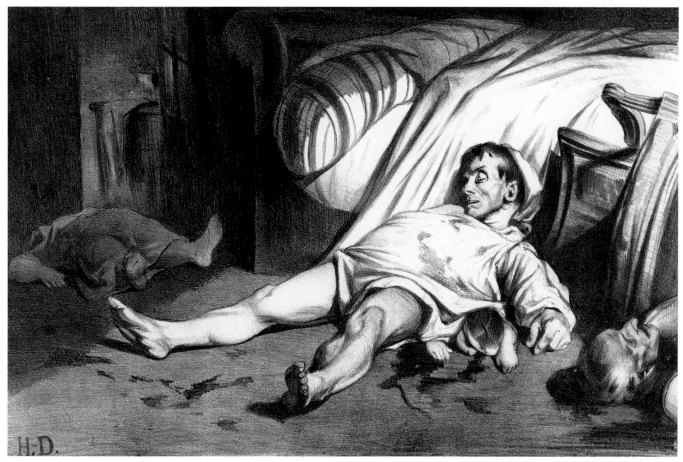

2.3.15 Honoré Daumier, *Rue Transnonain, April 15, 1834*, 1834. Lithograph, 11½ × 17⅝".
Metropolitan Museum of Art, New York

lithographic process to tell the citizens of Paris about an incident of police brutality. Daumier, who worked for the monthly magazine *L'Association Mensuelle*, depicted the aftermath of a horrible incident that took place at Rue Transnonain on April 15, 1834 (**2.3.15**). That night, police responded to a sniper attack they believed had come from that street by entering a property there, no. 12, and ruthlessly killing everyone inside. Daumier, a great critic of the French government's treatment of workers, drew the massacred in gruesome detail, including placing the most shocking—the dead child—in the center, under its father's body.

Serigraphy (Silkscreen Printing)

Serigraphy, also known as silkscreen printing, is another planographic printing process, as well as one of the most versatile, capable of placing a heavy coverage of ink on a wide variety of surfaces, from printed circuit boards to packaging; from solar panels to T-shirts. Artists value, amongst its many other virtues, its potential for printing strong colors. Unlike all the other printing processes discussed in

this chapter, only silkscreen printing produces right-reading reproductions of the original artwork. Relief, intaglio, and litho prints all make mirror images, so an artist making such a print needs to think in reverse.

Silkscreen printing was first developed in China during the Song Dynasty (960–1279) and uses a **stencil** process. A stencil **masks** out areas so that ink will take on the shape of the unmasked, open parts. It can be used to create a large number of prints. The silkscreen itself is nowadays a fine mesh, usually made out of nylon. The image area of the screen is open and allows ink to pass through, while the rest of the screen is masked off. As the printmaker moves the squeegee (like a heavy flat windshield wiper) over the screen, the mask prevents ink from passing through in unwanted areas. The mask can be a kind of thick glue painted on with a brush, or it can be a physical barrier, such as tape. Photographic silkscreen prints can be produced using a photosensitive masking material.

The American artist Andy Warhol (1928–1987) used photographic silkscreen techniques

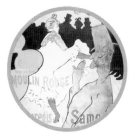

Henri de Toulouse-Lautrec used lithography for a more light-hearted purpose in his poster promoting a famous Parisian destination:
→ see **2.7.16**, p. 292

Stencil: a perforated template allowing ink or paint to pass through to print a design

Mask: in spray painting or silkscreen printing, a barrier, the shape of which blocks the paint or ink from passing through

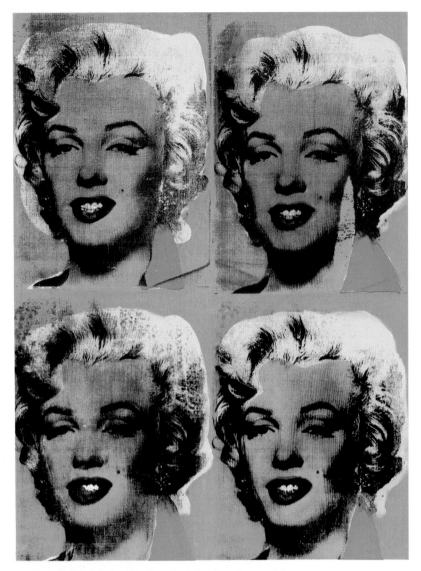

2.3.16 Andy Warhol, *Four Marilyns*, 1962. Acrylic, silkscreen ink, pencil on linen, 29 × 21½". Sold at Phillips, New York, 2014

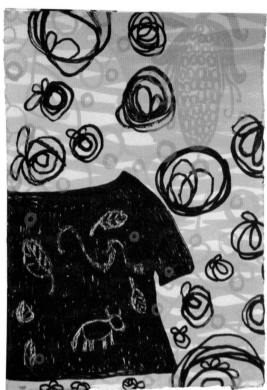

2.3.17 Melanie Yazzie, *Untitled*, 2016. Screen print. Mesa Contemporary Art, Arizona

over aluminum paint to create a distinctive style, seen in his work *Four Marilyns* (**2.3.16**). Warhol reproduces a sultry image of Marilyn Monroe from a photograph taken at the height of the actress's career, deliberately repeating her image to comment on the nature of mass-produced images in advertising, and on how public figures market their image. Silkscreen printing is particularly suited to printing large areas of flat, heavy color, and by using this technique, Warhol emphasizes the flatness and lack of depth in the image of Marilyn, showing how it has become a commodity rather than a genuine attempt to capture her individuality. The repeating "clones" of Marilyn also accentuate the degeneration that occurs when an original is copied.

Screen printing can be a spontaneous and expressive process, as evidenced in the work

of Navajo printmaker Melanie Yazzie (b. 1966). For her *Untitled* (**2.3.17**) screen print, Yazzie created irregular marks, printed the image, then after it had dried, created a new image and superimposed it over the previous layer. This kind of spontaneous imagery contrasts with the well-planned processes that most printmaking demands. Yazzie, who explores her Navajo heritage in her work, uses an impulsive approach to express the human condition combined with an intimate view of her people's history. The energetic character of her work projects an optimistic vision of the future, in contrast to the past hardships imposed on Indigenous people.

Editions

Prints are produced in limited numbers of identical impressions, called editions. The printmaker has the ethical responsibility for making sure that each print is similar enough to the others so that each person who buys a print has a high-quality image. When a print is deemed identical to others in the edition, it is assigned a number in the production sequence. For example, a print marked 2/25 is the second print in an edition of twenty-five. Some unnumbered prints bear the letters A/P.

These prints, called artist's proofs, are used by the printmaker to check the quality of the process and are not intended to be part of the edition. Some artist's proofs are sold as one-of-a-kind works, rather than as part of an edition, because variations in the process may produce visually engaging results. Even though most artists could create more prints than they do, they usually decide to print a set number: a limited edition. The artist afterward destroys the original plates so it is impossible to make any more copies. Destroying the plates protects the integrity of the edition, because no more can be made. It also limits the number in the edition so that each print is rarer and therefore more valuable.

Monotypes and Monoprints

Nearly all printmaking is done in editions, or multiple impressions, but some artists who like the way a printed image looks will opt to create unique prints. Monotypes and monoprints are print techniques that enable an artist to produce an image that is one of a kind.

A monotype image prints from a polished plate, perhaps glass or metal. The artist puts no permanent marks on it. They make an image on it in ink or another medium, then wipe away the ink in places where the artist wants the paper to show through. The image is then printed. Only one impression is possible. Hedda Sterne (1910–2011) was the sole woman in a group of **abstract** painters called the Irascibles. Although abstract, Sterne's *Untitled (Machine Series)* monotype makes associations with architectural and mechanical images (**2.3.18**). Sterne probably employed a straightedge to maintain the regularity of line in the print.

Monoprints can be made using any print process. The artist prepares the image for printing as described previously in this chapter, but will ink or modify each impression in a unique way. This includes varying colors, changing the spread of the ink across the

Abstract: art imagery that departs from recognizable images of the natural world

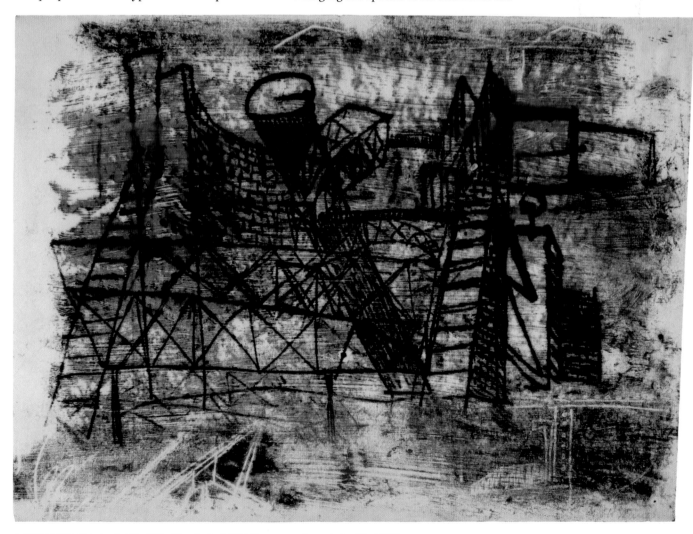

2.3.18 Hedda Sterne, *Untitled (Machine Series)*, 1949. Trace monotype, design 12 × 16⅜".
Harvard Art Museums, Fogg Art Museum, Cambridge, Massachusetts

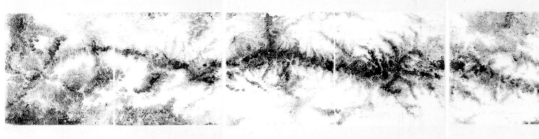

2.3.19 Kathy Strauss, *Kepler Underneath 1*, 2007. Monotype over India-inked calculations, Somerset velvet paper, each panel 30 × 23″. Collection of the artist

image area, and adding features by hand. The individual modifications possible are as infinite as for any hand-made work of art. Artists choose to make monoprints to explore themes and variations, where some elements of the work remain the same but others are different. If two prints are identical, they are not monoprints.

Kathy Strauss's (b. 1956) monoprint *Kepler Underneath 1* painstakingly depicts the Milky Way Galaxy (**2.3.19**). The artist has first incised a series of calculus problems into the metal plate. As with any other intaglio print, the plate was then completely covered with ink and wiped. Ink stayed in the incised grooves. Strauss then painted the image of the Milky Way in ink directly onto the same plate; when the inking was complete, she centered the paper over the image and ran it through the press. Because Strauss painted the ink on by hand, she cannot re-create the result exactly in a second print, so it is not part of an edition.

Contemporary Directions in Printmaking

The freedom of expression and changing technologies that artists have experienced over the past fifty years have inspired printmakers to innovate, developing new processes. Printmakers have reimagined the printmaking process so that it can be utilized by artists working in a variety of media, from sculpture to the digital realm. Much of this innovation has happened through collaborative print shops, where many craftspeople and artists have joined forces to redefine the nature of the print.

Print Shops and Digital Reproduction Services

Contemporary printmakers sometimes rely on the technical expertise of craftspeople who may not be artists themselves, but have developed the knowledge and expertise to bring creative ideas to a well-crafted artwork. For example, Skyline Art Editions is a commercial printing service, based in Austin and Dallas, that works with artists and other creative professionals to re-create original imagery (**2.3.20**). This studio, like many others, works with the individual artist to find the right paper, surface appearance, and archival qualities that meet their high standards. Although some print shops will provide traditional printmaking tools and equipment along with their expertise, Skyline Art Editions provides digital reproductions that replicate the character of the original work, be it a print, painting, or another two-dimensional piece.

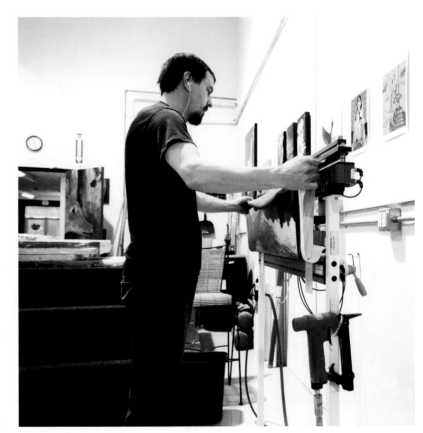

2.3.20 Drying racks at Skyline Art Editions, Austin, Texas

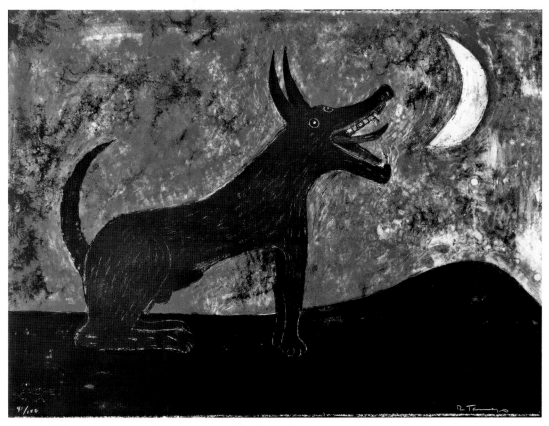

2.3.21 **Rufino Tamayo**, *Perro de Luna*, 1973. Mixograph, edition of 100, 22¼ × 30¼"

One of the first innovative print shops of the contemporary era was Mixografia®. Originally founded by Luis Remba (b. 1932) as Taller de Gráfica Mexicana (TGM) in Mexico City, the print shop worked with famous Mexican artists, beginning in the late 1960s, to create editions of their artwork for commercial distribution. While working on a series of lithographs with the Mexican artist Rufino Tamayo (1899–1991), the shop began incorporating paper pulp, creating their own bespoke surfaces to meet Tamayo's request for more texture. The technique was called the Mixografia® printing technique, which eventually lent its name to the current print shop, established in Los Angeles in 1984. One of Tamayo's first prints using this process was *Perro de Luna* ("Moon Dog"), which is a lithograph executed in heavily textured hand-made paper (**2.3.21**). Tamayo's print pushed the boundaries of printmaking beyond the traditional flat surface to such an extent that the print itself became a relief from which multiple copies could be produced.

Computer Graphics and Digital Printing

In the 1980s, the digital age thrust art into a new era with the introduction of computer graphics and other technical innovations that created new opportunities for artists. One of the most notable innovations in print technology was the inkjet printer. It allowed an electronic image to be re-created on a paper surface, but this model had serious weaknesses for use as an art medium because the ink color was not permanent and the paper size was limited. In the early 1990s, however, high-resolution commercial print devices overcame these disadvantages. While working at the digital printing company Nash Editions, the printmaker Jack Duganne (b. 1942) introduced the term *giclée* to identify and separate fine art print methods that used permanent ink color from their commercial counterparts. Duganne now leads his own print shop, Duganne Atelier, where he uses the giclée process to print the work of such significant contemporary artists as Ilana Raviv (b. 1945). Raviv, an Israeli artist, works in a number of different media and has her work reproduced for commercial distribution. A reproduction of one of her paintings, *Doll with Toys* (**2.3.22**, p. 226) has been replicated using the giclée process because the resolution and color permanence ensures that an art buyer will have a lasting piece of art that encapsulates Raviv's unique gestural style.

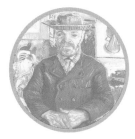

This commercially printed Van Gogh image uses color separations:
→ see **2.7.22**, p. 297

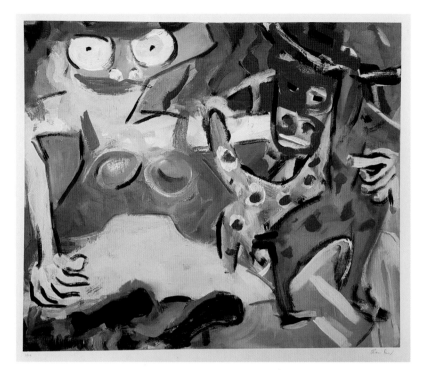

2.3.22 Ilana Raviv (Oppenheim), *Doll with Toys*, 2003. Acrylic on canvas, 29 × 37"

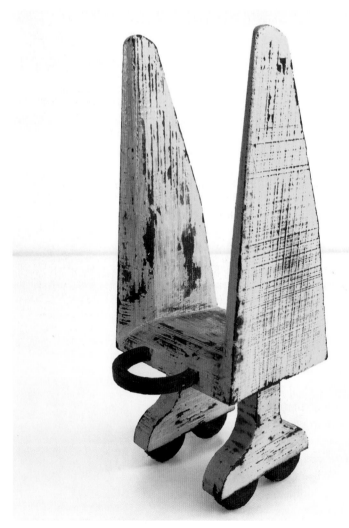

2.3.23 Kurt Dyrhaug, *Unterschieden Tonka*, 2017. Three-dimensional print, metal coating, and acrylic paint, 7 × 3 × 3". Museo de Arte Contemporano Costa da Morte, Corme, Spain

Technical innovations in computer graphics have pushed the boundaries of traditional image-making so that images giving the illusion of three dimensions can actually be fabricated as three-dimensional objects in real space through the use of **3-D modeling** software. Three-dimensional printing begins with the creation of a computer graphic that is described as if it has height, width, and depth. Of course, these dimensions do not exist, but are formulated within a computer application that allows the artist to draw the form. Once the object is created, the artist can print the object as a real object, add finishing touches, then exhibit. Like a traditional two-dimensional print, a three-dimensional print can be made many times and can even be considered an edition when all the works are identical.

The American sculptor Kurt Dyrhaug (b. 1966) creates three-dimensional prints of sculptures using 3D-modeling. His work *Unterschieden Tonka* (**2.3.23**) may look like a cast metal object, but in fact it has been printed. The original computer graphic information (designed by the artist) is passed to the printer, which uses a thick, glue-like liquid plastic that is organized into thin layers, each placed on top of the previous until the form takes shape. Dyrhaug, who has extensive training in iron and aluminum sculpting, coats the surface with an iron metal coating and acrylic paint after cleaning up any excess print material left on the object. Although it may seem very different from a traditional woodcut, this process is very much like a multiple-color print where one color must be printed over another.

From woodcuts to three-dimensional prints, printmaking has evolved with new advances in technology and to meet the needs of creative artists. These radical changes in the printed form may signal future trends in art production.

3-D modeling: a computer-generated illusion that emulates an object in three dimensions; it can be modified to show visual movement

Explore Further Printmaking

Relief	Intaglio	Planographic	Contemporary

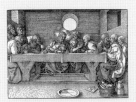

3.6.19 Albrecht Dürer, *The Last Supper*, 1523 ➜ p. 458

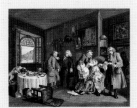

3.7.8 William Hogarth, "The Lady's Death", *c.* 1743 ➜ p. 471

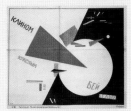

1.1.24 El Lissitzky, *Beat the Whites with the Red Wedge*, 1919 ➜ p. 46

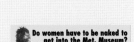

4.9.8 Guerrilla Girls, *Do Women Have to Be Naked…*, 1989 ➜ p. 654

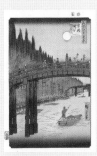

1.8.11 Ando Hiroshige, "Riverside Bamboo Market, Kyo-bashi," 1857 ➜ p. 146

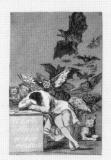

1.9.14 Francisco Goya, *The Sleep of Reason Produces Monsters*, 1799 ➜ p. 155

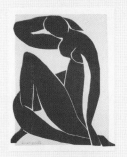

4.8.15 Henri Matisse, *Blue Nude II*, 1952 ➜ p. 640

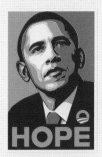

4.5.2 Shepard Fairey, Obama Hope Poster, 2008 ➜ p. 593

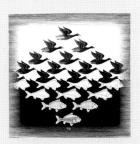

1.1.27 M. C. Escher, *Sky and Water I*, 1938 ➜ p. 47

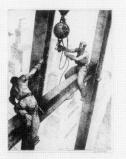

1.1.8 James Allen, *The Connectors*, 1934 ➜ p. 39

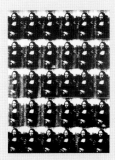

3.9.30 Andy Warhol, *Thirty Are Better than One*, 1963 ➜ p. 517

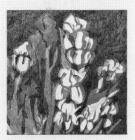

1.4.8 Analia Saban, *Layer Painting (CMY): Flowers*, 2008 ➜ p. 88

Your turn

What type of printmaking was used to make these artworks?

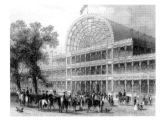

2.5.26 Joseph Paxton, Crystal Palace, 1851 ➜ p. 258

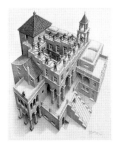

1.3.23 M. C. Escher, *Ascending and Descending*, 1960 ➜ p. 82

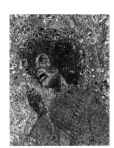

3.10.6 Wadsworth Jarrell, *Revolutionary*, 1972 ➜ p. 525

2.4
Sculpture

Renaissance: a period of cultural and artistic change in Europe from the fourteenth to the seventeenth century

Ceramic: fire-hardened clay, often painted, and normally sealed with a shiny protective coating

Three-dimensional: having height, width, and depth

In the round: a freestanding sculpted work that can be viewed from all sides

Relief: a sculpture that projects from a flat surface

Bas-relief (low relief): a sculpture carved with very little depth: the carved subjects rise only slightly above the surface of the work

High relief: a carved panel where the figures project with a great deal of depth from the background

Plane: a flat, two-dimensional surface on which an artist can create a drawing or painting. Planes can also be implied in a composition by areas that face toward, parallel to, or away from a light source

A great sculpture can roll down a hill without breaking.

(Michelangelo Buonarroti, Italian sculptor, painter, and architect)

Michelangelo is generally regarded as one of the finest sculptors in the Western tradition—some would say the greatest (see: Michelangelo, pp. 232–33). When the **Renaissance** Italian artist made the humorous remark above, he probably had in mind most of his own sculptures: statues chiseled out of durable marble. This might be the first response of most of us when asked to define what we mean by sculpture, although we might broaden our definition to include other materials, such as metal, **ceramics**, and wood. But, as we will see in this chapter, sculpture can be made from many materials: for example, glass, wax, ice, plastic, and fiber. In fact, the materials of modern sculpture can include, for example, neon lights and even animals. Sculptors' methods today still include chiseling (as Michelangelo did), carving, molding, assembling, and constructing, but inventive sculptors find new ways to create their art, and new materials to make it with.

It is probably because artists are so inventive that it is difficult to define sculpture exactly. Look up the word in a dictionary and then check whether the definition fits all the works in this chapter; it probably will not. But we can agree on a few things that are true of all sculptures. They exist in **three dimensions** and occupy physical space in our world. And they invite us to interact with them: by looking at them, by walking round them, or by entering them and being immersed in an environment created by the sculptor, including sights, sounds, textures, and other sensory

experiences. Antony Gormley (b. 1950), a British sculptor whose work is concerned with the human form, has said of his sculptures: "The figures in my work are corpographs: a three-dimensional equivalent of a photograph but which is left as a negative, as a void. I think of my works as objects that act on the space in which they are placed, allowing it to become a space for imagination and reflection."

Approaches to Three Dimensions in Sculpture

Sculptors planning new sculptures have two basic options for displaying them. The first approach invites us to examine them on all sides; sculpture made to be enjoyed in this way is known as freestanding, or sculpture **in the round**. Many freestanding sculptures are made so that we can move around them, but sculptures in the round can also be displayed in a way that prevents a viewer seeing every side of them. Sculptures can be made, for example, to be placed in a niche or standing against a wall. In such cases, the location of the statue determines the vantage points from which it can be viewed, and sculptors will design their work with the viewer's position in mind.

The second fundamental approach to the three-dimensional nature of sculpture is **relief**, a type of sculpture specifically designed for viewing from one side. The image in a relief either protrudes from or is sunk into a surface. It can have very little depth (**bas-relief**) or a great deal (**high relief**).

Freestanding Sculpture

Some freestanding sculpture is not intended to be experienced from every point of view. The Egyptian sculpture (1971–1926 BCE) of the Lady

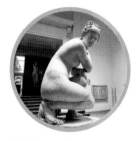

Sennuwy, wife of the very powerful governor of an Egyptian province, was designed to be seen from the front (**2.4.1**). (Many Egyptian sculptures were made to be displayed with their backs to a wall or a pillar.) In this work we can get a sense of the original block of granite from which the work was chiseled. Egyptian figure sculptures often sit, as this one does, very straight and upright on the stone from which they were carved, with the arms and legs drawn in close to the body.

Giambologna (1529–1608), a Flemish artist working in Florence, Italy, designed the *Rape of a Sabine* at the request of Florence's ruler, Francesco de' Medici (**2.4.2a** and **2.4.2b**). The sculpture forms a kind of spiral that draws the viewer around to view its many changing **planes**. With each step, the viewer can discover

2.4.1 Sculpture of the Lady Sennuwy, 1971–1926 BCE. Granite, 67 × 45¾ × 18″. Museum of Fine Arts, Boston, Massachusetts

To fully experience a freestanding sculpture it should be viewed from more than one angle, such as *Naked Aphrodite Crouching at Her Bath (Lely's Venus)*:
→ see **1.2.8a** and **1.2.8b**, p. 55

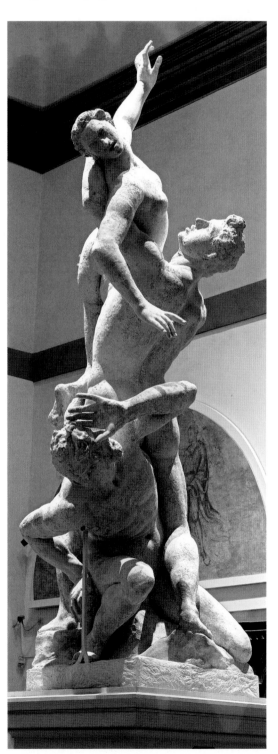

2.4.2a and 2.4.2b Giambologna, *Rape of a Sabine* (model), 1582. Gesso, height 13′8″. Galleria dell'Accademia, Florence, Italy

unexpected details as the surfaces spiral upward. This is a powerful and beautiful work, but Giambologna had more in mind when he created it than just a dramatic design. His statue was a piece of political propaganda. It recreates an ancient story about the foundation of Rome around 753 BCE. Most of the early founders of Rome were male. For the city to grow, the Romans needed wives. They solved this problem by inviting their neighbors, the Sabine people, to a festival, during which the Romans seized the Sabine women and forced them to marry. This story symbolized the ability of a small community to become the most powerful city in Italy—as Rome was by Giambologna's time—and with this dramatic sculpture Francesco de' Medici announced to the Florentines and their enemies that, like Rome, Florence had risen to become a force to be reckoned with.

Bas-Relief and High Relief

In bas-relief (the French word *bas* means "low"), the sculptor's marks are shallow. An example of this kind of sculpted surface was found in the North Palace of the Assyrian king Ashurbanipal in the ancient city of Nineveh in Mesopotamia (modern-day Iraq, eastern Syria, and southeastern Turkey). Assyrian kings ruled over a large territory and had powerful armies. They decorated the interior walls of their palaces with images depicting their strength and power. The artist who carved away the stone to create *Dying Lioness* intended to reflect the great strength and bravery of King Ashurbanipal as he hunted the most fearsome beast known to the Assyrians (**2.4.3**).

The Maya **lintel** showing Shield Jaguar and his wife Lady Xoc (**2.4.4**) is a relief sculpture, or a type of carved surface intended to be seen from one side, like a written document. The flat surface of the limestone was probably chiseled using stone hammers and wooden drills, since Maya craftspeople had no metal tools. Shield Jaguar was a Maya ruler from 681 to 742 CE, and his influence is recorded in such sculptures as these. Various degrees of relief were used to emphasize different areas of the scene. Sculpting deeper into the stone, to create what is called high relief, had the effect of accentuating the major shapes, such as that of Shield Jaguar, the figure on the left, and Lady Xoc, who is positioned in the right bottom corner. Surfaces within those deeply

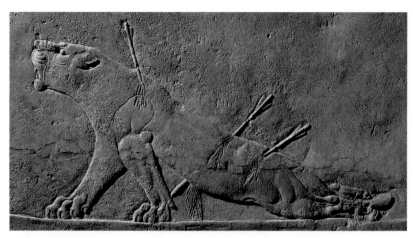

2.4.3 *Dying Lioness*, **limestone relief from the North Palace of Ashurbanipal**, Nineveh, Assyrian period, *c.* 650 BCE. British Museum, London, England

incised areas are more lightly carved, detailing the stately attire of these Maya royals. The use of different degrees of relief contributes to the realism of the image. For example, the texture on Lady Xoc's dress is not as prominent as her necklace, and the rope she holds is in higher relief and therefore is clearly in front of her. Originally the lintel would have been painted,

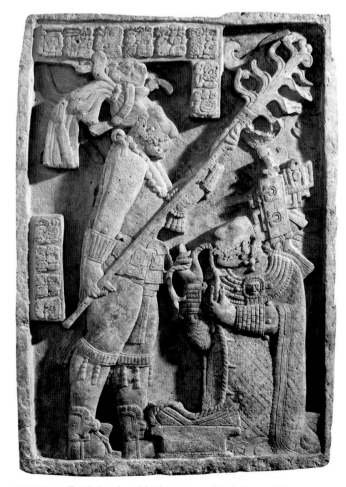

2.4.4 Maya lintel showing Shield Jaguar and Lady Xoc, *c.* 725 CE. Limestone, 43 × 30¾× 2⅜". British Museum, London, England

and analysis reveals traces of red and blue pigment.

Methods of Sculpture

Sculptural methods are either **subtractive** or **additive**. In the subtractive processes, a sculptor uses a tool to carve, drill, chisel, file, chip, whittle, or saw away unwanted material. In the additive processes of modeling, **casting**, or constructing, sculptors add material to make the final artwork.

Carving

The most ancient works of art that still exist were made using subtractive methods of sculpture. Most of these were made of stone or ivory (because wood eventually decays, we have few ancient wooden sculptures) and were worked by chipping, carving, sanding, and polishing.

The nearly 9-foot-tall figure of the Hawaiian war god Ku-ka'ili-moku was carved (the subtractive method) from large pieces of wood (**2.4.5**). The sculpture represents a god whose name translates from Hawaiian as "Ku, the land-grabber." Originally created for the powerful King Kamehameha I, the image of the god exhibits an open mouth (a disrespectful gesture) and was probably intended to gain divine favor. Another god, Lono (god of prosperity), is also symbolized by pigs' heads in Ku's hair. The combination of the two gods may have represented Kamehameha's invasions and conquests of adjacent kingdoms.

One of the largest and most famous sculptural portraits was executed using the subtractive method on a large standing granite rock near Avukana, Sri Lanka. The *Avukana Buddha* (**2.4.6**) was executed in the fifth century as an enormous carved sculpture. This rigidly

Lintel: the horizontal beam over the doorway of a portal

Subtractive (sculpture): the methodical removal of material to produce a sculptural form

Additive (sculpture): a sculpting process in which the artist builds a form by adding material

Cast: a sculpture or artwork made by pouring a liquid (for example molten metal or plaster) into a mold

2.4.6 *Avukana Buddha*, 5th century CE. Granite, height 38′10″ (without pedestal), Sri Lanka

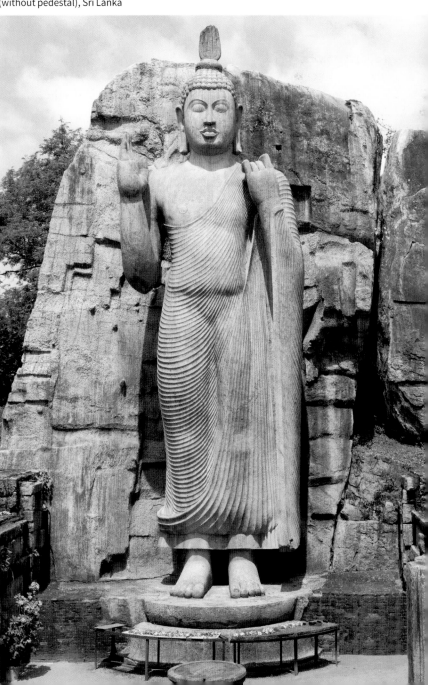

2.4.5 Figure of the war god Ku-ka'ili-moku, Hawaii, 18th or 19th century. Wood, height 8′11″. British Museum, London, England

Michelangelo

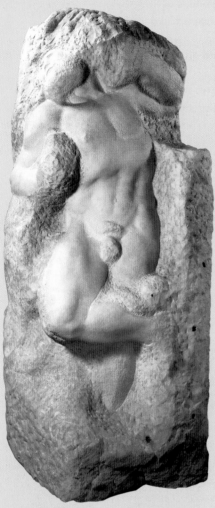

2.4.7 Michelangelo, *Prisoner*, known as the *Awakening Slave*, 1519–20. Marble, height 8'9⅛". Galleria dell'Accademia, Florence, Italy

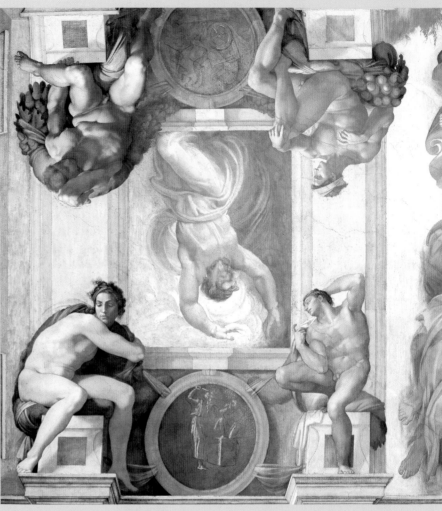

2.4.8 Michelangelo, *Separation of Light and Darkness*, 1508–12. detail of the vault, Sistine Chapel, Vatican City, Italy

One artist in history stands out because of his unique mastery of the materials and methods of sculpture. Michelangelo (b. Michelangelo Buonarroti, 1475–1564) used an unconventional technique to release the figure, as he saw it, from the stone. Rather than remove stone progressively from all sides, as most sculptors do, Michelangelo began on one side of the stone and sculpted through to the other side. He felt that he was freeing the figure from the stone in which it had been trapped. His unfinished sculpture, *Awakening Slave*, gives an insight into the artist's technique (**2.4.7**).

Michelangelo excelled in architecture and painting as well as sculpture. Yet he saw these arts through the eyes of a sculptor; he believed sculpture itself was the finest, the most challenging, and the most beautiful of all the visual arts. While painting the Sistine Chapel ceiling

(**2.4.8**), which many see as his grandest work, Michelangelo dreamed of finishing the ceiling quickly so that he could get back to work on several large sculptures intended for the tomb of Pope Julius II. He made many **sketches** of the figures intended for the nude male sculptures (which he called *ignudi*, from the Italian word for nude) that would cover the tomb. Unfortunately, the tomb was never completed in the way that Michelangelo intended, but some sculptures carved for the project survive, such as *Moses* (**2.4.9**). If we compare this polished statue with *Awakening Slave*, we can see how much refining of his sculptural work the artist did after the initial carving stage, through sanding, filing, and polishing.

The muscular figures painted on the Sistine Chapel ceiling have led many viewers to believe they are looking at sculptures. The figures have the appearance of mass, particularly the **nudes**, which

Sketch: a rough preliminary version of a work or part of a work

Nude: an artistic representation of an unclothed human figure, emphasizing the body's form rather than its exposure

really seem to be men perched on architectural platforms. The ceiling is smooth, however; the illusion of these three-dimensional forms was created through the use of shading. Michelangelo painted darker shades in the areas that would have been carved more deeply if the figures had been sculptures. Thus, even when he painted, he thought like a sculptor.

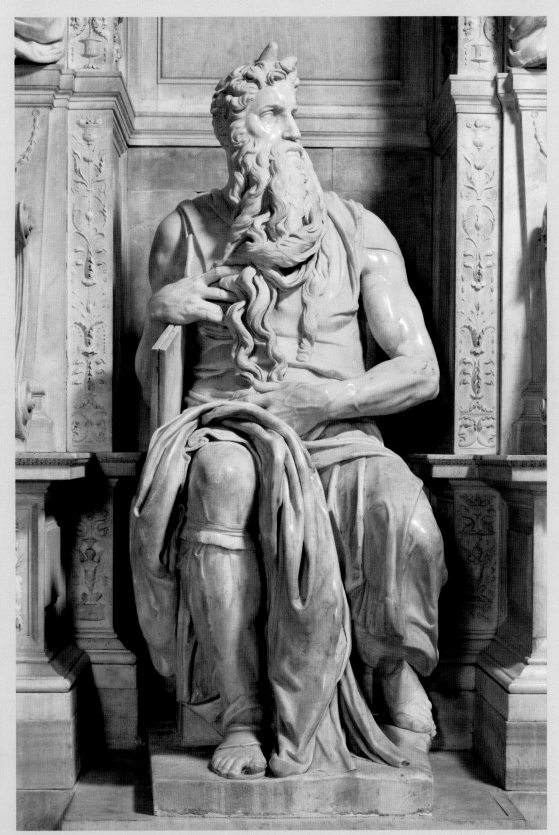

2.4.9 Michelangelo, Tomb of Julius II, detail of Moses, 1513–16. Marble, height 7'8½". San Pietro in Vincoli, Rome, Italy

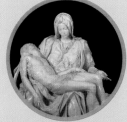

Another carved sculpture by Michelangelo is the Pietà: → see **0.0.22**, p. 31

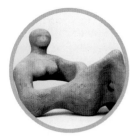

Carving is not limited to the ancient world. Twentieth-century sculptor Henry Moore also carved large stone sculptures, such as *Recumbent Figure*:

→ see **4.8.17**, p. 642

standing **form** is regarded as one of the best expressions of a hand position known as the Asisa **mudra**, or hand upright facing out. This gesture symbolizes fearlessness and reassurance. The sculptor, or team of sculptors, who created this work had to be careful to remove stone with the knowledge that they would not be able to repair a mistake. The sculpture is still attached to the native rock, but the lotus **pedestal** below the statue's feet was carved and placed after the work was completed.

Modeling

Modeling in clay and wax (for example) is an additive process; the artist builds up the work by adding material. Clay and wax are pliable enough for sculptors to model them with their hands. Sculptors also use specialized tools to manipulate them, such as wire or a rounded, flexible metal tool called a rib, or for wax, a heated surface. A sculptor may also cast clay in a mold. Because such materials as clay often cannot support their own weight, sometimes an artist will employ a skeletal structure, called an **armature**, to which the clay will be added; the armature will then later be removed (or burned away) when the work is dry. Permanent sculptures created from clay will most often

be dried, then fired in a kiln until the chemical structure of the clay changes. To achieve a glaze, a clay and chemical compound is added before re-firing the work. Because this process produces a very dry and hard material, many clay works from antiquity still exist.

Large sculptures, such as the Etruscan **sarcophagus** (a type of coffin) in **2.4.10**, are built from multiple pieces fired individually. Four separate **terra-cotta** (baked clay) pieces make up this sarcophagus, which contains the ashes of the deceased. The sculptor paid particular attention to the gestures and expressions of the couple, shown relaxed and enjoying themselves at an Etruscan banquet, although the expressions are **stylized** and not a likeness of the deceased. The **plastic** character of clay allowed the artist to make images that are **expressive** and capture the mood of the event.

The way the sculptor interpreted the figures tells us two interesting things about their culture. Women actively participated in social situations; this woman is shown gesturing, and even reclines in front of her husband. And, since this sculpture is part of a tomb, it suggests that celebrations took place upon the death of loved ones, although the figures' joyful expressions may simply indicate the deceased in an eternal state of happiness.

Form: an object that can be defined in three dimensions (height, width, and depth)

Mudra: hand gestures that signify meaning in Buddhism and Hinduism

Pedestal: a base upon which a statue or column rests

Armature: a framework or skeleton used to support a sculpture

Sarcophagus (plural **sarcophagi**): a coffin (usually made of stone or baked clay)

Terra-cotta: iron-rich clay, fired at a low temperature, which is traditionally brownish-orange in color

Stylized: art that represents objects in an exaggerated way to emphasize certain aspects of the object

Plastic, plasticity: referring to materials that are soft and can be manipulated, or to such properties in the materials

Expressive: capable of stirring the emotions of the viewer

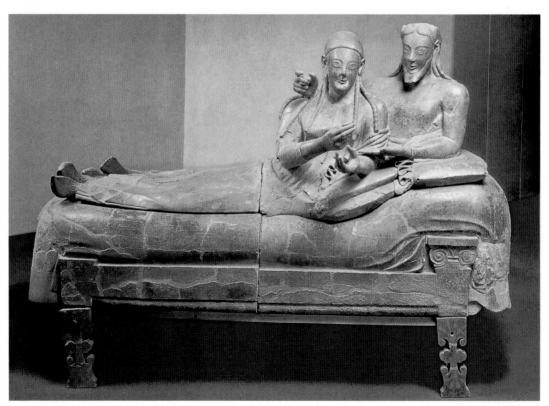

2.4.10 Sarcophagus from Cerveteri, *c.* 520 BCE. Painted terra-cotta, 3′9½″ × 6′7″. Museo Nazionale di Villa Giulia, Rome, Italy

Nkisi Nkondi
Synthesis and Spirit

For the other *nkisi nkondi*
GATEWAYS:
→ see p. 431 and p. 548

Nkisi nkondi (plural *minkisi minkondi*): combines the words for "sacred medicine" and "to hunt"; figurative sculpture(s) used in rituals by the Yombe of Central Africa

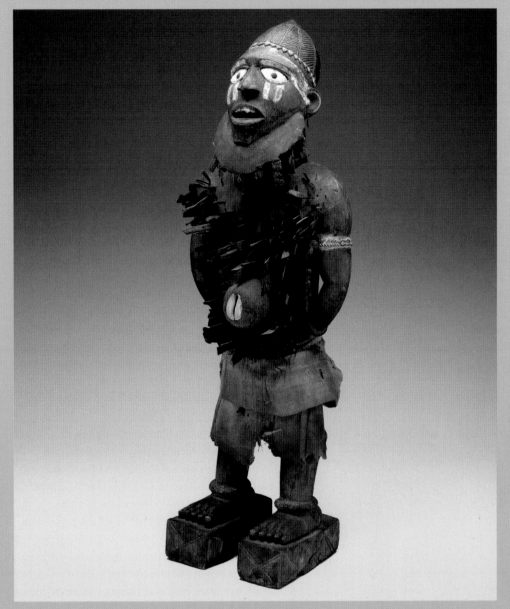

2.4.11 Standing power figure (*nkisi nkondi*), late 19th–early 20th century. Wood, iron, raffia, ceramic, pigment, kaolin, red camwood, resin, dirt, leaves, animal skin, and cowrie shell, 43¾ × 15½ × 11". Dallas Museum of Art, Texas

Sculptors of central Africa, like many contemporary artists, do not limit themselves to only one working or conceptual method to create a work. They synthesize, or integrate, various working processes to fit the needs of the object that they are constructing. This is true when Yombe sculptors fashion spiritually-charged *nkisi* figures, which act as containers of power. The crafter of these objects works with a spiritual advisor, or *nganga*, to fuse the spiritual with physical and visual attributes. A *nkisi nkondi* (**2.4.11**) is a figural form (either man or dog) that will hunt down and punish anyone who breaks agreements, laws, or commits evil.

In consultation with the nganga, the sculptor will start with a subtractive process, carving a wooden representation until it takes on the approved figural qualities. Then the artist will work in an additive method, adding pieces of clothing, paint, and ornament, making sure to leave a void somewhere on the figure where a spirit may reside. These works are also interactive, as the last part of the process involves awakening the spirit through the hammering of nails or blades. The act of hammering in a nail or blade during ritual may seal an agreement, or activate unseen forces to carry out punishments.

Casting

Casting, another additive process, involves adding a liquid or pliable material to a mold. It is done in order to set a form in a more durable material, or to make it possible to create multiple copies of a work. The first step in casting is to make a model of the final sculpture. This is used to make a mold. A casting liquid (often molten metal, but other materials, such as clay, plaster, acrylic polymers, or glass are also used) is poured into the mold. When it hardens, the result is a detailed replica of the original model.

Plaster casts are often used to create both models and finished products. To create a

2.4.12 *Riace Warrior A*, *c.* 460 BCE. Bronze with copper, silver, and ivory, height 6′6″. Museo Nazionale della Magna Grecia, Reggio Calabria, Italy

plaster cast, the artist makes a clay original, coats it with a release agent (usually a slick, oily substance), then creates a plaster coating to go over the original. The artist is careful to make divisions so that the plaster mold can be easily separated, in sections, from the clay original. After the plaster has cured—set in a permanent state—the sections are carefully detached, the inside of the parts of the mold coated with release agent, and the mold reassembled. Plaster, or another pliable casting material, can then be poured into the mold, allowed to set, and the cast form removed. Alternatively, an artist may create a finished sculpture of plaster by carving a cast block with chisels and files, and finish it by sanding.

The ancient Greeks cast bronze to produce many of their sculptures. Bronze is an **alloy**, or mixture, of copper and tin. It melts at a relatively low temperature (an average of 1,750°F depending on the composition of the alloy) and is comparatively easy to cast. Once formed and cooled it is light (compared to stone) and durable. The so-called *Riace Warrior A* is a fine example of the casting skills of ancient Greek artists (**2.4.12**). It is one of two sculptures found in 1972 by divers off the coast of Riace, southern Italy. This sculpture reflects great attention to detail and was made at a time when the Greeks emphasized the perfection of the human body. The figure is posed in a **contrapposto** (Italian for "opposite"), which uses the natural curvature of the body to enliven the design. By shifting the weight to the right leg, the hips are set at a slight angle, which is countered by small shifts in the shoulders, with the head fractionally tilted. The work may have been cast to celebrate the victory of the Athenians over the invading Persians, and the relaxed contrapposto of the figure reflects strength and confidence.

Riace Warrior A was created using the lost-wax method of casting. (Each numbered stage refers to **2.4.13**.) The artist begins by building an armature (1) and then adds clay to it to create the original form. A cast is made from the clay original (2), then a thick layer of wax is used to coat the inside of the emptied mold, filled with clay, and stabilized with metal rods called **chaplets** (3). Any detail the sculptor wishes to see in the final work is carved into the wax (4), then wax shafts are added before an **investment** made from sand and ground-up pieces of old molds is used to cover the surface of the wax

Alloy: a mixture of a metal combined with at least one other element

Contrapposto: a pose in sculpture in which the upper part of the body twists in one direction and the lower part in another

Chaplet: a metal support rod used in casting

Investment: a casting mold that is used in the final phase of lost-wax bronze casting

form, preserving all the detail (5). This hard coating needs to be strong enough to bear the heat and weight of the metal until it cools. The wax is exposed at the bottom of the investment, and is placed in a kiln (6). When heated, the wax melts out through the openings in the bottom of the investment, leaving a hollow space. Immediately after the mold has been removed from the kiln, very hot molten metal—in this case, bronze—is poured into it (7). When the metal has begun to cool, the mold is removed (usually by breaking it with a hammer) to reveal the bronze—which is still not finished (8).

The artist cuts off any extra metal, then sands and polishes (9). Over time, exposure to the elements can add surface color, called a **patina**, to bronze sculpture. Such a patina can enhance the beauty of the work. Patinas can also be applied using chemicals that react with the bronze and stabilize oxidation (10).

Lost-wax casting is called a substitution process because the molten metal takes the place of the wax. Other materials, such as foam or wood, are occasionally used as substitution materials instead of wax, because they can be burned out of the mold.

Patina: surface color or texture on a metal caused by aging

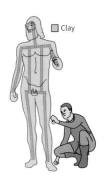

1. Original Form
The artist models the sculpture from clay using an armature for support.

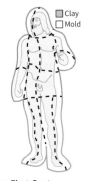

2. First Cast
A multi-part cast is created from the original form. The pieces of this cast are used to fabricate a wax impression.

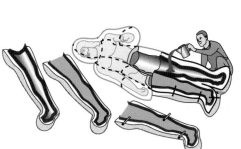

3. The clay original is removed from the mold and the void is coated with a thick layer of wax. The empty interior is filled with clay and fixed in place with chaplets (metal rods) to ensure that the shape will be stabilized.

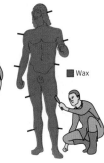

4. Investment Mold
The wax impression is refined and detailed by the artist.

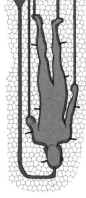

■ Wax ⊥ Investment ■ Clay

5. The wax impression is encased in an investment mold made of material that can withstand the high heat of molten bronze.

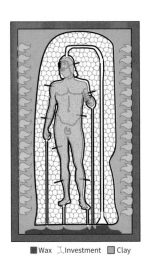

■ Wax ⊥ Investment ■ Clay

6. Heating and Pouring
The investment mold is heated to a high temperature allowing the wax to melt out, leaving an empty interior space.

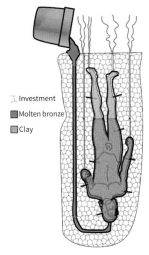

⊥ Investment
■ Molten bronze
■ Clay

7. Pouring
The hot investment mold is removed from the kiln and molten bronze is poured in the space left behind after the wax is "lost".

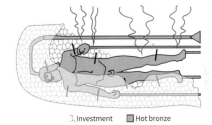

⊥ Investment ■ Hot bronze

8. Once the bronze has cooled to a hardened state, but is still hot, the artist(s) break away the investment, revealing the metal form.

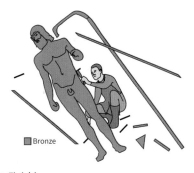

■ Bronze

9. Finishing
Once the investment has been cleared and the interior clay removed, excess bronze is stripped off the sculpture. The artist(s) fill imperfections and burnish the metal into the intended surface.

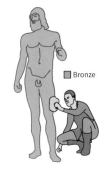

■ Bronze

10. Finishing
A patina, or surface treatment, may be added to protect the finished sculpture.

2.4.13 Steps in the lost-wax casting process

Pushing beyond Traditional Methods

The traditional processes used for sculpting were ideal for the creation of static objects, but artists have found other ways to enliven the **medium** that go beyond conventional additive and subtractive techniques. They have challenged conventional notions of what sculptures can be.

Earthworks

Prehistoric artists of the Americas made **monumental** sculptures that used the surface of the Earth itself as material: this was additive sculpture on a very large scale. The most prominent of these is the Great Serpent Mound near Locust Grove, Ohio. As can be readily seen from the air, it resembles a snake with its mouth open, ingesting an egg (**2.4.14**). The identity of the people who created it is still debated. The head of the serpent and the egg are aligned to the position of the setting sun on the summer solstice (the longest day of the year), suggesting that the Great Serpent Mound was used in making solar observations. The original artists heaped piles of earth to sculpt this work onto the Ohio landscape.

In the 1960s, artists again became interested in earthworks. The best-known modern earthwork is Robert Smithson's (1938–1973) *Spiral Jetty* in the Great Salt Lake in Utah (**2.4.15**). Smithson chose a spiral, a shape naturally found in shells, crystals, and even galaxies. The coiled artwork was made by dumping 6,550 tons of rock and dirt off dump trucks, gradually paving a spiraling roadbed out into the salt lake. The sculpture is not static in the way it interacts with nature: over the years the lake has repeatedly submerged and then

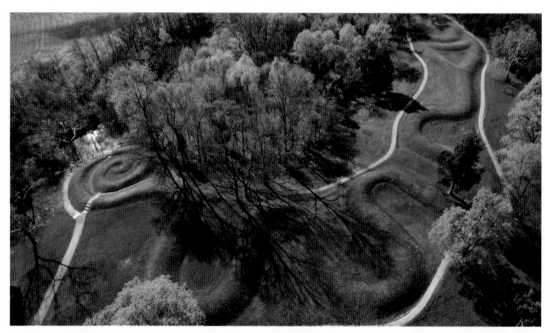

2.4.14 Great Serpent Mound, *c*. 800 BCE–100 CE, 1330 × 3', Locust Grove, Adams County, Ohio

2.4.15 Robert Smithson, *Spiral Jetty*, 1969–70. Black rock, salt crystals, and earth, diameter 160', coil length 1500 × 15'. Great Salt Lake, Utah

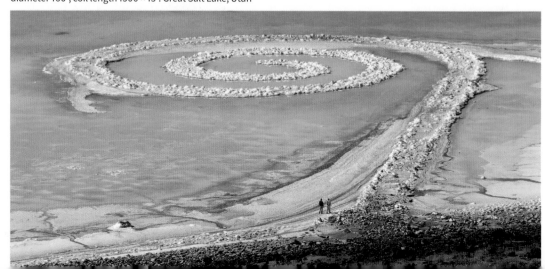

revealed it, so that it is constantly evolving as it drowns and rises with a new encrustation of salt crystals.

Because of their enormous size, earthwork projects need the collaboration of many artists and workers, and equipment. Such works as the Great Serpent Mound required a community effort. Today, earthwork projects are obliged to have permits and community approval, and to involve large groups of workers. Earthwork artists do not earn money from their works, but create them as a service to the community. Many believe their earthworks should represent a harmony between nature and humanity.

Construction

When engineers make a piece of machinery, they use a variety of methods—for example, sawing, grinding, and milling, or molding and casting—to create and put together its components. All the components are then assembled. Some artists construct sculptures in a similar way.

The idea of constructing sculptures is relatively new. Methods for doing so have proliferated with the growth of standardized, engineered materials, such as sheet metals and plastics. In the late nineteenth century, sculptors began to look beyond traditional carved or cast forms to the process of constructing. The **Constructivist** art movement in the Soviet Union created sculptural construction techniques based on practices associated more with a factory than with an art studio. Naum Gabo (b. Naum Neemia Pevsner, 1890–1977) used his *Constructed Head No. 2*

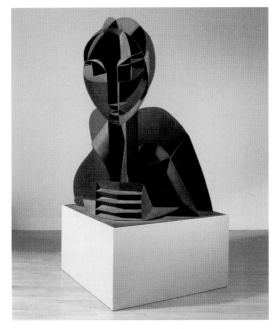

2.4.16 Naum Gabo, *Constructed Head No. 2*, 1916. Cor-ten steel, 69 × 52¾ × 48¼". Tate, London, England

(**2.4.16**) to investigate the sense of **space** and form implied by flat planes, in contrast to the solid **mass** of conventional sculpture. Here, Gabo is more interested in showing the interior construction of the work than the exterior surface, and has welded the intersecting planes of metal together.

Contemporary artists have adopted modern-day industrial techniques and unconventional materials to create their sculptures. The British artist Damien Hirst (b. 1965) made his work *The Physical Impossibility of Death in the Mind of Someone Living* out of a large tank full of formaldehyde, in which he suspended a dead shark (**2.4.17**). Of course, not every part

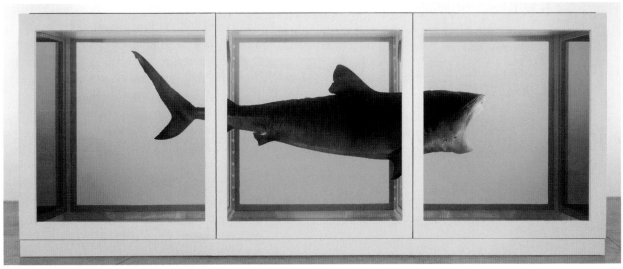

2.4.17 Damien Hirst, *The Physical Impossibility of Death in the Mind of Someone Living*, 1991. Glass, painted steel, silicone, monofilament, shark, and formaldehyde solution, 7'1½" × 17'9⅜" × 5'10⅞"

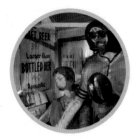

Another example of an assemblage is *Edward Kienholz, The Beanery*:
→ see **2.10.7a** and **2.10.7b**, p. 339

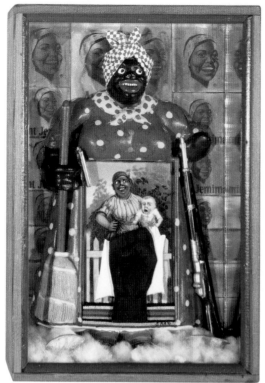

2.4.18 Betye Saar, *The Liberation of Aunt Jemima*, 1972. Mixed-media assemblage, 11¾ × 8 × 2¾". Collection University of California, Berkeley Art Museum, California

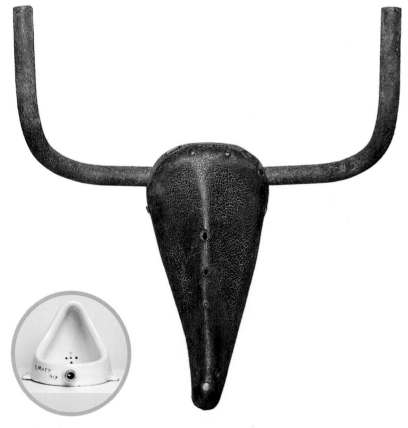

Marcel Duchamp's *Fountain* has become a classic example of readymade art:
→ see **3.10.1**, p. 523

2.4.19 Pablo Picasso, *Bull's Head*, 1942. Assemblage of bicycle seat and handlebars, 13¼ × 17⅛ × 7½". Musée Picasso, Paris, France

of his work was constructed; Hirst had the shark caught by fishermen. The entire work resembles a biology class dissection specimen. Hirst is known for creating his sculptures from unusual objects that contrast life and death.

Assemblage

The practice of gathering objects and fabricating them into a work of art is called **assemblage**. The gathered objects, sometimes called **found objects**, are repurposed so that they support the visual ideas and compositions of the artist. When the contemporary African American artist Betye Saar (b. 1926) created the work *The Liberation of Aunt Jemima* (**2.4.18**), she collected a variety of different found objects, such as cotton, syrup-bottle labels, and a stereotypical "Mammy" doll, and assembled them in a wooden box. The objects symbolize the relics and memorabilia of both personal and societal history as they relate to issues of gender and race; these pieces represent influences that were important to traditional African groups. Saar is interested in exploring themes of personal and communal identity: her art examines the survival of African traditions in black culture and often challenges stereotypes, for example those represented by such figures as Aunt Jemima.

Readymades

In the early twentieth century, a few artists began to create works using as raw materials **artifacts** that already existed. Sometimes they simply decided that found objects were works of art. The Spanish artist Pablo Picasso (1881–1973) once took the handlebars and the seat of a bicycle and combined them to make his *Bull's Head* (**2.4.19**). Such artworks are known as **readymades**. Although Picasso did not make the individual parts, he arranged them in such a way that they resemble a bull's head, yet they are also readily recognizable as parts of a bicycle. The artist's intent was both a serious and a humorous attempt to redefine art.

Picasso was following in the footsteps of the French artist Marcel Duchamp (1887–1968), who pioneered a practice known as **appropriation**, as a way of challenging traditional ideas about art. Duchamp argued that any object, by virtue of being chosen and presented by an artist, can become a work of art. This way of making art is known as appropriation because the artist appropriates a pre-existing image or object and alters its appearance in a way that changes its original meaning or purpose. For Duchamp, the act of discovery (of conceiving the artwork) was the most important part of the artist's process; he believed that the artist's original interpretation of the appropriated object is what makes it art. "I chose it!" Duchamp exclaimed, creating endless possibilities for artists to redefine art as ideas, and to help us see things differently.

Kinetic and Light Sculpture

Technological advances in our society have created more opportunities for creativity. Sculptors who work with movement and light express their ideas in ways that would not have been possible just a century or two before. These moving and lighted sculptural works, similarly to those of the Constructivists, rely on mechanical engineering as well as the creative input of the artist.

Sculpture that moves is called **kinetic sculpture**. The American artist George Rickey (1907–2002) designed works that were carefully balanced so that they could pivot in a variety of directions and provide an infinite number of changing views. His *Breaking Column* is moved by the slightest current of air; it also has a motor, and moves even when there is no wind (**2.4.20**). Although motorized, Rickey wanted to create a visual cue that illustrated the unseen forces of nature at work.

One of the first artists to merge movement, lighting, and performance into a single work was the Hungarian artist László Moholy-Nagy (1895–1946). Moholy-Nagy was interested in the work of the Constructivists and wanted to incorporate technology into his art. The sculpture *Light Prop for an Electric Stage* (**2.4.21**), initially created as a stage lighting device, eventually became the main character in a film, also by Moholy-Nagy. The work has a motor that

Assemblage: an artwork made of three-dimensional materials, including found objects

Found image or object: an image or object found by an artist and presented, with little or no alteration, as part of a work or as a finished work of art in itself

Artifact: an object made by a person

Readymade: an everyday object presented as a work of art

Appropriation: the deliberate incorporation in an artwork of material originally created by other artists

Kinetic art/sculpture: three-dimensional art that moves, impelled by air currents, motors, or people

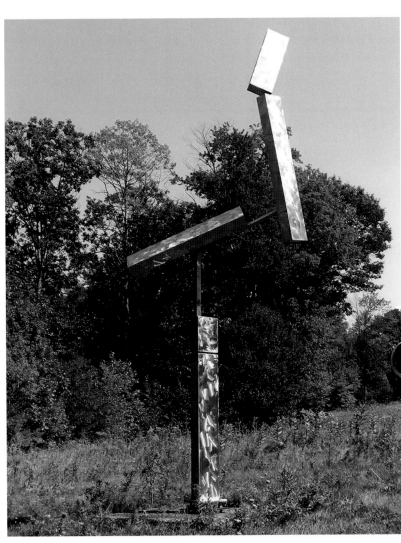

2.4.20 George Rickey, *Breaking Column*, 1986 (completed by the artist's estate, 2009). Stainless steel, 9′11⅜″ × 5½″. Contemporary Museum, Honolulu, Hawaii

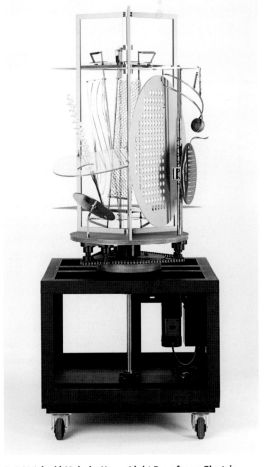

2.4.21 László Moholy-Nagy, *Light Prop for an Electric Stage*, 1929–30. Exhibition replica, constructed 2006, through the courtesy of Hattula Moholy-Nagy. Metal, plastics, glass, paint, and wood, with electric motor, 59½ × 27⅝ × 27⅝″. Harvard Art Museums, Busch-Reisinger Museum, Cambridge, Massachusetts

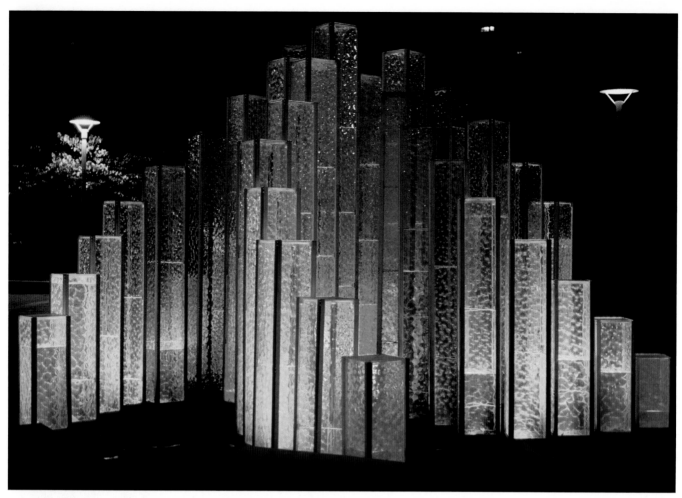

2.4.22 Athena Tacha in collaboration with EDAW of Alexandria, Virginia, *Star Fountain* **(night view)**, 2009. Sandstone, cast stone, granite, brick, glass, animated RGB-LEDs. Muhammad Ali Plaza, Louisville, Kentucky

moves a series of perforated discs so that they cross in front of the lighting unit. This creates a constantly changing sculptural object, and the changes in lighting also influence the surrounding environment.

Moholy-Nagy's investigations into the use of light influenced artists who were interested in the effects produced by controlling the lighting of an interior space. Through the use of light an artist can change how a viewer perceives a three-dimensional space. Carefully organized light projection can create the illusion that a surface exists in three dimensions even if it has only two.

Installations

Modern artists have explored many ways of expanding the range of sculpture as a

medium. **Installation** sculpture involves the construction of a space or the assembly of objects to create an environment; we are encouraged to experience the work physically using all our senses, perhaps even entering the work itself.

An installation work by the Greek-born artist Athena Tacha (b. 1936) deals with action. The movement in Tacha's work implies the action of dance, as the rhythms of her installations flow and repeat in graceful patterns. One gets the fullest impression of these rhythms at night, as her works are infused with constantly changing colored lighting. *Star Fountain* (**2.4.22**) is a series of vertical glass columns organized into a spiraling shape, with color changes over a four-minute time span.

Installation: originally referring to the hanging of pictures and arrangement of objects in an exhibition, installation may also refer to an intentional environment created as a completed artwork

Explore Further Sculpture

Subtractive sculpture

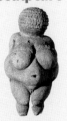

4.8.1 *Woman from Willendorf*, c. 24,000–22,000 BCE → p. 630

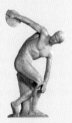

4.8.4 Myron, *Discus Thrower (Discobolos)*, c. 450 BCE → p. 633

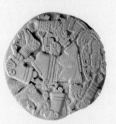

3.4.17 *The Dismemberment of Coyolxauhqui, Goddess of the Moon*, late Postclassic → p. 420

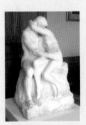

1.2.16 Auguste Rodin, *The Kiss*, c. 1882 → p. 59

Casting

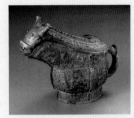

3.3.8 Ritual wine vessel (*guang*), late Shang Dynasty, c. 1700–1050 BCE → p. 396

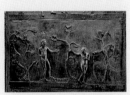

4.2.3b Hildesheim Doors (detail), Abbey Church of St. Michael's, 1015 → p. 556

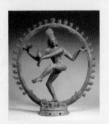

4.3.2 *Shiva Nataraja (Lord of the Dance)*, Chola Period, 11th century → p. 569

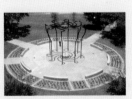

1.5.14 Nancy Holt, *Solar Rotary*, 1995 → p. 111

Modeling

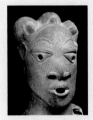

3.5.2 Head from Rafin Kura, Nigeria, c. 500 BCE–200 CE → p. 429

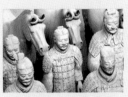

3.3.10b Soldiers from the mausoleum of Qin Shi Huangdi, c. 210 BCE → p. 397

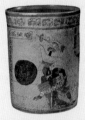

3.4.13 Cylindrical vessel with ritual ball-game scene, c. 700–850 → p. 418

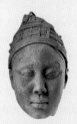

4.8.6 Head, possibly an Ife king, West Africa, 12th–14th century → p. 634

Construction

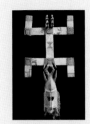

3.5.7 Kanaga mask, Mali, early 20th century → p. 432

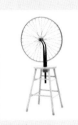

3.9.10 Marcel Duchamp, *Bicycle Wheel*, 1913 → p. 506

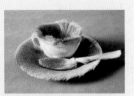

1.2.21 Méret Oppenheim, *Object*, 1936 → p. 64

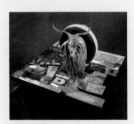

1.6.11 Robert Rauschenberg, *Monogram*, 1955–59 → p. 123

Your turn
What sculptural methods were used to create these works?

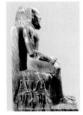

3.1.15 Statue of Khafre with Horus, Egypt, c. 2500 BCE → p. 357

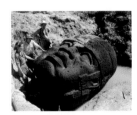

3.4.9 Colossal Olmec head, 1500–400 BCE → p. 416

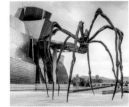

1.2.18 Louise Bourgeois, *Maman*, 1999 (cast 2001) → p. 61

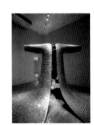

3.3.21 Do Ho Suh, *Some/One*, 2001 → p. 405

2.5 Architecture

Column: a freestanding pillar, usually circular in section

Form: an object that can be defined in three dimensions (height, width, and depth)

Architecture communicates important ideas; it has a special place in our lives. Architecture—three-dimensional art and design that surrounds and influences us—represents the safety of home, the strength of government, the energy of commercial enterprise, and the power of human innovation. It connects us to our history in a very real way: a historic building shows us how people lived in the past, while a new building adapts design ideas from previous eras to a contemporary context. Architecture suggests feelings of permanence and place. It is no wonder we all have an opinion about a new building, because a building inevitably affects all who see or enter it, whether or not they are aware of this.

Architectural space is the result of thoughtful design by an artist, or by a team of artists working to a common idea. The architect is the master planner who creates a building's overall design. Thoughtful design reflects a building's function and its intended role in the community. For example, an architect designing a college building will consider its users—the instructors and students—and will design classroom spaces that are well lit and flexible.

Sometimes an interior designer is responsible for making the space inside appropriate for the building's intended use. In the case of a college classroom, an interior designer will choose colors and furnishings and plan the organization of the space in a way that reflects the needs of students and teachers.

A landscape architect may be employed to organize the outdoor spaces around the building. This designer will plan the landscaping, parking, and entry and exit routes to be consistent with the rest of the structure.

The architect, interior designer, and landscape architect actively communicate with the building contractors to ensure that the final construction will accord with the design team's intentions. Some good architectural design even acts as a symbol that identifies the function of the space. For example, many American college buildings use such features as Greek **columns** to make reference to the foundations of European and North American culture and academic endeavor.

Structure, Function, and Form

Architecture is principally concerned with structure, function, and **form**. The engineering and science of architecture strives to understand and control the forces pushing or pulling the structure of the building. These forces, called stresses, are constantly at work. When stresses pull, they create tension, which lengthens and stretches the materials of the building. When stresses push, they create compression, which can squash and shorten the same materials. Architectural engineers work to create balances between tension and compression so that the amount of push equals the amount of pull. Each kind of building material resists the stress of compression or tension differently. Architects measure the strength of a material so that they can anticipate and control the balance of forces at work. If balanced correctly, a building can stand for many thousands of years; if not, it may collapse.

The Turkish architect Sinan (1489–1588) was chief architect to the Ottoman court under Sultan Süleyman, who commissioned him to design the magnificent mosque shown in **2.5.1**. Sinan's visionary ingenuity and grasp of engineering principles enabled him to develop new ways of opening up the architectural space, thus creating this extraordinary building, which includes not only the principal **dome**, but also four half-domes around it. The skillful design, which perfectly balances all of the different parts, has enabled this elaborate and complex structure to endure for more than 500 years. The integration of light in this building is striking, as the many windows illuminate the upper portion of the domes. This draws the worshiper's attention upward, as if toward the heavens, symbolically supporting the building's intended function as a place of worship.

The engineering of a building, or its structural integrity, dictates some of the design decisions. Wood-frame buildings may require waterproof external cladding to protect the timber from damp and rot. Tall office buildings may need to have a strong steel frame (or an alternative) to bear the combined weight of the whole structure (see p. 259).

An architect collects information about the planned location of the building, its place in the community, and its purpose; selects the appropriate building techniques; and decides which materials are needed to construct it. The location, or site, influences the design. Is the building going to sit on a plain or a mountainside, in a city or a rural community, on a waterfront or in a desert? Each of these sites presents different challenges that the design must answer. For example, a building facing the sea might need to be strong and resilient to resist the effects of storms, while one in a desert must be made of materials that can help keep the building cool.

Artists must consider the availability and cost of building materials when they plan their projects. The unique character of these materials—for example their flexibility, strength, **texture**, and appearance—also affects the architect's choices.

Although buildings can be some of the largest and most complicated human-made objects, they usually begin from the simplicity of a drawing. Fumihiko Maki (b. 1928) created a simple drawing as he began working on a design for the New World Trade Center in New York City (**2.5.2**). The drawing shows how his building was designed to fit in with other buildings on or around the site by continuing a spiral design.

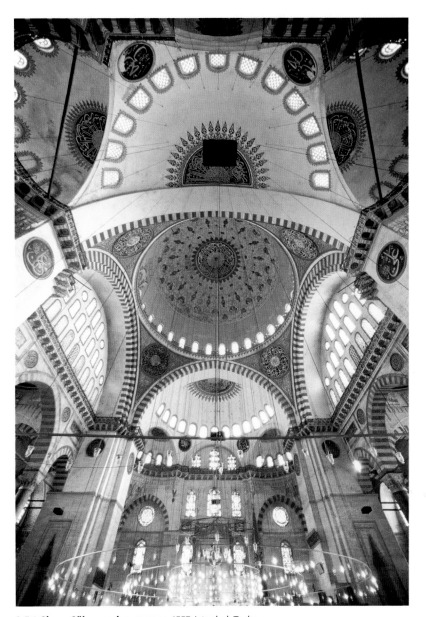

2.5.1 Sinan, **Süleymaniye mosque**, 1557. Istanbul, Turkey

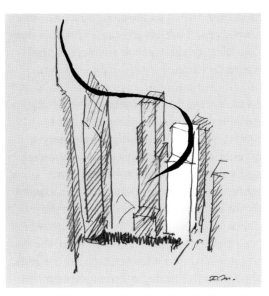

2.5.2 Fumihiko Maki, **sketch of Four World Trade Center**, 2006

Dome: an evenly curved vault forming the ceiling or roof of a building

Texture: the surface quality of a work, for example fine/coarse, detailed/lacking in detail

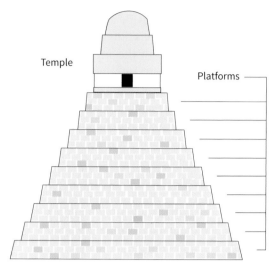

2.5.4 Load-bearing architecture: Maya pyramid

carefully organized stack of stones (**2.5.3**). The weight of the temple structure at the top, which is a three-room building where Maya priests conducted religious rites, bears down on the stone platform beneath it, which, in turn, bears down on the stone platform beneath *it*, and so on, holding all the stones securely in place (**2.5.4**). Construction on this scale required sophisticated engineering and mathematical skills to ensure that such an enormous structure formed a perfectly symmetrical shape that would stand for thousands of years. The ability of the ancient Maya to engineer these massive structures using only stones, with the few tools available at the time, has always been a cause of wonder.

Post-and-Lintel Construction

The **monumental** quality of ancient pyramids stands as a testament to the ingenuity and will of humankind. But these impressive structures did not provide the spacious interiors we have come to expect in everyday architecture. In order to create an interior space, an architect must create a **span**, or a distance between two supports in a structure. One of the oldest and most effective ways of doing this is a system called **post-and-lintel construction**.

In elementary post-and-lintel construction (**2.5.5**), the lintel rests on top of two posts. Ancient Egyptian architects built the Temple of Amun-Re at Karnak by placing a series of post-and-lintel spans side by side to create a spacious interior, as seen in the Great Court (**2.5.6**). The temple also includes an architectural space known as a hypostyle hall,

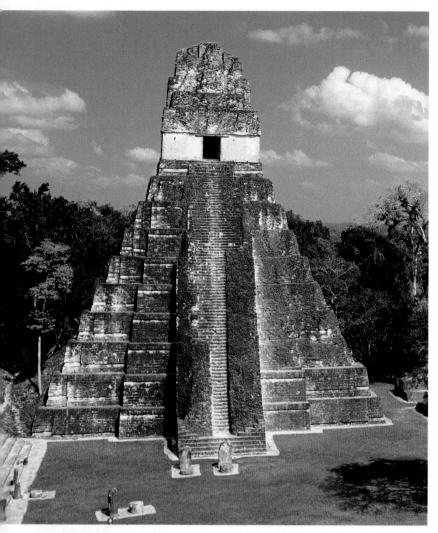

2.5.3 Temple I in the Great Plaza, Maya, *c*. 300–900 CE. Tikal, Guatemala

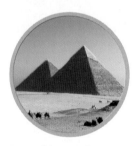

Some of the most famous load-bearing constructions are the Great Pyramids at Giza: → see **3.1.13**, p. 355

Monumental: having massive or impressive scale

Span: the distance bridged between two supports, such as columns or walls

Post-and-lintel construction: a horizontal beam (the lintel) supported by a post at either end

---

Ancient Construction

Ancient cultures derived their building materials from the earth. Stone, wood, and clay are plentiful and easily available, but they must be modified for use in architecture. When shaped and used with great care and skill, these raw materials can result in architecture that transcends time.

Load-Bearing Construction

Probably the most direct way to build something is the apparently simple process of piling one stone or brick on top of another, as, for example, in a Maya pyramid. Such massive load-bearing works have been created throughout history. Protruding out of the Guatemalan rainforest at Tikal are hundreds of such pyramids that rise sharply toward the sky, emphasizing their role as gateways to the gods. Maya pyramids primarily served as platforms for temples. The pyramid that makes up the support for Temple I at Tikal is essentially a

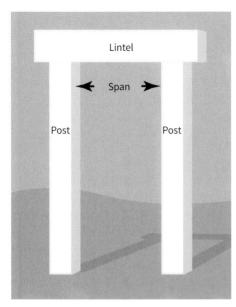

2.5.5 Post-and-lintel construction

a room created by using a series of columns, or a colonnade, to support a flat ceiling. The hall was used by Egyptian priests for rituals to worship the god Amun-Re, while ordinary people stood outside in an open courtyard. Amun-Re's temple, still one of the largest religious structures in the world, is just one of many at Karnak. The material used for the posts and lintels—in this instance, stone—needs to be strong enough to support the roof of the building, to absorb the stresses placed on the columns and lintel.

The architects of ancient Greece must have been aware of the majestic architecture of the Nile Valley, where such monuments as the Temple of Amun-Re can be found. Greek architects of the era adapted the systems invented by the Egyptians and went

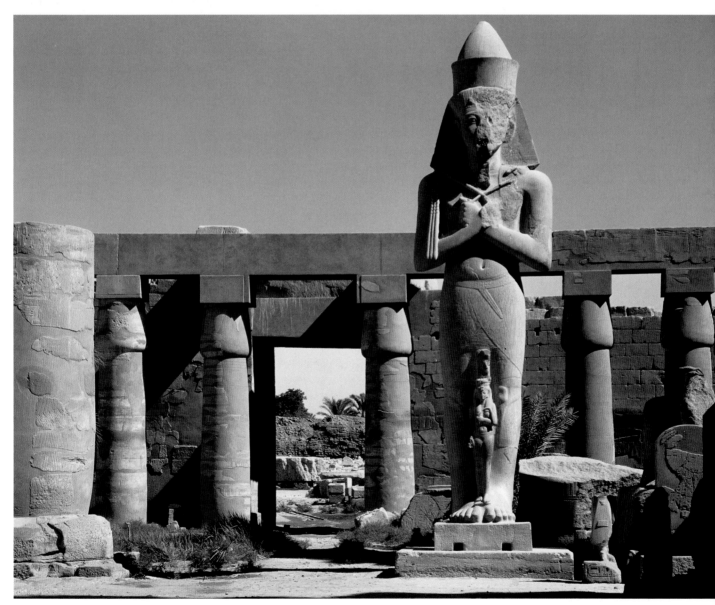

2.5.6 Great Court at Temple of Amun-Re, Middle Kingdom, *c.* 950–730 BCE. Karnak, Egypt

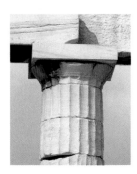

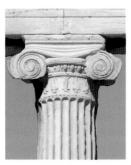

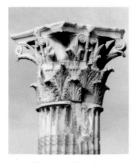

2.5.7 (from top) **Doric, Ionic, and Corinthian capitals**

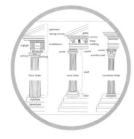

The use of post-and-lintel architecture by the ancient Greeks can be seen in three distinct styles: Doric, Ionic, and Corinthian:

→ see **3.1.23**, p. 363

Capital: the architectural feature that crowns a column

Shaft: the main vertical part of a column

Base: the projecting series of blocks between the shaft of a column and its plinth

Architectural order: a style of designing columns and related parts of a Greek or Roman building

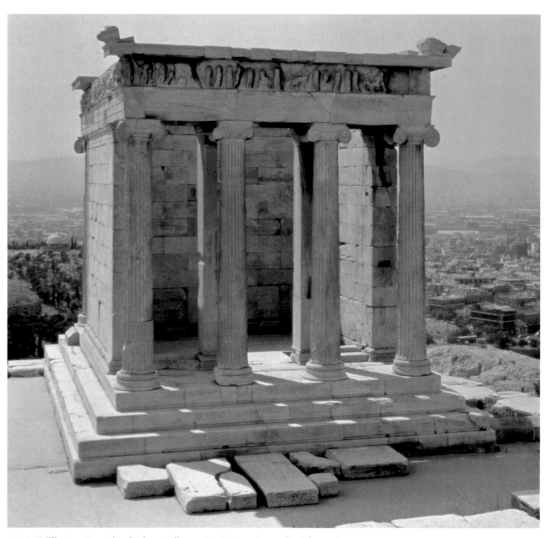

2.5.8 Kallikrates, **Temple of Athena Nike**, *c.* 421–415 BCE. Acropolis, Athens, Greece

on to become some of the world's greatest practitioners of post-and-lintel construction. They standardized the basic post, or column: an essential point of compression used to support the weight of a building (see **2.5.8**). Classical Greek architecture is dominated by the use of columns, a structural element with three main parts: **capital**, **shaft**, and **base**. The capital, or uppermost part of the column, serves as the transition point from the lintel to the shaft, or main vertical section of the post. The base acts as a stabilizing point where the building's weight is concentrated. Three different column styles help identify **architectural orders**. Doric columns have a plain, round, capital; Ionic are distinguished by a scroll-like formation called a volute; and Corinthian columns sport a leafy top modeled after the acanthus plant (**2.5.7**, bottom).

The ancient Greeks made a lasting impact on Western traditions in architectural style (**2.5.8**). The Romans quickly adopted Greek orders while adding their own new stylistic accents. Rome's architectural innovations then influenced the later styles of the **Renaissance** (see p. 254) and the **Baroque**, even being revived again in the eighteenth century to celebrate the rise of democratic government, especially in the US and France. The architectural character of Washington, D.C., with its many columns (the White House is a good example), reflects the ideals of democracy that the ancient Greeks instituted in order to allow the free citizens of Athens to decide their own destiny.

Arches in Ancient Architecture

A limitation of early post-and-lintel architecture is that the lintels could not span large spaces. Stone, while enormously strong in compression, is fairly weak in tension. Since stone cannot stretch, its use risks creating a weakness in the middle of a span that can snap under heavy pressure. Architects who want to design large interior spaces in stone have to be aware of the weight of the building constantly pressing down. The ancient Babylonians in Mesopotamia (modern-day Iraq) and the Mycenaeans of early Greece both employed the **corbeled arch** (**2.5.9**) as a solution to this problem. The stepping inward of successive layers of stonework over the doorway allows for the compression created by the weight of the building to be directed outward through **cantilevered** (secured at only one end) stones, rather than downward. This reduces the pressure on the structure and allows the architect to design and span larger spaces.

Early inhabitants of the Greek coastline experimented with ways to open up interior spaces using corbeled arches. The entrance to the Treasury of Atreus (also called the Tomb of Agamemnon; **2.5.10**), built around 1250 BCE, provides a glimpse into ancient corbeled arch construction. Although a lintel interrupts the space between the doorway and the arch above, the progressive cantilevering of stones above the lintel provides an additional opening so that more light can enter the chamber beyond.

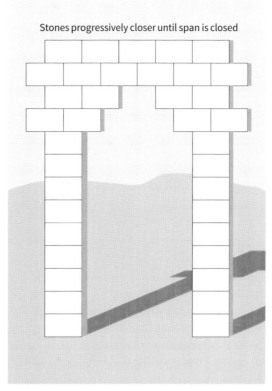

Stones progressively closer until span is closed

2.5.9 Corbeled arch

Renaissance: a period of cultural and artistic change in Europe from the fourteenth to the seventeenth century

Baroque: European artistic and architectural style of the late sixteenth to early eighteenth century, characterized by extravagance and emotional intensity

Corbeled: with a series of corbels—architectural feature made of stone, brick, wood, etc.—each projecting beyond the one below

Arch: a structure, usually curved, that spans an opening

Cantilever: a long beam or lintel that projects out from a structure beyond a support

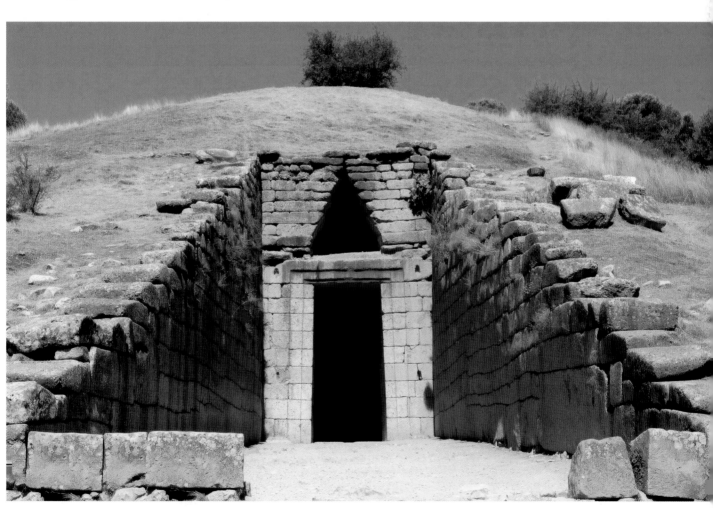

2.5.10 Entrance, Treasury of Atreus, *c.* 1250 BCE. Mycenae, Greece

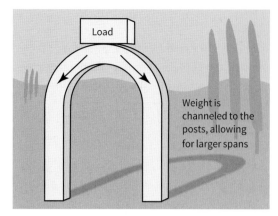

2.5.11 Arch construction

The Romans perfected the rounded arch (**2.5.11**), which was a more efficient way of distributing compressive stress over the whole of the structure, by spreading the weight of the building outward along the entire span of the arc. Its efficiency helped them span wider spaces than any previous architects had managed. The upper level of the Pont du Gard, in southern France, is a Roman **aqueduct**, built to move fresh water from mountain springs 30 miles away to the populated territories recently conquered by Rome (**2.5.12**). The lower level is a bridge across the river. The goal of the aqueduct was to create a consistent downhill path for the water: 1 in. down for every 33 in. along. The Romans made this impressive structure without any mortar

holding the stones together, so perfectly were they cut to fit. After conquering an area, the Romans often built aqueducts and roads. These structures benefited the local community, projected Roman imperial power, and enabled the army to move quickly across its new territory.

Vaults

Roman architects used three important architectural structures: the arch, **vault**, and dome. A vault is an arch that has been extended like a long hallway to create an open space overhead. The structural integrity of arches, vaults, and domes is created when the outward-pushing forces of the building weight are stopped by a heavy support, or buttress. The most common type of vault, the barrel vault,

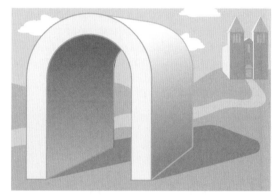

2.5.13 Barrel vault

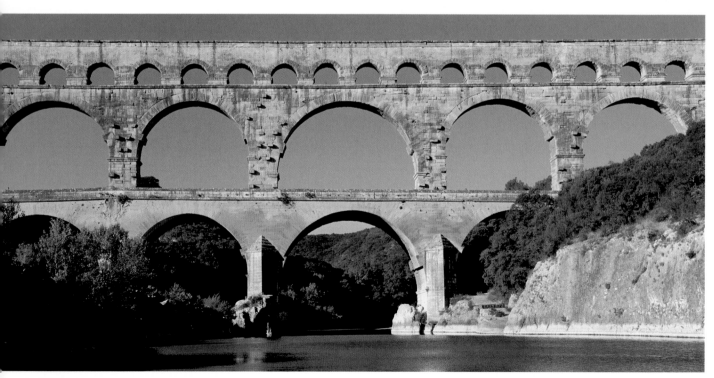

2.5.12 Pont du Gard, first century CE. Nîmes, France

consists of a long, semicircular arch (**2.5.13**). The vault helped to span larger areas of an interior space; this was especially important during the European **Middle Ages**, as churches became more significant centers of community activities that more people wished to attend.

The Church of Sainte-Madeleine at Vézelay (**2.5.14**) in France was a stop along the Christian pilgrimage route to the holy church Santiago de Compostela in Spain. The builders of the **Romanesque** church at Vézelay needed to create a space that could accommodate thousands of religious pilgrims. Their solution was to use the barrel vault, but they had to deal with an important limitation of vault construction. Because the weight of the vault thrusts outward,

Middle Ages: the time period roughly between the fall of the Roman empire and the start of the Renaissance

Romanesque: an early medieval European style of architecture based on Roman-style rounded arches and heavy construction

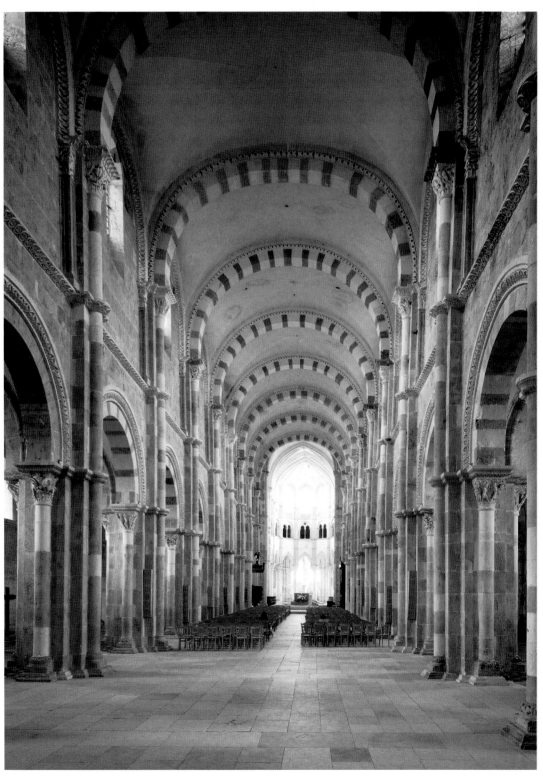

2.5.14 Church of Sainte-Madeleine, 12th century. Vézelay, France

Aisles: in a basilica or other church, the spaces between the columns of the nave and the side walls

Nave: the central space of a church or basilica

Groin vault: an architectural feature created by the intersection of two vaults into the nave

Flying buttress: an arch built on the exterior of a building that transfers some of the weight of the vault

Pointed arches: arches with two curved sides that meet to form a point at the apex

Emphasis: the principle of drawing attention to particular content in a work

Rib vault: an arch-like structure supporting a ceiling or roof, with a web of protruding stonework

the walls supporting it must be massive so as not to collapse. Vaulted **aisles** counteract this outward pressure on the walls and support both sides of the **nave**. **Groin vaults** can be seen as intersecting v-shapes in the ceiling between the arches of Vezelay and were an innovation that expanded the space where two vaults intersected, opening up even more architectural space.

Even though Romanesque churches are large enough for plenty of pilgrims and worshipers, the thick walls have only small windows, creating dark and gloomy interior spaces. One visionary church leader, named Abbot Suger (1081–1151), was not satisfied with the austere interiors of Romanesque architecture and embarked on the formulation of a new, more dynamic style that was to become one of the most important and influential movements in Western architecture. Suger had the Abbey Church of Saint-Denis, near Paris, France, rebuilt from its original Romanesque style to provide a much larger, grander place for worship. Two ideas were central to Suger's new church: the worshiper should be bathed in divine light, and should feel lifted up toward heaven.

Adding larger windows to the structure could indeed provide more light, but it would also weaken the walls and increase the chance

of a collapse. The walls of Saint-Denis therefore had to be supported by external structures. Suger's plan incorporated an architectural structure called a **flying buttress** (see **2.5.15a** and **2.5.15b**), designed to transfer the weight of the ceiling outward beyond the walls. This idea worked well: as the walls no longer needed to bear the weight of the building, the windows could be much larger to allow light into the interior.

Suger had seen small colored-glass windows in German churches and decided to create them on a larger scale by dividing up the window spaces into components of a larger design (**2.5.16**). The light would pass through enormous images based on biblical narratives and be projected onto the worshiper. This was Suger's "divine light."

The rounded arch of Romanesque churches tended to appear squat, and Suger wanted an arch that would raise the worshiper's gaze upward, toward heaven. He achieved this by adding a point to the arch. **Pointed arches** are structural features that help conduct the downward thrust of the vault outward, but they also have a strong upward visual **emphasis**. They could be arranged so that two vaults intersected to form **rib vaults**, which could be repeated in rows to open up long areas. Suger, through his role in creating this remarkable

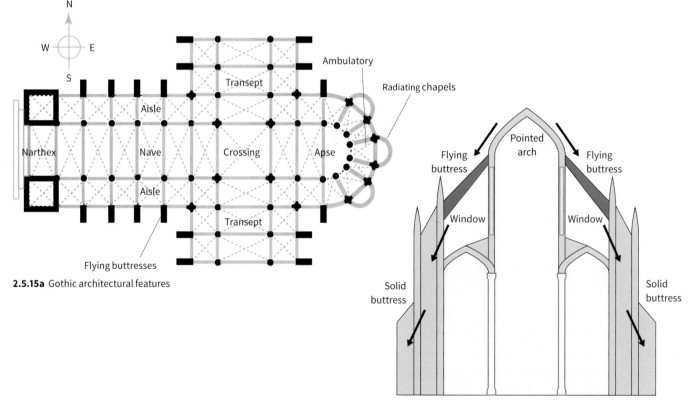

2.5.15a Gothic architectural features

2.5.15b Weight transfer in Gothic cathedral engineering

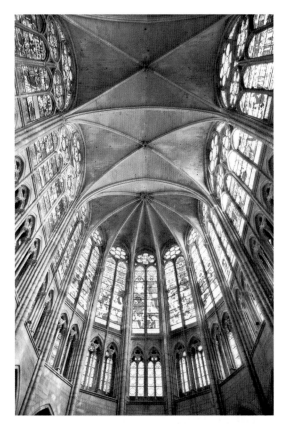

2.5.16 Rib vaults and elongated stained-glass windows, Abbey Church of Saint-Denis, 12th century. Near Paris, France

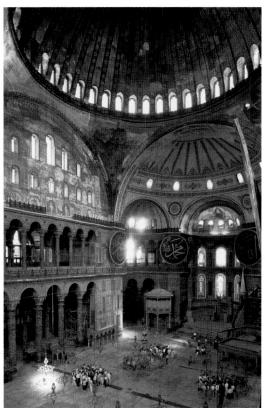

2.5.17 Hagia Sophia, 532–35 CE. Istanbul, Turkey

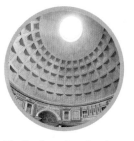

The Pantheon is an iconic Roman domed building that influenced similar structures that came after it: → see **3.1.34**, p. 369

building, was pivotal in establishing this highly influential architectural style, which came to be known as Gothic.

Domes

Abbot Suger wanted his church to be more impressive than the Church of Hagia Sophia (Holy Wisdom) in Constantinople (modern Istanbul, Turkey). Hagia Sophia is a magnificent Byzantine (Late Roman, with Eastern influences) structure that had already been standing for more than 500 years by Suger's time. Its most impressive feature is its enormous dome roof (**2.5.17**). Structurally, a dome is like an arch rotated 360 degrees on its vertical **axis**. Shaped like an umbrella, or a ball cut in half, it is a very strong structure. Domes can span large areas, because, as in other arch structures, the weight of the dome is dispersed outward toward the walls. Most dome constructions require the support of thick walls or another system for distributing the weight.

The dome of Hagia Sophia is so large and high that, for nearly 1,000 years, it was the largest interior space of any cathedral in the world. Prior to that, the Pantheon, a temple to the gods of Rome, had established the standard for all later domed buildings,

including Hagia Sophia. The inside of Hagia Sophia is illuminated by a series of **clerestory windows** in the lower portion of the dome and in the walls just below it. The dome rests on four arches. **Pendentives** (**2.5.18**) elegantly transfer the load of the circular dome to the four massive pillars of the square building beneath it.

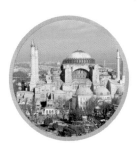

Hagia Sophia is an architectural marvel that has pendentives to transition from a round dome to a square support: → see **3.2.6**, p. 377

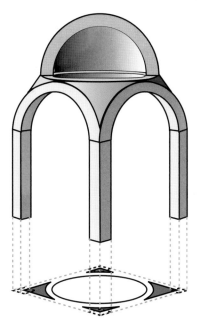

2.5.18 Pendentives (shown in green) allow transition from a square arched profile (below) to a dome (top)

Axis: an imaginary line showing the center of a shape, volume, or composition

Clerestory windows: a row of windows high up in a church to admit light

Pendentive: a curving triangular surface that links a dome to a square space below

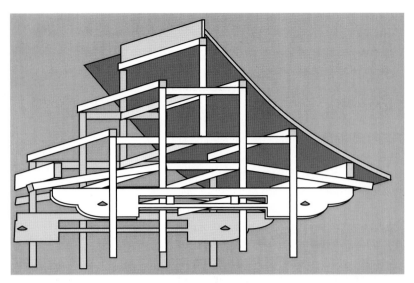

2.5.19 Post-and-beam architecture

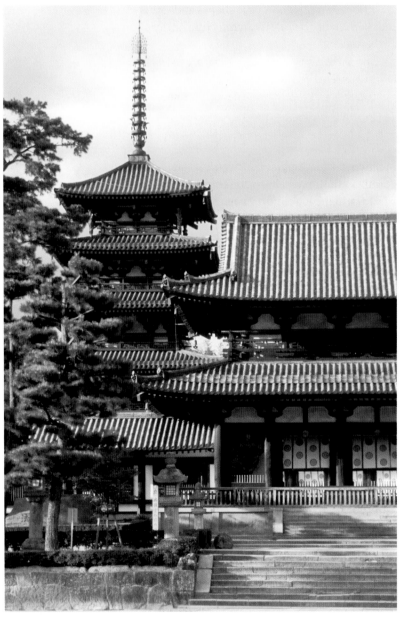

2.5.20 Horyu-ji (Horyu Temple), **Kondo and pagoda**,
c. 7th century. Nara, Japan

Post-and-Beam (Wooden) Architecture

The post-and-beam construction technique (**2.5.19**) has been used to build some of the world's finest wooden architecture. Two of the oldest wooden buildings in the world are in the grounds of the Buddhist Horyu-ji (Horyu Temple) in Nara, Japan (**2.5.20**). The construction of the Horyu-ji complex was the idea of the Japanese emperor Yomei, who hoped to gain spiritual favor so he could recover from illness, but he died before work started. In 607 Empress Suiko and Crown Prince Shotoku fulfilled the emperor's dying wish and built the first temple in the complex. Since then, it has withstood the ravages of time, and is an example of the durability of well-constructed wooden buildings.

These buildings use a complex post-and-beam design that is both beautiful and structurally sound. Crossbeams and counter-beams create a series of layers supporting the elaborate curved roof. The main building of the complex, the Kondo, is almost 61 ft. long by 50 ft. wide. This same structural design also enabled the architects to construct buildings that were very tall: the Goju-no-To (Five-story Pagoda) is 122 ft. tall. The pagoda's height was designed to impress rather than serve any practical purpose, since it is not possible to enter the top four floors.

Classical Architectural Styles

Since the fall of the Roman empire (about 410 CE), architects of European and North American countries have sought to revive the majesty displayed in the architectural style of the Greeks and Romans. The Romans had incorporated the unique architectural designs of the Greeks into their own after conquering Greek territory by 46 CE. These buildings endured a millennium of disrepair, surviving the ravages of time to a significant degree and affirming the great architectural engineering of the ancients. As Italian city-states, such as Florence, gained greater economic power in the fourteenth century, it became possible to erect large architectural projects in homage to the monumental Classical ruins that dotted the Italian and Greek landscapes. So, it was natural that the architects of the Renaissance looked to the Greeks and Romans for inspiration.

One of the great architects of the High Renaissance who drew inspiration from the

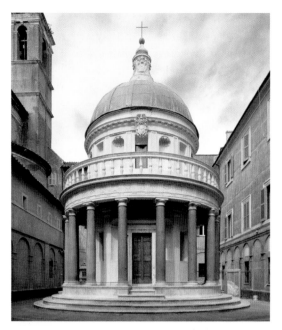

2.5.21 Donato Bramante, Tempietto of San Pietro in Montorio, *c.* 1502. Rome, Italy

temples. Bramante, like many Renaissance architects, particularly sought to design works that used geometric forms, such as circles, spheres, and cylinders.

The architectural style of the Greeks and Romans was once again revived during the mid-eighteenth century. This renewed Classical style, appropriately labeled **Neoclassicism**, was a reaction against such opulent and ornamented styles as **Rococo** (see the palace of Versailles, p. 467), which had dominated the previous century. Rococo was a **decorative** style characterized by asymmetrical balance, abundant curves, and opulent finishes, unlike the more reserved Classical architectural style that dominated the Italian Renaissance. Neoclassicism sprang from the orderly attention to simple geometric shapes and forms that had characterized the architectural styles of the ancients.

One of the first expressions of Neoclassical architecture was designed by an English aristocrat named Richard Boyle, better known as Lord Burlington. His design for Chiswick House (**2.5.22**) exemplifies the character of earlier Classical styles, but also integrates more contemporary elements, such as the chimneys that straddle the domed central roof. The design reflects an interest in the historical beginnings of European architecture combined with the practical concerns of the eighteenth century.

ancients was Donato Bramante (1444–1514). Bramante is credited with introducing the architectural style of the High Renaissance when he built a memorial at the place where St. Peter was believed to have been crucified. The Tempietto (Italian for "small temple") is a **central-plan church** with a dome, in Rome, Italy (**2.5.21**). The circular plan and dome reflect influences from Roman domed structures, for example the remains of Hadrian's villa at Tivoli, and colonnaded Greek

Central-plan church: a church design, often in the shape of a cross with all four arms of equal length

Neoclassicism: a European style that flourished during the late eighteenth and early nineteenth centuries, characterized by an extreme interest in the Classical world, strictly ordered scenes, and heroic subjects

Rococo: an eighteenth-century style in France characterized by organic forms, ornate extravagance, and whimsy

Decorative: intentionally making an artwork pleasant or attractive

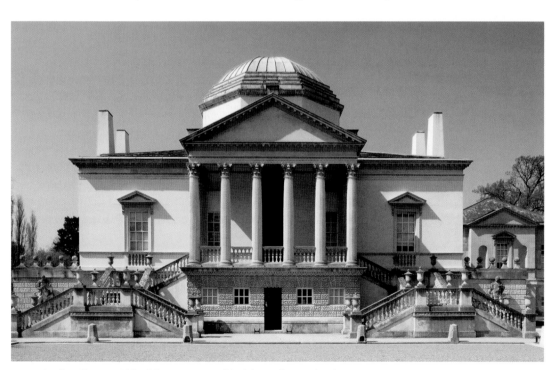

2.5.22 Lord Burlington, **Chiswick House**, 1729. Chiswick, London, England

The Taj Mahal
Engineering Eternity

For the other Taj Mahal
GATEWAYS:
→ see pp. 126–27 and p. 578

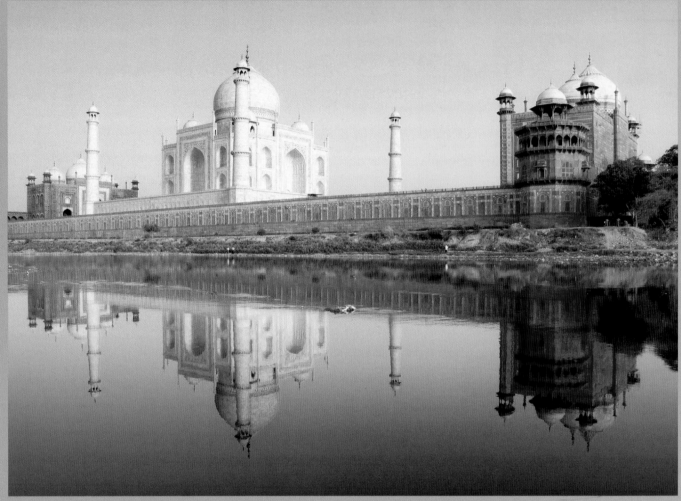

2.5.23 View of the Taj Mahal from the Yamuna River, Agra, India

In 1631, the Mughal Emperor Shah Jahan experienced a terrible personal tragedy when his third wife, Mumtaz Mahal, died in childbirth. Mumtaz, a Persian princess, had devoted her life to Shah Jahan, even accompanying him on multiple military campaigns while she was pregnant. The Shah's grief was so profound he dedicated all of his vast resources to the creation of a mausoleum complex in her honor that would endure throughout eternity.

The Shah assembled a team of architects and engineers who, under his supervision, would build a symbol of his love that could defy the instability of this world. The lead architect was probably Ustad Ahmad Lahauri, who borrowed design elements from Persia, India, and Turkey, incorporating them into a masterpiece of Islamic symmetry. The Taj Mahal (**2.5.23**) was built of white marble with a unique crystalline character that absorbs and radiates the light of northern India. When it was first constructed, many artists created lavish decorative work for the buildings on the site, including mosaic inlays, relief carvings, gold details, and inlaid precious stones.

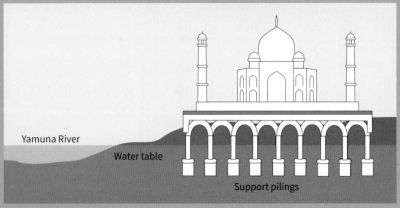

2.5.24 Diagram illustrating the support structure of the Taj Mahal

The central dome is 58 ft. in diameter and 213 ft. tall. The structure is completely symmetrical both when viewed from above and from any of its four sides. Four domed chambers emanate from this central dome, balanced on an octagon-shaped platform. Four towers called **minarets**, each 162 ft. high, frame the corners of the large structure. The minarets and pointed domes are characteristic of Islamic art.

Because Shah Jahan wished for a pastoral site, the complex was built next to the Yamuna River, away from the hustle and bustle of nearby Agra. As the building was so close to the river, which would rise and fall with the seasons, a clever combination of stone filler material and wooden supports was constructed to hold the foundation in place.

The promise of a masterwork that would endure throughout eternity has been challenged in recent years, as experts have reported threats to the longevity of the building. Discoloration of the marble has led some to believe that polluted air from increased industrial activity and urban transport, as India grows as a world economic power, is causing a yellowing of the marble surfaces. That concern is dwarfed by more serious issues regarding the integrity of the structure's foundation-support system as river conditions change. The support structure (**2.5.24**), which incorporates submerged sal (a teak-like timber) and ebony wood, may be in jeopardy as river levels drop, allowing the wood to dry out and contract. Recent water-management projects leave the riverbed nearly dry for months. Cracks have been observed in the Taj Mahal's marble structure and many fear that this building, which has so far transcended time, may not be able to survive the realities of the mortal world forever.

The Emergence of the Methods and Materials of the Modern World

A new and different type of construction, made of wood, was invented in the United States in 1832. Balloon framing (**2.5.25**) involves the fabrication of lightweight wooden frames to support the structure, instead of using heavy timbers. It was introduced when the advent of power sawing could efficiently and economically produce smaller cross-section lumber from saw logs. The Stick Style took advantage of balloon framing to support a decorative design that often used asymmetry with steep roofs to create a dynamic visual statement. Originally, balloon framing was a derisive term used by builders who stayed with traditional building methods and felt the new method was too fragile to support a building. Today, however, most houses in America are built using this method.

In the nineteenth century, iron, steel, and concrete became less costly and more widely available, and so came into common architectural use. New possibilities emerged as architects began to examine innovative

Minaret: a tall slender tower, particularly on a mosque, from which the faithful are called to prayer

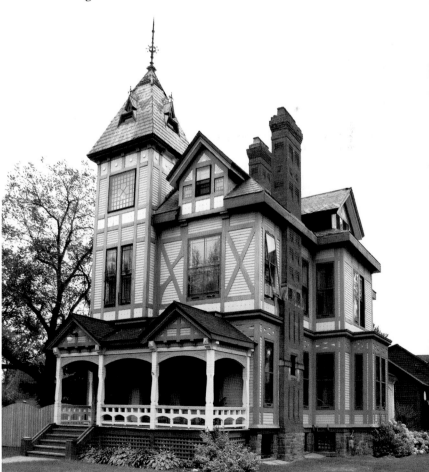

2.5.25 Stick Style house using balloon framing, Brockville, Ontario, Canada

Modernism, Modernist:
a radically new twentieth-century art and architectural movement that embraced modern industrial materials and a machine aesthetic

ways to control tension and compression. Buildings could be built taller and in different configurations. Architects found exciting new ways to distribute the stress forces in their buildings. New types of building emerged, and the use of previously untried materials made buildings look radically different.

Cast-Iron Architecture

Cast iron has been available to humankind since ancient times. Iron is a more flexible material than stone. Molten iron can be cast in a mold to almost any shape, but it was not until the eighteenth century that it could be smelted in large enough quantities to play a significant role in building.

An important example of the use of cast iron during the Industrial Revolution was the Crystal Palace, designed by Sir Joseph Paxton (1803–1865) for the Great Exhibition of 1851 in London (**2.5.26**). This event was intended to promote trade, and to showcase Great Britain's goods, services, horticulture, and technical innovation—for which the building was a very good advertisement. The walls and roof were of glass, supported by the skeletal cast-iron structure. The building was more than a third of a mile long; it was completed in only eight months by 2,000 men; and it used 4,500 tons of cast iron and 990,000 square feet of glass. Paxton's expertise in greenhouse building was applied to the design of this massive temporary space and the use of mass-produced parts heralded the later rise of **Modernist** architecture.

The Crystal Palace inspired other architects to work with iron, including the French engineer Gustave Eiffel (who designed the Eiffel Tower in Paris, France). The Crystal Palace was eventually dismantled and reassembled in south London, where it became an exhibition center and concert hall, but it was destroyed by fire in 1936.

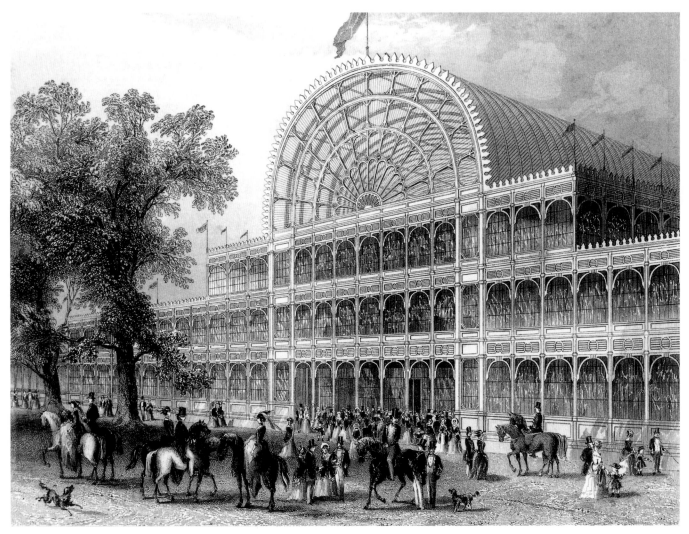

2.5.26 Joseph Paxton, Crystal Palace, 1851. London, England. 19th-century engraving

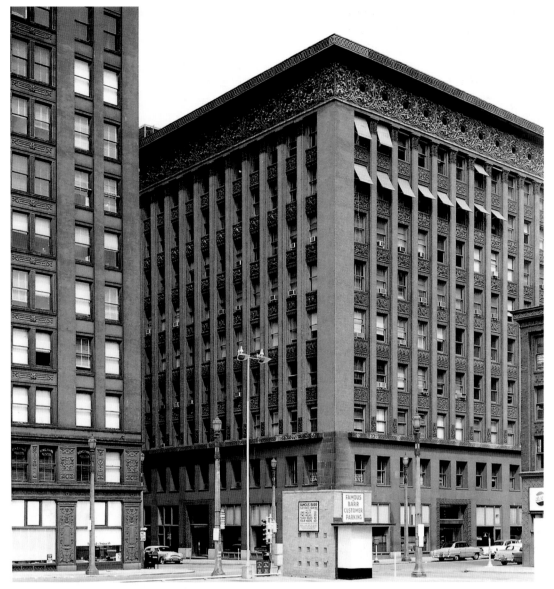

2.5.27 Louis Sullivan, **Wainwright Building**, 1890–91. St. Louis, Missouri

Steel-Frame Construction

While the use of cast iron for construction opened up new possibilities for architects, steel (made from iron and a small amount of carbon) was stronger than pure iron and had even greater potential. Paxton and Eiffel's successful use of iron, considered unsightly as a finish material in their own time, invited architects to think about new alternatives to past styles. Architects began to question traditions and to create structures that featured simplicity; mass-produced building materials like steel, glass, and concrete; and a lack of historical ornamentation, to usher in a new style called Modernism.

One architect who noted the advantages of steel was Louis Sullivan (1856–1924), called the "father of Modernism," who became a pioneer in the creation of the modern skyscraper. Sullivan attended Massachusetts Institute of Technology at the age of sixteen, and at only seventeen, participated in the rebuilding of Chicago after the Great Fire of 1871. Chicago provided fertile ground for creative young architects, and Sullivan pushed the use of steel frame to new heights. Although Sullivan was based in Chicago, one of his masterpieces is in St. Louis, Missouri. The Wainwright Building, a ten-story office building, is one of the world's oldest skyscrapers (**2.5.27**). In this building Sullivan obeys his famous phrase, "form follows function," by providing versatile interior space. Because the steel frame supports the building, and because it is mostly located at its outer edges, the interior can easily be reconfigured to meet the specific needs of the user.

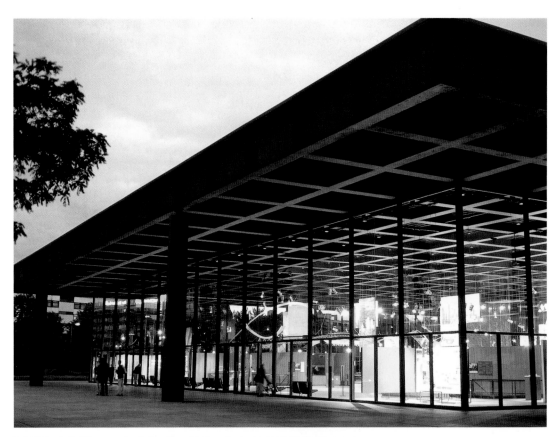

2.5.28 Ludwig Mies van der Rohe, **Neue Nationalgalerie**, 1968. Berlin, Germany

The skyscraper was a completely new idea, and such architects as Sullivan had no precedents on which to base their design. The Wainwright Building reflects the elements of a column (base, shaft, capital; see p. 248) in the organization of its exterior. Representing the capital, at the top of the building, is a **cornice**, or protruding ledge, which is highly ornamented with designs derived from Gothic cathedrals. The middle and tallest area shows strong vertical emphasis, with its projecting rectangular-section shafts and high, narrow windows. The lower section (base) shows little ornamentation and reflects ideas of the time about the frivolous nature of ornament. Later architects would avoid ornament altogether and rely on the **aesthetic** characteristics of the structure to provide visual interest.

Because steel frames carry the load of the building, many Modernist architects realized there was no need to use a facing material, such as brick; the entire side of the building could be sheathed in glass. The simplicity of this idea captured the imagination of such architects as Germany's Ludwig Mies van der Rohe (1886–1969) (**2.5.28**), who proclaimed that "less is more," and the Swiss Le Corbusier (1887–1965), who called a building a "machine for living"

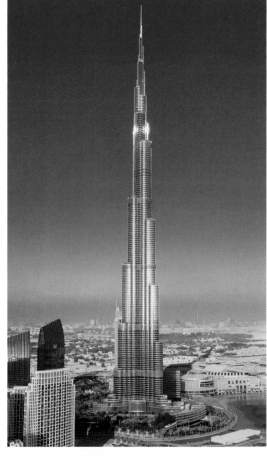

2.5.29 Adrian Smith and Bill Baker (Skidmore, Owings & Merrill), **Burj Khalifa**, 2010. Dubai, United Arab Emirates

(see: Geometric and Organic Ideas in Modern Architecture, pp. 262–63). A building could now reflect its surroundings while also giving people inside it a spectacular view of the landscape.

When it opened on January 4, 2010, the Burj Khalifa (**2.5.29**) became the most impressive piece of steel-frame construction in the world, as well as the tallest human-made structure. Designed and built by the architecture and engineering firm Skidmore, Owings & Merrill under the supervision of American architect Adrian Smith (b. 1944) and engineer Bill Baker (b. 1953), the Burj Khalifa is still the tallest building in the world. Its design was derived from the spiraling minarets—towers that surround mosques and are used to call the faithful to prayer—of Islamic architecture. The structural framing that supports the building is created from tubular steel to make the support lighter without compromising the integrity.

Reinforced Concrete

The character of architecture comes from its use of building materials, the sourcing or manufacture of which determines much of modern buildings' visual form. Steel and glass are produced in rectangular shapes that are a vital part of the visual aesthetic prizing the integration of form and function. But what aesthetic form would a material have if its raw manufactured state was liquid?

Architects began to use reinforced concrete as a way of avoiding the hard, right-angled edges of buildings made from blocks or bricks. Beginning with the architecture of the nineteenth century, steel, cast iron, and reinforced concrete came into widespread use. Concrete is a mixture of cement and ground stone. It is reinforced through the use of either a fibrous material (such as fiberglass) or steel rods called rebars. The inclusion of fibrous or metal reinforcing helps the concrete resist cracking. In architecture, steel rebar is shaped to the architect's design specifications; builders make a large wooden mold, and then pour the concrete into the form. Reinforced concrete gave rise to shell architecture, which is the use of a solid shell that also provides support for the structure.

When the Danish architect Jørn Utzon (1918–2008) designed the Sydney Opera House, overlooking the harbor of Sydney, Australia, he broke away from Modernist rectangular designs (**2.5.30**). The structure is a testament to the **expressive** character of reinforced concrete. The rooflines resemble billowing sails, a reference to the building's harbor location. The sails were created over precast ribs and then set into place, allowing the architect more freedom in the creation of the design and (in theory) reducing the cost. In fact, owing to a succession of technical problems with this innovative building, the project cost fourteen times its intended budget. As controversy surrounding the project escalated, Utzon resigned nine years before its completion.

Expressive: capable of stirring the emotions of the viewer

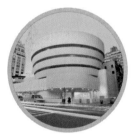

An architectural marvel at the time of its construction, the Guggenheim museum in New York is a masterpiece of steel and concrete:
→ see **4.1.4**, p. 542

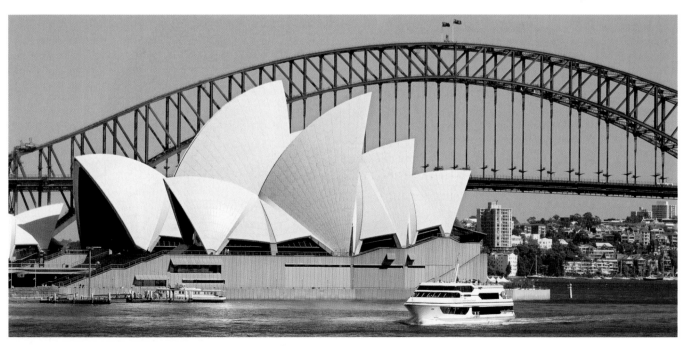

2.5.30 Jørn Utzon, **Sydney Opera House**, 1973. Sydney, Australia

Geometric and Organic Ideas in Modern Architecture
Le Corbusier's Villa Savoye and Frank Lloyd Wright's Fallingwater

A building's appearance can be a visual expression of an idea the architect wants to communicate. Two buildings constructed about the same time, the Villa Savoye and Fallingwater, share certain similarities, but are based on radically different ideas about architecture. Le Corbusier's design was inexpensive compared with Wright's, particularly since Wright's building materials needed to be specially collected from the surrounding countryside. In Wright's work, architecture becomes part of the natural surroundings, whereas Le Corbusier wants nature to be viewed from a comfortable vantage point. Each design creates a beautiful modern space.

LE CORBUSIER'S VILLA SAVOYE: INTERNATIONAL STYLE

Le Corbusier (b. Charles-Edouard Jeanneret, 1887–1965), a Swiss-French architect, (also a designer and painter) saw architecture as a "machine for living", and believed that the architecture of a building should be designed around the lifestyle of the occupants. The Villa Savoye in Poissy, France, was completed in 1931 as a weekend residence for a family that lived in Paris during the week (**2.5.31**). Villa Savoye was designed in the International Style, a style that was promoted as a universal aesthetic form that could be built in any geographical or cultural environment relatively inexpensively. The International Style claimed that its rational approach to design could (and should) be used universally, for rich and poor alike.

Design elements are not intended to complement or mimic surrounding environment

Preferences for unadorned, open interiors

International Style emphasized industrial and cheap materials, such as steel, glass, and concrete

The style favored a strongly geometric visual organization of spaces and elements of the building, including the shapes of the roofline, windows, and walls

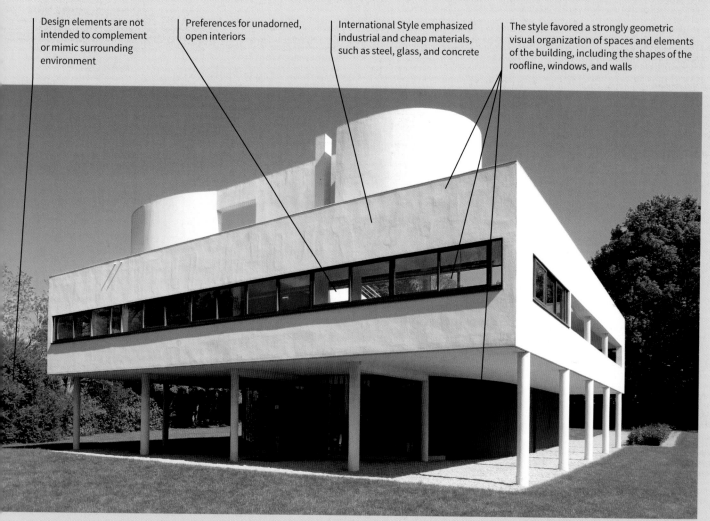

2.5.31 Le Corbusier, Villa Savoye, 1928–31, Poissy, France

FRANK LLOYD WRIGHT'S FALLINGWATER: ORGANIC STYLE

American architect Frank Lloyd Wright (1867–1959) was commissioned to build Fallingwater in Bear Run, Pennsylvania, as a weekend getaway for the Kaufmann family (**2.5.32**). It was completed in 1939. Wright did not think that a house should be a machine. He believed the design of a house should respond organically to its location. Rather than positioning the house so that the Kaufmanns could view the waterfall from inside, he placed the house right on top of it. Sometimes underlying rock juts into the living space of the house so that the occupants may take pleasure in stepping over or around the stone. The house is so integral to the environment that the bottom step of one of the stairways hovers just above the creek.

Wright believed so strongly in the organic relationship between site and building that he had many of the materials collected from the surrounding countryside.

The stone was quarried nearby and the wood for the supports between the windows came from the surrounding forest

The profile of the house features vertical and horizontal elements much like those of the Villa Savoye

The reinforced concrete is colored to fit in

The design mimics the layers in the rocks around the site

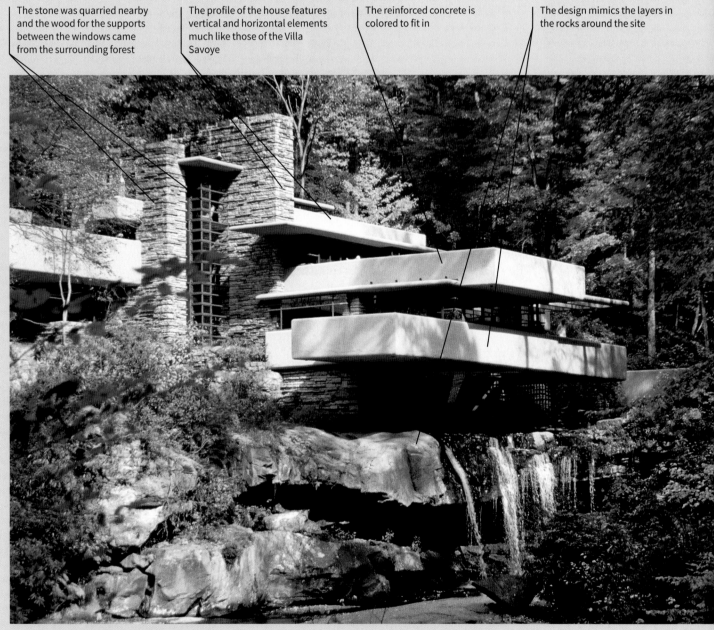

2.5.32 Frank Lloyd Wright, **Fallingwater**, 1939, Bear Run, Pennsylvania

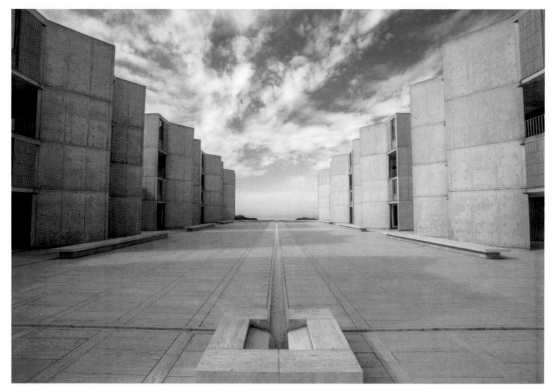

2.5.33 Louis I. Kahn, **Salk Institute**, 1965, La Jolla, California

Reinforced concrete was used by American master architect Louis I. Kahn (1904–71) when he designed the Salk Institute (**2.5.33**) in La Jolla, California. Jonas Salk, discoverer of the polio vaccine, tasked Kahn with creating "a facility worthy of a visit by Picasso" when he contacted him about the project. Kahn envisioned a scientific village, which faced the Pacific Ocean, where new discoveries could be cultivated. The concrete construction allowed the facility to be simple and durable, with an inspiring design.

The Postmodern Reaction to Modernism

Beginning in the 1980s, a new approach to architecture, known as **Postmodernism**, combined the hard, pure rectangles of Modernism with unusual materials and features of styles from the past. Postmodernism took hold as architects sought new ways to reflect a complex and changing world.

The Humana Building in downtown Louisville, Kentucky, designed by the American architect Michael Graves (1934–2015), is an intriguing mix of historical styles and references (**2.5.34**). The **facade** onto the street has a **stylized** Greek **portico**. The **negative space** of large windows and openings implies columns that rise up to support a cornice

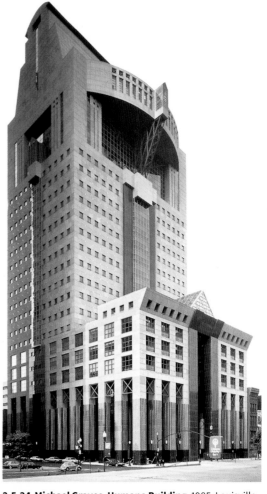

2.5.34 Michael Graves, **Humana Building**, 1985, Louisville, Kentucky

Postmodernism, Postmodernist: a late twentieth-century style of architecture and art that playfully adopts features of earlier styles and critically focuses on content

Facade: any side of a building, usually the front or entrance

Stylized: art that represents objects in an exaggerated way to emphasize certain aspects of the object

Portico: a roof supported by columns at the entrance to a building

Negative space: an unoccupied or empty space that is created after positive shapes are positioned in a work of art

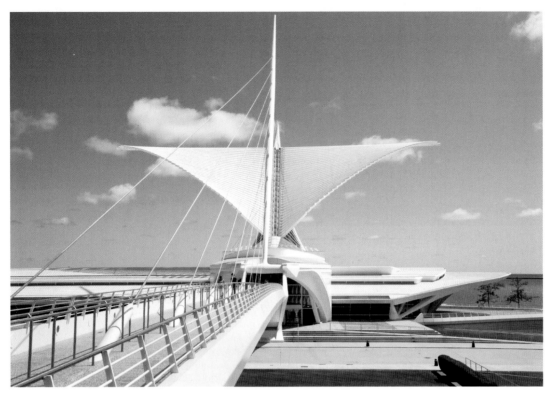

2.5.35 Santiago Calatrava, **Quadracci Pavilion**, **Milwaukee Art Museum**, 2001, Wisconsin

and triangular glass structure similar to the triangular **pediment** of a Greek temple. The upper portion of the building (set back from the street) suddenly changes from simple right angles to a series of curved surfaces that undulate in a manner similar to the architecture of the Baroque period. Graves also artfully varies the facing material, changing its color and texture at different intervals, seeking to avoid the austere simplicity and purity of Modernism. A work of Modernist architecture would not include influences from Greek or Baroque architecture because the Modernist idea was to create a new style that was not based on the past.

In Postmodernist architecture, form no longer follows function with the same dedication as it did during the Modernist period. In fact, sometimes the building seems like a huge toy, a playful exploration of what we expect a building to be. The Quadracci Pavilion at the Milwaukee Art Museum was designed by the Spanish architect Santiago Calatrava (b. 1951) to express the character of the site (**2.5.35**). Built on the shores of Lake Michigan, the pavilion reminds us of ships passing by; a cable-suspended bridge over a beautiful expanse of water also connects the museum to downtown Milwaukee. The building becomes a **kinetic sculpture** when a large moveable

sunscreen atop the structure slowly rises and lowers throughout the day, like the flapping wings of the many species of birds that flock near the lake. The inside is reminiscent of the curved interior of a sailing ship. The Quadracci Pavilion provides an exciting exhibition space for the display of contemporary art.

Currents in Architecture

Architects often face challenges when buildings are required to suit multiple purposes. When Iraqi-born architect Zaha Hadid (1950–2016) designed the new home for the Contemporary Arts Center in a small space in downtown Cincinnati (**2.5.36a** and **2.5.36b**, p. 266), the challenge was to design a building that provided spaces for many different activities: temporary exhibitions, site-specific installations and performances, an education facility, offices, art-preparation areas, a museum store, a café, and public areas. Hadid designed the gallery spaces as a three-dimensional "jigsaw puzzle" of interlocking solids and voids suspended above the lobby. The unique geometry, scale, and varying heights of the gallery spaces offer organizational flexibility to accommodate and respond to the size and media of the contemporary art that will be displayed. Hadid said of her design, "We wanted to give the

Pediment: the triangular space, situated above the row of columns, on the facade of a building in the Classical style

Kinetic art/sculpture: three-dimensional art that moves, impelled by air currents, motors, or people

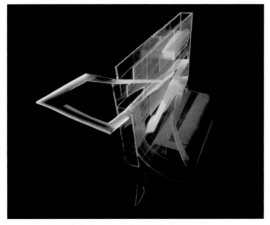

2.5.36a Zaha Hadid, Contemporary Arts Center, Cincinnati, Ohio. Study model by the architects, experimenting with different structural ideas

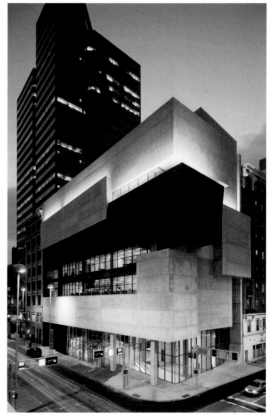

2.5.36b Zaha Hadid, Contemporary Arts Center, 2003, Cincinnati, Ohio

building a weightless quality, as if it were a sculpture, not just a building. The public and administrative spaces are glass, so that those outside are invited to look into the building, and those inside to look out at the cityscape. In this way the center's building is connected to the city it serves."

Architecture faces both challenges and opportunities as the twenty-first century unfolds. Concerns over limited resources, energy conservation, and sustainability have become important issues. The American architect Michelle Kaufmann (b. 1968) responded to these challenges by introducing the Glidehouse concept in 2004. The Glidehouse (**2.5.37**) was developed because Kaufmann was looking for an inexpensive alternative to the costly California homes in the Bay area. She developed a prefab module made of sustainable wood and finished it with double-pane windows, roof solar cells, and other materials that were reused or recyclable. The resulting plan was designed with the

everyday usage of the occupant in mind, so that it made life easier while also lowering costs. Because the Glidehouse is modular, it can be expanded into a larger living space by adding more modules, then modifying them to fit with the intended plan. Kaufmann's idea has influenced new trends in architecture, such as tiny houses and portable homes. In 2017, Kaufmann was Artist-in-Residence at Google, where she worked on new company buildings and proposed innovative new ideas through research and development.

2.5.37 Michelle Kaufmann, Glidehouse, 2004. Marin County, California

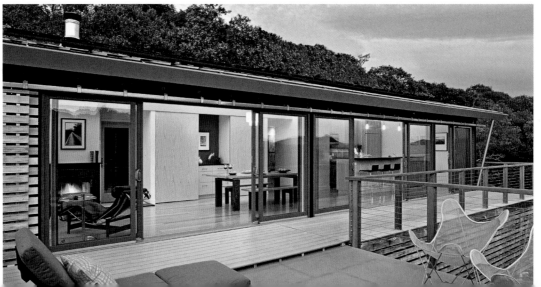

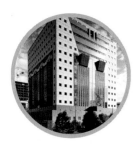

For more information about the roots of contemporary architecture:

→ see **3.9.35**, p. 520

Explore Further Architecture

Ancient

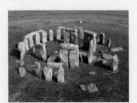

4.1.7 Stonehenge, England, *c.* 3200–1500 BCE → p. 544

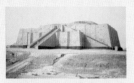

4.1.6 Ziggurat, Ur, Iraq, *c.* 2100 BCE → p. 543

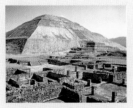

3.3.2 Great Stupa, Sanchi, India, 3rd century BCE → p. 392

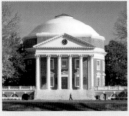

3.4.11 Pyramid of the Sun, Teotihuacan, Mexico, *c.* 225 CE → p. 417

Classical

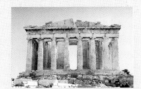

1.7.14a Iktinos and Kallikrates, Parthenon, Athens, 447–432 BCE → p. 138

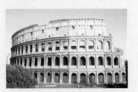

4.1.2 Colosseum, Rome, Italy, 72–80 CE → p. 541

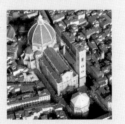

3.6.4 Arnolfo di Cambio and others, Florence Cathedral, begun 1296 → p. 445

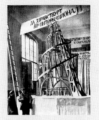

3.7.13 Thomas Jefferson, Rotunda, University of Virginia, 1769–1809 → p. 475

Modern

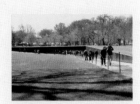

3.8.24 Victor Horta, Tassel House, 1892–93 → p. 498

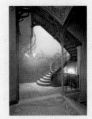

1.2.11 Vladimir Tatlin, Model for *Monument to the Third International*, 1919 → p. 57

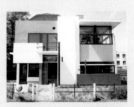

3.9.34 Gerrit Rietveld, Schröder House, Utrecht, 1924–25 → p. 520

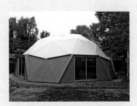

1.1.2b Buckminster Fuller Dome Home, Carbondale, Illinois, 1960 → p. 35

Postmodern

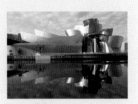

4.6.15a Maya Lin, Vietnam Veterans Memorial, Washington D.C., 1981–83 → p. 615

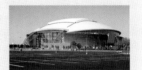

1.2.17 Frank Gehry, Guggenheim Museum, Bilbao, Spain, 1997 → p. 60

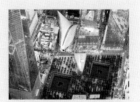

4.1.3 AT&T Stadium, Arlington, Texas, 2009 → p. 542

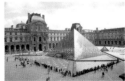

4.6.16a Michael Arad and Peter Walker, 9/11 Memorial, New York, 2011 → p. 616

Your turn

To which era of architectural history do these buildings belong?

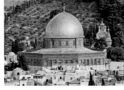

3.2.15 Dome of the Rock, Jerusalem, 688–91 → p. 382

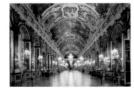

3.7.2 Jules Hardouin-Mansart, Hall of Mirrors, Versailles, 1678–84 → p. 467

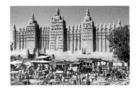

3.5.9 Great Mosque, Djenné, Mali, completed *c.* 1907 → p. 433

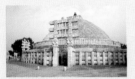

0.0.8 Pyramid at the Louvre Museum, Paris, 1988 → p. 20

2.6
The Tradition of Craft

Medieval: the time period roughly between the fall of the Roman empire and the start of the Renaissance

Ceramic: fire-hardened clay, often painted, and normally sealed with shiny protective coating

Renaissance: a period of cultural and artistic change in Europe from the fourteenth to the seventeenth century

Medium (plural media): the material on or from which an artist chooses to make a work of art, for example canvas and oil paint, marble, engraving, video, or architecture

Embroidery: decorative stitching generally made with colored thread applied to the surface of a fabric

Ceramist: a person who makes ceramics

Decorative: intentionally making an artwork pleasant or attractive

Life is so short, the craft so long to learn.

(Geoffrey Chaucer, English poet)

In Geoffrey Chaucer's (*c.* 1340–1400) time, the makers of the fine objects we can see today in the world's great art museums learned their trade in associations called guilds. Fourteenth-century aspiring craftspeople trained with masters, a process that lasted many years, as Chaucer's comment suggests. In **medieval** Europe, painting, for example, was not considered to be of higher status than turning **ceramics** into fine vessels or weaving exquisite tapestries.

Things gradually changed after 1400 during the **Renaissance**, and by the eighteenth century, certain **media**, notably painting and sculpture, came to be considered as art, while ceramics, weaving, and **embroidery** were termed crafts. Other materials, such as metals, were used to make fine sculpture (which was "art") as well as practical and household objects ("craft").

Crafts came to mean the disciplines that produced hand-made items to be used rather than simply looked at. This view was generally accepted, even though utilitarian objects require technical skill to produce, and craftspeople devote years to mastering their craft. Indeed, some hand-crafted objects, because of their ingenuity and refinement, stand out as artworks that transcend mere utility.

The distinction between art and craft was unique to western European and North American culture, and it has been broken down over the course of the twentieth and twenty-first centuries, as this chapter will show. Elsewhere in the world, the maker of a bronze vessel in China during the Shang Dynasty (*c.* 1500–*c.* 1050 BCE; see 3.3.8, p. 396), the maker of a fine embroidered wool mantle in Paracas, South America (*c.* 600–*c.* 200 BCE; see 3.4.3, p. 412), and the **ceramist** who made lamps for the Dome of the Rock in Jerusalem (sixteenth century; see 1.4.22, p. 96) probably did not consider themselves any less skillful or artistic than painters or sculptors.

Craftspeople working today still produce works using traditional craft materials and techniques, but they have updated their methods and subjects to reflect a changing world; they also sometimes apply traditional skills to new, contemporary materials to create their work. Examples of contemporary artists working in this way include Hyo-In Kim (opposite), Sheila Hicks (pp. 280–81), Toshiko Horiuchi (pp. 280–81), and Daniela Villegas (p. 276). Through the development of their craft, such artists are able to enhance their understanding of materials involved in a work's creation.

In this chapter we will examine examples of both craft objects and works of art, each of which are made with the same materials. However, if we try to define precisely the difference between art and craft, we will discover that it is difficult, perhaps impossible. As you read this chapter, ask yourself whether you think the objects discussed can be considered art or craft. At the same time, think about whether the makers of the objects, and the people they made them for, would have thought about such a distinction, or whether they would have been able to tell the difference. In the hands of skillful designers, great craft objects such as those discussed here possess artistry equal to great works of art.

Perspectives on Art: Hyo-In Kim
Art or Craft: What's the Difference?

When we look at a fine painting, we will almost certainly describe it as being art. But is a fine example of clothing, for example, art or craft? If craft is something that has a useful function, then presumably a dress is craft. Here, however, Professor Howard Risatti, an art historian at Virginia Commonwealth University, examines a work based on a traditional Korean dress that transforms a practical piece of clothing to comment on our modern globalized world (2.6.1). He asks: What makes something a work of art rather than a work of craft?

Only by understanding something essential about a work of art can we begin to appreciate its richness and complexity as an aesthetic object. So to begin, we must ask, "What is essential to a work of craft?" To my thinking, it is that craft is an object constructed around the idea of function, say the way a container functions to hold water, or a chair to support a person, or clothes to cover someone's body. The work shown here is from a series by the Korean American artist Hyo-In Kim (2.6.1). It is a *hanbok*, a traditional Korean dress worn with shoes and a hairpin by women of the upper and royal classes. Its gold-colored decoration indicates its prestige; such expensive materials were costly and well beyond the means of commoners, who mostly wore plain white garments.

The title, *To Be Modern #2*, however, suggests the artist has something more in mind than simply a fondness for traditional Korean clothes. Kim is faithful to the original dress design; she wants it to be correct to tradition. But she also wants it to indicate something important about tradition. That is why she has subtly transformed it by making it out of silver-colored wire mesh (instead of cloth) and by molding the **decorative** details out of porcelain, which she has then painted gold. And in keeping with the idea of transformation, instead of displaying it on a mannequin as if it were a dress in a store window, like something to be bought and sold, she decided to suspend it with its sleeves outstretched so that its transparency and weightlessness would be emphasized.

Kim intends us to see through the material so that the dress, like the hairpin, appears to float like

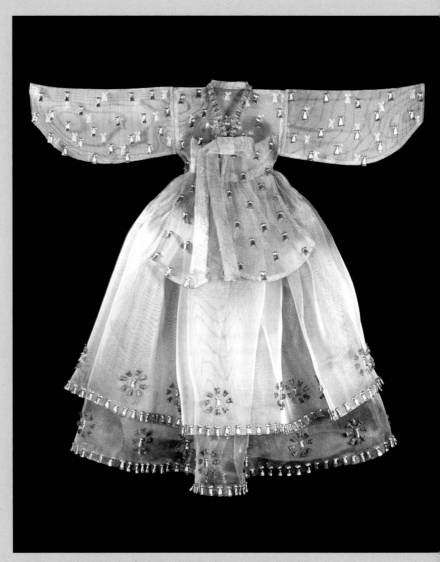

2.6.1 Hyo-In Kim, *To Be Modern #2*, 2004. Metal screen, wire, porcelain, acrylic paint, and found objects, slightly over lifesize

a ghostly, disembodied figure—something almost there and yet not quite. This apparitional effect, enhanced by the glittering gold of the decoration, is then undercut when, upon close-up inspection of the dress, the decoration turns out to be tiny versions of fashionable Western clothing: jeans, skirts, shoes, purses. What Kim wants us to see and appreciate, both literally and figuratively, is that those traditional cultural values that give structure and form to people's lives, including our own, are fading away and disappearing as globalization spreads.

Ceramics

Our word ceramic comes from the Greek word *keramos*, meaning "pottery," which was probably derived from a word in Sanskrit (a language of ancient India) meaning "to burn." The accepted interpretation of the word, burnt earth, aptly describes the ceramic process. The manufacture of a ceramic object requires the shaping of clay, a natural material dug from the earth, which is then baked at high temperatures to harden it.

We know that the basic techniques used to make ceramics date back thousands of years because archaeologists investigating the earliest known societies have found potsherds, small pieces of ancient ceramics.

The first step in making a ceramic object is to choose a clay. Ceramists can choose from a variety of clays, each with unique characteristics; they often select a mixture they have developed themselves that fits their own working methods. Clay used to make earthenware has good **plasticity**, or pliability, but it can be somewhat brittle after **firing**. Earthenware is often red in color and hardens at a lower temperature than other clays. Stoneware clays are less plastic than earthenware clays. Stoneware (as its name implies) is much harder than earthenware and is fired at a higher temperature. Stoneware is a good clay for the creation of items for everyday use, such as mugs and bowls. Porcelain, a durable, high-temperature ceramic commonly used for fine dinnerware, is made of a mixture of three clays: feldspar, kaolin, and silica. Porcelain is strong but sometimes hard to manipulate. Fine white china, bathroom fixtures, and dental crowns are made of porcelain.

When the ceramist has selected the clay, the next step in the making process is called wedging. This means the clay is kneaded to work out pockets of air (which can destroy a piece of ceramic ware when it is heated) and make the clay easier to work. Next, the ceramist uses one of a number of hand methods to shape the clay into the form of the finished object. For example, the artist can build up an object using slabs or coils of clay, or by modeling a lump of clay into the desired shape by pressing or pinching. Another method is to shape the clay as it turns on a rapidly turning potter's wheel, a process known as **throwing**.

Once it has been shaped, the clay is left to dry. The dried clay, called **greenware**, is very fragile. It is ready to be loaded into an oven called a kiln, and to be fired at a high temperature (between 2,000 and 3,000°F). The firing process takes an entire day of slowly raising the temperature to the appropriate level, then another day to allow for a slow cool-down to prevent cracking. The fired object, called **bisqueware**, is now permanently a hard ceramic and cannot be wetted and returned to a soft-clay state.

To add the finishing touches to a ceramic object, artists apply a glaze, a liquid mixture of

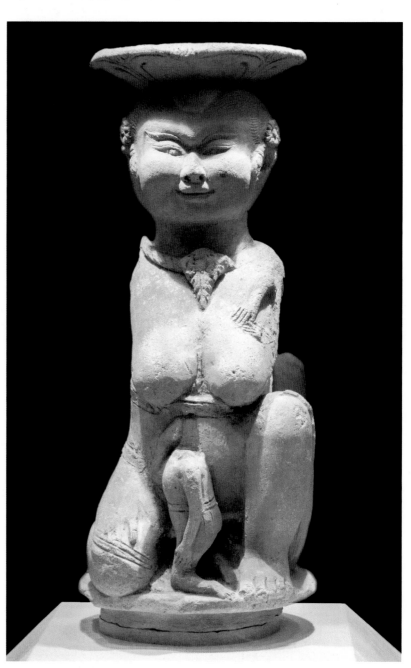

2.6.2 *The Mother Goddess Men Brajut (Hariti)*, **Indonesian**, *c.* 14th–15th century. Terra-cotta, 18⅞ × 8½ × 8″. Metropolitan Museum of Art, New York

clay, water, and chemical compounds that will give the object a glass-like finish and that adds color, **texture**, and protection to the object's surface. (A glaze can also make an object more watertight.) Some ceramists opt for a more matte finish, so they use a thin liquid clay called slip. The artist usually applies the slip or glaze with a brush. The object is again placed in the kiln and fired to melt and harden the glaze or slip, which fuses with the clay body.

Pinch Method

One of the most basic ways of working with clay is to squeeze it between the fingers. This process, called the pinch method, has for millennia provided artists with a spontaneous and effective way to create a clay object. To create an object using this method, artists will work the clay with their fingers, pushing and pulling it into the desired shape.

During the Majapahit period of Indonesia (1293–1520), artists squeezed and pinched clay into images that honored the manifested gods and goddesses of Hinduism. One such image made using this technique is the **terra-cotta** work *The Mother Goddess Men Brajut (Hariti)* (**2.6.2**), which was originally created as a pillar ornament for an open pavilion. The artist would have manipulated the clay carefully to portray Hariti (or *Men Brajut* in Javanese), the protector of children, as well as to create a hollow to hold a wooden pillar, which fulfilled the functional element of this piece.

Coil Method

The art of using coils to create a clay object has been a common hand-building method since ancient times. A coil is created by rolling the clay on a flat surface so that it extends into a long, rope-like shape. When making a round vessel, the artist wraps the coil around upon itself and then fuses the sections together by smoothing.

Seated Figure, a work from the Zapotec culture of Mexico, was made using the coil method (**2.6.3**). This figure was made to be buried in the tomb of a Zapotec ruler, and may portray a god or possibly a companion for the deceased. On its headdress and chest, the artist has carved two calendar dates in Zapotec writing. Most of the pottery made by Native American cultures was carefully crafted by hand. The coil method was preferred for constructing rounded objects because the

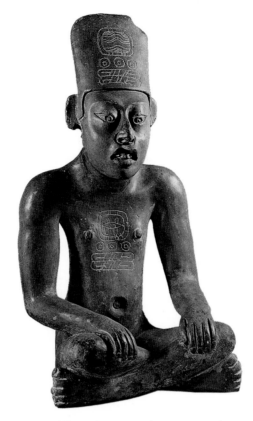

2.6.3 *Seated Figure*, **Oaxaca, Mexico, Zapotec style**, 300 BCE–700 CE. Ceramic, 12⅝ × 7 × 7⅜". Cleveland Museum of Art, Ohio

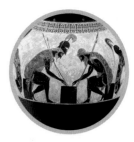

The ancient Greeks excelled in the creation of ceramic vessels, such as this amphora depicting Achilles and Ajax playing dice:
→ see **3.1.28**, p. 366

organic line of the coil could be controlled in a way that would complement the piece's essence or spirit.

Throwing

The use of a potter's wheel probably began when an artist, in order to make the process of **coiling** more efficient, placed a clay object on a round mat and turned it while adding coils of clay to a piece of pottery. A potter's wheel consists of a round disk that revolves while the ceramist shapes the object. No one is sure exactly when such wheels were invented, but by 3000 BCE, Chinese people were using them to produce ceramic objects.

The process of making pottery on a wheel is known as throwing. The potter centers a mound of clay on the turning wheel and then shapes a pot by poking a hole in the middle of the mound, and then pushing and pulling the wall of the pot up and out with both hands as it turns. To finish the surface of the pot, the potter can employ sponges and scrapers as it spins, or simply let the natural grooves made by the fingertips remain. Finally, a piece of wire is used to cut the finished piece from the wheel.

Plastic, plasticity: referring to materials that are soft and can be manipulated, or to such properties in the materials

Firing: heating ceramic, glass, or enamel objects in a kiln, to harden them, fuse the components, or fuse a glaze to the surface

Throwing: the process of making a ceramic object on a potter's wheel

Greenware: a clay form that has been shaped and dried, but not yet fired to become ceramic

Bisqueware: a ceramic form that has been fired but not glazed or that has not received other surface finishing

Texture: the surface quality of a work, for example fine/coarse, detailed/lacking in detail

Terra-cotta: iron-rich clay, fired at a low temperature, which is traditionally brownish-orange in color

Organic: having irregular forms and shapes, as though derived from living organisms

Coiling: the use of long coils of clay—rather than a wheel—to build the walls of a pottery vessel

The ceramic artists of China invented porcelain and used a greater variety of high-quality glazes than any ceramic tradition in the world, many of which are still in use today. This porcelain flask (**2.6.4**) was produced on a potter's wheel during the Ming Dynasty almost 600 years ago. Chinese ceramists of the Ming Dynasty were known for their use of multiple glaze layers. Their wares were so fine that the users of Ming Dynasty porcelain included the emperor of China himself. In this piece the artist used first a blue glaze, and then a clear glaze over that to complete the work. The clear glaze gave the flask a luxurious glossy finish.

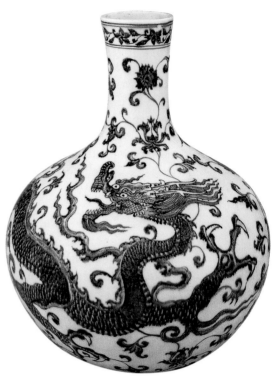

2.6.4 Porcelain flask with decoration in blue underglaze, Ming Dynasty, 1403–24. Height 16⅝". Palace Museum, Beijing, China

Slab Method

When artists use slab construction to make a ceramic object, they first roll out a flat sheet of clay. They then cut this clay into the shapes needed to make the object. To make a **three-dimensional** object, the ceramist takes care to join the corners. This style of working lends itself to making boxes and other forms that have large flat sides.

In *Gallas Rock*, by the American sculptor Peter Voulkos (1924–2002), we see slab construction (and wheel throwing) used in an organic and **Expressionist** way (**2.6.5**). The slabs are evident in the flat **planes** that dominate this 8-foot-tall sculptural object. Voulkos is known for using clay's naturalness—its tendency to take on organic forms—and plasticity.

Glass

As with ceramics, the manufacture of glass objects relies on heat and materials dug from the earth. The process of applying intense heat to melt silica (usually sand) together with lead (historically used to help the melted silica to flow) is the basis for most glass production. As in the making of ceramics, slow cooling of heated objects is critical to avoid serious cracking.

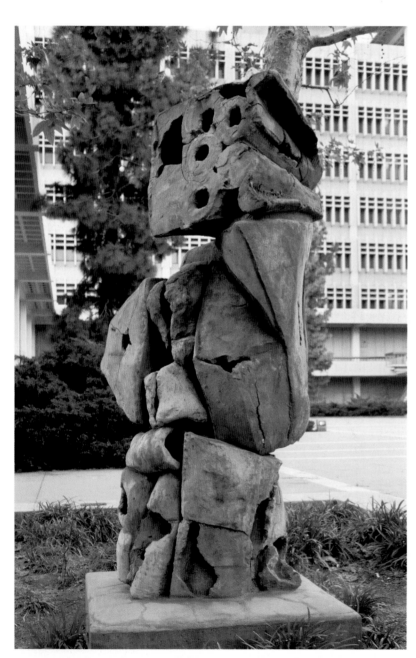

2.6.5 Peter Voulkos, *Gallas Rock*, 1960. Stoneware with slip and glaze, 84 × 37 × 26¾". University of California at Los Angeles, Franklin D. Murphy Sculpture Garden

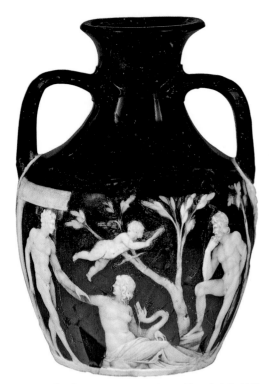

2.6.6 Portland Vase, **Roman**, *c.* 1–25 CE. Glass, height 9¾".
British Museum, London, England

Glass was probably first used in ancient Mesopotamia (an area of West Asia that includes present-day Iraq) and Egypt around 3500 BCE. At that time, glass was cast in small molds and core formed: that is, molten glass was wrapped around a lump of clay or dung attached to the end of a metal rod. The ancient Egyptians valued glass as highly as gold. Glassblowing—the process of forming a glass vessel by forcing air into molten glass, usually by blowing through a tube—was in use by the first century BCE in Syria and was later adopted and perfected by the Romans.

The Portland Vase (named after one of its owners, Margaret Bentinck, Duchess of Portland), is a beautiful vessel created in the Roman empire during the first century CE (**2.6.6**). Modern research has shown that it was made by the dip-overlay method: an elongated bubble of blue glass was partially dipped into a crucible of white glass, before the two were blown together. After cooling, the white layer was cut away to form the design. The cutting was probably performed by a skilled gem-cutter. The blue glass forms the **background** to the figures picked out in white. The amazing degree of detail attests to the artist's skill, as we can see from the four figures and a tree-like plant.

The designers of the **Gothic** cathedrals of medieval France adopted a type of colored

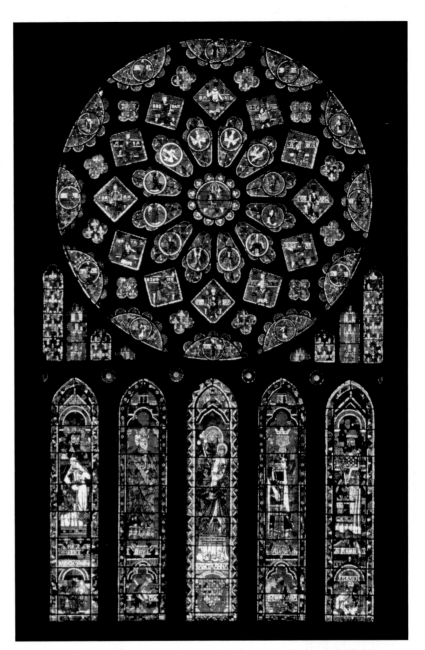

2.6.7 Rose window and lancets, **north transept**, 13th century. Chartres Cathedral, France

glass, known as **stained glass**, which had been used previously on a smaller scale in northern Europe. But the French did something extraordinary with stained glass by using it to make enormous decorative windows that bathed the cathedral in colored light. The windows of the cathedral in the northern French town of Chartres are magnificent examples of stained glass (**2.6.7**). The large (43 ft. in diameter) circular windows are accented by the **contrast** with smaller, tall thin windows with pointed tops. The brilliant blue color in these windows stands apart as one of the most extraordinary achievements of the early thirteenth century. They are so valued that to prevent them from being damaged during

Background: the part of a work depicted furthest from the viewer's space, often behind the main subject matter

Gothic: a Western European architectural style of the twelfth to sixteenth century, characterized by the use of pointed arches and ornate decoration

Stained glass: colored glass used for windows or decorative applications

Contrast: a drastic difference between such elements as color or value (lightness/darkness) when they are presented together

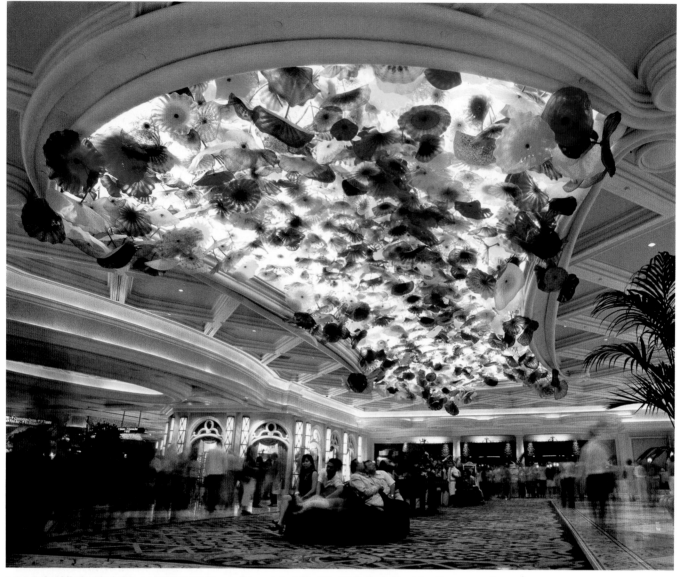

2.6.8 Dale Chihuly, *Fiori di Como*, 1998. Hand-blown glass and steel, 70 × 30 × 12'. Bellagio Hotel, Las Vegas, Nevada

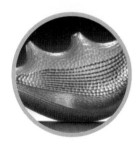

Lino Tagliapetra, another contemporary master of glass, made the work *Batman*: → see **1.2.5**, p. 53

Alloy: a mixture of a metal combined with at least one other element

World War II, they were removed and placed in storage until after the war had ended.

The contemporary American glass artist Dale Chihuly (b. 1941) makes comparable use of the kind of visual experience that glass can bring to an interior. To enhance the reception area at the Bellagio Hotel in Las Vegas, Chihuly created a dazzling ceiling made of 2,000 individually blown glass flowers (**2.6.8**). The strong color, reminiscent of stained glass, enlivens and invigorates the interior and becomes an inviting and memorable symbol of the hotel. The effect is mesmerizing.

Metalwork

As with ceramics, the use of metal in the creation of objects goes back to ancient times. Metal has been so important in human history that some archaeological periods, such as the

Bronze Age (more than 5,000 years ago) and Iron Age (more than 3,000 years ago), are named for the metal most commonly used at that time. Metalworking has been a measure of human development and, like most traditional crafts, an important medium for utilitarian purposes.

The properties of a metal object are derived from its basic components. Some metals, such as iron or copper, are natural materials and can be dug from the ground and then refined. Others are **alloys**, or combinations of two or more naturally occurring metals, combined to take advantage of the specific properties of each. For example, if tin is mixed with copper, it produces bronze. As a result of the addition of tin, the bronze is harder and has a lower melting point than copper, so it is easier to manipulate. Other common alloys include pewter, brass, and steel.

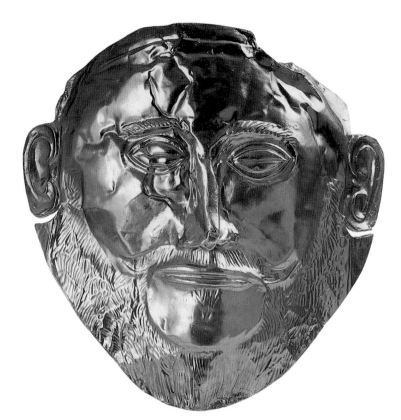

2.6.9 Death mask from Shaft Grave V, Grave Circle A, Mycenae. Also known as Mask of Agamemnon, *c.* 1550–1500 BCE. Gold, height 12″. National Archaeological Museum, Athens, Greece

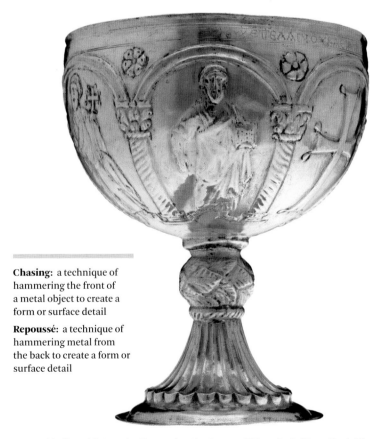

Chasing: a technique of hammering the front of a metal object to create a form or surface detail

Repoussé: a technique of hammering metal from the back to create a form or surface detail

2.6.10 *Chalice with Apostles Venerating the Cross*, *c.* 600 CE, Syria (Byzantine). Silver repoussé, partial gilt, diameter at rim 6⅝ × 5½″. Walters Art Museum, Baltimore, Maryland

Metal can be heated to a liquid state and poured into molds. It can also be heated and then hammered into shape, or it can be worked (usually, again, by hammering) when it is cold. Most metals are strong but malleable, and can be bent or stretched to fit the needs of the artist. Gold is particularly well suited for decorative metalwork because it is comparatively soft (for a metal) and easy to shape.

The gold mask in **2.6.9** was created by laying a thin piece of metal over an object carved to resemble a human face. The artist then carefully hammered the surface of the thin metal, a process called **chasing**, until the shape and texture of the design were imprinted in the metal. The artist has deftly given us the impression of a human face by placing objects, such as cowrie shells for the eyes, under the surface of the metal and forcing the gold sheet into its final shape. This process would have been repeated with different textures and objects to create the detailed ears, eyebrows, beard, and so on. This type of mask was used as a burial mask to cover the face of the departed.

The process of chasing involves hammering the front of a metal surface that has a form beneath it, in order to create a relief design; but reversing the process can have equal impact. This technique is known as **repoussé**. Take, for example, the *Chalice with Apostles Venerating the Cross* (**2.6.10**), a silver cup that was created in around 600 CE. In order to create this precious object, the artist hammered a blunt tool against the back of the image. Consequently, the opposite side was systematically pushed out to form the images of figures, columns, crosses, and arches. These symbols were used by early Christians to represent elements of their belief system.

Artists with good technical skills can control metals to make almost any object they can imagine. The Italian goldsmith Benvenuto Cellini (1500–1571) created the *Salt Cellar of Francis I* as an extremely elaborate object to go on the dining table of the king of France (**2.6.11**, p. 276). To make this salt cellar, Cellini first sculpted wax models of Neptune (the Roman god of the salty sea) and Mother Earth (from whence table salt was extracted) in harmony and at rest. Cellini then covered the wax model with a strong material, perhaps sand and lime, to make a mold. The mold was then heated so that the wax melted and left the center of the mold empty. Once the metal had reached the

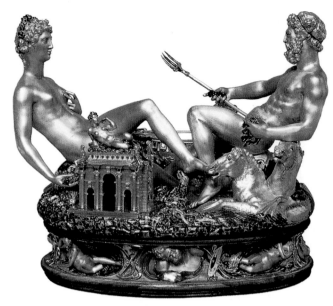

2.6.11 Benvenuto Cellini, *Salt Cellar of Francis I*, 1540–43. Gold, enamel, ebony, ivory, 11¼ × 8½ × 10⅜″. Kunsthistorisches Museum, Vienna, Austria

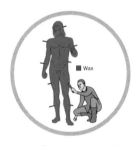

More information about the process of metal casting can be found in chapter 2.4:
→ see **2.4.13**, p. 237

required 2,000 °F, Cellini poured the molten gold into the mold. When it was cool, the artist could remove the mold and then carefully finish off the piece. The salt was held in a bowl shape next to Neptune, and the pepper inside the small triumphal arch next to the symbolic image of Earth. This magnificent example of Renaissance metalwork took more than two years to make.

Jewelry

Evidence of personal ornamentation dates back to about 100,000 BCE. The first pieces of jewelry

were Nassarius shells modified with small holes that allowed the shells to be worn as a necklace. The word jewelry is derived from the Latin word *jocale* and the French word *joule* which mean "plaything", but their precious nature and role as a signifier of wealth means these treasures have been tools of power and royal identity throughout history.

The ancient Egyptians were highly regarded as gold metalsmiths and added colored glass and precious stones to their jewelry. Egyptian metalsmithing involved working with temperatures of around 2,000 °F, the temperature at which gold melts. Melted gold was poured into a mold where it would take on its shape. The artist would then refine the metalwork using abrasive materials and applying more heat. The stones would be set by placing them into a prepared space and slightly wrapping the metal around them so that they would stay in place. The pectoral (to be worn on the chest) with the name of Senwosret II (**2.6.12**) uses this process to hold the carnelian, feldspar, garnet, and turquoise stones in place.

Jewelry in the form of rings, earrings, watches, and neckpieces are still common today. Jewelry artist Daniela Villegas expresses a refined and contemporary approach in her ring *Grannus* (**2.6.13**). Using a computer-aided design application to organize the placement of the precious stones, Villegas fashioned a crab-like sea creature to reflect prosperity and protection. Grannus, the Celtic god of the sun and warm waters, is interpreted as a dazzling sea creature offering up a large orange tourmaline gem to illuminate the moment.

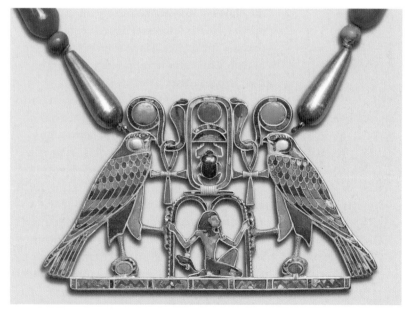

2.6.12 Pectoral of Sithathoryunet with the name Senwosret II, *c.* 1887–78 BCE, 12th Dynasty, reign of Senwosret II. Gold, carnelian, lapis lazuli, turquoise, garnet, 1¾ × 3¼″. Metropolitan Museum of Art, New York

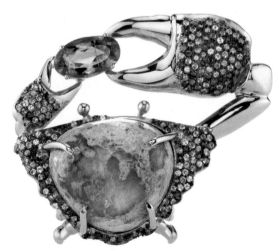

2.6.13 Daniela Villegas, *Grannus* ring, 2017. Orange tourmaline, Mexican fire opal, sapphires, 1⅜ × 1⅝″.

Fiber

Fibers are threads made from animal or vegetable materials (such as fur, wool, silk, cotton, flax, or linen) or, more recently, synthetic materials (such as nylon or polyester). Fiber art is most often associated with the creation of textiles. The fibers can be spun into yarn, string, or thread, then woven or knitted into lengths of textiles. In the case of embroidery, the thread, string, or yarn is applied using stitching techniques. Relatively stiff fibers, such as grass and rushes, can be woven together to make baskets and similar objects. Processing plant fibers begins with separating the fiber from the plant, then preparing it for use by spinning the fiber into a long thread. In the case of cotton, once the cotton bolls are collected, the fibers are separated and washed; then the individual fibers are spun, or twisted, into thread. Wool is sheared from sheep in the spring, washed and separated, then spun into yarn. Silk fibers are very fine and are the product of silkworms, which spin cocoons. Once the cocoons are complete, they are harvested. They are softened in warm water to loosen the gum that binds the fibers together. The silk can then easily be removed and spun into an exquisite fabric.

Embroidery is the process of stitching an image into a fabric surface using a needle and thread (or yarn). An embroiderer attaches the thread to the fabric by way of a variety of stitches, each with its own function in a design. The British artist Mary Linwood (1755–1845) practiced the art of crewel embroidery, a process that uses freeform, fine wool thread stitching on a drawn design. The detail from *Hanging Partridge* (**2.6.14**) shows that the

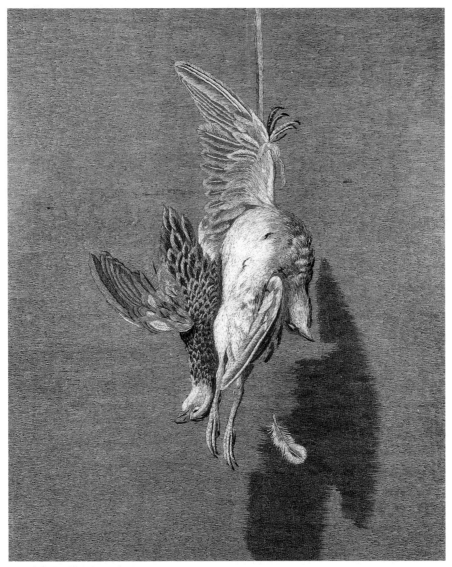

2.6.14 Mary Linwood, **detail from** *Hanging Partridge*, late 18th century. Crewelwork embroidery, approximately 24½ × 28″. Private collection

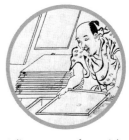

A diverse range of materials can be used in the creation of fiber art, including paper:
→ see **2.1.5**, p. 182

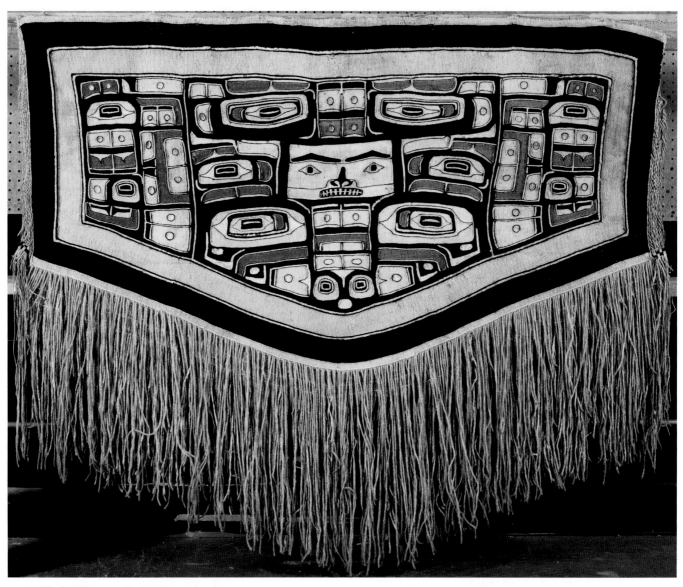

2.6.15 Tlingit Chilkat dancing blanket, 19th century

process is a lot like painting with thread, as the artist applies the thread colors the way a painter would apply color in a painting. This kind of needlework is intricate and slow (one of Linwood's pieces reportedly took ten years to complete), but it shows exceptional patience and skill. Linwood's work was held in high esteem, and indeed she was popular with royalty in England and Russia.

The Tlingit people, who live on the western coast of Canada and Alaska, combine both animal and plant material in their fiber art. The blanket shown in **2.6.15** has been woven entirely by hand (without a loom) from goat wool and cedar bark in their traditional **Chilkat** style. As Chilkat weaving is intended to be a two-dimensional portrayal of totem carving, the designs for the blankets come from pattern boards developed by wood carvers who use

symbols that convey subjects of significance to their tribe or family. In many cases these designs are **abstract** depictions of animals. The central figure here might be a bear or raccoon—note the large eyes on either side of the image, which imply the presence of even bigger creatures. Blankets like this are worn on civic and ceremonial occasions by high-ranking tribal members, their long fringe intended to sway against the body in both dances and rituals. They are very expensive, and are prized possessions of anyone fortunate enough to inherit or purchase one.

Contemporary art responds to current culture and trends. While the ancient process of weaving fibers is still used to create modern artworks, contemporary artists have developed interesting new techniques to respond to the culture of their time and locale. A modern

Chilkat: a traditional form of weaving practiced by Tlingit and other Northwest Coast peoples of Alaska and British Columbia

Abstract: art imagery that departs from recognizable images of the natural world

Faith Ringgold, *Tar Beach*

"There once was a little girl named Cassie who lived in an apartment in New York. On warm summer evenings, she and her family would lay out blankets and have picnics under the stars on their tar beach. The roof was a wonderful place to lie back and look at the city and its lights, and dream about wonderful things like flying through the sky. She could dream that her father, who had helped to build the building where she lived, could join the union, even though being half-Black and half-Indian made it impossible. She could dream that her mother owned an ice-cream factory andwas able to eat ice cream every night for dessert."

In this artwork, the African American artist Faith Ringgold (b. 1930) tells the story of a child called Cassie (**2.6.16**). Ringgold relates the African American experience, her personal history, and her family life by presenting her own childhood memories in a work that combines painting on canvas with the quilting skills of her family and ancestors. Ringgold began to paint on fabrics in the 1970s. As she did, the works evolved into a collaborative effort with her mother, who was a dressmaker and fashion designer. Ringgold would create the painted part of the work, and her mother would stitch the edges and sew patches of cloth and quilted areas together to form a border. Her great-great-great-grandmother had been a slave who made quilts for plantation owners in the South. Ringgold's works thus possess many layers of meaning that relate to this history and these craft skills. Together these layers communicate the richness of human experience.

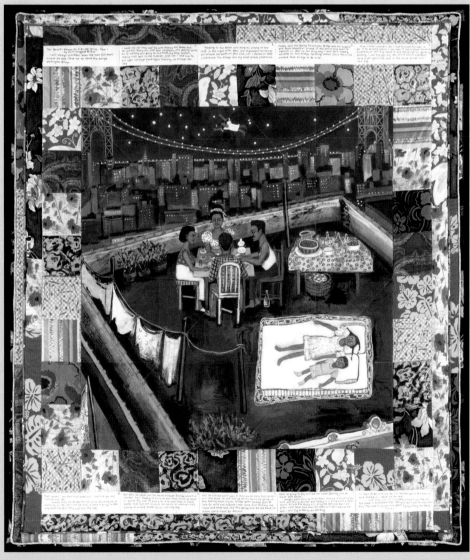

2.6.16 Faith Ringgold, *Tar Beach*, 1988. Acrylic on canvas, bordered with printed, painted, quilted, and pieced cloth, 6'2⅝" × 5'8½". Solomon R. Guggenheim Museum, New York

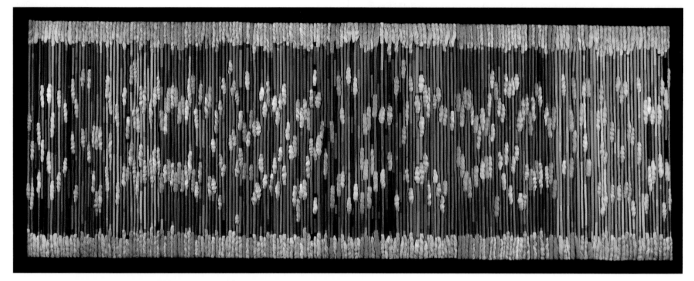

2.6.17a **Sheila Hicks**, ***The Silk Rainforest***, *c.* 1975. Silk, linen, and cotton, 96 × 270 × 3″, Smithsonian American Art Museum, Renwick Gallery, Washington, D.C.

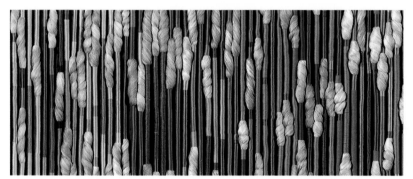

2.6.17b Detail of *The Silk Rainforest*

master of woven fiber is the American-born Sheila Hicks (b. 1934) who challenges the traditional nature of fiber by using it in more expressive ways on a massive scale. In her woven work *The Silk Rainforest* (**2.6.17a** and **2.6.17b**), Hicks created a huge work that challenged the kind of measured and controlled corporate **installations** being created in other media by keeping the raw irregularity of the frayed fiber. The rich fiber surface and the interplay of color display a unique sensitivity

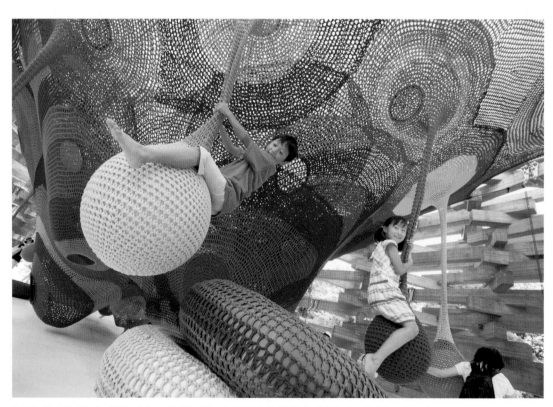

2.6.18 **Toshiko Horiuchi MacAdam**, ***Knitted Wonder Space II***, 2009. Braided nylon 6-6; hand crochet, 49′2″ × 29′6″ × 21′3″. Woods of Net Pavilion, Hakone Open Air Museum, Hakone, Japan

to the tactile characteristics of the silk, linen, and cotton for the viewers at the AT&T Headquarters in Basking Ridge, New Jersey, where it was originally installed. Hicks created a composition that conjured the physical sense of touch and paired it with a rich visual experience, making the viewer's experience more holistic.

Knitting is a process of creating a fabric using loops and stitching. Various materials can be knitted, including wool, cotton, and nylon. The Japanese artist Toshiko Horiuchi MacAdam (b. 1940) knits entire environments where viewers are invited to touch the artwork. Her early work in architectural fabric structures led her to create interactive environments. For example, *Knitted Wonder Space II* (**2.6.18**) is a knitted structure designed to be a children's playground. MacAdam builds these large-scale fiber constructions in her studio in Canada, and installs them as required: her work can be found in many countries worldwide. These works challenge preconceived ideas of what fiber art can be, as do others in which artists have knitted metals and plastics.

Wood

Wood, an organic plant-based material, deteriorates over time, so we have few ancient examples of art objects made from it. But we know that wood has been utilized for objects and architecture throughout history. Trees provide many colors and hardnesses of wood, the innate beauty of which can be brought out by cutting and carving. Sanding and polishing a piece of wood gives its surface a mesmerizing beauty.

Around 1480, the Italian artist Francesco di Giorgio Martini (1439–1501) used a decorative wood technique called **intarsia** in his design for a *studiolo* (a private room, often a library or study) in Gubbio, Italy. Intarsia is a kind of wood mosaic using woods of different colors. Giuliano da Maiano, who executed the work, took very thin, shaped pieces of wood and organized them to create a masterpiece of **illusionistic** depth and **value** (**2.6.19**). To the casual viewer, because the artists employed such skill, it is not clear where reality ends and the illusion begins. Federico da Montefeltro, the Duke of Urbino, who commissioned Martini

Installation: originally referring to the hanging of pictures and arrangement of objects in an exhibition, installation may also refer to an intentional environment created as a completed artwork

Intarsia: the art of setting pieces of wood into a surface to create a pattern

Illusionism, Illusionistic: the artistic skill or trick of making something look real

Value: the lightness or darkness of a plane or area

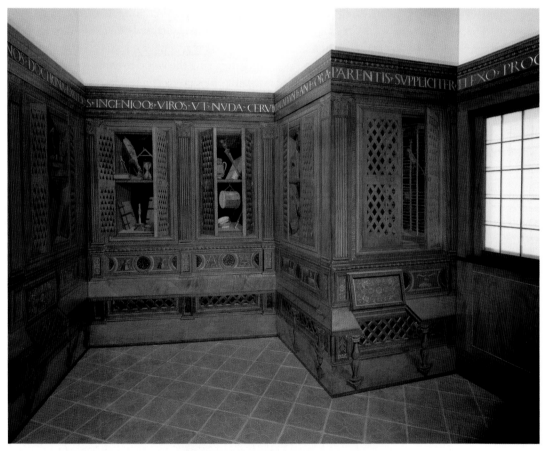

2.6.19 Detail of *studiolo* from the Ducal Palace in Gubbio, Italy, by Giuliano da Maiano, after a design by Francesco di Giorgio Martini, *c.* 1478–82. Walnut, beech, rosewood, oak, and fruit woods in walnut base, 15'11" × 16'11" × 12'7¼". Metropolitan Museum of Art, New York

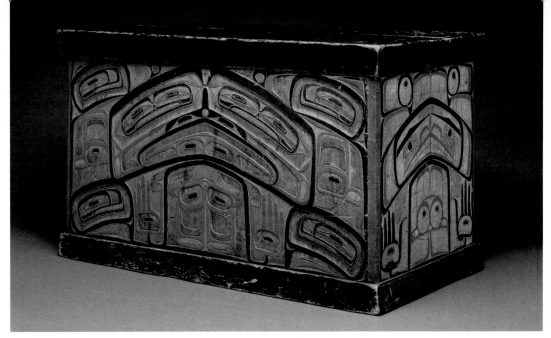

2.6.20 Captain Richard Carpenter, **bent-corner chest**, *c.* 1860. Yellow cedar, red cedar, and paint, 21¼ × 35¾ × 20½". Seattle Art Museum, Washington

to create this work, wanted the symbols in this magnificent design to reflect his achievements as a ruler, military commander, collector of books, and **patron** of the arts.

A Native American artist of the Heiltsuk tribe worked with wood to make the bent-corner chest shown in **2.6.20**. To create this vessel, a plank of cedar was smoothed, notches known as kerfs were cut at three corners, and then the wood was made flexible by exposing it to steam created by fire-baked rocks and water. The plank was then bent at the kerfs and joined at the juncture of the last corner. After that, the chest was carved and painted with an elaborate, symmetrical design that fills the whole surface. A separate base and top were then fitted to the whole.

The practice of wood turning, or fashioning a wooden object using a lathe (a power-driven spinning support), continues to grow in popularity. The artist who practices this craft must, naturally, be knowledgeable about wood and its attributes; prepare the wood by seasoning (careful aging and drying); and control the orientation of the grain of the wood on the turning axis. Andrew Early (b. 1970), a South African wood turner who was taught this craft by his father, John, has become one of today's most collected and exhibited wood turners. Early places emphasis on selecting and preparing the wood to capture its natural organic character, often aging the wood for many years. He leaves voids and irregularities that naturally occur in the lumber to preserve its rich innate personality or quality. Such works as the turned wood bowl in **2.6.21** reflect the sensitivity to the material that most craftspeople and artisans possess after having spent long hours in the study and execution of excellence. Early would probably agree with Chaucer that "life is so short, the craft so long to learn."

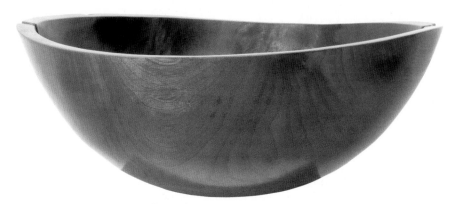

2.6.21 Andrew Early, **turned bowl**, 2010. Indian mahogany, 13¾ × 29½"

Explore Further The Tradition of Craft

Ceramic and Glass

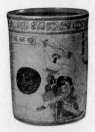

3.4.13 Cylindrical vessel with ritual ball-game scene, *c.* 700–850 ➔ p. 418

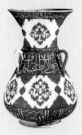

1.4.22 Mosque lamp from the Dome of the Rock, Jerusalem, 1549 ➔ p. 96

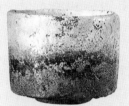

0.0.9 Hon'ami Koetsu, tea bowl, early 17th century ➔ p. 21

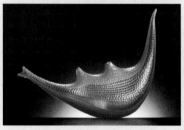

1.2.5 Lino Tagliapietra, *Batman*, 1998 ➔ p. 53

Metalwork and Jewelry

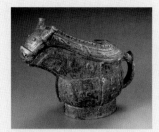

3.3.8 Ritual wine vessel (*guang*), *c.* 1700–1050 BCE ➔ p. 396

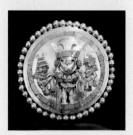

3.4.4 Moche earspool, Peru, *c.* 300 CE ➔ p. 412

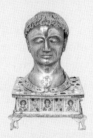

3.2.14 Reliquary of the Head of St. Alexander, 1145 ➔ p. 382

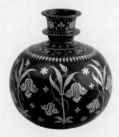

1.9.3 Huqqa base, India, last quarter of 17th century ➔ p. 149

Textile

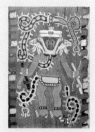

3.4.3 Paracas textile, Peru, 3rd century BCE ➔ p. 412

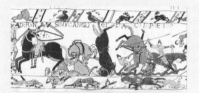

4.6.6 Detail of the Battle of Hastings, *Bayeux Tapestry*, *c.* 1066–82 ➔ p. 608

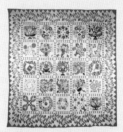

1.6.12 Alice A. Ryder, *Baltimore Album Quilt*, *c.* 1847 ➔ p. 123

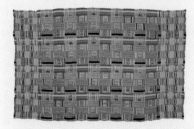

3.5.4 Asante textile wrapper (*kente*), 20th century ➔ p. 430

Your turn
What media were used to make these objects?

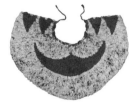

3.5.18a Feather cloak (*ahu'ula*), Hawaii, 18th century (?) ➔ p. 438

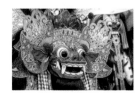

3.3.24 Barong dance mask of a lion, Bali, Indonesia ➔ p. 407

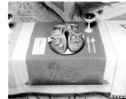

4.9.7 Judy Chicago, *The Dinner Party*, 1974–79 ➔ p. 653

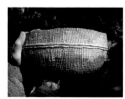

3.4.28 Julia Parker, basket for cooking acorns, *c.* 2011 ➔ p. 426

2.7
Visual Communication Design

Graphic design: the use of images, typography, and technology to communicate ideas for a client or to a particular audience

Medium (plural **media**): the material on or from which an artist chooses to make a work of art, for example canvas and oil paint, marble, engraving, video, or architecture

Typefaces: the particular unified style of a family of typographical characters

New Wave design: a design movement that exemplified the counter-cultural currents of the 1980s

Abstract: art imagery that departs from recognizable images of the natural world

Hieroglyph: written language involving sacred characters that may be pictures as well as letters or signifiers of sounds

Calligraphy: the art of emotive or carefully descriptive hand lettering or handwriting

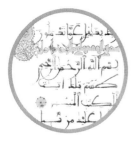

In early versions of the Koran, calligraphic writing was important to the stylistic use of Arabic:
→ see **3.2.10**, p. 379

The essence of visual communication design is the use of symbol to communicate information and ideas. Traditional communication design was known as **graphic design**: the design of books, magazines, posters, advertising, and other printed matter by arranging drawings, photographs, and type. Advances in printing processes, television, the computer, and the growth of the Web have expanded graphic design to include many more design possibilities. A better and more complete term for it now is visual communication design. Furthermore, while graphic design was the responsibility of specialists, the typographical power of the computer—both for print and the Web—means that many more people can, with a little practice, create effective and even innovative design work, provided they understand the principles of visual communication design.

The term visual communication design was first introduced by the designer April Greiman (b. 1948), shortly after she was named chair of the Department of Design at the California Institute of the Arts in 1981. Unlike other designers at that time, Greiman embraced the computer as a creative tool, and experimented with the possibilities that this new **medium** afforded. In 1986, Greiman forever changed the design world when she produced a six-page fold-out *Design Quarterly* cover, *Does It Make Sense?*, that was created on an Apple Macintosh computer (**2.7.18**, p. 294). Greiman's design integrated a nude self-portrait, graphic symbols, and creative **typefaces** into one dynamic piece of cover art that dazzled the industry and ushered in the digital age. The computer allowed the integration of elements that did not need to be rigidly set into a grid,

reflecting the looseness of 1980s punk culture, a style that came to be called **New Wave design**.

This chapter will discuss the development of the media, systems, and processes used in visual communication design, which enables us to express visual ideas with increasing clarity, style, and sophistication.

The Visual Character of Text

Early History of Writing

The people of ancient Mesopotamia—who inhabited a region that includes present-day Iraq—were the first (*c.* 3400 BCE) to employ picture symbols in a consistent language system. The ancient Egyptians later created their own version of picture symbols, known as **hieroglyphs**, as a written form of communication. In particular, the Egyptians wrote them on scrolls made of a paper-like substance created from the pith of the papyrus plant (**2.7.1**). While early Chinese written characters also frequently resembled the subject they identified, later forms of picture writing became increasingly **abstract**. The Latin alphabet has followed the same trajectory; while originally (for example) the letter A was supposed to be derived from the shape of a cow's skull, and B from a house, it has now lost any of its earliest connections with the representations of things.

Wherever literacy takes hold, **calligraphy** usually develops as a form of art concerned with expressing layers of meaning and feelings through the shape of written letterforms. For example, handwritten wedding invitations are created using calligraphy because the flowing line and distinctive character of the lettering communicate the upcoming event in an elegant and romantic way. In oral communication,

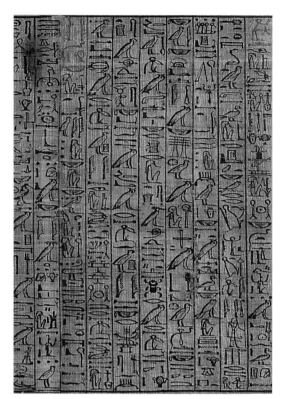

2.7.1 Section of papyrus from Book of the Dead of Ani, *c.* 1250 BCE. British Museum, London, England

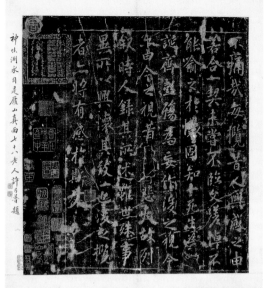

2.7.2 Rubbing of stela inscription, *Preface of the Lanting Gathering*, Ding Wu version (Inukai version), original by Wang Xizhi, Eastern Jin Dynasty, dated 353 CE. Album, ink on paper, 9⅝ × 8⅞". Tokyo National Museum, Japan

Typography: the art of designing, arranging, and choosing type

Illuminated manuscript: a hand-lettered text with hand-drawn pictures

changes in tone, volume, facial expression, hand gestures, and body movement work together; in calligraphy, the physical act of writing, the thought expressed, and the visual form of the text become one.

Chinese culture particularly exalts calligraphy executed in black ink with a brush. The Chinese calligrapher Wang Xizhi (303–361 CE) defined the art of calligraphy in China during the Jin Dynasty (265–420 CE). Although none of Wang's originals still exist, other calligraphers copied his work through the ages, perpetuating his ideal of perfect form. In ancient China, fine specimens of writing were carved on large standing stone tablets, from which visitors could take copies by making rubbings—a rudimentary printing technique (**2.7.2**).

Typography

The visual form of printed letters, words, and text is called **typography**. Type, a word derived from a Greek word meaning "to strike," first came into existence with Johannes Gutenberg's (*c.* 1398–1468) invention of the printing press in Germany around 1450. Gutenberg also created a technique for producing small cast-metal letter shapes, known as letterforms, that could be set next to each other in a row, inked,

and then printed in relief on paper using his press. Gutenberg's letterforms have angled thick and thin strokes that mimic the pen calligraphy used in **illuminated manuscripts** (called Black Letter; see p. 286). Scholars believe his intention was to emulate handwritten texts; his first bibles used exactly the same letterforms as those used in manuscripts, and the pages even included illustrations drawn by hand.

The German master printmaker Albrecht Dürer (1471–1528) wrote systematically on the subject of typography in order to teach

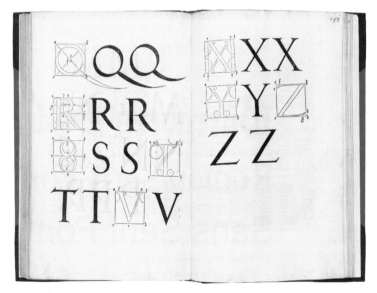

2.7.3 Albrecht Dürer, pages from *Course in the Art of Measurement with Compass and Ruler*, 1538. Victoria and Albert Museum, London, England

others. In *Course in the Art of Measurement with Compass and Ruler* (1538) (**2.7.3**, p. 285), he sought to create a set of rules for the design of letter shapes. His was the first text to standardize how to create each letter using such geometric elements as squares, circles, and lines. By following these careful instructions, a typographer could create letterforms similar to those used by the ancient Romans.

Dürer's Roman alphabet is notably different from Gutenberg's letterforms. A complete alphabet of letterforms and matching punctuation is called a font. A font is a group of letterforms designed to have a unified appearance. Roman-style fonts were derived directly from the letters chiseled into stone on the buildings and monuments of ancient Rome. Those characters had a vertical or horizontal mark at the edges of some letters. These marks, called serifs, were integrated into many early typefaces. The differences between these kinds of fonts are shown in **2.7.4**.

In books and newspapers, serif fonts are traditionally used in the main text because they are considered easier to read. Typographers often use a sans serif font, or a font without serifs, in headings. (Sans serif derives its name from the French word *sans*, meaning "without," and perhaps from the Dutch word *schreef*, meaning a stroke of a pen.) In the twenty-first century, sans serif has become the standard font style in electronic media, as tiny serifs may not fully appear in comparatively low-resolution electronic displays.

Typographers follow some simple rules to make sure a written message is clear. When using multiple fonts, the fonts must be different enough to avoid confusion between the typefaces. The visual weight, or thickness,

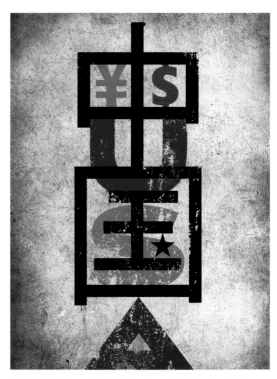

2.7.5 Kok Cheow Yeoh, *Hegemony*, 2016. Poster design for International Art and Design Exhibition (INAD), Selçuk University, Konya, Turkey

of the letters can be used for **contrast** and to emphasize a section of the text simply by changing the type to bold. The choice of larger or smaller font sizes also adds another level of contrast and **emphasis**. Finally, even more emphasis and contrast can be gained through the choice of **color**. Typographers use these options carefully to keep it simple and to create a message that is clear, concise, and easily understood.

Contemporary typographers coax expression from the printed word by carefully balancing message with visual form. The Malaysian-born American typographer Kok Cheow Yeoh (b. 1967) pushes the limits of text by considering the relationship between the message and the visual form. In the poster *Hegemony* (**2.7.5**), the designer has visually balanced most of the letters and symbols atop a large blue letter "A". In this work the word hegemony, meaning authority or dominance, refers to the economic leadership of the US and China, two of the world's strongest financial powers. Both countries compete economically, but also rely on each other for trade, resulting in a balanced tension that maintains their commercial and financial markets. The designer has integrated letters and **glyphs** from the dominant language of each country to illustrate this relationship.

𝕲ütenberg 𝕭ible

Roman Serif Font

Sans Serif Font

2.7.4 Some font styles (top to bottom):
1. Replica of Black Letter style used in Gutenberg's 1454 Bible
2. Times New Roman with some serifs circled
3. Helvetica font with no serifs (sans serif)

Influence of the Bauhaus on Visual Design

The Bauhaus was a German school of art and design that operated in the early twentieth century. From about 1919 to 1933, the students at the school were immersed in the creation of art and design relating to every object and idea that could be addressed using **Modernist** theory, or the idea that the design of an object and the material from which it is made should be determined by its purpose ("form follows function"). Although the Bauhaus was initially conceived as a school of architecture by its founder, Walter Gropius (1883–1969), the school worked to establish design ideals that could be applied universally with no constraints on culture or medium. Bauhaus artists designed and redesigned furniture, kitchenware, and household items, and set a new standard for visual communication design.

The mission of the school was to create designs that fit the modern world. Using inexpensive and common materials, the artists of the Bauhaus sought to imagine a style that was universal and did not favor one culture over another. This was evident in the printed materials that were generated by such professors as Herbert Bayer. Bayer created a sans serif typeface that he named "Universal" (**2.7.6**). Bayer's typeface had its own character that could not be immediately associated with any one culture, but that was easy to read

ABCDEFGHIJKLM NOPQRSTUVWXYZ

2.7.6 Herbert Bayer, *Universal* **typeface**, 1925

and facilitated visual communication. This same typeface was used to spell out the name of the Bauhaus on the outside of the building (**2.7.7**).

After the rise of the Nazi Party in Germany and the subsequent closure of the school in 1933, a number of artists and designers relocated outside of Europe, many moving to the United States. Amongst them was Ludwig Mies van der Rohe (1886–1969), who had been Head of the Bauhaus. He re-established the school and continued its ideals by founding the Armour Institute of Technology (later called the Illinois Institute of Technology) in Chicago. Mies van der Rohe is often best remembered for his emphasis on simplicity of design, and his quips, "Less is more" and "God is in the details," expressed two key ideas that inspired an entire generation of architects and designers in the mid-twentieth century, whose influence can still be seen in design practice today.

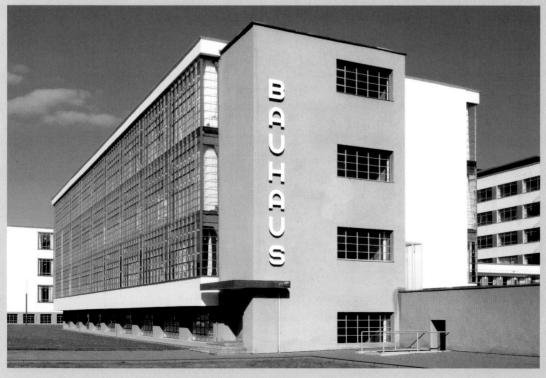

2.7.7 Walter Gropius, **Bauhaus building**, 1925–26, Dessau, Germany

Modernism, Modernist: a radically new twentieth-century art and architectural movement that embraced modern industrial materials and a machine aesthetic

Logos and Icons

Businesses and other organizations use **logos** as communication tools. A logo (from the Greek *logos*, meaning "word") is often simply a carefully designed piece of type, called a logotype, that is unique and easily identified. Sometimes a designer communicates an idea using a pictorial symbol instead of type. The Chevrolet logo was first used in 1913 and has been an identifying mark for the company ever since. Originally, the name Chevrolet was written across the simple stylized cross (called the "bowtie"). Over time, the symbol became associated in people's minds with the name, which was then removed from the design. It now communicates the company name without using any letter of the alphabet (**2.7.9**).

The immediacy and the universal communicative properties of logos have become the basis for a new kind of labeling system that is now used worldwide. Icons, or simple symbolic graphic shapes, are being used in place of written labels because they provide an immediate message that can be understood in any language. For example, on car dashboards, the icon in the shape of two concentric triangles (third row down, sixth icon on the right in Figure **2.7.10**) indicates the control button for the hazard blinkers. The triangular icon has provided

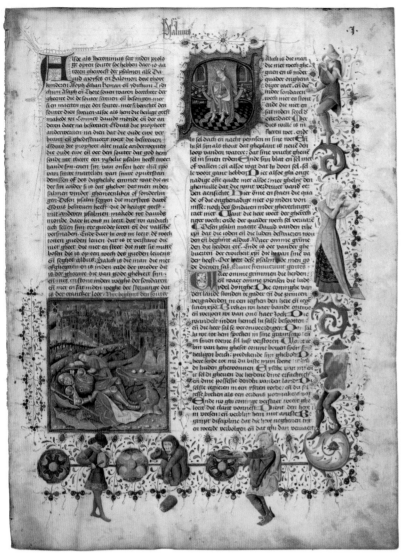

2.7.8 *Dutch History Bible*, **copied by Gherard Wessels van Deventer in Utrecht**, 1443, fol. 8r. National Library of the Netherlands, The Hague

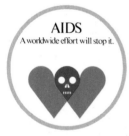

AIDS
A worldwide effort will stop it.

Milton Glaser used a simple and powerful visual communication method when he formed the letter W from heart and skull icons:

→ **see 1.8.3**, p. 141

Stencil: a perforated template allowing ink or paint to pass through to print a design

The Communicative Image

The first communicative graphic was probably created when a prehistoric person blew pigment through a reed to **stencil** a handprint on the wall of a cave. During the Middle Ages, European artists combined calligraphy and illustration to craft illuminated manuscripts (**2.7.8**). Illuminated manuscripts were executed in monasteries on prepared animal skins, called parchment. After being painted and lettered by hand, they were bound as books. This kind of design was very time-consuming as well as expensive to produce, and resulted in only one copy of the book. The invention of printing technology in the mid-fifteenth century simplified the design process and made it possible to print multiple copies. In other words, printing made graphic design possible.

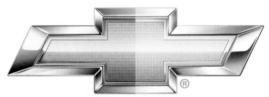

2.7.9 Chevrolet logo, first used in 1913

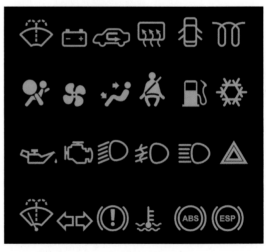

2.7.10 Illuminated car dashboard icon set

an accepted meaning across cultures and has therefore become recognized by drivers everywhere, so that no words need to be printed on the button.

Illustration

Illustrations are images created to inform as well as to embellish the printed page. Good illustration is critical in such fields as medicine and science, where it may communicate essential information more effectively than text or a photograph.

The nineteenth-century English artists and designers William Morris (1834–1896) and Edward Burne-Jones (1833–1898) believed that society should reject rampant industrialization and restore handcrafting. Their illustrated book of the works of the **medieval** poet Geoffrey Chaucer was handcrafted so that each page contained illustrations, **illuminated characters**, and patterns (**2.7.11**). The illustrations allow readers to experience and understand the works of Chaucer more richly. They support and enhance the written words.

Logo: a unique graphic image used to identify an idea or entity

Medieval: the time period roughly between the fall of the Roman empire and the start of the Renaissance

Illuminated characters: highly decorated letters, usually found at the beginning of a page or paragraph

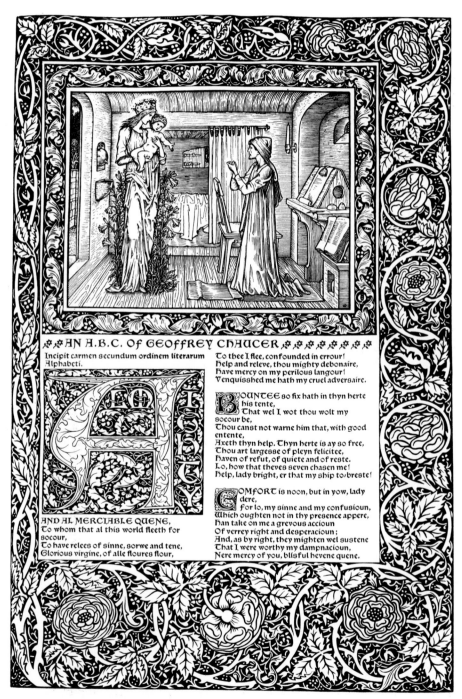

2.7.11 William Morris and Edward Burne-Jones, page from *Works of Geoffrey Chaucer*, Kelmscott Press, 1896. British Museum, London, England

Lithography, lithographic: a print process executed on a flat, unmarred surface, such as a stone, in which the image is created using oil-based ink with resistance to water

The American illustrator James Montgomery Flagg (1877–1960) brought a patriotic literary figure to life and created a memorable icon of the United States when he drew the first image of "Uncle Sam." Although Uncle Sam was a fictional character from the early nineteenth century, it was Flagg in his poster of 1917, "I Want YOU for U.S. Army," who created an image that would become a representation of the US government (**2.7.12**). The poster—which was inspired by a similar British poster featuring the former secretary of state for war, Lord Kitchener—helped to recruit soldiers for World Wars I and II. Flagg designed the image of Uncle Sam using his own face, its intimidating authoritarian stare and the outstretched pointing finger intended to confront and single out the viewer and challenge his commitment to the defense of the nation.

One of the most popular illustrations ever created, based on the number of printed copies made, was a striking image by the American painter-illustrator Maxfield Parrish (1870–1966). Parrish painted *Daybreak* (**2.7.13**) for use as a printed **lithograph** that could be commercially marketed. The work, a vivid image of two figures between a pair of columns, in a dramatic and colorful landscape, was so popular that experts estimate 25 percent of American households owned a copy in the 1920s. The image continues to influence artists and filmmakers because of its otherworldly visual qualities.

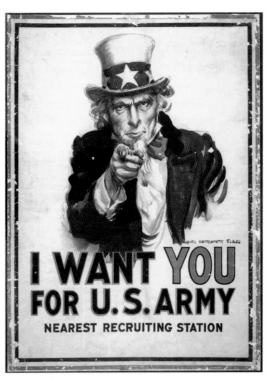

2.7.12 James Montgomery Flagg, *I Want YOU for U.S. Army*, recruitment poster, c. 1917

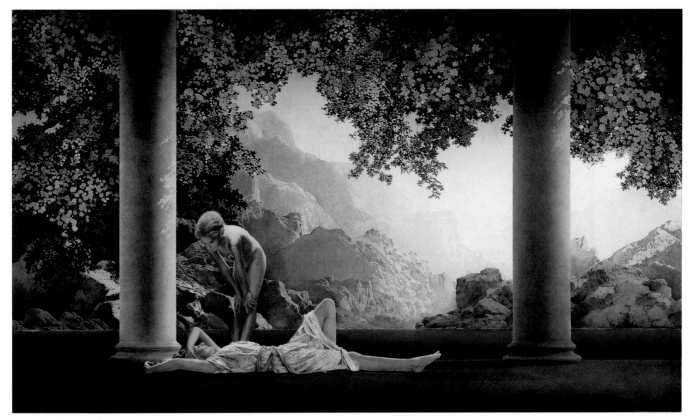

2.7.13 Maxfield Parrish, *Daybreak*, 1922. Oil on board, 26½ × 45". Private collection

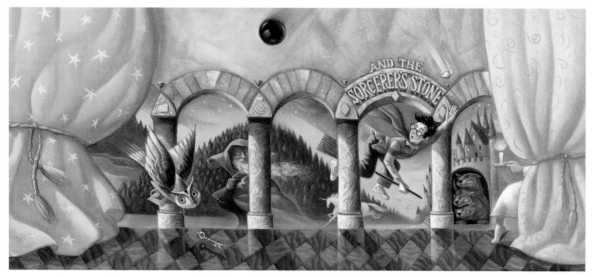

2.7.14 Mary Grandpré, cover art for *Harry Potter and the Sorcerer's Stone*, published by Scholastic, 1997

Such contemporary illustrators as Mary Grandpré (b. 1954) have continued, and built upon, the traditions of the past. In her illustrated cover for *Harry Potter and the Sorcerer's Stone*, (**2.7.14**) by J. K. Rowling, Grandpré has also integrated a colonnaded vista through which the bespectacled protagonist, Harry Potter, flies toward the viewer while attempting to catch a shiny object called a Golden Snitch. Grandpré introduces the reader to the main character and an exciting scene that will be encountered as the story unfolds. The imagery complements the written text and creates a visual introduction via the clues that are scattered, half-hidden, throughout the artwork.

Digital illustration has become a popular way for designers to incorporate illustrations into a printed design. Digital drawings are produced through the use of computer applications that use mathematical formulas dependent on the relative placement of points. In these math-based applications, the computer generates an image, called a vector graphic, from a series of lines plotted from the relationship between individual points. Since points and lines are the basic units of this system, it bears a resemblance to drawing processes. Most of the line art in this book was created using this type of digital illustration application.

The Portuguese-born illustrator Jorge Colombo (b. 1963) creates drawings digitally, using his iPhone on the streets of New York City. His images have become well known,

having graced several covers of *The New Yorker* magazine (**2.7.15**). The artist likes to create his work this way because passersby think that he is just checking his e-mail and do not disturb him as he works. The results are fresh and spontaneous enough to capture the vibrant energy of New York.

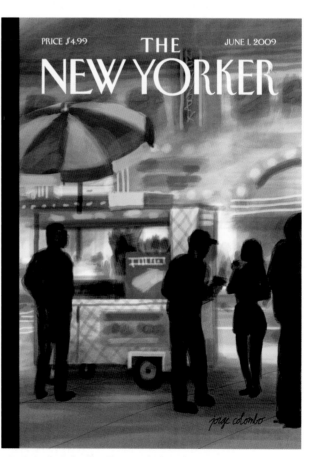

2.7.15 Jorge Colombo, *Finger Painting*. *The New Yorker* magazine cover, June 1, 2009. Digital sketch using iPhone

Layout Design

Graphic design is the art of improving visual communication. As you read this text, you may have noticed the way the information is organized. Headings, page numbers, illustrations, and the definitions of terms in the margin have all been carefully considered with you in mind. The use of **boldface** type and columns of text helps you read and understand. In other visual arts, it may be preferable to invite a viewer to consider and contemplate. But in graphic design, the communication is intended to be instantaneous, clear, and direct. Layout design is the art of organizing type, logos, and illustrations to optimize communication. Good layout design is essential if information is to be easily understood. One of the main considerations in layout design is spacing. Designers are very aware of **white space**—the **voids** that lie between text areas and images—and are careful in its organization and distribution in their layouts.

If you examine the way this page is designed, you will notice the relationships between columns of text, images, and other features, such as page numbers. The designer responsible for this page has made sure each feature has enough white space around it

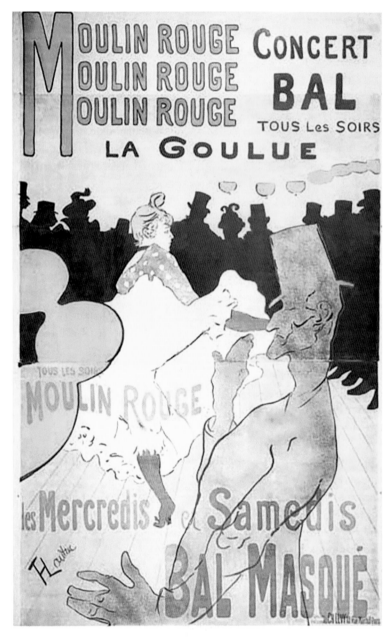

2.7.16 Henri de Toulouse-Lautrec, *La Goulue at the Moulin Rouge*, 1891. Lithograph in black, yellow, red, and blue on three sheets of tan wove paper, 6'2½" × 3'9⅝". Art Institute of Chicago, Illinois

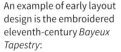

An example of early layout design is the embroidered eleventh-century *Bayeux Tapestry*:

→ see **4.6.6**, p. 608

to be easily identified and understood, but is close enough to related elements, such as the pictures, so that the text and images complement each other.

The French artist Henri de Toulouse-Lautrec (1864–1901) created posters for his favorite Parisian nightspot, the Moulin Rouge. In *La Goulue at the Moulin Rouge*, Toulouse-Lautrec uses a free, rounded writing style that is as casual as the spectators in the nightclub scene as they watch La Goulue (the nickname, meaning "The Glutton," of the dancer Louise Weber) dance the can-can (**2.7.16**). Here, the text is calligraphy rendered by hand directly (in mirror-writing) on the lithographic stone from which it is printed. Toulouse-Lautrec's skill as an illustrator and typographer is apparent in the excellent hand-rendered text and images.

The master graphic designer Michael Bierut (b. 1957) has used layout design creatively to communicate and inspire. One of his most famous and memorable advertising campaigns was done for the Yale University School of Architecture (**2.7.17**). Bierut incorporated various typefaces to differentiate between the visiting speakers, exhibitors, and symposia that highlight the school's unique contributions to architectural education.

Mirror writing: writing that reads correctly only when reflected in a mirror, as in the case of the journals and other writings of Leonardo da Vinci

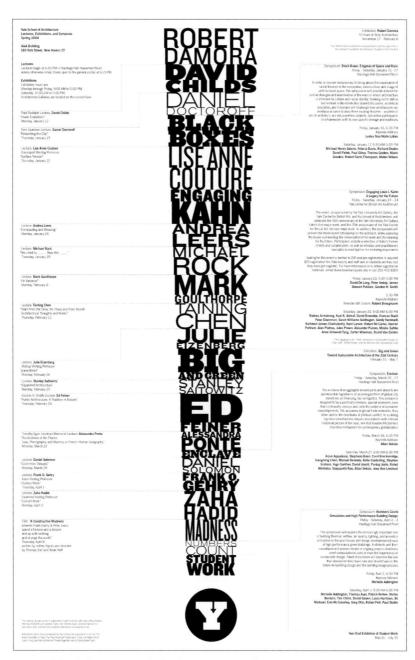

2.7.17 Michael Bierut, Poster design for Yale School of Architecture, Lectures, Exhibitions, and Symposia, Spring 2004

April Greiman, *Does It Make Sense?*
Design Quarterly #133, 1986

**For the other Greiman
GATEWAYS:**
→ see p. 526 and p. 652

New Wave design reflected the alternative counter-culture of the 1980s, exemplified by such movements as Punk, a reaction against the slick commercial style of the time. Here, the visual communication designer April Greiman talks about her issue of the Design Quarterly *magazine. She turned the magazine into a two-sided poster, the self-portrait* Does It Make Sense? (**2.7.18**). *The pixellation of the image shows it to be a product of the digital age, but its subjects, the human mind and body, are some of the oldest in art.*

I like to think of my process as one of jumping into a stream, to see where it takes me. The final product emerges after following questions and guidance from my internal voice, trying a thousand iterations of the work, and having solutions to problems come to me in dreams. I try to go into all my work with a sense of openness and a desire for discovery.

It seems crazy now, but the design community was very reluctant to begin using computers. Back in the 1980s, graphic designers were deeply focused on print and analog technology. As for me, I wouldn't even call myself a graphic designer. The term is too closely tied to print, which wasn't the only medium then and isn't the dominant medium now. So in 1986, when *Design Quarterly* asked me to design an issue of their magazine, I knew I wanted to create something using digital technology.

Back in 1984, I attended the first TED (Technology, Education, and Design) conference, co-founded by my friend Harry Marks. After the conference, Harry dragged me out to see the first Macintosh computer, which had only just been released. I got my hands on it and never looked back. When I was commissioned by *Design Quarterly*, I was using a 512k Mac, which is a minuscule amount of processing power—it probably couldn't handle the full text of this feature. I reimagined *Design Quarterly*, usually a thirty-two-page magazine, as a two-by-six-foot fold-out poster covered in images, text, and symbols. To make it, I used this little add-on device called the MacVision, which could port directly from a video camera to the computer so that the Mac could digitize the photos. There was no one-stop photo-editing tool, such as Photoshop, back then, so I was cutting out images and layering and resizing them across several different programs. The final image is 289kb, smaller than a photo you'd make on a smartphone today, but which at the time was large enough to generate dozens of error messages and take all night to print.

The shift from print to digital is really a shift from working with matter to working with light. When I created *Does It Make Sense?*, the images I was layering and manipulating weren't physical, they were light. Money, art, books—all these things that were once objects can now exist as nothing more than patterns of light on a screen. We can make art that has no real physical existence; the computer, in a way, changed my body to light, then the printer gave it physical form again.

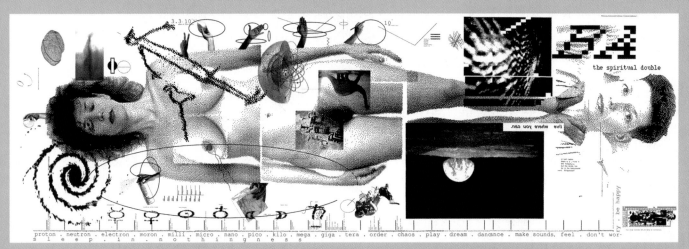

2.7.18 April Greiman, *Does It Make Sense?* from *Design Quarterly* Issue #133, 1986.

Advertising Design

Design specifically created to sell a product or service has become a common part of contemporary life. The same care that an artist puts into the expressive character of a great work of art is similar to the designer's process when creating an advertisement. In the early twentieth century, the Japanese cosmetic company Shiseido integrated traditional Japanese design with influences from European art movements to create a series of elegant and memorable designs. In the 1920s, the company produced a number of eye-catching designs in which type, illustration, symbol, and message come together within the advertising layout to promote cosmopolitan and elegant beauty goods—in this case a tooth whitening product (**2.7.19**). An image of a relaxed and elongated

figure dominates a design where both English and Japanese writing are organized along with a stylized camellia, the symbolic identity used by the company. Originally founded in 1872, Shiseido still produces beautiful, understated designs to advertise its cosmetics.

The thoughtful placement of text and visual elements to unify an advertising design has become a common contemporary practice. In fact, some of the biggest advertising firms have teamed up with illustrators and typographers to produce such designs. Chip Kidd (b. 1964), a New York graphic designer whose main focus was the creation of book covers, created a design for Michael Crichton's novel *Jurassic Park* that used a silhouetted Tyrannosaurus rex. The image had such a strong visual impact that, after reviewing many other professional

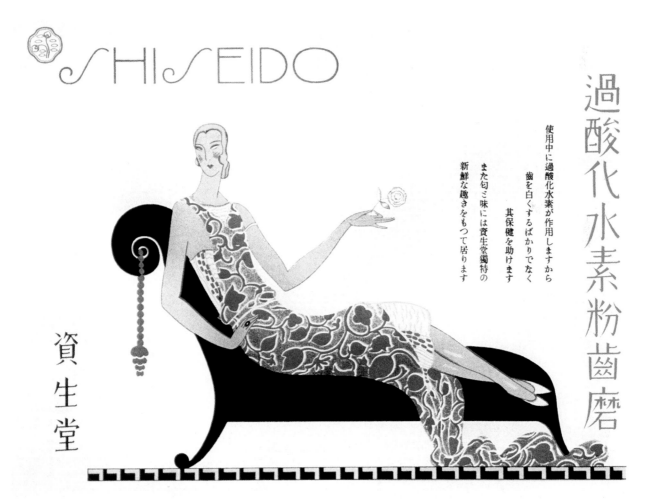

2.7.19 Poster for Hydrogen Peroxide Tooth Powder, *c*. 1927.
Shiseido Corporate Museum, Tokyo, Japan

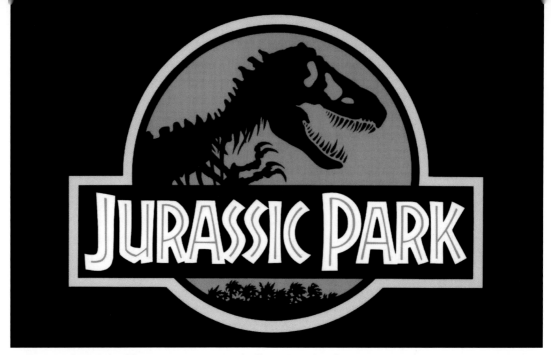

2.7.20 *Jurassic Park*, detail from a poster promoting the film, Universal Studios, 1993

logo designs, the creative director for the movie decided to use Kidd's original dinosaur. The collaboration between the film's creative director and Chip Kidd resulted in the enduring *Jurassic Park* (**2.7.20**) identity, which was distributed worldwide.

Web Design

In the past twenty-five years, visual communication design has been dramatically influenced by the Internet. The use of text and image in mass communication has evolved from the motionless design of print publications to the interactive designs used on the World Wide Web. The Web allows designers more freedom to add interactivity so that text and image can change as the reader progresses through the information presented.

Web design is strongly connected to layout design because the process of creating a good website design also involves the careful organization of text and image. This is

Color in Visual Communication Design

Artists who design images for commercial printing or to display on video screens take a different approach to color than painters or other kinds of artists. In this section we will look at how color is used in print and electronic displays.

COLOR IN PRINT

Most printed color images—from posters, to magazines, to this book—rely on four separate colors to create the range of colors that we see. Commercial printers use three **primary colors**—cyan (a kind of light blue-green), magenta (a light red-violet), and yellow—plus black (called "key"); the color system for printing is referred to as **CMYK** (**2.7.21**). An image is scanned and separated into the four colors. Figure **2.7.22** shows a typical set of color separations. The image is re-created when the separated colors are printed in sequence, overlapping each other. The four colored inks are printed on paper as dots in a regular pattern ("screen"): the smaller the dot, the less of each color is printed. In the darkest colors the dots are nearly joined together. Variations in color printing can be expected depending on the paper used. A coated paper supports more rich, lustrous

Primary colors: three basic colors from which all others are derived

CMYK: subtractive system based on the primary colors used in four-color printing: cyan, magenta, blue, and key (black)

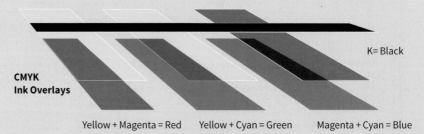

CMYK Ink Overlays

K= Black

Yellow + Magenta = Red   Yellow + Cyan = Green   Magenta + Cyan = Blue

2.7.21 Cyan, magenta, yellow, and black ink overlays, showing the resulting secondary color when they are combined

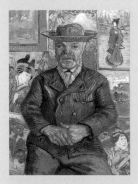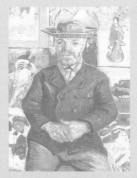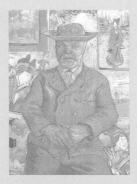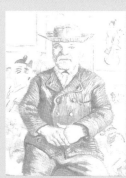

2.7.22 Color separation for a commercially printed reproduction of an artwork by Van Gogh. The image on the extreme left is Van Gogh's original; the other four show how it reproduces in each of the separate, different-colored ink printing screens

color than an uncoated one. The perception of color is important to comprehension, because color provides more levels of information by attracting attention and differentiating visual data. Because printed color relies on reflected light and computer monitors are directly lit, a printed color may not have the same appearance as one on an electronic display.

COLOR IN ELECTRONIC DISPLAYS

A computer-generated image produces color very differently. First, the digital display is illuminated by three colored light cells, called phosphors, which project the primary colors of red, green, and blue

(this color system is referred to as RGB) (**2.7.23**). Then, the electronic monitor turns a combination of phosphors on or off to produce the colors the designer wants. For example, if the red and blue phosphors are on, the color on the display will be magenta. If all three of the primaries are on, the combination will result in white light. Complex combinations of these color lighting cells will result in millions of color possibilities.

The brilliant illuminated color of a video display is a seductive medium for video-game developers. Activision/Blizzard developed the game *Starcraft2* using RGB primaries to create a dazzling illuminated array of colors reminiscent of a modern-day stained-glass window. *Starcraft 2*'s rich colors are displayed for a large audience each year at the annual Dreamhack (**2.7.24**) computer gaming conference in Bucharest, Romania. Teams of professional game players generate vivid animated scenes for audiences that fuse the experience of an animated movie with that of a sporting event. Digital works have a glow and rich color that bring new sensations to art and design, and they attract a growing number of artists and game developers.

RGB Light Overlays

R + G + B = White

Red + Green = Yellow   Green + Blue = Cyan   Red + Blue = Magenta

2.7.23 Combinations of Red, Green, and Blue (RGB) light, overlaid to reveal mixtures

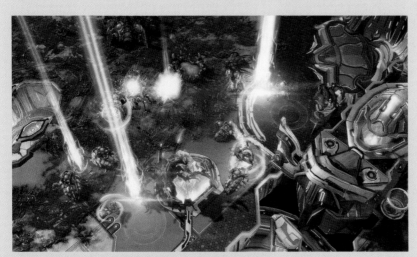

2.7.24 Blizzard, *Starcraft 2* video game screenshot, 2019

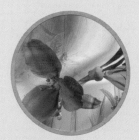

An example of a work that was produced on a computer monitor is Charles Csuri's *Wondrous Spring*: → **see 1.4.3**, p.85

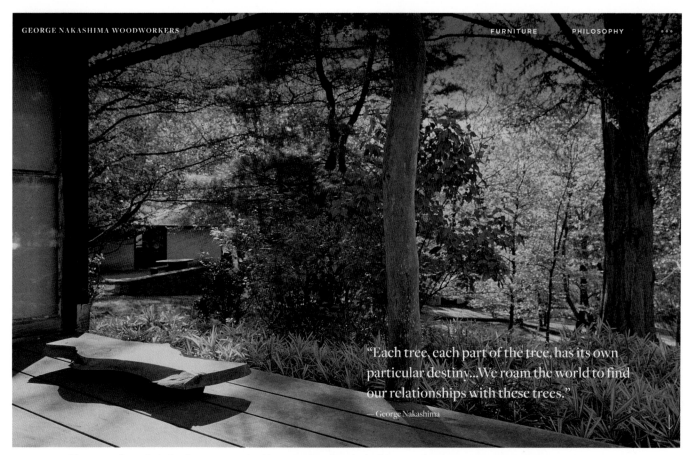

"Each tree, each part of the tree, has its own particular destiny...We roam the world to find our relationships with these trees."
— George Nakashima

2.7.25 For Office Use Only, web design for George Nakashima Woodworkers (nakashimawoodworkers.com), 2016. Screenshot of opening page

exemplified by Webby Award-winning website of furniture makers George Nakashima Woodworkers (**2.7.25**). In this website design, the emphasis is on simplicity and ease of use. George Nakashima (1905–1990) was an architect who believed that the natural material of wood should be celebrated in a work of architecture or furniture. Although Nakashima died in 1990, his studio continues to produce pieces based on his philosophy. The emphasis on elegance and natural forms is reflected in the studio's website design.

Contemporary website designers try to connect the subject to the design by incorporating interesting features. The digital design group Hello Monday did just that when it created a website for the music of the composer Alan Menken's (b. 1949) work (**2.7.26**). In this work, the designers have programmed the interactivity so that sounds, movement, and other features are revealed as the viewer enters the site and is invited to discover new aspects of it while being introduced to the artist's work. Menken's music, which has been featured in many of the animated films by the Walt Disney Company, is accompanied by clips from the animated features, backstory, and many interactive devices that hold a user's interest as he or she surveys the highlights of his music career.

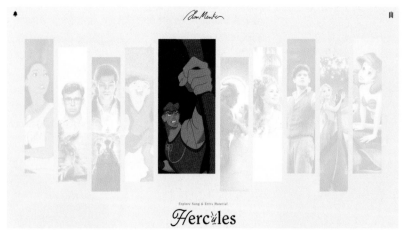

2.7.26 Hello Monday, web design for composer Alan Menken's website (alanmenken.com), 2020. Screenshot of projects page

Explore Further Visual Communication Design

Writing as Art

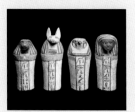

3.1.14 Hieroglyphs on canopic jars, Egypt, 700 BCE → p. 356

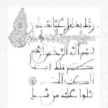

3.2.10 Page from the Koran, probably late 13th century → p. 379

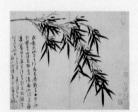

2.1.19 Wu Zhen, leaf from an album of bamboo drawings, 1350 → p. 189

Pictographs and Logos

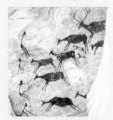

1.5.16 Cave paintings, Valltorta Gorge, Spain, c. 20,000 BCE → p. 113

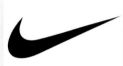

1.1.11 Carolyn Davidson, Nike Company logo, 1971 → p. 40

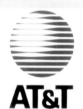

1.1.23 Saul Bass, Bass & Yager, AT&T logo, 1984 → p. 45

Illustration

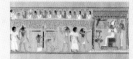

4.2.10 Book of the Dead of Hunefer, Egypt, c. 1275 BCE → p. 560

3.2.11a Cross-and-carpet page, Lindisfarne Gospels, 710–721 CE → p. 380

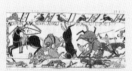

4.6.6 Detail of the Battle of Hastings, *Bayeux Tapestry*, c. 1066–82 → p. 608

Communication

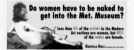

4.9.8 Guerrilla Girls, *Do Women Have to be Naked…*, 1989 → p. 654

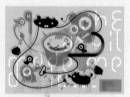

1.1.7 Sauerkids, *The Devil Made Me Do It*, 2006 → p. 38

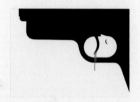

1.1.26 Noma Bar, *Gun Crime*, 2009 → p. 47

Your turn:

How do communication and design function in these works?

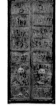

4.2.3a Doors, Church of St Michael's, Hildesheim, Germany, 1015 → p. 556

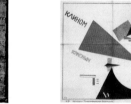

1.1.24 El Lissitzky, *Beat the Whites with the Red Wedge*, 1919 → p. 46

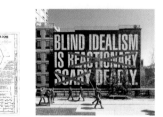

0.0.19 Keith Haring, *Ignorance = Fear*, 1989 → p. 28

0.0.7 FedEx logo, 1994 → p. 20

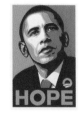

4.5.2 Shepard Fairey, Obama Hope Poster, 2008 → p. 593

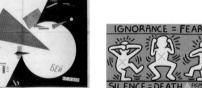

1.1.2a Plan drawing of Buckminster Fuller Dome Home, 2011 → p. 35

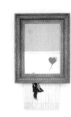

2.10.2 Barbara Kruger, *Untitled (Blind Idealism Is…)*, 2016–17 → p. 336

0.0.17 Banksy, *Love Is in the Bin*, 2018 → p. 27

2.8
Photography

Negative: a reversed image, in which light areas are dark and dark areas are light (opposite of a positive)

Positive: an image in which light areas are light and dark areas are dark (opposite of a negative)

Subject, subject matter: the person, object, or space depicted in a work of art

Recording the Image: Film to Digital

The word photography derives from two Greek words, *phos*, meaning "light," and *graphein*, meaning "to draw": or "writing with light." Traditional photographic processes recorded an image onto a light-sensitive material, which darkened when it was exposed to light. This **negative** image (meaning the lights and darks are the opposite of what we see in life, with the tones reversed) makes the image repeatable. The negative can be reversed again, with chemicals or by re-exposure to light, to make an infinite number of **positive** prints, called photographs, that match the original scene. Most photographs were created in this way until very recently.

With the development of digital cameras in the 1980s, it became possible to record images in the form of pixels, which can then be stored as files on a computer. Today, digital photography is the most common way of creating photographic images. Additional adjustments, often quite complex and involving a lot of skill, can be made afterward to produce the final image on a monitor or in the form of a print.

While a smartphone, a Polaroid, and an antique camera may look very different to one another, the mechanics of all cameras are very similar to those of the human eye. Light enters the eye through the pupil; similarly, light enters the camera through a small opening, the aperture. In both eye and camera, the lens adjusts, or is adjusted, to bring things into focus and give a clear vision of what is being viewed. The image is received by the retina, a piece of film, or an image sensor.

We now encounter photography everywhere. Many of us regularly take photographs and snapshots, and we have also become familiar with photographers producing enduring works of art. But—perhaps surprisingly—when photography was invented in the nineteenth century, its reliance on mechanical and chemical processes led many to refuse to consider it an art form. Because photography has a direct tie to the external world (we take a picture of something), it is easy to believe that photographs simply present facts. It is important to keep in mind that photographers can also make photographs to express ideas and many different messages; for example, by deciding the way the **subject** is photographed, by manipulating the image after it has been captured, or by combining the photograph with other images.

The invention of photography had an enormous impact on the development of modern art. Its ability to replicate the world precisely as we see it meant that an artist's rendering was no longer the only way to record reality. In fact, one of the first books illustrated with photographs was called *The Pencil of Nature* by William Henry Fox Talbot (see **2.8.6a** and **2.8.6b**, p. 303), as if photography meant that nature could draw itself. Photography's ability to record minute visual details opened up additional possibilities for art and allowed artists to experiment with other approaches that would revolutionize art from the late nineteenth century onward.

The Dawn of Photography

The basic principles of photography were known long before modern photographic processes were invented. A simple kind of camera, called the *camera obscura* (Latin for "dark room"), had been used by artists for

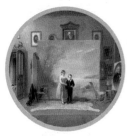

Photographic portraiture was a subject of fascination in the nineteenth century. Painters such as Thomas Le Clear were able to combine elements of the past and present while acknowledging the camera among the artist's important tools:

→ see **3.8.7**, p. 485

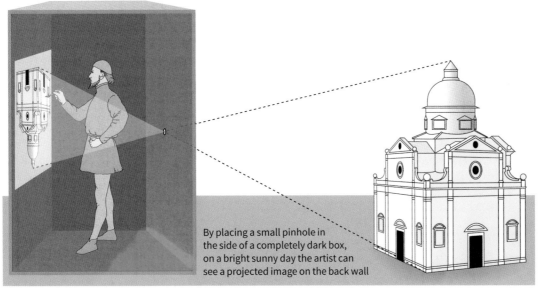

Color: the optical effect caused when reflected white light of the spectrum is divided into separate wavelengths

Fixing: the chemical process used to ensure a photographic image becomes permanent

By placing a small pinhole in the side of a completely dark box, on a bright sunny day the artist can see a projected image on the back wall

2.8.1 Diagram of a camera obscura

several centuries as an aid to drawing. It was not until the nineteenth century, however, that inventors discovered a number of ways to make permanent camera images that could be reproduced: in other words, photography.

The first cameras were actually room-sized, and the projections they created were used as guides for making drawings. An illustration of a camera obscura shows the basic principles of all cameras today (**2.8.1**). When a small hole, or aperture, is placed in an exterior wall of a darkened room, light rays project the outside scene onto the opposite wall inside the room. A person could stand inside a camera obscura and trace over the image projected onto the wall. Inside a camera, the image, no matter what size it was, would appear in **color**, but upside down and backward. Smaller, portable models used as drawing aids throughout Europe in the eighteenth century were adapted to make the first photographic cameras.

The images projected in a camera obscura are not permanent, but looking at the work of contemporary Cuban-American photographer Abelardo Morell (b. 1948) allows us to see what a camera obscura image looks like. Morell records camera obscura images using a second camera. He turned an entire hotel room into a camera obscura to capture a projected upside-down image of the Panthéon building in Paris, France (**2.8.2**). The image projected against the wall of Morell's hotel room was only temporary until he made a picture of it, showing that the principles of the camera obscura are the same as those in a photographic camera.

The earliest images projected in a camera obscura could be recorded only when traced over by hand. Photography did not exist until the image could be **fixed** (as photographers say). In 1819, the English scientist John Herschel (1792–1871) discovered a chemical compound that allowed the final step: fixing, or making permanent, camera obscura images. The first photographic image from nature was made using a camera obscura. The inventor Joseph Nicéphore Niépce (1765–1833) made his famous *View from the Window at Le Gras* (**2.8.3**, p. 302) using a method he kept secret, though he

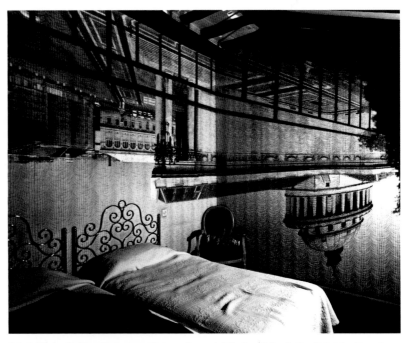

2.8.2 Abelardo Morell, *Camera Obscura Image of the Panthéon in the Hotel des Grands Hommes,* 1999. Gelatin silver print, 20 × 24″

went on to work with fellow Frenchman Louis-Jacques-Mandé Daguerre (1787–1851)—a painter and stage designer—and invent the process known as daguerreotypes (**2.8.4**). The pair worked together during the 1820s and 1830s to develop a method of producing and fixing a camera image. They placed a polished metal plate, made light sensitive by silver iodide, inside the camera. The camera's shutter was opened for twenty to thirty minutes to expose the plate to sunlight and record an image on its surface. Mercury vapor revealed the image before it was chemically fixed with table salt (later, daguerreotypes would be fixed with sodium thiosulfate, commonly known as hypo).

When Daguerre made *Boulevard du Temple* in 1838, exposure times were still too long to photograph people easily. Even when produced in full daylight, the exposure time for this photograph was approximately eight to ten minutes, a great improvement from the eight hours it took to expose Niépce's *View*

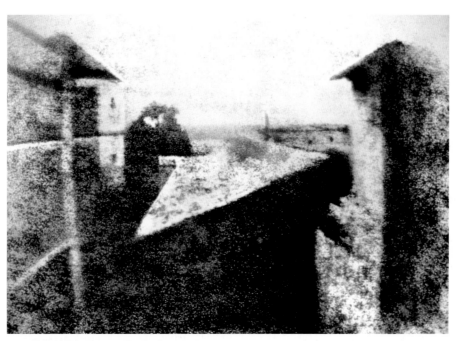

2.8.3 Joseph Nicéphore Niépce, ***View from the Window at Le Gras***, *c.* 1826. Gernsheim Collection, Harry Ransom Humanities Research Center, University of Texas at Austin

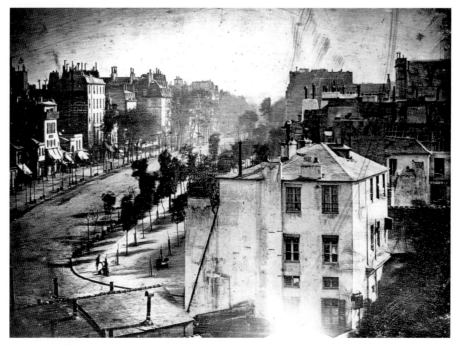

2.8.4 Louis-Jacques-Mandé Daguerre, ***Boulevard du Temple***, *c.* 1838

from the Window. The only person captured on this busy Parisian street was a man who had stopped on the corner to have his shoes shined for the duration of the exposure. After Daguerre publicly presented the process in 1839, advancements were quickly made that reduced exposure time to around one minute in the right lighting conditions. While the daguerreotype process created very detailed images captured through a camera, these single, positive images on metal plates could not be readily reproduced.

Negative/Positive Process

Using a process invented by John Herschel, the English botanist and photographer Anna Atkins (1799–1871) made **cyanotype** images in 1843. She placed pieces of algae directly on paper that had been treated with a special light-sensitive solution and exposed the sensitized paper to direct sunlight (**2.8.5**). The areas of the paper exposed to the light turned dark, but in the places where the plant's leaves and stems created a shadow, the paper remained white. Although Atkins made this image without a camera, the same principles are at work when a film camera is used, and her images look like film negatives.

At about this time, the Englishman William Henry Fox Talbot (1800–1877) captured on light-sensitive paper a negative image of a tree (**2.8.6a**). This image, known as a calotype, resembled Atkins's botanical specimens. Talbot also discovered how to reverse the negative, which enabled him to make numerous positive prints: the places that appeared light in the negative, such as the trunk and branches, would be dark in the print, while the dark areas, such as the sky, would change to light. The resulting print (**2.8.6b**) contained shades of gray that matched the **values** of the original scene. This negative/positive process is the basis of film photography (see: The Black-and-White Darkroom, p. 304).

Cyanotype: a photographic process using light-sensitive iron salts that oxidize and produce a brilliant blue color where light penetrates and remain white where light is blocked; a variant of this process was used historically to copy architectural drawings

Value: the lightness or darkness of a plane or area

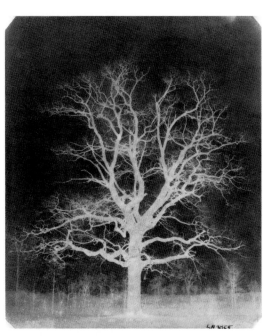

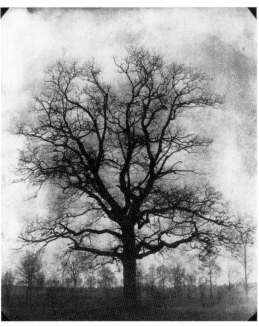

2.8.6a (top) and 2.8.6b William Henry Fox Talbot, *Oak Tree in Winter*. Top: Calotype, *c.* 1842–43; Bottom: salted paper print, *c.* 1892–93. British Library, London, England

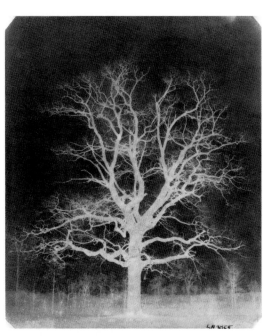

2.8.5 Anna Atkins, *Halydrys siliquosa ß minor*, 1843. Folio 19 from Volume 1 of Photographs of British Algae. Cyanotype, 5 × 4″. British Library, London, England

The Black-and-White Darkroom

Once a photographer captures an image with a camera (step 1 in **2.8.7** below), they must develop the film (2) to produce a negative (3), which can then be used to make photographic prints. Working in a darkroom prevents any further light from reaching the light-sensitive materials and damaging the image. Shining a light from an enlarger through the negative reverses the tones and projects a positive image onto light-sensitive paper (4). The enlarger also allows the photographer to choose the size of the final image. At this point, the image is not yet visible.

The paper then goes through a series of chemical solutions. First, a fluid called the **developer** reveals the image (5). Next, placing the paper in the stop bath halts the development process (6); then fix, or fixer—a compound that also stops and stabilizes the photographic image—makes it permanent (7). Finally, the print is washed and dried.

Artworks in this chapter that were made using black-and-white darkroom processes include:
• **2.8.2** Abelardo Morell, *Camera Obscura Image of the Panthéon in the Hotel des Grands Hommes*
• **2.8.11** Ansel Adams, *Sand Dunes, Sunrise—Death Valley National Monument, California*
• **2.8.12** Henri Cartier-Bresson, *Place de l'Europe. Gare Saint Lazare*
• **2.8.20** Sally Mann, *Jessie #34*
• **2.8.23** Lewis Wickes Hine, *Ten Year Old Spinner, Whitnel Cotton Mill*
• **2.8.26** Garry Winogrand, *Central Park Zoo, New York City*
• **2.8.27** Edward Steichen, *Gloria Swanson*
• **2.8.28** Diane Arbus, *Hermaphrodite and a dog in a carnival trailer, Md. 1970*

The same basic steps (but not the same chemicals, equipment, or processes) were used to make salted paper, albumen silver, gelatin silver, and Caffenol prints.

Developer: after an image has been recorded on light-sensitive film or photographic paper (usually in a camera), immersion in this liquid substance chemically transforms a latent (or invisible) image into a visible one

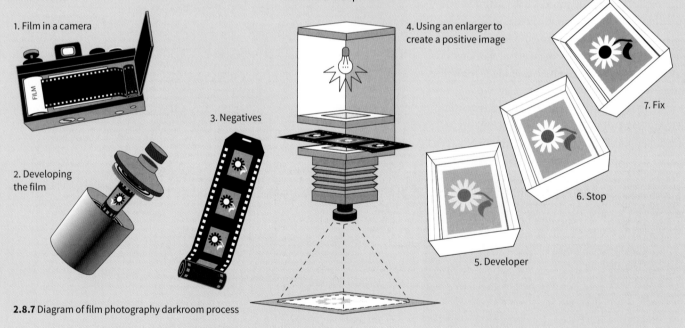

1. Film in a camera

2. Developing the film

3. Negatives

4. Using an enlarger to create a positive image

5. Developer

6. Stop

7. Fix

2.8.7 Diagram of film photography darkroom process

The photographs by British artist Roger Fenton (1819–1869), who photographed the Crimean War, illustrate some of the haunting effects made possible through early nineteenth-century processes. Fenton made his salt prints using paper negatives, which gave them a grainy appearance and allowed the landscape to take on symbolic associations. The title, *Valley of the Shadow of Death*, seems to derive from Psalm 23 in the Bible, referring to the comfort God offers for life's suffering. In fact, Fenton chose it some time after he had taken the photograph, as a result of the popularity of a now-famous poem by Alfred, Lord Tennyson (1809–1892), "The Charge of the Light Brigade". The poem's refrain, "Into the Valley of Death/Rode the six hundred," is echoed in Fenton's title (**2.8.8**). In black and white, the cannonballs littering the battlefield take on an eerie quality, like human skulls. Fenton's process captures the emptiness and desolation of the aftermath of combat in a poetic and thought-provoking scene.

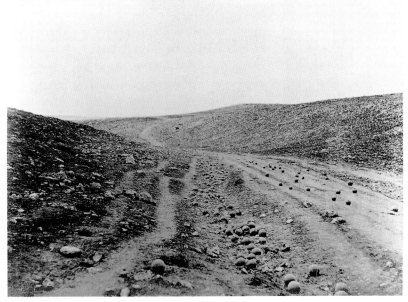

2.8.8 Roger Fenton, *Valley of the Shadow of Death*, 1855. Salted paper print from a paper negative, 10⅞ × 13¾". Gernsheim Collection, Harry Ransom Humanities Research Center, University of Texas at Austin

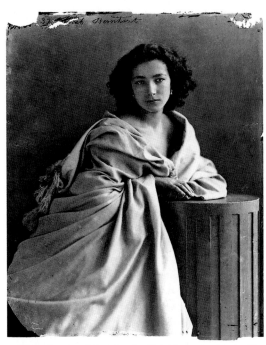

2.8.9 Nadar, *Sarah Bernhardt*, 1865. Albumen print, 4 × 6". Bibliothèque Nationale, Paris, France

Many inventors wanted to combine the detail of the daguerreotype with the reproducibility of the calotype. (Prints made from calotypes lose some sharpness and definition, while the daguerreotype's metal plate retains much more detail.) In 1850–51 Frederick Scott Archer (1813–1857) invented the **collodion** or wet-plate process. Even though it was very cumbersome, requiring a lot of equipment and chemistry that had to be wet to be light sensitive, this process allowed a crisp image to be recorded on glass. The collodion negative could be used in many ways, one of which was to make prints on paper. Photographers used this popular process until around the 1880s.

Before photography was invented, the only way to get a portrait was to have an artist paint one—an expensive and time-consuming process. Photography changed all that. The French photographer Nadar (1820–1910) made collodion negative/albumen print portraits of many well-known artists, writers, and politicians. His photographs of the actress Sarah Bernhardt helped to increase her celebrity (**2.8.9**). Rather than showing the actress posed with elaborate props, which was the norm for portraits at the time, Nadar placed her in the **foreground**, surrounded only by luxurious fabric and leaning on a plain column. Most photographs at this time had to be posed because, while shorter than those for the

daguerreotype, exposure times ranged from a second to a minute.

Also known for her portraits of celebrities, the British photographer Julia Margaret Cameron (1815–1879) intentionally avoided the sharp focus that many photographers sought from the collodion process (**2.8.10**). Cameron

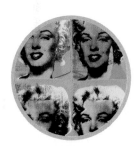

The negative/positive process made it possible to print multiple images of the same picture then to publish and distribute them widely. In *Four Marilyns*, Andy Warhol explored celebrity, one of the consequences of photographic reproduction:
→ see **2.3.16**, p. 222

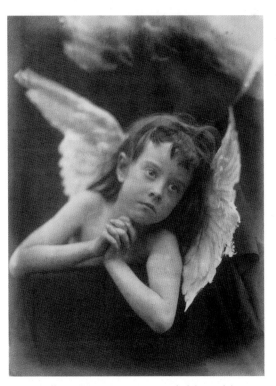

2.8.10 Julia Margaret Cameron, *Angel of the Nativity*, 1872. Albumen print, 12⅞ × 9½". The J. Paul Getty Museum, Los Angeles, California

Collodion (wet-plate) process: a black-and-white darkroom photography process invented by Frederick Scott Archer in 1850–51 and popular until the 1880s

Foreground: the part of a work depicted as nearest to the viewer

believed that photography could show—in addition to what was visible—allegorical, poetic, and intuitive aspects of life that we may not readily see in the course of our daily lives. In order to emphasize spiritual and literary aspects, she used specially designed lenses as well as long exposure times to create a **soft-focus** look. In *Angel of the Nativity* (**2.8.10**, p. 305) her characteristic technique helps transform her niece into a cherub, similar to those commonly featured in Renaissance and **Baroque** paintings.

The film/print process still used in many darkrooms today, **gelatin silver**, was introduced to the public in 1871. Much later, such artists as Ansel Adams (1902–1984) preferred this process because it allowed them to capture the subject the way they wanted to, with everything in the picture clearly in focus and detailed. In *Sand Dunes, Sunrise—Death*

Valley National Monument, California, Adams used a large-format camera to capture a full range of black, white, and gray tones that creates a balanced effect (**2.8.11**). He was also deeply involved with the Sierra Club, which is dedicated to preserving America's wilderness. Such landscape photographs as these can raise awareness of nature's grandeur.

Also using the gelatin silver process, the French photographer Henri Cartier-Bresson (1908–2004) emphasized the lived moment in his photographs using a hand-held 35mm camera. While Cartier-Bresson earned a living publishing his photos in news media, he believed that the most effective photographs captured the narrative effect of the moment, not simply the height of the action. When he photographed dignitaries giving speeches, for example, he turned his lens to the crowd instead of the speaker. His concept of the decisive moment comes through clearly in *Place de l'Europe, Gare Saint Lazare*, named after the location the photo was made (**2.8.12**). Cartier-Bresson waited for just the right moment, with all the visual elements in place, to snap the shutter. Just before or after this moment, the **composition** would have been very different,

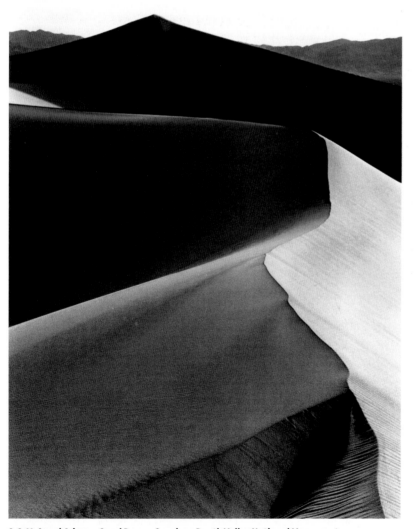

2.8.11 Ansel Adams, *Sand Dunes, Sunrise—Death Valley National Monument, California*, c. 1948. Gelatin silver print, 19½ × 14¾"

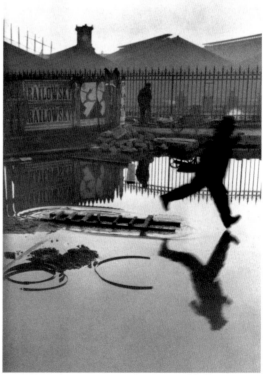

2.8.12 Henri Cartier-Bresson, *Place de l'Europe. Gare Saint Lazare*, 1932. Gelatin silver print, 14¼ × 9⅝".

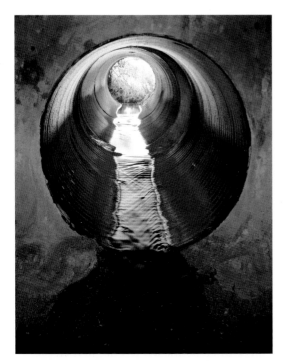

2.8.13 Maia Dery, *Storm Drain–Cape Fear River Basin*, 2013. Caffenol negative/Caffenol silver gelatin print, 9¾ × 7½"

and the man would not appear to be suspended above the water.

While very popular, the gelatin silver process uses toxic chemicals that are harsh on the environment. In 1995, Professor of Chemistry and Material Science Scott A. Williams (b. 1962) and his Technical Photography class at Rochester Institute of Technology, New York, discovered that successful negatives and photographic prints could be made using a coffee-based developer. The ingredients are simple: caffeinated instant coffee, washing soda, and vitamin C. The development time is longer, but no chemical stop bath is required. While no alternatives for chemical fix exist, using the Caffenol process, as it is now called, greatly reduces the environmental toxicity of traditional darkroom photography. In recent years, environmentally conscious photographers, such as the American Maia Dery (b. 1966), have begun to seek alternatives to traditional chemical developer. As seen in Dery's *Storm Drain—Cape Fear River Basin* (**2.8.13**), the use of Caffenol successfully allows the same expansive range of deep rich blacks and luminous lights.

In Living Color

By the early 1900s, shutter speeds allowed virtually instantaneous photographs of **form** frozen in time. Photographers still wanted more. Before color photography was made practicable in the 1880s, people would **hand-tint** photographs to make them look more lifelike. Even once color processes were available, they were hard to market (and it was hard to convince some artists to use them) because they tended to be complicated, and the results were not as chemically stable as black and white.

Autochromes, one of the first commercially viable color processes, are made using an **additive color process**. Potato starch grains colored with **RGB** dyes create a filter and transform an exposed glass plate into a **transparency**. The colors captured on the plate resemble a mosaic or a **pointillist** painting, though optical mixing prevents us from noticing the very tiny dots. Because they can be easily damaged by light, autochromes are best preserved by limiting their exposure to the sun.

The Belgian painter and photographer Alfonse van Besten (1865–1926) enjoyed the painterly potential of the autochrome in his landscapes and romantic views of figures in fancy dress, especially in gardens. Flowers are a common element in his autochromes, maximizing the visual potential of his chosen medium (**2.8.14**). *Fragility* includes the autochrome hallmarks of sharp contrast and dreamy atmosphere in the color-pop of the white, violet, and green cuttings against a dark floral wallpaper. Van Besten's title could be a general reference to the fragility of all living things, like a *memento mori*, or a specific

Form: an object that can be defined in three dimensions (height, width, and depth)

Hand-tint: an early process for adding color to monochrome photographic products by adding pigment in a manner very much like painting

Autochrome: an early additive color photography process patented by the Lumière brothers in 1904 and primarily used from 1907 to the 1930s

Additive color process: creates colors by mixing RGB colors on a screen to create a direct positive print; same principle used in LED, LCD, plasma, and CRT video screens

RGB: an additive system that mixes color based on the primary colors of light: red, green, and blue

Transparency: in film and photography, a positive image on film that visible when light is shone through it

Pointillism: a late nineteenth-century painting style using short strokes or points of differing colors that optically combine to form new perceived colors

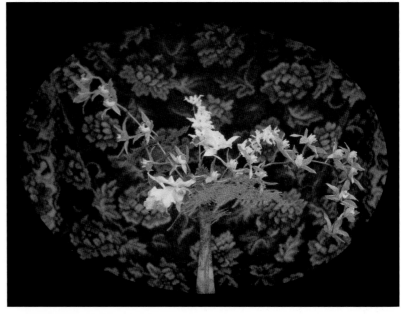

2.8.14 Alfonse van Besten, *Fragility*, c. 1912, autochrome

invocation of the symbolic language long associated with flowers.

Unlike the autochrome, the process used to make most color photographs in the twentieth century was a **subtractive process** known as **chromogenic** or **c-prints**. Such products as **Kodachrome** slide film and some photo papers create light-sensitive material by replacing silver with a color emulsion. The emulsion reacts chemically and forms color dyes that absorb the opposite colors in a negative (or reverse them to make a positive print). American photographer William Eggleston (b. 1939) is credited with bringing color photography into the realm of respected fine art. He used the dye transfer process because of the amount of control it gave him and because the prints would last longer than other color processes. The cyan, magenta, and yellow filters for each color record corresponding levels onto separate gelatin negatives. To make the image, they have to be aligned exactly, a technique known as registration. His photographs of everyday life in the US south, such as *Untitled:*

Devoe Money in Jackson, Mississippi (**2.8.15**), show the distinctive (and dated) color quality characteristic of dye transfer.

A more recent (though now virtually obsolete) process for color prints, is **Cibachrome** (also known as Ilfochrome). This additive method uses layers of **CMY** dyes that are bleached away based on the exposure in order to form a transparent, direct positive image. The Cibachrome photograph *Radioactive Cats* by the American artist Sandy Skoglund (b. 1946) displays the **tableau**'s vibrant, crisp color profile on a super high-gloss base (**2.8.16**). In *Radioactive Cats*, the outlandish color contributes to a **surreal** combination of factual and fictional elements that make us question whether seeing really should be believing.

In the later part of the twentieth century, most color film photography used by the general public was commercially processed. Black-and-white darkroom processes continued to be used by serious amateurs and professional photographers (though black-and-white film could also be processed commercially). Even

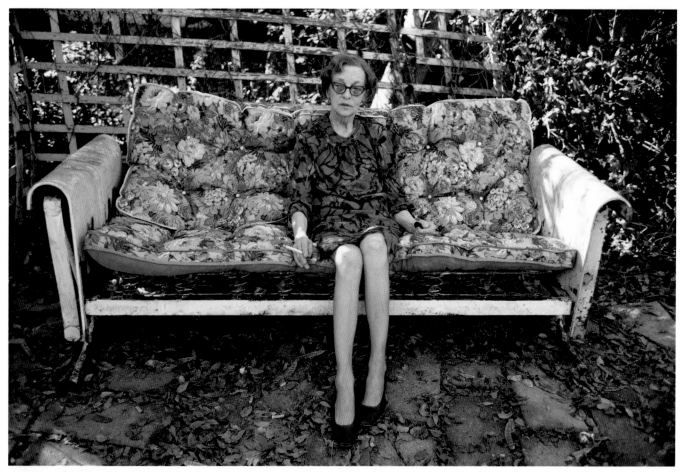

2.8.15 William Eggleston, *Untitled, Devoe Money in Jackson, Mississippi,* c. 1970

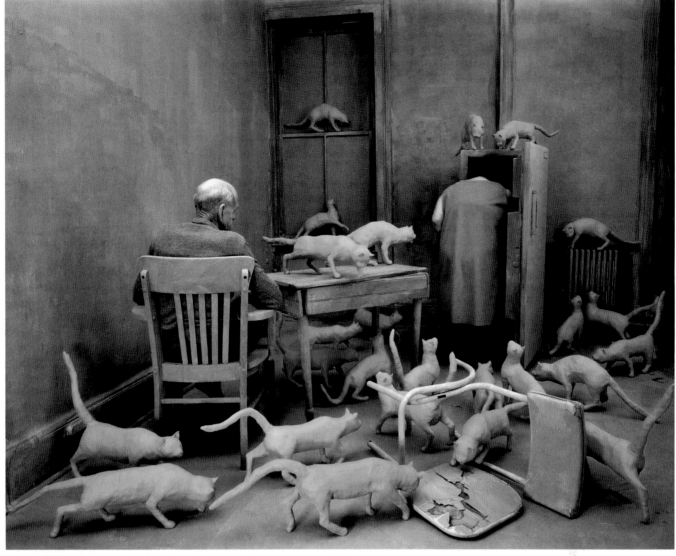

2.8.16 Sandy Skoglund, *Radioactive Cats* © 1980. Cibachrome or pigmented inkjet color photograph, 25⅝ × 35″

after color film became commercially viable in the 1930s, some people preferred to use black and white because it makes elements of the composition clearer: specifically the lines, contrast, and overall design. Today, the majority of images we see are in color. As a result, black-and-white photographs can sometimes give the impression of being old-fashioned. But, whether the image is captured in black and white or in color, digital technology now makes it easy to alter the tonality of photographs. Tonal manipulation can be achieved using a number of digital effects that replicate the results of early photographic processes, including black-and-white and sepia tones.

When digital cameras became available around 1985, they marked a huge shift in the medium of photography. By around 2000, when such cameras started being integrated in cell phones, people could have one at their fingertips. Digital photography records images not on film but in the form of pixels (tiny square dots arranged in a grid). Images recorded as pixels can be stored as digital files and printed on paper or projected on a screen or computer monitor. Some photographers present these images as they were originally taken, but others make alterations to them on a computer. When printing such images on paper, photographers often use archival inks to improve the longevity of the prints.

The Canadian photographer Edward Burtynsky (b. 1955) prints his powerful digital photographs about 4 × 6 ft. using high-quality Fujicolor archival paper. At this enormous scale, each minute detail contributes to the vast expanse of urban landscapes and the relative smallness of humankind. His series

Cibachrome: a dye-destruction process for making direct positive photographic images available in the 1960s

CMY: the primary colors used in inkjet printing: cyan, magenta, and blue

Tableau: a stationary scene arranged for artistic impact

Surreal: reminiscent of the Surrealist movement in the 1920s and later, whose art was inspired by dreams and the subconscious

Series: a group of related artworks that are created as a set

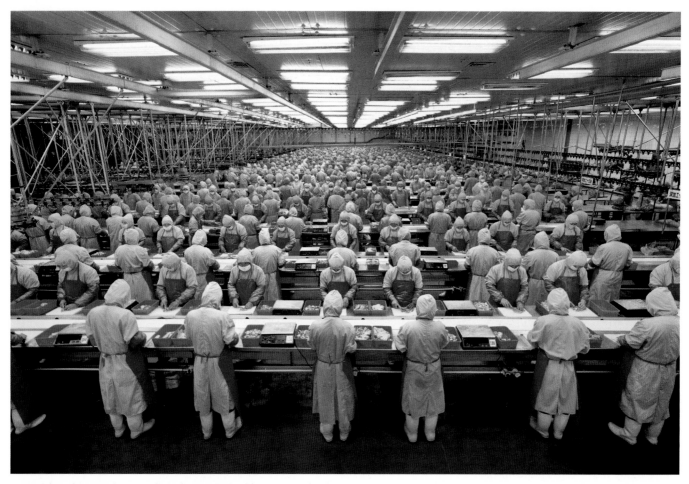

2.8.17 Edward Burtynsky, *Manufacturing #17: Deda Chicken Processing Plant, Dehui City, Jilin Province, China*, 2005

called *China* focuses on factories driven by mass consumerism, where raw and recycled materials are brought to be turned into commercial products and shipped all over the world. *Manufacturing #17: Deda Chicken Processing Plant* shows a vista of workers in the industrial grimness of a chicken-processing plant (**2.8.17**), evidence of the fact that chicken bones are expected to be a defining marker in the geologic profile of our present era, known as the Anthropocene. This prediction is due to the vast human consumption of chicken, the most common bird in the world.

The vivid pinks, bright-blue aprons, white boots, and the rows upon rows of hooded figures create a surreal effect, as if this were a scene from an alien world. Without passing judgment, Burtynsky's arresting images call our attention to things not usually in our consciousness. Burtynsky has said he wants viewers to come to their own conclusions about civilization's impact on the planet because "it's not a simple right or wrong. It needs a whole new way of thinking."

Postmodern Return to Historic Processes

A prominent characteristic of **Postmodernism** is its focus on historical references, including past artworks. In the 1960s, photography began to be taught in college art programs and many artists became interested in critically considering the medium, what it could do, and what could be done with it. A large number of photographers looked to alternative and vintage processes to reflect their artistic focus or to create a particular look.

In her series *From Here I Saw What Happened and I Cried*, American artist Carrie Mae Weems (b. 1953) investigates the collective African American experience through photographs (**2.8.18**). In this case, the historical stories are rooted in enslavement: Weems reinterprets a series of nineteenth-century daguerreotypes of enslaved African people in America (**2.8.19**). In the original photographs by J. T. Zealy (American, 1812–1893), the **sitters** were stripped and exposed to the scrutiny of racist theorists who sought to examine and investigate them

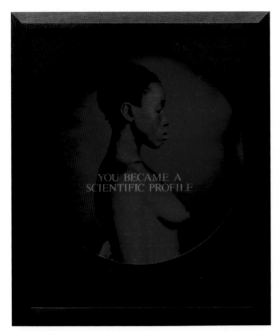

2.8.18 Carrie Mae Weems, "You Became a Scientific Profile," from the series *From Here I Saw What Happened and I Cried*, 1995. Chromogenic color prints with sand-blasted text on glass, 25⅝ × 22¾". MoMA, New York

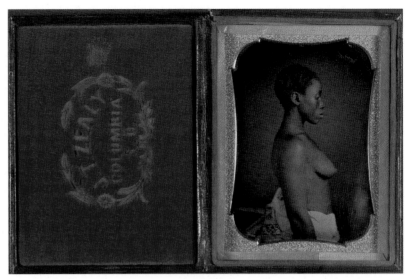

2.8.19 J. T. Zealy, *Delia, country born of African parents, daughter of Renty, Congo*, 1850. Daguerreotype in leatherette case, 4¾ × 3⅜ × ⅜". Peabody Museum of Archaeology and Ethnology at Harvard University, Cambridge, Massachusetts.

in a coldly analytical, supposedly scientific way. The original daguerreotypes were presented in leather cases to protect them. Weems rephotographed the images, colored them red, and framed them with circular mats to highlight the fact that they were being seen through the camera lens. The text she inscribes on the glass challenges ideas of race, gender, and class that were once taken for granted. Weems points out that these individuals had become "scientific profiles" used as evidence to support anthropological theories; her retelling of these images aims to restore some of the dignity that had been denied to the sitters and motivate viewers to understand and respect their humanity.

In the series *Faces*, the American photographer Sally Mann (b. 1951) made portraits of her children using a vintage process. As in other series, she uses black and white to transform ordinary moments into nostalgic and provocative statements. In *Jessie #34* (**2.8.20**) Mann adopted the collodion (wet plate) process used during the Civil War to make the negative and the silver gelatin method to create the print. Imperfections, caused by the chemicals on the glass during image capture, create what appear to be gashes on Jessie's face and make the photographic process itself visible. In an interview for the PBS series ART21 in 2000, Mann explained that she was "so

immersed in that whole glass-plate, nineteenth-century aesthetic, it was natural to want to learn how to do this....I'm surprised it took me this long to get to this process, because I've always admired that aesthetic and find it redolent with [the] past. I just need to inject a little of the present in it."

Today the processes of **photomontage** and **photocollage** can be made relatively easily by cutting, pasting, and merging image files on a computer, but it was not always so easy. Although it may not look like it, *Two Ways of Life*

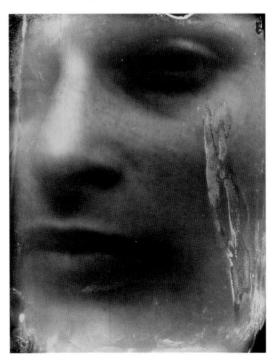

2.8.20 Sally Mann, *Jessie #34*, 2004. Gelatin silver print with soluvar matte varnish and diatomaceous earth, (edition of 5), 48⅝ × 38½"

Photomontage: a single photographic image that combines (digitally or using multiple film exposures) several separate images

Photocollage: an artwork made by assembling separate photographs or photographic images, often by gluing them onto a surface

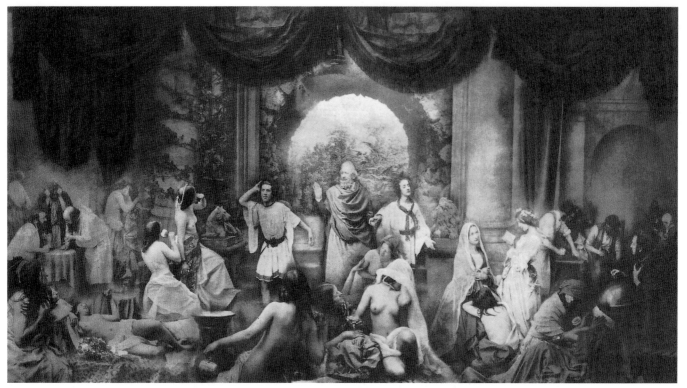

2.8.21 Oscar Gustav Rejlander, *The Two Ways of Life*, 1857. Albumen silver print, 16 × 31″. Royal Photographic Society, Bath, England

was made with thirty separate negatives, which were cut out like puzzle pieces (**2.8.21**). The Swedish photographer Oscar Gustav Rejlander (1813–1875) worked in a labor-intensive, time-consuming way, just as traditional artists do. By emulating the appearance and process of painting, Rejlander hoped his photographs would earn the respect that at that time was reserved for painting. He exposed the negatives one at a time, covering the rest of the print every time he exposed another negative. The resulting image, which took him six weeks to make, looks like one seamless scene.

While Rejlander used manual methods to create his images, the German photographer Loretta Lux (b. 1969) uses digital technology to assemble the elements in her compositions in a very similar way. She takes pictures of her friends' children and then subtly manipulates the colors and **proportions**, making the subjects look as if they just stepped out of a fairy tale. Sometimes she also paints **backgrounds**, which she then photographs and retouches digitally to contribute to the otherworldly effect. She works on each photograph for anywhere from several months to a year. *The Waiting Girl* shows a little girl and a cat on a vintage sofa (**2.8.22**). The girl's severely knotted hair, her uniform-like dress with its prim collar, and the emptiness of the background give the impression she spends her time in a confined environment, probably with people much older than herself. This picture, like the one Rejlander created, shows a scene that did not exist before the artist made it. Lux's subtle use of digital technology allowed her to alter certain attributes, such as **scale** and proportion, to create the effect she wanted.

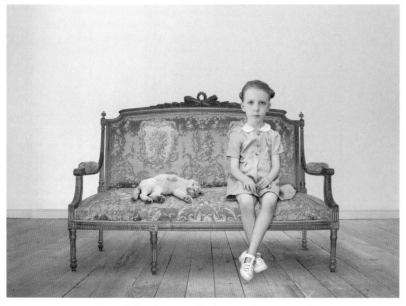

2.8.22 Loretta Lux, *The Waiting Girl*, 2006. Ilfochrome print, 11⅞ × 15⅞″

The Art of Photography

The process used by Rejlander was intended to make fine art products. He believed, like other photographers who used similar approaches, that the only way to make photography artistic was to emulate painting. Over time, photography has become appreciated in its own right. Soon after it was invented, there were heated debates about whether photography worked best for recording reality or as a way to make works of art. Even though photographs have been collected in major fine art museums since the early twentieth century, the immediacy of the medium still causes some people to have trouble considering photography as art. A walk through today's galleries in any major city will show that photography is a favored medium of many contemporary artists. Photographic processes and techniques range from direct capture, promoting immediacy as one of the distinct characteristics of the medium, to full-on construction. Regardless of the approach, reality and artifice exist in varying degrees in most photos.

Photojournalism

Photojournalism is the use of photography to tell a news story. Some of the earliest examples of photojournalism date back to the American Civil War, when collodion photographic equipment was portable enough to be used in the field. Although we now readily accept that photographs can distort, exaggerate, and even lie—because they can be manipulated, altered, cropped in particular ways, and only ever give a partial view—the medium was once believed to be inherently truthful. This credibility, even today, is crucial for news reportage. As a result, the question of what constitutes truth in photography affects its ethical use in photojournalism.

The American photographer Lewis Wickes Hine (1874–1940) used photography to expose the injustice of child labor in the early 1900s (**2.8.23**). He went into factories and mines under the guise of a salesman, repairman, or safety investigator, and then took photographs as well as detailed notes about the ages of the children he found there. When he later published his findings, the public was shocked by his photos of these children and their often grueling and dangerous working conditions. His efforts eventually led to the establishment

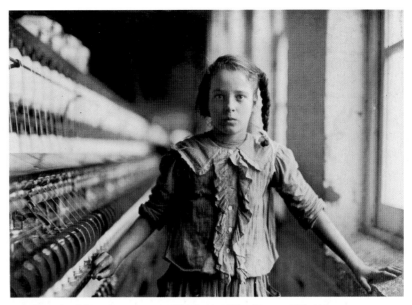

2.8.23 Lewis Wickes Hine, *Ten Year Old Spinner, Whitnel Cotton Mill*, 1908. Photographic print. Library of Congress, Washington, D.C.

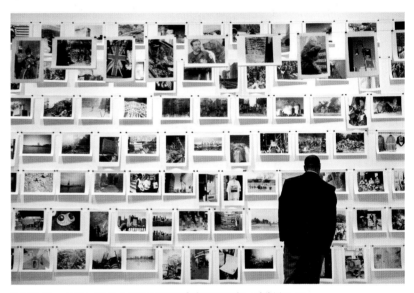

2.8.24 *Here Is New York: A Democracy of Photographs*, exhibition at the New York Historical Society, September 2007

of laws preventing children from working at such young ages.

Contemporary photojournalism communicates events almost immediately on television and the Internet, but those same images can also be used to record events for posterity. Photographs made during the attack on the World Trade Center on September 11, 2001, were published all over the world right after the event. In the days following 9/11, a group of photographers organized an exhibition called *Here Is New York: A Democracy of Photographs on the Streets of SoHo in New York City* (**2.8.24**). The collection of photos gave voice to almost 800 people who had experienced

Proportion: the relationship in size between a work's individual parts and the whole

Background: the part of a work depicted furthest from the viewer's space, often behind the main subject matter

Scale: the size of an object or an artwork relative to another object or artwork, or to a system of measurement

the attack at first hand, whether they were professional photographers or people who just happened to be carrying a camera that day. The exhibition traveled all over the world and was later donated to the New York Historical Society.

Recording Detail and Stopping Time

At a time when other photographers were trying to imitate traditional painting, the American Alfred Stieglitz (1864–1946) was amongst the first to emphasize what he considered to be the particular strengths of the photographic medium: its clarity and realism. In addition to making artistic photographs, Stieglitz actively promoted photography as a fine art medium in the journal *Camera Work* (first published in 1902) and in his New York galleries. *The Steerage* shows the decks of a passenger ship in the cheapest accommodations, separate from the first-class passengers, including Stieglitz himself (**2.8.25**). Stieglitz was struck by the composition of **shapes** and **rhythms** in the photograph, including the straw hat on the upper deck near the center, the crossed suspenders on the man below, the funnel leaning left, the stairway on the right, and the shapes of round machinery, draping chains, and the triangular mast. This composition

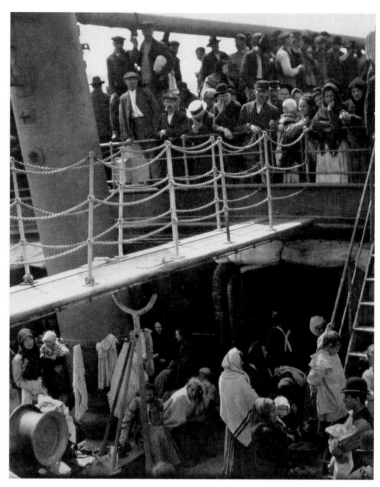

2.8.25 Alfred Stieglitz, ***The Steerage***, 1907. Photogravure, 13¼ × 10⅜″. J. Paul Getty Museum, Los Angeles, California

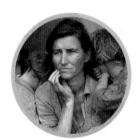

The impact of this famous photograph on its subject, Florence Owens Thompson, has raised issues about ethics in documentary photojournalism:
→ see **4.7.10**, p. 626

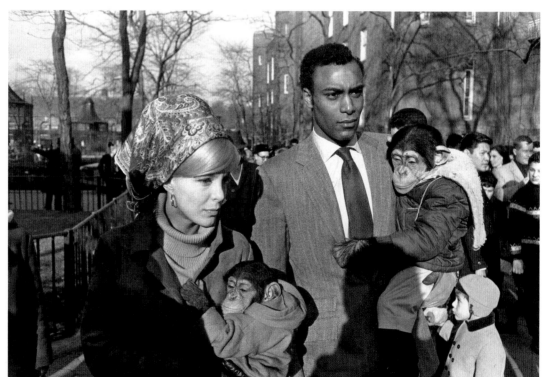

2.8.26 Garry Winogrand, ***Central Park Zoo, New York City***, 1967. Gelatin silver print, 11 × 14″

seemed thoroughly modern and reminiscent of the **abstract** paintings of that era.

In contrast to Stieglitz's concern with sharp focus and formal composition, the American photographer Garry Winogrand (1928–1984) was more interested in photography's ability to directly capture a fleeting moment in time. Winogrand used a small camera he could easily carry around. He generally did not pose his subjects or set up shots beforehand. Many of his photographs seem spontaneous, as in *Central Park Zoo, New York City*: he walked the city's streets and captured what he found there (**2.8.26**). Winogrand's subjective approach, known as the snapshot aesthetic, seems casual, but he intended his photographs to be serious and artistic with some room for interpretation on the viewer's part.

"Ideal-slash-reality:" Intimate Moments and Conversational Portraits

The American photographer Edward Steichen (1879–1973) was among the first to promote photography as a legitimate form of fine art. In addition to early forays into pictorialism and war photography, he began making fashion photographs in 1911. For fourteen years his photographs appeared in *Vanity Fair* and *Vogue* magazines and he served in the prestigious position of chief photographer for Condé Nast. In *Gloria Swanson* (**2.8.27**), the actress's gaze is powerfully focused on the camera, connecting

with the photographer, and transfixing the viewer. This portrait captures the interaction between two accomplished professionals as much as the actress's identity. The lace hung in front of Swanson's face suggests beauty and feminine mystique, enhancing her intrigue. The lace also underscores the camera as a mediating element between the actress and the photographer, emphasizing the way the photographic process veils and thus masks reality.

Also known for intimate portraits, Diane Arbus (American, 1923–71) started her career in magazine work. She photographed a wide variety of people, including eccentrics and marginalized people whose uncommon physical attributes and abilities were showcased in circuses and side shows. Arbus was drawn to the stories of her subjects and built trust in order to photograph people in their own private spaces, such as the carnival trailer in *Hermaphrodite and a dog* (**2.8.28**). This photo reveals the performer's dual nature through the feminine costume, make-up, and clean-shaven right side visibly juxtaposed with the masculine tattoo, wristwatch, and hairy body on the left. Arbus's photographs call attention to anomalies in a way that is objectifying: in person, staring would be impolite. At the same time, her work is celebratory. To her, the hermaphrodite, the giant, the twins, and others were individuals "in a fairy tale that stop you

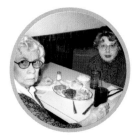

Nikki S. Lee's photographs confront ideas of fact and fiction as the artist takes on different identities:
→ see **4.9.14a and b**, p. 657

Shape: the two-dimensional area the boundaries of which are defined by lines or suggested by changes in color or value

Rhythm: the regular or ordered repetition of elements in the work

Abstract: art imagery that departs from recognizable images of the natural world

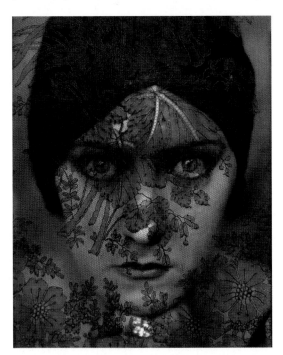

2.8.27 Edward Steichen, *Gloria Swanson*, 1924. Published in *Vanity Fair*, 1928. Gelatin silver print, 9½ × 7½", MoMA, NY

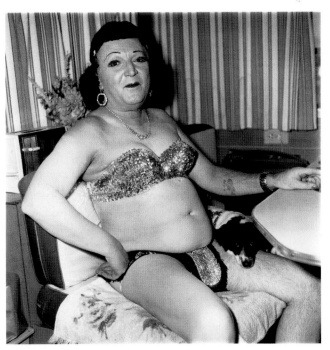

2.8.28 Diane Arbus, *Hermaphrodite and a dog in a carnival trailer, Md. 1970*, 1970, gelatin silver print, 20 × 16".

Nude: an artistic representation of an unclothed human figure, emphasizing the body's form rather than its exposure

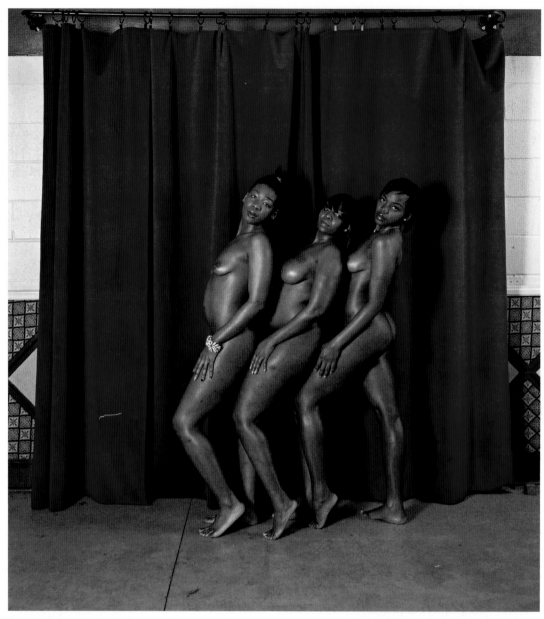

2.8.29 Deana Lawson, *Three Women*, 2013. Pigment print, 39¾ × 36½"

and demands that you answer a riddle...They've already passed their test in life."

In 2020, Deana Lawson (American, b. 1979) became the first photographer to win the Guggenheim Museum's prestigious Hugo Boss Prize, which recognizes artists who are transforming the field. Lawson's examinations of the majesty of people from the African diaspora started in her Brooklyn neighborhood and continued in Louisiana, Haiti, Democratic Republic of Congo, Jamaica, and Ethiopia. Lawson explores themes of intimacy even as she photographs strangers, such as those in *Three Women* (**2.8.29**). This trio, posed as embodiments of the Three Graces from Greek mythology, bring to life the goddesses of charm, beauty, and creativity. The Classical **nude**, a

quintessential art subject, is shown here as both ideal and real. The red drape does not quite extend to the edges of the frame, suggesting that the ideal can mask a more complex reality. Lawson's scenes are constructed, sometimes including props, and often shaped by the way the subjects themselves want to be seen. The mythical views of everyday Black life Lawson creates are populated by people who resemble those the artist grew up with, but was not seeing in popular visual culture.

Steichen, Arbus, and Lawson all feature reality and artifice in their portraits. They deliberately include more specific elements of the story told by the photograph, knowing that this will make the work intriguing, as well as more relatable to more people.

Explore Further Photography

Photographic Documents

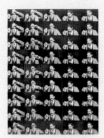

1.5.17 Thomas Edison and W. K. Dickson, *Fred Ott's Sneeze*, 1894 → p. 113

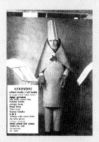

3.9.9 Hugo Ball, Performance of "Karawane" at Cabaret Voltaire, 1916 → p. 506

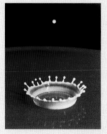

4.4.3 Harold "Doc" Edgerton, *Milk Drop Coronet*, 1957 → p. 581

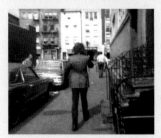

2.10.5 Vito Acconci, *Following Piece*, 1969 → p. 338

Creative Approaches

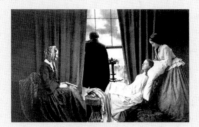

1.7.13a Henry Peach Robinson, *Fading Away*, 1858 → p. 138

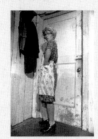

4.9.4 Cindy Sherman, "Untitled Film Still #35," 1979 → p. 650

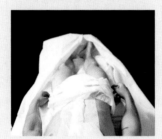

4.3.13 Andres Serrano, *The Morgue (Gun Murder)*, 1992 → p. 576

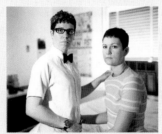

4.9.15 Catherine Opie, "Melissa & Lake, Durham, North Carolina," 1998 → p. 658

Historic Processes

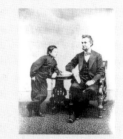

3.8.6 Alexander Gardner, *Abraham Lincoln and His Son Thomas (Tad)*, 1865 → p. 485

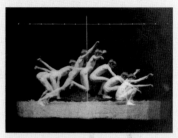

3.8.8 Thomas Eakins, *Motion Study: Male Nude, Standing Jump to Right*, 1884 → p. 486

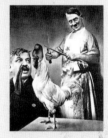

4.5.11 John Heartfield, *Have No Fear, He's a Vegetarian*, 1936 → p. 601

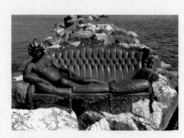

4.8.10 Kiluanji Kia Henda, *Great Italian Nude*, 2010 → p. 636

Your turn

How do these works relate to the ideas discussed in this chapter?

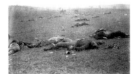

4.6.2 Timothy O'Sullivan, *Harvest of Death, Gettysburg...* → p. 605

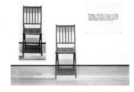

1.9.11 Edward Weston, *Artichoke Halved*, 1930 → p. 154

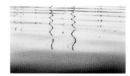

3.10.3 Joseph Kosuth, *One and Three Chairs*, 1965 → p. 524

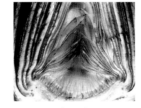

0.0.2 Marcia Smilack, *Cello Music*, 1992 → p. 17

2.9
Film/Video and Digital Art

Medium (plural media): the material on or from which an artist chooses to make a work of art, for example canvas and oil paint, marble, engraving, video, or architecture

Video: a recording of moving images, usually made digitally or on videotape

Motion: the effect of changing placement in time

Celluloid: tough, transparent plastic used to make motion-picture film, photographic film, and X-rays; until relatively recently most movies were filmed on celluloid

Frame: a single image from the sequence that makes up a motion picture; on average, a 90-minute film contains 129,600 separate frames

SLR (single-lens reflex) camera: hand-held digital or film camera that uses a mirror and prism system so the focus screen matches the image captured

Analog: photography or a movie made using a film camera that chemically records images using a continuous gradation of value ranges from light to dark, so that they directly match the actual appearance of the object or scene

The moving image is one of the youngest, most widely used, and most rapidly changing art **media**. The products of film, **video**, and digital art include home movies, artworks, independent films, television shows, video games, and major **motion** pictures. Historically, the dominant process for making movies has been film: flexible, **celluloid**, and light-sensitive. A movie camera captures movement by taking many separate **frames** per second, all exposed in sequence onto the same strip of film. After being developed and edited, the moving film passes in front of a bright light in a projector that shines the image onto a screen.

Because of the high costs of the medium, making a full-length movie requires serious, usually commercial, investment. Digital cameras have become the dominant process used by both individuals and professional production teams. Until around 2013, digital cameras could not match the resolution, or detail, that was possible with film cameras due to the number of megapixels required. Now, technological advancements in digital film have outpaced traditional film.

Digital filmmaking also has considerable advantages: streamlining the workflow for the director and editor; eliminating the costs of film and film processing; giving greater access to footage; and increasing the possibilities for more accessible and affordable manipulation than 35mm film. Nevertheless, even after technological advances made digital the industry standard, a number of talented and high-profile directors have continued to use film both for the way it looks and because they prefer the film process.

While cinematic films are made using a movie camera and viewed with a projector, most movies are now primarily made with digital video cameras (which have been commercially available since 1986), and videos are generally made with small, hand-held cameras. For various reasons (including the look and the process), sometimes moving images are recorded on film and transferred to a digital format for the purposes of editing and presentation, requiring the skills of many different people.

More common today, digital **single-lens reflex (SLR) cameras** record images in the form of pixels as files on a DVD, Blu-ray, or computer hard drive. Digital film editing can be done by single individuals, whereas the traditional film-editing process requires a production team. Video—initially an **analog** technology, like film—has the advantages of being less expensive and highly portable, yet its quality is still generally lower than film and digital SLRs.

Technological developments in both film- and video-making processes mean that today, viewing motion-picture productions no longer requires a dedicated room, projector, and screen. Over time, such shows transitioned to broadcasts and recordings seen on televisions and computer monitors in businesses and people's homes. Public viewing on a screen is still common, now with digital rather than film projectors, or via wireless technology. Accessing movies remotely, viewing videos on the Internet, and streaming from the **Cloud** have made viewing increasingly portable. Today, everything from full-length productions to clips can be watched on a variety of devices and screen sizes, almost anywhere and at any time: so much so that it is hard to imagine a time when they did not exist.

Moving Images before Film

How is the illusion of movement created? The principle was understood long before the invention of still or moving film images. Representations of movement adorn ancient examples of pottery from Asia and South America. By the nineteenth century, a child's toy developed in Europe, known as the **zoetrope**, was able to produce a convincing effect of a sequence of movement. The zoetrope contains a rotating cylinder with a series of images on the inside (**2.9.1**). By spinning the zoetrope and looking through the outer ring of the cylinder, which has slots cut into it, the viewer gets the impression of a single image in continuous motion.

A similar principle is at work in the sequential images on Laboratorio Paravicini's "Play Plates" (**2.9.2**), which create the impression of a single moving image when they are spun in rapid succession. The decorations on these contemporary plates utilize the same concept of implied motion, and consist of still images from stages of an action using animals, acrobats, children, dancers, hunters, and demons in a vintage style. The illusion of movement created in this way, known as **stroboscopic motion**, is the basis of modern film and video technique.

A theory known as persistence of vision explains that this illusion results from presenting the eye with separate images at regular intervals so that they appear to be a continuous sequence. Because visual

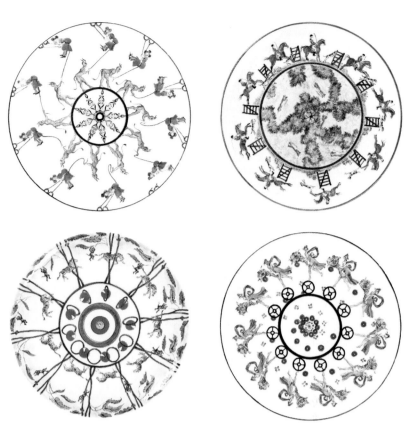

2.9.2 Costanza Paravicini/Laboratorio Paravicini, "Play Plates," 2016. Ceramic, diameter 9¾"

impressions persist even after the seen object is no longer there, the mind connects them together. This concept is illustrated in a rudimentary way by a flip book with separate still images in a sequence that, when flipped, become visually connected and appear to move. Images captured in the camera use the same concept: the faster the succession of images, the smoother the impression of movement. The earliest film projectors had a visible "blink" between frames. While higher resolutions are available even for personal use, a standard movie will show images at twenty-four frames per second; **IMAX** and other high-definition films can show forty-eight, to provide a heightened sense of reality.

As strange as it may seem, in order to make moving pictures it was first necessary to freeze movement in the form of still images. After many failed attempts, the English photographer Eadweard Muybridge (1830–1904) arranged a line of twelve cameras to take a sequence of twelve pictures of a running horse (**2.9.3**, p. 320). The cameras, connected to cables stretched across the racetrack, were tripped as the horse passed.

Muybridge's experiments cost about $42,000 and resolved a wager that a galloping horse has

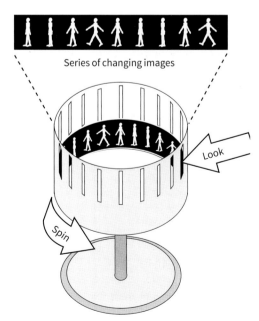

Series of changing images

Look

Spin

2.9.1 Diagram of a zoetrope

Cloud (the Cloud): can refer to any electronic network; generally refers to shared resources on the Internet rather than local servers or devices for storage and computer applications

Zoetrope: an antique, European toy; contains a rotating cylinder with a sequence of images on the inside that creates the impression of a single action in continuous motion when spun

Stroboscopic motion: the effect created when we see two or more repeated images in quick succession in such a way that they visually fuse together

IMAX: "Image Maximum," a format for film presentation that allows presentation of films at ten times larger sizes than the conventional one

Film: a thin, flexible material with light-sensitive emulsion exposed in a camera to produce photographs or motion pictures; when used to describe a movie, the word often has artistic or professional connotations

Moving picture(s): another term for movie or movies; used frequently in the early period of the medium

Motion picture(s): another term for a movie or movies

Movie: a recording of moving images presented to create the illusion of natural movement; can be watched on a theater screen, television, or other device

Science-fiction (Sci-fi): a genre of film in which fictional stories include advanced science and technology, often in futuristic settings

Fantasy: a fiction genre set in an imaginary universe; often uses magical or supernatural elements in the plots, themes, or settings

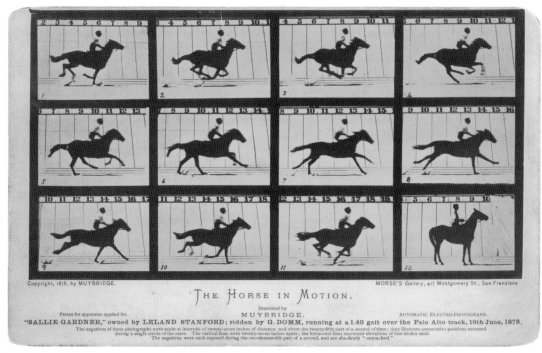

2.9.3 Eadweard Muybridge, *The Horse in Motion*, June 18, 1878. Albumen print, 8¾ × 5½". Library of Congress, Washington, D.C.

all four legs off the ground at once. The camera proved what the naked eye could not see: the horse does lift all of its hooves simultaneously (**2.9.3**, third frame). Before then, people thought the legs of a horse were extended, like those of a rocking horse, when off the ground. When prints of Muybridge's photographs were published in *Scientific American* magazine, they were accompanied by instructions to cut them out and place them in a zoetrope.

Silent and Black-and-White Film

The very earliest **films** were short clips usually documenting single instances of everyday occurrences—feeding a baby, doing a dance, leaving the factory gate at closing time. The earliest **moving pictures** were black and white and silent: they had no soundtrack. They were shown in nickelodeons, small storefront movie theaters popular in the early years of the twentieth century. Nickelodeons provided

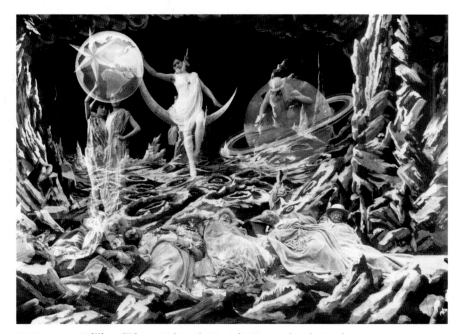

2.9.4 Georges Méliès, still from *A Trip to the Moon (Le Voyage dans la Lune)*, 1902, 14 minutes, Star Film

musical accompaniments with live piano and drums, and some provided lecturers to explain the action as the **motion pictures**, or **movies**, played. As movies grew into a business, they were shown in huge, ornate movie palaces that might also feature a pipe organ.

By 1896, movies were being shown all over Europe and the United States. Georges Méliès (1861–1938), a French magician and filmmaker, began showing films as part of his theatrical magic show. His silent **science-fiction** and **fantasy** films featured special effects and humor. In *A Trip to the Moon* (1902), Méliès's most famous film, a group of astronomers flies to the moon in a spaceship launched from a cannon (**2.9.4**). Their vessel crashes into the man-in-the-moon's right eye, and then the astronomers encounter wondrous sights and moon inhabitants called Selenites. Méliès was one of the first to use multiple settings, repeated scenes, and cuts to establish a sense of time moving forward.

The American filmmaker D. W. Griffith's (1875–1948) fictional silent film *Birth of a Nation* (1915) was Hollywood's first blockbuster (**2.9.5**). The film is now seen as extremely offensive for its reinforcement of racist views and stereotypes of the Old South; in fact, the Ku Klux Klan used it for recruitment. The

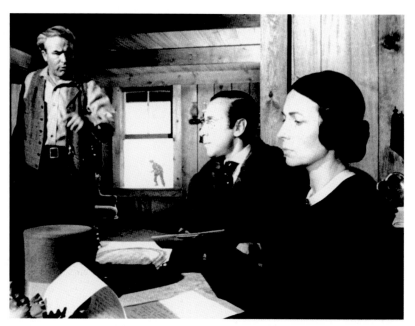

2.9.6 **Orson Welles**, **still from** *Citizen Kane*, 1941, 112 minutes, RKO Pictures

film introduced a number of new techniques, including original editing styles to transition between scenes, to tell an **epic** story of the Civil War. *Birth of a Nation* uses **symbolism**, gesture, and intertitles (onscreen text), rather than spoken dialogue, to move the story along. Alongside this troubling history, *Birth of a Nation* is important to the history of film for the epic scale of its production, its stylistic and technical innovations, and its use of the medium as a **propaganda** tool.

Another American filmmaker, Orson Welles (1915–1985), wrote, directed, and starred in *Citizen Kane* (1941), a box-office failure but hailed by critics as brilliant (**2.9.6**). It is now considered one of the most important films of all time. To tell the story of Charles Foster Kane (a character modeled on the real-life newspaper tycoon William Randolph Hearst), Welles used what were then highly innovative techniques. Fabricated newspaper headlines and newsreels give the impression of following a factual story. Parts of the plot are told using **flashbacks**, which was then a new mode of storytelling; these are now commonplace. Additional techniques that were revolutionary for the time include dramatic lighting, innovative editing, natural sound, elaborate sets, moving camera shots, deep focus, and low camera angles. The movie contrasts the simplicity of home and family with wealth and power, questions the values of the American Dream, and (controversially) criticizes Hearst, who was a powerful public figure.

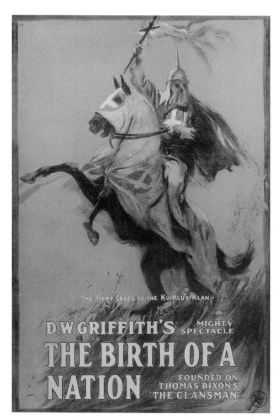

2.9.5 **D. W. Griffith**, *Birth of a Nation*, 1915, publicity poster

Epic: a style or genre in film/television that focuses on grand-scale storytelling with dramatic music, elaborate costumes, and high production values; may use historical events or people but does not focus on historical accuracy

Symbolism: using images or symbols in an artwork to convey meaning; often obvious when the work was made but requiring research for modern viewers to understand

Propaganda: art that promotes an ideology or a cause

Flashback: a transition to an earlier time in a story that disrupts the chronological order of events

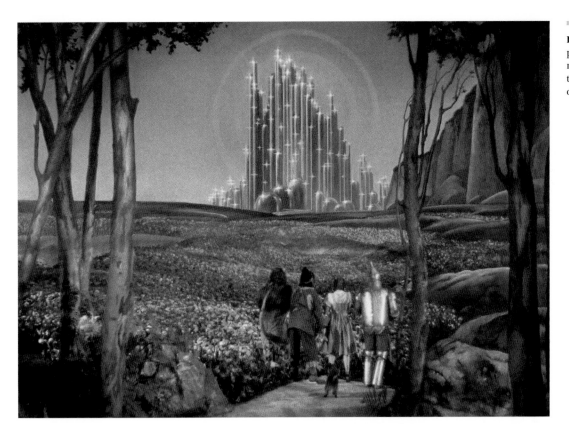

2.9.7 **Victor Fleming**, still from *The Wizard of Oz*, 1939, 101 minutes, Metro-Goldwyn-Mayer (MGM)

Dubbing: the post-production addition or mixing of voices (or sounds) that do not belong to the original recording

Sound and Color

From the late 1920s, movie studios promoted color as a novelty to attract audiences. One of the first popular films to make use of color combined both the new and old approaches. In *The Wizard of Oz* (1939), the character Dorothy is transported by a cyclone from Kansas to the Technicolor Land of Oz (**2.9.7**). The story's two separate locales are distinguished by the use or absence of color. The film opens with Dorothy in the black-and-white world of her home on a Kansas farm. Later, the brilliant colors of the Land of Oz transport us into a fantasy world clearly far removed from Kansas. Color features prominently throughout the film: Dorothy wears ruby slippers as she travels with her companions—her dog Toto, the Scarecrow, the Tin Man, and the Lion—along the yellow-brick road to the Emerald City to find the wizard.

Before 1927, any sound in a cinema was performed live by musicians in the theater building. After that, integrated sound made it possible to build dialogue, background noise, and music into the film itself. *Singin' in the Rain*, made in 1952, looked back to the silent era by telling the story of a silent-film company making the difficult transition to sound. Synchronizing sound with the actors' lip movements and **dubbing** was one of the great

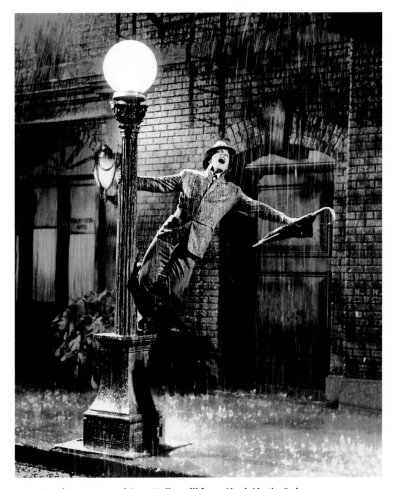

2.9.8 **Stanley Donen and Gene Kelly**, still from *Singin' in the Rain*, 1952, 103 minutes, produced by Loew's Incorporated, distributed by MGM

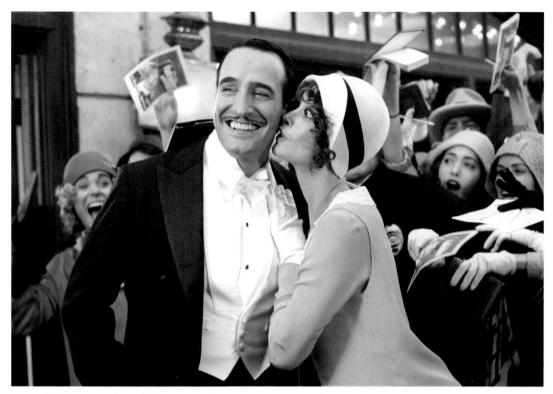

2.9.9 Michel Hazanavicius, still from *The Artist*, 2011, 100 minutes, Studio 37

technical challenges of early sound movies, as songs could not be performed on camera by the actors, but had to be recorded separately. *Singin' in the Rain* finds much humor in this situation. In the movie's most famous scene, actor Gene Kelly jubilantly performs the title song in the rainy streets (**2.9.8**). **Musicals** usually tell their story in a combination of dialogue, songs, and dance, with song being their dominant characteristic. Frequently, as in this scene, dialogue stops completely, and song and dance move the story along.

In 2011, the French film director Michel Hazanavicius (b. 1967) achieved a huge success with his film, *The Artist*, which harks back to the impact of sound on the silent-film industry (**2.9.9**). In the words of one critic, the film "uses old technology to dazzling effect to illustrate the insistent conquest of a new technology." All of the technical details, including lenses, lighting, and camera moves, were calculated to match the look of original silent films of the 1920s and 1930s as closely as possible. *The Artist* won eighteen major awards, including the Academy Award (Oscar) for Best Picture, for its witty, stylish, and ingenious story, told almost entirely in silence and in black and white. It shows how vividly actors can communicate through gesture, expression, and dance, without relying on a soundtrack.

The film's extraordinary success proved that cinema's appeal remains primarily visual, and that, despite all of the technological progress that has been made in the industry in the past century, audiences are still nostalgic for the "good old days" of black-and-white movies.

Animation and Special Effects

Animation creates the illusion of movement in films by taking a sequence of still images, changed slightly in each new frame until the desired sequence is acted out, and then presenting them all together in succession. Individual images can be made using drawings, photographs, objects, or a combination. The many thousands of images in modern animations are generated and manipulated on computers.

In 1981, Disney animators Ollie Johnston and Frank Thomas published twelve rules for animation that have been consistently relevant from the 1930s to today. "Squash and stretch" are among the most important principles of animation design. They serve to give the illusion of weight, mass, flexibility, and gravity. For example, imagine a rubber ball that stretches as it bounces up and squashes as it hits the ground. This rule, and the others, such as following through or easing in and out of an action, help make animations look believable

Musical: a genre of film in which the story is told through song, usually combined with dialogue and dancing

Animation: a genre of film made using stop-motion, hand-drawn, or digitally produced still images set into motion by showing them in sequence

Puppet: a figure in the form of an animal or person used for entertainment purposes that appears to move on its own but is actually controlled by a person's hand(s), strings, or another mechanism

Stop-motion animation: figures, puppets, or dolls are photographed in a pose, moved very slightly, and then photographed again; the process is repeated until the desired sequence of movements has been acted out

Background: the part of a work depicted furthest from the viewer's space, often behind the main subject matter

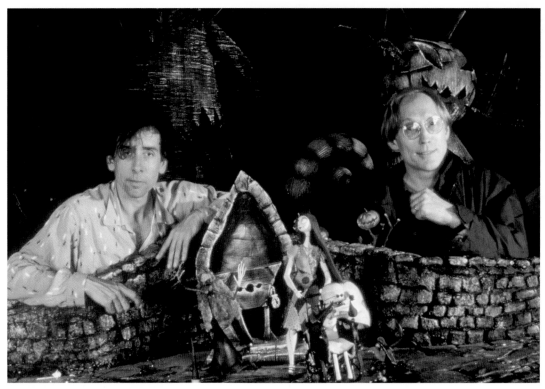

2.9.10 **Tim Burton (left) and director Henry Selick**, set of *The Nightmare Before Christmas*, 1993

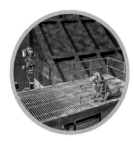

A process shot from the film *Isle of Dogs* shows stop-motion animation in progress:

→ see **1.5.6**, p. 107

and effective, regardless of the technology used to create them.

Special effects can be created by using models, props, or makeup during filming, or by the use of digital technology during or post-production. Some of the earliest film animations were made by laboriously posing **puppets** or dolls to create the individual images. One of the most famous **stop-motion animated** movies, *The Nightmare Before Christmas* (**2.9.10**), was made by the US animator Tim Burton (b. 1958) in 1993. After accidentally entering the portal to Christmastown, the "Pumpkin King" Jack Skellington plots to kidnap "Sandy

Claws," impersonates him, and leads the ghouls and goblins in a series of misadventures that inadvertently almost wreck Christmas. In common with many animated films, the dark nature of *The Nightmare Before Christmas* makes it more appropriate for older kids and adults than for young children. It was also the first stop-motion animated feature to be converted entirely to 3-D, in 2006.

For much of the twentieth century, the most common technique for making animated films was cel animation, in which the sequenced drawings are called cels (originally drawn on celluloid, then later on acetate). **Backgrounds** and stationary sections were overlaid by the moving parts on transparent sheets, greatly reducing the number of images that had to be generated. Digital animation more efficiently generates all the individual frames on a computer, but the original, physical images on which they are based may still be made using stop-motion or hand drawings. Digital processes also enable imagery, sound, and narrative components of the sequence to be imported and then manipulated.

The Oscar-winning film *Spirited Away* (2001), written and directed by Hayao Miyazaki (b. 1941), tells the story of a ten-year-old girl named Chihiro. She is introduced to a world filled with spirits from Japan's mythology,

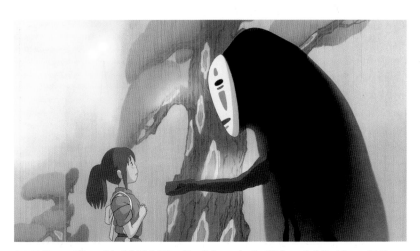

2.9.11 **Hayao Miyazaki with Kirk Wise (English version)**, still from *Spirited Away*, 2001, 125 minutes, Studio Ghibli

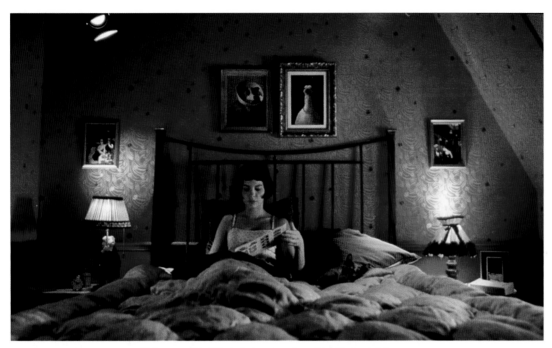

2.9.12 Jean-Pierre Jeunet, still from *Amélie (The Fabulous Destiny of Amélie Poulain)*, 2001, 122 minutes, Claudie Ossard Productions

but discovers that her parents have been transformed into pigs by a witch (**2.9.11**). She must go on a quest to conquer her fears in order to bring her family back together. Miyazaki personally created detailed **storyboards**, or series of drawings, to be used as the basis for the animations, which were then completed by a team of artists, with a separate drawing made for each stage in the movement of any moving object in a scene. At least twelve drawings, and sometimes thirty, were required for every second of *Spirited Away*. Thus, a film of this length (125 minutes) requires a minimum of 90,000 drawings, and perhaps as many as 200,000.

The French director Jean-Pierre Jeunet (b. 1953) adds animation and special effects to live-action film in order to tell the story of *Amélie* (2001), a shy twenty-three-year-old waitress (**2.9.12**). Amélie's heart beats out of her chest at one point; in another scene, when her crush Nino walks away, she melts into a puddle on the floor. Inanimate objects, such as the **Impressionist** artist Pierre-Auguste Renoir's painting *Luncheon of the Boating Party* (1881), take on so much significance that they almost function as additional characters. Jeunet creates an environment in which fantasy, reality, and rich color are mixed together to reveal the magical qualities of ordinary life.

Cutting-edge visual effects in the *Lord of the Rings* film trilogy (2001–3, **2.9.13a** and **b**)

brought to life the fictional world of J. R. R. Tolkien's (1892–1973) novels by combining live action and **CGI**. Directed by Peter Jackson (b. 1961), these adventure/fantasy films won many Oscars, including Best Picture and Best Visual Effects. One of the most remarkable actors from the series was deemed ineligible for the Best Supporting Actor award, though, because his on-screen character, Gollum, was computer-generated. Andy Serkis (b. 1964) acted out all of the scenes twice: once on set, which allowed him to interact directly with the other actors and greatly assisted the animators; and again on the performance-capture stage. Combining traditional acting, **motion capture**

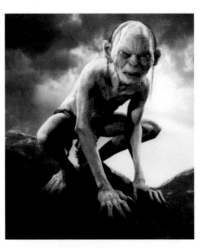

2.9.13a Gollum from Peter Jackson's *The Lord of the Rings: The Return of the King*, 2003. 201 minutes, New Line Cinema

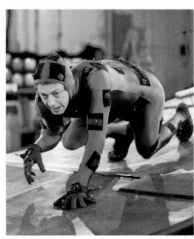

2.9.13b Andy Serkis playing Gollum in *The Lord of the Rings: The Two Towers*, 2002

Key-frame animation:
a technique in which an animator creates important frames in the sequence, and software fills in the gaps

Genre: a category of artistic subject matter, often with a strongly influential history and tradition

Biopic: a movie that tells the story of a person's life, often filling in facts with narration and plotlines

Historical drama: based on real-life events or time periods; can be factual or fictionalized

Documentary: non-fiction films based on actual people, settings, and events

(also known as mo-cap or performance capture), and the skills of animators enabled the transformation of Serkis into a fictional character. The motion-capture process involved putting dots on Serkis's face and body suit to track and record his movements with twenty-five cameras in order to register as much information as possible so the software could replicate the movements digitally. The animators then used **key-frame animation** to edit Gollum into the movie. Because Tolkien named Gollum for the gurgling sound his voice made, Serkis based the voice on the sounds and motions his cat made when coughing up a furball. Serkis's method of intense psychological and emotional character development, and his dedication to realizing the physicality of the character, make Gollum believable and haunting.

Film Genres

Over time, certain **genres**, or categories, of film have developed their own conventions, plotlines, and stock characters. As we have seen, musicals interweave singing and (usually) dancing into the narrative flow; animation and science-fiction films explore fantasy in a context of space and time beyond the everyday. Some genres reflect cross-cultural influence. For example, the narratives of many Indian films influenced the development of the "coming of age" genre in American and European film culture. There is also a great deal of crossover between the Japanese films of the 1950s and the American western. In addition to westerns, the New York Film Academy identified the following film genres: action, animation, crime, fantasy, historical, romance, horror, and science-fiction.

Within the historical genre, **biopics** and **historical dramas** comprise two approaches to films about individuals and time periods, past or present. A biopic focuses on a person's life, often filling in facts with added narration and plotlines to craft an effective story. Historical drama places more emphasis on portraying real-life events in believable ways, though the stories themselves can be fictionalized or based on facts. Both genres differ from **documentary**, which uses photographs, newsreels, home movies, shots on location, and interviews for the imagery instead of actors and stage sets.

The American director Julie Taymor's biopic *Frida* (2002) focuses on the Mexican painter Frida Kahlo (**2.9.14**). Based on the biography by the art historian Hayden Herrera (b. 1940), the movie effectively brings to life Frida's fearless

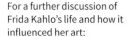

For a further discussion of Frida Kahlo's life and how it influenced her art:

→ see **4.8.19**, p. 643

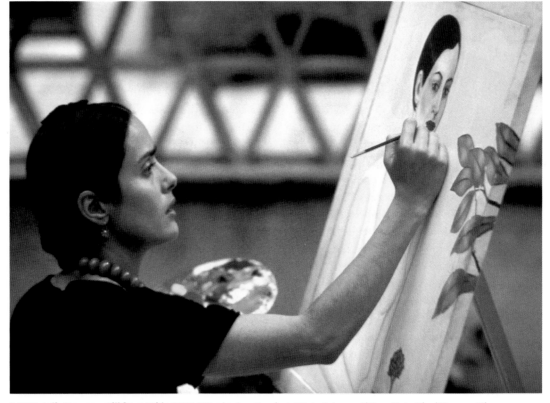

2.9.14 Julie Taymor, still from *Frida*, 2002. 123 minutes, Handprint Entertainment/Lions Gate Film/Miramax Films

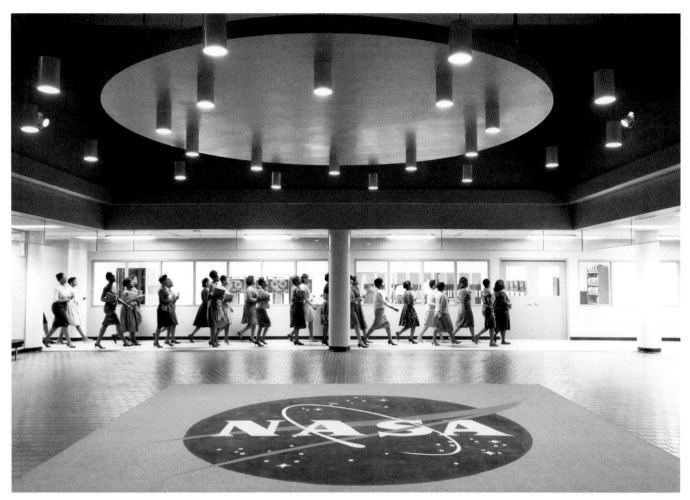

2.9.15 **Theodore Melfi, still from** *Hidden Figures*, 2016. 127 minutes, Fox 2000 Pictures

journey as an artist, activist, and individual while invoking Kahlo's artistic **style** and **subject matter**. Taymor selected actors with physical resemblance to the individuals they play, including Salma Hayek (b. 1966) as Frida and Alfred Molina (b. 1953) as the Mexican painter Diego Rivera. The film fleshes out Frida's recovery from a serious accident, her journey as an artist, and the turbulent relationship with her husband, Rivera; it also references her bisexuality.

Taymor intended *Frida* to transcend the biopic genre and produce an effective story beyond the historical figures who are its focus. In addition to realistic scenes based on photographs and personal accounts, Taymor included dream-like creations based on Frida's experiences. For example, the surgery scene at Calaca Hospital, which takes place after the fateful trolley accident that Kahlo endured when she was eighteen, allowed Taymor to apply her background in puppetry by using shadowy *dia de los muertos* (Day of the Dead) figures to re-enact the procedure.

It is hard to believe that the story of historical drama *Hidden Figures* (2016) is not already an integral part of established history. The film centers on three women who worked at NASA, Langley as "computers," or mathematicians, in the early 1960s (**2.9.15**). The book of the same name that served as inspiration for the film was written by Margot Lee Shetterly (b. 1969). Shetterly researched for five years and wrote *Hidden Figures* to tell the story of the Black scientists and engineers who worked with her father at NASA but who were omitted from former stories of the pioneering days of US space exploration. The movie, directed by Theodore Melfi (b. 1971), highlights the impact of Jim Crow segregation on Katherine Goble Johnson, Dorothy Vaughan, and Mary Jackson, as they performed their professional assignments and sought rightful advancement. During the 2017 Oscars ceremony, the ninety-eight-year-old Johnson was recognized for her long-overlooked contributions to the progress of aeronautical and scientific discovery.

Style: a characteristic way in which an artist or group of artists uses visual language to give a work an identifiable form of visual expression

Subject, subject matter: the person, object, space, or topic depicted in a work of art

Sondra Perry, *Typhoon coming on*
Oceans of History, Technology, and Racial Reckoning

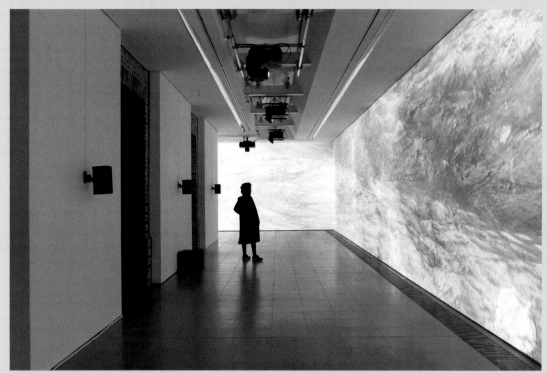

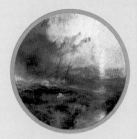

A key part of the Romanticism movement was to investigate incidents and draw attention to injustice, as J. M. W. Turner did in his painting *Slave Ship... Typhoon Coming On*:
→ see **3.7.17**, p. 478

2.9.16a Sondra Perry, *Typhoon coming on*, Installation view, Serpentine Sackler Gallery, London, England, March 6–May 20, 2018

The American artist Sondra Perry (b. 1986) uses the medium of video to create multi-layered symbols of personal experience and contemporary life. In her 2018 installation *Typhoon coming on* (**2.9.16a, b, and c**), she investigates various aspects of the ocean as the concept relates to historical events, painted narratives, digital technology, and Black and brown bodies. Perry used the open-source

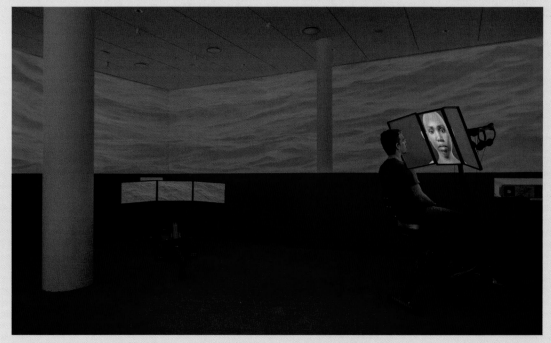

2.9.16b Sondra Perry, *Typhoon Coming On*, Installation view, Institute of Contemporary Art, Miami, Florida, July 14–Nov 4, 2018

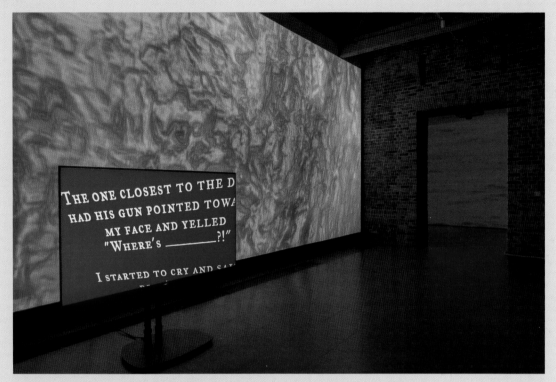

2.9.16c Sondra Perry, *Typhoon coming on*, Installation view, Serpentine Galleries, London, England, March 6–May 20, 2018

software Blender, particularly one of its tools called the Ocean Modifier, to animate oceans in three different chromatic versions.

The first ocean, as the title of the piece suggests, references a famous 1840 painting by J. M. W. Turner, *Slave Ship (Slavers Throwing Overboard the Dead and Dying, Typhoon Coming On)*. This painting recounts an incident from around sixty years before it was made: the captain of a ship called the *Zong*, which carried enslaved Africans, threw the sick overboard to collect insurance. The enslaved people were referred to as "cargo." Instead of actually showing the bodies, chains, and sharks that are painted in the right foreground of *Slave Ship*, Perry re-creates the easily recognizable colors of the sea, focusing on how nature seemingly reacted to the murders, and suggesting that the typhoon extends beyond that singular incident (**2.9.16a**). The swirling waters, for example, recall video footage of recent natural disasters, such as the floods in New Orleans that followed Hurricane Katrina in 2005.

Further modifications were made to generate a second, more vivid ocean, which foregrounds the color Chroma Key Blue. In the installation, this color also appears on a three-monitor workstation with a rowing machine and the artist's avatar (**2.9.16b**). Usually, the use of Chroma Key is seen only by artists and designers, since it serves as a placeholder in the program for a missing material or texture to be replaced by CGI (computer-generated imagery); for example, when an area of a scene needs to be adjusted because it is in darkness. Blue (and green) screens are used in this way because they are less present in human skin tones and environments, making digital substitutions easier. In a 2018 interview, the artist explained that in post-production, Chroma Key can be anything: it is "literally creating a space in which that imagining can happen. And imagining is very important because inflexible imaginations create terrible spaces for people to live."

A third ocean in the installation was generated by zooming in on the artist's own skin (**2.9.16c**). Looking somewhat like hot lava, this ocean serves as a backdrop for a monitor that displays excerpts of text and videos related to incidents of police brutality linked to racial bias: sourced from protests, the artist's family, and body-cam footage from the news. The references to skin tone range from symbolic in the ocean background to more overt in the written and spoken words, but again, no graphic violence is directly shown. As the Turner painting did for viewers in the nineteenth century, Perry's installation draws our attention to a sustained history of human rights violations that can easily be overlooked. She transforms systems of realistic and abstract representation into new expressions for our consideration, engagement, and interaction.

Film as Art

The category "indie," or independent film, generally refers to movies made outside the major production studios and distributed by independent film agencies. Regardless of budget or connections to preexisting genres, independent films tend to champion creative and non-mainstream approaches and content.

Auteur Films

Auteur theory, from the French word for "author," considers films to be works of art due to the fact that they are the realization of a director's creative vision. This theory, focusing on the director or screenwriter, has been controversial because the nature of movies is collaborative, and auteur theory does not acknowledge the creative contribution of actors, cinematographers, set and costume designers, and the many other people who help to make a film. Proponents of the theory, though, cite the films of François Truffaut, Jean-Luc Godard, Akira Kurosawa, Alfred Hitchcock, Jean Renoir, Woody Allen, Jane Campion, Julie Taymor, and Wes Anderson as especially guided by the artistic vision of their directors.

The distinctive vision of the Chinese director Wong Kar-wai (b. 1958) permeates *Chungking Express* (**2.9.17**). In the crowded urban metropolis of Hong Kong, we follow the stories (one after the other) of two police officers. Two tales overlap, like the strangers who brush past each other in a Hong Kong crowd depicted at the beginning of the film. In both cases the officers are transitioning from one romance to another, but the future of each new romance remains uncertain. The suspenseful story of drug dealing in the first tale in some ways contrasts with the odd comedy of the second; in other ways, however, the two stories resonate poetically, each evoking the other in its depiction of lost love and longing. Wong's work is characterized by complicated narratives in addition to a stylized, color-rich, impressionistic cinematography (by Christopher Doyle) that highlights the fast **pace** and isolation of contemporary life.

Experimental Films

Experimental films analyze and extend the medium of film by using new technology or subject matter, and by exploring new **aesthetic**

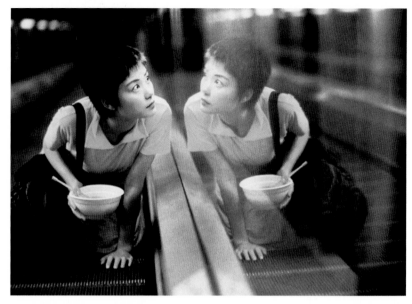

2.9.17 **Wong Kar-wai**, **still from** *Chungking Express*, 1994. 102 minutes, Jet Tone Production

ideas. They tend to be visually compelling and poetic, notable for their unusual content and idiosyncrasy. They are often the production of a single person or small group, and experimental filmmakers use inexpensive equipment and low-budget formats to create the desired effects. Such films frequently do not have integrated sound, or typically use it in unnatural ways. Experimental filmmakers tend to adopt innovative approaches, including dream sequences and fantastic imagery created by manipulating the filmstrip. Their films are also often autobiographical.

Auteur theory/auteur films: from the French word for "author," refers to films that notably reflect the director's creative vision above other criteria

Pace: the speed at which something moves; the rhythmic flow of dialogue or action related to an overall scene or sequence

Aesthetic: related to beauty, art, and taste

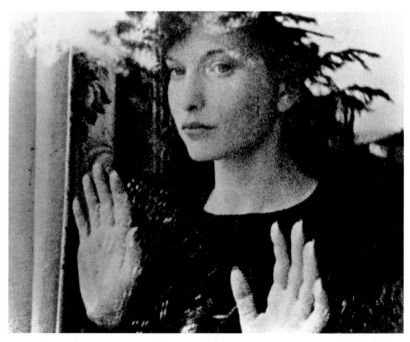

2.9.18 **Maya Deren**, **still from** *Meshes of the Afternoon*, 1943, 14 minutes, 16mm black-and-white silent film

The American dancer, choreographer, and filmmaker Maya Deren (1917–1961) wrote *Meshes of the Afternoon* (1943) and co-directed it with her husband, cinematographer Alexander Hammid (1907–2004). The short (14-minute) film follows a woman's experience of an afternoon, shuffled together with her dreams after she has drifted off to sleep (**2.9.18**). Two sequences are repeated: in one, a cloaked woman with a mirror over her face walks down the road; in the other, the woman (played by Deren) enters a house and walks up the stairs. These sequences seem to be replaying themselves in the woman's mind rather than representing actual events. Several objects are shown again and again: a flower, a key, a telephone, a knife, a record player, billowy curtains, rumpled sheets. Elements change each time the sequences occur. For instance, one moment the flower is placed on the pillow; the next, the knife appears in the same position. Toward the end of the film, a man replaces the female figures, in one sequence entering the house and in the next walking on the road.

Time is circular in this film, and the overall effect mimics a dream in which events that make sense to the dreamer seem illogical to others. Each object seems to have an unnamed symbolic significance, and it is impossible to separate actual occurrences from memories or fiction. Ultimately, the film reflects a state of mind, and can be best understood as visual poetry. This ability to express psychological states is one of film's particular strengths as an artistic medium.

Video

Typically, video artworks are made to be presented in art galleries or at art events. They may be shown on television monitors or projected onto walls. Sometimes artists incorporate video displays (along with other media) in a darkened area in ways that transform the space and create a total environment of sight and sound. Because high-quality video equipment is relatively inexpensive, artistic experimentation with video is widespread.

The Korean American artist Nam June Paik (1932–2006) was a pioneer of video art. In 1969 Paik worked with Shuya Abe, an engineer from Tokyo, to modulate video signals with a device called the Paik-Abe Synthesizer. The results combined both recognizable and distorted

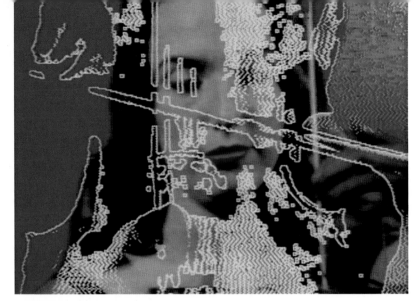

2.9.19 Nam June Paik and John J. Godfrey, still from *Global Groove*, 1973, single-channel videotape, color with sound. Courtesy Electronic Arts Intermix (EAI), New York

pictures that were recorded and could be replayed later. Paik's *Global Groove* (1973), a 30-minute video recording, comments on the increasing role of media and technology in daily life.

Global Groove replicates the variety of things that were available on television at the time the video was made, from Pepsi commercials and news footage to game shows and President Richard Nixon's face. All these scenes are interspersed, like glimpses of changing channels. Most of the clips integrate music and visuals, consisting of either performers or dancers. For example, the performance artist and musician Charlotte Moorman (1933–1991) is shown playing several experimental cellos designed by Paik. The close-up of her face (**2.9.19**) is surrounded by visual noise, static translated into changing designs that correspond to the rhythms of the music she is playing. *Global Groove* draws on contemporary culture, and foreshadows the music video by integrating visual and musical inputs.

Interactive Technology and Television

Artists and designers create artworks, installations, websites, video games, and television shows that provide new possibilities for sharing and accessing creative expressions. Developments in digital technology have allowed artists to involve viewers as active participants in the artwork by, for example, determining the appearance of the work or choosing different paths to follow. **GIFs**, developed in 1987 by the software engineer Steve

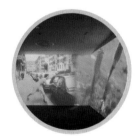

Some videos are projected to create visual connections as well as sensory experiences. The elements of *Ever Is Over All* juxtapose still life and narrative scenes with ambient music:
→ see **3.10.15**, p. 532

GIF (graphics interchange format): a compressed image file type intended to reduce transfer time

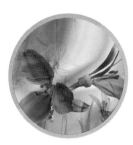

In addition to interactivity, the technology used in computer images enables an unprecedented range of colors and visual effects:
→ see **1.4.3**, p. 85

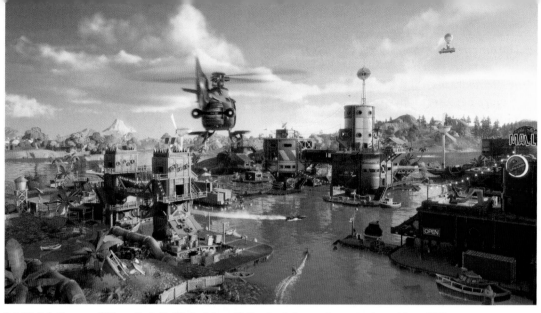

2.9.20 Epic Games, still from Fortnite "Splashdown!" Chapter 2, Season 3, event, released June 2017

Wilhite, are used extensively for animated and static images. These image files, compressed to reduce transfer times, are good for simple graphics or logos with solid areas of color. Activated by clicking or opening, GIFs enhance communication with quick, isolated, and repeated gestures or motions.

The video-game industry has grown so much that it rivals the film industry in revenue. Epic Games released the multiplayer online video game Fortnite in 2017 and it now has over 350 million registered users. Fortnite graphics combine visual detail and flow with an animation style that helps minimize on-screen violence. To increase engagement and discovery, the action-adventure game promotes narrative, incentives, and social interaction through live events and periodic releases of new

versions. In 2020, the second Fortnite concert, held with Travis Scott on April 26, drew over 12 million live viewers; "Waterworld," Chapter 2, Season 3 was released on June 17 (**2.9.20**).

Once seen as an inferior medium to film and cinema, television has created its own set of influential entertainment criteria. In 2013, Netflix began releasing complete seasons of shows simultaneously, allowing viewers to watch all of the episodes at once rather than one a week. This format generated the phenomenon of binge watching, which approximates the rhythms and time commitment of reading books. Streaming is now the industry standard for such giants as HBO (Home Box Office) and Showtime, as well as independent production companies. Created by Eugene and Dan Levy, *Schitt's Creek* (2015–2020) swept the 2020 Emmy's comedy genre for its sixth and final season (**2.9.21**). We pick up the story of the Rose family after they have lost their lavish lifestyle at the hands of a crooked business manager. They move, destitute, to a town once purchased as a joke, to live in adjoining rooms at the Rosebud motel. Humor ensues from the collision of expectations (wealth/nonwealth, fashion/kitsch, surface/heart, struggle/resilience), the endearing and quirky mannerisms of the characters, and the absurdity of daily life in relative isolation. Inspired by life, reality TV, celebrity culture, nostalgia, and imagination, the hopeful present becomes more important than the glamorous past. In his Emmy acceptance speech, Dan Levy said, "Our show…is about the transformational effects of love and acceptance…we need more of now than we've ever needed before."

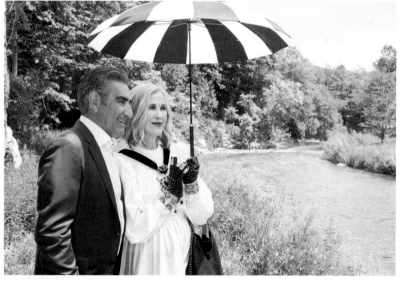

2.9.21 Eugene Levy and Catherine O'Hara in *Schitt's Creek* season 6 premiere, 2020. (CBC/Pop TV/Not A Real Company)

Explore Further Film/Video and Digital Art

Photographs of Moving Images before Film

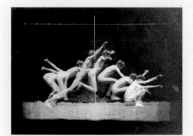

3.8.8 Thomas Eakins, *Motion Study: Male Nude, Standing Jump to Right*, 1884 → p. 486

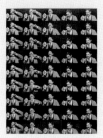

1.5.17 Thomas Edison and W. K. Dickson, *Fred Ott's Sneeze*, 1894 → p. 113

Film and Moving Images as Art

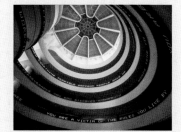

1.5.3 Jenny Holzer, *Untitled (Selections from Truisms …)*, 1989 → p. 106

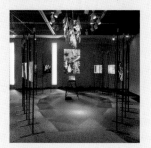

3.10.9 Jolene Rickard, *Corn Blue Room*, 1998 → p. 527

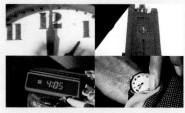

4.3.7 Christian Marclay, stills from *The Clock*, 2010 → p. 572

Historic Processes and Film Genres

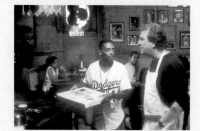

4.9.12 Spike Lee, still from *Do the Right Thing*, 1989 → p. 656

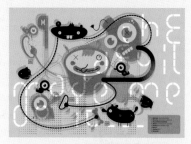

1.1.7 Sauerkids, *The Devil Made Me Do It*, 2006 → p. 38

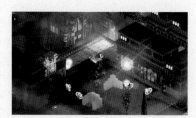

1.3.16 Supergiant Games, screenshot from *Transistor*, 2014 → p. 76

Your turn:

How do these works relate to the ideas discussed in this chapter?

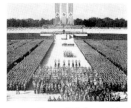

4.5.10b Leni Riefenstahl, *Triumph of the Will*, 1935 → p. 600

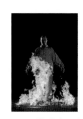

4.3.1 Bill Viola, *The Crossing*, 1996 → p. 568

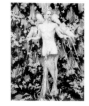

3.10.16 Matthew Barney, *Cremaster 5*, 1997 → p. 532

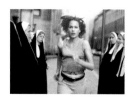

1.5.7 Tom Tykwer, still from *Run Lola Run*, 1998 → p. 108

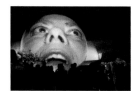

4.1.17 Krzysztof Wodiczko, *Tijuana Projection*, 2001 → p. 552

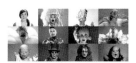

4.3.11 Jillian Mayer, *I Am Your Grandma* (selected video stills), 2011 → p. 575

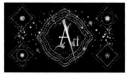

1.5.8 Oliver Harrison, still from *Apocalypse Rhyme*, 2014 → p. 108

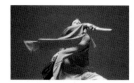

4.9.16a Wu Tsang, *Duilian*, 2016 → p. 658

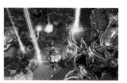

2.7.24 *Starcraft 2* video game screenshot, 2019 → p. 297

2.10
Alternative Media and Processes

Medium (plural media): the material on or from which an artist chooses to make a work of art, for example canvas and oil paint, marble, engraving, video, or architecture

Conceptual art: a work in which the communication of an idea of group of ideas is most important to the artwork

Performance art: a work involving the human body, usually including the artist, in front of an audience

Installation: originally referring to the hanging of pictures and arrangement of objects in an exhibition, installation may also refer to an intentional environment created as a completed artwork

Action painting: the application of paint to canvas by dripping, splashing, or smearing that emphasizes the artist's gestures

Dada: an anarchic anti-art and anti-war movement, dating back to World War I, that reveled in absurdity and irrationality

Readymade: an everyday object presented as a work of art

Assemblage: an artwork made of three-dimensional materials, including found objects

Many artists working today choose unconventional approaches and incorporate more than one **medium** (often several), making the categorization of these artworks much more complicated. Artworks made using alternative media and processes break down the traditional boundaries between art and life. They tend to draw our attention to actions or ideas rather than only to a physical product. The creative process produces events, ideas, and experiences as artworks in and of themselves. Many artworks that are interactive or involve the viewer in unusual and significant ways fall into this category.

In **conceptual art**, the idea behind an artwork is more important than any visible subject or material product. Artists generally plan the piece and make all of the major decisions beforehand; the execution of the piece itself is secondary. Conceptual art often produces no permanent artwork and very little that can be promoted and sold: sometimes a set of instructions, a documentary photograph, or nothing at all remains as evidence that the piece existed. For example, if an artist printed a set of instructions for the viewer, the actual, tangible result of the piece would be the actions that person performed. Yoko Ono's *Wish Tree* artworks (**2.10.3**, see p. 337) existed only in a potential state when the artist first made them. Each piece requires the viewer's participation in order to be realized. In Vito Acconci's *Following Piece* (**2.10.5**, see p. 338), there was no audience at the time, but the artist took pictures of each "following" he made.

Performance art has some similarities to theater because it is (usually) performed in front of a live audience; it includes varying amounts of music, dance, poetry, video, and multimedia technology. Unlike traditional theater, however, there is rarely a conventional story and the performance takes place in consciously artistic venues. The actions of the artist, or individuals chosen by the artist, become the focus. These actions, which occur in a gallery, on a stage, or in a public place, may last from a few minutes to a few days, and may not be repeated.

When artists design an entire exhibition space as an artwork, usually in a gallery or museum, it is called an **installation**. Often installations are designed to fit the dimensions or environment of a particular location: these installations are called "site-specific." The artist plans the space, considers how people will move through it, and arranges the elements to create a certain effect. Whether they are designed for an interior or exterior space, installations immerse viewers in the artwork.

Bringing together a number of these alternative approaches, socially engaged art draws attention to issues in the hopes of engaging communities, raising awareness, and inspiring action.

Context of Alternative Media

During the twentieth century, a way of making art emerged that focused on modes of creation, such as actions, texts, and environments. These approaches differed from the traditional western European practices of fine art, narrowly defined as paintings on canvas and sculptures on pedestals. The American artist Jackson Pollock's (1912–1956) **action paintings** of the 1950s brought the canvas off the easel and onto the floor to become a surface around which the artist moved as he splashed, dripped, and flung his paint. His unusual and exciting painting techniques galvanized public interest in difficult modern art. Pollock rocketed to popular fame following an article published on August 8, 1949 in *Life Magazine* that asked, "Is he the greatest living painter in the United States?" Not long after Pollock's early death in a car crash, though, there was a sense that artists had exhausted all they could say with paint on canvas. Artists began to turn to performance, conceptualism, and installations to explore radical new ideas about art.

Because this chapter focuses on the ideas expressed in the making of artworks rather than the finished objects themselves, we shall also look at the documentation about them—instructions used to plan an activity, notes taken by the artist related to a piece, or photographs or video made during a performance. The works themselves tend to last for a relatively short period of time.

Conceptual Art

Conceptual art is a form of art that emphasizes ideas and radically downplays the importance of the work of art as a craft object. It has flourished from the 1960s onward. In some ways conceptual art is similar to **Dada** absurdist events that took place in Zürich, Switzerland in 1916, where artists performed nonsense poetry as a release from and as a savage commentary on the events of World War I. The Dadaist Marcel Duchamp (1887–1968) also made artworks that challenged traditional notions of art. One of his works, *Fountain*, was rejected for an art exhibition in New York in 1917 because it was simply a factory-made white porcelain urinal, signed "R. Mutt." While the group hosting the exhibition was outraged, it missed Duchamp's entire point: the meaning of the artwork is not in what it's made of or how it's made. An artist can communicate worthwhile ideas using any sort of material because the message is what matters. As the first artist truly to promote this kind of art, now known as **readymades**, Duchamp was very influential for many artists later in the twentieth century. His approach opened up possibilities for making art from everyday things and materials, imagery from popular culture, or even simply *ideas*.

Imagine walking into an art museum and seeing a giant machine with wheels, gears, and pulleys. Then you hear a crashing and whirring as smoke rises from the mass, flames shoot out from a piano, a can of gasoline overturns onto

a burning candle, and a small carriage hurtles out straight toward you, making a shrieking noise. You have just encountered *Homage to New York* (**2.10.1**) by Swiss artist Jean Tinguely (1925–1991). This mechanized **assemblage** of discarded junk was designed to mimic the automatic processes and spontaneous painting techniques that had become popular amongst artists (methods such as those used by Jackson Pollock; see pp. 515–16). Once set in motion in the sculpture garden of the Museum of Modern Art, the piece behaved unpredictably in its one-off performance: a journalist ended up sending the hurtling carriage in another direction and eventually a firefighter had to put out the flames to keep the museum from being burned to the ground. Like Duchamp, Tinguely was interested in exploring impermanence, accident, and uncertainty as legitimate forces within the creation and experience of a work of art. *Homage to New York* revived many of Dada's (and Duchamp's) rebellious and humorous antics, in the form of a huge, self-destructing sculpture.

Many examples of conceptual art consist of words on a page or background. These words cut to the chase, directing our attention to the core concept, and allow us to make the words meaningful for ourselves. Since the 1980s, the American artist Barbara Kruger (b. 1945) has used her experience as a graphic designer to combine **found images** and words to give them new meanings. Her pieces address the powerful institutions of society and stereotypes that

Found image or object: an image or object found by an artist and presented, with little or no alteration, as part of a work or as a finished work of art in itself

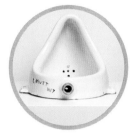

Marcel Duchamp pioneered the readymade: a regular object (e.g. a urinal) that becomes an artwork (here, *Fountain*) by the decision of the artist:
→ see **3.10.1**, p. 523

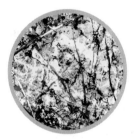

The painting method used by Jackson Pollock brought attention to the physical movement of the artist in the creation of art, in addition to the artwork itself: → see **3.9.28**, p. 516

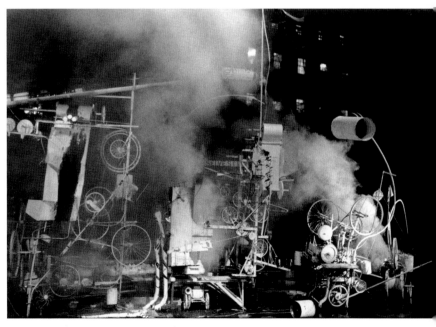

2.10.1 Jean Tinguely, *Homage to New York*, MoMA, New York, March 17, 1960. Photo David Gahr

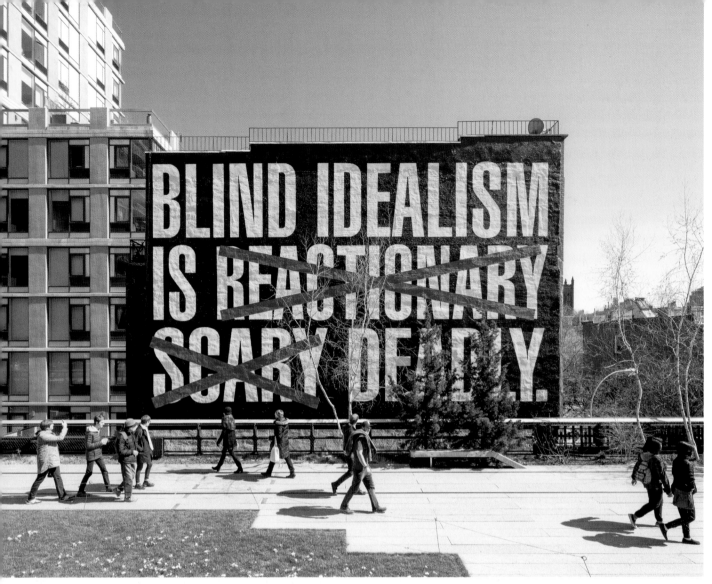

2.10.2 Barbara Kruger, *Untitled (Blind Idealism Is…)*, 2016. Wall painting. A High Line Commission, on view at The High Line, New York, March 2016–March 2017

are often seen in visual culture. *Untitled (Blind Idealism Is…)*, a large-scale **mural** hand-painted by a professional sign company, broadcasts the artist's trademark text and image combinations in bold black and white with red accents (**2.10.2**). The text addresses viewers directly and urges them to think about the nature of truth, power, consumerism, and feminist interventions. In an interview in 2018, Kruger said: "I've always had a very broad definition of art…I do know that art is the creation of commentary….The goal for every human being, including myself, is to live an examined life—to really think about what makes us who we are in the world and how culture constructs and contains us. That's what I'm interested in."

Yoko Ono (b. 1933), a Japanese-born American artist and musician, began making conceptual artworks in the early 1960s. Her first pieces were poetic instructions to be performed or just imagined. Sometimes they were typescripts framed and put on the wall. Other times, Ono painted right on the museum or gallery wall (highlighting the transient nature of some of these pieces: when the exhibition ended, those instructions would disappear).

She then started to ask viewers to complete her pieces by, for example, burning or walking on the paintings. Eventually she made "Instruction Paintings," consisting of typed instructions, rather than finished works of art. The instructions are open-ended and serve as a beginning point rather than a final product. They rely heavily on the interaction with and participation of the viewer. The instructions for *Wish Tree for Washington D.C.* (2007) state: "Make a wish, Write it down on a piece of paper, Fold it and tie it around the branch of a Wish Tree, Ask your friends to do the same, Keep wishing Until the branches are covered with your wishes."

Mural: a painting executed directly onto a wall

Happening: impromptu art action, initiated and planned by an artist, the outcome of which is not known in advance

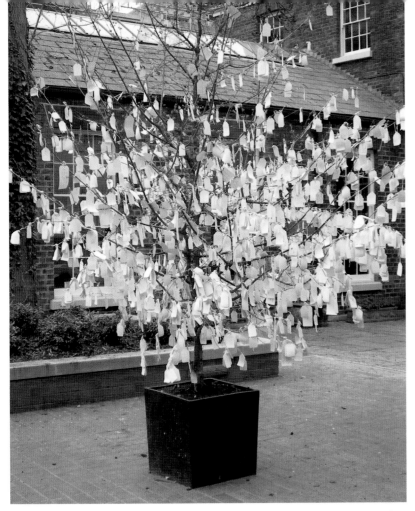

2.10.3 **Yoko Ono**, ***Wish Tree for Liverpool***, 2008. Bluecoat Arts Centre, Liverpool, England

Inspired by the Japanese practice of tying prayers to a tree, Ono has made *Wish Trees* like the one in **2.10.3** all over the world.

Performance Art

During the 1960s and 1970s, artists around the world began exploring theatrical actions or performances as a new form of creative activity, termed performance art. American composer John Cage (1912–1992) incorporated into his music chance operations, experimental techniques, and even silence. Heavily influenced by Zen Buddhism, Cage wanted to jolt his audiences into paying attention to the life around them. He was one of the first artists to conduct **happenings**. *Theater Piece No. 1* (1952) (**2.10.4**) was an unrecorded collaboration in poetry, music, dance, and paintings by the faculty and students of Black Mountain College in North Carolina. The performers mingled with the members of the audience, and the piece relied for its outcome on improvisation and chance rather than a script or musical score. Its lasting influence comes from its emphasis on performance rather than documentation. Happenings expanded the scope of art to include the lived moment—actions as they happen, here and now.

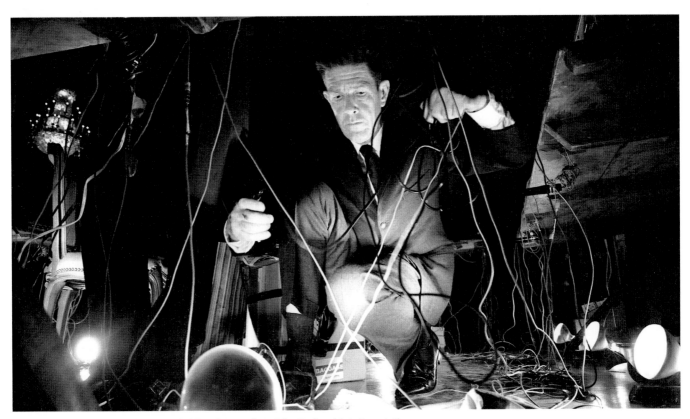

2.10.4 **John Cage, during his concert held at the opening of the National Arts Foundation**, Washington, D.C., 1966

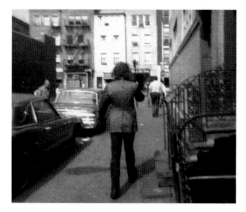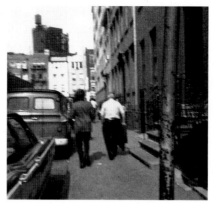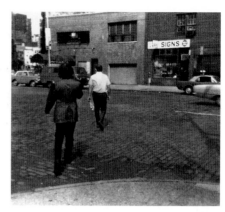

2.10.5 Vito Acconci, *Following Piece*, 1969, "Street Works IV," 23-day activity

Early in his career, the American artist Vito Acconci (b. 1940) was known for art actions and performances. These works consisted of situations he set up for himself, and records of how he completed them. His stated intentions for *Following Piece* (**2.10.5**) were: "Choosing a person at random, in the street, a new location, each day. Following him wherever he goes, however long or far he travels. (The activity ends when he enters a private place—his home, office, etc.)." Acconci performed this activity for twenty-three days; the longest following lasted nine hours. An exhibition of *Following Piece* includes documents of the events, such as the artist's handwritten note cards, and photographs of Acconci walking behind the person being followed. *Following Piece* examines both the relationship between the artist and the viewer and the way in which an artist's actions create interactions with another person. In this sense, Acconci's work is a conceptual performance: it is about ideas and a set of actions as much as about the production of a work of art. It is interesting to note how our view of such works can change through time. In 1969, when the piece was first developed, it was regarded as a new idea, but nowadays, we might look on the artist's actions in following and photographing someone without their knowledge as disturbing or even menacing.

Some performances put the body through extremes of endurance, as Serbian artist Marina Abramović (b. 1946) has done in a number of works dating back to the 1970s. In one piece she lay in a ring of fire until she fainted from asphyxiation (and had to be rescued by onlookers). In another, one of her longest pieces (it took almost three months), she and her partner Ulay started at opposite ends of the Great Wall of China and met in the middle after walking more than 1,242 miles.

In 2010, Abramović performed the longest-lasting work of her solo career so far, *The Artist Is Present*, for three months at the Museum of Modern Art, New York (MoMA) (**2.10.6**). Every day during that period she sat quietly at a table in the museum's gallery all day, from before it opened until after it closed. Museum visitors were invited to sit—one at a time, for as long as they wished—in the chair opposite her. The title of the piece illustrates its purpose: for the artist to be personally in the space and engage with people, creating what she has called an "energy dialogue," without talking, touching, or otherwise overtly communicating. Through this engagement, Abramović put her mental and physical abilities to the test. At the same time, the audience experienced the intensity of this seemingly simple interaction. Portraits were made of each person who sat in the chair, showing most of them staring intently forward, some of them smiling, and a number of people crying.

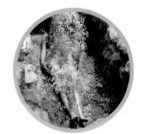

Ana Mendieta's *Silueta* series places the artist's body in various natural scenarios:

→ see **3.10.4**, p. 524

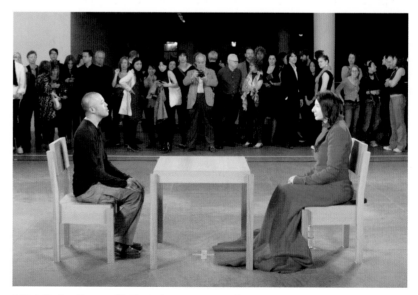

2.10.6 Marina Abramović, *The Artist Is Present*, Performance, 3 months. MoMA, New York, 2010

This piece was a part of a retrospective exhibition of Abramović's work, which was the first major performance exhibition at MoMA. The show revealed the numerous challenges institutions must deal with when displaying performance art, such as the unpredictability of audience members who have been invited to participate. Crowd control took on epic proportions for this retrospective, with around 1,400 museum visitors per day and an estimate of more than 500,000 over the whole course of the exhibition. In addition to photographs, video documentation, and written accounts of performance pieces made throughout Abramović's career, for the first time, performers re-enacted her earlier pieces so that visitors could experience them firsthand, and visitors shared their perspectives on personal blogs and through social media.

Installation and Environments

The Beanery by American Edward Kienholz (1927–1994) reflects the artist's desire to break down barriers between art and life (**2.10.7a** and **2.10.7b**). Kienholz meticulously replicated the interior of his local bar, Barney's Beanery, complete with lifesize figures inspired by people he knew. This very specific place has been transformed into an assemblage through the products, interior design, technology, clothing, newspapers, music, and even odors it contains. To keep the experience as true to the artist's intentions as possible, the original soundtrack on tape has been converted to CD, and "odor paste" that smells like a bar is replenished by the museum that holds

the work. By using clocks in place of the figures' faces, Kienholz reiterated the fact that time now stands still in this sculptural **tableau**.

The London-born Nigerian Yinka Shonibare (b. 1962) creates more disembodied and conceptual sculptural groupings that explore issues of race and colonialism. He uses parody and **masquerade** to suggest that things are not always what they seem. Here, his mannequin figures, headless to reflect the violence of capitalism, wear Victorian-style garments made out of distinctive African-style textiles. These fabrics, widely associated with Africa, in this context represent the multi-layered product of colonial exploitation. Wax-printed cotton, originally made in Indonesia, began to be industrially manufactured by a Dutch company

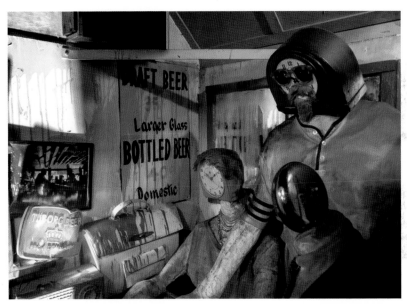

2.10.7b Edward Kienholz, detail of *The Beanery*

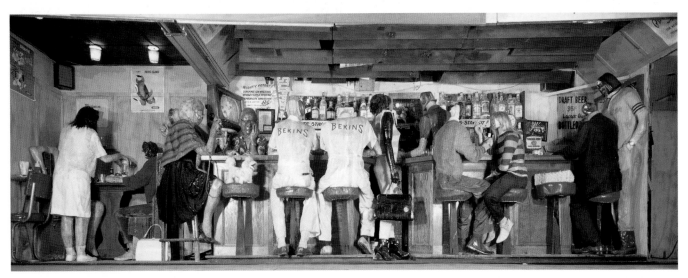

2.10.7a Edward Kienholz, ***The Beanery***, 1965 (restored 2012). Installation, 8′3½″ × 21′11¾″ × 6′2¾″. Stedelijk Museum, Amsterdam, The Netherlands

Kara Walker, *Insurrection!*
Out of the Shadows and into the Light, Enlivened Gallery Space

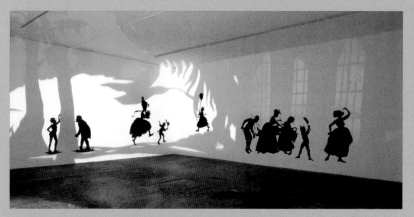

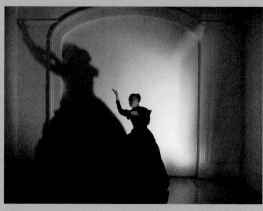

2.10.8 Kara Walker, *Insurrection! (Our Tools Were Rudimentary, Yet We Pressed On),* 2000. Cut paper and projection on wall, dimensions variable. Installation view, *Why I Like White Boys, an Illustrated Novel by Kara E. Walker Negress,* Centre d'Art Contemporain, Geneva, Switzerland

2.10.9 Yuki Kihara, *Taualuga: The Last Dance,* 2006. Performance/digital video. Still courtesy of Milford Galleries, Dunedin and Yuki Kihara. © Yuki Kihara

Several contemporary artists have used installations and performance as ways to call attention to historical media and ways of thinking while encouraging viewers to take a longer look and attend to the way things have (or should have) changed. From the seventeenth to nineteenth century, **silhouette** cutouts offered a cheaper alternative to individual painted portraits in Europe, America, and colonized countries. Also called "shades" or "likenesses," the process of making silhouettes involves an artist tracing the shadow of the sitter as it is cast from a strong light source. Still available but much less common today, silhouettes tend to carry a sense of nostalgia and an aura of the past.

The installations of American artist Kara Walker (b. 1969) combine silhouettes and projections in the gallery space to address overlooked history from the pre-Civil War South. These silhouettes provide a glimpse of the subject in an indirect way, a view of history that once existed but may never have been told. The addition of projectors in the installations enables Walker to cast more shadows on the walls, including those of viewers in the room. As their shadows appear on the wall, the viewers are included and even implicated in the events unfolding there. The combined projections and silhouettes can be seen in *Insurrection! (Our Tools Were Rudimentary, Yet We Pressed On)*, which presents a story that combines fact and fiction (**2.10.8**). Walker explains that this scene is intended to show "a slave revolt in the antebellum South where the house slaves got after their master with their instruments, their utensils of everyday life."

Each grouping of figures highlights the bodies of the individuals, the stories they represent, and the scenarios of which they become a part.

Projected silhouettes in the performance *Taualuga: The Last Dance* (2006) bring to light contemporary issues of race and identity within a cultural context of colonialism, (mis) representation, and consumerism (**2.10.9**). The Samoan/Japanese artist who lives in New Zealand, Yuki Kihara (b. 1975), created an alter ego named Salomé to embody a nineteenth-century Samoan woman she had seen in ethnographic photographs. Her Victorian mourning dress references the losses and struggles resulting from colonialism, natural disasters, tourism, and life. Traditionally her dance, called *taualuga*, is a carefully choreographed, celebratory method of narrative storytelling. Salomé embodies more than meets the eye, bringing together past and present, suggesting creation and destruction, and representing the artist's identity as a *fa'afafine*, Samoan third gender. The Samoan woman in colonial dress steps out of the mythical paradise of the untouched Pacific wilderness, passes through iconic cultural images (for example, paintings by Paul Gauguin), and dances into the present day by simultaneously embracing and dismantling stereotypes.

Kara Walker brought the silhouette into the contemporary art context through her installations and Yuki Kihara further extended its use in multimedia performances. Both artists train a postcolonial lens on historical subjects through their explorations of the interactions between art and life.

For the other Walker
GATEWAYS:
→ see p. 48 and p. 625

Silhouette: a shape represented in outline, which contains no detail inside its border

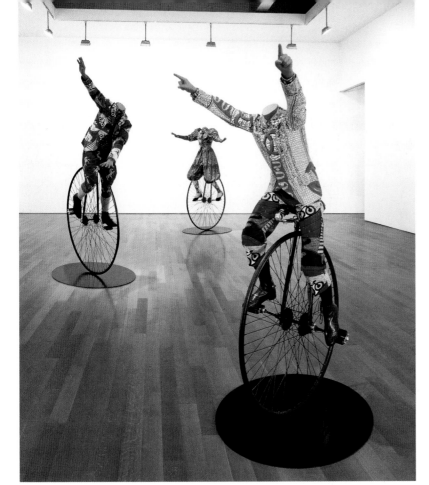

2.10.10 Yinka Shonibare, **installation view of** *Mobility*, James Cohan, New York, 2005. From left to right: *Man On Unicycle*, 2005. Metal, fabric, resin, and leather, 86 × 53 × 47½"; *Lady On Unicycle*, 2005. Metal, fabric, resin, and leather, 86 × 53 × 47½"; *Child On Unicycle*, 2005. Metal, fabric, resin, and leather, 79 × 46 × 38½"

Abstract: art imagery that departs from recognizable images of the natural world

Minimalism, minimalist: a mid-twentieth-century artistic style that references industrial production modes, often with unified arrangements of geometric shapes that become part of the viewer's space

Symbolism: using images or symbols in an artwork to convey meaning; often obvious when the work was made but requiring research for modern viewers to understand

at the end of the nineteenth century. When the material proved unpopular in Indonesia, these cheap fabrics were successfully marketed in West Africa. Shonibare inverts colonialist expectations by using cloth associated with poverty-stricken West Africans to outfit faceless and raceless aristocrats.

In *Mobility* (**2.10.10**), Shonibare created a family of three aristocrats riding unicycles with differing degrees of confidence and implied stability. The title of this piece brings in connotations of wealth (economic mobility), travel (the ability to go places, often for pleasure), and bodily movement (how able one is to get around). The playful and joyous mood of these artworks carries a serious message. In addition to commenting on economic disparities resulting from colonialism and capitalism, he is also referring to assumptions about physical ability. Having suffered complete paralysis after contracting a virus at age nineteen, Shonibare has been recovering ever since. A few years before he made this installation Shonibare began using his art to

confront his own mortality and the difficulty of living in his body. Like the unicyclists, for Shonibare the very act of getting around presents distinct challenges. Shonibare's work parallels his life and world views: just as he cannot be easily labeled as Nigerian or British, his figures and the textiles they wear cannot be easily categorized according to class, culture, or physical ability.

Art as Activism

In recent years some artists have moved away from asking "what does art mean?" and toward focusing on "what can art do?" Throughout its history, the products of the creative process have served as sites of contemplation—making viewers think. Once artists shifted into the realms of conceptualism and **abstraction**, the meaning of the art no longer had to be determined by the way it looked. An artwork's meaning could flourish in the realm of suggestion and even **symbolism**. In recent years, artists have built on performance art to generate a new form of activism, to call attention to issues facing the world, ranging from poverty to racial justice. The artists we'll look at here draw our attention to issues that may otherwise remain invisible: the AIDS epidemic, the COVID-19 pandemic, and the criminal phenomenon of human trafficking.

American artist (born Cuba) Félix González-Torres (1957–1996) built on **minimalist** form to draw attention to personal and political issues and to leave meaning open to viewer interpretation. *"Untitled" (Portrait of Ross in L.A.)* (**2.10.11**), one of González-Torres's most

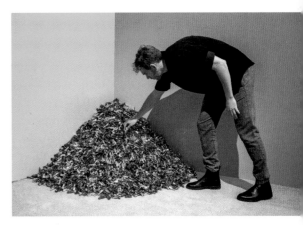

2.10.11 Félix González-Torres, *"Untitled" (Portrait of Ross in L.A.)*, 1991, candies in variously coloured wrappers, endless supply. Overall dimensions vary with installation. Ideal weight 175 lb. Installation view from *Objects of Wonder: from Pedestal to Interaction*, ARoS Aarhus Kunstmuseum, Denmark, 2019–2020, curated by Pernille Taagard Dinesen

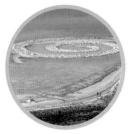

For more information on the movement called Minimalism, see the discussion of Dan Flavin, *Untitled* and Robert Smithson, *Spiral Jetty*
→ see **3.9.33**, p. 519 and **2.4.15**, p. 238

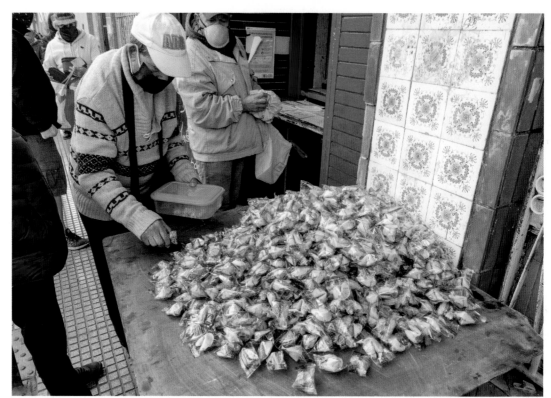

2.10.12 Félix González-Torres, *"Untitled" (Fortune Cookie Corner)*, 1990. Fortune cookies, endless supply. Overall dimensions vary with installation; original installation: approximately 10,000 fortune cookies. Installed by Sonia Becce and Gabriel Chaile in Buenos Aires, Argentina at Community Kitchen Nuestro Hogar.

famous candy spills, is situated in the corner of the gallery—an area unutilized before the days of the Minimalists. Viewers have the opportunity to take a piece of candy, and so the intact sculpture may diminish over time. Exhibitors of the work may choose to replenish the candy. The lighthearted presentation makes the experience of art more democratic, offering edible pieces of the sculpture to everyone. At the same time, the sculpture can be seen to draw indirect but critical attention to harsh realities, such as the horrifying and certain death faced by victims of the 1980s–90s AIDS epidemic in the US before antiretroviral medication was developed. The connection to AIDS happens conceptually: the candy's potential disappearance over time could poignantly represent loss. González-Torres's approach served as a strong influence for later artists who have used art as a site of social engagement.

Another work by González-Torres— *"Untitled" (Fortune Cookie Corner)*, 1990—was on view during the coronavirus outbreak. This piece was exhibited from May 25–July 5, 2020 in numerous locations around the world simultaneously. The project, curated by the New York gallerist Andrea Rosen, involved 1,000 international invitees to create the installations, and an untold number of viewers/participants. Individual sites replicated the isolation of quarantine just as the network of around one hundred installations indicated the global impact of the COVID-19 outbreak (which, in August 2021, tallied over 207 million cases). Installations included those in Buenos Aires, Argentina (**2.10.12**); Hamburg, Germany; Rio de Janeiro, Brazil; Shanghai, China; Caracas, Venezuela; Seoul, South Korea; Cape Town, South Africa; Sarvisalo, Finland; and multiple sites in the United States.

The sculptures diminished over time as anyone who passed by took a cookie, perhaps symbolizing the astounding loss inflicted by the virus (4.37 million deaths as of August 2021). Among other possible readings, a sense of community and hope was part of the unexpected fun of participating and the sense of renewal suggested when the cookie piles were replenished on June 14 2020 (as per the curator's stipulations). *"Untitled" (Fortune Cookie Corner)* serves as a profound reminder of the lasting impact of memory that art can invoke, including memorializing individuals lost to the pandemic, as well as the artist himself, who died in 1996 from AIDS and lives on in his work.

Perspectives on Art: Molly Gochman
Bringing Light to the Scars

Molly Gochman (b. 1978, San Antonio Texas) is an interdisciplinary artist and activist whose work hopes to prompt questioning by providing opportunities to pause and awaken sensations. Based in New York City, her work engages larger social issues and challenges the traditional role of the artist and the expected outcomes of artworks. Here Gochman describes how Red Sand Project, *a collective work of art* (2.10.13) *made by participants from across the United States and around the world, raises awareness about modern-day enslavement and human trafficking.*

As both an artist and activist, I believe all art documents moments in time. In a world where we tend to overlook so much, I think we have the opportunity to look ahead to what can be and to create cultural change through empathy. For me, art has served as my invitation for people to reflect upon and participate in the experience of humanity. Our experiences as humans are vastly different, but we don't often take the time to understand them. I hope to encourage people to stop, soften, and really feel the meaning that exists in the objects and communities that surround us.

That is one of the main reasons why I started *Red Sand Project*, a participatory artwork that uses sidewalk interventions, earthwork installations, and convenings to create opportunities for people to question, to connect, and to take action against vulnerabilities that can lead to human trafficking and exploitation.

Several hundred thousand *Red Sand Project* toolkits have been requested and used by people and groups of diverse backgrounds—from students to educators, businesses to outreach organizations, concerned citizens to celebrities.

Since its inception, installations and events have taken place in all fifty United States and in more than seventy countries around the world. In partnership with organizations, I've sought to create works that invite public participation from people of all different cultures, ethnicities, and backgrounds. With the goal, in so doing, that people will participate in a communal effort to raise awareness of vulnerabilities and social injustices facing people around the world.

The sidewalk interventions remind us that we can't merely walk over the most marginalized people in our communities—those who fall

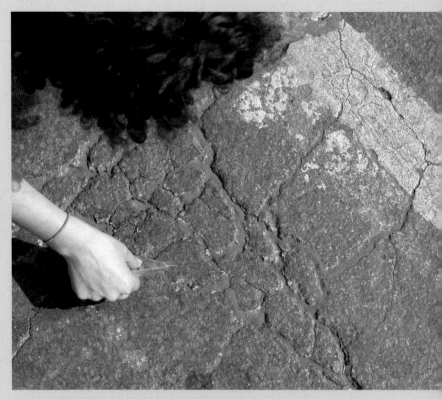

2.10.13 A *Red Sand Project* participant spreads sand in sidewalk cracks in their neighborhood, New York City, October, 2015

through the metaphoric cracks—and allow anyone anywhere to fill sidewalk cracks with red sand and to then document their images on social media using #RedSandProject, thereby expanding the reach of their artistic expression and participation.

While I was nervous, at first, about what this project might mean to some, specifically survivors, I have been so lucky to receive positive feedback. Many survivors of human trafficking have embraced the project and even brought it to their own communities. This project has shown me that while this is an incredibly sensitive issue, art gives space to share images and stories in a way that doesn't exploit the people being affected.

Whether through sidewalk interventions, gallery exhibits, earthworks, or panel discussions, I've used my work to bring new audiences together to find common ground around what's affecting them most deeply. The simple act of placing sand in a crack, posting a photo on social media, chatting with someone as they pass by or finding a brief moment of connection may seem inconsequential, but small actions build upon each other to make transformational change.

Explore Further   Alternative Media and Processes

Conceptual Art

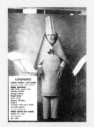

3.9.9 Hugo Ball, Performance of "Karawane" at Cabaret Voltaire, 1916 → p. 506

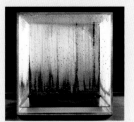

0.0.4 Hans Haacke, *Condensation Cube*, 1963–65 → p. 18

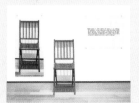

3.10.3 Joseph Kosuth, *One and Three Chairs*, 1965 → p. 524

Performance Art

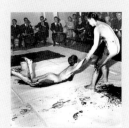

4.8.13a Yves Klein, *Anthropométries de l'époque bleue*, 1960 → p. 638

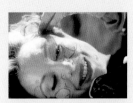

4.8.23b ORLAN, Seventh surgery-performance, entitled *Omnipresence*, 1993 → p. 646

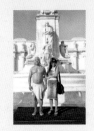

4.9.11 James Luna, *Take a Picture with a Real Indian*, 2010 → p. 655

Installations and Environments

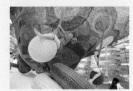

2.6.18 Toshiko Horiuchi MacAdam, *Knitted Wonder Space II*, 2009 → p. 280

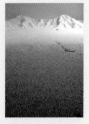

4.3.14b Motoi Yamamoto, "Labyrinth" from *Return to the Sea*, 2013 → p. 577

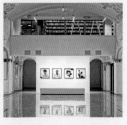

3.10.21b Theaster Gates, Stony Island Arts Bank after restoration, 2015 → p. 537

Art as Activism

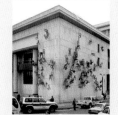

3.4.7 Doris Salcedo, *Noviembre 6 y 7*, 2002 → p. 415

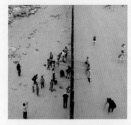

4.7.4 Ronald Rael and Virginia San Fratello, *Teeter-Totter Wall*, 2019 → p. 621

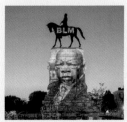

4.7.8 Dustin Klein, BLM projections on Robert E. Lee Monument, 2020 → p. 624

Your turn:
How do these artworks relate to the ideas discussed in this chapter?

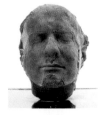

4.9.5 Marc Quinn, *Self*, 1991 → p. 651

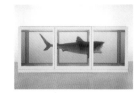

2.4.17 Damien Hirst, *The Physical Impossibility of Death …*, 1991 → p. 239

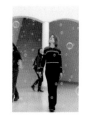

4.7.2 Teresa Margolles, *En el Aire (In the Air)*, 2003 → p. 619

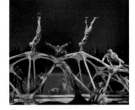

1.5.10 Cirque du Soleil performing *Totem*, 2010 → p. 109

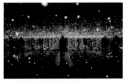

3.3.16 Yayoi Kusama, *Infinity Mirrored Room*, 2013 → p. 402

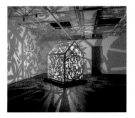

1.9.8 Quayyum Agha, *This is NOT a Refuge! 2*, 2019 → p. 153

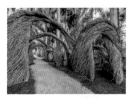

4.1.5 Patrick Dougherty, *Grand Central*, 2020 → p. 543

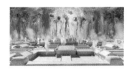

3.10.17b Cai Guo-Qiang, *Sleepwalking in the Forbidden City*, 2020 → p. 533

Part 3 History and Context

The history of art is an important aspect of the many ways in which we can understand a work. Art is not just the skillful application of design concepts and materials to produce an impressive work. Inevitably, an artwork is influenced by the time and place in which it was created. This influence is known as the context in which the art was made. In this part, as well as learning about context, you will discover how history has influenced art and how art, in turn, reflects history.

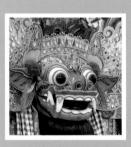

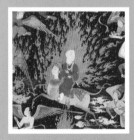

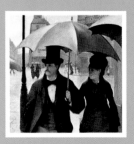

Art and Architecture

200,000 BCE

c. **73,000 BCE** *Africa:* Portable art objects made from such materials as shell
c. **65,000–c. 23,000 BCE** *Africa, Pacific Islands, Europe:* First cave paintings

c. **7000–c. 5700 BCE** *West Asia:* Çatalhöyük (modern Turkey)
c. **4000–c. 3000 BCE** *West Asia:* Incised stones rolled across clay or pressed into wax to create relief impressions
c. **3500 BCE** *West Asia and Africa:* Use of glass begins
c. **3300 BCE** *West Asia:* First written script developed in Mesopotamia
c. **3300 BCE** *Pacific Islands:* Earliest known preserved tattooed bodies in New Zealand
c. **3200–c. 1500 BCE** *Europe:* Stonehenge is built in England
c. **2580–c. 2510 BCE** *Africa:* Great Pyramids at Giza, Egypt
2500 BCE *East and South Asia:* Use of carbon ink begins in China and India
c. **2100 BCE** *West Asia:* Ziggurat of Ur is built (modern Iraq)
c. **1600–c. 1500 BCE** *Europe:* First fresco paintings, Palace of Knossos, Crete

1000 BCE

900 BCE *South America:* Chavín de Huantar (modern Peru)
800 BCE–100 CE *North America:* Great Serpent Mound (modern Ohio)
c. **700–c. 200 BCE** *Africa:* Nok-style terra-cotta sculptures made
c. **500 BCE–c. 500 CE** *South America:* Nazca lines carved into the ground (modern Peru)
c. **480–323 BCE** *Europe:* In the Greek Classical period, Polykleitos develops canon for ideal human proportions and the three architectural orders are perfected
447–432 BCE *Europe:* Parthenon built in Greece

c. **400 BCE** *Africa:* Museum of Alexandria founded in Egypt

300 BCE

3rd century BCE *Southeast Asia:* Great Stupa begun at Sanchi, india

c. **246–210 BCE** *East Asia:* Mausoleum of Qin Shi Huangdi, the first emperor of China

c. **200 BCE** *East Asia:* Printing ink on fabric first used in China
1st century BCE *Europe:* The Roman architect Vitruvius writes *Ten Books On Architecture*
72–80 CE *Europe:* Colosseum: Romans first to exploit concrete's full potential
End of 1st century CE *East Asia:* Paper invented in China

100 CE

c. **225** *Mesoamerica:* Pyramid of the Sun, Teotihuacan (modern Mexico)

244–45 *West Asia:* Dura Europos synagogue built (modern Syria)
3rd–4th century *Europe:* Catacombs of Saints Peter and Marcellinus (modern Italy)
532–35 *West Asia:* Hagia Sophia first built (modern Turkey)
7th century *East Asia:* Construction of Horyu Temple, Nara, Japan
688–691 *West Asia:* Dome of the Rock built in Jerusalem
8th and 9th centuries *Africa:* Icons in Egypt protected from destruction during iconoclastic controversy
c. **900–c. 1750** *Pacific Islands:* *Moai* heads and figures made on Rapa Nui (Easter Island)
960–1279 *East Asia:* Silkscreen printing develops in China

Politics, Society, Religion, and Philosophy

200,000 BCE

c. **200,000 years ago** *Africa:* First modern humans
c. **24,000–13,000 years ago** *North America:* First populated by humans
c. **4000–331 BCE** *West Asia:* Mesopotamian cultures include Sumerians, Akkadians, Assyrians, and Babylonians
c. **3100–332 BCE** *Africa:* Ancient Egyptian culture

c. **2700–1200 BCE** *Europe:* Minoan culture, Crete
c. **2000 BCE** *West Asia:* Judaism begins
2000 BCE–1500 CE *Mesoamerica:* Maya culture
c. **1500–c. 1050 BCE** *East Asia:* Shang Dynasty, China
c. **1500–400 BCE** *Mesoamerica:* Olmec culture
c. **1000 BCE** *Southeast Asia:* Hinduism first practiced

1000 BCE

900 BCE *South America:* Chavín culture flourishes (modern Peru)
604 BCE *East Asia:* Birth of Laozi, founder of Daoism
c. **600 BCE** *Pacific Islands:* First humans arrive in Hawaii
600–200 BCE *South America:* Paracas culture

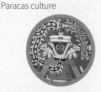

6th century–c. 280 BCE *Europe:* Etruscan culture (modern Italy)

c. **563–483 BCE** *Southeast Asia:* Life of Siddhartha Gautama (Buddha), founder of Buddhism
551–479 BCE *East Asia:* Life of Confucius, founder of Confucianism, in China
5th and 4th centuries BCE *Europe:* Lives of Greek philosophers Plato (*c.* 427–347 BCE) and Aristotle (384–322 BCE)

300 BCE

c. **268–232 BCE** *Southeast Asia:* King Ashoka reigns
221–206 BCE *East Asia:* Qin Dynasty: the first unified Chinese dynasty
206 BCE–220 CE *East Asia:* Han Dynasty, China

200 BCE–600 CE *South America:* Moche culture
27 BCE–476 CE *Europe:* Western Roman empire

c. **7–2 BCE to c. 30–36 CE** *West Asia:* Life of Jesus, the son of God for Christians

100 CE

265–420 *East Asia:* Jin Dynasty, China
306–337 *Europe:* Constantine the Great rules the Roman empire
320–550 *Southeast Asia:* Gupta period

c. **330–1453** *Europe and West Asia:* Byzantine empire
500 *Mesoamerica:* Peak of Teotihuacan culture
c. **570–632** *West Asia:* Life of Muhammad, primary messenger of Allah: beginning of Islam
800–1400 *Africa:* The Yoruba Kingdom of Ile-Ife
800–1527 *South America:* Inca culture
960–1279 *East Asia:* Song Dynasty, China

1000 CE	1600 CE	1800 CE	1900 CE	1950 CE

c. 1000–1500s Europe: Architectural styles: Romanesque (c. 1000–1150) and Gothic (c. 1150–1500s)

c. 1150–c. 1300 North America: Mesa Verde established by ancient Puebloans

12th century Southeast Asia: Angkor Wat built in Cambodia; Buddhist statues are added in the 14th century

1350–1450 Africa: Great Zimbabwe, center of Shona state in Zimbabwe, flourished

1377–1446 Europe: Life of Brunelleschi, who invents linear perspective in Florence, Italy

14th–17th centuries Europe: Renaissance art and architecture in Italy and Northern Europe

Early 15th century Europe: Woodblock printing and papermaking become common; in c. 1450 Gutenberg invents the printing press

1450–1700 Africa: Bronze plaques made in Benin, Nigeria

c. 1503–6 Europe: Leonardo da Vinci paints the *Mona Lisa*

Late 16th–early 18th century Europe: Baroque style in art and architecture

1632–43 Southeast Asia: Taj Mahal is built in Agra, India

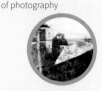

1678–84 Europe: Construction of palace of Versailles in France

18th century Europe: Rococo style in art and architecture

Late 18th–early 19th century Europe and North America: Neoclassical style in art and architecture; Thomas Jefferson designs Rotunda, U. of Virginia

1796 Europe: In Germany, Senefelder invents lithography

1799 Africa: Discovery of the Rosetta Stone, leading to the translation of Egyptian hieroglyphs

18th–19th centuries East Asia: *Ukiyo-e* woodblock printing flourished in Japan

19th century Europe and North America: In architecture, iron, steel, and concrete more commonly used

Early 19th century Europe: Romanticism in art and literature

1805 North America: Pennsylvania Academy of the Fine Arts is the first museum (and arts school) in the US

1820s–1830s Europe: Invention of photography

Mid-19th century Europe: Realism in art

1874–86 Europe: Impressionism

1880s–1905 Europe: Post-Impressionism

Late 19th century–1914 Europe: *Fin de siècle* and Art Nouveau in art and architecture

1890–91 North America: Wainwright Building in St. Louis is one of the world's first skyscrapers

1894 North America: Thomas Edison and William Dickson create one of the first American movies

Early 20th century Europe: Expressionist, Fauvist, and Cubist styles

c. 1907 Africa: World's largest mud-brick structure: latest version of the Great Mosque, Djenné, Mali

1910s–1930s Europe: Art movements include Dada, Surrealism, Futurism, De Stijl, and Suprematism

1911 Europe: The *Mona Lisa* is stolen from the Louvre

1911 Mesoamerica: Mexican Revolution; Mural Renaissance in the 1920s–30s

1913 North America: Armory Show brings European Modernist art to New York

c. 1919–33 Europe: Bauhaus school in Germany promotes Modernism

1922 Africa: King Tutankhamun's tomb is discovered in Egypt by archaeologist Howard Carter

1920s–1930s North America: The Harlem Renaissance

1930s–1950s Europe and North America: Modernist architecture pioneered by Mies van der Rohe, Le Corbusier, and Lloyd Wright

1937 Europe: Nazis hold Degenerate Art exhibition in Germany; many artworks stolen during World War II

1939 North America: *The Wizard of Oz* is one of the first popular color movies

1950s North America: Acrylic paint comes into wide use

1950s North America: Abstract Expressionist and Pop art styles pioneered

1960s Worldwide: Contemporary period in art begins: Minimalism and Conceptual art; performance art; earthworks; and Postmodernism in art and architecture

1960s North America: Black Arts movement begins

1980s North America and East Asia: Development of digital camera

1990 North America: NAGPRA laws legislate the repatriation of artifacts and sacred remains

2010 West Asia: World's tallest building (to date) completed in Dubai, UAE

2011 East Asia: Ai Weiwei arrested by Chinese government and imprisoned for 81 days

2018 North America: Amy Sherald paints portrait of US First Lady Michelle Obama

2019–20 North America: Over 100 Confederate monuments removed from their public locations in the US

1054 Europe: Christian Church splits in two: Greek Orthodox in the east and Roman Catholic in the west

1066 Europe: Battle of Hastings

12th century East Asia: beginning of Zen Buddhism in Japan

1368–1644 East Asia: Ming Dynasty, China

15th century Europe: Philosophy of Humanism

1400– c. 1530 Mesoamerica: Aztec culture

1450–1700 Africa: Kingdom of Benin (modern Nigeria) at its height

1453 Europe/West Asia: Ottomans take control of Constantinople: end of the Byzantine empire

Late 15th century North and South America: Arrival of Europeans

1517 Europe: Protestant Reformation begins, led by Martin Luther

1526–mid-19th century South Asia: Mughal empire

1527 Europe: Sack of Rome

1545–1648 Europe: Catholic Counter-Reformation

18th–19th century Europe: The Enlightenment period

1760–c. 1840 Europe: Industrial Revolution

1776 North America: Declaration of Independence in the US

1789 Europe: French Revolution

1789 North America: George Washington is first US president

1791 Africa: beginning of the Haitian Revolution

1828–1910 North America: Industrial Revolution

1830, 1848 Europe: Revolutions in France

1833 Europe: The UK abolishes enslavement

1856–1939 Europe: Life of Sigmund Freud, Austrian founder of psychoanalysis

1848 Europe: The Communist Manifesto published by Marx and Engels

1861–65 North America: American Civil War

1863 North America: Abraham Lincoln's Emancipation Proclamation frees enslaved people in the US

1865 North America: Abolition of enslavement in the US

1875–1961 Europe: Life of Carl Jung, Swiss founder of analytical psychology

1884–85 Europe and Africa: Berlin Conference assigns African territories to European powers

1914–18 Worldwide: World War I

1918 Europe and North America: Women partially gain the right to vote in Britain; and in the US in 1920

1929 North America: Great Depression; Works Progress Administration begins

1937 Europe: General Franco approves aerial attack of small town of Guernica, Spain

1939–45 Worldwide: World War II

c. 1947–91 Worldwide: Cold War

1948–91 Africa: Apartheid in South Africa segregates and discriminates against Black residents

1949 East Asia: Mao Zedong leads Communist Party to power in China

1955–68 North America: Civil Rights movement

1955–75 Southeast Asia: Vietnam War

1960s onward Worldwide: Feminist and LGBTQ+ movements promote gender and sexual equality

1966–76 East Asia: Cultural Revolution in China

1978–79 West Asia: Iranian Revolution

1989 East Asia: More than 100,000 people gather in Tiananmen Square, China to protest government corruption

2001 North America: World Trade Center attack, September 11, New York City

2010–2013 Africa and West Asia: Arab Spring uprisings

2013–present Worldwide: Black Lives Matter movement

2018 North America: Kehinde Wiley is the first Black painter to paint a presidential portrait, that of Barack Obama

2021 Europe and Africa: Germany begins negotiations to return looted Benin bronzes to Nigeria

3.1
Art of the Prehistoric and Ancient Mediterranean

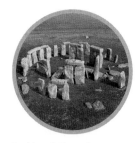

Prehistoric Stonehenge, made of monumental stones, functioned as a calendar: → see **4.1.7**, p. 544

Human prehistory is the long period during which humans and their ancestors developed societies for which no written record has been found. We know about the achievements of these early people from the material traces they left behind. In Europe, this takes us back thousands of years—and on the African continent, even 2.5 million years, if we include tools. Ancient people survived by gathering wild plants and hunting, and some found time to produce what we admire today as prehistoric art. Prehistoric art has been discovered in the Mediterranean region from as early as around 65,000 BCE.

As humans formed larger communities, the Mediterranean region—including West Asia

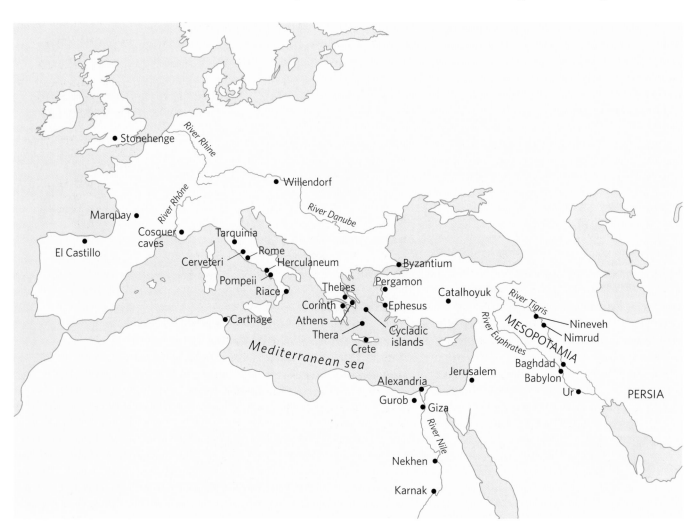

3.1.1 Map of prehistoric Europe and the ancient Mediterranean

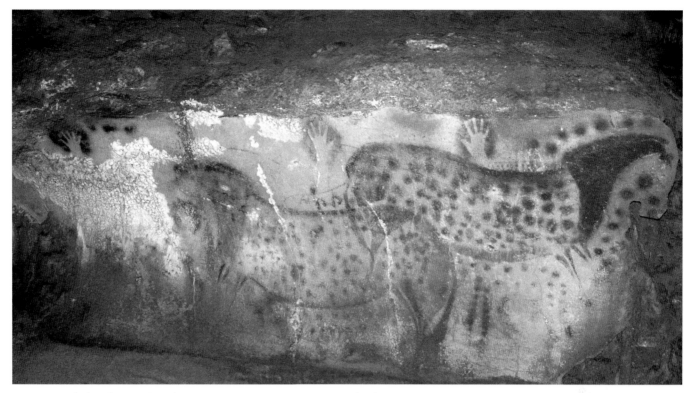

3.1.2 Cave paintings from Pech Merle cave, France, *c.* 23,000 BCE. Pigment with saliva.

(a region including present-day Turkey, Israel, Jordan, Syria, Iran, Iraq, and the countries on the Arabian peninsula), northern Africa, and southern Europe—flourished as an area of trade (**3.1.1**). The region thrived because it was surrounded by bodies of water; frequently, the most powerful were those who controlled access to the seas. Here, a succession of cultures arose that continue to shape the ways we live, even in the twenty-first century. It was here that humans invented agriculture, started to live in urban settlements, and eventually planned cities; it was here that people invented writing, and produced works of art we still regard as great wonders of the world. The achievements of these people remain evident in our own lives. For example, farmers who raise wheat crops today can do so because other farmers domesticated wheat and barley nearly 10,000 years ago.

Some of these achievements were matched independently elsewhere, for example in Asia and the Americas. This chapter first tells the story of the sculptures, cave paintings, and palaces made by prehistoric Europeans. Then it looks at the emergence of early cultures in West Asia and the rise of a great society in Egypt. Last we will study the powerful societies of ancient Greece and Rome and the beautiful sculptures, paintings, and buildings they produced.

Prehistoric Art in Europe and the Mediterranean

As long as 65,000 years ago, prehistoric people painted the interiors of caves; and sculptures still survive from around 40,000 years ago. Not surprisingly, such art is preoccupied with the basics of life: procreation and sources of food. Prehistoric artworks are particularly important records of the lives of our early ancestors because written records of these cultures do not exist. Often, what we know about their lives is based upon archaeological finds, and our modern interpretations of these discoveries.

The earliest found paintings were made on the walls of caves. The Pech Merle cave in France (**3.1.2**) shows examples of the two most common **subjects** used in cave paintings: hands and animals. To create these paintings, humans blew the **pigment** (made from natural materials, such as like charcoal or red **ocher**) through something like a hollow bone or a reed to create a spray for painting. In the example shown here, they created reverse **stencils** by blowing paint around hands (to judge from their size, these were probably female) that were placed on the rock wall. The same method was used to create the dots and outlines of thehorses.

The most common type of prehistoric artworks found throughout the world are small

Subject, subject matter: the person, object, or space depicted in a work of art

Pigment: the colored material used in paints. Often made from finely ground minerals

Ocher: a pigment found in nature containing hydrated iron oxide

Stencil: a perforated template allowing ink or paint to pass through to print a design

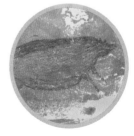

Prehistoric cave paintings have been found around the world, including in Indonesia:
→ see **2.2.1**, p. 195

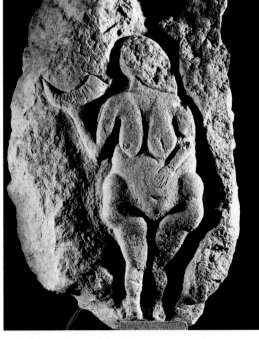

3.1.3 Venus of Laussel, found in Marquay, Dordogne, France, *c.* 23,000 BCE. Low relief on limestone block, height 18⅛″. Musée d'Aquitaine, Bordeaux, France

female sculptures. Like other similar figurines the Venus of Laussel (**3.1.3**) shows a faceless woman with large breasts, belly, and vulva. One possible interpretation suggests that such figurines were fertility symbols; they may also have been a general symbol of womanhood. Made approximately 25,000 years ago, the figure was carved into limestone and originally painted with red ocher. The carving is unique in that the woman holds a horn-shaped object that has thirteen short lines carved on it, which has led scholars to develop different opinions about the work. For example, the figure may represent a **shaman** and the horn could have been used for a ritual designed to ensure a

successful hunt, or as a musical instrument. Other experts have suggested the horn may be a phallic symbol, emphasizing the woman's role in procreation. Further, as the number thirteen corresponds to the number of menstrual cycles a woman may have in a year, some scholars have speculated that the horn may symbolize a waning crescent moon, which, with the number of stripes, could be intended to represent a woman's monthly cycle.

On the Cycladic Islands, now part of present-day Greece, human figures carved out of white marble have been found, many of them at grave sites (**3.1.4**). Cycladic sculptures of females far outnumber those of males. Curiously, however, the female Cycladic figures look similar to their male counterparts, with barely noticeable breasts and only minimal anatomical detail. The figures usually have a long head and protruding nose; they are generic renderings of females, rather than individual portraits. Originally, these figures were painted in black, red, and blue to show some facial details, body ornamentation, and probably jewelry. Little is known about the Cycladic culture because it did not have a written language, but these expressive, **geometric** figures are some of the most intriguing in the history of art.

Other significant early works of art from the Mediterranean region come from Çatalhöyük, Turkey. Here, fragments of wall paintings remain from a large building complex that stood between *c.* 7000 and 5700 BCE. Inhabitants of the Çatalhöyük settlements lived in mud-brick homes, which they entered from the rooftops; there was no organized street system. The deceased were buried beneath the floors, and sometimes homes were demolished

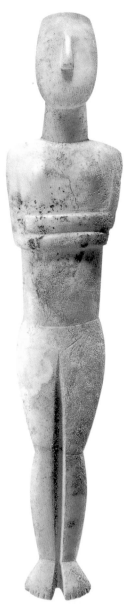

3.1.4 Attributed to the Steiner Master, reclining female figure of the Late Spedos variety, Cyclades, 2500–2400 BCE. Island marble, height 23⅜″. The J. Paul Getty Museum, Villa Collection, Malibu, California

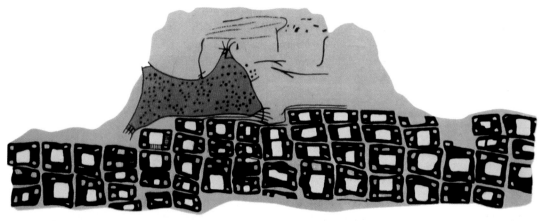

3.1.5 Landscape with erupting volcano, detail of watercolor copy of a wall painting from Level VII, Çatalhöyük, Turkey, *c.* 6150 BCE. Wall painting: Ankara Museum of Anatolian Civilizations, Turkey. Watercolor copy: Private collection

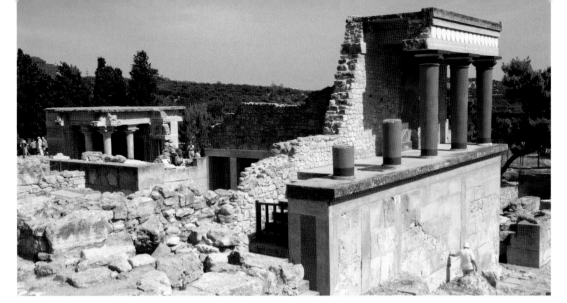

3.1.6 Ruins of the Palace of Knossos, Crete, Greece, c. 1700–1400 BCE. From 1900, parts of the palace were reconstructed, as seen here

Fresco: a technique in which the artist paints onto freshly applied plaster. From the Italian *fresco*, "fresh"

to create a higher base from which to build new ones. More than twelve layers of building have been discovered at the site.

While many paintings from Çatalhöyük depict humans and animals (often in hunting scenes), one intriguing but faint wall painting re-creates the design of the town (reproduced here in a watercolor copy for ease of reading), with rectangular houses closely aligned side by side (**3.1.5**). In the background is the double-peaked volcano, Hasan Da, which in reality is 8 miles away. The volcano appears to be erupting; lava falls in droplets down the mountain, and smoke fills the sky. Scholars have not determined an exact volcanic eruption that could be the one referred to in this image: this makes it possibly the first "pure" landscape (a picture of a setting in its own right, without life and narrative) ever created in the history of mankind.

Just over 100 miles south of the Cyclades and dating from a little later in time, there is ample archaeological evidence of a sophisticated and complex society, the Minoan, on the island of Crete from about 2700 to about 1200 BCE. Minoan cities, with their powerful fleets and their location at the hub of the eastern Mediterranean, grew wealthy as centers of trade. Some of our written evidence of Minoan culture comes from Greek legend. King Minos was the stepfather of the Minotaur: a ferocious creature with the body of a man and the head of a bull, trapped in a labyrinth. The powerful Minos required the Athenians to send seven young men and seven young women as tribute each year to satisfy the Minotaur's appetite.

The Minoans built palaces in the center of their cities, the largest being King Minos's Palace of Knossos (**3.1.6**). This complex—up to five stories high—was a maze of some 1,300 rooms, corridors, and courtyards. These spaces were used for governmental and ceremonial functions, as accommodation for the king's family and their servants, as large storerooms, and even as a theater. The palace complex was so full of twists and turns that it is easy to see how the Greeks developed the myth about a labyrinth.

The importance of bulls in Minoan culture can be seen from their inclusion in the Minotaur myth and in much of Minoan art. Several sculptures and **frescoes** with scenes of bulls were found throughout the Palace of Knossos, including the lively *Bull-Leapers* (**3.1.7**). In this scene, three young acrobats are jumping a spirited bull. The boy flips over the beast, while a figure that some scholars identify, due

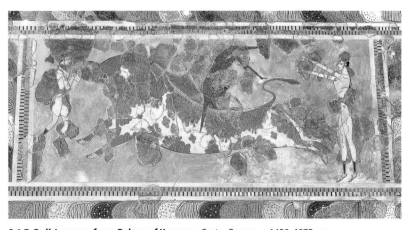

3.1.7 *Bull-Leapers*, from Palace of Knossos, Crete, Greece, c. 1450–1375 BCE. Archaeological Museum, Heraklion, Crete, Greece

to its lighter skin, as a young woman, prepares to take the next leap. The girl on the right has apparently just landed. The creature is depicted with great energy, yet the Cretans seem able to match it. Bull-leaping, boxing, and acrobatic scenes were common subjects in Minoan art, evidence of an athletic people; these activities may have been for pleasure, or for more ritualistic ceremonies.

Minoan society suffered a variety of upheavals, both natural and human-made, from around 1500 BCE, when, as some believe, a volcanic eruption on the nearby island of Thera created a huge tidal wave that destroyed the Minoans' cities and fleets. Some decades later, Mycenaean invaders from mainland Greece overran Crete, taking over such palace sites as Knossos.

Mesopotamia

Mesopotamia, from the Greek for "the land between the rivers" (a reference to the Tigris and Euphrates rivers), includes the regions of present-day Iraq and portions of Syria, Turkey, and Iran. Ancient Mesopotamia has historically been called the "Cradle of Civilization," for it was here that urban centers first developed as early as 4000 BCE.

The earliest forms of writing, using pictograms, also developed in Mesopotamia in the fourth millennium BCE. Here too, in the rich land of the Fertile Crescent, complex irrigation systems enabled people to raise plentiful crops. Mesopotamia was frequently conquered by rulers desiring the wealth of its farmland. Amongst the many cultures that battled for control of the region were the Sumerians, Akkadians, Assyrians, and Babylonians.

Sumerians

The Sumerian culture was the first great power in Mesopotamia. By the third millennium BCE, under the Sumerians, a writing system evolved from pictograms: it was called cuneiform, and consisted of wedge-shaped symbols drawn with a reed pen in soft clay. The Sumerians also seem to have invented the wheel, which was probably first used to help potters make circular pots. The people of Mesopotamia worshiped many gods and goddesses (a practice known as **polytheism**) in temples or shrines located on huge **ziggurats**—stepped pyramid structures made of baked and unbaked mud bricks—

which they constructed in the centers of their communities.

Ur was an important city of Sumer, and the treasures found at its Royal Cemetery reveal the wealth of the Sumerian elite. Buried with the bodies were gold jewelry and daggers inlaid with **lapis lazuli**. Whether the dead were royalty or religious leaders is unknown, but the chariots, weapons, and musical instruments buried with them indicate their importance. Servants and soldiers were also interred with their leaders, perhaps intended to protect and serve them in the afterlife.

The artists of Sumer excelled in the art of inlaying ivory and shell in wood, as seen in the Standard of Ur found in the Royal Cemetery of Ur (**3.1.8a** and **b**). When it was first discovered, scholars thought it must have been carried on the end of a pole, like a standard, but there is no real evidence for this. The wooden box is only 8 in. high and is decorated with inlaid pieces of shell, lapis lazuli, and red limestone. One side of the box shows war scenes (**3.1.8a**), while the other shows life during times of peace (**3.1.8b**). Each side is divided into three sections, known as **registers**. The bottom register of the war

Polytheism: the worship of more than one god or goddess

Ziggurat: a Mesopotamian stepped tower, roughly pyramid-shaped, that diminishes in size toward a platform summit

Lapis lazuli: a bright-blue semiprecious stone containing sodium aluminum silicate and sulphur

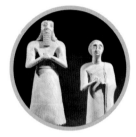

Sumerians created small figures that embodied themselves as individuals praying to the gods:
→ see **1.10.5**, p. 163

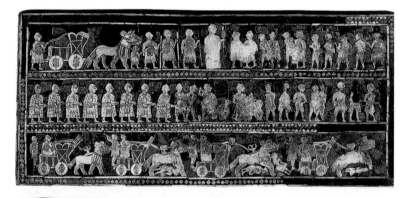

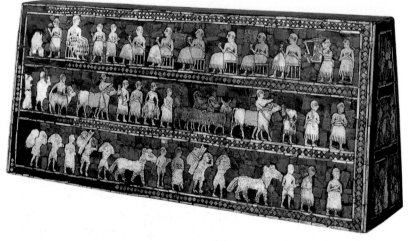

3.1.8a (top) and **3.1.8b** (above) **Standard of Ur**, c. 2600–2400 BCE. Wood inlaid with shell, lapis lazuli, and red limestone, 7⅞ × 18½". British Museum, London, England

Register: one of two or more horizontal sections into which a space is divided in order to depict the episodes of a story

Hierarchical scale: the use of size to denote the relative importance of subjects in an artwork

Relief: a sculpture that projects from a flat surface

side shows chariots running over the bodies of the enemy. The middle register shows soldiers (from left to right) marching, shaming their enemies by stripping them of their clothing, and forcing them to continue walking. In the center of the top register is the ruler. His larger size indicates his importance, a convention known as **hierarchical scale**. His status is reinforced by the fact that all the surrounding people are facing him. He has stepped out of his chariot while prisoners are brought before him. On the peace side, animals, fish, and other foods are brought to a banquet where seated figures drink, while a musician playing a lyre entertains them. The standard is a fine example of narrative art and a source of evidence about what food the Sumerians ate, their clothing and weapons, their musical instruments, and their success in war.

Akkadians

The next Mesopotamian empire was founded by the Akkadian king Sargon, who ruled between *c.* 2334 and 2279 BCE. He conquered the Sumerian city-states. Before King Sargon, most rulers of Mesopotamia were believed to be merely representatives of the gods on Earth. The Akkadian rulers who followed Sargon, however, elevated themselves to divine status. The bronze, lifesized Akkadian Head (**3.1.9**) is the portrait of a great king, probably Sargon's grandson Naram-Sin (*c.* 2254–2218 BCE). The figure's expression is one of proud majesty. The artist paid particular attention to the texture and patterning of the hair on the ruler's beard, eyebrows, and head. The eye sockets have been damaged from violent gouging, either to remove the materials (probably shells or lapis lazuli) used to make the eyes, or to make the figure's presence less powerful. The head was originally discovered in Nineveh in northern Iraq, and was one of the many objects missing after the looting of the National Museum of Iraq in Baghdad in 2003 during the US invasion of Iraq. More than 15,000 artifacts were stolen, of which fewer than half have been recovered—this Akkadian head being one of them.

Assyrians

The Assyrians, who had intermittently enjoyed considerable power in the second millennium BCE, ruled much of Mesopotamia during the Neo-Assyrian period (883–612 BCE). The first great Assyrian king, Ashurnasirpal II (who ruled between 883 and 859 BCE), used enslaved laborers to build the large city of Nimrud (near modern Mosul, Iraq), which became the capital of Assyria.

Ashurnasirpal II's grand palace was covered with **relief** sculptures of battles, hunting scenes, and religious rituals. An accompanying inscription refers to guardian figures (called *lamassu*) at gateways and entrances throughout the palace: "Beasts of the mountains and the seas, which I had fashioned out of white limestone and alabaster, I had set up in its gates. I made it [the palace] fittingly imposing."

These figures were meant to show the fearsome power of the Assyrian ruler and the authority given to him by the gods (**3.1.10**). Almost twice as tall as a human, this lamassu combines the head of a man with the body and strength of a lion, and the wings and all-seeing eyes of an eagle. The horned cap signifies

3.1.9 Head of an Akkadian ruler, *c.* 2300–2200 BCE. Bronze, height 15″. National Museum of Iraq, Baghdad

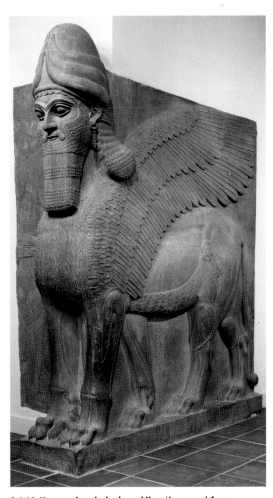

3.1.10 Human-headed winged lion (*lamassu*) from a gateway in Ashurnasirpal II's palace in Nimrud, Mesopotamia, Neo-Assyrian, 883–859 BCE. Alabaster (gypsum), height 10′3½″. Metropolitan Museum of Art, New York

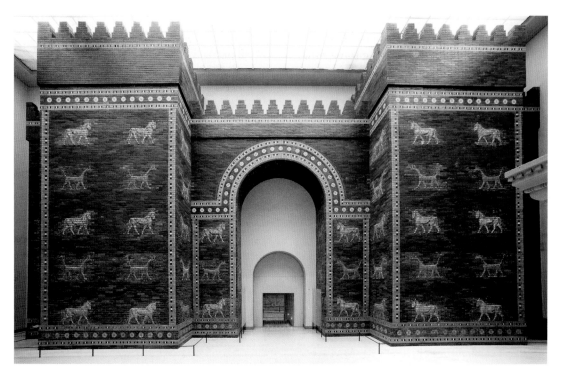

3.1.11 Ishtar Gate from Babylon (Iraq), reign of Nebuchadnezzar II (602–562 BCE). Colored glazed terra-cotta tiles, 48'4" × 51'6" × 14'3¾". Vorderasiatisches Museum, Staatliche Museen, Berlin, Germany

divinity, representing the gods' support and protection of the rulers of Assyria. Lamassu often have five legs, so they appear to be standing still when viewed from the front, and striding forward when seen from the side. The lion is an animal that is often associated with kingship, and at this time in this society, only Assyrian kings were considered powerful enough to protect the people from the lions that roamed the areas outside the cities—and only kings were allowed to hunt the creatures. Some of the reliefs decorating Ashurnasirpal II's palace show the king hunting lions.

Babylonians

In the late seventh century BCE, the Babylonians defeated the Assyrians and re-emerged as a powerful force in Mesopotamia. The ruler Nebuchadnezzar II (605–562 BCE) built a grand palace famous for its Hanging Gardens. Around the city, he built fortified walls with eight gateways. The dramatic Ishtar Gate was the main entrance to the streets and temples of Babylon (**3.1.11**). This enormous ceremonial entrance was actually two arched gates, the shorter of which (shown here) stood 47 ft. high. Golden reliefs of animals that symbolize Babylonian gods project out from a background of blue glazed bricks. A Processional Way ran through the Ishtar Gate, leading to the ziggurat

on the south side of the city, which some believe to be the inspiration for the Bible's Old Testament story of the Tower of Babel, in which God, after seeing that humans were trying to build a structure to heaven, spreads them throughout the world and takes away their common language. Walls on either side of the Processional Way were covered with 120 glazed reliefs of lions (60 on each side), symbols of the goddess Ishtar. The Ishtar Gate was taken to Germany in pieces in the early twentieth century and is now reconstructed at the Pergamon Museum in Berlin.

Ancient Egypt

At the time of the pharaohs, or Egyptian rulers, the African land of Egypt traded with groups throughout the Mediterranean, and thus many of the ideas and techniques invented by Egyptian artists were taken up by Mediterranean cultures. Indeed, some thousands of years after they were made, the ancient Egyptians' extraordinary artistic and architectural achievements continue to be a source of wonder and astonishment worldwide.

We know so much about Egyptian art and culture largely because we can translate **hieroglyphs**, the written language of the ancient Egyptians. This was made possible in 1799 through the discovery of the Rosetta

Stone (**3.1.12**), which was found by the French army during Napoleon's invasion of Egypt. The lettering on the stone is dated to 196 BCE and repeats the decrees of Ptolemy V, the Greek ruler of Egypt, in three separate forms of writing. Hieroglyphic and Demotic were different written forms of the Egyptian spoken language; Greek was familiar to many scholars and was the key to deciphering the other two. Hieroglyphs are often images of recognizable objects, but the image can represent the object itself, an idea, or even just a sound associated with that object. In 1822 Frenchman Jean-François Champollion was finally able to claim that, thanks to studying the Rosetta Stone, he understood the meaning of the complex hieroglyphic writing of the ancient Egyptians.

It is perhaps appropriate that our fascination with Egyptian art should be so long-lasting when so much of early Egyptian culture focused on eternity and the afterlife. The Egyptians believed that their pharaohs ruled with the authority of gods, and as a result, the Egyptian people took great care to ensure that, when a pharaoh died, his needs in the afterlife—where it was believed a person would require everything they had needed when living—would be met. So in the pharaohs' tombs were buried furniture, weapons, jewelry, and food. Family and servants were even killed to accompany the dead pharaohs, although as time went on the Egyptians came to believe that art portraying these objects and people would be enough.

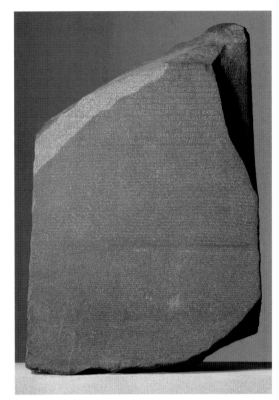

3.1.12 The Rosetta Stone, from Fort St Julien, el-Rashid (Rosetta), Egypt, 196 BCE. Granodiorite stone, 44¼ × 29⅞ × 11¼". British Museum, London, England

The great investment of time, labor, and wealth that was involved in creating the pyramids demonstrates further the importance the Egyptians placed on the afterlife. The three **pyramids** at Giza (**3.1.13**) were built to house the tombs of three Egyptian pharaohs: Khufu, his son Khafre, and Menkaure, son of Khafre. Construction on Khufu's pyramid, the largest

Hieroglyph: a written language involving sacred characters that may be pictures as well as letters or signifiers of sounds

Pyramid: an ancient structure, usually massive in scale, consisting of a square base with four sides that meet at a point or apex with each side forming a triangular shape

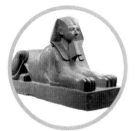

Around 1,000 years after the Great Pyramids were built, the female leader Hatshepsut ruled Egypt. To underline the legitimacy of her rule, she presented herself as a sphinx:
→ see **4.9.13**, p. 657

3.1.13 Pyramids at Giza, **Egypt**: from left to right, the pyramids of Khufu (*c.* 2580–2560 BCE), Khafre (*c.* 2570 BCE), and Menkaure (*c.* 2510 BCE)

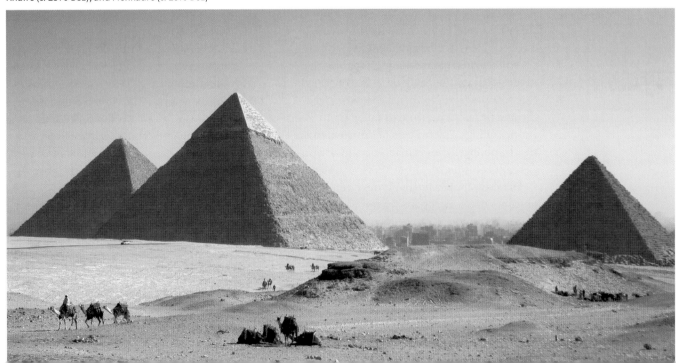

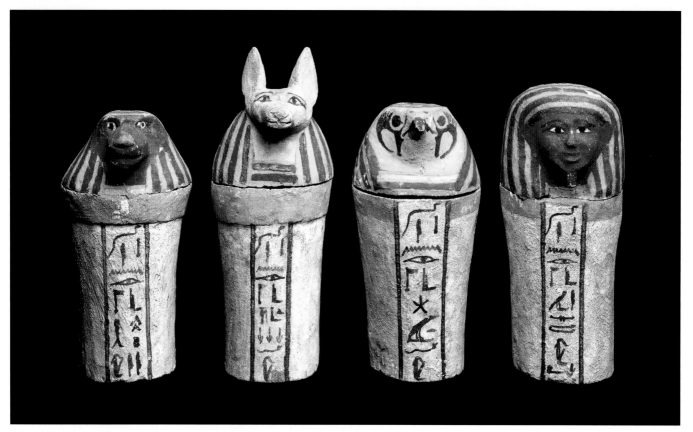

3.1.14 Painted wooden canopic jars, *c.* 700 BCE (25th Dynasty). Painted sycamore fig wood, height 12¼".
British Museum, London, England

of the three at 481 ft. high and 750 ft. long per side, began about 2551 BCE, and all three were completed over three generations. The sides of each pyramid are precisely the same length and all are placed precisely at the **cardinal points**, revealing the Egyptians' mastery of engineering and mathematics.

The pyramids were built of carefully stacked stones clad in white limestone. The pyramid of Khufu contains about 2,300,000 blocks of stone that have been calculated to weigh on average 2.5 tons each. The methods used by the Egyptians to move such massive stones are still debated today, although scholars have suggested that they probably used the River Nile for transportation, then either dragged the stones across the sand or rolled them over a series of logs. Once the stones made it to the site, tumbling, systems of levers, and ramps were probably used.

We know quite a bit about the burial practices of the Egyptians from the hieroglyphs written on the objects buried with the dead. When a pharaoh died, in order to preserve the body for its afterlife, it was mummified—a process that took several months. Mummification involved the removal

of some of the major organs, among them the liver, lungs, intestines, and stomach. The heart was left inside the body; Egyptians believed it to be the organ of thought and therefore necessary for the body to exist in the afterlife. The brain was deemed to be of no value and was removed through the nostrils. Canopic jars, such as the ones shown here (**3.1.14**), each only 12 in. high, were designed so that each one would hold an organ of the deceased. The hieroglyphic inscription painted down the vertical band on the front of each canopic jar identifies the figure it portrays and the organ it was meant to protect. Each jar represents one of the sons of the god Horus, who protects the organ contained within: the baboon-faced Hapy guards the lungs; the jackal-headed Duamutef guards the stomach; the falcon-headed Qebhsenuef guards the intestines; and the human-looking Imsety guards the liver. Once the organs were removed, the body was then soaked in a salt preservative called natron (a hydrated carbonate of sodium, found on some lake borders) for forty days and was finally wrapped in linen. An elaborate funerary mask was placed upon the face of the pharaoh, who was then buried inside layers of **sarcophagi**.

Cardinal points: North, South, East, and West

These complex burials were meant to protect the treasure and life force, or *ka*, of the buried.

Connected to Khafre's pyramid, the second largest, is an underground walkway that links to Khafre's temple. Next to the temple is the colossal stone sculpture known as the Great Sphinx, a mythical creature with the body of a lion and the head of a human ruler. As in Assyrian culture, the image of the lion was in part an expression of royal power, but for the Egyptians it was also a symbol of the sun god, Re, who was believed to carry away the dead in his boat to their afterlife. One theory is that the pyramids themselves may also have been seen to represent Re; for when the sun could be seen at the apex of a pyramid, the pyramid glistened and reflected the light of the sun. According to this theory, the corners of the pyramid extended the rays of the sun, and thus represented a ladder for the pharaoh to ascend to the afterlife. The funerary temples of these three pharaohs were placed on the east side of the pyramids, to symbolize that, just as the sun rises again in the east, they would be reborn into the afterlife.

Image **3.1.15** shows a statue of the pharaoh Khafre, which was found in the pharaoh's temple. When Khafre died, his body was taken to his temple and mummified before being taken to his pyramid. In this statue, Khafre and the chair in which he sits have been carved from a single block of hard stone called diorite. He seems to sit stiffly, as if attached to his throne. Egyptian sculptures portrayed people with gracefully proportioned bodies, but they only subtly suggested movement, in this case by showing one hand clenched in a fist. To signify the pharaoh's importance, the powerful sky god Horus, symbolized as a falcon, perches on the throne behind his head. In Egyptian belief, Khafre's statue provides a place for his *ka* to rest during the afterlife. In fact, in Egyptian writing, "sculptor" translates as "he who keeps alive."

Ancient Egypt was generally a polytheistic culture. However, the ruler Akhenaten, who ruled in the fourteenth century BCE, was unique in that he introduced worship centered on only one god: Aten, the disk of the sun. In one family portrait, Akhenaten is seated opposite Queen Nefertiti as he holds his eldest daughter lovingly in his arms (**3.1.16**). Nefertiti, with one child on her lap and one on her shoulder, is only slightly smaller in size than her husband. Some historians believe that Nefertiti ruled

Sarcophagus (plural **sarcophagi**): a coffin (usually made of stone or baked clay)

Ka: in Egyptian belief, the spirit of a person that leaves the body upon death and travels to the afterlife

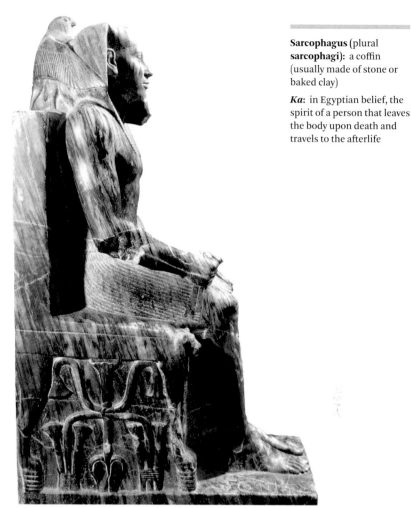

3.1.15 Khafre with the falcon god Horus embracing the back of his head, *c.* 2500 BCE. Diorite, height 5′6⅛″. Cairo Museum, Egypt

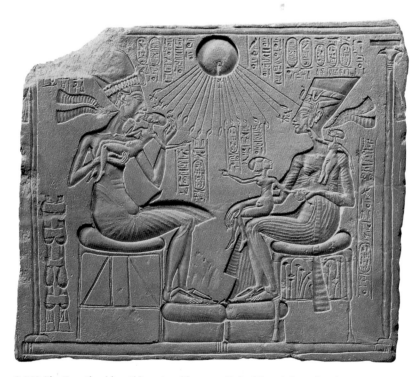

3.1.16 The Egyptian king Akhenaten, his queen Nefertiti, and three daughters, *c.* 1353–1335 BCE. Limestone, height 12¼″. Aegyptisches Museum, Staatliche Museen, Berlin, Germany

Perspectives On Art: Zahi Hawass
The Golden Mask of King Tutankhamun

Zahi Hawass is an Egyptian archaeologist and was formerly Secretary General of the Supreme Council of Antiquities. Amongst his responsibilities was the care of the fabulous treasures of King Tutankhamun, *discovered by the English archaeologist Howard Carter in 1922. Dr. Hawass is one of the few people to have studied the famous mask of the king up close. Here he describes how the mask was made.*

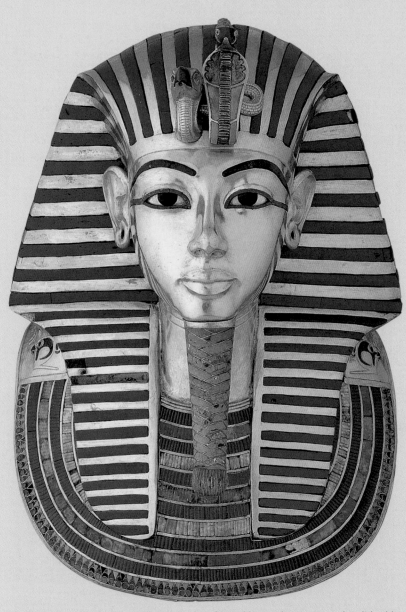

3.1.17 Funerary mask of Tutankhamun, reign of Tutankhamun (1333–1323 BCE). Solid gold, semiprecious stones, quartz, and vitreous paste, height 21¼". Cairo Museum, Egypt

Whenever a television program wants to interview me about the golden king, I go directly to the mask (**3.1.17**). While the film crew is setting up the cameras, I have a chance to look again at the mask and I always discover something new. Each time, its beauty makes my heart tremble.

This spectacular mask represents an idealized portrait of the king. Intrinsically beautiful owing to the precious materials and masterful workmanship that went into its creation, it was also an essential item of the royal burial equipment, serving as an image that the soul could enter and occupy during the afterlife if something happened to the body.

The artisans who crafted this masterpiece began by hammering together two thick sheets of gold, thought by the ancient Egyptians to echo the flesh of the gods. They then shaped this metal into the likeness of the king wearing the striped nemes headcloth, using inlays of semiprecious stones and colored glass to add color and detail. The whites of the eyes were inlaid with quartz, and obsidian was used for the pupils. Red paint was lightly brushed into the corners of the eyes, subtly increasing their realism.

The vulture and cobra adorning the king's brow, images of the protective goddesses of Upper and Lower Egypt respectively, were made of solid gold with inlays of lapis lazuli, carnelian, **faience**, and glass. The long curled beard on the king's chin, emblematic of divinity, is made of blue glass laid into a golden framework.

On the shoulders and the back of the mask is a magical text that refers to the different parts of the body and mask, and their connection to particular gods or goddesses. This served to protect the king's body and render it functional for the afterlife.

Faience: quartz or sand, ground and heated to create a shiny, glasslike material

the kingdom jointly with Akhenaten. The adults and three daughters all have stretched bodies with swollen bellies, known as the Amarna style, which is characteristic of art during Akhenaten's rule. The sun is carved more deeply than anything else in the **sunken relief**, which signifies visually its importance as a god. Its rays emanate toward the figures, suggesting that the sun god has brought great joy to the royal family. The flames at the end of the rays are small hands, some holding an *ankh*, the character that symbolizes life in ancient Egyptian writing. Akhenaten ruled for 17 years; shortly after his death, his son Tutankhamun ruled as a child, and polytheism was restored. In 1922, the revelation of the extraordinary riches hidden within the tomb of Tutankhamun fueled renewed interest in the ancient dynastic culture (see Perspectives on Art: Zahi Hawass).

Paintings made during the time of the ancient Egyptians are rich in details that tell us about the way people lived. Wealthy people filled their tombs with paintings showing what they wished to take with them into the afterlife. The image in **3.1.18** is from the tomb-chapel of Nebamun, a "scribe and grain accountant in the granary of divine offerings" in the Temple of Amun-Re at Karnak. The hieroglyphic writing on the right identifies him and tells us that he enjoyed hunting. Nebamun is depicted hunting

several species of birds; a cat holding birds in its mouth is shown underneath his right elbow. The artist included an Egyptian boat and the rich, lush growth of the reed-like papyrus plant. This scene highlights the importance of the River Nile to the Egyptians, and how the flooding of the Nile symbolized a cycle of regeneration and new life each year, just as Egyptians believed that after death they would be reborn.

The artist depicted the figures in hierarchical scale, that is, in proportion to their importance: Nebamun is shown the largest, his wife is smaller, and their daughter is the smallest of all. Nebamun's legs are shown in profile while his torso is shown frontally, and although his face is in profile, his eye looks straight at the viewer. This method of depicting figures is known as **twisted perspective**, also called composite view.

Art of Ancient Greece

> Man is the measure of all things.
>
> (Protagoras, Greek philosopher)

The Greeks, like the societies that came before them, worshiped gods. But, as the quote from Protagoras indicates, they also valued humanity. Although their gods were portrayed as idealized and beautiful beings, they looked like humans and had some human weaknesses. The emphasis on the individual led the Greeks to practice democracy (the word means rule by the *demos*, or people), although their society did not give equal rights to women or enslaved people. Their great advances in philosophy, mathematics, and the sciences continue to influence our thinking up to the present day.

Athleticism was important in Greek culture and the Greeks held sporting contests, the origins of the modern Olympic Games, at which individuals competed for glory and money. Sculptures of men were predominantly of the nude body, shown with ideal proportions (see Stylistic Changes in the Sculpture of Ancient Greece, pp. 360–61). For the Greeks, the idealized human form represented high intellectual and moral goals. Indeed, Greek architecture was based on mathematical systems of proportion similar to those applied to the human form. Greek pride in their own physical and intellectual achievements is evident in the art they produced.

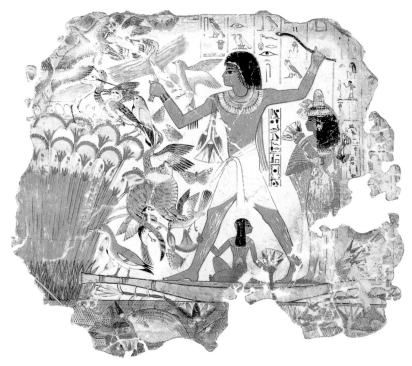

3.1.18 Fowling scene, from the tomb of Nebamun, Thebes, Egypt, 18th Dynasty, *c.* 1350 BCE. Painted plaster, 38⅝ × 8¾". British Museum, London, England

Stylistic Changes in the Sculpture of Ancient Greece

Greek sculptures are generally categorized into three types, referring to both the date of their making and to their style. The *Kouros* (**3.1.19**), *Doryphoros* (**3.1.20**), and *Laocoön and His Sons* (**3.1.21**) are all **freestanding** male nudes and exemplify characteristics of these three styles: **Archaic**, **Classical**, and **Hellenistic**.

	Kouros (male youth)	Doryphoros (Spear Bearer) by Polykleitos	Laocoön and His Sons
Style	Archaic, c. 620–480 BCE	Classical, c. 480–323 BCE	Hellenistic, c. 323–100 BCE
Medium	marble	marble Roman copy (original was bronze)	marble
Size	6'4"	6'6"	6'½"
Characteristics of Style	• Nude, muscular, youthful • Slight smile known as "archaic smile" • Long hair and hairless face represent youth • Attention given to patterned, long hair • Static and **symmetrical** except for one foot forward • Unlike Egyptian sculptures, stone is removed to show space between the arms and legs suggesting life and movement	• Idealized proportions to convey perfection • Nude, more muscular than archaic • Hair is short and carved with a linear pattern • **Contrapposto** – hip shifts to the side while opposing arm is raised, creating a natural, lifelike stance • Influential for Renaissance and Neoclassical artists	• Idealized bodies with enhanced muscularization • Beard suggesting wisdom rather than youth (older figures often shown in Hellenistic works) • Dramatic subject matter and heightened emotion, as seen in poses and facial expressions • Asymmetrical composition conveying complexity of subject matter • Dynamic movement using diagonals and curving lines • Influential for Mannerist and Baroque artists
Purpose	• Grave marker for a man named Kroisos who died in battle • Other examples are offerings at sanctuaries (usually for Apollo) • Female versions (*korai*) are always clothed and functioned as offerings to female goddesses	• Polykleitos created this sculpture to exemplify his canon (or treatise), which used mathematical ratios to create a harmoniously proportioned body • Usually depicted gods or heroes to show worship and respect • Female goddesses are not depicted in the nude until the end of the Classical period	• The priest Laocoön and his sons are shown struggling in agony as they are attacked by twisting sea serpents, sent by the god Poseidon as punishment for warning the leaders of Troy not to accept the Trojan Horse • Subject matter is often more narrative, complex, physical, sensual, and dramatic than in earlier periods

Freestanding: any sculpture that stands separate from walls or other surfaces so that it can be viewed from a 360-degree range

Archaic: Greek art of the period c. 620–480 BCE

Classical: Greek art of the period c. 480–323 BCE

Hellenistic: Greek art of the period c. 323–100 BCE

Symmetrical balance: an image or shape that looks exactly (or nearly exactly) the same on both sides when cut in half

Contrapposto: a pose in sculpture in which the upper part of the body twists in one direction and the lower part in another

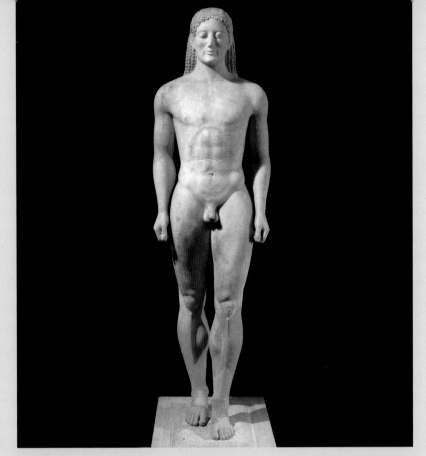

3.1.19 Kroisos *Kouros*, *c.* 530 BCE. Marble, height 76".
National Archaeological Museum in Athens, Greece

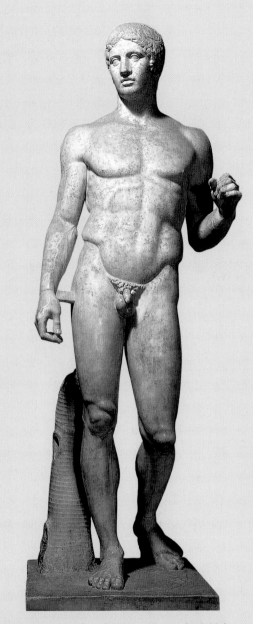

3.1.20 Roman version of the *Doryphoros* **of Polykleitos**,
120–50 BCE, after a bronze original of *c.* 460 BCE. Marble,
height 6'6". Minneapolis Institute of Arts, Minnesota

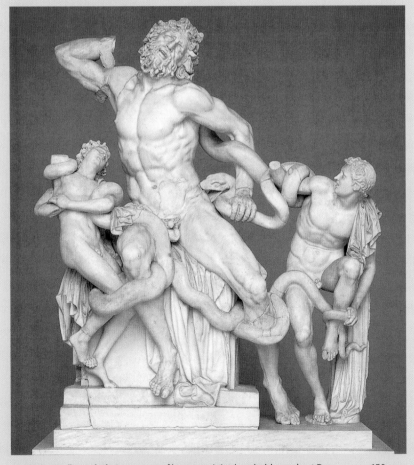

3.1.21 *Laocoön and His Sons*, copy of bronze original probably made at Pergamon *c.* 150 BCE.
Marble, height 6'1½". Vatican Museums, Vatican City, Italy

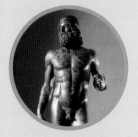

The Greeks often created
sculpture out of bronze
using lost-wax casting.
Many of these sculptures
do not survive because
they were melted down
for their materials:

→ see **2.4.12**, p. 236

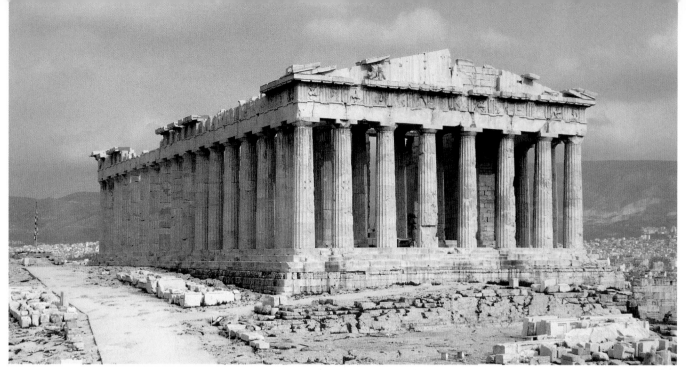

3.1.22 Iktinos and Kallikrates, Parthenon, 447–432 BCE, Acropolis, Athens, Greece

The Parthenon

Every large city in ancient Greece had its own government and was protected by its own god. Each had an acropolis, a complex of buildings on the highest point in the city that was both a fortress and a religious center, dedicated to the city's patron deity. The best-known acropolis is in Athens, and is dedicated to Athena, the goddess of war, wisdom, and the arts. According to Greek mythology—stories of the gods—the city was won by the goddess in a competition with Poseidon, god of the sea. Legend says that the goddess grew an olive tree, giving Athenians a source of wealth and defeating Poseidon, who had created a spring by striking the earth with his trident.

The original temple complex to Athena on the acropolis was burned by the Persian army in 480/479 BCE, less than a decade after it was begun. A new temple was built on the site because, according to legend, a new olive tree grew from the ashes of the old temple. This new temple, the Parthenon (**3.1.22**), was both the main temple to Athena and a war treasury. After the Persian attack, the Athenians formed an alliance with other Greek cities to protect one another from further attacks by the so-called "barbarians." The cities contributed funds to prepare for future wars; these were housed in the Parthenon.

The new Parthenon was so important that it was made of glistening white marble, which was transported several miles to Athens, and then carried up the steep slope to the acropolis. Its design was thought to epitomize ideal proportions, symbolizing for the Athenians their achievements as an enlightened society. For many, the Parthenon is the iconic example of Classical architecture (see: Classical Architectural Orders). Modern visitors to the Parthenon can see the basic architectural structure of the building, but can gain only a slight impression of its original appearance. Originally it had a timber roof covered with marble tiles, but this was destroyed in 1687, when Turkish army munitions stored there exploded. When it was first made, the structure was covered with sculptures. Both building and sculptures were painted in red, yellow, and blue. The bright paint has fallen off or faded over time, giving modern viewers the incorrect impression that Greek architecture and sculpture were intentionally made the natural color of marble. In several places there were statues of Athena to receive offerings and prayer. One enormous statue of the goddess, 38 ft. tall and made of gold and ivory, dominated the interior space.

Kallikrates and Iktinos, architects of the Parthenon, used their knowledge of mathematics to make the building appear as if it were harmoniously proportioned to the naked eye. Because of the temple's great size, the base and columns would appear warped unless the design was adjusted to counteract these naturally occurring optical illusions.

Classical Architectural Orders

The Greeks developed three types of designs, called architectural orders, for their temples (**3.1.23**). Elements of Greek temple design have been used in government buildings throughout the United States, particularly in state capitols and in Washington, D.C. See if you can recognize the architectural order used on **3.1.33** (p. 369), or **2.5.22** (p. 255), and **3.6.17a** (p. 456) or on buildings you see in person. The **Doric** and **Ionic** orders were first used as early as the sixth century BCE. The Parthenon is unusual in that it combines the two: its exterior columns and **frieze** are Doric, while the inner frieze (as viewed from the outside) is Ionic. The reason for this is debated, but it is likely that the blending of two styles popular in different parts of Greece marked a unity between different Greek cities. The **Corinthian** order was invented toward the end of the fifth century BCE. It was used for very few Greek buildings, but was widely applied by the Romans. The easiest way to recognize which order was used in a building is to look at the columns, and more specifically the **capitals**. Ionic and Corinthian columns both have a more decorative and slender quality, while the Doric is wider. The Doric column has the least amount of ornamental detail. The Ionic column has the most noticeable fluting (vertical grooves) on the **shaft** and a volute (inverted scroll) on the capital. The Corinthian column is the most ornate, with layers of acanthus leaves decorating the capital. The **entablatures** of the three architectural orders are also quite distinct. The Doric frieze is divided by **triglyphs** (a kind of architectural decoration so named because it always has three grooves) that alternate with **metopes** (panels often containing relief sculpture). The Ionic and Corinthian friezes have relief sculpture along the entire frieze, and do not contain metopes or triglyphs.

Doric architectural order: a Classical style of architecture characterized by weighty columns and a frieze with triglyphs and metopes

Ionic architectural order: a Classical style of architecture characterized by narrow columns and volutes (scrolls) on the capitals

Frieze: the strip that goes around the top of a building, often filled with sculptural ornamentation

Corinthian architectural order: a Classical style of architecture characterized by ornate leaves on the capitals

Capital: the architectural feature that crowns a column

Shaft: the main vertical part of a column

Entablature: the part of a Greek or Roman building that rests on top of a column

Triglyph: a projecting block carved with three raised bands, which alternates with figurative reliefs in a frieze

Metope: a square space between triglyphs, often decorated with sculpture

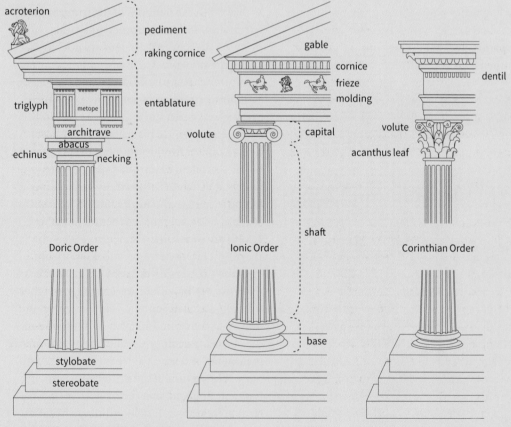

3.1.23 Diagram of the Classical architectural orders

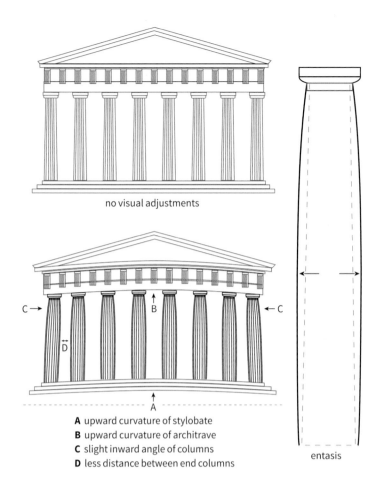

no visual adjustments

entasis

A upward curvature of stylobate
B upward curvature of architrave
C slight inward angle of columns
D less distance between end columns

3.1.24 Diagram showing the optical illusions utilized in the Parthenon

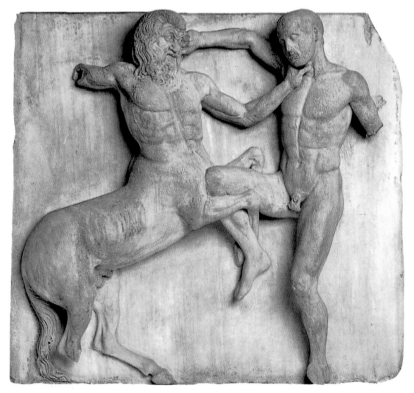

3.1.25 Metope of a Lapith and centaur in combat, from the south side of the Parthenon, designed by Pheidias, *c.* 445 BCE. Marble, height 52⅝".
British Museum, London, England

For example, the **stylobate**, or platform on which the columns stand, would appear to sag if it were constructed as a precisely straight horizonal base. To counteract this, the architects created a slight upward swelling in the center of the stylobate, which makes the base of the temple appear perfectly horizontal. For another example, the columns of the Parthenon actually swell at mid-height, an illusionistic technique called **entasis** (**3.1.24**). This optical trick prevents them from appearing to be hourglass-shaped, when seen from a distance, which would happen if the columns were flawlessly straight-sided. In addition, the columns are not precisely vertical but tilted slightly inward. If they were extended into the air, the **implied lines** created by the four corner columns would eventually intersect about a mile into space. Finally, the columns are not all spaced equidistantly, as they appear to be; those closer to the corners have less space between them. This is another visual trick used to compensate for the optical illusion that makes columns near the end of a row appear further apart than ones near the middle.

Placed in the metopes of the frieze in the Parthenon were sculptural reliefs of the battle in which the Lapiths, a legendary people in Greek mythology, tried to prevent the centaurs (creatures that are half-human and half-horse) from kidnapping the Lapith women (**3.1.25**). The scenes are intensely energetic, yet neither side seems to win. This subject was chosen as a metaphor for the Athenians (represented by the so-called "civilized" Lapiths) who were always at war with the Persians (represented by barbaric centaurs). The magnificent sculptures that once adorned the Parthenon (**3.1.25** and **3.1.26**) are now widely dispersed. Between 1801 and 1805, the British ambassador Lord Thomas Elgin removed many of the marbles from the Acropolis after receiving permission from the Ottoman empire, which controlled Athens at the time. Today, about one-third of the surviving sculptures (taken mostly from the **pediments** and metopes) form the Parthenon marble collection in the British Museum, in London, England; one-third of the sculptures remain in Athens; and one-third are in various other places around the globe.

The Greeks argue that since the Ottoman empire was occupying Greece when the sculptures were taken, the Turks did not have the authority to give Lord Elgin permission to

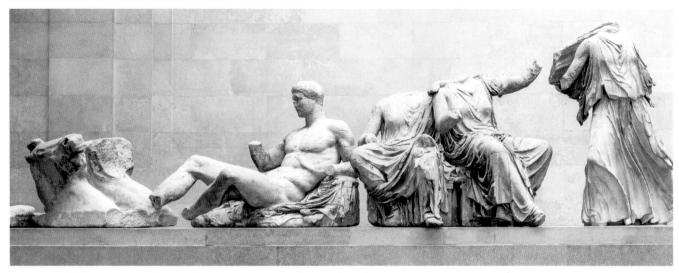

3.1.26 Marbles from the east pediment of the Parthenon celebrating the Birth of Athena, 438–432 BCE. British Museum, London, England.

take the artifacts. The British claim that the sculptures have been preserved because of their residence in the British Museum, where the marbles have been protected from warfare and environmental damage. The Greek government contends that the sculptures, as part of their national heritage, belong in Greece and have even built a museum to house them with the expectation that they will someday be returned.

Hellenistic sculpture

Artists during the Hellenistic period—the beginning of which is marked by the death of Alexander the Great in 323 BCE—chose subject matter that pushed beyond the idealism of the Classical period, with imagery that conveyed higher drama, eroticism, or the suffering of aging. Greek artists did not depict nude females until the end of the Classical period, but draped them in tightly-fitting cloth, as on the east pediment of the Parthenon (**3.1.26**). During the Hellenistic period, nude women, especially the goddess Aphrodite (Venus), were shown in a more sensual manner. The *Venus de Milo* (**3.1.27**) twists her body in an S-shaped pose, appearing unbothered by the falling of her drapery. It is thought that one of her now-missing arms may have been placed in front of her genital region, a pose called "Venus Pudica" or "modest Venus." The other hand would probably have held an apple, which refers to the mythological story in which the young man Paris had to choose which goddess (Aphrodite, Hera, or Athena) was the most beautiful. Paris awarded the golden apple to Venus to signify that she had won the contest.

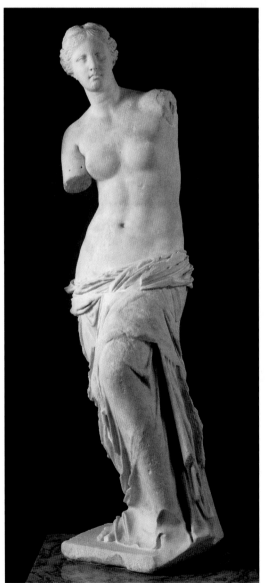

3.1.27 Alexandros of Antioch, *Venus de Milo*, Aphrodite or Venus from Milo, known as 'Venus de Milo', 2nd century BCE. Marble, height 6' 7½". Photo taken after 2010 restoration.

Stylobate: the uppermost platform of a Classical temple, on which the columns stand

Entasis: the slight swelling or bulge at the midpoint of a column

Implied line: a line not actually drawn but suggested by the positions of elements in the work, for example, an aligned series of dots

Pediment: the triangular space, situated above the row of columns, on the facade of a building in the Classical style

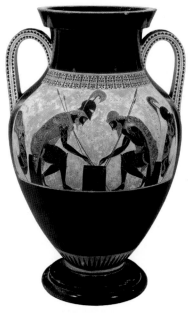

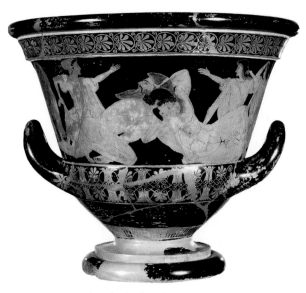

3.1.28 Exekias (potter and painter), black-figure amphora with Achilles and Ajax playing dice, Vulci, *c.* 530 BCE. Height 24″, diameter at mouth 11″. Vatican Museums, Vatican City, Italy

3.1.29 Euphronios (painter) and Euxitheos (potter), Attic red-figure calyx-krater showing Heracles and Antaios in battle, *c.* 515–510 BCE. 17⅝ × 21⅝″. Musée du Louvre, Paris, France

Ancient Greek painting

Ancient accounts tell us that Greek paintings were remarkably convincing scenes with **three-dimensional** figures that seemed to come to life. Unfortunately, only incomplete fragments survive. Several Roman mosaics were made as copies of Greek paintings, however. We can also surmise the skill of Greek painters by looking at the scenes painted on pottery.

The vase in **3.1.28** shows the Greek warriors Achilles and Ajax playing a game while waiting to battle with the Trojans. Through the layering of clothing, body parts, and even facial hair, the Athenian artist Exekias was able to represent figures that seem to fill a real space. The shields perched behind the figures also help to create a sense of depth. The long body of the pot and its two handles identify this as an ***amphora***. Greek pots were made in large workshops headed by both a master potter, who formed the vase, and a master painter. The two worked together closely, as the painting technique was intricately connected with the process of **firing** the pot. Exekias was particularly talented in that he was both a skilled painter and potter.

There were two main types of Greek vase painting: **black-figure** and **red-figure**. To make a black-figure vase, the painter used slip (watered-down clay) to paint the design on the pot, and then incised the details into the slip. A three-phase firing method then turned the slip-covered areas black, while the rest of the pot

remained the original red color. The red-figure technique was invented around 530 BCE, after the time of Exekias. It used the reverse process to black-figure: the slip was used to outline the figures and paint in the details. This can be seen on a ***krater***, showing Heracles and Antaios in battle (**3.1.29**). The red-figure method had the advantage of making the figures appear slightly more three-dimensional, which is advantageous for showing these two muscular figures actively struggling. Very close attention is also paid to their facial expressions and hair. Depth and space are created by the two smaller female figures in the background, who frame the scene with comparative calmness as they raise their arms.

As the Greeks developed a strong trade market through ports throughout the Mediterranean, a variety of Greek vases and pots have survived in great numbers outside of Greece, particularly in Etruscan tombs, where they were collected and buried with their owners.

Etruscan Art

During the sixth century BCE, the Etruscans were successful seafarers and traders who lived in central Italy, and formed the first urban society in the northern Mediterranean. Despite their prosperity, the Etruscans were eventually conquered by the Romans around 280 BCE. We understand much about Etruscan funerary

Three-dimensional: having height, width, and depth

Amphora: a type of pot used to carry and store such goods as wine or olive oil

Firing: heating ceramic, glass, or enamel objects in a kiln, to harden them, fuse the components, or fuse a glaze to the surface

Black-figure vase painting: in ancient Greece, figures painted in black slip on a red clay body

Red-figure vase painting: in ancient Greece, black slip is used on a red clay body to create the background as well as outline and linear details of the figures

Krater: a container for mixing wine with water, into which cups can then be dipped to ladle out the diluted wine for drinking

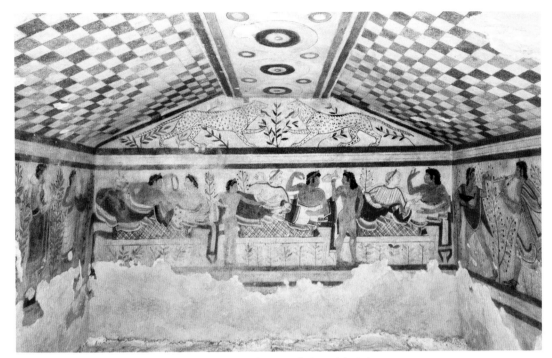

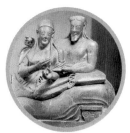

Etruscan husbands and wives were often buried in the same sarcophagus. In this work, a couple is shown celebrating the afterlife together:
→ see **2.4.10**, p. 234

3.1.30 Tomb of the Leopards, *c.* 530–520 BCE. Monterozzi Necropolis, Tarquinia, Italy

customs because they built necropolises, or large cemeteries, containing hundreds of tomb chambers, which were filled with sculptures or decorated with images of objects. The Etruscans were also very talented metalworkers; many intricate objects for personal use, such as gold jewelry and bronze mirrors, have been found in the tombs in Italy, and must have been buried with the deceased. These indicate that, like the ancient Egyptians, the Etruscans believed that such things would be needed in the afterlife.

Large Etruscan tomb chambers, often containing the remains of several generations of one family, were buried within mounds made of raised dirt and limestone. The tomb chambers were designed to mimic Etruscan houses, and portrayed settings in which celebrations could be held in the afterlife. The painting in the Tomb of the Leopards (**3.1.30**) shows a banquet in which men (portrayed as dark-skinned) and women (portrayed as light-skinned) are enjoying music, food, and drink. Etruscan women held a higher status within their own culture than other women were afforded in the ancient world. This is reflected here by their placement as equals, lounging with their husbands.

Roman Art

The first evidence of a settlement at Rome dates to about 900 BCE. This small village grew to become the center of an enormous empire that at its zenith covered much of Europe, northern Africa, and large parts of West Asia. In the process of conquering such extensive territories, the Romans absorbed many cultures, frequently adopting the gods of others but giving them Latin names. In fact, Roman emperors often associated themselves with the qualities of such gods.

The Romans used Greek methods to create ideal proportions in their architecture, and adopted the Corinthian architectural order that the Greeks had originally devised (see p. 363). The Romans also greatly admired Greek bronze sculptures and often remade them in marble. While the Greeks celebrated the idealized human body and mostly portrayed nude gods and mythological heroes, Roman art focused instead on emperors and civic leaders, who were usually portrayed clothed in togas or wearing armor. Roman sculpture often portrayed the individual character of its subject with recognizable, rather than ideal, facial features.

The Roman Republic

During the Roman Republic (509–27 BCE), in which power was held by a group of powerful families called patricians, aged members of Roman society were portrayed—and viewed— as wise and experienced, particularly in political settings.

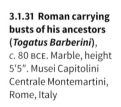

3.1.31 Roman carrying busts of his ancestors (*Togatus Barberini*), *c.* 80 BCE. Marble, height 5'5". Musei Capitolini Centrale Montemartini, Rome, Italy

Roman artists recognized individuals' accomplishments with naturalistic, lifelike portraits often made from death masks. Family members treasured such portraits as records of their loved one's likeness and character. In **3.1.31** a Roman patrician proudly displays the **busts** of his ancestors in order to reinforce his own social standing. His face shows individuality and believable signs of aging, and he wears clothing appropriate to his status.

The catastrophic eruption of Mount Vesuvius in 79 CE buried the buildings of the Roman cities of Pompeii and Herculaneum in a matter of hours under some 60 ft. of volcanic ash. Excavation of Pompeii began in the eighteenth century, and the remarkable discoveries there stimulated interest in ancient art throughout Europe. This unique act of accidental preservation has given us, centuries later, an incomparable opportunity to witness how Romans lived in their homes. Frescoes covered the walls of many rooms in the houses in Pompeii. One such house—the so-called Villa of the Mysteries—includes a room painted an intense red and decorated with scenes believed to describe rituals relating to the worship of Dionysus, the god of wine,

ecstasy, agriculture, and the theatre (**3.1.32**). The frescoes depict women who were part of the Dionysus cult who would have had to practice their faith in secret. In the scene shown here, women surround a table and pour liquid (perhaps wine) into a bowl. The woman with her back to us turns her head to see a naked drunken satyr called Silenus, who was a frequent companion of Dionysus. The rendering of the space itself is incredibly believable as it projects into the background, and figures appear to have a solid ground to walk upon.

The Roman Empire

From 27 BCE, Rome became an imperial state under the rule of Augustus. One of the Romans' most impressive works of architecture under the Roman empire (27 BCE–1453 CE) is the Pantheon ("Temple of all the Gods"). It was originally constructed in the first century BCE. Emperor Hadrian had it rebuilt from about 118 to 125 CE in order to enhance his own status. The entrance **facade** is a pediment atop Corinthian columns (**3.1.33**). Once inside, one is standing under a spectacular **coffered** dome 143 ft. in diameter and 143 ft. from the ground (**3.1.34**). The dome was made possible by the Romans' revolutionary use of concrete and their engineering genius. In the center of this

Bust: statue of a person depicting only the head and shoulders

Facade: any side of a building, usually the front or entrance

Coffered: decorated with recessed paneling

Oculus: a round opening at the center of a dome

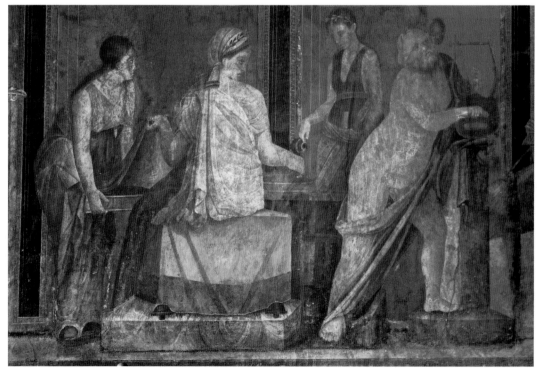

3.1.32 Detail from Dionysiac mystery frieze in Room 5 of the Villa of the Mysteries, Pompeii, Italy, *c.* 60 BCE. Wall painting, height 5'4"

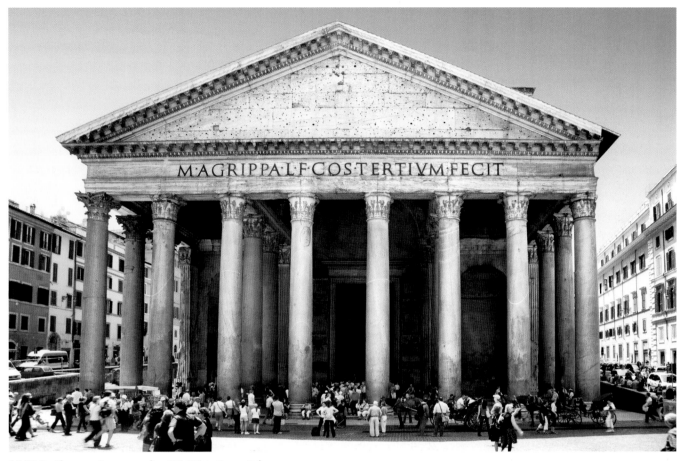

3.1.33 Pantheon, entrance porch, *c.* 118–125 CE. Rome, Italy

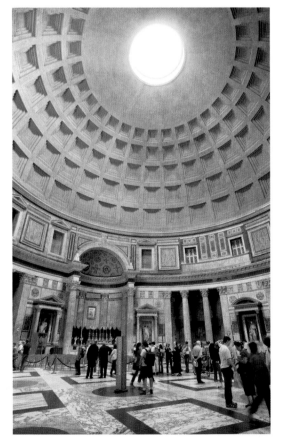

3.1.34 Pantheon, interior view, *c.* 118–125 CE. Rome, Italy

dome is an **oculus**, (the Latin word for "eye") open to the skies. One can tell the season and time of day from where the sunlight hits the interior. Any rain coming in runs quickly away into a central drain because the entire floor slopes gradually.

At the center of each Roman city was a forum, or marketplace, which was surrounded by temples, basilicas, and civic buildings. Emperors made a public show of their power by commissioning architects to create grand arches and tall columns, which usually celebrated the rulers' triumphs in battle.

The enormous Arch of Constantine (**3.1.35**, p. 370) was built between 312 and 315 CE by the emperor Constantine to commemorate the military victory (the Battle of the Milvian Bridge) that would ensure his future position as sole ruler of the empire. Constantine declared his place in history by placing the arch close to the famed Colosseum, built by an earlier family of powerful emperors (see p. 541). Constantine also had sculpture removed from other imperial monuments, often erasing the faces of previous emperors from such statues and replacing them with his own likeness; he then had the

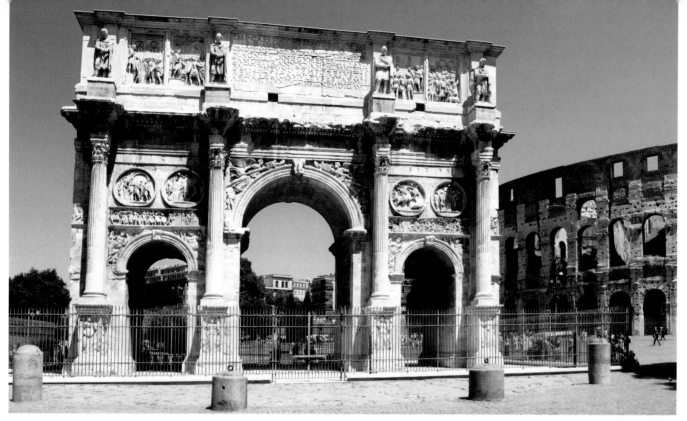

3.1.35 Arch of Constantine, south side, 312–15 CE. Rome, Italy

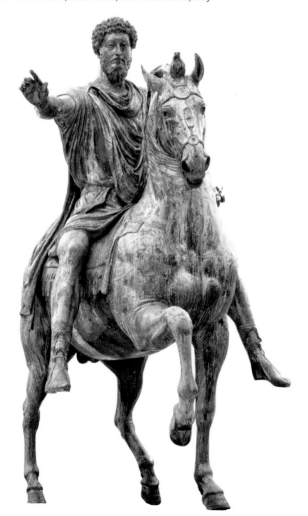

3.1.36 Equestrian statue of Marcus Aurelius, *c.* 175 CE. Bronze replica, height 11'6". Piazza del Campidoglio Rome, Italy (original in Musei Capitolini)

sculptures placed upon the triumphal arch. By doing so, he proclaimed both his lineage to previous great emperors and his belief in his superiority over them. Constantine associated himself with Apollo and other pagan gods, as well as with Christianity. He became known as Constantine the Great, and would eventually make it legal to practice all religions, opening the doors for Christianity to grow into the primary religion of the empire. He was baptized as a Christian on his deathbed.

The Romans also distributed statues of their emperors throughout the empire and placed them in town centers. In this sculpture, which is more than lifesize, the emperor, Marcus Aurelius, is shown exuding great physical strength, commanding his powerful, muscular horse (**3.1.36**). The sculptor has conveyed a sense of tension between action and stillness. The horse's front right leg appears in motion, ready to take another step, while Marcus Aurelius raises his arm as if he is about to orate to an audience. Although sculptures showing emperors powerfully atop a horse were common in ancient Rome, few have survived because they were melted down for their bronze to make weapons during the Middle Ages. The equestrian statue of Marcus Aurelius escaped destruction because it was thought to represent Emperor Constantine.

Explore Further The Prehistoric and Ancient Mediterranean

Mesopotamia	Egypt	Greece	Rome

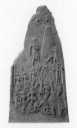

4.2.8 Stela of Naram-Sin, *c.* 2254–2218 BCE → p. 559

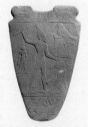

4.6.5b Palette of Narmer (back), Egypt, *c.* 2950–2775 BCE → p. 607

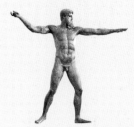

1.7.12a *Poseidon* (or *Zeus*), Greece, *c.* 460–450 BCE → p. 137

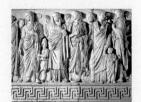

1.2.6 Imperial Procession, from the *Ara Pacis Augustae*, 13 BCE → p. 54

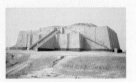

4.1.6 Ziggurat, Ur, Iraq, *c.* 2100 BCE → p. 543

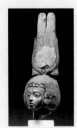

4.5.7 Queen of Tiye of Egypt portrait head, Egypt, *c.* 1355 BCE → p. 598

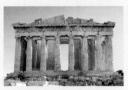

1.7.14a Iktinos and Kallikrates, Parthenon, Athens, 447–432 BCE → p. 138

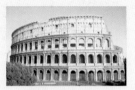

4.1.2 Colosseum, Rome, 72–80 CE → p. 541

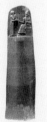

4.5.6 Stela of Hammurabi, *c.* 1792–1750 BCE → p. 597

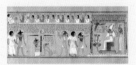

4.2.10 Book of the Dead of Hunefer, Egypt, *c.* 1275 BCE → p. 560

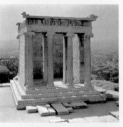

2.5.8 Kallikrates, Temple of Athena Nike, *c.* 421–415 BCE → p. 248

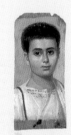

2.2.4 Portrait of a boy, *c.* 100–150 CE → p. 196

Your turn
With which regions are these artworks associated?

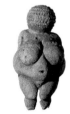

4.8.1 *Woman from Willendorf, c.* 24,000–22,000 BCE → p. 630

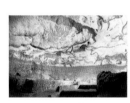

4.2.14b Hall of the Bulls, Lascaux Caves, *c.* 17,000–15,000 BCE → p. 563

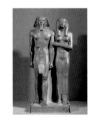

4.8.3b *Menkaure and His Wife, Queen Khamerernebty, c.* 2520 BCE → p. 632

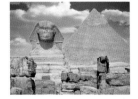

1.2.2 Great Sphinx of Giza, *c.* 2500 BCE → p. 51

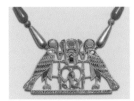

2.6.12 Pectoral with the name Senwosret II, *c.* 1879–78 BCE → p. 276

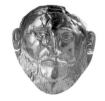

2.6.9 Gold death mask, Mycenae, *c.* 1550–1500 BCE → p. 275

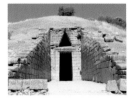

2.5.10 Entrance, Treasury of Atreus, *c.* 1250 BCE → p. 249

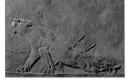

2.4.3 Dying Lioness relief, North Palace of Ashurbanipal, *c.* 650 BCE → p. 230

3.2
Art of the Middle Ages

The Roman empire dominated the Mediterranean region from the second century BCE, later extending its control of western Europe and West Asia, but by the fourth century CE the empire was crumbling in the west. In 330, the Roman emperor Constantine I (272–337 CE) moved the center of the Roman empire from Rome to Byzantium, which he renamed Constantinople (today's Istanbul,

Turkey) (see **3.2.1**). The eastern part of the empire became known as the **Byzantine** empire and lasted a millennium, until Constantinople fell to the Turks in 1453. In the west, however, a series of invasions had ended the Roman empire by 476. The period that followed is known as the **Middle Ages**, or the **medieval** period, because it comes between the ancient cultures of the Mediterranean region and the

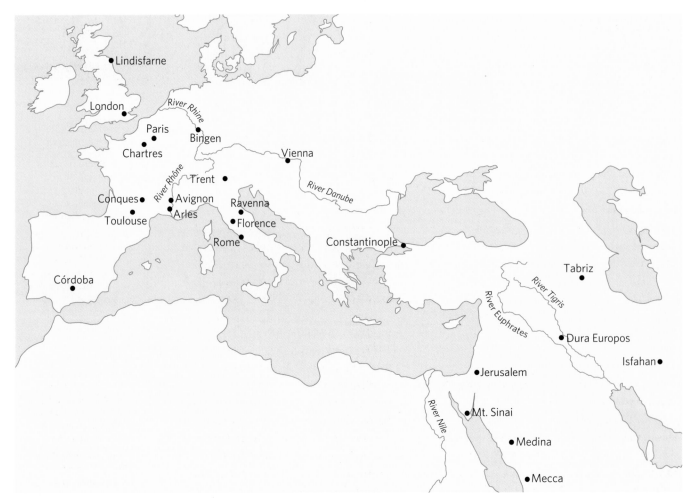

3.2.1 Map of Europe and West Asia in the Middle Ages

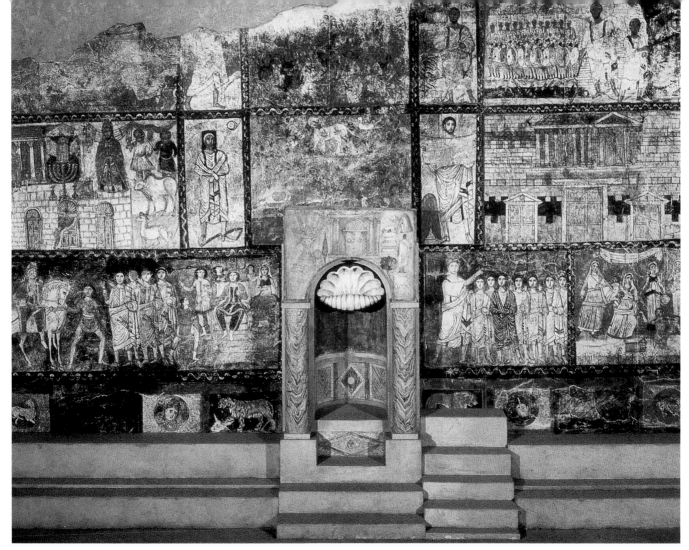

3.2.2 Interior west wall of synagogue at Dura Europos, Syria, 244–245 CE. Reconstruction in National Museum, Damascus, Syria

rebirth, or **Renaissance**, of Greek and Roman ideals in Europe in the fifteenth century.

In the study of the history of art, the Middle Ages is often broken down further because of the stylistic variations of its art, particularly its architecture. Beginning in the eleventh century, large stone churches, heavily ornamented with sculpture inside and out, were built throughout the Christian world. These churches were later given the name **Romanesque** for their similarity to the heavy, round-**arched** style of the Romans. This comparison is not obvious, but the term Romanesque was meant as a contrast to the architectural style that followed it, from around 1150, in which great **Gothic** cathedrals, the spires of which reached toward the heavens, were built. Religious belief was integral to the lives of the people—whether Christian, Jew, or Muslim—who lived in Europe and West Asia during this period (see Three Religions of the Middle Ages, p. 374). Much of the art from the period reflects their beliefs.

Art of Late Antiquity and Early Christianity

Jewish culture thrived periodically during the Middle Ages, although this was also a time of persecution. Partially as a result of the constant displacement of many Jews, few examples of Jewish art from the Middle Ages survive. The oldest surviving Jewish artwork (other than coins) can be found in a synagogue in the ancient Roman city of Dura Europos, on the River Euphrates in modern Syria. Here, more than fifty stories are displayed in **fresco** paintings on the wall. The paintings were used to teach the stories upon which Jewish history and belief are based. The didactic nature (with the aim of teaching) of these images explains why figures are shown, a feature that is uncommon in later Jewish art. On the center of the west wall facing Jerusalem is a shrine containing the Torah, the most important part of the Jewish Bible, which contains the commandments given to Moses by God (**3.2.2**).

Renaissance: a period of cultural and artistic change in Europe from the fourteenth to the seventeenth century

Romanesque: an early medieval European style of architecture based on Roman-style rounded arches and heavy construction

Arch: a structure, usually curved, that spans an opening

Gothic: a Western European architectural style of the twelfth to the sixteenth century, characterized by the use of pointed arches and ornate decoration

Fresco: a technique in which the artist paints onto freshly applied plaster. From the Italian *fresco*, "fresh"

Three Religions of the Middle Ages

> You shall not make for yourself an idol, whether in the form of anything that is in heaven above, or that is on the Earth beneath, or that is in the water under the Earth. You shall not bow down to them or worship them.
>
> (Second Commandment, Exodus 20:4–5)

Judaism, Islam, and Christianity all have their origins in West Asia. They have some similar beliefs—each religion considers Abraham to be a prophet, for example, and each considers their God to be the one true God. Importantly for the study of art, each also warns against the worship of false idols. Understanding some basic beliefs of followers of these faiths can help us to understand better some of the art produced during the Middle Ages.

- Judaism teaches that it began with a contract between Abraham and God (Yahweh) in about 2000 BCE. Abraham promised to exalt Yahweh as the one true God, and in exchange Yahweh promised Abraham many descendants, who are the Jewish people of today. The Torah (or "Teaching") is believed to have been written by Moses under divine inspiration and is the core of Jewish belief and law. Jewish art does not show any more than the hands of Yahweh, and rarely depicts human figures. Instead, it usually shows objects used in acts of worship, such as scroll holders and candelabra.

- Christians worship Jesus Christ (a Jew who lived from around 7–2 BCE to around 30–36 CE), who they believe was the son of God. The Bible contains both the writings of the Jewish Bible ("The Old Testament") and what Christians see as their fulfillment in the life of Jesus ("The New Testament"). For Christians, Jesus was a great teacher who demonstrated how to lead a good and pious life, but who also suffered, was sacrificed, and then rose again to show that the sins of humanity could be forgiven and that for those who were true believers, eternal life could be achieved after death. Christians have interpreted the Second Commandment in different ways, at times causing great conflict and even the destruction of images.

- Muslims (followers of Islam) call their one true God Allah. They believe that Jesus was a prophet but that Muhammad (c. 570–632 CE) was the primary messenger of Allah. The Koran is the word of Allah given to Muhammad and is Islam's primary sacred text. Islamic art never depicts the figure of God, and human figures are not shown within the holy space of a mosque. The majority of Islamic art is decorative and often makes beautiful use of **calligraphy** to illustrate the word of Allah.

Calligraphy: the art of emotive or carefully descriptive hand lettering or handwriting

Continuous narrative: when different parts of a story are shown within the same visual space

Catacombs: an underground system of tunnels used for burying and commemorating the dead

The fresco painting of the scene in **3.2.3** does show God, but not his face; only his hands are seen, reaching down from the sky. In the passage from the Book of Exodus in the Torah, God tells Moses to guide the Israelites out of Egypt toward Mount Sinai, where Moses will receive the Ten Commandments. When they arrive at the Red Sea, God tells Moses to place his rod in the water. This action parts the sea, creating a safe crossing for Moses and his people. When they are safely on the other side, Moses again places his rod in the water. The Red Sea floods, drowning the Egyptian soldiers who have been chasing the Israelites. The Exodus painting is a **continuous narrative**, in which different points in time in the story are shown within the same scene. Moses is shown in the center, while the soldiers on the left are lined up to follow him. A second Moses is shown slightly in front and to the side of the first. Behind the second Moses on the right side of the scene, the soldiers have been washed away as the sea has flooded.

The earliest examples of Christian art date from the early third century. From 200 CE to the sixth century, it was common practice in Italy amongst Christians, Jews, and others to bury the dead in underground cemeteries known as **catacombs**. The catacombs may also have served as sites for Christian worship. Scenes were often painted on burial-room walls and ceilings. One such scene in a catacomb in Rome shows Christ as the Good Shepherd in the center and tells the Old Testament story of Jonah in the semicircular areas around the central image (**3.2.4**). Christians believe

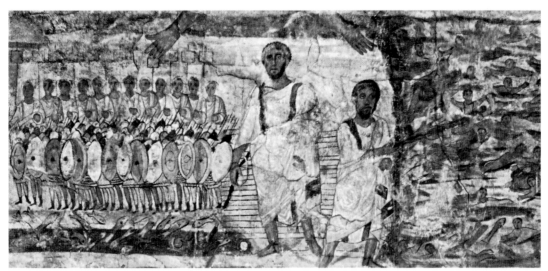

Motif: a design or color repeated as a unit in a pattern

Syncretism: the blending of multiple religious or philosophical beliefs

3.2.3 *Exodus and Crossing of the Red Sea*, **panel from west wall of synagogue at Dura Europos,** Syria, 244–45 CE. Reconstruction in National Museum, Damascus, Syria

that the story of Jonah, who was swallowed by a whale and then spat out alive three days later, foreshadows the death and resurrection of Christ.

In their depiction of Christian themes, early Christian artists often used **motifs** and figures adapted from other, older religions. Under the Roman empire, religious **syncretism**—the blending of multiple religious or philosophical beliefs—was common; as Christianity spread, rituals, symbols, and even objects were assimilated from the so-called "pagans". For example, statues of the Egyptian goddess Isis, mother to the god Horus, were altered and used as models for images of the Virgin Mary. The Good Shepherd in **3.2.4** was adapted from images of several pagan figures, including the Greek hero Orpheus (who could charm animals

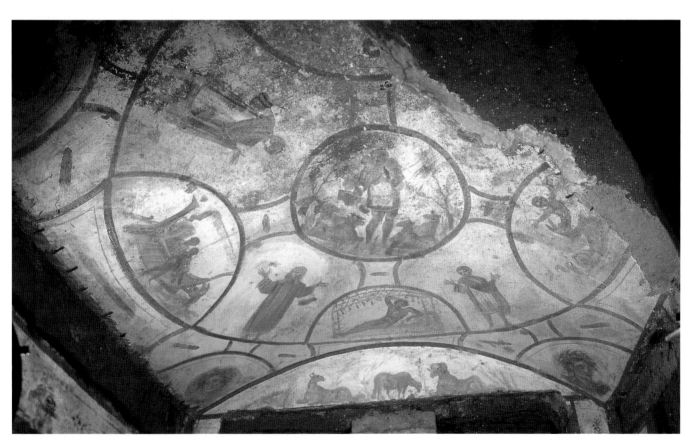

3.2.4 Painted ceiling, late 3rd–early 4th century CE. The catacombs of Saints Peter and Marcellinus, Rome, Italy

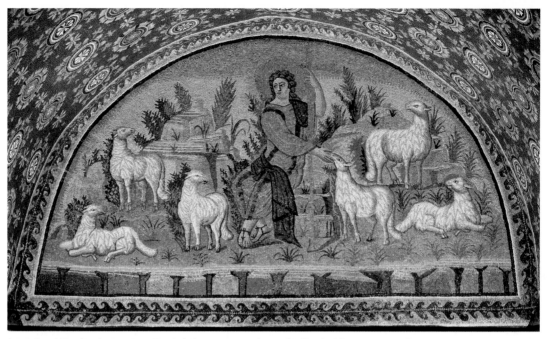

3.2.5 *Good Shepherd*, 425–46 CE. Mosaic in lunette. Mausoleum of Galla Placidia, Ravenna, Italy

Mosaic: a picture or pattern created by fixing together small pieces of stone, glass, tile, etc.

Tesserae: small pieces of stone or glass or other materials used to make a mosaic

Three-dimensional: having height, width, and depth

Patron: an organization or individual who sponsors the creation of works of art

Basilica: an early Christian church, either converted from or built to resemble a type of Roman civic building

Minaret: a tall slender tower, particularly on a mosque, from which the faithful are called to prayer

Central-plan church: a church design, often in the shape of a cross with all four arms of equal length

Icon: a small, often portable, religious image venerated by Christian believers; first used by the Eastern Orthodox Church

Iconoclasm, Iconoclastic: the destruction of images or artworks, often out of religious belief.

with his songs) and the Greek god Apollo (god of music, the sun, and healing, who was always shown as a beardless youth).

A century later, the depiction of Christ changed. Christian artists developed a range of symbols that were more varied and elaborate. The **mosaic** in **3.2.5** was made for the building known as the Mausoleum of Galla Placidia, which was the family tomb of the Roman emperor Flavius Honorius. We can see that Christ is still portrayed as a Good Shepherd, here flanked by three lambs on each side, but he is seated and more mature. Compared to the image on the catacomb ceiling, Christ's appearance is regal. He wears a fine gold robe with a purple (the traditional color for royalty) cloth draped over his shoulder, and he holds a golden cross. His hair is long, and a prominent gold halo shines behind him; the **tesserae**, small pieces of glass that make up the mosaic, create a beautiful glow that glitters and reflects light. Unlike figures in Roman art, Christ's body is sharply delineated and flat-looking rather than fully **three-dimensional**. These stylistic qualities foreshadow the art of Byzantium, the Christian empire that continued in the east after the fall of the western Roman empire.

Byzantine Art

The Byzantine emperor Justinian I (483–565) was a devoted **patron** of the arts. He funded hundreds of churches, mosaics, and paintings throughout his empire, including Hagia

Sophia in the center of Constantinople (**3.2.6**). Although Hagia Sophia was built as a Christian **basilica**, it was altered into a mosque when the Ottomans took control of Constantinople in 1453. The four **minarets** were added after that date. At the time, the dome of Hagia Sophia was the largest ever built, at 182 ft. high. At the base of the dome are forty closely aligned windows, making the dome appear to float on a bed of light from the inside. Hagia Sophia is based on a **central-plan** design where the width and length of the building are almost identical.

One of Justinian's greatest achievements was placing 2,000 **icons** at St. Catherine's Monastery, Mount Sinai, where they were protected from later destruction. Icons, paintings of religious figures on wooden panels, are still used in the Eastern Orthodox Church for meditation and prayer. Many early Christians believed icons had special healing powers; therefore, icons that survive are often faded from being kissed and touched by numerous worshipers. In the eighth and ninth centuries, an **iconoclastic** controversy arose in the Byzantine empire, provoked by divisions amongst Christians over the interpretation of the Bible's Second Commandment: "You shall not make for yourself an idol, whether in the form of anything in heaven above, or that is on the Earth beneath, or that is in the water under the Earth. You shall not bow down to them or worship them." Some Christians took this commandment to mean that icons should be

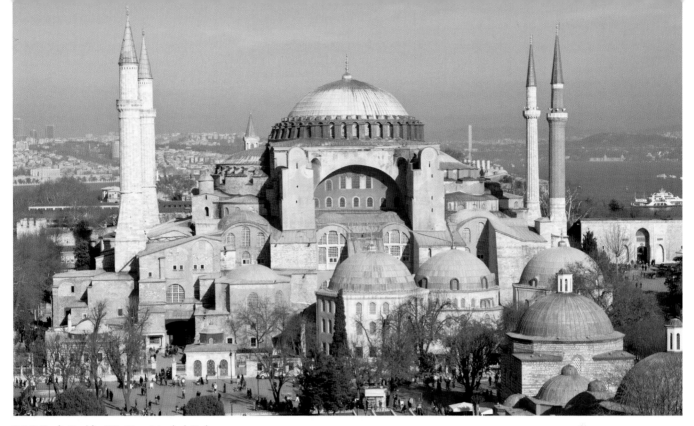

3.2.6 Hagia Sophia, 532–35 CE, Istanbul, Turkey

prohibited. Iconoclasts were concerned that the faithful were worshiping icons of religious figures rather than worshiping Mary and Christ directly. This fundamental disagreement led to the destruction of thousands of Byzantine icons, including almost all portrayals of Christ and Mary. The icons in St. Catherine's Monastery, however, remained safe due to the monastery's location in the Egyptian desert.

The sixth-century icon of Christ (**3.2.7**) from St. Catherine's Monastery is intended to show the dual nature of Christ as both human and God. As in the Good Shepherd mosaic (**3.2.5**), here Christ is shown as a regal figure, wearing a rich purple robe. He is now represented with a beard and long hair, which became the convention in subsequent Christian art. Christ's duality is brilliantly portrayed here by the differences on each side of his face; his right side (viewer's left) represents his heavenly half, and his left side his human half. The right side of Christ's face is ideally proportioned, with a healthy glow, and his hair is in place. By comparison, his left side seems to sag slightly, his eyes and mouth have wrinkles, and his hair is somewhat disheveled. His right hand makes a gesture of holy blessing, while his left hand holds sacred writings read by those on Earth.

One of the most beautiful Byzantine churches was built in Ravenna, Italy, in the

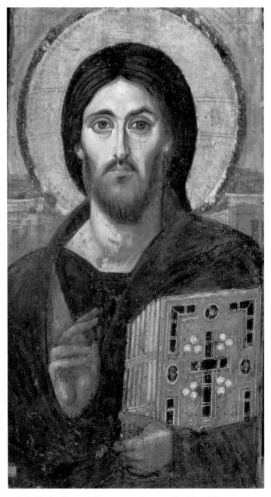

3.2.7 Christ icon, 6th century. Encaustic, 33 × 18″. St. Catherine's Monastery, Mount Sinai, Egypt

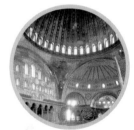

Hagia Sophia is known for its dome that seems to float because of the forty windows at its base::
→ see **2.5.17**, p. 253

Nave: the central space of a church or basilica

Apse: a semicircular vaulted space in a church

Altar: an area where sacrifices or offerings are made

Outline: the outermost line or implied line of an object or figure, by which it is defined or bounded

Composition: the overall design or organization of a work

Manuscripts: handwritten texts

Decorative: intentionally making an artwork pleasant or attractive

Illuminations: illustrations and decorations in a manuscript

Arabesque: an abstract pattern derived from geometric and vegetal lines and forms

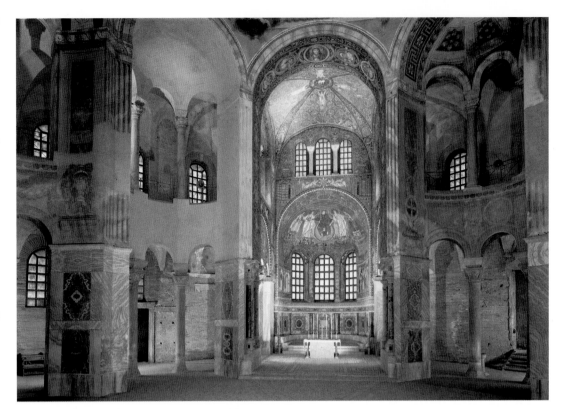

3.2.8a Church of San Vitale, *c.* 547 CE. Ravenna, Italy

sixth century (**3.2.8a**). The floor plan of the Church of San Vitale is a central plan, based on two octagons, one inside the other (**3.2.8b**). Central-plan churches were a common style in the Eastern Orthodox tradition, as opposed to the Latin-cross design of western Europe (see **3.2.21**, p. 385). The smaller octagon, the **nave**, is a space nearly 100 ft. high, filled with windows, and covered by a dome. Natural light glistens off the glass mosaics that cover the walls. Eight semicircular bays emanate from the center, with the **apse** that contains the **altar** on the southeast side; above the altar is a mosaic of Christ enthroned on Earth. Flanking either side of the apse are glorious glass mosaics of the emperor Justinian and the empress Theodora.

It is characteristic of Byzantine art that figures and their clothing are often boldly **outlined**. Such delineation creates a flatness to the figures and decreases their three-dimensionality. This lack of volume or mass, along with the way the figures seem to float, gives a timeless, spiritual quality to the image, as if it belongs somewhere between the heavenly and earthly realms. The figures in the image are even layered so that their repetition creates a sense of movement toward the altar.

Justinian stands in the center of his mosaic (**3.2.9**), wearing the imperial color purple. On either side of him are clergy in white robes.

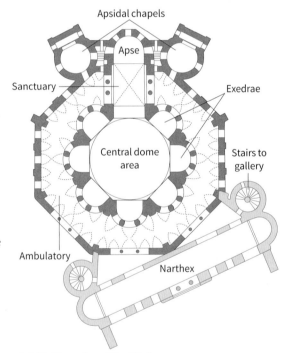

3.2.8b Floor plan of San Vitale

To his far right are soldiers, who display a large shield that bears the Greek letters for Christ (*chi-rho*), emphasizing Justinian's role as a Christian military leader. There are other Christian symbols in the mosaic: the men to the left of the emperor hold a cross, a copy of the gospels (the first four books of the New Testament), and a censer used to burn incense during church services. Justinian holds the

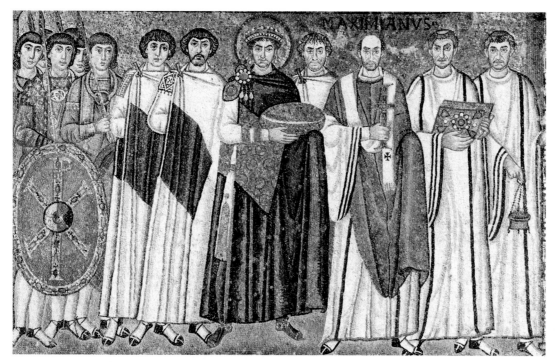

3.2.9 **Emperor Justinian**, *c.* 547. Glass mosaic. San Vitale, Ravenna, Italy

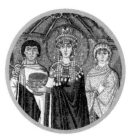

A mosaic featuring Empress Theodora holding a chalice of wine, representing Christ's blood, is placed across the apse from the mosaic of her husband, Emperor Justinian:

→ see **4.5.8**, p. 599

bread used to represent the body of Christ in the communion service, recalling that the mosaic itself is displayed near the altar where the service would take place. Interestingly, one other figure in this mosaic is given special recognition: the local bishop, Maximianus. It was Maximianus who arranged the commission and organized the **composition** so that his figure was the only one identified in writing on the image (his name is written above his portrait). The bishop also requested that his feet should be placed slightly in front of the figure of the emperor. Justinian himself needed no such label; the imperial robe, in addition to his crown and halo, were enough to identify the ruler.

Manuscripts and the Middle Ages

Manuscripts (books written and decorated by hand) in the Middle Ages are richly detailed objects that reflect the piety of the time. The production of manuscripts was intensely laborious, from making the pages out of animal hides to copying painstakingly in careful handwriting. Manuscripts were the work of many artists (usually monks and sometimes nuns), some specializing in **decorative** lettering (scribes), and others in painting images (**illuminators**). Jewelers and workers in fine metals often contributed to decorating the covers. The great effort required to create a manuscript was considered a tribute to God.

Islamic manuscripts rarely show human figures, and never the image of Allah (God). Rather, attention is paid to the word of Allah, recorded in the Koran, and revealed in elegant script. Islamic artworks often have an **arabesque** quality, and this is particularly apparent in manuscripts. *Surah* (chapters) from the Koran are written in Arabic, from right to left, but the script varies from region to region. In a beautiful page of the Koran (**3.2.10**) from

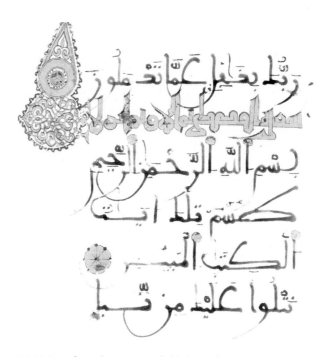

3.2.10 **Page from the Koran**, probably late 13th century. *Maghribi* on vellum, 7½ × 7½". British Library, London, England

Kufic: an Arabic script, angular in form; often used to copy the Koran.

Stained glass: colored glass used for windows or decorative applications

Vault: an arch-like structure supporting a ceiling or roof

Relic: an object that survives from the past; in religion, the mortal remains of a saint or an object that has been in contact with the saint

thirteenth-century Spain, the oldest Arabic script, *kufic*, is used for the headings, while the script *maghribi* is used for the rest of the text. This regional script derived its name from its popularity in the region of Maghreb, which in the Middle Ages included northern Africa and Islamic areas of Spain. The areas in the manuscript where the text is thicker and in gold signify the heading for a new chapter. The ornamental circular designs in gold break the reading into appropriate sections.

The Lindisfarne Gospels are an illuminated manuscript book of the Christian gospels of Matthew, Mark, Luke, and John (known as the Four Evangelists). They were made during the early eighth century. Each gospel is decorated with a "cross-and-carpet" page (named for its similarity to a carpet design). The design in the cross-and-carpet page at the beginning of St. Matthew's gospel appears to be made up of numerous intertwining lines (**3.2.11a**). Upon closer inspection, tiny animal heads can be

seen twisting throughout (**3.2.11b**). While the specific meaning of these animals is unclear, this decorative element was common in the Middle Ages, particularly in northeast England, where the Lindisfarne Gospels were made.

The Lindisfarne Gospels were scribed fully or in part by a bishop named Eadfrith, who signed his name to the manuscript. The pages, written in Latin, would have taken him at least five years to complete. Such beautiful pages as these are often called illuminations because their rich colors recall light shining through **stained glass** in a cathedral. (Similarly, because of their didactic nature, stained-glass windows have been called "books in glass," and the sculpture around cathedrals "books in stone.") Both the Lindisfarne Gospels and the Spanish Koran were made to be studied and enjoyed over long periods of contemplation.

Manuscripts often illustrated religious stories or the visions of spiritual leaders. Hildegard of Bingen was a Christian mystic and

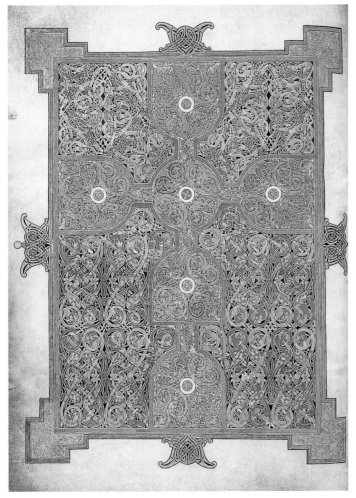

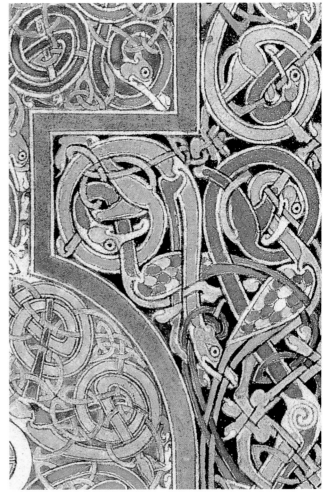

3.2.11a Cross-and-carpet page introducing the Gospel according to St. Matthew, Lindisfarne Gospels, fol. 26b, 710–721. Illuminated manuscript. British Library, London, England

3.2.11b Detail of **3.2.11a**

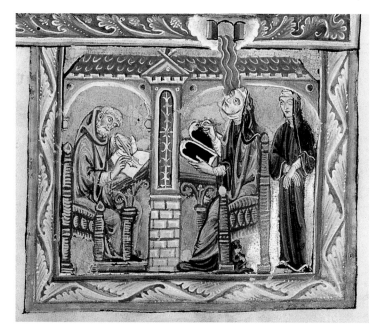

3.2.12 *The Fifth Vision of Hildegard of Bingen*, **frontispiece for** *Scivias*, *c.* 1230. Original manuscript lost. Biblioteca Governativa, Lucca, Italy

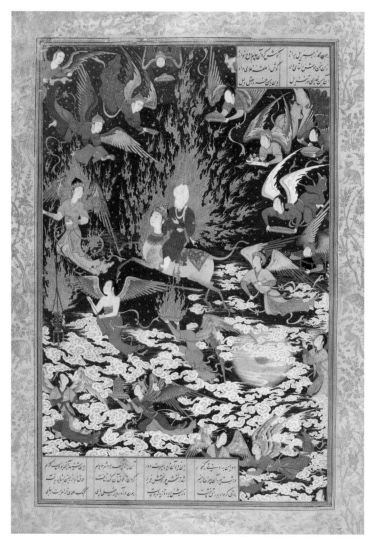

3.2.13 *The Ascent of the Prophet Muhammad on His Steed, Buraq, Guided by Jibra'il and Escorted by Angels*, 1539–43. Miniature painting from a manuscript of Nizami's *Khamsa (Five Poems)*, originally produced in Tabriz, Iran

visionary; she advised kings and popes, who often traveled long distances to meet with her. Born into an aristocratic family and educated as a nun, she eventually became abbess of a convent in Germany. Her visions included insights into medicine, astronomy, and politics, which she shared in a book called *Scivias* (*Know the Ways*), which was read throughout Europe. The original manuscript was destroyed during World War II; however, from copies of *Scivias* we know that Hildegard was repeatedly portrayed in the act of receiving a vision. Her assistant is also usually shown transcribing her vision (**3.2.12**). This misleadingly suggests that the scribe wrote on the pages after they were bound. In reality, the manuscript took months to make: it was carefully planned out on pieces of paper before being put together as a book. Hildegard described the experience of receiving visions as "a fiery light, flashing intensely, which came from the open **vault** of heaven and poured through my whole brain," which is an apt description for what is taking place in the manuscript shown here.

Islamic manuscripts often depict events from the life of Muhammad, the main prophet of Allah. The manuscript painting in **3.2.13** shows the ascension of Muhammad, which Muslims believe took place at the Dome of the Rock in Jerusalem (see **3.2.15**, p. 382). Muhammad's face is not shown, but is covered with a veil. He is surrounded by blinding flames, which signify his holiness, as he rides his half-human horse, Buraq, toward the heavens. On the left, guiding Muhammad, is the angel Gabriel (Jibra'il), whose head is also encircled with fire.

Pilgrimage in the Middle Ages

Pilgrimages were integral to the practice of Christianity, Islam, and Judaism. In medieval Europe, devout Christian pilgrims journeyed to holy sites where significant religious events had occurred or where **relics** were kept. Relics were holy objects (such as a piece of the wooden cross on which Christ was crucified), or body parts of saints or holy figures. Elaborately decorated containers called reliquaries were made to house individual relics, and they were designed to look like the relic they contained. Thus, the reliquary of the Head of St. Alexander (**3.2.14**, p. 382) houses a skull. This reliquary was made in 1145 for the Abbot Wibald of Stavelot in Belgium. The face is made of beaten silver

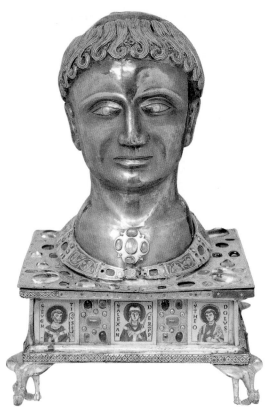

3.2.14 Reliquary of the Head of St. Alexander, 1145. Silver repoussé, gilt bronze, gems, pearls, and enamel, height 7½". Musées Royaux d'Art et d'Histoire, Brussels, Belgium

(**repoussé**), with the hair made from gilded bronze. The emphasis on the portrait itself recalls the Roman heads of antiquity. The head is placed upon a base covered with gems and pearls. Small plaques painted in enamel show a portrait of the sainted Pope Alexander in the center, flanked by two other saints.

Jerusalem

Throughout the Middle Ages, devout people made pilgrimages to the city of Jerusalem; a shining gold dome still marks a site in the city that is sacred to Jews, Christians, and Muslims alike (**3.2.15**). The Dome of the Rock surrounds the sacred Foundation Stone, which Jews believe is the site of the beginning of the world, and Muslims believe is the rock from which Muhammad ascended to heaven. To Jews and Christians, this site is also thought to be the place where Adam was created and where Abraham was asked to sacrifice his son.

The Dome of the Rock was built as a site for pilgrims (not as a mosque) between 688 and 691 under the order of Abd al-Malik, who wanted it to surpass all Christian churches in the Middle East. Although al-Malik was a caliph (an Islamic ruler), the Dome of the Rock was probably built by Christian laborers; its proportions, octagonal shape, dome, and mosaic designs show a clear Byzantine style. The glorious dome that crowns the shrine was originally solid gold, but was rebuilt in the twentieth century with aluminum. In 1993, King Hussein of Jordan spent more than $8 million of his own money to gild the aluminum with gold. The height and diameter of the dome are approximately 67 ft. each, as is the length of each of the eight walls. The walls of the octagon are covered with verses in Arabic calligraphy from the Koran. Although all religions are permitted on the Temple Mount, since 2006 only Muslims have been allowed within the domed shrine.

3.2.15 Dome of the Rock, 688–91, Jerusalem

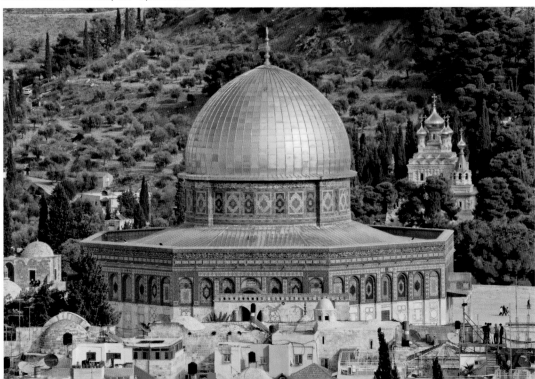

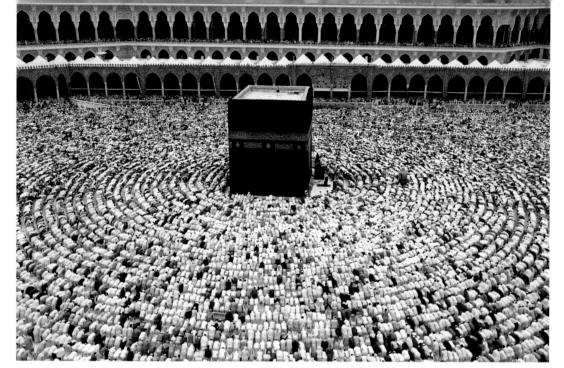

3.2.16 **Pilgrims surrounding the Kaaba**, Al Masjid al-Haram, Mecca, Saudi Arabia

Mecca and Mosques

Mecca, Saudi Arabia, is the most important pilgrimage site for Muslims because it was the birthplace of the Prophet Muhammad, and it is also the site of the Kaaba, a large cube-shaped building (today draped in black-and-gold cloth) surrounded by a large mosque (**3.2.16**). Muslims believe Abraham constructed the Kaaba as a kind of replica of the home of God. The Kaaba protects the Black Stone, perhaps a meteorite, that has been worshipped at the site since before the Islamic period. When Muhammad visited the Kaaba around 630, he destroyed the idols that had surrounded the shrine and, by so doing, transformed the site back into a holy site for Allah.

Similarly to Christian churches, mosques are designed to reflect religious belief and practice. In the center of each mosque complex is usually a large courtyard with a pool where the faithful can cleanse themselves before entering the mosque itself to pray. Muslims must pray five times a day in the direction of Mecca. They are called to prayer from the mosque's large minarets that rise above the city: nine distinctive minarets surround the mosque in Mecca.

One of the five important commitments of the Muslim faith (known as the Five Pillars of Islam) is the obligation to visit Mecca once in one's lifetime, unless sickness or some other factor makes this impossible, to honor the house of Allah. Although pilgrimage is important to many Christians, it has never been an obligation as it is in Islam.

For Muslims, there is only one God, called Allah, and the Prophet Muhammad specifically forbade the worship of idols. Medina is another holy place and destination for Muslim pilgrims because it is the location of the tomb of Muhammad. Many pilgrims do visit the mosque (**3.2.17**), often before or after a visit to Mecca, in order to greet the Prophet, but limit themselves to a greeting as Islam prohibits worship of any other than Allah.

The original mosque on the site was built by Muhammad himself and was his house as well as a place of worship. The building measured 100 cubits (about 183 ft.) on all sides,

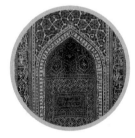

All mosques contain a *mihrab*, or a prayer niche, that faces in the direction of Mecca: → see **4.2.16**, p. 565

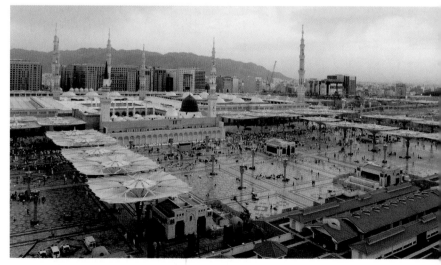

3.2.17 **Masjid al-Nabawi (The Prophet's Mosque)**, Medina, Saudi Arabia

and was built of mud-brick, with palm trunks to support a flat roof over the northern part of the building, where worshipers prayed toward Jerusalem. In 624, however, Allah revealed to Muhammad that the direction of prayer (known as the **qibla**) should be redirected to the south, toward Mecca. In the eighth century a curved prayer niche, called a **mihrab**, was built into the southern wall. All mosques include a mihrab within them, placed on the wall facing Mecca (known as the qibla wall). This enables Muslims to pray toward Mecca from any mosque in which they may happen to be.

Subsequent rulers substantially enlarged the mosque, making it one hundred times bigger than the original. They have added a courtyard, school, resting places for pilgrims, ten minarets, and twenty-four domes. The slightly taller green dome marks the spot of Muhammad's tomb (**3.2.17**, p. 383). Within the mosque, the most sacred spot is the Riad-ul Jannah. Placed between the Prophet's **minbar** (pulpit) and his tomb, it is believed to be a piece of the Garden of Paradise.

A centuries-old diagram, made of watercolors, gold, silver and ink, identifies the important original components of the Prophet's Mosque in Medina (**3.2.18**). This

image shows the tomb chamber of the Prophet (identifiable by its green dome) in the upper left-hand corner. A textile covering patterned in green and white chevrons is visible on the grille and tomb within the chamber.

At the center of the image is the garden that Fatima, the daughter of the Prophet, planted with two palm trees; her tomb is also shown there, while others—belonging to some of the Prophet's companions—can be seen outside the walls of the sanctuary. To the right of the diagram, standing in the **arcades**, we can see the Prophet's minbar, from which he preached.

Romanesque Art and Christian Pilgrimages

One of the most traveled pilgrimage journeys in the Middle Ages was the Way of St. James, a network of paths that led to the burial site of St. James at the Cathedral of Santiago de Compostela in Galicia, Spain. Pilgrims could start their journey at any point: some started from as far away as Jerusalem, although the majority came from France following one of four distinct routes (**3.2.19**). During the journey, which could take several months, pilgrims would stop at other important sites that held sacred relics. Along the way large churches were built to accommodate the crowds of pilgrims, even in small towns that could not otherwise have funded such expansive construction. One such town was Conques in France. Conques was a stop along one of the French routes to Santiago de Compostela, but was also a pilgrimage destination in its own right. In the

Qibla: the direction to Mecca, toward which Muslims face when praying

Mihrab: a niche in a mosque that is in a wall oriented toward Mecca

Minbar: a platform in a mosque, from which a leader delivers sermons

Arcade: a series of connected arches

3.2.18 View of the Sanctuary at Medina, 17th or 18th century. Opaque watercolor, gold, silver, and ink on paper, 25½ × 18¼". Nasser D. Khalili Collection of Islamic Art

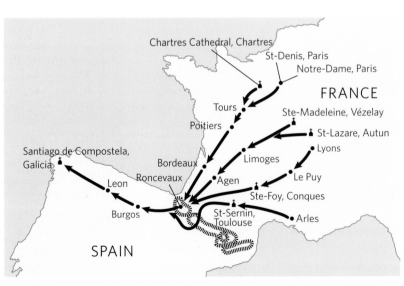

3.2.19 Pilgrimage map showing the routes from France toward Santiago de Compostela, with important churches along the routes, including Sainte-Foy at Conques

ninth century, a monk from Conques stole the relics of Sainte Foy (Saint Faith) from their original resting place in the much larger town of Agen. According to legend, Sainte Foy was a young woman who lived in Agen in the third century. She was tortured to death with a red-hot brazier during the persecution of Christians in about 290 or 303 CE. A number of miracles attributed to the relics made Conques a famous pilgrimage site, and by the eleventh century this meant that a new church was needed to house the relics and the crowds of pilgrims.

Sainte-Foy is a characteristically Romanesque church (**3.2.20**). Its arches, vaults, and **columns** recall architectural elements from ancient Rome. For example, the exterior arches are rounded. Churches in the Middle Ages in the Western tradition were often designed, as Sainte-Foy was, in the shape of a Latin cross (**3.2.21**). In this kind of plan the main and longer **axis** (the nave) usually runs from west to east, with a shorter axis (the **transept**) at right angles across it nearer the east end. Cathedral

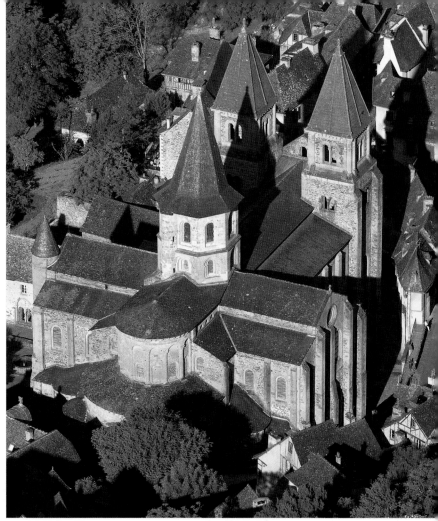

3.2.20 Church of Sainte-Foy, *c.* 1050–1130, Conques, France

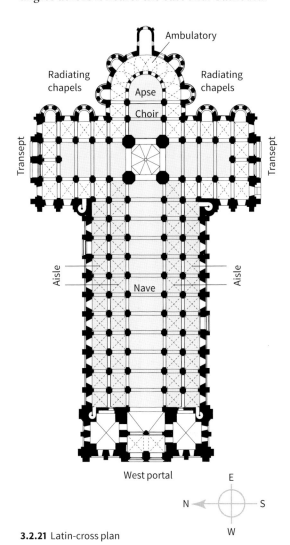

3.2.21 Latin-cross plan

floor plans were designed to guide the flow of visiting pilgrims and the congregation during services. Worshipers entered at the west end and walked eastward down the nave toward the altar. The **choir** continued the nave on the other side of the crossing. As it was closest to the apse, which contained the altar, it was reserved for the clergy and the choir of singers. Pilgrims could also circle around behind the apse through the **ambulatory** and visit individual chapels, most of which held sacred relics.

The west–east orientation of churches, like the shape of the cross, also has symbolic meaning. The crucifixion is often depicted in a painting or sculpture at the east end, while an artwork of the Last Judgment may be displayed at the western **portal**, where parishioners and pilgrims would enter and exit. The orientation of the church also mimics the natural course of the sun: thus to the east, Christ, as "light of the world," rises like the sun in the morning, while to the west, the setting sun reminds worshipers of their own mortality and the impending Judgment Day.

Column: a freestanding pillar, usually circular in section

Axis: an imaginary line showing the center of a shape, volume, or composition

Transept: the structure crossing the main body of a Latin-cross-plan church

Choir: the part of a church traditionally reserved for singers and clergy, situated between the nave and the apse

Ambulatory: a covered walkway, particularly around the apse of a church

Portal: an entrance; a royal portal (main entrance) is usually on the west front of a church and features sculpted forms of kings and queens

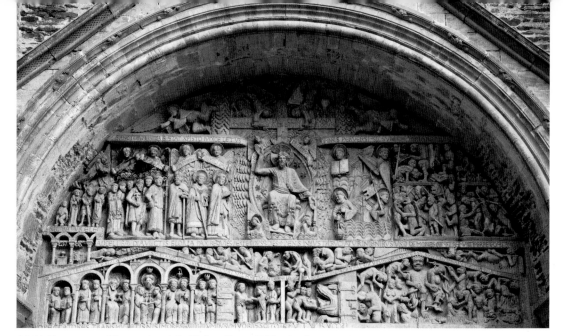

3.2.22 Tympanum of the west portal of Sainte-Foy, c. 1050–1130, Conques, France

Most people in the Middle Ages were illiterate, so pictures taught religious stories to pilgrims and parishioners alike, and thus reinforced their faith. Portals, or gateways, served as both entrances and exits to the church for the public (see **3.2.23**). In many Romanesque churches, the **tympanum**, **lintel**, **trumeau**, and **door jambs** were all covered with **relief** sculptures, often of scenes from the Bible, and originally colorfully painted.

The tympanum above the entryway to Sainte-Foy (**3.2.22**) shows the Last Judgment, using **hierarchical scale** to highlight the importance of Christ in the center; he is larger than the angels, prophets, and ancestors that surround him. He raises his right hand to show the salvation of those to his right, and lowers his left hand, marking the damnation of those to his left. He is enclosed within a **mandorla**, an oval, pointed, full-body halo that is a decorative hallmark of the Romanesque style.

The entire scene is divided into three **registers**. The top register contains four angels, two of whom hold the cross and two who herald the Last Judgment with their horns. In the middle register, Christ is surrounded by more angels. To the left of Christ (Christ's right) are the Virgin Mary, with a faint amount of surviving blue paint, and St. Peter holding his keys. The other figures are people who played an important role in the history of the monastery of Conques, including King Charlemagne, its most significant patron.

Sainte Foy is shown on the left side, between the middle and bottom register, slightly to

3.2.23 Diagram of the west portal tympanum in **3.2.22**

the right of some arches. She is bowing down, praying before a large hand, which represents God. To the right of Christ (from the viewer's perspective) are the damned, suffering a variety of tortures, often based on the kind of sin the damned person performed during his or her lifetime. Below Christ are scenes of souls being guided either to heaven, through an arched doorway, or to hell, represented by the head of a monster and a door designed to bolt in the damned for eternity.

The Rise of the Gothic

Gothic cathedrals have been called books or bibles in stone. Stories from the bible were carved into the stone and captured in the dazzling glass that covers and illuminates these cathedrals. First built in the twelfth century, the structures are distinguished by their immense height that reach toward the heavens, and glorious stained-glass windows, which symbolically fill the space with the light of God. The grand interior of Chartres Cathedral in France (**3.2.24**) combines all of the characteristic elements of Gothic architecture. The vaulted ceiling is 118 ft. above the floor and the nave is more than 50 ft. wide, surrounding receptive visitors with height and light to transport them beyond the cares and concerns of the mundane world.

Rib vaults make the great height of Gothic cathedrals possible: the weight of the structure is spread through the ribs of the ceiling vaults (see **3.2.25**), before further dividing the burden between the walls and **flying buttresses** (see **3.2.24**). Flying buttresses function like many long, outstretched fingers to prevent the walls from falling outward. Because these engineering achievements distributed the weight previously carried by very thick walls, it was possible to build with walls that became progressively thinner. In addition, large stained-glass windows now filled cathedrals with light, as the walls no longer needed to bear all the weight of the structure. The cathedral at Chartres is famous for the beautiful blue cast from its stained-glass windows.

Cathedrals were built by hired mason-workers headed by one main architect. Funding for the cathedral was donated by townspeople and pilgrims, but part of the money came from bishops, the centralized Catholic Church, and wealthy individuals. By offering gifts to the Church, benefactors were not only acknowledged by others, but would also often be pardoned by religious officials for their sins.

Upon entering Chartres, pilgrims walked the labyrinth on the floor, symbolic of their physical and spiritual journey (**3.2.25**). Again, as at Sainte-Foy, the architects created a pathway through the cathedral that guided the pilgrims to the numerous chapels containing relics. The site of Chartres was particularly important for holding the tunic said to have been worn by the Virgin Mary at Christ's birth. When the tunic survived a fire in 1194, the townspeople

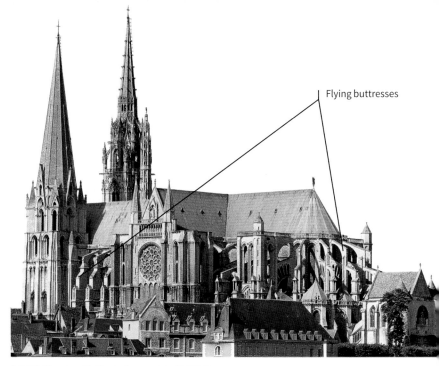

Flying buttresses

3.2.24 Chartres Cathedral, completed 1260, France

believed this to be a sign that Mary continued to protect them and wished for them to rebuild the cathedral.

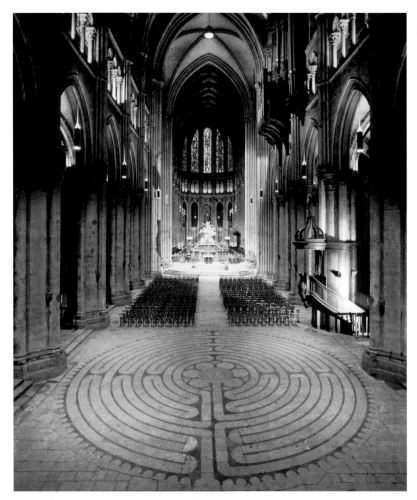

3.2.25 Chartres Cathedral, interior view showing labyrinth

From the Gothic to the Early Renaissance in Italy

How did artists represent in two dimensions the equivalent of the soaring spirituality of the Gothic style of architecture? And how did this evolve into a new style of painting that would come to be known as Renaissance art? Two paintings of the Virgin Mary and Christ Child, one by Cimabue (*c.* 1240–1302) and the other made thirty years later by his student Giotto di Bondone (*c.* 1266–1337), illustrate some of the characteristics that mark the transition from the Gothic to the early Renaissance style.

Cimabue's Gothic painting is reminiscent of Byzantine icons, with the rich gold throughout, the **stylized** quality of Mary's robe, the organization of the angels' faces and halos in orderly rows, the elongation of the bodies, and the flatness of the figures appearing somewhat like paper cutouts (**3.2.26**). Cimabue's figures seem to float in space and rise up toward the top of the composition in much the same way that Gothic cathedrals emphasized height to inspire worshipers to look up toward the heavens.

While Giotto's *Virgin and Child Enthroned* (**3.2.27**) clearly shows architectural elements that recall Gothic churches (such as the pointed arch on Mary's throne), his painting makes many innovations, such as the three-dimensionality of his **forms** and the emphasis on creating a believable sense of the space in which Mary sits. We can also see through the spaces in the framework of the throne: the figures nearer to us overlap those that are behind them, and light seems to shine in a natural way and cast consistent shadows, helping to create the illusion that this is a three-dimensional space. Mary, Jesus, and the angels also look more three-dimensional than the more delineated figures in Cimabue's painting. Cimabue's *Virgin and Child Enthroned* seems to focus only on the spirituality of the scene; Giotto appears to wish to create a realistic space, more like the world in which we live. This shift in approach was revolutionary, and Giotto's artistic inventions were at the forefront of the stylistic changes that would take place in the fifteenth and sixteenth centuries.

3.2.26 Cimabue, *Virgin and Child Enthroned*, *c.* 1280. Tempera and gold on wood, 12'7½" × 7'4". Uffizi Gallery, Florence, Italy

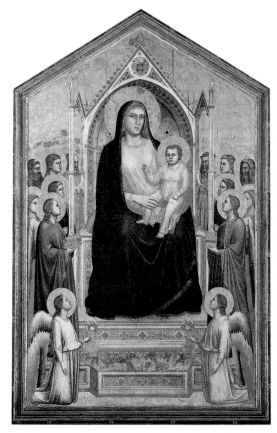

3.2.27 Giotto, *Virgin and Child Enthroned*, *c.* 1310. Tempera on wood, 10'7" × 6'9". Uffizi Gallery, Florence, Italy

Explore Further Art of the Middle Ages

Early Christian and Byzantine

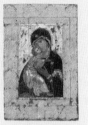

4.2.15b Catacombs of Priscilla, 2nd and 3rd centuries CE → p. 564

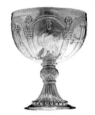

4.2.9 *Virgin of Vladimir*, 12th century (before 1132) → p. 559

Medieval and Romanesque

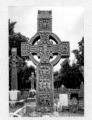

1.6.13 Muiredach's High Cross (West face), *c.* 10th century → p. 124

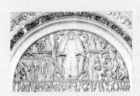

4.2.11 Gislebertus, *The Last Judgment*, *c.* 1120–35 → p. 561

Islamic

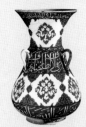

1.4.22 Mosque lamp from the Dome of the Rock in Jerusalem, 1549 → p. 96

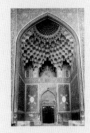

4.4.7 *Iwan* with *muqarnas* vaulting, Masjid-i-Shah, early 17th century → p. 584

Gothic

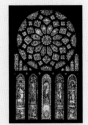

2.6.7 Rose window with lancets, Chartres Cathedral, France, 13th century → p. 273

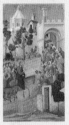

2.2.10 Duccio di Buoninsegna, *Entry into Jerusalem*, 1308–11 → p. 200

Your turn

To which periods of art history do these artworks belong?

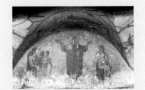

2.6.10 *Chalice with Apostles Venerating the Cross*, *c.* 600 CE → p. 275

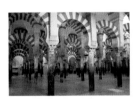

1.9.10 Great Mosque of Córdoba, Spain, 784–86 CE → p. 153

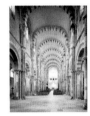

2.5.14 Church of Sainte-Madeleine, Vézelay, France, 9th–13th century → p. 251

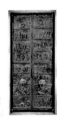

4.2.3a Doors, Church of St. Michael's, Hildesheim, Germany, 1015 → p. 556

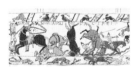

4.6.6 Detail of the Battle of Hastings, *Bayeux Tapestry*, *c.* 1066–82 → p. 608

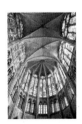

2.5.16 Stained-glass windows, Abbey Church of St. Denis, France, 12th century → p. 253

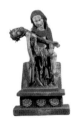

1.2.4 *Roettgen Pietà* (*Vesperbild*), Germany, *c.* 1330 → p. 52

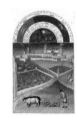

4.3.6a Limbourg Brothers, *Très Riches Heures du Duc de Berry*, 1412 → p. 571

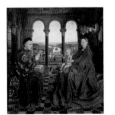

2.2.13 Jan van Eyck, *The Madonna of Chancellor Rolin*, 1430–34 → p. 202

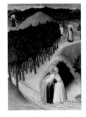

1.5.13 *The Meeting of St. Anthony and St. Paul*, *c.* 1430–35 → p. 111

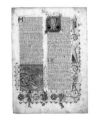

2.7.8 *Dutch History Bible*, Utrecht, The Netherlands, 1443 → p. 288

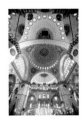

2.5.1 Sinan, Süleymaniye mosque, Istanbul, Turkey, 1557 → p. 245

3.3
Art of India, China, Japan, Korea, and Southeast Asia

Asia is home to artistic traditions that date back many thousands of years. India and China are large landmasses, both bordered by land and by great expanses of ocean (see **3.3.1**). Southeast Asia lies east of India and south of China; the arts of the region have been influenced by these large neighbors. Japan, on the other hand, is a country of more than 3,000 islands off the eastern coast of mainland Asia. Trade by sea and along the famed Silk Road—a network of trade routes between Asia and the Mediterranean world—led to the spread of cultural ideas and a sharing of religious and philosophical beliefs.

Religion and philosophy have been integral to the arts of the entire region (see: Philosophical and Religious Traditions in Asia), yet certain stylistic characteristics make the art of each of these cultures distinctive.

In Indian art, there is a noticeable tendency toward elaborate decoration and an emphasis on the human body, frequently showing sensual movement and suggesting fertility. Chinese art combines an interest in religious subject matter with a great respect for Chinese heritage and ancestors. In general, Chinese artworks are also very precise and symmetrically balanced; Chinese artists aim to create uniformity and convey control of their material. In contrast, Japanese artworks tend to be more asymmetrical, organic, individual, and to convey spontaneity. Japanese art is also distinctively contemplative and reveals a great reverence for nature. Korea, in East Asia, was divided into two states (North and South) in 1945 as a consequence of the Allied victory of World War II. In South Korea, Christianity, Buddhism, and Korean Shamanism survive, while in North Korea religious practice is minimal and is not supported by the government. Southeast Asia is an immensely diverse region; strong influences of Hinduism and Buddhism from India often feature in Southeast Asian art and architecture. For example, many Hindu temples were built to represent cosmic mountains, homes for Hindu gods who were believed to support local rulers. This chapter highlights both the individuality of these places and the themes and ideas that unite their artistic traditions.

India

The landmass of India occupies a peninsula in southern Asia that is bordered on the north by the Himalayan Mountains. It is about one-third the size of the United States. Buddhist and Hindu beliefs have been important influences on India's rich visual history. The shrines and

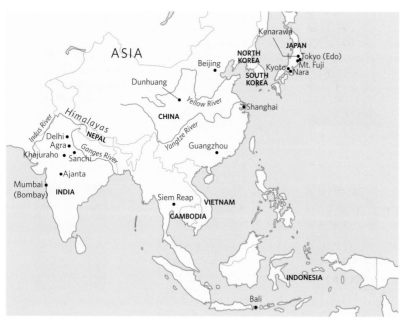

3.3.1 Map of Asia

Philosophical and Religious Traditions in Asia

The arts of India, China, Japan, Korea, and Southeast Asia can be fully understood only in relation to each country's religions and philosophies. All have a long tradition of religious pluralism; in other words, the acceptance of beliefs from different religions and philosophies. They can also be described as **syncretic**, meaning that their religions blend two or more belief systems. For one example, it is common in Japan to be a follower of Shinto, and a Buddhist, and to practice Confucianism all at the same time. This is possible partly because of the similar values of the various religions and philosophies. For instance, many of these religions strive for harmony with nature, and have a component of ancestral worship.

Buddhist beliefs are founded on the teachings of Siddhartha Gautama (the Buddha) (*c.* 563–483 BCE). Buddhism emphasizes an acceptance of the difficulties of life and of samsara (the cycle of birth, suffering, death, and rebirth). Once one attains enlightenment, the ultimate wisdom, one arrives at nirvana, the end of suffering for eternity. Chan Buddhism, influenced by Daoism, originated in China and became Zen Buddhism in Japan; it promotes meditation and introspection, and a focus on individual moments and daily tasks.

Confucianism is based on the philosophy of Chinese Master Kong (Confucius) (551–479 BCE), who promoted the use of ethics to attain social order. His teachings emphasize self-discipline, moral duty, and paying respect both to one's ancestors and (by extension) to the elders of society. Confucianism is common in China and Japan, and is also practiced in Korea.

Daoism (The Way) comes from the teachings of Laozi (b. 604 BCE), who explained in *Dao de jing* ("The Book of the Way") how to live in harmony with nature and the universe. Yin and yang is the concept that seemingly opposing forces are interconnected and need each other for balance. Such opposing forces might be male and female, or light and dark. Daoism is found throughout Asia, but most prominently in China.

Hinduism encompasses a number of beliefs, including reincarnation, rebirth of the soul or of the body, and karma, the idea that one's actions will cause a reaction or consequence in the universe. Hindus believe that, while on Earth, their main goals should be to practice righteous living (*dharma*), achieve physical and emotional love, and attain spiritual salvation. Hindus believe in the existence of several gods (including Brahma, Shiva, and Vishnu), although individual practice and worship vary greatly amongst adherents. Hinduism originated in India and has been adopted throughout Asia, although India still holds the largest Hindu population.

Islam: Muslims base their beliefs on a sacred text called the Koran that records the will of Allah (God) as revealed to the prophet Muhammad (*c.* 570–632 CE). Islam originated at the birthplace of Muhammad (Mecca, Saudi Arabia) but today is practiced worldwide, with many followers in Asia, including India and China. (See also: Three Religions of the Middle Ages, p. 374.)

Shinto is a native religion of Japan. Its name means "The Way of the Gods." Shinto worships several gods, of whom the most significant is Amaterasu-omikami, the sun goddess, and emphasizes respect for nature and ancestors. Followers believe that non-human entities (animals, plants, and inanimate objects) all possess a spiritual essence. *Kami*, for example, are believed to be forces in nature (such as wind or trees), or spirits of ancestors.

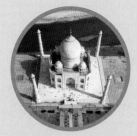

The Taj Mahal was built by the Mughals, Muslims who ruled for centuries:
→ see **1.6.15a**, p. 126

Syncretism: the blending of multiple religious or philosophical beliefs

temples built for both of these religions are designed to be small replicas, or microcosms, of the universe, and places to meditate and worship the gods.

Buddhism in Indian Art

Siddhartha Gautama (*c.* 563–483 BCE), who would become the Buddha or "The Enlightened One," was born a prince in what is now Nepal. Traditions tell how Siddhartha was raised in comfort in the royal palace, but, at the age of twenty-nine, he witnessed the lives of the poor and sick and became an ascetic: a person who practices self-discipline and rejects personal wealth and worldly pleasures. Buddhists believe that Siddhartha achieved enlightenment through meditation and self-discipline; he spent the second half of his life teaching others to try to do the same. After his death, his life and teachings were spread by

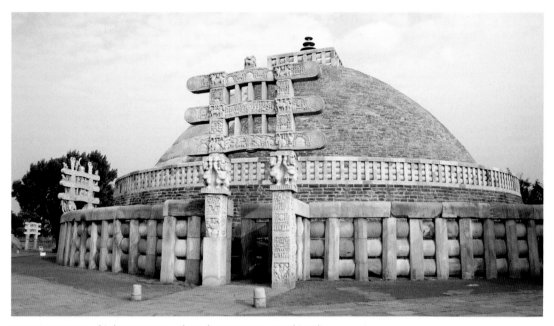

3.3.2 Great Stupa, third century BCE, enlarged *c.* 150–50 BCE. Sanchi, India

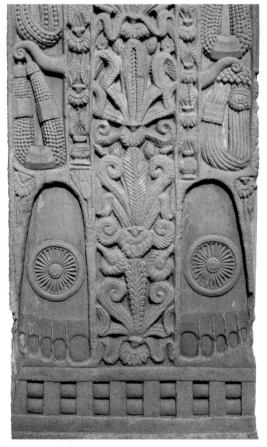

3.3.3 Detail of North gate showing footprints of Buddha and Wheel of Law (dharma wheel), Great Stupa, Sanchi, Madhya Pradesh, India

Stupa: a burial mound believed to contain some of the Buddha's remains

Torana: a gateway used in Hindu and Buddhist architecture

Cardinal points: North, South, East, and West

Circumambulation: the act of walking around a sacred object

The Great Stupa in Sanchi, India, was built by King Ashoka as part of a large Buddhist monastery (**3.3.2**). Ashoka (304–232 BCE) was emperor of India in the mid-third century BCE. He was born a Hindu, but it is said that he became a Buddhist after feeling ashamed of the murderous destruction caused by a war in which his army killed more than 100,000 people. He became known as "the pious Ashoka" and gained a reputation as a charitable and peace-loving ruler who built hospitals and schools throughout India. When Ashoka converted to Buddhism, he disinterred the Buddha's remains and distributed them to be reburied within several thousand more stupas he built throughout India.

Surrounding the Great Stupa at Sanchi are four gateways, or ***toranas***, placed at the four **cardinal points** surrounding the large mound. At a height of 35 ft., the columns and horizontal crossbeams of these toranas are covered with scenes of the Buddha's multiple lives (*jatakas*). The Buddha himself is not shown, but there are signs of his presence, such as an empty throne, his footprints, and the Wheel of Law (the Buddha's teaching of the path to nirvana), the last two of which can be seen in **3.3.3**. In this way, Buddhists are invited to **circumambulate** the structure, symbolically following in the footsteps of the Buddha. Pilgrims enter through the east gate and circle the stupa in a clockwise direction, following the path of the sun. Stone railings added after Ashoka's time allow pilgrims safely to climb higher as they encircle

word of mouth throughout India. The Buddha's remains were cremated and buried within eight large dirt mounds, called ***stupas***, the locations of which were relevant to important periods in his life.

the mound in which the Buddha's remains are interred, a ritual that emulates the Buddha's path toward enlightenment. The stupa and its four gateways represent a three-dimensional **mandala**, or a re-creation of the universe.

Representations of the Buddha first appeared in India during the first few centuries CE. The Silk Road—an immense system of trade routes used for many centuries across Asia and Europe—was a channel for the spread of Buddhism, and therefore also for the dispersal and development of the image of the Buddha (**3.3.4**). While certain attributes of the Buddha—hair in a knotted bun, and stretched earlobes—remain consistent, stylistic changes often reflect the regions in which the depictions were made. A Buddha sculpture from the Gupta period (320–550 CE) (**3.3.5**) sits

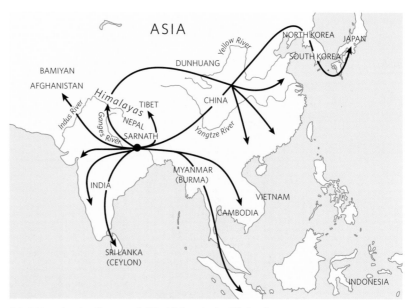

3.3.4 Map showing the spread of Buddhism via the Silk Road

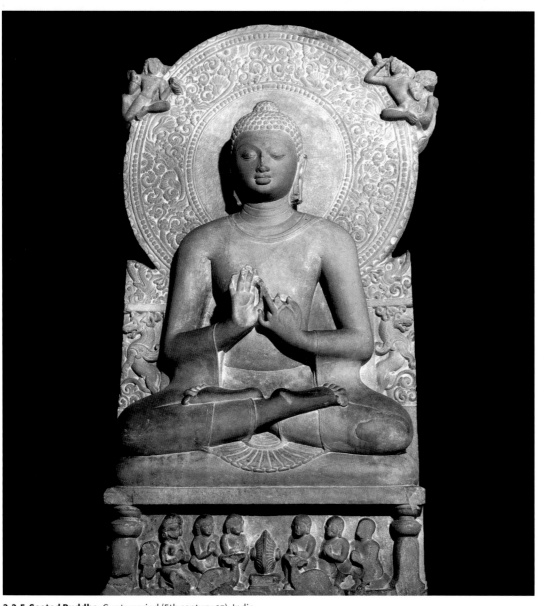

3.3.5 Seated Buddha, Gupta period (5th century CE). India

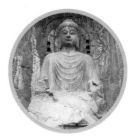

The Longmen Grottoes in China helped to spread Buddhism along the Silk Road:

→ see **4.5.9**, p. 599

Mandala: a sacred diagram of the universe, often involving a square and a circle

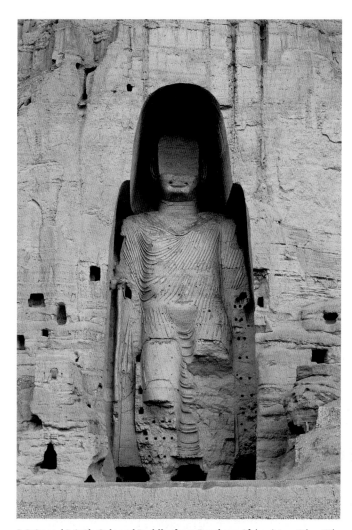
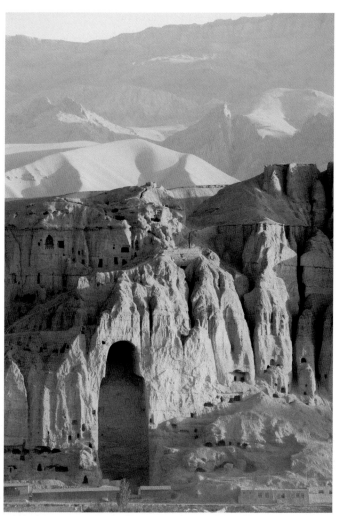

3.3.6a and **3.3.6b Colossal Buddha from Bamiyan**, Afghanistan, 6th or 7th century CE, destroyed by Taliban, 2001. Before (left) and after (right) destruction

in a meditative, serene pose, with his eyes closed, spiritually turning inward to develop inner strength and enlightenment. His body is graceful, with a solid posture and elegantly crossed legs. The soft facial features and overall idealized beauty of the sculpture are typical of the Gupta period. The meaning of depictions of the Buddha is often communicated through the figure's hand gestures (**mudras**). The Buddha is presented here as a compassionate teacher, with the orb of the sun—symbolizing the Wheel of Law—behind him. The Buddha is setting the Wheel of Law into motion while teaching the principles of his Eightfold Path of Righteousness; the sculpture also represents his eternal guidance. This statue was found in Sarnath, the site of the Buddha's first sermon, and the figures carved below the Buddha are his disciples, giving him their rapt attention.

Through the Silk Road, Buddhism also spread as far as Bamiyan, Afghanistan. Between the fifth and ninth centuries, more than 800 caves were carved into the cliffs, which were used as Buddhist temples and monasteries. Two colossal standing Buddhas, the taller one reaching 175 ft. in height (**3.3.6a** and **3.3.6b**), were the largest Buddhas in the world until the Taliban destroyed them with dynamite in 2001, claiming that the statues lead to the worship of false idols. The elegant folds of the drapery on these Buddhas show the influence of a **Classical** Greek style that had been passed through India. The feet of these standing Buddhas were carved away from the cliff wall so that pilgrims could circumambulate the sacred figures. The larger statue was the Vairocana Buddha, which embodies emptiness and impermanence—a meaning that now holds a strong sense of irony, since the sculpture was destroyed so violently.

Hinduism in Indian Art

Hinduism has been practiced at least as far back as 1000 BCE. Today, it is the world's third largest religion, with the majority of its

Mudra: hand gestures that signify meaning in Buddhism and Hinduism

Classical: Greek art of the period *c.* 480–323 BCE

followers living in India. The kinds of personal practices and gods that are worshiped vary greatly amongst Hindus, but they all share the belief that one's spirit is eternal. Just as Buddhism grew because powerful people promoted it, the increase in popularity of Hinduism was largely due to the efforts of rulers to encourage Hindu worship, particularly by building religious temples.

Around 1020 CE, King Vidyadhara built a large complex containing Hindu temples in Khajuraho, in northern India. The largest of these, the Kandariya Mahadeva (**3.3.7a**), is dedicated to Shiva, the Hindu god of creation and destruction. Hindus see their temples as cosmic mountains, or links between heaven and Earth. The large towers on Hindu temples are called *shikhara*s and represent mountain peaks. The vertical towers pull the eye upward to the heavens, suggesting a desire for *moksha*, or the release from suffering. Every temple

has a central room underneath the shikhara that contains an image of the god to whom the temple is dedicated. A Hindu priest's job is to maintain the sculpture (which embodies the god itself) through prayer, meditation, incense burning, feeding and clothing the sculpture, and pouring milk or honey on it.

The temple is aligned with the rising and setting of the sun, with stairs for entrance on the east. Horizontal decoration encourages the viewer to walk around the temple and view the intricate carving and **relief** sculpture. The exterior is covered with more than 600 sculptures in poses that suggest dancing, which creates a rhythmic pulsing effect over the entire structure (**3.3.7b**). Many of the scenes are sensual and erotic, depicting the physical union of males and females. The sexual joining of these male and female forces represents the balance of opposing elements in the universe, or the unity of the cosmos.

Relief: a sculpture that projects from a flat surface

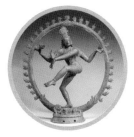

Shiva is often portrayed in the act of balancing opposing forces of the universe:

→ see **4.3.2**, p. 569

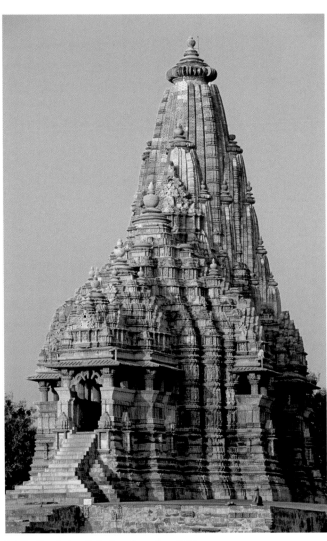

3.3.7a Kandariya Mahadeva temple, *c.* 1000 Khajuraho, Madhya Pradesh, India

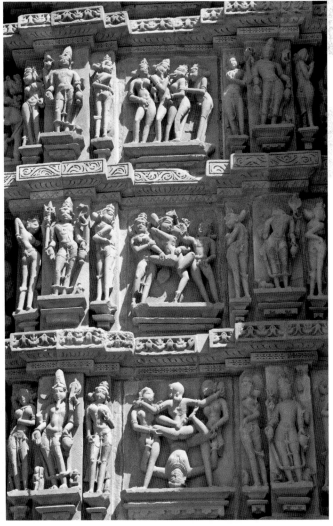

3.3.7b **Detail of exterior sculpture, Kandariya Mahadeva temple**

China

The earliest traces of settled communities in China have been found along the Yellow and Yangtze rivers. The first Chinese emperor, Qin Shi Huangdi, established the first unified Chinese dynasty in 221 BCE. China's boundaries have changed throughout its subsequent history according to its military success or failure, but today it is approximately the same size as the United States.

Buddhism and Daoism are the largest religious and philosophical systems in China. Each faith integrates the beliefs of the other and of Confucianism (see: Philosophical and Religious Traditions in Asia, p. 391) as well: the Chinese believe a person may practice more than one belief system. This affects the whole of Chinese culture. In Chinese art, for example, scroll paintings are intended to enhance meditation, as well as respect for nature and one's elders—virtues that are valued by all three faiths. Many great Chinese artworks have been discovered in tombs, providing evidence both of a widespread reverence for ancestors, and of the importance of the idea of the afterlife.

Death and the Afterlife

For thousands of years, Chinese people have worshiped their ancestors, who they believe are transformed after death into supernatural entities with the power to communicate with the gods and protect the living. To show the ancestors due respect, and so that the deceased would have what they needed in the afterlife, both valuable and everyday items were buried with them in their tombs. Humans and animals were also sacrificed in the belief that they would serve the dead in the next realm. Today, similar customs persist: the Chinese often burn money, food, and other objects in the hope that these will reach their ancestors in the spirit world.

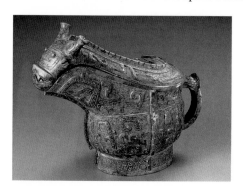

3.3.8 Ritual wine vessel (guang), late Shang Dynasty, c. 1700–1050 BCE. Bronze, 6½ × 3½ × 8½". Brooklyn Museum, New York

The tombs of the Shang Dynasty's rulers have preserved many lavishly made objects in jade, gold, ivory, and in particular, bronze. This bronze *guang* (lidded vessel; **3.3.8**) was found buried in a tomb. It was used to pour wine during a ritual, perhaps for a burial ceremony. The container depicts a horn-headed dragon with sharp teeth at its spout. The dragon was one of the most commonly used **motifs** in Chinese art, symbolizing good fortune, power, and immortality. The mazelike design on the side of the vessel is called a *t'ao t'ieh* (monster mask). It was believed to ward off evil spirits and connect the living with their ancestors.

The tomb of Lady Dai (d. 168 BCE), a noblewoman of the Han Dynasty (206 BCE–

Motif: a design or color repeated as a unit in a pattern:

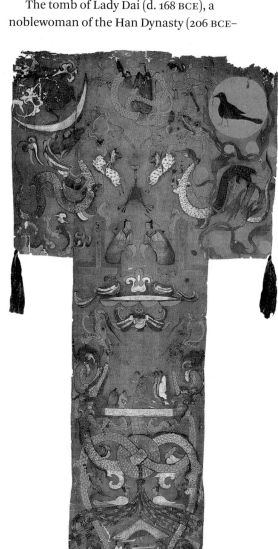

3.3.9 Painted banner from tomb of Lady Dai Hou Fu-ren, Han Dynasty, c. 168 BCE. Silk, length 80½", width at top 36", width at bottom 18¾". Hunan Museum, Changsha, China

220 CE), was excavated in 1972, revealing a wealth of objects intended to accompany her into the afterlife. An exquisite, richly painted silk textile (**3.3.9**) had been placed over Lady Dai's coffin, protected by several additional layers of wooden coffins. The silk banner is in the shape of a T; the wide horizontal section represents heaven, with twisting dragons, a toad on a gold moon, and a crow on a red sun. At the top in the center, surrounded by a red serpent, is probably an imperial ancestor. Lady Dai stands with relatives and attendants upon a central white platform about halfway down the banner, awaiting her ascent to the heavenly realm. Above her is a bird and, at the cross of the T, are two kneeling figures who are thought to be guardians or guides of some kind. A jade circle, crossed by two writhing dragons and known as a *bi*—frequently used as a symbol for heaven—sits below Lady Dai on her platform. Scholars have hypothesized that this banner either shows Lady Dai's funeral and her journey to heaven, or views of the three spiritual realms of heaven, Earth, and the underworld.

The emperors of ancient China sought to take their riches with them to the afterlife. Ancient records described how the first emperor of China, Qin Shi Huangdi, prepared for his death by constructing a burial mound with a vast underground city palace that matched the one he occupied in life. These accounts were believed to be sheer legend until 1974 when, in a spectacular archaeological discovery, excavations of a tomb mound revealed evidence that the ancient stories were true (**3.3.10a** and **3.3.10b**).

Soon after he came to the throne at the age of thirteen, Qin Shi Huangdi began overseeing the elaborate preparations for his own resting place, which continued for thirty-six years until his death in 210 BCE. Artisans filled the

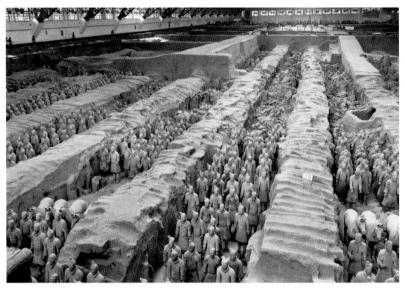

3.3.10a Building housing pit number 1 of the terra-cotta army, mausoleum of Qin Shi Huangdi, China, *c.* 210 BCE. Xi'an, Shaanxi Province, China

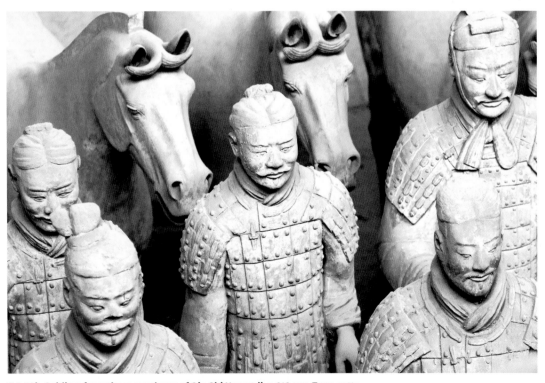

3.3.10b Soldiers from the mausoleum of Qin Shi Huangdi, *c.* 210 BCE. Terra-cotta and pigment, figures approximately lifesize. Xi'an, Shaanxi Province, China

Ai Weiwei, *Dropping a Han Dynasty Urn*
The Value of Art: Questions of History and Authenticity

For the other Ai Weiwei
GATEWAYS:
→ see p. 112 and p. 620

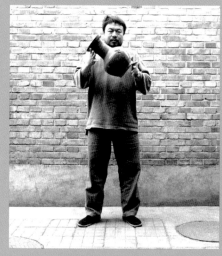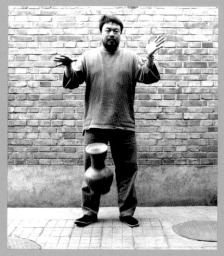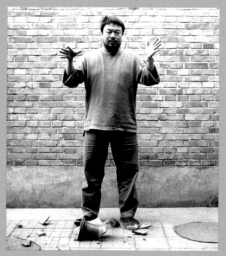

3.3.11 Ai Weiwei, *Dropping a Han Dynasty Urn*, 1995. Three black-and-white photographs, each 53½ × 42⅞"

Triptych: an artwork comprising three panels, normally joined together and sharing a common theme

Piece-mold casting: A process for casting metal objects in which a mold is broken into several pieces that are then reassembled into a final sculpture

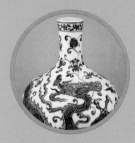

Cobalt imported from Persia was combined in innovative ways with white porcelain during the Ming Dynasty:
→ see **2.6.4**, p. 272

The significant value about any act or art really exists in the viewer's mind.

Ai Weiwei

When Chinese artist Ai Weiwei (b. 1957) damaged and altered numerous ancient pots, he was highlighting his belief that the value of an object is based on personal perception. In exhibitions, Ai's work is often installed according to the dates of the objects he has appropriated. The vase shown in this group of photos (**3.3.11**), for example, was made during the Han Dynasty (206 BCE–220 CE). Ai began collecting ancient vases in the 1990s, and is thought to have paid around $2,000 for the one smashed in the third photograph of the *Dropping a Han Dynasty Urn* **triptych**. Some scholars have questioned whether the vases shown are authentic historical specimens, or fakes. This speculation only furthers Ai's desire to inspire questions about how value is determined and by whom.

The Chinese ceramics appropriated by Ai Weiwei reference long-standing traditions and an impressive history of significant technical innovations. Vases produced in China have traditionally been made for utilitarian purposes or buried with the dead. Pottery from the Neolithic period (*c.* 5000–2000 BCE) is notable for its painted decoration. Artists from the Shang Dynasty (*c.* 1500–*c.* 1050 BCE) were distinctively skilled in the process of **piece-mold casting** (see **3.3.8**). The Han Dynasty is known for developing prolific numbers of high-quality ceramics covered with a low-fired lead glaze. High-quality Imperial pottery production was a focus of the Ming Dynasty (1368–1644 CE), when artists developed a formula for adding manganese (a chemical element) to cobalt (a blue pigment) to create distinctive blue-and-white porcelain pieces in such a way that the blue does not bleed into the white.

Ceramics artists today still learn and use these once innovative, now traditional, methods. In fact, imitation of past styles is part of the tradition of Chinese ceramics, which has led to the production of countless replicas. Knowing this, Ai Weiwei's art leads us to consider whether such old objects should still be considered important if they can be reproduced almost identically. Further, are copies of ancient pots authentic works in their own right? What if another artist alters the original object? Interestingly, in 2012, a collector purchased a work made by Ai Weiwei—one in which the artist had painted a Coca-Cola logo on a Han vase—and purposely let it fall and shatter to the ground, in an exact mimicry of Ai's photo triptych.

The artist has said, "To have other layers of color and images above the previous ones calls into question both the identity and authenticity of the object. It makes both conditions non-absolute: you cover something so that it is no longer visible but is still there underneath, and what appears on the surface is not supposed to be there but is still there." The questions raised by Ai Weiwei's works are not meant to be definitively answered, but to trigger thoughts about the value of art.

complex surrounding Qin Shi Huangdi's tomb with the treasures he would need in the afterlife, including an army of **terra-cotta** soldiers, chariots, and horses, all of which were originally painted.

The 8,000 lifesize figures found in the largest pit were intended to guard the body of the emperor. They have similar rigid and upright poses because molds were used for the various body parts, which were then pieced together. The unique portions of each soldier (clothing, weaponry, and facial features) were added individually, however, with a layer of moist clay.

Chinese Painting

The earliest known painting in China dates back some 10,000 years. Archaeologists have found painted pots, and paint on the walls and floors of caves and huts. From 200 BCE until today, however, many Chinese paintings have been made with ink on silk or paper, the same materials used in the arts of **calligraphy** (fine hand lettering) and poetry. These three arts are inextricably linked in Chinese society, and talented calligraphers are accorded the highest respect. Chinese calligraphers can convey a mood through the handling of a brush, the thickness of a line, or the quickness of a stroke. Skilled calligraphers can communicate elegance, formality, sadness, or joyful exuberance through their script. Historically, many poets became calligraphers so that they could express most eloquently the moods of their poems. Many painters, too, were calligraphers, because both art forms require great skill in handling the brush.

Most Chinese paintings are made as hanging or hand scrolls; their subject matter typically includes battles, scenes of daily life, landscapes, and animals. Chinese scroll paintings are meant to be experienced as though we are on a slow, contemplative journey. Artists who paint scrolls do not intend their work to be viewed from one position, as is usual in artworks created in the European tradition. Instead, the complexity and (in the case of a hand scroll) length of a painting invite us to view one portion of it at a time.

During the Song Dynasty (960–1279), painters called **literati** wrote poems—either their own or the work of other poets—next to their paintings. The tradition continues to this day. Room for calligraphic inscriptions is often left on paintings, not only for the artist's signature but also to describe a scene, dedicate the painting, or add poetry.

The Chinese believe that any inscriptions on a painting become part of the work, whether or not they are written by the painter. Frequently, red seals or stamps are pressed onto part of a work to claim authorship, or to show admiration for that part. Colophons are inscriptions—often poems or historical information about the artwork—usually written in black ink by the artist or admirers of the work. Therefore, a scroll painting with many inscriptions and colophons is one that has been much enjoyed, and this becomes part of the story of the painting.

The calligraphy in the upper right of the hanging scroll by Wang Meng (**3.3.12**) tells

3.3.12 Wang Meng, *Ge Zhichuan Moving His Dwelling*, *c.* 1360. Hanging scroll, ink and color on paper, 54¾ × 22⅞". Palace Museum, Beijing, China

Terra-cotta: iron-rich clay, fired at a low temperature, which is traditionally brownish-orange in color

Calligraphy: the art of emotive or carefully descriptive hand lettering or handwriting

Literati: Chinese scholar-painters who created expressive paintings rather than formal academic works

us that *Ge Zhichuan Moving His Dwelling* is a historical scene from the life of a well-known Chinese writer. Ge Zhichuan was one of the first alchemists (someone who seeks to make gold or silver from lead or iron). He is also considered a great teacher of Daoism. In the painting, Ge Zhichuan is traveling to Guangzhou to find the red, mercury-based mineral cinnabar. He is shown in the lower left on a bridge. His family follows in the lower center. The scene shows the power of nature compared to the small scale of man.

The fantastic landscape, full of twisting trees, steep cliffs, and high waterfalls, shows the mystical nature of Ge Zhichuan's journey; it also symbolizes the wondrous path we all take through life. We cannot view the entire scroll at one time, just as we cannot see everything going on around us. This is a metaphor for the Zen-like philosophy in which one can comprehend the universe in its entirety only through the mind, thus achieving Enlightenment. As Ge Zhichuan follows his meandering path, he will eventually arrive at a new village, seen in the upper left. His destination is higher in the scroll than his present location; this is a device used in Daoist painting to symbolize the growth that the subject will experience along his spiritual path. Just like the people in the painting, the viewer may wander in any direction, exploring new territory and facing challenges; all of this is a metaphor for the journey of life. The mountain ridges high in the distance speak of the journeys yet to come.

Fang Zhaoling (1914–2016) was born in eastern China, lived in Britain and the United States, and survived the Japanese invasion upon her return to Hong Kong in 1941. While raising eight young children alone after her husband died, she delved into the practice and study of Chinese painting. She protects and honors traditional Chinese painting, while infusing her work with influences from western **Abstract Expressionism**.

Both Wang Meng's (**3.3.12**) and Fang Zhaoling's (**3.3.13**) scroll paintings focus on the beauty and mystery of the landscape, and the smallness of humans within each landscape. However, Fang's *Yellow-Earth Highland* combines traditional Chinese painting with modern **abstraction**. *Yellow Earth* is the name of a popular Chinese film that came out the year before Fang painted the work shown here. The film describes the

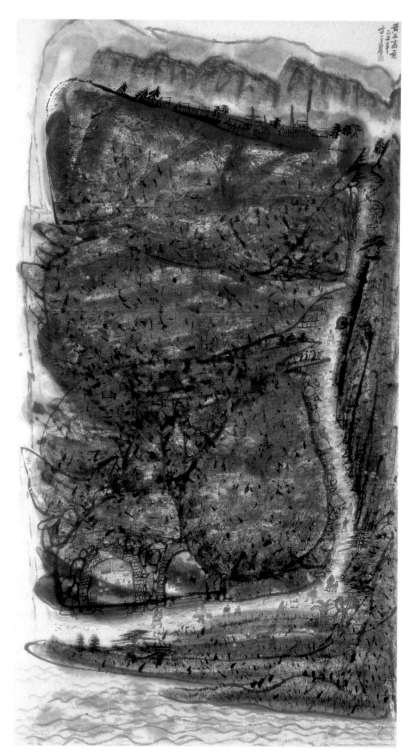

3.3.13 **Fang Zhaolin**, *Yellow-Earth Highland*, 1985. Ink and color on paper, 68⅞ × 38¼". Hong Kong Museum of Art

struggles of a girl struggling to move beyond traditional customs, just as Fang grapples with developing a more modern painting style. In this painting, large, red bulbous shapes suggest boulders or hills. Surrounding these rock formations, Fang has altered the oft-used device of a vertical element—a waterfall in Wang's work—to a steep path that lessens the three-dimensionality of the hillside. Poetry and

Abstract Expressionism: a mid-twentieth-century artistic style characterized by its capacity to convey intense emotions using non-representational images

Abstract: art imagery that departs from recognizable images of the natural world

calligraphy are incorporated in the upper right and calligraphic marks are made throughout, sometimes to represent houses and trees. People go about their daily tasks, such as the workers and families gathering in cave-like dwellings below.

Japan

Japan is a country of many islands off the eastern coast of Asia. In size, it covers about the same area as California. Combining its own cultural and religious traditions with influences from mainland Asia, Japanese art reflects stories of the Buddha and of emperors, and (in modern times) the lives of ordinary people as well. Since the islands are vulnerable to frequent tsunamis, earthquakes, and volcanic eruptions, the Japanese have a great respect for nature. According to the long-established Shinto religion, spirits called *kami* are present everywhere, including within nature. Many Japanese combine aspects of Shinto with a belief in Buddhism, which came to Japan in the sixth century CE, having developed in India and then spread through China and Korea, changing and adapting to each culture as it went. The other primary religion in Japan is Confucianism (see: Philosophical and Religious Traditions in Asia, p. 391). The reverence for

nature, and the desire for meditation, quiet reflection, and mental discipline, are all seen in Japanese art.

Spaces for Contemplation

Zen dry gardens, such as the one at Ryoan-ji in Kyoto, Japan (**3.3.14**), have been popular since the fifteenth century CE. They are a microcosm of the larger earthly landscape: white quartz gravel represents water, and the bigger rocks are surrounded by moss, mimicking islands. The garden is maintained to create a serene space for contemplation. Practitioners of Zen Buddhism cultivate mental calm on the path to enlightenment by emphasizing rigorous discipline and personal responsibility, here achieved by raking the gravel regularly. This practice reinforces the impermanence of earthly existence; any design—however beautiful—that is raked into the garden will soon disappear or be replaced. The garden features fifteen stones of assorted shape and size, but due to their placement, the viewer can catch sight of only fourteen at any one time; only those who have reached enlightenment possess the ability to see all fifteen stones at once. Zen gardens are designed to be places to embrace the present moment and meditate on nature and life.

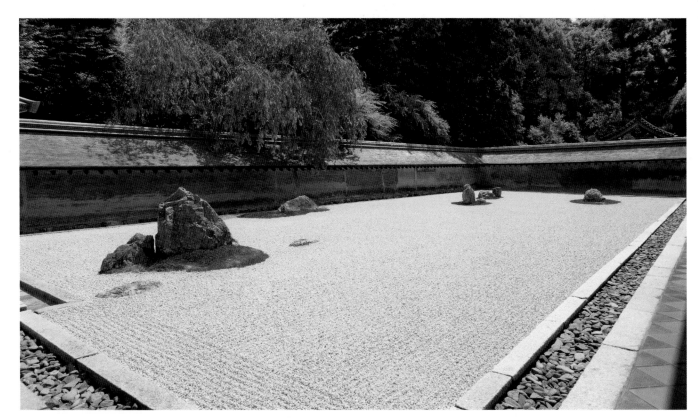

3.3.14 Garden at Ryoan-ji, *c.* 1480. Stone and gravel. Kyoto, Japan

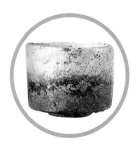

During *chanoyu*, participants slowly meditate on the design and texture of tea bowls:
→ see **0.0.9**, p. 21

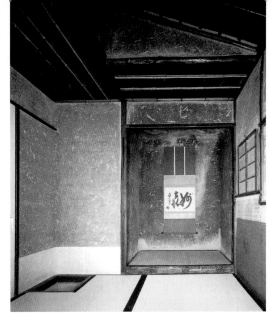

3.3.15 Sen no Rikyu, Taian teahouse, interior, *c.* 1582. Myoki-an Temple, Kyoto, Japan

Chanoyu (Way of the Tea) is the Japanese word for the traditional tea ceremony. Rooted in Zen Buddhism, chanoyu is a set of rituals that helps one find peace and solace from the ordinary world. It is a tenet of Buddhism that disciplined observation of the mundane things in life leads one toward enlightenment, and chanoyu is designed to facilitate such observation. It also helps create an environment for intense concentration. Tea masters train for many years in the practice of creating a meditative environment through the serving of tea and the preparation of the teahouse. In the sixteenth century, the tea master Sen no Rikyu developed an influential tea ritual; the Taian tearoom in Kyoto is the only remaining teahouse by this master (**3.3.15**). The

modest room is made with natural materials, such as mud for the walls, and bamboo and other wood for the trim and ceilings. The windows are made of paper, and the *tatami* (floor mats) are made of straw. The simple room has no decoration except for a scroll or small floral arrangement, placed in a niche called a *tokonoma*.

Chanoyu can take hours. It involves preparing and drinking the tea, and quiet conversation. The ceremony begins as one removes one's shoes and enters the house on hands and knees, showing humility. The contemplative environment invites participants to enjoy conversation, and also to appreciate each object involved in the ceremony.

Yayoi Kusama (b. 1929) is a contemporary Japanese artist who has used art to represent and cope with her experience of extreme hallucinations. Kusama began using dots in many of her artworks, and compares these dots to the cosmos; for her, the Earth, the moon, the stars, and each of us are all dots. Like the cosmos, her paintings and installations have no apparent visual boundaries. Later, she began creating *Infinity Rooms*, in which she fills the floors and ceiling with multiples of the same object (such as dots, pumpkins, or lanterns) and covers the walls with mirrors.

In *The Souls of Millions of Light Years Away*, (**3.3.16**) the room is covered with LED lights in various colors and shapes. When a visitor enters the room, the endless repetition of themselves and of the lights gives them a feeling of their own smallness, but also a sense of connection—that everyone is linked in a

3.3.16 Yayoi Kusama, *Infinity Mirrored Room—The Souls of Millions of Light Years Away*, 2013. Exhibited October 2017, Kunstmuseum (Museum of Art), Wolfsburg, Germany

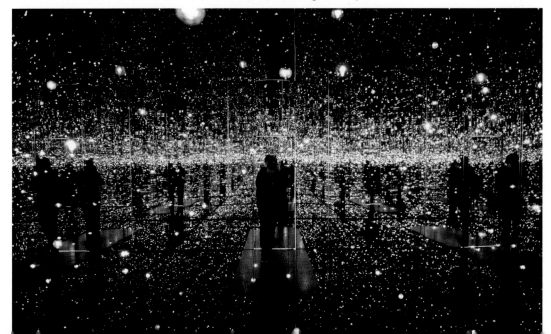

universal way. The beauty of the space creates a setting for contemplation, but the moment passes quickly: to prevent crowding in galleries, visitors are often only permitted to enter for a few minutes at a time.

Storytelling

One of the oldest examples of storytelling in Japanese art appears on a wooden shrine in the Buddhist Horyu-ji Temple in Nara (**3.3.17**). One side of the shrine is painted with a *jataka* (a story from the life of Buddha) known as *The Hungry Tigress*. The painting is a **continuous narrative**, meaning that it shows multiple scenes from a story in one pictorial space. In this story, Buddha sacrificed his own body to save a starving tigress and her cubs. Buddha is shown first at the top of a cliff carefully hanging his clothes from a tree, his slender body reflecting the curves of the natural elements that surround him. He then jumps off the cliff, and is finally devoured by the tigers in the valley below.

The *Tale of Genji* is one of the greatest works of Japanese literature. Written in the eleventh century by Murasaki Shikibu, a noblewoman at the court of the emperor at Heian-kyo (modern-day Kyoto), it tells of the love affairs of Prince Genji. The chapters are filled with undercurrents of sadness, reflecting the Buddhist view that earthly happiness is fleeting, and that there will always be consequences to our actions. Some of the earliest surviving Japanese painting illustrates the *Tale of Genji*, including the scroll section shown in **3.3.18**.

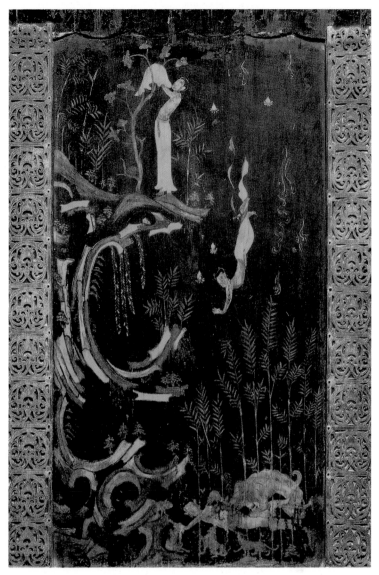

3.3.17 *The Hungry Tigress*, **panel from the Tamamushi Shrine, Horyu-ji Temple,** Nara, Asuka period, *c.* 650. Lacquer on wood, shrine height 7'7¾".
Horyu-ji Treasure House, Japan

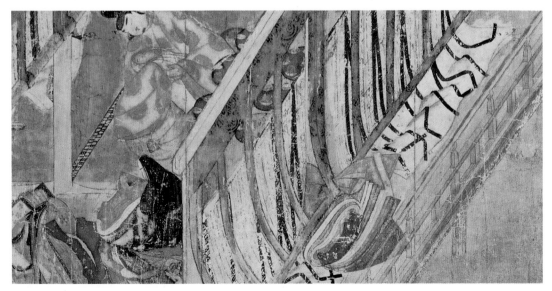

3.3.18 Scene from the *Tale of Genji*, Heian period, first half of 12th century. Hand scroll, ink and color on paper, 8⅝ × 18⅞". Tokugawa Art Museum, Nogoya, Japan

Continuous narrative: when different parts of a story are shown within the same visual space

Katsushika Hokusai, "The Great Wave off Shore at Kanagawa"

Mount Fuji: The Sacred Mountain of Japan

For the other Hokusai
GATEWAYS:
→ see p. 117 and p. 215

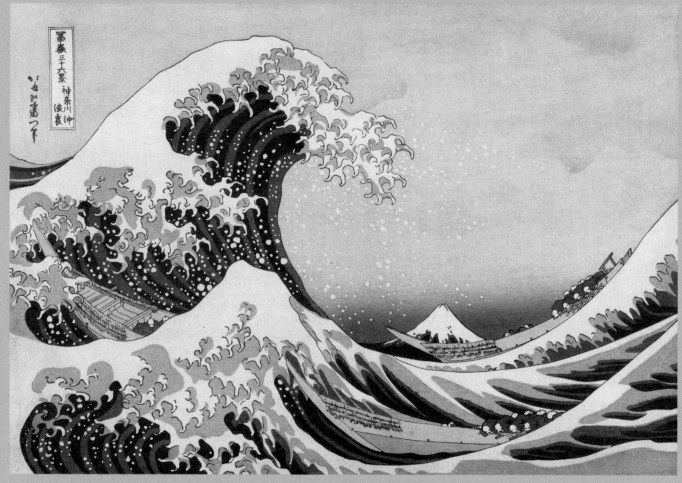

3.3.19 Katsushika Hokusai, "The Great Wave off Shore at Kanagawa" from *Thirty-Six Views of Mount Fuji*, 1826–33 (printed later). Print, color woodcut. Library of Congress, Washington, D.C.

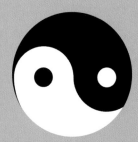

3.3.20 Yin and yang symbol

Series: a group of related artworks that are created as a set

Katsushika Hokusai's **series** *Thirty-Six Views of Mount Fuji* was so popular in his time that, after the initial thirty-six scenes, he later added ten more. Mount Fuji is the largest mountain in Japan (12,388 ft. high), and has become a recognizable symbol of the country. The mountain is sacred to believers of both Buddhism and Shinto. Because it is an active volcano, it is believed to have a particularly powerful *kami*, or spirit, although it has not erupted since 1708. In one print from Hokusai's series, "The Great Wave off Shore at Kanagawa" (**3.3.19**), the mountain is the only part of the scene that is not in motion; it is therefore a powerful stabilizing force. Indeed, the fierce movement of the wave thrashing the boats around contrasts markedly with the eternal and still form of the mountain.

As one looks at the print, an abstract yin and yang (**3.3.20**), symbolic of the Daoist belief that the forces may seem opposed, but are dependent on each other (see: Philosophical and Religious Traditions in Asia, p. 391), appears in the intertwining of the large wave with the sky. Two smaller focal points then become Mount Fuji, the reduced size of which serves to make the curling wave seem to tower even higher, and the boat on the left. All of the views in this series contrast the stable form of Mount Fuji with the daily actions (fleeting life) of people. In "The Great Wave," Hokusai shows the hard lifestyle of the fishermen who worked in the area of Edo, and their courage in the face of the power of the sea. The rhythmic composition also highlights the balance and harmony of man and nature.

The scroll is designed so that different portions of the tale are revealed as the scroll is unrolled from right to left. In this scene we see the prince from a so-called "blown-off roof" perspective, in which we as viewers peer, almost voyeuristically, into the private space of the palace. The flat figures and use of strong **diagonal** lines to guide the viewer through the scene are both qualities frequently used in Japanese painting. The strict diagonal and vertical lines not only powerfully divide the space within the scene, but also create a sense of drama and tension.

This scene specifically shows Genji at the naming ceremony of his first son. Unbeknownst to anyone but Genji and his wife, however, the baby he holds is actually his father's son, and Genji is being forced to raise the child as his own. The claustrophobic positioning of Genji, trapped between two rows of curtains and crushed against the top edge of the page, reflects the trapped feeling of the character in the story. In the tale, he is being punished for his past deeds because he had an affair with one of his father's wives.

Ukiyo-e

An important artistic development in Japanese art history was *ukiyo-e*, or "pictures of the floating world." These were **woodblock** prints that were first produced in the seventeenth century and showed characters and scenes from the entertainment districts of Edo, modern Tokyo. Later, the prints came to include landscapes and images of women from different social classes, such as courtesans. One of the best-known ukiyo-e series is Katsushika Hokusai's *Thirty-Six Views of Mount Fuji* (see Gateway: Hokusai, **3.3.19**).

Korea

Korea, located between China and Japan, has been influenced by the arts and culture of both of those countries, but it is unique in its elegantly simplified and organic forms.

The South Korean contemporary artist Do Ho Suh (b. 1962) explores issues of identity, individuality, and collectivism in his immense sculpture *Some/One*. The work recalls traditional armor of the type worn by the successful sixteenth-century military leader Yi Sun-sin, who defeated the Japanese in several naval invasions of Korea. All Korean men are required to serve in the military (a law

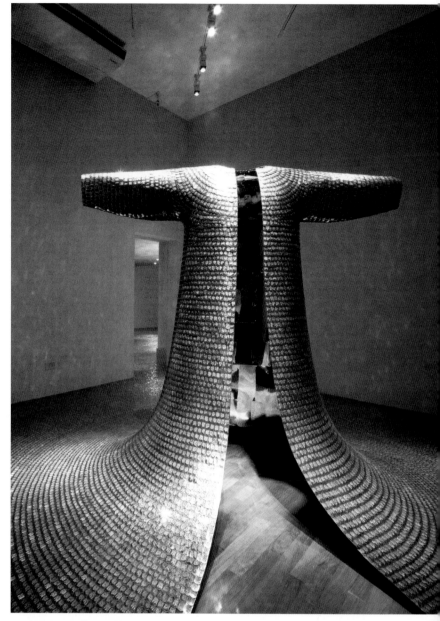

3.3.21 Do Ho Suh, ***Some/One***, 2001 (installation at the 49th Venice Biennale, Korean Pavilion). Stainless-steel military dog tags, nickel-plated copper sheets, glass-fiber reinforced resin, and rubber sheets, dimensions variable

that has been in place since 1957), and Do Ho Suh's work comments on his experience in the Korean army. He describes it as dehumanizing, a feeling that as an individual you are beaten down to become part of a larger collective. At the same time, by pushing himself physically and psychologically to extremes, he felt he was made into something strong and invincible. *Some/One* reflects this in its **medium**: it is made of a huge collection of stainless-steel dog tags (**3.3.21**). Each of the tags loses its individuality when it becomes part of the whole; but at the same time, viewers of the artwork are able to consider their own identities, as they look inside the opening at the front

Diagonal: a line that runs obliquely, rather than horizontally or vertically

Woodblock: a relief print process where the image is carved into a block of wood

Medium (plural **media**): the material on or from which an artist chooses to make a work of art, for example canvas and oil paint, marble, engraving, video, or architecture

Bas-relief (low relief): a sculpture carved with very little depth: the carved subjects rise only slightly above the surface of the work

and see themselves reflected in a smooth, mirrored surface.

Southeast Asia

Covering more than 500 acres (three-quarters of a square mile, or some 380 football fields), the largest religious monument in the world is in Cambodia, Southeast Asia (**3.3.22**). Angkor Wat was created in the twelfth century by Suryavarman II, ruler of the Khmer empire. The temple complex was built to worship the Hindu god Vishnu, believed to be the preserver of the universe who restores the balance of good and evil during difficult times, and as a burial site for the king. Therefore, the temple is oriented toward the west where the sun sets (representing the end of life). Angkor Wat was designed as a re-creation of the heavens on Earth: the site is tiered, with the center being the highest point. In the center is a temple mount, in which five towers represent Mount Meru, in Hindu belief the home of the gods.

Each of the towers resembles a lotus flower, a plant often associated with Vishnu. The huge moat that surrounds this complex symbolizes the ocean, encompassing the water-floating lotus flowers. Emanating from the temple mount is a richly modeled complex built of sandstone and covered with **bas-reliefs**.

The bas-reliefs that adorn Angkor Wat show military and religious scenes, all designed to convey Suryavarman's power. *Vishnu Churning the Ocean of Milk*, which is 161 ft. long, depicts the story of the creation of Amrita, the elixir of life (a liquid that grants immortality) (**3.3.23**). Vishnu is in the center, with two arms holding weapons (a sword and disk). The gods, on the right, and the demons, on the left, struggle against one another as they each pull on one side of a serpent wrapped around the mountain that is behind Vishnu. Vishnu uses the tortoise shell on his back to help hold up the mountain as it churns. The movement of the serpent causes the mountain to move and release

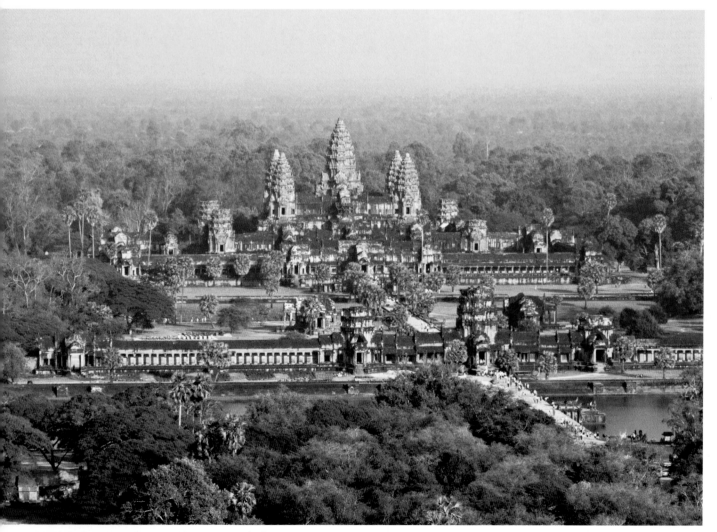

3.3.22 Angkor Wat, 12th century. Siem Reap, Cambodia

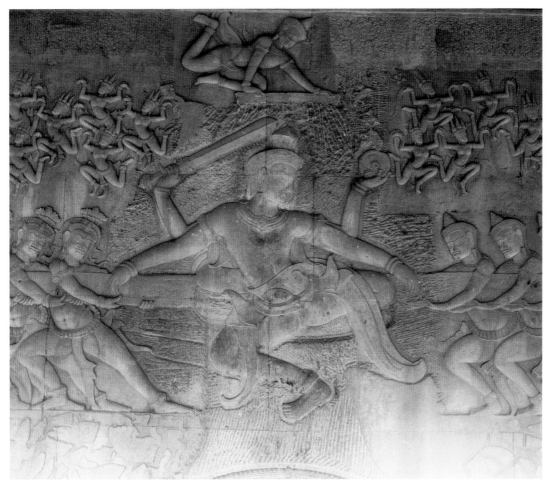

3.3.23 *Vishnu Churning the Ocean of Milk*, relief sculpture, length 161'.
Angkor Wat, Siem Reap, Cambodia

Amrita, allowing it to rise from the depths of the ocean. In the original story that inspired the bas-reliefs, this is how Vishnu and the gods trick the demons into helping them release the powerful elixir, which transforms the ocean into milk. Milk, of course, gives nutrients and life to newborns. In fact, the process of churning milk into butter is very similar to the scene shown here.

Angkor Wat is an example of the way in which, throughout Asia, different religions have frequently been expressed and blended in architectural sites: this is often described as their syncretic nature. Although Angkor Wat was originally built under Hindu rule, Cambodia has been primarily Buddhist since 1200. The lotus-shaped towers hold a different symbolic meaning for Buddhists, for whom the flower represents strength and beauty in the face of adversity, since it must grow through the muck of the earth in order to bloom into a work of beauty. Similarly, Buddhists believe they must experience difficulties and struggles in life in order to gain enlightenment. During

the fourteenth century, because of the many Buddhist pilgrims who visited Angkor, statues of Buddha were added to the artworks of Vishnu there.

In Indonesia, a tropical nation of volcanic islands, religious stories are kept alive through mask-making and theatrical dances (**3.3.24**)

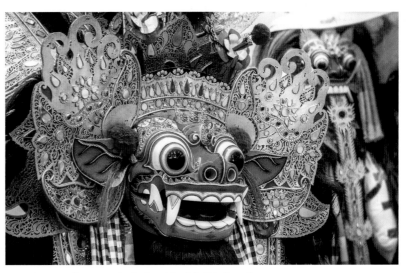

3.3.24 Barong dance mask of a lion, Ubud, Bali, Indonesia

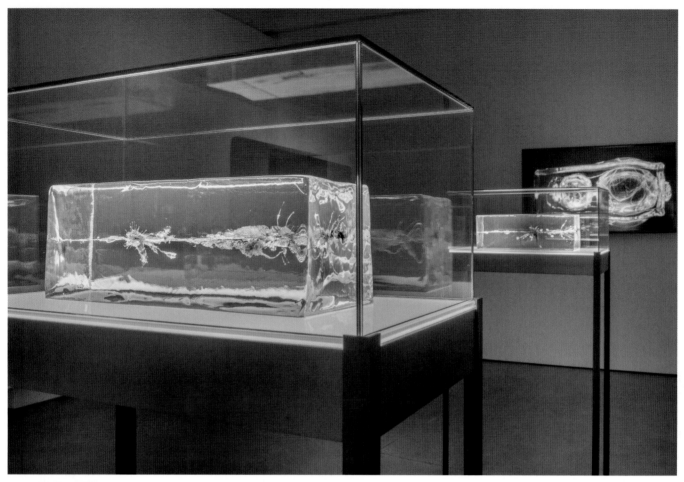

3.3.25 The Propeller Group, *AK47 vs. M16*, 2015. Fragments of AK-47 and M16 bullets, ballistics gel, custom vitrine and digital video, 7⅛ × 16⅞ × 7¼". Installation view, The Propeller Group, Luckman Gallery at California State University, Los Angeles, December 1, 2018–March 9, 2019

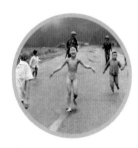

This photograph persuaded many Americans to further protest their country's involvement in the Vietnam War: → see **4.6.3**, p. 605

in village temples. Barong is a protector spirit from the ancient mythology of the people of Bali, Indonesia. He is portrayed in animal masks, often with characteristics similar to a lion (see **3.3.24**, p. 407). Such masks are used in sacred performances in which Barong battles with Rangda, an evil witch. The characters are played by important individuals in the community, and performers or audience members are often placed into a trance as the presence of either Barong or Rangda comes forth. Although today similar masks are sold to tourists, true Barong masks are sacred objects. Each village or region has its own Barong mask to protect its people.

The Propeller Group, founded in 2006, is a collaboration of multimedia artists based in Ho Chi Minh City, Vietnam. The work *AK47 vs. M16* (**3.3.25**) contrasts the two types of assault rifles created during the Vietnam War, the former made and used by the Soviet Union and the latter by the United States. The Vietnam War (1955–1975), a battle between the northern (backed by the Soviet Union) and southern (backed by the United States) regions, killed almost 1.4 million Vietnamese citizens. In this work, bullets from each gun are shot from opposite angles into ballistics gel that is designed to mimic the consistency of human tissue. Through watching the film, one repeatedly witnesses the moment when two bullets (one from each gun) meet, each cancelling out the other's power. The resulting blocks are displayed alongside the video, leaving the viewer to imagine the damage these weapons caused to the human body. Because these weapons are also eternally linked to the Vietnam War, the artists are also commenting on the involvement of two foreign powers in their internal national war, which resulted in an seemingly endless violent stalemate.

Explore Further Art of India, China, Japan, Korea, and Southeast Asia

India

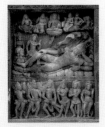

1.6.9 *Vishnu Dreaming the Universe*, c. 450–500 CE
→ p. 122

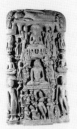

4.2.1 Life of Buddha, stela, Gupta period, c. 475 CE
→ p. 554

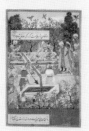

1.8.10 *The Emperor Babur Overseeing His Gardeners*, c. 1590 → p. 146

China

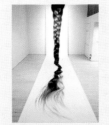

2.1.14 Zhang Chun Hong, *Life Strands*, 2004 → p. 186

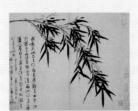

2.1.19 Wu Zhen, leaf from an album of bamboo drawings, 1350 → p. 189

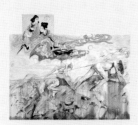

2.2.17 Hung Liu, *Interregnum*, 2002 → p. 204

Japan

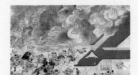

4.6.7 *Night Attack on the Sanjo Palace*, late 13th century → p. 608

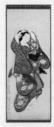

4.8.7 Kaigetsudō Dohan, *Beautiful Woman*, 18th century → p. 635

4.3.14b Motoi Yamamoto, *Labyrinth (Return to the Sea)*, 2010 → p. 577

Korea

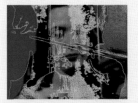

2.9.19 Nam June Paik and John J. Godfrey, still from *Global Groove*, 1973→ p. 331

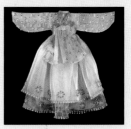

2.6.1 Hyo-In Kim, *To Be Modern #2*, 2004
→ p. 269

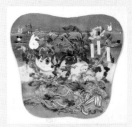

3.10.10 Jiha Moon, *Mystery Myo…*, 2010
→ p. 528

Your turn

With which regions are these artworks associated?

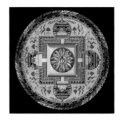

4.2.17 Ise Jingu (shrine), 4th century, rebuilt 1993
→ p. 565

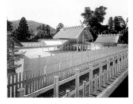

1.6.17 Amitayus Mandala, Drepung Loseling Monastery → p. 128

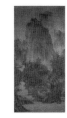

1.3.10 Li Cheng, *A Solitary Temple Amid Clearing Peaks*, c. 960–1127 → p. 72

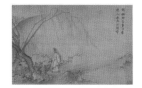

1.6.14 Ma Yuan, *Walking on a Mountain Path in Spring*, c. 960–1279 → p. 125

1.8.11 Ando Hiroshige, "Riverside Bamboo Market, Kyo-bashi," 1857 → p. 146

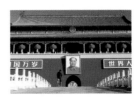

4.5.12 Mao Zedong's portrait, 1949 → p. 601

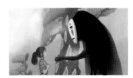

2.9.11 Hayao Miyazaki with Kirk Wise, *Spirited Away* (still), 2001 → p. 324

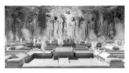

3.10.17b Cai Guo-Qiang, *Sleepwalking…*, 2020
→ p. 533

3·4
Art of the Americas

When's the Beginning?

We may never be sure when the first human arrived in the Americas, but, since 2000, scholars have found evidence that humans were in the Americas much earlier than previously thought. Most scholars agree that groups of people crossed a land bridge called Beringia that linked Asia to North America. For many years, habitation dates were traced to expertly made spear points discovered in 1933 on a farm in Clovis, New Mexico , dated to around 13,400 years ago. Similar Clovis points, as they are called, have been found all over North America, indicating that the continent was populated with people using the same type of hunting technologies and sharing genetic similarities. Many scholars are becoming

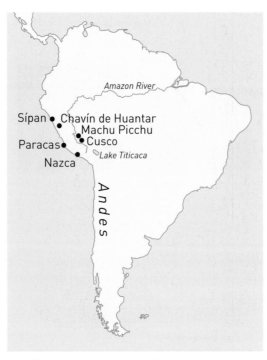

3.4.1 Map showing sites of ancient South America

convinced that the Americas were inhabited long before the Clovis spear points were made. Archaeological discoveries and scientific testing have continued to suggest that even earlier dates of habitation may be possible, in such sites as Monte Verde, Chile (*c.* 14,600 years ago); old Buttermilk Creek Complex, central Texas (*c.* 15,500 years ago), and, most recently, Chiquihuite Cave, central Mexico (*c.* 33,000 years ago).

We can trace the early cultures of South America (see **3.4.1**), ancient Mexico and Central America (Mesoamerica), and North America through their art and architecture. Some descendants of these people still live in the Americas, speaking their inherited languages, continuing ancient cultural practices, and following artistic traditions hundreds of years old. The arrival of Europeans, such as Hernán Cortés, from the fifteenth century onward drastically altered the ways of life of Indigenous people. Direct impacts included widespread disease and forced relocation to reservations, or areas of public land set aside for use by Native Americans. European settlers destroyed many great cities and magnificent works of art, especially those made of gold and silver, which they melted down for their monetary value. Enough remains, however, to tell us much about how people lived in the Americas. Although they were spread over the two continents and their cultures were enormously varied, these people shared some common interests. Their art reflects the ways in which their societies were organized; their cultural and spiritual beliefs; and their connections with nature.

As is the case when looking at all prehistoric and ancient art, understanding the art of the ancient Americas requires careful interpretation of a variety of clues. In addition to the artwork itself, scholars use scientific testing and written accounts to piece together the story of ancient American artifacts. Indigenous narratives include oral histories, handwritten accounts with painted pictures and **glyphs** in bark books, and inscriptions on stone monuments that have survived for many generations. The intricate writing of the Maya has been deciphered and has provided vast amounts of information about their beliefs and the way they lived their lives. European explorers wrote firsthand descriptions, translated Indigenous writing, and continued to interpret the art and culture well after the conquest. The legacy of European conquest persists in the form of language (some find the term "Indian" offensive, while others embrace it); legal rights over citizenship and land use; and in striking a balance between celebrating Indigenous cultures and exploiting them.

South America

From about 3000 BCE, the region around the Andes Mountains was home to a host of cultures, including the Chavín, Paracas, Nazca, Moche, Tiwanaku, and Inca. The objects created by Andean artists frequently reflected the local environment and resources, with animals, plants, and people represented, often in a **stylized** form. Beliefs about the relationship between humans and the parallel supernatural realm were communicated both in myths about the origin of the world and in the images that artists created. History, culture, and current events continue to affect the production of contemporary art in South America as well.

The Chavín and the Paracas

The Chavín culture is one of the oldest in South America. The Chavín established a pilgrimage center in Chavín de Huantar, Peru, around 900 BCE. This site is marked by remarkable temples and elaborate stone monuments.

The Raimondi Stela (**3.4.2a**) contains a complex depiction of a deity with both human and animal attributes. (The carving on the stone surface is so delicate that the design is easier to see in drawings; see **3.4.2b**.) At the bottom of the **stela** is a creature with eagle talons for feet. The figure's hands hold two staffs, which have faces, snakes, swirls, and vegetation tangling along their surfaces. A

Glyph: a carved figure referring to a sound, word, or idea

Stylized: art that represents objects in an exaggerated way to emphasize certain aspects of the object

Stela (plural **stelae**): an upright stone slab decorated with inscriptions or pictorial relief carvings

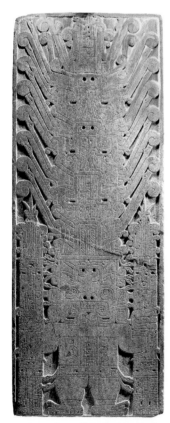
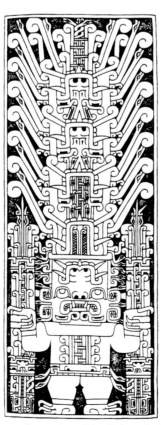

3.4.2a Raimondi Stela, Chavín de Huantar, 7th century BCE. Granite, 6'5"× 2'5". Museo Arqueología, Lima, Peru

3.4.2b Drawings of details from the Raimondi Stela

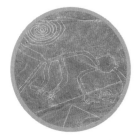

The designs of many Andean art forms, including the giant drawings on the Nazca plain, were inspired by organic forms from the natural world. This 330-ft. monkey on the desert floor was also influenced by textile designs:

→ see **1.1.1**, p. 35

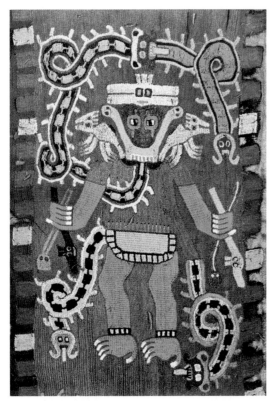

3.4.3 Paracas textile, embroidered with mythological figure, 3rd century BCE. Wool embroidery. Museo Arqueología, Lima, Peru

multiple interpretations. Some of the most spectacular textiles were made by the Paracas people, who lived on the coast of Peru from about 600 to 200 BCE. The dry conditions of their necropolis (burial place) have preserved a great number of these textiles. They show a continuation of the style (contour rivalry with single lines describing more than one thing and readable in more than one direction) and content (natural life and mythical beings) developed by the Chavín culture. This Paracas textile (**3.4.3**) is a detail from a mantle, a cape-like garment often made by the Paracas people for burial purposes. Intricately **embroidered** stitches form each figure; their repetition creates a pattern. Outlines merge into body parts, and costumes resemble animals (in **3.4.3**, a kind of mythical being with deer on its shoulders—a shaman with its animal self as a disguise). Plant forms and animals appear frequently in Paracas imagery, and deer shown here represent revered creatures associated with the hunt.

The Moche

Visually and conceptually intricate designs were also common for the Moche culture of northern Peru. Moche art, made from about 200 BCE to 600 CE, tells us much about their society. The earspool (a large-gauge ornament worn through the earlobe) in **3.4.4** was found in a royal tomb at Sipán. It shows a figure dressed almost exactly like the man found buried in the tomb, who is believed to be a warrior-priest.

headdress, with scroll-ended projections, takes up more than half of the composition. Its eyes, resembling those of a stalking jaguar, are looking up. When we turn the stela upside down, though, the second creature seems to descend from above; its eyes look down over a crocodile snout with an additional face above it with thin eyes, a scroll nose, and fanged smile. What was formerly the headdress repeats the crocodile face menacingly. Such designs, with lines that describe more than one object at the same time, possess what is known as **contour rivalry**. They allow marks to serve dual purposes and figures to project multiple readings.

The Chavín culture's principal deity, known as the Staff God, has a close connection to nature, agriculture, and fertility, as does the crocodile. In Chavín culture generally, and in this artwork in particular, animals feature prominently and are associated with all three realms of the cosmos: snakes with the earth; crocodiles, or caymans, with the watery underworld; and birds with the celestial realm of the sky.

Andean textile design is closely related to carved stone **relief** sculpture, such as the Raimondi Stela. They both use contour rivalry to create complex patterns that encourage

Contour rivalry: a design in which the lines can be read in more than one way at the same time, depending on the angle from which it is viewed

Relief: a sculpture that projects from a flat surface

Embroidery: decorative stitching generally made with colored thread applied to the surface of a fabric

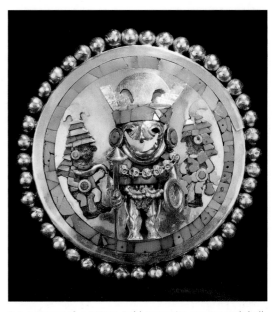

3.4.4 Earspool, c. 300 CE. Gold, turquoise, quartz, and shell, diameter 5″. Royal Tombs of Sipán Museum, Sipán, Peru

Pictured standing next to him on the earspool (and also lying next to him in the tomb) are two attendants dressed for battle. The detailed depiction includes replica turquoise-and-gold earspools, a war-club and shield, a necklace of owls' heads, and a crescent-shaped helmet. Although gold was not considered as valuable as textiles in the ancient Andes, its symbolic associations with the sun's energy and power made it nonetheless very important.

The Inca

The Inca, like the Moche metalworkers who integrated into their designs the world they saw around them, were inspired by nature. The Inca culture may have existed as early as 800 CE. It became an empire when the powerful Inca ruler Pachacuti centralized the government. By the early 1500s, a series of rulers had increased the area of land under their control until it covered more than 3,000 miles of the western coast of South America, thus becoming the largest empire in pre-Columbian America. Pachacuti selected a ridge high on a mountaintop in Peru for Machu Picchu, his private estate and religious retreat (**3.4.5**).

The location, on what is now known as the Inca trail, offered privacy and protection as well as breathtaking views; the site is now one of the world's most popular tourist destinations. The condor, a majestic bird of prey, is depicted throughout the site, which includes a building known as the Condor Temple, and a stone carved in the shape of a curved beak. The walls, terraces, platforms, and buildings are constructed of huge stones precisely stacked and fitted together without mortar. Machu Picchu was abandoned around 1527, probably after a devastating smallpox epidemic caused by contact with Europeans. Because of its elevated location, the site was not excavated until 1911, when the Yale archaeologist Hiram Bingham led an expedition to the Inca trail.

After more than one hundred years in the collection of Yale University, the artifacts gathered by Bingham and his crew were returned to Peru in 2011 and 2012. When collected artifacts are returned to Indigenous cultures (a process known as **repatriation**), the focus is usually on legal rights. This case is different: with the return of these items, the focus has been on stewardship (careful and responsible management), preservation, research, and exhibition of the materials, rather than ownership. (For further discussion of Indigenous rights see: "We Are the Mirrors":

Repatriation: the return of cultural artifacts, often sacred remains, to their country of origin

3.4.5 Machu Picchu, 1450–1530, Peru

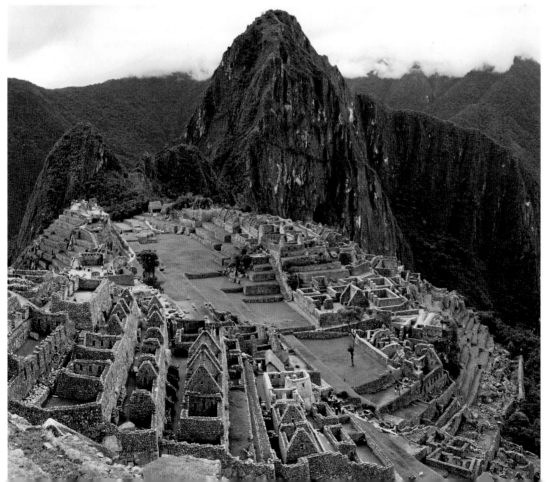

Legislation and Activism to Protect Native Rights and Land, p. 425.)

In the Andes, stone architecture was a hallmark of the Inca culture. Similarly, textiles had a cultural significance more valuable than gold or silver. Weaving was such a sacred art that it had its own god, Spider Woman, who featured prominently in the Inca creation story. Textiles were thus considered sacred and were made exclusively by women. This scale of values was not shared by the Spaniards who conquered Peru in the sixteenth century: they demanded gold and silver from the Inca and melted down fine works of art to ship the precious metals home to Spain.

The checkerboard tunic in **3.4.6** was worn by an Inca ruler. Its square designs contain a number of patterns that together indicate the high status and importance of the person who wore it. The little checkerboard designs would have decorated tunics worn by warriors serving the ruler; similarly, the diagonal lines and dots indicate the clothing of administrators.

3.4.6 Tunic, c. 1500. Interlocked tapestry of cotton and wool, 35⅞ × 30⅛". Dumbarton Oaks Research Library and Collections, Washington, D.C.

The other patterns do not directly represent specific roles or people as such, but through the complexity and variety of designs, they stand for the conquest of all possible ethnicities. The tunic refers to an important Inca creation myth, when the great god Viracocha sent out all the different peoples with their ethnic patterns painted on their bodies.

Contemporary Colombia: Collective Memory

Today the largest concentrations of Colombia's population live in the high plateau of the Andes Mountains, where the capital, Bogotá, is located. Contemporary artist Doris Salcedo (b. 1958) draws inspiration from the political landscape of her home country (with a history of civil conflict, inequal wealth distribution, and disruption from the illicit drug trade), and from the experiences of individuals affected by violence both in Colombia and around the world. Her pieces generally begin in the form of research, interviews, and careful listening to the stories of witnesses and people who have experienced trauma and loss resulting from brutal social, political, and economic conditions. The intricate objects and installations she envisions are brought to fruition by a team of architects, engineers, and craftspeople. Salcedo sees her artworks as a collective act of mourning, completed when they are experienced by viewers.

For many Bogotá residents, *Noviembre 6 y 7* calls to mind memories of the 1985 siege in their supreme court building (**3.4.7**). A guerilla group called M-19 violently overtook the government building, and the Colombian army, who knew the attack would be taking place, retaliated equally violently. Around 300 hostages were taken and over 100 people were killed, including rebels, soldiers, and supreme court justices. At 11:35 a.m., on the seventeenth anniversary of the seizure of the Palace of Justice, a chair was lowered on the facade of the new building to commemorate the moment the first guard was shot (the old building had been demolished). For 53 hours, marking the duration of the building's seizure, 280 chairs were lowered at the times that individuals and groups of people died, according to the forensic reports and autopsies. The empty chairs serve as a poetic reminder of those who died on that day. Salcedo believes that this kind of memorial is important because, while "art cannot explain things, it can expose them."

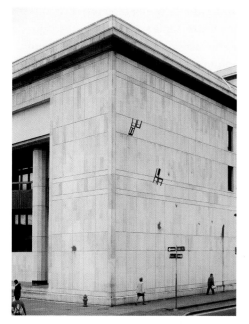
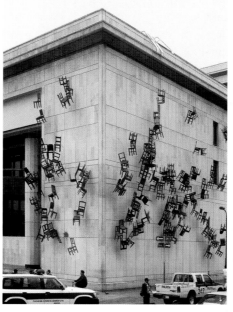
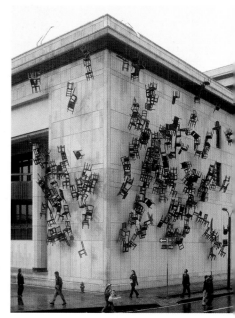

3.4.7 Doris Salcedo, *Noviembre 6 y 7*, 2002, 280 wooden chairs, ephemeral public project, dimensions variable. Palace of Justice, Bogotá, Colombia

Mesoamerica

Mesoamerica is the name given by archaeologists to the area occupied by modern-day Mexico and Central America (**3.4.8**). The many different groups and cultures that inhabited the region founded powerful city-states and produced diverse artworks. Mesoamericans were skilled astronomers and mathematicians, and developed an accurate calendar that they used to calculate the dates of important ceremonies and rituals and to predict astronomical events. They shared similar religious beliefs and many cultural traditions, including a ball game played with a hard rubber ball (see **3.4.13**, p. 418).

The Olmec

The art and architecture of the Olmec, who lived on the fertile lowlands of Mexico's Gulf Coast from around 1500 to 400 BCE, influenced such later Mesoamerican people as the inhabitants of the city of Teotihuacan, the Maya, and the Aztecs. The Olmec used images to record information, a tradition also common amongst other people of Mesoamerica. Eventually the Olmecs, and later the Teotihuacanos, used images as a form of writing, although scholars have not yet been able to interpret their scripts. The Maya also developed a system of writing, called **hieroglyphs**, much of which can now be read. Some Aztec **pictographs** can also be deciphered.

Amongst the most spectacular and mysterious products of the Olmec creative vision were the colossal sculpted heads (see **3.4.9**, p. 416). Olmec artists carved these giant heads out of a hard volcanic stone called basalt. Today we often see Olmec art (and replicas of it) in modern museums, but centuries ago these massive monuments were displayed in the ceremonial centers of Olmec cities. They were then forgotten for hundreds of years, as they lay buried in remote locations.

In 1938 the archaeologists Matthew and Marion Stirling found a colossal Olmec head at Tres Zapotes. A few years later they found

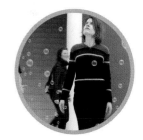

Teresa Margolles uses art to examine and raise awareness about violent death: → see **4.7.2**, p. 619

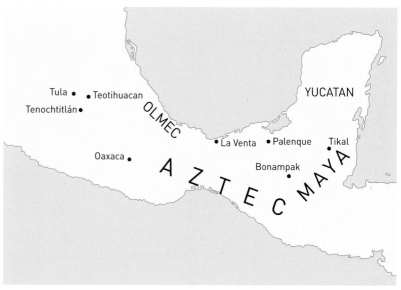

3.4.8 Map of Mesoamerica

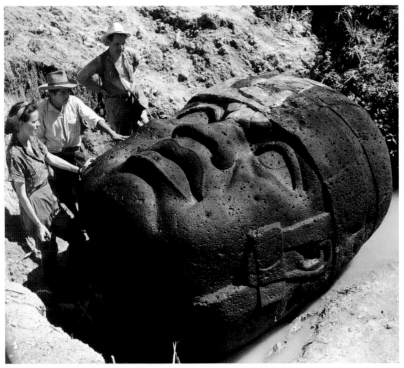

3.4.9 Colossal head, **San Lorenzo**, **Olmec**, *c.* 800–400 BCE. Basalt, height approx. 9′. With the help of local villagers, Matthew and Marion Stirling discovered this 8-foot-tall colossal head in San Lorenzo in the state of Veracruz, Mexico, in 1945—a few years after their discoveries at La Venta

Monumental: having massive or impressive scale

Pyramid: ancient structure, usually massive in scale, consisting of a square base with four sides that meet at a point or apex with each side forming a triangular shape

Stepped pyramid: a pyramid consisting of several rectangular structures placed one on top of another

several more Olmec heads *in situ*, or in their original positions. According to the Stirlings, after ten days of exploring La Venta, they finally found a colossal head in a densely overgrown area of the forest. Then, a small boy standing nearby took the couple about a half mile to another location, where they found three more heads "positioned about 100 yards north of the pyramid" in an east–west row about thirty yards from one another. In total, seventeen of these colossal heads have been found at four sites in

Mexico. They range in size from 5 to 12 ft. tall and each head weighs approximately 6 to 25 tons; astonishingly, they were carved using only stone hammers and wooden drills. In terms of scale, the eye of one of these sculptures would be the size of a human head. All portray adult men with flat noses, large cheeks, and slightly crossed eyes. Because of their **monumental** scale and individual appearance, many scholars believe that the impressive heads depict mighty Olmec rulers.

Teotihuacan

The main components of Olmec sites are a **pyramid** and a plaza, a layout that also features, on a much larger scale, at Teotihuacan, in the Central Highlands of Mexico about 30 miles from modern-day Mexico City. Teotihuacan was one of the largest cities in the world at the time. Around 500 CE, at the peak of its power, it had 600 pyramids and 2,000 apartment compounds. A wide street, the Avenue of the Dead, runs north–south and is about 3 miles long. At its northern end lies the Pyramid of the Moon. The Pyramid of the Sun lies on its east and the Temple of the Feathered Serpent is located to the south (**3.4.10a** and **3.4.10b**).

The Pyramid of the Sun, Teotihuacan's largest structure, is a **stepped pyramid** (**3.4.11**). Covering 13 acres, its base is about 700 ft. across on each side, and it is 210 ft. tall. The location of the Pyramid of the Sun was of utmost importance. It faced west—toward the setting sun and the Avenue of the Dead—and was built on top of a cave and a spring. Caves had religious significance throughout Mesoamerica

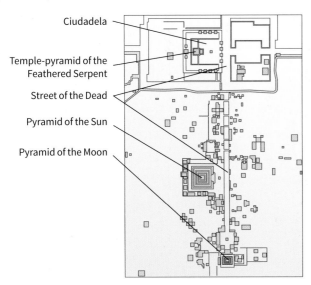

Ciudadela

Temple-pyramid of the Feathered Serpent

Street of the Dead

Pyramid of the Sun

Pyramid of the Moon

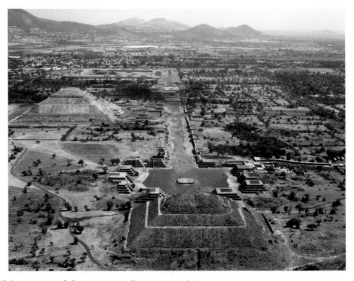

3.4.10a and 3.4.10b Plan and aerial view of the ceremonial center, Teotihuacan, Mexico

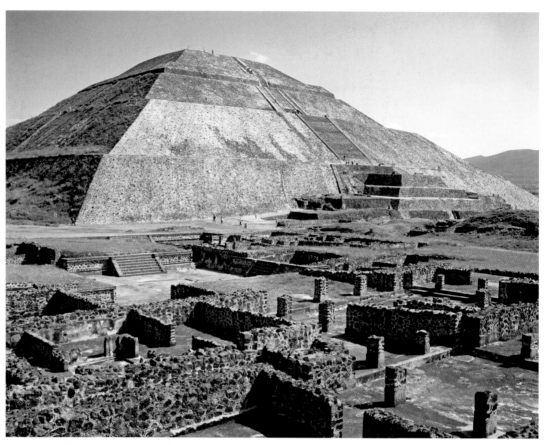

3.4.11 Pyramid of the Sun, *c.* 225 CE, Teotihuacan, Mexico

because they were thought to connect the world of humans with the world of the gods. The Aztecs, who established a powerful empire in central Mexico about 800 years after

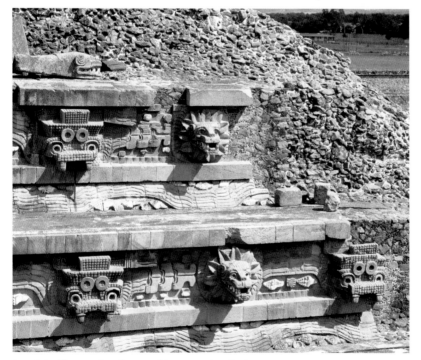

3.4.12 Architectural sculpture with serpent heads and masks on the Temple of Quetzalcoatl, Teotihuacan, Mexico (also known as the Temple of the Feathered Serpent)

Teotihuacan was abandoned, admired the cultural achievement of the Teotihuacanos. In fact, the name Teotihuacan is Aztec for "The Place of the Gods," and the Pyramid of the Sun was a place of pilgrimage for the Aztecs. The Temple of the Feathered Serpent at Teotihuacan is located in an enclosed compound. The plaza next to it is below ground level, to symbolize the underworld. Sculpted heads on the temple depict serpents with feathers and jaguar features alongside square heads with goggle eyes and fang-like teeth (**3.4.12**). To the Aztecs, these sculptures looked like images of their gods Quetzalcoatl, the feathered serpent, and Tlaloc, the goggle-eyed rain god. These figures symbolized warfare and fertility, or perhaps cycles of wet and dry seasons.

The Maya

The Maya culture existed from about 2000 BCE to 1500 CE. At the peak of the Maya empire, from about 300 to 900 CE, there were Maya centers in Mexico, Guatemala, Belize, Honduras, and El Salvador. By 900 most of them had faded away, but the culture continued to exist in isolated locations. Surviving Spanish colonization, the Maya continue to speak their

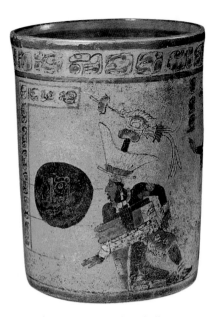

3.4.13 Cylindrical vessel with ritual ball-game scene, c. 700–850. Ceramic, 6¼ × 4″. Dallas Museum of Art, Texas

The twentieth-century Mexican artist Diego Rivera was influenced by the style, appearance, symbolism, and narrative techniques of Mesoamerican murals, one of the world's richest painting traditions:

→ see **4.1.16**, p. 551

own language and now number an estimated seven million.

Mythology and cosmology and their associated rituals were important to ancient Maya society. The ball game was a common ritual event in Mesoamerica and could also be played for sport, gambling, or as a gladiatorial contest to the death (**3.4.13**). The rubber ball, magnified on the cylindrical vessel shown

here, was about 8 in. in diameter. The game was played on a court; the objective was to get the ball through a ring or into a goal area without using one's hands. The rings were very high off the ground and it was virtually impossible to get the ball through. Players' uniforms offered both physical and symbolic fortification: yokes were fitted around the waist to strike the ball and protect the body. *Hachas* (stone objects often shaped like a human head) and *palmas* (thin flat stones) were worn on the yokes to guide and deflect the ball. The elaborate quality of the yokes and helmet-like headdresses of the players on the vessel in **3.4.13** indicate that this was a ceremonial game played for the purposes of ritual.

Mesoamerican ball games often served as the arena for the final stages of warfare in which captured enemies met their fate. The murals at the Maya city of Bonampak in southern Mexico show the victory of the Lord of Bonampak, Chaan Muan, in 790 CE, and the treatment of his defeated opponents. The wall illustrated in **3.4.14** shows the ritual presentation of captives on the steps of a temple. Chaan Muan is shown at the center of the composition, wearing a headdress with long green feathers; his ministers and aides stand beside him, well armed and in full regalia. The prisoners have been stripped of their own clothing and weapons, leaving them naked and vulnerable. They have been tortured, perhaps starved, and probably made to play a fixed and fatal ball game in which the losers are eventually executed. The man sprawled out at the ruler's feet has an incision in his side, indicating that he is already dead. To the left of this figure are several prisoners with blood dripping from their fingers, their fingernails recently ripped out. The Maya considered blood on the steps a sign of their triumph and a sacrifice to please the gods, so they wanted as much of it on the building as could be spilled.

The Aztecs

The Aztecs formed a powerful empire in Mesoamerica, which they dominated at approximately the same time the Inca were in power in South America (from 1400 until Spanish occupation in the 1520s and 1530s). At its peak, the empire covered central Mexico, Guatemala, El Salvador, and Honduras; the Aztecs were overthrown by Spanish conquistador Hernán Cortés in 1524.

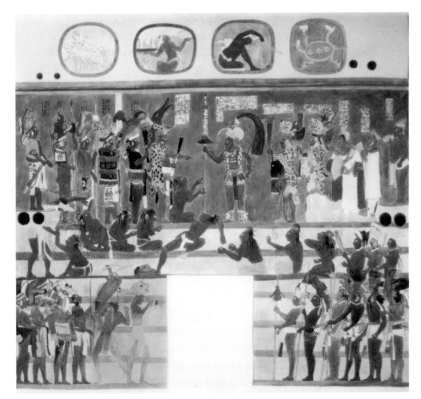

3.4.14 Bonampak mural, copy of fresco from Room 2, original 8th century. Peabody Museum, Harvard University, Cambridge, Massachusetts

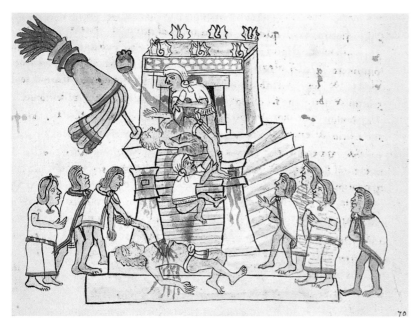

3.4.15 A human sacrifice, fol. 70r of the *Codex Magliabechiano*, 16th century. European paper, 6½ × 8⅞". Biblioteca Nazionale Centrale, Florence, Italy

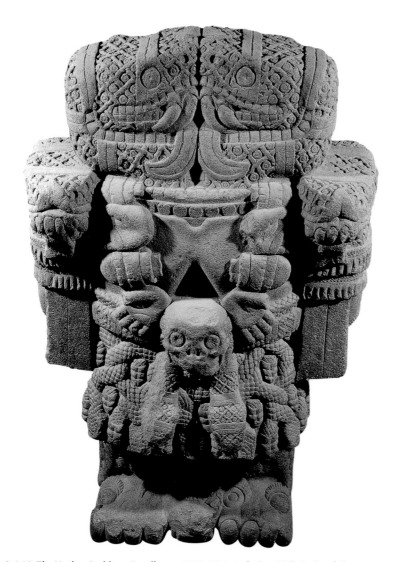

3.4.16 *The Mother Goddess, Coatlicue*, *c.* 1487–1520. Andesite, 11'6". National Museum of Anthropology, Mexico City, Mexico

In a manner similar to the Olmec, Teotihuacan, and Maya societies before them, the Aztecs placed pyramid structures in the center of their cities, emphasizing their importance as the site of rituals. Amongst the most notorious of these rituals was the practice of sacrificing a person by extracting from the body their still-beating heart (**3.4.15**). Sacrifices to the gods were performed at specific times of the year, such as planting season, and at certain points in the ceremonial calendar, for example the end of a 52-year cycle. Important events, such as the dedication of a new temple, might also be the occasion for sacrifices. Capturing victims for this purpose was one of the major goals of warfare, another being to expand the empire. People sometimes sacrificed members of their own community. In some cases it was considered an honor to die by the sacrificial blade; other individuals were selected because they had been born on an unlucky day.

The Aztecs based some of their sacrifice rituals on the story of their origins, which they traced to a mythical place called Aztlan. The Aztecs believed that their ancestors had journeyed from Aztlan to their future capital at Tenochtitlán (modern Mexico City). During their journey they met Coatlicue, or "Serpent Skirt," the guardian at Serpent Mountain. Coatlicue had been impregnated by a ball of feathers that fell from the sky; her son Huitzilopochtli, the god of war, was miraculously born fully armed. When Coatlicue's other children attempted to murder their dishonored mother, Huitzilopochtli defended her by attacking his sister Coyolxauhqui, or "She of the Golden Bells." Coyolxauhqui's dismembered body was rolled in pieces down Serpent Mountain.

The events of Huitzilopochtli's birth are the source for many Aztec artworks, including a colossal sculpture of Coatlicue (**3.4.16**). A ferocious face, created by the profiles of two facing serpent heads, enhances her imposing presence. She also has a necklace made of human hearts and hands, with a skull pendant. Coatlicue was the Mother Goddess, associated with the Earth, fertility, and transformation, who was seen as both creator and destroyer.

Coyolxauhqui's dismemberment was commemorated on a stone disk (**3.4.17**, p. 420) placed at the base of an early temple built on the site of Templo Mayor, the Great Temple of the Aztecs, in Tenochtitlán. The goddess is shown in a simplified but realistic way, with parts of her body scattered across the circular surface. Each limb, like her waist, is tied with a rope that has snake heads on the ends. The incorporation of skulls throughout the scene—at her waist, elbows, and knees—evokes her

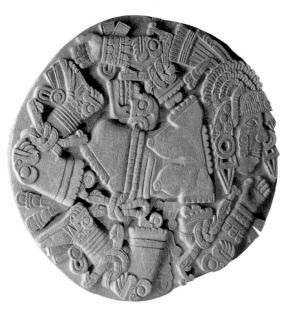

3.4.17 *The Dismemberment of Coyolxauhqui, Goddess of the Moon*, late Postclassic. Stone, diameter 9'10⅛". Museo del Templo Mayor, Mexico City, Mexico

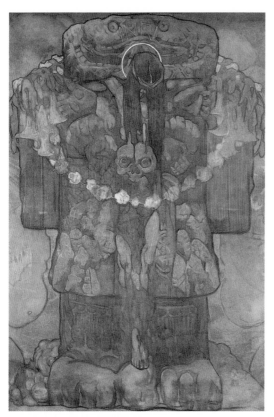

3.4.18 Saturnino Herrán, *Coatlicue Transformed* (central panel of *Our Gods*), 1915. Crayon and watercolor on paper, 34⅞ × 24⅝". Museo de Aguascalientes, Mexico

violent murder. The placement of the disk also symbolized the treatment of sacrificial victims: as a sign of their defeat, their bodies were thrown down the steps of the Great Temple to land where the disk of Coyolxauhqui lay.

This story poetically explains astronomical phenomena observed by the Aztecs. Coatlicue (the Earth) gives birth to Huitzilopochtli (the sun), who then slices up his sister (the moon), as their siblings (the stars) stand by. It is a metaphor for the phases of the moon, when the sun—with the help of the Earth's shadow—appears to cut across the moon during an eclipse.

The profound cultural resonance of the Aztec creation myth can be seen in *Coatlicue Transformed*, the central panel of an unfinished **triptych** (**3.4.18**) by the Mexican painter Saturnino Herrán (1887–1918). Made during the Mexican Revolution, Herrán's **Expressionist** depiction of Coatlicue includes, in the middle, the image of the crucified Christ. The side panels (not shown here) include Aztec and Spanish worshipers paying homage to the goddess of life, death, and rebirth. The combined Indigenous and Christian imagery reflects the complex and **syncretic** (the blending of two or more belief systems) nature of Mexican identity, in which traditional gods persist even while much of the Mexican population has practiced Catholicism since Spain colonized the country in the 1500s.

Contemporary Borderlands: Ciudad Juárez/El Paso

The Mexican-born and Canada-based artist Rafael Lozano-Hemmer (b. 1967) mixes technology, architecture, and interactive performance to investigate human interactions, make complexity visible, and pose critical questions. In 2019 he devised a response to the controversial border wall built by then-US president, Donald Trump, to separate the United States and Mexico. *Border Tuner* (**3.4.19**) bridged the space between Ciudad Juárez and El Paso to show that the people in the neighboring, international cities are more connected than divided. He used high-powered search lights that could be seen from up to 10 miles away, and advanced sound technology so that people from the two communities could talk to each other. Participants shared their personal stories and, significantly, listened to stories from across the border. More

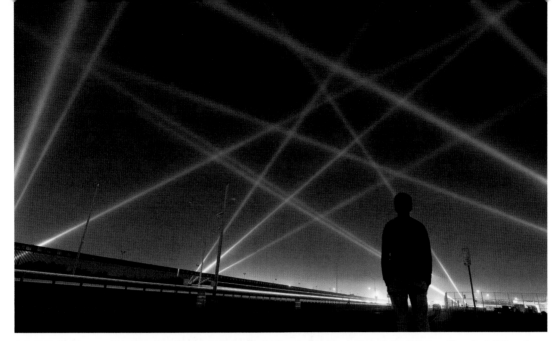

3.4.19 Rafael Lozano-Hemmer, *Border Tuner/Sintonizador Fronterizo, Bowie High-School/Parque Chamizal, El Paso/Ciudad Juárez, Texas/Chihuahua, United States/México*, 2019. Interactive light and sound installation

remotely, people contributed SMS messages, listened live on the Internet, or accessed archived recordings. *Border Tuner* inverted the narrative of power to prioritize local voices over politicized rhetoric.

North America

During the thousands of years before Europeans arrived, the people who lived in the North American continent (see **3.4.20**) occupied arctic regions, ocean coasts, dry desert, semi-arid plains, and lush forests. The resources available to these original Americans were therefore very diverse. Groups who lived east of the Mississippi River used the plentiful trees, earth, and water surrounding them. In present-day Arizona, New Mexico, and Colorado, some groups lived in permanent dwellings made of adobe (sun-dried bricks of clay and straw). Others, from the Midwest to modern-day Mississippi and Louisiana, constructed settlements of wood and earth and made large ceremonial mounds. On the northwest coast, fishing communities built villages using abundant local wood. Still others lived nomadic lives, moving to find their food and other essential materials. Not surprisingly, the people of North America spoke many different languages and developed diverse cultural traditions. Their structures and domestic objects met their practical needs, but many were so beautifully designed that today we call them art. Although European invaders killed many Indigenous people and displaced others,

some survived, maintained their cultural traditions, and continued to make artworks.

Ancient Puebloans (The Anasazi)
The people of North America used local materials to build practical structures that

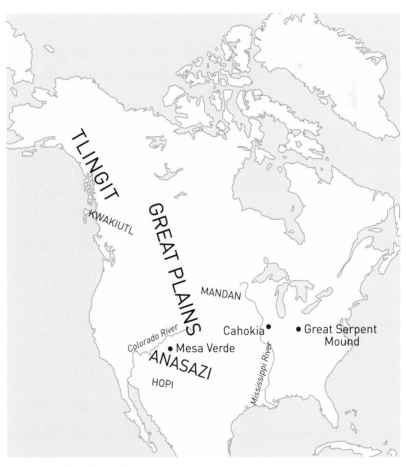

3.4.20 Map of North America

San Ildefonso-Style Pottery

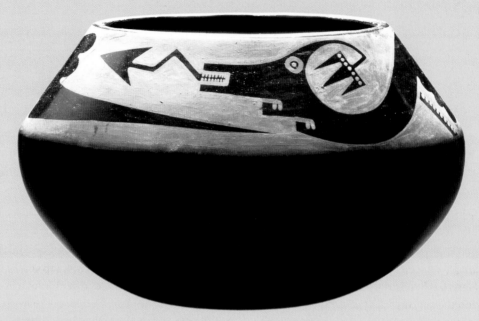

3.4.21 Maria Martinez and Julian Martinez, bowl with plumed serpent, *c.* 1925. coiled and burnished earthenware, 6″ × 9½″. Newark Museum, New Jersey

In the twentieth century, a family of Native American potters revived and perfected the distinctive pottery tradition of the Tewa people. Dr. Edgar Lee Hewett discovered sherds of pottery near San Ildefonso Pueblo in New Mexico and asked a local potter to produce replicas of the originals. That potter, Maria Martinez (1887–1980), whose Tewa name was Po've'ka ("Pond Lily"), and her husband Julian (1879–1943) re-created ceramic objects that their distant ancestors had made. They were asked to demonstrate the process at the Panama California Fair in 1915, and then in other major public venues.

Maria and Julian Martinez went on to develop their own distinctive San Ildefonso style, which became internationally famous (**3.4.21**). Maria would carefully craft the pottery objects from the volcanic ash-laden clays of the region (**3.4.22**), then Julian would apply the designs. Matte slip was painted over the stone-burnished surfaces, leaving a shiny finish. Then the pieces were fired in a mound of wood and manure that reduces exposure to oxygen and gives the pieces their rich black color. The Martinez family and other Pueblo potters adopted the techniques Maria developed. As a result of her mastery, creativity, and innovations, Pueblo pottery continues to develop as a living tradition within Native American art.

According to family members, Julian was the first painter at San Ildefonso to use the *avanyu* for decoration (see **3.4.21**). An avanyu is a water guardian serpent god of the Tewa peoples. Avanyu imagery was frequently used to decorate Southwest pottery and has also been found in the many caves that dot the canyons in this area. It bears a close resemblance to the Mesoamerican serpent god Quezalcoatl (see **3.4.12**, p. 417).

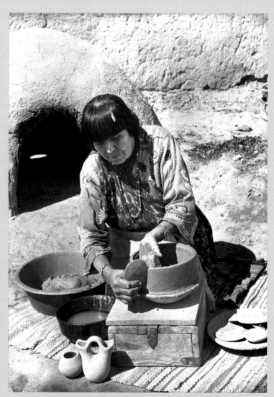

3.4.22 Maria Martinez, San Ildefonso Pueblo, New Mexico, *c.* 1930–40

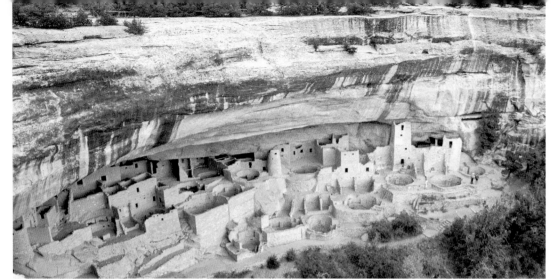

3.4.23 Cliff Palace, 1100–1300. Mesa Verde, Colorado

provided shelter. Late in the twelfth century (*c.* 1150 CE), a drought forced the Ancient Puebloans, also referred to as the Anasazi, to abandon their homes, called pueblos, on the canyon floors of New Mexico, and move north to what is now southwestern Colorado. When they arrived at Mesa Verde they constructed communal dwellings of stone, timber, and adobe in ridges high on cliff faces, often hundreds of feet above the canyon floor (**3.4.23**). These locations took advantage of the sun's orientation to heat the pueblo in the winter and shade it during the hot summer months. Exactly why elevated locations were used or even how the cliff dwellings were constructed, we do not know. Similarly, we do not know what happened to the Ancient Puebloans after the four-corners area (the place where today Utah, Colorado, New Mexico, and Arizona meet) was abandoned between about 1300 and 1540. Although modern descendants of the Ancient Puebloans—the Hopi, Zuni, Tewa, and Taos Indians—have many cultural and symbolic connections with their ancestors, even they do not know the full story.

Plains Indians

Pushed westward by European expansion, many Native Americans were forced into the Great Plains region. Groups belonging to the Sioux clan, such as the Lakota and Crow, became nomadic, living in portable homes called tipis (also spelled teepees), made of wooden poles covered with bark or deer and buffalo hides. The Mandan had been living on the Plains in what is now North and South Dakota for more than 1,000 years. They had established permanent villages, but had used tipis when hunting or traveling. The painted buffalo hide in **3.4.24a** and **3.4.24b** shows a detailed, **naturalistic** representation of a battle in 1797 between the Mandan of North Dakota and the encroaching Sioux. Sixty-four combatants, twenty of them on horseback,

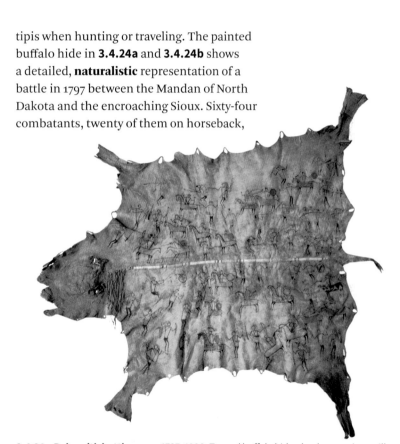

3.4.24a Robe with battle scene, 1797–1800. Tanned buffalo hide, dyed porcupine quills, and pigments, 37 × 40¼″. Peabody Museum of Archaeology, Harvard University, Cambridge, Massachusetts

3.4.24b Detail of robe with battle scene

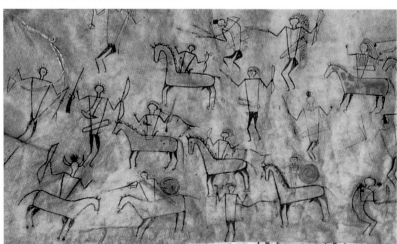

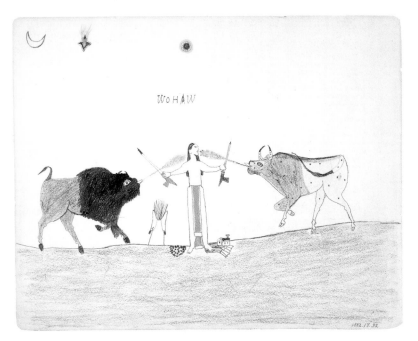

3.4.25 Wo-Haw, *Wo-Haw between Two Worlds*, 1877. Graphite and colored pencil on paper, 8½ × 11". Missouri Historical Society, St. Louis

are engaged in battle with spears, bows and arrows, tomahawks, and guns. This hide was meant to be draped over the shoulders of its wearer, likely someone who played a key role in the battle it depicted. Hides used for tipis and as garments were decorated with different **motifs**. This narrative scene would have served a commemorative purpose for the individual wearer, and as an aid to the oral storytelling tradition of the Mandan people.

While the Mandan robe tells us something of a battle between two Native North American tribes, *Wo-Haw between Two Worlds* offers a window into the changing existence of one individual as a result of westward European expansion (**3.4.25**). It is a drawing from a sketchbook kept during the artist's imprisonment in Fort Marion, Florida, between 1875 and 1878. Wo-Haw was one of about seventy Kiowa, Cheyenne, and other Plains individuals arrested in Oklahoma for allegedly committing crimes against white settlers. Twenty-six of the men made art while they were in captivity. No traditional materials, such as the buffalo hide and mineral pigments used in the Mandan robe, were available, so they used the pencils and paper provided for them.

Wo-Haw's self-portrait shows him caught between the two worlds referenced in the drawing's title: that of his ancestry on his

Motif: a distinctive visual element, design or color repeated as a unit in a pattern or reused in multiple artworks

right side (our left) and the new presence of European settlers on his left. His Kiowa heritage is represented by a buffalo and a tipi underneath a crescent moon and a shooting star. The world of white people is represented by a domesticated bull, cultivated fields, and a European-style frame house. Wo-Haw holds peace pipes toward both the Native American and European worlds, expressing the hope that they can learn to live in peace (see **3.4.27**).

The Kwakiutl

The Kwakiutl, an Indigenous group in southern British Columbia, Canada, continue to practice ceremonies that have been passed down through the generations. They are known for their masks, which they use ceremonially in different ways, depending on the time of year. The late nineteenth-century *Eagle Transformation Mask* (**3.4.26**) was probably used in a public summer performance for a male coming-of-age ceremony. The eagle was probably the spirit guardian revealed during a vision quest undertaken at the onset of puberty. As such, the *Eagle Transformation Mask* showed the deep, inner reality of the wearer, who used the strings to open and close the mask, giving the impression he was transforming into an animal. In flickering firelight, the mask's movement would have created an impressive spectacle as its human aspects (such as the large nose) combined with animal features (in this case a curved beak). The dancer thus transformed himself from human to eagle and back again as he danced. This performance

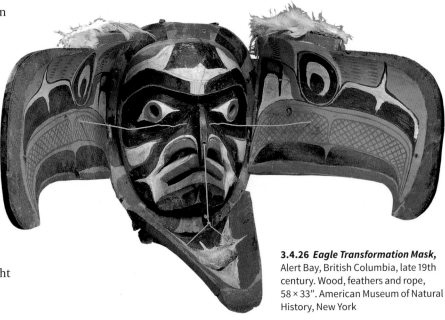

3.4.26 *Eagle Transformation Mask,* Alert Bay, British Columbia, late 19th century. Wood, feathers and rope, 58 × 33". American Museum of Natural History, New York

"We Are the Mirrors": Legislation and Activism to Protect Native Rights and Land

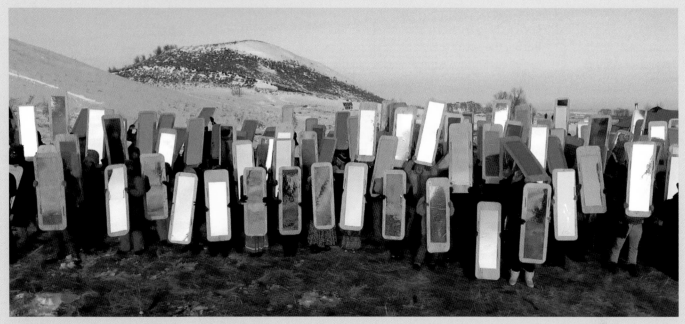

3.4.27 Cannupa Hanska Luger, *The Mirror Shield Project*, 2016. Oceti Sakowin Camp, Standing Rock, North Dakota

In North America, a federal law known as NAGPRA (Native American Graves Protection and Repatriation Act) was enacted on November 16, 1990 to legislate the repatriation of artifacts and sacred remains, such as those at Machu Picchu (see p. 413). According to the National Park Service, NAGPRA addresses "rights of lineal descendants, Indian tribes, and Native Hawaiian organizations to Native American cultural items, including human remains, funerary objects, sacred objects, and objects of cultural patrimony." Since the time of European contact in the Americas, issues of ownership have extended to include occupation, access, and treatment of the land itself.

Still being contested in the courts as of 2021, the 2016 construction of an oil pipeline under the Missouri River in North Dakota drew a great deal of media attention. The Standing Rock and Cheyenne River Sioux (and thousands of allied protesters) opposed the Dakota Access Pipeline (DAPL) that the developer, Energy Transfer Partners, was running through Indigenous land, because of its potential to harm their access to clean water, necessary for life in both physical and spiritual ways. The situation came to a head on November 20, when police attacked unarmed protestors with rubber bullets, tear gas, and water canons in sub-freezing temperatures.

In response to the situation, artists made posters to raise awareness, sold artwork to donate to the Standing Rock cause, and made narrative videos telling the tale of a mythical beast (oil) devouring the natural world. One artist incited people to create "mirror shields" to be used on the frontlines of the protest (**3.4.27**). Born on the Standing Rock Reservation, the artist Cannupa Hanska Luger is of Mandan, Hidatsa, Arikara, Lakota, Austrian, and Norwegian descent. Luger was inspired by Ukrainian activists to use mirrors as a way of drawing the oppressors' attention to their own actions. Actual battle regalia using mirrors as spiritual (and physical) protection can be traced back to the Bronze Age and in antiquity all over the world, including parts of Europe, Asia, and West Asia. Using social media, Luger shared directions for making "Mirror Shields for Water Protectors" using inexpensive materials and asked contributors to mail them to the camps. In an interview in the *LA Times*, Luger explained that artists "live on the periphery. But we are the mirrors. We are the reflective points that break through a barrier." According to the artist, the mirror shields are "designed to let them [the people reflected in the mirrors] know that we love them and they stand with water as well. The wall the mirror shields create is not a wall of division, but a wall of unity."

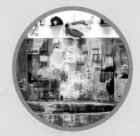

The artist Jaune Quick-to-See Smith also features the (mis)treatment and (mis)representation of Native Americans in her collages:
→ see **1.9.15**, p. 156

served a ritual function, highlighting the powerful nature of the eagle, and transferring that bravery and strength to the human wearer and his community. It also represented the ancestral connections between humans and eagles. The transformation that was enacted during the performance also symbolized the changes the wearer experienced during initiation.

The Great Basin and California Indians

Basket-making, a long-standing tradition for California Indians, served functional, symbolic, and metaphorical purposes for their communities. Although in the past several groups developed unique approaches in isolation, many of today's basket-weavers share their techniques with each other and work to revive the practices used by their ancestors. **Coiling** and **twining** are the two most common methods of construction.

The plants chosen for a basket's construction were often determined by what grew in the region, but also by the characteristics of the material that made it suitable for its purpose. For example, willow bark was commonly used for storage containers and baskets for other uses in the home because it contains salicin, a natural insect repellent (which would help protect the contents from the ravages of mites and weevils) and an agent that would prevent the basket from catching fire if placed near a stove or other source of heat. Indigenous weavers even made baskets, such as

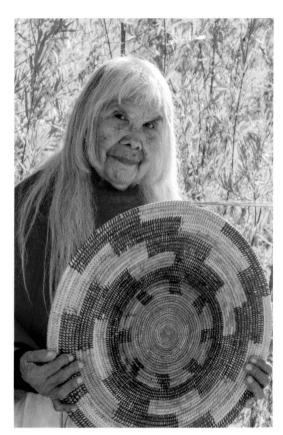

3.4.29 **Julia Parker holding one of her baskets**

the one shown in **3.4.28**, that were watertight and could be filled with boiling water to cook acorn mush, a staple in the diet of Native Californians for centuries.

The names of many weavers of the baskets in museum collections are unknown because little information was recorded when they were collected. Julia Parker (b. 1928), a Coast Miwok-Kashaya Pomo weaver, learned from talented elders, including her husband's Paiute grandmother Lucy Telles, how to make such baskets as the one in **3.4.29**. The collective nature of basket-making is reflected in Parker's practice, which she has taught to her family (her daughter Lucy Ann Parker, granddaughter Ursula Min-ne-ah Jones, and great-granddaughter Naomi Kashaya Jones are also basket-weavers) and shared with the public as a cultural specialist at Yosemite Museum, giving basket demonstrations and workshops. Because it is so time-consuming, basket-making has become increasingly rare, though it is now highly valued for its intricacy, craft, and visual appeal.

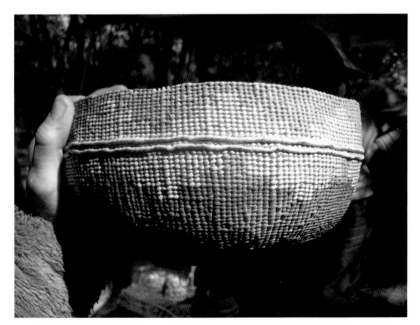

3.4.28 **Julia Parker**, **basket for cooking acorns**, *c.* 2011. Collection Julia Parker

Explore Further Art of the Americas

Architecture and Land Art

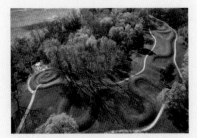

2.4.14 Great Serpent Mound, *c.* 800 BCE–100 CE, Ohio → p. 238

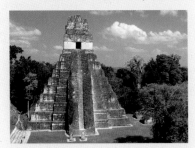

2.5.3 Maya Temple I, Tikal, Guatemala, *c.* 300–900 → p. 246

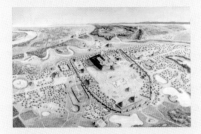

4.1.9 Monks Mound, Cahokia, Illinois, *c.* 1150 → p. 546

Art by and about Indigenous People

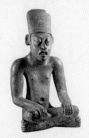

2.6.3 *Seated Figure*, Zapotec, Oaxaca, Mexico, 300 BCE–700 CE → p. 271

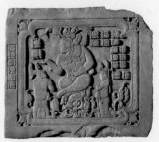

1.7.4 Maya ruler Tajal Chan Ahk, Guatemala, *c.* 8th century → p. 133

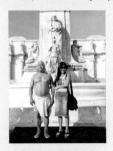

4.9.11 James Luna, *Take a Picture with a Real Indian*, 2010 → p. 655

Art about Indigenous Beliefs

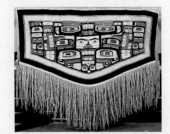

2.6.15 Tlingit Chilkat dancing blanket, 19th century → p. 278

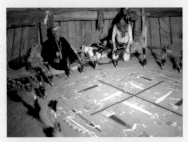

4.2.6 Navajo Whirling Log dry painting, early 20th century → p. 558

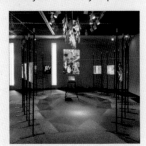

3.10.9 Jolene Rickard, *Corn Blue Room*, 1998 → p. 527

Your turn:

How do these artworks relate to the cultures or ideas discussed in this chapter?

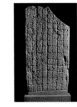

1.2.7 Limestone stela with Mayan glyphs, Belize, *c.* 600–800 → p. 54

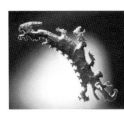

4.4.10 Maya flint depicting crocodile canoe, 600–900 → p. 586

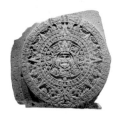

4.3.3 Aztec calendar stone, Mexico, 1502–1521 → p. 569

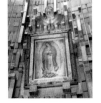

0.0.10 *The Virgin of Guadalupe*, Mexico City, 1531 → p. 22

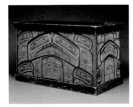

2.6.20 Captain Richard Carpenter, bent-corner chest, *c.* 1860 → p. 282

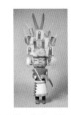

4.2.5 Hopi, *kachina* doll, *c.* 1925 → p. 557

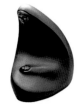

0.0.24 Allan Houser, *Reverie*, 1981 → p. 32

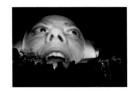

4.1.17 Krzysztof Wodiczko, *Tijuana Projection*, 2001 → p. 552

3·5
Art of Africa and the Pacific Islands

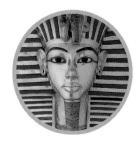

King Tutankhamun ruled Egypt from 1333 to 1323 BCE. Egypt is located on the African continent, but its proximity to the Middle East and Mediterranean Sea also gave it a position of unique influence on Western and European art:
→ see **3.1.17**, p. 358

As diverse as they may at first seem, the artworks produced on the expansive continent of Africa (see **3.5.1**) and in the remote islands of the Pacific Ocean (see **3.5.2**) have some intriguing similarities. In both areas, traditional art integrates and responds to the environment, incorporates important mythological beliefs, and follows conventional methods of construction and decoration. Perhaps the most striking similarity between art made in Africa and that of the Pacific Islands is the continuity of traditional techniques. Historically, artists have had to undergo apprenticeships lasting several years. In these cultures, learning traditional ways to make objects was more important than building an individual reputation. Although some past artists earned legendary status while alive, the names of most have been forgotten over time.

Both of these regions' artistic traditions have relied on such natural materials as wood, reeds, shells, and earth. Cowrie shells feature prominently in the *nkisi nkondi* (see p. 431) from the Democratic Republic of Congo, and in the decoration of the Abelam cult house in Papua New Guinea (see **3.5.21**, p. 440). In both parts of the world, shells are symbols of fertility. Natural materials often have symbolic significance, but because they are usually perishable (wood in particular), few examples of ancient artworks made from such substances remain.

As we find elsewhere in the world, traditional artists in Africa and the Pacific Islands have tended to serve as communicators for and within their communities. They record events and relate important cultural beliefs, such as rules of behavior, or fables that seek to explain the mysteries of the world. Communication beyond the human realm, enhanced by the ritualistic use of hallucinogens that induce trances, reflects belief in supernatural powers that infuse the natural world.

All around the world, contemporary art tends to focus on both personal and communal expression, but artists from Africa and the Pacific Islands often incorporate references to their culture's mythology, religion, history, and life experience, along with industrial materials, found objects, and references to popular

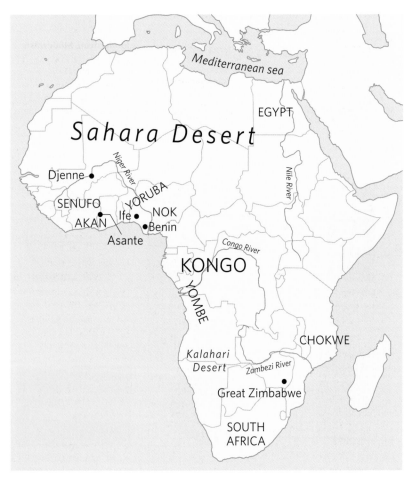

3.5.1 Map of Africa

culture. Many scholars consider that the study of African art extends into the African Diaspora (the regions affected by the mass dispersal of Africans, whether by the trade in enslaved people or by choice, and which include the Americas, the Caribbean, Asia, and Europe). During the **Modernist** period (*c.* 1860–1960) art from Africa and the Pacific Islands, as well as the Americas, served as an inspiration for European **abstraction**. Today, contemporary African and Pacific Island artists do not exclusively focus on their own communities, but actively participate in the global art world.

Art of Africa

Modern Africa includes 54 different countries, more than 1.3 billion inhabitants, and at least 1,500 different languages. Archaeological evidence from about 200,000 years ago suggests that the first modern humans lived on the African continent before moving to other parts of the world. In more recent records of human activity, oral history has been more important for African communities than written documentation; records of specific events do not exist in many areas, especially south of the Sahara. Art has therefore been a particularly important form of communication and cultural expression. Amongst the earliest examples of African art are portable objects, such as beads made from shells that date back to 75,000 years ago. Wooden sculpture and architecture also have long traditions, although ancient examples have largely perished.

Sculpture, the Body, and Power

For thousands of years, people have used art to tell stories about and create images of their daily lives. African rulers, similarly to rulers and members of the elite everywhere, have used art to assert and reinforce their power. Some of the art they commissioned has also emphasized their connection with the supernatural realm, thereby encouraging a belief that gods or ancestor spirits have bestowed upon them the authority to rule. It is also believed that artworks can act as conduits to the spirit world, and permit the entry of supernatural forces into the human world to bestow good or ill fortune.

The objects themselves are invested with power, and a certain amount of power is also associated with the owner. Often objects or artworks communicate the rules and customs that members of society are expected to follow.

These objects can be symbolic, related to a particular position or role; or they can tell a tale, illustrating a proverb or a story with a specific message.

We do not know the exact meanings and uses of some of the oldest known **figurative** sculptures in Africa, yet they have a strong physical presence. The Nok of Nigeria made hollow, lifesize **terra-cotta** figures (**3.5.2**). These sculptures were made using a **coiling** technique commonly used to make pottery vessels. The features and details of the sculptures were carved in a manner similar to woodcarving. Although clay is durable, it is still a breakable material, and therefore very few of the sculptures have been found undamaged. In many cases only the heads remain intact.

As with many Nok heads, the piece in **3.5.2** has a distinctive hairstyle or headdress, with three conical buns on top. Also characteristic of Nok sculpture, the head has triangular-shaped eyes and holes in the pupils, nostrils, mouth, and ears, which probably facilitated air flow during **firing**. In the lifesize sculptures that have survived, Nok figures are shown standing, kneeling, and sitting, wearing detailed jewelry and costumes. The heads are proportionally much larger than the bodies, a feature that is also common in later traditions in African

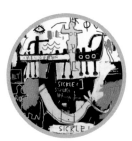

Jean-Michel Basquiat made Africa and the African Diaspora the subject of his painting *The Nile*, also known as *The History of Black People* or *The Grand Spectacle*:
→ see **3.10.12**, p. 529

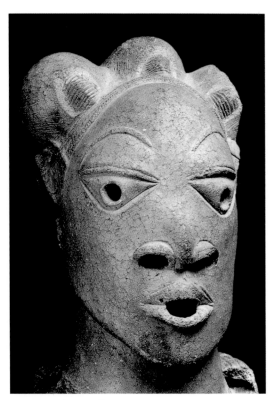

3.5.2 Head from Rafin Kura, *c.* 500 BCE–200 CE. Terra-cotta, height 14¼″. National Museum, Lagos, Nigeria

Modernism, Modernist: a radically new twentieth-century art and architectural movement that embraced modern industrial materials and a machine aesthetic

Abstract: an artwork the form of which is simplified, distorted, or exaggerated in appearance. It may represent a recognizable form that has been slightly altered, or it may be a completely non-representational depiction

Figurative: art that portrays items perceived in the visible world, especially human or animal forms

Terra-cotta: iron-rich clay, fired at a low temperature, which is traditionally brownish-orange in color

Coiling: the use of long coils of clay—rather than a wheel—to build the walls of a pottery vessel

Firing: heating ceramic, glass, or enamel objects in a kiln, to harden them, fuse the components, or fuse a glaze to the surface

Representational: art that
depicts figures and objects
so that we recognize what is
represented

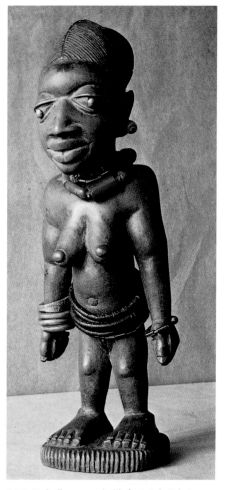

3.5.3 Twin figure, probably from Ado Odo in
Yorubaland, pre-1877 (probably 19th century).
Wood, 10″ high. Linden Museum, Stuttgart,
Germany

art: the head, because of its association with
knowledge, identity, and the fact that it is often
considered the location of a person's spirit, is
emphasized in many figurative sculptures.

The Yoruba of western Nigeria contributed
much to the rich tradition of figurative
sculpture in Africa. Sculptors working in the
Yoruba city of Ile-Ife produced impressive terra-
cotta and metal sculpture; and the twin figure
in **3.5.3** displays Yoruba skill at woodcarving.
Its features, characteristic of the regional style,
include small size, large eyes, and elongated
breasts. Such figures, known as *ere ibeji*, were
sometimes carved when a twin died at birth
or in infancy, in order to harness the life force
of the deceased and bring prosperity to their
families. This twin figure shows how Yoruba
hand-made objects are invested with spiritual
powers of their own.

Textiles, Abstraction, and Identity

Because many kinds of information have
traditionally been communicated visually
rather than verbally in Africa, objects are often
made with a specific purpose or even a specific
person in mind. Artworks that contain abstract
designs and patterns can convey information
that is just as important, recognizable, and
specific as **representational** images. They
can also communicate a great deal about the
maker or the user of an object. The symbols

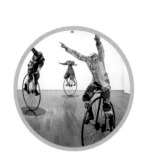

Distinctive fabrics
associated with Africa
also feature prominently
in contemporary
British-Nigerian artist
Yinka Shonibare's
sculptural installations:
→ see **2.10.10**, p. 341

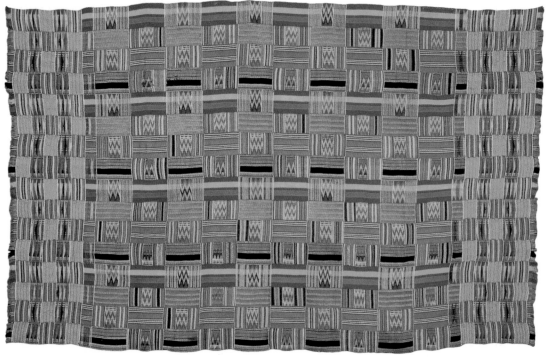

3.5.4 Textile wrapper (kente), 20th century. Silk, length 6′10½″. National Museum
of African Art, Smithsonian Institution, Washington, D.C.

Nkisi Nkondi
Mystical Hunter Activated to Restore Balance

For the other *nkisi nkondi*
GATEWAYS:
→ see p. 235 and p. 548

Known for a strong sculptural tradition, the Yombe people of western Central Africa use power figures as reminders of social obligations and enforcers of proper behavior. Objects called *minkisi* (the singular *nkisi* means "sacred medicine") can take the form of shells, bags, pots, or wooden statues. Substances, or actual medicines, might be placed inside the minkisi to give them certain properties. In carved figures, these medicines were placed in the head or stomach area. A particular type of nkisi, called a **nkisi nkondi**, is a standing figure with its feet spread apart in a powerful, assertive pose (**3.5.5**). Nkondi means "hunter," as in, to hunt down and call to account those who have done wrong in society. White kaolin clay, shells, and other reflective objects on such figures as this symbolized contact with the supernatural. Ritual specialists, believed to have the power to release the object's spiritual presence, activated all minkisi.

Each figure served a specific function, but generally a nkisi nkondi was responsible for making sure that oaths sworn in its presence were honored. Each time the figure was needed, the ritual specialists would drive nails, blades, and other metal objects into its wooden surface to make it "angry" and "rouse it into action." As a mediator between the ancestral spirit world and the living world of human beings, the nkisi nkondi was believed to bring protection and healing to the community. The nkisi nkondi shown here has been activated many times by iron blades that have been thrust into it. The giant cowrie shell on its abdomen is a symbol of fertility and wealth for the Yombe people as well as other cultures; such shells are

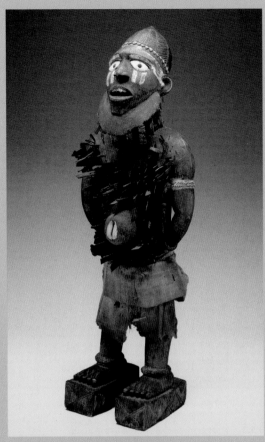

3.5.5 Standing power figure (*nkisi nkondi*), late 19th century. Wood, iron, raffia, ceramic, kaolin pigment, red camwood powder (tukula), resin, dirt, leaves, animal skin, and cowrie shell, 43¾ × 15½ × 11". Dallas Museum of Art, Texas

also widely used as currency. This nkisi nkondi has wide, staring eyes and an imposing stance to help ensure that no other forces will interfere with the fulfillment of its ritual function.

Nkisi nkondi (plural *minkisi minkondi*): combines the words for "sacred medicine" and "to hunt"; figurative sculpture(s) used in rituals by the Yombe of central Africa

that decorate utilitarian objects, from clothing and pipes to bowls and chairs, and the care that went into making them, give them significance.

The colors, materials, and designs of textiles can indicate a person's age, station in life, and cultural connections. In the West African kingdom of Asante in Ghana, woven fabrics called *kente* were traditionally worn only by royalty and state officials: the cloth was too expensive for ordinary people to afford. More recently, kente have become accessible to the general public, though they are typically reserved for special and ceremonial occasions.

Making kente requires a loom that allows the weaver to integrate vertical and horizontal designs in a strip ranging from 2 in. to 4 in. wide. The strips are sewn together to make a complete cloth of **geometric** shapes and bright colors. Women wear the cloth in two parts, as a floor-length skirt and as a shawl, while men drape it around themselves like a toga. The kente in **3.5.4** contains yellow, representing things that are holy and precious; gold, a symbol of royalty, wealth, and spiritual purity; green, for growth and good health; and red, for strong political and spiritual feelings.

Kente **cloth:** an African textile made of interwoven strips of silk and cotton fabric; native to the Asante and Akan groups of Ghana and traditionally worn by royalty and state officials

Geometric: predictable and mathematical

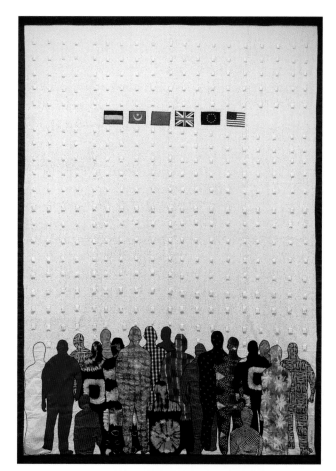

3.5.6 Abdoulaye Konaté, *Generation Biométrique, No. 5*, 2008–2013. Textile, 124⅞ × 89⅜″

Contemporary artist Abdoulaye Konaté (b. 1953, Mali) has been using textiles as his primary **medium** since the 1990s. His wall tapestries build on the function, formal appearance, and recognizability of distinctly African fabrics. He also uses traditional textiles, including Ghanaian kente at times, to tell current stories and raise awareness about socio-political and environmental issues. *Generation Biométrique, No. 5* (**3.5.6**) was inspired by the inhumane treatment of African immigrants seeking more hospitable living conditions in the European Union. The piece comments on global environmental policy and the increasing instances of personal data being collected and tracked. The flags at the top represent desirable, wealthy nations. The fabrics on the figures at the bottom reference the colors, textures, and appearance of textiles that symbolically communicate cultural heritage and individual identity. Even though this information is far more richly layered than a person's fingerprints, it tends to be stripped away and overlooked, while strictly biological data is gathered as displaced persons enter a new country. Small

fabric packets are attached throughout the white background, a reference to the charms and amulets on Malian hunting tunics, believed to bring magical protection to the refugees and help them evade danger.

Masking and Masquerade

Another highly recognizable and influential African art form, masks appear widely in ceremonies. Like kente cloth, masks emphasize geometric shapes, though unlike kente, they also reference human features. In museums, masks are often presented as lifeless objects on display, isolated from the vibrant sights, sounds, smells, and movements of the **masquerade**. For African groups, though, the mask is most meaningful when being worn in live performance. In fact, sometimes masks are created for a particular event and discarded afterward because they are no longer considered alive.

The Dogon of Mali in West Africa traditionally used the Kanaga mask in ceremonies designed to assist the deceased in their journey into the spiritual realm (**3.5.7** and **3.5.8**). One interpretation is that the two cross-bars on the mask represent the lower earthly realm and the upper cosmic realm of the sky.

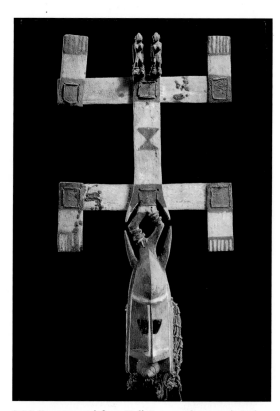

3.5.7 Kanaga mask from Mali, **Dogon culture**, early 20th century. Polychrome wood, leather cords, and hide, height 45¼″. Musée Barbier-Mueller, Geneva, Switzerland

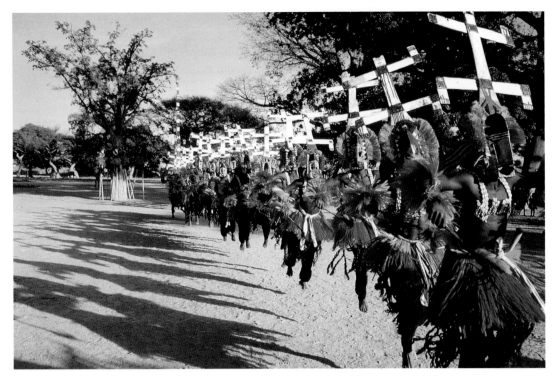

3.5.8 Dogon Kanaga mask ceremony, Bandiagara, Mali

In performance, dancers swoop down and touch the mask to the ground; loud noises, like the crack of gunfire, scare away any souls that might linger in the village. Today such funeral rituals, called *dama*, continue to be performed (though rarely) and still include masks.

African Architecture

The early history of architecture in Africa is difficult to track because so many buildings were made of perishable materials, such as mud-brick and wood. Some ceremonial structures, places of worship, and royal residences have been maintained over time, but others have fallen into ruin. Contemporary architects in Africa combine traditional approaches and non-local, European/North American solutions to create innovative, customized buildings. Whether they are designing rural schools, open-access train stations, luxury homes, or high-profile business or government headquarters, sustainability is a key concern in postcolonial Africa as populations grow rapidly.

The town of Djenné in Mali has long been a trade center and site of Islamic learning and pilgrimage. The town's Great Mosque (**3.5.9**) is located next to Djenné's bustling marketplace.

3.5.9 Monday market, Great Mosque, Djenné, Mali

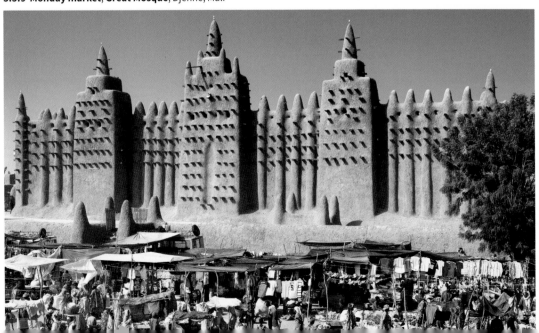

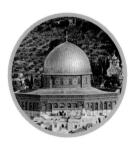

For further discussion of the form and context of mosques as religious architecture:
→ see **3.2.15**, p. 383

433

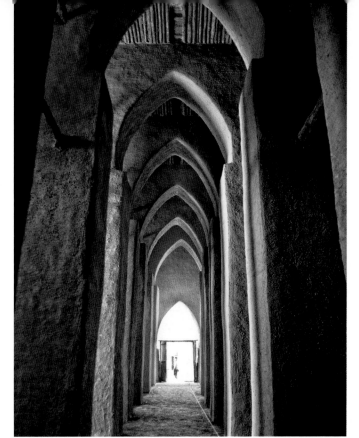

3.5.10 Interior, Great Mosque, current structure 1907; on this site since 1240. Djenné, Mali

An earlier building on this site was a mosque adapted from the palace of King Koi Konboro when he converted to Islam in 1240. Several centuries later, in 1834, Sheikh Amadou Labbo ordered that the mosque be demolished. He considered the original too lavish and built a more modest one on the site. The current building, more in keeping with the thirteenth-century version, was finished around 1907 while Mali was under French occupation. It is considered the largest mud-brick structure in the world.

The Great Mosque combines characteristics of Islamic mosques with West African architectural practices. Three **minarets**, or towers, are used to call the faithful to prayer. Spiral staircases inside lead to the roofs, which feature cone-shaped spires topped by ostrich eggs. These ostrich eggs are important symbols of fertility and purity for the people of Djenné.

The clay-mud and palm-wood exterior (**3.5.9**, p. 433) of the building is similar to the houses of Mali. Numerous wooden beams support the mosque and line the ceiling (**3.5.10**), not only to give it a distinctive look, but also for functional purposes. Some beams structurally support the ceiling, but most are used to access the walls for annual maintenance. The area's hot climate has also affected the building's design, with roof ventilation to cool the building, and mud-brick walls to regulate the temperature. The walls' thickness ranges from 16 to 24 in.; they are thickest where they are tallest. They absorb heat to keep the interior cool during the day and release it at night to keep it warm.

Amongst the largest and most impressive examples of ancient architecture south of the Sahara Desert are the massive stone walls of Great Zimbabwe, built and expanded from the thirteenth to the fifteenth century, in southern Africa (**3.5.11**). The remnants of altars, stone

3.5.11 Conical Tower, c. 1350–1450, Great Zimbabwe, Zimbabwe

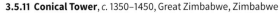

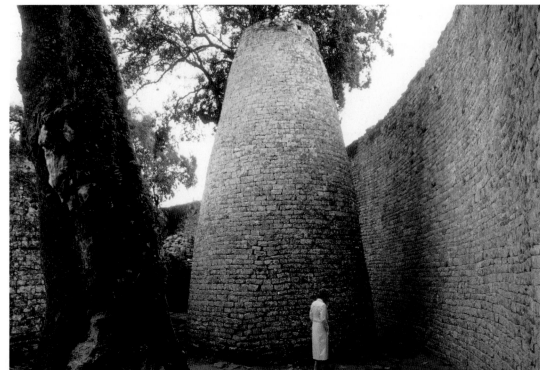

Minaret: a tall slender tower, particularly on a mosque, from which the faithful are called to prayer

Monolith: a monument or sculpture made from a single piece of stone

Ocher: a pigment found in nature containing hydrated iron oxide

Syncretism: the blending of multiple religious or philosophical beliefs

monoliths, and soapstone sculptures found at Great Zimbabwe suggest that it served as both a political and religious center for the Shona state. Indeed, the name of the site comes from the Shona phrase for "houses of stone" or "royal court," and we know that it included three main areas: the seat of the king's rule, a royal residence, and a residential area for at least 10,000 goldsmiths, potters, weavers, blacksmiths, and masons. During its prime, from about 1350 to 1450, Great Zimbabwe also functioned as an important cattle farm and international trade center. By the end of the fifteenth century, when centers of trade moved to the north, the site had been abandoned.

Many of the original mud-and-thatch buildings and platforms have long since disintegrated, but the sturdily built stone walls remain. Made from slab-like granite quarried from the nearby hills and stacked without mortar, the stability of the walls is increased by their design; they slope slightly inward at the top. The Conical Tower is an imposing structure, 18 ft. in diameter and 30 ft. tall, it rises above the high wall of the Great Enclosure and is completely solid. Its purpose remains unknown. Like the walls, the Conical Tower probably served as a symbolic display of authority, a way to distinguish the areas used by royalty from the rest of the village.

Eight carved pieces of soapstone, each about 16 in. tall, were found integrated into buildings on top of columns at Great Zimbabwe. The image of the creature in **3.5.12** combines the features of a human-like bird and crocodile (the crocodile's eyes and zigzag mouth are visible just below the bird's leg and tail feathers). The bird's beak has been replaced with human lips, and its claws look more like feet, suggesting that these figures have supernatural significance. In fact, the Shona believe that royal ancestral spirits visit the living world through birds, especially eagles. Birds are considered messengers from the spirits because they traverse freely between the realms of the sky and the Earth. These sculptures reflect some of the core beliefs in many African cultures: the symbolic use of emblems of royal authority, reminders of familial relationships, and expectations of spiritual reward in the afterlife.

Many contemporary African architects combine features of the past and the present in their designs. In the plan for the South

African Embassy in Berlin, Mphethi Morojele (b. Maseru, Lesotho) included a central courtyard as a reference to South African *kraal* (or corral) spaces, like the 820-ft. one seen in the Great Enclosure, Great Zimbabwe complex. The kraal, a roughly circular area within an African village or settlement, was used to hold cattle or other livestock. Within the embassy's predominantly glass and European Modernist-styled building, traditional African design features include the geometric wall decoration made of red **ocher** and white chalk (**3.5.13**), as well as fittings, artwork, and furniture.

South Africans lived under apartheid, a political system of severe racial segregation and discrimination, from 1948 to 1991. When Morojele founded MMA Architects in 1995 he was one of the first Black men in the country to own an architectural practice. Focused on building a post-apartheid architectural language, Morojele says he is inspired by the "**syncretic**" (a word typically used in religious contexts; the blending of ideas from two or more cultures or belief systems) nature of African design and its ability to absorb many influences, yet remain "of Africa, her people, her landscapes."

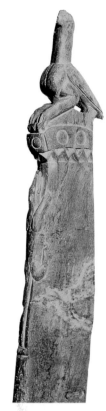

3.5.12 Bird on top of stone monolith, 15th century. Soapstone, height 14½" (bird image). Great Zimbabwe Site Museum, Zimbabwe

3.5.13 Mphethi Morojele (MMA Architects), South African Embassy, Berlin, Germany, 2003

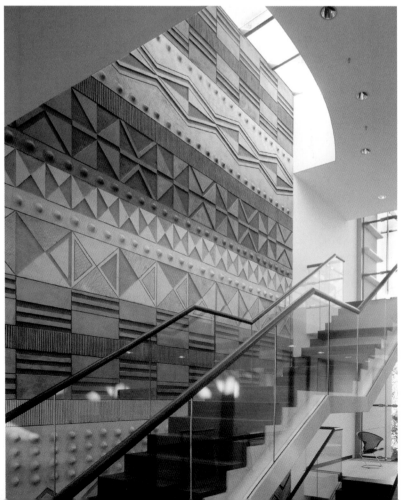

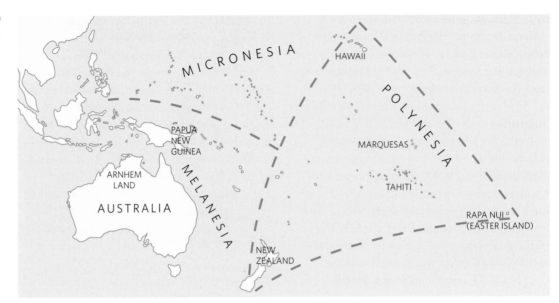

3.5.14 Map of the Pacific Islands, showing the regions of Micronesia, Melanesia, and Polynesia

Tattoos: designs marked on the body by injecting dye under the skin

Petroglyph: an ancient or prehistoric image made in rock by carving, engraving, or scratching the surface to reveal the underlying layer

Pictograph: a picture used as a symbol in writing; conveys meaning through resemblance to physical shape

Art of the Pacific Islands

The geographic area of the Pacific Islands includes Polynesia, Melanesia, Micronesia, and Australia (**3.5.14**). The islands are separated by enormous expanses of ocean, but since ancient times the people living there have been connected by shared beliefs, languages, and similarities in their cultures, which strongly value customary ways of life and behavior, such as farming, ancestor worship, and the preservation of social and artistic traditions. *Mana*, or pervasive magical power and its associated prestige, has been a strong influence in Polynesian, Melanesian, and Maori belief.

The art of the Pacific Islands includes such portable objects as jewelry, furniture, and weapons; body ornamentation; wooden sculpture; paintings on rock; monumental sculptures; masks; and ceremonial architecture. The works often combine practical usefulness with sacred significance, thus linking the everyday world and living people with their ancestors and gods. Contemporary artists work in all types of artistic media—from traditional to technological.

New Zealand

The Maori of New Zealand have one of the most elaborate traditions of tattooing in the world. Their words for it are *ta moko*. **Tattoos** (or moko) are made by injecting a pigment or dye under the skin so that a permanent mark is left on the body. It is not known when the first tattoos were made. The earliest known preserved tattooed bodies date back to *c.* 3300 BCE and feature abstract tattoos composed of designs with dots and line patterns; Maori designs are part of this tradition (**3.5.15**).

The designs mark specific events in the wearer's life, such as reaching puberty, becoming a warrior, making a kill, getting married, having a child, and so on. Tattoos covering the entire face and body were originally worn by chiefs and their families, indicating lineage and social status. When comparing two *ta moko*, the patterns may seem

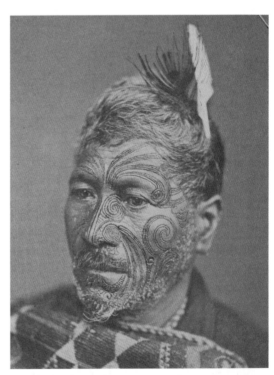

3.5.15 E. Pulman, *Maori chief, Ngapuhi, Hati Wira Takahi Bay of Islands*, 1873. Albumen silver print. The J. Paul Getty Museum, Los Angeles, California

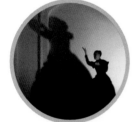

The contemporary New Zealand artist Yuki Kihara examines the challenges to Samoan cultural identity as a result of colonialism, natural disasters, and stereotypes by performing the traditional narrative dance form *taualuga*:
→ see **2.10.9**, p. 340

to be the same at first: however, upon closer inspection, no two designs are exactly alike. In fact, elaborate facial designs were so distinctive and specific to an individual that at times they were used as a form of legal signature.

Australia

Australia has over 100,000 surviving rock art sites—places with paintings, drawings, stencils, carvings, and figures made out of beeswax. Made as early as 40,000 years ago, most surviving prehistoric art from this region is less than 15,000 years old. Australian rock art relating to nature and to the life experience, myths, and beliefs of Aboriginal people has been found on the walls and ceilings of rock shelters, in caves, on boulders, and on rock platforms.

For at least a decade, scholars who study the Indigenous rock art of Australia have been working to raise awareness about its cultural importance, the threats it faces, and access to historical monuments. **Petroglyphs** (rock engravings) and **pictographs** (paintings and drawings) made from natural materials date back to 20,000 years ago (**3.5.16**). Australian rock art charts changes in animal habitation (including of some now-extinct species), records early contact by Europeans, and contains cultural touchstones for people living in the area. The sites are sacred to Aboriginal Australians because they are believed to be inhabited by their ancestral spirits, often depicted in the rock art. The factors endangering the preservation of these sites include natural erosion over time, pollution, vandalism, mining, fires, and development.

Many contemporary Aboriginal artists in Australia tell stories of their homeland and connect to the belief in the ongoing presence of ancestral beings in the landscape and the animals that live there. Abie Loy Kemarre (b. 1972) and other Anmatyerre people identify their traditional country as Artenya (also called Iylenty or Mosquito Bore). Kemarre inherited custodial rights to the Bush Hen Dreaming story from her grandfather. "Dreaming" is the English word for the creation period of Aboriginal Australia. The Bush Hen Dreaming story conveys the mythological and foundational Anmatyerre beliefs connected to ecology, ancestral spirits, and non-linear time. Kemarre's paintings focus on the journey of the bush hen in search of its favorite food, the bush

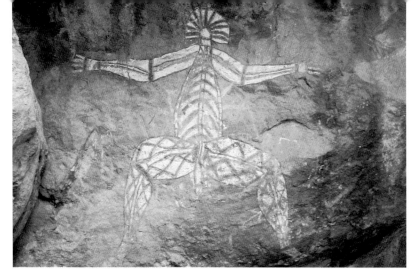

3.5.16 Indigenous rock art at Anbangbang gallery of Burrungkuy (Nourlangie) rock, Kakadu National Park, Northern Territory, Australia. The traditional owners of this particular area are the Kunbim people

tomato, while faithfully tending to its young in the sandhills near Utopia in the central Australian desert. For aboriginal artists, it is more important to connect to the embedded memory of and deep familiarity with place than it is to give a visual representation of the story's narrative. In *Sandhill Country* (**3.5.17**), Kemarre uses abstraction to depict the wind patterns in the sandhills as parallel concentric lines, referring to the physical location and spiritual resonance of the Dreaming Ancestors that inhabit their homeland.

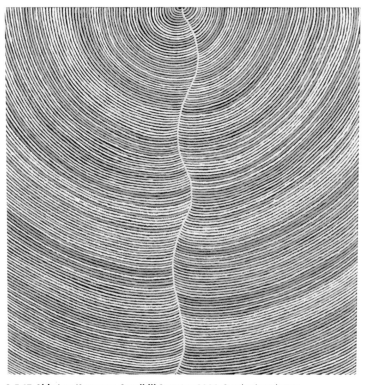

3.5.17 Abie Loy Kemarre, *Sandhill Country*, 2006. Synthetic polymer paint on canvas, 84 × 84", Art Gallery of South Australia, Adelaide

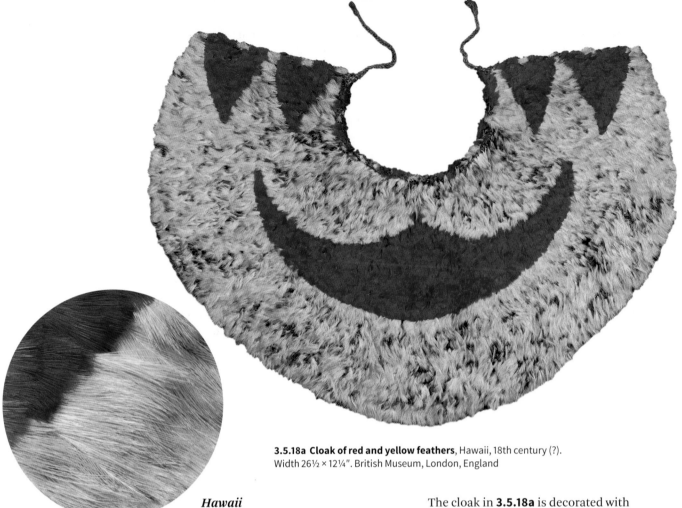

3.5.18a Cloak of red and yellow feathers, Hawaii, 18th century (?). Width 26½ × 12¼". British Museum, London, England

3.5.18b Detail of Hawaiian feather cloak

Hawaii

The first inhabitants of Hawaii (*c.* 600 CE) were Polynesians from the Marquesas Islands, more than 2,000 miles away. Five hundred years later, Tahitian settlers introduced a strict social hierarchy based on a system of *kapu* (or taboo) and a belief in a new host of gods and demigods. King Kamehameha unified the islands' warring factions during the eighteenth century. Hawaii became the fiftieth state of the United States in 1959, though it has also kept cultural connections with its Polynesian and Tahitian roots.

The ceremonial and warfare attire for Hawaiian nobility included thickly woven cloaks called *ahu'ula*, made of feathers (**3.5.18a** and **3.5.18b**). These garments were used as a kind of armor in hand-to-hand combat; more importantly, however, they were believed to offer the protection of the gods. Ahu'ula cloaks were generally made by men. This was a time-consuming task that required a great degree of skill, and was by and large considered a sacred activity. The feathers were tied to a plant-fiber netting with cording, based on an ancient belief that knots reflected a metaphorical binding between humans and gods.

The cloak in **3.5.18a** is decorated with geometric designs, and identifies the wearer as a high-ranking member of society. The red feathers on the ahu'ula came from the 'i'iwi bird, and the yellow feathers from the 'o'o bird. Because the yellow birds were very rare, cloaks with more yellow feathers were considered more valuable, and all-yellow cloaks were the most valuable of all.

These feather cloaks were prized possessions that were passed from generation to generation, unless they had been collected by enemies as war trophies or presented as political gifts. One famous cloak was presented by King Kamehameha III to American naval officer Lawrence Kearny as a gesture of gratitude for his diplomatic service on behalf of Hawaii.

Rapa Nui (Easter Island)

Rapa Nui (Easter Island) is small, measuring 15 miles long and 7½ miles wide. It is also extremely isolated, almost 1,300 miles away from the nearest inhabited landmass, the coast of Chile. Rapa Nui's famous stone sculptures are called *moai* (meaning "seamount," "image," "statue," or "bearers of the gift"). These monolithic heads and torsos are unique, but their abstracted and symmetrical features resemble the style of other faces made throughout Polynesia (**3.5.19**). Between around 900 and 1750 CE, about one thousand of these huge figures were carved out of volcanic rock and scattered around the island, especially along the coast. They represent deified ancestors who were chiefs. The large quantities and size of the moai also suggest they have ritual, ceremonial, or cultural importance. Measuring from 10 to 60 ft. in height and weighing as much as 50 tons, these figures have unique individual features as well as common general characteristics.

While their heights and body shapes vary, they all have deep eye sockets (perhaps originally inlaid), angular noses, pointed chins, elongated earlobes, and an upright posture; their arms are by their sides, and they have no visible legs. Many of the moai (887 have been documented to date) were originally placed on platforms along the coastline, facing inland; a small number of them wore flat cylindrical hats of red volcanic stone, each weighing more than 10 tons. Scholars believe it likely that the hats on the sculptures represented crowns, identifying them as ancestor chiefs and thus providing a connection between the present and the past, and the natural and the cosmic realms. During a period of civil strife from 1722 to 1868, all the moai on the coastline were torn down by islanders. Thanks to recent archaeological efforts, many of the statues have been put back in their original places, appearing to emerge from the sea.

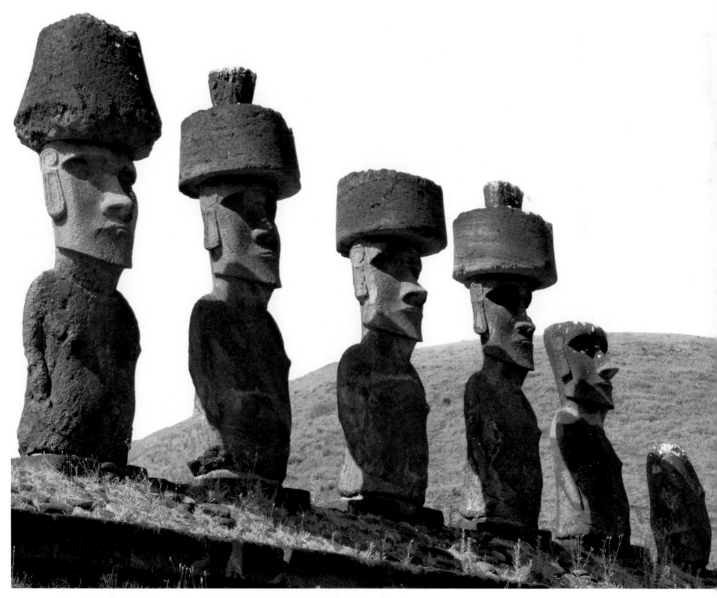

3.5.19 *Moai* **ancestor figures**, Ahu Nau Nau, Rapa Nui (Chile), Polynesia, before the 15th century

and intrigue of Abelam deities and traditions (**3.5.21**). The interior space is filled with detailed wooden figures representing supernatural beings, and with meaningful objects.

Colors and shapes have symbolic meaning in Abelam art; for example, white is believed to make long yams grow, and the pointed oval shape represents the belly of a woman. The use of yellow, red, and white is common. As in African art, certain objects, such as large cowrie shells, represent fertility and prosperity. Abelam see individual carvings, as well as the entire ceremonial house, as temporary. They are important during use, but are discarded afterward. Because of the powerful nature of the objects and imagery, they must be taken far away from the village, and are sometimes abandoned in the jungle or sold to collectors or museums.

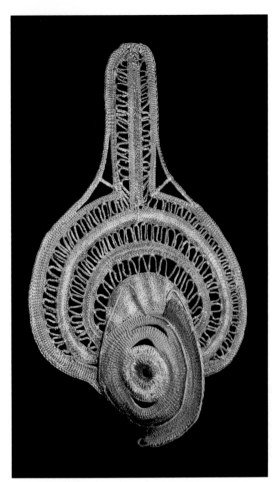

3.5.20 Yam mask, Abelam, Maprik district, Papua New Guinea. Painted cane, height 18″. Musée Barbier-Mueller, Geneva, Switzerland

Papua New Guinea

The Abelam live in the wetland areas of the northern part of Papua New Guinea. One of the principal activities of their society is farming, especially yams, taro, bananas, and sweet potatoes. Yams are the main crop of Abelam society. Symbolically, they are associated with male fertility. The Abelam hold yam festivals each year to display the most impressive yams, with the grower of the largest yam achieving higher social status and helping to secure the prosperity of the village as a whole. In the festivals associated with these contests, the yams themselves actually wear masks made of baskets and wood (**3.5.20**).

Another important ceremony for the Abelam has traditionally been the initiation cycle for male members of the community. Eight separate rituals take place over the course of twenty or thirty years before a man is fully initiated. The elaborate ceremonial houses where some rites of passage take place are meant to impress the initiate with the power

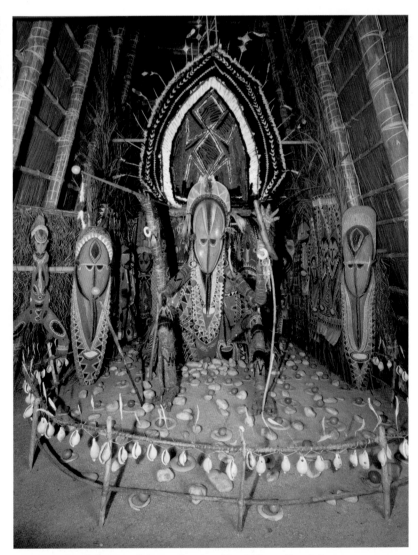

3.5.21 Interior of Abelam cult house, Bongiora, Maprik, Papua New Guinea, Melanesia. Museum der Kulturen, Basel, Switzerland

Explore Further Art of Africa and the Pacific Islands

Art by and about African People and Cultures

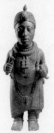

1.7.9 Nigerian Ife artist, Figure of Oni, Ife culture, early 14th–15th century → p. 135

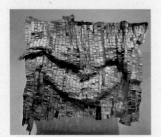

1.4.14 Kane Kwei, *Coffin in the Shape of a Cocoa Pod*, c. 1970 → p. 91

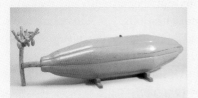

1.10.1a El Anatsui, *Man's Cloth*, 2001 → p. 159

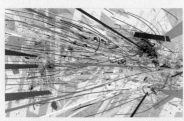

2.2.22 Julie Mehretu, *Excerpt (Suprematist Evasion)*, 2003 → p. 207

The African Diaspora and the History of Enslavement

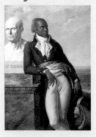

3.7.14 Anne-Louis Girodet, *Jean-Baptiste Belley*, 1797, France → p. 476

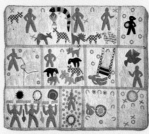

0.0.5 Harriet Powers, *Bible Quilt*, 1885–86 → p. 19

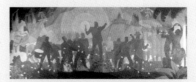

3.9.24 Aaron Douglas, *Aspects of Negro Life ...*, 1934 → p. 514

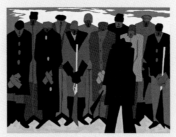

1.8.7 Jacob Lawrence, "John Brown Remained a Full Winter in Canada...," 1977 → p. 143

Art by and about Pacific Islanders and Their Cultures

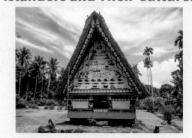

1.9.12 Bai-ra-Irrai, Republic of Palau, c. 1700 → p. 154

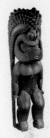

2.4.5 Figure of the war god Ku-ka'ili-moku, Hawaii, 18th or 19th century → p. 231

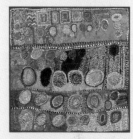

0.0.15 Loongkoonan, *Bush Tucker Nyikina Country*, 2006 → p. 26

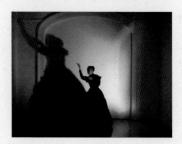

2.10.9 Yuki Kihara, *Tualuga: The Last Dance*, 2006 → p. 340

Your turn

How do these artworks relate to the cultures discussed in this chapter?

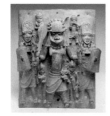

4.6.8 Benin plaque with, warrior and attendants, 16th–17th century → p. 609

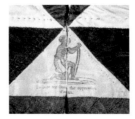

1.9.5b Deborah Coates, detail of quilt, Pennsylvania, c. 1840–50 → p. 150

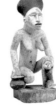

4.3.10 Kneeling figure with bowl and child, late 19th/ early 20th century → p. 574

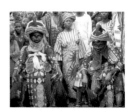

4.1.10 Yoruba culture, Gèlèdé masqueraders in Benin, 1971 → p. 547

3.6
Art of Renaissance and Baroque Europe (1400–1750)

The thousand years of European history known as the **Middle Ages** were followed by the period known as the **Renaissance** (*c.* 1400–1600). The term means "rebirth," a reference to a renewed interest in the **Classical** world of Greece and Rome. The influence of Classical **subject matter** is evident in the numbers of **nudes** and mythological figures in Italian Renaissance art. Although Christian subjects remained popular, the emphasis switched from a belief in faith as the only factor in attaining immortality after death, to a concentration on how human actions could enhance the quality of life on Earth. Mathematics and science, derived from a renewed study of Classical Greek and Roman works, encouraged the systematic understanding of the world. Renaissance artists used and refined new

systems of **perspective** to translate their careful observations more consistently into realistic artistic representations. The Renaissance was also marked by an interest in education and the natural world. Improved literacy, means of travel, and printed books (made possible by the invention of moveable type in the 1400s) expanded the transmission of ideas and artistic developments throughout Europe (**3.6.1**). **Humanism** became influential as a philosophical approach to life that stressed study of the Classical world and promoted the success of individuals as a reflection of what were believed to be their gifts from God.

Italian artist and historian Giorgio Vasari (1511–1574) used the term Renaissance (*rinascità*) in the first art history book, *The Lives of the Most Excellent Painters, Sculptors, and Architects* (sometimes known as *Lives of the Great Artists*). Published in 1550, it began with a biography of Giotto (see **3.6.2**) as the father of the Italian Renaissance and culminated in Vasari's attribution of Michelangelo as the master of the period. Vasari's text emphasized the ability needed to make paintings, sculptures, and architecture as both intellectual and divinely inspired. During this period, artists began to be seen as creative geniuses rather than manual laborers making craft works. This humanist focus on individual achievement and earthly **naturalism** contrasts with the art of the Middle Ages, in which artists were often unidentified and scenes depicted a spiritual, otherworldly space.

Giotto (*c.* 1266–1337) lived during the cusp of the end of the Middle Ages and the beginning of the Renaissance. The *Lamentation* (**3.6.2**), part of a series of **frescoes** for the Arena Chapel in Padua, Italy, depicts the grief over

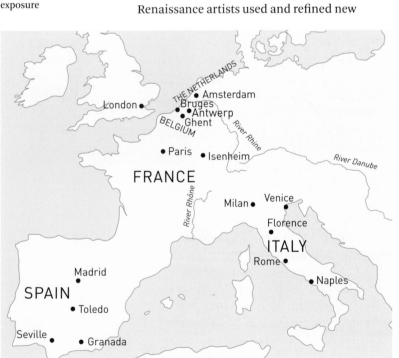

3.6.1 Map of Renaissance and Baroque Europe

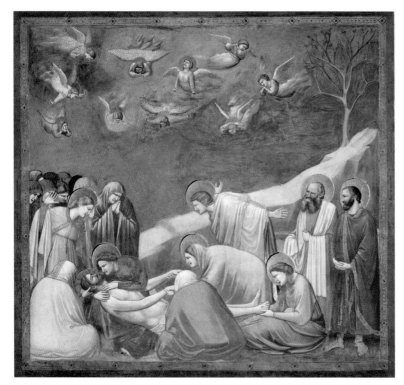

3.6.2 **Giotto**, *Lamentation*, *c.* 1305. Arena (Scrovegni) Chapel, Padua, Italy

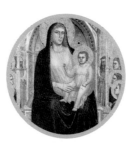

Toward the end of the Middle Ages, the artist Giotto created believable three-dimensional space with figures that convey mass and volume:
→ see **3.2.27**, p. 388

Perspective: the creation of the illusion of depth in a two-dimensional image by using mathematical principles

Humanism, humanist: the study of such subjects as history, philosophy, languages, and literature, particularly in relation to those of ancient Greece and Rome

Naturalism, naturalistic: a very realistic or lifelike style of making images

Fresco: a technique in which the artist paints onto freshly applied plaster. From the Italian *fresco*, "fresh"

Mass: a volume that has, or gives the illusion of having, weight, density, and bulk.

Depth: the impression of three dimensions in a two-dimensional artwork.

Narrative: an artwork that tells a story

Intercessor: one who pleads with God on behalf of others

Oil paint: paint made of pigment suspended in oil

Baroque: a European artistic and architectural style of the late sixteenth to early eighteenth century, characterized by extravagance and emotional intensity

Patron: an organization or individual who sponsors the creation of works of art

Pigment: the colored material used in paints. Often made from finely ground minerals

Christ's death and suffering as recounted in Christian belief and tradition. The gold haloes and layering of figures are characteristics of Byzantine and Gothic art (periods of the Middle Ages), but in this work, Giotto invents new artistic strategies that herald the Renaissance to come. The figures appear to have substantial **mass**, and he has given the scene a sense of **depth**. Giotto has also indicated a **narrative** in the scene through the gestures and expressions of the figures, as if they were putting on a play.

In general, when looking at art from the Renaissance, one can see that different religious and stylistic parameters are in play in Italy as opposed to the north of Europe. Italian artists often depicted grand-scale imagery (frequently frescoes) that promoted saints or other intermediaries (people who act as interpreters or go-betweens, in this case between ordinary people and God) and therefore highlighted the role of the Catholic Church as an essential **intercessor** to God. Even when artworks from the Italian Renaissance depicted Classical mythological subjects, they often conveyed a Christian message.

In the Northern Renaissance, which occurred in areas of Europe north of Italy, artists preferred to depict clothed religious or everyday figures in smaller scenes or on altarpieces. Northern Renaissance paintings often include more intricate details, due to the use of **oil paint**, and convey symbolic messages, often about Christian morality.

The period that followed the Renaissance is known as the **Baroque** (*c.* 1600–1750). Like the word Renaissance, Baroque refers to both a historical period and a style of art. The seventeenth century is noted for an increase in trade and advancements in science. Baroque art draws on much of the same subject matter as the Renaissance, but Baroque images tend to include more motion, emotion, and theatricality. The Renaissance and Baroque periods were both marked by constant warfare throughout Europe, and art was often used to memorialize battles or to inspire people to support their rulers. Throughout this time, artworks were commissioned by wealthy **patrons**, often a church or ruling family, such as the wealthy Florentine Medici family, who determined such things as the size, subject matter, and even how much of an expensive **pigment**, such as ultramarine blue, the artist could use. This period is also marked by a split in the Church between Catholicism and Protestantism, beginning with the Protestant Reformation in 1517 and continued into the mid-seventeenth century. Catholic artwork highlighted the power of intermediaries—such as saints and the Church—between Christians and God, while Protestants believed artworks should be more individual and direct, without the need for intermediaries.

The Early Renaissance in Italy

Following the renewed interest in the Classical past and the influence of humanist thought, Italian artists during the early Renaissance were preoccupied with making pictures that their viewers would find entirely believable. The real was balanced by the **ideal**, however, especially when the subjects were mythological or religious. Whereas during the Middle Ages, depictions of the nude body had been avoided

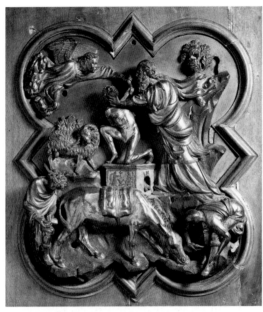

3.6.3a Filippo Brunelleschi, *Sacrifice of Isaac*, 1401. Bronze. Museo Nazionale del Bargello, Florence, Italy

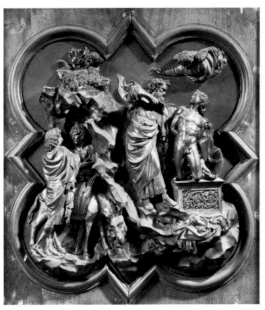

3.6.3b Lorenzo Ghiberti, *Sacrifice of Isaac*, 1401, bronze. Museo Nazionale del Bargello, Florence, Italy

except to show the weakness and mortality of such sinners as Adam and Eve, during the Renaissance, artists portrayed the idealized nude figure as the embodiment of spiritual and intellectual perfection.

Artists' interest in exploration and high individual achievement meant that competitions between them were common. In 1401, seven artists submitted **relief** panels portraying the Biblical narrative of the Sacrifice of Isaac to compete for the commission to create a large set of bronze panels for the Florence Baptistry's north doors. The requirements for the submissions were very specific. Each Old Testament scene depicting Abraham, who, at the behest of God, is about to kill his son Isaac, should also include an altar for the boy, a rocky landscape, an angel, a ram, a donkey, and two shepherds, all encased in a so-called **quatrefoil** frame.

Filippo Brunelleschi (1377–1446) and Lorenzo Ghiberti (1378–1455) took very different approaches to the scene. Brunelleschi (**3.6.3a**) shows a father terrified at the prospect of killing his son, and a boy who, although he tries to hold up his adolescent body, appears to shrink in fear. The extraordinary emotion conveyed by these two figures shows what a heart-wrenching act God had asked Abraham to commit. Ghiberti's depiction (**3.6.3b**) instead shows a very muscular boy and a father who looks like an ancient god himself. They appear proud and willing to accept their fate. In both scenes, an angel swoops down at the last minute to stop Abraham. The committee chose Ghiberti's depiction, probably in part because of the Classical-looking figures and the fearlessness of Abraham and Isaac. In addition, Ghiberti used only one piece of bronze with small attachments for his panel, so it required less bronze than Brunelleschi's, which was made by casting seven separate pieces. Ghiberti created twenty-eight panels for the north doors of the baptistry over the next nineteen years. He was then commissioned to create ten very intricate scenes for the northern doors of the baptistry, which Michelangelo called the Gates of Paradise.

In the end, it was fortunate that Brunelleschi lost the competition, because shortly thereafter he went to Rome and, among other pursuits, studied its Classical architecture. When he returned to Florence, he won a competition in 1419 to complete the 140-ft.-diameter **dome**

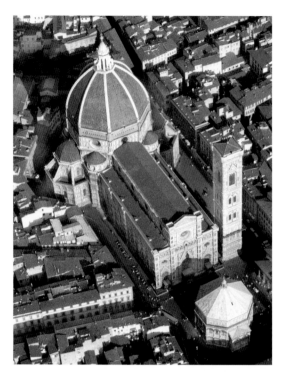

3.6.4 Arnolfo di Cambio and others, Florence Cathedral (Italy), begun 1296, view from the south

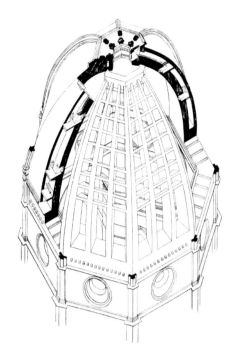

3.6.5 Modern diagram showing Filippo Brunelleschi's dome of Florence Cathedral, 1420–23

Linear perspective: a system using converging imaginary sight lines to create the illusion of depth

Three-dimensional: having height, width, and depth

Foreground: the part of a work depicted as nearest to the viewer

Scale: the size of an object or artwork relative to another object or artwork, or to a system of measurement

Vanishing point(s): the point or points in a work of art at which imaginary sight lines appear to converge, suggesting depth

Focal point: the center of interest or activity in a work of art, often drawing the viewer's attention to the most important element

Atmospheric perspective (also called **Aerial perspective**): the use of shades of color to create the illusion of dept: closer objects have warmer tones and clear outlines, while objects set further away are smaller and become hazy

Chiaroscuro: the use of light and dark in a painting to create the impression of volume

Composition: the overall design or organization of a work

for Santa Maria del Fiore (Florence Cathedral). The dome was a great technological challenge and Brunelleschi's proposal was radical. He not only designed the dome, but also devised the machinery used to build it and oversaw the construction itself, thus earning himself the right to be called the first Renaissance architect (**3.6.4**).

Existing construction techniques required temporary wooden scaffolding to form the dome shape (170 ft. above the ground at its top) until the stonework was finished—which in this case would have been too costly and heavy. The enormous weight of the bricks and stone could not be held up by external stone supports either, because of the existing buildings around the cathedral. Brunelleschi invented equipment to hoist the building materials and came up with an ingenious system that used each stage of the structure to support the next as the dome was built, layer by layer (**3.6.5**). The dome's construction began in 1420 and took sixteen years to complete.

Brunelleschi is also credited with inventing a new method for creating the illusion of depth, known as **linear perspective**, a technique for creating the illusion of **three-dimensional** space. He shared the process with other Florentine artists, including his close friend, a painter nicknamed Masaccio, or "Big Clumsy Tom" (1401–1428).

Masaccio applied these rules of linear perspective in several large-scale fresco paintings, including *Tribute Money* (**3.6.6**, p. 446). This painting depicts the biblical story from the gospel of Matthew, in which, as advised by Jesus, St. Peter has to pay the local tax collector. Here, figures, architecture, and landscape are integrated into a believable scene. The buildings in the **foreground** appear on the same **scale** as the group of figures standing next to them. To show how the buildings and people are perceived as being further away from us, they are depicted as smaller, and lead, in a naturalistic way, toward a **vanishing point** on the horizon. The **focal point** converges on Jesus, and the vanishing point lies behind his head, making him the visual and symbolic center of the scene. Masaccio uses **atmospheric perspective** to show the distant landscape, where the mountains fade from greenish to gray.

Notable Renaissance characteristics in this painting include consistent lighting throughout, a wide range of colors, and the use of **chiaroscuro** (extremes of light and dark) to enhance the illusion of three-dimensional form. *Tribute Money* is one of Masaccio's most original paintings: it also shows three scenes in a sequence within one setting. While the fresco maintains the medieval tradition of narrative painting, the **composition** deviates

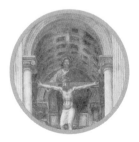

Masaccio's *Trinity* was the first painting to use linear perspective:
→ see **1.3.20**, p. 79

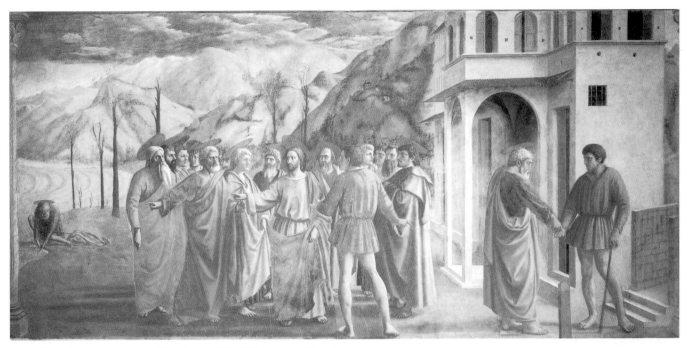

3.6.6 Masaccio, _Tribute Money_, c. 1427. Fresco, 8'1" × 19'7". Brancacci Chapel, Santa Maria del Carmine, Florence, Italy

from the earlier practice in an important way. Rather than showing each scene on a separate panel, events that take place at different times are shown together in a unified space, or a **continuous narrative**. In the center, the tax collector, with his back to us, demands the Jewish temple tax as the disciples look on. The tax collector is shown in a natural stance called **contrapposto**, which was found in ancient sculpture and imitated by Renaissance artists. On the left of the scene we see Peter following the instructions of Jesus to retrieve the money from the mouth of the first fish he catches. On the right, Peter pays the collector double the amount owed, using the money miraculously obtained from the fish's mouth. This story would have been particularly relevant for contemporary Florentines, who were required to pay a tax for military defense in 1427, the same year the painting was made. Similarly to other Early Renaissance artists, Masaccio used both linear and atmospheric perspective to convince viewers they were looking at reality rather than a symbolic representation. He incorporated an understanding of the movement of the human bodies beneath the drapery to increase the sense of volume. This series of frescoes, which was displayed in the Brancacci family chapel, was a major influence on later artists, including Michelangelo (see **3.6.8a** and **3.6.8b**, p. 448), who specifically went to the chapel to study Masaccio's paintings.

The High Renaissance in Italy

The Italian artists Leonardo da Vinci (1452–1519), Michelangelo Buonarroti (1475–1564), and Raphael (1483–1520) dominated the art world in Europe at the beginning of the sixteenth century. All three of them, like other artists of the high Renaissance, utilized the rules of perspective and **illusionism**, but willingly departed from exact mechanical precision in order to create desired visual effects. Leonardo was the eldest amongst these three great artists of the period. He was a great observer of the world around him and known not only as a virtuoso painter, but also as a scientist and engineer. He died at the age of sixty-seven while staying with the King of France, which is how the _Mona Lisa_, a project Leonardo worked on throughout his life, ended up in a French museum. Michelangelo was younger than Leonardo, but lived until he was a month shy of ninety years old. Raphael, known as the most charming and handsome of the three, died at the young age of thirty-seven.

As part of Pope Julius II's (1443–1513) campaign to restore Rome to its ancient grandeur, he assigned Michelangelo to paint the ceiling of the Vatican's Sistine Chapel. Also under the direction of Julius II, Raphael was working on the _School of Athens_ fresco nearby in the Vatican apartments between 1510 and 1511 (see Gateway: Raphael, p. 448). Michelangelo's enormous painting, which took the artist four

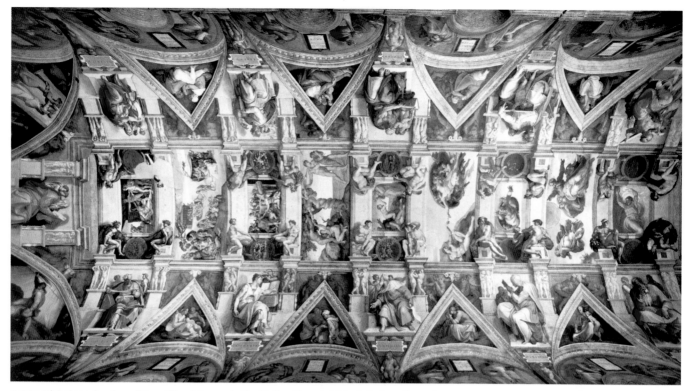

3.6.7a Michelangelo, view of the ceiling frescoes in the Sistine Chapel, 1508–12. Vatican City, Italy

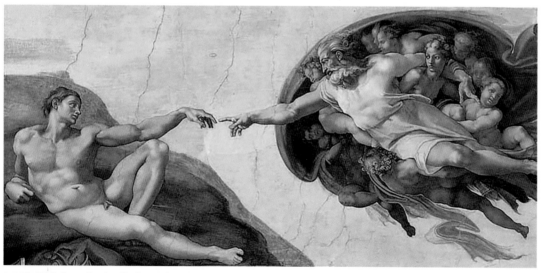

3.6.7b Michelangelo, detail of *Creation of Adam*, Sistine Chapel ceiling

years to complete, is so believable that we could be fooled into thinking the beams, **pedestals**, and structural elements are real (**3.6.7a**). The only part of the ceiling that is actual architecture, and not a painted illusion, are the frames of the **pendentives**. Michelangelo preferred stone carving to painting, which perhaps explains why he painted the ceiling with such apparently three-dimensional figures and surrounded them with architectural elements and sculpture. The nine panels at the ceiling's center detail the Old Testament stories of Genesis, from the creation of the heavens and Earth, to the creation and fall of Adam and Eve, and ending with scenes from the Great Flood. The ceiling is covered with idealized depictions of the human (mostly male) nude, Michelangelo's specialty. In the *Creation of Adam* panel (**3.6.7b**), for example, the muscular form of Adam echoes that of God, his creator. Just as God's spiritual energy is about to bring life to Adam through the touching of their fingers, Renaissance thinkers believed that human perfection in body and mind was a reflection of the ideals God wished humans to achieve.

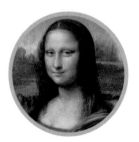

In the *Mona Lisa*, Leonardo da Vinci used a new painting technique he had invented, **sfumato**, as well as a mystical landscape and the gaze of the sitter to create a sense of mystery about the woman's mood:

→ see **0.0.12**, p. 23

Raphael, *The School of Athens*
Paying Homage to Humanists in the Past and Present

For the other *Raphael*
GATEWAYS:
→ see p. 80 and p. 180

Apollo: god of music and lyric poetry; made to look like Michelangelo's *Dying Slave*

Socrates, in green, engaging youths in debate, talking to Alexander the Great

Plato, a great Classical philosopher, modeled after Leonardo da Vinci

Aristotle holding *Nicomachean Ethics* and pointing to the ground—the material world

Architecture and coffered ceiling use rules of perspective as a reference to man's design ability and perhaps dominance over nature

The sky (and Plato pointing to it) as a reference to the heavens as the realm of the ideal

Athena: Goddess of Wisdom

Ptolemy holding the Celestial Globe

Self-portrait of Raphael, second from the right, listening to Ptolemy. In a group because he was gregarious. Perhaps representing Apelles

Euclid bending with compass and slate, modeled after Bramante

Pythagoras with a book

Poetic thinkers

Heraclitus, modeled after Michelangelo, leaning on a block of marble. Shown by himself because he was a solitary person

Diogenes

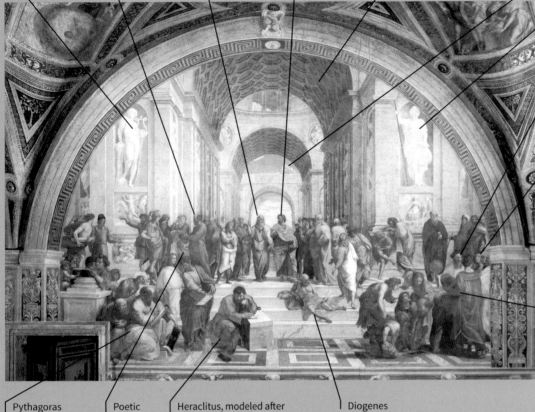

3.6.8 Raphael, *The School of Athens*, 1510–11. Fresco, 16'8" × 25'. Stanza della Segnatura, Vatican City, Italy

In *The School of Athens* (**3.6.8**), Raphael links a gathering of great philosophers and scientists from the Classical past—Plato, Aristotle, and Pythagoras, for example—to sixteenth-century Italy by using people he knew as models for the figures from ancient Greece and Rome. The two figures in the center combine spiritual and intangible thought, represented by Plato pointing toward the heavens, and the study of things observable in nature, represented by Aristotle (384–322 BCE) whose hand is open toward the ground. During the Renaissance, writings by Plato (*c.* 427–347 BCE) were combined with Christian doctrine to form a philosophy termed Neoplatonism. Renaissance humanists believed that individuals' achievements in the arts and sciences reflected the beauty, joy, and reflection found in God and Heaven.

By using the Renaissance painter Leonardo da Vinci as the model for the Greek philosopher Plato, Raphael expresses admiration for Leonardo's accomplishments. Using the face of Leonardo also allows us to see Plato in the flesh as a believable individual. Raphael pays homage to his contemporary Michelangelo, too, who is shown sitting by himself on the steps, in the guise of the pessimistic philosopher Heraclitus. This is appropriate because Raphael frequently saw a brooding Michelangelo working down the hall on the Sistine ceiling. Raphael subtly includes a self-portrait of himself as the Greek painter

Apelles in the group on the right listening to the mathematician and astronomer Ptolemy (holding a globe), showing himself to be a gregarious, intellectual person.

The left side is filled with great thinkers in the fields of grammar, arithmetic, and music, while those on the right are involved with the scientific pursuits of geometry and astronomy. The setting for this symposium is a grand Roman building with majestic **arches** and **vaults** that open up to the heavens. The Classical past is further invoked through the sculptures of Apollo (on our left) and Athena (on our right) in the niches behind the crowd. Despite its sixteenth-century references, the scene is utterly convincing, with calm, orderly groups of scholars and thinkers from throughout history gathered according to Raphael's carefully organized plan.

Arch: a structure, usually curved, that spans an opening

Vault: an arch-like structure supporting a ceiling or roof

Michelangelo also painted *The Last Judgment* on the west wall of the Sistine Chapel more than twenty years later for Pope Clement VII (a member of the influential Medici family).(**3.6.9a**). The muscular, dynamic figures on both the ceiling and the altar wall highlight Michelangelo's first love of sculpting the nude male body. After years of wishing he could be sculpting rather than painting, and of enduring frequent unsolicited advice regarding his compositions and choice of nude figures, Michelangelo painted the mask on St. Bartholomew's flayed skin within *The Last Judgment* as a self-portrait of a tortured artist who would have preferred his chisel andhammer (**3.6.9b**). Some scholars speculate that the location of Bartholomew (and Michelangelo's self-portrait) on the side of the damned is a cloaked reference to the artist's homosexuality because, at that time, the Catholic Church considered homosexuality a sin.

The energetic, whirlpool effect of the judgment scene is much more chaotic and psychologically dark than many other Last Judgment scenes by previous artists. The multitude of nude figures include saints (surrounding Christ), and the blessed and damned souls as they face their last moments on Earth. The Pope's Master of Ceremonies, Biagio da Cesena, criticized the artist for the prolific nudity. Michelangelo responded by painting the official as King Minos, Judge of the Damned, with donkey ears and with a serpent coiling around him (**3.6.9c**).

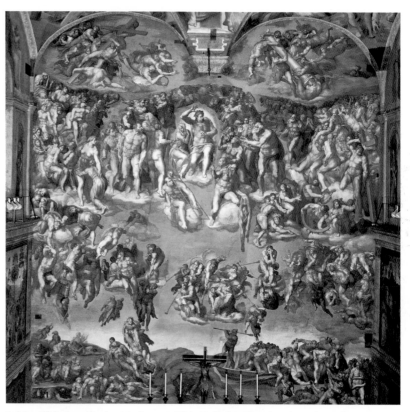

3.6.9a Michelangelo, *Last Judgment*, 1534–41. Sistine Chapel, Vatican City, Italy

3.6.9b (right) **Michelangelo, detail of *Last Judgment* showing self-portrait in St. Bartholomew's skin**, 1534–41. Sistine Chapel, Vatican City, Italy

3.6.9c (far right) **Michelangelo, detail of *Last Judgment* showing Minos, Judge of the Damned**, 1534–41. Sistine Chapel, Vatican City, Italy

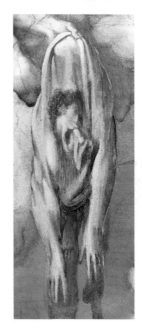

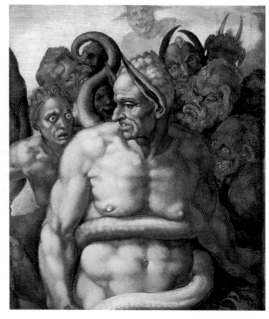

Van Eyck, Panofsky, and Iconographic Analysis

One of the most important Northern Renaissance paintings, *The Arnolfini Portrait* by Jan van Eyck, has been a source of mystery for scholars for generations (**3.6.10a**). Like many works from this time and region, it depicts an intimate, domestic scene, and the young couple and the room in which they stand are painted in such detail that viewers feel as if they are looking into a real room with real people. Indeed, since the nineteenth century, the portrait was thought to depict Giovanni Arnolfini, a wealthy merchant, and his wife. In 1934, the art historian Erwin Panofsky (1892–1968) suggested it could have been some kind of legal document, perhaps certifying their wedding ceremony. An inscription on the wall above the mirror says "Johannes de eyck fuit hic 1434," or "Jan van Eyck was here 1434," which Panofsky argued announces the painter's presence and suggests he was declaring himself as one of two witnesses, visible in the convex mirror behind the principal figures, at the event (**3.6.10b**). Fifteenth-century viewers would probably have paid careful attention to the mirror, with its circular mini-pictures, or roundels, depicting scenes from the crucifixion of Christ, since such an object would have been very expensive and a truly luxurious possession. The mirror helps extend the illusion of reality by showing in its reflective surface the room in front ofthe couple, which is otherwise not in the picture.

Through intense study of the culture in which this artwork was made, Panofsky argued that

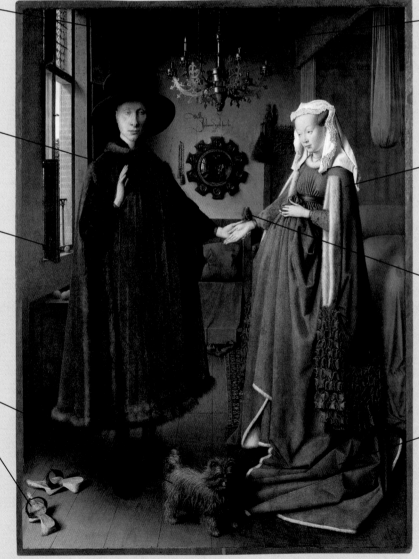

A single candle burning in the chandelier: possibly a symbolic reference to Christ; or a unity candle used in a marriage ceremony; or a sign of a legal event

The man stands near the window to show that he is part of the world outside

Fruit on the windowsill: a sign of fertility. Indicates wealth (oranges and lemons were expensive because they had to be imported from Spain); also a reference to innocence and purity before humans sinned in the Garden of Eden

Dog: a sign of fidelity and wealth

Shoes/clogs: given to a woman as a wedding gift; a symbol of stability; removed to show that the event taking place here is sacred and makes the ground sacred too

The chandelier is very ornamental and expensive, a clear sign of wealth

The woman stands near the elaborate bed to indicate her domestic role and the hope that she will bear children

The figure carved on the chair: St. Margaret, protector of women in childbirth

The full-skirted dress: fashion of the day because the current queen was pregnant (the woman in the painting is not pregnant herself, because she never had children)

3.6.10a Jan van Eyck, *The Arnolfini Portrait*, 1434. Oil on panel, 32⅜ × 23⅝". National Gallery, London, England

numerous objects in this painting had symbolic meanings that are lost to modern viewers, and that the image is about the sacramental nature of marriage. For example, the shoes on the left and in the back behind the couple can be interpreted as having been taken off because the ground is considered sacred for the event; the dog is, traditionally, a sign of fidelity; the single candle lit in the chandelier suggests unity; and the exotic, ripe fruit near the window indicates the hope of fertility.

While Panofsky's **iconographic analysis** has been adopted as a valid approach by many art historians, scholars still debate the meaning of this specific painting. Recent discoveries prove that not all of the above interpretations can be true. In 1997, documents were found that show that the Arnolfini couple were not married until 1447, six years after the death of Van Eyck. The artist, therefore, cannot have painted this portrait as a depiction of their wedding, although some argue that it could be a statement of intent to marry.

Iconographic analysis: the study of art by interpreting symbols, themes, and subject matter as sources of meaning

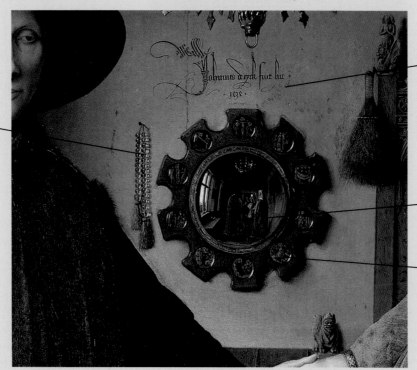

Crystal prayer beads beside the mirror indicate the couple's piety

"Johannes de eyck fuit hic 1434": the innovative signature of the artist (seen by some as evidence that this is a legal contract)

The reflection in the mirror includes the entire room and probably the artist

The roundels around the mirror show scenes from the Passion of Christ

3.6.10b Detail of Jan van Eyck, *The Arnolfini Portrait*

The Renaissance in Northern Europe

The Renaissance that took place in northern Europe in the countries we now know as The Netherlands, Germany, France, and Belgium differed significantly, visually, from the developments in Italy. Unlike Renaissance works from Italy, Northern Renaissance artworks are less concerned with idealized figures and precise perspective, but often contain messages expressed through **symbolism**. Artists in the northern countries are known for their skilled use of oil paint as opposed to the more common use of fresco and **tempera** painting in Italy. While a fresco painting had to be completed quickly (it dries within a day), the slow drying process of oil paint allowed artists to create fine details

and the illusion of **texture** in their work. The development of oil paint was attributed to Dutch artist Jan van Eyck (*c.* 1395–1441) by Giorgio Vasari, but it was actually used in the Middle Ages to decorate stone, metal, and, occasionally, plaster walls. The technique of **glazing**, which Van Eyck developed with such virtuosity, was widely adopted throughout Europe after 1450 (see: Van Eyck, Panofsky, and Iconographic Analysis).

In the Northern Renaissance, it was common to infuse works of art with religious meaning. Instead of conveying such meaning through mythological subjects, as was often the practice in Italy, northern artists frequently depicted people from everyday life. On the surface, Quentin Metsys's *The Moneylender and*

Symbolism: using images or symbols in an artwork to convey meaning; often obvious when the work was made but requiring research for modern viewers to understand

Tempera: a fast-drying painting medium made from pigment mixed with water-soluble binder, such as egg yolk

Texture: the surface quality of a work, for example fine/coarse, detailed/lacking in detail

Glazing: in oil painting, adding a transparent layer of paint to achieve a richness in texture, volume, and form

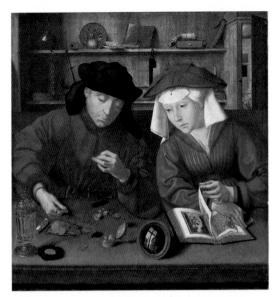

3.6.11 Quentin Metsys, *The Moneylender and His Wife*, 1514. Oil on panel, 27¾ × 26⅜". Musée du Louvre, Paris, France

His Wife (**3.6.11**) shows a shopkeeper weighing the coins of his trade as his wife looks on. The scene depicts a businessman enjoying his growing wealth thanks to the increasing commerce in their port town of Antwerp (in modern-day Belgium). But the artist has also created a scene in which the couple's morals are being questioned. The woman, who was in the process of reading her daily devotional, has been distracted by the beautiful material objects featured to her right on the table. The glass pitcher filled with water and the rosary are symbols of the Virgin's purity, and the wife's devotional was turned to a page discussing Mary. But the tempting fruit and the candle above the woman's head are symbols of the presence of the devil. Thus, the scale used to weigh the gold coins, pearls, and jewels is also symbolic of the struggle taking place between morals and greed; in a sense, the couple's spiritual future hangs in the balance. The artist also created an intricate sense of a larger space, by showing the shelves behind the couple, the front of the tablecloth, the two men outside the door on the right (just visible here), and the extraordinarily illusionistic **convex** mirror reflecting a figure by a window, which some scholars relate to Van Eyck's self-portrait in *The Arnolfini Portrait* (see **3.6.10b**, p. 451).

Altarpieces were extremely common in the Northern Renaissance. They often depicted the Annunciation, when Mary learns that she will bear Jesus, or scenes surrounding the Crucifixion, when Christ dies on a cross. In the

Mérode Altarpiece (**3.6.12**) **triptych**, the central scene shows the Annunciation at the moment when the angel Gabriel is about to tell Mary the news of her pregnancy. A tiny white body carrying a cross can be seeing flying through the window above Gabriel; this represents the soul of Jesus, or the Holy Spirit. The breeze created by the entrance of the Holy Spirit and Gabriel blows out the single candle on the table. The fact that the soul can go through the glass without breaking the window is symbolic of the Immaculate Conception, in which, according to Christian belief, Mary was impregnated without having sexual relations. Other symbols of Mary's purity are depicted, such as the white lily on the table, the religious text next to it—the pages of which are blowing from the breeze as well—and the towel and basin in the background.

The left wing of the triptych shows the patrons of the work, who are kneeling as they peek into the sacred scene. The right wing depicts Joseph, Mary's fiancé, in his carpentry workshop. On the window behind him is a mouse trap, which refers to the writings of St. Augustine that compare the cross (or death and suffering of Christ) to a mousetrap for the devil. The precise details throughout the scene, such as on the wings of the angel or the intricate scene of a town outside the window behind Joseph, demonstrate the importance of textural illusion for artists in the north. In contrast to artists in Italy, northern artists are less interested in using perspective to create a believable sense of **space**. The angle of the bench next to Mary and the odd opening of the shutters on the window are examples of this. Also, the table in this scene is tilted so that in reality, the objects might slide off, but the artist angled the table in this way because he believed that highlighting the symbols on the table was his top priority.

Some eighty or so years after the creation of the Mérode Altarpiece, the German artist Matthias Grünewald (*c.* 1475/80–1528) painted an equally complex altarpiece for the chapel in a hospital that cared for patients with skin diseases, the Abbey of St. Anthony in Isenheim (in what is now northeastern France). The Crucifixion scene, which forms the center panel when the altarpiece is closed, is one of the most graphic images of Christ's crucifixion in the history of art (**3.6.13**). The vivid details offered patients who were suffering from a

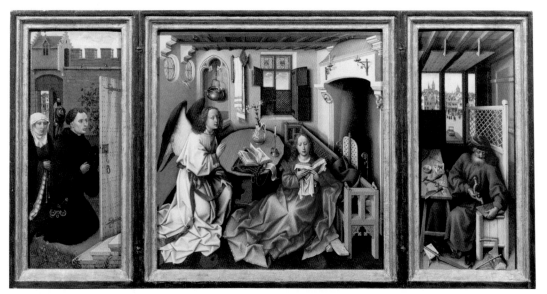

3.6.12 Robert Campin, *Mérode Altarpiece*, 1427–32. Oil on wood. Dimensions: overall (when open), 25⅜ × 46⅜"; central panel, 25¼ × 24⅞"; each wing, 25⅜ × 10¾". Metropolitan Museum of Art, New York

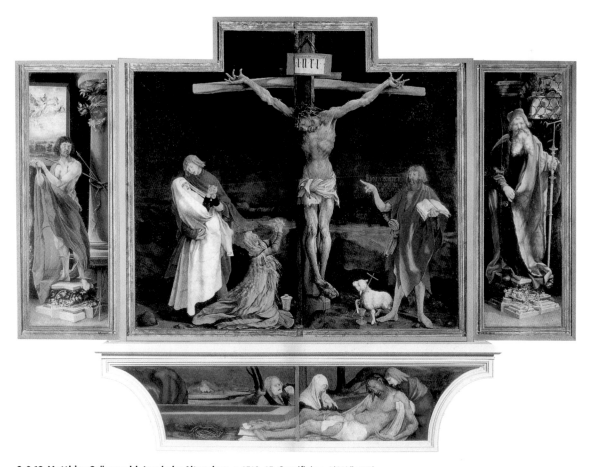

3.6.13 Matthias Grünewald, *Isenheim Altarpiece*, *c.* 1510–15. Crucifixion, 8'9½" × 10'; predella: Lamentation, 29¾" × 11'1¾"; side panels: Saints Sebastian and Anthony, 7'6½" × 29½" each. Musée d'Unterlinden, Colmar, France

variety of serious diseases a way to identify with Christ in his human form, as well as comfort that they were not alone in their own suffering. St. Anthony, shown on the right wing of the altarpiece, was the patron saint of sufferers from skin disease. Indeed, a common disease that caused a swollen stomach, convulsions, gangrene, and boils on the skin was named "St. Anthony's Fire." When patients prayed before this altarpiece they saw the green pallor of Christ's skin, the thorns that drew blood from his body, and the deformations of his

Mannerism: from Italian *maniera*, meaning 'stylish style;' a mid- to late sixteenth-century style of painting, usually with elongated human figures elevating grace as an ideal

Expressionistic: devoted to representing subjective emotions and experiences instead of objective or external reality

Modeling: the representation of three-dimensional objects in two dimensions so that they appear solid

bones caused by hanging on the cross for so long. The altarpiece can be opened to reveal additional scenes inside that also relate to St. Anthony.

Christ's suffering was further emphasized when the altarpiece was opened on certain occasions, such as Easter Sunday. When the left door was swung open, Christ's arm would appear to separate from the rest of his body. Similarly, opening the left side of the Lamentation scene at the bottom of the altarpiece would make his legs appear to be cut off. As limbs were often amputated to prevent the further spread of disease, many patients could directly identify with Christ's experience.

Late Renaissance and Mannerism

Compared to the art that came before it, works in the late phase of the Renaissance are often depicted in a style called **Mannerism** (*c.* 1520–1600), which tends to feature compositions that are more chaotic, emphasize movement,

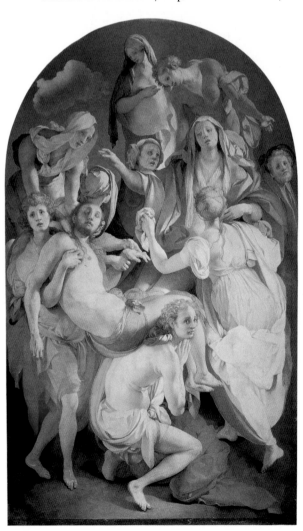

3.6.14 Jacopo da Pontormo, *Deposition,* 1525–28. Oil on wood, 10′3¼″ × 6′3½″. Capponi Chapel, Santa Felicita, Florence, Italy

and possess greater emotional intensity. The successes of the high Renaissance could not be rivaled: Leonardo, Raphael, and Michelangelo were thought to have achieved perfection in the arts. Artists were faced with the predicament of where to go from there. In reaction, instead of harmony, many artworks stressed dissonance. Distortion and disproportion were intentionally used to emphasize certain anatomical features and themes. Rather than mathematically precise depictions, artists created ambiguous spaces with multiple focal points.

Pope Julius II's building campaign and patronage of the arts had helped make Rome the center of artistic and intellectual activity in Italy. The Sack of Rome by the troops of Charles V of Spain in 1527 happened as the high Renaissance came to a close, and forced many artists to flee the city. When Pope Clement VII, one of Julius's successors, humiliatingly had to crown Charles as Holy Roman Emperor in 1530, it was further evidence of the end of those days of supremacy and assuredness. The disorder of the period was reflected in its art.

In Jacopo da Pontormo's (1494–1556) Mannerist painting of the Deposition, in which Christ is removed from the cross, the arrangement of the group of figures appears to be very unstable (**3.6.14**). Pontormo has stacked the figures vertically and placed them in an oddly swirling pattern, almost as if they are supported by the figure at the bottom of the composition, who is crouching unsteadily on tiptoe. Far from being a realistic depiction of observable reality, the figures no longer have ideal anatomy, but their bodies appear stretched. The color palette, as well, is unrealistic, with an unusual preference for pastels. We would expect to see grief and sorrow in a deposition scene, but here the faces show expressions of loss and bewilderment. Everything contributes to an unsettling sense of disorder.

Another artist working in the Mannerist style, Domenikos Theotokopoulos (*c.* 1541–1614), called El Greco ("The Greek"), lived in Venice and Rome before moving to Spain. *Laocoön* is a subject from Greek mythology. The Trojan priest Laocoön attempted to warn the inhabitants of Troy that Greek soldiers were trying to infiltrate their fortifications by hiding inside the Trojan Horse, seen in the middle ground at the center of this painting. El Greco shows the priest and his

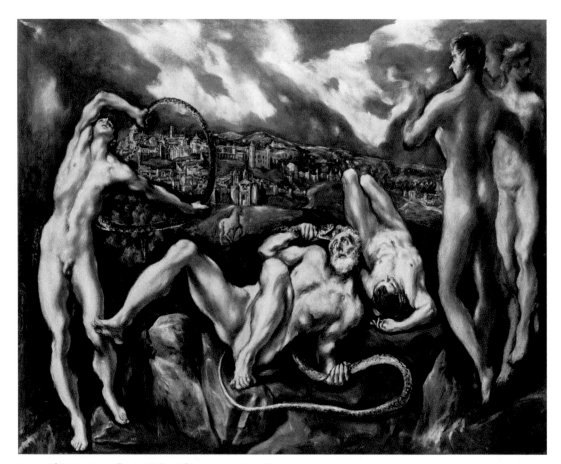

3.6.15 El Greco, *Laocoön*, *c.* 1610/14. Oil on canvas, 54 × 68". National Gallery of Art, Washington, D.C.

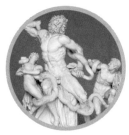

This sculpture of *Laocoön and His Sons* from ancient Greece would have been known to El Greco:
→ see **3.1.21**, p. 361

sons being attacked by snakes sent by the god Poseidon (who supported the Greeks) to stop Laocoön's warning (**3.6.15**). The landscape in the background is a view of Toledo, Spain, where El Greco lived and made his best-known works late in his life. El Greco combined Mannerist exaggeration, seen in the elongated forms and distorted figures, with his own **expressionistic** use of color and **modeling**. Like other Mannerist artworks, this intricate composition combines carefully observed factual information with mythological stories according to the dictates of the artist's imagination.

The Late Renaissance artist Sofonisba Anguissola (*c.* 1532–1625) achieved a level of success rarely enjoyed by women during this time. Known primarily for her portraits, she gained an international reputation that led to an official appointment at the court of the Queen of Spain. Anguissola emphasized emotion and heightened the realism in her artworks. *Portrait of the Artist's Sisters Playing Chess* (**3.6.16**) shows an everyday scene in the outdoors, as indicated by the tree behind the girls and the landscape in the distance.

Anguissola concentrates on the rich details of the textures of the girls' clothing, jewelry, and hair. Rather than focusing on creating a unified and mechanically precise scene, Anguissola has emphasized the individuality of each one of her

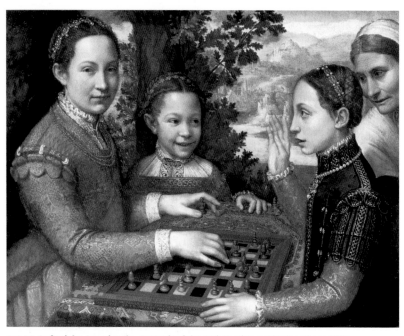

3.6.16 Sofonisba Anguissola, *Portrait of the Artist's Sisters Playing Chess*, 1555. Oil on canvas, 28¼ × 38¼". National Museum, Poznań, Poland

sitters, from the expressions on their faces to the elegant placement of their fingers. As the older sisters play their game, the clear sense of joy in the youngest sister's face is balanced by the expression of the maid, who looks on with care and concern.

Like all Renaissance architects, the Italian architect Andrea Palladio (1508–1580) was influenced by Classical architecture and in particular, by the writings of the Roman architect Vitruvius. The Villa Rotonda (**3.6.17a** and **3.6.17b**) shows Classical architectural features including **columns**, **pediments**, and a **hemispherical** dome. The bishop Paolo Almerico commissioned Palladio to build him this retirement home in the Venetian countryside. The hilltop location with panoramic views of this aristocratic refuge inspired Palladio. The building's plan consists of a square, made up of several rectangles and other symmetrical shapes, surrounding a circle in the center (see **3.6.17b**). This configuration creates a clear, balanced design that allows a visitor to look out from a central point in the circular courtyard toward four different views. In addition, people approaching the building would see four identical **facades** (see **3.6.17a**), each with a stately set of stairs topped by six columns that hold up a triangular pediment. The central plan and repeated facades create a building that expresses **symmetrical balance**, **proportion**, and clarity. Palladio's designs were tremendously influential in the design of churches and domestic architecture in sixteenth-century Italy and subsequently.

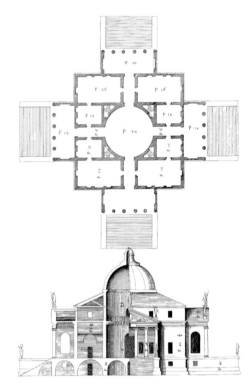

3.6.17b Andrea Palladio, plan and part elevation/section of the Villa Rotonda

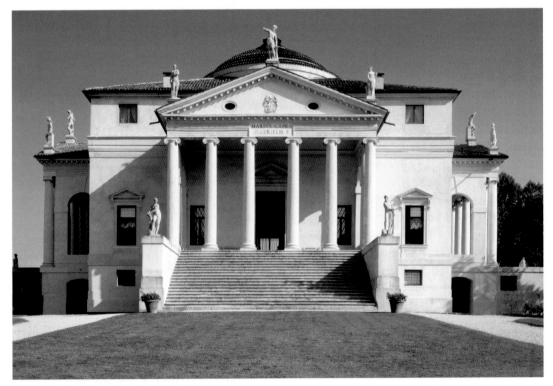

3.6.17a Andrea Palladio, Villa Rotonda, Vicenza, Italy. Completed after 1580 by Vincenzo Scamozzi

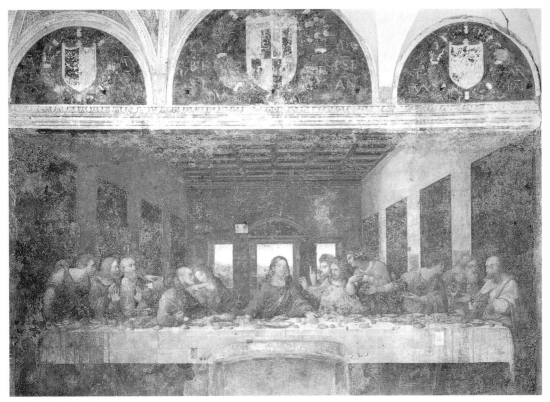

3.6.18 Leonardo da Vinci, *The Last Supper*, *c.* 1497. Fresco: tempera on plaster, 15'1" × 28'10½",
Refectory of Santa Maria delle Grazie, Milan, Italy

Protestant Reformation and Catholic Counter-Reformation

The Protestant Reformation (beginning in 1517 with Martin Luther's ninety-five criticisms of the Catholic Church) resulted in thousands breaking away from the Catholic Church, as well as a period of **iconoclasm**. Protestantism was based on a more individual and direct relationship with God rather than one strictly guided by and through the Church. Since the Catholic leadership was based in the Vatican in Rome, much of the artwork of the Italian Renaissance reflects Catholic doctrine, whereas artworks from the Northern Renaissance reflect Protestant beliefs. The differences in beliefs between Catholicism and Protestantism can be seen in a comparison of works depicting the Last Supper created during this period.

In Leonardo da Vinci's *Last Supper*, the best-known depiction of the episode in the Bible that describes Christ sharing a last meal with his disciples before his crucifixion, the artist used an experimental mixture of **media** (**3.6.18**), which is why it survives only in poor condition today. Leonardo was commissioned by Dominican friars to paint *The Last Supper* for their dining hall in the monastery of Santa Maria delle Grazie in Milan, Italy. In

this masterpiece, Christ is emphasized as the most important figure in four ways. First, he is depicted in the center of the painting. Second, he is shown as a stable, triangular form, in contrast to the agitated activity of the other figures. Third, his head is framed by the natural light of the middle of the three windows behind him. Finally, Leonardo arranged the linear perspective of this painting so that the vanishing point is directly behind Christ's head.

This work is not simply a representation of a meal, however, for Leonardo highlights two important aspects of religious doctrine related to this event: the Eucharist, or communion ceremony, and the betrayal of Judas. The painting portrays the tradition accepted by Catholics, who believe that communion bread and wine are the body and blood of Christ. The artist also invites the viewer to locate Judas by depicting the moment when Christ has just announced, "One of you is about to betray me" (Matthew 26:21). Through gesture and facial expression, Leonardo shows the individual reaction of each disciple. Judas has his elbow on the table and is in the group of three to Christ's right (our left). The betrayer clutches a money bag in his right hand and has just knocked down a salt dish, which is a bad omen.

Iconoclasm, iconoclastic: the destruction of images or artworks, often out of religious belief

Medium (plural **media**): the material on or from which an artist chooses to make a work of art, for example canvas and oil paint, marble, engraving, video, or architecture

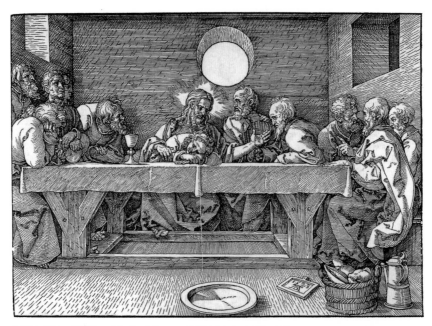

3.6.19 Albrecht Dürer, *The Last Supper*, 1523. Woodcut, 8½ × 11″.
British Museum, London, England

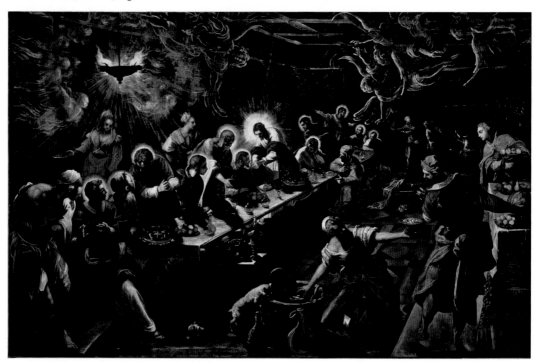

3.6.20 Tintoretto, *The Last Supper*, 1592–94. Oil on canvas, 11′11¾″ × 18′½″.
San Giorgio Maggiore, Venice, Italy

Print: a picture reproduced on paper, often in multiple copies

Symmetry: the correspondence in size, form, and arrangement of items on opposite sides of a plane, line, or point that creates direct visual balance

Balance: a principle of art in which elements are used to create a symmetrical or asymmetrical sense of visual weight in an artwork

Tenebrism: the dramatic use of intense darkness and light to heighten the impact of a painting

A quarter of a century after Leonardo's famous painting, the German artist Albrecht Dürer (1471–1528) interpreted the same subject as a **print**. Prints were common during the Reformation because they could be distributed to the masses and not solely owned by wealthy individuals. Like Leonardo, Dürer draws attention to Christ in his composition by placing him centrally and surrounding his head with white light (**3.6.19**). Only eleven disciples are there; the absence of Judas tells us that he has already left to betray Jesus to the authorities. Dürer's print reflects the ideas of the Protestant Reformation and, in particular, the doctrine of the Lutheran Church. While Lutherans accepted the communion ceremony, they insisted it was only a re-enactment of the Last Supper, not a literal receiving of Christ's body and blood. To emphasize this important doctrinal point, Dürer displays an empty plate in the foreground, signifying that the meal has already taken place. The still, quiet, and somewhat bare scene reflects the Protestant contemplative practice of direct connection with Jesus. Rather than being created for a religious space, this work is a print that individual believers could carry with them.

The Catholic Church's Counter-Reformation (1545–1648) was an attempt to define further the beliefs of Catholics in opposition to Protestants. In particular, the Council of Trent, active between 1545 and 1563, regulated the types of subjects that could be depicted in Catholic art and the way in which they should be portrayed. Catholicism had long believed that images should be used as powerful teaching tools, and this belief now became more apparent in the art of the time. For example, the intensely dramatic quality of *The Last Supper* by the Venetian artist Tintoretto (1519–1594) highlights the urgency of the Catholic mission to encourage believers to remain in the Church rather than converting to Protestantism (**3.6.20**). Tintoretto depicts the Last Supper as a glorious and spiritual event. There are many ordinary people busy in service and discussion—we can almost hear the buzz of conversation and clatter of dishes. At the same time, the heavens seem to be opening up to send down angels, depicted as otherworldly, turbulent figures, twisting through the darkness overhead to witness the event.

This scene is a marked change from the **symmetry** and emotional **balance** of both Leonardo's and Dürer's versions. Tintoretto still makes Christ the focal point by placing him in the center with the largest and brightest halo, reaching out with a glass to one of the disciples; Judas is easy to find, too, alone without a halo across the table from Jesus. But Tintoretto's picture conveys a dynamic—even disturbed— sense of motion and drama, with the table placed at an angle pointing off-center and deep into space, dramatic contrasts of lighting, and the theatrical gestures of the characters. The combination of the domestic, earthly setting with the hovering, shadowy angels above hints at the imminent spiritual crisis that is about to occur when Judas, tempted by the worldly offer of money, will betray Jesus and cause his death.

Italian Baroque

The Baroque period was a time of exploration, increased trade, and discovery in the sciences. Western Europe now accepted the theory of astronomer Nicolaus Copernicus that the Sun, rather than the Earth, was the center of the universe—a theory the Catholic Church had previously rejected. Light, both heavenly and otherwise, became a prominent feature in many Baroque artworks. The seventeenth century was also a time of battles throughout Europe, largely the result of the divisions in the Catholic Church after the Reformation. Baroque artworks give us a sense of this turmoil: their theatrical, dynamic compositions feature movement and light, and both visually and physically invade the space of the viewer. The painter Caravaggio and the sculptor and architect Gianlorenzo Bernini (see Depictions of David, p. 460) who both created intensely emotional and dramatic scenes, are regarded as the masters of the Baroque period.

Michelangelo Merisi da Caravaggio (1571–1610) painted *Narcissus* (**3.6.21**) early in his career, while he was in Rome, but already shows his signature technique of **tenebrism**, in which extreme shadows are contrasted with severe spotlighting. The heightened emotion

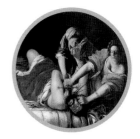

The artist Artemisia Gentileschi created a dramatic series of paintings utilizing tenebrism:

→ see **1.8.1**, p. 140

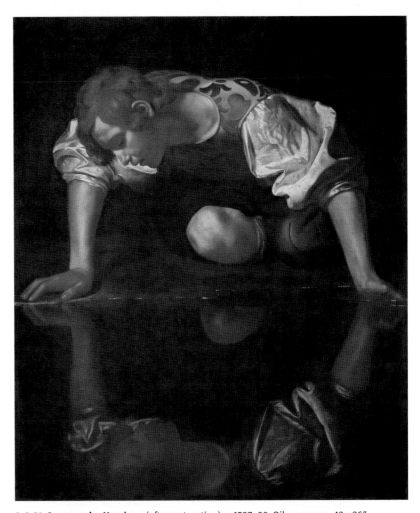

3.6.21 Caravaggio, *Narcissus* (after restoration), *c.* 1597–99. Oil on canvas. 43 × 36″. Galleria Nazionale d'Arte Antica, Palazzo Barberini, Rome, Italy

Depictions of David

The biblical story of David and Goliath inspired three renowned Renaissance and Baroque sculptors in three centuries. Donatello, Michelangelo, and Bernini each took a different approach to the appearance of the hero, David. Each work displays the characteristic cultural and artistic concerns of their respective eras. In the Bible, David is a young Israelite who battles the giant Goliath. Goliath challenges the Israelites to send a champion to fight in single combat. Only David is brave enough to face him. Armed with just his shepherd's hook, slingshot, and a handful of stones, he fells Goliath with a single slingshot to the forehead and then uses the giant's own sword to cut off his head. David's triumph against a powerful opponent became an emblem for the city of Florence after its forces defeated a much stronger army from Milan in 1428. Our comparison of statues of David considers two sculptures made for Florence and one made in Rome.

Donatello (*c.* 1386/87–1466) was a skilled sculptor of both bronze and marble. At the time he made *David*, he was reinvigorating the ancient technique of bronze casting. His *David*, the first nearly full-scale male nude since antiquity, also reflects

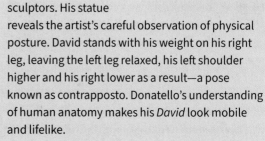

3.6.22 Donatello, *David*, *c.* 1430. Bronze, height 5'2¼". Museo Nazionale del Bargello, Florence, Italy

the sculptor's familiarity with and admiration for the Classical ideal depictions of the human body (**3.6.22**). Rather than emphasizing the mortal and corruptible nature of the body, as was common during the Middle Ages, Donatello follows the idealized nude model used by Greek and Roman sculptors. His statue reveals the artist's careful observation of physical posture. David stands with his weight on his right leg, leaving the left leg relaxed, his left shoulder higher and his right lower as a result—a pose known as contrapposto. Donatello's understanding of human anatomy makes his *David* look mobile and lifelike.

Michelangelo's *David* was carved from a single block of marble (**3.6.23**). It was originally intended to be placed in a high niche of Florence Cathedral as a symbol of the city's power and (temporary) freedom from the tyranny of the Medici. The sculpture was so popular that, on its completion in 1504, it was instead placed near the entrance to the main piazza, or plaza, where it could be viewed by masses of people. Its Classical attributes include athletic musculature and essentially ideal proportions. By presenting David as nude, with a scarcely noticeable slingshot over his shoulder—the only reference to his identity—Michelangelo creates a sculpture of a man as well as a hero. David's facial expression is idealized and calm, but his gaze, which is purposefully directed off to the side, reveals a mood of concentration and intensity.

Gianlorenzo Bernini (1598–1680) created his *David* in the Baroque period. It is a dynamic, three-dimensional sculpture that emphasizes movement and action (**3.6.24**). Whereas Donatello's sculpture shows David as triumphant and Michelangelo's sculpture shows him as contemplative, Bernini's

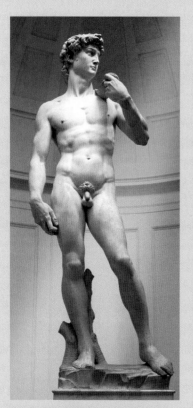

3.6.23 Michelangelo, *David*, 1501–4. Marble, height 14'2". Galleria dell'Accademia, Florence, Italy

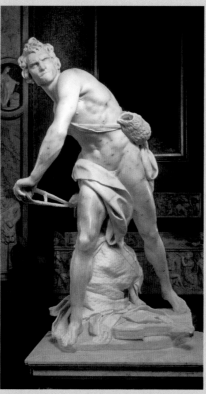

3.6.24 Gianlorenzo Bernini, *David*, 1623. Marble, height 5'7". Galleria Borghese, Rome, Italy

shows David at a moment of dramatic, heightened tension, when he is about to launch the stone. The energy of David's entire body is focused on the physical movement he is about to make. Even the muscles in his face tighten. Bernini is said to have studied his own reflection to create the perfect facial expression for such an energetic feat. Unlike Michelangelo's and Donatello's sculptures, which are meant to be viewed from the front, Bernini's is intended to be seen and understood **in the round**.

These three sculptures are clearly different in several ways. Michelangelo's sculpture is more than twice the size of the other two, in order to allow viewers to see all of the detail had the sculpture been installed in its originally planned location, high above the ground. Donatello's sculpture is the only one to include weaponry other than a slingshot: his David holds the sword with which he has just beheaded his opponent, whose head lies at his feet. Bernini's sculpture, like Michelangelo's, features the slingshot, but it is in action, and a pile of cast-off armor lies beneath. Such a prop was

necessary to allow for the wide stance and gesture of the figure, as marble sculptures are prone to snap if their weight is unsupported.

The moment each artist chose to depict has a strong influence on the resulting appearance and effect of their sculptures. Donatello shows a triumphant, boyish David standing in calm repose after the fight. Michelangelo presents David as an adult: the sheer size and mass of his form are much more adult-like than Donatello's slim, youthful figure. Michelangelo's David stands poised at a moment of anticipation and determined contemplation before the battle; a concentrated expression is visible on his face. Bernini's David, more mature, is dynamically focused on casting a lethal strike at the giant Goliath—the time of calculation and reflection has passed; now it is time for action.

Religious stories were common subjects for artworks during the Renaissance and Baroque. These three artists' *David* sculptures show the stylistic characteristics of their time as well as their individual originality.

In the round: a freestanding sculpted work that can be viewed from all sides

and intensity created by this technique may reflect what was supposed to have been the impassioned personality of the artist (he was frequently involved in violent altercations and was accused of emotional instability and even murder). Narcissus, the subject of this painting, is a Classical mythological character who found himself so beautiful when he looked at his reflection in a river that he died there, because he could not pull himself away. Psychologically, the story warns against being so fixated on one's self that life passes one by. In Caravaggio's version, the repeated circular shapes in the composition (Narcissus's head, his knee, and the circle formed by the curve of his back and arms above and reflected below in the pool) convey this intense concentration, while the darkness of the work suggests the deathly nature of the boy's attraction to his own image. The artist also skillfully mimics the subject matter by making us, too, as viewers, have to peer deep into the picture to decipher it.

During the seventeenth century, popes and powerful royal patrons commissioned numerous important buildings in Italy. Architecture at this time evolved so that, instead of the harmonious proportions and austere simplicity that were common in

Renaissance designs, architectural works now incorporated much more ornate decorations and more complex forms. The result was that Baroque buildings became stages for dramatic expressions of the architect's art.

One example is the Baroque church of San Carlo alle Quattro Fontane (**3.6.25a**, p. 462) in Rome, designed by Italian architect Francesco Borromini (1599–1677). Borromini, similarly to his Renaissance predecessors, incorporated **geometric** shapes into his design, but he did not aim to achieve the perfectly balanced symmetry of such buildings as Palladio's Villa Rotonda (**3.6.17b**, p. 456). Instead, this church takes on the qualities of a dramatic sculpture. At the center of the plan is an oval (**3.6.25b**, p. 462), which is less symmetrical than the flawless equilibrium of a central circle found at the heart of Renaissance designs. In the interior of the building, columns divide the walls into undulating spaces. The irregular shapes of the interior are echoed in the curving, wavelike walls of the facade. Because the walls are curving instead of flat, they create dramatic shadows. The surfaces and spaces of this church are typically Baroque in that they are very ornamental and spectacular. The complexity of this design influenced later

Geometric: predictable and mathematical

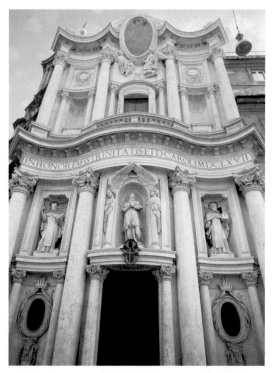

3.6.25a Francesco Borromini, Church of San Carlo alle Quattro Fontane, Rome, Italy, 1638–46. Facade added *c.* 1677

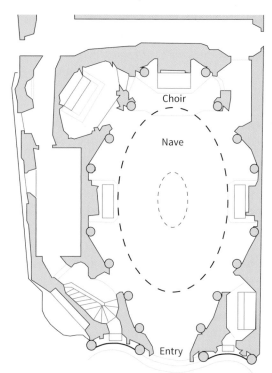

3.6.25b Plan of the Church of San Carlo alle Quattro Fontane

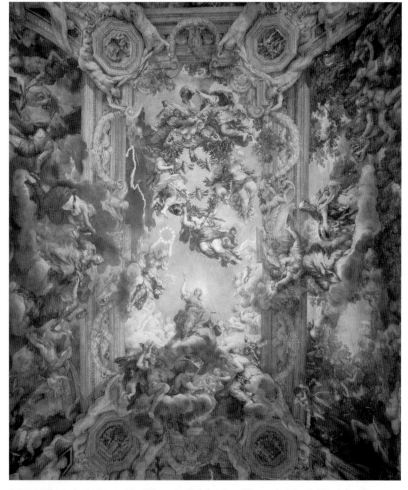

3.6.26 Pietro da Cortona, *The Triumph of Divine Providence and the Fulfilment of its Purposes under Pope Urban VIII ("The Glorification")*, *c.* 1633–39. Fresco, ceiling of the Salone di Pietro da Cortona, Palazzo Barberini, Rome

Baroque architects. In addition to the new emphasis on opulence, light was emphasized both through the use of windows and in the imagery of frescoes in Baroque church interiors.

Along with pulsing and theatrical enhancements to the architecture, grandiose ***trompe l'oeil*** ceiling paintings were created as ornamentation for Baroque buildings. Pietro da Cortona, who was also an architect, painted the *Glorification of Urban VIII* (**3.3.26**) to appear as if the room in the palace had an excessively high open roof filled with at least one hundred mythological figures. The illusion was created through extreme **foreshortening**, as the architecture and flying figures appear to be perpendicular to the surface below. The scene suggests that the heavens (symbolizing the Christian God) support Pope Urban VIII, member of the Barberini family, in his recent rise to power. On the sunny half of the central scene, dressed in a yellow-and-orange billowing cloth, Divine Providence (symbolizing the support of the heavens for the pope) is seated on a cloud. On the blue half of the central scene, symbols of the papacy, such as a gold crown (red on the inside) and two crossed gold keys, are carried by numerous mythological figures. The three outsize bees in the center are a symbol from the Barberini coat of arms.

Northern Baroque

Baroque in northern Europe also included some of the characteristics that were common in Italy, such as drama, a sense of grandeur, and use of intense light and darkness (tenebrism). Just as their Italian counterparts did, Northern Baroque artists utilized ways of including the viewer in the visual space of artworks. Northern Baroque painters also excelled at depictions of non-religious subject matter, such as landscapes, still lifes, **genre scenes**, or portrayals of people from their contemporary world.

Peter Paul Rubens (1577–1640) produced about 2,000 paintings in his lifetime, an impressive output made possible because he operated a large workshop in Antwerp. His assistants were responsible for producing some of his paintings, but Rubens generally finished works for important clients himself. Rubens frequently made several **preparatory studies**, which were studied and copied by his students, before determining a final composition for a painting. *Four Studies of a Head of a Moor* (**3.3.27**), showing a man from different angles and with a variety of expressions, was made for this purpose. Although paintings of Black figures were extremely rare in Renaissance and Baroque Europe, one of the three Magi (the wise men who brought gifts after the birth of Jesus) was often depicted as a dark-skinned man. In at least four of the Adoration of the Magi paintings by Rubens, he has used the same figure depicted in this study.

The Raising of the Cross, also by Rubens, was one of several paintings commissioned by wealthy merchants to be installed in a church (**3.6.28**). In this painting, we can sense the physical exertions of these muscular men as they raise Christ onto the cross. A dynamic tension is created along the diagonal line of the cross that visually connects the men at its base as they strain to pull Christ up toward the right side of the painting. The muscular arms and shoulders of the men holding the cross project out toward the **picture plane** into the viewer's space. Although, in fact, Christ would have been tortured and close to death at this point, the artist has painted his flesh as almost immaculate, and lighter than that of those around him. In this way, and by bathing him in light, Rubens makes Christ the focal point and emphasizes his holiness.

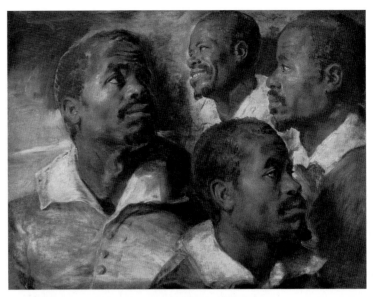

3.6.27 Peter Paul Rubens, *Four Studies of a Head of a Moor*, c. 1614–16. Canvas transferred from wood, 26 × 20". Royal Museums of Fine Arts of Belgium, Brussels

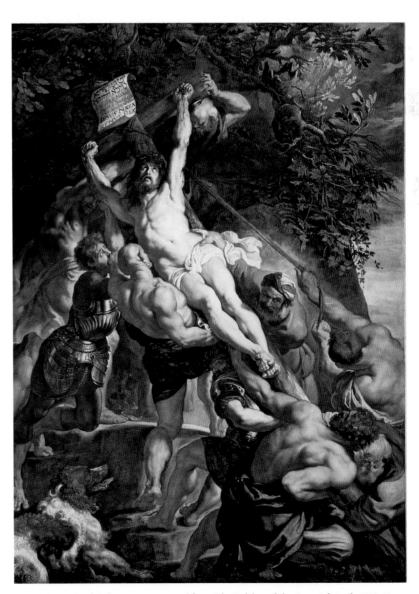

3.6.28 Peter Paul Rubens, center panel from *The Raising of the Cross* triptych, 1610–11. Oil on panel, 15'1" × 11'1½". Onze Lieve Vrouwkerk, Antwerp Cathedral, Belgium

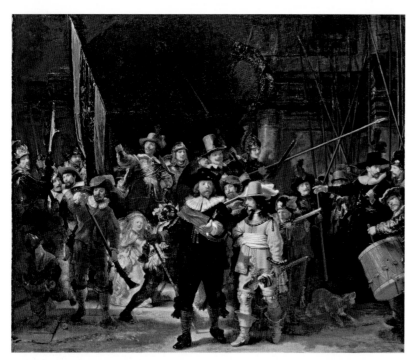

3.6.29 Rembrandt van Rijn, *The Company of Frans Banning Cocq and Willem van Ruytenburch (The Night Watch)*, 1642. Oil on canvas, 11'11" × 14'4". Rijksmuseum, Amsterdam, The Netherlands

Rembrandt Harmenszoon van Rijn (1606–1669) was an extremely popular painter who also had a large workshop at one point in his life. Yet, despite his impressive reputation, he filed for bankruptcy in old age. In *The Night Watch*, the gathering of officers and guardsmen probably commemorates a visit by Queen Marie de'Medici to Amsterdam in 1638 (**3.6.29**). The painting was commissioned by the civic militia, and scholars believe that all of those

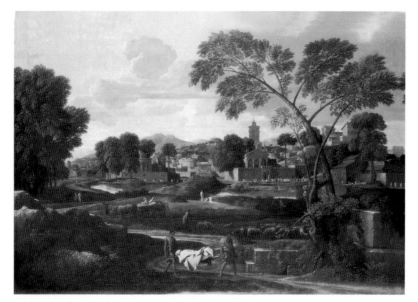

3.6.30 Nicolas Poussin, *The Funeral of Phocion*, 1648. Oil on canvas, 44 × 68". National Museum of Wales, Cardiff

portrayed in this scene contributed to the artist's fee. *The Night Watch* is a fine example of Rembrandt's innovative approach to a group portrait. His painting is not only convincing but also full of the vitality and energy typical of a group getting ready for an important occasion. The various members of the company are shown busily organizing themselves. This painting came to be known as *The Night Watch* because its dark atmosphere made it look like a night scene. Rembrandt made skillful use of chiaroscuro, tenebrism, and dramatic lighting to enliven his composition, but the impression of night-time was actually created by years of accumulated dirt and layers of varnish. The painting was revealed to be a daytime scene when it was cleaned after World War II.

French artist Nicolas Poussin (1594–1665) specialized in paintings of subjects from Classical antiquity. Everything in his paintings was carefully constructed and positioned to create a sense of refined balance and order. He would even arrange miniature figures on a small stage when choreographing the scenes for his landscapes. Although these and his Classical buildings look detailed and realistic, their appearance and placement were always invented from his imagination. *The Funeral of Phocion* depicts two men carrying the deceased Phocion, an Athenian general, over a winding road that leads away from the city (**3.6.30**). Phocion had been executed after being falsely accused of treason; because he was considered a traitor, he was buried outside the city.

Poussin's landscapes were designed to create a sense of depth, and often the Classical subject of the scene was secondary to this goal. The two figures carrying Phocion's body, covered with a white sheet, are prominently placed in the foreground. The winding road emphasizes the distance of Phocion's burial from the city and also creates a sense of deep space, skillfully guiding our gaze into the landscape. In a further effort to create the illusion of depth, the artist uses size differentiation, in which the same object—such as a tree or person— becomes smaller the further into the distance it is shown. Atmospheric perspective is also used to show the layers of air between the men in the foreground and the mountains in the distance.

In the next two centuries, the center of European art would move to France, with the work of Poussin greatly influencing the training of artists.

Explore Further Art of Renaissance and Baroque Europe (1400–1750)

Italian Renaissance

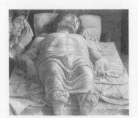

4.3.12 Andrea Mantegna, *Dead Christ, c.* 1480 ➔ p. 576

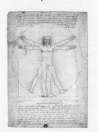

4.4.1 Leonardo da Vinci, *Vitruvian Man, c.* 1490 ➔ p. 580

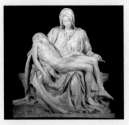

0.0.22 Michelangelo, *Pietà*, 1498–99. St. Peter's Basilica, Vatican City ➔ p. 31

Northern Renaissance

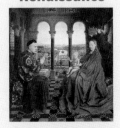

2.2.13 Jan van Eyck, *The Madonna of Chancellor Rolin*, 1430–34 ➔ p. 202

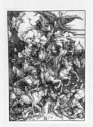

2.3.2 Albrecht Dürer, "The Four Horsemen," 1498 ➔ p. 213

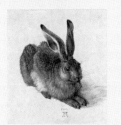

2.2.20 Albrecht Dürer, *A Young Hare*, 1502 ➔ p. 206

Italian Baroque

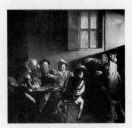

1.3.6 Caravaggio, *The Calling of St. Matthew, c.* 1599–1600 ➔ p. 69

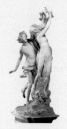

1.5.1 Gianlorenzo Bernini, *Apollo and Daphne*, 1622–24 ➔ p. 104

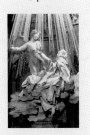

4.2.13 Gianlorenzo Bernini, *The Ecstasy of St. Teresa*, 1647–52 ➔ p. 562

Northern Baroque

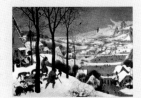

1.9.7 Pieter Bruegel, *Hunters in the Snow*, 1565 ➔ p. 152

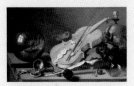

4.3.8 Pieter Claesz (attr.), *Vanitas (Still Life with Glass Globe), c.* 1628 ➔ p. 573

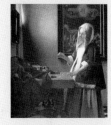

4.2.12 Johannes Vermeer, *Woman Holding a Balance, c.* 1664 ➔ p. 561

Your turn

How do these works relate to art of Renaissance and Baroque Europe?

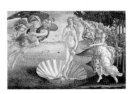

2.6.19 Giuliano da Maiano *Studiolo*, Ducal Palace, Italy, *c.* 1478–82 ➔ p. 281

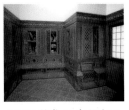

4.8.5 Sandro Botticelli, *The Birth of Venus, c.* 1482–86 ➔ p. 634

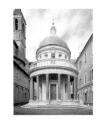

2.5.21 Donato Bramante, Tempietto of San Pietro in Montorio, *c.* 1502 ➔ p. 255

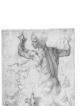

2.1.15 Michelangelo, *Studies for the Libyan Sibyl*, 1510–11 ➔ p. 186

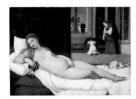

4.8.8 Titian, *Venus of Urbino*, 1538 ➔ p. 635

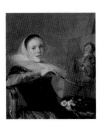

0.0.11 Judith Leyster, *Self-Portrait, c.* 1630 ➔ p. 22

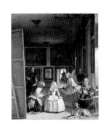

1.10.12a Diego de Silva y Velázquez, *Las Meninas, c.* 1656 ➔ p. 171

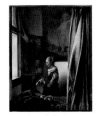

4.4.16b Johannes Vermeer's *Reading a Letter at an Open Window*, 1657–59 ➔ p. 590

3·7
Art of Europe and America (1700–1865): Rococo to Romanticism

Enlightenment: historical period, also called the Age of Reason, in which reason was prized above faith, liberty above oppression, and there was a movement to secure equal rights for all men

Patron: an organization or individual who sponsors the creation of works of art

The eighteenth and nineteenth centuries in Europe are characterized by concerns about social equality, and a transition in power from the wealthy to the growing middle class. There was resentment against the monarchs who inflicted their will on the people of both their own countries and their colonies. Thus this period is often called an Age of Revolutions, beginning with the American Declaration of Independence in 1776. There were three revolutions in France during this period (1789, 1830, and 1848), all of which called for government by and for the people and equality for the lower classes, and all of which inspired revolutions elsewhere in Europe. At the same time, the Industrial Revolution, instigated by advancements in technology, began in Britain and spread throughout Europe, creating a shift from agrarian societies to more urban ones, and offering new working opportunities for the majority of people. Within Europe, the development of the telegraph in the 1830s allowed for quicker communication, and the invention of the steam engine in 1869 led to expansive railroads, enabling more people to travel greater distances faster. Europe and America therefore became more aware of the wider world. As a result of these factors, as well as through colonization and trade, the Western art world was influenced by other cultures.

This was an age also known as the **Enlightenment**, sometimes called the Age of Reason. Enlightenment thinkers called for reason over faith, liberty over oppressive systems of government, and equal rights for all people. The English philosopher John Locke promoted a theory of empiricism, according to which humans are born with minds like blank slates, which are influenced by their experiences rather than being innately fully formed. This notion had significant ramifications, particularly on education and the impact of social experience on individuals.

Artworks of this time both reflect and promote contemporary changes in economics, politics, and personal expression. While art historians have determined stylistic tendencies, it is important to note that the various styles in this period often overlapped; that is, each style did not strictly follow another chronologically. At times, artworks possess qualities of more than one style, or will not seem to fit easily into any single category. This complexity reflects the richness of ideas that were being exchanged in the eighteenth century and the first half of the nineteenth century.

Absolute Monarchy

At the end of the seventeenth century and beginning of the eighteenth century, most European countries were governed by absolute monarchs—rulers who, it was believed, derived their power and authority from God. The monarchy was characterised by wasteful extravagance in France, epitomized by King Louis XIV (1638–1715), whose grandiose view of himself and his role in the world demonstrated the power of the absolute monarch. Louis called himself the Sun King to associate himself with the Greek sun god Apollo, and to imply that the activities of France began when—like the sun—Louis arose in the morning, and stopped when he retired at night. The exaggerated self-regard, even pomposity, of the royal circle would eventually prove its downfall and lead to its demise by the end of the eighteenth century.

The regal portrait by Hyacinthe Rigaud (1659–1743) is meant to demonstrate the king's power (**3.7.1**) and exudes the extravagant wealth of the late Baroque style. Louis is dressed in royal attire, with the gold fleur-de-lis (or "lily flower," the symbol of the French monarchy) embroidered on a rich blue velvet gown, lined in expensive white fur known as ermine. Insisting on the finest of everything, Louis XIV dressed in the most opulent textiles from around the world. He invented the high heels shown here, which he used to increase his height (5 ft. 4 in.) and to show off his trim legs. This painting was in fact made when the monarch was in his sixties. It was common practice for painters to depict royal figures in the best light, often portraying them as decades younger than they actually were.

In this portrait, the Sun King stands at the entrance to the famed Baroque Hall of Mirrors (**3.7.2**), an opulent chamber filled with mirrors (highly expensive at the time) that reflect the gardens and fountains surrounding his grand new palace of Versailles, near Paris. Louis XIV was a great **patron** of the arts, and had commissioned artists from throughout Europe to construct and decorate Versailles to be the largest and finest palace in the world. The Hall of Mirrors was used for greeting dignitaries, for formal celebrations, and as a ballroom. The 239-foot-long hallway is lavishly decorated with gilding, chandeliers, sculpture, and paintings depicting scenes of Louis XIV's political successes. The bright light that fills the room and is reflected in the numerous mirrors is not only a characteristic of the Baroque period, but also symbolizes Louis's identity and power as

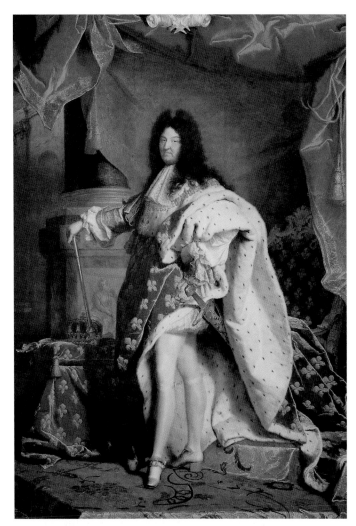

3.7.1 Hyacinthe Rigaud, *Louis XIV*, 1701. Oil on canvas, 9'1" × 6'4¾". Musée du Louvre, Paris, France

the Sun King. One of his greatest contributions to the art world was his development of a French art academy (1648) based on those

3.7.2 Jules Hardouin-Mansart, **Château de Versailles**, **Hall of Mirrors (Galerie des Glaces)**, 1678–84. Versailles, France

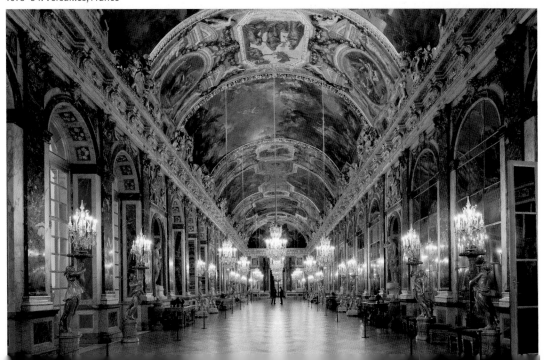

in Italy, which would define much of the art produced in the following centuries (see: The French Academy of Painting and Sculpture: Making a Living as an Artist, p. 472).

Rococo

The undisputed power of the European ruling classes during the seventeenth and much of the eighteenth century inspired a period of extravagance amongst the very wealthy. Desiring the finest in everything, the ruling classes financed endless commissions of artworks in a style known as the **Rococo**. Stylistically, in its abundance of rich decoration, the Rococo is an outgrowth of the **Baroque**, but while the Baroque's **subject matter** was very formal and moralistic, the Rococo's was more whimsical. Rococo artworks tend to be lighthearted, indulgent, and even somewhat superficial, featuring elaborately curved lines and **organic** forms. Rococo paintings were usually commissioned by the aristocracy and are often playful, with erotic undertones. The delicate brushstrokes and pastel colors create a sense of lightness and ease, and the frequently frivolous subject matter suggests that those who commissioned such artworks had ample time to amuse themselves.

At first sight, *The Swing* by Jean-Honoré Fragonard (1732–1806) appears to be an

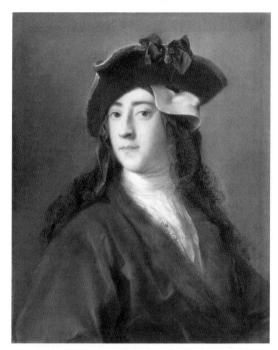

3.7.4 Rosalba Carriera, *Gustavus Hamilton, Second Viscount Boyne, in Masquerade Costume*, 1730–31. Pastel on paper, laid down on canvas, 22¼ × 16⅞", Metropolitan Museum of Art, New York

innocent scene of a refined young lady enjoying her swinging (**3.7.3**). Upon closer inspection, however, we see that the woman has flirtatiously kicked her foot into the air, causing her shoe to fly off, which allows the man in the bushes below (thought by some to be the patron of this painting) a view up her skirt. Represented in a statue on the left side of the canvas, Cupid puts his finger to his lips, suggesting a secret tryst between the young couple. The feathery brushstrokes, pastel colors, abundance of delicate greenery, and soft plumes of clouds support the romantic and trivial nature of the subject matter. A bishop, standing in the shadows in the lower right-hand part of the canvas, holds a rope that controls the swing, and he appears to be completely unaware of the couple's mischievous behavior. The artist's inclusion of this figure has been interpreted by some as a comment on the Church's ignorance of immoral behavior, and by others as a chiding of the Catholic Church for not condemning such conduct.

The Venetian-born painter Rosalba Carriera (1673–1757) was one of the most admired artists of the Rococo period. As a child, to help her family earn income, she created lace patterns and painted tiny scenes on ivory lids for snuff boxes. By the time she was in her twenties, wealthy travelers on the **Grand Tour** hired her to

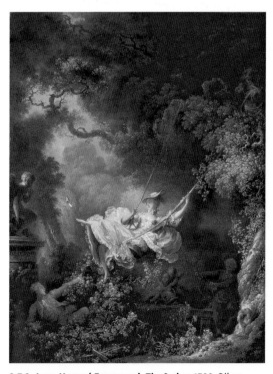

3.7.3 Jean-Honoré Fragonard, *The Swing*, 1766. Oil on canvas, 32 × 25¼". Wallace Collection, London, England

depict their likenesses, which she was able to do much more quickly in **pastel** than was possible in oil paint. In one such **portrait**, she depicts Gustavus Hamilton, the 2nd Viscount Boyne, in a remarkable fur-trimmed blue coat, with a rich black hat. Placed slightly under the hat is a white mask, referring to the count's delight in wearing such masks at Venetian masquerades (**3.7.4**). While the delicate **medium** of pastel has sometimes historically been considered a material more appropriate for female artists, her exceptionally accomplished pastel portraits led to a trend of many male artists trying to mimic her skills. In fact, she was one of the few female artists elected to the prestigious Accademia di San Luca in Rome.

Enlightenment in Art

In his treatise called *The Social Contract* (1762), the writer and political theorist Jean-Jacques Rousseau (1712–1778) states that, "Man is born free, and everywhere he is in chains." Influenced by the ideas of John Locke, Rousseau believed that society should be governed by the consent and involvement of all the people. For this kind of community to work, Rousseau argues, society must support equal

rights and education. At the same time, the Enlightenment was a period of intense interest in learning, reason, and the natural world. The English painter Joseph Wright of Derby (1734–1797) was a member of the Lunar Society, an informal club of scientists, intellectuals, and manufacturers who met monthly to discuss developments in science and technology. He often painted scientific and industrial subjects, employing a notably dramatic use of light and dark, called **tenebrism**.

Wright's work *An Experiment on a Bird in the Air Pump* shows a traveling scientist lecturing on pneumatics, or the study of air and other gases (**3.7.5**). He is using an air pump that adds and removes oxygen from the prominently placed glass container, inside of which a white bird lies on the bottom. The artist has chosen to depict the climactic moment when the bird runs out of air due to the vacuum. Wright has also increased the drama by using a rare cockatoo—in reality, a more common bird would have been used in the experiment—and through his use of shadows and light, which highlights reactions ranging from concern to indifference, contempt, resignation, pity or fear. Light was also a symbol of knowledge during

Grand Tour: in the seventeenth to mid-nineteenth century, a trip for the cultured and wealthy to study Classical and Renaissance artworks and culture found mostly in Italy

Pastel: a powdered pigment mixed with gum and used in stick form for drawing.

Portrait: an image of a person or animal, usually focusing on the face

Medium (plural **media**): the material on or from which an artist chooses to make a work of art, for example canvas and oil paint, marble, engraving, video, or architecture

Tenebrism: the dramatic use of intense darkness and light to heighten the impact

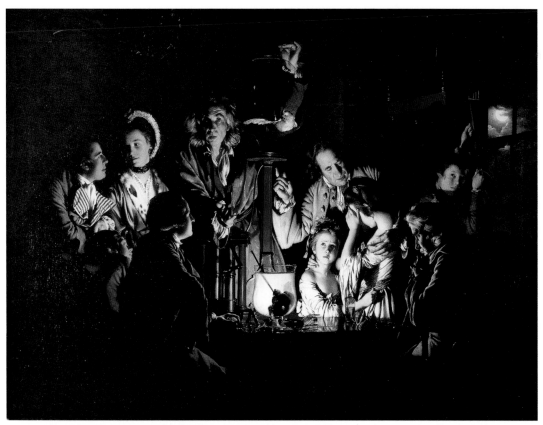

3.7.5 Joseph Wright of Derby, *An Experiment on a Bird in the Air Pump*, 1768.
Oil on canvas, 6 × 8′. National Gallery, London, England

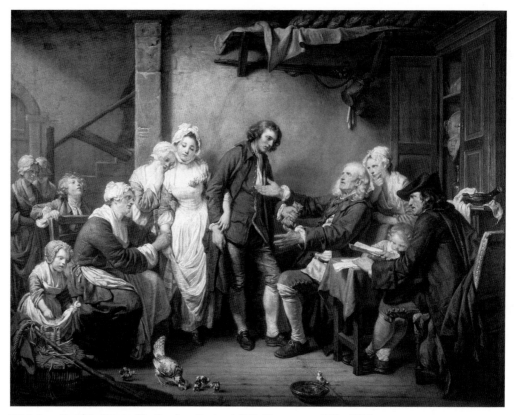

3.7.6 Jean-Baptiste Greuze, *The Marriage Contract*, 1761. Oil on canvas, 25¼ × 31½".
Musée du Louvre, Paris, France

the Enlightenment, so the light shining on the children's faces represents the knowledge they are believed to be gaining from the experiment. The luminous moon visible through the window is a symbol of the Lunar Society.

Jean-Baptiste Greuze (1725–1805) was known for his images that **idealized** the virtues of simple life among the lower classes. In *The Marriage Contract*, a loving young couple are about to be married (**3.7.6**). A notary on the right documents the formal agreement. The bride's humble father has just given the man her dowry, and her family members are crying over how much they will miss her. The scene emphasizes the rustic surroundings, highlighting the family's lack of wealth and suggesting that the poor are closer to nature. The family's situation is echoed by the hen feeding her chicks in the lower portion of the canvas. One chick goes off to the right to sit upon a saucer, just as the young bride is about to leave and start her own family. While the family is financially poor, it is depicted as rich in love. The simplicity of the setting and the people contrasts with the frivolous materialism of the Rococo.

Wealthy patrons during the Rococo were also preoccupied with depictions of poor people maintaining good moral conduct despite difficult circumstances. Criticizing immoral behavior in society was a technique used by some artists to promote Enlightenment values. British painter and **engraver** William Hogarth (1697–1764), for example, frequently satirized the behavior of the upper classes. Many of his paintings were reproduced as **prints**, which were released one at a time to spur interest and curiosity; these were effectively the soap operas of the eighteenth century. Hogarth's prints (often engraved by others) made his work affordable for the lower and middle classes, who were a receptive audience for his **satire**. The prints were extremely popular and forged copies were rampant, so much so that Hogarth requested protection from Parliament for his original creations, leading to the Engraving Copyright Act of 1734, also called Hogarth's Act.

The series *Marriage à-la-Mode (A Fashionable Marriage)* includes six paintings on which the highly successful engravings were based. "The Marriage Settlement" is the first in the series (**3.7.7**), and shows quite a different marriage arrangement than that in Greuze's depiction (**3.7.6**). The betrothed couple sits together on the left, completely uninterested in each other. The miserable bride toys with her handkerchief while her father's lawyer, Silvertongue, flirts

Idealized: represented as perfect in form or character, corresponding to an ideal

Engraving: a printmaking technique where the artist gouges or scratches the image into the surface of the printing plate

Print: a picture reproduced on paper, often in multiple copies

Satire: a work of art that exposes the weaknesses and mistakes of its subjects to ridicule

Foreground: the part of a work depicted as nearest to the viewer

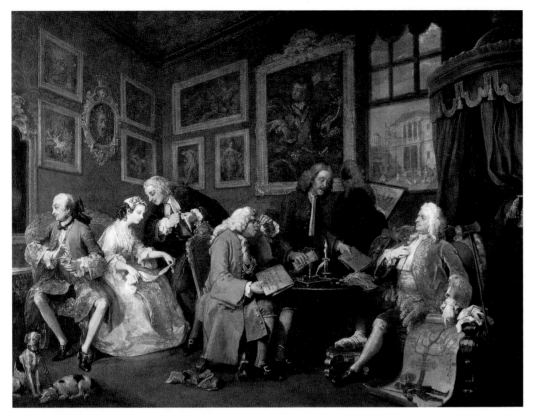

3.7.7 William Hogarth, "The Marriage Settlement" (from the series *Marriage à-la-Mode*), c. 1743. Oil on canvas, 27½ × 35¾". National Gallery, London, England

with her. The bridegroom admires himself in a mirror, too much of a snob to even look at his bride. The two dogs shackled together in the **foreground** echo the attitudes of the bride and groom. The marriage contract is being arranged by their fathers. The groom's father, on the far right, proudly displays in his family tree his aristocratic lineage as Earl Squander. The bride's merchant father offers a pile of coins as a dowry, which will finance the earl's building project (seen through the window).

Much of Hogarth's artwork addresses the need for social change, and the *Marriage à-la-Mode* series condemns the devastating effects of immorality. In the rest of the series, both husband and wife have affairs and fritter away their fortune; Silvertongue becomes the wife's lover, kills her husband, and is executed for the murder. The final scene of the series, called "The Lady's Death," is shown here as an engraving, the way most of the public would have seen it (**3.7.8**). The wife has poisoned herself, devastated by her lover's death. The bride's father has just removed the ring from her finger, while the old earl's completed building project is seen through the window. The disastrous coupling is recalled through the emaciated dog on the table, eating a pig's

carcass. Much of Hogarth's work addressed the need for protection of children. In this scene, it is the child who suffers. Shown kissing her mother goodbye, the sore on her face indicates that she has contracted syphilis from her promiscuous parents.

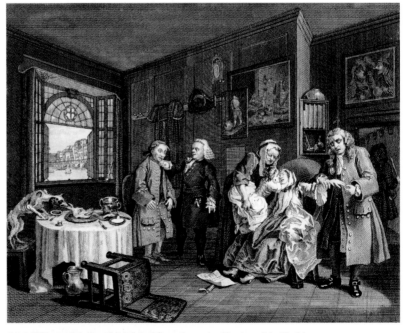

3.7.8 "The Lady's Death" (plate 6 from the series *Marriage à-la-Mode*). Engraving after the original painting by William Hogarth, c. 1743

The French Academy of Painting and Sculpture: Making a Living as an Artist

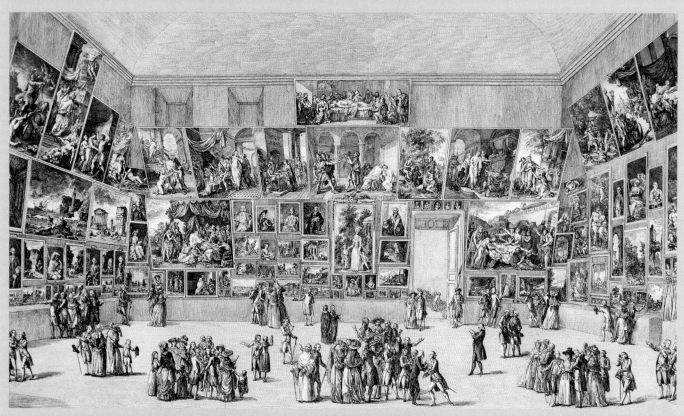

3.7.9 Pietro Antonio Martini, *The Salon*, 1785.
Musée du Château de Versailles, France

Throughout the eighteenth and much of the nineteenth centuries in Europe, France was the artistic center of Europe at this time, and the French Academy of Painting and Sculpture, founded in 1648 (renamed the Academy of Fine Arts in 1816), was vastly influential in determining artistic success. Its strict curriculum required artists to copy ancient works of art before they were allowed to draw a living model. Students also studied history, mythology, literature, and anatomy—important subjects of academic art. The Academy thrived on the notion of competition. The winner of the most important competition, the Prix de Rome (Rome Prize), was sent to Rome to study Classical works and the **Renaissance** masters.

The French Academy also developed a hierarchy for the relative importance of a painting's subject matter. History painting (see **3.7.10**, opposite, and **3.7.15**, p. 477), which depicted historical, biblical, or mythological scenes, usually containing large groups of people, was considered the finest of the **genres**. Portraits were the next most valued type of painting, then **genre scenes** of everyday life (see **3.7.6**, p. 470), landscapes, and

finally **still-life** paintings (**3.7.11**, p. 474). History paintings highlighted an artist's academic training in that they showed subjects, often with idealized nude bodies, that the artists had studied in their readings. Painters of other genres often tried to increase the importance of their artworks by including elements such as references to Classical stories and messages of morality. While artists who excelled in any of these subjects could belong to the Academy, only history painters were allowed to teach there.

The Royal Academy of Painting and Sculpture held a highly competitive exhibition in Paris called the **Salon** every one or two years. In Pietro Antonio Martini's print of the Salon of 1785, paintings fill the walls from floor to ceiling (**3.7.9**). The history paintings (always much larger in scale) were given prominent places, and the still lifes were usually hung lower. Martini's print highlights the prominent placement (at the center of the middle wall) of David's history painting *The Oath of the Horatii* (see **3.7.10**). Critics from around the world reviewed these exhibitions, making or breaking artists' reputations.

Neoclassicism

> Those marks of heroism and civic virtue presented to the eyes of the people will electrify the soul, and sow the seeds of glory and loyalty to the fatherland.
>
> (Jacques-Louis David)

This statement by the French painter David summarizes the moral objectives of **Neoclassical** (literally, "new **Classical**") art. This was a movement that developed during the late eighteenth century as an even bolder reaction against the artificiality of the Rococo. Neoclassical artworks recall, in their imagery and subject matter, the ancient Classical cultures of Greece and Rome. This interest in the ancient world was fueled by such archaeological discoveries around this time as the remains of the Roman city of Pompeii. Ancient Greece and Rome were thought to embody such virtues as civic responsibility and an emphasis on rational thought. At a time of public unrest, Neoclassical artworks used historical or mythological stories to convey a moral message, and sought to convey rationalism and stability visually through structure and stillness, creating visions of balance and order.

Jacques-Louis David (1748–1825) lived through one of the most tumultuous periods in French history. He made paintings purchased by the monarchy, then supported revolutionary leaders who opposed the king, and later painted numerous portraits of the French emperor, Napoleon. Although David's painting *The Oath of the Horatii* (**3.7.10**), because of its promotion of civic duty or accepting personal sacrifice in the service of one's nation, is often linked to the ideas that fueled the French Revolution that began in 1789, the image was in fact made for King Louis XVI, five years before the revolution that removed him from the throne.

The Oath of the Horatii was an exceptionally popular work when it was shown at the 1785 Salon and is often credited with pioneering Neoclassicism (see: The French Academy of Painting and Sculpture: Making a Living as an Artist). The painting is based on a story from early Roman history in which three brothers are shown making a vow to their father to fight for

Neoclassicism: a European style that flourished during the late eighteenth and early nineteenth centuries, characterized by an extreme interest in the Classical world, strictly ordered scenes, and heroic subjects

Classical: ancient Greek and Roman; art that conforms to Greek and Roman models, or is based on rational construction and emotional equilibrium

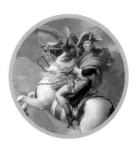

Jacques Louis David would later paint for French Revolutionary leaders and Napoleon:
→ see **4.5.3**, p. 594

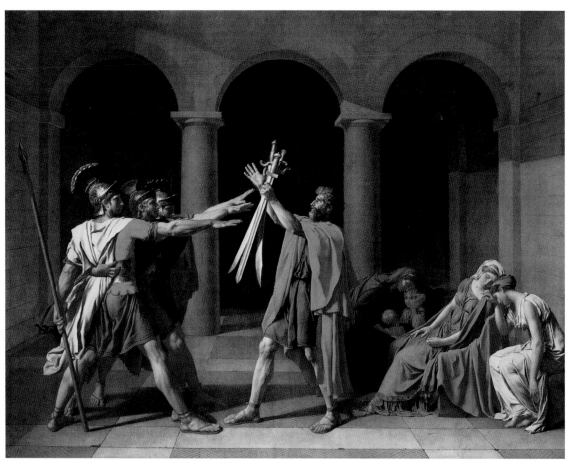

3.7.10 Jacques-Louis David, *The Oath of the Horatii*, 1784. Oil on canvas, 10'10" × 13'11½". Musée du Louvre, Paris, France

Linear outline: a line that clearly separates a figure from its surroundings

Linear perspective: a system using converging imaginary sight lines to create the illusion of depth

Orthogonals: in perspective systems, imaginary sightlines extending from forms to the vanishing point

Vanishing point(s): the point or points in a work of art at which imaginary sight lines appear to converge, suggesting depth

Rome. The scene is Neoclassical in its muscular Classical figures, with distinct **linear outlines**, and its stable, balanced composition, created in part by the pyramidal groupings of the figures and the strict vertical columns. David used **linear perspective**, with **orthogonal** lines in the geometric floor that lead to the **vanishing point** at the father's hand as he holds the swords. The three Roman archways separate the empty, dark background from the figures and organize the people into three groups. The brothers on the left are contrasted with the women of the family on the right, and the father is central. While the soldiers stand heroically, the women mourn the losses they know will come. Personal sacrifice and civic duty are common themes shown in history paintings.

During the eighteenth and nineteenth centuries, only four women were allowed into the French Academy. It was very difficult for women to become artists since few workshops would accept women as students, and women were not allowed to study nude models, which was considered a critical skill in the Academy, particularly for the creation of history paintings. The female artists who did become successful academic painters tended to do so in one of the so-called lesser genres, and thanks to familial or royal support.

Anne Vallayer-Coster (1744–1818), trained by her father and other artists, was a brilliant painter of still lifes. Although she often painted fruits or flowers, she chose the subject of *Attributes of Painting, Sculpture, and Architecture*, which highlights the traits and tools needed to be successful in these arts and to gain entrance into the French Academy (**3.7.11**). The painting, Neoclassical in its powerfully structured composition, was sized to be an "overdoor," meaning that it would have been hung high above a doorway. The dynamism of the composition is enhanced when one stands below the work and feels a sense of anxiety that the precariously arranged objects could fall. Vallayer-Coster chose objects referencing intellectualism in other artistic endeavors, including architectural plans, tools, and a Classically styled sculpture that seems to point its missing head to the upper left corner of the painting. Unlike other paintings of the attributes of the arts, however, the artist includes an unfinished bust. We know it is unfinished because of its darker shade, signifying that the clay is moist, and the temporarily removed cloth that would have been used to prevent it from drying. The bust might be interpreted as a self-portrait, in which the artist is presenting herself as an unfinished work, ready to be molded by the Academy.

The Swiss-Austrian artist Angelica Kauffmann (1741–1807) used purely Neoclassical elements, such as Classical subject matter, Classical architecture, and stable compositions, in her paintings. Kauffmann was one of only

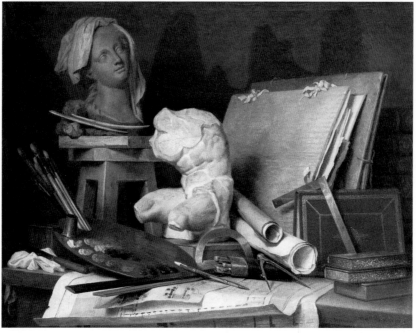

3.7.11 Anne Vallayer-Coster, *Attributes of Painting, Sculpture, and Architecture*, 1769. Oil on canvas, 35½ × 47¾". Musée du Louvre, Paris, France

two women amongst the thirty-four original members of the British Royal Academy of the Arts. Kauffmann was trained in painting by her father in her youth, and became a well-respected artist with commissions from international patrons. She was fortunate to have traveled extensively and her works were appreciated by those who had experienced a Grand Tour. Her best-known works are Neoclassical scenes that portray strong female characters. In *Cornelia Pointing to Her Children as Her Treasures*, a Roman woman is represented as a model of motherhood and morality (**3.7.12**). While the woman on the right displays her fine jewelry, Cornelia gestures to her sons as her source of pride, her own jewels; they will grow up to be the political leaders Tiberius and Gaius Gracchus. Cornelia's daughter, curious, strokes the woman's jewels, but Cornelia holds her hand firmly and models strength of character rather than pride in material wealth.

Neoclassicism represented the ideals of Americans in the late eighteenth century: equality, patriotism, and civic responsibility. Thomas Jefferson (1743–1826), author of the Declaration of Independence and America's third president, founded the University of Virginia in 1819 to educate its students about these Enlightenment ideals, which is ironic considering that the university was built using the labor of enslaved people. Jefferson designed the university's Rotunda to house the library and to reflect his belief in Classical, rather

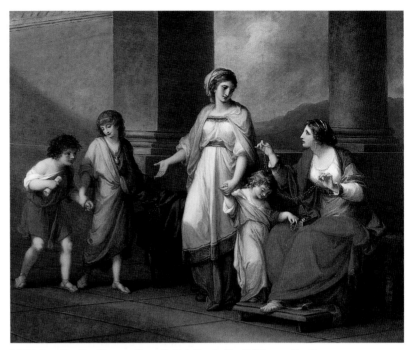

3.7.12 Angelica Kauffmann, *Cornelia Pointing to Her Children as Her Treasures*, c. 1785. Oil on canvas, 40 × 50″. Virginia Museum of Fine Arts, Richmond

than church-centered, education (**3.7.13**). The building, inspired by the Roman Pantheon, contains Classical architectural elements such as a **pediment**, **Corinthian columns**, and a dome with an **oculus**.

Although revolutions based on equality took place in Europe and America in the late eighteenth century, it took longer for freedom to come to enslaved people taken from Africa. Black men and women were rarely depicted in Europe and American art of this period,

Pediment: the triangular space, situated above the row of columns, on the facade of a building in the Classical style

Corinthian column: a type of Classical column with an ornate capital, common in ancient Roman architecture.

Oculus: a round opening at the center of a dome

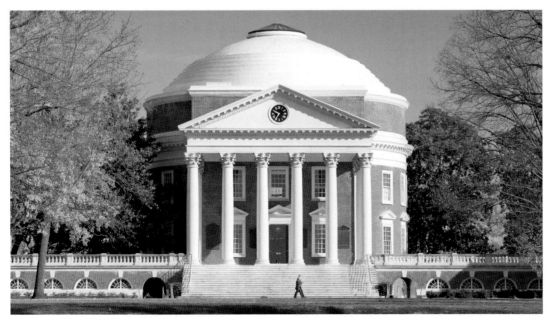

3.7.13 Thomas Jefferson, **Rotunda**, **University of Virginia**, Charlottesville, Virginia, 1769–1809

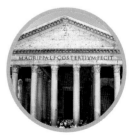

Thomas Jefferson's Rotunda was inspired by the Pantheon in Rome:
→ see **3.1.33**, p. 369

and when they were, they were often shown as enslaved people and depicted in an objectified manner. Jean-Baptiste Belley, born in Senegal around 1747, was sold into enslavement in Saint-Domingue, Haiti, at the age of two, and he bought his freedom as an adult. Knowing first-hand the abuses experienced by enslaved people, in 1793 Belley became the first Black man elected to the French National Convention. He argued for the abolition of enslavement, which led to a unanimous vote to end the brutal practice in France and its colonies.

Both the subject and the compositional balance of Anne-Louis Girodet's portrait of Belley convey a Neoclassical rationalism (**3.7.14**). Belley stands in a confident pose, reflecting his democratic triumph and his status as a symbol of liberty. The dark skin of Belley contrasts with the white marble bust of the recently deceased Enlightenment philosopher Guillaume Thomas Raynal, who had also argued vehemently against enslavement in his treatise of 1770. Belley is leaning on the base of the sculpture, thus symbolically leaning on the writings of Raynal. The figures balance one another further by staring in opposite directions, giving the sense that the living man is carrying on the ideas of

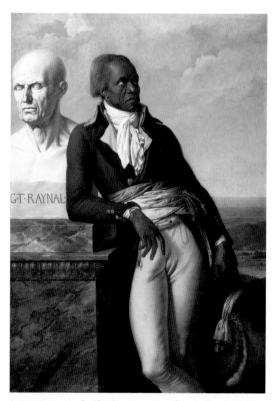

3.7.14 Anne-Louis Girodet, *Jean-Baptiste Belley*, 1797. Oil on canvas, 62⅝ × 44". Châteaux de Versailles et de Trianon, Versailles, France

the deceased, who has empty eyes and appears somewhat ghost-like next to the colorful, confident, and robust figure of Belley.

Romanticism

While the style and subject matter of Neoclassical art were designed to express rationalism, stability, and traditional notions of duty, Romantic artworks, by contrast, emphasize individuality, and surge with drama, fantasy, and heightened emotion. Additionally, many Romantic images portray the power and beauty of nature and humanity's relationship with it, both as a rejection of the encroaching industrialization of the period and as a symbol for the natural impulses and creativity of humans. Romantic artists valued emotion over reason, and **Romanticism** in art, which emerged in the first half of the nineteenth century, reflects the turmoil of the European and American revolutions, when the people rose up against the ruling classes and demanded their freedom. Romantic art challenged the traditional norms and structures of society and often showed citizens' sacrifices for ideals of liberty, equality, and humanity, in images charged with energy created by the use of **implied lines** in all directions, frequent **asymmetry**, and visual movement and **rhythm**.

Liberty Leading the People, by Eugène Delacroix (1798–1863), depicts the French people bravely rising up against their government in the three-day July Revolution of 1830 (**3.7.15**). The bare-breasted symbol of freedom, Liberty, carries the flag of the revolution in one hand and a musket in the other. This **personification** of France's symbol of Liberty was shocking at the time for its portrayal of a modern, dirty figure rather than an idealized goddess. Although partly an imagined scene, the painting accurately shows the chaos of the event and the sacrifice of people of all ages and social classes. A little boy fearlessly marches forward carrying two pistols, while an upper-class man in a top hat holds a rifle. Crowds of people with muskets and swords follow Liberty as she climbs over those who have died, signifying that such sacrifice is worth the greater good. In contrast to David's *Oath of the Horatii* (**3.7.10**, p. 473), which glorifies a Roman story for a modern purpose, Delacroix's Romantic image highlights the emotion felt by many Parisians about a contemporary event.

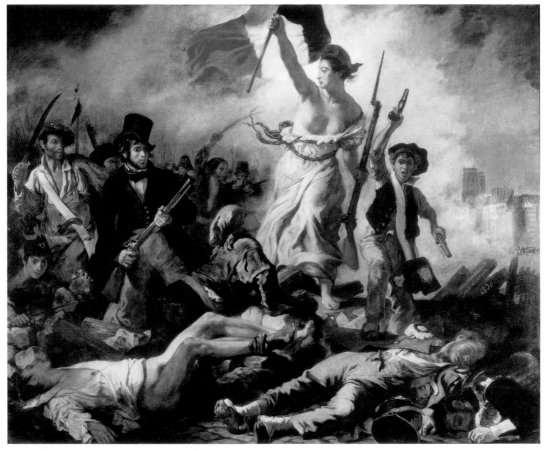

3.7.15 Eugène Delacroix, *Liberty Leading the People*, 1830. Oil on canvas, 8′6¼″ × 10′8″.
Musée du Louvre, Paris, France

The British artist and poet William Blake (1757–1827) conveys in both his visual and literary works emotionally charged messages about his beliefs in personal and creative freedom. In *Elohim Creating Adam* (**3.7.16**), Blake transforms Michelangelo's famous *Creation of Adam* (see p. 447) from the Sistine Chapel ceiling in Rome into a Romantic image filled with anguish and struggle. In Blake's vision, God ("Elohim" in Hebrew) has enormous wings

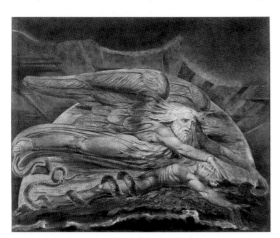

3.7.16 William Blake, *Elohim Creating Adam*, 1795.
Color print finished in ink and watercolor on paper, 17 × 21″.
Tate, London, England

that seem to grow from the tendons in his shoulders. The process of creation is shown to be painful for both creator and created, rather than a cause for joy and celebration. The sadness evident in Elohim's face may convey his knowledge that the creation of man will inevitably bring about humanity's fall from grace, implied in the image by the presence of a snake. Blake believed that man's spiritual freedom was suppressed on the day of his creation, and his painting shows it: Adam's body is restrained by the serpent, while his mind is restrained by the hand of God. Blake resisted any controls on either his creativity or behavior, rejecting many of the accepted Christian values of the time, as well as rebelling against the philosophies of the British Royal Academy. Blake often passionately protested the inequalities faced by the less fortunate, whether they were struggling artists, atheists, women, or enslaved people.

The British painter J. M. W. Turner (1775–1851) used his art to express his views against enslavement and as a force for social protest. In his dramatic painting in the Romantic style, *Slave Ship (Slavers Throwing Overboard the*

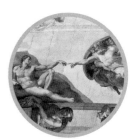

William Blake knew about Michelangelo's frescoes in the Sistine Chapel through engravings. For the paintings, see:

→ **3.6.7a–b**, p. 447

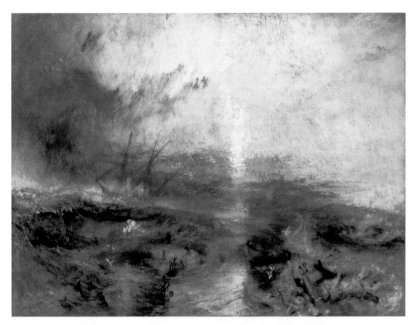

3.7.17 J. M. W. Turner, *Slave Ship (Slavers Throwing Overboard the Dead and Dying, Typhoon Coming On)*, 1840. Oil on canvas, 35¾ × 48¼". Museum of Fine Arts, Boston, Massachusetts

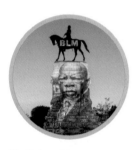

The Robert E. Lee Monument in Richmond, Virginia, is a site of controversy today because of General Lee's association with the Confederacy and their practices of enslavement:

→ see **4.7.8**, p. 624

Abstract: an artwork the form of which is simplified, distorted, or exaggerated in appearance. It may represent a recognizable form that has been slightly altered, or it may be a completely non-representational depiction

Dead and Dying, Typhoon Coming On) (**3.7.17**), Turner condemns the trade in enslaved people. Although enslavement was illegal in Britain by this time, Turner was highlighting the injustice of the trade and protesting any consideration of its renewal. His powerful canvas portrays an infamous incident aboard the ship *Zong* in 1781. It was common practice for the captains of ships used to transport enslaved people to fill their vessels with more people than they would need, knowing that disease might spread amongst them. The captain knew that he would be paid for any enslaved people lost at sea, but not for those who were sick when they arrived. He therefore had sick people thrown overboard while the ship was still far from land.

Turner's chaotic canvas displays several aspects of the Romantic style. Humans versus nature was a common theme in Romantic art, and here the immense power of nature, expressed as a fierce storm, overpowers the enslaved people. Body parts, still shackled and being attacked by sharp-teethed fish, can be seen in the central and right foreground. Turner uses intense colors and turbulent brushstrokes to convey the heightened emotion and fearful horror of the event. His canvas also has an **abstract** quality, making its subject matter difficult to understand. Beside his painting, Turner placed a quotation from the book that had inspired it, Thomas Clarkson's *History and Abolition of the Slave Trade*, in order to help viewers understand his artwork's meaning.

Edmonia Lewis (1843/45–1907) is thought to be the first African American sculptor to have an exhibition—which took place in San Francisco in 1872—devoted to her work, and to achieve international acclaim. Her works often include African American and Native American figures and stories, which reflect her personal experiences and heritage. Her father was a formerly enslaved African American and her mother was a Chippewa Indian whose tribe raised Edmonia when she was orphaned at a young age. *Forever Free* (**3.7.18**), made in 1867, four years after the Emancipation Proclamation, shows a man standing with his arm raised, his wrist still wrapped by the chains that bound him as an enslaved man. Below him is a clothed woman clasping her hands in prayer. The sculpture is made of white marble, a material that was typical of Neoclassicism, but the representation of women, particularly non-Caucasian women, as clothed and without being sexualized was unique for the time. It is not uncommon for artworks to contain characteristics of both Neoclassicism and Romanticism. While *Forever Free* is Neoclassical in its use of white marble and the theatrical poses of the figures, the subject matter contains the emotional charge of a Romantic work.

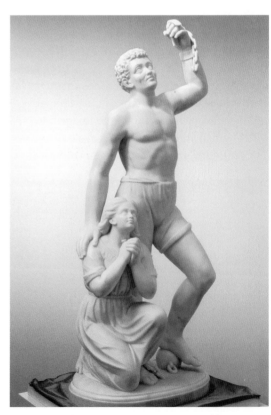

3.7.18 Edmonia Lewis, *Forever Free*, 1867. Marble, 41¾ × 21½ × 12⅜". Howard University Art Gallery, Washington, D.C.

Explore Further Art of Europe and America (1700–1865): Rococo to Romanticism

Neoclassicism

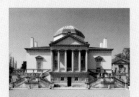

2.5.22 Lord Burlington, Chiswick House, 1729 → p. 255

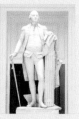

4.5.1 Jean-Antoine Houdon, *George Washington*, 1788–92 → p. 592

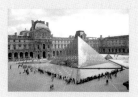

0.0.8 Louvre Museum, Paris → p. 20

Romanticism

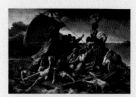

4.7.1 Théodore Géricault, *Raft of the Medusa*, 1819, → p. 619

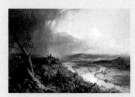

0.0.3 Thomas Cole, *View from Mount Holyoke, Massachusetts, after a Thunderstorm— The Oxbow*, 1836 → p. 17

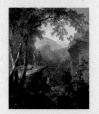

1.3.13 Asher Brown Durand, *Kindred Spirits*, 1849 → p. 74

Enlightenment versus Enslavement

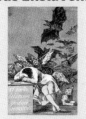

1.9.14 Francisco Goya, *The Sleep of Reason Produces Monsters*, 1799 → p. 155

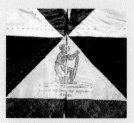

1.9.5b Deborah Coates, detail of quilt, *c.* 1840–50 → p. 150

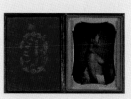

2.8.19 J. T. Zealy, *Delia*, front, 1850 → p. 311

Revolution and War

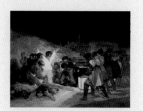

4.6.9 Francisco Goya, *Third of May, 1808*, 1814 → p. 610

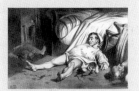

2.3.15 Honoré Daumier, *Rue Transnonain*, 1834 → p. 221

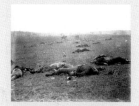

4.6.2 Timothy O'Sullivan, *Harvest of Death, Gettysburg, Pennsylvania*, 1863 → p. 605

Your turn
To which periods of art history do these works belong?

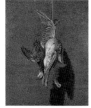

2.6.14 Mary Linwood, detail from *Hanging Partridge*, late 18th century → p. 277

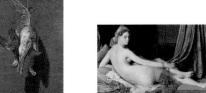

1.10.8 Jean-Auguste-Dominique Ingres, *Grande Odalisque*, 1814 → p. 167

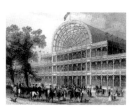

2.5.26 Joseph Paxton, Crystal Palace (engraving), 1851 → p. 258

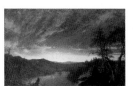

1.4.12 Frederic Edwin Church, *Twilight in the Wilderness*, 1860 → p. 90

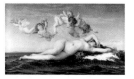

3.8.1 Alexandre Cabanel, *Birth of Venus*, 1863 → p. 481

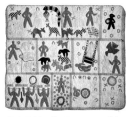

0.0.5 Harriet Powers, *Bible Quilt*, 1885–86 → p. 19

3.8
The Modern Aesthetic: Realism to *Fin de Siècle*

Fin de Siècle: French for "end of the century"; usually refers to the end of the nineteenth century

Impressionism, Impressionist: in the visual arts, a late nineteenth-century style conveying the fleeting impression of the effects of light; Impressionists were artists working in this style

Post-Impressionists: artists either from or living in France, *c.* 1885–1905, who moved away from the Impressionist style—notably Cézanne, Gauguin, Seurat, and Van Gogh

Representational: art that depicts figures and objects so that we recognize what is represented

Symbolist: an artist or artistic style belonging to the movement in European art and literature, *c.* 1885–1910, that conveyed meaning by the use of powerful yet ambiguous symbols

Art Nouveau: French for "new art," a visual style of the late nineteenth and early twentieth century, characterized by organic flowing lines, simulating forms in nature and involving decorative pattern

Modernism, Modernist: a radically new twentieth-century art and architectural movement that embraced modern industrial materials and a machine aesthetic

In the second half of the nineteenth century, art entered a period of great experimentation. European and North American cultures and lifestyles were changing radically: railways expanded rapidly, steamships crossed the world's oceans, and industrial growth brought the rural poor to cities, in search of work. Increasingly, the city, which offered modern forms of transport, such as the tram, and new technologies, such as electricity, became the center of economic activity and growth. The expanding economy in turn created a prosperous middle class of people who had the time and money for leisure and cultural pursuits. Thanks to the revolutionary invention of photography, those who could not afford hand-painted or drawn portraits of themselves could purchase mass-produced photographic prints; the culture people consumed became a central part of their identity, and an indication of their desired status.

At the approach of the turn of the century (**Fin de Siècle**), curiosity and anxiety grew about what the new century would bring. Artists responded to the continuing pace of change in society with multiple forms of experimentation. Some, such as the **Impressionists** and **Post-Impressionists**, continued to be interested in **representational** art, but chose to explore the impact of the formal qualities of their artwork, leading towards greater abstraction in many works. They sought to capture the impression of the fleeting moment through quick brushstrokes, dabs of paint, and the use of vibrant color and light. **Symbolists** then did the complete opposite, attempting to portray what could be felt but not seen. **Art Nouveau** imitated organic forms, especially in architecture and the decorative arts.

Art Academies and Modernism

Much of the art of the late nineteenth and the early twentieth centuries that is most familiar to us today is from experimental artists who pushed traditional boundaries and fought against long-held artistic conventions with a view toward conveying the spirit of their time. **Modernism** itself is often defined as a movement that essentially broke with tradition. It is important to remember that much of the art respected today was considered shocking in its time, particularly to those who admired artists using classic conventions established and maintained by the Art Academies. Often, these were government-sponsored institutions set up to train artists to produce work in a particular style and following certain prescribed ideas about what was suitable subject matter for artworks. Indeed, modern artists were often held up for comparison, frequently in a negative manner, with those who were supported and exhibited by the academic system. By the end of the nineteenth century, this division led to artists establishing new avenues for selling and exhibiting their artworks outside of the traditional **Salon**.

The contrast between art produced within the traditions established by the Academy and the work of artists experimenting with other forms of representation can be understood by comparing two very different French paintings from 1863. Alexandre Cabanel's (1823–1889) *Birth of Venus* (**3.8.1**) is an example of the kind of work that was highly appreciated in academic circles. A nude Venus, the mythical Greek goddess of love, lounges invitingly on the ocean, her sensual body on full display, offered submissively to the viewer's gaze, her eyes almost covered by her arm, and barely open.

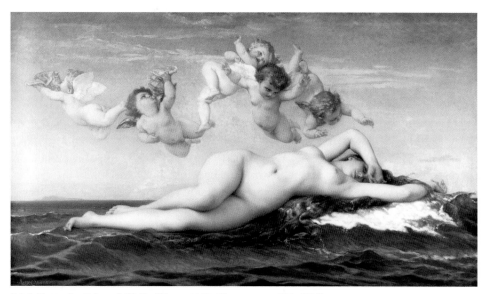

3.8.1 Alexandre Cabanel, *Birth of Venus*, 1863. Oil on canvas, 51⅛× 88½"
Musée d'Orsay, Paris, France

Salon: an official annual exhibition of Frenchpainting, first held in 1667

Putto (plural ***putti***): a representation of a nude or scantily clad infant angel or boy, common in Renaissance and Baroque art

Flying young boys, known as ***putti***, accompany her, creating a fluttering decorative ribbon effect above her reclining form.

The French painter Édouard Manet's (1832–1883) *Le Déjeuner sur l'Herbe (Luncheon on the Grass)* (**3.8.2**) also includes a naked woman, but a very different one from Cabanel's Venus. Manet's nude is completely awake, self-possessed, and looks self-confidently and directly at the viewer. She is accompanied, not by naked *putti*, but by fully clothed, middle-class men with whom she appears to be having a picnic. Far from being submissive, Manet's woman sits up, at ease with her nudity—she has casually discarded her clothes—and her businesslike gaze suggests she may be a modern sex worker, or perhaps an artist's model, rather than a mythological goddess. Viewers were shocked to see two men dressed in contemporary clothing and casually placed in a

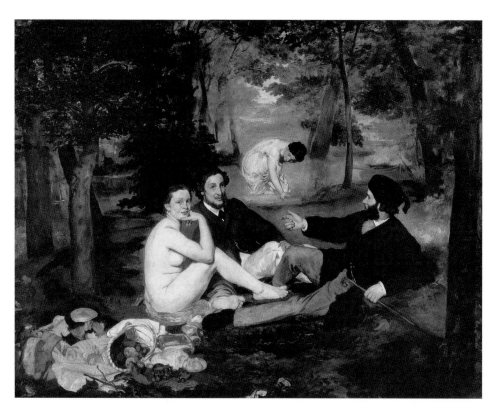

3.8.2 Édouard Manet, *Le Déjeuner sur l'Herbe (Luncheon on the Grass)*, 1863. Oil on canvas, 6'9⅞" × 8'8⅛". Musée d'Orsay, Paris, France

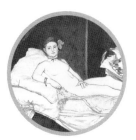

In 1865, Manet again showed a nude woman boldly staring out at the viewer:

→ see **4.8.9**, p. 636

local park next to a naked woman who (despite the speculation about her profession) does not seem to be portrayed for the erotic pleasure of the audience—her body is much less fully displayed than the Venus Cabanel depicted.

The artworks of Cabanel and Manet also differ in their painting and **compositional** techniques. Cabanel's artwork has a sense of depth and **illusionism**: for example, **atmospheric perspective** is used to show the land in the far distance. His Venus is fully rounded to give maximum appeal to the viewer. Manet, instead, flattens the visible **space** in his scene. In the small area of distant landscape in the center of the painting, he further destroys the illusion of depth by using thick brushstrokes and obscuring access to the objects in the distance with trees and the figure of an enigmatic woman stooping in the stream.

Manet's figures appear almost as cutouts, much less **volumetric** than Cabanel's erotic and fleshy nude, and whereas Cabanel uses different degrees of **value** to **model** the flesh of his Venus, Manet's female appears as if sitting in an unnatural spotlight: unlike Cabanel's painting, there is no gradual, soft gradation from light to dark, and the **outline** of her body is harsh. Although shocked by the composition, contemporary viewers would have realized that Manet had based both his arrangement of figures and the fact that some were naked and some were clothed on already esteemed artworks, depicting mythological themes, in the Louvre Museum. Manet is not interested in re-creating a mythological subject in an **idealized** way, however, but rather in portraying figures from his own era, and reflecting on the act of painting itself. By thinly disguising his use of **Classical** models to portray a controversial scene of leisure, Manet highlights in *Luncheon on the Grass* how distant the artistic standards of the Academy were from the styles adopted by modern painters.

Alexandre Cabanel had been supported by the Academy throughout his career, having been sent to study in Rome, and winning awards at previous Salons. Inclusion in the Salon was important to a successful artistic career, and could lead to both government and private commissions, but the jury that selected the works for the Salon was very conservative and increasingly out of step with developments in both technique and subject matter. Unhappiness with the traditional Academy

and its Salon came to a head in 1863. While Cabanel's *Birth of Venus* was praised in the Salon of that year and purchased by Emperor Napoleon III for his personal collection, more unconventional works by Manet, Gustave Courbet and Camille Pissarro were rejected. Manet's *Luncheon on the Grass* was instead placed in an exhibition called the Salon des Refusés (Salon of the Rejected), which was arranged by Napoleon III to address the many complaints that year about the large number of artworks not accepted in the official Salon. Installed near the Salon, this second exhibition was designed to appease artists who felt unfairly excluded from that show. The Academy also anticipated that visitors to the exhibition would heap ridicule upon the artists and works its jury had rejected, but in this sense it was not entirely successful. Such paintings as Manet's *Luncheon on the Grass* were indeed mocked by some critics, but the public, thousands of whom flocked to the Salon des Refusés due to the controversy, was now exposed to art that had not been approved by the Academy. Artists were emboldened to exhibit independently in venues throughout Paris, and the power of the Salon was weakened. With this painting, Manet proved that it was possible for an artist to create arresting work that did not conform to convention, and to break away from or alter traditional subjects and modes of representation. It is regarded by some as the work that marks the beginning of modern art, and Manet himself came to epitomize the notion of a modern painter.

Realism

Show me an angel, and I'll paint one!
(Gustave Courbet, French painter, defending Realism)

Beginning around the mid-nineteenth century, a significant shift took place in the objectives of the visual arts and in the way art looked. To varying degrees, a number of artists broke away from the traditions of earlier eighteenth- and nineteenth-century art to create objective representations of the real world. The movement called **Realism** refers specifically to writers and artists in France who were concerned about achieving social change after the Revolution of 1848. They created depictions of individuals in modern society, with underlying political messages about the inequality of the poor. Realism in general, however, can also refer to artists (in France and elsewhere) who observed their modern subjects in great detail yet did not have a social or political agenda. Realist artists also began to allow the process of creating art to show through in their final works, and they were less concerned with illusionistic surfaces.

Gustave Courbet (1819–1877) is credited with being the first to use the term "realist" to describe his own work. As a reaction to the **Neoclassical**, moralizing images of historic scenes, or the extremely emotional paintings of the **Romantics**, Courbet argued that it was more meaningful to paint people and things in everyday life. The painting *Stonebreakers* was shocking for its depiction of working-class people on a large-sized canvas, a scale normally reserved for the heroic subject matter of history paintings (**3.8.3**). Courbet's painting highlights the backbreaking, monotonous work of the poor. The breaking of stones was a job taught by older generations to young men, and it was a job a man would have for a lifetime. The painting shows an older worker and his young assistant as powerful and unrelenting—qualities that alarmed the upper classes: a year before Courbet painted this work, in the Revolution of 1848, workers throughout Europe had rebelled and demanded an end to bad working conditions and low pay.

Realist tendencies took a different form in the case of a group of English painters and

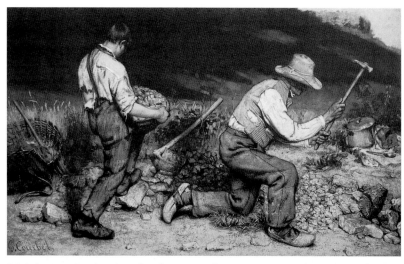

3.8.3 Gustave Courbet, *Stonebreakers*, 1849. Oil on canvas, 5′3″ × 6′8″. Formerly in the Gemäldegalerie, Dresden, Germany. Pre-war color photograph (painting destroyed 1945)

writers, formed in 1848, who called themselves the **Pre-Raphaelite Brotherhood**. While many Realist painters in France were rejecting the traditions of their Academy, the Pre-Raphaelites (as they became known) were opposed to the values of the Royal Academy of Arts in Britain, which promoted artwork inspired by ancient Greece and Rome and by the **Renaissance**. Pre-Raphaelite artists were instead inspired by medieval subjects. They were realist in their intense attention to visual details and their true-to-life depictions of nature and people.

Ophelia (**3.8.4**) by the Pre-Raphaelite John Everett Millais (1829–1896) depicts a scene from Shakespeare's tragedy *Hamlet*, in which

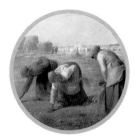

As with Courbet's work, Jean-François Millet's *The Gleaners* highlights respect for the struggling working class: → see **1.7.3**, p. 132

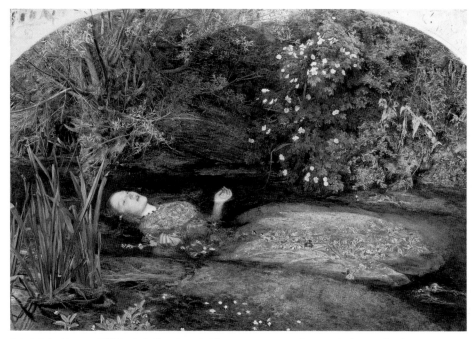

3.8.4 John Everett Millais, *Ophelia*, 1851–52. Oil on canvas, 30 × 44″. Tate, London, England

Romanticism, Romantic: a movement in nineteenth-century European culture, concerned with the power of the imagination and greatly valuing intense feeling

Pre-Raphaelite Brotherhood: an English art movement formed in 1848 by painters who rejected the academic rules of art, and often painted medieval subjects in a naïve style

Renaissance: a period of cultural and artistic change in Europe from the fourteenth to the seventeenth century

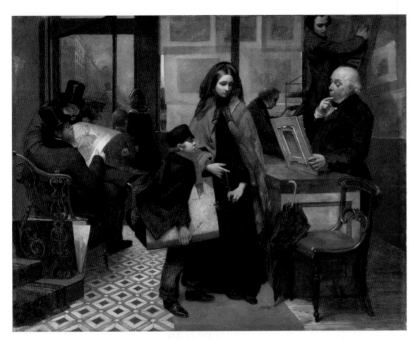

3.8.5 Emily Mary Osborn, *Nameless and Friendless*, 1857. Oil on canvas, 32½ × 40⅞". Tate, London, England

the young female character, Ophelia, drowns herself because her lover, Prince Hamlet, has harshly rejected her and accidentally killed her father. Millais's depiction of nature is painstakingly detailed. To make this painting, he selected a single spot on a nearby river and painted the plants growing there so carefully that botanists can identify each one. He worked at the site almost every day over a five-month period. Millais also included flowers that were not growing by the river but that are mentioned in *Hamlet*. He then took realism to the extreme by having his model pose for the painting in a filled bathtub so that he could study the way her hair and dress floated. Although she often had oil lamps around her to keep her warm, the model caught a severe cold from spending so many hours in the water in the middle of winter.

Emily Mary Osborn (1828–1925) exhibited *Nameless and Friendless* (**3.8.5**) at the Royal Academy of Arts, London, in 1857, the same year she became a member of the Society of Female Artists, which was an organization designed to support the unique challenges of being a woman artist. Osborn was actively involved in women's suffrage, and, in 1859, petitioned to allow women to become students at the Academy. *Nameless and Friendless* shows the experience of a female artist, wearing black (indicating that she was in mourning), trying to sell her work to a local dealer. She is accompanied by a boy who carries her work, suggesting that she does not have a man in

her life to escort her. As she humbly looks down and plays with some string in her hand, she awaits the shopkeeper's assessment. The two men on the left look up from studying an artwork depicting a ballet dancer to leer at the woman, implying that they are thinking of her scantily clad, like the dancer. Osborn is making a statement in this work about the roles to which women are restricted in society. A third woman, one of higher status, is exiting the shop with her son; despite her social standing, she is barely noticed, as Osborn argued was the case for many women at this time.

A Revolutionary Invention: Photography and Art in the Nineteenth Century

Realism was partly inspired and fueled by the invention of photography in the first decades of the nineteenth century, which led many artists to feel the need to capture the truth of everyday life, as photographers could. The advent of photography also affected artists directly in terms of their income. A client who wanted a portrait, for example, had previously had only one option: to pay a portrait artist to paint a likeness, which was a time-consuming task for both the artist and the **sitter**, expensive for the client, and lucrative for the artist. Photography provided another, much less laborious and less expensive way to record a likeness or an event in a very realistic manner.

By the 1860s, photographic portraits were commonly taken of celebrities, and portraits of families were common. Exposure times, while still taking several seconds, no longer took minutes, so sitters did not have to remain still for very long. President Lincoln had more than forty individual photographic portraits taken of himself while in office, and credited these photos, often reproduced in small sizes for the public, with helping Americans feel like they knew him, and with fueling support for his political decisions. Figure **3.8.6** shows Lincoln, donning a rare, slight smile, sitting with a book while one of his sons stands casually nearby.

Since portraits had long been produced by professionally trained painters and sculptors, the ability of the camera to record such scenes as Lincoln's portrait raised some important questions. Could portraits made with a camera be considered art? In other words, were photographers artists, or simply technicians creating reproductions? The notion

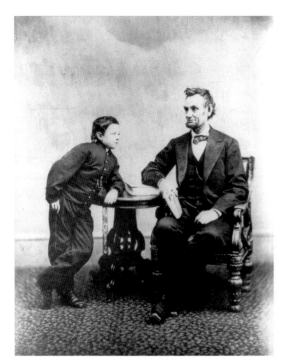

3.8.6 **Alexander Gardner**, *Abraham Lincoln and His Son Thomas (Tad)*, February 5, 1865. Silver gelatin print, 8 × 10″. Library of Congress Prints, Washington, D.C.

that photographers could replace the role of painters sparked a debate that raged during the second half of the nineteenth century.

Thomas Le Clear's *Interior with Portraits* at first seems to be self-explanatory (**3.8.7**).

A young brother and sister are posed before a painted landscape while a photographer on the far right snaps their picture. Le Clear, however, is highlighting the tension between photographers and painters as they competed for **patrons** in this period. While photographs are often thought to be accurate accounts of reality, Le Clear shows that in some ways paintings can be more truthful. The date of the painting, believed to be 1865, is the year of death of the boy shown, James Sidney. Yet Sidney did not die as a child, but as a firefighter at the age of twenty-six. His sister, Parnell, however, had died years earlier in 1849. Therefore, the children shown in the painting were neither this age nor even alive when this canvas was painted. The scene is effectively a memorial to the lost pair, and the painting is able to create an apparent reality and transcend time in a way that the camera, used to capture particular real-life moments, could not. While post-mortem photographs of deceased children, which helped the bereaved remember their loved ones' faces, were common during this period, Le Clear shows that, in this case, a painting could keep these children alive in the memory of their loved ones better than a photograph.

In the decades that followed Le Clear's painting, some artists responded to the advent

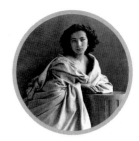

Nadar took many artistically composed portraits of famous figures:
→ see **2.8.9**, p. 305

Patron: an organization or individual who sponsors the creation of works of art

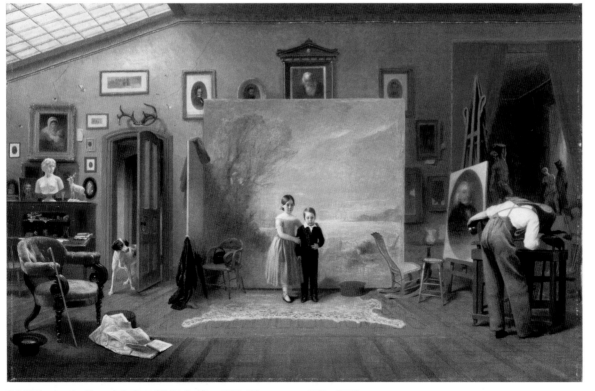

3.8.7 **Thomas Le Clear**, *Interior with Portraits*, *c*. 1865. Oil on canvas, 25⅞ × 40½″. Smithsonian American Art Museum, Washington, D.C.

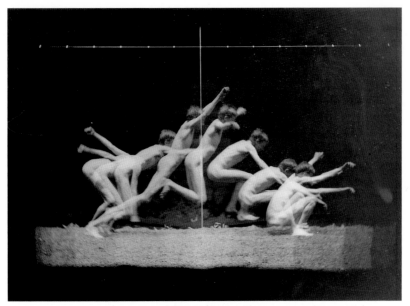

3.8.8 Thomas Eakins, *Motion Study: Male Nude, Standing Jump to Right*, 1884. Dry plate negative, 3⅝ × 4½". Pennsylvania Academy of the Fine Arts, Philadelphia

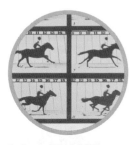

Eadweard Muybridge studied horse movements using photography in 1878:

→ see **2.9.3**, p. 320

En plein air: French for "in the open air"; used to describe painting out of doors from start to finish rather than working in a studio for all or part of the process

Palette: a smooth slab or board used for mixing paints or cosmetics

Hue: the general classification of a color; the distinctive characteristics of a color as seen in the visible spectrum, such as green or red

Optical mixture: when the eye blends two colors that are placed near one another, creating a new color

of photography and the restrictions of their traditional academic training by continuing to question what the purpose of art should be. The French poet Charles Baudelaire declared that "As the photographic industry became the refuge of all failed painters with too little talent, or too lazy to complete their studies...the badly applied advances of photography...have greatly contributed to the impoverishment of French artistic genius." Others, however, saw positive opportunities, and experimented with the artistic potential of the new medium.

For instance, the American artist Thomas Eakins (1844–1916) was a student at the first American art academy, the Pennsylvania Academy of the Fine Arts. When he started teaching there in 1876, and later became its director in 1882, his methods were controversial because of their deviation from traditional European approaches. Rather than following the standard artistic norm—intense study of the nude figure, Classical statuary and the work of earlier artists—Eakins promoted the study of anatomy through photographs and through observation of dissections.

Influenced by the photography of Eadweard Muybridge and his study of horses and humans in motion, he, too, observed the human body in motion through photography. Eakins superimposed several exposures of a jumping man onto one negative (**3.8.8**), creating a tool with which to improve his understanding of anatomy for his paintings. Due to his unconventional teaching methods, which

included allowing women to study the full male nude, Eakins was forced to resign in 1886.

Impressionism

The artists who came to be called Impressionists worked in individual, sometimes very different styles, but they were united in rejecting the formal approach of the art taught at the Academy in Paris. Their art attempted not so much to portray exactly and realistically such scenes as a landscape or life in a city (although they did depict those subjects) as to capture the light and sensations produced by the scene. The Impressionists formed a group to show their work together outside of the official Salon, in eight exhibitions held between 1874 and 1886. Their subject matter was scenes of everyday life: rural landscapes, and life in the modern and growing cities of France—especially scenes of the middle classes engaged in leisure pursuits. The Impressionists were often intent on capturing the essence of moments in time, and many of them painted *en plein air*, made possible by the advent of tubed containers for oil paint.

Before the Impressionists, artists who followed traditional methods of painting gave their work a smooth surface, often finishing paintings with a topcoat of varnish, so that the application of the paint was not evident. Impressionists, on the other hand, chose to reveal their brushstrokes. The almost sketchy, unfinished appearance of many Impressionist works breaks away from the academic tradition of simply creating an illusion of three-dimensional space on the canvas. Instead, Impressionists flattened space, welcomed the texture created by paint, and often allowed the canvas to be seen beneath the painting. Many Impressionist paintings do indeed have an apparently unfinished quality, because the artists were interested in capturing instantaneous moments rather than creating a highly finished, technically flawless piece of work.

The Impressionists lived during a time in which great strides were made in the studies of optics and color theory, which changed the way these artists painted. They discovered that if they applied individual colors in their purest form to the canvas, rather than mixing them beforehand on a **palette**, the colors remained more intense. Through observation they realized that objects are not one single color, but are made up of many variations of color. To imitate this, Impressionist artists placed brushstrokes of different colors next to one another, knowing that the viewer's eye would blend the disparate **hues**—a process known as **optical mixture**. Often, too, Impressionists reinterpreted the bright natural light of day in their paintings by applying a layer of white paint as a base coat.

The Impressionists were also influenced by the formal qualities of photography and Japanese **woodblock** prints, such as sharp framing and **cropping** of scenes (see: The Influence of Japanese Woodcuts on the Impressionists, p. 488). They adopted unusual vantage points and cropped scenes in ways resembling these media, including arranging space within an image using **asymmetry** and the layering of objects. While photographers could capture a single moment in time, the Impressionists tried to capture the sensations of such moments: the atmosphere, colors, light, and individual impressions.

Whereas many painters in the past, working within their studios, had taken the upper classes as their subject, the Impressionists instead often painted outdoors and chose to capture the urban middle classes in such places as bustling cafés. In a period when prosperous people had more leisure time than ever before, the Impressionists depicted Parisians, for example, dancing, drinking, swimming, and attending the opera or the ballet. Such paintings as *Bal du Moulin de la Galette* by Pierre-Auguste Renoir (1841–1919) were intended to transport viewers into a world of beauty and pleasure (**3.8.9**). Renoir shows people at a popular outdoor café in the Montmartre district of Paris. The dappled sunlight falls through the trees onto the scene as if to create a **rhythm** that reflects the joyfulness of the gathering. The absence of strong outlines, the feathery

Woodblock: a relief print process where the image is carved into a block of wood

Cropping: trimming the edges of an image, or composing it so that part of the subject matter is cut off

Asymmetry: a type of design in which balance is achieved by elements that contrast and complement one another without being the same on either side of an axis

Rhythm: the regular or ordered repetition of elements in the work

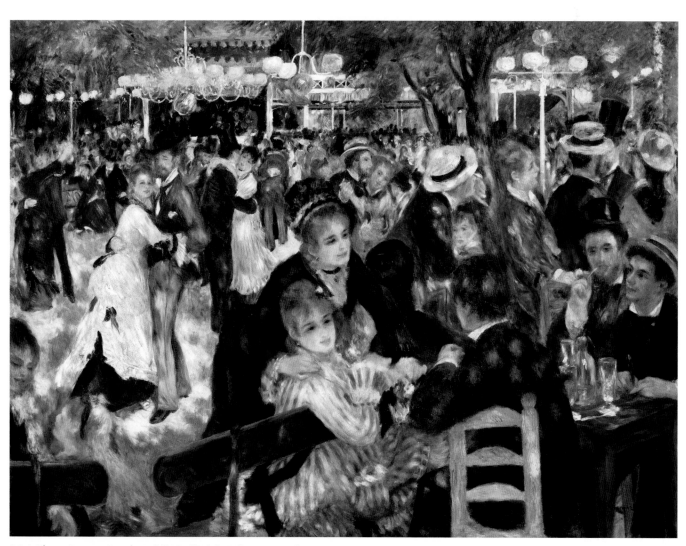

3.8.9 Pierre-Auguste Renoir, *Bal du Moulin de la Galette*, 1876. Oil on canvas, 51⅝ × 68⅞". Musée d'Orsay, Paris, France

The Influence of Japanese Woodcuts on the Impressionists

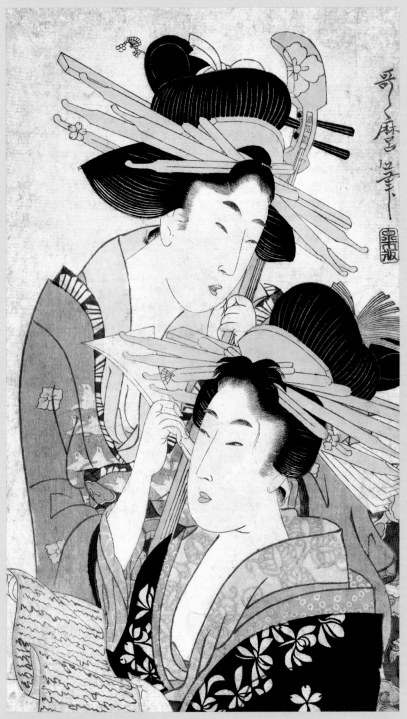

3.8.10 Kitagawa Utamaro, *Two Courtesans*, second half of 18th century. Woodblock print, 12⅝ × 7½". Victoria and Albert Museum, London, England

The art of the Impressionists reflected the world they lived in, and they were inspired by other new art forms that surrounded them in Paris. The influx of woodblock prints from Japan changed the way Impressionist artists perceived and composed their own works.

Japanese prints depicted cropped, asymmetrical scenes, which had a flattened sense of space because objects were emphasized with bold outlines rather than shadows. After studying such prints, the Impressionist painters and other modern artists began to incorporate slanted viewpoints, bright colors, and busy patterns into their work. This influence is known as *Japonisme*.

The American painter Mary Cassatt (1844–1926) lived most of her life in France and exhibited with the Impressionists. After seeing more than one hundred of the Japanese printmaker Kitagawa Utamaro's prints exhibited in Paris in 1890, Cassatt wrote to friends raving about him; later, she began creating prints very much in his style. Cassatt herself had always focused on the daily lives of women in her paintings. A comparison between one of Utamaro's prints (**3.8.10**) and a painting by Cassatt (**3.8.11**), made three years after she had seen the Japanese artist's work in Paris, highlights the techniques Cassatt emulated.

The composition of the two scenes is very similar. Each creates a strong diagonal line from the upper right to the lower left. The musical instrument is gently being played by the lady in the background of Utamaro's print, while in Cassatt's painting the child's foot is gently stroked by her mother's hand. The mother's right arm and that of the musician are both, in contrast to the objects that they hold, strictly vertical.

Both artists use bold lines to create a flattening of space and absence of modeling. In Utamaro's print, lines in the ladies' dresses suggest folds, but also make the women appear as two-dimensional as the writing on the paper one of them holds. Cassatt creates a similar effect with the striped lines on the mother's dress, which lengthen the figure but give her body less volume than the child she holds. The child, in contrast,

brushstrokes, and the use of dark blues and purples instead of black, are characteristic of Renoir's style.

Edgar Degas (1834–1917) was a prolific artist who reveled in experimentation in pastel, charcoal, oil, photography, **lithography**, and sculpture. For his artworks he frequently studied female subjects, including sex workers, singers, and bathers. One of his favorite subjects was ballet dancers, whom he studied during performances, in practice, and backstage (**3.8.12**). Degas's scenes of dancers evoke the everyday quality of a dancer's life, and his composition gives the impression of immediacy, as if the viewer has caught the dancers off guard, primping before their performance. The artist masterfully drew on the surface by holding the pastel in his hand (rather than using a paintbrush), to create a rich texture in which light bounces off the flesh and dresses of the dancers.

Like many of the Impressionists, Degas was inspired by the formal qualities of Japanese prints and photography. Influence from Japanese prints is evident in Degas's dynamic composition, which uses diagonal lines to guide the viewer's eyes around the scene.

Lithography: a print process executed on a flat, unmarred surface, like a stone, in which the image is created using oil-based ink with resistance to water

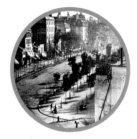

Photographs such as this one by Daguerre, which views a street from above, influenced the Impressionists to look at scenes from various angles:
→ see **2.8.4**, p. 302

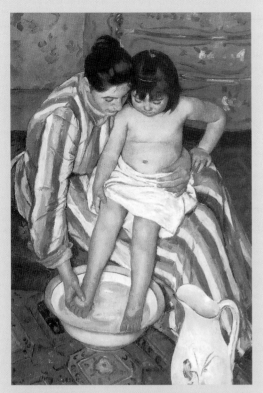

3.8.11 Mary Cassatt, *The Child's Bath*, 1893. Oil on canvas, 39½ × 26″. Art Institute of Chicago, Illinois

has softer body outlines, and skin with a range of values.

The background of Utamaro's print is mostly empty, creating a space behind the ladies apart from some twisting flowers on one of the robes, and crowded calligraphy on the pages at the left. Cassatt fills her background space, but her busy floral patterns echo the flowers in the Japanese work.

Last, Japanese prints often look at their subject from multiple vantage points. Utamaro's ladies are viewed from up close and at the same height, but the bottom of the rearmost lady's dress, the music, and parts of the instrument are seen from above. Similarly, in Cassatt's painting, the viewer looks at the child's torso, the dresser in the background, and at the pitcher in the lower right corner from directly in front at the same height. Yet, simultaneously, the bowl of water and the rug are viewed from above.

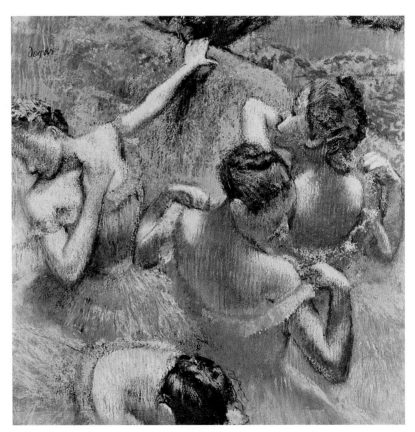

3.8.12 Edgar Degas, *Blue Dancers*, *c.* 1898. Pastel on paper, 25½ × 25½″. The Pushkin State Museum of Fine Arts, Moscow, Russia

The head of the girl on the left and the body of the girl at the bottom of the composition are cropped, a device he learned from studying both Japanese prints and photography. The formal qualities of photography, such as sharp framing and the cropping of the scene, viewing the scene from above (a **bird's eye view**), the lack of even focus across the **picture plane**, and a tendency to flatten the illusion of depth, were mimicked by many modern artists, including Degas. Here the ballet dancers' bodies are cropped and viewed from above; a lack of focus is suggested by the sketchy brushstrokes; and the lack of finish flattens the space.

Berthe Morisot's (1841–1895) sketch-like *The Beach at Nice* (**3.8.13**) shows how painters tried to compete with the photograph's ability to capture instantaneous moments. Morisot exhibited in all but one of the Impressionist exhibitions and was particularly close friends with Édouard Manet, who became her brother-in-law (see **3.8.2**, p. 481). As a female of upper-class status, Morisot did not have access to many of the modern subjects painted by her fellow Impressionists. Therefore, her images are usually of women, children, gardens, or domestic spaces, all subjects she would

see in her daily life. As with many of the Impressionists, Morisot portrayed people doing everyday things, who were unaware of or uninterested in the fact that they were being watched. *The Beach at Nice* shows a young girl playing in the sand at the beach next to a woman reading. Morisot captures the sensations of being at the beach: the bright light, the brisk breeze, and quiet relaxation. Her seemingly quick brushstrokes appear to blur into nothing when one stands close to the painting but transform into objects and shadows when one steps away. The exquisitely painted blue hat in the center of the painting draws the viewer's eye to the little girl, probably Morisot's daughter, Julie. Although the painting appears to have been created *en plein air*, Julie wrote in her journal about how her mother painted watercolors at the beach and then painted this scene back in their hotel room.

Another perspective on the everyday life of the French middle class can be seen in a painting by Gustave Caillebotte (1848–1894) of the newly renovated busy streets of Paris. The artist was a wealthy lawyer as well as a painter, and he supported other Impressionists financially. Caillebotte's *Paris Street: Rainy Day*

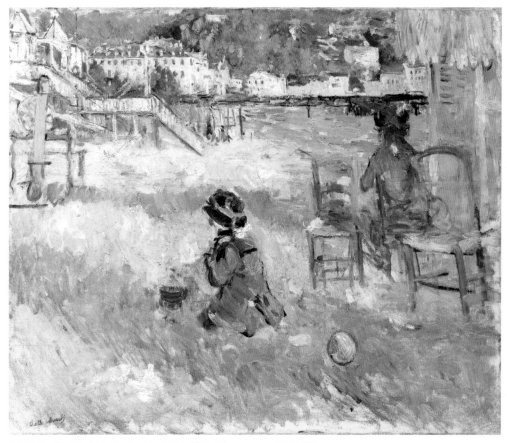

3.8.13 Berthe Morisot, *The Beach at Nice*, 1882. Oil on canvas, 18¼ × 22"

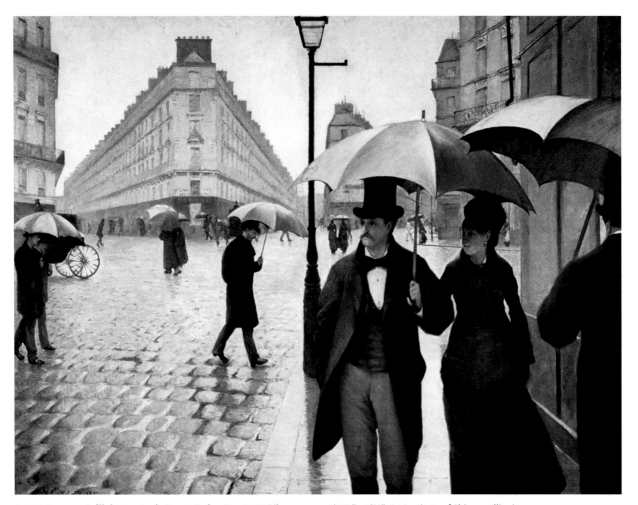

3.8.14 **Gustave Caillebotte**, *Paris Street, Rainy Day*, 1877. Oil on canvas, 6′11½″ × 9′¾″. Art Institute of Chicago, Illinois

(**3.8.14**) shows the results of the massive rebuilding of Paris organized by Baron Haussmann, the prefect or state representative of the region. Under the direction of Napoleon III, Haussmannization involved tearing down much of the medieval city—an action that displaced thousands—and building glorious new boulevards, townhouses, and parks. Caillebotte makes use of **linear perspective** to show how the modern boulevards extend in every direction, like spokes on a wheel. A green lamppost and its shadow extend beyond the height of the canvas, creating a strong vertical line that divides the composition. To the left of the post, very **foreshortened**, is a newly designed apartment building. To the right is a well-dressed couple who, although surrounded by the different classes of people in the city, seem to be alone and in their own world. Caillebotte captures the mood of a rainy day with the cloudy atmosphere and soaked streets and pavement.

The works of Claude Monet (1840–1926) most exemplified the impressionistic brushstrokes for which the group of painters was known. At the first Impressionist exhibition in 1874, his painting *Impression, Sunrise* (1872)—which indicated with only a few brushstrokes the sea, the reflection of the sun, and the boats in the background—helped to give the group their famous name. As his work evolved, Monet made several series of paintings that focused on individual subjects, such as cathedrals, haystacks, poplars, and train stations. Within these series, rather than altering the subject, each work varied slightly in the way it captured mood, light, color, time of day, and atmosphere. In 1890, Monet purchased a house and land in the French town of Giverny, where he designed his own pond filled with water lilies. He created more than 300 water-lily paintings based on his pond. While at first these paintings might seem similar, they are each unique. Monet would paint his garden from different viewpoints, at times including a willow tree or a Japanese bridge from his garden (**3.8.15**, p. 492). The pond flowers might be seen from a distance or up close, from above or horizontally, and

Linear perspective: a system using converging imaginary sight lines to create the illusion of depth

Foreshortening: a perspective technique that depicts a form—often distorting or reducing it—at an angle that is not parallel to the picture plane, in order to convey the illusion of depth

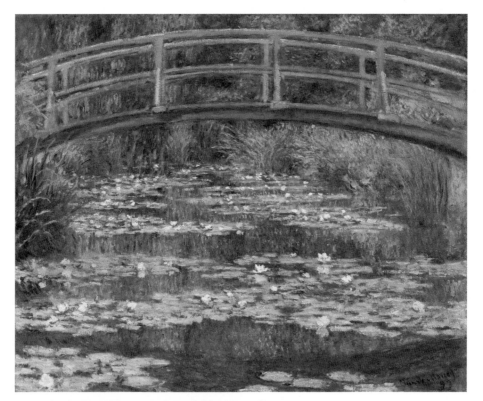

3.8.15 Claude Monet, *The Japanese Footbridge*, 1899. Oil on canvas, 32 × 40 ". National Gallery of Art, Washington, D.C.

he might focus on single flowers or large groups. Eventually, Monet's paintings would grow so large that viewers would feel as if they were part of the pond itself, foreshadowing twentieth-century movements such as **Abstract Expressionism**. To honor the sacrifices of the French people during World War I, and memorialize those that were lost, Monet created his largest water-lily project, which he envisioned as a bouquet for France (**3.8.16**). The project consists of eight panels placed in two elliptical rooms, creating a symbol for infinity, as the space forever changes with and responds to nature. Rather than looking at the water lilies and the pond, the display places viewers within the pond itself.

3.8.16 Claude Monet, *Waterlilies*, *c.* 1914–18. Oil on canvas. Musée de l'Orangerie, Paris, France

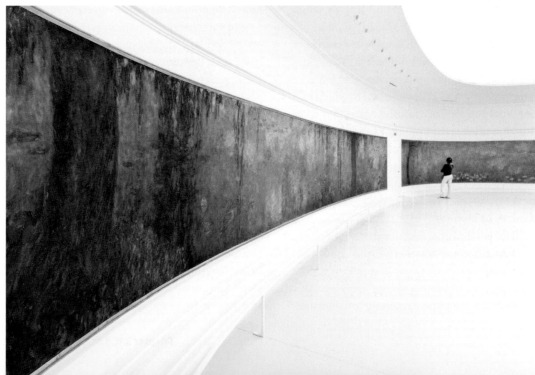

Post-Impressionism

By the 1880s, the once-revolutionary Impressionism had gained great public popularity amongst the newly risen middle class. Yet the Academy critics accused the Impressionists of lacking discipline and training, and of having no intellectual substance other than a shallow preoccupation with the depiction of beauty. Impressionist artists responded to these criticisms in different ways: Monet developed his serial approach, in which he analyzed atmosphere rather than subject matter; Renoir returned to Classical models and created a series of bathers. The movement that resulted—that of Post-Impressionism—consisted of artists who had been exposed to, and often participated in, the Impressionist movement, but who wanted to differentiate themselves from what was then perceived to be the simplicity of the Impressionists. They preferred instead to emphasize **abstract** qualities or subjective content in their artworks.

The French painter Paul Cézanne (1839–1906) developed a new type of landscape painting through intense study of Mont Sainte-Victoire, a mountain he could see from his studio (and childhood home) in Aix-en-Provence, where he worked for much of his adult life. Cézanne made several paintings of this mountain, and worked on some of them for years. By gradually adding brushstrokes to reflect the mountain's changing atmosphere and weather conditions, Cézanne sought to construct the essence of the mountain as it appeared over time, rather than at a single moment.

Cézanne created the structure of his landscape in a very different way from earlier painters. He conceived a view of nature in which the subject was analyzed from multiple views, forms became abstracted, and planes shifted. For example, Cézanne utilized his understanding of atmospheric perspective to blend warm and cool colors within the same structure, as in the mountain (**3.8.17**). This creates a push–pull effect for viewers, as the warm hues of the mountain come toward us, and cool colors recede. The tree in the foreground creates a similar experience as we look at it, a feeling of being pulled into the depth of the painting and then being pushed forward, as if the image has been flattened. The upper branch seems to echo the outline of the distant mountain, bringing it closer to us.

The French painter Paul Gauguin (1848–1903) was a successful stockbroker, but in his mid-30s, he gave up his career and left his wife and children to become a painter. Modern

Abstract: art imagery that departs from recognizable images of the natural world

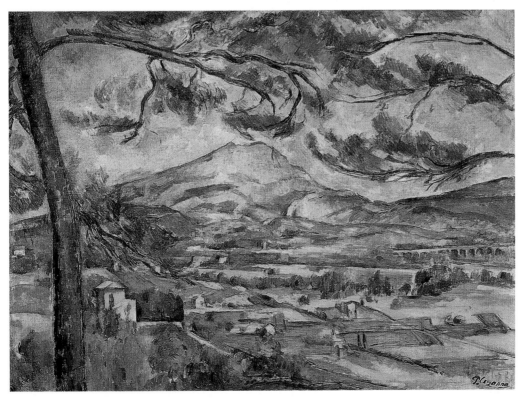

3.8.17 Paul Cézanne, *Mont Sainte-Victoire*, *c.* 1886–88. Oil on canvas, 26 × 36¼".
Courtauld Gallery, London, England

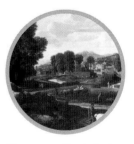

Cézanne greatly admired the earlier French painter Nicolas Poussin. Compare how the two artists created structure in their landscapes:
→ see **3.6.30**, p. 464

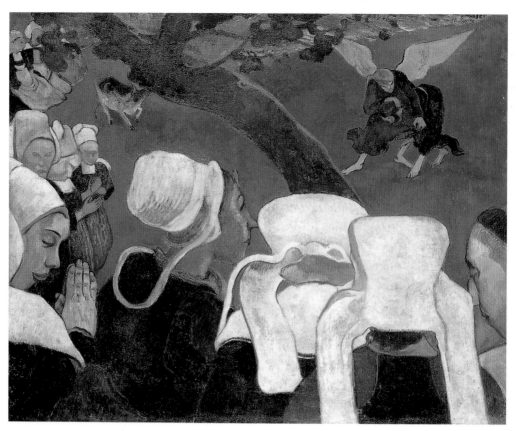

3.8.18 Paul Gauguin, *The Vision after the Sermon (Jacob Wrestling with the Angel)*, 1888. Oil on canvas, 28½ × 35⅞". Scottish National Gallery, Edinburgh, Scotland

so-called civilization was, in Gauguin's view, materialistic and lacking in spirituality. This belief led him to seek to portray people whom he considered pure, untouched by materialistic values. *The Vision after the Sermon* shows the pious people of the small town of Pont-Aven dressed in their Sunday clothes (**3.8.18**). The scene in the upper right depicts the sermon the townspeople have just heard, that of the biblical story of Jacob wrestling with the angel. The spaces are abruptly flattened, the figures lack volume and are closely cropped. Yet rather than just showing a scene from everyday life, Gauguin expresses what is in these people's minds: a vision. The way the tree slices the scene in two (one section for the dreamers and one for the dream) is a device Gauguin observed in Japanese prints. Some scholars believe that Gauguin depicted himself as the figure with closed eyes in the lower right of the canvas, as if he too is experiencing the vision. Gauguin once said, "I shut my eyes in order to see." The bold red charges this image with a vivid power that speaks to the intense spirituality of the women and the drama of their vision, but also suggests the violence of the struggle they are witnessing between Jacob and the angel. Gauguin's ability

to use color as an expressive element would greatly influence later artists, particularly the Symbolists (see pp. 496–97).

After leaving Pont-Aven in 1888, Gauguin shared a house with the Dutch painter Vincent van Gogh (1853–1890) for two months in the southern French town of Arles. The two artists challenged and annoyed each other. While Van Gogh had envisioned an artistic exchange, a brotherhood of painters, Gauguin made it clear that he felt his work was superior to the gentler Van Gogh's. Van Gogh's mood fluctuated between pure joy in their working closely alongside each other and frustration at Gauguin's intense bouts of criticism and anger.

Shortly before Christmas of the same year, Vincent van Gogh was hospitalized with a severed left earlobe. Scholars debate over whether this was a self-inflicted injury or whether it was the result of a fight with Gauguin. After this, he and Gauguin never spoke again. Gauguin took his desire to study people of a supposedly pure and primitive nature to Tahiti, where he painted the locals, including what are now considered highly controversial nudes of his teenage female lovers.

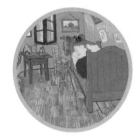

Van Gogh depicted the bedroom he lived in Arles: see **1.1.12**, p. 40

Famous to us now, yet largely unremarked upon in their time, the paintings of Vincent van Gogh express strong emotions. Yet, unlike Gauguin, Van Gogh claimed he could not invent images, but instead painted emotion into what he saw. He once stated:

I cannot work without a model. I won't say that I don't turn my back on nature to transform a study into a picture, arranging the colors, exaggerating, simplifying, but when it comes to form I'm too fearful of departing from the possible and the true…I exaggerate, sometimes I make changes…but I do not invent the whole picture.

Van Gogh, who struggled with mental illness all his life, painted *Starry Night* during a stay in an asylum; the scene includes elements of the real-life view from his window (**3.8.19**). The artist infused the scene with his own emotions: one can sense the very physical act of applying the thick paint (**impasto**), and Van Gogh's intense energy, in swirls that show movement in the sky and the light emanating from the stars. A cypress tree, resembling flames reaching

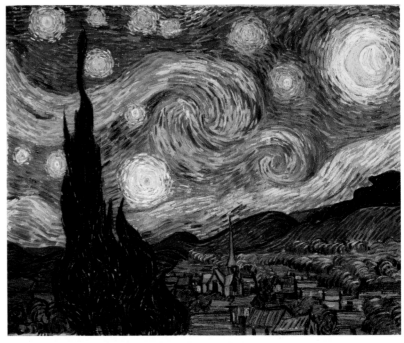

3.8.19 Vincent van Gogh, *Starry Night*, 1889. Oil on canvas, 29 × 36½". MoMA, New York

up to the sky, fills much of the left side of the canvas. The church in the distance may hint at Van Gogh's personal trials with religion; some believe it relates to his childhood church in The Netherlands.

In a letter to his brother Theo, Van Gogh wrote of how looking at stars put him into a state of dreaming:

Why, I say to myself, should spots of light in the firmament be less accessible to us than the black spots on the map of France? Just as we take the train to go to Tarascon or Rouen [French towns], we take death to go to a star.

His use of color, bold texture, and form in this work have been variously interpreted as exuberant and hopeful, but also as expressing his emotional suffering; in 1890, the year after this painting, Van Gogh shot himself in the chest with a revolver and died two days later.

Camille Claudel (1864–1943) was one of the most talented sculptors of the late nineteenth and early twentieth centuries. In *The Waltz* (**3.8.20**) one can see her ability to vary texture, in the smooth skin of the woman's back compared to the folds of the cloth that falls from her waist. In addition to technical acumen, she created intensely lyrical compositions. In *The Waltz*, the physicality and sensuality of the couple create a rhythmic energy as they seem to glide through their dance.

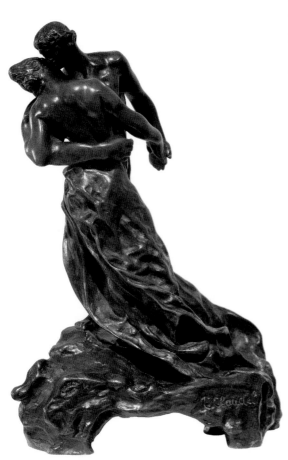

3.8.20 Camille Claudel, *The Waltz*, 1889–1905 (dated 1895). Bronze, 9⅞ × 5¾ × 4". Cast Eugène Blot, Paris, No. 4. Loan of the Bayerische Landesbrandversicherung AG to the Bayerische Staatsgemäldesammlungen, Munich, Germany

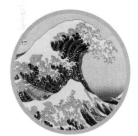

Van Gogh admired Japanese woodblock prints, for example "The Great Wave off Shore at Kanagawa" by Hokusai. Its form seems echoed in the turbulent night sky of *Starry Night*: → see **2.3.5**, p. 215

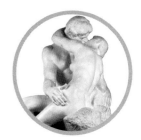

Auguste Rodin epitomizes the modern sculptor because he studied live models rather than copying Classical nudes: → see **1.2.16**, p. 59

Impasto: paint applied in thick layers

Claudel trained in the workshop of Auguste Rodin, and quickly became his lover as well. Through Rodin's connections, she met important people, and received commissions she might not otherwise have had. However, there was a clear discrepancy, based on gender, in the way that Rodin and Claudel were treated professionally. Rodin's works were often of nude and sexualized figures, yet his works were judged more on their technical skill than were Claudel's. A government representative who had purchased many of Rodin's erotic nudes remarked that *The Waltz* was too erotic, and suggested that Claudel should put clothes on the figures. One writer proclaimed, "In this group of a waltzing couple, they seem to want to finish the dance so they can go to bed and make love."

3.8.21 Henry Ossawa Tanner, *Banjo Lesson*, 1893. Oil on canvas, 48 × 35½".
Hampton University Museum, Hampton, Virginia

Additionally, while there is no evidence that *The Waltz* was made in reference to the love affair between the two sculptors, Claudel's work was often disproportionately seen as an emotional response to her relationship with Rodin, while no one ever thought to view his work in such a light. Unfortunately, Camille Claudel's family forcibly placed her in an asylum for the last thirty years of her life. The degree and legitimacy of her mental illness is difficult for scholars to determine, but the fact that she was institutionalized has further clouded all interpretations of her work.

Henry Ossawa Tanner (1859–1937) was born into a middle-class African American family. He was educated at the Pennsylvania Academy of the Fine Arts, where his professor, the painter Thomas Eakins, encouraged him to study anatomy and observe nature closely. Later Tanner moved to Paris, where he was influenced by French painters, including Courbet. Just as Courbet's *Stonebreakers* showed an older man training a younger worker, Tanner's *Banjo Lesson* shows the passing of knowledge between generations (**3.8.21**). In a humble home, a young African American boy is patiently being taught by his grandfather to play the banjo.

Tanner's painting challenges the stereotype then common in America, of smiling Black men as simple-minded entertainers. The artist creates a dignified image of a poor African American family by showing a thoughtful Black man as a teacher, and an intelligent Black child engaged in learning. Tanner sets a calm scene with natural objects and earthy colors, but he symbolizes the boy's spiritual and mental growth with the light coming in through the window, creating a soft rhythm, which can be likened to the act of playing the banjo.

Symbolism

Symbolist painters were inspired by the use of emotionally charged and often dreamlike images. Although they frequently made use of psychologically potent symbols, such as biblical or mythological subjects, and women in the guise of a virgin or seductress, they also engaged in individual explorations of otherworldliness. They created works that often look like visions and express spiritualism. Like Gauguin, who greatly inspired the Symbolists, these artists often saw the role of the artist as a guide who reveals universal inner truths.

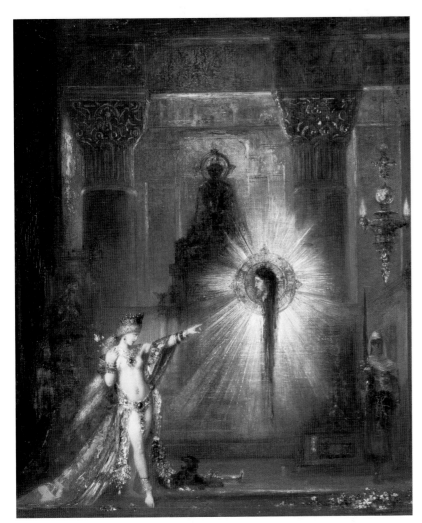

3.8.22 Gustave Moreau, *The Apparition*, *c.* 1876. Oil on canvas, 22 × 18⅜".
Fogg Art Museum, Harvard Art Museums, Cambridge, Massachusetts

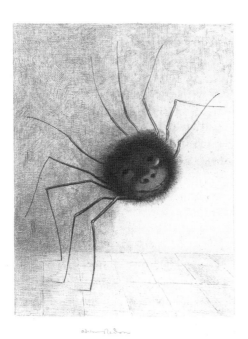

3.8.23 Odilon Redon, *The Spider*, 1887, Print, 11 × 8⅝".
Rijksmuseum, Amsterdam

Gustave Moreau (1826–1898) painted the biblical figure Salome sensually dancing—a true *femme fatale* (a woman whose sexual allure is believed to be dangerous to men)—in front of King Herod (shown on the left, **3.8.22**). She points toward the head of St. John the Baptist, dripping with blood. Light emanates from the floating head, suggesting it may be an apparition or a vision of her desire. However, the scene is ambiguous. The soldier on the right holds a bloodied sword, implying that John the Baptist has just been killed and offered to the temptress. Symbolist writers and painters often influenced one another. This painting was given a lengthy description by Joris-Karl Huysmans (1848–1907) in his famous novel *À rebours* (*About Nature*):

> She was no longer the mere performer who wrests a cry of desire and of passion from an old man by a perverted twisting of her loins; who destroys the energy and breaks the will of a king by trembling breasts and quivering belly. She became, in a sense, the symbolic deity of indestructible lust.

The French painter Odilon Redon (1840–1916) was also discussed in Huysman's novel. Between 1970 and 1890, Redon rose to fame with his studies in black. Redon stated that "black is the most essential color," believing that the absence of color was the best way to access one's innermost curiosities and dreams. These so-called *noirs* were explorations of darkness and shadows through fantastical, sometimes frightening, subject matter. *The Spider* (**3.8.23**) was created purely with black on a white page, filled by a ten-legged spider that grimaces disconcertingly. Redon's process for this series often began with close study of animals or insects and then transforming them into monsters that expressed different emotions. This grinning spider bares its teeth, while another of his spiders has teary eyes and appears to be crying. Ironically, Redon switched fully to oil and pastels in 1890 and created some of the most colorful artworks seen during the turn of the century.

Fin de Siècle and Art Nouveau

Fin de siècle (from the French, "end of the century") refers to the period from the end of the nineteenth century to the start of World War I in 1914. This was a time of great social change in Europe. A growing middle class had sufficient income to enjoy the pleasures that

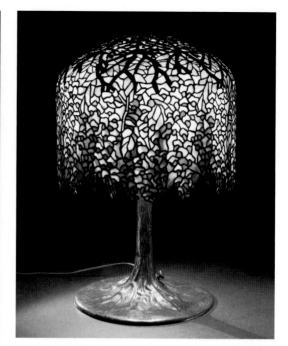

3.8.25 Tiffany Studios, "Wisteria" table lamp, *c.* 1905. Leaded glass and patinated bronze, height 26⅞"

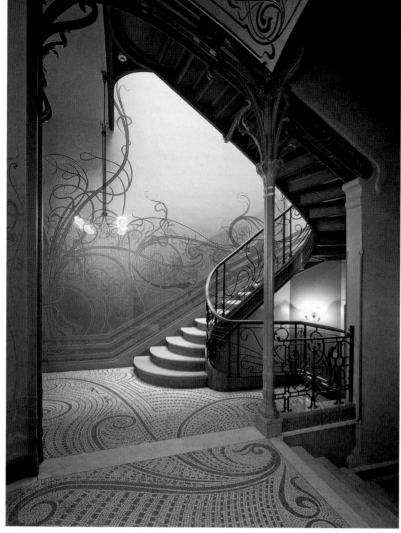

3.8.24 Victor Horta, stairway of Tassel House, Brussels, Belgium, 1892–93

Decorative: intentionally making an artwork pleasant or attractive

Organic: having irregular forms and shapes, as though derived from living organisms

Mosaic: a picture or pattern created by fixing together small pieces of stone, glass, tile, etc.

Cartoon: a full-scale preparatory drawing for a painting or tapestry; from the Italian *cartone*, meaning "large sheet of paper"

life had to offer. As they faced the new century, however, some were anxious (and rightly so, in view of the war that came a decade later) about the changes it would bring. In art and design, the Art Nouveau style emphasized **decorative** pattern and applied it to traditional fine arts (such as painting and sculpture), decorative arts (such as furniture, glass, and ceramics), and architecture and interior design. Art Nouveau is characterized by **organic** flowing lines, gold decoration, and the simulation of natural forms.

The Belgian architect Victor Horta (1861–1947) designed a home for Emile Tassel infused with elements that would come to epitomize Art Nouveau (**3.8.24**). Horta used new, modern materials, such as cast steel and glass. He created a home in which form and light seem to be in constant motion, even alive, like the organic forms that inspired him. The elegant staircase twists like a roller coaster and widens as it spills onto the floor. Further spirals flood the walls and the **mosaic** floor, creating an eternally active space.

Louis Comfort Tiffany brought Art Nouveau to America with works whose designs were derived from complex forms found in nature. His "Wisteria" lamp from *c.* 1905 is made with leaded glass (**3.8.25**). This process involved creating a **cartoon** of the design, transferring it to a form (made of wood or plaster) in the shape of the shade, cutting the glass pieces, wrapping them in copper foil, and soldering them together. The Wisteria lamp used 2,000 separate pieces of glass. The thick bronze vine at the top of the shade highlighted the fact that there was no opening at the top, because electrical lighting no longer required venting of a flame. The bronze base mimics a tree trunk from which the glorious colors of the wisteria grow forth. It was not known until the twenty-first century that Clara Driscoll, who had been the head of Tiffany's Women's Glass Cutting Department, was also the designer of many of his lamps, including Wisteria. When they were made, Tiffany lamps sold for about $400. In 2014, two Wisteria lamps sold for more than $1 million each.

By the beginning of the twentieth century, artists had begun to move away from purely realistic forms, to more abstracted and symbolic scenes.

Explore Further   The Modern Aesthetic: Realism to *Fin de Siècle*

Realism

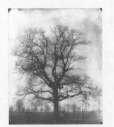

2.8.6b William Henry Fox Talbot, *Oak Tree in Winter*, c. 1842 → p. 303

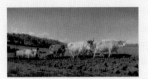

1.9.13a Rosa Bonheur, *Plowing in the Nivernais: The Dressing of the Vines*, 1849 → p. 155

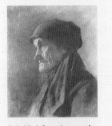

2.1.13 Léon Augustin Lhermitte, *An Elderly Peasant Woman*, c. 1878 → p. 185

Impressionism

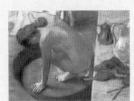

2.1.16 Edgar Degas, *The Tub*, 1886 → p. 187

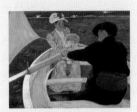

1.4.13 Mary Cassatt, *The Boating Party*, 1893–94 → p. 90

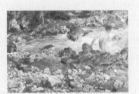

2.2.19 John Singer Sargent, *Mountain Stream*, c. 1912–14 → p. 205

Post-Impressionism and Symbolism

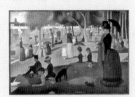

4.4.12 Georges Seurat, *Sunday on La Grande Jatte*, 1884–86 → p. 587

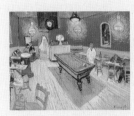

1.4.28 Vincent van Gogh, *The Night Café*, 1888 → p. 99

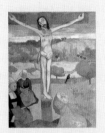

1.4.31 Paul Gauguin, *The Yellow Christ*, 1889 → p. 101

Art Nouveau

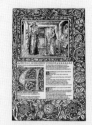

2.7.11 Morris and Burne-Jones, *Works of Geoffrey Chaucer*, 1896 → p. 289

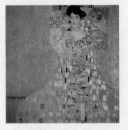

0.0.14 Gustav Klimt, *Portrait of Adele Bloch-Bauer I*, 1907 → p. 25

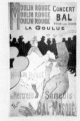

2.7.16 Henri de Toulouse-Lautrec, *La Goulue at the Moulin Rouge*, 1891 → p. 292

Your turn

How do these works relate to the ideas discussed in this chapter?

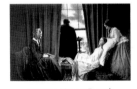

1.7.13a Henry Peach Robinson, *Fading Away*, 1858 → p. 138

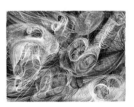

1.1.17 Georgiana Houghton, *Glory be to God*, 1864 → p. 43

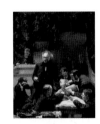

4.4.2 Thomas Eakins, *Portrait of Dr. Samuel D. Gross (The Gross Clinic)*, 1875 → p. 581

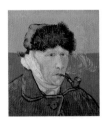

4.9.3 Vincent van Gogh, *Self-Portrait with Bandaged Ear and Pipe*, 1889 → p. 650

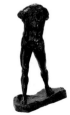

4.8.16 Auguste Rodin, *Walking Man*, c. 1890–95 → p. 641

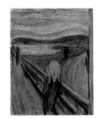

1.10.11 Edvard Munch, *The Scream*, 1893 → p. 170

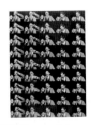

1.5.17 Thomas Edison and W. K. Dickson, *Fred Ott's Sneeze*, 1894 → p. 113

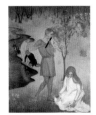

1.3.9 Beda Stjernschantz, *Pastoral (Primavera)*, 1897 → p. 71

3.9
Late Modern and Early Contemporary Art in the Twentieth Century

Modernism, Modernist: a radically new twentieth-century art and architectural movement that embraced modern subjects, industrial materials, and a machine aesthetic

Dada: an anarchic anti-art and anti-war art movement in Europe and the US that, in reaction to World War I, reveled in absurdity and irrationality

Surrealism: an artistic movement in the 1920s and later; its works were inspired by dreams and the subconscious

American Scene: a naturalistic style of painting in the US from the 1920s to 1950s that celebrated American themes, locations, and virtues

Abstract: art imagery that departs from recognizable images of the natural world

Expressionism, Expressionistic: an artistic style, at its height in 1920s Europe, devoted to representing subjective emotions and experiences instead of objective or external reality

Avant-garde: an early twentieth-century emphasis on artistic innovation, which challenged accepted values, traditions, and techniques

Experiments in **Modernism** occurred on both sides of the Atlantic in the first decades of the twentieth century with artistic experiments in both form and content that responded to personal experience and cultural events. The devastation of World War I spurred the creation of European movements in the 1920s that were very distinct from those inspired by the 1929 Great Depression in the United States. The art of the European **Dadaists** and **Surrealists** reacted against the evils of war and what these artists saw as the corruption pervading modern society by making attacks on art itself and by exploring the psyche, while **American Scene** artists chose to respond to the suffering surrounding them through the portrayal of subjects and spaces close to their heart. After World War II, the center of the art world shifted to the US, where many European Modernists had emigrated to escape persecution.

The world that emerged from World War II was radically changed. Millions of people had been killed and hundreds of thousands displaced. When the war was over, the great powers of Europe—Great Britain, Germany, France, Spain, and Italy—found their societies devastated by the destruction of years of war. Two new super-powers now dominated the global markets. The United States had become an economic powerhouse based on free enterprise and capitalism. On the other hand, the Soviet Union, which now controlled much of central Europe, adopted a centrally planned system of economic management and Communism, and focused on rivaling the industrial might of America in what came to be called the Cold War.

After World War II, the global expansion in commerce and politics was paralleled by the fact that territories that until then had been colonized by European countries (for example, India under Britain) gained political independence to become new nations in their own right. These developing nations promoted their own cultural traditions, including Muslim, Hindu, and Buddhist religions. People emigrated (forcibly or by choice) from Africa, Asia, Latin America, and throughout Europe, bringing their belief systems and customs to different countries, the populations of which had previously been unfamiliar with them.

The Modern period of art (c. 1860–1960) was followed by the Contemporary period (1960–present). Artists continued to respond to events occurring in the wider world, and also reacted to the styles and approaches of earlier art movements. Modernist artists since the Impressionists had been moving away from producing strictly recognizable imagery. During this time period, formal experiments, such as **abstraction**, allowed artists revolutionary ways to express their ideas though unconventional depictions of the world. Artists working in the contemporary period experimented seemingly without limit and in a variety of ways.

Expressionism

From around 1905 to around 1920, some artists developed a style that came to be known as **Expressionism**, in which they explored ways of portraying emotions to their fullest intensity by exaggerating and emphasizing the colors and shapes of objects. Expressionists were concerned with the representation of objects and the world, but they emphasized inner states of feeling. Expressionist artists tried to depict what they felt rather than what they saw, with sometimes unconventional results.

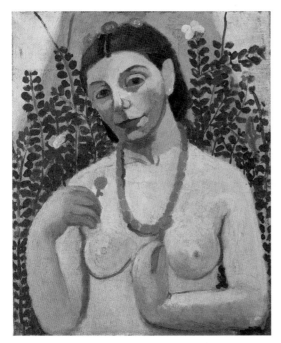

3.9.1 Paula Modersohn-Becker, *Self-Portrait as a Half-Length Nude with Amber Necklace II*, 1906. Oil on canvas, 24 × 19⅞". Kunstmuseum Basel, Switzerland.

Making self-portraits was central to Expressionism because artists could explore a great variety and intensity of emotions through repeated studies. Self-portraits also allow artists to express both the inner and outer worlds that they know most fully. For instance, when making a portrait of someone else, an artist can only guess at the other person's mood, thoughts, or motivations. While making a self-portrait, however, the artist can decide which moods or motivations to show and how best to do so.

The German Expressionist artist Paula Modersohn-Becker (1876–1907) made several self-portraits (**3.9.1**). She also has the distinction of being one of the first women to make nude self-portraits. Her style reflects the flattened forms, reduced details, heavy outlines, and solid geometry she saw in earlier **avant-garde** styles of such artists as Paul Cézanne and Paul Gauguin in Paris (see pp. 493–94). At the same time, her work balances delicate details in gesture and mood with the physical substance of her body.

Two important groups of German Expressionist artists were **Der Blaue Reiter** and **Die Brücke**. Both groups rejected **Classical** approaches in favor of radical experimentation. They were among the first artists to make **non-objective**, or completely abstract, art that focuses on shapes, designs, and colors

rather than recognizable imagery. The daring approaches of the German Expressionists were part of the revolutionary artistic developments of the early twentieth century.

German artist Ernst Ludwig Kirchner (1880–1938) adopted a deliberately raw painting style in his search for meaning beyond surface appearance. Kirchner used flat **planes** of intense color, simplified forms, and rough, even aggressive, brushwork. His painting *Street, Berlin* reflects his belief that art should come from direct experience (**3.9.2**). The figures he saw in this street scene appear dressed for a night on the town (the women are likely prostitutes), but the similar clothing and mask-like faces in the background drain them of individuality, almost as if they were clones. In this painting, Kirchner seems to ask why the modern city is so alienating. Kirchner made this painting shortly after Die Brücke disbanded. This group intended their new mode of expression to form a bridge between the past, present, and future. They also believed the decadence and dehumanization of society could only be counteracted by the younger generation—such artists as themselves.

Der Blaue Reiter: ("The Blue Rider") a German Expressionist movement (1911–14) in Munich; used abstract forms to suggest spiritual content as a contrast to corruption and materialism of the times

Die Brücke: ("The Bridge") a German Expressionist movement of painters and printmakers formed in Dresden (1905–13) with the aim of defying anything Classical and using art as a bridge between the past, present, and a utopian future

Classical: ancient Greek and Roman; art that conforms to Greek and Roman models, or is based on rational construction and emotional equilibrium

Non-objective: art that does not depict a recognizable subject

Plane: a flat, two-dimensional surface; planes can be implied in a composition by areas that face toward, parallel to, or away from a light source

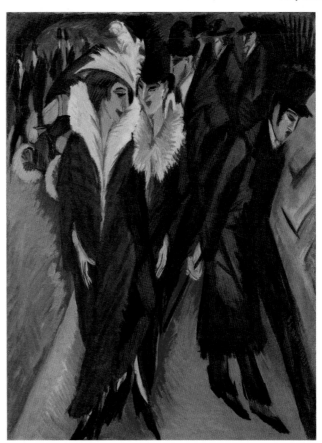

3.9.2 Ernst Ludwig Kirchner, *Street, Berlin*, 1913. Oil on canvas, 47½ × 35⅞". MoMA, New York

The Revolution of Color and Form

Henri Matisse (1869–1954) and Pablo Picasso (1881–1973) are very important figures now permanently associated with the development of modern art. Matisse, who was French, had earned some professional notoriety by the time Picasso moved from Spain to Paris in 1904. Picasso left behind his academic training in **representational** art to embrace the brave new world of experimental approaches he found there. Meanwhile, Matisse was working in Paris, exploring the expressive potential of color and its relation to form—as he was to do throughout his career. Matisse and Picasso developed a mutual respect for each other, but they were also rivals because each wanted to be considered the leader of the progressive art world. As it turns out, both artists enjoyed extremely productive careers and have been extraordinarily influential: Matisse for his expressive forms, **decorative** style, and bold use of color; Picasso for his radical handling of form and shape.

Henri Matisse

The colors in Matisse's *Joy of Life*—orange and green bodies, pink trees, a multicolored sky—are not strictly **naturalistic** (**3.9.3**). These departures from everyday appearances are intentional. Artists' inspired choice of colors varies according to what they see or imagine. For Matisse, color was principally a way to express emotions. In fact, Matisse founded a movement now known as **Fauvism** (from the French *fauve*, "wild beast"). The group's name derived from a comment by a critic who mocked their fiercely unconventional work, especially in comparison to Classical approaches, because the bold colors the Fauves used did not correspond to natural appearances. Matisse continued to explore the potential of pure color throughout his career. He often emphasized colors and made them vibrant and intense rather than rendering them as subdued or blending them to make a scene look more natural. Matisse was interested in making an artwork, not in imitating nature or copying external appearances. He was not trying, as many artists from earlier times had primarily done, to persuade us into believing that we are looking through a window onto a real world. In response to a viewer who complained that one of his portraits did not resemble the dimensions of an actual woman, Matisse said, "I did not create a woman. I made a picture."

In *The Red Studio* Matisse has included a lot of information about his working environment, but he has also left a lot out

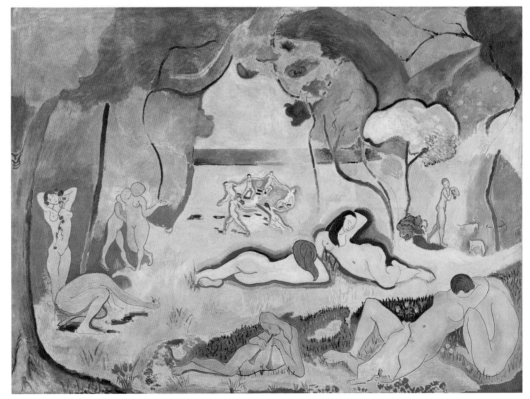

3.9.3 Henri Matisse, *Joy of Life*, 1905–6. Oil on canvas, 5'9⅛" × 7'10⅞".
Barnes Foundation, Merion, Pennsylvania

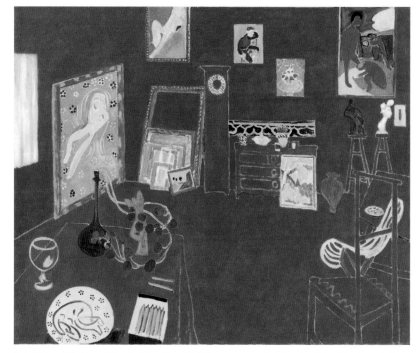

3.9.4 Henri Matisse, *The Red Studio*, 1911. Oil on canvas, 5'11¼" × 7'2¼". MoMA, New York

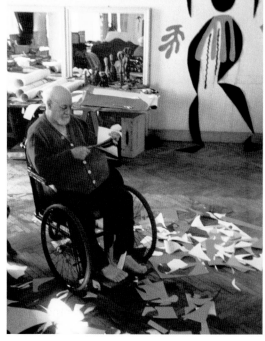

3.9.5 Henri Matisse in his studio, 1953

(**3.9.4**). He accurately shows a number of the paintings, sculptures, and ceramics he had been working on. The space is filled with an intense red; this makes the artworks stand out against the walls and floor, which have been collapsed into a single flat plane. The furniture is also red, with subtle gold outlines indicating the edges and details. Matisse is keenly concerned with the use of color to convey his experience of place.

When Matisse worked on a painting he generally started with complex **sketches** and, over time, simplified the image by eliminating details and paring down the composition. He also used paper cutouts as preparatory sketches, pinning them on a canvas to help him place the figures in a composition. In early 1941 Matisse was diagnosed with cancer of the intestines. After his treatment, he used a wheelchair (**3.9.5**), making painting any large-scale work impossible. So Matisse began to present the cutouts as the completed works themselves. He created his cutouts from paper his assistants would paint in bright colors; the artist would then use scissors as if drawing the elegant lines of the shapes he was making, creating images filled with movement and life.

There seems to have been no limit to the ideas Matisse could fashion in this way. He used cutouts to design tapestries, the interior decoration of buildings, and stained-glass windows. His final cutout compositions were on a large scale, some covering an area of more than 87 sq. ft. Toward the end of a long career, Matisse found that simple scissors and paper offered a way to help him continue, once again, finding new ways to experiment with line and color.

Picasso, Braque, and Cubism

In the early twentieth century, shortly after Matisse was experimenting with new ways of using color in the 1900s, Picasso and the French artist Georges Braque (1882–1963) revolutionized the way artworks were made. They concentrated on their underlying **geometric form** and the construction of pictorial space, and together eventually developed the style known as **Cubism**. Instead of showing conventionally realistic objects in the illusion of **three-dimensional** space, in the way that had fascinated European artists since the **Renaissance**, they enabled us to see what an object might look like if we could see more than one side of it at the same time. They broke up objects and figures into geometric shapes and changed them according to their own conception of deeper truth.

Picasso explored new methods of depicting the human figure in his painting *Les Demoiselles d'Avignon* (**3.9.6**, p. 504). Rather than re-creating the way we actually see a room with people standing in it, Picasso has treated the space in the picture, and the figures within it, in a

Sketch: a rough preliminary version of a work or part of a work

Geometric form: a three-dimensional form composed of predictable and mathematically derived planes and curves

Cubism, Cubist: a twentieth-century movement and style in art, especially painting, in which perspective with a single viewpoint was abandoned and use was made of simple geometric shapes, interlocking planes, and, later, collage

Three-dimensional: having height, width, and depth

Renaissance: a period of cultural and artistic change in Europe from the fourteenth to the seventeenth century

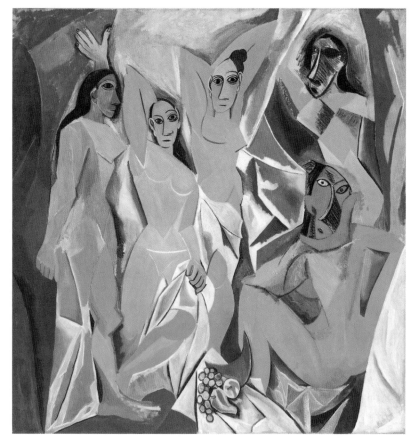

3.9.6 Pablo Picasso, *Les Demoiselles d'Avignon*, 1907.
Oil on canvas, 8′ × 7′8″. MoMA, New York

revolutionary way. He simplified the forms into abstract planes, made the figures more angular, and transformed faces and bodies into geometric pieces. The blue and white planes of what would usually be called the **background** clash violently with the angular pink figures of the women, in a complex struggle for dominance.

The three figures on the left are shown in historical, even Classical poses. The forms of the two women near the center of the painting are simplified, with almond-shaped eyes, triangular noses, and outlines for bodies, but they are still recognizable as female figures. The heads of the standing figures on the far left and far right have been dramatically replaced by African masks. Picasso, along with Matisse and other European artists in the early twentieth century, studied and collected art from outside the European tradition, especially Africa and the Pacific Islands. These formal interests, reflected in the masked faces, are studied as examples of **cultural appropriation**.

The crouching figure at the bottom right has the most abstract features. Her body is splayed out, and the geometric shapes that make up the

woman's face do not correspond to the usual orientation. The eye on our left is shown from the front, while the eye on our right can be read as if it is in **profile**. The nose is also in profile with the mouth off to the side and a crescent shape in place of the jawline. The **composite view** of this figure shows us more parts of her body than we could see from one vantage point. Yet the figures are still fairly recognizable. Picasso's later Cubist pieces became far more abstract, but always intentionally retained a connection to the visible world.

Together, Picasso and Braque developed the movement known as Cubism. Cubist art is never totally non-objective or non-representational: though it can be hard to recognize without referring to the artwork's title, some element of the artist's subject is always identifiable. Cubist artists select which portions of each object to represent, often including views of a single object that would not normally be visible simultaneously. Georges Braque's *Man with a Guitar* is part of the first phase of Cubism (**3.9.7**). At this time, Cubist artists analyzed (or broke down) form, fractured planes of space, and used only a **monochromatic palette**.

The man and the guitar are suggested in lines and shapes placed in predictable

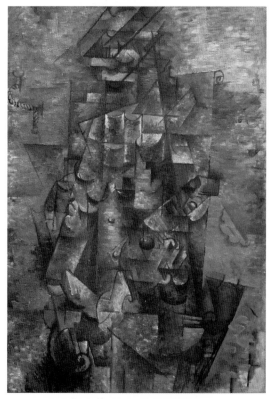

3.9.7 Georges Braque, *Man with a Guitar*, 1911–12.
Oil on canvas, 45¾ × 31⅞″. MoMA, New York

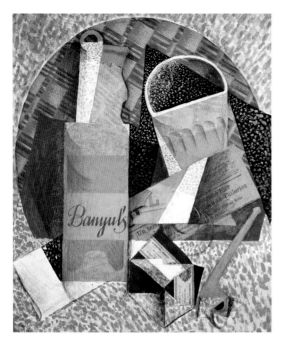

3.9.8 Juan Gris, *Bottle of Banyuls*, 1914. Pasted papers, oil, charcoal, and gouache, and pencil on canvas, 21½ × 18". Kunstmuseum, Bern, Switzerland

Dada

The devastating effects of World War I had a profound impact on how people thought about the world, progress, and society. Improvements in science and industrial manufacturing may have led to some positive developments in life, but to many people they seemed primarily to have resulted, disastrously, in arms production on an unprecedented scale, and in mass slaughter in the trenches of northern Europe. The war inevitably also affected artists and the way they made art. Artists who adopted the term Dada for their art protested against the kinds of so-called rational thought processes that had led to war. Dadaism also took the **Impressionists'** and Cubists' questioning of representation still further and radically rejected existing traditions and the notion of art altogether.

In the folklore of Dada, the name was notoriously chosen at random from the dictionary. It is both a nonsense word and one that has contradictory meanings in several languages. Dada was anti-art and refused to call itself a movement. It was founded by a group of artists and writers who avoided the draft in World War I by taking refuge in the neutral country of Switzerland. Dada soon spread to the United States and later to Berlin, Cologne, Paris, Russia, Eastern Europe, and Japan. Dada works, performances, and publications were critical and playful. They emphasized individuality, irrationality, chance, and imagination.

In keeping with its activist nature, Dada was inspired by revolutionary thinking and initially took the form of events, posters, and pamphlets. In February 1916, German actor and anarchist Hugo Ball (1886–1927) opened the Cabaret Voltaire in Zürich, Switzerland, with his future wife, Emmy Hennings (1885–1948). The Cabaret was a **bohemian**, avant-garde nightclub that provided artists and writers with a place to meet, perform, and be entertained. Ball organized and promoted many of the events. The performances were lively and highly theatrical. At a particularly flamboyant recital of one of his sound poems, "Karawane," Ball wore a costume that made him look like a figure from a Cubist painting (**3.9.9**, p. 506). His poems were made of nonsense words and sounds, intended to be chanted, screamed, and howled. Sometimes several poets would recite at the same time, while others yapped like dogs.

Collage: a work of art assembled by gluing materials, often paper, onto a surface; from the French *coller*, to glue

Impressionism: in the visual arts, a late nineteenth-century style conveying the fleeting impression of the effects of light; Impressionists were artists working in this style

Bohemian: derived from the gypsies of the former Czech Kingdom of Bohemia who moved around; a wanderer; an artist or writer who functions outside the bounds of conventional rules and practices

locations: head in the top center, body down the middle, and musical instrument in the lower third. Scattered around the figure are scrolls recalling parts of an instrument and musical notation. We can also clearly see a guitar's sound hole, body, and strings. In the upper left, Braque included a segment of a rope hanging from a nail to remind us of the three-dimensional world. Cubist artists were much more interested in emphasizing the two-dimensional painted surface, like a visual puzzle, than in re-creating a unified scene.

During the second phase of Cubism, artists synthesized (or brought together) elements directly from life into their art. They cut newspaper, wallpaper, and fine art papers into shapes and glued them to a support to make paper **collage**. This kind of construction is very familiar to us today, but in the early twentieth century it was a completely new technique for making art. *Bottle of Banyuls* (**3.9.8**) by Spanish painter and sculptor Juan Gris (1887–1927) includes some shapes that relate to a table (the patchwork circle around the objects near the center), glass (suggested by the transparent paper he used), and a bottle (the layered rectangular shape on the left). By using an actual bottle label from the southern French wine Banyuls, the artist is able to make the shapes identifiable as a bottle and to bring everyday materials into the picture.

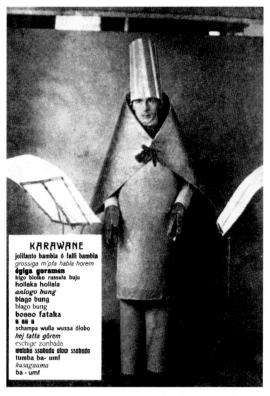

3.9.9 Hugo Ball, performance of "Karawane" at Cabaret Voltaire, Zürich, Switzerland, 1916

The French artist Marcel Duchamp (1887–1968) was a key figure in the New York branch of Dada (he became an American citizen in 1955). Following his early career as a painter (see **3.9.17**, p. 511), one of his first and most enduring anti-art statements was his *Bicycle Wheel* (**3.9.10**). Its date of production, 1913, shows that the spirit of Dada pre-dates the war. This **assemblage** of **found objects** resembles a sculpture, with a stool serving as the base, and the wheel itself as the main subject. Duchamp first made the piece for his own pleasure, because he "enjoyed looking at it, just as I enjoy looking at the flames dancing in the fireplace."

The original *Bicycle Wheel* was lost when Duchamp moved to the United States in 1915. Usually, an artwork's value partly depends on the existence of an original creation that is unique, but Duchamp unflinchingly re-created the piece for an exhibition in 1916. This version, too, was lost. According to the Museum of Modern Art in New York, the *Bicycle Wheel* in its collection is the third remake. Duchamp, in true Dada style, subverts the institution and originality of art.

Duchamp was responsible for three major innovations in art in the twentieth century: **readymades** (ordinary objects turned into

artworks simply by the decision of the artist), **kinetic** sculptures (sculptures with moving parts), and what came to be known as **conceptual art** (see Chapter 3.10, p. 522). For Duchamp, the making of the work and its appearance were secondary. What mattered were the choices of the artist and art's effects in our mind.

A member of Berlin Dada, the German artist Hannah Höch (1889–1978) was one of the first to make **photomontages**. She used them to protest social conditions, especially during and after World War I. In *Cut with the Kitchen Knife Dada through the Last Weimar Beer-Belly Cultural Epoch of Germany*, Höch's Dada combination of text and images, like the image's title, is at once complex and apparently nonsensical (**3.9.11**). The disorder of the image reflects the chaos of life at that time, as seemingly unrelated pictures

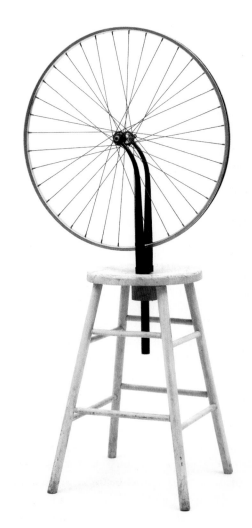

3.9.10 Marcel Duchamp, *Bicycle Wheel*, 1951. Metal wheel mounted on painted wood stool, 50½ × 25½ × 16⅝″. MoMA, New York

Assemblage: an artwork built up from three-dimensional materials including found objects

Found image or object: an image or object chosen by an artist and presented, with little or no alteration, as part of a work or as a finished work of art in itself

Readymade: an everyday object presented as a work of art

Kinetic art/sculpture: art, usually three-dimensional, with moving parts activated by wind, personal interaction, or motors

Conceptual art: a work in which the communication of an idea or group of ideas is most important to the artwork

Photomontage: a single photographic image that combines (digitally or using multiple film exposures) several separate images

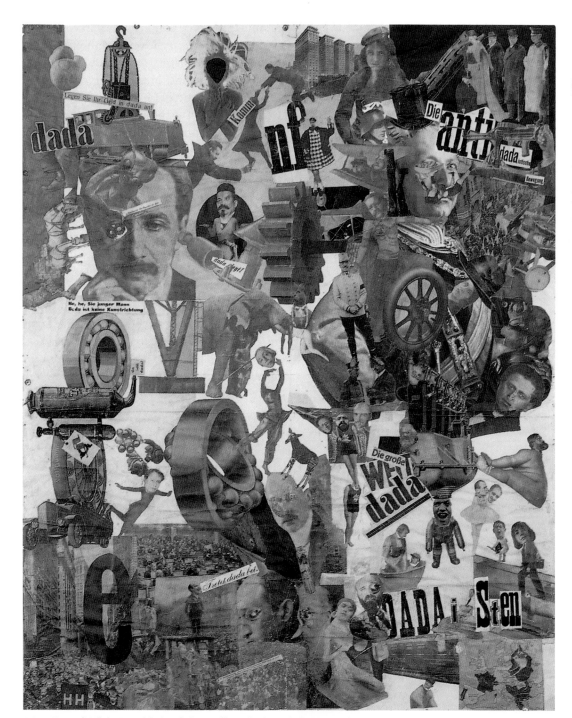

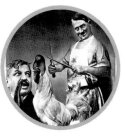

John Heartfield used photomontage to make anti-Nazi statements that were distributed through magazines and posters:
→ see **4.5.11**, p. 601

3.9.11 Hannah Höch, *Cut with the Kitchen Knife Dada through the Last Weimar Beer-Belly Cultural Epoch of Germany*, 1919–20. Photomontage and collage with watercolor, 44⅞ × 35½".
Nationalgalerie, Staatliche Museen, Berlin, Germany

of political figures and modern technology from mass-media publications are collected together. Höch also expresses her concern about women's issues in post-war Germany, highlighting their traditional tool of the kitchen knife and also including, in the lower right corner, a map showing where women had obtained the right to vote. Höch is purposely subverting conventional pictorial space by making a flat image with no perspective and leaving the viewer to unpack the meaning.

Surrealism

Similarly to Dada, Surrealism was opposed to rationality and convention. Surrealists believed that art was a model for human freedom, meaning, and creativity in an absurd world. The movement began in the early 1920s amongst a group of writers and poets in Paris, and developed during the time between the two World Wars; the group's ideas were then taken up by visual artists. Surrealism was the first artistic style based directly on the ideas

Psychoanalysis: a method of treating mental illness by making conscious the patient's subconscious fears or fantasies

Narrative: the story that the artwork expresses

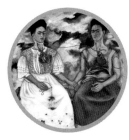

Like De Chirico, Frida Kahlo's work is often called Surrealist even though neither artist was part of the movement. An unexpected and fantastical element creates an internal logic, like the dreams that inspired the Surrealists:

→ see **4.8.19**, p. 643

of Austrian **psychoanalyst** Sigmund Freud. In order to make artwork that was not fully under their conscious control, Surrealists used techniques that Freud had originally pioneered to access his patients' unconscious minds: dreams and dreamlike images were therefore very important to their work. Sometimes the Surrealists used extremely realistic images in surprising ways to jolt our expectations. Surrealists challenged the very idea of objective reality (that universal truths exist independently of the human mind), which they considered absurd.

One artist whose work influenced the Surrealists was the Greek-born Italian Giorgio de Chirico (1888–1978). He was not a member of the Surrealist movement, but he was interested in intuitive and irrational approaches to art, which the Surrealists would likewise become interested in later. In his work *The Melancholy and Mystery of the Street*, De Chirico creates a dreamlike environment in which more questions are posed than resolved (**3.9.12**). The little girl with the hoop, herself a shadow, seems unaware of the figure with a pole looming

around the corner. Although the **narrative** remains unclear, a vague sense of threat fills the still air. The crisp clarity of the forms, the Classical architecture, and the gradation of colors in the otherwise empty sky are all characteristic of De Chirico's work and enhance the enigma.

Spanish artist Salvador Dalí (1904–1989) was a notable Surrealist inspired by Freud's dream theory and his studies on sexual urges and behavior. Dalí developed an approach he called the paranoiac-critical method, which used various methods from scribbling to self-induced hallucinations, to "systematize confusion and thus help to discredit completely the world of reality." Dalí's paintings, such as the famous *Persistence of Memory* (**3.9.13**), use this method to create their own dreamlike logic.

The stretched form in the center (a nose with long eyelashes and a tongue hanging out) is, unexpectedly, a unexpected self-portrait. The cliffs in the background resemble the Catalan coast in Spain where Dalí lived. After a late night, Dalí was playing with some melted cheese from dinner and it inspired the three warped, melting watch faces. The limp watches may be interpreted as symbols of both impotence and recent sexual satisfaction. Scholars have remarked on a link between this work and the physicist Albert Einstein's theory of relativity, which addresses the complexities of time. In Dalí's painting, the clocks each display a different time, conveying a distorted sense of time as well as space. Dalí also painted a fly on the drooping watch on the ledge, a visual metaphor for the phrase "time flies." The fly, along with the ants on the closed watch, also symbolizes death and decay.

German-born artist Max Ernst (1891–1976) was first involved with Dada and then Surrealism. Ernst used different techniques— such as collage, rubbing, scraping, and assemblage—to encourage chance events that would reduce his conscious control over his work. These processes, as he stated, would liberate the human imagination. He deliberately embraced the bizarre, strange, irrational, and humorous to express truths that he believed were buried by logic in the conscious mind. For the sculpture *Capricorn*, Ernst collected everyday objects—including egg crates, milk cartons, and car parts—to make plaster molds for the hybrid figures (**3.9.14**). Resembling giant chess pieces brought to life,

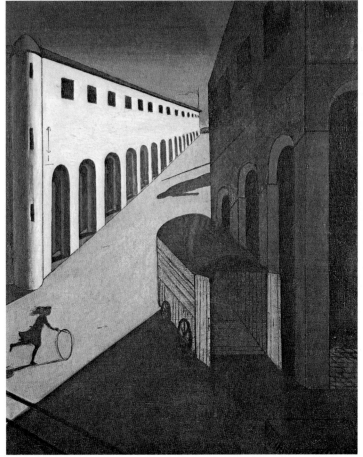

3.9.12 Giorgio de Chirico, *The Melancholy and Mystery of the Street*, 1914. Oil on canvas, 34¼ × 28⅛". Private collection

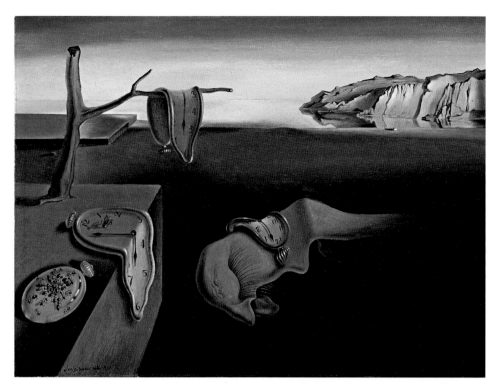

3.9.13 Salvador Dalí, *The Persistence of Memory*, 1931. Oil on canvas, 9½ × 13″. MoMA, New York

the King and Queen figures seem poised for a royal portrait in timeless, perhaps comical posterity. Their awkward anatomy hints at male/female duality: the king is shorter than the queen, perhaps hinting at her dominance in life, if not in the game. The zodiac sign of Capricorn is typically represented by a goat with the tail of a fish and in this sculpture, these traits are distributed between the couple, granting him goat horns and casting her as a mermaid. Ernst highlights the mystery of creativity through both subject matter and process to activate the viewer's imagination.

Introduced to Surrealism as a young woman, Leonora Carrington (British-born, Mexican, 1917–2011) met Max Ernst at the age of nineteen and created Surrealist art throughout the rest of her life. Her 1974 serigraph print, *Bird Bath*, recalls several significant periods of her life spent in a barren landscape under brilliantly dreary skies (**3.9.15,** p. 510). The large, **silhouetted** shell of a house represents Crookey Hall, the Gothic-revival mansion she lived in as a child. She rebelled against the trappings of wealth and never returned to Crookey Hall after she moved to Mexico in 1942. The bird cutout on the upper story of the house, perhaps a crane, is brought to life in the strange ritual in the foreground. Two figures in black cloaks

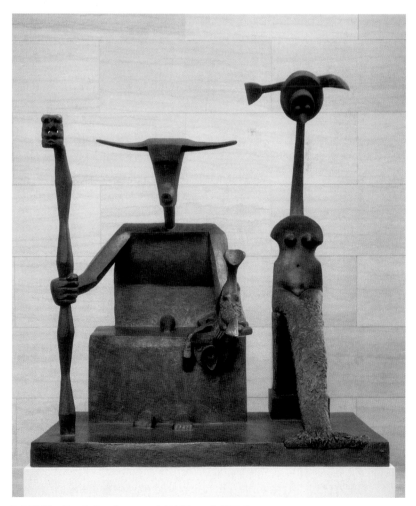

3.9.14 Max Ernst, *Capricorn*, model 1947, cast in 1975. Bronze, 95½ × 81⁷⁄₁₆ × 59⁷⁄₁₆″. National Gallery of Art, Washington, D.C.

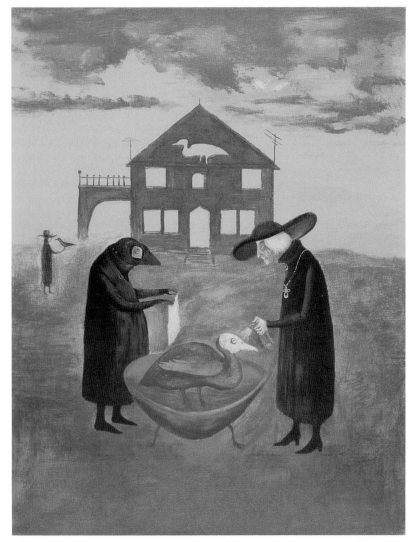

3.9.15 Leonora Carrington, *Bird Bath/Baño de pajaros*, 1974. Color serigraph on paper (ed. 13/50), 35 × 27½". Museum of Latin American Art, Long Beach, California

Futurism: an artistic movement originating in Italy in 1909 that violently rejected traditional forms in favor of celebrating and incorporating into art the energy and dynamism of modern technology; Futurists were artists working in this style

Monumental: having massive or impressive scale

Armory Show: an exhibition in 1913 in New York City that introduced America to Modernist European abstraction; continues as an annual international exhibition

stand on either side of the red bird, possibly referencing nun's habits and Carrington's upbringing in a Catholic school. The left figure wears a bird mask and holds out a white cloth. The white-haired figure in a hat, perhaps a future self-portrait of the artist as an elderly woman, sprays white paint onto the bird's face. The cloaked figure in the middle distance holds a bird as if taming or talking to it. Mysterious ceremonies and animal familiars populated Carrington's writing and imagery as she wove fantasy, reality, and nightmares into intricate and visionary worlds.

The Influence of Cubism

Cubism's ground-breaking approach to art (see pp. 503–5) had a huge impact throughout Europe. Many artists adopted the Cubist style, while others explored ways of making art and depicting objects that had not been conceived of before Cubism.

Futurism, De Stijl, and Suprematism

In Italy, during the period from 1909 to the late 1920s, some artists were influenced by Cubism's clashing planes and geometry to develop a style known as **Futurism**. Unlike Cubist artworks, though, Futurist works celebrated dynamic movement, progress, and modern technology. Some Futurist artists held political beliefs that were later known as Fascist. They also expressed contempt for the past. Italian Umberto Boccioni (1882–1916) explored some of these concepts in his Futurist sculpture *Unique Forms of Continuity in Space* (**3.9.16**). Looking like a flame, the figure forcefully strides through space. Boccioni made the sculpture in plaster; it was not cast in bronze during his lifetime. The shiny, golden appearance of the metal version embodies the words of the founder of Futurism, Filippo Marinetti: "War is beautiful because it inaugurates the long dreamed-of metallization of the human body." At the same time, the figure has heroic **monumentality** as it leaves behind the artistic traditions of the past.

As we have seen, Marcel Duchamp (see p. 506) had a significant impact on the development of modern art. It was his *Nude Descending a Staircase, No. 2* and the scandal it caused at the **Armory Show** in New York

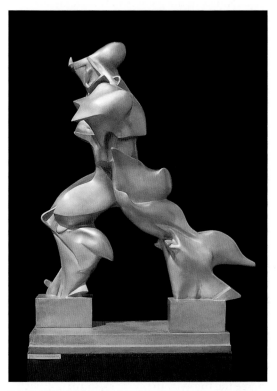

3.9.16 Umberto Boccioni, *Unique Forms of Continuity in Space*, 1913 (cast 1931). Bronze, 49¾ × 35 × 16". Private collection

in 1913 that earned him an international reputation (**3.9.17**). For this short period in his career, Duchamp combined Cubism's figures—broken into geometric planes—with Futurism's emphasis on movement. The mechanization of the figure in this painting reflected a widespread contemporary interest in machines, industrial progress, and stop-motion photography. As did many other works at the Armory Show, this painting shocked the audience, who at that time would only have been familiar with more realistic representational imagery, or pictures of something as it would have been seen in the physical world.

The Dutch painter Piet Mondrian (1872–1944) was the founder of the movement called **De Stijl** ("The Style") in the Netherlands. He painted in a naturalistic style early in his career and was influenced by avant-garde movements, including Cubism, to move away from directly depicting visible reality. Always interested in the underlying structure in his subjects, Mondrian increasingly began to concentrate on creating non-representational works. In 1914, he began making compositions entirely of intersecting lines, right-angled shapes, and linear planes. In 1921, he restricted his palette to the **primary colors**, and black, white, and gray. Using these select formal elements for decades, Mondrian is known for his geometric abstractions (**3.9.18**). The subtle adjustments in the proportions and arrangements in his paintings result from mathematical principles and the ratios of the **Golden Section**. Mondrian believed that the clarity and organization of his compositions reflected rational beauty that is objective and appeals to the mind in a universal way, as opposed to subjective beauty, which appeals to the senses.

Along with Mondrian and Kandinsky (see p. 87), the Russian artist Kazimir Malevich (1878–1935) was one of the first artists to make completely non-objective paintings. Unlike Kandinsky, Malevich concentrated solely on direct geometric forms. He called his approach **Suprematism** because he considered it morally, spiritually, and **aesthetically** superior to what had been done in the past. Malevich believed that recognizable objects were a burden for the viewer and that geometric abstraction helped to free the mind from the thoughts of politics, religion, and tradition that were so prevalent in the early twentieth century, partly as a result of

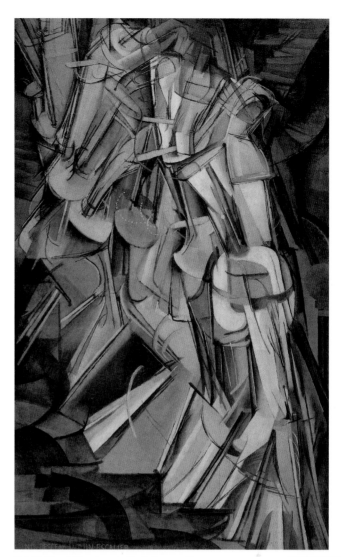

3.9.17 Marcel Duchamp, *Nude Descending a Staircase, No. 2*, 1913/1951. Oil on canvas, 57⅞ × 35⅛". Philadelphia Museum of Art, Pennsylvania

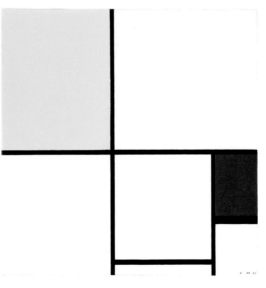

3.9.18 Piet Mondrian, *Composition with Yellow and Blue*, 1932. Oil on canvas, 21⅝ × 21⅝". Bayeler Collection, Bayeler Foundation, Riehen/Basel, Switzerland

De Stijl: a group of artists originating in The Netherlands in the early twentieth century, associated with a utopian style of design that emphasized primary colors and straight lines

Primary colors: the three basic colors from which all others are derived

Golden Section: a unique ratio of a line divided into two segments so that the sum of both segments (a + b) is to the longer segment (a) as the longer segment (a) is to the shorter segment (b). The result is 1:1.618

Suprematism: a Russian art movement of the early twentieth century, focused on geometric shapes and limited colors, which emphasized feeling over visual phenomena

Aesthetic: related to beauty, art, and taste

3.9.19 **Kazimir Malevich,** *Suprematist Composition: White on White*, 1918. Oil on canvas, 31¾ × 31¾". MoMA, New York

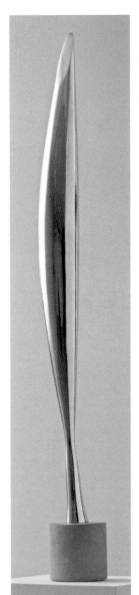

3.9.20 **Constantin Brancusi,** *Bird in Space (L'Oiseau dans L'Espace)*, 1928. Bronze, 54 × 8½ × 6½". MoMA, New York

the cataclysmic conflict of World War I. Most of Malevich's Suprematist works consist of rectangular shapes floating on a white **ground**. While they look like Cubist collages, the shapes are in fact painted. In *Suprematist Composition: White on White* the palette has been reduced to two shades of white, and the inner square is tilted to suggest movement (**3.9.19**).

Twentieth-Century Abstraction

The road to abstraction began with the Impressionist emphasis on the immediate effects of color and light instead of details in line work and shading. From there, **Post-Impressionists** emphasized visual structure and emotion; Matisse and the Fauvists released color from its representational obligations; Expressionists explored non-representational approaches; and the Cubists revolutionized form by showing multiple viewpoints at one time. Twentieth-century abstract artists continued where these avant-garde pioneers left off.

The Romanian-born French sculptor Constantin Brancusi (1876–1957) devoted his working life to finding the very simplest and most elegant way to express the essence of his chosen subject. His *Bird in Space* distills the vital qualities of a bird to what, at first sight, looks like a totally abstract form (**3.9.20**). The shape exquisitely reminds us of a bird's body, a feather, or even the soaring quality of flight.

This sculpture, with the polished bronze form stacked on top of a small stone cylinder with a lighter-colored stone rectangular prism underneath, shows Brancusi's careful consideration of even the *base* of the sculpture. He chose the materials of the base—usually wood, metal, stone, or marble—so that they would contrast in texture with the different material used for the rest of the sculpture. In this case, the solidity and bulk of the stone suggest heaviness and earth, while the contrasting thinness of the smooth and shiny bronze makes it look as if it would slip easily through the air.

Abstraction has continued to be a guiding principle for many artists, such as Canadian-born artist Agnes Martin (1912–2004). Her painting *Starlight* has an overall field of a soft, nebulous blue color with a superimposed **grid** so uniform that no one area of the work dominates (**3.9.21**). Martin, who grew up in Vancouver, became interested in Eastern philosophy, especially Daoism, and for many years lived a life of solitude and simplicity in New Mexico. She explored the idea that art could enable people to experience a profound sense of calm and so "leave themselves behind." In the work *Starlight*, Martin's Daoist ideas about the importance of harmony in the universe are reflected in the emphasis on the work as a whole, held together by the essential simplicity of the grid, the structure of which, with its faint but regular and insistent lines, permeates the entire painting. The resulting effect allows us to immerse ourselves in the work, as if it were a place for reflective meditation.

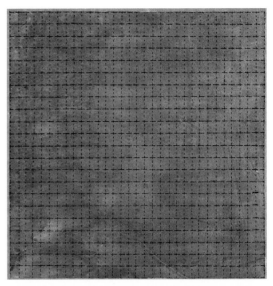

3.9.21 **Agnes Martin,** *Starlight*, 1963. Watercolor and ink on paper, 11¾ × 10½". Private collection

Early Twentieth-Century Art in America

The move toward abstraction in the US happened after the Armory Show of 1913 in New York City, when the American public was introduced to the work of such artists as Matisse, Picasso, Kandinsky, and Duchamp. While European artists and some Americans continued experiments with abstraction during the 1930s, another group, inspired by the harsh realities presented by the advent of the Great Depression in 1929, chose to focus on distinctly American subjects and representational styles with a shared sense of nationalism. This approach came to be known as the American Scene. The **Regionalists** focused on rural environments and promoted American virtues, such as patriotism and hard work. The **Social Realists** were interested in promoting social justice through their artwork. **Harlem Renaissance** artists specifically focused on the expression of African American experience through music, writing, and visual art.

An American Regionalist, Grant Wood (1891–1942) made study trips to Europe but was largely self-taught. His work focuses on his home in the Midwest and the places he knew best. Wood's sister and his dentist were the models for the farmer and his daughter in Wood's now-famous *American Gothic* (**3.9.22**). They stand in front of an Iowa farmhouse built in a style called Carpenter Gothic, inspiring the painting's title. Their full-frontal posture and the clarity of detail and light come from Flemish Renaissance art (see Chapter 3.6) that Wood had studied while in Europe. While this painting has been the subject of many artistic parodies, it was meant to be a serious reflection of hope in spite of the Depression, and an affirmation of the Midwestern American values of individuality, morality, and hard work.

Also focused on distinctively American subjects, Isabel Bishop (1902–1988) was part of a group called the 14th Street School and is associated with the Social Realists due to her scenes of urban life in Union Square. She came to New York at age sixteen to attend the School of Applied Design for Women and entered the Art Students League a few years later. In addition to street scenes, Bishop's most frequently cited subject is women. She created a distinctive style of detailed realistic figures emerging from light-filled background settings and patterned, washy environments

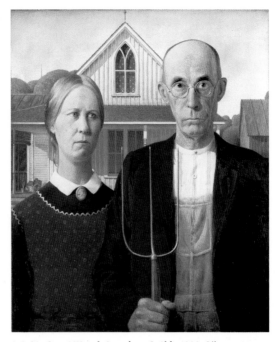

3.9.22 Grant Wood, *American Gothic*, 1930. Oil on beaverboard, 30¾ × 35¾". Art Institute of Chicago, Illinois

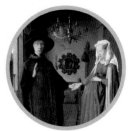

Among the artists that inspired Grant Wood were 15th- and 16th-century German and Flemish painters, such as Jan van Eyck:

→ see **3.6.10a**, p. 450

using layers of **tempera** and oil glazes on **gessoed** Prestwood panels (a thin, engineered wood board). Her direct observations capture in-between moments of working women on breaks, often with awkward expressions and unique gestures. As seen in images such as *Waiting* (**3.9.23**), Bishop's quick brushstrokes suggest busy **rhythms** and show an enduring sympathy for the underprivileged at the same

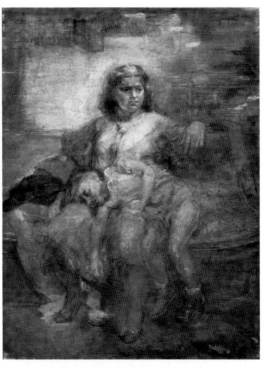

3.9.23 Isabel Bishop, *Waiting*, 1938. Oil and tempera on gesso panel, 29 × 22½". Newark Museum, New Jersey

Regionalism: a branch of American Scene painting that promoted rural, small-town virtues and values, especially related to the Deep South and Midwest US

Social Realism: a branch of American Scene painting that focused on Depression-era social issues and the hardships of daily life

Harlem Renaissance: a movement in literature, music, and the visual arts from the end of WWI into the 1930s celebrating Black experience and culture

Tempera: fast-drying painting medium made from pigment mixed with water-soluble binder, such as egg yolk

Gesso: a substance similar to white acrylic paint, used to make a surface smooth for painting

Rhythm: the regular or ordered repetition of elements in the work

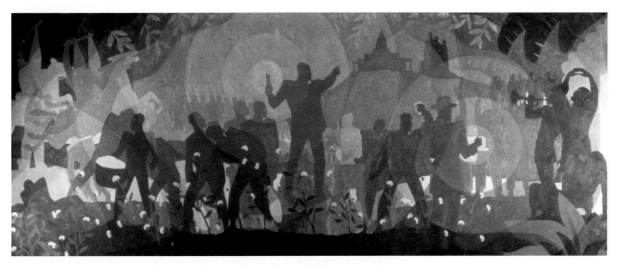

3.9.24 Aaron Douglas, *Aspects of Negro Life: From Slavery Through Reconstruction*, 1934. Oil on canvas, 57¾ × 108¼". The New York Public Library, Schomburg Center for Research in Black Culture, New York

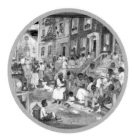

Palmer Hayden's *Midsummer Night in Harlem* is another example of a Harlem Renaissance painting that focuses in a more realistic way on daily life:

→ see **1.10.6**, p. 165

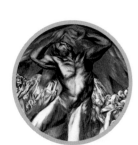

The lasting influence of Mexican muralists, such as Diego Rivera and José Clemente Orozco, includes the promotion of equitable access to art in public spaces and the use of art to combat injustice:

→ see **2.2.8**, p. 199 and **4.1.16**, p. 551

time as raising consciousness about the experience of everyday life in the city.

In the 1920s and 1930s the Harlem Renaissance was known as the "New Negro" movement. Interested in art at an early age, American Aaron Douglas (1899–1979) moved to New York City and soon became a leading figure of the movement. As seen in *Aspects of Negro Life: From Slavery Through Reconstruction* (**3.9.24**), Douglas's work depicts African American life and post-enslavement/pre-Civil Rights struggles. Part of a series of four paintings commissioned by the Works Progress Administration (WPA) for the 135th

St. branch of the New York Public Library, each panel depicts a different aspect of Black life, from Africa to the migration to northern US cities. The *Slavery to Reconstruction* panel combines the past and the present—jungle plants and animals referencing Africa alongside a trumpet and drum referencing jazz and its importance to society at the time the painting was made. The silhouettes, which became a signature aspect of Douglas's work, combine the influences of Egyptian wall paintings, Art Deco (a style similar to **Art Nouveau**) designs, African art, and Modernist abstraction. The lively atmosphere, dancing, and jazz music shown here also represent the intersections of African heritage, African American culture, and nationalistic identity in relation to Black American experience in the 1930s.

Also an active member of the Harlem arts community, Augusta Savage (1892–1962) came to New York to become an artist. She studied at Cooper Union School of Art and in Paris. In 1939 she was commissioned to make a sculpture celebrating African American contributions to music for the World's Fair in New York (**3.9.25**). She used the 1900 song "Lift Every Voice and Sing" by James Weldon and J. Rosamund Johnson as her inspiration. The figures of the 16-ft. plaster sculpture seem to personify the lyrics:

> Sing a song full of faith that the dark past
>   has taught us,
> Sing a song full of hope that the present has
>   brought us;
> Facing the rising sun of our new day begun,
> Let us march on till victory is won.

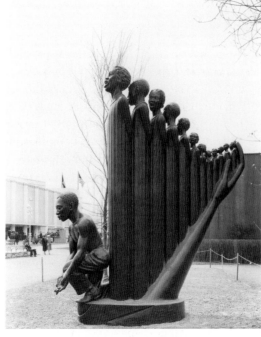

3.9.25 Augusta Savage, *The Harp ("Lift Every Voice and Sing")*, 1939, plaster sculpture for the New York World's Fair (destroyed)

Along with dozens of other sculptures made for the fair, the original was destroyed because there was no budget for casting or storage. In addition to being an accomplished practicing artist, Savage was a teacher and mentor, including serving as the first director of the Harlem Community Art Center. The center was funded by the WPA and it invited African Americans to learn more about their culture by studying the fine arts.

Abstract Expressionism

European refugees, including numerous artists, intellectuals, and scientists, came to the US during World War II to escape persecution. Many of them settled in New York City, which became a globally important cultural center. As described in Chapter 3.8 and earlier in this chapter, the late nineteenth- and early twentieth-century avant-garde artistic developments began in Europe. **Abstract Expressionism** was the first Modernist art movement to originate in the US, a sign of increasing national self-confidence. In this distinctly American movement, Abstract Expressionist artists wanted to create, with energy and emotion, a universal visual experience that anyone could respond to, without needing to refer to their own life experience or religious or political beliefs.

American artist Mark Rothko (1903–1970) emigrated to the US from Russia with his family. He became interested in Surrealist art as a way to move beyond depicting familiar subjects and to explore archetypes (a psychoanalytical term used to describe an original model after which later examples follow) and mythic narratives that might generally appeal to any viewer regardless of his or her background. Eventually, Rothko entirely eliminated representation from his work and created what we see in the example shown: compositions consisting solely of form and color, known as **Color Field painting**.

For about twenty years, from *c.* 1950 to 1970, Rothko's works consisted of luminous rectangles floating in fields of color, such as *No. 3/No. 13 (Magenta, Black, Green on Orange)* (**3.9.26**). This painting includes subtle color shifts that become visible next to one another. Bold expanses of color in the large fields contain nuances, visible in the layered undertones around the edges. Not only is the green made more vibrant through its proximity

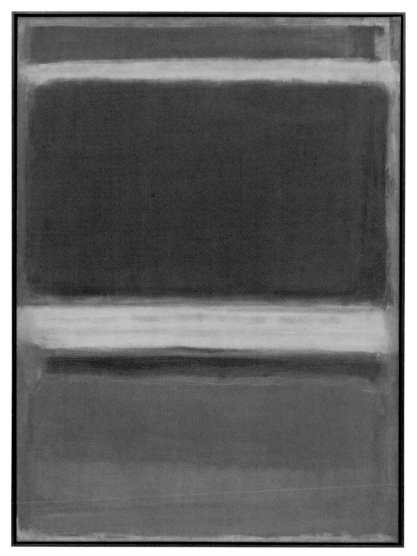

3.9.26 Mark Rothko, *No. 3/No. 13 (Magenta, Black, Green on Orange)*, 1949, 85⅜" × 65", oil on canvas, MoMA, New York

to orange, but the bright orange field also pops out in contrast to the duller orange ground. By reducing the formal elements he uses and eliminating narrative titles, Rothko creates an opportunity for viewers to be transported away from the specificity of scenes from daily life and to lose themselves in contemplation. He made these kinds of abstract paintings for over twenty years and hoped viewers would probe more deeply beyond their surfaces. Rothko famously said, "I'm not an abstractionist. I'm not interested in the relationship of color or form or anything else. I'm interested only in expressing basic human emotions: tragedy, ecstasy, doom, and so on."

To make his enormous paintings, American artist Jackson Pollock (1912–1956) started by unrolling the canvas onto the floor. Then he could move about freely, almost dancing

Art Nouveau: French for "new art," a visual style of the late nineteenth and early twentieth century, characterized by organic flowing lines, simulating forms in nature and involving decorative pattern

Abstract Expressionism: a mid-twentieth-century artistic style characterized by its capacity to convey intense emotions using non-representational images

Color Field painting: a branch of Abstract Expressionism focusing on non-objective abstractions

around and over the piece (**3.9.27**). Pollock used sticks as well as brushes to drip and pour the paint onto the surface. The absence of any recognizable subject fixes our attention on the actions and gestures of the artist. The process becomes the subject, making the painting about the act of creation itself. The results of Pollock's process, known as **action painting**, are complex abstract paintings so large that when we stand before them,

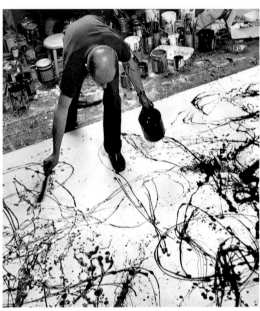

3.9.27 Jackson Pollock painting in his Long Island studio, 1950. Photo by Hans Namuth

they completely dominate our field of vision (**3.9.28**). Pollock's artworks evolved **organically** and spontaneously rather than from precise pre-planning. The improvisational process and the tension between the rhythms and cross-rhythms of Pollock's paintings—seen, for example in the longer black and white lines, in contrast to the built-up textures around them— also have some similarities to jazz music, which he liked to listen to as he worked.

One of the few women to receive recognition in the Abstract Expressionism movement, Helen Frankenthaler (1928–2011) pioneered a new and influential technique in the early 1950s. Inspired by the Color Field work of artists such as Rothko and Barnett Newman (see p. 93), and Pollock's drip technique, she began pouring paint directly onto unstretched and unprimed canvas. *Mountains and Sea* (**3.9.29**), Frankenthaler's first major painting, was inspired by the landscape she experienced while on a trip to Nova Scotia. She applied **oil paint** thinned with turpentine for this painting then tilted and lifted the canvas rather than using brushes to move the paint around. Because the canvas was not primed with gesso, the paint soaked into the weave of the fabric. Frankenthaler, like other second-generation Abstract Expressionists, saw abstraction as a way to focus attention on formal elements

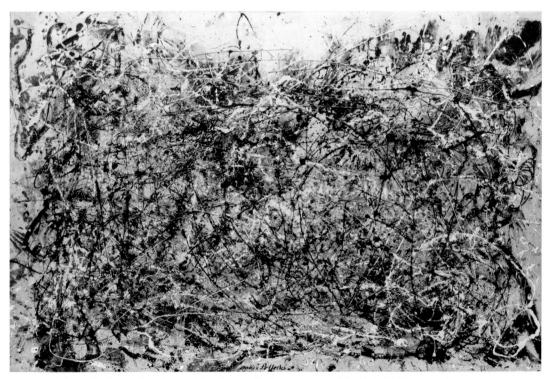

3.9.28 Jackson Pollock, *Number 1A*, 1948. Oil and enamel paint on canvas, 5'8" × 8'8". MoMA, New York

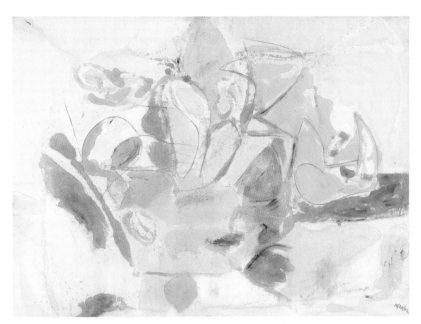

3.9.29 Helen Frankenthaler, *Mountains and Sea*, 1952. Oil and charcoal on unsized, unprimed canvas, 86⅜ × 117¼". Helen Frankenthaler Foundation, New York, on extended loan to the National Gallery of Art, Washington, D.C.

such as line and color in and of themselves rather than using them to represent other things. Water and geography informed many of her artworks, though she was not focused on context or speculation: as she said, "sentiment and nuance are being squeezed out."

Pop Art

Unlike the Abstract Expressionists, the artists who began producing **Pop art** in the late 1950s embraced everyday subject matter in their work. Consumer culture and futuristic high-tech gadgets promised ways for everyone to live a life of plenty and leisure. In reality, however, middle-class suburban living was out of reach for those who lived in the inner cities—primarily African Americans at the time—not to mention countries outside Europe and North America. In addition, even the latest movie idols and pop music playing on the radio could not fully tune out the threat of atomic war.

Pop art embraced the objects and experiences of daily life in a way that was entirely new to the art world at the time. Jasper Johns (b. 1930) and Robert Rauschenberg (1925–2008), who believed that Abstract Expressionist art was too obscure and personal, served as inspiration for Pop artists by highlighting common objects taken directly from the life they were living. Because Pop artists wanted their subjects to be immediately familiar to their audiences, they borrowed imagery from popular culture, including famous

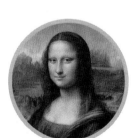

For further discussion of the masterpiece Warhol reproduced in his painting:
→ see **0.0.12**, p. 23

artworks, comic-books, advertising, car design, television, movies, and the news. At the time there was a division between fine art (a supposedly sophisticated part of high culture) and its opposite, popular culture (considered unrefined and ordinary). Pop artists bridged this gap by combining fine art materials with commercial elements, such as pictures from magazines, sometimes printing by **silkscreen**, and then selling their pieces in fine art galleries.

The American artist Andy Warhol (1928–1987) began his professional career as an illustrator and graphic designer in advertising. Around 1960, using the expressive brushwork and drips of paint that were characteristic of Abstract Expressionism, Warhol made **acrylic** paintings of the comic-book heroes Superman, Batman, and Dick Tracy. He then quickly turned to the imagery of advertising, using as his subjects such familiar products as Campbell's soup and Coca-Cola. He also began using the silkscreen printing technique. This process allowed him not only to make art more quickly, but also to give it a depersonalized and mass-produced quality, very different from some art's emphasis on personal expression or technique. Warhol even borrowed, or appropriated, the famous image of the Italian Renaissance artist Leonardo da Vinci's *Mona Lisa* (**3.9.30**). The title of this piece, *Thirty Are Better than One*,

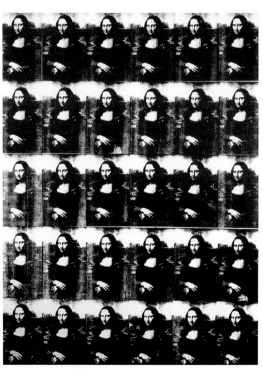

3.9.30 Andy Warhol, *Thirty Are Better than One*, 1963. Silkscreen ink on synthetic polymer paint on canvas, 9'2" × 7'10". Private collection

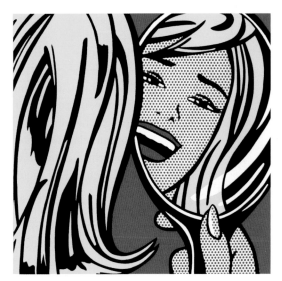

3.9.31 Roy Lichtenstein, *Girl in Mirror*, 1964. Enamel on steel, 42 × 42". Private collection

Ben-Day dots: a technique used in printing to create gradations and suggest a range of tones; named for its inventor

Value: the lightness or darkness of a plane or area

Pointillism: a late nineteenth-century painting style using short strokes or points of differing colors that optically combine to form new perceived colors

Graphic design: the use of images, typography, and technology to communicate ideas for a client or to a particular audience

Minimalism, Minimalist: a mid-twentieth-century artistic style that references industrial production modes through materials and seriality, often with unified arrangements of geometric shapes and massive forms that become part of the viewer's space

clearly echoes the language of advertising and consumerism—"more is better." It refers to the multiple reproductions of the painting in Warhol's work while also undermining the high art tendency to value an artwork financially and aesthetically only if it is original and unique.

The American artist Roy Lichtenstein (1923–1997) also made works based on comics. Lichtenstein challenged traditional notions of the subject matter and appearance of fine art painting by embracing everyday subjects. In his painting *Girl in Mirror* he uses strong black outlines filled with bold primary colors (**3.9.31**). In order to create gradations of a color, Lichtenstein borrowed a technique from older kinds of newspaper printing and comics. The regular pattern of dots, called **Ben-Day dots**, emulates the screen visible on printed pictures, where areas of light **value** have small dots, and those of dark value have large ones nearly joined together. Lichtenstein created the dots using a stencil, which gives a commercial edge to the technique of **pointillism**, while his use of black, white, and primary colors references the color palette of such geometric abstract artists as Piet Mondrian (see **3.9.18**, p. 511).

Warhol's and Lichtenstein's work used appropriation to bring recognizable and familiar imagery into galleries and museums. By combining the practices of what was then considered high art at the time with the so-called low art of **graphic design**, these artists were able to bridge the gap between the two and expand the boundaries of acceptable fine art practices to include popular imagery and commercial printing processes.

Minimalism

Minimalist artists in the 1960s reacted against both what they saw as the excessive emphasis on the artist's personality in Abstract Expressionism, and the commercial nature of Pop. Minimalism is an approach to making art

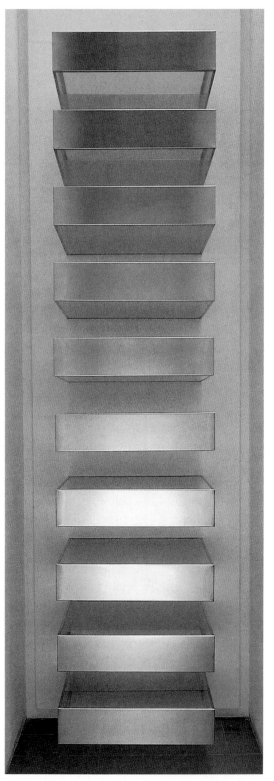

3.9.32 Donald Judd, *Untitled*, 1967. Stainless steel and Plexiglas, 190⅛ × 40 × 31". Modern Art Museum of Fort Worth, Texas

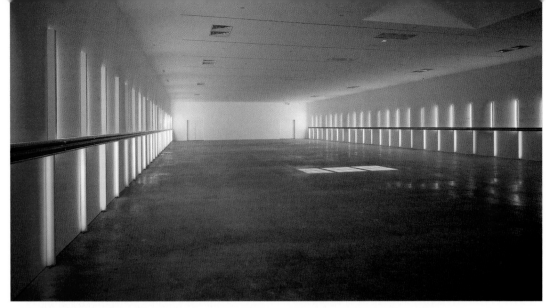

3.9.33 Dan Flavin, *Untitled*, 1996. Installation of 4′ fixtures in two opposing banks for the east and west interior walls of Richmond Hall, Houston, Texas. Pink, yellow, green, blue, and ultraviolet fluorescent tubes and metal fixtures, two sections, each 8′ high, approximately 128′ wide. Menil Collection, Houston, Texas

that by its very nature is non-representational. Minimalists sought instead to use neutral textures, geometric shapes, flat colors, and even mechanical construction in order to strip away any traces of emotion or underlying meaning in their work.

American sculptor Donald Judd (1928–1994) produced Minimalist pieces that were totally abstract, usually rectangles and cubes. Although during the early stages of his career Judd was a painter, and he did go on to paint some of his sculptures, he generally preferred the medium of sculpture to painting because it existed in "actual space." According to Judd, any painting, no matter how abstract, shows something, whereas a sculpture *is* something, in real space. His sculptures had an industrial appearance and were commercially manufactured to allow the artist to focus on new materials rather than fine art conventions, which he believed had become limiting.

For his *Untitled* piece (**3.9.32**), Judd ordered from a factory ten boxes made with stainless steel around the edges and Plexiglas on the top and bottom, each measuring 9⅛ × 40 × 31 in. Then, when the piece was installed, it was placed according to his specifications. Even though the work includes multiple pieces, they are spaced in an orderly way to focus the viewer's attention on "the thing as a whole, its quality as a whole." Judd preferred to have his pieces made in this way because it made them stand on their own, limited the role of the artist as creator, and downplayed any underlying message.

American artist Dan Flavin's (1933–1996) work, like that of other Minimalists, is made from industrial materials and has a clean, geometric quality. Flavin created individual artworks and **installations** with fluorescent light tubes. The sculptures have a physical aspect (the fixtures and tubes), but they also focus our attention on the use of light itself as a means of affecting the space. The light from the bulbs, which are commonly used in offices, stores, and even homes, takes on a new significance in the form of a sculpture on the walls of an art gallery. When the fluorescent tubes are placed together in an installation (**3.9.33**), the noticeable glow transforms the space. Flavin's work promotes the idea that a simple object that has been commercially purchased can become a work of art and cause us to look at such familiar objects in new ways.

The Transition from Modernism and Postmodernism in Architecture

The spirit of innovation in twentieth-century arts included the design of products, media, and buildings. Around the 1960s, the shift to **Postmodernism** began as a form of architecture reacting and responding to Modernism, the predominant art and architectural style from the late nineteenth century until that time. Modernist architecture was characterized by straight lines and geometric shapes (see, for example, Le Corbusier's [1887–1965] Villa Savoye, p. 262). Its designs were intended to be direct, clean, uncluttered, and progressive. As early as the 1960s, Postmodernist architects

Installation: originally referring to the hanging of pictures and arrangement of objects in an exhibition, installation may also refer to an intentional environment created as a completed artwork

Postmodernism, Postmodernist: a late twentieth-century style of architecture and art that playfully adopts features of earlier styles and critically focuses on content

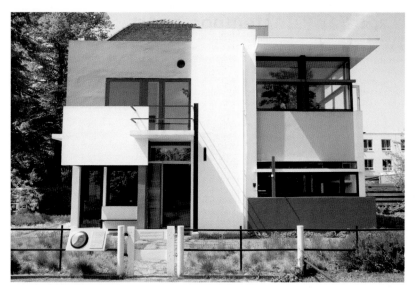

3.9.34 Gerrit Rietveld, *Schröder House*, 1924–25. Utrecht, The Netherlands

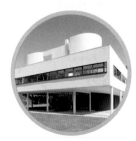

Villa Savoye, a Modernist building, and the Postmodern Guggenheim Museum in Bilbao offer a good comparison of the two movements' characteristics:
→ see **2.5.31**, p. 262 and **1.2.17**, p. 60

Column: a freestanding pillar, usually circular in section

Asymmetry: a type of design in which balance is achieved by elements that contrast and complement one another without being the same on either side of an axis

Facade: any side of a building, usually the front or entrance

Capital: the architectural feature that crowns a column

reacted against the Modernists' use of angular lines, severe geometry, and subdued colors, considering the aims of Modernists to be too idealistic and inaccessible. As a result, Postmodern designs often combine dynamic forms (see, for example, Frank Gehry's [b. 1929] Guggenheim Museum, Bilbao, pp. 60–61) and incorporate familiar elements from different historical periods, such as **columns** reminiscent of buildings in ancient Greece.

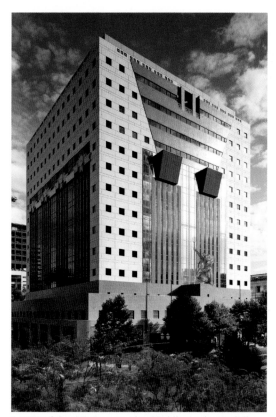

3.9.35 Michael Graves, *Portland Public Services Building*, 1980–82. Portland, Oregon

Similarly to his fellow Dutch De Stijl artists, Modernist designer Gerrit Rietveld (1888–1964) emphasized geometric shapes, horizontals and verticals, and a limited color palette of black, white, and primary colors. His Schröder House, created in 1924–25, integrates Modernist design into a building that served the specific needs of Rietveld's client (**3.9.34**). The lower floor consists of traditional kitchen, dining, and living areas, while upstairs Rietveld took an innovative approach to the bedrooms. Modular partition walls separate the areas of the upper floor, providing private quarters for sleeping but allowing a more open space to be used during the day. The balconies, windows, concrete planes, and linear elements on the building's exterior, which resembles a three-dimensional version of an abstract painting, show how architects achieve balance through **asymmetry**. Rietveld's emphasis on geometry and function influenced the International Style of architecture, developed in the 1920s and 1930s, which stressed logical planning, followed an industrial or machine aesthetic, and eliminated all arbitrary decoration.

Postmodern architects reacted against the severity of International Style Modernism, incorporated references to earlier buildings, and included ornamentation that was not required by the structural design. The Portland Public Services Building, designed by American architect Michael Graves (1934–2015) in 1980–82, was the first public building to employ the Postmodern approach (**3.9.35**). Its distinctive design includes a brightly colored exterior, small square windows, and Classical architectural forms. Columns have been extended up to ten stories tall on either side of the entrance and on the sides of the building. On the **facade**, the shape of the exaggerated **capitals** has been repeated on the upper floors. While this building has generated some controversy due to strong negative opinions about its appearance, and claims of shoddy workmanship, it stands as a significant example of Postmodern ingenuity and of Postmodernism's potential to integrate diverse ideas. More recently, Graves has become well known for a line of kitchenware and domestic merchandise. The line of household products, which Graves originally designed for Target, features sleek shapes and stylish colors that incorporate many Postmodern design principles into functional items.

Explore Further Late Modern and Early Contemporary Art in the Twentieth Century

Revolution of Color and Form

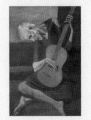

1.4.17 Pablo Picasso, *The Old Guitarist*, 1903–4 → p. 93

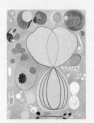

1.4.32 Hilma af Klint, *Group IV, No. 7, Adulthood*, 1907 → p. 102

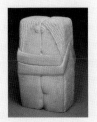

1.2.15 Constantin Brancusi, *The Kiss*, 1916 → p. 59

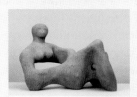

4.8.17 Henry Moore, *Recumbent Figure*, 1938 → p. 642

Ideas and Conceptual Approaches

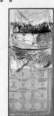

2.2.24 Robert Rauschenberg, *Bed*, 1955 → p. 208

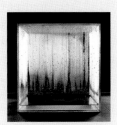

0.0.4 Hans Haacke, *Condensation Cube*, 1963–65 → p. 18

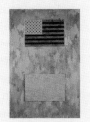

4.4.13 Jasper Johns, *Flags*, 1965 → p. 588

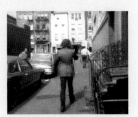

2.10.5 Vito Acconci, *Following Piece*, 1969 → p. 338

Specific Art Movements

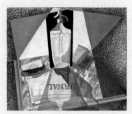

1.6.4 Marie Marevna, *Nature morte à la bouteille*, 1917 → p. 119

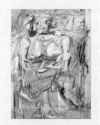

1.3.1 René Magritte, *The Treachery of Images*, 1929 → p. 66

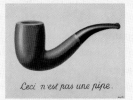

4.8.2 Willem de Kooning, *Woman I*, 1950–52 → p. 631

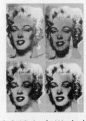

2.3.16 Andy Warhol, *Four Marilyns*, 1962 → p. 222

Also at this Time

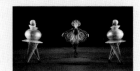

1.5.9 Costumes by Oskar Schlemmer for *Triadic Ballet*, 1922 → p. 109

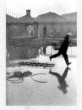

2.8.12 Henri Cartier-Bresson, *Place de l'Europe. Gare Saint Lazare*. 1932 → p. 306

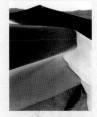

2.8.11 Ansel Adams, *Sand Dunes, Sunrise…*, c. 1948 → p. 306

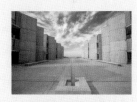

2.5.33 Louis I. Kahn, Salk Institute, 1965 → p. 264

Your Turn:
How do these artworks relate to the culture or ideas discussed in this chapter?

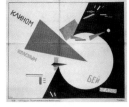

1.1.24 El Lissitzky, *Beat the Whites with the Red Wedge*, 1919 → p. 46

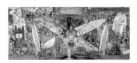

4.1.16 Diego Rivera, *Man, Controller of the Universe…*, 1934 → p. 551

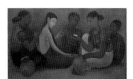

1.8.2 Amrita Sher-Gil, *Bride's Toilet*, 1937 → p. 141

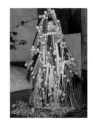

1.6.5 Atsuko Tanaka wearing *Electric Dress*, c. 1956 → p. 119

3.10
The Late Twentieth Century and Art of the Present Day

Postmodernism, Postmodernist: a late twentieth-century style of architecture and art that playfully adopts features of earlier styles and critically focuses on content

Postcolonialism: a theoretical approach that aims to explain the relationships between colonized and colonizing nations and people

Abstraction: the degree to which an image is altered from an easily recognizable subject

Figurative: art that portrays items perceived in the visible world, especially human or animal forms

Conceptual art: a work in which the communication of an idea or group of ideas is most important to the artwork

Sketch: a rough preliminary version of a work or part of a work

Artist's book: a book produced by an artist, usually an expensive limited edition, often using specialized printing processes

In the Contemporary period (1960–present), ideas, concepts, actions, and experiences sometimes take precedence over the physical objects created by artists. Artists look to a wide range of influences, from current popular culture to traditional cultural identity, for inspiration. Recognizing cultural diversity has meant that artists now represent a wider range of perspectives than the male Eurocentric viewsthat had previously dominated the art world.

Postmodernism, which began in the 1960s (see Chapter 3.9, pp. 519–20) and **postcolonialism** are hallmarks of the history and art of this period. Some artists have continued the formal explorations of Modernist **abstraction**, but more often Postmodern artworks embrace complexity, ambiguity, even contradictions. Indeed, some have reintroduced realistic, **figurative** imagery into their artworks and frequently refer to past artistic styles, earlier artworks or buildings, philosophical ideas, historical events, or political issues.

Postcolonial art explores new social structures in addition to diverse perspectives, and in the process inevitably—and often deliberately—challenges or raises questions about existing conventions and preconceptions. Artists have responded to the feminist and Civil Rights movements of the 1960s and 1970s by increasingly focusing on identity politics, referencing their own personal history, or examining the history of the nation or culture to which they are connected. Our current times are playing out on a dynamic world stage to which artists regularly respond, including such issues as the effects of political and ideological divisiveness; systemic transitions related to economics, environmental concerns, and climate change; civil unrest in reaction to police violence against BIPOC (Black, Indigenous, and People of Color) in the US, and the global impact of the COVID-19 pandemic.

Conceptual Art

Conceptual art, or art centered on ideas above all other things, takes the non-representational tendencies that are apparent in Minimalism even further, often eliminating the art object altogether. Instead of painting a canvas or carving a block of marble, for example, an artist might arrange certain objects together in a way that makes people reconsider each one in a new light. Some conceptual artists focus their efforts on planning, rather than producing, artwork. The results of conceptual art include documentation, **sketches**, **artist's books**, photographs, performances, and mail art (any artwork, often in the form of postcards or small packages, distributed through the mail).

The work of American Conceptual artist Joseph Kosuth (b. 1945) provokes questions in the minds of viewers. His processes, approach, and materials were inspired by Marcel Duchamp's readymades (see: Borrowing an Image) as well as by his interest in art that appeals to the mind rather than the senses. On one level, Kosuth's *One and Three Chairs* simply presents three things that a chair could be: on our left, a photographic representation of a chair; in the center, an actual wooden chair; and on our right, an enlarged dictionary definition of the word "chair" (**3.10.3**, p. 524). On another level, this piece represents a sophisticated investigation into how we know and understand the world around us. Which of these chairs is more familiar? Which is

Borrowing an Image

Many artworks are personal statements, and those statements can take many forms. Some artworks are created by borrowing objects, figures, or entire compositions from the work of other artists. This practice, known as appropriation, can be traced to the invention by the French artist Marcel Duchamp (1887–1968) of **readymades** (**3.10.1**), which consist of ordinary objects transformed into artworks simply through a decision taken by the artist. When Duchamp introduced such readymades as *Fountain* into the realm of art, he was challenging existing artistic practice and shifting the focus to the ideas behind the work rather than its physical appearance.

Duchamp appropriated such objects as urinals, bicycle wheels, snow shovels, and even existing artworks as viable material for his art. Over time, other artists followed in his footsteps by continuing to appropriate artworks (including works by Duchamp). Some also borrowed images from the realms of popular culture, advertising, and even social stereotypes. Thus, an artist can make a personal statement by appropriating the work of another.

The American artist Sherrie Levine (b. 1947) is known for her appropriation of famous paintings, sculptures, and photographs from the past. These pieces raise many questions: Who can be an artist? What role does the artist play? How has that role changed over time? What is originality? Who can be original? The pieces Levine appropriates are generally by male artists who worked at a time when very few women artists were recognized in the art world, as has been the case throughout most of history. As feminist statements, Levine's work leads us to reconsider the structures of art institutions as they existed in the past and highlights the historic exclusion/absence of women. Her sculpture *Fountain (After Marcel Duchamp: A. P.)* (**3.10.2**) recalls Duchamp's famous porcelain urinal from 1917. Unlike Duchamp, though, who took an existing urinal and declared it to be art, Levine had a urinal cast in bronze, a material traditionally used for fine art sculptures. Levine encourages viewers not just to interact with her own piece, but also to consider their attitudes toward Duchamp's urinal; so her quotation of a past artwork makes Levine's sculpture most meaningful for viewers who are familiar with Duchamp's work.

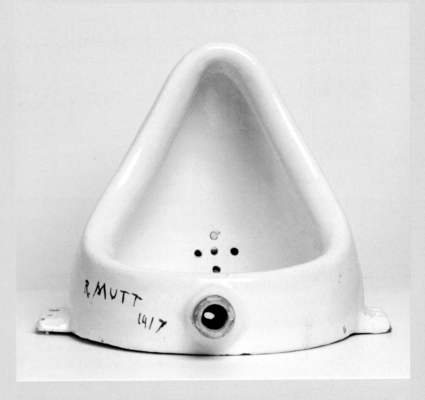

3.10.1 Marcel Duchamp, *Fountain*, 1950 (replica of original from 1917). Porcelain urinal, 12 × 15 × 18". Philadelphia Museum of Art, Pennsylvania

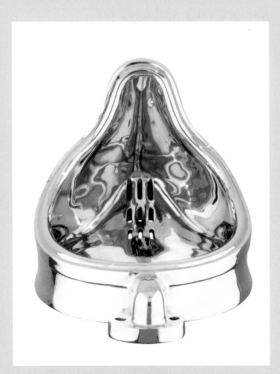

3.10.2 Sherrie Levine, *Fountain (After Marcel Duchamp: A. P.)*, 1991. Bronze, 26 × 14½ × 14"

Readymade: an everyday object presented as a work of art

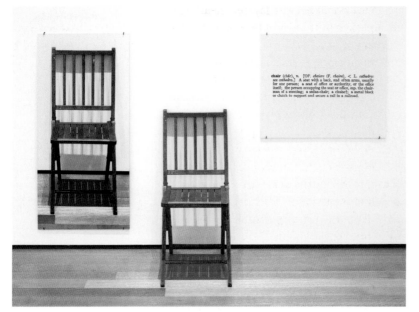

3.10.3 Joseph Kosuth, *One and Three Chairs*, 1965. Mounted photograph of a chair, wooden folding chair, and photographic enlargement of a dictionary definition of "chair," photographic panel 36 × 24⅛", chair 32⅜ × 14⅞ × 20⅞", text panel 24 × 24⅛". MoMA, New York

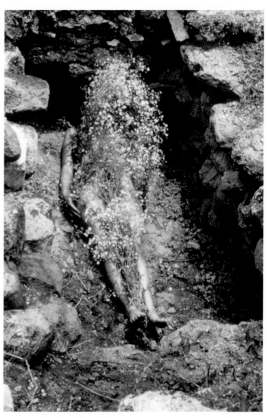

3.10.4 Ana Mendieta, "Untitled" (*Silueta* series, Mexico, 1973–80). Color photograph from 35mm slide, 20 × 16"

more real? Which one provides us with the most information? Ultimately, our experience of a chair, its meaning, our awareness of how we communicate ideas, and the way all these things impact art is changed after seeing this piece.

Performance and Body Art

Performance art and Body art are closely related to Conceptual art and focus attention on the physical form and actions of the artist and/or other participants. The Cuban-born artist Ana Mendieta (1948–1985) is known for using her own body as an integral part of her art-making. Her performances and art actions explore personal themes (such as the displacement she experienced by moving away from the country of her birth to the United States). She also incorporates references to natural elements (water, earth, fire, blood) and biological cycles (life, death, spiritual rebirth). For her *Silueta* series of 1973–80 (**3.10.4**), Mendieta situated her body in various outdoor environments: on the ground, in front of a tree, on a sandy beach. In the example shown here, the artist's body is camouflaged by the flowers and mud that cover it. Whether her body or its **silhouette** is shown in the photograph, Mendieta reinforces the powerful connection between body and nature, while calling attention to the ways women are sources of strength, endurance, and nourishment.

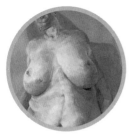

While the human body has been a crucial subject for art throughout its long history, contemporary artists have explored such body issues as sexuality, gender presentation, and perceptions of the ideal:
→ see **1.10.9**, p. 168 and **4.8.22**, p. 645

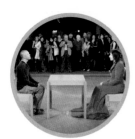

Marina Abramović used performance to test the limits of human endurance and bring the worlds of art and life together:
→ see **2.10.6**, p. 338

Earthworks

Minimalist and Conceptual art expanded the existing notion of art. Similarly, artists who create earthworks (a term coined by Robert Smithson [1938–1973]) make art using the Earth itself, or natural elements of it, on such a large scale that it cannot be displayed in commercial art galleries. Also known as land art, this art is difficult (but not quite impossible) to sell and required a great effort to see. These works unite sculpture and nature and blur the boundary between art and life. The media that earthwork artists have used range from collections of natural materials big and small, to expanses of mesas in Nevada, lakes in Utah, fields in New Mexico, and beyond. Since almost all land art is in a specific location, it cannot be shown in traditional art venues, although photographic documentation and fragments of an earthwork can be displayed in galleries and museums.

Not all earthworks are made on an enormous scale, however. In fact, the British artist Andy Goldsworthy (b. 1956) creates both intimate and larger-scale site-specific structures out of grass, rocks, leaves, flowers, bark, snow, ice, and water. *Japanese maple ...* (**3.10.5**)

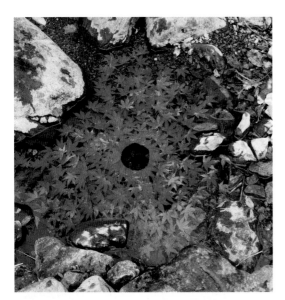

3.10.5 Andy Goldsworthy, *Japanese maple / leaves stitched together to make a floating chain / the next day it became a hole / supported underneath by a woven briar ring / Ouchiyama-Mura / Japan, 21–22 November / 1987*. Print size 24 × 24"

create hybrid pieces with layered meaning to be unpacked by the viewer (see Gateway: April Greiman, pp. 526–27).

A disillusionment with government structures and institutions inspired some Postmodernist thinkers to suggest that power does not come from a single leader, but instead from the masses. As a result, art became noticeably concerned with social issues and with addressing the concerns of a culturally diverse world. By the 1980s, artists and art institutions recognized the need to be more inclusive in their consideration of artists from all cultural backgrounds. Postmodern artists are driven by a desire to have their voices heard so that their artwork reveals the specificity of their cultural backgrounds and identity, rather than a reflection of the old Modernist ideal of shared, universal experience.

Soon after the 1964 race riots in Chicago, Wadsworth Jarrell (American, b. 1929) became part of several seminal Black Arts movement groups, OBAC (Organization of Black American Culture) and AFRICOBRA (African Commune of Bad Relevant Artists), which he co-founded. Their use of art to promote Black pride and Black empowerment messages gained international acclaim. Jarrell's dynamic 1972 screenprint, *Revolutionary* (**3.10.6**), features high key "coolade" [*sic*] colors, named for the

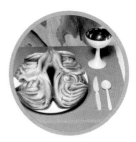

Feminist artists, such as Judy Chicago, challenged the status quo of Eurocentric male artists:
→ see **4.9.7**, p. 653

consists of a ring of leaves invisibly stitched together and placed in a rocky pool supported by a briar ring. This piece draws attention to the splendor of nature in the unrivaled vibrancy of the leaves' red **hue**, configured to **contrast** with the gray of the stones, almost as if they had arranged themselves. An environmentalist as well as an artist, Goldsworthy meticulously creates his pieces, then photographs them before they disintegrate and return to nature due to the impact of time and weather.

Postmodernism, Identity, and Cultural Diversity

Art and society in the second half of the twentieth century responded to earlier political and cultural events, including the atrocities resulting from the Nazis' totalitarian regime, the Cold War, and debates over US involvement in Vietnam. Those who in the past had been oppressed or discriminated against began to claim their rights. The Civil Rights movement in the US claimed equality for African Americans, while feminism asserted the right of women to the same treatment, privileges, opportunities, pay, and status as men. Reacting against the principally Eurocentric, white male perspective of Modernism, some artists and scholars promoted the idea that meaning is ultimately unreliable and that truth arises from multiple sources. Such artists as April Greiman were using Postmodern style and content to

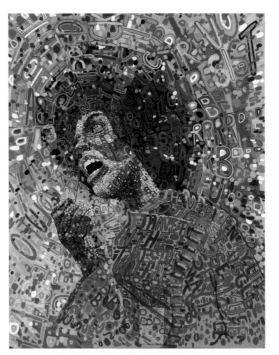

3.10.6 **Wadsworth Jarrell**, *Revolutionary*, 1972, screenprint on paper, 34 × 26½". Brooklyn Museum, New York

Silhouette: a solidly colored-in shape represented in outline, which contains no detail inside its border

Hue: the general classification of a color; the distinctive characteristics of a color as seen in the visible spectrum, such as green or red

Contrast: a drastic difference between such elements as color or value (lightness/darkness) when they are presented together

April Greiman, *Does It Make Sense?*
Pioneering Postmodern Design

For the other Greiman
GATEWAYS:
→ see p. 294 and p. 652

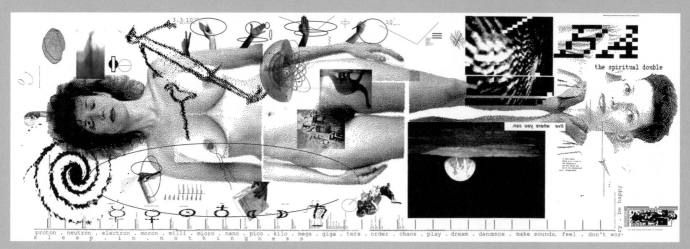

3.10.7 April Greiman, *Does It Make Sense? Design Quarterly* Issue #133, 1986

In both cases there is a picture in the foreground, but the sense lies far in the background; that is, the application of the picture is not easy to survey.

—Ludwig Wittgenstein (philosopher)

American April Greiman (b. 1948) is known for being one of the first artists to explore the Postmodern design aesthetic. She calls herself a transmedia artist because she feels "graphic design" is too limiting for the variety of media, technology, and ideas she uses. Her work moved beyond conventional modernist linear compositional grids and advanced women's position in print media. Her 1986 *Does It Make Sense?* (**3.10.7**) comprised an entire issue of *Design Quarterly* in which Greiman converted the 32-page magazine into a 2-by-6-ft. foldout featuring a lifesize double self-portrait.

Because she was a well-known designer at the time, the publication of her nude self-portrait was surprising, even shocking. The presentation of women's bodies was being actively reconsidered by feminists during the 1980s. *Does It Make Sense?* is an updated version of the centerfold, used since 1953 in *Playboy* magazine. We do not see a nude body passively presented for a male consumer, however. The design here clearly highlights intellectual exploration and creative experimentation rather than exploitation or pornography. Greiman used her subject matter and format to propose a new,

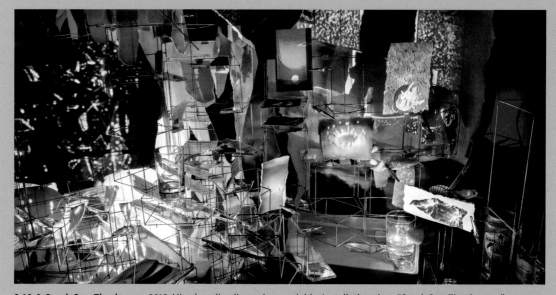

3.10.8 Sarah Sze, *Timekeeper*, 2016. Mixed media, dimensions variable. Installation view, "Sarah Sze: Timekeeper," The Rose Art Museum, Brandies University, Waltham, Massachusetts, 2016

generative model for women in print media, science, marketing, design, and technology.

It took her about a year to make the piece and, as the artist explained in a 1986 interview, it covers the "personal history of mankind and technology [that] starts with the birth of our solar system and evolves through the camera obscura, industrial revolution, photography, electricity, first satellite communications, first shot into space, [and] finally the Macintosh computer." In keeping with the quote by twentieth-century philosopher Wittgenstein included in the piece (under the shorter-haired version of herself), it may take the viewer some time to become oriented and unpack the complexity of this piece because multiple meanings lie beneath the surface.

Other snippets of language range from lists to charts to hand gestures. Her imagery encompasses the past, present, and future in a relatively small space, with the Paleolithic depiction of the bird-headed man and his bird staff from the caves of Lascaux (see pp. 562–63) like a floating tattoo above her dreaming body. Greiman uses blur, bitmapping (binary data in a matrix of pixels, or bits used to make digital images and displays), variations in typography, and collage as playful design elements. At a time when the Xerox machine was cutting edge, this piece was very daring.

Timekeeper by American Sarah Sze (b. 1969) (**3.10.8**) takes Greiman's transmedia approach to two-dimensional explorations of design into three-dimensional space and time. Sze's approach has been called a post-medium condition, because the lived experience of the piece and references to the omnipresence of information overload in today's world eclipse the use of a certain artistic medium, such as painting, sculpture, or video. The internal logic of the artwork comes from the amalgamation, not the distinction, of art media.

A large mass within a darkened room, *Timekeeper* consists of surfaces, metal structures, and surrounding walls punctuated by found objects, moving images, and points of light—all combined into a transfixing constellation. The artist considers the sculpture a tool for the images seen here and incorporated the location and sound of its making directly in the installation (the desk she used to edit it is included, and the sounds of the machines during its making serve as the audio). In order to experience the piece, the viewer walks through the structure and becomes immersed in the video.

In much the same way that Greiman's *Does it Make Sense?* used design and technology as her subject, source material, and visual vocabulary, Sze's *Timekeeper* serves as a treatise on moving pictures explored through the visual history and lived experience of the passage of time in art. In both of these works, the floating frames and extreme scale shifts reference the proliferation of information we encounter in our contemporary lives by mimicking how we actually see things.

flavored drink mix (Kool-Aid) known for its distinctive hues. Such words as "resist," "love," "black," "nation," "revolution," and "beautiful" radiate from the head and body of political activist Angela Davis to signal the intensity and necessity of the message, like a call to action.

Throughout her artistic career, Native American artist Jolene Rickard (b. 1956) has told complex stories as she examines her heritage through myths, stories, cultural practices, and experiences, both past and present. As a member of the Tuscarora nation (from the Iroquois language family), Rickard creates work that often combines spiritual experiences and events from daily life, which are familiar to the Tuscarora, but less so to outside audiences. Her installation *Corn Blue Room* (**3.10.9**), part of an exhibition called "Reservation X: The Power of Place," explores the importance of home in the formation of identity, and also the changing

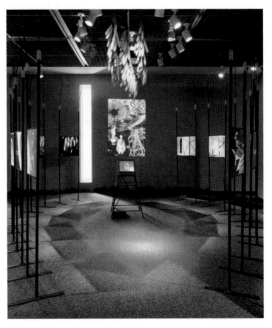

3.10.9 Jolene Rickard, *Corn Blue Room*, 1998. Mixed-media installation, Denver Art Museum, Colorado

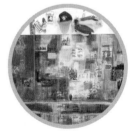

Jaune Quick-to-See Smith also confronts issues related to the Native American community, such as environmental awareness and preservation, racial and gender stereotyping, cultural commodification, and problems of alcoholism:
→ see **1.9.15**, p. 156

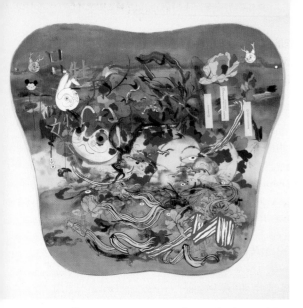

3.10.10 Jiha Moon, *Mystery Myo—frustration is one of the great things in what you do*, 2010. Ink and acrylic on hanji, 51 × 44¾″

Iranian-born artist Shirin Neshat (b. 1957) has lived in the United States since 1974, when she was seventeen years old. Her photographs and films explore the experience of a woman caught between the tradition and heritage of her native Iran and her perspective as a woman living outside of that culture. When she was allowed to return to Iran in 1990, following the Islamic Revolution, the country had become a conservative, theocratic republic. One of the most striking changes was the requirement for women to wear the *chador*, a loose robe that covers them from head to toe, leaving only their faces and hands exposed. Neshat made art as a way to process her feelings of displacement, exile, and loss. Over time her work has taken a more critical stance against the erosion of individual freedom in the

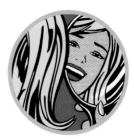

The bold colors and dot patterns of Lichtenstein's Modernist style influenced Jiha Moon and have become so iconic that they are now recognizable even when used in isolation:
→ see **3.9.31**, p. 518

nature of the reservation as a community and home. Ears of corn hang from above, saturated with blue light. The projected photographs and images relate to nature on one side (corn, the seasons, community) and technology on the other (the towers of a hydroelectric plant owned by the New York Power Authority), both of which have significantly affected the Tuscarora community's land in upper New York State. The installation invites viewers to walk into the space and interact with it. By looking at the imagery, they can experience the importance of song and dance as ways of expressing kinship and of passing knowledge from one generation to the next.

In such works as *Mystery Myo—frustration is one of the great things in what you do* (**3.10.10**), Jiha Moon (b. 1973 in Daegu, South Korea; lives in Atlanta, Georgia) visually communicates the complexity of identity through densely collaged works and wide-ranging **symbolism**. The mashup of styles ranges from smoky shadows and traditional brush painting to bold colors and graphic outlines of cartoons and Roy Lichtenstein-inspired Pop art-style marks. Moon is interested in the simplifications, stereotypes, and shortcuts people take as they access people outside their own cultural background, sometimes referred to as "the other" or "foreign." While her work has a light and humorous tone, it uses these unexpected combinations of visual categories to take a critical stance toward misunderstandings about identity, refuse simplistic labels, and create an intriguing and empowering expression.

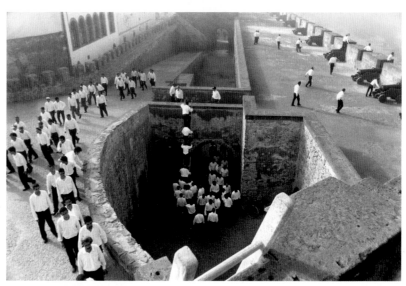

3.10.11a Shirin Neshat, *Rapture*, 1999. Production still

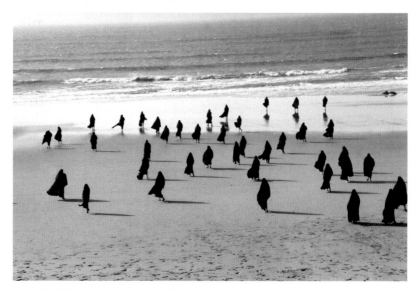

3.10.11b Shirin Neshat, *Rapture* series, 1999. Gelatin silver print, 42½ × 67½″

extremist environment she knows the people of her country are enduring.

In such artworks as the film *Rapture* (**3.10.11a** and **3.10.11b**) Neshat projects two images into a gallery space at the same time. One screen shows men wearing white shirts and black pants in a stone fortress (**3.10.11a**). The motivation behind their collective actions is never explained, but they seem to revolve around the cannons located on the building's rooftop. On the other screen, women wearing black chadors are shown making their way to a beach where they will later push a small group of women out to sea in a rowboat (**3.10.11b**). Whether the women are being persecuted or liberated, whether they chose to leave or were forced to go, is unclear. This scene in *Rapture* takes on added resonance in relation to the worldwide refugee crisis. Because she deals with social, political, and cultural issues in a very poetic way, Neshat's work has a broad appeal to audiences from diverse communities and backgrounds.

Recontextualizing Historical Events

Art in a Postmodern and postcolonial world involves revisiting histories and introducing elements once overlooked, as well as perspectives not previously supported. Unlike much of the art made during the modern period, artists directly engage with difficult narratives rather than focusing exclusively on formal abstraction or absurdity.

The American Jean-Michel Basquiat (1960–1988) was an outsider of sorts, because he was not formally trained, and started as a **graffiti** artist. His style has been called **Neo-Expressionist** because, like earlier Expressionist styles, it used aggressive lines, rough **textures**, and personal narrative. His painting *The Nile* (**3.10.12**), also known as *The History of Black People* or *The Grand Spectacle*, is an expansive collage of images inspiring us to reconsider many groups that were potentially outsiders, and with which Basquiat was connected. The scribbled text and intentionally "primitive" figures acknowledge his beginnings as an untrained artist tagging buildings (anonymously signing them with recognizable marks) on the streets of New York. Numerous references to Egypt, including a female figure in the center, the boats, pharaoh, and guard dog to the right, together with the African masks on the left, make connections to African heritage. By referring to Memphis both in connection with Thebes (Egypt) and Tennessee, Basquiat reinforces the spread of African culture and traditions into other parts of the world, a development known as the African Diaspora. Spanish words used throughout the artwork refer to Basquiat's immigrant parents, who came from Puerto Rico and Haiti. Notably, the

Symbolism: using images or symbols in an artwork to convey meaning; often obvious when the work was made but requiring research for modern viewers to understand

Graffiti: markings that are scratched, scribbled, or sprayed on a wall without the consent of the owner

Neo-Expressionist: a broad term, first used in the late 1970s to early 1980s; describes figurative and allegorical, not totally abstract, art with materials used aggressively to give clear evidence of the artist's gestures

Texture: the surface quality of a work, for example fine/coarse, detailed/lacking in detail

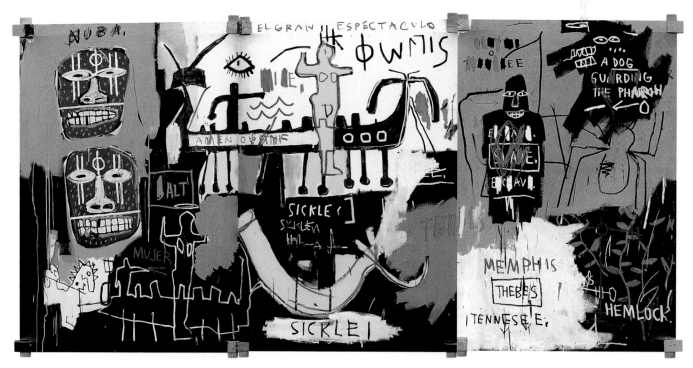

3.10.12 Jean-Michel Basquiat, *The Nile*, 1983. Acrylic and oilstick on canvas mounted on wood supports, triptych, 5'8" × 11'11". Private collection

word "slave" written on the figure on the right has been crossed out, suggesting that, while the sufferings of enslavement cannot be erased or ignored, new terminology and expectations beyond its history are needed.

Fred Wilson (b. 1954), an American artist with African, Native American, and European ancestry, draws on his background as an art educator to rearrange objects in museum collections. He takes on the role of the curator—the person responsible for overseeing, preserving, and exhibiting objects in a particular collection—and converts the role into an art action. Wilson's employment at the Metropolitan Museum of Art, the American Museum of Natural History, and the American Crafts Museum gave him insight into the ways in which museum displays create certain experiences that have specific effects on audiences. In his own art, Wilson looks critically at the assumptions behind the ways in which museums exhibit artworks.

In *Mining the Museum*, Wilson selected and presented objects only from the collection of the Maryland Historical Society (**3.10.13**). He included objects rarely seen because they were usually in storage (like a broadsheet offering $50 reward for a runaway enslaved man named Jack) and arranged them in unusual ways (such as a KKK robe in a baby carriage). He also provided provocative wall labels, and installed audio loops to accompany certain

3.10.13 Fred Wilson, *Portraits of Cigar Store Owners*, from *Mining the Museum*, installation, Maryland Historical Society, April 4, 1992–February 28, 1993

pieces. One section of the installation displays five "cigar store Indians" with their backs to the viewer. (Since the nineteenth century, "cigar store Indians" have been used as sidewalk displays for tobacco shops in America.) The title *Portraits of Cigar Store Owners*, is ironic because Native Americans would never have owned cigar stores at the time; it is also critical of the degradation of the dignity of Native Americans that is involved in turning them into advertising signs. Throughout *Mining the Museum*, the museum's unconscious racial biases are exposed. As a result of this installation, the Maryland Historical Society realized it had never staged an exhibition about enslavement or institutionalized racism, despite the fact that eight out of ten Baltimore residents are African American.

American artist Mark Bradford (b. 1961) uses art to create dialogues with historical accounts and the clear acknowledgment that all interpretations are subjective. His site-specific installation on the cylindrical walls of the Hirshhorn Museum was inspired by the space's similarities to a painting of 1883 by Paul Philippoteaux. Made twenty years after the Battle of Gettysburg, Philippoteaux's original painting is a **cyclorama** (a theatrical precursor to the IMAX in which a painting covers cylindrical walls to create a 360-degree panorama). To make *Pickett's Charge* (**3.10.14a**), Bradford crafted billboard-sized reproductions of Philippoteaux's painting into eight new paintings, totaling nearly 400 linear feet. Using his signature process of **décollage** (to take away) and **collage** (to combine), Bradford combined the reproductions with paper, glue, rope, and twine; then he scraped away, built up, and sanded them until they were five to ten layers deep. The linework created by the ropes makes them look as if they were tightened to dig rows into the surface and create the distressed, dynamic texture (**3.10.14b**).

Bradford explains that the materials he uses are invested with meaning that he doesn't want to erase. It begins with the romanticized painting of a battle (in which an estimated 1,500 union soldiers and over 6,000 confederates died) that was once visited by middle-class and working people for entertainment. Another critical layer is created by the accounts included in history books, once accepted as facts but which over time have been recognized as selective and incomplete. Finally, the

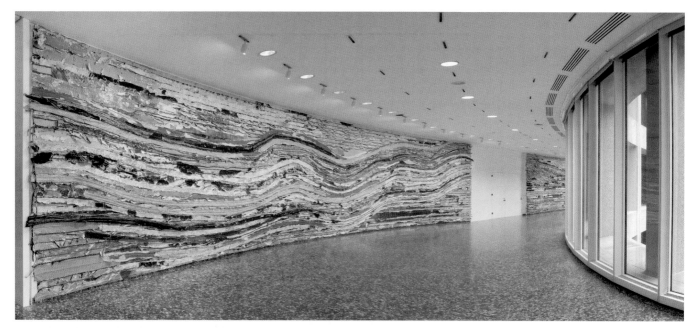

3.10.14a Mark Bradford, *Pickett's Charge (The High-Water Mark)*, 2017. Mixed media on canvas, 144 × 200". Installation view, "Mark Bradford. Pickett's Charge," Hirschhorn Museum and Sculpture Garden, Washington, DC

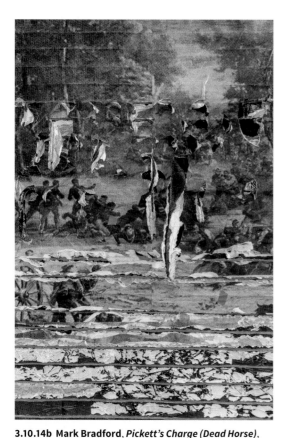

3.10.14b Mark Bradford, *Pickett's Charge (Dead Horse)*, 2017 (detail)

accumulated and scraped-down layers bring the artist and viewers to a contemporary experience of the legacy of the "troubling history" of American race relations dating back to the US Civil War. In 2017, when the catalog for *Pickett's Charge* was being written, Bradford observed

that "the world is on fire." He found himself contemplating civil rights that he, and many other American citizens, had previously taken for granted.

Complexity, Chaos, and Imagination

Since the late twentieth and early twenty-first century, computers, televisions, and smartphones bombard us with an increasing and overwhelming number of images and ideas twenty-four hours a day, seven days a week. Many contemporary artists acknowledge and embrace the complexity and chaos of the world in which we live. The Internet and—until very recently—increasingly easy international travel have made the world seem smaller, and have hugely expanded our awareness of and interest in other cultures. Some artists bring order to their experiences of this global culture by creating their own systems of symbols and signs. Others incorporate widely ranging styles, techniques, and messages into single artworks. Reflecting the experience of living in the twenty-first century, contemporary artists assimilate approaches from all kinds of sources, past and present, real and imagined. Artworks made in response to the complexity of today's world, not surprisingly, contain many elements that operate on more than one level. The more you learn, the more each individual element makes sense and comes alive. Many artists navigate this complexity by integrating and fusing the once-distinct realms of fact and fiction.

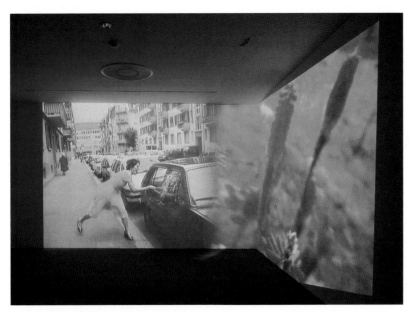

3.10.15 Pipilotti Rist, *Ever Is Over All*, 1997. Video installation with two monitors, dimensions variable. MoMA, New York

A captivating video installation called *Ever Is Over All* (**3.10.15**), created in 1997 by the Swiss artist Pipilotti Rist (b. 1962), provides a multi-sensory experience that subtly comments on decorum and the breaking of rules that normally govern society. It is a two-part projection into the corner of the room, and also has an ambient sound component that pulses throughout the gallery or museum space. On one screen we see a woman whose brilliant aquamarine dress and ruby-red slippers contrast with the drab backdrop of an urban street. On the other screen, the vibrant oranges, yellows, and greens of a luminous field of torch lilies, also called red-hot pokers, directly illuminate the room.

In her fairytale attire, the woman carries a torch lily like a staff. As she saunters down the street, she occasionally stops to smash out a car window with her flower, which is magically strong instead of fragile. The violence of her destruction does not have any effect on her happy-go-lucky demeanor. In fact, she does not even react when a police officer passes her on the sidewalk. The police officer does not react to her apparent vandalism either. They just exchange a pleasant greeting.

In 2016, the video for the song *Hold Up* by Beyoncé pays tribute to *Ever Is Over All* as Beyoncé strides down an inner-city street in a flowing yellow dress. Rist's torch lily has been replaced by a baseball bat and Beyoncé delivers blows to car windows, a fire hydrant (allowing it to sprinkle water joyously on kids in the street),

shop windows, and a video surveillance camera. Both artists create for the contemporary viewer an enigmatic story crossing the boundaries between fantasy and reality, where beauty coexists with aggression and empowerment delivers what might otherwise be seen as transgression.

From 1994 to 2002, American artist Matthew Barney (b. 1967) produced, created, and starred in five full-length films called the *Cremaster* cycle. "Cremaster" literally refers to the set of muscles that control the height of male testicles. Barney adopted the cremaster as a metaphor because it expresses the sense that identity changes over time: from prenatal sexual differentiation (in *Cremaster 1*) to a fully formed, or "descended," being (in *Cremaster 5*). The films do not use narrative or dialogue in the conventional sense, but visually and conceptually incorporate the history of the place in which the films are set, episodes of invented mythology, Barney's personal interests, and a system of symbols that he developed.

In the still shown here from *Cremaster 5* (**3.10.16**), Barney plays a fictional character known as the Queen's Giant, who is undergoing the final stages of his transformation into a fully formed man. In an interview in 2004, Barney explained that he was not searching for coherence in the *Cremaster* cycle, but that the

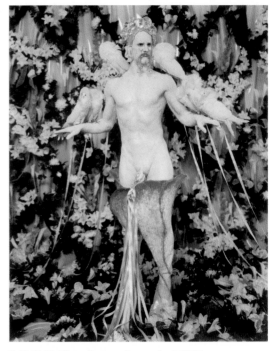

3.10.16 Matthew Barney, *Cremaster 5*, 1997. Production still

films' ambiguity mimics his own wandering interests and the way he absorbs things on a day-to-day basis. The intricate symbolism that Barney invests in the people, places, and things in the films recalls all the simultaneous meanings that these elements can have (whether we are aware of them or not), and suggests that we can access them at the touch of a button, or at the whim of an artist.

In 2020, Chinese artist Cai Guo-Qiang (b. 1957) created a high-tech spectacle called *Sleepwalking in the Forbidden City* (**3.10.17a** and **3.10.17b**). Known for using gunpowder as an art medium since the 1980s, Cai has gone on to make gigantic installations with actual cars, lifesize replicas of wild animals, and outdoor explosion events to call attention to the beauty, power, and uncertainty of the physical world we live in. In *Sleepwalking...* he combined fireworks and VR (virtual reality) technology with more conventional sculptural modeling and video animation in order to do what is impossible in real life. Due to the cultural importance of the fifteenth-century imperial palace (as the political and ritual center of China since the 1400s), fireworks could not be set off on the site. Instead, Cai and his crew filmed an elaborate and brightly colored fireworks display on the banks of the Liuyang River (**3.10.17a**). An enormous alabaster replica of the palace complex, handcrafted by Quanzhou Xinwen Craft, was used to make animations and was installed in the gallery for the exhibition. Finally, all of the parts came together in a dazzling and captivating video that can also be viewed on site through VR headsets (**3.10.17b**). About this piece, Cai said: "The [COVID-19] pandemic further prompted me to consider what my methodology can be when employing an unfamiliar medium that is high tech, to dialogue with the invisible world on a spiritual level." The artist has also said that "art can help

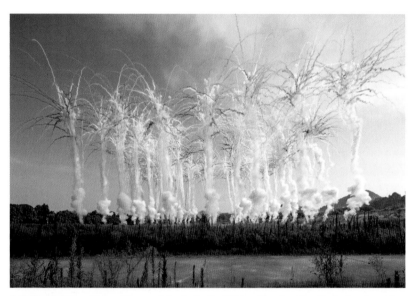

3.10.17a Cai Guo-Qiang, *Sleepwalking in the Forbidden City: Daytime Explosion Event for Virtual Reality*, 2020. 9 minutes 6 seconds. Realized at Tanghua Fireworks, Liuyang, Hunan, August 4, 2020

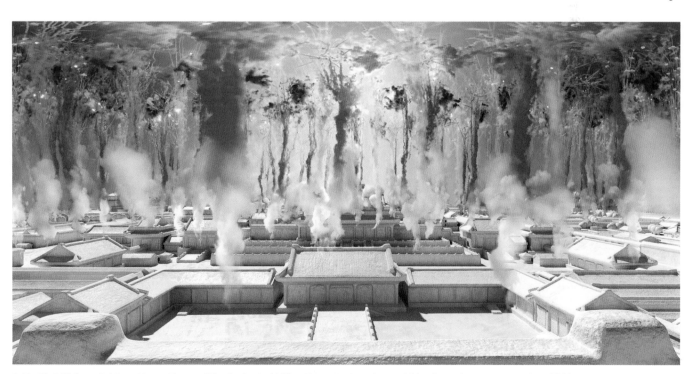

3.10.17b Still from Cai Guo-Qiang, *Sleepwalking in the Forbidden City*, 2020. Duration variable. Fireworks ceremony over Forbidden City (replica) in virtual reality experience through VR headsets. Virtual Reality in Partnership with HTC VIVE Arts. Collection of the artist

make the political climate more open and help society become more free."

Transforming Space

Many contemporary artists continue practices established from previous artistic styles, movements, or individual approaches. Minimalism comes to mind when viewing the work of American artist Tara Donovan (b. 1969), both in materials and aesthetic effect. Donovan's *Untitled* (**3.10.18**) fills the entire room. From far away, it takes up the panorama of the space and viewers are uncertain whether they are seeing fabric or a giant lamp in the **contours** of cloud-like shapes across the ceiling. Upon closer inspection, the details of the medium become clear: Styrofoam cups—lots of cups. The artist has also made sculptures out of toothpicks, pencils, tar paper, paper plates, short pieces of wire, buttons, and plastic straws (more than two million of them, in another piece called *Haze*). Donovan states that the value of mass-produced objects in an art context is now widely accepted; the excitement comes from what happens to them. Donovan calls her work "site-responsive"

because she selects her materials for their unique properties—here, the soft white color and curves of the cups—and the way in which these interact with aspects of a given space, for example, the ceiling, lighting, and shape of the room, to produce a very specific effect on the viewer.

Art as Social Practice

In the early 2000s the term "social practice" was adopted from social theory to describe art that directly engages a community in confronting societal issues and challenges. Collaboration, interaction, and impactful results building on the vision of the artist (or artists) are more important than appearance, style, or medium. While aspects of the work may be brought into art museums or galleries, social practice art tends to exist in the neighborhoods where people live, and they evolve over time.

The American conceptual artist Mel Chin (b. 1951) challenges the traditional role of the artist and the expected outcomes of artworks by engaging specialists and the community to generate solutions for an important environmental issue in his *Operation Paydirt/*

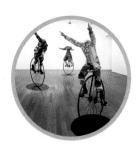

The installation *Mobility* by Yinka Shonibare consists of three headless sculptural figures on unicycles occupying a gallery space:
→ see **2.10.10**, p. 341

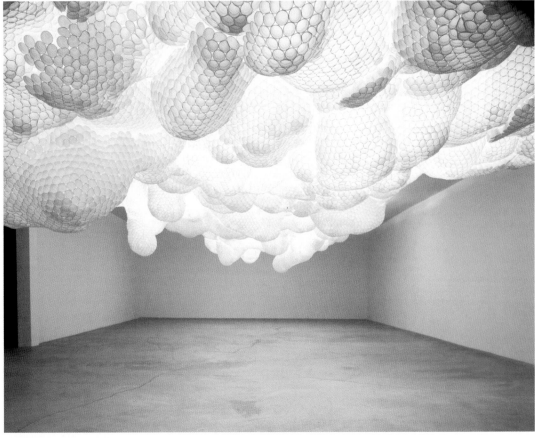

3.10.18 Tara Donovan, ***Untitled***, 2003. Styrofoam cups and hot glue, 16 × 16′. Installation at Ace Gallery, Los Angeles, California, 2005

Perspectives on Art: Gabriel Dawe
Materializing Light, Inverting Constructs

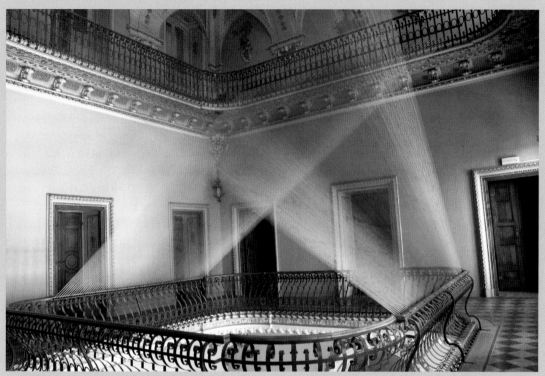

3.10.19 **Gabriel Dawe**, *Plexus no. 19*, site-specific installation at Villa Olmo, Como, Italy for *Miniartextil: Agora*, 2012. Gütermann thread, painted wood, and hooks, 23 × 23 × 23'

Gabriel Dawe (b. 1973) was born in Mexico City where he grew up surrounded by the intensity and color of Mexican culture. Here the artist describes what his colorful thread installations mean to him.

One of the first ideas I began developing...is related to the human need for shelter. I decided to create an architectural structure by using the core material of clothing....By reversing scale and material to create an actual structure made of thread, the sheltering quality goes through a transformation, from protecting the body on a physical level, to soothing the human spirit in a subtle, yet powerful way....The fineness of the thread makes these installations ethereal, almost immaterial, yet not, almost disappearing to the eye and leaving a color haze behind. This color mist alludes to a symbolic quest to materialize light, to give it density, so that I can offer the viewer an approximation of things otherwise inaccessible to us—a glimmer of hope that brings us closer to the transcendent, to show that there can be beauty in this messed-up world we live in.

The choice to use thread is a natural extension of my attempt to explore and subvert social constructs of gender. My growing up in Mexico,

where machismo is ingrained in the very structure of society, led to many frustrations as a boy, one that looked up to his older sister—a sister who was privy to certain activities that were a definite no-no for boys....Eventually, I grew out of that frustration, but the memory of it led me to explore [embroidery] as an adult, and in doing so, to question the many social constructs that we sometimes presume to be permanent, rigid and inflexible. Eventually, I came to see the structures I was making with thread as symbolic representations of these social constructs, the viewer navigating and negotiating the installation in a dance that is analogous to what we all do in real life, without any particular thought, on a daily basis.

"Plexus" [see **3.10.19**] literally means the network of nerves or vessels informing and sustaining the body. It was the perfect name [for this series] because it not only refers to the connection of the body with its environment, but it also relates directly to the intricate network of threads forming the installation itself, and to the tension inherent in the thread, vibrating with an almost tangible luminosity. Plexus evokes the intrinsic order within the apparent chaos that exists in nature.

Fundred Dollar Bill projects (**3.10.20a** and **3.10.20b**). After the devastation caused by Hurricane Katrina in 2005, Chin learned about the presence and severity of lead-toxic soil in and around New Orleans and its effects, especially on children. Chin responded by initiating a collective art project that involves hundreds of thousands of contributors, including many schoolchildren, drawing their interpretations of $100 bills. The Fundred organization planned to make the money for the bioremediation of the lead-toxic soil by requesting from the US government the equivalent of the drawings' value in exchange for the needed goods and services. The organization continues to raise awareness of lead poisoning through Fundreds and to work toward municipal and government implementation of Operation Paydirt. In 2016, the Fundred headquarters moved to Washington D.C. to be closer to policy makers. The organization also participated in the National Lead Summit to create a Blueprint for Action and ignite a national movement for the eradication of lead poisoning in the US. In 2021, the Fundred Reserve, housing nearly half a million Fundreds, was gifted to the Brooklyn Museum.

The American artist Theaster Gates (b. 1973) has similarly expanded the realm of art into life by focusing his art practice on community restoration. In 2006 he bought his first building (a house) on Dorchester Avenue. Located in a rough region of Southside Chicago, this block was known for violence, urban decay, and abandonment. Over a number of years, Gates has expanded his Dorchester Projects to include a record store, cinema house, housing collaborative, and an Arts Bank (**3.10.21a** and **3.10.21b**). When he learned that the area's historic bank building was set for demolition, he was determined to save it. The city effectively gave him the building because it was in such a bad state, including being flooded with about 6 ft. of water. At the time, ironically, no banks would finance construction plans in this neighborhood; however, Gates's belief in the power of art to make something out of nothing helped to finance the restoration work. As he had done with previous renovations,

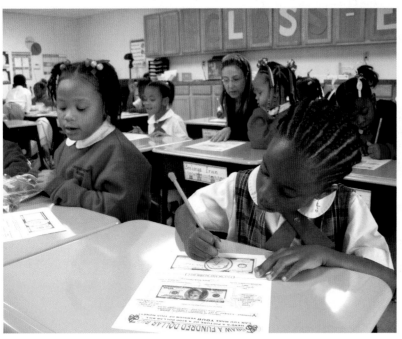

3.10.20a Mel Chin, *Operation Paydirt/Fundred Dollar Bill* **project**. Children making Fundreds at Langston Hughes Charter, New Orleans, Louisiana, 2008

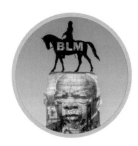

Projections and graffiti added during the 2020 Black Lives Matter protests at the Robert E. Lee Monument in Richmond, Virginia, brought people together and inspired reconsideration of the Confederate monument, including government plans for the sculpture's removal:

→ see **4.7.8**, p. 624

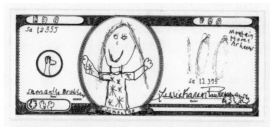
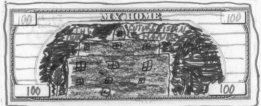
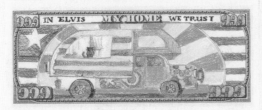
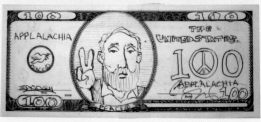

3.10.20b Mel Chin, *Operation Paydirt/Fundred Dollar Bill* **project**. Examples of the Fundreds drawn by students in New Orleans, Louisiana (top left and right); Marfa, Texas (bottom left); and Collowhee, Tennessee (bottom right)

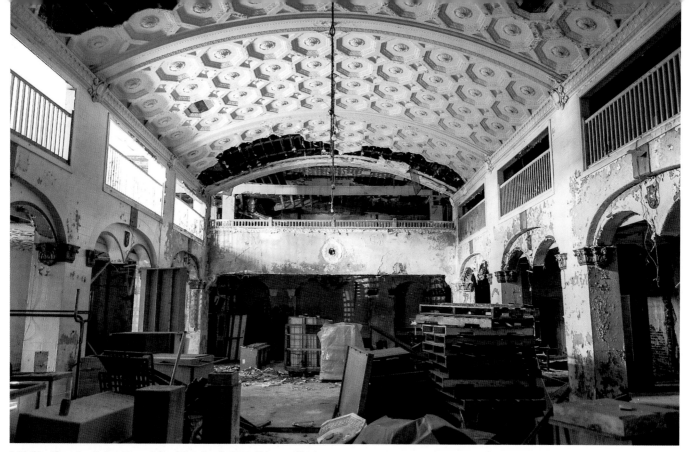

3.10.21a **Theaster Gates**, **Stony Island Arts Bank**, 2015, Chicago, Illinois

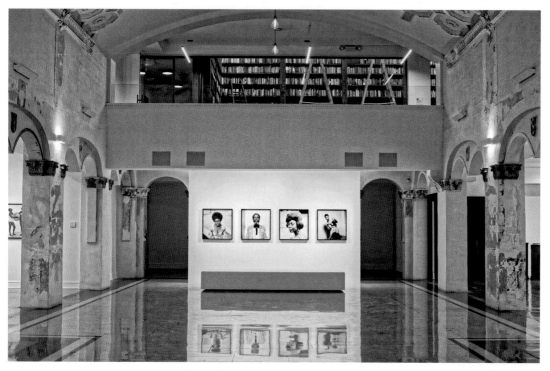

3.10.21b **Theaster Gates**, **Stony Island Arts Bank after restoration**

Gates used the materials in the bank to create pieces of art—such as "Bank Bonds" made out of marble from the bathroom walls—to in turn generate the proceeds needed to fund the million-dollar restoration. Now known as the Stony Island Arts Bank, the site serves as a repository for black historical experience, with archives and collections that would otherwise be lost to either demolition or renovation and gentrification.

Explore Further The Late Twentieth Century and Art of the Present Day

Identity

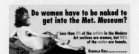

4.9.8 Guerrilla Girls, *Do Women Have to be Naked …?*, 1989 → p. 654

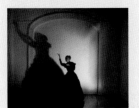

2.10.9 Yuki Kihara, *Taualuga: The Last Dance*, 2006 → p. 340

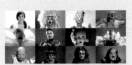

4.3.11 Jillian Mayer, *I Am Your Grandma* (selected video stills), 2011 → p. 575

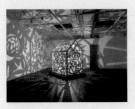

1.9.8 Anila Quayyum Agha, *This is NOT a Refuge! 2*, 2019 → p. 153

Transforming Materials

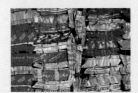

1.10.1b El Anatsui, *Man's Cloth* (detail), 2001→ p. 159

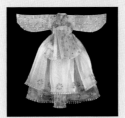

2.6.1 Hyo-In Kim, *To Be Modern #2*, 2004 → p. 269

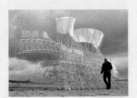

1.5.12 Theo Jansen, *Animaris Umeris (Strandbeest #48)*, 2009 → p. 110

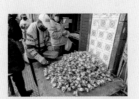

2.10.12 Félix Gonzàlez-Torres, *"Untitled" (Fortune Cookie Corner)*, 1990/2020 → p. 342

Postmodern and Conceptual

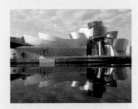

1.2.17 Frank Gehry, Guggenheim Museum, Bilbao, Spain, 1997 → p. 60

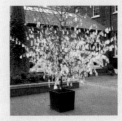

1.7.1 Claes Oldenburg and Coosje van Bruggen, *Plantoir*, 2001 → p. 131

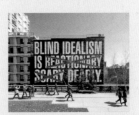

2.10.3 Yoko Ono, *Wish Tree for Liverpool*, 2008 → p. 337

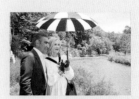

2.10.2 Barbara Kruger, *Untitled (Blind Idealism Is…)*, 2016–17 → p. 336

Contemporary

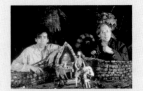

2.9.10 Tim Burton, set of *The Nightmare Before Christmas*, 1993 → p. 324

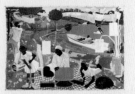

1.10.10 Kerry James Marshall, *Past Times*, 1997 → p. 169

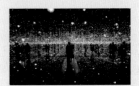

3.3.16 Yayoi Kusama, *Infinity Mirrored Room…* 2013 → p. 402

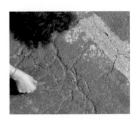

2.9.21 Eugene Levy and Catherine O'Hara in *Schitt's Creek*, 2020 → p. 332

Your Turn:
How do these artworks relate to the culture or ideas discussed in this chapter?

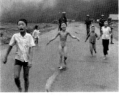

4.6.3 Nick Ut, *Vietnamese Girl Kim Phuc Running,* 1972 → p. 605

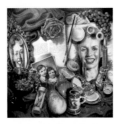

4.3.9 Audrey Flack, *Marilyn (Vanitas)*, 1977 → p. 573

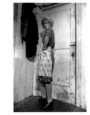

4.9.4 Cindy Sherman, *"Untitled Film Still #35,"* 1979 → p. 650

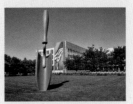

2.10.13 *Red Sand Project*, 2015 → p. 343

Part 4 Themes

Artworks reveal the concerns of humanity. Throughout the world, similar issues, or themes, are explored by artists. By comparing artworks in terms of their meaning, we come closer to understanding the uniqueness of different cultures and artists. Exploring topics commonly addressed by artists throughout space and time, and through a variety of methods and materials, also makes us more aware of shared concerns. Artworks deal with belief systems, survival, the natural world, and technology; and with issues related to status, power, and identity. By studying art in this way we can better understand various cultures and ourselves.

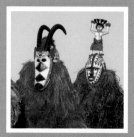

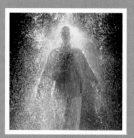

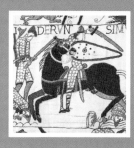

4.1
Art and the Community

Patron: an organization or individual who sponsors the creation of works of art

Gothic: a Western European architectural style of the twelfth to the sixteenth century, characterized by the use of pointed arches and ornate decoration

Relic: an object that survives from the past; in religion, the mortal remains of a saint or an object that has been in contact with the saint

Stained glass: colored glass used for windows or decorative applications

Vaulted: covered with an arch-shaped ceiling or roof

Concrete: a hard, strong, and versatile construction material made up of powdered lime, sand, and rubble

Travertine: a light-colored limestone deposited in mineral springs and used as a building material

Pilaster: a vertical element, rectangular in shape, that provides architectural support for crossing horizontal elements in post-and-lintel construction; also used for decoration

The community mural process makes art more accessible; it brings art into the lives of people who didn't have it.

(Susan Cervantes, San Francisco muralist)

This is a way of getting your art on the street. Lots of people stop to look at it. It's not like being famous, but it's a way of getting your art looked at. You have an audience.

(Aliseo Purpura-Pontoniere, urban youth arts student)

We tend to think of art as the work of a single individual, but art often involves large numbers of people, even whole communities. As the statements above by professional artist Susan Cervantes and a student who worked with her demonstrate, artists can create art not just for the enjoyment and benefit of a single **patron**, or for a larger audience in an art gallery, but also for an entire community. Community art may require many people to become involved in its construction. Other times, artworks play important roles for performers in ceremonies and group events. Still other community artworks, situated in public places, are there to be contemplated by countless viewers. A community—whether a small rural town, an apartment complex, a college campus, or an online discussion group—shares a common interest, if not a physical space. Studying the art made by and for communities throughout history tells us a great deal about the interaction between artists and their environments.

In this chapter we will examine the many ways in which art has been used to pursue community objectives. Because buildings have such a direct impact on shaping a community,

often becoming symbols of a particular place, we will look at several examples of architecture, as well as at paintings and ritual performances. We will look first at an example of architecture built to unite communities through religion. We will then turn our attention to other types of community art, including artworks made by, for, and about the community; those that reflect shared beliefs or experiences; and art made to exist in public places.

Places to Gather

Structures designed to house ceremonies, civic events, and entertainments often draw crowds of people, whether they were originally intended to or not (see: Massive Undertakings and Mysteries for the Masses, pp. 544–45). Throughout history and in places as varied as ancient Rome, medieval France, and present-day New York City, communities have come together to build, visit, or acknowledge important locations. Whether because of their distinctive features, or because they reflect the concerns and practices of the communities that use them, buildings often become iconic destinations for people to see when they travel.

Gothic churches, such as the magnificent Notre Dame Cathedral (**4.1.1**) in Paris, were originally built using resources from the entire community and remain a source of great civic pride. Started in 1163, Notre Dame originally took almost 200 years and 1,000 laborers to build. Pilgrims traveled to Notre Dame to experience a sense of religious community, both because the building was so impressive and because it contained sacred Christian **relics**. The cathedral made international news in April 2019 when it caught fire, either due to an electrical short circuit or an improperly

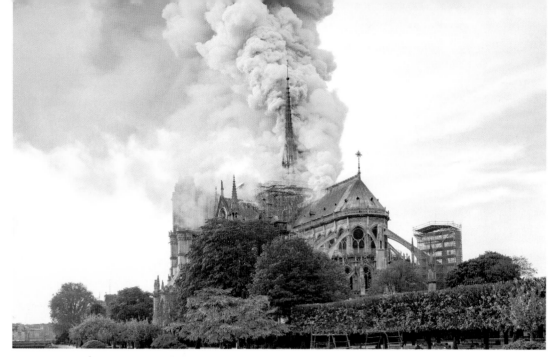

4.1.1 Fire at Notre Dame Cathedral (photograph April 15, 2019), built 1163–1250, Île de la Cité, Paris, France

extinguished cigarette. Saved from the fire's destruction were what are believed to be a piece of the True Cross on which, according to the Bible, Jesus Christ was crucified; a fragment of the Holy Lance used to pierce his side; and the Crown of Thorns that the Romans made to mock Christ as King of the Jews. While the **stained-glass** windows also survived, up to 10 percent of the artwork was destroyed and the roof collapsed, causing the spire to pierce the **vaulted** ceiling 102 ft. above the floor. Even while the fifteen-hour fire raged in 2019, the French President Emmanuel Macron vowed to rebuild. Scientists, architects, engineers, and construction workers will be working until at least 2024 to restore the building's soaring height and spiritual light. Within days of its destruction, people from around the globe contributed $1 billion for its reconstruction. But in addition to widespread support for the rebuilding initiative, the donations sparked debates about income inequality and questionable philanthropic motivations.

While cathedrals, churches, and other places of worship have become noteworthy as centers of community activity, people have designed buildings for the entertainment of their communities since antiquity. Among the most famous arenas of the ancient world is the Colosseum, one of imperial Rome's largest public buildings and an extraordinary feat of architecture and engineering (**4.1.2**). Measuring 615 ft. long by 510 ft. across and standing 159 ft.

tall, the Colosseum could hold between 45,000 and 55,000 people. The Romans were the first to exploit fully the structural possibilities of **concrete**, which they used to construct the Colosseum's massive foundations and parts of its vaulted ceilings. The exterior was covered with marble and **travertine** limestone (a light-colored form of limestone deposited in mineral springs) and decorated with columns, and **pilasters** made of another type of local limestone. There were seventy-six entrance doors, called *vomitoria*, a word that offers a vivid mental image of crowds spilling from the doors after an event. Roman citizens flocked to the Colosseum to see gladiatorial fights between men; staged combats with hunts of wild animals; and even mock sea battles.

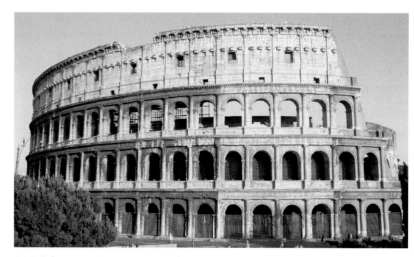

4.1.2 Colosseum, 72–80 CE, Rome, Italy

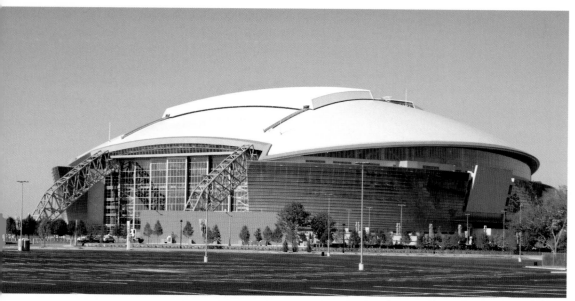

4.1.3 AT&T Stadium, Arlington, Texas, 2009

Atrium: a central, normally public, interior space, first used in Roman houses

Pyramid: an ancient structure, usually massive in scale, consisting of a square base with four sides that meet at a point or apex with each side forming a triangular shape

Ziggurat: a Mesopotamian stepped tower, roughly pyramid-shaped, that diminishes in size toward a platform summit

The Colosseum was designed almost 2,000 years ago for the entertainment of enormous crowds, but today's stadiums are built to hold far more people. The AT&T Stadium (**4.1.3**) was built in Arlington, Texas in 2009 to be the home of the Dallas Cowboys. It has the fourth-largest seating capacity in the NFL, 80,000, with a maximum capacity of 105,000 including standing room. This stadium is truly a community venue: it is city owned and supported by taxpayers. The Cowboys owner, Jerry Jones, funded much of the $1.15 billion construction cost and the NFL loaned a considerable amount toward the project. With an inside measuring 3 million sq. ft., AT&T Stadium is the world's largest domed structure and column-free interior. The roof retracts and glass doors at the end zones can be opened. A feat of twenty-first-century engineering, the building boasts LCD screens throughout and had the world's largest HDTV at the time of its construction. To attract an even wider audience, the building also houses an art museum with site-specific works commissioned from eighteen contemporary artists.

Art by and for the Community

In addition to attracting members of the public seeking entertainment, cultural instruction, and reflection, museums also serve as centers of local distinction, in much the same way as cathedrals and sports arenas do. In a bid to keep pace with the expanding attractions of other destination sites, many art museums,

such as the Solomon R. Guggenheim Museum in New York City (**4.1.4**), have broadened their own appeal by hosting community programming, including festivals, concerts, and film screenings. For many visitors, however, the design of a museum itself can be as much of an attraction as the art collected inside. The design of the Guggenheim Museum employs strong geometric shapes, which is characteristic of many modern buildings, but this white, circular building is distinctive amongst the city's rectangular blocks and glass skyscrapers. The

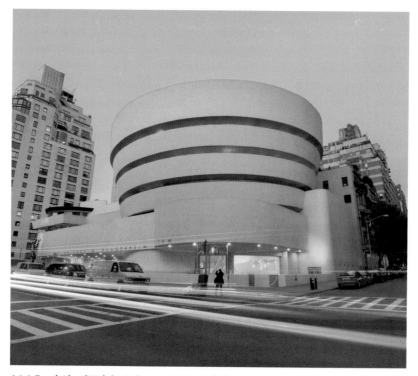

4.1.4 Frank Lloyd Wright, Solomon R. Guggenheim Museum, 1956–59, New York

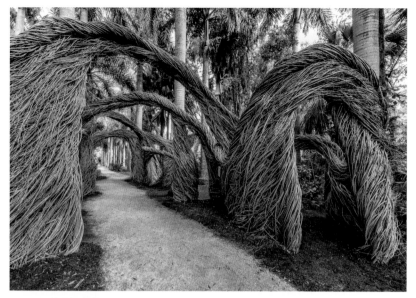

4.1.5 Patrick Dougherty, *Grand Central*, McKee Botanical Garden, Vero Beach, Florida, January 2020, 64 × 26 × 13'

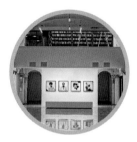

Theaster Gates has been regenerating neighborhoods in Chicago through art since 2006, by renovating buildings and creating cultural centers for the community:
→ see **3.10.21b**, p. 537

architect Frank Lloyd Wright (1867–1959) sought to provide what the director of the museum had asked for, "a temple of spirit, a monument." The interior is open, with a continuous spiral ramp around the central **atrium** connecting each successive floor. The space is filled with light from the domed skylight above.

Art can also form a center of community activity in its own right. The American artist Patrick Dougherty (b. 1945) makes site-specific "stickworks" throughout the United States and all over the world. The process of making a stickwork takes several weeks and the lifespan of Dougherty's temporary sculptures is usually two years before the natural materials break down. A key part of the construction is the

involvement of hundreds of community members. They collect saplings (from the location in which the work is to be installed, if possible) and together build the sculpture using a technique similar to weaving. *Grand Central* (**4.1.5**) was made by Dougherty and the team using willow to transform twigs and branches into a sculptural spectacle amidst the forest of Royal Palms in the McKee Botanical Garden in Vero Beach, Florida. Visitors are encouraged to enter and explore the sculpture's winding pathways and portals.

Constructed Mountains

Buildings and other structures intended to shape and dominate the environment—as Wright surely intended with his design for the Guggenheim (**4.1.4**)—have been made since ancient times. Earthen mounds and **pyramids** are amongst the most intriguing kinds of architecture. Mysteries surround their creation, function, and symbolic significance. Why were such substantial human and material resources devoted to making these figurative mountains? Whether they were built as memorials for the dead, for administrative purposes, or for religious worship and rituals, these structures had a dramatic and lasting impact on the geography of their locations.

While they resemble the Egyptian pyramids in form, the **ziggurats** of ancient West Asia, such as the one in the city-state of Ur in Sumer (now part of Iraq), were built for the benefit of the living community rather than to bury the dead (**4.1.6**). The ziggurat was part of a

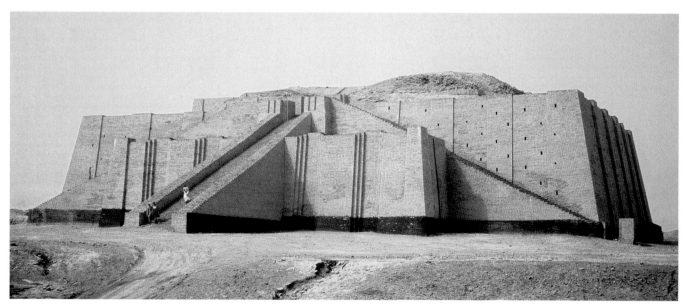

4.1.6 Ziggurat, Ur (near Nasiriyah, Iraq), originally built *c.* 2100 BCE and heavily restored

Massive Undertakings and Mysteries for the Masses

Two famous works of art, made more than 4,000 years apart, occupied public spaces used by large numbers of people. Both structures were created by the efforts of masses of laborers. Considering these enormous works together can help us understand how a work of art can change a public place and how people interact with such works.

Very little is known about the makers of Stonehenge (**4.1.7**), but the creators of *The Gates* (**4.1.8**), Christo (b. 1935–2020) and Jeanne-Claude (1935–2009), explained themselves in countless statements and interviews. We know about the construction methods they used from descriptions and from video documentation, but the techniques used to erect Stonehenge, and the intentions of its builders, remain shrouded in mystery. Stonehenge is still standing after thousands of years, while *The Gates* was designed to be in place only temporarily. Despite their differences, both works share a common aim: to focus the attention and movements of crowds of people in directions calculated by the artists who designed them.

The oldest parts of Stonehenge, on Salisbury Plain in England, are the circular embankment and ditch that surround the monument. This site was used for hundreds of years before the stones were imported from as far as 23 miles away. Stonehenge is 106 ft. in diameter and up to 20 ft. tall in places. The massive stones in the **sarsen** circle weigh up to 50 tons apiece, each one equaling the weight of 500 people or 5 buses. We will probably never know how the builders moved those stones, but most scholars believe that Stonehenge served as a giant observatory or calendar. People who gathered at Stonehenge on the longest day of the year, the summer solstice, would have seen the sun rise precisely over the great stone known as the Heelstone, which stands outside the circle. For a farming community, such as the one that built Stonehenge, the precise date of the summer solstice was important: it signaled the time to begin preparing for the fall harvest.

The Gates, installed in 2005, meandered through the 23 miles of walkways in New York's Central Park for just sixteen days. The installation was intended for public enjoyment, and an estimated four million people visited Central Park during the exhibition. The piece required

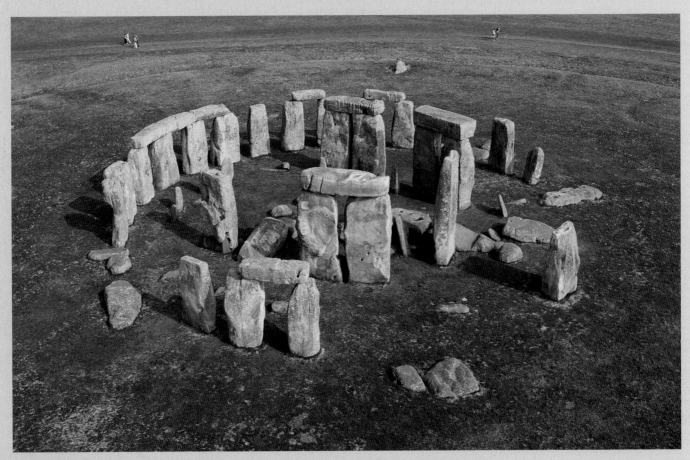

4.1.7 Stonehenge, *c.* 3200–1500 BCE, Salisbury Plain, Wiltshire, England

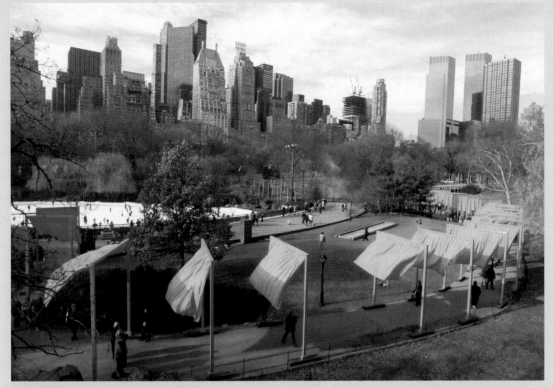

4.1.8 Christo and Jeanne-Claude, *The Gates*, Central Park, New York, 1979–2005. Steel, vinyl tubing, and nylon fabric, height *c.* 16'

community support garnered through petitions and meetings between the artists and New York City officials. Discussions about *The Gates* began in 1979 and the project was finally approved in 2003. The negotiation process was integral to the production of Christo's and Jeanne-Claude's installation, emphasizing the important role that the community plays in the conception and creation of their artworks. Facts and figures provided on the artists' website indicate the mind-boggling amounts of material and labor involved in the making of *The Gates*. A total of 60 miles of saffron-colored nylon fabric hung from 7,503 gates. Each gate was 16 ft. tall, with fabric coming down to approximately 7 ft. above the ground. The gates ranged from about 5 ft. to 18 ft. across, depending on the width of the walkway. The artists employed engineers; project directors; fabricators for the materials in the United States and Germany; 600 paid workers to install, monitor, and remove the pieces; and security guards to protect the work

at night. After *The Gates* was taken down, the materials were recycled, reflecting the artists' environmentally sustainable practices.

Although these two works were made at different times on different continents, they have in common the fact that their construction required the organized efforts of significant numbers of people and that they were used or viewed by an entire community. While it is uncertain how or why Stonehenge was built, it is clear that a highly organized social structure must have been in place to see such a venture through. *The Gates* similarly required teams of experts and construction crews to carry out the artists' vision. Keen on involving the community and having their work enliven public spaces, but interested in maintaining creative freedom, Christo and Jeanne-Claude did not accept any government or public funding and themselves paid for the creation, installation, and maintenance of the work.

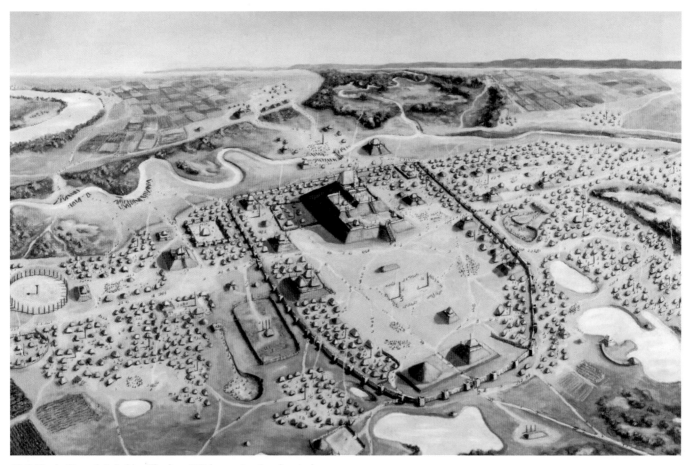

4.1.9 Monks Mound, Cahokia, Illinois, *c.* 1150 (reconstruction drawing)

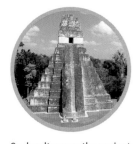

Such cultures as the ancient Egyptians and Maya created pyramid structures that resembled mountains, which became icons of their communities over time:
→ see **1.2.2**, p. 51 and **2.5.3**, p. 246

temple complex with civic and ceremonial purposes. The mud-brick structures are made up of at least three stepped levels, accessed by stairways or ramps. The lowest level is about 50 ft. high and about 210 by 150 ft. in area, with the others decreasing in size as they get closer to the heavens. The topmost platform, more than 100 ft. high, served as an elevated stage for the priest, who was one of the few people allowed access to that part of the ziggurat, and who served both as the principal human intermediary to the god who was believed to protect the city, and the chief administrator of the ziggurat. The city of Ur and its ziggurat were dedicated to the moon god Nanna, one of the three important sky deities in Sumerian religion. Festivals were organized around the phases of the moon, especially when it appeared as a crescent, and offerings were left on the high platform to please Nanna in the hope that this would ensure the abundance of such liquids as water, milk, and blood, which were believed to be sacred.

More than 3,000 years after the construction of the ziggurat at Ur, builders made the largest earthen mound ever discovered in North America (**4.1.9**). Cahokia, located in what is now southern Illinois, near St. Louis, covered 6 square miles and had an estimated population of 10,000–20,000. As with other communities that built such impressive structures, there is evidence of a highly organized society, advanced engineering knowledge, and a productive work force at this site.

The focal point of the settlement at Cahokia is Monks Mound, which was originally surrounded by about 120 smaller mounds. The base of Monks Mound measures 1,080 by 710 ft. and is topped by two smaller platforms. Though its exact purpose is uncertain, Monks Mound may have served as an elite residence, a temple, a burial structure, or perhaps all three. Monks Mound is aligned with the sun at the equinoxes, the two times of the year (in spring and fall) when day and night are exactly the same length. These alignments suggest that it may have functioned as a calendar and also served a ceremonial purpose. The site was abandoned around 600 years ago due to climate changes and the depletion of natural resources. Because Monks Mound has suffered from slumping and erosion, the enormous earthen mound's appearance is much less dramatic and impressive than it must have been at the height of Cahokia's occupation.

Rituals and Art of Healing and Community Solidarity

The production of art is often deeply connected to philosophical, religious, and ideological beliefs. Artworks made to be used in a ritual context often have symbolic meanings in addition to their appearance and visual impact. With such artifacts as temporary constructions and masks, it is important to keep in mind that the way they were experienced in their original context would have been very different from the way we now see them, in the pages of a book, on a screen, or inside glass museum cases. The objects themselves are suggestive of sights, sounds, and even smells to which we no longer have access.

Masks and **masquerades** serve the important communal function of mediating between the human and what are believed to be spiritual realms. Masquerades have been created in the belief that they enable humans to communicate with the spirit world, as it is thought the masker's personality is temporarily replaced with that of the spirit being evoked. The spirit's message will then have a direct impact upon the functions and behavior of the community. At the same time, the ritual performance of masquerades is often designed to reinforce the cultural beliefs of a community. While the mask is generally the focal point of the performance, it must be combined with costumes, music, and dance in order to invoke a particular spirit. **Gèlèdé rituals** performed by Yoruba men in Nigeria, Africa celebrate female strength, honor women as mothers, and commemorate their life-giving powers in the hope that they will continue to use them to help sustain and improve the community (**4.1.10**). The dramatic performance starts at midnight, when the mask of Efe appears, and continues into the next day. Incantations and recognition of community members occur, and the ritual then shifts toward spectators joining in the dancing. Drumming undergirds the entire ceremony. These ceremonies also acknowledge the important part played by female ancestors in Yoruba society and promote general spiritual well-being and social harmony.

Masquerade: a performance in which participants wear masks and costumes for a ritual or cultural purpose

Gèlèdé ritual: a ritual performed in Nigeria's Yoruba society to celebrate and honor women

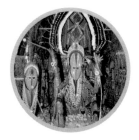

For coming-of-age rituals, the Abelam of Papua New Guinea carefully construct and decorate ceremonial houses; after the rituals take place, they no longer need them:

→ see **3.5.21**, p. 440

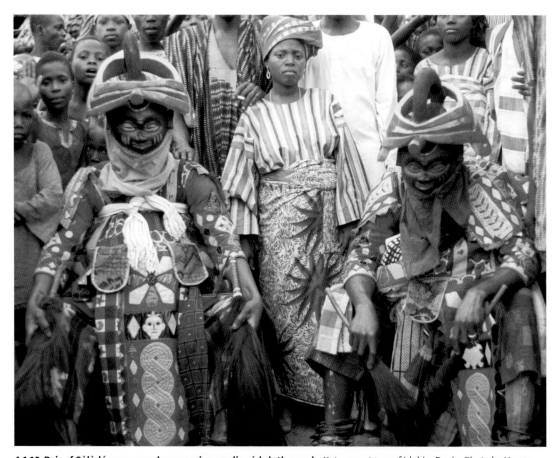

4.1.10 **Pair of Gèlèdé masqueraders wearing appliquéd cloth panels**, Ketu area, town of Idahin, Benin. Photo by Henry John Drewal, 1971

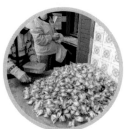

In 2020 during the COVID-19 pandemic, an earlier artwork by Félix Gonzàlez-Torres, *"Untitled" (Fortune Cookie Corner)*, was re-created internationally by 1,000 participants to encourage solidarity and bring art into spaces all over the world:

→ see **2.10.12**, p. 342

Nkisi Nkondi
Exploring the Past, Bringing It to Life

For the other *nkisi nkondi*
GATEWAYS:
→ see p. 235 and p. 431

Nkisi nkondi (plural *minkisi minkondi*): combines the words for "sacred medicine" and "to hunt"; figurative sculpture(s) used in rituals by the Yombe of Central Africa

Even in a museum, a *nkisi nkondi* has a powerful presence. When San Francisco-based choreographer and dancer Byb Chanel Bibene saw *minkisi minkondi* on a trip to Paris, it inspired him to look more deeply into his own cultural heritage. Born and raised in the Republic of Congo, Bibene did not previously know about the nineteenth-century Congolese sculptures connected to spirituality, medicine, and justice. He began researching them and in 2018 developed his piece *Nkisi Nkondi: A Divine Sculpture from Central Africa* (**4.1.13**), which presented his research and included demonstrations of traditional dances. Bibene builds on the aesthetic tradition of his country of origin to explore the meaning and impact of the nkisi nkonde in a postcolonial world that has relegated them to the status of historical artifact.

The way most people experience minkisi minkonde today would be very different from their original existence. Created by a sculptor in collaboration with a ritual specialist, they were used by individuals, families, and whole communities. An agreement struck between two or more people, for example, would have been sealed by driving nails and other metals into the wood body, similar to a paper contract today. The perceived supernatural power of the figure could be called on if one of the people broke the agreement.

Three dancers shown in this photograph of Bibene's performance wear raffia skirts while the fourth dancer is shirtless in flowing ocher pants, each resembling different parts of the sculptures, like the nail figure in the collection of the Field Museum of Natural History (**4.1.12**). The staccato

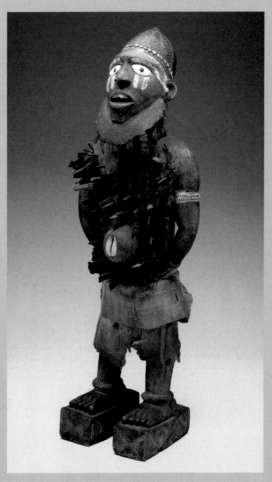

4.1.11 Standing power figure (*nkisi nkondi*), late 19th century. Wood, iron, raffia, ceramic, kaolin pigment, red camwood powder (tukula), resin, dirt, leaves, animal skin, and cowrie shell, 43¾ × 15½ × 11". Dallas Museum of Art, Texas

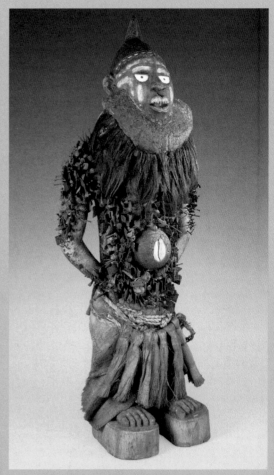

4.1.12 *Nail Figure/Nkisi Nkondi*, Yombe group, Kongo peoples, Shilango River area, Zaire, 9th century. Wood, metal, raffia cloth, pigment, clay, resin, cowrie shell, height 44½". Field Museum of Natural History, Chicago, Illinois

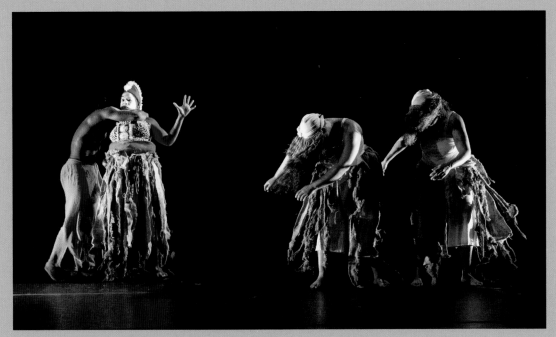

4.1.13 From left: **Byb Chanel Bibene, Sevan Kelle Boult, Nafi Thompson and Afia Thompson** appear in **"Nkisi Nkondi: Sacred Kongo Sculpture."** (Courtesy Jen Philip; published in Leslie Katz, "Striking Congo Sculptures Inspire Dance Premiere," San Francisco Examiner, May 10, 2018, sfexaminer.com)

flute and powerful percussion accompanying the performance recall the pounding required to drive the metal into the sculpture. The rhythms drive and synchronize the dancers' movements and bring to life the dynamic actions only approximated by the static sculpture that remains. Bibene's *Nkisi Nkondi* performance evokes these actions and more. It calls attention to the need for healing and protection in our community in much the same way that the sculptures that inspired it were once believed to be able to provide social bonds, protection, cures, and resolutions for the Yombe.

The Chinese artist Wenda Gu (b. 1956) says that he makes his so-called "hair monuments" in an effort to unite the people of the world through a chain of artworks. The monuments are made of walls or screens woven from human hair donated by people from countries around the globe. Gu then paints what appear to be ideograms (symbols that convey the meaning of words, such as numerals or Chinese characters) with a brush that is itself made from strands of human hair. The signs he paints are suggestive of particular cultures rather than literal transcriptions. "China Monument: Temple of Heaven" (**4.1.14**) is reminiscent of a Buddhist temple in which one partakes of a tea ceremony, and includes ancient-looking Chinese tables and chairs. Video monitors in the seats of the chairs show clouds and poetic text by the artist, so that the people experiencing this artwork are given the sense that they have entered a spiritual realm.

The space also unites a variety of cultures by including symbols that imitate Arabic, Hindi, and Chinese, as well as the Latin alphabet used by many European and North American languages. Gu's *United Nations* series of hair monuments has been made in more than

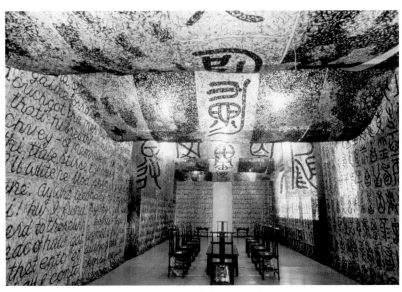

4.1.14 Wenda Gu, **"China Monument: Temple of Heaven"** (*United Nations* series), 1998. Mixed media, 52' × 20' × 13'. Hong Kong Museum of Art, China

twenty countries on five continents. More than one million people have contributed their hair to it. Gu has therefore been able to unite humans from all over the world in his work, through their common biology. The artist hopes someday to create monuments in every country in the world, linking all of the different human cultures.

Art in the Public Sphere

Not all art exists in galleries and museums. Public art generally appears in plazas and parks, or on the exterior walls of buildings. Public artworks are therefore accessible to a wide audience, as we have seen on pp. 544–45, and they are often much beloved by the community. But they can also cause problems. Sometimes public art can be taken out of context or misunderstood. People can have different views about what should be seen in public or about what is appropriate in a particular environment. Public artworks can provoke strong reactions, favorable and disapproving, and can sometimes spark fierce controversies.

American Minimalist sculptor Richard Serra (b. 1939) was chosen by a panel of experts in the federal General Services Administration (GSA) to install a sculpture on Federal Plaza in downtown New York City in 1981 (**4.1.15**). *Tilted Arc* became the subject of controversy shortly after it was installed. The 12 by 120 ft. sculpture, a curving wall of **Cor-ten steel**, cut across the plaza. Some of the people who worked in the GSA building complained that it interfered with their use of the plaza and caused a safety hazard, attracting graffiti artists, trash and rats, criminals, and potentially even terrorists. As a result, a public hearing was held to decide whether or not to leave the sculpture in place. Although no evidence supported the sculpture being a safety hazard and the majority of testimonies were in favor of keeping the work, it was ordered to be removed. During the hearing, Serra explained his approach to making sculpture in public spaces:

> My works become part of and are built into the structure of the site, and they often restructure, both conceptually and perceptually, the organization of the site. My sculptures are not objects for the viewer to stop and stare at. The historical purpose of placing sculpture on a pedestal was to

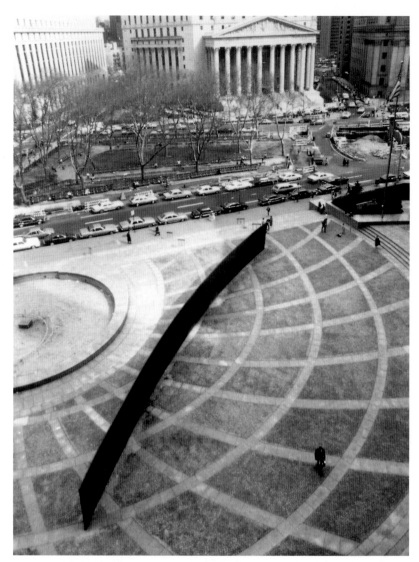

4.1.15 Richard Serra, *Tilted Arc*, 1981 (destroyed March 15, 1989). Weatherproof steel, 12′ × 120′ × 2½″. Collection General Services Administration, Washington, D.C. Installed at Federal Plaza, New York

establish a separation between the sculpture and the viewer. I am interested in creating a behavioral space in which the viewer interacts with the sculpture in its context. ...When a known space is changed through the inclusion of a site-specific sculpture, one is called on to relate to the space differently. This is a condition that can be engendered only by sculpture. This experience of space may startle some people....To remove *Tilted Arc*, therefore, would be to destroy it... If the government can destroy works of art when confronted with ... pressure [from the public], its capacity to foster artistic diversity and its power to safeguard freedom of creative expression will be in jeopardy.

The artist's lawsuit against the GSA failed to reverse the decision and the sculpture was

Cor-ten steel: a type of steel that forms a coating of rust that protects it from the weather and further corrosion

dismantled in 1989. Serra had argued that *Tilted Arc* was designed specifically for Federal Plaza and that relocating it was the equivalent of destroying it, so the metal was sent to a scrap yard. Even though the sculpture was demolished, the artist's hope of making people aware of their environment, pay attention to the path they follow on the way to work, and think about their surroundings was in some ways achieved by the attention generated by the controversy.

The dispute over Serra's *Tilted Arc* raises many questions that have a bearing on the form and functions of all public art. What is the desired impact of public art? Does it need to please its audience, or can it be used as a tool to challenge beliefs and experiences? How much weight should be given to the artist's freedom of expression? Should consideration be given to whether the artwork is in keeping with the kind of work an artist is known to produce? How much power should public voices be given, whether they belong to specialists in the art world or members of the general community? What bearing does the issue of funding—which may come from the government through special programs aimed at promoting public art or from individual patrons—have on how one answers such questions?

The subject matter of public art, especially when it has political implications, has also been a source of debate. One of the most infamous scandals surrounding a public art project occurred in 1932 when the Mexican artist

Diego Rivera (1886–1957) was commissioned by American industrialist and millionaire Nelson Rockefeller to paint a **mural** in the Radio Corporation Arts (RCA) Building at Rockefeller Center in Manhattan. Rivera was inspired by Mexico's tradition of adorning walls with paintings and sculptures, which originated long before European contact. Such murals create an environment rich with stories related to all aspects of life. Rivera's written plan for *Man at the Crossroads Looking with Hope and High Vision to the Choosing of a New and Better Future*, which Rockefeller approved, included depictions of forces of nature as well as technology, and looked forward to "the liquidation of Tyranny" and a more perfect society. In the course of painting, however, Rivera made some changes inspired by his Communist inclinations. The most notable was on the right side of the mural, where he included a portrait of the Russian revolutionary Vladimir Lenin leading a demonstration of workers in a May Day parade.

When he was asked to remove Lenin's portrait, Rivera refused, and offered instead to balance it with a depiction of Abraham Lincoln. Rockefeller rejected this proposal, paid Rivera his full fee, and banned him from the building. Rockefeller then made plans to remove the mural. An outpouring of public support for the project followed: picket lines were formed, newspaper editorials were published, and Rivera made a speech at a rally outside City Hall. Despite suggestions that the mural be moved a few blocks away to the Museum of Modern Art,

Mural: a painting applied directly to a wall, usually large and in a public space

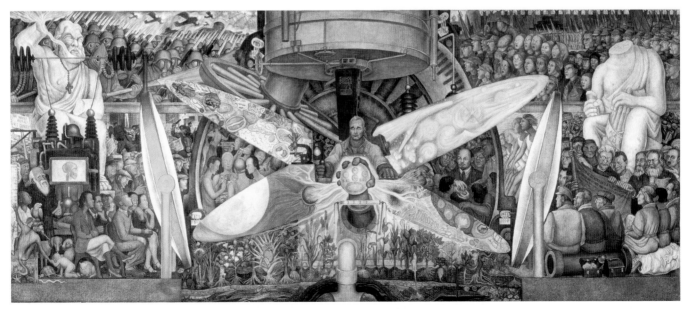

4.1.16 Diego Rivera, *Man, Controller of the Universe*, or *Man in the Time Machine*, 1934. Fresco, 15' × 37'6⅞". Full composite view of the fresco. Palacio de Bellas Artes, Mexico City, Mexico

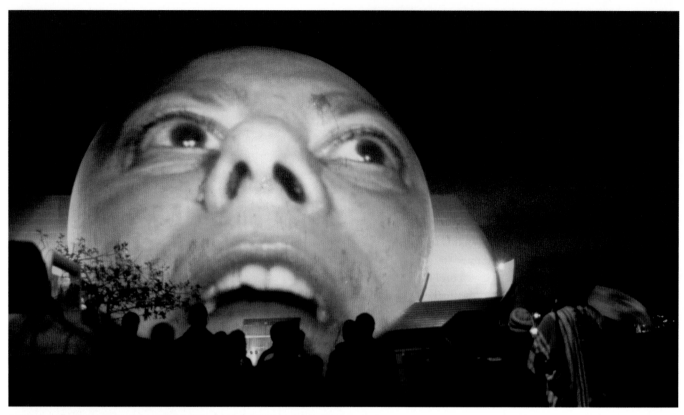

4.1.17 Krzysztof Wodiczko, *Tijuana Projection*, 2001. Public video projection at the Centro Cultural Tijuana, Mexico. Organized as part of the event InSite 2000

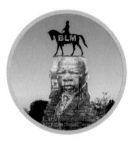

BLM (Black Lives Matter) projections on the Robert E. Lee monument in Richmond, Virginia (July 2020) follow Wodiczko's use of public projections to raise consciousness about social justice issues:

→ see **4.7.8**, p. 624

it was ultimately demolished with pickaxes in February 1934. The same year, Rivera re-created the mural in Mexico City with the new title *Man, Controller of the Universe* (**4.1.16**, p. 551). Rivera rather bluntly described the conflict that can arise between the vision of artists with strong opinions and their audiences: "[The artist] must try to raise the level of taste of the masses, not debase himself to the level of unformed and impoverished taste."

Over the course of his career, the Polish-born artist Krzysztof Wodiczko (b. 1943) has created more than ninety video projection pieces intended to draw attention to situations of social injustice around the world. Images and text telling the stories of individuals who have been overlooked or mistreated are projected onto architectural facades and monuments, which were made by or for powerful figures in the community. The projections of socially conscious messages about human rights and democracy onto public buildings associated with collective memory and history reclaim these spaces for the people and build community solidarity. *Tijuana Projection* (**4.1.17**) gave voice to women in the maquiladora industry, which consists of assembly plants and factories close to the

border between Mexico and the United States, where cheap labor can be hired, and which is notorious for atrocious working conditions. The women were recorded recalling a traumatic event and their testimonies were projected live for two consecutive nights on the spherical Centro Cultural Tijuana to a public plaza filled with more than 1,500 people. They told of terrible home and working conditions, including instances of rape, incest, poisoning through exposure to toxic chemicals, and police abuse. Wodiczko commented, "Their situation is incomparably worse than anything I have tried to understand before." In collaboration with support organizations based in Tijuana, Factor X and Yeuani, this project was created to raise awareness through the strength of participant testimonies, inspire public response, and catalyze change that would lead to the chance of a better life.

We can see from the work of Serra, Rivera, and Wodiczko that art displayed in public places often raises our awareness, either by drawing our attention to existing spaces and specific ideas, or by reflecting issues that resonate for the community and need to be addressed. Their work encourages much-needed dialog across differing perspectives.

Explore Further Art and Community

Places to Gather

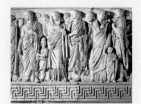

1.2.6 Imperial Procession from the *Ara Pacis Augustae*, 13 BCE → p. 54

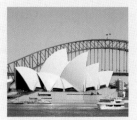

2.5.30 Jørn Utzon, Sydney Opera House, Australia, 1973 → p. 261

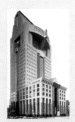

2.5.34 Michael Graves, Humana Building, Louisville, 1985 → p. 264

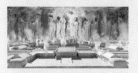

3.10.17b Cai Guo-Qiang, *Sleepwalking in the Forbidden City*, 2020 → p. 533

Constructed Mountains

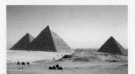

3.1.13 Pyramids at Giza, Egypt, *c.* 2580–2510 BCE → p. 355

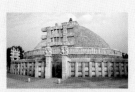

3.3.2 Great Stupa, Sanchi, India, 3rd century BCE → p. 392

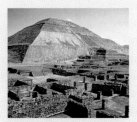

3.4.11 Pyramid of the Sun, Teotihuacan, Mexico, *c.* 225 CE → p. 417

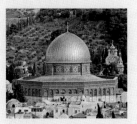

3.2.15 Dome of the Rock, Jerusalem, 688–91 → p. 382

Community Healing and Solidarity

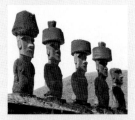

2.2.1 Cave paintings from Sulawesi, Indonesia, *c.* 42,000 BCE → p. 195

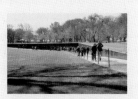

3.5.19 *Moai* ancestor figures, Rapa Nui, Polynesia, before the 15th century → p. 439

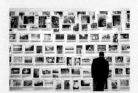

4.6.15a Maya Lin, Vietnam Veterans Memorial, 1981–83 → p. 615

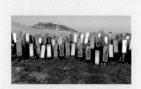

3.4.27 Cannupa Hanska Luger, mirror shields, Standing Rock, North Dakota, 2016 → p. 425

Art in the Public Sphere

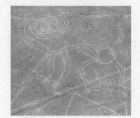

1.1.1 Monkey, Nazca, Peru, *c.* 500 BCE–500 CE → p. 35

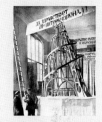

1.2.11 Vladimir Tatlin, Model for *Monument to the Third International*, 1919 → p. 57

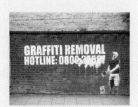

2.8.24 *Here Is New York: A Democracy of Photographs*, 2007 → p. 313

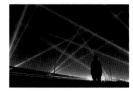

2.2.27 Banksy, *Graffiti Removal Hotline*, London, 2008 → p. 210

Your Turn:
How do these artworks relate to art and community?

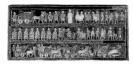

3.1.8 Standard of Ur, *c.* 2600–2400 BCE, 1919 → p. 552

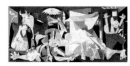

3.5.8 Dogon Kanaga mask ceremony, Mali → p. 433

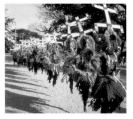

4.6.10 Pablo Picasso, *Guernica*, 1937 → p. 611

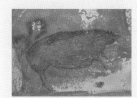

3.4.19 Rafael Lozano-Hemmer, *Border Tuner*, November 14–24, 2019 → p. 421

4.2
Spirituality and Art

Stela (plural **stelae**): an upright stone slab decorated with inscriptions or pictorial relief carvings

For as long as art has been made, artists have been inspired by beliefs in ancient deities, spirit beings, and the sacred figures of the world's religions. Through these works, artists have sought to express things that cannot be seen and are little understood. In this chapter we use the term spirituality to examine the ways in which beliefs, including both narrative stories and their interpretations, have inspired artists for thousands of years. Spirituality encompasses our sense of being connected to others, our awareness of both mind and body, and our wish to understand life's meaning in this world and beyond. It may serve as a source of inspiration and a way for us to share our beliefs. This chapter investigates six broad categories of artworks with a spiritual context: depictions of specific gods, deities, or central figures; references to spirits of the natural world or ancestors; suggestions of communication with the spirit world; reactions to places that are believed to have a sacred resonance; personal paths to spirituality; and depictions of judgment at the end of earthly life.

Gods, Deities, and Enlightened Beings

Artists communicate the stories of specific religious figures or deities to help explain their importance. Depictions of individuals considered divine or singly important in Buddhist scripture, Greek mythology, and the Christian Bible can make those individuals more accessible and memorable.

Buddha, the Awakened One, was a Hindu prince named Siddhartha Gautama who lived in Nepal and northern India from about 563 to 483 BCE. He did not believe in an eternal god, but focused on how to achieve spiritual

perfection to break the cycle of reincarnation: his insights are the core of Buddhism. Buddhist art focuses on his life and teachings. The large central panels of the **stela** in **4.2.1** show the cycle of Buddha's life. In the bottom section we see his miraculous birth as he emerges from his mother's right side. The second section, above the birth scene, is the moment of his

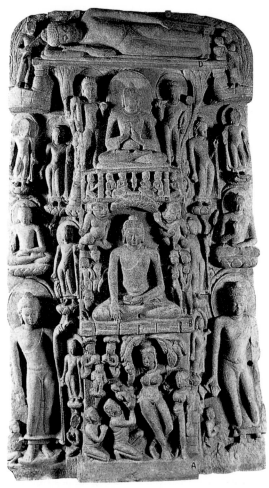

4.2.1 Life of Buddha stela, Gupta period, *c.* 475 CE. Sandstone, height 41″. India Museum, Calcutta, India

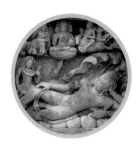

Vishnu, one of the three main gods of Hinduism, is the preserver and protector of creation, bringing order to a world that is threatened by chaos and destruction. Vishnu is often depicted (as in this example) sustaining the universe by dreaming about it:

→ see **1.6.9**, p. 122

Pediment: the triangular space, situated above the row of columns, on the facade of a building in the Classical style

Idealized: represented as perfect in form or character, corresponding to an ideal

enlightenment as he touches the Earth with a symbolic gesture of strength and renewal. In the third section he is shown giving his first sermon, seated with his legs crossed and his hands posed in prayer, with the wheel of law behind him. At the top of the sculpture, he is shown reclining as he achieves eternal tranquility, a state called nirvana. The smaller carvings along the sides of the stela show noteworthy moments after he decided to leave his princely life at the age of thirty to become a holy man.

The ancient Greeks often made artworks to honor their gods and deities. The sculptures in **4.2.2** are from the west **pediment** of the temple dedicated to the god Zeus at Olympia, Greece, where the Olympic games were first held. The scene depicts the legendary battle between the Lapiths of Thessaly and the centaurs—half-human and half-horse creatures, which, according to Greek mythology, lived in the nearby mountains. During the wedding feast of the Lapith king, the centaurs, who were amongst the guests, drank too much wine and tried to abduct the bride and the other women. The supposedly civilized Lapiths are depicted as **idealized**, rigid, and without emotion. The centaurs, which were perceived as barbarian, by contrast are shown with more dramatic gestures and ferocious expressions. Apollo, the

god of the sun, who was also associated with the poetic arts and medicine, stands at the center and brings order to the violent struggle. He is the appropriate deity for this scene because he represents reason, order, and male beauty. The centaurs represent the opposite attributes: change, chaos, and even madness. Their drinking associates them with Dionysus, the god of wine.

Similarly to Buddhist and Greek texts, important themes and events from the Bible inspired visual artists to illustrate Christian stories. In the eleventh century, Bishop Bernward was directing the building of the Abbey Church of St. Michael's at Hildesheim, Germany. He commissioned a set of doors that show scenes from the book of Genesis on the left side and scenes from the life of Christ on the right. In chronological order, the doors are read counterclockwise, beginning at the top of the left door. The panels are also arranged so that events from the Old Testament are paired with related episodes from the New Testament (**4.2.3 a–c**, p. 556). For example, the third panel from the top matches the Tree of Knowledge on the left with the Tree of Life on the right. In the left scene Eve accepts the forbidden fruit from the Tree of Knowledge, therefore committing the first, or original, sin; as a consequence, she and Adam were expelled from the Garden

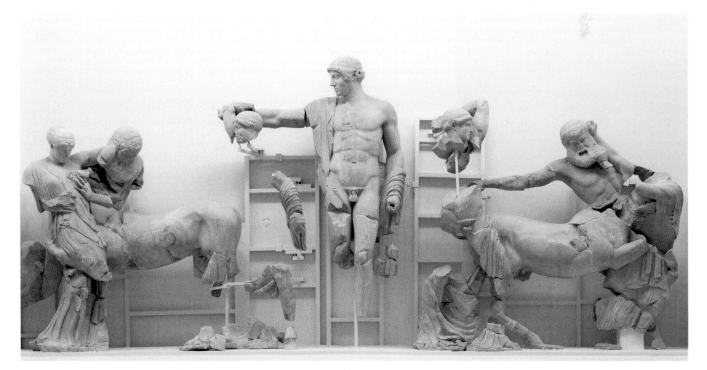

4.2.2 Apollo, centaur, and Lapith, fragments of relief sculptures from the west pediment of Temple of Zeus, Olympia, Greece, *c.* 460 BCE. Marble, 8′8″ × 10′10″. Archaeological Museum, Olympia, Greece

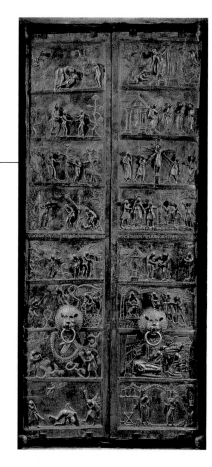

4.2.3a Doors depicting scenes from Genesis and the life of Christ, commissioned by Bishop Bernward for the Abbey Church of St. Michael's, Hildesheim, 1015. Bronze, height 16'6". Dom-Museum, Hildesheim, Germany

Old Testament		New Testament	
Paradise Lost	Formation of Eve	Noli Me Tangere	Paradise Gained
Salutations	Eve Presented to Adam	The Three Marys at the Tomb	Salutations
Tree of Knowledge (sin)	Temptation and Fall	The Crucifixion	Tree of Life, The Cross, Salvation
Judgment	Accusation and Judgment of Adam and Eve	Judgment of Jesus by Pilate	Judgment
Separation from God	Expulsion from Paradise	Presentation of Jesus in Temple	Reunion with God
Firstborn Son of Eve (Cain), and Poverty	Adam and Eve Working	Adoration of the Magi	Firstborn Son of Mary (Jesus) and Wealth
Abel's Sacrificial Lamb	Offerings by Cain (grain) and Abel (lamb)	The Nativity	Jesus, Lamb of God
Despair, Sin, Murder	Cain Slaying Abel	The Annunciation	Hope and Everlasting Life

4.2.3c Diagram with identification of panels on Hildesheim Doors

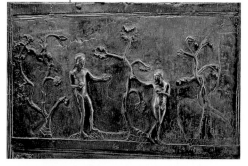

4.2.3b Detail of Hildesheim Doors: Temptation in the Garden of Eden

of Eden into the world of suffering and death. On the right, the cross on which Jesus was crucified—understood as the Tree of Life—offers eternal life to believers who ask for forgiveness of their sins and accept Christ as their savior. The elongated and frail appearance of the figures and the non-naturalistic settings reflect the Christian emphasis on internal, spiritual matters and themes instead of the exterior, physical body.

Spirits and Ancestors

In African and Native American cultures, artworks often reflect the spiritual importance of gods and ancestors. According to some belief systems, objects can be infused with a spiritual presence. Through ritual, these objects help to continue and preserve cultural practices, ideas, and family ties; to establish or restore balance; and to enhance, or even transform, mundane life.

Creator deities, nature spirits, and ancestors feature prominently in the religion of the Senufo people of West Africa. They believe in a supreme being who created the world, a dual female–male deity. Divination, governed by the Sandogo society, is also important to their religious practices. **Masqueraders** serve as intermediaries between the spiritual and human worlds during ritual performances. The masquerades feature exquisitely carved wooden masks, full-body garments (raffia, as shown in **4.2.4**), dynamic music, dances, and protocols specific to the society and the occasion. Some Senufo masks honor deceased elders while others, like the helmet masks shown here, are connected with fraternal organizations in the region, such as the *Poro*. Mask designs reference powerful animals and scarification patterns in the belief that these

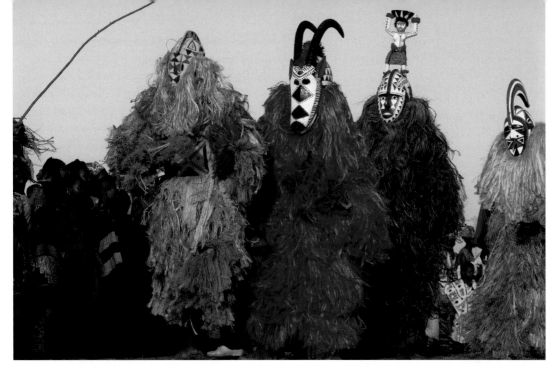

4.2.4 Senufo Mask Dancers, 2 Nov 2006, Sikasso, Mali

will offer fierce protection against malevolent forces.

For the Hopi of the southwestern United States, rituals highlight the cycles of nature that are central to their daily activities. *Kachinas*, or supernatural spirits, personify events and such natural elements as the solstices (the longest and the shortest days of the year, which mark the beginning of a new stage in the seasonal ritual cycle), patterns of stars (constellations), plants, and animals. During the planting season, masked dancers assume the likeness of the kachinas in annual festivals dedicated to rain, fertility, and good hunting. Along with the masqueraders, dolls give a physical form to these spirits. The kachina doll shown in **4.2.5** represents the Jemez kachina, which appears near the end of the season when the kachinas are about to leave the mesas (steep-sided, elevated plateaus where the Hopi live) for six months. The elaborate headdress on the Jemez kachina contains cloud symbols, denoting its effectiveness in bringing rain. The doll carries a rattle in one hand and a sprig of Douglas fir (here represented by a feather) in the other. As the first kachina to bring mature corn to the Hopi, this figure is believed to ensure a successful corn crop.

Ancient rituals passed from generation to generation often reflect ideas that are central to that community's belief system. The **sand-painting** ritual of the Navajo of New Mexico produces temporary works of art that are constructed as part of a prayer or ceremony (**4.2.6**, p. 558). The paintings are closely connected to nature, both in terms of the materials used (such as corn, pollen, charcoal, sand, and powdered stones) and imagery. The subject matter, from Navajo creation mythology,

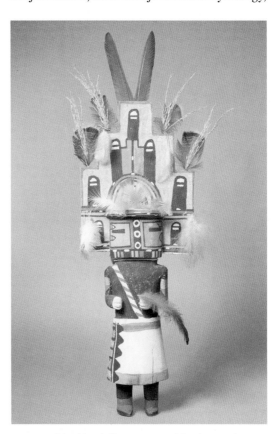

4.2.5 Hopi *kachina* doll, *c.* 1925. Wood, feathers, and pigment, height 25¼". Gustav Heye Center, New York (National Museum of the American Indian)

Sand painting: also known as dry painting, a labor-intensive method of painting using colored grains of sand or other natural materials as the medium

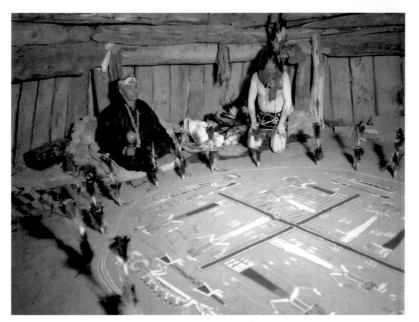

4.2.6 Navajo Yebashi Ceremony, *Whirling Log Dry Painting*, *c.* 1930–1950, Navajo Nation, Arizona, New Mexico and Utah

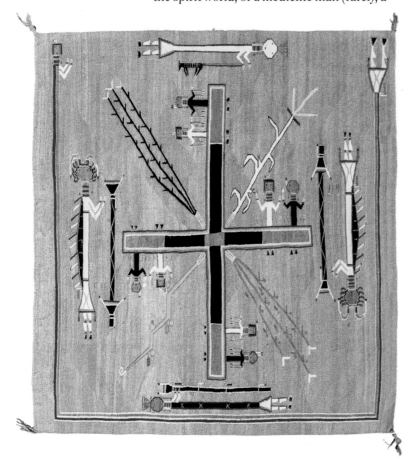

4.2.7 Navajo *Whirling Log Ceremony*, *c.* 1925, tapestry woven by Mrs. Sam Manuelito, based on a sand painting by Hosteen Klah. Heard Museum, Phoenix, Arizona

includes logs, holy plants, animals, and deities. After an image has been meticulously created over the course of days or weeks, a healing ceremony takes place, overseen by a priest with the ability to communicate directly with the spirit world, or a medicine man (rarely, a woman). In the ritual, the paintings are believed to transform into vehicles of power, restoring harmony to the tribe or an individual. When the person to be healed sits in the center, they absorb power from Navajo ancestors and from the gods depicted in the painting. The careful production of sand paintings and the choice of an impermanent medium are believed to channel forces of nature and ancestry to benefit the community in the physical realm by promoting food, health, harmony, and well-being.

Navajo healer, artist, and ceremonial singer Hosteen Klah started making weavings in 1919 that showed the kinds of designs made in sand paintings. While Klah was greatly respected, many Navajos attacked him for making outsiders aware of these private ceremonies. One **tapestry**, *Whirling Log Ceremony* (**4.2.7**)—woven by someone else based on a design by Klah—shows part of the Navajo creation myth in which a human, Tsil-ol-ne, partakes in a symbolic journey through life. Over time he comes to the Colorado River, where he will be pulled ashore by the gods, shown one on each side holding a staff. Guides (male and female pairs placed in each quadrant, standing on the edges of the crossed logs) will teach him everything he needs before he returns home. All the while, Tsil-ol-ne is protected by the guardian god Rainbow Maiden, shown as a stretched figure that surrounds the scene. The Rainbow Maiden, however, does not border the East horizon (shown at the top of the picture) in order to allow for sunrise the next day, and symbolically a new beginning after the transformation of Tsil-ol-ne.

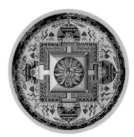

The Tibetan Buddhist tradition of dry painting involves the painstakingly detailed creation of intricate designs over a period of weeks, even years. Once complete, mandalas are destroyed to signify impermanence and are often dispersed into nature: → see **1.6.17**, p. 128

Tapestry: hand-woven fabric—usually silk or wool—with a non-repeating, usually figurative, design woven into it

Icon: a small, often portable, religious image venerated by Christian believers; first used by the Eastern Orthodox Church

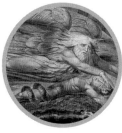

Because he was very religious but opposed to organized religion, William Blake interpreted the creation of man as anguished and full of suffering. Many of his artworks were inspired by his visions of angels, spirits, demons, and devils:
→ see **3.7.16**, p. 477

Connecting with the Gods

Communication with the gods has been an important subject for art in many cultures, whether in the worship of multiple gods or just one. Sometimes individuals perceived as possessing special qualities serve as intermediaries between people and a deity. Rulers have been depicted interacting directly with divine beings or traveling into supernatural realms. Artworks showing such interactions reinforce the power of rulers by convincing their people that they are blessed, aided by the gods, and worthy of their exalted position. This has made such works a significant element in many cultures.

The interaction between a ruler and a deity is the focal point of the Stela of Naram-Sin (**4.2.8**). Naram-Sin, an Akkadian king who ruled central Mesopotamia (part of modern-day Iraq) around 2254–2218 BCE, was head of both church and state. His stela commemorates the Akkadian military victory over the Lullubi people. The lower portions of the scene show signs of the battle that has taken place on a mountain. Above, Naram-Sin stands victorious near the summit, his horned helmet and larger size emphasizing his importance. The

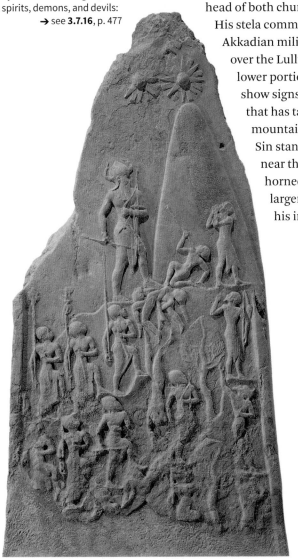

4.2.8 Stela of Naram-Sin, *c.* 2254–2218 BCE. Pink sandstone, 6'7" × 3'5". Musée du Louvre, Paris, France

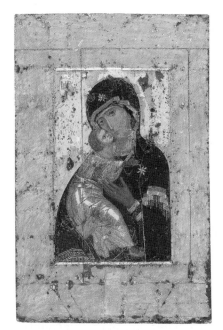

4.2.9 *Virgin of Vladimir*, 12th century (before 1132). Tempera on panel, 30¾ × 21½". Tretyakov Gallery, Moscow, Russia

sun god is not depicted in human form but appears symbolically as a sunburst. Naram-Sin's location, as close as possible to the sun god, illustrates his own supreme, divine status in society and suggests that he was looked upon with approval by the many gods the Akkadians worshiped. As the godlike representative of his community, a ruler such as Naram-Sin needed to maintain a favorable connection with the supernatural realm in order to ensure continued prosperity for his kingdom.

In much Christian art, saints and mythological figures interact with God to provide role models or to help educate viewers about religious practices. During the Middle Ages, Christians in the Eastern Orthodox Church (which separated from the Roman Catholic Church in 1054 CE) used **icons**, such as **4.2.9**, as a focus of devotion and a source of inspiration. Many were painted on wood panels so they could be carried around, but some were attached to chapel screens in churches. The portable icons could be transported from Constantinople in the Byzantine empire to distant places, such as Russia, in order to help spread and support Christian beliefs. The icons themselves were not worshiped as divine, but they were believed to have miraculous powers. They became the subjects of intense reverence because they depicted individuals whose saintliness meant that they were close to God, and therefore able to spread goodness.

Judgment and the Afterlife

Lintel: the horizontal beam over the doorway of a portal

Romanesque: an early medieval European style of architecture based on Roman-style rounded arches and heavy construction

Portal: an entrance. A royal portal (main entrance) is usually on the west front of a church and features sculpted forms of kings and queens

Tympanum: an arched recess above a doorway, often decorated with carvings

As we live our lives, our choices determine the impact we will have and how we will be perceived. In many belief systems, the moral implications of our decisions have lasting consequences. As a result, the act of judging a life before the deceased is allowed to pass into the afterlife has been the theme of numerous artworks. In many judgment scenes, including those discussed here, scales are featured as a symbol of justice in which a life is "held in the balance" before the soul is allowed to pass on.

In ancient Egypt, the deceased were buried with a set of belongings that reflected their position in life. One of the most important of these possessions was a Book of the Dead, a scroll with spells and incantations designed to help the deceased navigate the passage into the afterlife. As we can see in the Book of the Dead that belonged to a scribe named Hunefer, who lived more than 3,000 years ago, a successful journey required proof that one had lived an honorable life and that proper respect had been paid to the gods (**4.2.10**).

At the top of the scroll, Hunefer pleads his case to the forty-two judges of the dead (represented here by just fourteen mummified deities, probably because the artist did not have room to show them all). In the bottom panel, Hunefer is escorted by Anubis (the jackal-headed god associated with mummification and the afterlife) to the scales where his soul will be weighed. As Ammit ("Eater of the Dead," with the head of a crocodile, mane and forequarters of a lion, and hindquarters of a hippopotamus) anxiously looks on, Anubis determines that Hunefer's soul, in the form of his heart in a canopic jar, is lighter than the ostrich feather it is weighed against. Having been proven worthy, Hunefer is presented by Horus (the falcon-headed god of the sun, sky, and war) to Osiris (god of goodness, vegetation, and death), who is seated on his throne. This Book of the Dead was placed in Hunefer's coffin in the hope that its script would be followed and he would successfully gain immortality in the afterlife.

In twelfth-century Europe, depictions of the Last Judgment took on an ominous tone in scenes showing the fate of the blessed and the damned side by side. In Gislebertus's version of *The Last Judgment* (**4.2.11**), the **lintel** underneath the main panel contains a row of figures awaiting judgment. The **Romanesque** characteristic of elongated and somewhat angular figures on the sculpture throughout the whole **portal** creates a visually dynamic tension.

A pair of hands comes down from above to gather the eighth figure from the right for weighing. In the center of the carved **tympanum**, Christ is shown as larger than all the rest of the figures, indicating his key role in the judgment of humankind. On his right (our left) are the angels and the souls of the blessed, who will go on to live

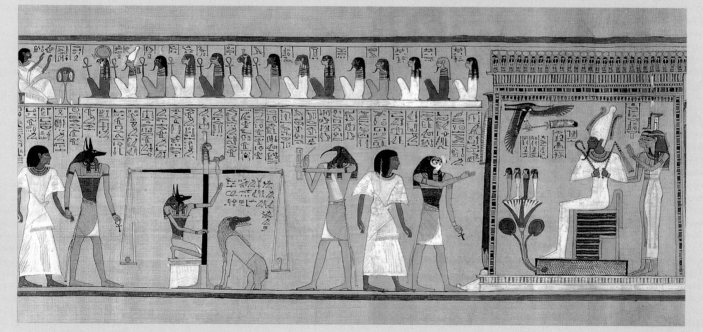

4.2.10 Book of the Dead of Hunefer: Last Judgment before Osiris, *c.* 1275 BCE. Painted papyrus, height 15⅜". British Museum, London, England

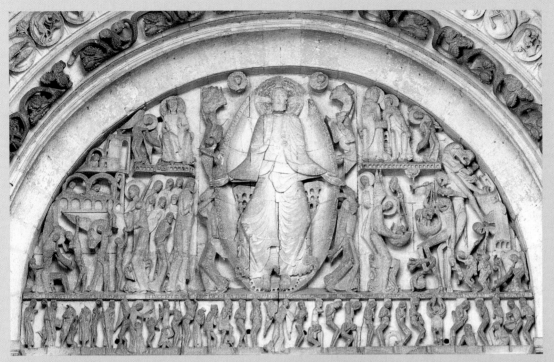

4.2.11 Gislebertus, *The Last Judgment*, *c.* 1120–35. Tympanum from the west portal, Cathedral of Saint-Lazare, Autun, France

out eternity in heaven. Their bodies are smooth, elegant, and peaceful. On Christ's left are the scales in which souls are weighed, and the ravaged bodies of the damned. Their horrid, grotesque appearance was meant to send a strong message to churchgoers about the consequences of living a sinful life, and to give them a glimpse of the misery of spending the afterlife in hell.

The Dutch painter Johannes Vermeer (1632–1675) subtly includes religion in a scene from everyday life in his *Woman Holding a Balance* (**4.2.12**). Following a style that was popular at the time, Vermeer focuses on an ordinary moment, in which the woman is standing at a table by a window near her open jewelry boxes. The painting on the wall behind her provides a symbolic backdrop for her actions. It shows the Last Judgment, with Christ in the sky above and the souls to be judged below, and serves as a reminder that life is short and that it is important to be honest and decent. The scales the woman holds are empty, but perfectly balanced, suggesting that one's actions rather than one's possessions are the true indication of a person's worth.

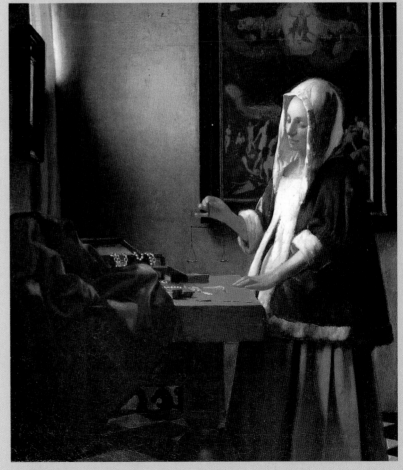

4.2.12 Johannes Vermeer, *Woman Holding a Balance*, *c.* 1664. Oil on canvas, 16¾ × 16″. National Gallery of Art, Washington, D.C.

The Orthodox Church required the form and content of icons to follow traditional rules. As a result, although each painting is unique, it has a family resemblance to other icons: gold backgrounds, **linear outlines**, and **stylized** but believable poses. It was important that the figures in the icons could be recognized by anyone who saw them. Thus the Madonna and Child were always shown with haloes to represent their holiness. The *Virgin of Vladimir* portrays Mary with her face touching Jesus to emphasize her virtue as the "Virgin of Loving Kindness" (**4.2.9**, p. 559). This icon, probably made in the city of Constantinople (modern-day Istanbul), was intended to bless and protect the city in which it was housed (it has been in Moscow almost continuously since 1395). Only the faces are original; the rest of the panel, probably damaged by people touching it during devotions or prayer, has been repainted.

4.2.13 Gianlorenzo Bernini, *The Ecstasy of St. Teresa*, 1647–52. Polychromed marble, gilt, bronze, yellow glass, fresco, and stucco, height 4′11″ (figures only). Cornaro Chapel, Santa Maria della Vittoria, Rome, Italy

The Ecstasy of St. Teresa by Gianlorenzo Bernini (1598–1680) is another Christian artwork that is meant to inspire devotion and reverence (**4.2.13**). It was made between 1647 and 1652 to decorate a funerary chapel for the Cornaro family in the Church of Santa Maria della Vittoria in Rome, Italy. This massive sculpture (more than 11 ft. tall) depicts one of St. Teresa of Ávila's mystical visions: she is about to be pierced by an angel's arrow that will infuse her with divine love. The theatrical staging and the emphasis on dramatic light—created by the use of gilt bronze rays behind the figures and by the light falling from a hidden window above the sculpture—are typical of the **Baroque** style. Bernini's sculpture is executed with great attention to detail. The whole scene seems to take place in the clouds and the angel almost hovers above St. Teresa. The marble is carved to suggest several different textures, including smooth skin, gauzy fabric, clinging draperies, and the heavy wool of the nun's habit worn by the saint. The combination of accurate and believable details with an exaggerated picture of devotion reflects the Catholic Church's new emphasis at that time on believers establishing a strongly personal relationship with Christ. In Bernini's sculpture, Christ's **Passion** is relived in the intensity of St. Teresa's piety, which serves as an example for the devout.

Sacred Places

We all have places that restore our souls. Whether it is the mountains, the beach, or the family dinner table, there are places that allow us to feel connected and at peace. In addition to the places themselves, certain artworks represent personal retreat or communal worship as sites of reverence, renewal, and contemplation. By marking these sites and communicating these experiences, artists and architects give us a sense of their connectedness to nature, religion, or community. Places that people returned to again and again, such as the **prehistoric** caves of Lascaux and the **catacombs** of Rome, were clearly important for their users. Whether for memorial or religious purposes, such places were adorned with artworks, giving their sacred nature an added dimension.

The walls of the Lascaux Caves in southern France (**4.2.14a**) were painted sometime between around 17,000 and 15,000 BCE. One section is densely packed with paintings of animals. The effort required to paint the walls of the caves with so many images suggests that these animals, encountered on a daily basis, were extremely important. Some of the most magnificent paintings are found in the Hall of Bulls in the main cave, which is 66 ft. wide and 16 ft. high (**4.2.14b**). The hall is near the entrance to the system of caves and, as its name suggests, it is decorated with outlines and realistic details of numerous bulls—one of them more than 15 ft. long.

The images in this area overlap, indicating that the site was visited repeatedly, that it was painted over a period of time, and that making these paintings in this particular place was significant. Because the makers of the paintings at Lascaux had no system of writing, we must interpret the stories of these images from the pictures themselves. In addition to telling stories, prehistoric cave paintings may also have been used to teach hunting and to represent spiritual or ritual practices. Paintings similar to those at Lascaux have been found in other places in France and also in Spain, indicating that these paintings were part of a wider cultural practice for people who either moved from place to place or shared ideas with others.

The human desire to decorate important or sacred places can also be seen in the catacombs constructed outside the city of Rome, Italy, between the second and fourth centuries CE

Catacombs: an underground system of tunnels used for burying and commemorating the dead

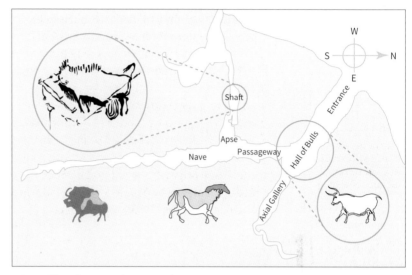

4.2.14a Plan of Lascaux Caves, Dordogne, France, c. 15,000–17,000 BCE

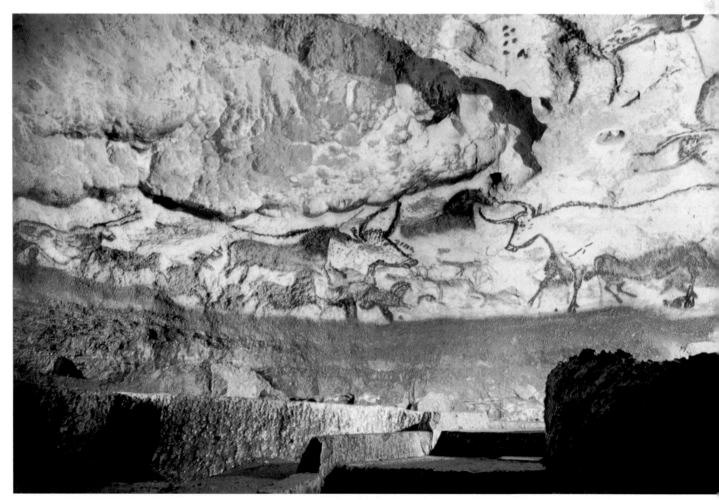

4.2.14b Hall of the Bulls, pigment on limestone rock, Lascaux Caves, Dordogne, France

(**4.2.15a** and **4.2.15b**). The catacombs were an underground system of tunnels measuring between 60 and 90 miles in length and containing the ancient remains of four million people. They were sacred spaces for Romans, who held a variety of religious beliefs and went there to visit their ancestors' burial places. While pagan Romans practiced both cremation and burial of the dead, burial was especially important for Jews and Christians.

The catacombs were also used as temples for religious observances, a space where Christians could gather, and hiding places for fugitives.

As with Lascaux, the catacombs contain paintings in areas used for different purposes. The paintings in the catacombs include pagan, Jewish, and Christian scenes. Banquet scenes or images of shepherds, for example, could be seen by Romans of all three faiths and interpreted differently according to the viewer's religion. The central figure in the Christian **fresco** from the catacombs of Priscilla stands in a praying position (**4.2.15b**). Such a pose appears in pagan art, but it has a distinct meaning for Christians, who understand the figure to be praying to their God. Using familiar imagery, such as this prayerful person, probably made it easier for people to convert from other religions to Christianity while also conveying a clear message to existing believers.

Mosques are the sacred place of worship for Muslims to gather and pray to Allah. Because mosques are often the largest structures in a city, they have also played a significant role in community activities when used as schools or hospitals. All mosques include a special prayer niche, a **mihrab**, orientated toward Mecca (**4.2.16**). This mihrab from the Madrasa Imami in Isfahan, Iran, shows the decorative

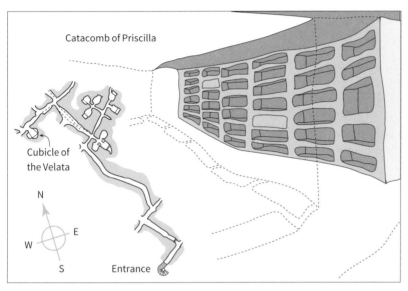

4.2.15a Plan and section showing part of the catacomb of Priscilla, 2nd and 3rd centuries CE. Via Salaria, Rome, Italy

Fresco: a technique where the artist paints onto freshly applied plaster. From the Italian *fresco*, "fresh"

Mihrab: a niche in a mosque that is in a wall oriented toward Mecca

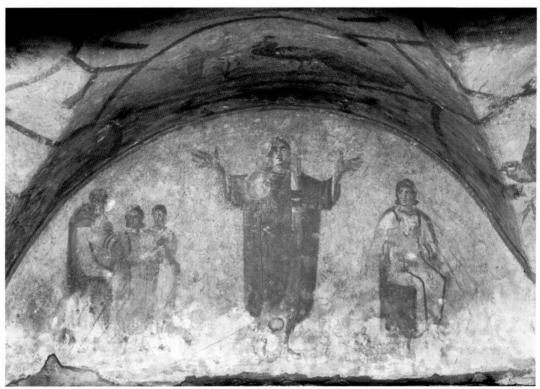

4.2.15b Fresco from the Cubicle of the Velata, the catacomb of Priscilla, 2nd and 3rd centuries CE. Via Salaria, Rome, Italy

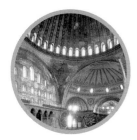

The structure of the Hagia Sophia is so impressive that it has transcended religious affiliations. It was built in Constantinople as a Byzantine basilica for the Eastern Orthodox Christian Church. It later became a mosque, then a museum, and has recently been declared a mosque again:
→ see **2.5.17**, p. 253

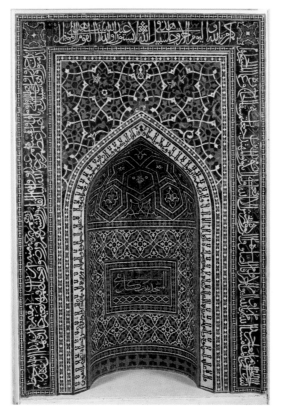

4.2.16 Mihrab from the Madrasa Imami, Isfahan, Iran, *c.* 1354. Mosaic of polychrome, glazed cut tiles on stonepaste body, set into plaster, 11′3″ × 9′5¾″. Metropolitan Museum of Art, New York

attention given to a space of such importance. **Geometric** lines, **abstract** floral designs, and **calligraphy** are created using small glazed tiles. The words of God are emphasized in the decoration of this mihrab. Inside the central rectangle, proclaimed in elegant cursive, are the words, "the mosque is the house of every pious person." Script bordering the edges of the mihrab's rectangular frame quotes from

the Koran (IX: 14–22), and describes both the importance of a mosque and the duties of a believer. The **kufic** script that borders the pointed arch refers to the five central elements, or pillars, of the Islamic faith: devotion to God, prayer, charity, fasting, and pilgrimage to Mecca.

Nature, Contemplation, and Personal Paths to Spirituality

Unlike paganism, Christianity, and Islam, the Shinto religion in Japan focuses on the here and now and reveres nature itself as a deity. For example, Shinto recognizes a mountain as a sacred object because it is the source of water for rice cultivation. Such a mountain was once worshiped directly, but over time shrines were built as places to worship a god, known as a *kami*, that was important to a particular area or community. Marking a site as sacred is a common practice in Shinto, which emphasizes the ways in which such natural elements as the sun, mountains, water, and trees are connected to well-being. These sites, such as the Grand Shrine of Ise, or Ise Jingu, started with small piles of stones in an area surrounded by stone enclosures, which have gradually evolved to include buildings, fences, and gates.

Ise Jingu (**4.2.17**) is one of thousands of shrines throughout Japan dedicated to the sun goddess Amaterasu Omikami. Local residents visit the shrine to revere the goddess and seek her assistance. The site is now marked by a stately **A-framed** wooden building that is simple in design and made with natural materials.

Geometric: predictable and mathematical

Abstract: art imagery that departs from recognizable images of the natural world

Calligraphy: the art of emotive or carefully descriptive hand lettering or handwriting

Kufic: an Arabic script, angular in form; often used to copy the Koran.

A-frame: an ancient form of structural support, made out of beams arranged so that the shape of the building resembles a capital letter A

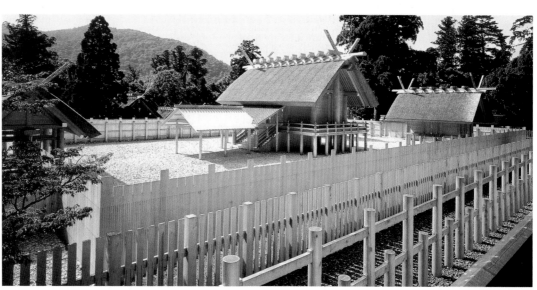

4.2.17 Ise Jingu, site dates from 4th century CE, rebuilt 1993. Mie Prefecture, Japan

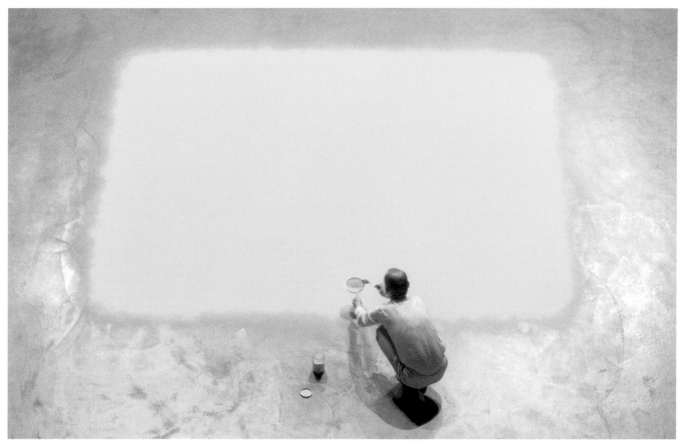

4.2.18 Wolfgang Laib, *Pollen from Hazelnut*, 1992. Pollen, 11′ 5⅞″ × 13′ 1½″. Installation, Centre Pompidou, Forum, Paris, France

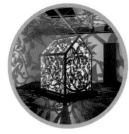

In a 2014 interview Anila Quayyum Agha explained that she does not subscribe to any organized religion, but instead believes in ethics, compassion, tolerance, and generosity. She uses art to evoke the extreme beauty of deep sorrow and joy simultaneously:

→ see **1.9.8**, p. 153

Abstraction: the degree to which an image is altered from an easily recognizable subject

Because nature is cyclical, the shrine must also be renewed and refreshed. Since 690 CE, Ise Jingu has been rebuilt every twenty years with a special ceremony in which meals are shared with the kami, infusing the everyday act of eating with ritual significance.

As we have seen in this chapter, many people develop their own approaches to spirituality, whether within an organized religion or independently. For some people, art works as an effective channel not only for expressing those beliefs, but also for exploring them. The possible methods of expression and exploration are endless but include **abstraction**, visionary constructions, focus on personal journeys, and the search for one's inner light.

German artist Wolfgang Laib (b. 1950) is influenced by many religious traditions—including Buddhism, Jainism, Hinduism, and Christianity—but his work is not connected to any one religion in particular. Among his inspirations is the first chapter of the *Tao Te Ching* by Lao Tsu:

Something mysteriously formed,
Born before heaven and earth.

In the silence and the void,
Standing alone and unchanging,
Ever present and in motion.
Perhaps it is the mother of ten
    thousand things.
I do not know its name.
Call it Tao.
For lack of a better word, I call it great.

Along with the Taoist ideas of mystery and creation, Laib also considers both the simplicity and complexity of nature to be vital. After completing medical school, Laib determined that he could contribute more to the benefit of humankind by becoming an artist than he could as a doctor or a monk. His solitary processes take an inordinate amount of time. *Pollen from Hazelnut* (**4.2.18**) was made from five jars of pollen, each taking a month to collect and representing multiple growing seasons. He spends all this time in the hopes of inspiring a meditative contemplation and an embodied experience for viewers that mimics the passage of time in the natural world—as if they, too, were spending an entire summer sitting in a dandelion field.

Explore Further Spirituality and Art

Deities and Enlightened Beings

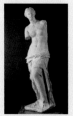

3.1.27 Alexandros of Antioch, *Venus de Milo*, 150 BCE ➔ p. 365

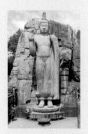

2.4.6 *Avukana Buddha*, Sri Lanka, 5th century ➔ p. 231

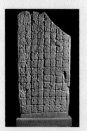

1.2.7 Limestone stela with Mayan glyphs, Pusilhà, Belize, *c.* 600–800 CE ➔ p. 54

Connecting with Gods and Ancestors

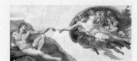

3.6.7b Michelangelo, detail of *Creation of Adam*, 1508–12 ➔ p. 447

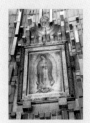

0.0.10 *The Virgin of Guadalupe*, Mexico City, 1531 ➔ p. 22

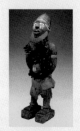

3.5.5 *Nkisi nkondi* figure, late 19th–early 20th century ➔ p. 431

Sacred Places

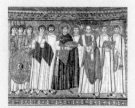

3.2.9 Emperor Justinian, glass mosaic, Ravenna, Italy, *c.* 547 CE ➔ p. 379

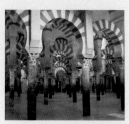

1.9.10 Great Mosque of Córdoba, Spain, 784–86 CE ➔ p. 153

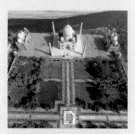

1.6.15a Taj Mahal, Agra, India, 1632–43 ➔ p. 126

Nature and Paths to Spirituality

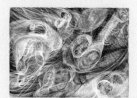

1.1.17 Georgiana Houghton, *Glory Be to God*, *c.* 1864, ➔ p. 43

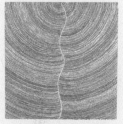

4.1.14 Wenda Gu, "China Monument: Temple of Heaven", 1998 ➔ p. 549

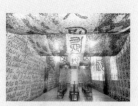

3.5.17 Abie Loy Kemarre, *Sandhill Country*, 2006 ➔ p. 437

Your turn

How do these artworks relate to the culture or ideas discussed in this chapter?

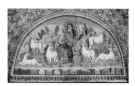

3.2.5 *Good Shepherd* mosaic, Ravenna, Italy, 425–46 CE ➔ p. 376

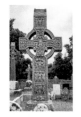

1.6.13 Muiredach's High Cross, 10th century ➔ p. 124

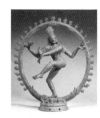

4.3.2 *Shiva Nataraja (Lord of the Dance)*, Chola period, India, 11th century ➔ p. 569

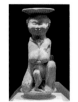

2.6.2 *The Mother Goddess Men Brajut*, Indonesian, *c.* 14th–15th century ➔ p. 270

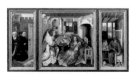

3.6.12 Robert Campin, *Mérode Altarpiece*, 1427–32 ➔ p. 453

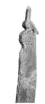

3.5.12 Bird on top of stone monolith, Great Zimbabwe, 15th century ➔ p. 435

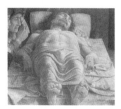

4.3.12 Andrea Mantegna, *Dead Christ*, *c.* 1480 ➔ p. 576

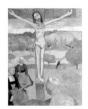

1.4.31 Paul Gauguin, *The Yellow Christ*, 1889, ➔ p. 101

4.3
The Cycle of Life: Nature and Time

Human cultures from the earliest times to the twenty-first century have been deeply concerned with fundamental questions of existence: Where do we come from? What happens when we die? What lies beyond death? These persistent concerns, not surprisingly, have also been a frequent subject of works of art. In this chapter, we look at the ways in which artists have examined the cycle of life of both nature and humans. Visual artists have dealt with topics as unfathomable as the beginning of human existence, as miraculous as the birth of a child, as enduring as natural forces or the passage of time, and as overwhelming as the

finality of death. Life's mysteries are examined through both metaphorical and direct portrayals of life's beginnings, its endings, and what happens in between.

Creation, Destruction, and Renewal

Stories about the beginning of human society and the creation of humankind are found throughout history in cultures across the globe. Creation myths use forces of nature, such as floods or the movement of the stars, to symbolize the creation of humans.

The Crossing (**4.3.1**) by American artist Bill Viola (1951) highlights the creative and

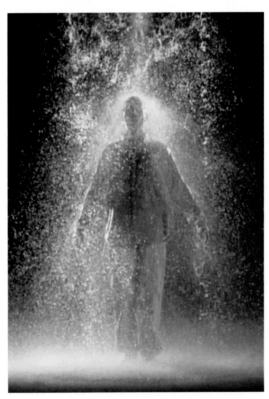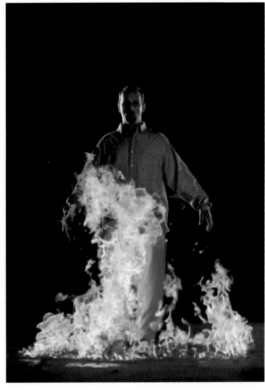

4.3.1 **Bill Viola**, ***The Crossing***, 1996. Video/sound installation. Projected image size: 13′2″ × 9′5″. 10.57 minutes. Dallas Museum of Art and Guggenheim, New York.

destructive forces of water and fire. They both have the ability to renew nature: water nourishes the land, and fire, though initially destructive, has the potential to regenerate it so that more can grow. They are also opposing destructive forces—each can only be destroyed by the other. In *The Crossing*, two 57-foot-high screens are placed facing each other on opposite walls within a dark, enclosed space. Each screen simultaneously plays one of two eleven-minute videos, and the viewer, in the middle, must decide which screen to watch. Both films begin in silence, with a man walking forward before stopping. On one screen, a single drop of water falls on the man's face, then more drops begin to fall, slowly leading to a torrential downfall that engulfs him. On the opposite screen, a small flame transforms into a roaring fire that also destroys the man. At the climax of the videos, the sound is deafening, and one wonders how the man could possibly withstand the ordeal: he is not screaming out in pain, yet he remains calm and still until he vanishes. In this work, Viola captures the cyclical and transformative power of nature and links these cycles to human life.

In the Hindu religion, creative and destructive forces symbolize the belief of reincarnation. One of the principal Hindu deities, Shiva, embodies a balancing of contradictory qualities: half-male and half-female, benevolent and fearsome, giver and taker of life. As Nataraja, or "Lord of the Dance" (**4.3.2**), Shiva is responsible for dancing the world into existence and generating *samsara*, the endless cycle of death and rebirth in which Hindus believe. The flames surrounding Shiva's agile form represent the periodic chaos and destruction that occur when the dance ceases. Shiva dances while poised on top of a dwarf who represents the evil and ignorance that are stamped out during the dances. Shiva's dance creates a balance between creation and destruction that, over the course of time, manifests itself in the cycle of life.

The Aztecs, a culture active from *c.* 1300 to 1521 in the region of present-day central Mexico, were skillful observers of the skies. The Aztec Sun Stone is a store of astronomical and mathematical knowledge (**4.3.3**). Originally painted in shades of brown, red, white, blue, and green, the heavy Sun Stone (weighing 24 tons) stood atop the main temple at Tenochtitlan, the capital of the Aztec empire

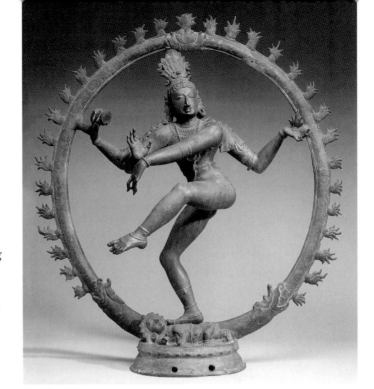

4.3.2 *Shiva Nataraja (Lord of the Dance)*, Chola Period, India, 11th century. Bronze, height 43⅞". Cleveland Museum of Art, Ohio

(present-day Mexico City). Later it was buried, to be uncovered again only in 1790.

The Sun Stone, also known as a calendar stone, reveals how the Aztecs counted time, and illustrates their belief that the Earth endures recurring cycles of destruction and creation. The center of the stone shows the face of Tonatiuh, the sun god to whom Aztecs offered

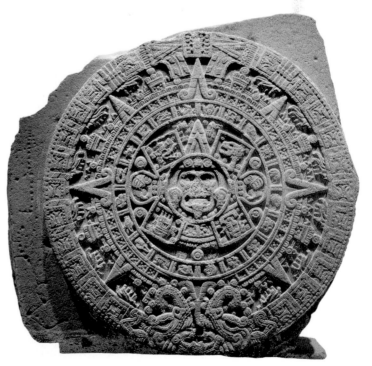

4.3.3 **Calendar stone (Sun Stone)**, *c.* 1502–1521. Basalt, 12' diameter. National Museum of Anthropology, Mexico City, Mexico

frequent human and animal sacrifices. Each of the four squares emanating from Tonatiuh's face frames a symbol representing the ways in which the Earth was believed to have previously come to an end: by wind, by fire, by floods, and by wild beasts. The Aztecs believed that the Earth would be destroyed again by an earthquake. In the ring surrounding these symbols are twenty animals, each framed by a rectangle. These represent the days of the Aztec month. Priests used the calendar stone to determine sacrificial periods. Such sacrifices and periods of disaster were considered essential in order for creation and growth to occur.

Life's Beginnings

Artists have depicted birth as a way of celebrating the existence of life forces whose beginnings are often hard to comprehend. Symbolically, the stages of life in humans are frequently linked to weather seasons or the cycles of farming. In many cultures, the creation of a human, and the mother's role in carrying and birthing a child, are often linked to planting and growth stages of crops.

For the Aztecs, it was important to mark the physical, if still mystical, beginnings of human life. In Aztec culture, a woman giving birth was seen as a female warrior going to battle on behalf of the state. Women who died in childbirth were afforded the same respect as men who died on the battlefield; they resided in the same final resting place as heroes, accompanying the sun on its daily journey through the sky. The goddess Tlazolteotl, an Earth Mother and patron of childbirth, was known as the "filth eater" because she visited people at the end of their lives and absolved or ate their sins. A stone sculpture of Tlazolteotl shows her in the act of giving birth to her daughter Centeotl (**4.3.4**). Centeotl was the goddess of maize (corn), the main crop that nourished the Aztecs. Without the Earth Mother's suffering through childbirth, the Maize god would not have been born.

While the Tlazolteotl sculpture shows a semi-symbolic representation of childbirth, the Dutch artist Rineke Dijkstra (b. 1959) highlights some of the stark realities of birth in her *Mothers* series. "Julie" (**4.3.5**) captures a mother and her newborn baby just one hour after delivery, at a time and in a way that defies most expectations of mother-and-child imagery. They

are standing against a cold, anonymous wall. Their position starkly exposes the vulnerability, even shock, that both mother and baby probably feel. Dijkstra makes public a time in a

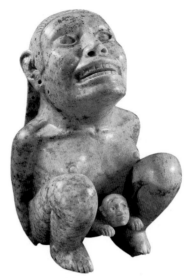

4.3.4 **Tlazolteotl giving birth to the maize god**, *c.* 1500. Aztec granite carving, 8 × 4¾ × 5⅞". Dumbarton Oaks Museum, Washington, D.C.

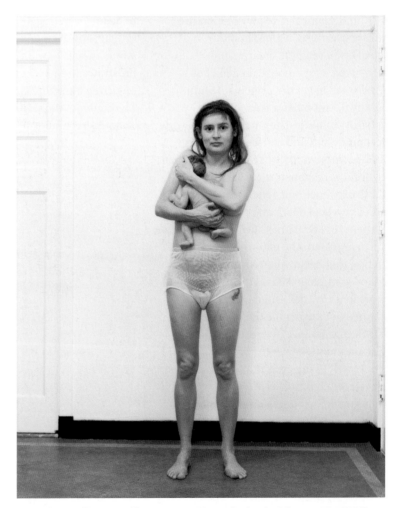

4.3.5 **Rineke Dijkstra, "Julie, Den Haag, The Netherlands, February 29, 1994,"** from the *Mothers* series. C-print, 60¼ × 50¾"

woman's life that is now generally considered private and personal. Her photographs capture the awkwardness and enduring strength of the early moments of a new life and of a mother's instinct to protect her child.

Marking Time

The invention of time is one way that humanity has marked the cycles experienced in nature, the most obvious being the rotation of the Earth around the sun. Although we have a standard understanding of time today, throughout history different cultures devised diverse systems, some of which were linear while others emphasized recurring or simultaneous moments (see Perspectives on Art: Christian Marclay; Darian Leader, p. 572). Artworks about time often remind viewers of the brevity of life and encourage them to live in the moment.

Much like a calendar today, a medieval "book of hours" was filled with prayers that corresponded to the times of day and tracked months of the year. The now-famous French **illuminated manuscript**, *Très Riches Heures*, made by the Limbourg Brothers for the Duke of Berry (**4.3.6a** and **4.3.6b**) is unique for its prominent inclusion of the labors of the peasants, although one of the Duke's castles also remains prominent in the background of each monthly scene. On the page for March, crops are being planted and a man in the front directs an ox while ploughing the same fields that will be harvested in September. The page for September shows grapes being harvested at the Château de Saumur to make the region's celebrated wine. Some figures show the drudgery of the work as they bend down, including one in the lower center who is bent over, showing his underwear. The hemisphere at the top of each panel shows the solar chariot with Apollo the sun god and relevant signs and degrees of the zodiac.

Illuminated manuscript: a hand-lettered text with hand-drawn pictures

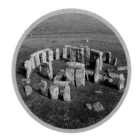

While many mysteries surround Stonehenge, the way that certain stones align with the sunrise on the summer solstice indicate that it was used as a giant calendar:
→ see **4.1.7**, p. 544

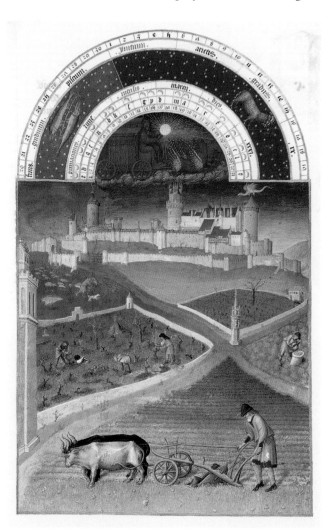

4.3.6a Limbourg Brothers, March from *Très Riches Heures du Duc de Berry*, 1412. Ink/colors on vellum, 11¼ × 8½". Musée Condé, Chantilly, France

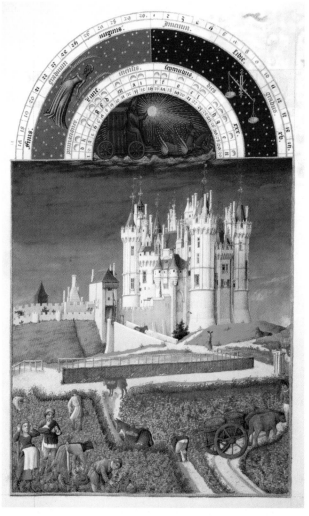

4.3.6b Limbourg Brothers, September from *Très Riches Heures du Duc de Berry*, 1412. Ink/colors on vellum, 11¼ × 8½". Musée Condé, Chantilly, France

Perspectives on Art: Christian Marclay, *The Clock*
"Glue" by Darian Leader

In addition to tracking planting seasons, months, and days, technology helps us mark time to the hour, minute, and second. This kind of time-keeping became the subject of The Clock *(**4.3.7**), made by Swiss-American artist and composer Christian Marclay (b. 1955) and discussed here in an excerpt from an essay called "Glue" by psychoanalyst and author Darian Leader (British, b. 1965).*

Christian Marclay's *The Clock* (2010) is just that: a mechanism that allows us to tell the time. Unlike other clocks, however, this one is made up of the representation of clocks. Thousands of brief film extracts in which the face of a clock or watch appears, or a time is referred to in the dialogue, mark out a twenty-four-hour cycle. The fragments are taken from films of every genre and period: black-and-white comedies from the 1940s, 1950s sci-fi movies, continental art-house films, 1970s heist movies and modern horror. Spliced together with grace and invention, they form both a history of film and, as the title makes clear, a timepiece.

Marclay's clock is synchronized to the time zone in which it is being exhibited, so that it does exactly what a timepiece is meant to do: we can consult it to learn the time. One glance is enough to give us our temporal bearings. We'll just look at the screen and know how much time we've got left before our next rendezvous, or before our plane or train departs. If works of art are often deemed artificial or illusory, this one can't be: the time displayed or spoken is the real thing—the one that controls and regulates our lives.

Although Marclay's work is quite literally a clock, it is also much more than that, and it complicates the transparency that we ascribe to timepieces. Although a watch or a clock can be a status symbol or the vehicle of memories, it offers immediate access to its referent. We hardly ever have to decipher or interpret clock faces…. Clocks simply tell us—albeit in different ways—what the time is. Yet Marclay's clock not only marks the passing of minutes and hours, but invites us to reflect on our relation to time, as well as offering a rich and sometimes painful questioning of the nature of images, narrative…and indeed, the glue that holds all these together.

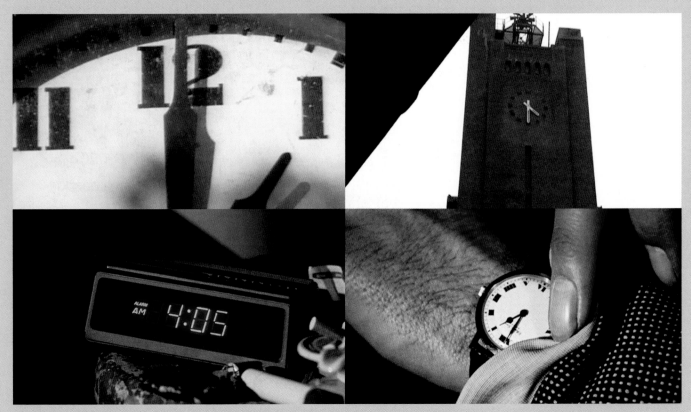

4.3.7 Christian Marclay, stills from *The Clock*, 2010. Single-channel video installation, duration 24 hours

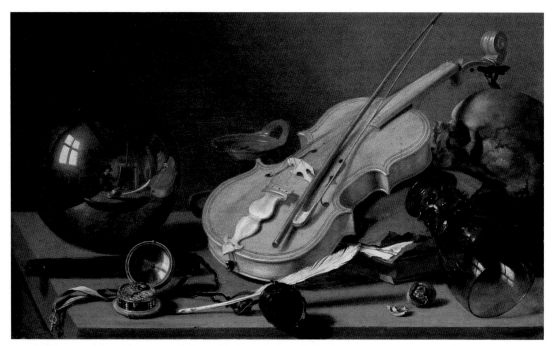

4.3.8 **Pieter Claesz (attr.)**, *Vanitas (Still Life with Glass Globe)*, c. 1628. Oil on panel, 14⅛ × 23¼". Germanisches Nationalmuseum, Nürnberg, Germany

Vanitas: a genre of painting that emphasizes the transient nature of earthly materials and beauty; often seen in still-life painting

Still life: a scene of inanimate objects, such as fruits, flowers, or dead animals

Trompe l'oeil: from the French meaning to "deceive the eye"; a visual illusion in art, in which a painted image appears as a three-dimensional object

Memento mori: a Latin phrase that means "remember you must die." In artworks, such symbols as skulls, flowers, and clocks are used to represent the transient nature of life on Earth

Photorealist: a style of art that began in the 1960s and involves the artist creating artworks that resemble, and were inspired by, photographs

In seventeenth-century Dutch still-life paintings, *vanitas* artworks are based on the theme of the fleeting nature of life, for example *Vanitas (Still Life with Glass Globe)* (**4.3.8**), attributed to Pieter Claesz (1597–1660). The word vanitas refers to vanity (excessive pride in or admiration of one's own appearance or achievements), materialism (both physical limitations and the desire to own possessions), and inevitable mortality.

Still-life images, because they depict inanimate objects, give the artist the chance to display a great degree of technical ability using ***trompe-l'oeil*** techniques to trick viewers into thinking that they are seeing a real scene. The passing of time is suggested in *Vanitas (Still Life with Glass Globe)* by the timepiece, and the skull is an obvious ***memento mori*** (literally meaning "remember that you must die"). The tipped glass and cracked walnut tell us that a person was here enjoying wine and food, but is now gone. The instrument reminds us that music, too, is only transient; it is not fixed in time and will at some point end. Claesz includes his own presence in the painting by showing his reflection in the glass ball on the left side of the table. The tiny self-portrait displays the artist's virtuosity; it also simultaneously expresses the fragility of life (the ball could easily roll off the table and shatter) while also presenting a challenge to death, as the painter lives on through his work.

American **photorealist** artist Audrey Flack (b. 1931) built on the Dutch tradition. In addition to commenting on human mortality, *Marilyn (Vanitas)* (**4.3.9**) is a homage to the American film actress Marilyn Monroe. The

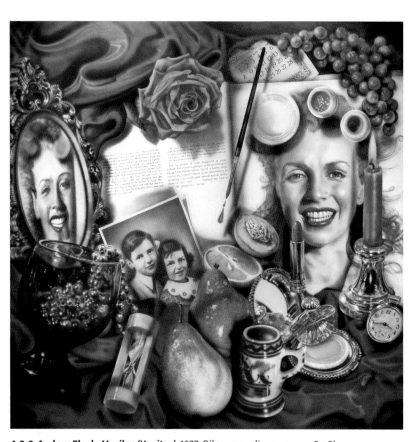

4.3.9 **Audrey Flack**, *Marilyn (Vanitas)*, 1977. Oil over acrylic on canvas, 8 × 8'. Collection of the University of Arizona Museum of Art, Tucson

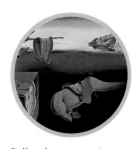

Dalí explores concepts of space and time using what he describes as a paranoiac-critical method:
→ see **3.9.13**, pp. 508–9

photograph on the right is reflected in the mirror on the left, showing Monroe's public persona as a blonde beauty. Mirrors in art often symbolize the transience of youth, beauty, and life. As with similar objects in Claez's work, the calendar, clock, and hourglass further represent the passing of time. They, too, are reminders of the brevity of life—as are the burning candle, the flower and the fruit, all of which last only a short time.

The hyper-realistic colors and floating objects within Flack's painting give it an otherworldly quality—a dramatic contrast to the objects that symbolize time. By including a childhood portrait of herself with her brother, the artist further wishes to remind herself (and us) that the pleasures of her life are as fleeting as those of the movie idol. The mirrored compact, makeup, and pearls refer to Marilyn Monroe's mask to the world. Made fifteen years after the celebrity died of a drug overdose in 1962, this painting helps to preserve the past in the face of earthly beauty, to reflect on the glamorization of famous figures, and to promote art as a response to the inevitability of time's passing.

Lineage and Ancestors

One way to make sense of one's place in the world and the passage of time in our lives is to explore connections with the past, such as genealogy. Some people use family albums to chronicle their own life stories and consult pictures to find out what their ancestors looked like and what events and details occurred during their lifetimes. Artists have explored similar connections, sometimes factual and sometimes fabricated. In addition to telling stories and satisfying curiosity, artworks related to family lineage can serve to legitimize a person's status and rank in society.

In many African cultures, an important connection between past and present exists in the reverence people show for their ancestors and the nature spirits that they believe influence their lives. The rituals people in certain cultures perform are as crucial to their livelihood as the chores and tasks of daily life. It is still important to link oneself to ancestors in many African cultures, and many of these artwork types continue today. A painted wooden maternity sculpture (called a *pfemba*) from the Yombe (possibly Kongo) people shows a woman kneeling as she holds a bowl in one hand and supports a child with the other (**4.3.10**). This sculpture is a simple representation of a routine daily event—a woman goes to collect water and takes her child with her—but the artist has given us clues that it has further significance. She is frequently thought to symbolize an ancestor that protects and nourishes the village. This example is unlike other pfemba figures, because they usually show the woman nursing the child. The bowl and the child may be gifts bestowed by the ancestor or god, or they may represent sacrifices the woman is prepared to make. White paint (as has been used on this sculpture) often identifies nature spirits, who are associated with ancestors. This woman thus provides a role model for the living members of the community: they must honor their ancestors with gifts of sustenance and with children who will continue the traditions they have worked so hard to establish.

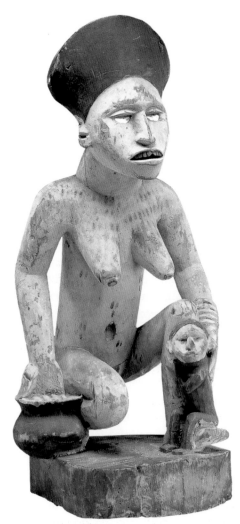

4.3.10 Kneeling female figure with bowl and child, late 19th/early 20th century. Wood, pigment, and glass. 21½ × 10 × 9½". Dallas Museum of Art, Texas

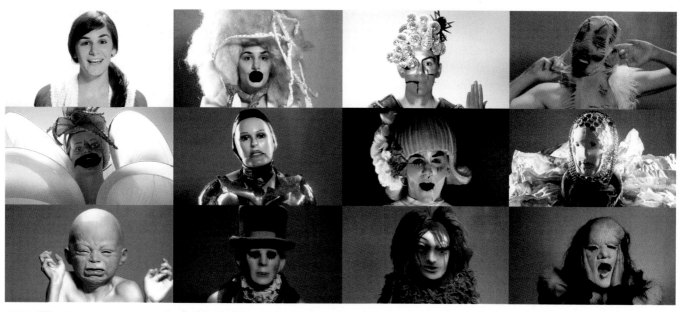

4.3.11 Jillian Mayer, *I Am Your Grandma* (**selected video stills**), 2011. Duration 1 min. 3 secs. Music by Jillian Mayer and Michael-John Hancock

Contemporary American artist Jillian Mayer (b. 1984) was inspired by genealogy (which was an obsession for one of her family members) to wonder what her descendants would know about her in the future. As she said, "we only know our grandparents as old." Her musings resulted in *I Am Your Grandma* (**4.3.11**), a minute-long video that went viral on YouTube (more than 4.6 million views as of July 2021). Like a self-portrait in the future tense, the video mixes fast-paced shots of Mayer wearing thirteen different masks and costumes and rapping over a catchy tune:

One day, I'm gonna have a baby, and you will call her mom. That baby will have a baby and you will have this song to know that I am your grandma....This is a gift I give to you, like I already said, that there was a time I was aware that one day I'd be dead. I wish we could have met. I would have loved you so, but you are in the future. You get love by video. I am your grandma...

Funny but somewhat unnerving, this "message to [her] future unborn grandchild" shows the artist to be anything but old. Mayer is interested in what she calls "legacy leaving," and she acknowledges the importance of "using technology to deal with identity." In the video, viewers can also find visual references to figures from art history—such as Pablo Picasso's images of the harlequin, a comic figure from European theater tradition—as well as from

popular culture—for example, the singer Lady Gaga's Mother Monster—based on the artist's experience and imagination. Whether or not we recognize the specific references, *I Am Your Grandma* embraces play, ambiguity, and uncertainty as ways to connect with the real world: a world in which attachments are sometimes made to people we have never met, including distant or long-dead relatives, characters in theater or art, or favorite singers.

Mortality and Immortality

There are many questions about death, mortality and immortality, often unanswerable, that artists confront. After we die, do we leave the world of the living? Is it important for the body to stay intact? Is there a place to which the soul is believed to go? Images of death in art capture the body as it is remembered and, in a sense, allow the person's memory to become immortal.

Christian artists during the **Renaissance** often depicted the damaged body of Christ after his crucifixion. Such images were important because they emphasized what Christians believe to be the miraculous nature of Christ's later resurrection, and also the concept of eternal life after death, which is at the core of Christianity. The Italian artist Andrea Mantegna (*c.* 1431–1506) created a direct and intimate view of the body in *Dead Christ* (**4.3.12**, p. 576). Because Mantegna has dramatically **foreshortened** the scene, we are first confronted by the stigmata (the wounds Christ suffered

Renaissance: a period of cultural and artistic change in Europe from the fourteenth to the seventeenth century

Foreshortening: a perspective technique that depicts a form—often distorting or reducing it—at an angle that is not parallel to the picture plane, in order to convey the illusion of depth

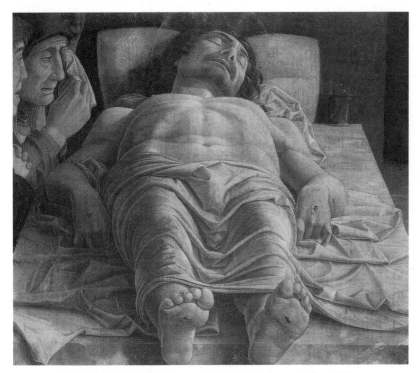

4.3.12 Andrea Mantegna, *Dead Christ*, *c.* 1480. Tempera on canvas, 26¾ × 31⅞".
Pinoteca di Brera, Milan, Italy

while hanging on the cross) in his feet and, further into the picture, in his hands. His body, covered in carefully depicted drapery, extends away from us on a marble slab, suggesting a tomb. Beyond the muscular torso, we see his lifeless face. By Christ's side are the Virgin Mother and Mary Magdalene, who are mostly cropped out of the picture. While their grief adds to the atmosphere of the scene, the artist focuses our attention on the immediacy of Christ's body and his death.

Perhaps because we are somewhat detached from death, or perhaps out of a sense of propriety, contemporary images of the deceased are not as common as they were during the Renaissance. Photographs of the dead can be especially shocking because today we no longer have such a direct relationship with death. In the past, loved ones most often died at home, not in hospitals; bodies were laid out for burial by family members, not by funeral homes.

The American artist Andres Serrano (b. 1950) made a series of photographs in a morgue in which the subjects are identified only by the manner of their deaths. The composition of *The Morgue (Gun Murder)* (**4.3.13**), with the feet pointing away from the viewer, is the opposite of Mantegna's *Dead Christ*. The dark background, the white bandages and body bag, and the strong lighting create a sense of drama and contrast. The formal beauty of the image itself contradicts the shocking reality that this person, whose identity we will never know, was murdered.

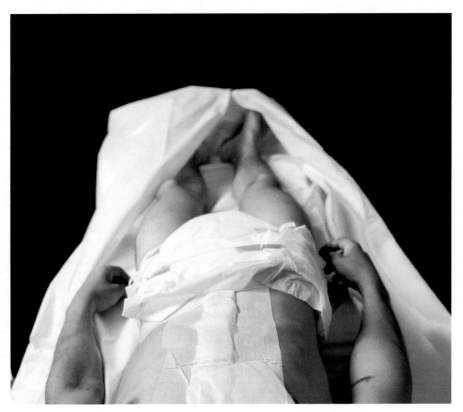

4.3.13 Andres Serrano, *The Morgue (Gun Murder)*, 1992. Cibachrome print, 50 × 60"

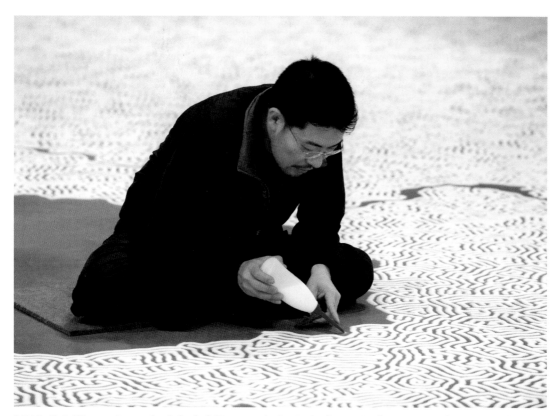

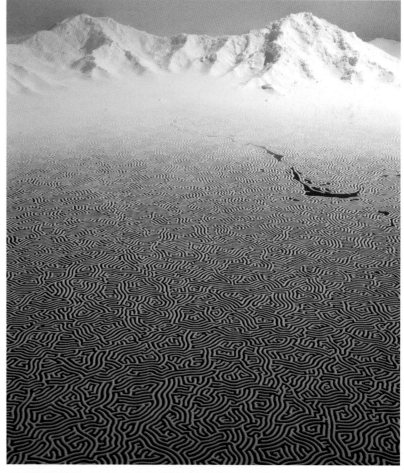

The making of the Amitayus Mandala over many days was an act of meditation for its creators:
→ see **1.6.17**, p. 128

Installation: originally referring to the hanging of pictures and arrangement of objects in an exhibition, installation may also refer to an intentional environment created as a completed artwork

4.3.14a Motoi Yamamoto creating *Labyrinth* **(***Return to the Sea Project)*. Kunst Station St. Peter, Cologne, 2010. Salt, dimensions variable

As Serrano's photograph demonstrates, the visceral quality of art can often challenge us intellectually and emotionally to grapple with the finality of death. Some of the most moving works of art were created to honor someone who was loved (see Gateway: The Taj Mahal, p. 578). Japanese artist Motoi Yamamoto (b. 1966) expresses the painful loss of his younger sister, who died of brain cancer, through **installations** of complex patterns made of salt (**4.3.14a** and **4.3.14b**). The labyrinths he creates symbolize the elaborate and intricate organization of the brain. Yamamoto's use of salt as medium is also symbolic, since the mineral serves a dual purpose in life and death: it is needed for a living body to function, and it is also used to preserve the dead. Yamamoto's painstaking and meticulous process of creating these works puts him in an almost meditative state as he explores grief, memory, and time. It is physically demanding, as he is seated on the ground carefully pouring salt over a period of several weeks. When the process is complete, he destroys the pattern, acknowledging the intertwining relationship between creation and destruction. Visitors are invited to take small jars of the salt and dump them into the ocean, where the regenerative cycle of nature will continue.

4.3.14b Motoi Yamamoto, *Labyrinth* **(***Return to the Sea Project)*. Kunst Station St. Peter, Cologne, 2010. Salt, dimensions variable

The Taj Mahal
Mumtaz Mahal: A Life Remembered

For the other Taj Mahal
GATEWAYS:
→ see pp. 126–27 and
pp. 256–57

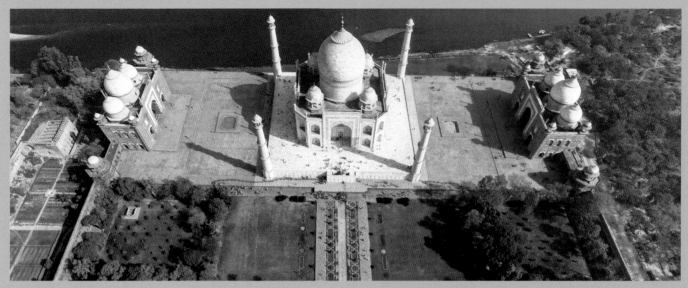

4.3.15 The Taj Mahal, designed by Ustad Ahmad Lahauri, Abd al-Karim Ma'mur Khan, and Makramat Khan; commissioned by Shah Jahan, 1632–43. Marble architecture. Agra, India

When Shah Jahan commissioned the Taj Mahal (**4.3.15**) he was grieving the loss of his wife Mumtaz Mahal, the love of his life. She was a princess of Persian nobility, born Arjumand Banu Begum in 1593. Most of what is known about her relates to her life as a Mughal empress, but she became legendary for her beauty, grace, and compassion as well as for the love she and Shah Jahan were said to have shared. Arjumand was Shah Jahan's third wife and by all accounts his favorite. They became engaged when she was fourteen and married five years later on May 10, 1612, a date the court astrologers calculated as auspicious and most likely to ensure a happy marriage. Shah Jahan bestowed on her the name Mumtaz Mahal meaning "Chosen One of the Palace" and he also gave her the royal seal Muhr Uzah, which was a great honor.

Mumtaz died in 1631 at the age of thirty-nine from giving birth to their fourteenth child. (Maternal death and infant mortality were common in India at the time: seven of Mumtaz and Shah Jahan's children died at birth or when they were very young.) The entire kingdom was ordered into mourning for two years. Perhaps responding to a deathbed wish, Shah Jahan set about building the world's richest mausoleum in history, which took twenty-two years in total. In keeping with the symmetry of the grounds, he planned to have a matching black marble mausoleum made for himself on the other side of the river. His successor, Aurangzeb, abandoned that scheme, and Shah Jahan's sarcophagus (the larger of the two in **4.3.16**) now rests beside Mumtaz Mahal's in the crypt of the Taj Mahal. The surfaces of the crypt and sarcophagi are covered with calligraphy and floral motifs. The Arabic script on Mumtaz's sacred tomb includes the ninety names of God and a Koranic prayer recited by angels asking for the faithful to be allowed into paradise.

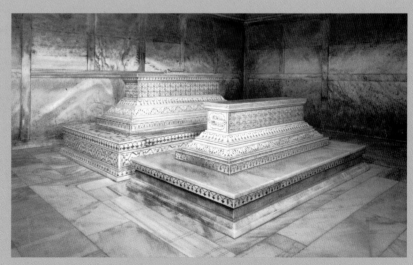

4.3.16 The crypt of the Taj Mahal, with the sarcophagi of Mumtaz Mahal and Shah Jahan

Explore Further The Cycle of Life: Nature and Time

Cycles of Nature

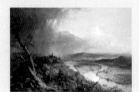

0.0.3 Thomas Cole, *View from Mount Holyoke…*, 1836 → p. 17

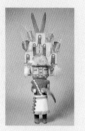

4.2.5 Hopi *kachina* doll, *c.* 1925 → p. 557

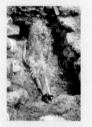

3.10.4 Ana Mendieta, "Untitled" (*Silueta* series, Mexico), 1973–80 → p. 524

Marking Time

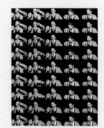

1.5.17 Thomas Edison and W. K. Dickson, *Fred Ott's Sneeze*, 1894 → p. 113

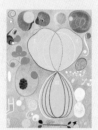

1.4.32 Hilma af Klint, *Group IV, No. 7, Adulthood*, 1907 → p. 102

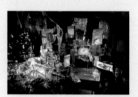

3.10.8 Sarah Sze, *Timekeeper*, 2016 → p. 526

Ancestors and Lineage

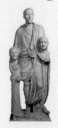

3.1.31 Roman carrying busts of his ancestors, Italy, *c.* 80 BCE → p. 368

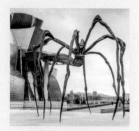

1.2.18 Louise Bourgeois, *Maman*, 1999 (cast 2001) → p. 61

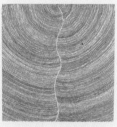

3.5.17 Abie Loy Kemarre, *Sandhill Country*, 2006 → p. 437

Death and Immortality

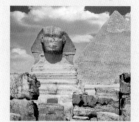

1.2.2 Great Sphinx of Giza, Egypt *c.* 2500 BCE → p. 51

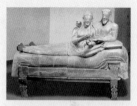

2.4.10 Sarcophagus from Cerveteri, Italy, *c.* 520 BCE → p. 234

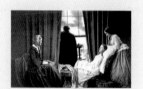

1.7.13a Henry Peach Robinson, *Fading Away*, 1858 → p. 138

Your turn

How do these artworks relate to the themes of nature, time, life and death?

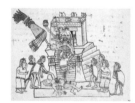

1.6.14 Ma Yuan, *Walking on a Mountain Path…*, *c.* 960–1279 → p. 125

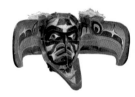

3.4.15 Aztec sacrifice, *Codex Magliabechiano*, 16th century → p. 419

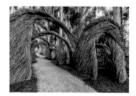

3.4.26 Eagle Transformation Mask, late 19th century → p. 424

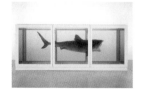

2.4.17 Damien Hirst, *The Physical Impossibility of Death…*, 1991 → p. 239

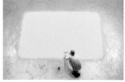

4.2.18 Wolfgang Laib, *Pollen from Hazelnut*, 1992 → p. 566

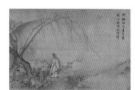

1.5.14 Nancy Holt, *Solar Rotary*, 1995 → p. 111

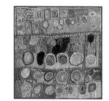

0.0.15 Loongkoonan, *Bush Tucker Nyikina Country*, 2006 → p. 26

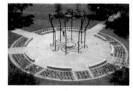

4.1.5 Patrick Dougherty, *Grand Central*, McKee Botanical Garden, 2020 → p. 543

4·4
Art, Science, and Mathematics

Conservation: scientific efforts to preserve artworks

Renaissance: a period of cultural and artistic change in Europe from the fourteenth to the seventeenth century

Mirror writing: writing that reads correctly only when reflected in a mirror, as in the case of the journals and other writings of Leonardo da Vinci

Some consider science and art to be separate disciplines, even complete opposites. We tend to think of art as intuitive and emotional, and science as rational and objective. Both fields, however, are exploratory in nature and involve extensive trial and error; art and science interact more often than we might suppose. In fact, many medical schools require students to take a course in art observation to hone their skills of diagnosis and empathy. The making of art has also been used for therapeutic purposes.

Some artworks openly celebrate scientific achievements, while some artists have even used scientific methods to make art. The appreciation of art relies, of course, on the human senses, and artists have always been particularly keen on manipulating the perception of those viewing an artwork. Science and technology also play an important role in the restoration and **conservation** of works of art.

Art Celebrating Science

The **Renaissance** artist Leonardo da Vinci (1452–1519) was not only a painter, but also an engineer, anatomist, botanist, and mapmaker. The drawing *Vitruvian Man* (**4.4.1**) shows Leonardo's interest in the proportions of the human body. The **mirror writing** above and below the drawing—readable when reflected— consists of Leonardo's notes based on the ideas of the first-century BCE Roman architect Vitruvius. Vitruvius was an architect, engineer, and the author of *Ten Books on Architecture*, the only surviving treatise on architecture from the ancient world.

In this treatise, Vitruvius outlined the ideal proportions of a man, and argued that architecture should imitate these proportions. Thus, in Leonardo's drawing, the length of both arms combined is equal to the height of a man, the distance from an elbow to the tip of a finger is one-quarter the height, and a man's foot is one-seventh his height. Leonardo also made his own observations of the human body, frequently studying corpses to determine whether the writings of Vitruvius were accurate. Inspired by the writing of Vitruvius, architects often combine the geometric shapes of squares and circles to suggest harmony in both a building and between Heaven and Earth. By placing the figure inside both a circle (representing the cosmos or Heaven) and a

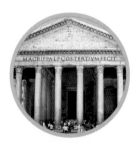

The Pantheon, built shortly after the death of Vitruvius, combines circular and square shapes to represent the interrelationship between heaven and earth:
→ see **3.1.33**, p. 369

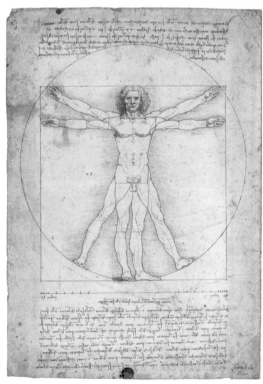

4.4.1 Leonardo da Vinci, *Vitruvian Man: Study of the Human Body*, *c.* 1490. Pen and ink with wash over metalpoint, 13½ × 10″. Gallerie dell'Accademia, Venice, Italy

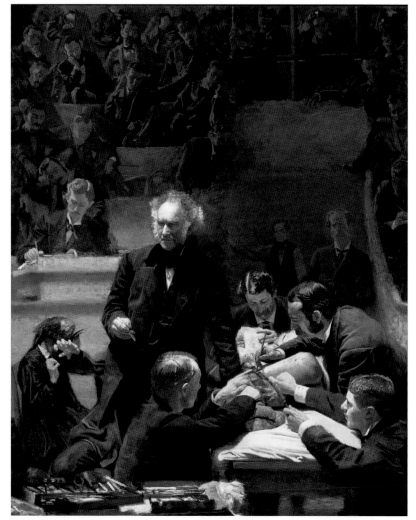

4.4.2 Thomas Eakins, *Portrait of Dr. Samuel D. Gross* (*The Gross Clinic*), 1875. Oil on canvas, 8′ × 6′6″. Philadelphia Museum of Art and Pennsylvania Academy of the Fine Arts

is a picture that even strong men find difficult to look at long, if they can look at it at all." Eakins's meticulous attention to detail makes his painting a useful historical document of early surgical procedure. For instance, he shows us the use of anesthesia (the anesthetist holds a white cloth over the patient's face), without which this procedure would not have been possible. Although the center of the auditorium would have been lit in a similar way from a skylight, the artist also uses theatrical lighting to heighten the emotional impact of the painting. Eakins also includes the patient's distraught mother, seen on the left, who in actuality was probably not present at the surgery.

Is It Art or Is It Science?

Artists and scientists are both keen observers of phenomena and events, which often leads to an interweaving of the two fields. In the examples shown here, enhancements were made to photographic processes out of scientific curiosity; biological organisms are used in an art **installation**; and a sculptor uses DNA from discarded objects to determine the genetic profiles of humans. In each of these scientific experiments, artworks were created that either show the process or that were made as a result of the project.

American Harold "Doc" Edgerton (1903–1990) was an electrical engineer but his work led to some stunningly beautiful photographic

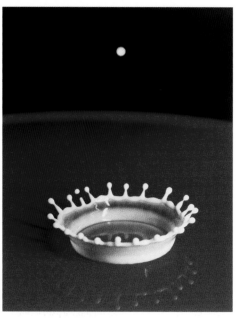

4.4.3 Harold E. Edgerton, *Milk Drop Coronet*, 1957. Dye transfer print, 18⅜ × 13⅜", print made 1984

square (representing the Earth) Leonardo is suggesting an equilibrium in the human body as well.

Artists study anatomy to learn how to depict figures, and many artists have become interested in dissection and medical procedures. The American painter Thomas Eakins (1844–1916) depicted a demonstration by a famous surgeon, Dr. Samuel Gross, that he witnessed in Philadelphia, in which the doctor removed dead tissue from a bone infection in the patient's thigh (a procedure developed by Dr. Gross) (**4.4.2**). In Eakins's painting, assistants surround the body while the white-haired doctor lectures to medical students, who are dimly lit in the seating in the background. Eakins himself can just be glimpsed, seated on the right, taking copious notes. The artist's detailed observation of the procedure created such a brutally **realistic** depiction that a critic for the *New York Daily Tribune* commented: "It

Realism: an artistic style that aims to represent appearances as accurately as possible

Installation: originally referring to the hanging of pictures and arrangement of objects in an exhibition, installation may also refer to an intentional environment created as completed artwork

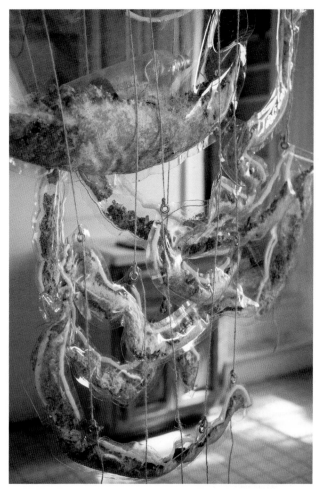

4.4.4 Elizabeth Demaray, *Home Is Where The Plastic Eating Stomach Is*, 2019. White rot fungi, cleaned plastic debris, sterilized woodchips, vinyl, documentation. Plastomach dimensions 80 × 50 × 24″, installation dimensions variable. Exhibition view: Swale House, Governors Island, New York, 2019

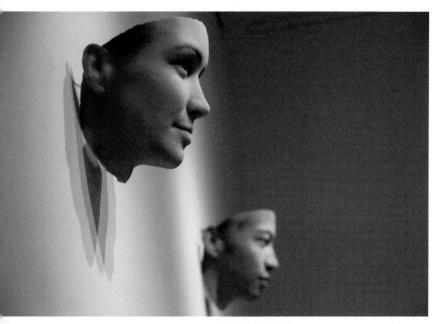

4.4.5 Heather Dewey-Hagborg, *Stranger Visions*, 2012–13. Found genetic materials, custom software, 3-D prints, documentation. Portrait dimensions 8 × 6 × 6″, overall dimensions variable. Exhibition view from *Stranger Visions*, Saint-Gaudens National Historic Site, Cornish, New Hampshire, 2014

images. Edgerton explored the changing processes of phenomena such as the movement of a bullet, the explosion of a hydrogen bomb, or the flapping of a hummingbird's wings. To capture details that could not be seen by the naked eye, he invented an electronic **stroboscope**, which produces short bursts of light, and combined this technology with camera-shutter motors. In *Milk Drop Coronet* (**4.4.3**, p. 581), this stop-motion technique was able to capture on film the microsecond when a drop of milk hit a table or, in the example shown here, a red plate. He worked on studies of droplets, which were originally produced only in black and white, over a period of two decades.

Continual advancements in the biological sciences have led to the field of **bioart**. In order to illustrate that white-rot fungi can be used by society to consume plastic debris, artist Elizabeth Demaray developed, with her students and the John Dighton Lab at Rutgers University, the "plastomach," or plastic-eating stomach (**4.4.4**). Shown in the Kitchen Gallery of Swale House, an art and science collaborative on Governors Island, New York, the exhibition invited people to bring their plastic waste and feed it to the living sculpture. Titled *Home Is Where The Plastic Eating Stomach Is*, this community art action encourages us to view our waste products as a resource: expanding the habitat of fungi into our own living spaces may allow us to eliminate our plastic footprint. Demaray creates many projects that explore trans-species giving, a concept that suggests that the similarities between living organisms mean that we can help other life forms, and vice versa. The fascination created by looking at the changes within the piece, and the high level of participation by an audience, blur the lines between artwork and scientific project.

For the project *Stranger Visions* (**4.4.5**), the American artist Heather Dewey-Hagborg (b. 1982) gathered objects from the streets of New York City that had been touched by humans (such as gum and cigarettes) or discarded material from the human body itself (such as hair), and analyzed the DNA found on these samples. From the DNA, she was able to determine genetic characteristics (such as eye color, hair color, gender, and race) of the people connected with these items and to print 3-D models of their faces. Dewey-Hagborg explains, "I was really struck by this idea that the very things that make us human—hair, skin, saliva, and fingernails—become a real liability for us as we constantly shed them in public." Because Dewey-Hagborg was able to gather and reproduce only general qualities from the DNA due to her limited skill and equipment, her work highlights concerns about privacy and DNA profiling as the field of genetic research continues to grow.

Art and Mental Health

When hearing the phrase "mental health" as it relates to art, one might think of such artists as Vincent van Gogh or Frida Kahlo, whose emotional state often came through in their paintings. But art therapy, the act of creating art as a form of psychotherapy, has been used to help all kinds of people with varying degrees of stress or trauma. Art therapy as an intentional exercise was begun by the British artist Adrian Hill, who, after realizing the healing effects of making art as he recovered from tuberculosis, began prescribing art projects to his fellow patients. The success of art-making as therapy seems to be due in part to the distraction it creates (both mentally and physically), as well as the fact that the act of creation stimulates portions of the brain that help in processing stress.

The Collection de l'**Art Brut** in Lausanne, Switzerland, collects art made by people on the fringes of society, usually self-taught artists. The museum was founded in 1945 by the French artist Jean Dubuffet (1901–1985) with an initial collection of 5,000 works made by those with severe mental illness, such as schizophrenia or those deemed criminally insane. Dubuffet studied and collected works that he considered raw or, in his view, made from impulses that had not been influenced by cultural norms. The museum now holds over 70,000 artworks, including Carlo Zinelli's (1916–1974) *Untitled* (**4.4.6**). At the age of twenty-three, while serving in the Spanish Civil War, Zinelli was diagnosed with schizophrenia. It was not until 1955, when he was almost forty, that an art studio was created in his asylum to help patients cope with their illnesses. Carlo (who is known as an artist by his first name only) thrived in this environment and, now creating art nearly all day long, made almost 2,000 watercolor paintings. Carlo's work exemplifies many of the characteristics commonly found in art created by the mentally ill, particularly the deceptively simple nature of the figures—almost like cut-outs—and the strong use of repetition, symbols, and rhythm.

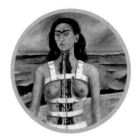

Frida Kahlo conveyed her physical pain from lifelong surgeries in *The Broken Column*:

→ see **4.8.20**, p. 643

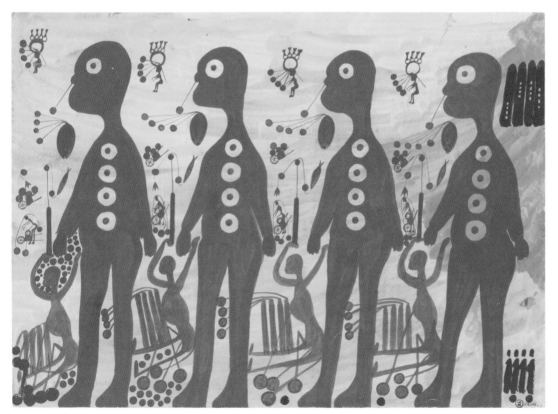

4.4.6 Carlo Zinelli, *Untitled*, 1963, Gouache on paper, 19¾ × 27⅝".
Collection de l'Art Brut, Lausanne, Switzerland

Stroboscopic motion: the effect created when we see two or more repeated images in quick succession in such a way that they visually fuse together

Bioart: art that is created with living, changing organisms

Art Brut: literally "raw art," or art that is outside of the academic tradition; a term invented by Jean Dubuffet

Using Science and Mathematics to Create Art

Advancements in science and mathematics throughout history have enabled artists to create new kinds of art. In the examples shown here, Islamic artists used geometry and mathematics to mimic complex forms found in nature; the advent of the microscope enabled one artist to create minuscule artworks; and the ancient Maya used astronomy to make art.

The Arabic term *muqarnas* means "stalactite vaults," or the drips of calcium salt found within caves. Muqarnas are decorative elements in Islamic architecture made by combining individual cells (*bayt*) in various mathematical combinations to create a structure resembling a honeycomb. A spectacular example of muqarnas can be seen in the entrance portal (*iwan*) to the Masjid-i-Shah mosque in Isfahan, Iran (**4.4.7**). The seemingly inexplicable complexity of the design helps visitors to the holy space feel as if they are entering an otherworldly gateway, and muqarnas are in fact used to mark transitions into holy spaces and frequently cover domes inside of large mosques. The geometric shapes resemble a series of small **domes** lined up in rows and stacked on top of one another. One description suggests that the muqarnas sanctify the space by symbolizing "the rotating dome of heaven". The repetitive forms and glossy tiles reflect light in multiple directions, symbolizing spiritual light filling the space.

As early as in ancient Greece, artists desired to create artworks that would fool viewers into believing what they saw in a painting was actually real (***trompe l'oeil***). The Greek painter Zeuxis was said to have painted such convincing grapes that birds flew into the canvas trying to eat them. Beginning with the invention of **linear perspective** in the Renaissance, artists tried to create canvases that were **illusionistic** windows, a phrase coined by the architect Alberti to describe the intention to suggest in a painting a **depth** that appeared to be as real as that in nature.

The British artist Julian Beever (b. 1960) applied a special form of *trompe l'oeil* known as **anamorphosis** to his sidewalk art. An anamorphic image is one that is stretched and distorted, but that becomes clear and realistic when viewed from a single, oblique angle. Beever's chalk drawings confront passersby with what appear to be convincing scenes taking place in three-dimensional space. When his *Woman in Pool* is viewed from the right vantage point, it appears that a woman is lying back in a swimming pool, drink in hand, kicking her leg in the air (**4.4.8a**). But when it is viewed from the opposite direction, the illusion is destroyed and one can see that Beever used extreme foreshortening to represent the woman's leg (**4.4.8b**). The only genuinely three-dimensional element in the photograph of

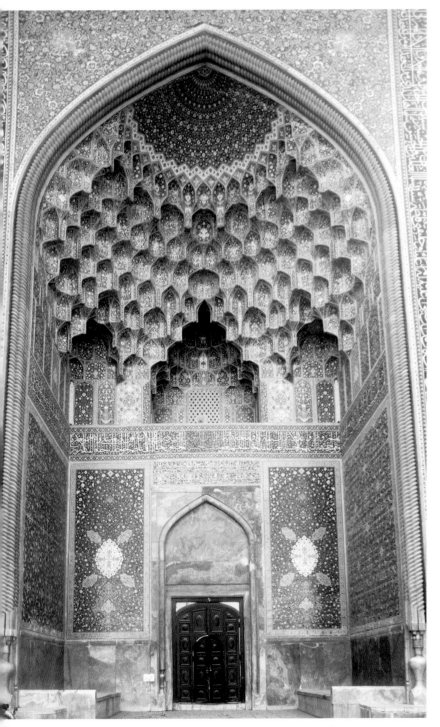

4.4.7 Main entrance portal (*iwan*) with *muqarnas* vaulting, Masjid-i-Shah, early 17th century, Isfahan, Iran

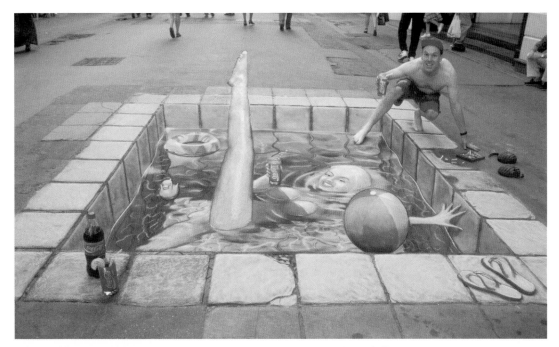

4.4.8a Julian Beever, *Woman in Pool*, drawn in Glasgow, Scotland, 1994. Colored chalks, 14'9¼" × 13'1½" (correct viewing point)

Dome: an evenly curved vault forming the ceiling or roof of a building

Trompe l'oeil: from the French meaning to "deceive the eye"; a visual illusion in art, in which a painted image appears as a three-dimensional object

Linear perspective: a system using converging imaginary sight lines to create the illusion of depth

Illusionism, Illusionistic: the artistic skill or trick of making something look real

Depth: the impression of three dimensions in a two-dimensional artwork

Anamorphosis: the distorted representation of an object so that it appears correctly proportioned only when viewed from one particular position

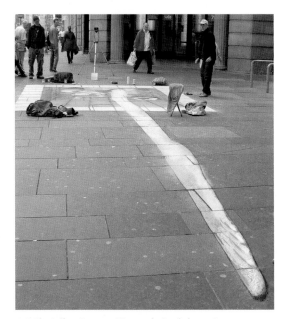

4.4.8b Julian Beever, *Woman in Pool*, drawn in Glasgow, Scotland, 1994. Colored chalks, 14'9¼" × 13'1½" (incorrect viewing point)

the illusionistic drawing (**4.4.8a**) is the artist himself, who is holding a drink and has his foot placed flat on the pavement.

Another British artist, Willard Wigan (b. 1957), has created artworks that are possible only because he uses a microscope—his creations can barely be seen by the naked eye. He carves his artworks on individual pieces of sand or grains of rice and places them on equally tiny bases, such as the head of a pin or a strand of human hair; the Statue of

Liberty in **4.4.9** was re-created inside the eye of a needle. Wigan then paints his artworks using an eyelash for a brush. To create one of these microscopic works, Wigan puts himself into a very calm state of mind, which slows his heartbeat and decreases hand tremors: "I need to work between heartbeats, or else the pulse in my finger will cause a mistake," he says. He works through the night so that daylight activity, such as cars frequently driving by, will not disturb his steady hand. Wigan found that the intense concentration required for this sculpting helped him come to terms with his difficulties as a dyslexic child. As he recalled:

> I became obsessed with making more and more tiny things. I think I was trying to find a way of compensating for my embarrassment at having learning difficulties: people had made me feel small so I wanted to show them how significant small could be.

For millennia, the regular yet ever-changing night sky has been a source of endless fascination and study. In ancient Mexico, amongst the Maya and Aztecs, the planets were regarded as gods, and their movements were closely monitored. Some of the most fascinating artworks of the Maya and Aztecs reflect this interest in astronomy.

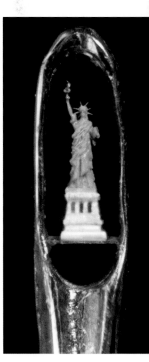

4.4.9 Willard Wigan, *Statue of Liberty*

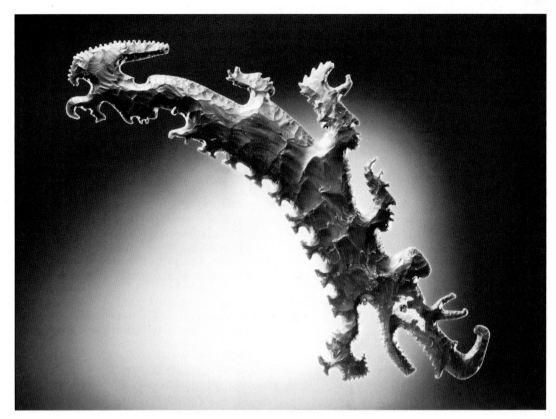

4.4.10 Maya flint depicting a crocodile canoe with passengers, 600–900 CE. 9¾ × 16¼ × ¾".
Dallas Museum of Art, Texas

The **flint** in **4.4.10** incorporates elements of the cosmology (beliefs about the origin of the world) and astronomical knowledge of the Maya. The delicate carving of this very hard stone reveals a high level of craftsmanship. Light enough to be held in one hand, the flint depicts the story of creation, said by the Maya to have occurred precisely on August 13, 3114 BCE, when, according to Maya belief, the First Father was sacrificed after losing a ball game against the Lords of Death. The First Father's soul is seen riding a crocodile to the Maya underworld (called the Place of Creation, ruled by a water-monster god) accompanied by other Maya lords. The **profiles** of the First Father and two of the lords appear on top of the crocodile, leaning back to suggest the speed of the journey. Two additional figures are shown facing downward toward the underside of the crocodile. The serrated edge on the bottom of the flint represents the forceful waves encountered on the journey. The moment shown here is the transformation of the crocodile into a sacred canoe just before it dives into the rough waters, signifying the death of the First Father. Soon thereafter, the First Father will rise from the waters, transform into the maize god, and become the creator of humans.

The flint, however, is more than a depiction of a Maya story; it is also an instrument for astronomical observations. When the object was held up to the sky each year on August 13, the five heads on this flint align with the brightest stars of the Milky Way galaxy. For the Maya, the stars re-enact the story of man's creation when, at midnight, the stars of the Milky Way align horizontally east to west. Over the next several hours, the galaxy appears to pivot and fall out of the sky, resembling a canoe diving into water. Then, immediately before the sunrise, the three stars of the constellation known as Orion's belt appear, symbolizing for the Maya the three hearthstones at the site of the First Father's rebirth.

The fascination with outer space continues in modern times, as many contemporary artists have depicted space exploration and astronomical discoveries, and images of the planets, the galaxy, and beyond are posted by NASA. This infrared image of the Orion Nebula from the Hershel Space Observatory (**4.4.11**) shows how scientific instruments and data-visualization techniques can combine to produce beautiful imagery of astronomical phenomena that we are otherwise unable to perceive. The light-blue areas indicate what

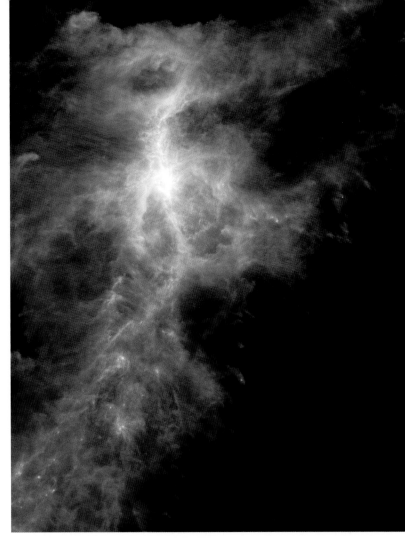

4.4.11 NASA photo of Orion Nebula from Herschel Space Observatory, 2016

can be observed in visible light, while the red and orange filaments of dust (which would normally appear dark and opaque to the human eye) were mapped using spectrographic data, and the resulting effect is that of a **painterly** sky or seascape, reminiscent of Turner (see, for example, **3.7.17**, p. 478).

Perception and the Senses

Since art is a visual medium, artists expect viewers to respond to an artwork through their sense of sight. It is not surprising, therefore, that artists have often been keenly aware of scientific studies of visual perception. Some artists have experimented with ways to use their images to trigger responses from the other senses, such as hearing or smell. Other artists have tried to express visually their personal experiences or portray their subconscious.

Sunday on La Grande Jatte (**4.4.12**) is a picture of people engaged in the activities of everyday life. Its artist, the French Georges Seurat (1859–1891), also applied to this artwork recent scientific studies on the way that the human eye perceives color. Seurat developed a process called **pointillism**, a meticulous way of applying **color theory** in his paintings. He relied on two optical effects (**optical mixture** and **afterimage effect**) to create scenes in which the figures are very distinct, almost like cutouts, because of

Painterly: a loosely executed style in which paint and brushstrokes are evident

Pointillism: a late nineteenth-century painting style using short strokes or points of differing colors that optically combine to form new perceived colors

Color theory: the understanding of how colors relate to one another, especially when mixed or placed together in close proximity

Optical mixture: when the eye blends two colors that are placed near each other, creating a new color

Afterimage effect: when the eye sees the complementary color of something that the viewer has spent an extended time viewing (also known as successive contrast)

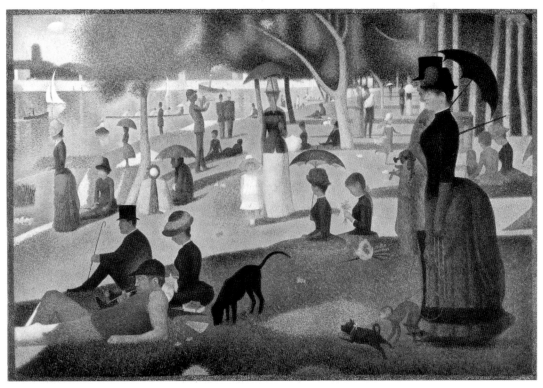

4.4.12 Georges Seurat, *Sunday on La Grande Jatte*, 1884–86. Oil on canvas, 6'9¾" × 10'¼". Art Institute of Chicago, Illinois

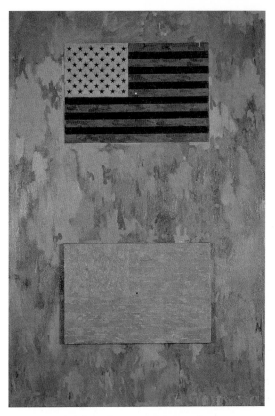

4.4.13 Jasper Johns, *Flags*, 1965. Private collection

up of dots not only of various shades of green but also of oranges and purples. Seurat took three years to paint this work, meticulously applying dots while considering the effects of color theory on his **palette** choices. To ensure that the optical arrangement would not be disrupted when the painting was framed, Seurat also painted a border using the same pointillist technique.

The American artist Jasper Johns (b. 1930) makes us take a second look at familiar subjects, objects the artist says are "seen but not looked at." He uses such **iconic** images as numbers, letters, targets, and, perhaps most famously, the American flag, of which he painted several versions. In the version of *Flags* reproduced here, Johns uses his knowledge of color theory to create an optical illusion that forces a viewer to stare intently at an image of the flag (**4.4.13**). The top flag is made up of black and green stripes, while black stars are placed on a background of orange; these colors are **complementary** to the white, red, and blue colors of the American flag. (Johns's optical effect depends on the use of these complementary colors.) The rectangle in the bottom half of the painting is just a faded ghost of a flag. For the optical illusion to work, stare at the top flag for a full minute. Focus your attention on the white dot in the center. After

the precise way in which he applied tiny dots of color to the canvas. The colors we see when we view *Sunday on La Grande Jatte* from several feet away are quite different from the colors we see up close. For example, the green grass is made

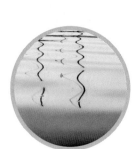

Marcia Smilack experienced synesthesia when she heard music while looking at bodies of water:

→ see **0.0.2**, p. 17

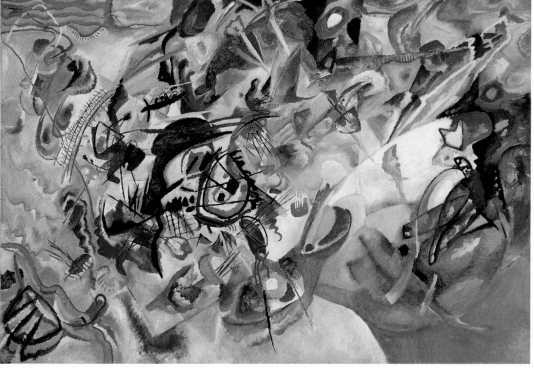

4.4.14 Kandinsky, *Composition no. 7*, 1913. Oil on canvas, 6'5¾" × 9'10⅛". Tretyakov Gallery, Moscow, Russia.

a minute has passed, blink and look at the black dot in the center of the lower flag. The red, white, and blue of the American flag will appear. Johns is utilizing the science that lies behind afterimage effect. While looking at the top flag, your eyes became fatigued from the colors. Therefore, when you blinked your eyes and looked at the lower flag, your eyes produced the complementary colors of each aspect of the upper flag.

Artists often draw upon other senses in addition to sight. The process whereby stimulation in one sense causes experiences in a different sense—such as visualizing color when we hear music—is called **synesthesia**. For Vasily Kandinsky (1866–1944), music and color were intertwined, both being perceived by vision and sound simultaneously. He titled many of his paintings "compositions" or "improvisations" and associated different colors with specific instrumental sounds, creating an orchestra with his paintbrush (**4.4.14**). In his treatise *Concerning the Spiritual in Art* (1911), Kandinsky associates each color with specific sensations. For example, he describes yellow as aggressive with a shrill sound, whereas blue he perceives as having the potential for profound feeling. Each **hue** is also influenced by the addition of black or white. Light blue is described as sounding like a flute, while a **shade** of blue would sound like a cello or even a double bass. *Composition no. 7* is a complex **abstraction** that combines color and form into a harmonious symphony.

Science as a Tool to Understand and Care for Art

Scientific advancements have not only enabled the creation of artworks, but have also helped to improve the way experts can restore and understand them. Through the use of new technology, scientists have been able to study the layers of painting, both by using X-rays and by analyzing minute paint samples. The impetus for such studies is usually to determine how best to preserve or restore works. Scientists, however, often make discoveries that offer new information to art historians about an artist's creative process or the circumstances surrounding a commission.

Some of the most momentous restorations in recent times have been the cleaning of the **frescoes** at the Vatican in Rome, Italy. The restoration of Michelangelo's Sistine

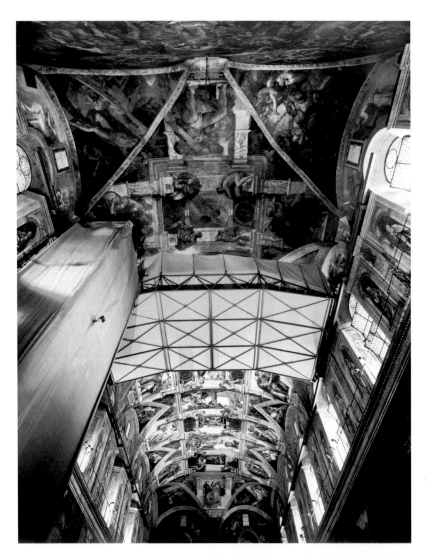

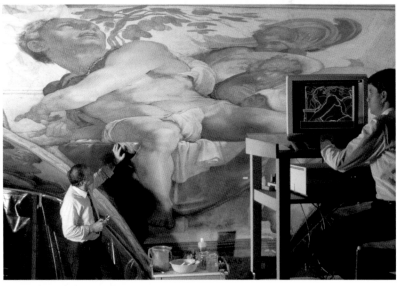

4.4.15a and **4.4.15b Sistine Chapel ceiling during restoration**, Vatican City, Italy, 1980–89

Chapel ceiling, which began in 1980, took nine years to complete, twice as long as it took Michelangelo to paint the ceiling originally (**4.4.15a** and **4.4.15b**). In order to decide how

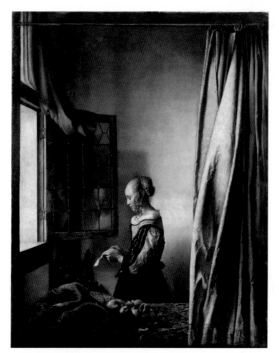

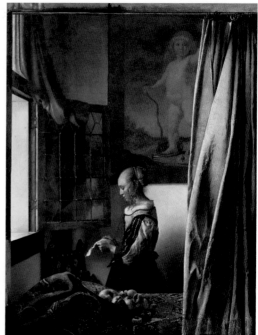

4.4.16a Johannes Vermeer, *Girl Reading a Letter at an Open Window*, *c.* 1657–59 (before restoration). Gemäldegalerie Alte Meister, Dresden, Germany

4.4.16b Johannes Vermeer, *Reading a Letter at an Open Window*, *c.* 1657–59 (after restoration)

best to clean the frescoes, restorers first had to determine what was original and what was due to the effects of time, such as candle smoke, the interventions of previous restorers, rain damage, the settling of building foundations, and even bacteria introduced by the visits of millions of tourists. They analyzed the chemical composition of minuscule samples of the paint, glue, wax, and varnish taken from the many layers they found on the ceiling. This analysis, along with their ability to examine the entire work at close range, led them to believe that Michelangelo had painted the ceiling almost entirely in *buon fresco* (when the plaster was still wet) with only slight corrections executed *a secco* (when the plaster had dried), and that all other layers were later additions.

The most shocking discovery, revealed after centuries of dirt were removed, was the bright colors that Michelangelo had used. Critics denounced the cleaning as a disaster, accusing the restorers of removing Michelangelo's original varnish. An international committee of the world's leading art conservators, however, reviewed the approach taken by the restoration team, and after a lengthy inspection of the restorers' research, methods, and handiwork, the panel declared that the team had been thorough and painstaking, and that their approach was accurate and correct: the original paintings had indeed been this bright.

Johannes Vermeer is known as a meticulous painter who created still, peaceful images, frequently showing women alone in their homes. As a father of fifteen children, Vermeer had difficulty making a living as a painter, particularly considering the amount of time he took to finish a work. He created fewer than fifty paintings in his lifetime, including *Girl Reading a Letter at an Open Window* (**4.4.16a**). As the girl gazes down at her letter, we notice the **implied texture** of the tapestry beside her and on the curtains in the room, the fruit on the tapestry, the nail heads on the chair, and the reflection of the girl and the curtain in the window beside her. The wall in the background is empty except for a shadow created by the open window. In 1979, X-rays revealed an image that had been on the back wall but had since been covered up. Scholars assumed, because of the harmonious final composition, that Vermeer had decided intentionally to cover up an idea he had planned for that wall. However, when restorers began to study the chemistry of the paint in 2017, they realized that the layer that showed a blank wall was painted not by Vermeer, but by someone else decades later, after Vermeer died. Science revealed that Vermeer painted a cupid in the background, now viewable in the restored painting (**4.4.16b**). This new discovery adds a clue to the meaning of the portrait, suggesting that the girl is probably reading a love letter.

Implied texture: a visual illusion expressing texture

Explore Further   Art, Science, and Mathematics

Mathematics and Perspective

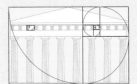

1.7.14b The Golden Section in the design of the Parthenon → p. 138

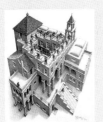

1.3.23 M. C. Escher, *Ascending and Descending*, 1960 → p. 82

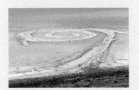

2.4.15 Robert Smithson, *Spiral Jetty*, 1969–70 → p. 238

Psychology and the Senses

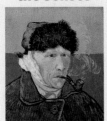

4.9.3 Vincent van Gogh, *Self-Portrait with Bandaged Ear and Pipe*, 1889 → p. 650

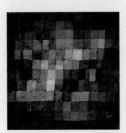

1.4.21 Paul Klee, *Ancient Sound*, 1925 → p. 95

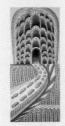

2.1.11 Martin Ramirez, *Untitled*, 1954 → p. 184

Anatomy and the Body

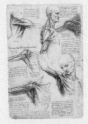

2.1.2 Leonardo da Vinci, *The muscles of the shoulder*, c. 1510 → p. 179

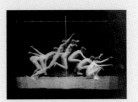

3.8.8 Thomas Eakins, *Motion Study: Male Nude, Standing Jump to Right*, 1885 → p. 486

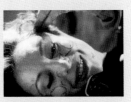

4.8.23b ORLAN, Seventh surgery-performance, *Omnipresence*, 1993 → p. 646

Exploration

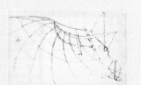

2.1.1 Leonardo da Vinci, *Drawing for a wing of a flying machine* → p. 178

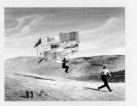

1.4.16 Mark Tansey, *Picasso and Braque*, 1992 → p. 92

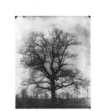

1.5.12 Theo Jansen, *Animaris Umeris (Strandbeest #48)*, 2009 → p. 110

Your turn
How do these artworks relate to science and mathematics?

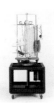

1.3.20 One-point perspective in Masaccio's *Trinity*, c. 1425–26 → p. 79

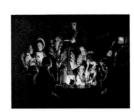

3.7.5 Joseph Wright of Derby, *An Experiment on a Bird in the Air Pump*, 1768 → p. 469

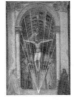

2.8.6b William Henry Fox Talbot, *Oak Tree in Winter*, c. 1842–43 → p. 303

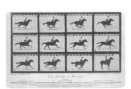

2.9.3 Eadweard Muybridge, *The Horse in Motion*, 1878 → p. 320

1.1.25 Georgia O'Keefe, *Music—Pink and Blue II*, 1919 → p. 46

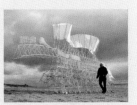

2.4.21 László Moholy-Nagy, *Light Prop for an Electric Stage*, 1929–30 → p. 241

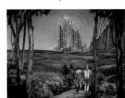

2.9.7 Victor Fleming, still from *The Wizard of Oz*, 1939 → p. 322

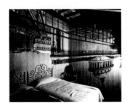

2.8.2 Abelardo Morell, *Camera Obscura Image of the Pantheon ...*, 1999 → p. 301

4.5
Art of Political Leaders and Rulers

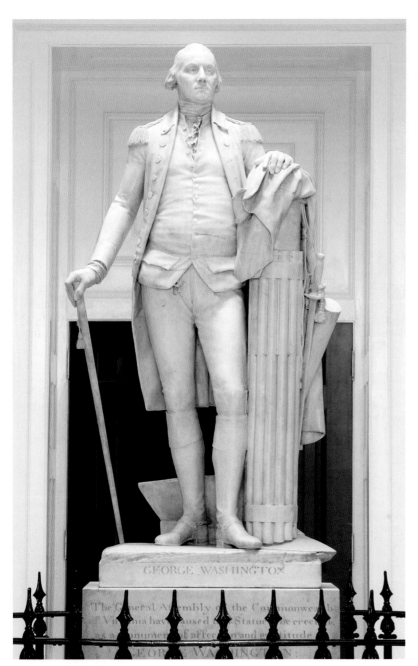

4.5.1 Jean-Antoine Houdon, *George Washington*, 1788–92. Marble, height 6′2″. Virginia State Capitol, Richmond, Virginia

Political leaders have always made use of works of art to help define and assert their power and to influence their people. Seeking to demonstrate supreme control, leaders have used artworks to highlight their right to rule, sometimes even to claim that their authority has been granted by the gods. Leaders are often portrayed in an **idealized** way—dressed in elaborate clothing, placed centrally in the **composition**, or depicted as larger than other figures. National leaders have frequently commissioned artworks to reinforce their reputations as skillful commanders and to project an image of military strength. **Portraits** and other forms of art can also be a potent **propaganda** tool for sustaining a leader's support and power. Such images are, additionally, potentially revealing of what a society might be looking for, or expecting, from its leader. This chapter explores how heads of state and other political leaders have seen themselves and how they wished to be viewed by both friend and foe, and also looks at how some artists have tried to challenge those portrayals.

Iconic Portraiture of Leaders

What image comes to mind when you think of a great leader? Artists have endeavored for centuries to develop ways to show leaders as figures with power and authority, deserving the respect and trust of the people they govern. Portraits vary in the degree to which they depict the physical characteristics of the **sitter** accurately, often instead conveying the qualities a leader wishes to be perceived as embodying. The following portraits of leaders have become **iconic**—recognizable worldwide and often mimicked by later artists.

It was a unique challenge to portray George Washington (1732–1799), the first president of the United States. Initially, attempts had been made to depict Washington in the manner of an ancient god, sculpted in white marble, wrapped in **Classical** drapery, and seated high atop a throne. Washington and many citizens argued that such godlike images of a ruler enthroned and partially nude did not represent the ideals of the young country of America. More fittingly, Washington requested that Jean-Antoine Houdon (1741–1828), one of the most respected sculptors of contemporary figures, carve a portrait of him in his military uniform (**4.5.1**).

Houdon did, however, maintain certain elements adopted from ancient sculpture: white marble was used, and Washington stood using a **contrapposto** stance adopted from ancient Greek figures. Washington's left hand is placed upon a *fasces* (a bundle of wooden rods), which was a symbol of power in ancient Rome. There are thirteen rods, representing the number of US colonies; they are bound together in unity. Washington is shown with his sword set aside and his cape removed. He resigned from the position of Commander-in-Chief of the Continental Army after the Revolutionary War (1775–83) and returned to his farm (a plow is behind him in this sculpture), before being appointed America's first president in 1789. Washington's gaze—slightly to the left, upward, and into the distance—has become so iconic that it has often been repeated in other portraits, particularly of democratic leaders.

Shepard Fairey's (b. 1970) portrait of former US president Barack Obama (**4.5.2**), in which he combined the power of both posters and digital media to reach the masses, has become one of the most iconic images of a leader in modern times. The colors red, white, and blue symbolize America's flag. Obama tilts his head slightly as he looks up and into the distance, very much in the same way as Houdon's sculpture of Washington, suggesting that he has a vision for the country's future. At first, only 350 copies were printed, and they included the word "Progress." The Obama campaign of 2008 requested that the word be changed to "Hope" and, in the end, over 400,000 copies were distributed. The image, however, became even more visually recognizable through its dispersal and replication online. An image becomes iconic when it is copied and mimicked

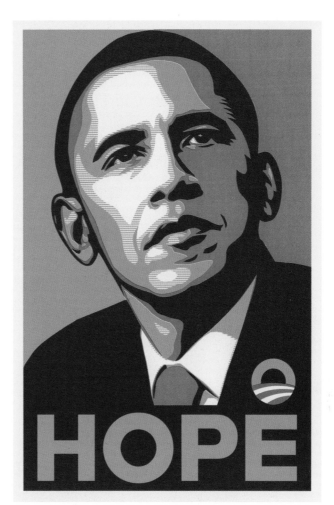

4.5.2 Shepard Fairey, Obama Hope Poster, 2008

profusely, which has been the case with Fairey's poster. Interestingly, Fairey did not invent this pose but copied it from a photograph of Obama taken by Mannie Garcia, who was working for the Associated Press (AP). The AP sued Fairey for copyright infringement, but they came to an agreement outside of court in which the AP and Fairey would share in the profits from the image.

During his reign as emperor of France from 1804 to 1815, Napoleon Bonaparte had painters create hundreds of portraits of him in an effort to persuade the French people of his leadership skills, military might, and humanitarian efforts. Many of these artworks were masterpieces of propaganda, fueling the peoples' support of the emperor. Jacques-Louis David (1748–1825) became Napoleon's favorite painter, and for the French, his portrait *Napoleon Crossing the Alps* (**4.5.3**, p. 594) became representative of Napoleon's leadership as he conquered much of the world.

In *Napoleon Crossing the Alps*, David displays the powerful force of nature, a characteristic of

Idealized: represented as perfect in form or character, corresponding to an ideal

Composition: the overall design or organization of a work

Portrait: an image of a person or animal, usually focusing on the face

Propaganda: art that promotes an ideology or cause

Sitter: the person who poses, or "sits," for an artist to paint, sculpt, or photograph

Iconic: possessing established and widely recognizable characteristics

Classical: art that conforms to Greek and Roman models, or is based on rational construction and emotional equilibrium

Contrapposto: a pose in sculpture in which the upper part of the body twists in one direction and the lower part in another

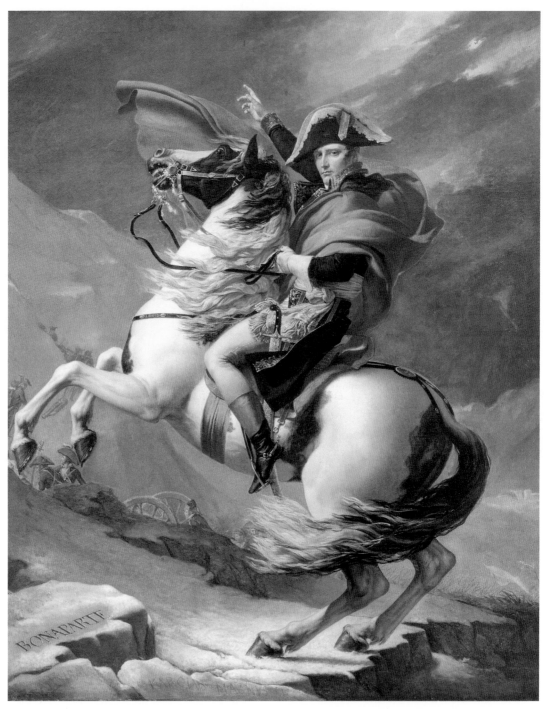

4.5.3 Jacques-Louis David, *Napoleon Crossing the Alps* (or *Bonaparte Crossing the St. Bernard Pass, 20 May, 1800*), 1801. Oil on canvas, 8′9¼ × 7′3¾″. Châteaux de Versailles et de Trianon, Versailles, France

Romanticism, and the French leader's ability to withstand the wind and snow. Here the painter commemorates an actual event, as Napoleon and his men victoriously crossed the dangerous Alpine pass of St. Bernard to enter and eventually conquer Italy. Although the journey was real, the artist deliberately glamorizes the moment, heightening its dramatic impact. In reality, Napoleon did not lead his army over the Alps but sent them ahead on foot while he followed on a mule. In the painting, the horse struggles against the powerful wind, yet Napoleon fearlessly points toward the snow-covered mountains that his troops must cross: by implication, the artist suggests that the leader can master not only his horse but also nature. Napoleon's name is carved into the rock ("Bonaparte"), above the names of two earlier military leaders—the great Carthaginian general Hannibal and the Holy Roman Emperor Karolus Magnus, also known as Charlemagne—who had crossed the same treacherous path.

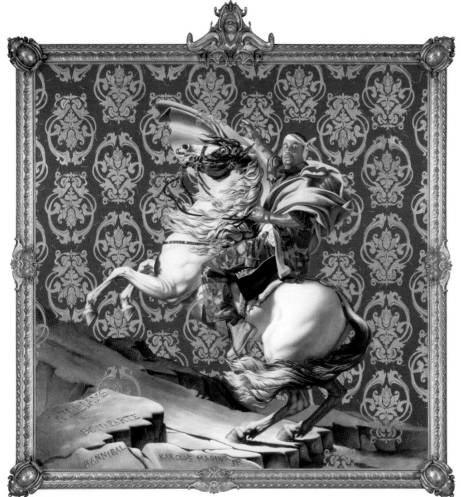

4.5.4a Kehinde Wiley, *Napoleon Leading the Army over the Alps*, 2005. Oil on canvas, 9 × 9'. Brooklyn Museum, New York

4.5.4b Kehinde Wiley, *Napoleon Leading the Army over the Alps*: detail of sperm in the painting's background

> Painting is about the world that we live in. Black men live in the world. My choice is to include them. This is my way of saying yes to us.
>
> (Kehinde Wiley)

Kehinde Wiley (b. 1977) is an American artist who noticed that the paintings in many museums rarely showed dark-skinned figures. After studying many seminal portraits in the history of European art, he began to copy such artworks, replacing the main characters with people who looked more like him. He says, "When I watch television or participate in the media culture in America, sometimes the way that I've seen Black people being portrayed in this country feels very strange and exotic because it has nothing to do with the life that I've lived or the people I've known." Wiley found strangers on the street to model for his portraits, asking them to wear their own clothing but to mimic the poses of sitters in famous artworks. In Wiley's *Napoleon Leading the Army over the Alps* (**4.5.4a**), the Caucasian Napoleon has been supplanted by a Black man wearing camouflage fatigues and fashionable hiking boots, with sweat bands on his wrists and tattoos on his right arm. The two men's poses and facial expressions are identical, but Wiley has replaced Jacques-Louis David's mountain background with a rich red-and-gold design, removing the specific location and time referenced in the original portrait. The ornate background also highlights the artificiality of painting: the way that some of the gold **motifs** overlap the figure and the rocky floor in the foreground makes clear to the viewer that this is an artistic imagining, not a real scene.

In many of Wiley's works, Black men are shown in settings that, historically, were not available to them in European and North American society. By placing a figure of a different race within such an iconic scene, the artist forces the viewer to acknowledge the different cultural experiences of these two men. The tiny white sperm painted onto the luxurious background (**4.5.4b**) somewhat mockingly highlight how royal portraits have

Motif: a design or color repeated as a unit in a pattern

been designed to convey strength through masculinity. The artist pushes the viewer to confront racial and gender stereotypes and constructs a place for Black men to be viewed in traditional, preconceived realms of power. Adding to the names of earlier leaders on the rocks beneath the man and horse, Wiley has carved the name "Williams," a typical African American name, and perhaps the name of this sitter. By doing so, the artist attempts to conquer the restrictive past that limited Black culture, and to challenge today's perceptions of culture, race, and masculinity.

Elizabeth I became queen of England in 1558 and maintained her rule until her death in 1603, despite the challenges of inheriting a religiously divided country and a poor economy, and being declared an illegitimate child of Henry VIII after her mother's execution. For all these obstacles, Elizabeth's reign was relatively peaceful, culturally rich, and saw England united under Protestantism. As an unmarried woman, she risked being seen as weak and unable to rule; however, Elizabeth used her status to her own advantage, and through art she was able to promote belief in her chastity as evidence of her commitment first and foremost to her country. One of the great successes of her reign came in 1588 when the Spanish Armada, a fleet of more than a hundred ships—commanded by Philip II, whose marriage proposal Elizabeth had rejected—tried to invade England, only to be defeated by the waiting English navy.

In the *Armada Portrait* (**4.5.5**), painted to commemorate the English victory, the queen is shown in a rich gown covered with bows and pearls. The largest pearl hangs over her genital region, symbolizing the chastity she is

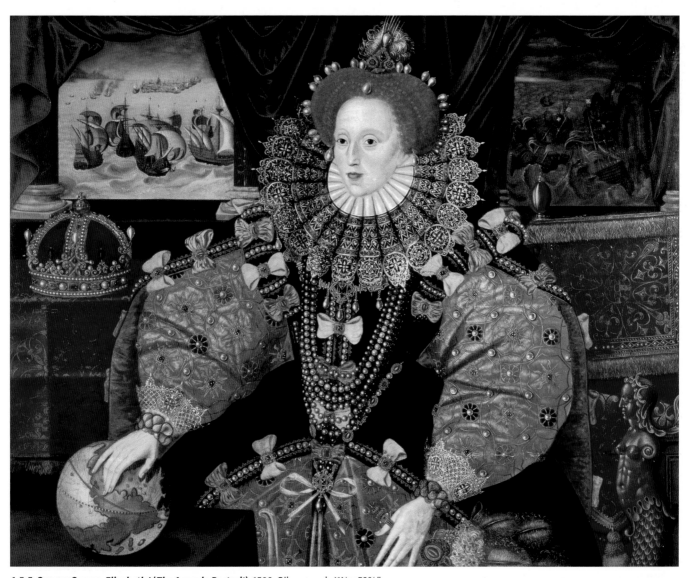

4.5.5 George Gower, *Elizabeth I* (*The Armada Portrait*), 1588. Oil on panel, 41¼ × 52⅜". Woburn Abbey, Bedfordshire, England

believed to have maintained. She sits next to her royal crown, with her right hand on a globe, signifying English naval might throughout the world, and her desire to expand to the Americas. The scenes behind her depict events from the Armada. On the left, the English ships are stationed ready to attack the arriving Spanish fleet. On the right, in a now stormy sky, we see Spanish ships wrecking along a coastal shore, which in real life many of them did while trying to escape England's fire power. Although Elizabeth I's right to rule began quite tenuously, she became a famously powerful and independent queen, a status that she conveyed through portraits such as this one.

Rulers' Connection to the Divine

In many cases throughout history, rulers are thought to be placed in their positions by gods, giving them absolute authority as both religious and political leaders. The following artworks from ancient Babylon, Egypt, China, and Byzantium, and the Maya use imagery to show that rulers are supported by their god or gods, which in turn persuaded people to agree with the decisions made by these rulers.

King Hammurabi of Babylon (now part of Iraq) is best known today for the code of law that he established around 1790 BCE. His code was carved in **cuneiform** writing into a **stela** for public viewing (**4.5.6**). King Hammurabi's code has often been described as "an eye for an eye," because it frequently called for a person to be punished for wrongdoing by suffering in the same way as the person who had been wronged. Yet Hammurabi's laws tended to be more complex and less even-handed when they pertained to people with low status, such as enslaved people, freedmen, and women.

The scene at the top of the stela highlights the belief that Hammurabi's power had been given to him by the gods. Shamash, the god of justice and the sun, is enthroned and shown with flames radiating from his shoulders. The repeated arches below his feet symbolize that he is high atop a mountain. The sun god reaches toward Hammurabi and hands him rings and a scepter (symbols of power) as he dictates to the king the laws he will implement. Below this scene is a long description of the gods' support for Hammurabi and the king's law code. Monuments similar to this stela were placed in town centers throughout Mesopotamia to enforce Hammurabi's judicial system.

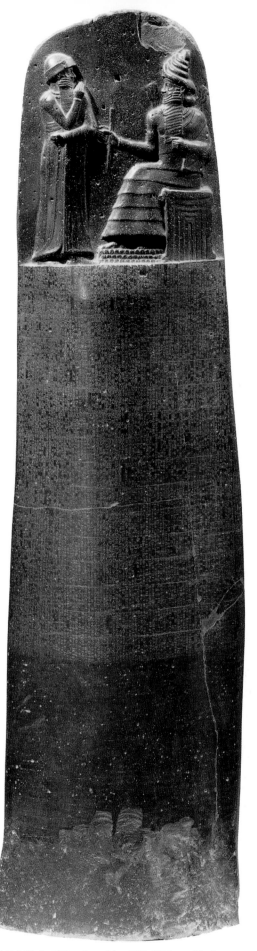

4.5.6 Stela of Hammurabi, *c.* 1792–1750 BCE. Diorite, 88⅝ × 25⅝". Musée du Louvre, Paris, France

Cuneiform: a form of writing from ancient Mesopotamia that uses wedge shapes

Stela (plural **stelae**): an upright stone slab decorated with inscriptions or pictorial relief carvings

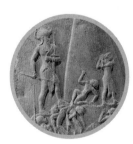

It was common in Mesopotamian art for rulers to derive their power from gods. As with Hammurabi of Babylon, the Akkadian ruler Naram-Sin was portrayed as having been given his power from a sun god:
→ see **4.2.8**, p. 559

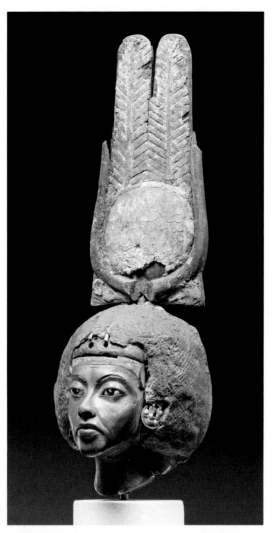

4.5.7 *Queen Tiye of Egypt portrait head*, *c.* 1355 BCE, (18th Dynasty). From Medinet el-Gurob, Egypt. Yew wood, ebony, gold, silver, lapis lazuli, textiles, faience. Head 4 × 3 × 3¼″, base 4 × 4¾ × 4¾″. Aegyptisches Museum, Staatliche Museen, Berlin, Germany

The portrait of Queen Tiye (**4.5.7**), the grandmother of the now-famous pharaoh King Tutankhamun, reflects the history of the stages of her power in ancient Egypt. Through her role as an advisor to her husband, and later to her son, Tiye appears to have played an active part in Egyptian politics and foreign policy; her name is mentioned frequently in documents and correspondence. Tiye was also portrayed in art more frequently than previous queens had been—sometimes as the goddess Hathor, or even as a sphinx—although she was more often shown or mentioned along with her husband.

This portrait head is extraordinarily well preserved, considering it was made out of wood thousands of years ago. Its preservation is due to the fact that it was found buried underground, and protected by the dry Egyptian desert. Originally the portrait had a

gold crown, the remnants of which can be seen on the queen's forehead, which was designed to symbolize her role as a trusted advisor to her husband. When her husband died, her son Akhenaten, who also valued her counsel, changed her status by pronouncing her a goddess, thus greatly increasing her power. To reflect her new deified status, the earlier gold crown was covered with a finely woven linen cap and decorated with blue **faience** beads. The tall headdress with a gold disk framed by horns, along with two long gold feathers, was also added, all to signify her new status as a goddess. The inclusion of the sun disk is further significant because Tiye's son had rejected the **polytheism** of the pharaohs who ruled before him and worshipped only the sun god Aten.

The sixth-century depiction of the **Byzantine** empress Theodora (500–548 CE) in (**4.5.8**), third from left, and her attendants is filled with rich details, such as the Three Magi on the hem of the empress's stunning robe in purple, the color of royalty. The **mosaic** is positioned on the wall of the **apse**—a sacred part of a church, where the **altar** is placed—in the Church of San Vitale in Ravenna, Italy. The glass **tesserae** are each laid at slightly different angles, rather than flat against the wall, making the light refract in multiple directions, so the mosaic appears to glow. Theodora carries a jeweled chalice of wine that she raises in the direction of the actual altar, which is located to the left of the mosaic. The figures in the image are layered so that their repetition creates a sense of movement toward the altar. Born to the lower classes, and having been both an actress and a sex worker before she met her husband, who would become Emperor Justinian, she was inspirational to many as someone who had so dramatically changed her circumstances. The emperor thought of Theodora as his partner and confidante, heeding her advice on many political and social decisions, including convincing him not to flee when a mob rioted outside the palace.

Less than a century after the rule of Justinian and Theodora, Empress Wu Zhao (also known as Wu Zetian) became the first and only female emperor in China. Ruling jointly with her husband Emperor Gaozong for almost twenty years, she ruled independently after his death, from 690 to 705, frequently claiming that she had divine connections to justify her power.

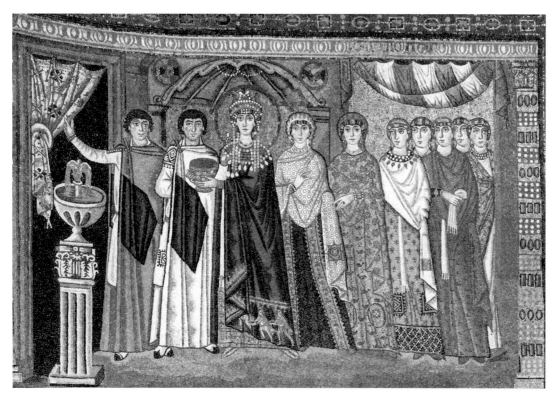

4.5.8 *Theodora and Attendants*, *c.* 547 CE. Mosaic. San Vitale, Ravenna, Italy

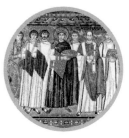

Compare the mosaic of Emperor Justinian, placed opposite Theodora's in the apse of the same church:
→ see **3.2.9**, p. 379

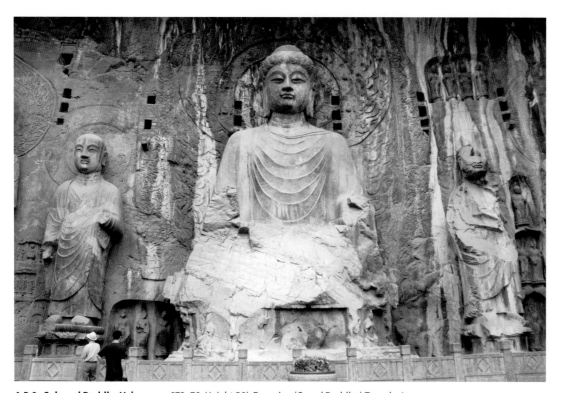

4.5.9 Colossal Buddha Vairocana, 672–76. Height 56′. Fengxian (Grand Buddha) Temple, Longmen Grottoes, Luoyang, Henan province, China

One extraordinary example of the couple's promotion of Buddhism is the addition of many colossal sculptures at Longmen Grottoes, carved into cliffs along the Silk Road (**4.5.9**). Between 672 and 676, her husband created Fengxian, the Ancestor Worshipping Cave, and dedicated it to the empress. Upon her husband's death, Wu and her supporters claimed that she was a reincarnation of the Jingguang (Pure Radiance), a *bodhisattva* that was prophesied to return in the body of a woman and become a powerful monarch.

Symmetry: the correspondence in size, form, and arrangement of items on opposite sides of a plane, line, or point that creates direct visual balance

Dada: an anarchic anti-art and anti-war movement, dating back to World War I, that reveled in absurdity and irrationality

Photomontage: a single photographic image that combines (digitally or using multiple film exposures) several separate images

Later, Wu would spread the notion that she was also an incarnation of male Buddhist deities, including Vairocana. The 56-foot-high Buddha at the Longmen Grottoes is the largest of the 110,000 statues carved at the site, and is thought to convey a portrait of the empress.

Using Art to Influence Society

Strong leaders understand the power of art as a tool for propaganda, both to convey their power and to persuade people to obey their laws. The

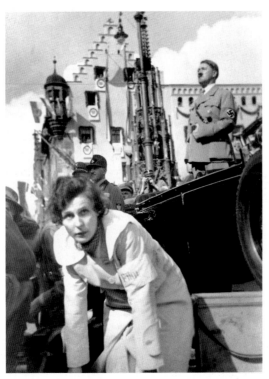

4.5.10a **Leni Riefenstahl filming** *Triumph of the Will*

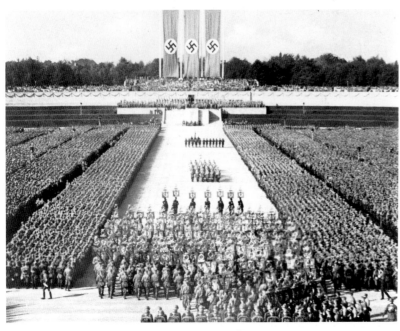

4.5.10b **Leni Riefenstahl**, **still from** *Triumph of the Will*, 1935.

following artworks are examples of ways in which artists have used visual media to convey messages to the masses.

In 1934, German dictator Adolf Hitler (1889–1945) commissioned filmmaker Leni Riefenstahl (1902–2003) to record a four-day Nazi Party rally in Nuremberg. The resulting film, *Triumph of the Will* (**4.5.10a** and **4.5.10b**), was designed to promote the Nazi ideology and create the impression that Hitler was wholeheartedly supported by the entire German nation. Hitler is depicted as a savior, with religious references made throughout. At the beginning of the film, he descends from the clouds in an airplane with a cathedral behind him, with ringing church bells frequently shown. During his speech, Hitler is filmed from below, visually emphasizing his importance and psychologically placing the viewers of the film in the audience that stood before him at the rally. When Hitler speaks, the crowd appears wildly excited, but there is no sound other than Hitler's voice—an effect that gives his words great authority. This technique of viewing leaders from below has often been used in later films to convince an audience of the speaker's power. In democratic societies, leaders are more often filmed or photographed from a head-on view, in which the audience and the leader are symbolically on an equal level.

Through the moving camera, viewers witness the adoration of Hitler, with people frenetically crying and cheering. The enormity and unifying **symmetry** of the militaristic event was emphasized by aerial views of the grand stage, with three large Nazi banners, and the organization of the orderly audience as they salute. While considered a pioneering work of modern filmmaking, *Triumph of the Will*, is also political propaganda and must be viewed as part of the Nazi Party's attempts to consolidate its power and promote its ideology of German superiority over those it considered inferior, such as Jews, homosexuals, the mentally and physically ill, and others (including modern artists) that the Nazis defined as outside of their Aryan norm. Hitler, who had aspired to be an artist himself, understood the power to fuel protest that art could wield. He therefore threatened and publicly shamed many modern artists, particularly in the 1937 Degenerate Art exhibition (see pp. 621–22).

A member of the Berlin **Dada** movement, John Heartfield (1891–1968) published artworks criticizing Adolf Hitler. *Have No Fear, He's a Vegetarian* (**4.5.11**) is a **photomontage** and, like many of Heartfield's works, was copied and distributed in posters and magazines. In this work, Hitler is shown wearing a blood-splattered apron and grinning maniacally while he sharpens a large carving knife to kill a cock, a rooster that is a symbol of France. Heartfield is simultaneously warning the French people of Hitler's intentions to invade and satirically criticizing the French prime minister Pierre Laval, who looks on in the left of the poster, who appeased and collaborated with Hitler. The cock symbolizes France, a country Hitler would invade four years later, and the scene overall warns the French people to question Laval's pronouncements that France would not be invaded. The scene foreshadows many of the disasters that would be the result of, or actively perpetrated by, Hitler's rule, including widespread starvation and genocide (the deliberate mass killing of a specific race or group of people). Heartfield fled Germany to Prague and then England to escape arrest and persecution, but he continued his artistic political statements from abroad.

As we have seen, art is often used by leaders seeking to manipulate the people they govern. Mao Zedong (1893–1976) led the Communist Party to power in the Chinese civil war that ended in 1949. Mao, who ruled the most populous country in the world for twenty-seven years, understood the power of imagery and, like leaders for centuries before him, used artwork to promote his political and social agenda to his thousands of subjects. Mao installed a huge portrait of himself at Tiananmen in Beijing, the capital of China, when he declared the country to be the People's Republic of China (**4.5.12**). Tiananmen, the site of many important political and cultural events in China's history, was built in the fifteenth century as a gateway to the Forbidden City, the home of the Chinese emperors for centuries.

As well as displaying Mao's portrait, Tiananmen Square has also been the site of bloody protests against China's Communist rule. The most famous example took place in 1989, when more than 100,000 people gathered in peaceful protest against government corruption and unfair wages. Catastrophically, the police responded with violence, and several thousand people were killed. Mao's portrait is a powerful national symbol of China, even

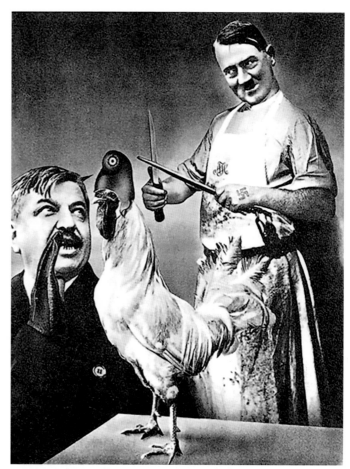

4.5.11 John Heartfield, *Have No Fear, He's a Vegetarian*, published in *Regards*, no. 121 (153), Paris, May 7, 1936. Stiftung Archiv der Akademie der Kunste, Berlin, Germany

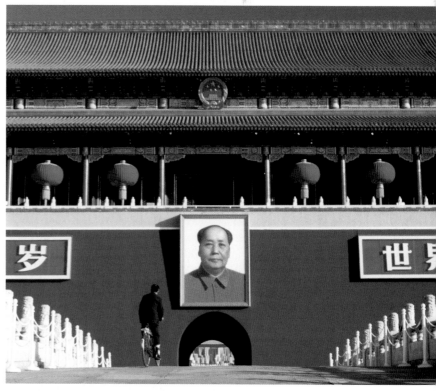

4.5.12 Mao Zedong's portrait, The Gate of Heavenly Peace, Tiananmen (south entrance to the old Forbidden City), Beijing, China

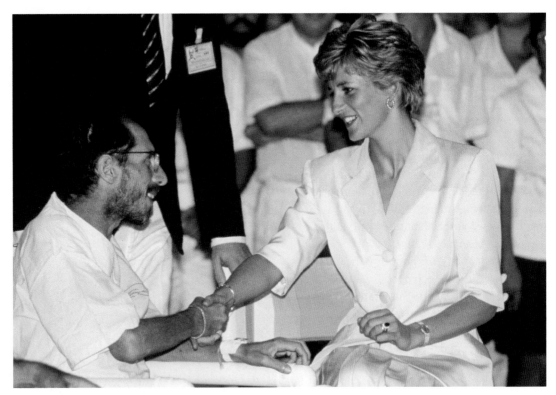

4.5.13 Diana, Princess of Wales, visiting patients suffering from AIDS at the Hospital Universidade in Rio de Janeiro, Brazil, 25th April 1991

though his legacy remains very controversial. His "Great Leap Forward" campaign in 1958, an attempt to transform and industrialize China, resulted in widespread famine, and the Cultural Revolution that followed in 1966 led to the imprisonment and persecution of millions of people. Yet he maintained a hold on the Chinese people in part because of the image he projected as the benevolent leader of the Chinese Republic. Pictures of Mao's face, typically similar in appearance to the portrait hanging in Tiananmen, decorated bank notes, stamps, statues, posters, and massive portraits in public spaces, conveying the idea that he was always watching over his citizens. The Mao portrait that currently hangs over Tiananmen is in fact not the same painting that was erected in 1949; it has been replaced with near-identical portraits almost annually, or whenever the current portrait is damaged by acts of protest. In this way, Mao's image functions like an **icon**: while the original portrait is no longer on display, copies are believed to hold the same power and essence of Mao himself.

Not all power is wielded in either a formal or domineering way. Princess Diana (1961–1997) was daughter-in-law to Queen Elizabeth II and ex-wife of Prince Charles, Prince of Wales, who himself is next in line to become King

of England. When Diana Spencer married Prince Charles in 1981, their wedding was an event celebrated globally, with over 750 million people watching worldwide. Beyond the normal excitement a royal wedding invoked, Diana's charm, fashion sense, and beauty were the obsession of millions. Because cameras followed her everywhere, Diana gradually came to use this limelight strategically, to promote social causes she believed in. During the 1980s, people suffering with HIV, the virus that can lead to AIDS, were often vilified by others in society. Some people were uneducated as to how AIDS could be contracted, and some falsely believed the virus affected only the LGBTQ+ community and claimed it was divine punishment for their gender or sexual identity. On April 19, 1987, Princess Diana publicly spoke with and touched patients in a London hospital who were being treated for HIV and AIDS (**4.5.13**). Photographs and videos of these gentle interchanges inspired people worldwide to reach out to victims of the disease and helped to increase funding for research globally. Princess Diana continued to wield her very significant public power for social change, promoting the rights of those affected by issues such as childhood hunger and poverty, leprosy, cancer, and detonated landmines.

Icon: a religious image venerated by believers

Explore Further   Art of Political Leaders and Rulers

Power and Propaganda

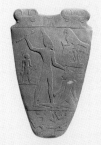

4.6.5b Palette of Narmer (back), Egypt, c. 2950–2775 BCE → p. 607

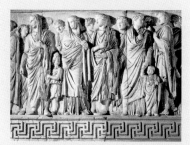

1.2.6 Imperial Procession from the *Ara Pacis Augustae*, 13 BCE → p. 54

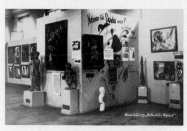

4.7.5 Nazi-curated exhibition "Degenerate Art", 1937 → p. 622

Female Rulers

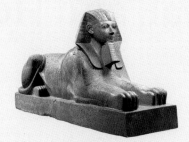

4.9.13 Sphinx of Hatshepsut, Egypt, 1479–1458 BCE, → p. 657

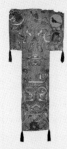

3.3.9 Painted banner from tomb of Lady Dai, Han Dynasty, c. 168 BCE → p. 396

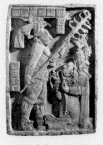

2.4.4 Maya Lintel showing Shield Jaguar and Lady Xoc, c. 725 CE → p. 230

Rulers and the Afterlife

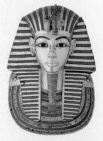

3.1.17 Funerary mask of Tutankhamun, 1333–1323 BCE → p. 358

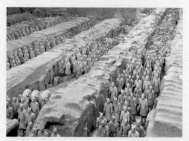

3.3.10a Terra-cotta army, mausoleum of Qin Shi Huangdi, China, c. 210 BCE → p. 397

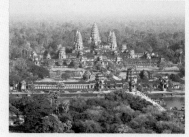

3.3.22 Angkor Wat, Siem Reap, Cambodia, 12th century → p. 406

Your turn:

How do these artworks relate to the ideas discussed in this chapter?

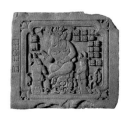

3.1.9 Head of an Akkadian ruler, c. 2300–2200 BCE → p. 353

1.7.4 Maya panel portraying the ruler Tajal Chan Ahk, 8th century → p. 133

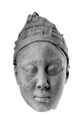

4.8.6 Head, possibly an Ife king, West Africa, 12th–14th century → p. 634

3.4.6 Inca tunic, Andes, c. 1500 → p. 414

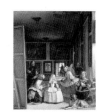

1.10.12a Diego de Silva y Velázquez, *Las Meninas*, c. 1656 → p. 171

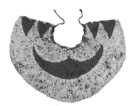

3.5.18a Feather cloak (*ahu'ula*), Hawaii, 18th century (?) → p. 438

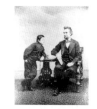

3.8.6 Alexander Gardner, *Abraham Lincoln and His Son…*, 1865 → p. 485

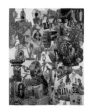

3.9.11 Hannah Höch, *Cut with the Kitchen Knife…*, 1919–20 → p. 507

4.6
Art, War, and Healing

Relief: a sculpture that projects from a flat surface

Composition: the overall design or organization of a work

Iconoclasm: the destruction of images or artworks, often out of religious belief

War has been a theme of artworks for millennia because it reflects some of the most emotionally charged moments of human existence. Artists re-create the terror of battle, the tragedy of death, the joy of victory, and the sorrow of defeat. Artists choose the subject of war for a variety of reasons: to educate us about the realities of conflict, to inspire us through the depiction of heroism, or to shock us into opposing violence. Artworks about historical events can be rich sources of information, skillfully documenting the kinds of weapons used in a particular battle or the uniforms the soldiers wore; but artists may also manipulate scenes in order, for example, to inspire support for one side over another. Art about war, revolutions, or uprisings should therefore be treated with caution, for just as we bring our own biases when we engage with an artwork,

so artists may also be promoting a specific political point of view.

Documenting the Tragedies of War

When art is looted, censored, or even destroyed during times of war, it highlights the importance of art to our society. In 2015, the terrorist group ISIL (the Islamic State of Iraq and the Levant; also referred to as ISIS, IS, or Daesh) videotaped themselves toppling and disfiguring ancient Assyrian **relief** sculptures made for King Ashurnasirpal II in Nimrud, now northern Iraq (**4.6.1**). ISIL claimed these acts of **iconoclasm** were due to the Islamic belief that one must not worship false idols. However, many have argued that these objects no longer held spiritual significance today but were instead treasures of cultural heritage. The fact that their destruction was filmed and announced suggests that its purpose had more to do with creating a sense of power and instilling fear and devastation in others.

As a viewer, do you question certain visual documents of history more than others? One often assumes that a photograph or video can be trusted as an accurate documentation of an event. Yet photographers, like other artists, can manipulate their scenes through lighting, **composition**, point of view, and digital editing. Art that seems to be documentary evidence may not be entirely factual.

American Timothy O'Sullivan (1840–1882) took the famous Civil War photograph *Harvest of Death* after a day at Gettysburg, the battle that caused the most casualties of the entire conflict (**4.6.2**). His photograph shows a field covered with bodies, highlighting the tragic loss of life. O'Sullivan has focused the photograph's composition on the face of a soldier in the

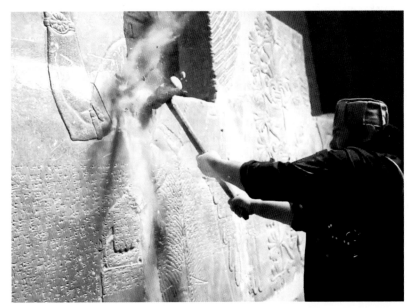

4.6.1 Militant destroying ancient Assyrian relief sculptures, April 2015 (still from ISIL video). Ruins of the Palace of Nimrud, near Mosul, Iraq

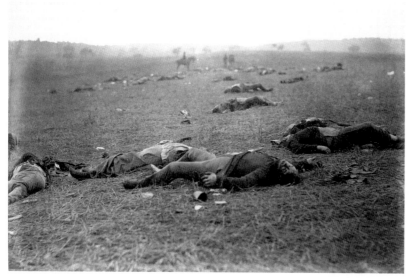

4.6.2 Timothy O'Sullivan, *Harvest of Death, Gettysburg, Pennsylvania, July 1863*. Photograph. Library of Congress, Washington, D.C.

foreground, whose arms are flung out from his sides. By concentrating on this individual, whose features we can see, O'Sullivan brings home the human aspect of the great loss of life at Gettysburg. The clothes of some of the soldiers have been partly removed, suggesting that thieves have been searching their bodies. We do not know, however, whether O'Sullivan may have arranged these corpses or their clothing in order to heighten the emotional impact of this powerful image, but he was known to have done so with some of his other photographs. Does the knowledge that he might have staged the scene in some way

cause us to doubt the truth of the tragedy he represents?

The photograph by the Vietnamese Nick Ut (b. 1951) of children running from their village in Vietnam after a napalm attack was so shocking that some, including the US president Richard Nixon, questioned its authenticity when it appeared in newspapers on June 12, 1972 (**4.6.3**). The image also moved many Americans to question their nation's involvement in the Vietnam War. The photographer defended its authenticity for years:

> The picture for me and unquestionably for many others could not have been more real. The photo was as authentic as the Vietnam War itself. The horror of the Vietnam War recorded by me did not have to be fixed. That terrified little girl is still alive today and has become an eloquent testimony to the authenticity of that photo.

Although the photograph records an actual event, Ut's disapproval of the war and his concern for its victims influenced the way his shot was composed. He focused on the young girl, Kim Phuc, screaming in terror and running naked, her clothes having been burned off her body. Her two brothers are running on the left side of the image, while her two cousins hold hands behind her on the right. The soldiers in the background appear strangely calm, a dramatic contrast to the horrified expressions of the running children.

The story of the people in the photograph did not end with that moment. The nine-year-old girl kept screaming; the photographer gave her his water and rushed her to a hospital. Physicians predicted Phuc would die. But because of the photograph's fame, money poured in to save her. She underwent seventeen surgical operations and later emigrated to Canada. Nick Ut became "Uncle Nick" to the girl and the two have remained in close contact throughout their lives. Kim Phuc was embarrassed for many years by the photo and her notoriety, but as an adult she created her own foundation that assists children who are victims of war.

Warriors and Battle Scenes

Artists have often recorded and celebrated the bravery of warriors, both their successes and defeats, in great detail. Although at times, as we

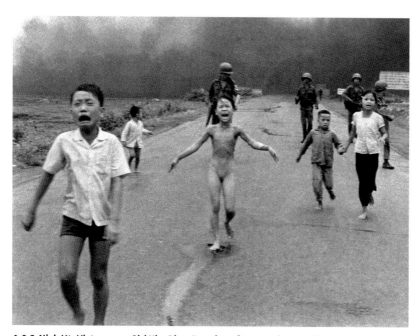

4.6.3 Nick Ut, *Vietnamese Girl Kim Phuc Running after Napalm Attack*, June 8, 1972

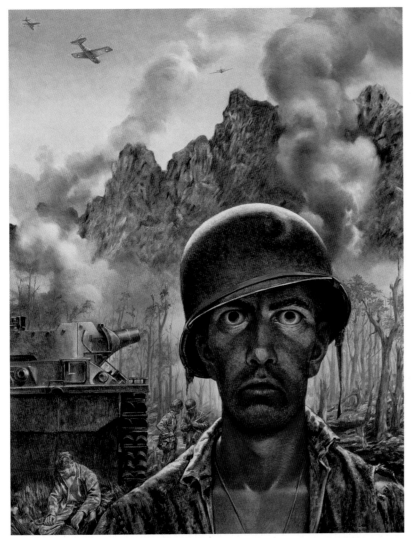

4.6.4 Thomas Calloway "Tom" Lea III, *The 2000 Yard Stare*, 1944. Oil on canvas, 36 × 28″. U. S. Army Center of Military History, Fort Belvoir, Virginia

is not known, as having been fighting for two years under constant emotional stress caused by experiencing illness, violence, and extreme lack of sleep, as well as witnessing the death of the majority of his comrades. Appreciation of the psychological effects of war on humans is generally a modern phenomenon, while earlier depictions of war more often focus on the physical injuries experienced by warriors.

The Palette of Narmer, one of the earliest surviving ancient Egyptian artworks, records the unification of Egypt after a great war, and highlights the importance of the first pharaoh, Narmer, who was to rule over all of Egypt and keep the peace (**4.6.5a** and **4.6.5b**). Before the reign of Narmer, Egypt was divided into Upper Egypt (to the south) and Lower Egypt (named so because of the flow of the Nile towards the more fertile north). **Palettes** were used to grind **pigment** that both men and women painted around their eyes to protect them from the sun. The round area on the front of the Palette of Narmer (**4.6.5a**), in which the necks of two creatures intertwine, would have been used for mixing the paint.

The front of the palette is divided into four **registers**. The top register shows a pair of horned bull heads, which represents the aggressive strength of the king. In the next register the king is shown larger than the other figures in order to indicate his importance, a convention known as **hierarchical scale**. On the far right of this register are ten bodies with severed heads between their legs, indicating the scores of enemies Narmer has killed. The intertwining of the fantastical long-necked creatures in the next register embodies the unification of Upper and Lower Egypt. In the bottom register, Narmer is again represented as a bull, who bows his head toward a fortified city and tramples on an enemy.

The back of the palette (**4.6.5b**) features a large scene in which the pharaoh, wearing the White Crown that symbolizes Upper Egypt, prepares to club an enemy who kneels before him. The falcon represents the god Horus, suggesting that Narmer was supported by the gods. At the very bottom is a scene showing two fallen enemies, viewed as if from above. Much of the **hieroglyphic** writing on the palette has not yet been interpreted, but it seems to record the names of places conquered by Narmer. As a whole, the palette shows this pharaoh's military might as he unifies all of Egypt under his rule.

have seen, an artist's interpretation of historical events is skewed and presented through an emotional lens, artworks can be valuable records of critical historical moments. They can teach us the significance of certain battles, and provide accurate studies of the weapons used and the uniforms worn by those who took part in them.

Some soldiers who have been traumatized by battle and the atrocities they have seen convey a seemingly wide-eyed, faraway gaze that is called the "thousand-yard stare". This condition was captured by the artist Thomas Lea (1907–2001) in a painting that was reproduced in *Life* magazine in 1945 (**4.6.4**), bringing widespread awareness to the American public of the shock and trauma experienced by soldiers. The Texan artist-turned-World War II war correspondent witnessed this soldier at the Battle of Peleliu, which was fought between Japan and the U.S. in 1944. Lea described the man, whose name

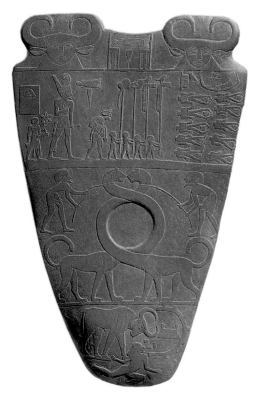

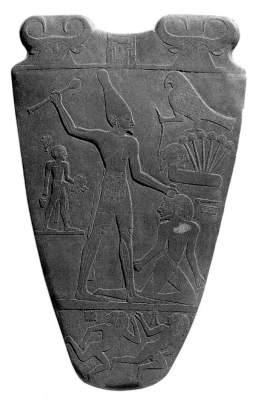

4.6.5a Palette of Narmer (front), Early Dynastic Period, Egypt, *c.* 2950–2775 BCE. Green schist, 25¼ × 16⅝". Egyptian Museum, Cairo, Egypt

4.6.5b Palette of Narmer (back)

Some artists have focused on the heat of battle, and conveyed the sounds and sensations of war using completely different **media**. Both the *Bayeux Tapestry* and the *Tale of the Heiji Rebellion* (*Heiji Monogatari*) portray rousing battle scenes (**4.6.6** and **4.6.7**, p. 608). We can almost hear the clanking of weapons and smell the odor of burning flesh. While a few figures illustrate the courage of the enemy, both artworks are skewed toward celebrating the overwhelming prowess of the victors. Both artworks, too, consist of multiple scenes and are meant to be viewed slowly, unraveling their historical stories one incident at a time. Their very long horizontal formats take the viewer on a visual journey through history.

The 275-foot-long *Bayeux Tapestry* (**4.6.6**, p. 608) records the events surrounding the Battle of Hastings (1066), in which the Normans, led by William the Conqueror, seized control of England from the Anglo-Saxons. It was probably commissioned by William's brother Odo, the Bishop of Bayeux in France, shortly after the Norman victory. The so-called **tapestry** is in fact an **embroidery** that was worked by women (legend tells that William's wife was one of the embroiderers), and took more than ten years to complete. It shows the events that led to the battle, the preparations of the Norman fleet, the Battle of Hastings itself, and finally the coronation of William the Conqueror as King of England. More than 600 men, but only three women, are shown in the fifty scenes on the tapestry. The embroiderers were highly skilled: to establish a sense of depth, each figure is given a border, which is filled in with stitches running in the opposite direction to the rest of the embroidery, and then outlined in boldly contrasting colors. The process creates clearly delineated figures, a flat sense of space (to guide the viewer in a horizontal direction), and, through repeated patterns, a sense of overall **rhythm**.

The *Night Attack on the Sanjo Palace* (**4.6.7**, p. 608) is a single scene from one of five long painted scrolls that depict battles from the *Tale of the Heiji Rebellion*, a Japanese war epic about the short-lived Heiji era (1159–60). In this period several clans fought for control of Kyoto, the historical capital of Japan. This scene shows the burning of the palace by samurai warriors of the Fujiwara and Minamoto clans during the raid in which they captured the emperor Nijo. Soon afterward, another clan, the Taira, rescued the emperor and regained control of Kyoto. Like the *Bayeux Tapestry*, the *Night Attack on the*

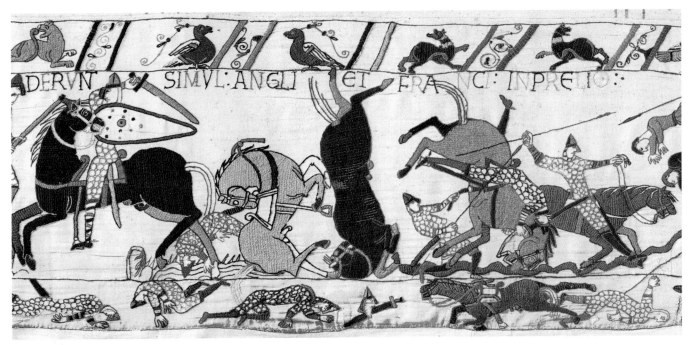

4.6.6 Detail of the Battle of Hastings, *Bayeux Tapestry, c.* 1066–82. Linen with wool, 275' long. Bayeux Tapestry Museum, Bayeux, France

Sanjo Palace is representative of the visual style of its period. The almost 23-foot-long Japanese scroll employs **isometric perspective** from a **bird's-eye view**. The horses and warriors are carefully delineated and detailed. The precise lines and limited use of blurry brushwork (as in the horses' tails and the billowing smoke) demonstrate the artist's skill. The story in the scroll is read from right to left, and the artist guides the viewer in that direction using the diagonal lines of the buildings, the layering of the figures, and the movement of the billowing

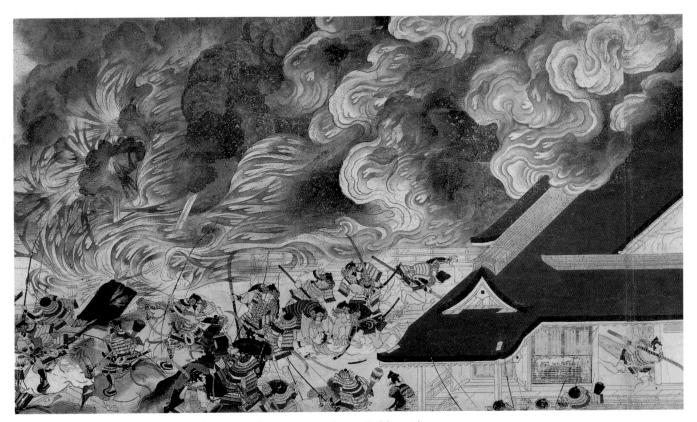

4.6.7 *Night Attack on the Sanjo Palace,* **detail from** *Heiji Monogatari,* Kamakura period, late 13th century. Hand scroll, ink and color on paper, 16⅛" × 22'11¼" (whole scroll). Museum of Fine Arts, Boston, Massachusetts

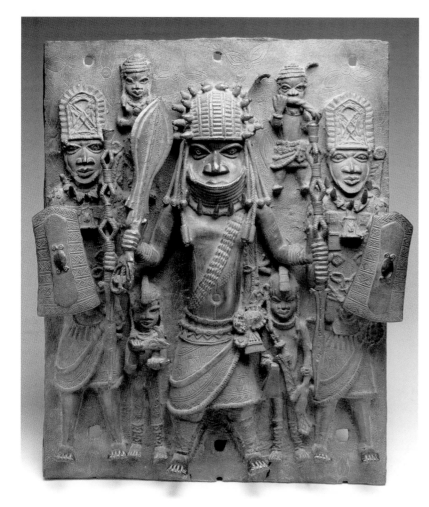

4.6.8 Benin plaque with warrior and attendants, 16th–17th century. Brass, height 18¾". Metropolitan Museum of Art, New York

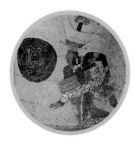

The Maya played ball games to the death with enemies captured during times of war: → see **3.4.13**, p. 418

Isometric perspective: a system using diagonal parallel lines to communicate depth

Bird's-eye view: an artistic technique in which a scene or subject is presented from some point above it

High relief: a carved panel where the figures project with a great deal of depth from the background

smoke. In the section of the scroll shown here, the building on the right shows the palace under attack; then, moving left, prisoners are beheaded. The emperor is shown captured on a black cart in the lower left. Later in the scroll, the emperor is shown imprisoned with the decapitated heads displayed on pikes.

The attention to detail in both the Japanese scroll and the Norman tapestry gives us a strong sense of the equipment and weapons used by the warriors of these peoples. The Japanese samurai are shown covered in intricately detailed armor atop their fine and powerful horses. Lengthy bows and arching swords are their weapons of choice. The soldiers of the Bayeux tapestry wear patterned armor and conical helmets, and carry broadswords, kite-shaped shields, and spears.

A plaque from the palace of an African king, or *oba*, suggests that military strength is often needed to bring peace to a kingdom (**4.6.8**). The Benin kingdom, from the region that is now southern Nigeria, was at its height

between 1450 and 1700. The central warrior in this plaque is larger than the two beside him, signifying his importance; he is in **higher relief** than the others, making him seem closer to us. The ceremonial sword he carries in his left hand and his elaborate helmet tell us that he is a high-ranking chief. His spear and the shields of those beside him are imposing, emphasizing their physical power and that of their ruler, the oba. The chief wears a leopard-tooth necklace and has dotted markings on his stomach and arms resembling the spots of a leopard. Leopards, known for their power and speed, were a symbol of the oba.

The obas commissioned hundreds of brass artworks to reflect their power, including at least 900 plaques like this one that originally covered the royal palace. Many of them were stolen in a raid in 1897 in which British soldiers were avenging the murder of a British official. Most of the plaques are now owned by museums in North America and Europe: Benin City has been fighting for the return of these brass plaques for decades. Some museums, such as the Humboldt Forum in Berlin and the British Museum, are returning theirs, which will be displayed in a museum in Benin City scheduled to open in 2023.

The Artist's Response to War

Artists have often created artworks that attempt to convey their personal experience of war. This is sometimes a cathartic exercise, releasing emotion, and it is sometimes meant to inspire awareness of the realities of war. But by no means have all powerful responses to war been created by artists who actually witnessed the events they portray. Artists can produce powerful visual statements about the horrors of war from both their experiences and their own imagination (see Perspectives on Art: Wafaa Bilal, p. 613).

Francisco Goya's (1746–1828) painting *The Third of May, 1808* (**4.6.9**, p. 610) is considered one of the most powerful portrayals of the horrors of war. The Spanish War of Independence (1808–14) was known for its guerrilla fighting and for the heroism of the civilian population. *The Third of May, 1808* documents the French emperor Napoleon's troops executing Spanish citizens during the French occupation of Madrid in 1808. The painting was commissioned in 1813 by the Spanish king Ferdinand VII to memorialize

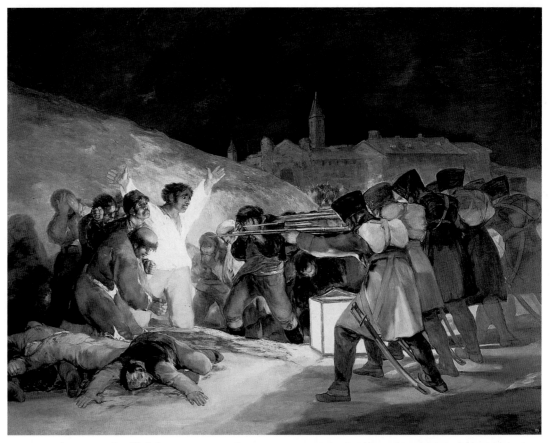

4.6.9 Francisco Goya, *The Third of May, 1808*, 1814. Oil on canvas, 8′4⅜ × 11′3⅞″. Museo Nacional del Prado, Madrid, Spain

the event. Goya, a Spanish citizen who lived through the Napoleonic occupation, had complex views about the political situation as he watched it unfold, but in this work he made choices about how the image needed to be organized to evoke the drama and brutality of this event.

The figure given the most emphasis stands with his arms held high in a bright white shirt that glows from the light of a single lamp. He is about to be executed, which is suggested by the repetition of his pose in the dead figure lying bloodied on the ground. Terror is on the faces that surround this martyr, making him seem calm in comparison. Goya continually brings our attention back to this figure by using directional lines, such as the strong horizontals created by the rifles. The viewer identifies with the victims, not the line of faceless executioners.

Another famous Spanish artist, Pablo Picasso (1881–1973), painted *Guernica* as a passionate response to the aerial attack carried out on April 26, 1937, on a small town of that name in northern Spain (**4.6.10**). During the Spanish Civil War, the Nationalist general Francisco Franco, who would later become

the country's ruler, allowed German and Italian planes to test their bombing tactics on Guernica and study the psychological effects of air warfare. News of the attack quickly spread to Paris, where Picasso read stories and saw photographs of the devastation in newspapers. The absence of color and the small dashes on the body of the horse recall black-and-white newspaper print.

While the general meaning of *Guernica* is clearly outrage against the violence directed at the citizens of the small Spanish town, Picasso never explained the specific symbolism of the figures in the painting. He stated:

> A picture is not thought out and settled beforehand. While it is being done it changes as one's thoughts change. And when it is finished, it still goes on changing, according to the state of mind of whoever is looking at it.

Expressive faces with distorted necks scream and cry in despair. On the right, a figure reaches to the sky as it escapes from a burning building; flames appear like scales on the back of a dragon. The tortured figure on the left

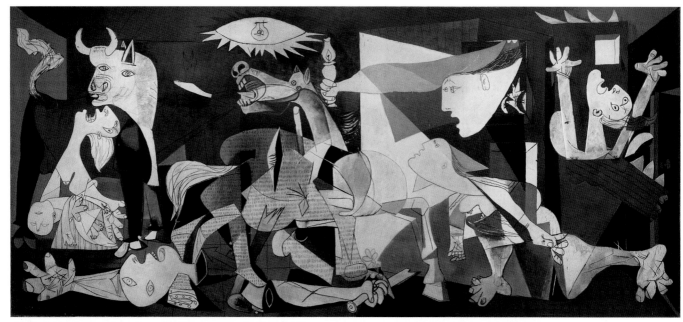

4.6.10 Pablo Picasso, *Guernica*, 1937. Oil on canvas, 11′5½″ × 25′5¾″. Museo Nacional Centro de Arte Reina Sofia, Madrid, Spain

experiences the horror of her child's murder. The bull, often associated with the violence of Spanish bullfighting, is seen by many as a symbol of Franco. The terrified horse, as it tramples upon a man lying on the ground, may represent the chaos inflicted on the people by the attack. The lightbulb shining powerfully at the top of the canvas may symbolize awareness and knowledge, as if illuminating the situation.

Picasso exhibited this large protest statement at the Spanish Pavilion during the 1937 World's Fair in Paris, France, and declared that neither he nor the painting would go to Spain as long as Franco ruled. The artwork traveled the world before residing in New York's Museum of Modern Art. Franco died in 1975, two years after Picasso. In 1981, *Guernica* was finally sent to Madrid, Spain, to be exhibited there permanently.

The German artist Anselm Kiefer (b. 1945) was born in Germany just months before World War II ended. He grew up in a society ashamed of its past, and his artworks urge viewers to acknowledge the horrors of the Nazi regime that ruled Germany from 1933 until 1945. His attempts to confront this past have often shocked and angered Germans. For example, he photographed himself making the Nazi salute—a gesture that has been illegal in Germany since 1945.

Kiefer's *Breaking of the Vessels* (**4.6.11**) conveys the loss of life and the destruction of knowledge caused by the extermination of

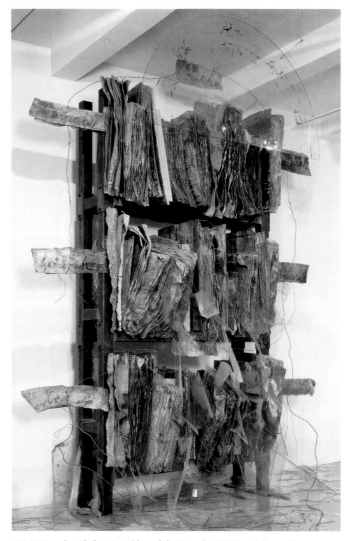

4.6.11 Anselm Kiefer, *Breaking of the Vessels*, 1990. Lead, iron, glass, copper wire, charcoal, and Aquatec, 12′5″ × 27′5½″ × 17′. St. Louis Art Museum, Missouri

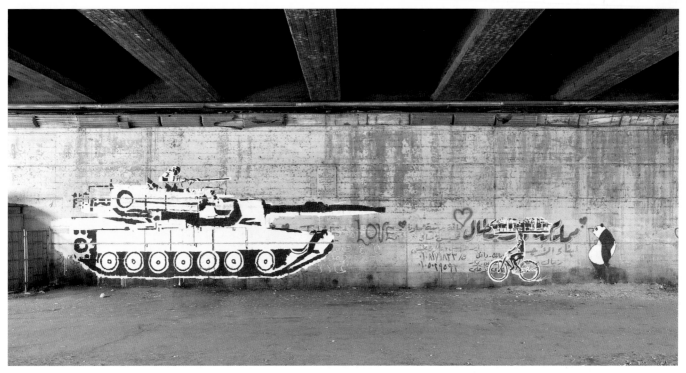

4.6.12 Ganzeer, *Tank vs. Bread-Biker*, with graffiti by Sad Panda, 2011. Cairo, Egypt

millions of Jews during the Holocaust. The imposing 27-foot-tall artwork is made of lead and glass. The heavy lead books appear to be scorched, just as so many human beings (also holders of knowledge) were incinerated in concentration camps. The shattered glass also recalls *Kristallnacht* (Night of the Broken Glass), when the Nazis destroyed hundreds of Jewish stores and synagogues in 1938. The splintered glass on the ground makes any access to these books of knowledge a dangerous and frightening proposition. Symbolically, Kiefer has conveyed the fear and pain one must face in order to confront the past.

In *Breaking of the Vessels*, Kiefer draws upon the Jewish religion and more specifically the Kabbalah, a collection of Jewish mystical writings. The words "Ain-Sof," which mean the infinite presence of God, are written on the arched piece of glass above the bookshelf. Ten lead labels are placed around and on the bookshelf; these represent the ten vessels that, as described in the Kabbalah, are believed to contain the essence of God. In this way, the books represent the potential presence of God even in the midst of destruction and tragedy.

The Egyptian artist Mohamad Fahmy, known as Ganzeer, became internationally famous for his **graffiti** art criticizing the Supreme Council of the Armed Forces (SCAF),

a council of military officials that ruled his country after the Egyptian Revolution in February 2011. Immediately following the revolution, Ganzeer began a series called the *Martyr Murals*, in which he created portraits of those killed during the revolution. As is the case with much **street art**, this artwork was collaborative, and was the result of many artists who wished to raise their voices in protest against the massacre.

During Mad Graffiti Weekend (May 20–21, 2011) Ganzeer produced his best-known work, *Tank vs. Bread-Biker*, in which an enormous tank points its gun at a young Egyptian boy on a pushbike, who is balancing a huge tray full of bread upon his head (**4.6.12**). Ganzeer was assisted by a team of volunteers to create the stencils for this work. Later, the artist known as Sad Panda added his trademark figure of a panda behind the boy. Since then, other artists have added to the image and it continues to evolve. For example, the graffiti artist Khaled painted bodies being crushed under the tank. This recorded an actual event that took place in October 2011, when a group of peaceful civilians, protesting the demolition of a church, were attacked by security forces and the army. Graffiti and other street art was a major form of protest throughout the uprisings against governments across West Asia and North Africa in the early 2010s (known as the Arab Spring).

Graffiti: markings that are scratched, scribbled, or sprayed on a wall without the consent of the owner

Street art: art created in public spaces (examples include graffiti, posters, and stickers)

Perspectives On Art: Wafaa Bilal
Domestic Tension: An Artist's Protest against War

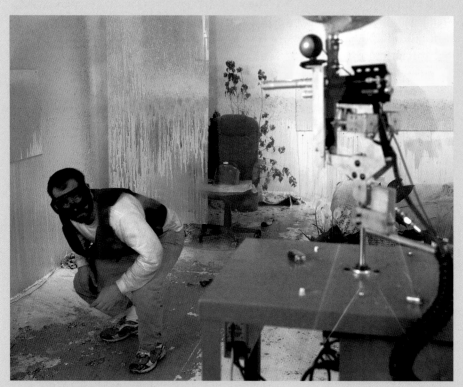

4.6.13 Wafaa Bilal, *Domestic Tension*, 2007. Flatfile Gallery, Chicago, Illinois

Iraqi-born Wafaa Bilal teaches in the Photography and Imaging department at the Tisch School of the Arts at NYU. His art reflects his concerns with the injustices committed in Iraq under the dictatorial regime of Saddam Hussein and, since then, during American military operations in the country.

As an Iraqi artist living in the US since 1992, I have created many provocative works to raise awareness and create dialogue about US–Iraq conflicts. But when my brother Haji was killed by an American bomb at a checkpoint in our hometown of Kufa, Iraq, in 2004, the war became deeply personal.

I had to find an unconventional new approach to translate this tragic event into a work of art that empowered its audience. Not something that lectured the audience, nor something dogmatic, but a dynamic encounter between me and my audience.

A TV news segment about a soldier in Colorado remotely dropping bombs on Iraq highlighted the anonymous and detached nature of this current war, and the complete disconnect between the comfort zone here in the US and the conflict zone in my home country. I needed to create a platform for people to be nudged out of their comfort zone.

The result was an interactive performance entitled *Domestic Tension* (**4.7.13**). I stayed in a Chicago gallery for a month with a paintball gun aimed at me. People could control the paintball gun, and command it to shoot at me, over the Internet.

I wanted to create a virtual and physical platform, turning the virtual to physical and vice versa, and, by putting my body on the line, create a physical impact in viewers by enabling them to identify with the physical effect on my body.

The project generated worldwide attention, with more than 60,000 shots taken and 80 million hits to the website from 137 countries.

I never anticipated how many people would be drawn to the project and how it would become a truly dynamic artwork in which the viewers had control over the **narrative**. It achieved an unexpected goal of democratizing the process of the viewing and the making of the artwork, by enabling the audience to participate.

As evidenced by dialogue on the website's chat room, the experience had a profound impact on many people from all sides of the political spectrum. At the conclusion of the project, I felt fulfilled in my mantra that "Today we silenced one gun; hopefully one day we will silence all guns."

Narrative: an artwork that tells a story

Remembrance and Memorials

Art can serve as a way of acknowledging historical tragedy, mistreatment, or suffering, often in the hope that similar events will not be repeated. Memorials may address the history of a single individual or of many people. While memorials are often designed to promote healing and hope, they can also cause controversy and inflame unresolved issues in society.

The Asmat people live on the island of New Guinea in the southern Pacific Ocean. Sculpted mangrove trees known as *bis* poles (**4.6.14**), 12 to 30 ft. high, are made to care for and honor the souls of those who have died, especially warriors. When bark is ritually removed from the trunk of the tree, the red sap on the white wood symbolizes the blood that has been lost. The carvings depict stacked human figures, sometimes groups of deceased people and sometimes one deceased person along with their ancestors. The lower part of the sculpture, called the "canoe," is believed to carry the deceased into the afterlife. The projection at the top is actually the root of the tree, which is turned upside down before carving, and which is also a phallic symbol of fertility.

In the past, when a community member died, it was believed that an enemy's head needed to be captured and hung on the pole to avenge that person's death, and therefore bring order and balance back to society. While headhunting ended in the mid-twentieth century, bis poles are still used today as monuments to the dead and in healing rituals. Once a bis pole has served its ritual function, it is placed in sago palm groves to decay and nourish future harvests of the trees, which are an important food source for Asmat people. This final step in the ritual shows the Asmat belief in a connection between fertilization of the land and memorialization of ancestors.

The Vietnam Veterans Memorial was built in Washington, D.C. to pay tribute to many fallen men and women, in the hope of laying to rest some of the lingering controversy over the war (**4.6.15a**). The design itself was immediately controversial, however. Maya Lin (b. 1959), who was only twenty years old when she won the competition to design the memorial, envisaged her monument as a place for mourning and healing. A black-granite V-shaped wall descends into the earth, and then ascends, giving one a sense of coming into the light. The wall also becomes taller as one descends, creating a powerful visual expression for the enormous loss of life during the war.

It symbolizes the eternal wound in America caused by the conflict, but also the healing that Lin hoped would take place as those who experienced the monument walked through it and physically rose again. The names of the

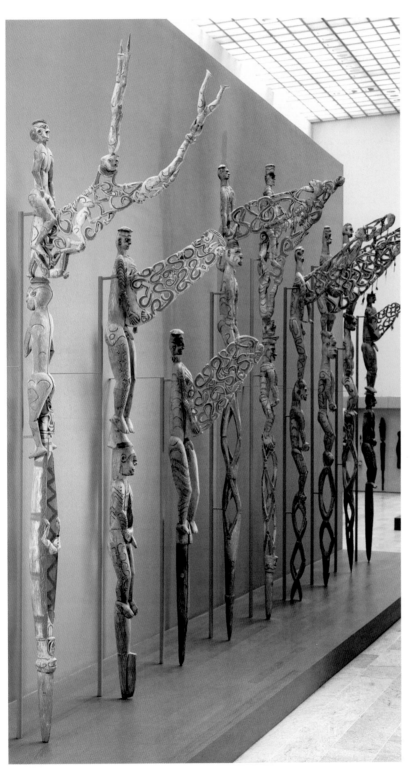

4.6.14 *Bis* **poles**, late 1950s. Wood, paint, and fiber, 18′ × 3′6″ × 5′3″. Metropolitan Museum of Art, New York

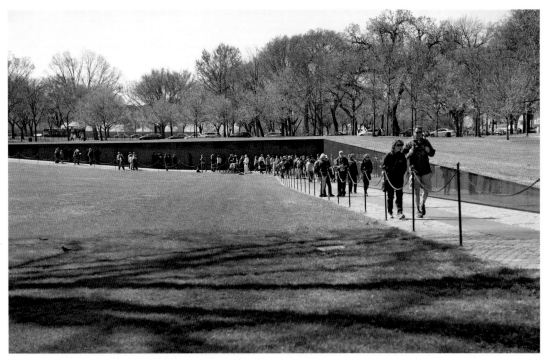

4.6.15a Maya Lin, Vietnam Veterans Memorial, Washington, D.C., 1981–83.
Granite, each wing 246′ long, height 10′1″ at highest point

dead are carved into the wall and organized by date of death (**4.6.15b**). The surface is polished because, the artist explained, "the point is to see yourself reflected in the names." The walls are aligned toward two other monuments, the Washington Monument and the Lincoln Memorial. The integration of the Vietnam Veterans Memorial with these important structures acknowledges the significance of the Vietnam War to American history.

Lin intended the memorial as a tribute, and most visitors are moved upon experiencing it. Some veterans, however, saw it as part of a continued condemnation of the war. They said that rather than uplifting and instilling pride in the soldiers who fought, the monument's descent into the ground symbolized a moral criticism of both the war and its soldiers. The veterans also perceived the use of dark granite, rather than the white marble more conventionally used for memorials, as a criticism. In response to these protests, a bronze sculpture of three soldiers, more traditional in style, was later placed a short distance from Lin's wall.

On September 11, 2001, the United States suffered the worst terrorist attack in its history in which almost 3,000 people were murdered. Two planes hijacked by members of Al Qaeda, an Islamic fundamentalist group, destroyed the Twin Towers of New York's World Trade

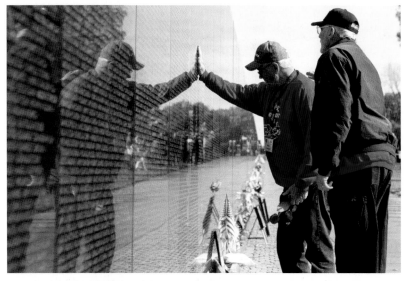

4.6.15b Maya Lin, detail of the Vietnam Veterans Memorial: visitors interacting with the wall

Center; a third plane damaged the Pentagon in Washington, D.C.; and another crashed in a Pennsylvania field. Some criticized the idea of making a monument at the site of the tragedy because the remains of many of the deceased are still buried underground, making the site sacred ground in the minds of some family members and therefore inappropriate as a site for a gift shop, admission prices, or gawkers.

However, like the Vietnam memorial, a competition was held to win the contract to build a memorial and museum to commemorate those who lost their lives on

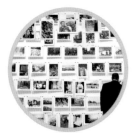

Here Is New York… is an installation of photographs taken by people who recorded what they saw on 9/11:

→ see **2.8.24**, p. 313

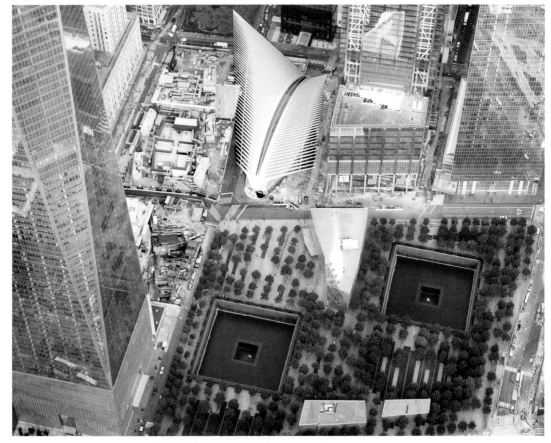

4.6.16a Michael Arad and Peter Walker, **National September 11 Memorial & Museum**, New York. Aerial view, September 8, 2016

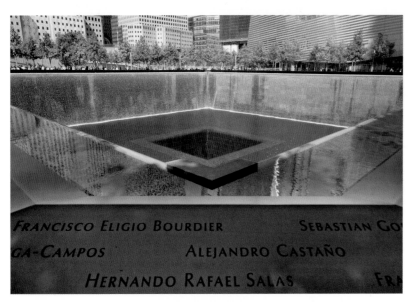

4.6.16b Michael Arad and Peter Walker, **National September 11 Memorial & Museum**, New York

September 11. After considering over 5,000 submissions, the design by Israeli-American Michael Arad and American landscape architect Peter Walker was chosen (**4.6.16a** and **4.6.16b**).

Square footprints of the fallen towers, framed in steel, are now filled with waterfalls that represent the loss of so many lives. The edges of the squares are covered with bronze plaques inscribed with the names of the 2,977 who were killed, including those on the hijacked flights on 9/11, those at the Pentagon, and the rescuers who tried to help people escape, as well as victims of the World Trade Center bombing in 1993. Every effort was made to align the names most accurately to the location closest to where they perished in the buildings, and the victims of the other sites were placed together.

Located between and to the side of the tower waterfalls is the entrance to the 9/11 Memorial Museum, which is entirely underground. It contains artifacts from and information about the events of September 11. The entryway is designed so that visitors experience the sadness of the event as they descend underground and are introduced to the personal lives of the victims. When visitors rise above the earth again and visit the sites of the towers, the sound and sight of the rushing waters and trees are meant to invite contemplation and promote healing.

Explore Further Art, War, and Healing

Warriors

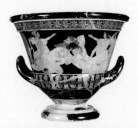

3.1.29 Krater showing Heracles and Antaios in battle, *c.* 515– 510 BCE ➔ p. 366

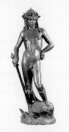

3.3.10b Terra-cotta army, mausoleum of Qin Shi Huangdi, *c.* 210 BCE ➔ p. 397

3.6.22 Donatello, *David*, *c.* 1430 ➔ p. 460

Battle Scenes

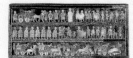

3.1.8a Standard of Ur, *c.* 2600–2400 BCE ➔ p. 352

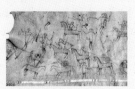

3.4.24b Hide robe with battle scene, 1797–1800 ➔ p. 423

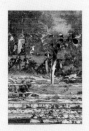

3.10.14b Mark Bradford, detail of *Pickett's Charge*, 2017 ➔ p. 531

Responses to War

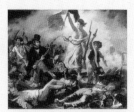

3.7.15 Eugène Delacroix, *Liberty Leading the People*, 1830 ➔ p. 477

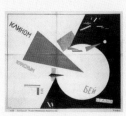

1.1.24 El Lissitzky, *Beat the Whites with the Red Wedge*, 1919 ➔ p. 46

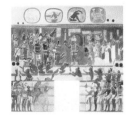

3.3.25 The Propeller Group, *AK47 vs. M16*, 2015 ➔ p. 408

War and Religious Belief

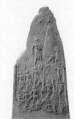

4.2.8 Stela of Naram-Sin, *c.* 2254–2218 BCE ➔ p. 559

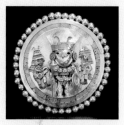

3.4.4 Moche earspool, Peru, *c.* 300 CE ➔ p. 412

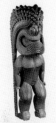

2.4.5 Figure of the war god Ku-ka'ili-moku, Hawaii, 18th or 19th century ➔ p. 231

Your turn

How do these works relate to war or healing?

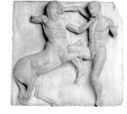

3.1.25 Metope of a Lapith and centaur, Parthenon, Athens, *c.* 445 BCE ➔ p. 364

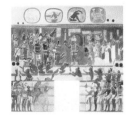

3.4.14 Bonampak mural (copy), Mexico, original 8th century ➔ p. 418

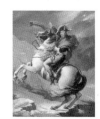

4.5.3 Jacques-Louis David, *Napoleon Crossing the Alps*, 1801 ➔ p. 594

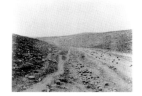

2.8.8 Roger Fenton, *Valley of the Shadow of Death*, 1855 ➔ p. 305

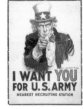

2.7.12 James Montgomery Flagg, recruitment poster, *c.* 1917 ➔ p. 290

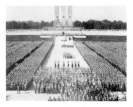

4.5.10b Leni Riefenstahl, *Triumph of the Will*, 1935 ➔ p. 600

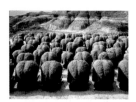

1.10.7 Magdalena Abakanowicz, *80 Backs*, 1976–80 ➔ p. 166

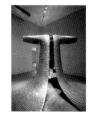

3.3.21 Do Ho Suh, *Some/One*, 2001 ➔ p. 405

4·7
Art of Protest and Social Conscience

The visual language of art can be an extremely effective means of communicating a point of view on social issues. While words can describe an event, art can demonstrate it visually with raw power. Art often reflects historical, social, and political concerns. It can even provoke change. Art is able to arouse such strong emotions that artworks themselves can become the focus of protest, sometimes suffering damage or destruction as a result. Art can also inspire us toward a better and more just world. This chapter is concerned with the ways that artists have expressed their convictions through artworks that have, at times, caused powerful, even violent, reactions (see Gateway: Ai Weiwei, p. 620).

Art as Protest and Activism

By creating potent artworks that activate emotional responses, artists can instigate social change. Here we examine artworks that have sought to combat cruelty, poverty, and inequality; for example, the injustices of enslavement and colonialism. While considering this section's protest artworks, think about your own response. Does the artist inspire you to agree with their point of view?

The painting *Raft of the Medusa* (**4.7.1**) by the French artist Théodore Géricault (1791–1824) memorializes on a grand scale a scandalous event in history. On July 2, 1816, the French naval vessel *Medusa* ran aground off the coast of West Africa. While the captain and approximately 250 crew boarded the lifeboats, the rest of the passengers—146 men and one woman, some of them enslaved people—got onto a makeshift raft that had been built from the wreckage. Although the raft was pulled by the lifeboats initially, the captain soon abandoned it. Left

to battle starvation, sunburn, disease, and dehydration, only fifteen men survived the horrors of the sea; some cannibalized their shipmates. Géricault's painting shows with emotional intensity the moment when the raft's survivors are about to be rescued.

Géricault interviewed the survivors, studied corpses, and even had a replica of the raft built in his studio in preparation for this project. The survivors told him of their despair and madness when they saw a ship on the horizon on the thirteenth day. They had seen ships in the distance before, but those ships' crews had not seen them, and many feared this ship, too, would disappear. But the survivors, all close to death, were rescued, and they told the world the story of their abandonment.

In *Raft of the Medusa*, Géricault depicts the emotions of the survivors. Several men, their arms reaching out toward the tiny ship in the distance, convey desperate hope. Another is shown still slouched in despair and surrounded by corpses; he even holds one on his lap. The artist painted the skin of the men with a green pallor to indicate that they are near to death, yet the musculature of their bodies gives them nobility. The dramatic intensity is heightened by the use of diagonal lines that compose the figures into a large X. From the bottom left corner of the **composition**, the bodies of the men are arranged in a line that leads the viewer's eye to the Black man who is higher than anyone else. An opposing diagonal is made from the mast in the upper left to the near-naked male body on the lower right, which appears to be falling from the raft.

Despite being exhibited among over 1,000 other paintings, *Raft of Medusa* received tremendous public attention at the **Salon**

Composition: the overall design or organization of a work

Salon: an official exhibition of French painting, first held in 1667

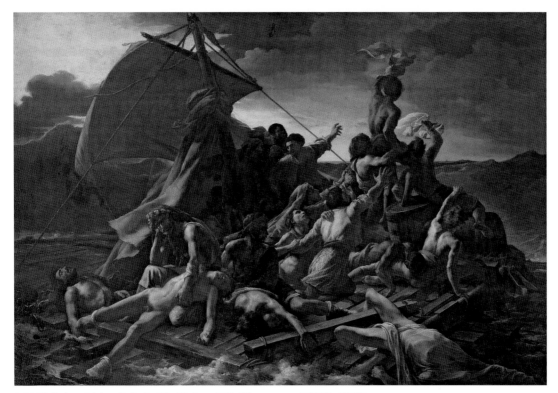

4.7.1 Théodore Géricault, *Raft of the Medusa*, 1819. Oil on canvas, 12'1⅜" × 17'9⅞".
Musée du Louvre, Paris, France

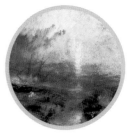

In a similar manner to Géricault, the British Romantic artist J. M. W. Turner used the sublime power of nature to convey the horror of human tragedy: → see **3.7.17**, p. 478

exhibition of 1819. Some critics were shocked and repulsed by the pile of dead bodies. Others commented on the dark-skinned man at the painting's apex, atop a pyramid of bodies, waving a piece of his clothing to get the attention of the ship in the distance. Gericault included this Black man in a prominent position in the composition not only to criticize the *Medusa* disaster, but also as a comment on colonization and enslavement. Although the event had happened three years prior, the exhibition of Géricault's painting re-ignited anger towards the captain of the ship, who had been hired without experience under King Louis XVIII because of his political leanings. The captain was court-martialed in 1817 and served three years in prison.

En el aire (In the Air) by Teresa Margolles is a seemingly peaceful, even playful, room filled with bubbles (**4.7.2**). Yet visitors to her **installation** are shocked when they discover that the bubbles are made from the water used to cleanse the bodies of corpses. Using her experience as a trained medical examiner who worked in a morgue in Mexico City, Margolles wishes to activate greater awareness of the large number of violent deaths in Mexico due to narco (drug-related) crimes. Margolles states that "each bubble is a body," and she stuns

visitors by creating a tactile experience in which they touch the remains of the deceased. The beauty of the bubbles and the cleanliness of the

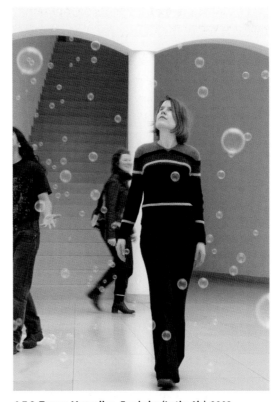

4.7.2 Teresa Margolles, *En el aire (In the Air)*, 2003. Installation view, "Muerte sin Fin," Museum für Moderne Kunst, Frankfurt, Germany, 2004

Installation: originally referring to the hanging of pictures and arrangement of objects in an exhibition, installation may also refer to an intentional environment created as a completed artwork

Ai Weiwei: *Dropping a Han Dynasty Urn* and *Colored Vases*

The Art of Activism: Speaking Out At all Costs

For the other Ai Weiwei
GATEWAYS:
→ see p. 112 and p. 398

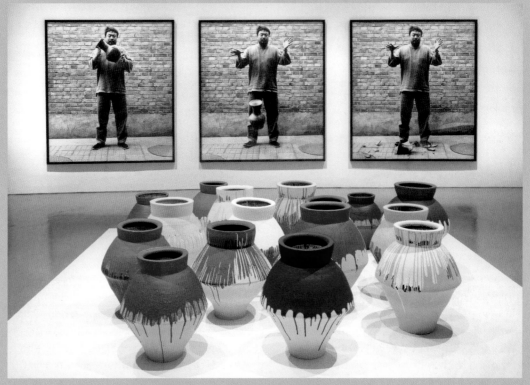

4.7.3 **Installation view showing Ai Weiwei's** *Colored Vases* **in front of his** *Dropping a Han Dynasty Urn*, displayed at the "According to What?" exhibition, held at the Hirshhorn Museum and Sculpture Garden, Washington, D.C.

Current news stories report on strict Chinese government controls over what the public has access to on the Internet, in the press, and in much of their daily lives. Similarly, artistic expression in China is forcefully restricted. The artist Ai Weiwei (b. 1957) has become internationally famous for his works that question the Chinese government's conduct and for the price he has had to pay for such expression. In both *Colored Vases* and the three photos shown here, Ai Weiwei has vandalised, even destroyed ancient Chinese vases as a protest statement. The vases were dipped in bright-colored paint, covering up their original designs.

Ai Weiwei was raised in an activist family. His father, regarded as one of the finest modern Chinese poets, was imprisoned and exiled for opposing the Nationalist Party of China. After studying film and the arts in Beijing, he lived in the United States from 1981 to 1993, where he was particularly influenced by the ideas of Marcel Duchamp and Andy Warhol. The photographs *Dropping a Han Dynasty Urn* (**4.7.3**) were made in the same year that he photographed himself raising a middle finger toward Tiananmen Square, the symbol of Chinese government. In 2005, he began a blog in China that criticized government policies. His blog was shut down by the police in 2009 after he exposed poor construction standards as the cause of the high number of deaths from the 2008 Sichuan province earthquake (more than 69,000 people were killed and at least 4.8 million were left homeless). He also posted the names of all 5,385 children killed in the earthquake. Also in 2009, Ai Weiwei was beaten by the police for his intention to testify about the earthquake aftermath. His injuries were so severe that brain surgery was required to treat them. In 2011, he filmed the government's destruction of his studio and two months later, he was imprisoned, just as his father had been.

Ai Weiwei's work has been shown prolifically around the world, but only rarely in China. Shortly before the opening of a Shanghai exhibition of Chinese Contemporary art in 2014, his works were forcibly removed and records of his previous awards were destroyed. Ai Weiwei continues to protest the Chinese government through his art.

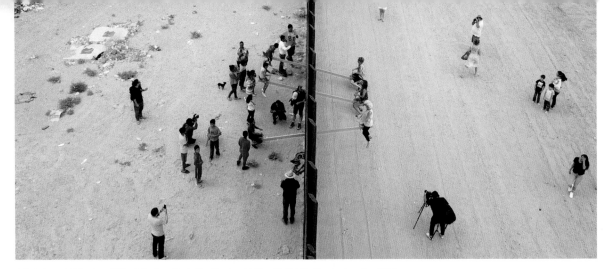

4.7.4 Ronald Rael and Virginia San Fratello, *Teeter-Totter Wall*, US–Mexico border, 2019

space create a setting in which the visitor's body can become traumatized by the knowledge of the material used to make the bubbles. Such trauma is necessary, Margolles argues, in order to trigger disgust and horror at the tragedy of the numerous violent deaths. Visitors to the exhibition are forced to acknowledge these deaths and are asked to become involved in working to prevent further murders.

Inspired by the ongoing immigration crisis at the American border, and in particular the separation of children from their parents, Ronald Rael and Virginia San Fratello built *Teeter-Totter Wall* in 2019 (**4.7.4**). Built at the site where a border wall separates Juárez in Mexico from El Paso in the US, the steel pink beams slice through the wall, literally and conceptually dismantling the separation of people that the wall enforces. The bright pink color was chosen to commemorate the suffering and murder of women in Juárez, but pink also has a childlike and playful connotation that contrasts strikingly with the dark brown wall. The form of the teeter-totter requires interaction on both sides for play to take place, and this symbolizes the interconnectedness of the US and Mexico. The wall was designed to highlight the interdependency between the two countries, who need one another for balance in trade and labor. The human interaction created by the work reduces the foreboding impact of the border wall, which the artists hope will be dismantled completely.

Art as the Target of Protest: Censorship and Destruction

Art can inspire a forceful response. When the ideas an artwork represents are considered harmful or incompatible with a desired message or point of view, artworks might be censored or removed from public eyes. **Censorship** has the ability to cause shifts in public opinion. For this reason, artworks and the artists who create them are often amongst the first to be targeted by dictatorial governments. They are also some of the first victims in times of war.

As a young man in his late teens, Adolf Hitler sold realistic watercolors and painted postcards on the streets of Vienna. He failed twice to be accepted into the Academy of Fine Arts Vienna, an institution that did accept several artists with more abstract styles, such as Egon Schiele. Hitler never got over the disappointment of being unable to become a successful artist, and he abhorred modern art—in particular, that of the German Expressionists.

In Germany in the 1930s, Hitler's National Socialist (Nazi) regime launched a systematic and large-scale attack on modern art that did not conform to Nazi party goals. The Nazis initially confiscated around 5,000 works of art from museums; they later took a further 16,500 from private collections. Some 4,000 of these were burned; others became the property of Nazi collectors, or were sold to foreign collectors for Nazi profit. The artists who made them were banned from working. The Nazis also dismissed museum directors, closed art schools, such as the famous Bauhaus, and burned books.

On July 18, 1937, the Nazis opened an exhibition of "Great German Art," which displayed the kind of art approved by the regime. The next day they opened another show of 730 works called "Degenerate Art," to suggest that these were the works of mentally deficient artists. Works were deliberately displayed

Censorship: the suppression or prohibition of a work of art

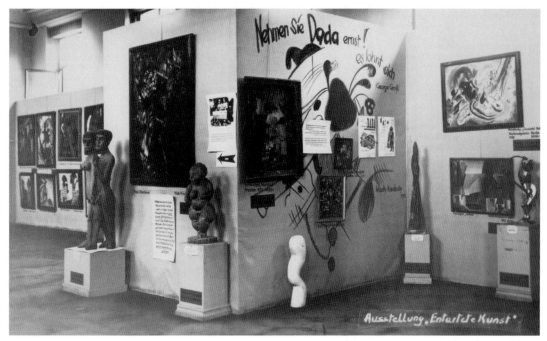

4.7.5 The Dadaist section of the Nazi-curated traveling exhibition "Degenerate Art" *(Entartete Kunst)*, which opened in Munich, Germany in 1937

awkwardly, and labels on the walls ridiculed the artworks (**4.7.5**). One read: "We act as if we were painters, poets, or whatever, but what we are is simply and ecstatically impudent. In our impudence we take the world for a ride and train snobs to lick our boots!" Artists vilified in the exhibition included Egon Schiele, Otto Dix, Paul Klee, Kathë Kollwitz, Ernst Kirchner, Marc Chagall, Max Ernst, Pablo Picasso, Henri Matisse, and Vincent van Gogh. Dozens of German artists whose work featured in the show fled Germany or committed suicide, and many were later sent to concentration camps.

Attendance at the Degenerate Art exhibition was unparalleled for its time, with more than two million visitors in Munich alone, and one million more when the show went on tour through the rest of Germany and Austria. Although there are records of people spitting on the artworks, there remains little other evidence of what visitors actually thought of the art in this propaganda spectacle. In general, the Nazi regime disliked works that contained unnaturalistic forms or colors, works that did not promote Nazi beliefs, or those that criticized war and the sacrifices that go with it.

When the exhibitions ended, the Nazis sold some artworks to raise money for their impending war effort, but most of the artworks were destroyed, along with thousands of others considered degenerate. The freedom to create art and to have opinions about it are

emblems of a peaceful society; the Degenerate Art show and the book burnings perpetrated by the Nazis are two examples of how extreme censorship can result in the end of peace and freedom for many.

Sometimes the impact of a work of art is so powerful that viewers wish to destroy it, along with the message or attitude they see represented in it. The *Rokeby Venus* (or *The Toilet of Venus*) by the Spanish artist Diego de Silva y Velázquez (1599–1660) (**4.7.6a**) may seem inoffensive to the modern viewer, but in 1914 it was the target of a violent protest at the National Gallery in London. A woman called Mary Richardson, armed with a meat cleaver hidden inside her coat, slashed the *Rokeby Venus* seven times (**4.7.6b**). Richardson was a member of the Suffragette movement, which campaigned for women's right to vote. For her, the painting represented a sexist definition of ideal beauty, showing a woman solely as an object of male desire. Richardson was more specifically protesting the imprisonment of the Suffragette leader Emmeline Pankhurst, and later explained that she believed justice to be more valuable than art:

I have tried to destroy the picture of the most beautiful woman in mythological history as a protest against the Government for destroying Mrs. Pankhurst, who is the most beautiful character in modern history.

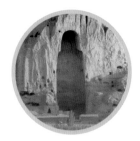

Iconoclasm refers to images being destroyed for religious reasons, such as the Colossal Buddha from Bamiyan, Afghanistan, destroyed by the Taliban in 2001: → see **3.3.6b**, p. 394

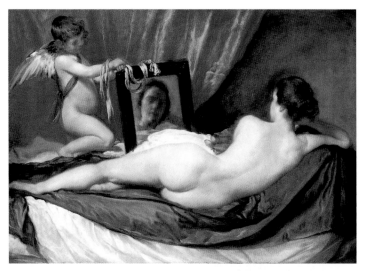

4.7.6a Diego de Silva y Velázquez, *The Toilet of Venus* (*Rokeby Venus*), 1647–51. Oil on canvas, 48½ × 69¾". National Gallery, London, England

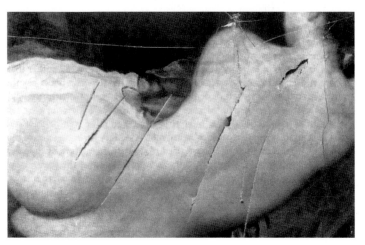

4.7.6b Photograph of damage to the *Rokeby Venus,* 1914

Richardson's attack on the painting did not have its intended effect on perceptions of the *Rokeby Venus*. The seven slashes were soon completely repaired, and many still consider the painting to be a defining representation of female sensuality and beauty. Richardson was imprisoned briefly after the attack, and the incident did not seem to help the Suffragette movement either (although some women did gain the right to vote in Britain in 1918). For a while after the incident, in fact, women were forbidden to enter the National Gallery unless they were accompanied by a male chaperone.

While Velázquez's *Venus* was the subject of protest centuries after its creation, the American artist Eric Fischl's (b. 1948) *Falling Woman* provoked an instantaneous reaction (**4.7.7**). When the bronze sculpture, intended as a tribute to the victims of the terrorist attacks of September 11, 2001, was unveiled in New York City, it was considered so offensive that it was covered over almost immediately. It shows a woman in freefall, with her legs above her head and her arms flailing. Fischl placed a poem next to his artwork:

> We watched,
> disbelieving and helpless,
> on that savage day.
> People we love
> began falling,
> helpless and in disbelief.

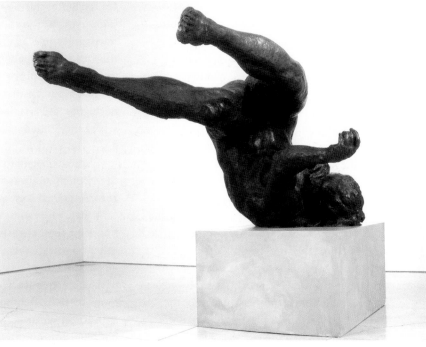

4.7.7 Eric Fischl, *Falling Woman*, 2001–2. Bronze, 38 × 72 × 48". Private collection

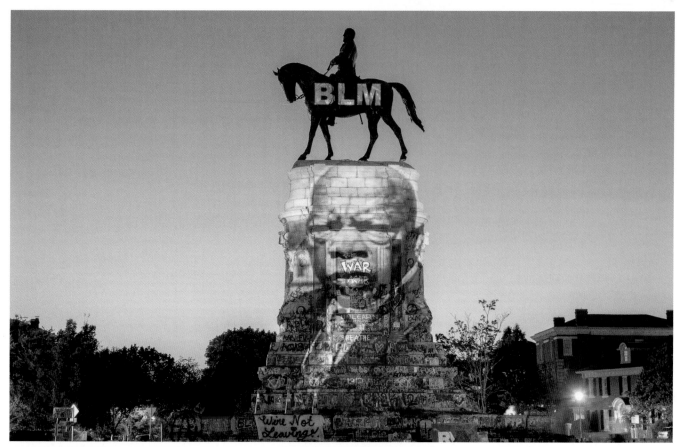

4.7.8 Dustin Klein, projected image of late Rep. John Lewis on the Confederate General Robert E. Lee Monument in Richmond, Virginia, July 19, 2020. The monument was removed on September 8 2021

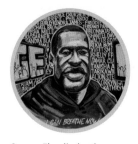

George Floyd's death fueled protest against racial and social inequity:
→ see **0.0.18**, p. 28

Appropriation: the deliberate incorporation in an artwork of material originally created by other artists

Many New Yorkers had witnessed firsthand the tragedy of desperate victims, who had been trapped in the World Trade Center towers, jumping to their deaths to escape the fire. Perhaps because of this, Fischl's sculpture, displayed only a year after the terrorist attack, was seen as too potent and heart-wrenching. The artwork and the response to it reflect one of the challenges artists face when they address contemporary issues. Would Fischl's sculpture have been accepted if it had been unveiled many years later, when the event was no longer fresh in the minds of so many? Or was it simply too graphic, depicting a moment too shocking and unbelievable for people ever to want to remember?

Some viewers, however, were upset that the sculpture was covered up, considering it a powerful reminder and a valid, even cathartic (emotionally releasing) response to what happened. "The sculpture was not meant to hurt anybody," said the artist. "It was a sincere expression of the deepest sympathy for the vulnerability of the human condition. Both specifically towards the victims of Sept. 11 and towards humanity in general."

Confederate monuments have become a frequent target of protest in the United States, leading to the removal of hundreds of statues. The Confederacy was composed of eleven southern states that seceded from the United States during the American Civil War (1861–1865). At the end of the war, when the north and south again became a single country, the 13th Amendment to the US Constitution was ratified, ending the practice of enslaving people. Many southerners, who lost loved ones in the war and lost their way of life, continued to revere the Confederacy. Interestingly, however, it was not until decades later that Confederate monuments began to appear, coinciding with the implementation of Jim Crow laws, which enforced racial segregation.

Today, while some see these monuments as honoring their ancestors and southern society, others associate them with the institution of enslavement and see them as a glorification of racial inequality. The Robert E. Lee monument in Richmond, Virginia (**4.7.8**), an equestrian statue of the Confederate general, has been **appropriated** as a gathering place for expressing African American rights. The

Kara Walker, *Insurrection!*
Using Narrative to Explore Truth and Fiction

**For the other Walker
GATEWAYS:**
→ see p. 48 and p. 340

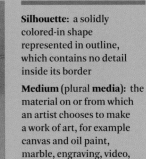

Silhouette: a solidly colored-in shape represented in outline, which contains no detail inside its border

Medium (plural **media**): the material on or from which an artist chooses to make a work of art, for example canvas and oil paint, marble, engraving, video, or architecture

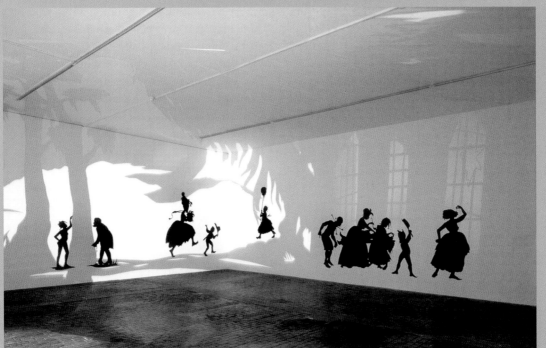

4.7.9a Kara Walker, *Insurrection! (Our Tools Were Rudimentary, Yet We Pressed On)*, 2000.
Cut paper and projection on wall, dimensions variable. Installation view: *Why I Like White Boys, an Illustrated Novel by Kara E. Walker, Negress*, Centre d'Art Contemporain, Geneva, Switzerland, 2000

The combined projections and **silhouettes** in Kara Walker's *Insurrection! (Our Tools Were Rudimentary, Yet We Pressed On)* (**4.7.9a** and **4.7.9b**) present a story that combines fact and fiction, tasking the viewer with questioning the narrative of American history. The artist explains that this scene is intended to show "a slave revolt in the antebellum South where the house slaves got after their master with their instruments, their utensils of everyday life." The installation, shown on three walls in one room, is designed to engulf viewers, making them part of the reimagining, their own shadows falling on the walls that surround them. In the various scenes, young and old figures rise up, fight, and escape their oppressors. A young girl carries a severed head, which at first glance looks like a balloon that will carry her away. What at first seems like a sexual encounter between a Black woman and her white owner, instead shows her beheading him, as another child removes his shoes. Walker's works have been criticized for their stereotyped depictions of enslaved people and their violence. But the **media** used—cut black paper and colorful light projecting on a white wall—signify the complexity, and often inaccurate retelling, of the history of enslavement in America.

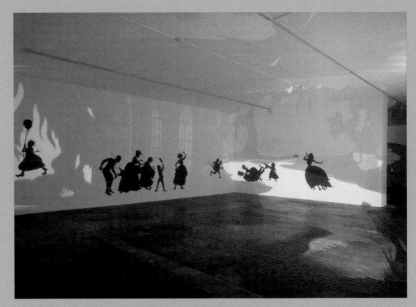

4.7.9b Kara Walker, *Insurrection!* (alternative view)

Walker has appropriated the silhouette, an art form used by the wealthy white class in the eighteenth century to convey elegance and beauty. It is reused here—still breathtakingly beautiful in its form—to show both the ugliness and the bravery of some of the ancestors of America. In this way, Walker insists that conversations about racial issues continue.

45-ft.-tall base has been covered with graffiti, particularly after the killing of George Floyd in May 2020. In the evenings, Dustin Klein and other artists projected images of George Floyd and other important African Americans (such as pioneer of the civil rights movement and long-time member of the U.S. House of Representatives, John Lewis, shown here) on the colossal base. The letters "BLM"—signifying Black Lives Matter—shine on the sculpted horse's body.

Art that Raises Social Awareness

Because of the power of visual language, artists can make people more aware of a social problem, spur people to become involved in an issue, or even call for change. These artists have used art to shine light on social, racial, and environmental issues.

Dorothea Lange's (1895–1965) famous photograph of Florence Owens Thompson,

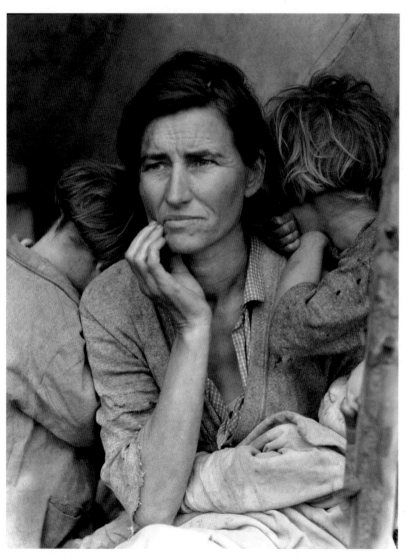

4.7.10 Dorothea Lange, *Migrant Mother*, 1936. Library of Congress, Washington, D.C.

known as *Migrant Mother*, was used to demonstrate the plight of the poor and remains a powerful symbol of the struggle against poverty (**4.7.10**). The picture was taken in 1936 when Florence and her children were living in the remains of a Californian pea-pickers' camp. Lange's image had an immediate impact. The photograph was published in several newspapers and *Time* magazine, and the federal government sent 20,000 pounds of food to the camp. Unfortunately, the Thompson family had migrated elsewhere before the supplies arrived.

While the photograph had an incalculable effect on people's understanding of the devastation of the Great Depression, Thompson herself was always ashamed and irritated by the portrait. To her mind, it never had a positive effect on her life. When the photograph was taken, she was recently widowed, had six children, and worked wherever she could to support her family. The identity of Thompson was not discovered until 1978, and she was quoted as saying, "I wish she hadn't taken my picture," and complained about never being compensated. Her experience raises questions about the role of an artist when depicting an actual event. To what extent should the subject's privacy be protected, and to what extent should they be compensated, if at all, when their image has demonstrable effects on the social conscience? More than eighty years after it was taken, Lange's photograph remains a memorable symbol of the plight of the poor, and since 1936 it has been published many times in books and newspapers and has twice featured on US postage stamps.

The series *Women of Allah* (1993–1997) by the Iranian-born artist Shirin Neshat contains black-and-white photographs of armed and veiled Islamic women. These works explore Western stereotypes of Muslim women as well as the women's religious and personal convictions. These beautiful images show women as powerful, and speak to the seemingly contradictory perception of Muslim women as both suppressed and as soldiers of Islam. In "Speechless" (**4.7.11**), the muzzle of a gun is placed beside a woman's face, and at first it appears to be an earring. Written on her face in Farsi calligraphy is text written by the female poet Tahereh Saffarzadeh, in which a woman addresses her brothers in the Iranian Revolution (1978–79), asking if she can participate as well. Neshat herself was

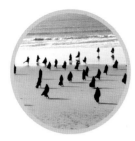

Shirin Neshat's *Rapture* series of films also considers gender roles in Iranian society:
→ see **3.10.11b**, p. 528

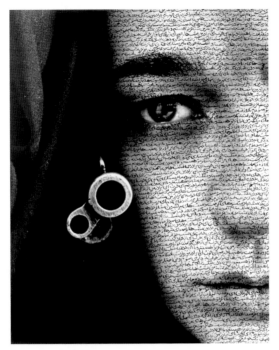

4.7.11 Shirin Neshat, **"Speechless" (from *Women of Allah* series)**, 1996. RC print and ink, 46¾ × 33⅞"

exiled from Iran, but disagrees with Western interventions in her home country. Her works address the complexities surrounding the identity of Muslim women.

Vik Muniz (b. 1961) made a series of artworks—called the Wasteland Project— from the trash he found at the world's largest landfill, located near Rio de Janeiro, Brazil. The film *Wasteland* documents the people Muniz met for this project, and the artworks they inspired. Muniz spent time with the *catadores*, people who survive by going through the trash looking for items to recycle. Discarded waste is, by definition, material that is considered useless and unwanted. The people who live at this landfill are also treated as discarded members of society. Muniz took this rejected material and arranged it on his studio floor to create large-scale portraits showing the beauty of the human spirit. The artworks were then photographed from high above. Figure **4.7.12** shows a woman who worked at the landfill

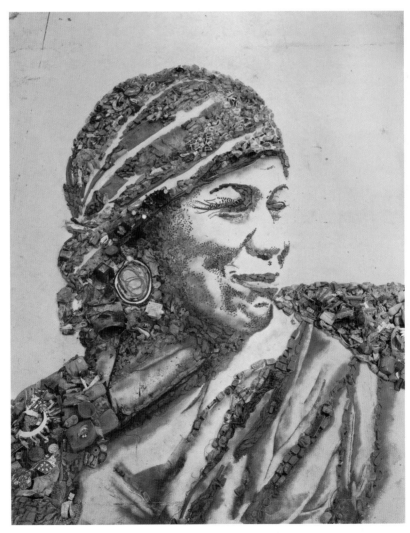

4.7.12 Vik Muniz, **"The Gipsy (Magna)"**, from *Pictures of Garbage* series, 2008–11, C-print

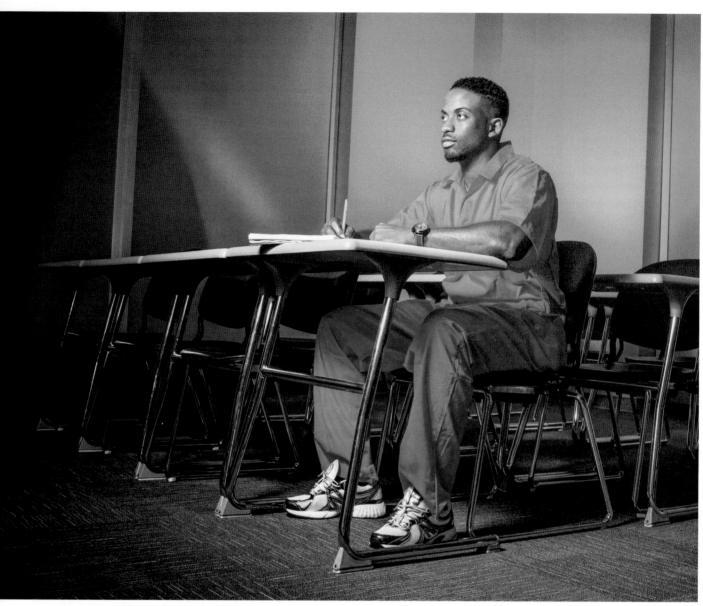

4.7.13 Sherrill Roland III, *The Jumpsuit Project*, 2016–2017,
Year-long socially engaged performance art project

every day, always smiling and bringing joy to those around her. The shadows and features of her face are made with old shoes, bottle caps and computer keyboards. Her scarves are made of plastic bottles—designed to hold everything from detergent to gasoline—and the arms, legs, and heads of dolls. Her earring is made of used hoses. The lighter portions of her skin and some of her clothing are actually the bare floor of the warehouse in which Muniz worked. Muniz's portraits bring to light the impact our combined trash has on society; the trash doesn't disappear, but instead becomes a burden for others.

The artist Sherrill Roland (b. 1984) was a graduate student at the University of North Carolina in Greensboro in 2013 when he was wrongfully imprisoned for more than ten months. By the time he was exonerated, both he and the kind of art he wished to produce had radically changed. He returned to graduate school in 2016 and initiated *The Jumpsuit Project*, a performance piece in which he goes about his daily activities wearing an orange jumpsuit like the one he was forced to wear in prison (**4.7.13**). This act altered his interactions with others, just as being jailed had, and served to trigger conversations about the impact of the prevalence of false incarcerations, especially for African American males. Roland wants to raise awareness of the many lives affected by this social issue: "Incarceration happens every day. I could be anybody. It could be me today, it could be you tomorrow."

Explore Further Art of Protest and Social Conscience

Racial Injustice

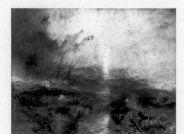

3.7.17 J. M. W. Turner, *Slave Ship…*, 1840 → p. 478

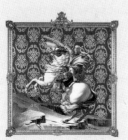

4.5.4a Kehinde Wiley, *Napoleon Leading the Army…*, 2005 → p. 595

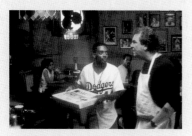

4.9.12 Spike Lee, still from *Do the Right Thing*, 1989 → p. 656

Immigration and Refugees

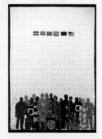

3.5.6 Abdoulaye Konaté, *Generation Biométrique, No. 5*, 2008–2013 → p. 432

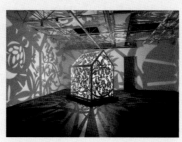

1.9.8 Anila Quayyum Agha, *This Is NOT a Refuge! 2*, 2019 → p. 153

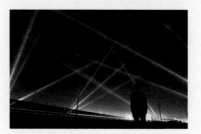

3.4.19 Rafael Lozano-Hemmer, *Border Tuner*, 2019 → p. 421

Environmental Awareness

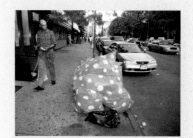

1.4.33 Adrian Kondratowicz, *TRASH project*, 2008–ongoing → p. 102

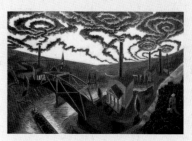

2.2.23 Ralph M. Larmann, *Coalopolis*, 2010 → p. 208

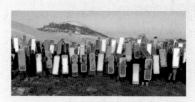

3.4.27 Cannupa Hanska Luger, mirror shields, Standing Rock, 2016 → p. 425

Your turn

How do these artworks relate to protest and social conscience?

2.3.15 Honoré Daumier, *Rue Transnonain*, 1834 → p. 221

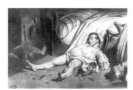

2.2.8 José Clemente Orozco, *Prometheus*, 1930 → p. 199

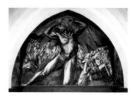

0.0.19 Keith Haring, *Ignorance = Fear*, 1989 → p. 28

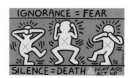

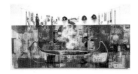

1.9.15 Jaune Quick-to-See Smith, *Trade…*, 1992 → p. 156

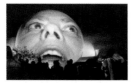

4.1.17 Krzysztof Wodiczko, *Tijuana Projection*, 2001 → p. 552

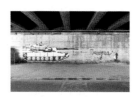

3.4.7 Doris Salcedo, *Noviembre 6 y 7*, 2002 → p. 415

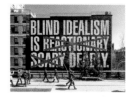

4.6.12 Ganzeer, *Tank vs. Bread-Biker*, 2011 → p. 612

2.10.2 Barbara Kruger, *Untitled*, 2016–17 → p. 336

4.8
The Body in Art

The human **form** is one of the most common **subjects** in art, perhaps because making art about the body allows us to reflect on, come to terms with, and literally express ourselves. Some of the earliest sculptures made during **prehistoric** times depict human figures. Since then, artists have continued to portray the body, both clothed and unclothed, in motion and in repose. The body is not always portrayed as it actually looks, and it may even be altered so much that it does not resemble a human body at all. In art, the reality of the body can be distorted to suggest great beauty, or to emphasize such qualities as power, status, wisdom, or even godlike perfection. Personal and cultural preferences often determine the way an artist chooses to portray a body. Of course, the body itself can also participate in art: through performances, dances, rituals, and so on. As a subject, it offers endless expressive possibilities.

Archetypal Images of the Body

Female figurines have been discovered all over the world and are commonly amongst the oldest known created objects in a number of societies. The *Woman from Willendorf* is one of the earliest artworks on record, dating to about 26,000 years ago (**4.8.1**). The small size of this figurine, just over 4 in. tall, made it easily portable, which was a benefit for nomadic people. Some interpretations of the *Woman from Willendorf* suggest that it was connected to fertility, while more recently, these female figurines have been seen as representations of women's accumulated knowledge and cultural continuity across generations. It almost certainly celebrates the woman as a potential mother and bringer of life. These types of

ancient figures have served as impactful **iconic** artistic models for the idea and image of woman since their rediscovery through **archaeological** expeditions (the *Woman from Willendorf*, for example, was rediscovered in the early twentieth century).

The Dutch-born American artist Willem de Kooning (1904–1997) made a series of paintings of women that incorporate bold, apparently aggressive—even violent—marks and slashing strokes. De Kooning said that his *Woman* series referred to "the female painted through all the

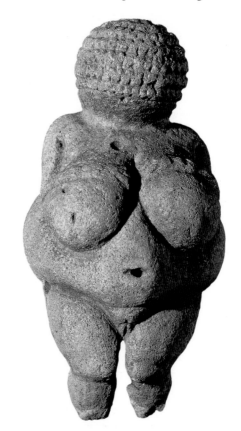

4.8.1 *Woman from Willendorf*, c. 24,000–22,000 BCE. Oolitic limestone, height 4⅜". Naturhistorisches Museum, Vienna, Austria

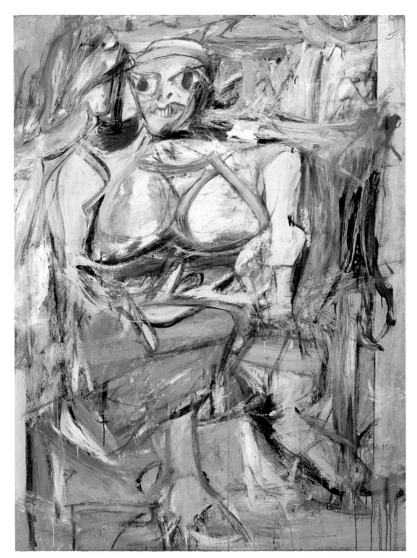

4.8.2 **Willem de Kooning**, *Woman I*, 1950–52. Oil on canvas, 6′3⅞″ × 4′10″. MoMA, New York

Composition: the overall design or organization of a work

Abstract: art imagery that departs from recognizable images of the natural world

Canon of proportions: a set of ideal mathematical ratios in art, used to measure the various parts of the human body in relation to one another

Figurative: art that portrays items perceived in the visible world, especially human or animal forms

ages, all those idols." In De Kooning's *Woman I* (**4.8.2**), the exaggerated form and emphasis on characteristically female elements of human anatomy visually connect the modern artwork to the *Woman from Willendorf*. In this large painting, made thousands of years after the tiny sculpture was created, the most prominent parts of the body are the breasts, while the arms and legs are minimized in a manner similar to the ancient figurine.

While both artworks convey the power of women as potential givers and protectors of life, they do so very differently. De Kooning's woman seems strong to the point of being ferocious. The painting is physically big, over lifesize, making literal the larger-than-life feeling conveyed by the small sculpture, and features a woman's glaring eyes and grinning mouth at the top of the **composition**. By contrast, the *Woman from Willendorf* does not include facial features at all. Both figures, however, have an

abstracted form, visible in the rough shapes of the *Woman from Willendorf* and the jagged brushstrokes of *Woman I*. Their appearance shifts away from representations of individual people and toward reflections of a universal idea of women. As De Kooning's statement suggests, *Woman I* embodies "the female... through all the ages."

Ideal Proportion

Long after the Paleolithic sculptor and long before De Kooning searched to find something universal about the female figure, the ancient Egyptians applied formal mathematical systems in consistent ways to depict their ideal of the human form. They developed a standardized method for depicting men and women, known as the **canon of proportions**, and used it for thousands of years. A similar system of proportion was later adopted by the Greeks for their **figurative** sculpture, and this influenced European artists during the **Renaissance**. These **idealized** proportions, clearly visible in figurative paintings, reliefs, and three-dimensional sculpture, were applied to architectural construction as well.

Egyptians systematically depicted the human body to match their cultural notions of perfection. The Egyptian canon of proportions is calculated in the form of a grid that provides consistent measurements of the parts of the body (**4.8.3a**). Each square of the grid represents a standard small measurement, or a unit, based on the width of the pharaoh's clenched hand. Sometimes other ratios are used to make the grid, resulting in a slightly different but still standardized appearance. The pharaoh's body was used as the standard for measurement because all measure was believed to come from the king. In fact, the **hierarchical scale** used in Egyptian depictions of multiple figures shows the pharaoh and nobles as significantly larger than workers, members of

lower classes, and animals, because they were viewed as being of greater importance.

Thus, in ancient Egyptian art, the portrayal of the body followed **conventions**, or prescribed methods, which produced consistent results. Egyptian depictions of the human body, as a result, look very similar even when they have been produced thousands of years apart. In sculpture, royal figures are shown either seated or standing, firmly connected to the stone from which they are carved, with their arms and hands close to their sides. In standing poses, the feet are firmly planted on the ground with the legs slightly apart and one foot in front of the other, as if the figure is about to take a step. Any suggestion of movement is potential, however, as if the figure is frozen; if it were in motion, its weight would shift to one side or the other. In the Egyptian figure, the feet are flat, the hips are even and immobile, and the shoulders are entirely square. The use of the canon gives the sculpture of *Menkaure and His*

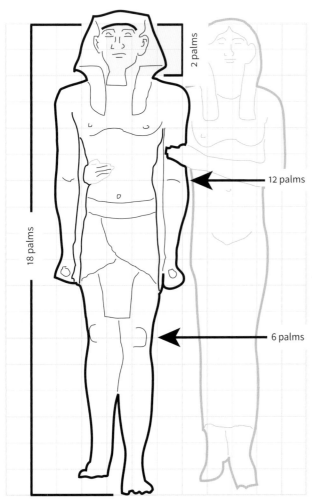

4.8.3a Canon of proportions: diagram showing the measurements used for *Menkaure and His Wife, Queen Khamerernebty*

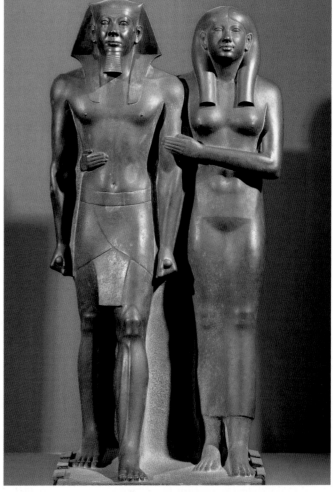

4.8.3b *Menkaure and His Wife*, *Queen Khamerernebty*, 4th Dynasty, *c.* 2520 BCE. Graywacke, 54¾ × 22½ × 21¼″. Museum of Fine Arts, Boston, Massachusetts

Wife, Queen Khamerernebty an austere strength (**4.8.3b**). Their poses make the figures look rigid, calm, and enduring. They stand close together, as a single unit, his hands close to his sides and hers embracing his arm and torso. Their bodies do not twist, and the features are bilaterally symmetrical (meaning that the left side matches the right). The strong, frontal pose suggests that the power of the pharaoh is changeless, unwavering, and eternal. This representation is idealized: the couple's appearance is based on abstract concepts rather than direct observation.

Notions of Beauty

Ideal proportions inform many cultural notions of preferred body type. Our notions of beauty are formed by our personal experiences and by the society in which we live. If we look at the ways in which artists have depicted the human form, we soon realize that in different times and places, beauty can mean very different things. In some cultures, small feet or long necks are admired. Some groups may favor plump, even voluptuous, bodies, while others prefer slender, very thin and angular physiques. Our bodies can also express many things about our personalities: we can appear calm or agitated, elegant or unkempt, smart or stupid, sensuous or intellectual. The complex relationship between internal characteristics and outward appearance has led artists to explore these aspects of beauty through the human form.

The notions of beauty held by the ancient Greeks were based upon the combination of an underlying canon of mathematical proportions with the finely honed physiques possessed by male athletes, who competed in the nude. (It was far more common to see a Greek male than a Greek female figure sculpted in the nude.) Depicting the body without clothes allowed artists to study musculature and to reflect observations and knowledge of the anatomy in a way that a clothed body does not. Because the Greeks hoped to model themselves after gods, they aimed for perfect balance between mind and body in both their lives and their art. Such sculptures as the *Discus Thrower* not only demonstrate the ideal musculature of the athletic body, celebrating the strength and virility inherent in the masculine form, but also show the competitor immersed in concentration, his mind in complete harmony with his physique (**4.8.4**).

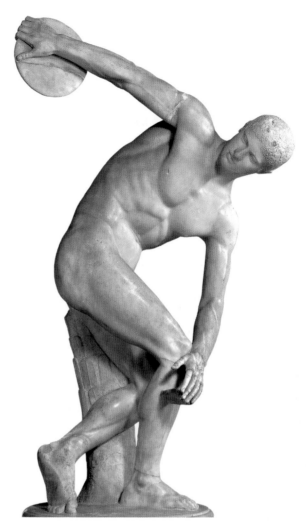

4.8.4 Myron, *Discus Thrower (Discobolos)*, Roman copy of Greek bronze original from *c.* 450 BCE. Marble, height 5'1". Museo delle Terme, Rome, Italy

In ancient Greece, although the male **nude** was certainly more common, the female nude eventually began to gain respectability in the late fourth century BCE. Years later, during the Renaissance, such Italian artists as Sandro Botticelli (*c.* 1445–1510) revived the appearance of the female nude as it had been depicted in antiquity. In Botticelli's day, the female nude became an acceptable subject as long as it appeared in a historical or mythological context. According to Classical mythology, Venus, the goddess of love and beauty, first emerged from the sea as a fully formed adult on a shell. In his painting *The Birth of Venus* (**4.8.5**, p. 634), Botticelli focuses on the moment when Venus has been blown to shore. She is wafted toward the land by Zephyr, the god of the west wind, who is accompanied by the earth nymph Chloris. Awaiting Venus is a goddess or nymph who will wrap her in a blanket of flowers. Venus has smooth ivory-

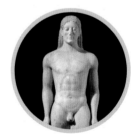

Archaic Greek artists closely copied the Egyptian canon and began developing their own lifelike and idealized sculptures:
→ see **3.1.19**, p. 361

Nude: an artistic representation of an unclothed human figure, emphasizing the body's form rather than its exposure

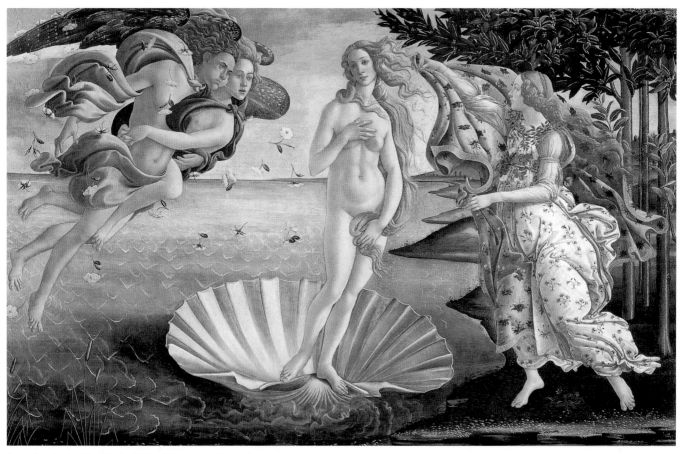

4.8.5 **Sandro Botticelli**, *The Birth of Venus*, *c*. 1482–86. Tempera on canvas, 5′8″ × 9′1⅝″. Uffizi Gallery, Florence, Italy

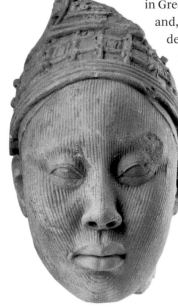

4.8.6 **Head, possibly an Ife king from West Africa**, 12th–14th century. Terra-cotta with residue of red pigment and traces of mica, 10½ × 5¾ × 7⅜″. Kimbell Art Museum, Fort Worth, Texas

colored skin and long flowing hair, and stands in an elegant pose. She discreetly covers her nudity, indicating that chastity is part of her appeal. Chastity was an important virtue in Greek, Roman, and Christian traditions, and, in the Renaissance, the nude body was depicted to suggest not only purity, but also fertility and reproduction (by contrast, medieval and early Christian artists had avoided depictions of nudity). The graceful shape and the flawless quality of Venus' body reflect the purity of the newborn goddess and create a harmonious and pleasing composition. Botticelli has modeled his figure on an ancient sculpture, thus basing his conception of beauty on Classical Greek standards.

In African societies, notions of beauty are often closely tied to the community's core values of composure and wisdom, believed to reflect, and even increase, a person's power. In other words, beauty is about more than external appearance. It is also about internal and societal principles. Being calm, wise, and composed were important attributes for the kings of Ife in West Africa. The elegant lines, delicate features, and elaborate headdress of the terra-cotta head in **4.8.6** indicate that it probably represents an Ife king, or *oni*. As the head was considered the seat of intelligence and the source of power, this sculpture's exquisite features draw our attention to the details of the face. The lifelike details—the folds of the ears, the **contours** of the nose, and the plumpness of the lips—are extremely naturalistic, but also graceful and refined. The fine lines on the face resemble scarification patterns, or scars created by cutting or branding the skin. Beauty in this case is a balance of invisible internal characteristics and an idealized, visible, outward appearance.

Many cultures determine beauty by a person's ability to conform to expectations, whether through clothes, cosmetics, or body shape. In Japan, traditional female performers called *geisha* are known for their social skills and artistic talents, such as singing, dancing, and serving tea. Geisha, not to be confused with courtesans or prostitutes, have a professional relationship with their clients and are strongly discouraged from becoming too intimate with them. A geisha's appearance changes over the course of her career. Early on she wears dramatic hairstyles, heavy makeup, dark eyeliner, and red lip pencil applied to make her lips look smaller. While an apprentice, the source of a geisha's beauty lies in her appearance, but later it is seen to derive from her maturity and her *gei*, or art. After three years of apprenticeship, a geisha adopts less elaborate kimonos tied with simpler knots, lighter makeup, and a subdued hairstyle, such as the one seen in Kaigetsudo Dohan's *Beautiful Woman* (**4.8.7**). In common with other Japanese artists working at the time, Kaigetsudo Dohan (working 1710–16) celebrated beautiful women, here emphasizing the experienced geisha's impressive attire and relatively natural appearance. In addition to her musical skills and gift for intelligent conversation, this mature geisha would have been appreciated for her inner beauty.

Reclining Nudes

The tradition of depicting the nude female figure lying down, or reclining, was established during the Renaissance.

These types of pictures recall the ancient Greek emphasis on the beauty and honesty conveyed by the nude human form. In some cases, they also suggest the sensuality of the nude.

The Venetian painter known as Titian (*c.* 1485/90–1576) was influenced by the Classical tradition when he painted a female nude for the duke of the Italian town of Urbino (**4.8.8**). The roses in the woman's right hand hint at her identity: they are a symbol of Venus (hence the name by which the painting is commonly known, the *Venus of Urbino*). She looks out from her couch with a coy expression and casually covers her pubic area, at once modest and inviting, as if she exists simply to be looked at. The presence of the maids in the background preparing her clothes, however, connects her to the concerns of a real woman. By suggesting that his painting depicted a mythological figure, Titian was able to explore in depth such secular themes as the nature of love and desire.

It is clear that the French artist Édouard Manet (1832–1883) was familiar with the *Venus of Urbino* when he painted *Olympia* (**4.8.9**, p. 636). The composition

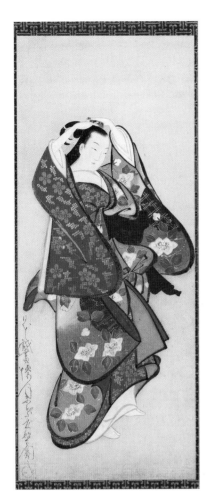

4.8.7 Kaigetsudō Dohan, ***Beautiful Woman***, Edo Period, Japan, 18th century. Hanging scroll, ink and color on paper, 64⅜ × 20⅛". Metropolitan Museum of Art, New York

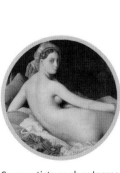

Some artists, such as Ingres, have used the reclining nude to express beauty and grace by exaggerating anatomy rather than rendering bodies in realistic proportion:

→ see **1.10.8**, p. 167

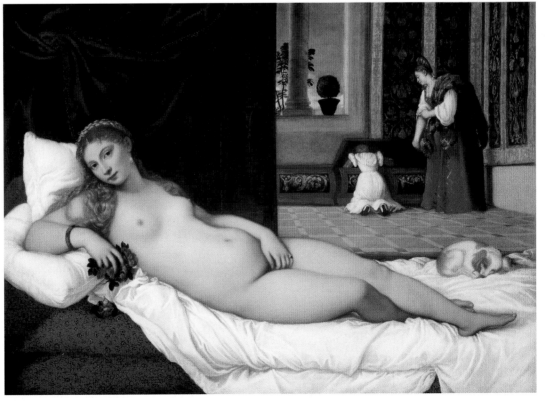

4.8.8 Titian, ***Venus of Urbino***, 1538. Oil on canvas, 3'10⅞" × 5'5". Uffizi Gallery, Florence, Italy

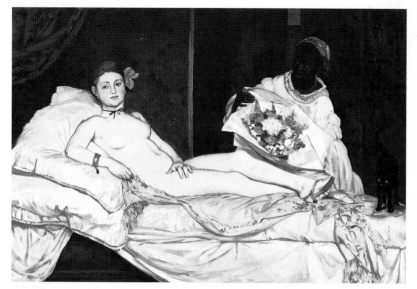

4.8.9 Édouard Manet, *Olympia*, 1863. Oil on canvas, 3'3⅜" × 6'2¾". Musée d'Orsay, Paris, France

of the paintings and the posture of the women within them are almost identical. Manet, however, has replaced the sleeping dog at the foot of the bed with a hissing black cat. And instead of the maids in the background, there is a Black woman, perhaps a servant, who brings Olympia flowers. In this painting, as in others, Manet took a Classical subject and updated it for his own time. In modernizing the reclining nude, Manet considered the reality of the situation. Why would a woman be naked and on display? One obvious answer is because she is a prostitute. Not only was Olympia a common name for a prostitute, but Manet also depicted her as a real woman, thin (at least by the standards of the time) and probably

poor. Olympia's pose would have seemed confrontational because she stares out at the viewer in an assertive way, while people at that time were used to seeing more passive women with voluptuous bodies and docile expressions similar to those of the figure depicted in the *Venus of Urbino*.

Although it was revolutionary at the time for showing a so-called "real" woman, eventually Manet's *Olympia* stood beside other European modernists in representing what has come to be known as "the male gaze" with a passive female body on display, presumably for a male spectator who has more power than she does.

In the late twentieth century, Angolan conceptual artist Kiluanji Kia Henda (b. 1979) revisited the theme of the reclining nude from a postcolonial perspective. *Great Italian Nude* (**4.8.10**) presents a black man lounging on a lavish red leather couch. The blackness of his face is exaggerated by makeup or a mask and he wears an elaborate headdress. This scene not only reverses the male gaze, but also focuses on the reclined body of an exotic other or outsider (a Black, African man rather than a white European) instead of leaving the black body in the shadowy background as in Manet's *Olympia*. Notably, we see a starkly different backdrop with the couch balancing on rocky ground surrounded by water. This setting recalls the Atlantic coastline of the artist's native Luanda and the Mediterranean lagoons, canals, and rivers in and around the city of Venice, where Henda made this piece during an artist's residency.

Despite living through decades of civil war in Angola, Henda is inspired to see humor as an important way of getting people's attention and allowing meaningful engagement with each other, as well as with (often troubling) history. According to Henda, he wants to create a "trap" for people who have narrow ideas about Africa and use art to "make the distance shorter" between cultures. In this piece, assumptions about cultural ideals are questioned; new models of understanding, communication, and inclusion are suggested; and possibilities for interconnection are expanded.

Performance Art: The Body Becomes the Artwork

Geisha are considered living works of art. Similarly, in **performance art**, and in some **installations**, the body and its actions become

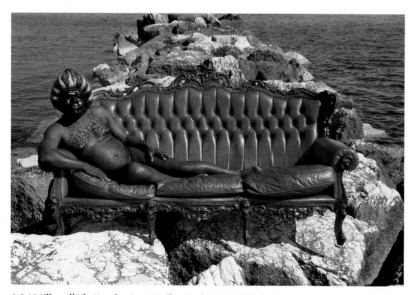

4.8.10 Kiluanji Kia Henda, *Great Italian Nude*, 2010. Digital print on matt paper mounted on aluminium, 43⅜ × 67".

Perspectives on Art: Spencer Tunick
Human Bodies as Installations

*American artist Spencer Tunick (b. 1967) is well known for his installation photographs involving crowds of people (**4.8.11** and **4.8.12**). He explains how he came to make such work, and how complicated it can be to organize the people.*

I didn't start out photographing hundreds or thousands of nude people. From 1990 to 1996, I worked on individual portraits of nudes on the streets of New York. I gained confidence in my ability to work on a public street, to deal with traffic, traffic light intervals, and the police. I switched to multiples when I had so many people to work with. I would carry the photographs round in my wallet and show them to people. By 1994 I had phone numbers for twenty-eight people and I decided to photograph them all at once outside the UN building in New York. Then in 1997 I gathered 1,000 people on an air-force base in Maine at a music concert.

I travel with a team of eight. In each city a contemporary art museum commissions my work and I can work wherever in the city I like. The museum provides team leaders and volunteers. Mexico City took three years to organize and one day to make the art. There were 250 team leaders and volunteers and 250 police officers. In Caracas, Venezuela, there were almost 1,000 police and military.

I know 75 percent of what I am going to do before we start but I like to keep an element of mystery. I have control of thousands of people, but in a way I don't like that control. I like to keep the event loose, personal, and intimate. Participants are not involving themselves in a spectacle but in a work of art. After ten minutes, once they get used to being nude, they get excited and start raising their hands in the air and so on, and then they calm down and we get organized.

I consider my works to be installations, not performances or photographs. I document the installations with photos and videos. I have two videographers and could have people take the photographs also, but I like to frame the photos and tweak them on location.

I still do individual portraits in streets. I am interested in the body and its relationship to the background. Instead of the body creating a meaning for the background, the background creates a new meaning for the body.

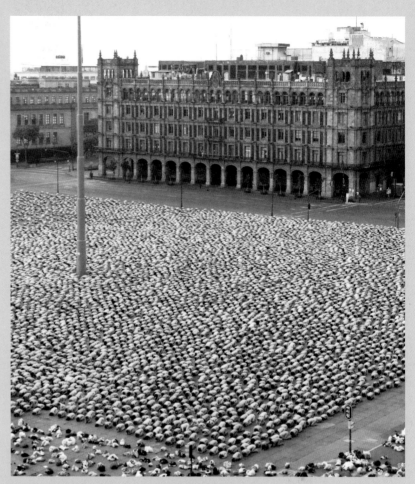

4.8.11 Photograph of Spencer Tunick's installation process in the Zócalo, Mexico City, Mexico, May 6, 2007. More than 18,000 people participated

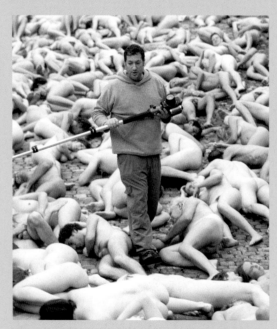

4.8.12 Spencer Tunick steps through 300 people whom he arranged as a living sculpture near City Hall, Fribourg, Switzerland, 2001

the artwork (see Perspectives on Art: Spencer Tunick, p. 637) A performance, by definition, involves the human form in action, but by engaging all of a viewer's senses through movement, expression, sound, smell, and so on, it also activates the space itself. The performers share a space with the audience, and the art becomes part of the viewer's lived experience. Because performances are not permanent or static, once they are finished they can be re-experienced only indirectly, through documentation. Written accounts, photographs, and videos taken at the time remind us later of the performances themselves.

Perhaps inspired by his deep interest in the martial art of judo, the French artist Yves Klein (1928–1962) began experimenting with "living brushes," or women using their nude bodies as the vehicle for applying paint to canvas under the direction of the male artist. In the late 1950s, Klein became one of the first artists to make

monochromatic (one-color) paintings. He used a bright, dense, ultramarine blue, a color that he eventually patented as "International Klein Blue" (IKB). Klein integrated performance in an innovative way to make the blue paintings for which he was known. The first paintings made by the "living brushes" were solid blue monochromes similar to those Klein himself had produced. Later, the women left imprints of their bodies on the canvas or paper (**4.8.13b**).

Klein devised the pieces, directed the women, and hired an orchestra for the first public performance of the living brushes, called *Anthropométries de l'époque bleue* (or *Anthropometries of the Blue Period*) (**4.8.13a**). In order to create a musical accompaniment that was suitable for monochromatic paintings, Klein had the musicians play a single chord for twenty minutes and then sit in silence for twenty minutes. In an art gallery, works of art are usually inert, still objects and it is the viewers who move around (often in silence).

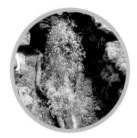

Ana Mendieta used her body as a medium to draw attention to issues of nature, gender, and identity:
→ see **3.10.4**, p. 524

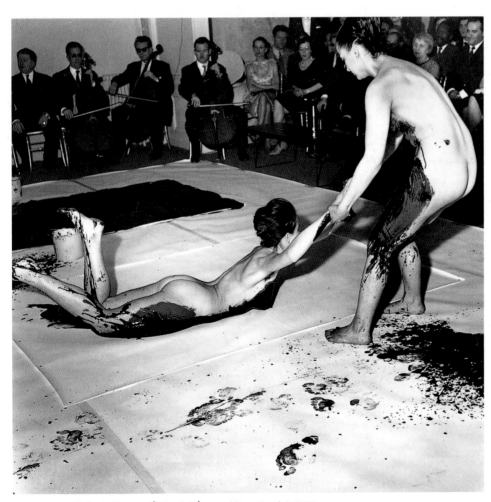

4.8.13a **Yves Klein,** *Anthropométries de l'époque bleue*, March 9, 1960. Galerie Internationale d'Art Contemporain, Paris, France

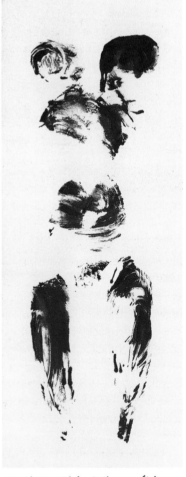

4.8.13b **Yves Klein,** *Anthropométrie sans titre*, 1960. Pure pigment and synthetic resin on paper mounted on canvas, 50⅞ × 14⅝". Private collection

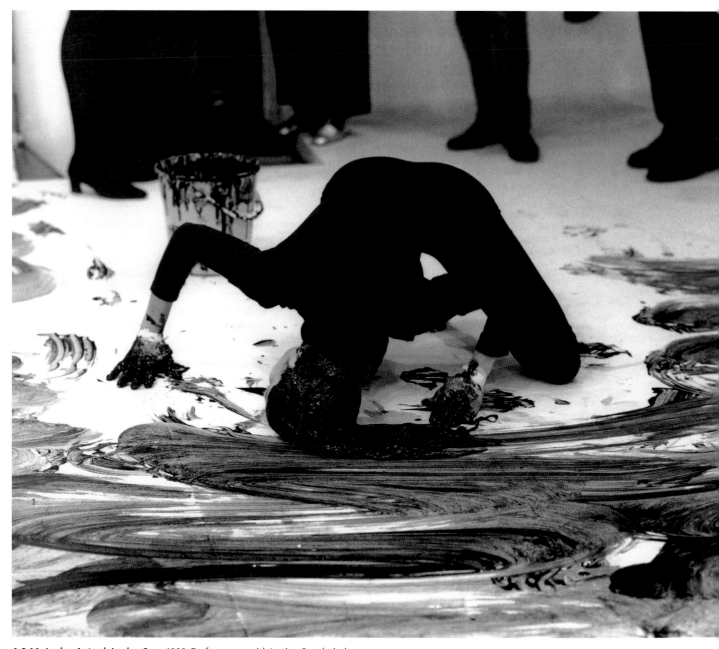

4.8.14 Janine Antoni, *Loving Care*, 1993. Performance with Loving Care hair dye Natural Black, dimensions variable. Photographed by Prudence Cuming Associates at Anthony d'Offay Gallery, London, England, 1993

In the case of Klein's performances, the artwork itself moved and made sounds while the audience sat still, giving the work a very physical presence in the usually quiet and austere gallery. At the same time, attention was brought to the odd circumstance of living nude figures as art, now active in the gallery space instead of represented in artworks, and surrounded by a fully clothed audience.

Unlike Klein, who directed rather than participated in his artworks, artist Janine Antoni (b. 1964 in the Bahamas) uses her own body and her own actions as the basis for most of her performances. In *Loving Care*, named for a brand of hair-care products, Antoni dipped her head in a bucket of hair color and proceeded to mop the floor with it, using her hair as a paintbrush (**4.8.14**). As more and more of the floor became covered with gestural marks, viewers were pushed out of the gallery space. The artwork comments on several actions typically regarded as feminine, including the domesticity of mopping and the messiness of using cosmetics for beautification. Antoni takes the dynamic creative role here, bringing attention to the actions she is performing as well as to the status of women in the art world and in society.

Perspectives on Art: Henri Matisse
The Blue Nude: Cutouts and the Essence of Form

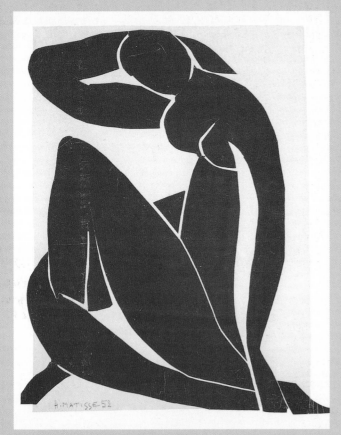

4.8.15 **Henri Matisse**, *Blue Nude II*, 1952. Gouache on paper, cut and pasted on white paper, 45¾ × 32¼". Musée National d'Art Moderne, Centre Georges Pompidou, Paris, France

---

Palette: the range of colors used by an artist

Plane: a flat, two-dimensional surface onto which an artist can create a drawing or painting. Planes can also be implied in a composition by areas that face towards, parallel to, or away from a light source

Silhouette: a solidly colored-in shape represented in outline, which contains no detail inside its border

Experimental artists, such as the French Henri Matisse (1869–1954), have consistently used the female nude as a subject for creative innovation. Throughout his career, Matisse was moving toward a more economical use of artistic elements. Early on, he made very detailed recordings of the world he observed around him. After the 1940s, he chose to isolate forms and reduce the range of his **palette**, emphasizing the elements he thought to be the most important for a particular subject, because, as he wrote, "exactitude is not truth." Even his sketches for individual artworks went from complex recordings of very detailed observations to pictures with selected details and limited colors. This approach suited the technique of making cutouts, as seen in *Blue Nude II* (**4.8.15**).

Matisse gives us enough information to know that we are looking at a human body. The shapes are rough, but energetic. The palette in *Blue Nude II* is restricted to blue only. The color blue is not used to shade the female figure or to make her look as if she is bathed in blue light. Instead, her form is made entirely of flat **planes** of color. Matisse started the cutout design for *Blue Nude II* by shaping the figure with scissors. The work focuses on expressing the essence of the body's energy within a form that is, at the same time, a simple **silhouette**.

An essay by Matisse in 1947, describing a series of self-portraits made using a mirror, helps explain how he arrived at this technique and what he hoped to communicate by making art in this way:

> These drawings sum up, in my opinion, observations that I have made for many years about the character of drawing, a character that does not depend on forms being copied exactly as they are in nature, or on the patient assembling of exact details, but on the profound feeling of the artist before the objects that he has chosen, on which his attention is focused, and whose spirit he has penetrated.
>
> My conviction about these things crystallized when I realized for example that in the leaves of a fig tree—of a fig tree particularly—the great difference of forms that exists among them does not keep them from sharing a common quality. Fig leaves, whatever their fantastic variations of form, always remain unmistakably fig leaves. I have made the same observation about other growing things: fruits, vegetables, etc.
>
> Thus there exists an essential truth that must be disengaged from the outward appearance of the objects to be represented. This is the only truth that matters…
>
> Exactitude is not truth.

The Body in Pieces

Artists have used exaggeration, stylization, and innovation to create abstract representations of the human body. Approaches originating outside the Western European art tradition, such as African masks, Aztec sculptures, and an emphasis on the unconscious mind, have influenced some modern European artists to make works suggesting forms that are altered but recognizable. Others have taken certain elements of anatomy out of their usual context by distorting or fragmenting the body. We do not have to see a whole body to read it as a human figure (see Perspectives on Art: Henri Matisse, opposite). Recognizing this fact, artists have focused attention away from identifying a particular individual or illustrating a coherent story in order to emphasize ways in which the body can be broken down and presented as a product of the human imagination.

In his artworks, the French artist Auguste Rodin (1840–1917) altered the appearance of the human body, which is one of the reasons he is now known as a pioneer in the field of modern sculpture. Although he had been formally trained, Rodin chose not to make his sculptures in the traditional, academic way. Instead of idealizing figures to look like perfected versions of actual people, Rodin intentionally left his surfaces rough, as seen in his sculpture *Walking Man* (**4.8.16**). The scrapes and gouges on the figure's chest, torso, and hips stand as evidence of the material the artist touched and manipulated to make the sculpture. Rodin also considered fragmentary representations, such as this one, which has no head or arms, to be completed sculptures rather than preparatory **sketches**. At the time, Rodin's pieces were harshly criticized because they looked so different from the smooth, idealized figures people had come to expect. Since then, his approach has been praised for allowing the figures to be more expressive, emotional, and individual.

Following Rodin, the British sculptor Henry Moore (1898–1986) created figures that did not match the way the human body actually looks. Instead, Moore emphasized natural forms in the shapes of bodies and their parts, which in his work often resemble mountains, hills, cliffs, and valleys. The organic lines in his sculptures mimic the organic contours of the materials he used, usually wood and stone. In addition to nature, Moore was inspired by other works of

art. He studied a range of artistic traditions of Egypt, Africa, and Mexico, as well as Classical and **avant-garde** European approaches. As a result of these influences, he departed from visible reality for the sake of making a strong artistic statement. A consistent characteristic of his sculptures is his use of the **void**, an empty space that opens up the figure and creates

Sketch: a rough preliminary version of a work or part of a work

Avant-garde: an early twentieth-century emphasis on artistic innovation, which challenged accepted values, traditions, and techniques

Void: in an artwork, an area that seems empty

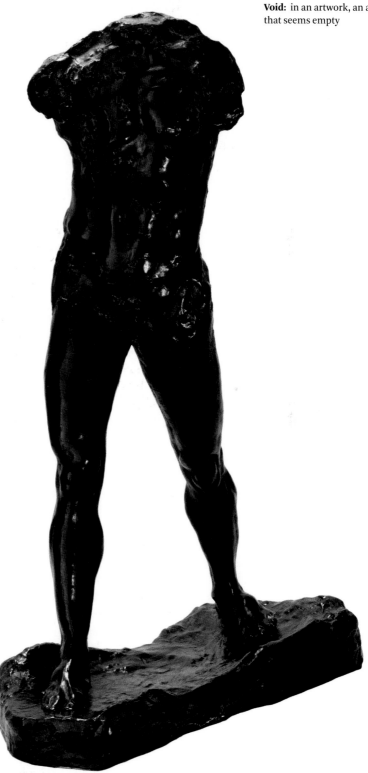

4.8.16 Auguste Rodin, *Walking Man*, c. 1890–95. Bronze, 33¾ × 22 × 11". MoMA, New York

Surrealist: an artistic movement in the 1920s and later; its works were inspired by dreams and the subconscious

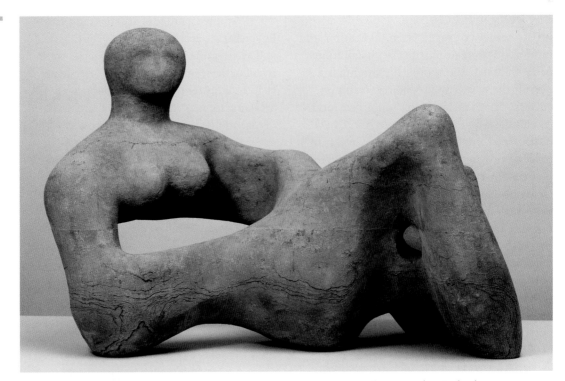

4.8.17 Henry Moore, *Recumbent Figure*, 1938. Green Hornton stone, 35 × 52¼ × 29″. Tate, London, England

visual interest. In *Recumbent Figure* the large hole in the center of the piece is surrounded by the masses that make up the body (**4.8.17**). The legs look like peaks while the abdomen is in the place of a valley. The breasts help to identify the shape as a female figure.

Also influenced by Rodin, the Swiss artist Alberto Giacometti (1901–1966) too stretched the boundaries of the recognizable form: first through **Surrealist** examinations of the human body, and then, after World War II, through the existential views represented in such sculptures as *Man Pointing* (**4.8.18**). Giacometti's obsessive nature at times caused him to reduce figures to the point where they were almost nonexistent. Eventually he began to accept his own artistic vision, in which the bodies look as if they are being seen from an extreme distance. The figures seem to have stepped out of the artist's dreams and into reality, carrying with them an air of mystery.

Man Pointing is an imposing figure, despite its apparent fragility. At 5 ft. 8 in. tall, it is hard to believe that it can support its own weight. Giacometti struck a delicate balance between the figure and its surroundings in this sculpture, which he first made in clay and then cast in bronze. Nothing indicates why the man is pointing, but the space around him seems almost heavy. The sculpture looks like a trace of the shadow the man casts rather than the man

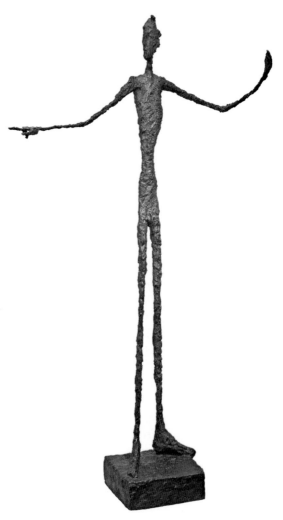

4.8.18 Alberto Giacometti, *Man Pointing*, 1947. Bronze, 70½ × 40¾ × 16⅜″. MoMA, New York

Frida Kahlo, *The Two Fridas*
A Body in Pain

For the other Kahlo
GATEWAYS:
→ see p. 41 and p. 190

A terrible accident brought art into Frida Kahlo's life (1907–1954) in a new way. At around the age of eighteen, she was riding in a bus with a friend when it collided with a trolley car. Her right leg and foot were crushed; her ribs, collarbone, and spine were broken; and her abdomen and uterus were pierced by an iron handrail. After the devastating accident she could not leave her bed for three months. Afterward, she endured as many as thirty-five surgeries and she experienced pain for the rest of her life. While she was recuperating in a full body cast, her father brought her art supplies and she began painting.

Throughout her life, she continued to create very personal portrayals of the psychological and physical suffering that plagued her (even before the accident, she had suffered polio as a child, compromising her right foot). Such paintings include *The Two Fridas* (**4.8.19**) and *The Broken Column* (**4.8.20**). Kahlo's self-portraits, which comprise up to a third of her artistic output, combine depictions of her outward appearance with metaphorical references to her feelings and graphic depictions of the physical agony she suffered. In *The Two Fridas*, for example, the presentation of the hearts—one of which is

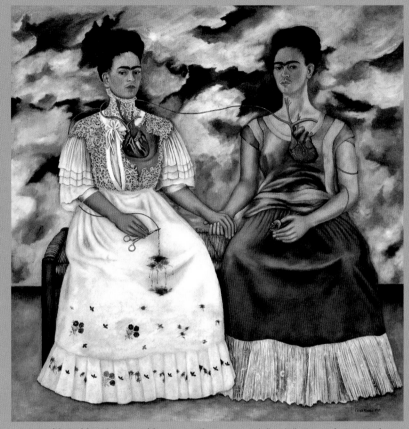

4.8.19 Frida Kahlo, *The Two Fridas*, 1939. Oil on canvas, 5′8″ × 5′8″. Museo de Arte Moderno, Mexico City, Mexico

radically torn open—on the outside of the bodies emphasizes the sensitive emotional content of the painting.

A few years later, around the time she painted *The Broken Column*, Kahlo said, "I am disintegration." In this later painting, nails pierce her skin all over, the front of her body is cracked open, and her spine is exposed. The nails recall depictions of the Catholic martyr St. Sebastian, and her spine takes the form of a Greek temple column. The Ionic column, considered the feminine architectural order, is ancient, ideal, and crumbling. No longer suited to supporting the body, the spinal column is reinforced by a metal corset.

We see subtle signs of Kahlo's constant anguish in the tears on her cheeks, but not in the expression on her face. It has the iconic, serene appearance seen in the numerous photographs taken of her and the many other self-portraits she made, including both faces in *The Two Fridas*. Like the column, Frida is fractured but whole, showing evidence of disintegration but still somehow surviving, even appearing almost ideal.

4.8.20 Frida Kahlo, *The Broken Column*, 1944. Oil on masonite, 13 × 17″. Museo Dolores Olmedo Patino, Mexico City, Mexico

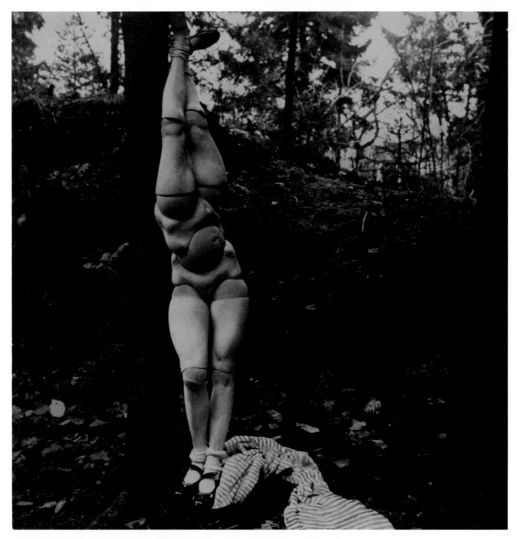

4.8.21 Hans Bellmer, *La poupée (The puppet)*, c. 1938–1939, Gelatin silver photo, hand-coloured, 5⅝ × 5½". Art Gallery of New South Wales, Sydney, Australia

himself, emphasizing the figure's loneliness and isolation.

The female nude in the work of German Surrealist Hans Bellmer (1902–1975) takes the form of dismembered, mutilated dolls. He creates a strong sense of attraction/repulsion in *La Poupée* (**4.8.21**). Beautiful and intriguing, the doll is at the same time startling and repulsive. Hand-coloring creates a nostalgic, fairytale atmosphere while the misaligned body parts take the mystery to a sinister level, almost like a crime scene. Bellmer's fragmented dolls have been interpreted as Surrealist fetish objects, meaning that the idea of woman becomes an unusual, even dangerous, object of desire. They are also seen as referencing the destruction and devastation resulting from Nazi political campaigns and genocide. The collection of prosthetic limbs serves as a reminder of the ravages to humanity resulting from both deviant sexual obsession and Nazi warfare.

The Body Reframed

In the late twentieth century, a number of artists, many of them women, began to focus very deliberately on the female body with a view to challenging traditional preconceptions about women that they perceived as limiting. Some of the new artworks these artists created include their own bodies, in more confrontational ways than had previously been attempted in art. Many of the works react to the frequently submissive images created by men in earlier eras. They expose the degree to which those images had created a disturbing view of the female nude, and they express a whole new range of ways in which the female form could be presented. In so doing, these artists rejected unrealistic notions of ideal body image: now, the female body could be seen as its own source of power, action, and inquiry.

The British painter Jenny Saville (b. 1970) is an artist who has chosen an unconventional

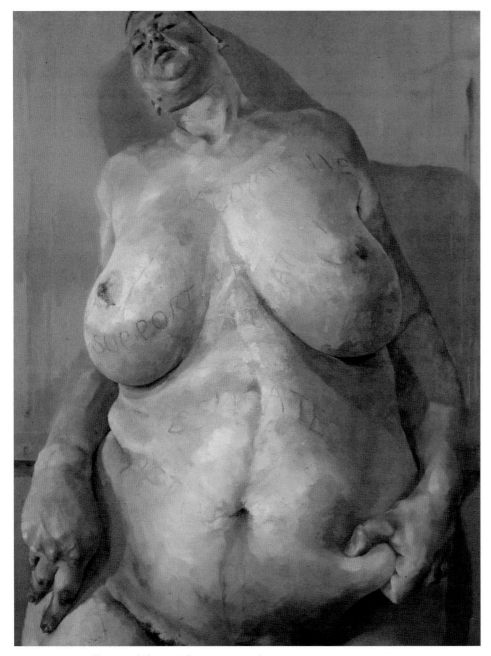

4.8.22 Jenny Saville, *Branded*, 1992. Oil on canvas, 7 × 6′

approach to depicting the female body. In such larger-than-lifesize self-portraits as *Branded*, which is 7 ft. tall, she appears as a **monumental** nude (**4.8.22**). From this vantage point, Saville's breasts and stomach are far more prominent than her head, which is barely squeezed into the frame. She glances down with a look of disdain as she pinches a roll of flesh with her left hand, as if peering into a mirror. Not only does her nude figure appear fat, countering contemporary society's bias toward thin women (and noticeably exaggerating Saville's actual size), but also her discolored skin is far from ideal. To make her paintings, Saville refers to photographs and medical illustrations of flesh tones, bruises, dimples, and pockmarks. Such words as "delicate," "supportive," "irrational," "decorative," and "petite," inscribed on her body, comment on society's expectations of the kind of body a woman should have. Saville has said that she uses her body as a prop that she is willing to distort and manipulate. The results are direct, if harsh and critical. By confronting—even exaggerating—the imperfections of reality, Saville comments on the conflicted relationship women sometimes have with their own body image, and on society's unreasonable expectations of how they should appear in order to be perceived as "acceptable" or "attractive."

Monumental: having massive or impressive scale

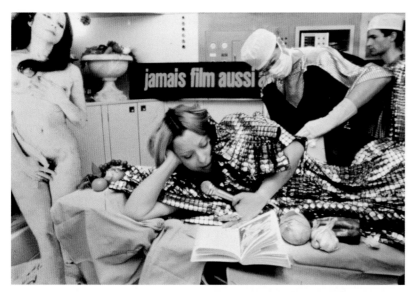

4.8.23a ORLAN, **Fourth surgery-performance**, entitled *Successful Operation*, December 8, 1991, Paris, France

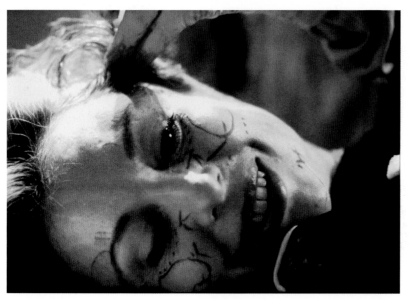

4.8.23b ORLAN, **Seventh surgery-performance**, entitled *Omnipresence*, November 21, 1993. *Smile of Delight (Sourire de Plaisir)*. Cibachrome in diasec mount, 43¼ × 65"

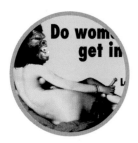

Feminist artists, such as the Guerrilla Girls, draw attention to the ways women have been overlooked and objectified in society and in the art world: → see **4.9.8**, p. 654

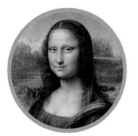

One of the famous artworks ORLAN copied for her constructed self was the Mona Lisa:
→ see **0.0.12**, p. 23

The French performance artist ORLAN (b. 1947) adopted an even more extreme approach to constructing the female body. ORLAN's artistic medium is literally her own body: in order to create a new persona, she underwent plastic surgeries that transformed her appearance, and documented the entire process (**4.8.23a** and **4.8.23b**). An operating room became the stage for ORLAN's performance. She was the star, the medical team the cast, with costumes created by famous fashion designers. Because she was given only a local anesthetic, ORLAN was able to remain conscious and read aloud from philosophical and poetic texts while the procedures were carried out. Video cameras in the operating room transmitted a live feed of the surgery to CBS News, the Sandra Gering Gallery in New York, and the Centre Georges Pompidou in Paris. ORLAN also documented the stages of her transformation with photographs taken as she healed.

In her final incarnation, ORLAN became a composite woman. Her features were modeled after famously beautiful paintings of women: her chin was copied from Botticelli's Venus (see **4.8.5** on p. 634); her mouth from the Roman deity Diana in a renowned French Renaissance canvas; her nose from Psyche, the mythical lover of Cupid, in a French painting by François Gérard; and her brow from Leonardo da Vinci's *Mona Lisa*. ORLAN has said that her work aims to intervene in the historical representation of women in art by actively determining her own appearance; to comment on the ways technology empowers us to transcend our human limitations; to critique the cult of beauty that imposes unfair standards on women; and to make a statement about the impossibility of physical perfection even in an age when plastic surgery is performed routinely. The measures she takes expose the tyranny of societal preconceptions about physical appearance because, by having herself operated on, she shows how extreme the insistence on stereotypical notions of female beauty has been. Ultimately, she has used the platform of art to make a statement that she is taking possession of her own body and asserting the right to do with it as she sees fit. ORLAN's performances broach the subject of body image for a world of women, young and old, trying to live up to impossible standards.

Explore Further   The Body in Art

Ancient Archetypes and Ideal Proportions

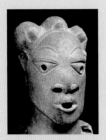

3.5.2 Head from Rafin Kura, Nok culture, Africa, *c.* 500 BCE–200 CE → p. 429

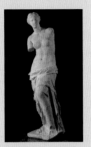

3.1.27 *Venus de Milo*, 2nd century BCE → p. 365

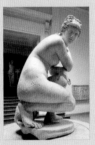

1.2.8b *Naked Aphrodite…* (*Lely's Venus*), Roman, 2nd century CE → p. 55

The Body in Pieces

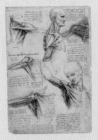

2.1.2 Leonardo da Vinci, *The muscles of the shoulder, c.* 1510 → p. 179

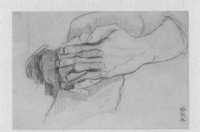

2.1.10 Paula Modersohn-Becker, *Gefaltete Hände (study)*, 1897–98 → p. 184

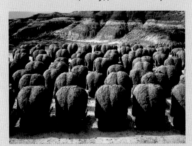

1.10.7 Magdalena Abakanowicz, *80 Backs*, 1976–80 → p. 166

The Body Reconsidered

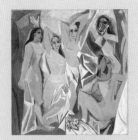

3.9.6 Pablo Picasso, *Les Demoiselles d'Avignon*, 1907 → p. 504

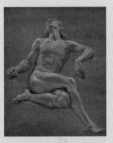

1.3.5a Paul Cadmus, *Male Nude NM32*, 1967 → p. 68

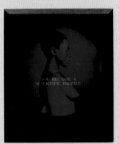

2.8.18 Carrie Mae Weems, "You Became a Scientific Profile," 1995 → p. 311

Your turn:
How do these artworks relate to the ideas discussed in this chapter?

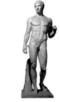

3.1.20 *Doryphoros* (Roman version), 120–50 BCE → p. 361

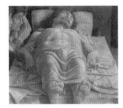

4.3.12 Andrea Mantegna, *Dead Christ, c.* 1480 → p. 576

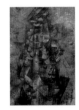

3.9.7 Georges Braque *Man with a Guitar*, 1911–12 → p. 504

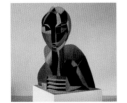

2.4.16 Naum Gabo, *Constructed Head No. 2*, 1916 → p. 239

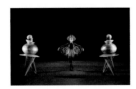

1.5.9 Oskar Schlemmer, *Triadic Ballet*, 1922 → p. 109

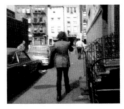

2.10.5 Vito Acconci, *Following Piece*, 1969 → p. 338

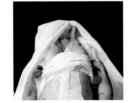

4.3.13 Andres Serrano, *The Morgue (Gun Murder)*, 1992 → p. 576

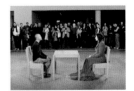

2.10.6 Marina Abramović, *The Artist Is Present*, 2010 → p. 338

4.9
Identity, Race, and Gender in Art

Harlem Renaissance: a movement in literature, music, and the visual arts from the end of WWI into the 1930s, celebrating black experience and culture

While personal identity affects everyone on some level, it became a central issue for artists during the late twentieth century (see the discussion of Postmodernism in Chapter 3.10). At that time, groups that had been neglected by or indeed excluded from mainstream culture, which was male-dominated and Eurocentric, began to celebrate their differences, whether these lay in being part of a non-white ethnic minority, or being female, homosexual, or transgender, for example. Earlier in the same century, social and cultural movements encouraged people to reconsider the status of women and communities of color in society by emphasizing their role as both the creators and the subjects of important artworks. The **Harlem Renaissance** (1920s and 1930s) and the Civil Rights movement (1955–68) in the US brought well-deserved attention to Black artists, while feminist and LGBTQ+ (lesbian, gay, bisexual, transgender, transsexual, and queer, among others) movements have since the 1960s, and even more recently, inspired a great deal of discussion and exploration of the effect gender has on our personalities and relationships, and on the assumptions we make.

The artworks in this chapter illustrate some of the ways in which artists have explored, reinforced, and challenged traditional expectations with regards to identity. (Of course, due to its limited space, this chapter cannot cover all of the various kinds and aspects of identity.) By presenting their personal experiences of daily life, their interpretations of historical events, and their response to particular social or political agendas, artists encourage us to question common assumptions about identity and to become aware of the possibilities of individual experience beyond simplistic labels and stereotypes.

Self-Portraits

One obvious way for artists to explore their identity is to make a self-portrait. In a self-portrait, the maker and the subject are the same person, while in a portrait the artist depicts someone else. In addition to the more familiar practice of providing a physical likeness of the artist, self-portraits often tell us something about the artist's personality, experiences, or choices. Another form of self-portraiture involves the artist assuming the role or persona of someone else, much as an actor portrays another person on the stage. We will see that some artists have become very inventive with their self-portraits to the point where the connection between artwork and artist ranges from very direct to not at all obvious.

The Italian artist Artemisia Gentileschi (1593–*c.* 1656) brought the characters of her paintings to life by using them to respond to intense personal experiences. The powerful biblical heroines in her paintings, such as Judith, who beheads Holofernes with steadfast determination, have a strong connection to events in the artist's own life. Gentileschi was the victim of a sexual assault by Agostino Tassi, who was her painting teacher and a colleague of her father. During the public rape trial that followed, Tassi claimed that Gentileschi was not only a willing lover, but also quite promiscuous. Gentileschi and her father felt that, in addition to the physical violence she had suffered in the assault, their family name and reputation had been attacked. They feared that her prospects of marrying had been damaged both by the

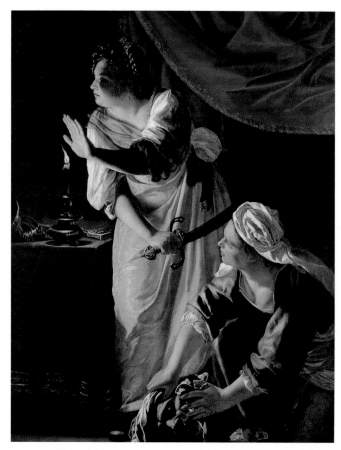

4.9.1 Artemisia Gentileschi, *Judith and Her Maidservant with the Head of Holofernes*, 1623–25. Oil on canvas, 6'⅜" × 4'7¾". Detroit Institute of Arts, Michigan

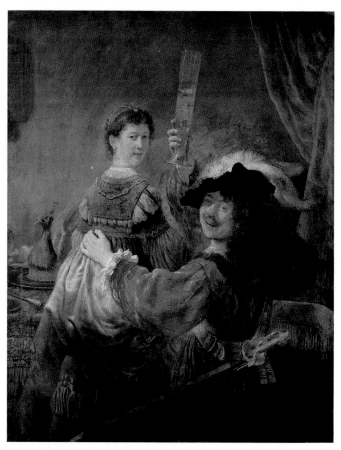

4.9.2 Rembrandt van Rijn, *Self-Portrait with Saskia in the Scene of the Prodigal Son in the Tavern*, c. 1635. Oil on canvas, 5'3⅜" × 4'3⅝". Gemäldegalerie Alte Meister, Dresden, Germany

rape and the trial. Tassi was eventually found guilty and sentenced to exile. Gentileschi went on to marry another man, with whom she had five children.

Gentileschi is known to have painted seven works showing different events from the biblical story of Judith's encounter with Holofernes. The first, depicting Judith and her maidservant cutting off his head, was painted about a year after the Tassi trial. Another, made about a decade later, shows Judith and her maidservant by candlelight while making their escape from the murder scene with the bloody head (**4.9.1**). Gentileschi's paintings of this violent assault by a brave and beautiful woman on the enemy commander who had conquered her city and tried to seduce her has been interpreted, using feminist analysis, both as an expression of the artist's anger at her own attacker and as a way of healing the effects of her ordeal. In fact, Gentileschi's heroines in the Judith paintings have features that resemble her own. While there may indeed be an element of autobiography, at least in Gentileschi's earlier versions, the numerous paintings of

the story that she made over a thirty-year period were probably created for a variety of other reasons, including the popularity of the theme at the time and the fact that her previous renditions of this subject had already attracted admiration.

The Dutch artist Rembrandt Harmenszoon van Rijn (1606–1669), known as Rembrandt, was one of the first artists to dedicate a significant portion of his output to self-portraits, producing more than ninety of them over the course of forty years. In them we can observe the changes that occurred both in his appearance and in his artistic style during the course of his lifetime. In Rembrandt's self-portraits, he is shown in many guises, from a peasant to an aristocrat, which demonstrates his interest in exploring different facial expressions and character types. In *Self-Portrait with Saskia in the Scene of the Prodigal Son in the Tavern*, Rembrandt appears as the prodigal son from the biblical story of the young man who rebels against his father's wishes by squandering his inheritance (**4.9.2**). Rembrandt creates a lively mood in the tavern: he raises

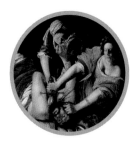

Artemisia Gentileschi painted another version of this heroine's story, *Judith Decapitating Holofernes*, in about 1620, just a year or so after the trial and sentencing of the person who had sexually assaulted her: → see **1.8.1**, p. 140

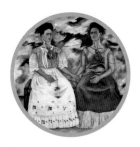

Frida Kahlo is perhaps best known for her self-portraits, which comprise up to one-third of her artistic output:
→ see **4.8.19**, p. 643

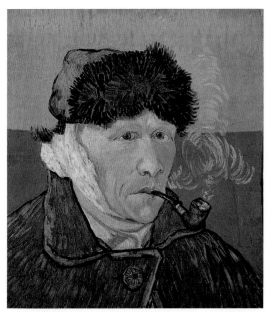

4.9.3 Vincent van Gogh, *Self-Portrait with Bandaged Ear and Pipe*, 1889. Oil on canvas, 25¼ × 19¾". Private collection

his glass toward the viewer, while the barmaid, modeled on his wife Saskia, looks on.

More than two centuries after Rembrandt, another Dutch painter, Vincent van Gogh (1853–1890), specialized in self-portraits in which he emphasized the internal reality of what he felt rather than simply recording what he saw. His *Self-Portrait with Bandaged Ear and Pipe*, one of around thirty self-portraits that he made, refers to a famous incident in his life (**4.9.3**). At the time this painting was made Van Gogh lived in Arles, in the south of France, and was hoping to realize his dream of starting an artists' colony there. When he learned that his fellow artist and close friend Paul Gauguin was planning to return to Paris, they had an intense argument, during which Van Gogh threatened Gauguin's life. Afterward, Van Gogh cut off a portion of his own ear. He then wrapped the severed lobe in newspaper and presented it to a prostitute in a brothel before he was hospitalized and treated for acute blood loss. In its restrained but nervous lines and bold, contrasting colors, the *Self-Portrait with Bandaged Ear and Pipe* displays some of the agitation that the artist experienced during the episode.

The American photographer Cindy Sherman (b. 1954) plays the roles of all of the women portrayed in her acclaimed *Untitled Film Stills* series, creating an intriguing visual puzzle as we try to uncover the real Cindy Sherman. She makes images of herself that are not, however, intended conventionally to reflect

her own identity: Sherman has explained that the images are not about her, but about the representations of the women being shown and the ways that each viewer interprets them (see Perspectives on Art: Cindy Sherman). At the time Sherman made "Untitled Film Still #35," feminism was beginning to have a significant impact on artistic representations of women as well as on the possibilities for women in society. Sherman made sixty-nine photographs in the series. The women in them always seem as if they are being watched, the object of an unseen voyeur's gaze, so that these images call attention to and question the way we look at women. For the *Untitled Film Stills*, Sherman fabricated backdrops and costumes for imagined characters from nonexistent 1950s B-movies. At that time, the film roles for women were limited to such stereotyped characters as housewife, starlet, country girl come to the city, and so on. In "Untitled Film Still #35" we see a woman—perhaps a housewife or a maid—with a distinctly bad attitude (**4.9.4**). The circumstances of the scene are far from clear, though. Is she sulking about something, planning to leave, or about to pull a wallet from the jacket hanging on the hook? Why are there so many scuff marks on the door? More

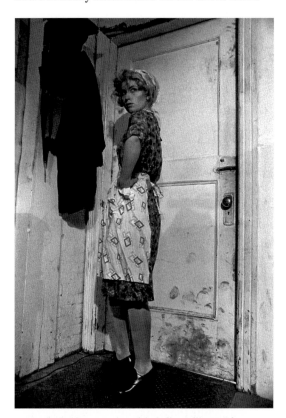

4.9.4 Cindy Sherman, "**Untitled Film Still #35,**" from the *Untitled Film Stills* series, 1979. Black-and-white photograph, 10 × 8". MoMA, New York

Perspectives on Art: Cindy Sherman
The Artist and Her Identity

The American photographer and film director Cindy Sherman is best known for her photographs in which she is dressed in costumes as if she were another person (see 4.9.4). Here she explains her general working process and one specific image, "Untitled Film Still #35," inspired by the Italian film actress Sophia Loren.

There is a stereotype of a girl who dreams all her life of being a movie star. She tries to make it on the stage, in films, and either succeeds or fails. I was more interested in the types of characters that fail. Maybe I related to that. But why should I try to do it myself? I'd rather look at the reality of these kinds of fantasies, the fantasy of going away and becoming a star…

The black-and-white photographs were… fun to do. I think they were easy partly because throughout my childhood I had stored up so many images of role models. It was real easy to think of a different one in every scene. But they were so clichéd that after three years I couldn't do them anymore. I was really thinking about the movies, the characters are almost typecast from movies.

For the woman standing in front of my studio door, I was thinking of a film with Sophia Loren called *Two Women*. She plays this Italian peasant. Her husband is killed and she and her daughter are both raped. She is this tough strong woman, but all beaten-up and dirty. I liked that combination of Sophia Loren looking very dirty and very strong. So that's what I was thinking of…

I realized I had to become more specific in details, because that's what makes a person different from other people.

questions are raised than answered in the scenarios Sherman invents. Her *Untitled Film Stills*, which were created between 1977 and 1980, reimagine these 1950s-inspired women in order to make it clear how narrow the representations of and expectations for women had been only a few short years before.

British artist Marc Quinn (b. 1964) combines the elements of self-portraiture in a very literal way. As the artist states on his website, "it depends on my life to be created—it's made from the substance of me; and so I think of it as the purest form of sculpture to sculpt your own body, from your own body." From 1991 to 2011, Quinn **cast** a lifesize mold of his head every five years and created a series of unique self-portraits. Each bust was created using about ten pints of the artist's blood, then frozen and displayed in a clear refrigeration device (**4.9.5**). These works have an immediate impact, partly because they use blood as the **medium**, a substance we recognize as viscerally related to the life force and that we all depend on for survival. Looking at *Self*, we are likely to contemplate our own mortality and our fear of it because the piece is so much like a death mask (cast directly from the face of someone who has deceased). This effect is underscored by our knowledge that if the refrigerator should fail, the sculpture would dissolve. In this fascinating way, Quinn's self-portrait calls attention to humans' physical vulnerability, to change over time, and to our ingenious ability to counteract our impermanence.

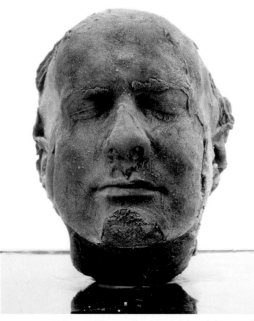

4.9.5 Marc Quinn, *Self*, 1991. Blood (artist's), stainless steel, Perspex, and refrigeration equipment, 81⅞ × 24 × 24¾". Private collection

Cast: a sculpture or artwork made by pouring a liquid (for example molten metal or plaster) into a mold that then hardens when cooled or dried

Medium (plural **media**): the material on or from which an artist chooses to make a work of art

April Greiman, *Does It Make Sense?*
The Identity of the Artist

For the other Greiman
GATEWAYS:
→ see p. 294 and p. 526

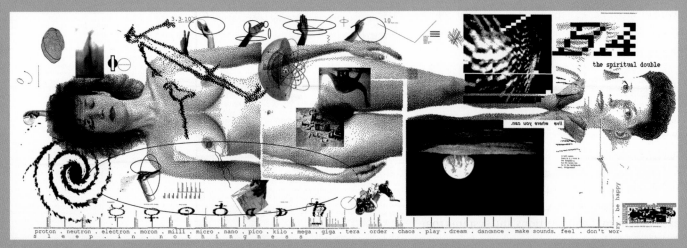

4.9.6a April Greiman, *Does It Make Sense? Design Quarterly* Issue #133, 1986

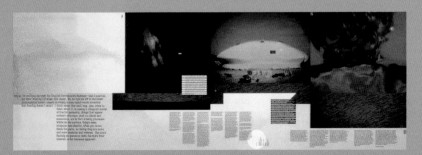

4.9.6b April Greiman, *Does It Make Sense?* (reverse view)

When she was hired to design an issue of *Design Quarterly* (**4.9.6a**), April Greiman was a well-established designer, but she also faced a great deal of criticism. For several years prior to the commission, she served as head of the graphic design program at California Institute of the Arts (CalArts), which was known for being innovative and rigorous. Not content with the limitations of the name Graphic Design, Greiman successfully lobbied to have the program name changed to Visual Communications.

Beginning in the 1970s, Greiman embraced technology, computers, and digitization, while other designers saw them as threatening. In a 2019 interview she explained, "there was this backlash from the established New York male graphic design community, who were saying it wasn't graphic design at all, it was fine art. So the chatter—the dialogue, that conversation in my own head—had to do with them saying my work was personal and not real, serious design." She faced discrimination as a female designer in a predominantly male-dominated field: she was called an airhead, her contemporaries said that her business would not last five years, and they claimed her work marked the end of design. At that time, she was questioning her own creativity and considering whether to join the establishment or chart her own path.

She ultimately focused on her own abilities and skill set, embraced technology (including video), and went on to become an award-winning and internationally acclaimed designer, business owner, and educator. For Greiman, *Does It Make Sense?* includes elements important to her personal journey, "'What's personal and what's professional design or commercial design?' That timeline [of running dates at the bottom of the piece] was to help me give it sense."

The back of *Does It Make Sense?* (**4.9.6b**) is visually less dense than the front, with text along the bottom and a layered collage of four main images across the top. The narrative at the far left recounts a conversation about order and chaos, concluding that: "While on the surface, things seem irregular and chaotic, when you break down the parts, in reality they are more and more modular and ordered. The more finitely we perceive them, the more their inherent order becomes apparent." This statement relates back to Greiman's design aesthetic and underlying philosophy. By embracing the abstraction resulting from pixilated digital imagery, she gives us the means to investigate and uncover the mysterious potential of her chosen medium as evocatively as dreams, space, and simultaneity.

Challenging the Status Quo

In Western countries, for many centuries marginalized individuals had far fewer opportunities to become artists, because they were discriminated against on grounds of their gender, race, and/or social class, and they were rarely given the recognition granted to their white male counterparts. For example, women were not allowed to draw from the **nude** in their art classes until the nineteenth century. It was also believed that genius was a trait exclusively available to men, and language with a gender bias—such as using the word "masterpiece" to describe a great artwork—reinforced that belief. Before the 1970s few people even noticed that women and people of color had largely been excluded from the institutions and systems that produced acclaimed artists.

The feminist movement of the 1960s and 1970s significantly affected the production and understanding of artworks. Feminist artists and feminist critiques of art have expanded the subject matter and interpretation of art, making it more relevant to a wider set of issues and a wider range of experiences. As has been the case throughout history, artists give voice to experiences shared by many people. Acknowledging that women and artists of color had been left out of much of the history of art introduces the possibility that this situation can be rectified. By the late twentieth and early twenty-first centuries, an increased number of artworks made by diverse artists were being included in museums and galleries.

The American artist Judy Chicago (b. 1939) appreciated the achievements of such women as Artemisia Gentileschi (who was well respected during her lifetime in the seventeenth century, only to be subsequently overlooked and then rediscovered in the early twentieth century). Chicago realized that many women had been forgotten over time and, likewise, that women who seem prominent today might in the future also be omitted from history. From 1974 to 1979, Chicago worked on an epic sculpture called *The Dinner Party* (**4.9.7**), which honors women from different eras of history. The enormous triangular dinner table has thirteen place settings on each side. Every setting features a placemat, on which is **embroidered** the name of a famous historical or mythical woman, and an elaborate plate designed intentionally to resemble the shape of a butterfly or a vagina. The appearance of

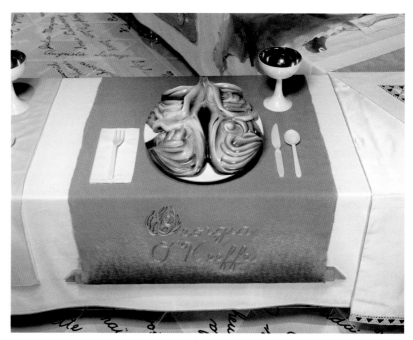

4.9.7 Judy Chicago, *The Dinner Party*, 1974–79. Installation view showing Georgia O'Keeffe place setting. Embroidery on linen and china paint on porcelain, entire work 48 × 48'. Brooklyn Museum, New York

all the elements on each setting was inspired by the woman whose place it is. Layers of lace designate the place of the nineteenth-century poet Emily Dickinson, while the plate for the artist Georgia O'Keeffe resembles a sculpted version of one of her **abstract** flower paintings. Artemisia Gentileschi's place setting has a brightly colored plate surrounded by lush fabric similar to the kind shown in her paintings.

Chicago made the table in the form of an equilateral triangle not only because the shape was an ancient sign for both woman and goddess, but also because it could be used here to symbolize the world of fairness and equality that feminists sought. She chose to have thirteen guests to a side both because there were thirteen witches in a coven and because it was an important number for those ancient religions that worshiped a mother goddess. (Both witches and goddesses were embraced by feminists as powerful symbols associated with women and counter to the patriarchy.) The number thirteen is also a reference to the biblical Last Supper, here reconfigured with women as the guests instead of Jesus and his twelve disciples. The idea of a dinner party—as well as the media, such as needlework and **ceramics**, which are included in her piece—evokes the role of woman as homemaker, which Chicago and other feminists believed should be admired and praised.

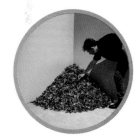

Félix Gonzàles-Torres used abstraction and audience participation to raise awareness about loss as a result of the AIDS epidemic:
→ see **2.10.11**, p. 341

Nude: an artistic representation of an unclothed human figure, emphasizing the body's form rather than its exposure

Embroidery: decorative stitching generally made with colored thread applied to the surface of a fabric

Abstract: art imagery that departs from recognizable images of the natural world

Ceramics: fire-hardened clay, often painted, and normally sealed with shiny protective coating

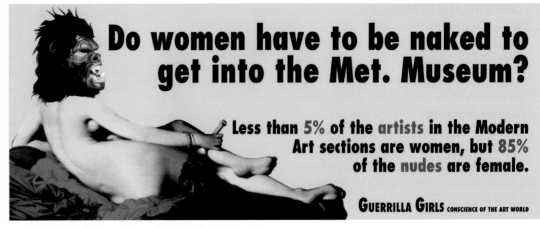

Do women have to be naked to get into the Met. Museum?

Less than 5% of the artists in the Modern Art sections are women, but 85% of the nudes are female.

GUERRILLA GIRLS CONSCIENCE OF THE ART WORLD

4.9.8 Guerrilla Girls, *Do Women Have to Be Naked to Get into the Met. Museum?*, 1989. Poster, dimensions variable

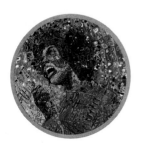

As seen in the work of Wadsworth Jarrell, art has often been used to draw attention to causes and inspire change, even revolution:
→ see **3.10.6**, p. 525

In 1985, a group of **intersectional** women artists in New York City formed a collective organization called the Guerrilla Girls to protest the unequal treatment of female artists in the art world. Their name indicates their willingness to engage in unconventional tactics in their fight for equality. The Guerrilla Girls, who are still active, are known for the gorilla masks their members wear to avoid being recognized by the art-world establishment and the institutions they might criticize. Their productions take the form of public protests and lectures as well as flyers and posters. One of their best-known posters, *Do Women Have to Be Naked to Get into the Met. Museum?* (**4.9.8**), includes statistics from the time the artwork was made to highlight the disproportionate representation of women artists (5 percent) compared to female nudes (85 percent) in the collection of the Metropolitan Museum

of Art in New York. As this poster shows, one of their principal goals is to oppose the lack of representation of women artists in major museum collections. In 2012, the Guerilla Girls updated their count and found that only 4 percent of the artists on display were women—worse than in 1989.

Also in the late twentieth century, nearly one hundred years after the Emancipation Proclamation, Black people in southern US states were still experiencing legalized discrimination and segregation that led directly to disenfranchisement, oppression, and violence. Using methods similar to those deployed by feminists, artists have brought attention to the experience of people of color and other marginalized groups.

The American artist and philosopher Adrian Piper (b. 1948) directly confronts racism and racial "passing" in her work of 1986, *My Calling (Card) #1 (for Dinners and Cocktail Parties)*. From 1986 to 1990, she performed this piece by handing out cards (**4.9.9**) in such social situations as dinner and cocktail parties. Many people assume, because of Piper's light skin tone, that she is white. For that reason, she has frequently encountered racist remarks that would likely be considered in poor taste to make (and therefore avoided) in the company of a Black person. After hearing a racist remark, she would hand the card to the person, to make them feel a similar discomfort to the way that their remarks have made her feel.

In the later part of the twentieth century, some contemporary artists adopted elements of **Minimalism** and **earthworks** (see Chapters 3.9, p. 518 and 2.4, p. 238) to inspire new ways of thinking. The art of these earlier movements—

Dear Friend,
    I am black.
    I am sure you did not realize this when you made/laughed at/agreed with that racist remark. In the past, I have attempted to alert white people to my racial identity in advance. Unfortunately, this invariably causes them to react to me as pushy, manipulative, or socially inappropriate. Therefore, my policy is to assume that white people do not make these remarks, even when they believe there are no black people present, and to distribute this card when they do.
    I regret any discomfort my presence is causing you, just as I am sure you regret the discomfort your racism is causing me.

4.9.9 Adrian Piper, *My Calling (Card) #1 (for Dinners and Cocktail Parties)*, 1986–present. Performance utensil: Business card with printed text on cardboard, 2 × 3½". Collection of the Adrian Piper Research Archive Foundation, Berlin, Germany

recognizable for featuring geometric shapes and a clean, industrial aesthetic—had itself challenged traditional notions of where art could be viewed and how works were made. Throughout his career, the American artist David Hammons (b. 1943) has been disrupting and extending the confines of the art world and the definitions associated with that sphere. His work references cultural stereotypes of race and class and focuses on the power of symbols. Hammons often uses such found objects as discarded bottles from the streets of Harlem and Brooklyn. In *Untitled (Night Train)*, empty bottles of inexpensive "bum wine" take the shape of an elegant abstract spiral. In this new context, the bottles are transformed (**4.9.10**). While the historical remnants remain intact—cheap (under $3), strong (18 percent ABV), and, emptied of its content, trash—the bottles take the form of high art in the pristine setting of an art gallery with a value that is dramatically heightened (for example, another sculpture by Hammons sold for $8 million in 2013).

Culture on Display

Puyukitchum/Ipai and Mexican American artist James Luna (1950–2018) used performance as a way of bringing cultural preconceptions/misconceptions to light in simultaneously humorous and serious ways. Luna sees his role as similar to that of the Native American ceremonial clowns, who call attention to norms of behavior by mimicking strangers and reversing the usual societal order to provoke laughter and send a strong message. Luna lived on the La Jolla Indian Reservation and built on his heritage and experience to comment on perceptions of Native Americans, which tend to be stereotypical and often offensive. In a performance of *Take a Picture with a Real Indian* (**4.9.11**), Luna wore an "outfit," as he called it, and stood stoically for the snapshots. The performance lasted until he felt "mad enough or humiliated enough. It's a dual humiliation." Even as these interactions can be lively and fun, they contrast simplistic preconceptions with his embodied reality as a living person, hopefully leaving people with the idea that "This isn't a joke."

The work of American filmmaker, director, producer, writer, and actor, Shelton Jackson "Spike" Lee (b. 1957) is characterized by its strong commitment to social justice issues,

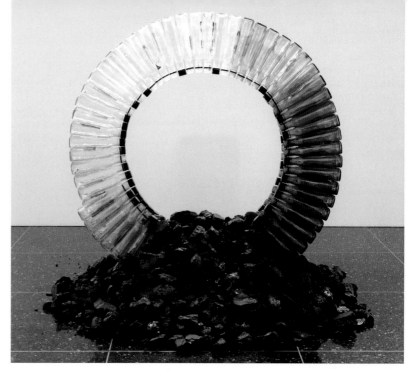

4.9.10 David Hammons, *Untitled (Night Train)*, 1989. Glass, silicon glue, and coal, 42 × 42 × 30". MoMA, New York

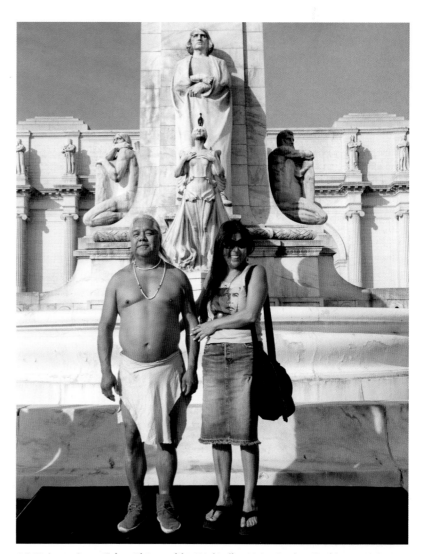

4.9.11 James Luna, *Take a Picture with a Real Indian*, Union Station, Washington, D.C., Columbus Day, October 11, 2010

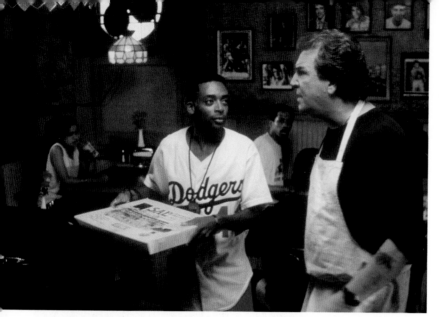

4.9.12 Spike Lee, still from *Do the Right Thing*, 1989. Duration 120 minutes. 40 Acres & A Mule Filmworks

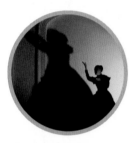

Yuki Kihara calls attention to issues of race and identity within a cultural context of colonialism, (mis)representation, and consumerism:

→ see **2.10.9**, p. 340

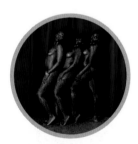

Contemporary artists have concentrated on bringing into the world of visual art the historical and lived experience of Black, Indigenous, People of Color (BIPOC): for example, see Kerry James Marshall → **1.10.10**, p. 169, Deana Lawson → **2.8.29**, p. 316, and Cannupa Hanska Luger → **3.4.27**, p. 425

and includes a film biography of Civil Rights leader Malcolm X (1992). Lee's landmark film *Do the Right Thing*, nominated for two academy awards, focuses on race relations between the Italian-American owner of Sal's Famous Pizzeria and the African-American residents of the neighborhood (**4.9.12**).

Modeled after Bedford-Stuyvesant, Lee's own Brooklyn neighborhood, and inspired by racial incidents in New York City in the 1980s, the movie also highlights the pervasiveness of institutionalized racism in America decades after the advancements of the Civil Rights movement. This movie makes a frank statement about race relations as tension builds over the course of a hot summer's day, with tragic consequences. The heavy content of the film is combined with inventive visuals, strong storytelling, humor, and music. Effective character development, which is sympathetic to all parties, highlights the complexity of the characters' various viewpoints, prejudices, and relationships with each other in a way that promotes understanding rather than perpetuating racial polarization.

Identity and Ambiguity

Our expectations of people are often based on stereotypes and on our ideas of what is normal for their culture, gender, or race. These stereotypes are frequently challenged, of course: women have been primary breadwinners, worked in mines, and gone to war; men have been nurturers and raised children; and a Black man has been elected

President of the United States. In recent years, it has become more acceptable to address the ways in which people transcend the conventional boundaries of identity. Public awareness of such issues as transgender and non-binary identity has been raised by increasingly open discussion. Investigations of the ways that bodies and identities can be transformed and racial identity can be transcended, however, are not entirely new to art. The question of identity is one that artists from many cultures and eras of history have sought to address. When the artworks are effective, they lead to a greater understanding of individuality.

Almost 3,500 years ago, ancient Egypt was governed by a woman called Hatshepsut, who abandoned the confines of gender that were customary during her lifetime. She was arguably the most powerful of the handful of female rulers in Egyptian history. Hatshepsut controlled the kingdom for about twenty years in the fifteenth century BCE, first as regent for her stepson and nephew Thutmose III, and then as pharaoh in her own right. To legitimize her reign in a society that equated masculinity with ruling power, Hatshepsut emphasized the fact that she was her father's choice as successor, ahead of her two brothers and half-brother. She also claimed direct lineage from Amun, the chief god who was worshiped at that time.

We may never fully know the extent to which she was subverting gender norms or playing with gender identity, but the fact that she wanted (or needed) to look like a man in order to shape perceptions about her identity and power seems clear. As did all Egyptian rulers, Hatshepsut commissioned many sculptures and relief carvings to replicate and immortalize her image. A few show her as a woman, but she is most often depicted in the conventional poses and clothing of a male king. The image in **4.9.13** is one of a group of sphinxes that all possess Hatshepsut's face. It was not uncommon for pharaohs to be represented in the form of a sphinx, a creature with the body of a lion and the head of a human. The artist has clearly followed the guidelines for depicting male pharaohs, including the traditional headcloth and royal beard. But, although the portrait is idealized, the sculptor has not attempted to disguise the delicate lines of Hatshepsut's own features.

For her *Projects* series, the Korean artist Nikki S. Lee (b. 1970) joined a number of different U.S. communities, from yuppies to lesbians, in places from trailer parks to tourist destinations. She shopped in the stores they frequented, listened to their music, and adopted their mannerisms. After radically changing her physical presentation, and once she felt she had become a genuine member of the group, she had a snapshot self-portrait taken with her new peers. Although she told the people in the close-knit groups she joined that she was an artist, most of them did not believe her. For her *Seniors Project* of 1999, Lee used a makeup artist and thoroughly convinced them she was a legitimate elderly acquaintance; they considered her story about being an artist to be a sign of her senility (**4.9.14a**). For the *Exotic Dancers* project in 2000, Lee went on a diet and then immersed herself in a radically different subculture: adult entertainment and striptease (**4.9.14b**). Such guises as the ones in *Projects* may be seen as a sign of connection for Lee, who genuinely likes people and considers her identity to be very fluid. However, what seemed a post-ethnic rejection of essentializing identity in the 1990s has been revisited by some artworld viewers, after the racial reckoning of 2020, as a more problematic example of **cultural appropriation**. In a 2006 interview Lee said, "Western culture is very much about the individual, while Eastern culture is more about identity in the context of society. You simply cannot think of yourself out of context."

American artist Catherine Opie (b. 1961) uses photography to investigate the nuances of gender and identity. Her pictures include studio portraits of her lesbian friends dressed

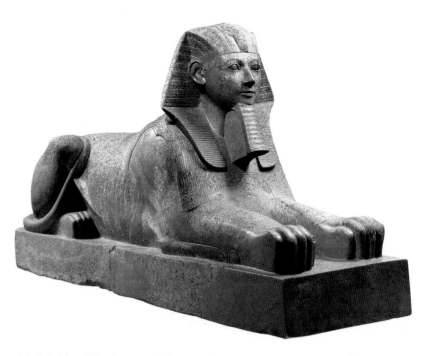

4.9.13 Sphinx of Hatshepsut, 18th Dynasty, Egypt, 1479–1458 BCE. Granite and paint, 5'4⅝" × 11'3". Metropolitan Museum of Art, New York

in leather or wearing false facial hair; staged depictions of radical performance artists; high school football games; and landscapes.

Opie created her *Domestic* series while traveling across the US in order to photograph lesbian couples, such as Melissa and Lake, in their everyday settings (**4.9.15**, p. 658). This photograph accentuates some of the similarities in the couple's appearance, such as their short haircuts with bangs. The point of the picture, however, is their bond, not their gender or sexual identity. Opie's portraits, by highlighting the lesbian community, introduce some viewers to new ways of life. They remind others that the familiar people, places, and things we see each day can be thought of in new

Cultural appropriation: when objects from or elements of a non-dominant culture or identity are adopted by a dominant culture without respect for their original meaning or significance

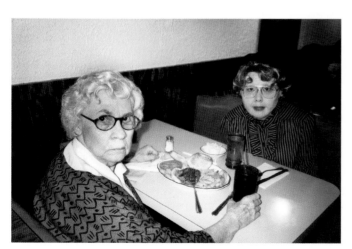

4.9.14a Nikki S. Lee, *Seniors Project*, 1999. Fujiflex print

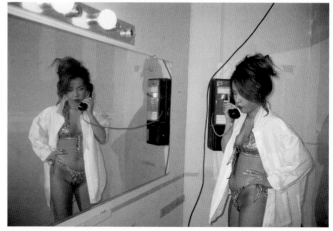

4.9.14b Nikki S. Lee, *The Exotic Dancers Project (31)*, 2000. Color photograph

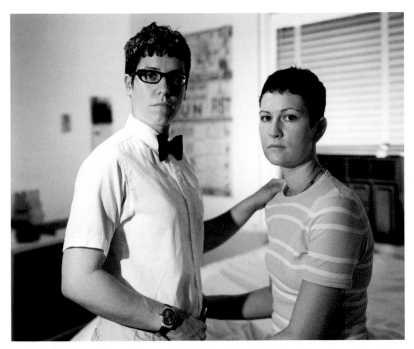

4.9.15 **Catherine Opie**, "**Melissa & Lake**, **Durham**, **North Carolina**," from *Domestic* series, 1998. Chromogenic print, 40 × 50″

ways. Such pictures are not about difference—they are celebrations of individuality.

American Wu Tsang (b. 1982) started her career in filmmaking as a community organizer and activist for marginalized voices, especially the LGBTQ+ community. Tsang now uses performance to explore the elusiveness of identity in order to shift the way people think about others. Like most works by Tsang, the 2016 film *Duilian* (**4.9.16a** and **b**) is a hybrid documentary/fiction. During a trip to China to investigate her personal roots, Tsang learned about the nineteenth-century feminist poet and revolutionary Qiu Jin. Tsang became fascinated with her life and eventually cast her own artistic collaborator, performance artist boychild (Tosh Basco) to play Qiu Jin. In a twist of art mimicking life, Tsang played the role of Qiu Jin's intimate friend and collaborator, calligrapher Wu Zhiying. This love story transcends space and time, set in a country where it was illegal to be gay until 1997 and where trans people are still virtually invisible.

The film's title, *Duilian*, refers to a form of poetry consisting of antithetical couplets and the wushu style of martial arts, like a dance with swords. Set in contemporary Hong Kong, the performance brings in the past through nineteenth-century clothing, abstract imagery, and voiceovers that include lines of Qiu Jin's poetry: "The bones I bring from a former existence regret the flesh that covers them"; and "My body will not allow me to mingle with men but my heart is far braver than that of a man...How could they with their vulgar minds understand me?"

Duilian was not meant to be a strict account of Qiu Jin's life or of her relationship with Wu Zhiying. Rather, it was interpreted through the artist's imagination and complemented by her lived experience. Tsang's artistic translation operates similarly to history: both modes construct identity through language and storytelling.

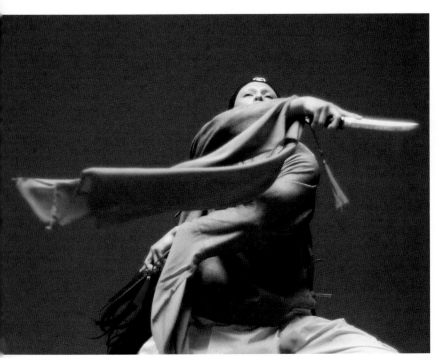

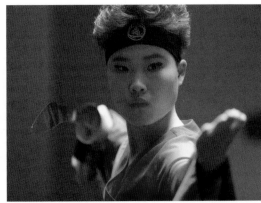

4.9.16a and b **Wu Tsang**, *Duilian*, 2016. Single-channel HD video with Dolby 5.1 Surround Sound, 26 minutes.

Explore Further   Identity, Race, and Gender in Art

Self-Portraits

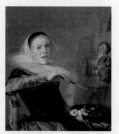

0.0.11 Judith Leyster, *Self-Portrait*, c. 1630 → p. 22

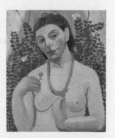

3.9.1 Paula Modersohn-Becker, *Self-Portrait as a Half-Length Nude…*, 1906 → p. 501

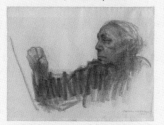

2.1.12 Käthe Kollwitz, *Self-Portrait, Drawing*, 1933 → p. 185

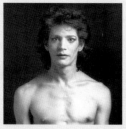

1.10.9 Robert Mapplethorpe, *Self-Portrait (#385)*, 1980 → p. 168

Challenging the Status Quo

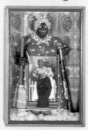

2.4.18 Betye Saar, *The Liberation of Aunt Jemima*, 1972 → p. 240

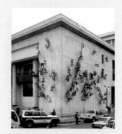

3.4.7 Doris Salcedo, *Noviembre 6 y 7*, 2002 → p. 415

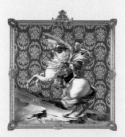

4.5.4a Kehinde Wiley, *Napoleon Leading the Army…*, 2005 → p. 595

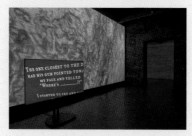

2.9.16c Sondra Perry, *Typhoon coming on*, 2018 → p. 329

Culture on Display

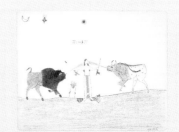

3.4.25 Wo-Haw, *Wo-Haw between Two Worlds*, c. 1875–77 → p. 424

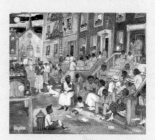

1.10.6 Palmer Hayden, *Midsummer Night in Harlem*, 1936 → p. 165

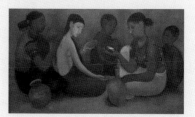

1.8.2 Amrita Sher-Gil, *Bride's Toilet*, 1937 → p. 141

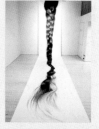

2.1.14 Zhang Chun Hong, *Life Strands*, 2004 → p. 186

Your turn

How do these artworks relate to the ideas discussed in this chapter?

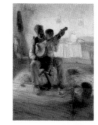

3.8.21 Henry Ossawa Tanner, *Banjo Lesson*, 1893 → p. 496

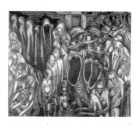

2.1.4 John Biggers, *Night of the Poor*, preparatory study, 1949 → p. 181

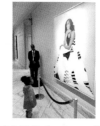

0.0.13 Parker Curry with Sherald's *Portrait of Michelle Obama*, 2018 → p. 24

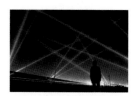

3.4.19 Rafael Lozano-Hemmer, *Border Tuner*, 2019 → p. 421

Glossary

NOTE: Some terms have more than one definition, depending on the context in which they are used.

3-D modeling: a computer-generated illusion that emulates an object in three dimensions; it can be modified to show visual movement

A-frame: an ancient form of structural support, made out of beams arranged so that the shape of the building resembles a capital letter A

Abstract: (1) art imagery that departs from recognizable images of the natural world; (2) an artwork the form of which is simplified, distorted, or exaggerated in appearance. It may represent a recognizable form that has been slightly altered, or it may be a completely non-representational depiction

Abstract Expressionism: a mid-twentieth-century artistic style characterized by its capacity to convey intense emotions using non-representational images

Abstraction: the degree to which an image is altered from an easily recognizable subject

Academies: institutions training artists in both the theory of art and practical techniques

Acrylic: a liquid polymer, or plastic, which is used as a binder for pigment in acrylic paint

Action painting: the application of paint to canvas by dripping, splashing, or smearing that emphasizes the artist's gestures

Actual line: a continuous, uninterrupted line

Additive (sculpture): a sculpting process in which the artist builds a form by adding material

Additive color: the colors produced from light

Additive color process: creates colors by mixing RGB colors on a screen to create a direct positive print; same principle used in LED, LCD, plasma, and CRT video screens

Aesthetic: related to beauty, art, and taste

Afterimage effect: when the eye sees the complementary color of something that the viewer has spent an extended time viewing (also known as successive contrast)

Aisles: in a basilica or other church, the spaces between the columns of the nave and the side walls

Alloy: a mixture of a metal combined with at least one other element

Altar: an area where sacrifices or offerings are made

Altarpiece: an artwork that is placed behind an altar in a church

Ambulatory: a covered walkway, particularly around the apse of a church

American Scene: a naturalistic style of painting in the US from the 1920s to 1950s that celebrated American themes, locations, and virtues

Amphora: a type of pot used to carry and store such goods as wine or olive oil

Analog: photography or a movie made using a film camera that chemically records images using a continuous gradation of value ranges from light to dark so that they directly match the actual appearance of the object or scene

Analogous colors: colors adjacent to each other on the color wheel

Analysis: a detailed examination of the structure of an artwork

Anamorphosis: the distorted representation of an object so that it appears correctly proportioned only when viewed from one particular position

Animation: a genre of film made using stop-motion, hand-drawn, or digitally produced still images set into motion by showing them in sequence

Appropriation: the deliberate incorporation in an artwork of material originally created by other artists

Apse: a semicircular vaulted space in a church

Aquatint: an intaglio printmaking process that uses melted rosin or spray paint to create an acid-resistant ground

Aqueduct: a structure designed to carry water, often over long distances

Arabesque: an abstract pattern derived from geometric and vegetal lines and forms

Arcade: a series of connected arches

Archaeology: the study of human history and prehistory by excavating sites of habitation to analyze artifacts and other cultural remains

Archaic: Greek art of the period *c.* 620–480 BCE

Arch: a structure, usually curved, that spans an opening

Architectural order: a style of designing columns and related parts of a Greek or Roman building

Architrave: a beam that rests on the top of a row of columns

Armature: a framework or skeleton used to support a sculpture

Armory Show: an exhibition in 1913 in New York City that introduced America to Modernist European abstraction; continues as an annual international exhibition

Art Brut: literally "raw art," or art that is outside of the academic tradition; a term invented by Jean Dubuffet

Art market: the economic space in which artworks are bought and sold

Art Nouveau: French for "new art," a visual style of the late nineteenth and early twentieth century, characterized by organic flowing lines, simulating forms in nature and involving decorative pattern

Artifact: an object made by a person

Artist's book: a book produced by an artist, usually an expensive limited edition, often using specialized printing processes

Assemblage: an artwork made of three-dimensional materials, including found objects

Asymmetry: a type of design in which balance is achieved by elements that contrast and complement one another without being the same on either side of an axis

Atmospheric perspective (also called **Aerial perspective):** the use of shades of color and clarity to create the illusion of depth. Closer objects have warmer tones and clear outlines, while objects set further away are cooler and become hazy

Atrium: a central, normally public, interior space, first used in Roman houses

Auction: an event in which artworks are sold to the highest bidder

Auteur theory/auteur films: from the French word for "author," refers to films that notably reflect the director's creative vision above other criteria

Autochrome: an early additive color photography process patented by the Lumière brothers in 1904 and primarily used from 1907 to the 1930s

Automatic: suppressing conscious control to access subconscious sources of creativity and truth

Avant-garde: an early twentieth-century emphasis on artistic innovation, which challenged accepted values, traditions, and techniques

Axis: an imaginary line showing the center of a shape, volume, or composition

Background: the part of a work depicted furthest from the viewer's space, often behind the main subject matter

Balance: a principle of art in which elements are used to create a symmetrical or asymmetrical sense of visual weight in an artwork

Baroque: a European artistic and architectural style of the late sixteenth to early eighteenth century, characterized by extravagance and emotional intensity

Bas-relief (low relief): a sculpture carved with very little depth: the carved subjects rise only slightly above the surface of the work

Base: the projecting series of blocks between the shaft of a column and its plinth

Basilica: an early Christian church, either converted from or built to resemble a type of Roman civic building

Bauhaus: design school founded in Weimar, Germany, in 1919

Ben-Day dots: a technique used in printing to create gradations and suggest a range of tones; named for its inventor

Binder: a substance that makes pigments adhere to a surface

Bioart: art that is created with living, changing organisms

Biopic: a movie that tells the story of a person's life, often filling in facts with narration and plotlines

Bird's-eye view: an artistic technique in which a scene or subject is presented from some point above it

Bisqueware: a ceramic form that has been fired but not glazed or that has not received other surface finishing

Black-figure vase painting: in ancient Greece, figures painted in black slip on a red clay body

Blueprint: a paper with a plan drawing for a building printed on it

Bohemian: derived from the gypsies of the former Czech Kingdom of Bohemia who moved around; a wanderer; an artist or writer who functions outside the bounds of conventional rules and practices

Boldface: a darker and heavier typeface than its normal instance

Bust: a statue of a person depicting only the head and shoulders

Byzantine: relating to the East Roman empire, centered on Constantinople (modern-day Istanbul) from the fifth century CE to 1453

Calligram: a word or piece of text that is laid out so that it creates a visual image related to the meaning of the word or piece of text

Calligraphy: the art of emotive or carefully descriptive hand lettering or handwriting

Canon of proportions: a set of ideal mathematical ratios in art, used to measure the various parts of the human body in relation to one another

Cantilever: a long beam or lintel that projects out from a structure beyond a support

Capital: the architectural feature that crowns a column

Cardinal points: North, South, East, and West

Caricature: a picture of a person in which certain striking characteristics are exaggerated in order to create a comic or grotesque effect

Cartoon: a full-scale preparatory drawing for a painting or tapestry; from the Italian *cartone*, meaning "large sheet of paper"

Cast: a sculpture or artwork made by pouring a liquid (for example molten metal or plaster) into a mold

Catacombs: an underground system of tunnels used for burying and commemorating the dead

Celluloid: tough, transparent plastic used to make motion-picture film, photographic film, and X-rays; until relatively recently most movies were filmed on celluloid

Censorship: the suppression or prohibition of a work of art

Central-plan church: a church design, often in the shape of a cross with all four arms of equal length

Ceramic: fire-hardened clay, often painted, and normally sealed with a shiny protective coating

Ceramist: a person who makes ceramics

CGI: computer-generated imagery

Chaplet: a metal support rod used in casting

Chasing: a technique of hammering the front of a metal object to create a form or surface detail

Chiaroscuro: the use of light and dark in a painting to create the impression of volume

Chilkat: traditional form of weaving practiced by Tlingit and other Northwest Coast peoples of Alaska and British Columbia

Choir: part of a church traditionally reserved for singers and clergy, situated between the nave and the apse

Chroma (also known as **Saturation**): the degree of purity of a color

Chromogenic prints (c-prints): the most widespread color process until digital prints; dyes couple with developers to create a negative image, reversed to make positive prints

Cibachrome: a dye-destruction process for making direct positive photographic images available in the 1960s

Circumambulation: the act of walking around a sacred object

Classical: (1) Greek art of the period *c.* 480–323 BCE; (2) ancient Greek and Roman; (3) art that conforms to Greek and Roman models, or is based on rational construction and emotional equilibrium

Clerestory windows: a row of windows high up in a church to admit light into the nave

Cloud (or the Cloud): can refer to any electronic network; generally refers to shared resources on the Internet rather than local servers or devices for storage and computer applications

CMY: the primary colors used in inkjet printing: cyan, magenta, and blue

CMYK: a subtractive system based on the primary colors used in four-color printing: cyan, magenta, blue, and key (black)

Coffered: decorated with recessed paneling

Coiling: (1) the use of long coils of clay—rather than a wheel—to build the walls of a pottery vessel; (2) a basket-weaving technique using a central foundation that is spiraled or coiled, and wrapped with another fiber that is stitched back into the previous row

Collage: a work of art assembled by gluing materials, often paper, onto a surface. From the French *coller*, to glue

Collagraphy, collagraphic, collagraph: a type of relief print that is created by building up or collaging material on or to a stiff surface, inking that surface, then printing

Collodion (wet plate) process: a black-and-white darkroom photography process invented by Frederick Scott Archer in 1850–51 and popular until the 1880s

Color: the optical effect caused when reflected white light of the spectrum is divided into separate wavelengths

Color Field painting: a branch of Abstract Expressionism focusing on non-objective abstractions

Color theory: the understanding of how colors relate to one another, especially when mixed or placed together in close proximity

Column: a freestanding pillar, usually circular in section

Complementary colors: colors opposite one another on the color wheel

Composite view: the representation of a subject from multiple viewpoints at one time

Composition: the overall design or organization of a work

Conceptual art: a work in which the ideas are most important to the work

Concrete: a hard, strong, and versatile construction material made up of powdered lime, sand, and rubble

Conservation: scientific efforts to preserve artworks

Constructivism: an art movement in the Soviet Union in the 1920s, primarily concerned with making art that is of use to the working class

Content: the meaning, message, or feeling expressed in a work of art

Context: circumstances surrounding the creation of a work of art, including historical events, social conditions, biographical facts about the artist and their intentions

Continuous narrative: when different parts of a story are shown within the same visual space

Contour: the outline that defines a form, but not necessarily the complete outline of a shape

Contour rivalry: a design in which the lines can be read in more than one way at the same time, depending on the angle from which it is viewed

Contrapposto: a pose in sculpture in which the upper part of the body twists in one direction and the lower part in another

Contrast: a drastic difference between such elements as color or value (lightness/darkness) when they are presented together

Convention: a widely accepted way of doing something; using a particular style, following a certain method, or representing something in a specific way

Convex: curved outward, like the exterior of a sphere

Corbeled: with a series of corbels—architectural feature made of stone, brick, wood, etc.—each projecting beyond the one below

Corinthian column: a type of Classical column with an ornate capital, common in ancient Roman architecture

Corinthian architectural order: a Classical style of architecture characterized by ornate leaves on the capitals

Cornice: a horizontally projecting molding round the top of a building

Cor-ten steel: a type of steel that forms a coating of rust that protects it from the weather and further corrosion

Critique: detailed assessment or evaluation of an artwork

Cropping: trimming the edges of an image, or composing it so that part of the subject matter is cut off

Cross-hatching: the use of overlapping parallel lines to convey darkness or lightness

Cubism, Cubist: a twentieth-century movement and style in art, especially painting, in which perspective with a single viewpoint was abandoned and use was made of simple geometric shapes, interlocking planes, and, later, collage; the Cubists were artists who formed part of the movement. The term Cubist is also used to describe their style of painting

Cultural appropriation: when objects from or elements of a non-dominant culture or identity are adopted by a dominant culture without respect for their original meaning or significance

Cuneiform: a form of writing from ancient Mesopotamia that uses wedge shapes

Cyanotype: a photographic process using light-sensitive iron salts that oxidize and produce a brilliant blue color where light penetrates and remain white where light is blocked; a variant of this process was used historically to copy architectural drawings

Cyclorama: a theatrical precursor to the IMAX, in which a painting covers cylindrical walls to create a 360-degree panorama

Dada: anarchic anti-art and anti-war movement, dating back to World War I, that reveled in absurdity and irrationality

De Stijl: a group of artists originating in The Netherlands in the early twentieth century, associated with a utopian style of design that emphasized primary colors and straight lines

Décollage: a work of art created by cutting, tearing off or removing parts of an image

Decorative: intentionally making an artwork pleasant or attractive

Depth: (1) the degree of recession in perspective; (2) the impression of three dimensions in a two-dimensional artwork

Der Blaue Reiter: ("The Blue Rider") a German Expressionist movement (1911–14) in Munich; used abstract forms to suggest spiritual content as a contrast to the corruption and materialism of the times

Developer: after an image has been recorded on light-sensitive film or photographic paper (usually in a camera), immersion in this liquid substance chemically transforms a latent (or invisible) image into a visible one

Diagonal: a line that runs obliquely, rather than horizontally or vertically

Die Brücke: ("The Bridge") a German Expressionist movement of painters and printmakers formed in Dresden (1905–13) with the aim of defying anything Classical and using art as a bridge between the past, present, and a utopian future

Documentary: non-fiction films based on actual people, settings, and events

Dome: an evenly curved vault forming the ceiling or roof of a building

Door jamb: vertical sections, often containing sculpture, that form the sides of a portal

Doric architectural order: a Classical style of architecture characterized by weighty columns and a frieze with triglyphs and metopes

Drypoint: an intaglio printmaking process where the artist raises a burr when gouging the printing plate

Dubbing: the post-production addition or mixing of voices (or sounds) that do not belong to the original recording

Earthworks: artworks made using the earth or natural elements; typically situated outdoors, most people experience earthworks only through photographs

Edition: all the copies of a print made from a single printing

Elements of art: the basic vocabulary of art—line, shape, form, volume, mass, texture, value (lightness/darkness), space, color, and motion and time

Embroidery: decorative stitching generally made with colored thread applied to the surface of a fabric

Emphasis: the principle of drawing attention to particular content in a work

En plein air: French for "in the open air"; used to describe painting out of doors from start to finish rather than working in a studio for all or part of the process

Encaustic: a painting medium that primarily uses wax, usually beeswax, as the binding agent

Engraving: a printmaking technique where the artist gouges or scratches the image into the surface of the printing plate

Enlightenment: an intellectual movement in eighteenth-century Europe that argued for science, reason, and individualism. Challenging received ideas passed down by tradition, the Enlightenment also promoted the notion of equal rights for all people

Entablature: the part of a Greek or Roman building that rests on top of a column

Entasis: the slight swelling or bulge at the midpoint of a column

Epic: a style or genre in film/television that focuses on grand-scale storytelling with dramatic music, elaborate costumes, and high production values; may use historical events or people but does not focus on historical accuracy

Etching: an intaglio printmaking process that uses acid to bite (or etch) the engraved design into the printing surface

Exhibition: the display of art objects, often only for a limited time

Expressionism, Expressionist: an artistic style, at its height in 1920s Europe, devoted to representing subjective emotions and experiences instead of objective or external reality

Expressionistic: devoted to representing subjective emotions and experiences instead of objective or external reality

Expressive: capable of stirring the emotions of the viewer

Facade: any side of a building, usually the front or entrance

Faience: quartz or sand, ground and heated to create a shiny, glasslike material

Fantasy: a fiction genre set in an imaginary universe; often uses magical or supernatural elements in the plots, themes, or settings

Fauves, Fauvism: an early twentieth-century art movement that emphasized bold, exaggerated colors and simplified forms to favor creative expression over accuracy. From the French *fauve*, "wild beast"

Figurative: art that portrays items perceived in the visible world, especially human or animal forms

Figure–ground reversal: the reversal of the relationship between one shape (the figure) and its background (the ground), so that the figure becomes the background and the ground becomes the figure

Film: a thin, flexible material with light-sensitive emulsion exposed in a camera to produce photographs or motion pictures; when used to describe a movie, the word often has artistic or professional connotations

Fin de Siècle: French for "end of the century"; usually refers to the end of the nineteenth century

Firing: heating ceramic, glass, or enamel objects in a kiln, to harden them, fuse the components, or fuse a glaze to the surface

Fixing: the chemical process used to ensure a photographic image becomes permanent

Flashback: a transition to an earlier time in a story that disrupts the chronological order of events

Flint: an object or tool made from the very hard, sharp-edged stone of the same name

Flying buttress: an arch built on the exterior of a building that transfers some of the weight of the vault

Focal point: the center of interest or activity in a work of art, often drawing the viewer's attention to the most important element

Foreground: the part of a work depicted as nearest to the viewer

Foreshortening: a perspective technique that depicts a form—often distorting or reducing it—at an angle that is not parallel to the picture plane, in order to convey the illusion of depth

Form: an object that can be defined in three dimensions (height, width, and depth)

Formal: in art, refers to the visual elements and principles in a work

Formal analysis: a visual study that includes careful description of the artwork and its use of elements and principles

Format: the shape of the area an artist uses for making a two-dimensional artwork

Found image or object: an image or object found by an artist and presented, with little or no alteration, as part of a work or as a finished work of art in itself

Frame: a single image from the sequence that makes up a motion picture; on average, a 90-minute film contains 129,600 separate frames

Freestanding: any sculpture that stands separate from walls or other surfaces so that it can be viewed from a 360-degree range

Fresco: a technique in which the artist paints onto freshly applied plaster. From the Italian *fresco*, "fresh"

Frieze: the strip that goes around the top of a building, often filled with sculptural ornamentation

Frontispiece: an illustration facing the title page of a book

Futurism, Futurist: an artistic movement originating in Italy in 1909 that violently rejected traditional forms in favor of celebrating and incorporating into art the energy and dynamism of modern technology; Futurists were artists working in this style

Gelatin silver print process (or **silver gelatin**): process for making glossy black-and-white photographic prints in the

darkroom based on silver halide gelatin emulsions
Gèlèdé ritual: a ritual performed in Nigeria's Yoruba society to celebrate and honor women
Genre: a category of artistic subject matter, often with a strongly influential history and tradition
Genre scenes: in painting, scenes that depict everyday life
Geometric: (1) predictable and mathematical; (2) in art, inspired by geometric shapes, such as circles, squares, and triangles
Geometric form: a three-dimensional form composed of predictable and mathematically derived planes and curves
Gesso: a substance similar to white acrylic paint, used to make a surface smooth for painting
Gestalt: complete order and indivisible unity of all aspects of an artwork's design
GIF (graphics interchange format): a compressed image file type intended to reduce transfer time
Glazing: in oil painting, adding a transparent layer of paint to achieve a richness in texture, volume, and form
Glyph: a carved figure referring to a sound, word, or idea
Golden Section: a unique ratio of a line divided into two segments so that the sum of both segments (a + b) is to the longer segment (a) as the longer segment (a) is to the shorter segment (b). The result is 1:1.618
Gothic: a Western European architectural style of the twelfth to sixteenth century, characterized by the use of pointed arches and ornate decoration
Gouache: a type of paint medium in which pigments are bound with gum and a white filler added (for example, clay) to produce a paint that is used for opaque watercolor
Graffiti: markings that are scratched, scribbled, or sprayed on a wall without the consent of the owner
Grand Tour: in the seventeenth to mid-nineteenth century, a trip for the cultured and wealthy to study Classical and Renaissance artworks and culture found mostly in Italy
Graphic design: the use of images, typography, and technology to communicate ideas for a client or to a particular audience
Greenware: a clay form that has been shaped and dried, but not yet fired to become ceramic
Grid: a network of horizontal and vertical lines; in an artwork's composition, the lines are implied
Grisaille: a painting in gray or grayish monochrome, either as a base or underpainting for the finished work, or as the final artwork itself
Groin vault: an architectural feature created by the intersection of two vaults into the nave
Ground: the surface or background onto which an artist paints or draws
Guilds: medieval European associations of artists, craftspeople, or tradespeople

Hand-tint: an early process for adding color to monochrome photographic products by adding pigment in a manner very much like painting
Happening: impromptu art actions, initiated and planned by an artist, the outcome of which is not known in advance
Harlem Renaissance: a movement in literature, music, and the visual arts from the end of WWI into the 1930s, celebrating Black experience and culture
Hatching: the use of non-overlapping parallel lines to convey darkness or lightness
Hellenistic: Greek art of the period *c.* 323–100 BCE
Hemispherical: having half the form of a spherical shape divided into identical, symmetrical parts
Hierarchical scale: the use of size to denote the relative importance of subjects in an artwork
Hieroglyph: a written language involving sacred characters that may be pictures as well as letters or signifiers of sounds
High relief: a carved panel where the figures project with a great deal of depth from the background
Highlight: an area of lightest value in a work
Historical drama: based on real-life events or time periods; can be factual or fictionalized
Hue: the general classification of a color; the distinctive characteristics of a color as seen in the visible spectrum, such as green or red
Humanism, humanist: the study of such subjects as history, philosophy, languages, and literature, particularly in relation to those of ancient Greece and Rome

Icon: (1) a religious image venerated by believers; (2) a small, often portable, religious image venerated by Christian believers; first used by the Eastern Orthodox Church
Iconic: Possessing established and widely recognizable characteristics
Iconoclasm: the destruction of images or artworks, often out of religious belief
Iconography: the study of the symbolic meaning of an artwork or the general study of symbolism
Iconographic analysis: the study of art by interpreting symbols, themes, and subject matter as sources of meaning
Ideal: more beautiful, harmonious, or perfect than reality; or exists as an idea
Idealism: elevating depictions of nature to achieve more beautiful, harmonious, and perfect depictions
Idealized: represented as perfect in form or character, corresponding to an ideal
Illuminated characters: highly decorated letters, usually found at the beginning of a page or paragraph
Illuminated manuscript: a hand-lettered text with hand-drawn pictures
Illuminations: illustrations and decorations in a manuscript
Illusionism, Illusionistic: the artistic skill or trick of making something look real
IMAX: "Image Maximum," a format for film presentation that allows presentation of films at ten times larger sizes than the conventional one
Impasto: paint applied in thick layers
Implied line: a line not actually drawn but suggested by the position of elements in the work, for example, an aligned series of dots
Implied texture: a visual illusion expressing texture
Impression: an individual print, or pull, from a printing press
Impressionism, Impressionist: in the visual arts, a late nineteenth-century style conveying the fleeting impression of the effects of light; Impressionists were artists working in this style
In situ: in the location for which it was originally made
In the round: a freestanding sculpted work that can be viewed from all sides
Incised: cut into a surface
Installation: originally referring to the hanging of pictures and arrangement of objects in an exhibition, installation may also refer to an intentional environment created as a completed artwork
Intaglio: any print process where the inked image is lower than the surface of the printing plate; from the Italian for "cut into"
Intarsia: the art of setting pieces of wood into a surface to create a pattern
Intensity: the relative clarity of color in its purest raw form, demonstrated through luminous or muted variations
Intercessor: one who pleads with God on behalf of others
Investment: a casting mold that is used in the final phase of lost-wax bronze casting
Interpretation: explaining the meaning of an artwork
Intersectional: an analytical framework for understanding how aspects of a person's social and political identities create modes of discrimination and privilege
Ionic architectural order: a Classical style of architecture characterized by narrow columns and volutes (scrolls) on the capitals
Isometric perspective: a system using diagonal parallel lines to communicate depth

Ka: in Egyptian belief, the spirit of a person that leaves the body upon death and travels to the afterlife
Kente cloth: an African textile made of interwoven strips of silk and cotton fabric; native to the Asante and Akan groups of Ghana and traditionally worn by royalty and state officials
Key-frame animation: a technique in which an animator creates important frames in the sequence, and software fills in the gaps
Kinetic art/sculpture: three-dimensional art that moves, impelled by air currents, motors, or people
Kinetic typography: an animation design process that features moving text
Kodachrome: created by Kodak Research Laboratories, Kodachrome is a subtractive reversal process for making color photographic film slides
***Krater*:** a container for mixing wine with water, into which cups can then be dipped to ladle out the diluted wine for drinking
Kufic: an Arabic script, angular in form; often used to copy the Koran.

Lapis lazuli: a bright-blue semiprecious stone containing sodium aluminum silicate and sulphur
Light: depicting a light source, applying contrasts of light and dark, or manipulating the emission of light in an artwork
Line: a mark, or implied mark, between two endpoints
Linear outline: a line that clearly separates a figure from its surroundings
Linear perspective: a system using converging imaginary sight lines to create the illusion of depth
Lintel: the horizontal beam over the doorway of a portal
Literati: Chinese scholar-painters who created expressive paintings rather than formal academic works
Lithography, lithographic: a print process executed on a flat, unmarred surface, such as a stone, in which the image is created using oil-based ink with resistance to water
Logo: a unique graphic image used to identify an idea or entity
Low relief: carving in which the design stands out only slightly from the background surface
Luminosity: a bright, glowing quality
Mandala: a sacred diagram of the universe, often involving a square and a circle
Mandorla: in art, an almond-shaped light, resembling a halo, which surrounds a holy person
Mannerism: from Italian *maniera*, meaning 'stylish style'; a mid- to late sixteenth-century style of painting, usually with elongated human figures, elevating grace as an ideal
Manuscripts: handwritten texts
Mask: in spray painting or silkscreen printing, a barrier, the shape of which blocks the paint or ink from passing through
Masquerade: a performance in which participants wear masks and costumes for a ritual or cultural purpose
Mass: a volume that has, or gives the illusion of having, weight, density, and bulk
Matrix: an origination point, such as a woodblock, from which a print is derived
Medieval: *see* Middle Ages
Medium (plural **media**): the material on or from which an artist chooses to make a work of art, for example canvas and oil paint, marble, engraving, video, or architecture
***Memento mori*:** a Latin phrase that means "remember that you must die." In artworks, such symbols as skulls, flowers, and clocks are used to represent the transient nature of life on Earth
Metope: a square space between triglyphs, often decorated with sculpture
Mezzotint: an intaglio print-making process based on roughening the entire printing plate to accept ink; the artist smooths non-image areas
Middle Ages: the time period roughly between the fall of the Roman empire and the start of the Renaissance
Middle ground: the part of a work between the foreground and the background
***Mihrab*:** a niche in a mosque that is in a wall oriented toward Mecca
Minaret: a tall slender tower, particularly on a mosque, from which the faithful are called to prayer
***Minbar*:** a platform in a mosque, from which a leader delivers sermons
Minimalism, Minimalist: a mid-twentieth-century artistic style that references industrial production modes through materials and seriality, often with unified arrangements of geometric shapes and massive forms that become part of the viewer's space
Mirror writing: writing that reads correctly only when reflected in a mirror, as in the case of the journals and other writings of Leonardo da Vinci
Mixed media: the use of a variety of materials to make a work of art
Mobile: suspended moving sculptures, usually impelled by natural air currents
Modeling: the representation of three-dimensional objects in two dimensions so that they appear solid
Modernism, Modernist: a radically new twentieth-century art and architectural movement that embraced modern industrial materials and a machine aesthetic
Monochromatic: having one or more values of one color
Monolith: a monument or sculpture made from a single piece of stone
Monumental: having massive or impressive scale
Mosaic: a picture or pattern created by fixing together small pieces of stone, glass, tile, etc.
Motif: (1) a design or color repeated as a unit in a pattern; (2) a distinctive visual

element, the recurrence of which is often characteristic of an artist's work
Motion: the effect of changing placement in time
Motion capture: also known as mo-cap or performance capture; technology developed to animate CGI characters by translating into a digital performance the live, exact motions of people or objects, using specially designed suits or equipment with sensors
Motion picture(s): another term for a movie or movies
Movie: a recording of moving images presented to create the illusion of natural movement; can be watched on a theater screen, television, or other device
Moving picture(s): another term for movie or movies; used frequently in the early period of the medium
Mudra: hand gestures that signify meaning in Buddhism and Hinduism
Mural: a painting applied directly to a wall, usually large and in a public space
Musical: a genre of film in which the story is told through song, usually combined with dialogue and dancing

Narrative: (1) an artwork that tells a story; (2) the story that the artwork expresses
Naturalism; naturalistic: a very realistic or lifelike style of making images
Nave: the central space of a church or basilica
Negative: a reversed image, in which light areas are dark and dark areas are light (opposite of a positive)
Negative space: an unoccupied or empty space that is created after positive shapes are positioned in a work of art
Neoclassicism: a European style that flourished during the late eighteenth and early nineteenth centuries, characterized by an extreme interest in the Classical world, strictly ordered scenes, and heroic subjects
Neo-Expressionist: a broad term, first used in the late 1970s to early 1980s; describes figurative and allegorical, not totally abstract, art with materials used aggressively to give clear evidence of the artist's gestures
Neutral: colors (such as blacks, whites, grays, and dull gray-browns) made by mixing complementary hues
New Wave design: A design movement that exemplified the counter cultural currents of the 1980s
Nkisi nkondi (plural ***minkisi minkondi***): combines the words for "sacred medicine" and "to hunt"; figurative sculpture(s) used in rituals by the Yombe of Central Africa
Non-objective: art that does not depict a recognizable subject
Nude: an artistic representation of an unclothed human figure, emphasizing the body's form rather than its exposure

Ocher: a pigment found in nature containing hydrated iron oxide
Oculus: a round opening at the center of a dome
Oil paint: paint made of pigment suspended in oil
One-point perspective: a perspective system with a single vanishing point on the horizon
Op art: a style of art that exploits the physiology of seeing in order to create illusory optical effects
Opaque: not transparent
Optical mixture: when the eye blends two colors that are placed near one another, creating a new color
Organic: having irregular forms and shapes, as though derived from living organisms
Orthogonals: in perspective systems, imaginary sightlines extending from forms to the vanishing point
Outline: the outermost line or implied line of an object or figure, by which it is defined or bounded

Painterly: a loosely executed style in which paint and brushstrokes are evident
Palette: (1) the range of colors used by an artist; (2) a smooth slab or board used for mixing paints or cosmetics
Passion: the arrest, trial, and execution of Jesus Christ, and his sufferings during them
Pastel: a powdered pigment mixed with gum and used in stick form for drawing
Patina: surface color or texture on a metal caused by aging
Patron: an organization or individual who sponsors the creation of works of art
Pattern: an arrangement of predictably repeated elements
Pedestal: a base upon which a statue or column rests
Pediment: the triangular space, situated above the row of columns, on the facade of a building in the Classical style
Pendentive: a curving triangular surface that links a vault or dome to a square or rectangular space below
Performance art: a work involving the human body, usually including the artist, in front of an audience
Personification: the representation of a thing, an idea, or an abstract quality, such as freedom, as a person or in human form
Perspective: the creation of the illusion of depth in a two-dimensional image by using predictable principles
Petroglyph: an ancient or prehistoric image made in rock by carving, engraving, or scratching the surface to reveal the underlying layer
Photocollage: an artwork made by assembling separate photographs or photographic images, often by gluing them onto a surface
Photomontage: a single photographic image that combines (digitally or using multiple film exposures) several separate images
Photorealist: a style of art that began in the 1960s and involves the artist creating artworks that resemble, and were inspired by, photographs
Pictograph: a picture used as a symbol in writing; conveys meaning through resemblance to physical shape
Pictographic: conveys meaning through resemblance to physical shape
Picture plane: (1) the surface of a painting or drawing; (2) the transparent division between the space depicted by the artist and the real space in which the viewer is placed
Piece-mold casting: a process for casting metal objects in which a mold is broken into several pieces that are then reassembled into a final sculpture
Pigment: the colored material used in paints. Often made from finely ground minerals
Pilaster: a vertical element, rectangular in shape, that provides architectural support for crossing horizontal elements in post-and-lintel construction; also used for decoration
Plane: a flat, two-dimensional surface on which an artist can create a drawing or painting. Planes can also be implied in a composition by areas that face toward, parallel to, or away from a light source
Planography: a print process—lithography and silkscreen printing—where the inked image area and non-inked areas are at the same height
Plastic, plasticity: referring to materials that are soft and can be manipulated, or to such properties in the materials
Pointed arches: arches with two curved sides that meet to form a point at the apex
Pointillism: a late nineteenth-century painting style using short strokes or points of differing colors that optically combine to form new perceived colors
Polymer: a chemical compound commonly referred to as plastic
Polytheism: the worship of more than one god or goddess
Pop art: a mid-twentieth-century artistic movement inspired by commercial art forms and popular culture
Portal: an entrance. A royal portal (main entrance) is usually on the west front of a church and features sculpted forms of kings and queens
Portico: a roof supported by columns at the entrance to a building
Portrait: an image of a person or animal, usually focusing on the face
Positive: an image in which light areas are light and dark areas are dark (opposite of a negative)
Positive–negative: the relationship between contrasting opposites
Positive shape: a shape defined by its surrounding empty space
Post-and-lintel construction: a horizontal beam (the lintel) supported by a post at either end
Post-Impressionists: artists either from or living in France, *c.* 1885–1905, who moved away from the Impressionist style—notably Cézanne, Gauguin, Seurat, and Van Gogh
Postcolonialism: a theoretical approach that aims to explain the relationships between colonized and colonizing nations and people
Postmodernism, Postmodernist: a late twentieth-century style of architecture and art that playfully adopts features of earlier styles and critically focuses on content
Pre-Raphaelite Brotherhood: an English art movement formed in 1848 by painters who rejected the academic rules of art, and often painted medieval subjects in a naïve style
Prehistoric: dating from the period of human existence before the invention of writing
Preparatory study: a drawing or painting that was used to practice or to prepare for a larger artwork
Primary colors: three basic colors from which all others are derived
Primary sources: immediate or first-hand accounts of an artwork
Principles: the principles, or "grammar" of art—contrast, unity, variety, balance, scale, proportion, focal point, emphasis, pattern, and rhythm—describe the ways the elements of art are arranged in an artwork
Print: a picture reproduced on paper, often in multiple copies
Prism: a transparent material with flat, polished surfaces—a form with at least three sides—that can be used to disperse light to reveal the range of color present in the visible spectrum
Profile: the outline of an object, especially a face or head, represented from the side
Propaganda: art that promotes an ideology or a cause
Proportion: the relationship in size between a work's individual parts and the whole
Provenance: the history of ownership of a work
Psychoanalysis: a method of treating mental illness by making conscious the patient's subconscious fears or fantasies
Puppet: a figure in the form of an animal or person used for entertainment purposes that appears to move on its own but is actually controlled by a person's hand(s), strings, or another mechanism
Putto (plural putti): a representation of a nude or scantily clad infant angel or boy, common in Renaissance and Baroque art
Pyramid: an ancient structure, usually massive in scale, consisting of a square base with four sides that meet at a point or apex with each side forming a triangular shape

***Qibla*:** the direction to Mecca, toward which Muslims face when praying
Quatrefoil: a symmetrical framework that has four lobes or leaves

Readymade: an everyday object presented as a work of art
Realism: (1) a nineteenth-century artistic style that aimed to depict nature and everyday subjects in an unidealized manner. "Realism" is also used to describe a historical movement from the same period, which tried to achieve social change and equality by highlighting, in art and literature, the predicament of the poor; (2) an artistic style that aims to represent appearances as accurately as possible
Red-figure vase painting: in ancient Greece, black slip was used on a red clay body to create the background as well as the outlines and linear details of the figures
Regionalism: a branch of American Scene painting that promoted rural, small-town virtues and values, especially related to the Deep South and Midwest US
Register: one of two or more horizontal sections into which a space is divided in order to depict different episodes of a story
Relative placement: the arrangement of shapes or lines to form a visual relationship to one another in a design
Relic: an object that survives from the past; in religion, the mortal remains of a saint or an object that has been in contact with the saint
Relief: a sculpture that projects from a flat surface
Relief printing: a print process where the inked image is higher than the non-printing areas
Renaissance: a period of cultural and artistic change in Europe from the fourteenth to the seventeenth century
Repatriation: the return of cultural artifacts, often sacred remains, to their country of origin
Repoussé: a technique of hammering metal from the back to create a form or surface detail
Representational: art that depicts figures and objects so that we recognize what is represented
RGB: an additive system that mixes color based on the primary colors of light: red, green, and blue
Rhythm: the regular or ordered repetition of elements in the work
Rib vault: an arch-like structure supporting a ceiling or roof, with a web of protruding stonework
Rococo: an eighteenth-century style in France characterized by organic forms, ornate extravagance, and whimsy
Romanesque: an early medieval European style of architecture based on Roman-style rounded arches and heavy construction

Romanticism, Romantic: a movement in nineteenth-century European culture, concerned with the power of the imagination and greatly valuing intense feeling

Rosin: a dry powdered resin that melts when heated, used in the aquatint process

Salon: an official exhibition of French painting, first held in 1667

Sand painting: also known as dry painting, a labor-intensive method of painting using colored grains of sand or other natural materials as the medium

Sarcophagus (plural sarcophagi): a coffin (usually made of stone or baked clay)

Sarsen: a type of hard, gray sandstone

Satire: a work of art that exposes the weaknesses and mistakes of its subjects to ridicule

Saturation (also known as Chroma): the degree of purity of a color

Scale: the size of an object or artwork relative to another object or artwork, or to a system of measurement

Science-fiction (Sci-fi): a genre of film in which fictional stories include advanced science and technology, often in futuristic settings

Sculpture: a work of art created by carving, chiseling, casting, or modeling

Secondary colors: colors mixed from two primary colors

Secondary sources: sources that are one step removed from primary references

Series: a group of related artworks that are created as a set

Serigraphy: printing that is achieved by creating a solid stencil in a porous screen and forcing ink through the screen onto the printing surface

Sfumato: in painting, the application of layers of translucent paint to create a hazy or smoky appearance and unify the composition

Shade: a color darker in value than its purest state

Shaft: the main vertical part of a column

Shaman: a priest or priestess regarded as having the ability to communicate directly with the spiritual world

Shape: a two-dimensional area, the boundaries of which are defined by lines or suggested by changes in color or value

Silhouette: a shape represented in outline, which contains no detail inside its border

Silkscreen: a method of printmaking using a stencil and paint pushed through a screen

Sitter: the person who poses, or "sits," for an artist to paint, sculpt, or photograph

Sketch: a rough preliminary version of a work or part of a work

SLR (single-lens reflex camera): a hand-held digital or film camera that uses a mirror and prism system, so the focus screen matches the image captured

Social Realism: a branch of American Scene painting that focused on Depression-era social issues and hardships of daily life

Soft focus: the deliberate blurring of the edges or lack of sharp focus in a photograph or movie

Space: the distance between identifiable points or planes

Span: the distance bridged between two supports, such as columns or walls

Spectral color: a color in the visible light spectrum

Spectrum: an arrangement of entities

Stained glass: colored glass used for windows or decorative applications

Stela (plural stelae): an upright stone slab decorated with inscriptions or pictorial relief carvings

Stencil: a perforated template allowing ink or paint to pass through to print a design

Stepped pyramid: a pyramid consisting of several rectangular structures placed one on top of another

Still life: a scene of inanimate objects, such as fruits, flowers, or dead animals

Stop-motion animation: figures, puppets, or dolls are photographed in a pose, moved very slightly, and then photographed again; the process is repeated until the desired sequence of movements has been acted out

Storyboard: sequences of drawings, often with directions and dialog, that indicate the shots or scenes planned for a movie or television production

Street art: art created in public spaces (examples include graffiti, posters, and stickers)

Stroboscopic motion: the effect created when we see two or more repeated images in quick succession in such a way that they visually fuse together

Stupa: a burial mound believed to contain some of the Buddha's remains

Style: a characteristic way in which an artist or group of artists uses visual language to give a work an identifiable form of visual expression

Stylized: art that represents objects in an exaggerated way to emphasize certain aspects of the object

Stylobate: the uppermost platform of a Classical temple, on which the columns stand

Subject, subject matter: the person, object, or space depicted in a work of art

Sublime: a feeling of awe or terror, provoked by the experience of limitless nature and the awareness of the smallness of an individual

Subordination: the opposite of emphasis; it draws our attention away from particular areas of a work

Subtractive (sculpture): the methodical removal of material to produce a sculptural form

Subtractive color: the colors produced from pigment

Subtractive color process: colors subtracted from white light by CMY dyes or pigments; in photography, light-sensitive film or paper absorbs the opposite colors of cyan, magenta, and yellow dyes to create a negative image, reversed to make a positive print

Sunken relief: a carved panel where the figures are cut deeper into the stone than the background

Support: the material on which a painting is executed

Suprematism: a Russian art movement of the early twentieth century, focused on geometric shapes and limited colors, which emphasized feeling over visual phenomena

Surreal: reminiscent of the Surrealist movement of the 1920s and later, whose art was inspired by dreams and the subconscious

Surrealism, Surrealist: an artistic movement in the 1920s and later; its works were inspired by dreams and the subconscious

Symbolism: using images or symbols in an artwork to convey meaning; often obvious when the work was made but requiring research for modern viewers to understand

Symbolist: an artist or artistic style belonging to the movement in European art and literature, c. 1885–1910, that conveyed meaning by the use of powerful yet ambiguous symbols

Symmetrical balance: an image or shape that looks exactly (or nearly exactly) the same on both sides when cut in half

Symmetry: the correspondence in size, form, and arrangement of items on opposite sides of a plane, line, or point that creates direct visual balance

Syncretism: the blending of multiple religious or philosophical beliefs

Synesthesia: when one of the five senses perceives something that was stimulated by a trigger from one of the other senses

Tableau: a stationary scene arranged for artistic impact

Tapestry: hand-woven fabric—usually silk or wool—with a non-repeating, usually figurative, design woven into it

Tattoos: designs marked on the body by injecting dye under the skin

Tempera: a fast-drying painting medium made from pigment mixed with water-soluble binder, such as egg yolk

Temperature: a description of color based on our associations with warmth or coolness

Temporal art: an artist's image or action that is transitory, existing in a passage of time

Tenebrism: the dramatic use of intense darkness and light to heighten the impact of a painting

Terra-cotta: iron-rich clay, fired at a low temperature, which is traditionally brownish-orange in color

Tertiary colors: colors that can be mixed from a secondary and a primary color

Tesserae: small pieces of stone or glass or other materials used to make a mosaic

Tetrahedron: a pyramid shape in which all four faces are equally sized triangles

Texture: the surface quality of a work, for example fine/coarse, detailed/lacking in detail

Three-dimensional: having height, width, and depth

Three-point perspective: a perspective system with two vanishing points on the horizon and one not on the horizon

Throwing: the process of making a ceramic object on a potter's wheel

Tint: a color lighter in value than its purest state

Tone: a color that is weaker than its brightest, or most pure, state

Tooth: the textural quality of a paper surface, for holding drawing media in place

Torana: a gateway used in Hindu and Buddhist architecture

Transept: a structure crossing the main body of a Latin-cross-plan church

Translucent: semi-transparent

Transparency: in film and photography, a positive image on film that is visible when light is shone through it

Travertine: a light-colored limestone deposited in mineral springs and used as a building material

Triglyph: a projecting block carved with three raised bands, which alternates with figurative reliefs in a frieze

Triptych: an artwork comprising three panels, normally joined together and sharing a common theme

Trompe l'oeil: from the French meaning to "deceive the eye"; a visual illusion in art, in which a painted image appears as a three-dimensional object

Trumeau: within a portal, a central column that supports a tympanum

Twining: a basket-weaving technique consisting of twisting two strands of material around a foundation of parallel sticks

Twisted perspective (also known as **composite view**): a representation of a figure, part in profile and part frontally

Two-dimensional: having height and width

Tympanum: an arched recess above a doorway, often decorated with carvings

Typefaces: the particular unified style of a family of typographical characters

Typography: the art of designing, arranging, and choosing type

Underpainting: in oil painting, the process of painting the canvas in a base, often monochrome, color as a first step in creating the areas of light and dark value

Unity: the appearance of oneness or harmony in a work of art: all of the elements appearing to be part of a cohesive whole

Value: the lightness or darkness of a plane or area

Vanishing point(s): the point or points in a work of art at which imaginary sight lines appear to converge, suggesting depth

Vanitas: a genre of painting that emphasizes the transient nature of earthly materials and beauty; often seen in still-life painting

Variety: the diversity of different ideas, media, and elements in a work

Vault: an arch-like structure supporting a ceiling or roof

Vaulted: covered with an arch-shaped ceiling or roof

Verdaccio: a mixture of black, white, and yellow pigments resulting in a grayish or yellowish soft greenish brown. It is used in oil painting, and sometimes in frescoes, as a base layer to refine the values in the work

Video: a recording of moving images, usually made digitally or on videotape

Void: an area in an artwork that seems empty

Volume: the space filled or enclosed by a three-dimensional figure or object

Voussoir: a wedge-shaped stone that is used to construct an arch

Wavelength: a term from physics that measures light as the distance between two corresponding points on a wave of energy, e.g. between two high points of a wave

White space: in typography, the empty space around type or other features in a layout

Woodblock: a relief print process where the image is carved into a block of wood

Woodcut: a relief print made from a design cut into a block of wood

Ziggurat: a Mesopotamian stepped tower, roughly pyramid-shaped, that diminishes in size toward a platform summit

Zoetrope: an antique, European toy; contains a rotating cylinder with a sequence of images on the inside that creates the impression of a single action in continuous motion when spun

Further Reading

GATEWAY IMAGES

Bouquillard, Jocelyn, *Hokusai's Mount Fuji: The Complete Views in Color.* New York (Harry N. Abrams) 2007.

Brougher, Kerry, Mami Kataoka, and Charles Merewether, *Ai Weiwei: According to What?* Munich (Prestel) 2012.

Burrus, Christina, *Frida Kahlo: "I Paint my Reality."* London (Thames & Hudson) 2008.

Driskell, David C., Michael D. Harris, Wyatt Macgaffey, and Sylvia H. Williams, *Astonishment and Power: The Eyes of Understanding: Kongo Minkisi.* Washington (Smithsonian Institution Press) 1993.

Greiman, April. *Something from Nothing.* Hove (Rotovision) 2002.

Hall, Marcia, ed., *Raphael's School of Athens.* Cambridge, England (Cambridge University Press) 1997.

Koch, Ebba, *The Complete Taj Mahal.* London (Thames & Hudson) 2006.

McEvilley, Thomas, *Kara Walker: My Complement, My Enemy, My Oppressor, My Love.* Minneapolis (Walker Art Center) 2007.

PART 1

Chapter 1.1 Line, Shape, and the Principle of Contrast
de Zegher, Catherine and Cornelia Butler, *On Line: Drawing Through the Twentieth Century.* New York (The Museum of Modern Art) 2010.

Ocvirk, Otto, Robert Stinson, Philip Wigg, and Robert Bone, *Art Fundamentals: Theory and Practice*, 11th edn. New York (McGraw-Hill) 2008.

Chapter 1.2 Form, Volume, Mass, and Texture
Ching, Francis D. K., *Architecture: Form, Space, and Order*, 3rd edn. Hoboken, NJ (Wiley) 2007.

Wong, Wucius, *Principles of Three-Dimensional Design.* New York (Van Nostrand Reinhold) 1977.

Chapter 1.3 Implied Depth: Value and Space
Auvil, Kenneth W., *Perspective Drawing*, 2nd edn. New York (McGraw-Hill) 1996.

Curtis, Brian, *Drawing from Observation*, 2nd edn. New York (McGraw-Hill) 2009.

Robertson, Jean, Deborah Hutton, et al., *The History of Art – A Global View*, New York (Thames & Hudson) 2021.

Chapter 1.4 Color
Albers, Josef and Nicholas Fox Weber, *Interaction of Color: Revised and Expanded Edition.* New Haven, CT (Yale University Press) 2006.

Bleicher, Steven, *Contemporary Color: Theory and Use*, 2nd edn. Clifton Park, NY (Delmar Cengage Learning) 2011.

Finlay, Victoria, *Color: A Natural History of the Palette.* London/New York (Random House Trade Paperbacks) 2003.

Stewart, Jude, *ROY G. BIV: An Exceedingly Surprising Book about Color.* New York (Bloomsbury) 2013.

Chapter 1.5 Motion and Time
Krasner, Jon, *Motion Graphic Design: Applied History and Aesthetics*, 2nd edn. Burlington, MA (Focal Press [Elsevier]) 2008.

Stewart, Mary, *Launching the Imagination*, 3rd edn. New York (McGraw-Hill) 2007.

Chapter 1.6 Unity, Variety, and Balance
Bevlin, Marjorie Elliott, *Design Through Discovery: An Introduction*, 6th edn. Orlando, FL (Harcourt Brace & Co./Wadsworth Publishing) 1993.

Lauer, David A. and Stephen Pentak, *Design Basics*, 8th edn. Boston, MA (Wadsworth Publishing) 2011.

Chapter 1.7 Scale and Proportion
Bridgman, George B., *Bridgman's Life Drawing.* Mineola, NY (Dover Publications) 1971.

Elam, Kimberly, *Geometry of Design: Studies in Proportion and Composition*, 1st edn. New York (Princeton Architectural Press) 2001.

Chapter 1.8 Focal Point and Emphasis
Lauer, David A. and Stephen Pentak, *Design Basics*, 8th edn. Boston, MA (Wadsworth Publishing) 2011.

Robertson, Jean, Deborah Hutton, et al., *The History of Art – A Global View.* New York (Thames & Hudson) 2021.

Stewart, Mary, *Launching the Imagination*, 3rd edn. New York (McGraw-Hill) 2007.

Chapter 1.9 Pattern and Rhythm
Ocvirk, Otto, Robert Stinson, Philip Wigg, and Robert Bone, *Art Fundamentals: Theory and Practice*, 11th edn. New York (McGraw-Hill) 2008.

Wong, Wucius, *Principles of Two-Dimensional Design*, 1st edn. New York (Wiley) 1972.

Chapter 1.10 Engaging with Form and Content
Barnet, Sylvan, *Short Guide to Writing About Art.* Harlow, UK (Pearson Education) 2010.

Brown, Jonathan, *Velázquez: Painter and Courtier.* New Haven, CT (Yale University Press) 1988.

Hatt, Michael and Charlotte Klonk, *Art History: A Critical Introduction to Its Methods.* New York (Manchester University Press; distributed exclusively in the USA by Palgrave) 2006.

PART 2

Chapter 2.1 Drawing
Faber, David L. and Daniel M. Mendelowitz, *A Guide to Drawing*, 8th edn. Boston, MA (Wadsworth Publishing) 2011.

Gardner, Stephen C. P., *Gateways to Drawing*, New York (Thames & Hudson) 2018.

Sale, Teel and Claudia Betti, *Drawing: A Contemporary Approach*, 6th edn. Boston, MA (Wadsworth Publishing) 2007.

Chapter 2.2 Painting
Gottsegen, Mark David, *Painter's Handbook: Revised and Expanded.* New York (Watson-Guptill) 2006.

Robertson, Jean and Craig McDaniel, *Painting as a Language: Material, Technique, Form, Content*, 1st edn. Boston, MA (Wadsworth Publishing) 1999.

Chapter 2.3 Printmaking
Hunter, Dard, *Papermaking.* Mineola, NY (Dover Publications) 2011.

Robertson, Jean, Deborah Hutton, et al., *The History of Art – A Global View.* New York (Thames & Hudson) 2021.

Ross, John, *Complete Printmaker*, revised expanded edn. New York (Free Press) 1991.

Chapter 2.4 Sculpture
Rich, Jack C., *The Materials and Methods of Sculpture*, 10th edn. Mineola, NY (Dover Publications) 1988.

Tucker, William, *The Language of Sculpture.* London (Thames & Hudson) 1985.

Chapter 2.5 Architecture
Ching, Francis D. K., *Architecture: Form, Space, and Order*, 3rd edn. Hoboken, NJ (Wiley) 2007.

Glancey, Jonathan, *Story of Architecture.* New York (Dorling Kindersley/Prentice Hall) 2006.

Robertson, Jean, Deborah Hutton, et al., *The History of Art – A Global View.* New York (Thames & Hudson) 2021.

Chapter 2.6 The Tradition of Craft
Speight, Charlotte and John Toki, *Hands in Clay: An Introduction to Ceramics*, 5th edn. New York (McGraw-Hill) 2003.

Wight, Karol, *Molten Color: Glassmaking in Antiquity.* Los Angeles, CA (J. Paul Getty Museum) 2011.

Chapter 2.7 Visual Communication Design
Craig, James, William Bevington, and Irene Korol Scala, *Designing with Type, 5th Edition: The Essential Guide to Typography.* New York (Watson-Guptill) 2006.

Meggs, Philip B. and Alston W. Purvis, *Meggs' History of Graphic Design*, 4th edn. Hoboken, NJ (Wiley) 2005.

Chapter 2.8 Photography
Heiferman, Marvin and Merry A. Foresta, *Photography Changes Everything.* New York (Aperture/co-published with the Smithsonian Institution) 2012.

Hirsch, Robert, *Light and Lens: Photography in the Digital Age.* London (Elsevier) 2007.

Jeffrey, Ian, *How to Read a Photograph.* New York (Abrams) 2010.

London, Barbara, John Upton, and Jim Stone, *Photography*, 10th edn. Upper Saddle River, NJ (Pearson) 2010.

Marien, Mary Warner, *Photography: A Cultural History*, 3rd edn. Upper Saddle River, NJ (Prentice Hall) 2010.

Rosenblum, Naomi, *A World History of Photography*, 4th edn. New York (Abbeville Press) 2008.

Trachtenberg, Alan, ed., *Classic Essays on Photography.* New York (Leete's Island Books) 1980.

Chapter 2.9 Film/Video and Digital Art
Cook, David A., *A History of Narrative Film*, 4th edn. New York (W. W. Norton) 2004.

Corrigan, Timothy and Patricia White, *The Film Experience*, 2nd edn. New York (Bedford/St. Martin's) 2008.

Monaco, James, *How to Read a Film: Movies, Media, and Beyond.* New York (Oxford University Press) 2009.

Sondra Perry Interview with Serpentine Gallery, May 16, 2018 https://www.youtube.com/watch?v=Qunkb4piXGw

Wands, Bruce, *Art of the Digital Age.* New York (Thames & Hudson) 2007.

Chapter 2.10 Alternative Media and Processes
Alberro, Alexander and Blake Stimson, *Conceptual Art: A Critical Anthology.* Cambridge, MA (MIT Press) 2000.

Bishop, Claire, *Installation Art*, 2nd edn. London (Tate Publishing) 2010.

Forester, Ian, "Resisting Reductivism & Breaking the Bubble: An Interview with Barbara Kruger," *ART21 Magazine*, Winter 2018, magazine.art.21.org

Goldberg, Rosalee, *Performance Art: From Futurism to the Present*, 2nd edn. New York (Thames & Hudson) 2011.

Helguda, Pablo, *Education for Socially Engaged Art: A Materials and Techniques Handbook.* New York (Jorge Pinto Books, Inc.) 2011.

Lippard, Lucy, *Six Years: The Dematerialization of the Art Object from 1966 to 1972.* Berkeley, CA (University of California Press) 1997.

Osborne, Peter, *Conceptual Art (Themes and Movements).* New York and London (Phaidon) 2011.

Rosenthal, Mark, *Understanding Installation Art: From Duchamp to Holzer.* New York (Prestel) 2003.

PART 3

Chapter 3.1 The Prehistoric and Ancient Mediterranean
Alfred, Cyril, *Egyptian Art.* New York (Oxford University Press) 1980.

Aruz, Joan, *Art of the First Cities: The Third Millennium B.C. from the Mediterranean to the Indus.* New York (The Metropolitan Museum of Art); New Haven, CT (Yale University Press) 2003.

Boardman, John, *The World of Ancient Art.* New York (Thames & Hudson) 2006.

Pedley, John Griffiths, *Greek Art and Archaeology*, 5th edn. Upper Saddle River, NJ (Pearson/Prentice Hall) 2007.

Wheeler, Mortimer, *Roman Art and Architecture.* New York (Thames & Hudson) 1985.

Chapter 3.2 Art of the Middle Ages
Benton, Janetta, *Art of the Middle Ages.* New York (Thames & Hudson) 2002.

Bloom, Jonathan and Sheila Blair, *Islamic Arts.* London (Phaidon) 1997.

Camille, Michael, *Gothic Art: Glorious Visions.* New York (Abrams) 1996.

Lowden, John, *Early Christian & Byzantine Art.* London (Phaidon) 1997.

Chapter 3.3 Art of India, China, Japan, Korea, and Southeast Asia
Craven, Roy, *Indian Art.* New York (Thames & Hudson) 1997.

Lee, Sherman, *History of Far Eastern Art.* New York (Abrams) 1994.

Stanley-Baker, Joan, *Japanese Art.* New York (Thames & Hudson) 2000.

Tregear, Mary, *Chinese Art.* New York (Thames & Hudson) 1997.

Chapter 3.4 Art of the Americas

Berlo, Janet Catherine and Ruth B. Phillips, *Native North American Art*. New York (Oxford University Press) 1998.

Coe, Michael D., Javier Urcid, and Rex Koontz, *Mexico: From the Olmecs to the Aztecs*, 8th edn. New York (Thames & Hudson) 2019.

Deats, Suzanne and Kitty Leaken, *Contemporary Native American Artists*. Layton, OH (Gibbs Smith) 2012.

Miller, Mary Ellen, *The Art of Ancient Mesoamerica*, 4th edn. New York (Thames & Hudson) 2006.

Passalacqua, Veronica and Kate Morris, *Native Art Now!: Developments in Contemporary Native American Art Since 1992*. Indianapolis, IN (Eiteljorg Museum) 2017.

Rushing, Jackson III, *Native American Art in the Twentieth Century: Makers, Meanings, Histories*. New York (Taylor and Francis) 1999.

Stone, Rebecca, *Art of the Andes: From Chavin to Inca*, 3rd edn. New York (Thames & Hudson) 2002.

Chapter 3.5 Art of Africa and the Pacific Islands

Bacquart, Jean-Baptiste, *The Tribal Arts of Africa*. New York (Thames & Hudson) 2002.

Berlo, Janet Catherine and Lee Anne Wilson, *Arts of Africa, Oceania, and the Americas*. Upper Saddle River, NJ (Prentice Hall) 1992.

D'Alleva, Anne, *Arts of the Pacific Islands*. New Haven, CT (Yale University Press) 2010.

Enwezor, Okuwui, *Contemporary African Art Since 1980*. Bologna, Italy (Damiani) 2009.

Kasfir, Sidney Littlefield, *Contemporary African Art*. New York (Thames & Hudson) 2000.

PBS, "Skin Stories: The Art and Culture of Polynesian Tattoo", https://www.pbs.org/skinstories/history/newzealand.html

Willet, Frank, *African Art*, 3rd edn. New York (Thames & Hudson) 2003.

Wu, Katherine J., "New Research Rewrites the Demise of Easter Island," February 11, 2020, smithsonianmag.com, https://www.smithsonianmag.com/smart-news/new-research-rewrites-demise-easter-island-180974172/

Chapter 3.6 Art of Renaissance and Baroque Europe (1400–1750)

Bazin, Germain and Jonathan Griffin, *Baroque and Rococo*. New York (Thames & Hudson) 1985.

Garrard, Mary, *Artemisia Gentileschi*. Princeton, NJ (Princeton University Press) 1991.

Hartt, Frederick, *History of Italian Renaissance Art*, 7th edn. Upper Saddle River, NJ (Pearson) 2010.

Welch, Evelyn, *Art in Renaissance Italy: 1350–1500*. New York (Oxford University Press) 2001.

Chapter 3.7 Art of Europe and America (1700–1865): Rococo to Romanticism

Chu, Petra ten-Doesschate, *Nineteenth-Century European Art*. New York (Abrams) 2003.

Irwin, David, *Neoclassicism*. London (Phaidon) 1997.

Levey, Michael, *Rococo to Revolution: Major Trends in Eighteenth-Century Painting*. New York (Thames & Hudson) 1985.

Vaughan, William, *Romanticism and Art*. London (Thames & Hudson) 1994.

Chapter 3.8 The Modern Aesthetic: Realism to *Fin de Siècle*

Chipp, Herschel, *Theories of Modern Art: A Sourcebook by Artists and Critics* (University of California) 1984.

Chu, Petra ten-Doesschate, *Nineteenth-Century European Art*. New York (Abrams) 2003.

Denvir, Bernard, *Post-Impressionism*. New York (Thames & Hudson) 1992.

Thomson, Belinda, *Impressionism: Origins, Practice, Reception*. New York (Thames & Hudson) 2000.

Chapter 3.9 Late Modern and Early Contemporary Art in the Twentieth Century

Arnason, H. H. and Elizabeth C. Mansfield, *History of Modern Art*, 6th edn. Upper Saddle River, NJ (Pearson) 2009.

Dempsey, Amy, *Styles, Schools, and Movements*, 2nd edn. New York (Thames & Hudson) 2011.

Fineberg, Jonathan, *Art Since 1940: Strategies of Being*, 3rd edn. Upper Saddle River, NJ (Prentice Hall) 2010.

Jones, Amelia, *A Companion to Contemporary Art Since 1945*. Malden, MA (Blackwell Publishing) 2006.

Stiles, Kristine and Peter Selz, *Theories and Documents of Contemporary Art: A Sourcebook of Artists' Writings*, 2nd edn, revised and expanded. Berkeley, CA (University of California Press) 2012.

Chapter 3.10 The Late Twentieth Century and Art of the Present Day

Barrett, Terry, *Why Is that Art?: Aesthetics and Criticism of Contemporary Art*. New York (Oxford University Press) 2007.

Evans, David, *Appropriation*. Cambridge, MA (MIT Press) and London (Whitechapel Gallery) 2009.

Ilić , Mirko and Steven Heller, *Head to Toe: Nudity in Graphic Design*. New York (Rizzoli) 2018.

Krauss, Rosalind, *A Voyage on the North Sea: Art in the Age of the Post-Medium Condition*. London (Thames & Hudson) 2000.

Rickard, Jolene, "Visualizing Sovereignty," *The South Atlantic Quarterly*, 110: 2 (Spring, 2011), 465–486.

Thompson, Nato, *Living as Form: Socially Engaged Art from 1991–2011*. Cambridge, MA (MIT Press) 2012.

PART 4

Chapter 4.1 Art and the Community

Art in Action: Nature, Creativity, and Our Collective Future. San Rafael, CA (Earth Aware Editions) 2007.

Christo and Jeanne-Claude, "Selected Works: The Gates," *The Art of Christo and Jeanne-Claude* (© 2005; access date September 7, 2007) www.christojeanneclaude.net.

Iosifidis, Kiriakos, *Mural Art: Murals on Huge Public Surfaces Around the World from Graffiti to Trompe l'oeil*. Vancouver, BC (Adbusters) 2009.

Kwon, Miwon, *One Place after Another: Site-Specific Art and Location Identity*. Cambridge, MA (MIT Press) 2004.

Musiker, Cy, "A Wild Mix of Movement in ODC's Walking Distance Dance Festival," May 9, 2018, kqed.org

Sholette, Gregory, Chloë Bass, and Social Practice Queens, eds., *Art As Social Action*. New York (Allworth Press) 2018.

Waxman, Olivia B. "Notre Dame Cathedral's History has always been one of destruction and restoration," April 15, 2019, time.com

Chapter 4.2 Spirituality and Art

Azara, Nancy J., *Spirit Taking Form: Making a Spiritual Practice of Making Art*. Boston, MA (Red Wheel) 2002.

Bloom, Jonathan, and Sheila S. Blair, *Islamic Arts*. London (Phaidon) 1997.

Fanning, Leesa K. (ed.) *Encountering the Spiritual in Contemporary Art* (Nelson Atkins Museum/Yale University Press, 2018).

Fisher, Robert E., *Buddhist Art and Architecture*. New York (Thames & Hudson) 1993.

Guo, Xi, *Essay on Landscape Painting*. London (John Murray) 1959.

Lyle, Emily, *Sacred Architecture in the Traditions of India, China, Judaism, and Islam*. Edinburgh (Edinburgh University Press) 1992.

Williamson, Beth, *Christian Art: A Very Short Introduction*. New York (Oxford University Press) 2004.

Chapter 4.3 The Cycle of Life: Nature and Time

Dijkstra, Rineke, *Portraits*. Boston, MA (Institute of Contemporary Art) 2005.

Germer, Renate, Fiona Elliot, and Artwig Altenmuller, *Mummies: Life after Death in Ancient Egypt*. New York (Prestel) 1997.

Miller, Mary Ellen and Karl Taube, *An Illustrated Dictionary of the Gods and Symbols of Ancient Mexico and the Maya*. New York (Thames & Hudson) 1997.

Ravenal, John B., *Vanitas: Meditations on Life and Death in Contemporary Art*. Richmond, VA (Virginia Museum of Fine Arts) 2000.

Steinberg, Leo, *The Sexuality of Christ in Renaissance Art and in Modern Oblivion*. Chicago, IL (University of Chicago Press) 1996.

Chapter 4.4 Art, Science, and Mathematics

Bordin, Giorgio, *Medicine in Art*. Los Angeles (J. Paul Getty Museum) 2010.

Brouger, Kerry, et al., *Visual Music: Synaesthesia in Art and Music Since 1900*. London (Thames & Hudson); Washington, D.C. (Hirshhorn Museum); Los Angeles, CA (Museum of Contemporary Art) 2005.

Gamwell, Lynn and Neil deGrasse Tyson, *Exploring the Invisible: Art, Science, and the Spiritual*. Princeton, NJ (Princeton University Press) 2002.

Milbrath, Susan, *Star Gods of the Maya: Astronomy in Art, Folklore, and Calendars*. Austin, TX (University of Texas Press) 2000.

Pietrangeli, Carlo, et al., *The Sistine Chapel: A Glorious Restoration*. New York (Abrams) 1999.

Rhodes, Colin, *Outsider Art: Spontaneous Alternatives*. New York (Thames & Hudson) 2000.

Chapter 4.5 Art of Political Leaders and Rulers

Cooper, Pia, *Art Mao: The Big Little Red Book of Maoist Art Since 1949*. Jericho, NY (CN Times Books Inc.) 2015.

Freed, Rita, *Pharaohs of the Sun: Akhenaten, Nefertiti: Tutankhamen*. Boston, MA (Museum of Fine Arts in association with Bulfinch Press/Little, Brown and Co.) 1999.

Rapelli, Paola, *Symbols of Power in Art*. Los Angeles, CA (J. Paul Getty Museum, Getty Publications) 2011.

Spike, John T., *Europe in the Age of Monarchy*. New York (The Metropolitan Museum of Art) 1987.

Chapter 4.6 Art, War, and Healing

Auping, Michael, *Anselm Kiefer Heaven and Earth*. Fort Worth, TX (Modern Art Museum of Fort Worth, in association with Prestel) 2005.

Blais, Allison, et al., *A Place of Remembrance: Official Book of the National September 11 Memorial*. Washington, D.C. (National Geographic) 2011.

Bourke, Joanna, ed., *War and Art: A Visual History of Modern Conflict*. London (Reaktion) 2017.

Hughes, Robert, *Goya*. New York (Alfred A. Knopf) 2003.

Steel, Andy, *Photojournalism: And the Stories Behind Their Greatest Images (The World's Top Photographers)*. Mies, Switzerland, and Hove, UK (RotoVision) 2006.

Van Hensbergen, Gijs, *Guernica: The Biography of a Twentieth-Century Icon*. New York (Bloomsbury) 2005.

Wilson, David, *The Bayeux Tapestry*. London (Thames & Hudson) 2004.

Chapter 4.7 Art of Protest and Social Conscience

Alhadeff, Albert, *The Raft of the Medusa: Géricault, Art, and Race*. Munich and London (Prestel) 2002.

Barron, Stephanie, *Degenerate Art*. Los Angeles, CA (Los Angeles County Museum of Art) and New York (Abrams) 1991.

Kammen, Michael, *Visual Shock: A History of Art Controversies in American Culture*. New York (Alfred A. Knopf) 2007.

Chapter 4.8 The Body in Art

Clark, Kenneth, *The Nude: A Study in Ideal Form*. Princeton, NJ (Yale University Press) 1956/1990.

Dijkstra, Bram, *Naked: The Nude in America*. New York (Rizzoli) 2010.

Jones, Amelia, *Body Art/Performing the Self*. Minneapolis, MN (University of Minnesota Press) 1998.

Nairne, Sandy and Sarah Howgate, *The Portrait Now*. New Haven, CT (Yale University Press) and London (National Portrait Gallery) 2006.

Chapter 4.9 Identity, Race, and Gender in Art

Broude, Norma and Mary Garrard, *Feminism and Art History: Questioning the Litany*. New York (Harper & Row) 1982.

Doy, Gen, *Picturing the Self: Changing Views of the Subject in Visual Culture*. London (I. B. Tauris) 2004.

Hickey, Dave, *The Invisible Dragon: Essays on Beauty*, revised and expanded edition. Chicago, IL (University of Chicago Press) 2009.

hooks, bell, *Feminism is for Everybody: Passionate Politics*. Cambridge, MA (South End Press) 2000.

Jones, Amelia, *The Feminism and Visual Culture Reader*. New York (Routledge) 2010.

Miller, Meg, "Don't Call April Greiman the 'Queen of New Wave,'" *Eye on Design* Magazine, (March 22, 2019), https://eyeondesign.aiga.org/april-greiman-is-still-ahead-of-the-curve/.

Patton, Sharon F., *African American Art.* Oxford (Oxford University Press) 1998.

Perry, Gill, *Gender and Art.* New Haven, CT (Yale University Press) 1999.

Powell, Richard, *Black Art: A Cultural History*, 2nd edn. New York (Thames & Hudson) 2003.

Powell, Richard, Virginia Mecklenberg, and Theresa Slowik, *African American Art: Harlem Renaissance, Civil Rights Era, and Beyond.* New York (Skira Rizzoli) 2012.

Rebel, Ernst, *Self-Portraits.* Los Angeles, CA (Taschen) 2008.

Reilly, Maura, "Taking the Measure of Sexism: Fact, Figures, and Fixes," *ARTnews* (May 26, 2015).

Rugg, Linda Haverty, *Picturing Ourselves: Photography and Autobiography.* Chicago, IL (University of Chicago Press) 1997.

Valenti, Jessica, *Full Frontal Feminism: A Young Woman's Guide to Why Feminism Matters.* Emeryville, CA (Seal Press) 2007.

Sources of Quotations

INTRODUCTION

p. 17: Marcia Smilack from www.marciasmilack.com/artist-statement.php and www.marciasmilack.com/sprintview.php?id=60

PART I

Chapter 1.1

p. 42: Barbara Hepworth from Abraham Marie Hammacher, *The Sculpture of Barbara Hepworth* (New York: Harry N. Abrams, 1968), 98.

Chapter 1.2

p. 50: Vivant Denon from http://www.ancient-egypt-history.com/2011/04/napoleon-bonapartes-wise-men-at.html.

p. 53: Lino Tagliapietra from the artist's website at http://www.linotagliapietra.com/batman/index.htm.

Chapter 1.3

p. 66: Albert Einstein from Thomas Campbell, *My Big TOE: Inner Workings* (Huntsville, AL: Lightning Strike Books, 2003), 191.

Chapter 1.4

p. 84: Vasily Kandinsky from Robert L. Herbert, *Modern Artists on Art* (New York: Dover Publications, 1999), 19.

p. 88: Analia Saban from www.artnet.com/magazineus/reviews/taubman/endless-summer10-15-09.asp

p. 98: Van Gogh quoted in Ian Chilvers, Harold Osborne, and Denis Farr (eds.), *The Oxford Dictionary of Art* (New York: Oxford University Press, 2009), 298.

p. 102: Kathleen Hall, *Hilma af Klint* (2014) from https://www.theosophyforward.com/theosophy-and-the-society-in-the-public-eye/1138-hilma-af-klint

Chapter 1.5

p. 104: William Faulkner from Philip Gourevitch (ed.), *The Paris Review: Interviews, Volume 2* (New York: Picador USA, 2007), 54.

p. 112: Gabrielle Cram and Daniela Zyman (eds.), "Interview with Ai Weiwei," in *Shooting Back* (Vienna: Thyssen-Bornemisza Art Contemporary, 2007), 36.

Chapter 1.7

p. 130: Baudelaire from Charles Baudelaire, *Flowers of Evil and Other Works*, ed. and trans. Wallace Fowlie (New York: Dover Publications, 1992), 201.

Chapter 1.9

p. 151: Elvis Presley from Dave Marsh and James Bernard, *The New Book of Rock Lists* (New York: Simon & Schuster [Fireside], 1994), 9.

Chapter 1.10

p. 161: Edward Hopper from Art Institute of Chicago website: www.artic.edu/aic/collections/artwork/111628.

p. 162: José de Sigüenza from Ian Chilvers, ed., "Bosch, Hieronymus," in *The Oxford Dictionary of Art and Artists* (Oxford University Press, 2009; and Oxford Reference Online, Oxford University Press).

p. 167: Magdalena Abakanowicz from Magdalena Abakanowicz, "Solitude," (1985) sent by the artist to the editors, Kristine Stiles and Peter Selz (eds.), *Theories and Documents of Contemporary Art: A Sourcebook of Artists' Writings* (Berkeley: University of California Press, 1996), 260.

pp. 168–69: Kerry James Marshall, from "Identity" Art21, Season 1 (PBS: September 28 2001), and "The World of Groundbreaking Artist Kerry James Marshall," artsy.net (April 20, 2016)

p. 174: Clive King from artist's statement https://www.clivedraw.com

PART 2

Chapter 2.1

p. 178: William Blake from *The Complete Poetry and Prose of William Blake* (Berkeley and Los Angeles, CA: Anchor/University of California Press, 1997), 574.

Chapter 2.2

p. 199: José Clemente Orozco from *The Artist in New York: Letters to Jean Charlot and Unpublished Writings, 1925–1929* (Austin, TX: University of Texas Press, 1974), 90–91.

p. 201: Andrew Wyeth from William Scheller, *America, a History in Art: The American Journey Told by Painters, Sculptors...* (New York: Black Dog & Leventhal Publishers, 2008), 22.

Chapter 2.4

p. 228: Michelangelo quoted by Henry Moore from Henry Moore and Alan G. Wilkinson, *Henry Moore–Writings and Conversations* (Berkeley, CA: University of California Press, 2002), 238.

p. 228: Anthony Gormley, from interview with Thames & Hudson.

Chapter 2.5

p. 259: Louis Sullivan, "The Tall Office Building Artistically Considered," *Lippincott's Magazine* 57, (March 1896).

p. 264: Jonas Salk, from Salk Institute website, www.salk.edu/about/history-of-salk

pp. 265–66: Zaha Hadid, from www.zaha-hadid.com/wp-content/uploads/2012/cac.pdf

pp. 260, 262: Le Corbusier from Nicholas Fox Weber, *Le Corbusier: A Life* (New York: Alfred A. Knopf, 2008), 171.

p. 260: Mies van der Rohe from E. C. Relph, *The Modern Urban Landscape*

(Baltimore, MD: The Johns Hopkins University Press, 1987), 191.

Chapter 2.6

pp. 268, 282: Geoffrey Chaucer from *The Works of Geoffrey Chaucer, Volume 5* (New York: Macmillan and Co., Limited, 1904), 341.

Chapter 2.7

p. 287: Mies van der Rohe, from www.moma.org/artists/7166

Chapter 2.8

p. 304: Alfred, Lord Tennyson from "The Charge of the Light Brigade", originally published in *The Examiner* (December 9, 1854).

p. 310: Edward Burtynsky from *Manufactured Landscapes (U.S. Edition)*, directed by Jennifer Baichwal (Zeitgeist Films, 2006).

p. 311: "Sally Mann: Collodion Process" PBS.org (November, 2011).

pp. 315–16: Diane Arbus from *Diane Arbus: An Aperture Monograph* (first published 1972).

Chapter 2.9

p. 323: *The Artist* from Rick Groen, "The Artist: Mostly mute, it speaks volumes about silent film," *The Globe and Mail* (Toronto), December 9, 2011.

p. 329: Jonathan Jones, "Sondra Perry's Typhoon wrenches my soul but Ian Cheng's AI is merely soulless—review," *The Guardian*, March 7, 2018.

Chapter 2.10

p. 336: Cedar Pasori, "An Interview with Barbara Kruger Discussing Her New Installation and Art in the Digital Age," August 21, 2012 complex.com (accessed March 6, 2017): http://www.complex.com/style/2012/08/interview-barbara-kruger-talks-her-new-installation-and-art-in-the-digital-age

p. 336: Yoko Ono's text accompanying *Wish Tree* from Jessica Dawson, "Yoko Ono's Peaceful Message Takes Root," *Washington Post* (April 3, 2007): washingtonpost.com.

p. 338: Vito Acconci's description of *Following Piece* from documentation accompanying the photographs; reprinted in Lucy Lippard, *Six Years: The Dematerialization of the Art Object* (Berkeley, CA: University of California Press, 1973/1997), 117.

p. 340: Kara Walker from "Interview: Projecting Fictions: 'Insurrection! Our Tools Were Rudimentary, Yet We Pressed On,'" *ART21* "Stories" Episode, Season 2 (PBS: 2003): http://www.pbs.org/art21/artists/walker/clip1.html.

PART 3

Chapter 3.1

p. 353: Inscription from Assyrian palace from Met Museum website and object

file: http://www.metmuseum.org/works_of_art/collection_database/ancient_near_eastern_art/huzman_headed_winged_bull_and_winged_lion_lamassu/objectview.aspx?collID=3&OID=30009052.

p. 359: Protagoras from Kenneth Clark, *Protagoras* (New York: Harper & Row, 1969), 57.

Chapter 3.2

p. 381: Hildegard of Bingen from *Hildegard von Bingen's Mystical Visions*, trans. by Bruce Hozeski from *Scivias* (I,1), 8.

Chapter 3.3

p. 398: "Ai Weiwei in Conversation with Virginia Trioli," National Gallery of Victoria, (December 15, 2015).

p. 398: Gabrielle Cram and Daniela Zyman (eds.), "Interview with Ai Weiwei," in *Shooting Back* (Vienna: Thyssen-Bornemisza Art Contemporary, 2007), 36.

Chapter 3.4

p. 415: Doris Salcedo from Jess Gormey, Antonio Ribeiro, and Chris Michael, "Artist Doris Salcedo on Bogotá: 'The forces at work here are brutal,'" (July 26, 2016), theguardian.com

p. 416: David Grove from David Grove, *In Search of the Olmec* (unpublished work), © David Grove.

p. 425: Carolina A. Miranda, "The artist who made protesters' mirrored shields says the 'struggle porn' media miss point of Standing Rock," *LA Times* (January 12, 2017).

p. 425: Cannupa Hanska Luger, Mirror Shield Community Workshop statement: http://www.allmyrelationsarts.com/mirror-shield-community-workshop/ (November 30, 2016).

p. 425: National Park Service, from "The Native American Graves Protection and Repatriation Act (NAGPRA)" reproduced from *Archaeological Method and Theory: An Encyclopedia*, ed. Linda Ellis (New York: Garland Publishing Co., 2000).

Chapter 3.5

p. 434: Mphethi Morojele, "Architect Profile: MMA Design Studio," *African Design Magazine* (September, 2015), pp. 72–79.

Chapter 3.7

p. 469: Jean-Jacques Rousseau, *On the Social Contract; or, Principles of Political Right*, 1762.

p. 473: Jacques-Louis David from the Revolutionary Convention, 1793, quoted in Robert Cumming, *Art Explained* (New York: DK Publishing, 2005), 70.

Chapter 3.8

p. 482: Gustave Courbet from Robert Williams, *Art Theory: An Historical Introduction* (Malden, MA: Blackwell Publishing, 2004), 127.

p. 486: Charles Baudelaire from *The Painter of Modern Life*, trans. and ed. Jonathan Mayne (London: Phaidon Press, 1995).

p. 494: Paul Gauguin from Charles Estienne, *Gauguin: Biographical and Critical Studies* (Geneva: Skira, 1953), 17.

p. 495: Vincent van Gogh from Letter to Emile Bernard, October 7, 1888 in Arles, France, in *The Complete Letters of Vincent Van Gogh*, vol. 3, no. B19 (New York: Bulfinch Press, 1958/2000).

p. 495: Vincent van Gogh from Letter to Brother Theo, July 10, 1888 in Arles, France, in *The Complete Letters of Vincent Van Gogh*, vol. 3, no. B19 (New York: Bulfinch Press, 1958/2000).

p. 496: Unspecified critic on Claudel from Ruth Butler, *Rodin: The Shape of Genius* (New Haven, CT and London: Yale University Press, 1993), 271.

p. 497: Joris-Karl Huysmans from John Howard (trans.) *Against the Grain* (Lieber & Lewis, 1922).

p. 497: Odilon Redon, from *À soi-même, journal (1867–1915)*, quoted in Met Museum online catalog, https://www.metmuseum.org/art/collection/search/459400.

Chapter 3.9

p. 502: Henri Matisse from Jack Flam, *Matisse: The Man and His Art, 1869–1918* (Ithaca, NY: Cornell University Press, 1986), 196.

p. 506: Marcel Duchamp from Arturo Schwarz, *The Complete Works of Marcel Duchamp* (New York: Delano Greenidge Editions, 1997), II, 442.

p. 508: Salvador Dalí, "L'Âne pourri," *La Surréaliste au service de la Révolution*, June 1930, in Haim Finkelstein, "Dali's Paranoia-Criticism or the Exercise of Freedom," *Twentieth-Century Literature*, v. 21, no. 1 (February, 1975), p. 60.

p. 510: Filippo Marinetti from his "Manifesto for the Italo-Abyssinian War," (1936), quoted in Walter Benjamin, "The Work of Art in the Age of Mechanical Reproduction," in Walter Benjamin, *Illuminations: Essays and Reflections*, ed. Hannah Arendt (New York: Schocken Books, 1968), 241.

p. 512: Agnes Martin quoted in Ann Wilson, "Linear Webs: Agnes Martin," *Art and Artists I, no. 7* (1966), pp. 48–49; reproduced in Olivia Laing, "Agnes Martin: the artist mystic who disappeared into the desert," May 22, 2015, theguardian.com

p. 514: James Weldon and J. Rosamund Johnson, "Lift Every Voice and Sing," 1900.

p. 515: Mark Rothko from Selden Rodman, *Conversations with Artists* (New York: Devin-Adair, Co.,), 1957).

p. 517: Henry Geldzahler, "Interview with Helen Frankenthaler" *Artforum* 4, no. 2 (October 1965), 36–38; reprinted in Kristine Stiles and Peter Selz (eds.), *Theories and Documents of Contemporary Art*, second edition (Berkeley: University of California Press, 2012), 32.

p. 519: Donald Judd, "Specific Objects," *Arts Yearbook, 8*, New York (1965).

Chapter 3.10

p. 526: Ludwig Wittgenstein, from G.E.M. Anscombe (trans.), *Philosophical Investigations* (Oxford: Basil Blackwell, 1958).

p. 526: April Greiman from 1986 interview with Archie Boston, "20 Outstanding Los Angeles Graphic Designers: Interview with April Greiman," *LA Design History*, www.youtube.com/watch?v=DoDItJ4zI98.

p. 531: Evelyn C. Hankins and Stéphane Aquin, *Mark Bradford: Pickett's Charge*, exhibition catalogue, Washington, DC: Hirshhorn Museum and Sculpture Garden, Smithsonian Institution, in association with Yale University Press, 2018.

p. 531: "Meet the Artist: Mark Bradford", Interview with Melissa Chio, February 8, 2018, YouTube, accessed January 10, 2021.

p. 533: Cai Guo-Qiang Returns to China with a (virtual) Bang in major new show at Beijing's Forbidden City Palace Museum," December 21, 2020, theartnewspaper.com

pp. 533–34: Interview with Leslie Hook, "Explosive artist Cai Guo-Qiang on politics and pyrotechnics," *Financial Times*, August 25, 2017.

p. 534: Tara Donovan from Richard McCoy, "Prelude: A Discussion with Tara Donovan," *ART21* Magazine (April 8, 2010): http://blog.art21.org/2010/04/08/prelude-a-discussion-with-tara-donovan/#.VTAZECMp3dk.

PART 4

Chapter 4.1

p. 540: Susan Cervantes from Tyce Hendricks, "Celebrating Art that Draws People Together," *San Francisco Chronicle* (May 6, 2005), F1.

p. 540: Aliseo Purpura-Pontoniere from Tyce Hendricks, "Celebrating Art that Draws People Together," *San Francisco Chronicle* (May 6, 2005), F1.

p. 543: Hilla Rebay (the curator of the foundation and director of the Guggenheim Museum) from the Solomon R. Guggenheim website: http://www.guggenheim.org/guggenheim-foundation/architecture/new-york/.

p. 550: Richard Serra, from Richard Serra's defense of his sculpture at a public hearing in 1985.

p. 551: Diego Rivera from Bertram D. Wolfe, *The Fabulous Life of Diego Rivera* (New York: Stein and Day, 1963), 423.

p. 552: Kryzstof Wodiczko, quoted in "Kryzstof Wodiczko, Tijuana Projection, 2001," *ART21* on pbs.org: http://www.art21.org/images/krzysztof-wodiczko/the-tijuana-projection-2001-0.

Chapter 4.2

p. 566: Lao Tsu, *Tao Te Ching*, translated by Gai-fu Feng and Jane English (Knopf Doubleday Publishing Group, 1974).

p. 566: Anila Quayyum Agha, from Laura C. Mallonee, "ArtPrize Winnter Anila Quayyum Agha Talks Sacred Spaces and Religion," *Hyperallergic* (October 16, 2014). https://hyperallergic.com/155821/artprize-winner-anila-quayyum-agha-talks-sacred-spaces-and-religion/.

Chapter 4.3

p. 572: Darian Leader, "Glue," *The Clock* (London: White Cube, 2010).

p. 575: Jillian Mayer, *I Am Your Grandma*: https://www.youtube.com/watch?v=YfY1lfFu8j8.

Chapter 4.4

pp. 582–83: Wang, Linda, "Guarding Our DNA: Art project exposes the vulnerability of the genetic material we unintentionally leave behind," *Chemical & Engineering News* 91 (25).

p. 584: Description of the Mosque of the Imam, Isfahan, from The Metropolitan Museum of Art, "Works of Art: Islamic Highlights: Signatures, Inscriptions, and Markings," accessed September 13, 2010: www.metmuseum.org/works_of_art/collection_database/islamic?art/mihrab/objectview.aspx?collID=14OID=140006815.

p. 585: Willard Wigan from *The Telegraph* article by Benjamin Secher on July 7, 2007: http://www.telegraph.co.uk/culture/art/3666432/The-tiny-world-of-Willard-Wigan-nano-sculptor.html.

p. 588: Jasper Johns from Martin Friedman, *Visions of America: Landscape as Metaphor in the Late Twentieth Century* (Denver, CO: Denver Art Museum, 1994), 146.

Chapter 4.5

p. 595: Dána-Ain Davis and Christa Craven, *Feminist Ethnography: Thinking Through Methodologies, Challenges & Possibilities* (Lanham, MD: Rowman & Littlefield, 2016), 4.

Chapter 4.6

p. 605: Nick Ut from William Kelly, *Art and Humanist Ideals: Contemporary Perspectives* (Australia: Palgrave Macmillan, 2003), 284.

p. 610: Picasso from Charles Harrison and Paul Wood, *Art in Theory, 1900–2000: An Anthology of Changing Ideas* (Oxford: Blackwell Publishing, 2003), 508.

p. 615: Maya Lin from Marilyn Stokstad, *Art History* (New York: Pearson Education, 2008), xliv.

Chapter 4.7

p. 619: Quote from Teresa Margolles in her lecture "Global Feminisms", Brooklyn Museum (2007): https://www.youtube.com/watch?v=HEO_iyYcFJ4.

p. 620: Interview by Zhuang Hui in *Ai Weiwei: Dropping the Urn* (Pennsylvania: Arcadia University Art Gallery, 2010), 23.

p. 622: Label from Nazi exhibition from Stephanie Barron, *Degenerate Art: The Fate of the Avant-Garde in Nazi Germany* (New York: Harry N. Abrams, 1991), 390.

p. 622: Mary Richardson from June Purvis, *Emmeline Pankhurst: A Biography* (London and New York: Routledge, 2002), 255.

pp. 623–24: Eric Fischl poem from Laura Brandon, *Art and War* (London: I. B. Tauris & Co. Ltd, 2007), 129; and Fischl's remarks from Daniel Sherman and Terry Nardin, *Terror, Culture, Politics: Rethinking 9/11* (Indiana: Indiana University Press, 2006), 60.

p. 626: Florence Owens Thompson from Kiku Adatto, *Picture Perfect: Life in the Age of the Photo Op.* (Princeton, NJ: Princeton University Press, 2008), 247–48.

p. 628: John Newsom, "UNCG grad student sheds light on going to jail with jumpsuit", *The Washington Times* (December 3, 2016).

Chapter 4.8

p. 631: Willem de Kooning from an interview with David Sylvester (BBC, 1960), "Content is a Glimpse..." in *Location I* (Spring, 1963) and reprinted in David Sylvester, "The Birth of 'Woman I,'" *Burlington Magazine* 137, no. 1105 (April, 1995), 223.

p. 640: Matisse from "Exactitude is not Truth," 1947, essay by Matisse written for an exhibition catalog (Liège: Association pour le progrès intellectuel et artistique de la Wallonie, with the participation of Galerie Maight, Paris); English translation (Philadelphia Museum of Art, 1948); reprinted in Jack Flam, *Matisse on Art* (Berkeley, CA: University of California Press, 1995/1973), 179–81.

Chapter 4.9

p. 651: Cindy Sherman from "Interview with Els Barents," in *Cindy Sherman* (Munich: Schirmer und Mosel, 1982); reprinted in Kristine Stiles and Peter Selz (eds.), *Theories and Documents of Contemporary Art: A Sourcebook of Artists' Writings* (Berkeley, CA: University of California Press, 1996), 792–93.

p. 651: Marc Quinn from Marc Quinn, "Exhibition: Selfs," Beyeler Foundation, Riehen/Basel, June 8–July 19, 2009 http://marcquinn.com/exhibitions/solo-exhibitions/selfs

p. 652: April Greiman, from an interview with Meg Miller, "Don't Call April Greiman the 'Queen of New Wave,'" *AIGA Eye On Design* (March 22, 2019), https://eyeondesign.aiga.org/april-greiman-is-still-ahead-of-the-curve/

p. 655: Jess Righthand, "Q and A: James Luna," *Smithsonian Magazine* (January 2011).

p. 657: Nikki S. Lee from Erica Schlaikjer, "Woman's Art Requires Becoming a Chameleon," *The Daily Northwestern* (February 24, 2006), Campus Section.

Illustration Credits

0.0.1 Photo Studio Kobra Collection © Kobra/DACS, London 2022; 0.0.2 Courtesy Marcia Smilack; 0.0.3 Metropolitan Museum of Art, Gift of Mrs. Russell Sage, 1908, 08.228; 0.0.4 Photo Hans Haacke. Courtesy the artist and Paula Cooper Gallery, New York. © Hans Haacke/DACS 2022; 0.0.5 Division of Cultural and Community Life, National Museum of American History, Smithsonian Institution, Washington, D.C.; 0.0.6 Photo The Maas Gallery, London/ Bridgeman Images; 0.0.7 © 2015 FedEx Corporation. All Rights Reserved; 0.0.8 Photo Charles Platiau/Reuters/ Alamy Stock Photo; 0.0.9 Sakai Collection, Tokyo; 0.0.10 Robert Harding Picture Library/agefotostock.com; 0.0.11 National Gallery of Art, Washington, D.C., Gift of Mr. and Mrs. Robert Woods Bliss. Courtesy National Gallery of Art, Washington, D.C.; 0.0.12 Musée du Louvre, Paris; 0.0.13 Photo Ben Hines. Artwork © Amy Sherald. Courtesy the artist and Hauser & Wirth; 0.0.14 Photo Erich Lessing/ akg-images; 0.0.15 Collection of Diane and Dan Mossenson, Perth, Western Australia. © Mossenson Galleries and the artist; 0.0.16 Photo Diane Mossenson. © Mossenson Galleries; 0.0.17 Courtesy of Pest Control Office, Banksy, Love Is in the Bin, 2018; 0.0.18 Photo Kerem Yucel/ AFP via Getty Images; 0.0.19 Keith Haring artwork © Keith Haring Foundation; 0.0.20a, 0.0.20b Photos © Jens Weber. Artwork © Ai Weiwei Studio; 0.0.21 Photo © Tate (Andrew Dunkley). © Mona Hatoum; 0.0.22 Photo Manuel Cohen/ Scala, Florence; 0.0.23 Whitney Museum of American Art, New York; purchased with funds from Eli and Edythe L. Broad, the Mrs. Percy Uris Purchase Fund, and the Painting and Sculpture Committee, 88.17a-b. © The Estate of Eva Hesse. Courtesy Hauser & Wirth; 0.0.24 Allan Houser archives © Chiinde LLC; p. 33 (above) Photo Michael Runkel/ Alamy Stock Photo; (center) Courtesy National Gallery of Modern Art, New Delhi; (below) Kunsthistorisches Museum, Vienna; 1.1.1 © Tomasz Pado/ Dreamstime.com; 1.1.2a First Place prize winner of the National Park Service's 'Leicester B. Holland Prize', 2011. Library of Congress, Washington, D.C., HABS IL-1234. Image courtesy Thad Heckman; 1.1.2b Photo courtesy Thad Heckman and the R. Buckminster Fuller Dome Not-For-Profit (fullerdomehome.com); 1.1.3 Musée des Beaux-Arts de Lyon. © Succession H. Matisse/DACS 2022; 1.1.4 The Museum of Modern Art, New York, The Louis E. Stern Collection, 988.1964.6. Digital image, The Museum of Modern Art, New York/Scala, Florence. © Succession Picasso/DACS, London 2022; 1.1.5 Ralph Larmann; 1.1.6 Axis Images/Alamy Stock Photo; 1.1.7 © Sauerkids; 1.1.8 British Museum, London; 1.1.9 © CLAMP/Kodansha Ltd; 1.1.10 Ralph Larmann; 1.1.11 Nike; 1.1.12 Art Institute of Chicago, Illinois/ Helen Birch Bartlett Memorial Collection/Bridgeman Images; 1.1.13 Museo de Arte Moderno, Mexico City. © Banco de México Diego Rivera Frida Kahlo Museums Trust, Mexico, D.F./DACS 2022; 1.1.14 Image courtesy Peter Freeman, Inc., New York;

1.1.15 © Bowness, Hepworth Estate; 1.1.16 © ADAGP, Paris and DACS, London 2022; 1.1.17 Courtesy the Victorian Spiritualists' Union, Melbourne; 1.1.18 National Gallery of Art, Washington, D.C., Collection of Mr. and Mrs. Paul Mellon, 1983.1.81; 1.1.19, 1.1.20 Ralph Larmann; 1.1.21 Courtesy Flomenhaft Gallery, New York. © Estate of Miriam Schapiro/ARS, NY and DACS, London 2022; 1.1.22 Ralph Larmann; 1.1.23 Courtesy AT&T Archives and History Center; 1.1.24 Photo Christie's Images/Bridgeman Images; 1.1.25 © Georgia O'Keeffe Museum/DACS 2022; 1.1.26 Noma Bar/Dutch Uncle; 1.1.27 © 2012 The M.C. Escher Company-Holland. All rights reserved. www. mcescher.com; 1.1.28 Photo Sarina Basta. Artwork © Kara Walker, courtesy of Sikkema Jenkins & Co., New York; 1.2.1 Ralph Larmann; 1.2.2 iStockphoto. com; 1.2.3 Photo courtesy the Marlborough Gallery Inc., New York. © Estate of David Smith/VAGA at ARS, NY and DACS, London 2022; 1.2.4 Rheinisches Landesmuseum, Bonn; 1.2.5 Photo Russell Johnson. Courtesy Lino Tagliapietra, Inc.; 1.2.6 Museo dell'Ara Pacis, Rome; 1.2.7 Photo Trustees of the British Museum, London; 1.2.8a Photo Mary Cameron-Sarani; 1.2.8b Prisma/SuperStock; 1.2.9 Ralph Larmann; 1.2.10a, 1.2.10b Photo Clements/Howcroft, MA. Courtesy the artists; 1.2.11 Photo Nationalmuseum, Stockholm; 1.2.12 Photo Andrew Hawthorne. Courtesy the artists; 1.2.13 Photo Sue Ormerod. © Rachel Whiteread. Courtesy Gagosian Gallery, London; 1.2.14 © Estate of Marisol/ARS, NY and DACS, London; 1.2.15 Philadelphia Museum of Art, The Louise and Walter Arensberg Collection, 1950-134-4. © Succession Brancusi - All rights reserved. ADAGP, Paris and DACS, London 2022; 1.2.16 Photo Szilas; 1.2.17 Petter Oftedal/Alamy Stock Photo; 1.2.18 Photo Stefano Politi Markovina/ Alamy Stock Photo. Bourgeois © The Easton Foundation/VAGA at ARS, NY and DACS, London 2022; 1.2.19 Photononstop/ SuperStock; 1.2.20a, 1.2.20b © Wangechi Mutu. Courtesy the artist and Victoria Miro, London; 1.2.21 Museum of Modern Art, New York, Purchase, 130.1946.a–c. Photo 2012, Museum of Modern Art, New York/Scala, Florence. © DACS 2022; 1.3.1 Los Angeles County Museum of Art (LACMA), California. Purchased with funds provided by the Mr. and Mrs. William Preston Harrison Collection, 78.7 (www.lacma.org). Magritte © ADAGP, Paris and DACS, London 2022; 1.3.2 Photo Franck Fotos/Alamy Stock Photo; 1.3.3, 1.3.4 Ralph Larmann; 1.3.5a, 1.3.5b Photo courtesy of DC Moore Gallery, New York. © Jon F. Anderson, Estate of Paul Cadmus/VAGA at ARS, NY and DACS, London 2022. Line artwork Ralph Larmann; 1.3.6 Contarelli Chapel, Church of San Luigi dei Francesci, Rome; 1.3.7 Ralph Larmann; 1.3.8 Musée du Louvre, Paris; 1.3.9 Courtesy K.H. Renlund Museum – Provincial Museum of Central Ostrobothnia, Kokkola, Finland; 1.3.10 The Nelson-Atkins Museum of Art, Kansas City, Missouri. Purchase William Rockhill Nelson Trust, 47-71. Photo John Lamberton; 1.3.11 © Benton

Testamentary Trusts/UMB Bank Trustee/ VAGA at ARS, NY and DACS, London 2022; 1.3.12 Ralph Larmann; 1.3.13 Crystal Bridges Museum of American Art, Bentonville, Arkansas; 1.3.14 Metropolitan Museum of Art, New York, Purchase, The Dillon Fund Gift, 1988; 1.3.15 Ralph Larmann; 1.3.16 © Supergiant Games, LLC 2014; 1.3.17a Ralph Larmann; 1.3.17b JTB Photo/SuperStock; 1.3.18 Private Collection; 1.3.19 Ralph Larmann; 1.3.20 Santa Maria Novella, Florence; 1.3.21a, 1.3.21b Stanza della Segnatura, Vatican Museums, Rome; 1.3.22 Ralph Larmann; 1.3.23 © 2012 The M.C. Escher Company-Holland. All rights reserved. www.mcescher.com; 1.3.24 From Trinity: Volume 1, TM and © DC Comics; 1.4.1, 1.4.2 Ralph Larmann; 1.4.3 Courtesy Charles Csuri; 1.4.4 Ralph Larmann; 1.4.5 akg-images; 1.4.6, 1.4.7 Ralph Larmann; 1.4.8 Photo Joshua White. Courtesy the artist and Thomas Solomon Gallery, Los Angeles. © Analia Saban 2008; 1.4.9, 1.4.10, 1.4.11 Ralph Larmann; 1.4.12 Cleveland Museum of Art, Mr. and Mrs. William H. Marlatt Fund, 1965.233; 1.4.13 National Gallery of Art, Washington, D.C., Chester Dale Collection, 1963.10.94; 1.4.14 Fine Arts Museum of San Francisco, Gift of Vivian Burns, Inc., 74.8; 1.4.15 Ralph Larmann; 1.4.16 © Mark Tansey; 1.4.17 The Art Institute of Chicago, Illinois/Helen Birch Bartlett Memorial Collection/Bridgeman Images. © Succession Picasso/DACS, London 2022; 1.4.18 Museum of Modern Art, New York, Gift of Mr. and Mrs. Ben Heller, 240.1969. Photo 2012, Museum of Modern Art, New York/Scala, Florence. © The Barnett Newman Foundation, New York/DACS, London 2022; 1.4.19 The Museum of Fine Arts, Houston, Gift of Audrey Jones Beck. © ADAGP, Paris and DACS, London 2022; 1.4.20 Ralph Larmann; 1.4.21 Kunstmuseum Basel, Switzerland; 1.4.22 British Museum, London; 1.4.23 Ralph Larmann; 1.4.24a, 1.4.24b Musée d'Orsay, Paris; 1.4.25a, 1.4.25b Yale University Press. 1.4.26 Ralph Larmann; 1.4.27 Los Angeles County Museum of Art (LACMA), California. Gift of Dr. and Mrs. Sam K. Lee, M.86.330 (www.lacma.org); 1.4.28 Yale University Art Gallery, New Haven, Bequest of Stephen Carlton Clark, B.A. 1903, 1961.18.34; 1.4.29 Photo Edwin Medina. Courtesy the artist and Embajada Gallery; 1.4.30 National Gallery of Art, Washington, D.C. Collection of Mr. and Mrs. John Hay Whitney, 1998.74.7. © Succession H. Matisse/DACS 2022; 1.4.31 Albright-Knox Art Gallery, Buffalo, New York, General Purchase Funds, 1946; 1.4.32 Photo Albin Dahlström/Moderna Museet-Stockholm. Courtesy Hilma af Klint Foundation; 1.4.33 Courtesy the artist; 1.5.1 Galleria Borghese, Rome; 1.5.2 Albright-Knox Art Gallery, Buffalo, New York, Bequest of A. Conger Goodyear and Gift of George F. Goodyear, 1964. © DACS 2022; 1.5.3 Solomon R. Guggenheim Museum, New York, Partial gift of the artist, 1989, 89.3626. Photo David Heald © Solomon R. Guggenheim Foundation, New York. © Jenny Holzer. ARS, NY and DACS, London 2022; 1.5.4 © Bridget Riley, 2012. All rights reserved; 1.5.5 © Gregory Barsamian 2013. Photo the artist; 1.5.6 American

Empirical Pictures/AA Film Archive/ Alamy Stock Photo; 1.5.7 Arte/Bavaria/ WDR/Spauke, Bernd/The Kobal Collection; 1.5.8 Courtesy Oliver Harrison; 1.5.9 Costumes: Akademie der Künste, Berlin (Gerhard-Bohner-Archive). Dancers: Members of the Bavarian Junior Ballet Munich. Music: Hans-Joachim Hespos. Costume Reconstruction and New Version: Ulrike Dietrich. Photo © Wilfried Hösl; 1.5.10 Photo OSA Images; 1.5.11 © Board of Trustees, National Gallery of Art, Washington, D.C.; 1.5.12 Courtesy the artist; 1.5.13 National Gallery of Art, Washington, D.C., Samuel H. Kress Collection, 1939.1.293; 1.5.14 Photo University of South Florida. © Holt-Smithson Foundation/VAGA at ARS, NY and DACS, London 2022; 1.5.15 © Ai Weiwei Studio; 1.5.16 Rotger/Iberfoto/ photoaisa.com; 1.5.17 Library of Congress, Washington, D.C., Prints & Photographs Division, LC-USZ62-536; 1.5.18 © Suzanne Anker; 1.5.19 © the artist. Courtesy Catherine Person Gallery, Seattle, Washington; 1.6.1 Ralph Larmann; 1.6.2 Library of Congress, Washington, D.C. Prints & Photographs Division, H. Irving Olds collection, LC-DIG- jpd-02018; 1.6.3a Photo Malono Yllera (instagram.com/manoloyllera); 1.6.3b Ralph Larmann; 1.6.4 Courtesy Galerie Berès, Paris. © ADAGP, Paris and DACS, London 2022; 1.6.5 © Kanayama Akira and Tanaka Atsuko Association; 1.6.6 Lito and Kim Camacho Collection, Manila. © Kanayama Akira and Tanaka Atsuko Association; 1.6.7 Museum of Modern Art, New York, Blanchette Hooker Rockefeller Fund, 377.1971. Photo 2012, Museum of Modern Art, New York/ Scala, Florence. © Romare Bearden Foundation/VAGA at ARS, NY and DACS, London 2022; 1.6.8 © The Joseph and Robert Cornell Memorial Foundation/ VAGA at ARS, NY and DACS, London 2022; 1.6.9 Photo M. Borchi/DEA/Getty Images; 1.6.10 Ralph Larmann; 1.6.11 © Robert Rauschenberg Foundation/VAGA at ARS, NY and DACS, London 2022; 1.6.12 American Museum & Gardens, Bath; 1.6.13 Photo Valery Egorov/iStock. com; 1.6.14 Collection National Palace Museum, Taipei, Taiwan; 1.6.15a © Airpano (www.airpano.com); 1.6.15b Ralph Larmann; 1.6.16a © Tibor Bognar/Photononstop/Corbis; 1.6.16b Ralph Larmann; 1.6.17 Courtesy Drepung Loseling Monastery, Inc.; 1.7.1 Photographs in the Carol M. Highsmith Archive, Library of Congress, Prints and Photographs Division, Washington, D.C. (LC-DIG-highsm-39254). © Oldenburg/van Bruggen. Courtesy Pace Gallery 1.7.2 © Golsa Golchini; 1.7.3 Musée d'Orsay, Paris. Photo akg-images; 1.7.4 Photo © Jorge Pérez de Lara; 1.7.5 Gemäldegalerie, Staatliche Museen, Berlin; 1.7.6 Purchased with assistance from the Art Fund and the American Fund for the Tate Gallery 1997. Photo Tate, London, 2012. © ADAGP, Paris and DACS, London 2022; 1.7.7, 1.7.8 Ralph Larmann; 1.7.9 National Museum, Ife, Nigeria; 1.7.10 The National Gallery, London/Scala, Florence. Line artwork Ralph Larmann; 1.7.11 Ralph Larmann; 1.7.12a National Archaeological Museum, Athens; 1.7.12b Ralph Larmann;

A. Cooke/Corbis; **2.5.33** Courtesy Salk Institute, La Jolla, CA; **2.5.34** Photo courtesy Michael Graves & Associates; **2.5.35** © Chuck Eckert/Alamy; **2.5.36a** Courtesy Zaha Hadid Architects; **2.5.36b** © Roland Halbe/artur; **2.5.37** Photo © John Swain; **2.6.1** Courtesy Trudy Labell Fine Art, Florida. © the artist; **2.6.2** Metropolitan Museum of Art, New York, Gift of Jaap Polak, 2009, 2009.321; **2.6.3** Cleveland Museum of Art, Gift of the Hanna Fund, 1954.857; **2.6.4** Palace Museum, Beijing; **2.6.5** Courtesy the Voulkos & Co. Catalogue Project, www.voulkos.com; **2.6.6** British Museum, London; **2.6.7** © Angelo Hornak/Corbis; **2.6.8** Photo Teresa Nouri Rishel © ARS, NY and DACS, London 2022; **2.6.9** National Archaeological Museum, Athens; **2.6.10** The Walters Art Museum, Baltimore. Acquired by Henry Walters, 1929; **2.6.11** Kunsthistorisches Museum, Vienna; **2.6.12** Metropolitan Museum of Art, New York, Purchase, Rogers Fund and Henry Walters Gift, 1916, 16.1.3a, b; **2.6.13** Courtesy Daniela Villegas; **2.6.14** Private Collection; **2.6.15** ©Christie's Images/Corbis; **2.6.16** The Solomon R. Guggenheim Foundation, New York, 88.3620. © Faith Ringgold/ARS, NY and DACS, London, Courtesy ACA Galleries, New York 2022; **2.6.17a, 2.6.17b** Photo Smithsonian American Art Museum/Art Resource/Scala, Florence. © ADAGP, Paris and DACS, London 2022; **2.6.18** Collaborators: Charles MacAdam with Interplay Design & Manufacturing, Inc, Nova Scotia, Canada (design & production); Norihide Imagawa with T.I.S. & Partners., Co. Ltd, Tokyo (structural design). Photo Masaki Koizumi. Courtesy the artist; **2.6.19** Metropolitan Museum of Art, Rogers Fund, 1939, 39.153. Photo Metropolitan Museum of Art/Art Resource/Scala, Florence; **2.6.20** Seattle Art Museum, Gift of John H. Hauberg and John and Grace Putnam, 86.278. Photo Paul Macapia; **2.6.21** Photo courtesy Andrew Early; **2.7.1** British Museum, London; **2.7.2** Tokyo National Museum **2.7.3** V&A Images/Victoria & Albert Museum; **2.7.4** Ralph Larmann; **2.7.5** © Kok Cheow Yeoh (www.yeoh.com); **2.7.6** © DACS 2022; **2.7.7** © Lianem/Dreamstime.com; **2.7.8** Koninklijke Bibliotheek, The Hague, folio 8r., shelf no. 69B 10; **2.7.9** General Motors Corp. Used with permission, GM Media Archives; **2.7.10** © Annsunnyday/Dreamstime.com; **2.7.11** from *Works of Geoffrey Chaucer*, Kelmscott Press, 1896; **2.7.12** Library of Congress Prints, Washington, D.C., Prints & Photographs Division, LC-DIG- ppmsc-03521; **2.7.13** © Maxfield Parrish Family, LLC/VAGA at ARS, NY and DACS, London 2022; **2.7.14** Harry Potter characters, names and related indicia are © & TM Warner Bros. Entertainment Inc. Publishing Rights © J. K. Rowling. (s18); **2.7.15** © Jorge Colombo, courtesy *The New Yorker*; **2.7.16** The Art Institute of Chicago, Mr. and Mrs. Carter H. Harrison Collection, 1954.1193; **2.7.17** Courtesy Pentagram Design, New York; **2.7.18** Video-computer graphic © April Greiman; **2.7.19** Shiseido Corporate Museum, Kakegawa-shi, Shizuoka-ken; **2.7.20** AA Film Archive/Alamy Stock Photo. Courtesy of Universal Studios Licensing LLC; **2.7.21** Ralph Larmann; **2.7.22** Private Collection; **2.7.23** Ralph Larmann; **2.7.24** Image provided courtesy of Blizzard Entertainment; **2.7.25** Photo Martien Mulder; **2.7.26** Courtesy Hello Monday/alanmenken.com; **2.8.1** Ralph Larmann; **2.8.2** Image appears courtesy Abelardo Morell; **2.8.3** Gernsheim Collection, Harry Ransom Humanities Research Centre, University of Texas at Austin; **2.8.5** British Library, London; **2.8.6a, 2.8.6b** British Library, London/British Library Board. All Rights Reserved/Bridgeman Images; **2.8.7** Ralph Larmann; **2.8.8** Gernsheim Collection, Harry Ransom Humanities Research Centre, University of Texas at Austin; **2.8.9** Bibliothèque nationale, Paris; **2.8.10** J. Paul Getty Museum, Los Angeles (84.XM.443.3). Digital image courtesy the Getty's Open Content Program; **2.8.11** © Ansel Adams Publishing Rights Trust/Corbis; **2.8.12** © Henri Cartier-Bresson © Fondation Henri Cartier-Bresson/Magnum; **2.8.13** © Maia Dery; **2.8.14** Photo Collection F. Van Hoof-Williame; **2.8.15** © Eggleston Artistic Trust. Courtesy Eggleston Artistic Trust and David Zwirner; **2.8.16** Sandy Skoglund, Radioactive Cats © 1980; **2.8.17** Photo © Edward Burtynsky, courtesy Flowers, London & Nicholas Metivier, Toronto; **2.8.18** Museum of Modern Art, New York, Gift on behalf of The Friends of Education of The Museum of Modern Art, 70.1997.2. Photo 2012, Museum of Modern Art, New York/Scala, Florence. © Carrie Mae Weems. Courtesy the artist and Jack Shainman Gallery, New York; **2.8.19** Courtesy of the Peabody Museum of Archaeology and Ethnology, Harvard University, 35-5-10/53039; **2.8.20** © Sally Mann. Courtesy Gagosian; **2.8.21** Royal Photographic Society, Bath; **2.8.22** Courtesy Yossi Milo Gallery, New York. © DACS 2022; **2.8.23** Library of Congress, Washington, D.C., Prints & Photographs Division, LC-DIG-nclc-01555; **2.8.24** © Hiroko Masuike/New York Times/Eyevine; **2.8.25** J. Paul Getty Museum, Los Angeles (84.XM.695.19). Digital image courtesy of the Getty's Open Content Program; **2.8.26** © Estate of Garry Winogrand, courtesy Fraenkel Gallery, San Francisco; **2.8.27** Museum of Modern Art, New York, Gift of the photographer, 219.1961. Photo 2021. Digital image, The Museum of Modern Art, New York/Scala, Florence. © The Estate of Edward Steichen/ARS, NY and DACS, London 2022; **2.8.28** © The Estate of Diane Arbus; **2.8.29** Inv.# DLA 19.061. Courtesy David Kordansky Gallery, Los Angeles; **2.9.1** Ralph Larmann; **2.9.2** Courtesy Laboratorio Paravicini; **2.9.3** Library of Congress, Washington, D.C., Prints & Photographs Division, LC-USZ62-45683; **2.9.4** Gainew Gallery/Alamy Stock Photo; **2.9.5** akg-images; **2.9.6** Courtesy Everett Collection/Mary Evans; **2.9.7** British Film Institute (BFI); **2.9.8** M.G.M./Album/akg-images; **2.9.9** La Classe Americane/uFilm/France 3/The Kobal Collection; **2.9.10** Album/akg-images; **2.9.11** Disney Enterprises/Album/akg-images; **2.9.12** British Film Institute (BFI); **2.9.13a** New Line Cinema/The Kobal Collection; **2.9.13b** Album/akg-images; **2.9.14** Handprint Entertainment/Lions Gate Film/Miramax Films/Ronald Grant Archive/Mary Evans; **2.9.15** Fox 200 Pictures/Levantine Fils/Album/akg-images; **2.9.16a** Image © Mike Din, courtesy the artist, Serpentine Sackler Gallery, London and Bridget Donahue, NYC**; 2.9.16b** Courtesy ICA Miami. Photo Fredrik Nilsen Studio. © Sondra Perry. Courtesy of the artist, ICA Miami and Bridget Donahue, NYC; **2.9.16c** Image © Mike Din, courtesy the artist, Serpentine Sackler Gallery, London and Bridget Donahue, NYC; **2.9.17** © AF Archive/Alamy; **2.9.18** British Film Institute (BFI); **2.9.19** Courtesy Electronic Arts Intermix (EAI), New York; **2.9.20** Courtesy Epic Games; **2.9.21** Photo CBS/Not A Real Company/Album/Alamy Stock Photo; **2.10.1** Photo © Estate of David Gahr. © ADAGP, Paris and DACS, London 2022; **2.10.2** Photo Timothy Schenck. Courtesy of Friends of the High Line; **2.10.3** Photo Karla Merrifield. © Yoko Ono; **2.10.4** Rowland Scherman/Hulton Archive/Getty Images; **2.10.5** Photo Betsy Jackson. © ARS, NY and DACS, London 2021; **2.10.6** Photo Marco Anelli. © Marina Abramović. Courtesy of the Marina Abramović Archives/DACS 2022 **2.10.7a** Photo SuperStock. Copyright Kienholz, courtesy L.A. Louver; **2.10.7b** Photo © Ed Jansen. Copyright Kienholz, courtesy L.A. Louver; **2.10.8** Photo Sarina Basta. Artwork © Kara Walker, courtesy of Sikkema Jenkins & Co., New York; **2.10.9** Still courtesy of Milford Galleries, Dunedin and Yuki Kihara. © Yuki Kihara; **2.10.10** Photo courtesy James Cohan, New York. © Yinka Shonibare CBE. All Rights Reserved, DACS 2022; **2.10.11** Photo Lise Balsby © Felix Gonzalez-Torres. Courtesy of the Felix Gonzalez-Torres Foundation; **2.10.12** Photo Santiago Orti. © Felix Gonzalez-Torres. Courtesy of the Felix Gonzalez-Torres Foundation; **2.10.13** Photo Red Sand Project; **p. 345** (above) Photo © acarapi/123RF.com; (center) British Library/akg-images; (below) Art Institute of Chicago, Charles H. and Mary F.S. Worcester Collection, 1964.336; **p. 346** (top half of page, from left to right) see ill. 3.1.2 on p. 349; see ill. 3.1.22 on p. 362; see ill. 3.3.2 on p. 392; see ill. 3.3.10b on p. 397; see ill. 3.4.11 on p. 417; see ill. 1.6.14 on p. 125; (bottom half of page, from left to right) see ill. 3.1.17 on p. 358; see ill. 3.4.3 on p. 412; see ill. 2.4.10 on p. 234; see ill. 3.3.9 on p. 396; see ill. 1.2.6 on p. 54; see ill. 3.3.5 on p. 393; **p. 347** (top half of page, from left to right) see ill. 4.6.8 on p. 609; see ill. 1.6.15a on p. 126; see ill. 1.6.2 on p. 117; see ill. 2.8.3 on p. 302; see ill. 4.7.8 on p. 624; (bottom half of page, from left to right) see ill. 1.8.10 on p. 146; see ill. 3.7.5 on p. 469; see ill. 4.5.1 on p. 592; see ill. 3.7.15 on p. 477; see ill. 4.6.10 on p. 611; see ill. 4.5.12 on p. 601; see ill. 4.9.7 on p. 653; **3.1.1** Drazen Tomic; **3.1.2** Photo courtesy Dean Snow; **3.1.3** Erich Lessing/akg-images; **3.1.4** J. Paul Getty Museum, Los Angeles (88.AA.80). Digital image courtesy of the Getty's Open Content Program; **3.1.5** Image courtesy the Mellaarts/Çatalhöyük Research Project; **3.1.6** Photo Jeff Morgan Travel/Alamy; **3.1.7** Archaeological Museum, Heraklion; **3.1.8a, 3.1.8b** British Museum, London; **3.1.9** Iraq Museum, Baghdad; **3.1.10** Metropolitan Museum of Art, New York, Gift of John D. Rockefeller Jr., 1932, 32.143.2; **3.1.11** Photo Scala, Florence/BPK, Bildagentur für Kunst, Kultur und Geschichte, Berlin; **3.1.12** Photo Trustees of the British Museum, London; **3.1.13** National Geographic/SuperStock; **3.1.14** Photo Trustees of the British Museum, London; **3.1.15** Gianni Dagli Orti/Egyptian Museum, Cairo/The Art Archive; **3.1.16** Ägyptisches Museum, Staatliche Museen, Berlin; **3.1.17** Egyptian Museum, Cairo; **3.1.18** British Museum, London; **p. 360 left, 3.1.19** Photo G. Dagli Orti/DeAgostini/Diomedia; **p. 360 center, 3.1.20** Minneapolis Institute of Arts, Minnesota; **p. 360 right, 3.1.21** Vatican Museums, Rome; **3.1.22** Photo G. Nimatallah/DeAgostini/Diomedia; **3.1.23, 3.1.24** Ralph Larmann; **3.1.25** British Museum, London; **3.1.26** © Grant Rooney/Alamy Stock Photo; **3.1.27** Photo © Musée du Louvre, Dist. RMN-Grand Palais/Anne Chauvet; **3.1.28, 3.1.29** Photos Scala, Florence; **3.1.30** Raimund Kutter/imagebroker.net; **3.1.31** Palazzo Torlonia, Rome; **3.1.32** Giovanni Caselli; **3.1.33** Image Source Pink/Alamy; **3.1.34, 3.1.35** iStockphoto.com; **3.1.36** Photo © Viacheslav Lopatin/123RF.com; **3.2.1** Drazen Tomic; **3.2.2, 3.2.3** Zev Radovan/www.BibleLandPictures.com; **3.2.4** Canali Photobank, Milan, Italy; **3.2.5** Photo Scala, Florence; **3.2.6** © Alp S/Alamy Stock Photo; **3.2.7** Monastery of St. Catherine, Sinai, Egypt; **3.2.8a** Photo Scala, Florence; **3.2.8b** Ralph Larmann; **3.2.9** Photo Scala, Florence; **3.2.10, 3.2.11a, 3.2.11b** British Library, London; **3.2.12** Biblioteca Governativa, Lucca; **3.2.13** British Library/akg-images; **3.2.14** Musées Royaux d'Art et d'Histoire, Brussels; **3.2.15** © Hanan Isachar/Corbis; **3.2.16** Mohamed Amin/Robert Harding; **3.2.17** Photo © Dilek Mermer/Anadolu Agency/Getty Images; **3.2.18** Nasser D. Khalili Collection of Islamic Art, MSS 745.2. © Nour Foundation, courtesy the Khalili Family Trust; **3.2.19** Drazen Tomic; **3.2.20** Photo © Gérard Labriet/Photononstop/Diomedia; **3.2.21** Ralph Larmann; **3.2.22** Photononstop/SuperStock; **3.2.23** Ralph Larmann; **3.2.24** Hervé Champollion/akg-images; **3.2.25** Sonia Halliday Photographs; **3.2.26, 3.2.27** Galleria degli Uffizi, Florence; **3.3.1** Drazen Tomic; **3.3.2** iStockphoto.com; **3.3.3** robertharding/Alamy Stock Photo; **3.3.4** Drazen Tomic; **3.3.5** Robert Harding Picture Library/SuperStock; **3.3.6a** © Reuters/Corbis; **3.3.6b** © Ton Koene/ZUMA Press/Corbis; **3.3.7a** © Frédéric Soltan/Sygma/Corbis; **3.3.7b** © Pep Roig/Alamy; **3.3.8** Brooklyn Museum, Gift of Mr & Mrs Alastair B. Martin, the Guennol Collection, 72.163a–b; **3.3.9** Hunan Museum, Changsha, China; **3.3.10a** Melvyn Longhurst/SuperStock; **3.3.10b** Hemis.fr/SuperStock; **3.3.11** © Ai Weiwei Studio; **3.3.12** Palace Museum, Beijing, China; **3.3.13** Collection Hong Kong Museum of Art; **3.3.14** Aflo Diversion/Diomedia; **3.3.16** Photo Silas Stein/dpa picture alliance/Alamy Stock Photo. Courtesy Victoria Miro, London/Venice © Yayoi Kusama; **3.3.17** Horyu-ji Treasure House, Ikaruga, Nara Prefecture, Japan; **3.3.18** The Tokugawa Art Museum, Nagoya, Japan; **3.3.19** Library of Congress, Washington, D.C., Prints & Photographs Division, H. Irving Olds collection, LC-DIG-jpd-02018; **3.3.20** iStockphoto.com; **3.3.21** © Do Ho Suh. Courtesy the artist and Lehmann Maupin, New York and Hong Kong; **3.3.22** © Shirley Hu/Dreamstime.com; **3.3.23** © Kevin R. Morris/Corbis; **3.3.24** Photo © acarapi/ 123RF.com; **3.3.25** © The Propeller Group 2021. Image courtesy the artists and James Cohan, New York. Photo Michael Underwood. **3.4.1** Drazen Tomic; **3.4.2a** G. Dagli Orti/DeAgostini Picture Library/The Art Archive; **3.4.2b, 3.4.2c** Anton, F., *Ancient Peruvian Textiles*, Thames & Hudson Ltd, London, 1987; **3.4.3** Museo Arqueología, Lima, Peru/Bridgeman Art Library; **3.4.4** Royal Tombs of Sipán Museum, Lambayeque; **3.4.5** iStockphoto.com; **3.4.6** Dumbarton Oaks Research Library and Collections, Washington, D.C.; **3.4.7a, 3.4.7b, 3.4.7c** © Doris Salcedo and White Cube; **3.4.8** Drazen Tomic; **3.4.9** Richard Hewitt Stewart/National

Geographic Stock; **3.4.10a** Drazen Tomic; **3.4.10b** © aerialarchives.com/Alamy; **3.4.11** © Ken Welsh/Alamy; **3.4.12** © Gianni Dagli Orti/Corbis; **3.4.13** Dallas Museum of Art, Gift of Patsy R. and Raymond D. Nasher, 1983.148; **3.4.14** Peabody Museum, Harvard University, Cambridge, Massachusetts, 48-63-20/17561; **3.4.15** Biblioteca Nazionale Centrale di Firenze; **3.4.16** Museo Nacional de Antropología, Mexico City; **3.4.17** Museo del Templo Mayor, Mexico City; **3.4.18** Museo de Aguascalientes – ICA, INBA; **3.4.19** Photo © Monica Lozano; **3.4.20** Drazen Tomic; **3.4.21** Newark Museum, Gift of Amelia Elizabeth White, 1937. 37.236 © 2014. Photo The Newark Museum/Art Resource/Scala, Florence; **3.4.22** Photo Tyler Dingee. Courtesy Palace of the Governors Photo Archives (NMHM/DCA), Neg. No. 073453; **3.4.23** © Chris Howes/Wild Places Photography/Alamy; **3.4.24a**, **3.4.24b** Peabody Museum, Harvard University, Cambridge, Massachusetts, 99-12-10/53121; **3.4.25** Missouri Historical Society, St. Louis, 1882.18.32; **3.4.26** American Museum of Natural History, New York; **3.4.27** Photo © Rory Wakemup. © Cannupa Hanska Luger; **3.4.28** Photo Keith Walklet. Courtesy Yosemite Conservancy; **3.4.29** Photo Jennifer Bresee; **3.5.1** Drazen Tomic; **3.5.2** National Museum, Lagos; **3.5.3** Linden Museum, Stuttgart; **3.5.4** National Museum of African Art, Smithsonian Institution, Washington, D.C.; **3.5.5** Dallas Museum of Art, Foundation for the Arts Collection, Gift of the McDermott Foundation, 1996.184. FA; **3.5.6** Courtesy the Artist & Primo Marella Gallery; **3.5.7** Musée Barbier-Mueller, Geneva; **3.5.8** © Michel Renaudeau; **3.5.9** © JTB Photo Communications, Inc./Alamy; **3.5.10** Photo © Alice Mutasa/placesandseasons.com; **3.5.11** Photo © Ed Kashi/National Geographic Creative; **3.5.12** Photo Barney Wayne; **3.5.13** Courtesy MMA Design Studio; **3.5.14** Drazen Tomic; **3.5.15** J. Paul Getty Museum, Los Angeles (84.XD.879.180). Digital image courtesy the Getty's Open Content Program; **3.5.16** Photo © Helen Davidson; **3.5.17** Gift of Colin Cowan, Beverley Anderson, Mark Livesey QC, David McKee, Hon. Graham Prior, Adam Wynn and Peter LeMessurier through the Art Gallery of South Australia Foundation Collectors Club 2006. Art Gallery of South Australia, Adelaide (20068P61). © estate of the artist licensed by Aboriginal Artists Agency Ltd; **3.5.18a** Photo Trustees of the British Museum, London; **3.5.18b** Chris Johns/National Geographic/Getty Images; **3.5.19** © Albertoloyo/Dreamstime.com; **3.5.20** Musée Barbier-Mueller, Geneva; **3.5.21** Collected by G.F.N. Gerrits, Vb 28418-28471 (1972). Photo Peter Horner 1981 Museum der Kulturen, Basel, Switzerland; **3.6.1** Drazen Tomic; **3.6.2** Photo A. Dagli Orti/DeAgostini; **3.6.3a** G. Nimatallah/DeAgostini Picture Library/Diomedia; **3.6.3b** A. Dagli Orti/DeAgostini Picture Library/Diomedia; **3.6.4** © Michael S. Yamashita/Corbis; **3.6.5** Libreria dello Stato, Rome; **3.6.6** Brancacci Chapel, Church of Santa Maria del Carmine, Florence; **3.6.7a** Rabatti - Domingie/akg-images; **3.6.7b** Vatican Museums, Rome; **3.6.8** Stanza della Segnatura, Vatican Museums, Rome; **3.6.9a** Vatican Museums, Rome; **3.6.9b** 1998/Mondadori Portfolio/akg-images; **3.6.9c** Mondadori Portfolio/akg-images; **3.6.10a**, **3.6.10b** National Gallery, London/Scala, Florence; **3.6.11** Photo RMN-Grand Palais (Musée du Louvre)/Tony Querrec; **3.6.12** Metropolitan Museum of Art, New York, The Cloisters Collection, 1956, 56.70a–c; **3.6.13** Musée d'Unterlinden, Colmar; **3.6.14** Capponi Chapel, Church of Santa Felicità, Florence; **3.6.15** National Gallery of Art, Washington, D.C., Samuel H. Kress Collection, 1946.18.1; **3.6.16** Muzeum Narodowe, Poznan/Bridgeman Art Library; **3.6.17a** Cameraphoto/akg-images; **3.6.17b** pl. XIII, Book II from Wade, I. (ed.) *Palladio: Four Books of Architecture*, 1738; **3.6.18** Refectory of Santa Maria delle Grazie, Milan; **3.6.19** British Museum, London; **3.6.20** Cameraphoto/Scala, Florence; **3.6.21** Galleria Nazionale d'Arte Antica, Rome. Palazzo Barberini, Inv. 1569. Last restoration 1995. Photo 2021, Scala, Florence; **3.6.22** Photo Scala, Florence, courtesy Ministero Beni e Att. Culturali; **3.6.23** © nagelestock.com/Alamy; **3.6.24** Photo Scala, Florence, courtesy Ministero Beni e Att. Culturali; **3.6.25a** Prisma/Album/akg-images; **3.6.25b** Ralph Larmann; **3.6.26** Photo Pirozzi/akg-images; **3.6.27** akg-images; **3.6.28** Peter Willi/Bridgeman Images; **3.6.29** Rijksmuseum, Amsterdam; **3.6.30** The Earl of Plymouth. On loan to the National Museum of Wales, Cardiff; **3.7.1** Musée du Louvre, Paris; **3.7.2** © Bertrand Rieger/Hemis/Corbis; **3.7.3** The Wallace Collection, London; **3.7.4** Metropolitan Museum of Art, New York, Purchase, George Delacorte Fund Gift, in memory of George T. Delacorte Jr., and Gwynne Andrews, Victor Wilbour Memorial, and Marquand Funds, 2002, 2002.22; **3.7.5** National Gallery, London/Scala, Florence; **3.7.6** Photo Scala, Florence; **3.7.7** National Gallery, London/Scala, Florence; **3.7.8** Classic Image/Alamy; **3.7.9** Gianni Dagli Orti/Musée du Château de Versailles/The Art Archive; **3.7.10** Musée du Louvre, Paris; **3.7.11** DeAgostini Picture Library/The Art Archive; **3.7.12** Virginia Museum of Fine Arts, Richmond, The Adolf D. and Wilkins C. Williams Fund; **3.7.13** Photo Philip Scalia/Alamy Stock Photo; **3.7.14** Photo RMN-Grand Palais (Château de Versailles)/Gérard Blot; **3.7.15** Musée du Louvre, Paris; **3.7.16** Photo Tate, London 2012; **3.7.17** Museum of Fine Arts, Boston, Henry Lillie Pierce Fund, BJ385; **3.7.18** Howard University Art Gallery, Washington, D.C.; **3.8.1**, **3.8.2** Musée d'Orsay, Paris; **3.8.4** Photo Tate, London 2012; **3.8.5** Photo Tate, London 2018; **3.8.6** Library of Congress Prints, Washington, D.C., Prints & Photographs Division, LC-USZ62-7990; **3.8.7** Museum purchase made possible by the Pauline Edwards Bequest. Photo Smithsonian American Art Museum/Art Resource/Scala, Florence; **3.8.8** Courtesy the Pennsylvania Academy of the Fine Arts, Philadelphia. Charles Bregler's Thomas Eakins Collection, purchased with the partial support of the Pew Memorial Trust, 1985.68.2.985; **3.8.9** Musée d'Orsay, Paris; **3.8.10** V&A Images/Alamy; **3.8.11** The Art Institute of Chicago, Robert A. Waller Fund, 1910.2; **3.8.12** Pushkin Museum, Moscow; **3.8.13** Photo courtesy Sotheby's, Inc. 2013; **3.8.14** Art Institute of Chicago, Charles H. and Mary F.S. Worcester Collection, 1964.336; **3.8.15** National Gallery of Art, Washington, D.C., Gift of Victoria Nebeker Coberly, in memory of her son John W. Mudd, and Walter H. and Leonore Annenberg, 1992.9.1; **3.8.16** Martin Bache/Alamy Stock Photo; **3.8.17** Courtauld Gallery, London; **3.8.18** National Gallery of Scotland, Edinburgh; **3.8.19** Museum of Modern Art, New York. Acquired through the Lillie P. Bliss Bequest, 472.1941. Photo 2012, Museum of Modern Art, New York/Scala, Florence; **3.8.20** akg-images; **3.8.21** Hampton University Museum, Virginia; **3.8.22** Fogg Art Museum, Harvard Art Museums/Bequest of Grenville L. Winthrop/Bridgeman Images; **3.8.23** Rijksmuseum, Amsterdam; **3.8.24** Photo © Bastin & Evrard, Brussels; **3.8.25** Photo courtesy Sotheby's, Inc. 2013; **3.9.1** Kunstmuseum Basel, Switzerland; **3.9.2** Museum of Modern Art (MoMA) Purchase, 274.1939. Digital image, Museum of Modern Art, New York/Scala, Florence; **3.9.3** The Barnes Foundation, Merion, PA. © Succession H. Matisse/DACS 2022; **3.9.4** Museum of Modern Art, New York, Mrs. Simon Guggenheim Fund, 8.1949. Photo 2012, Museum of Modern Art, New York/Scala, Florence. © Succession H. Matisse/DACS 2022; **3.9.5** Photograph by Hélène Adant/RAPHO/GAMMA, Camera Press, London; **3.9.6** Museum of Modern Art, New York, acquired through the Lillie P. Bliss Bequest, 333.1939. Photo 2012, Museum of Modern Art, New York/Scala, Florence. © Succession Picasso/DACS, London 2022; **3.9.7** Acquired through the Lillie P. Bliss Bequest, 175.1945. Digital image, Museum of Modern Art, New York/Scala, Florence. © ADAGP, Paris and DACS, London 2022; **3.9.8** Kunstmuseum, Bern/SuperStock/The Art Archive; **3.9.10** Museum of Modern Art, New York, The Sidney and Harriet Janis Collection, 595.1967 a–b. Photo 2012, Museum of Modern Art, New York/Scala, Florence. © Association Marcel Duchamp/ADAGP, Paris and DACS, London 2022; **3.9.11** Nationalgalerie, Staatliche Museen, Berlin. © DACS 2022; **3.9.12** © DACS 2022; **3.9.13** Museum of Modern Art, New York. Given anonymously, 162.1934. Photo 2012, Museum of Modern Art, New York/Scala, Florence. © Salvador Dalí, Fundació Gala-Salvador Dalí, DACS 2022; **3.9.14** National Gallery of Art, Washington, D.C., Gift of the Collectors Committee, 1979.30.1. © ADAGP, Paris and DACS, London 2022; **3.9.15** Museum of Latin American Art, Long Beach, California, Robert Gumbiner Foundation Collection. © Estate of Leonora Carrington/ARS, NY and DACS, London 2022; **3.9.16** Photo Francis Carr © Thames & Hudson Ltd, London; **3.9.17** Philadelphia Museum of Art, The Louise and Walter Arensberg Collection. © Association Marcel Duchamp/ADAGP, Paris and DACS, London 2022; **3.9.18** Fondation Beyeler, Riehen/Basel, Sammlung Beyeler; acquired with the contribution of Hartmann P. and Cécile Koechlin-Tanner, Riehen. Welsh/Joosten B 234, Photo Robert Bayer, Basel; **3.9.19** The Museum of Modern Art, New York. Acquisition confirmed in 1999 by agreement with the Estate of Kazimir Malevich and made possible with funds from the Mrs. John Hay Whitney Bequest (by exchange), 817.1935. Digital image, The Museum of Modern Art, New York/Scala, Florence; **3.9.20** The Museum of Modern Art, New York. Given anonymously, 153.1934. Digital image, The Museum of Modern Art, New York/Scala, Florence. © Succession Brancusi - All rights reserved. ADAGP, Paris and DACS, London 2022; **3.9.21** Christie's Images/Corbis. © Agnes Martin Foundation, New York/DACS 2022; **3.9.22** Art Institute of Chicago, Friends of American Art Collection, 1930.934; **3.9.23** Photo The Newark Museum/Art Resource/Scala, Florence; **3.9.24** New York Public Library/Aaron Douglas/Science Photo Library. © Heirs of Aaron Douglas/VAGA at ARS, NY and DACS, London 2022; **3.9.25** New York World's Fair 1939–1940 records, Manuscripts and Archives Division, The New York Public Library, Astor, Lenox and Tilden Foundations; **3.9.26** Museum of Modern Art (MoMA), New York, Bequest of Mrs Mark Rothko through The Mark Rothko Foundation, Inc., 428.1981. Photo 2021. Digital image, Museum of Modern Art, New York/Scala, Florence. Rothko © 1998 Kate Rothko Prizel & Christopher Rothko ARS, NY and DACS, London; **3.9.27** Courtesy Center for Creative Photography, University of Arizona © 1991 Hans Namuth Estate; **3.9.28** The Museum of Modern Art, New York. Purchase, 77.1950. Digital image, The Museum of Modern Art, New York/Scala, Florence. © The Pollock-Krasner Foundation ARS, NY and DACS, London 2022; **3.9.29** Photo National Gallery of Art, Washington, D.C. © Helen Frankenthaler Foundation, Inc./ARS, NY and DACS, London 2022; **3.9.30** © 2022 The Andy Warhol Foundation for the Visual Arts, Inc./Licensed by DACS, London; **3.9.31** © Estate of Roy Lichtenstein/DACS 2022; **3.9.32** Collection the Modern Art Museum of Fort Worth, Museum purchase, The Benjamin J. Tillar Memorial Trust. Acquired in 1970. © Judd Foundation/ARS, NY and DACS, London 2022; **3.9.33** Photo Hickey-Robertson, Houston. The Menil Collection, Houston. © Stephen Flavin/Artists Rights Society, New York and DACS, London 2022; **3.9.34** © EggImages/Alamy; **3.9.35** Photo courtesy Michael Graves & Associates; **3.10.1** Philadelphia Museum of Art, 125th Anniversary Acquisition. Gift (by exchange) of Mrs. Herbert Cameron Morris, 1998, 1998-74-1. © Association Marcel Duchamp/ADAGP, Paris and DACS, London 2022; **3.10.2** © Sherrie Levine. Courtesy Simon Lee Gallery, London; **3.10.3** Museum of Modern Art, New York, Larry Aldrich Foundation Fund, 393.1970.a-c. Photo 2012, Museum of Modern Art, New York/Scala, Florence. © Joseph Kosuth. ARS, NY and DACS, London 2022; **3.10.4** © The Estate of Ana Mendieta. Courtesy Galerie Lelong, New York; **3.10.5** Copyright © Andy Goldsworthy; **3.10.6** Brooklyn Museum, Gift of R.M. Atwater, Anna Wolfrom Dove, Alice Fiebiger, Belle Campbell Harriss, and Emma L. Hyde, by exchange, Designated Purchase Fund. Mary Smith Dorward Fund, Dick S. Ramsey Fund, and Carl H. de Silver Fund, 2012.80. © Wadsworth Jarrell; **3.10.7** Video-computer graphic © April Greiman; **3.10.8** Courtesy the artist and Tanya Bonakdar Gallery, New York/Los Angeles; **3.10.9** William Sr. and Dorothy Harmsen Collection, by exchange, 2007.47. Denver Art Museum. All Rights Reserved; **3.10.10** © the artist; **3.10.11a**, **3.10.11b** Courtesy Gladstone Gallery, New York. © Shirin Neshat; **3.10.12** Photo courtesy Galerie Enrico Navarra. © The Estate of Jean-Michel Basquiat/ADAGP, Paris and DACS, London 2022; **3.10.13** Photo courtesy PaceWildenstein, New York. © Fred Wilson, courtesy PaceWildenstein, New York; **3.10.14a** Hirshhorn Museum and Sculpture Garden, Washington, D.C., 2017. Photo Cathy Carver. © Mark Bradford. Courtesy the artist and Hauser & Wirth; **3.10.14b** Hirshhorn Museum

Index